Aerial view of Wharram Percy village site, seen from the north (NMR APR 1449/20, 21 August 1979. © Crown copyright.NMR)

Words at Wharram Percy

No silence here.
The place is loud with peace.
Blackcap and robin
give voice in the soft June rain,
conspire in their different octaves
with leaf and lawn and stone.
The air retains
millennia of sound. Listen.
An axe-note falls through countless autumns
down the valley's terraced side.
A wife calls out, in Middle English,
to a man who mows in the glebe,
but his blade lisps on as though he has not heard.
Shadow crawls slowly around a mass-dial
scratched on the porch of the church,
dislodging a grain of sand
which falls ringing onto the path.
There is only utterance.
Low-skimming birds pick flies from the tensile
surface of the pond, and each touch rings
as if struck from a vanished bell.
Hillside pasture lies fizzing under the rain,
through which a partridge
hurries her brood to safety
among cowslip, oat grass, Yorkshire fog, black medick.

Peter Didsbury

(first published in the *Times Literary Supplement*, January 2005)

WHARRAM

A Study of Settlement on the Yorkshire Wolds, XIII

A HISTORY OF WHARRAM PERCY AND ITS NEIGHBOURS

edited by

S. Wrathmell

with contributions by M. Atha, J. Bayley, E. Bentz, E. Blakelock, P. Brears, V. Castagnino, N. Chabot, E.A. Clark, A.B. Daoust, A. David, A. Deegan, C. Dyer, P. Everson, D. Hall, N. Linford, P. Linford, G. McDonnell, E. Marlow-Mann, A. Oswald, J.D. Richards, J. Richardson, I. Riddler, S. Roskams, S. Rubinson, A.M. Slowikowski, D. Stocker, M. Watts and C. Whittick

Illustrations by

E. Marlow-Mann, M. Chisnall, A. Deegan, C. Philo and J. Prudhoe

York University
Archaeological Publications 15

© Wharram Research Project and Department of Archaeology, University of York, 2012, except where otherwise indicated

ISBN 978 0 946722 22 8

Published by: The University of York
Sub-edited, designed
and typeset by: Chris Philo
Printed by: Short Run Press Limited, Exeter

This publication has been made possible by a grant from English Heritage

Further information relating to Wharram excavation sites which have not been fully published, together with data created during the analysis phase of the project, are available through the Archaeology Data Service. The Digital Object Identifier is: doi:10.5284/1000415

Wharram: A Study of Settlement on the Yorkshire Wolds
General Editor: S. Wrathmell

Vol. I   *Domestic Settlement 1: Areas 10 and 6* (1979)
               Society for Medieval Archaeology Monograph 8. £7.00

Vol. II   *Wharram Percy: The Memorial Stones of the Churchyard* (1983)
               York University Archaeological Publications 1. £4.00

Vol. III   *Wharram Percy: The Church of St Martin* (1987)
               Society for Medieval Archaeology Monograph 11. £17.50

Vol. IV   *Two Roman Villas at Wharram le Street* (1986)
               York University Archaeological Publications 2. £5.00

Vol. V   *An Archaeological Survey of the Parish of Wharram Percy, East Yorkshire.
               1. The Evolution of the Roman Landscape* (1987)
               British Archaeological Reports, British Series 172. £12.00

Vol. VI   *Domestic Settlement 2: Medieval Peasant Farmsteads* (1989)
               York University Archaeological Publications 8. £10.95

Vol. VII   *Two Anglo-Saxon Buildings and Associated Finds* (1992)
               York University Archaeological Publications 9. £7.50

Vol. VIII   *The South Manor Area* (2000)
               York University Archaeological Publications 10. £18.00

Vol. IX   *The North Manor Area and North-west Enclosure* (2004)
               York University Archaeological Publications 11. £22.00

Vol. X   *Water Resources and their Management* (2005)
               York University Archaeological Publications 12. £19.50

Vol. XI   *The Churchyard* (2007)
               York University Archaeological Publications 13. £25.00

Vol. XII   *The Post-medieval Farm and Vicarage Sites* (2010)
               York University Archaeological Publications 14. £27.50

Vol. XIII   *A History of Wharram Percy and its Neighbours* (2012)
               York University Archaeological Publications 15. £33.50

Volumes VIII to XIII are available from Oxbow Books, 10 Hythe Bridge Street, Oxford, OX1 2EW
Volumes I and III are available from Maney Publishing, Customer Sales and Service Department, Suite 1C, Joseph's Well, Hanover Walk, Leeds LS3 1AB

Cover: St Martin's church in the valley viewed from the western plateau (Photograph by P. Gwilliam)

Contents

Contents iii
List of Plates v
List of Figures vi
List of Tables viii
Summaries ix
Preface x

Part One: Old Excavations, New Surveys 1
1   The Excavations, 1950-1990 by E. Marlow-Mann and S. Wrathmell 3
2   The Danish Connection: Axel Steensberg and Wharram Percy by E. Bentz 10
3   A New Earthwork Survey of Wharram Percy by A. Oswald 23
4   A New Geophysical Survey of Wharram Percy by P. Linford, N. Linford and A. David 44

Part Two: Wharram and the Wolds in Prehistoric, Roman and Early Anglo-Saxon Times 55
5   The 2005 Excavation of the North-west Enclosure by S. Roskams 57
6   Prehistoric and Roman Transitions at Wharram Percy by M. Atha and S. Roskams 63
7   Early Anglo-Saxon Grazing Grounds by S. Wrathmell 82

Part Three: New Communities in the Middle and Late Saxon Periods 97
8   Resettlement of the Wolds by S. Wrathmell, with contributions from A. Deegan, J.D. Richards
     and S. Roskams 99
          Investigations of Anglo-Saxon occupation in Burdale: an interim note by J.D. Richards
          and S. Roskams 113
9   Characterising Middle Saxon Wharram Percy: the Structural Evidence by S. Wrathmell and
     E. Marlow-Mann with contributions from E.A. Clark and J. Bayley 118
10   Characterising Middle Saxon Wharram: Artefacts and the Iron Economy 135
          Early and Middle Saxon artefacts by I. Riddler, with contributions from E.A. Clark and
          A.M. Slowikowski 135
          The iron economy of Wharram Percy by G. McDonnell, E. Blakelock and
          S. Rubinson with contributions from N. Chabot, A. Daoust, and V. Castagnino 154
11   Wharram and its Neighbours in the Middle Saxon Period: a Debate and some Conclusions ... 163
          Introduction by S. Wrathmell 163
          Wharram before the village moment by P. Everson and D. Stocker 164
          Wharram before the village moment: a response by S. Wrathmell 172
          The Anglo-Saxon faunal assemblage of Wharram and its comparison with
          Burdale by J. Richardson 173
          Burdale and Wharram Percy in Middle Saxon times: some comparisons
          by J. Richards 178
          Conclusions by S. Wrathmell 178
12   Lordship, Local Administration and Ecclesiastical Provision in the Late Saxon Period
     by S. Wrathmell 180

13   The First Two Centuries of the Medieval Village: Wharram in the Late Saxon Period
         by I. Riddler, D. Stocker and P. Everson, with contributions from E.A. Clark,
         A.M. Slowikowski, M. Watts and S. Wrathmell   196
                  The Late Saxon material culture by I. Riddler   196
                        Ceramics of the Late Saxon period by A.M. Slowikowski 200
                  Dating the foundation of the medieval village by S. Wrathmell   203
                  The Mill and Dam Site at Wharram: some further thoughts by M. Watts   206
                  Graveyard, church and parish by S. Wrathmell 207
                  Why at Wharram? The foundation of the nucleated settlement by P. Everson and
                  D. Stocker   208

Part Four: Wharram and the Wolds from the 12th to the 16th Centuries   221
14   Lords and Manors from the 12th to the 15th centuries by S. Wrathmell, with contributions
         from C. Whittick   222
15   A New Understanding of the Church Fabric by D. Stocker with contributions from P. Everson... 240
16   Who at Wharram? by P. Everson and D. Stocker 262
17   Field Systems and Landholdings by D. Hall with contributions from S. Wrathmell   278
                  Permanent pastures on the northern Wolds by S. Wrathmell 288
                  Open fields and land holdings at Wharram Percy by S. Wrathmell with contributions
                  from A. Deegan   290
18   Rural Settlement in eastern Yorkshire by S. Wrathmell with contributions from A. Deegan   ... 297
19   The Late Medieval Village of Wharram Percy: Farming the Land by C. Dyer with contributions
         from E.A. Clark, J. Richardson and A.M. Slowikowski 312
20   The Late Medieval Village of Wharram Percy: Living and Consuming by C. Dyer with
         contributions from E.A. Clark, J. Richardson and A.M. Slowikowski   327
21   The Houses of Wharram's Tenant Farmers at the end of the Middle Ages 340
                  Observations on the structure and form of Wharram's late medieval farmhouses
                  by S. Wrathmell   340
                  The inventory of William Akclum and its context by C. Dyer   342
                  The interiors of Wharram's farmhouses and their contents: two artist's
                  impressions and a commentary by P. Brears   349
22   The Desertion of Wharram Percy Village by S. Wrathmell   356

Part Five: Wharram and the Wolds: Future Research Potential   365

Bibliography   369

Index by H.E.M. Cool   391

List of Plates

1 Open-area excavation at Wharram Percy:
   House 6 (Site 12) in 1962... 1
2 Axel Steensberg (1906-1999) guiding visitors
   at the Borup Ris site 10
3 Open area excavation at Store Valby, showing
   the excavation of farm no. 3 in 1949-50 15
4 Open-area excavation at Wharram, showing
   the excavation of House 10 in 1953 18
5 Aerial view of the Wharram Percy
   village earthworks, viewed from the east ... 37
6 Foundations of buildings and toft boundaries in
   the West Row (north), showing as parch marks 43
7 Sledmere Green Lane (Route 4) between
   Fimber and Wetwang 89
8 Aerial view of the east-west trans-valley trackway
   (Track C) 89
9 The white chalk surface of Track C, seen from
   the North Manor area 90
10 A stretch of the Track C hollow way
   descending from Bella towards the Beck and
   the village site 90
11 Aerial view showing crop marks of
   'Butterwick-type' settlement enclosures
   between East and West Lutton 108
12 Aerial view showing crop marks of 'Butterwick-
   type' settlement enclosures at Burdale 113
13 Site 70, general view of Period 3 and Period 4
   features 128
14 Site 78 general view of Period 2 features ...133
15 Selected Early and Middle Saxon objects of
   Phases 1-2, and glass beads of *Phases 1-5* ...138
16 Middle Saxon Objects, *Phases 3-4* 139
17 Aerial view of Weaverthorpe's manorial *curia* 183
18 Late Saxon objects from Wharram, *Phases 6-7* 198
19 Weaverthorpe soke estate, looking westwards
   along the Great Wold valley from
   Weaverthorpe *curia* 231

20 The South Manor undercroft from the
   south-east 232
21 The South Manor undercroft from the
   north-west 233
22 The South Manor undercroft entrance from
   the south 233
23 The present south doorway of St Martin's ...248
24 The blocked south arcade of St Martin's... ...249
25 The blocked north arcade of St Martin's ...253
26 Broad and narrow ridges in the fields of Great
   Kelk, Holderness in 1946... 282
27 Settrington village, the north-south rows along
   the Beck, depicted on the plan of 1600 301
28 Settrington village, the east-west rows
   depicted on the plan of 1600 301
29 Aerial view of the east-west rows of
   Settrington, marked by surviving farmsteads
   and earthworks 303
30 Aerial view of farmstead earthworks at
   Buckton Garths, Settrington 304
31 Aerial photograph of Wharram le Street
   village 307
32 Aerial view of Thirkleby deserted
   village 309
33 Aerial view of farmstead earthworks east
   of Duggleby village 310
34 Aerial view of farmstead earthworks at Kirby
   Grindalythe 311
35 William Acklum's inventory of 1481 343
36 Artist's impression of the interior of Building 1
   in Area 6 (Site 12) 348
37 Artist's impression of the interior of a late
   medieval house... 350
38 Deposition of 1555 referring to Wharram
   township having been laid to grass 357
39 Aerial view of Towthorpe deserted
   village 262

List of Figures

1   Wharram Percy and other locations mentioned in the text xiv
2   Plan of Wharram Percy showing excavated sites 4
3   Sites in Denmark excavated by Axel Steensberg 33
4   Plan showing the remains of Store Valby ... 14
5   Example of finds recording at Wharram Percy, House 10 19
6   Detail from the documentation of farm no. 4 at Store Valby 19
7   Inspiration sheet compiled by John Hurst ... 22
8   English Heritage's earthwork plan of Wharram Percy published in 2004 ... ... opposite 24
9   Schematic plan of the network of roads and tracks 25
10 Plan of the North Manor ... ...
11 Interpretative phase plan of the North Manor ... 27
12 Plan of the South Manor 29
13 Interpretative plan of the South Manor 32
14 Plan of the East Row 34
15 Plan of the North Row 35
16 Plan of the West Row (north) 36
17 Plan of the West Row (south) 40
18 Linear greyscale plot of the 2002 magnetometer survey 46
19 Interpretation of anomalies in the 2002 magnetometer survey 47
20 Interpretation of potential Iron Age and Roman anomalies detected in the 2002 magnetometer survey 48
21 Interpretation of potential medieval anomalies detected in the 2002 magnetometer survey ... 50
22 Interpretation of other potential archaeological anomalies detected in the 2002 magnetometer survey 52
23 Topographic model of the Wolds with main routeways 56
24 Geophysical survey of the North-west Enclosure and the 2005 excavation area 57
25 Summary plan of the 2005 excavation 59
26 The location of Wharram Percy and other places mentioned in Chapter 6 65
27 Prehistoric and Roman period features in and around Wharram Percy township 68-9
28 Late prehistoric and early Roman features excavated in the vicinity of Sites 45/60 72
29 Late Roman features excavated in the vicinity of Sites 45/60 74
30 Late Iron Age/Early Roman and Late Roman features across the North Manor area 75

31 The open field furlongs of Butterwick, and crop marks of earlier enclosures and fields ... 83
32 Topographic model of the Wolds, viewed from the north 88
33 Trackways running through the northern part of the village site 91
34 The chronological development of the trackway running through Site 60 (Track C) 92-3
35 Section along the west side of Site 60 94
36 Townships in the study area, showing place-names and routeways 100
37 Topographic model showing early Anglo-Saxon estates and later vills carved out of their territories 103
38 Township boundaries and the successive tracks of Route 3 104
39 'Butterwick-type' settlement enclosures south-west of Butterwick 106
40 'Butterwick-type' settlement enclosures between East and West Lutton 107
41 'Butterwick-type' settlement enclosures just north of Rudston 109
42 'Butterwick-type' settlement enclosures between Boynton and Caythorpe 109
43 'Butterwick-type' settlement enclosures north of Huggate 110
44 'Butterwick-type' settlement enclosures between Sledmere and Garton 110
45 'Butterwick-type' settlement enclosures north-east of Binnington 111
46 'Butterwick-type' settlement enclosures east of West Heslerton 112
47 'Butterwick-type' settlement enclosures just west of Wharram Percy 112
48 Roman and 'Butterwick-type' settlement enclosures south-east of Burdale House Farm... 114
49 Burdale 2006: plan of excavated features ... 115
50 Burdale 2007: plan of excavated features ... 116
51 Location of sites discussed in Chapter 9 ... 119
52 Middle Saxon and earlier features north-west of the South Manor area (Sites 94, 95, 98) ... 121
53 Plan of excavated features in Sites 94 and 95 ... 122
54 Plan of excavated features in Sites 98a and 98B 123
55 Middle Saxon features in the South Manor area 124
56 Middle Saxon features south-west of the South Manor area (Sites 18, 32, 70, 72 and 78) ... 126
57 Plan of excavated features in Site 70, Period 3 127
58 Plan of excavated features in Site 70, Period 4 129
59 Plan of excavated features in Site 78, Period 1 131

60   Plan of excavated features in Site 78, Period 2, phases 2, 3 and 4 132

61   Plan of excavated features in Site 78, Period 3, phases 1 and 2 134

62   Middle Saxon artefact phases at Wharram   ...136

63   Numbers and distribution of Middle Saxon objects from Wharram: *Phase 2-3* objects (*c.* 630-725) 142

64   Numbers and distribution of Middle Saxon objects from Wharram: *Phase 4-5* objects (*c.* 725-850) 145

65   Dimensions of Anglo-Saxon knives from Yorkshire 149

66   Smithing bar compositions from Wharram and from Coppergate, York 157

67   Stages of smithing 158

68   Manufacturing typology for iron knives 159

69   Burdale and Wharram: kill-off curves for sheep by period and site 175

70   Wharram: kill-off curves for cattle by period ...176

71   Burdale and Wharram: scattergram of adult sheep metacarpals showing size variation by period and site 176

72   Proportion of the main domestic animals from Wharram by area and period, with comparison to nearby sites 177

73   The Domesday hundreds of Acklam, Scard and Thorshowe 181

74   Landholding in 1066 and 1086 in the hundreds of Acklam, Scard and Thorshowe 182

75   The putative descendants of Thorbrandr the Hold 185

76   The 1066 landholdings of Ormr and Thorbrandr/Gamall 187

77   Map showing places mentioned in Chapter 12   190

78   Medieval parishes in the Wharram area 191

79   Wharram: Late Saxon pottery types 201

80   Wharram: distribution of Middle Saxon and Late Saxon pottery and small finds 205

81   Wharram: village development between the mid-10th and mid-11th centuries 210

82   Map showing places mentioned in Chapter 13   216

83   The successors and rival claimants to the lands once held by the descendants of Thorbrandr the Hold 223

84   The Percys of Bolton Percy and the Chamberlains 225

85   Manors and lands in eastern Yorkshire held by the Chamberlains and by the Percys of Bolton Percy, and other places mentioned in Chapter 14... 226

86   Wharram Grange and its watercourse 227

87   The phasing of St Martin's church 241

88   Phased elevations of the south wall of the nave 242

89   Phased elevations of the west wall of the nave and the tower 243

90   Phased elevations of the north wall of the nave 244

91   Phased elevations of the east wall of the nave   245

92   Location and plan form of the late 12th-century south doorway 247

93. Reconstruction of the late 12th-century south doorway   ...251

94   Reconstruction of the early 12th-century 'tub' font 260

95   Early Norman fonts in the old East Riding of Yorkshire 262

96   Proposed layout of the *camera* and hall in the South Manor enclosure 264

97   The South Manor and the late 12th-century village the North Manor and the mid-13th-century village 266

98   Map showing places mentioned in Chapter 17   279

99   The fields of Great Kelk, Holderness 282

100 Ridge and furrow in Burdale township 285

101 Ridge and furrow in Towthorpe township   ...285

102 Ridge and furrow in Wharram le Street township 286

103 Ridge and furrow in Settrington township   ...287

104 Southern part of the Wolds study area, showing stretches of permanent pasture 289

105 The bovate holdings in Middlegates furlong, Wharram Percy... 291

106 Ridge and furrow in Wharram Percy township, and the approximate positions of glebe lands ...293

107 Map showing places mentioned in Chapter 18   298

108 Village settlements in the Vale of Pickering in the mid-19th century... 299

109 Settrington and Buckton townships 300

110 The village of Preston in Holderness in the mid-19th century 305

111 Reconstruction of the original village boundaries and toft partitions of Wharram le Street... 306

112 Medieval settlement enclosures along the Gypsey Race 308

113 Map showing places mentioned in Chapters 19 and 20 313

114 Key to the items recorded in William Akclum's inventory of 1481 and shown in Plate 37   ...351

115 Reconstruction of the 17th and 18th-century infield and outfield of Wharram Percy 360

116 Arable and pasture lands in Wharram Percy in 1836 361

List of Tables

1   Anglo-Saxon glass beads from Wharram... ... 140
2   Anglo-Saxon bone pin head forms from Wharram 143
3   Anglo-Saxon strap-ends from Wharram 146
4   Anglo-Saxon knives from Wharram 148
5   Concordance of knife typologies 150
6   Knife forms from Early and Middle Saxon settlements 151
7   Selected object categories from Middle Saxon sites 152
8   Comparison of smithing slag debris from a range of sites 160
9   Proportion of the main domestic animals from the South Manor Area by period 174
10 The Wharram parishes: landholding recorded in Domesday Book 189
11 Late Saxon hones 199
12 Ceramic Group 2 pottery types 201
13 Comparative numbers of Middle and Late Saxon pottery 204

14 Comparative numbers of Middle and Late Saxon small finds 204
15 Provisional categorisation of morphology types of settlements in Buckrose wapentake ...218
16 Stints on common pasture for one oxgang (bovate) in the vicinity of Wharram Percy ...317
17 Animals attached for trespassing at Bishop Wilton, 1379-80 317
18 Crops from manors in the vicinity of Wharram Percy 319
19 Crops on an oxgang holding at Wharram Percy, c. 1300 322
20 Carbonised grain from Wharram Percy: samples most likely to reflect peasant crops ...332
21 Animal bones from Wharram Percy 333
22 Inventories of ten Yorkshire peasants, dated 1438-94 344
23 Crops in selected inventories 345
24 Livestock in inventories 346

Summary

This final volume in the series *Wharram: a Study of Settlement on the Yorkshire Wolds* charts the history of Wharram Percy from later prehistoric times down to the 16th century. The first part of the volume summarises the excavation programme and discusses key influences on the methods and techniques adopted at Wharram. It also introduces the results of earthwork and geophysical surveys carried out since the end of the excavations, and explores their role in generating new understandings of Wharram's settlement history. Part Two reviews the evidence for fields and farms in the Wharram area in later prehistoric and Roman times, and identifies some key social changes that took place during those periods. It also presents arguments in support of the hypothesis that the northern Wolds reverted to grazing grounds for surrounding lowland communities in the immediate post-Roman centuries. Evidence for the re-establishment, in the Middle Saxon period, of permanent settlement at Wharram and in neighbouring parts of the Wolds is presented and debated in Part Three. The creation of the earliest elements of the medieval village plan, along with the burial ground, church and mill in the Late Saxon period is examined and debated in the context of Scandinavian overlordship in the locality. The fourth part of the volume outlines the history of lordship at Wharram Percy from the 12th century onwards, and discusses the impact of lordship on the fabric of the village and its church. Evidence for the fields and farms, homes and daily lives of peasant farmers both at Wharram and in nearby communities is also explored, and the circumstances of depopulation and desertion are re-examined.

Zusammenfassung

Der vorliegende Band ist der letzte Bericht aus der Reihe *Wharram: a Study of Settlement on the Yorkshire Wolds*. Er behandelt die Geschichte Wharram Percys von der jüngeren vorrömischen Eisenzeit bis in das 16. Jahrhundert. Der erste Teil des Bandes fasst die Ausgrabungsstrategien zusammen und diskutiert zentrale Einflüsse auf die in Wharram angewandten Methoden und Techniken. In diesem ersten Teil werden auch die Ergebnisse der seit Abschluss der Ausgrabungen erfolgten Sondierungen und geophysikalischen Prospektionen vorgestellt. Diese eröffnen neue Einblicke in die Siedlungsgeschichte Wharrams. Im zweiten Teil werden die frühen Nachweise für Felder und Gehöfte in Wharram und Umgebung während der jüngeren vorrömischen Eisenzeit und der römischen Zeit vorgestellt: In diesen Perioden lassen sich einige wesentliche gesellschaftliche Veränderungen festmachen. Für die Hypothese, dass die nördlichen Yorkshire Wolds in unmittelbar post-römischer Zeit wieder in Weideland für die umliegenden ländlichen Ansiedlungen der Lowlands umwandelt wurden, werden unterstützende Argumente vorgelegt. Die Belege für eine erneute und permanente Besiedlung in Wharram und den benachbarten Gebieten der Wolds während des 7.-9. Jahrhunderts (*Middle Saxon Period*) werden im dritten Teil vorgelegt und erörtert. Die Errichtung der frühesten mittelalterlichen Dorfstrukturen im 9.-11. Jahrhundert (*Late Saxon Period*), einschließlich Friedhof, Kirche und Mühle, wird im Kontext einer ortsansässigen skandinavischen Obrigkeit debattiert. Der vierte Teil des Bandes umreißt die Geschichte der Herrschaftsstrukturen in Wharram Percy ab dem 12. Jahrhundert und diskutiert ihren Einfluss auf die Entwicklung des Dorfes und seiner Kirche. Auch werden sowohl für Wharram als auch für die nahe gelegenen umgebenden Dörfer Nachweise für Felder und Gehöfte, für das Zuhause und das tägliche Leben der Bauern, sowie der Umstände der Entvölkerung und das Auflassen der Siedlungen abschließend diskutiert.

Résumé

Le dernier volume de la série *Wharram: Une étude de peuplement dans les Yorkshire Wolds* trace l'histoire de Wharram Percy de la fin de la préhistoire au 16ème siècle. La première partie de ce volume donne un résumé du programme de fouilles et traite des influences clés au niveau des méthodes et des techniques adoptées à Wharram. Elle introduit également les résultats des ouvrages de terre et des levés géophysiques exécutés depuis la fin des fouilles, et elle explore leur rôle dans la génération de nouvelles conceptions au niveau de l'histoire du peuplement de Wharram. La deuxième partie fait le bilan des indices concernant les champs et les fermes de la région de Wharram à la fin de l'époque préhistorique et durant l'époque romaine, et elle identifie certains changements sociaux clés qui se produisirent lors de ces époques. Elle présente également des arguments à l'appui de l'hypothèse selon laquelle le nord des Wolds retourna à l'état de pâturages pour les communautés de basses terres des alentours durant les siècles immédiatement postérieurs à l'époque romaine. La troisième partie présente et discute les indices de rétablissement, au milieu de l'époque saxonne, d'un peuplement permanent à Wharram et dans les régions voisines des Wolds. La création des premiers éléments du plan du village médiéval, ainsi que du cimetière, de l'église et du moulin à la fin de l'époque saxonne, est présentée et discutée dans le contexte de la suzeraineté scandinave de la localité. La quatrième partie du volume trace les grandes lignes de l'histoire de la seigneurie à Wharram Percy à partir du 12ème siècle, et discute des conséquences de la seigneurie au niveau des structures du village et de son église. Les indices relatifs aux champs et aux fermes, aux foyers et à la vie quotidienne des paysans, et à Wharram et dans les communautés avoisinantes, sont également explorés, et les circonstances du dépeuplement et de l'abandon sont remises en cause.

Preface

Wharram Percy is unquestionably the best known deserted medieval village site in Britain. It lies on the northern edge of the Yorkshire Wolds, some 18 miles (29 km) to the north-east of York and about 7 miles (11 km) south-east of the town of Malton (SE 8583 6436; Fig. 1). Its topographical and geological contexts are discussed in Chapter 6 below. Though now in the District of Ryedale and county of North Yorkshire, it was until the 1970s – and had been since its first appearance in documentary records – part of the East Riding of Yorkshire. Archaeological excavation began at Wharram in 1950 and continued for forty years. It has been described by Christopher Taylor as 'the most important archaeological excavation of any period since 1945' (Taylor 2010, 5).

The work was carried out under the auspices of the Deserted Medieval Village Research Group (founded at Wharram in 1952), which later changed its name to the Medieval Village Research Group, and finally to the Medieval Settlement Research Group, to reflect its widening agenda. In 1974 the site of the village earthworks was placed in the Guardianship of the Ancient Monuments Directorate of the Department of the Environment by Birdsall Estates Co. Ltd, through the generosity of the 11th and 12th Barons Middleton, and is now in the care of English Heritage. The site is a nationally designated heritage asset (National Heritage List for England, no. 1011377; formerly Scheduled Monument 13302), and is entered on the Historic Environment Record for North Yorkshire under the number MNY 12309.

By the time excavations ended, in 1990, numerous summary discussions of the findings had appeared in journals and books, but the extent of definitive publication was very limited. There were two Society for Medieval Archaeology monographs, one dealing with the excavation of peasant houses and the South Manor buildings, the other concerned with the investigation of St Martin's church (*Wharram I* and *Wharram III*), and the prehistoric and Roman elements of the parish survey had been published in the British Archaeological Reports series (*Wharram V*). In addition, reports on the churchyard gravestones (*Wharram II*) and on trial excavations at two nearby Roman villas (*Wharram IV*), had appeared in the York University Archaeological Publications series, along with a second report on medieval peasant houses (*Wharram VI*). At that point it was decided that all future Wharram monographs should appear in the York University series.

The 1990s saw much progress in the sorting and analysis of finds and the preparation of archive reports, thanks in particular to the support of Jim Lang, English Heritage's inspector charged with overseeing this work.

Nevertheless, only one definitive report emerged in that decade (*Wharram VII*). It dealt with early Anglo-Saxon and Middle Saxon discoveries in a number of small trenches on the Plateau.

The post-excavation and publication programme was re-engineered in 1997-8, with the preparation of an Updated Project Design based on the methodology of English Heritage's *Management of Archaeological Projects* (MAP2, 1991). For the first time a comprehensive list of tasks, timescales, contributors and costs was developed, with a view to publishing a further six definitive reports on the excavations. The proposed monographs were to focus, like the earlier ones, on the main unpublished excavation areas: the South Manor Area, the North Manor Area, the Pond and Dam, the Churchyard, the Plateau sites, and the Vicarage and Post-medieval Farmstead. A seventh 'Synthesis' volume was also proposed, though inevitably its content could not yet, in 1998, be clearly envisaged.

In the event, English Heritage and its (then) Ancient Monuments Advisory Committee decided that the Plateau sites did not really provide a coherent focus of interest for a separate publication. It was agreed that the northernmost Plateau site should be added to the North Manor Area volume (as it concerned a further element of the Romano-British settlement featured in that volume), and that the rest should, where appropriate, be integrated into the other volumes, particularly the Synthesis; the remainder of the Plateau data would be prepared to Archive Report level. The Committee also advised that proposals to carry out detailed analysis on the site's early prehistoric worked flint should be withdrawn, and that publication of 18th and 19th-century material should be minimal.

The excavation data still requiring publication in 1998 could have been dealt with in several different ways, the most obvious being the creation of chronologically arranged or thematic volumes. The principal reason such alternatives were not adopted was what would now be termed 'risk management': every excavation area report, including its artefact and environmental analyses, would have had to be completed before the first of the volumes could be produced; and a gap in publication lasting seven or eight years or more might have damaged the credibility of the post-excavation and publication project. It would certainly have been much harder to persuade a wide range of contributors to maintain the flow of reports. Furthermore, if funding had, for some unanticipated reason, ceased before the final excavation report had been completed, the project would have had precious little to show for its efforts other than an extensive and very interesting archive.

The decision to prepare volumes that focus on particular major excavation areas has not, however, prevented them from being aligned with more general topics and themes: the South Manor Area (*Wharram VIII*) was central to discussions about the Middle Saxon and Anglo-Scandinavian settlement, and the North Manor Area (*Wharram IX*) to the Late Iron Age and Roman settlement; the Water Resources volume (*Wharram X*) focused inevitably on environmental and other organic evidence from the pond and dam, and the Churchyard (*Wharram XI*) on the large assemblage of human skeletal material. The Vicarage and Post-medieval Farmstead volume (*Wharram XII*) was effectively a report on the entire settlement at Wharram Percy from the early 16th to the early 19th centuries. This final volume (*Wharram XIII*) attempts to chart the chronological development of settlement at Wharram and in neighbouring communities from later prehistoric times to the 16th century. The thirteen definitive excavation reports amount in total to over 3,000 pages, contributed by more than 130 authors and specialists.

Wharram XIII is not a summary of what has already appeared in print; it is, instead, an attempt to write a history of Wharram (not *the* history of Wharram), and to do so specifically in the context of what was happening in neighbouring communities. One reason for adopting this approach is the failure to bring to fruition in its entirety the Wharram parish survey, covering the five townships that constituted the medieval ecclesiastical parish of Wharram Percy and the adjacent Wharram le Street. This was a major disappointment to Maurice Beresford, whose extensive notes and extracts from relevant documentary sources have been used in the present volume.

There is a second reason for adopting the approach taken here. Beresford was initially drawn to Wharram Percy because he had a specific question to answer – the date of village depopulation – which could be set against an early 16th-century record of the destruction of four farms there. Had that initial question been the wider one that came to dominate the first two decades of the project – the daily lives of the medieval peasants who lived and farmed there – an alternative village site might have been preferred; one that offered far better documentary evidence than a township for which there are virtually no medieval sources other than those concerned with manorial interests, their value and their succession.

Given the rather threadbare and patchy history that could be woven out of the material available for Wharram Percy itself, and particularly in the absence of a completed parish survey, a rather different approach was adopted: the informal application of the technique of historical research known as 'prosopography'. One of its leading exponents, Dr Katharine Keats-Rohan has defined it (in *History and Computing* 12.1.2) thus:

'Prosopography is about what the analysis of the sum of data about many individuals can tell us about the different types of connection between them, and hence about how they operated within and upon the institutions – social, political, legal, economic, intellectual – of their time'.

In terms of the present volume, we start with the understanding that it is impossible, on the basis of our present sources of information, to construct the equivalent of a biography for the 'medieval' community of Wharram Percy from its creation to its extinction. We know also that the same is true of all the surrounding communities; but that in each case the pattern of gaps and blocks of data may be different from those of its neighbours. Therefore, if we assemble the fragmentary histories of a number of communities that on geographical, topographical and socio-economic grounds will have had connections with one another, and will have shared similar experiences, we can learn more about individual communities through our knowledge of the group as a whole.

It is important to understand what this application of prosopography does *not* involve. It is not an attempt to construct individual histories for a geographically discrete group of townships: it is no substitute *Victoria County History* volume – though the existing East Riding volumes, and particularly the recent published and unpublished work of David and Susan Neave, have been invaluable in the present exercise. Nor is it the usual trawl of 'comparable' sites, a standard component of the 'wider discussion' section of any excavation report. The need for a chapter comparing the results at Wharram with those from a range of excavations at other village sites has been at least partly met by the Medieval Settlement Research Group's recent comprehensive review of investigations carried out across Britain and Ireland over the past 60 years (Christie and Stamper 2012).

The 'population' of communities explored in this volume, in Parts 3 and 4, is primarily, though not exclusively, a group of about forty townships on and adjacent to the northern Wolds of Yorkshire. The 'study area', as it is called here, stretches from the Vale of Pickering (on the south side of the river Derwent) in the north, to the High Wolds in the south, and from Langton and Birdsall in the west to Binnington and Boythorpe in the east (see Fig. 36). This territory has been selected because it encompasses lands of largely regular formation – bands of Vale and Wolds land running east to west. Regularity means that it is easier than it would otherwise be to detect patterns (for example in tracks and boundaries) that are culturally rather than topographically constrained. In simple terms, it is easier to see 'planning' and purpose against a uniform or at least regular background than against one that is highly irregular.

The study area has been explored in an attempt to understand various aspects of Wharram's history that are difficult or impossible to detect at the level of the individual township. Furthermore, the boundaries of the study area have been transgressed where it seemed appropriate to do so. One clear example of this is the use of Henry Best's account of farming an estate at Elmswell, south of the study area, in the early 17th century; another is the exploration of a network of 11th-century Anglo-Scandinavian estates held by the descendants of Thorbrandr the Hold, extending northwards across the

Derwent to the North York Moors. In the latter case, it had become evident that what was happening in the study area could not be understood without taking into account the wider patterns of contemporary landholding, and it was these wider patterns that offered some pointers to Wharram's socio-economic context in the period from the 8th to the 11th centuries.

There is, however, a further problem that afflicts some of the topics discussed in Parts 2 and 3 of this volume: even with the assistance of its neighbours in the study area, Wharram's history cannot be reconstructed in a conventional narrative fashion. For some parts of its story there are too many competing possibilities, and too few criteria that can be used to distinguish the more plausible of them from the less likely. Here, a different approach has been adopted. Instead of trying to persuade the reader that any one scenario is more likely, or more probable, than any other on grounds that are usually unstated and often based on nothing more than personal preference, a hypothesis is first sketched out and then data are related to it.

It is an approach that was used in an earlier volume dealing with the structural characteristics of Wharram's medieval peasant buildings (Wrathmell 1989c, 3-5), though subsequent references to that particular analysis as 'demonstrating' that peasant houses were cruck-built clearly indicates that the approach was not understood by all. A more recent deployment of explicit hypotheses, for similar reasons, can be found in Stephen Baxter's study of the Leofwinesons, earls of Mercia (Baxter 2007, 150-51).

This volume does not claim to be 'the final word' on the history of Wharram Percy and its neighbours; it is much more of an interim statement, drawing together the results of investigations carried out thus far. Most of the archaeological resource remains, both on the site and in the Site Archive, and further research on topics such as those outlined in the final part of the volume will undoubtedly overturn or at least modify many of the hypotheses presented here. One need only compare the interpretations put forward in this volume with those published at the end of the excavations (Beresford and Hurst 1990), to appreciate the impermanence of our efforts to achieve an understanding of Wharram's history. They will continue to be challenged and changed as long as archaeologists and historians continue to think analytically about Wharram.

In their 1976 contribution to Peter Sawyer's volume entitled *Medieval Settlement. Continuity and Change*, Maurice Beresford and John Hurst commented: 'We have been asked how anything new of significance can be found after twenty-five years [of excavation at Wharram Percy]' (Beresford and Hurst 1976, 144). Those who asked the question then would be astonished to find that, even after another thirty-six years, the authors of the following chapters are still claiming to have identified much that is both new and significant.

The Wharram Research Project could not have taken place without the generosity of three successive owners of the village site and its former township: the 11th Lord Middleton; the 12th Lord Middleton who succeeded in 1970 and died in 2011, sadly before he could be presented with a copy of this final volume, and the 13th Lord Middleton who has maintained the Willoughby family's interest in and support for the project.

Equally fundamental to the project's success has been the practical support and funding provided by English Heritage through four decades of excavation and post-excavation work. The editor and finds co-ordinator acknowledge their debt to Jim Lang, the English Heritage inspector who supported the post-excavation project during a challenging period in the 1990s, and to Kath Buxton who provided invaluable guidance at the end of that decade, when the post-excavation project was provided with clearer tasks and targets and the funding to achieve them. Over the past decade English Heritage's successive project monitors, Kath Buxton and Dave MacLeod, have ensured that the final six volumes of reports achieved publication within the agreed levels of funding – despite being subject to some delays. During this final phase of analysis and reporting, the project has been hosted by Archaeological Services (WYAS), part of West Yorkshire Joint Services.

Additional support from English Heritage, in relation to the site finds, their storage and access, has been provided by Martin Allfrey, Kevin Booth, Susan Harrison and Andrew Morrison. A succession of curators of archaeology at Hull Museum and the late Pat Wiggle, voluntary curator of Malton Museum, are thanked for bringing the Wharram objects into the public arena through exhibitions.

This volume is the final definitive publication of the Wharram Research Project, and it is therefore appropriate to acknowledge the contribution made by all those who have participated in the field investigations and in the post-excavation analysis and reporting – though they are too numerous to name individually. Particular mention should, however, be made of those who supervised and assisted in the excavation of the major sites that are reported here for the first time: Paul Herbert, who supervised work on Sites 70, 72, 78 and 86 with the assistance of Mark Atkinson, Tim Quine, Simon Ware and Jonathan Watt, and Julian Richards who directed Sites 88, 89, 92, 98A and 98B, with the assistance of Julie Dunk and Ian Lawton.

As for the 2005 excavation in the North-west Enclosure, summarised in Chapter 5, Steve Roskams thanks Lord Middleton and Birdsall Estates Co. Ltd for allowing access and for continuing support of the fieldwork, and Mr Hoddy, tenant farmer of Wharram Percy, for facilitating the work; Julian Richards and Dave Haldenby for the metal-detecting survey of the site; Ben Gourley, who masterminded fieldwalking, remote sensing, kite photography and spatial recording; Madeleine Hummler, who co-directed the excavation work and also prepared an initial report of the excavation, on which the following account has drawn extensively; Mick Atha, Frank Clough, Rob Collins, Pat Gibbs, Dan Hull and Ian Milsted for supervising the excavations; Yvonne Luke and Tania Holmes for supervising finds processing and indexing; and finally the many undergraduate students of the University of York who made the greatest input, working in good spirits even in the worst downpours. The University's involvement in the Wharram Research Project was, of course, established by Professor Philip Rahtz, and it is our sad duty to record his death only a few months before this volume was published.

The other excavations summarised here for the first time are those carried out at Burdale as part of the University of York's training excavations (see Chapter 8). Steve Roskams thanks Madelaine Hummler, Steve Dobson and Ben Gourley for providing additional supervision. Initial interest in the site was prompted by Cath Neal's doctoral research. Metal detecting support was provided by Mark Ainsley, Geoff Bambrook, Ian Postlethwaite, and colleagues in Historia Detectum. Permission to carry out the fieldwork was granted by Lester Bell, tenant farmer, and by the landowners, Lord Middleton and Birdsall Estates Co. Ltd.

Other contributors to this volume offer their own acknowledgements. Emma Bentz (Chapter 2) thanks Ann Clark and Peggy Pullan for their help during her researches in the Wharram Site Archive in 2006. She is also indebted to Mona Rasmussen (Danmarks Nyere Tid, The National Museum of Denmark, Copenhagen) for her assistance with archival work on Axel Steensberg; Mette Svart Kristiansen (Department of Anthropology, Archaeology and Linguistics, Aarhus University), who shares a common interest in the life and work of Axel Steensberg, and Jes Wienberg (Institute of Archaeology and Ancient History, Lund University), who read and commented on an earlier version of the chapter.

The authors of Chapter 4 are grateful to English Heritage Geophysics Team colleagues, both past and present, who have contributed to the Wharram Percy surveys over the years. They include A. Bartlett, D. Bolton, A. Clark, P. Cottrell, M. Dabas (CNRS Garchy), D. Haddon-Reece, L. Martin, S. Noon, A. Payne and D. Shiel. Thanks are also due to Lord Middleton and Mr P. Hoddy for their patience in allowing access to the village site and surrounding fields over the years to carry out the geophysical surveys. Chapter 14 owes much to Christopher Whittick, who has identified many new sources of information relating to the lords of Wharram Percy in The National Archives and in the Borthwick Institute for Archives, and who has provided partial transcripts and calendars of those records. He, and Phillipa Hoskins and Dr Henry Summerson, have provided advice on their interpretation.

Chapter 15, the reinterpretation of the fabric history of St Martin's, was originally written as a brief appendix to accompany the analysis of the impact of the later medieval lords of Wharram on the physical form of the settlement (see Chapter 16). David Stocker acknowledges the help of Paul Everson during several days looking at the fabric and its phasing, and developing the complex arguments in relation to its interpretation. Paul was not only characteristically generous with his time and with his understandings, but also read the script at draft stage and offered several vital observations: the chapter could not exist without his input. The author is also grateful to Richard Morris who read an early draft of the script.

The editor's thanks are due first to the post-excavation team, whose members have maintained the project's momentum in the face of many obstacles: to Ann Clark, who has co-ordinated the specialists' work on finds and environmental evidence, as well as supervising the archiving of the finds; to Peggy Pullan, who has assisted Ann in organising the Wharram Site Archive; to Emmeline Marlow-Mann, who has prepared many of the illustrations which appear in this volume as well as site archive reports and the digital archives which have been made available through the Archaeology Data Service, and to Chris Philo who has prepared this and five previous volumes for publication. Hilary Cool created the index and the summary has been translated into German by Emma Bentz and into French by Charlette Sheil-Small.

There are also other contributors to this volume whose roles have been more significant than may be apparent in the chapter headings. Alison Deegan prepared new transcriptions of aerial photographic evidence for the Wharram area, as well as identifying photographs recording further archaeological sites in the study area, some of which are published here. The late Anna Slowikowski made available her analyses of Wharram's entire (surviving) medieval pottery assemblage, which it is hoped will also be the subject of an additional journal article. It is a great tragedy that she did not live to see the final publication of her nationally important work on the Wharram pottery assemblage. Jane Richardson pulled together a comprehensive analysis of the faunal assemblages from the Wharram excavations as far as this was possible, and made her conclusions available to the contributors of several chapters which appear below.

The editor's thanks are also due to the individuals and institutions that gave permission for photographs to be reproduced in this volume: Dr Anthony Crawshaw for the aerial photographs that form Plates 17 and 31; Sir Richard Storey, Bt, for the extracts from the plan of Settrington dated March 1600 (Plates 27 and 28); the Borthwick Institute for Archives (Plates 35 and 38); the Department of Geography, University of Cambridge (Plates 5 and 8), and the Anthony Laughton Pacitto Collection for Plate 33. Plates 11, 12, 26, 29, 30, 32, 34 and 39 were made available by English Heritage's National Monuments Record, and the editor thanks Liz Jenkins and Graham Deacon of the NMR Enquiry and Research Services for making the necessary arrangements.

Finally, the editor owes a considerable debt to those who read and commented on the draft volume: to Mark Gardiner for his valuable advice on many of the chapters which appear below, and to English Heritage's anonymous reader, whose recommendations with regard to the overall structure and length of the draft volume have made the complex and overlapping debates presented below rather easier to follow than they might otherwise have been.

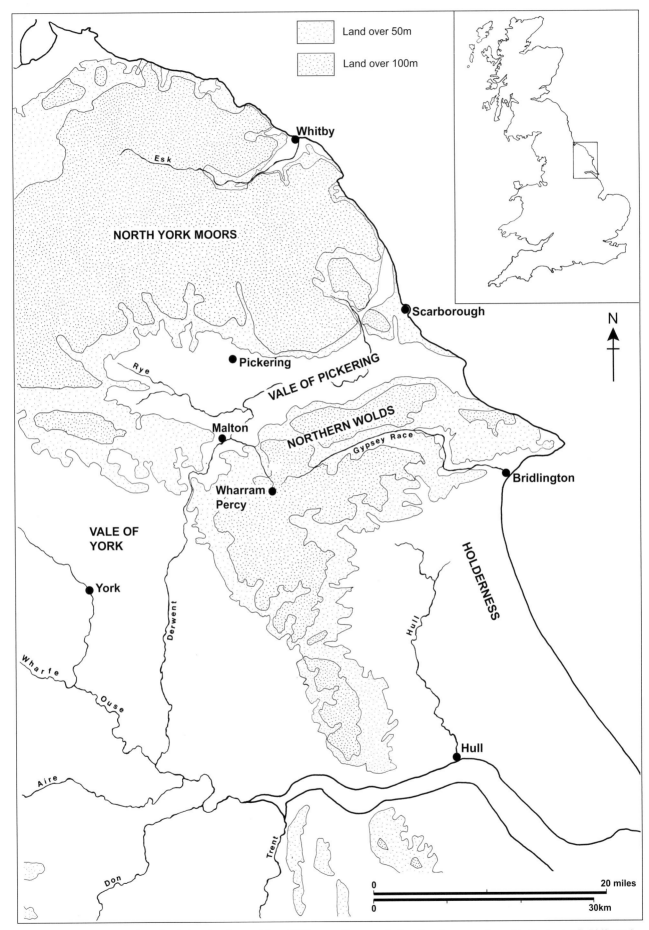

Fig. 1. Map of north-east England showing the position of Wharram Percy and other locations mentioned in the text. (C. Philo and E. Marlow-Mann)

Part One
Old Excavations, New Surveys

When, in 1990, the Wharram Research Project ceased working on site, the assemblages of records and finds from a large proportion of its excavations still awaited detailed analysis. Although some post-excavation work was carried out during the 1990s, it was not until the year 2000 that substantial progress began to be made. The results of much of that analysis have been published in the five most recent volumes in the series, *Wharram VIII-XII*, and *Wharram XIII* makes no attempt to summarise the contents of these or earlier publications. On the other hand, it is recognised that many readers of this volume will not have ready access to the earlier monographs, and might welcome brief notes on the one hundred excavation sites – ranging from open areas to small trenches – that were opened up between 1951 and 1990. Chapter 1, the first in this part of the volume, is intended to perform that function.

Plate 1. Open-area excavation at Wharram Percy: House 6 (Site 12) in 1962. (R. Glasscock)

By the end of its forty-year excavation campaign, the Wharram Research Project had become something of an institution, with its own traditions and folklore, and because of this it is hard, now, to appreciate that in its early years it occupied – and was intended to occupy – a spot on the frontier of research into medieval rural settlements. John Hurst designed it as a test-bed for the introduction to Britain of methodologies and lines of research that had been developed on the Continent. For example, the decision to attempt a complete excavation of the church was a response to similar excavations that had already taken place in Holland and Germany (Beresford and Hurst 1976, 128; *Interim Rep.* 11 (1963), 4), and experimentation with open-area excavation techniques, in 1953, came in response to the methodologies pioneered in Denmark by Axel Steensberg (*Interim Rep.* 2 (1954), 1;

Hurst 1956, 271-3). Steensberg's influence on the techniques employed at Wharram has frequently been asserted but never analysed in depth. Emma Bentz's recent study of Wharram's 'Danish connection' has rectified this omission; it is the subject of Chapter 2.

Though the chapters on the excavations are, inevitably, retrospective, Chapters 3 and 4 present new earthwork and geophysical surveys that have, in several important respects, revolutionised our understanding of Wharram's settlement history. Earthwork survey has a long and distinguished history at Wharram Percy – in fact, longer than most, as the first recorded survey of the late medieval vicarage earthworks was conducted on 26 July, 1555 by the vicars of three neighbouring parishes (Wrathmell 2010b, 20). Some of the main village earthworks were included on the Ordnance Survey's first edition (1854) six-inch scale map, surveyed 1850-51, and this depiction was substantially revised for the 25-inch scale map (1890) surveyed in 1888. A much more detailed plan was created in 1954 by G.L. Worsley of the Ordnance Survey as part of the Wharram Research Project. During the remaining years of the project, this plan was augmented with additional surveys, carried out by W.J. Hopkins, also of the Ordnance Survey, by C. Mahany and others, and with transcriptions of ridge-and-furrow cultivation and other earthworks visible on aerial photographs. All these sources of information were combined into a single plan by the Project's chief surveyor, R.T. Porter, again of the Ordnance Survey. Once redrawn, this final product, which makes its last appearance in this series as Figure 2, seemed consistent and comprehensive, serving as the standard depiction of the site in countless publications.

In reality, the plan had developed organically over the course of 25 years and was a composite of differing theoretical expectations, observational skills and survey methods (including working scales). There had been occasional revisions of the field survey in the light of discoveries made using other techniques; this methodological dialogue was certainly productive, but further eroded the consistency of the end-product. Therefore, in 1998 the Wharram Post-excavation and Publication Project submitted a request to the Royal Commission on the Historical Monuments of England (RCHME), which in the following year merged with English Heritage, for a fresh and comprehensive analytical earthwork survey and investigation to inform the forthcoming synthesis of the excavated evidence.

While the timetable for this work was still under discussion, English Heritage began the preparation in

2001 of Conservation Statements to lay the foundations for more detailed Conservation Plans for monuments in Guardianship in the Yorkshire Region. Accordingly, in November 2001, Alastair Oswald, Stewart Ainsworth and Trevor Pearson of English Heritage's Archaeological Survey and Investigation Team carried out a rapid examination of the site (at Level 1 standard, as defined in Ainsworth *et al.* 2007). This assessment noted several potentially important features not recorded by the earlier surveys and specific places where stratigraphic relationships visible on the ground were not accurately conveyed by the existing plan. It was suspected, too, that certain fundamental issues could be addressed through a more analytical approach to the village plan as a whole.

The parallel needs of the Wharram Project and English Heritage (as curators of the site) culminated, in 2002, in a thorough and detailed re-examination of the earthworks at Level 3 standard (as defined in Ainsworth *et al.* 2007). The full report on this work was published by English Heritage (Oswald 2004), and a shortened and updated version is now available on the Archaeology Data Service (doi:10.5284/1000415). The summary version published here as Chapter 3, which itself reflects developments in other strands of research in the five years after 2004, focuses on the most significant findings in relation to our understanding of settlement development at Wharram Percy.

The story of geophysical survey at Wharram follows a similar course. The first geophysical survey was undertaken in 1970, and visits to the site continued until 1989, prior to the final season of excavation, by which time a total of eight separate surveys had been carried out. During subsequent assessment of the survey evidence to produce this synthesis it was realised that the conclusions could be strengthened if magnetometer survey coverage were extended to the southern part of the plateau area, above the valley due west of St Martin's church. This part of the site had not previously been comprehensively surveyed and the extent of pre-village occupation there was unclear.

Furthermore, between 1970 and 1989 several generations of magnetometer had been employed. Development of the technique over this period meant that the instrument used for the 1989 survey was ten times more sensitive than those used earlier. In addition, digital recording of the magnetometer results had first been possible for the 1987 and 1989 surveys owing to advances in computer technology. Prior to this, measurements were recorded as a continuous paper trace using a portable chart recorder, making the results almost impossible to reanalyse quantitatively or to integrate with other surveys. Finally, different grid alignments had been used over the course of the project and combining the results of the various, often overlapping, survey areas would not be straightforward.

It was thus decided that the most desirable course of action would be for the English Heritage Geophysics Team to carry out a new magnetometer survey, using modern instruments, over all parts of the Guardianship area where survey was practicable. Those areas of the surrounding arable fields adjacent to the Guardianship area would also be covered, so that, where necessary, archaeological anomalies could be traced beyond the immediate area of the medieval village. This strategy offered the benefit of providing a complete magnetic map for all the open areas of Wharram Percy. The data were referenced to a single survey grid established to a high degree of accuracy using modern satellite global positioning system (GPS) equipment. As a result, the site was visited by the Geophysics Team between 16 and 25 September 2002, during which period the entire site was surveyed. Full details of the remarkably informative 2002 survey, summarised in Chapter 4, have been reported by Linford and Linford (2003) where the results of the survey visits made in 1984, 1987 and 1989 are also recorded. Once again, a shortened and updated version is now available on the Archaeology Data Service (doi:10.5284/1000415). Results of the five earlier surveys up until 1982 have been reported by David (1982).

Most readers of this volume would expect earthwork and geophysical survey to be carried out prior to an excavation, and the results of these surveys then to inform excavation strategy. Simply because of the longevity of the excavation programme at Wharram, and because of the technological advances in survey equipment and methodologies that took place during this period, the role of English Heritage's new surveys has been to explain the results of excavation, instead of informing their planning. This is best exemplified in Sites 70 and 78, which were dug in places where small plantations of trees were due to be established on the boundaries of the Guardianship site. Both provided evidence of Middle Saxon occupation to the west of the known village site, evidence that lacked an intelligible framework until the 2002 geophysical survey. Similarly, the findings of the new earthwork survey have encouraged us to rethink the late medieval history of the village.

This is as it should be: Wharram is a settlement site which retains the potential to yield new understandings that could and should, one day (but preferably not too soon), overturn the ideas presented in this volume. All too often, the cessation of a programme of excavation on a settlement site seems to have signalled the end of its relevance for research. It has been abandoned twice: first by its inhabitants and secondly by the archaeological research community. For those sites that were investigated in advance of complete destruction this is inevitable; but for sites that have substantially, or even partially survived, this need not be the end of the story. The Wharram Site Archive, and of course the site itself, still have the potential to generate new data, and will continue to do so as long as archaeologists remain engaged with them. Only when Wharram is no longer interrogated will it cease to play an active role in the development of new ideas about medieval rural settlement.

1 The Excavations, 1950-1990

by Emmeline Marlow-Mann and Stuart Wrathmell

Introduction

The current phase of post-excavation and publication work began in the year 2000, and at that stage a policy decision was made with regard to the content of this final volume. It would attempt to provide readers with a history of human activity at Wharram from the later prehistoric times to the end of the Middle Ages, and to set that activity in the context of the experience of neighbouring communities; but it would not attempt to summarise in any consistent way the excavation data presented in the previous twelve volumes. Excavation data are included here for one of two reasons: either they relate to sites for which definitive information has not previously been made available in print; or they relate to artefacts and structural remains that seemed to the contributors to be worthy of elaboration or in need of reinterpretation.

Nevertheless, it is recognised that this approach will make it difficult for readers to follow up data or interpretations published in previous site reports. For this reason, the following summaries have been provided, site by site, for all the excavations, with a reference to the definitive publication(s) where appropriate, or in the case of sites not fully published in print, to the Archive Report disseminated through the Archaeology Data Service (doi:10.5284/1000415). The location of each site is shown on the accompanying earthwork plan (Fig. 2). The excavation sites are marked in red against the earthwork plan that was in use during the later stages of the excavations, because it was this plan, not the more recent English Heritage survey (Ch. 3), that framed many of the questions which these excavations were intended to answer.

Before moving on to the site summaries, it is worth noting some overall quantities in relation to the effort put into the project and its products. Over the forty years, the excavations totalled just under 10,000 sq.m, representing about 6.5% of the Scheduled area (which includes the village green and part of the valley floor, but excludes the western and, potentially, northern parts of the Middle Saxon settlement). Not all the excavations reached chalk bedrock or clay 'natural': those in the areas of the Vicarage and Farmstead were mainly taken down only as far as late medieval levels.

A more remarkable aspect of the excavations at Wharram, in comparison with those carried out on other medieval village sites, is the quantity of artefacts and faunal material recovered. Wharram produced just over 220,000 fragments of animal bone, a figure that can be compared with those of other northern village excavations at Hillam, West Yorkshire (under 2700 fragments) and Thrislington, County Durham (over 5000 fragments). The Wharram project generated about 75,000 sherds of pottery (Hillam under 14,500, Thrislington under 7000). The number of iron objects was over 13,000

(Hillam under 300, Thrislington just over 100), and there were nearly 2000 non-ferrous metal objects (Hillam under 20, Thrislington under 100: information derived or estimated from Grassam 2010 and Austin 1989). These comments are not intended to cast doubt on the efficacy of the finds recovery strategies at Hillam, Thrislington or any other deserted village excavations; rather, they are made to emphasise that, despite the relatively small areas of Wharram so far excavated, the size of the artefact collection is exceptional. It is hoped that future scholars will find value in exploring further the extensive Site Archive in decades to come.

Excavation site summaries

Sites 1 and 2 (*Wharram IX*, 10, fig. 6)
Excavations across earthworks in the North Manor Area in 1950 revealed some wall foundations, up to three courses high. No detailed records survive.

Site 3 (*Wharram VI*, 15, fig. 6)
Also in 1950, trenches were opened along the inner faces of Area 15, Building 15 to investigate its construction. The building measured 12.5m by 4.3m; the walls were chalk rubble blocks laid roughly in courses, between 0.53m and 0.61m thick.

Site 4 (unpublished)
This trench was opened in the same year to investigate an area of disturbance suggested by a patch of heavy vegetation. No archaeological features were encountered and very little pottery was recovered.

Site 5 (unpublished)
Also in 1950, a trench was cut across the bank marking the south side of the east-west hollow way. No archaeological features were encountered and it was considered that any road surfaces would be at a much deeper level.

Site 6 (*Wharram VI*, 15, fig. 5)
In 1951, several trenches were excavated within Area 12, Building 12 to establish the size and construction of the walls. The building was found to be 14.6m by 4m, the side walls having a thickness of 0.53m.

Site 7 (unpublished)
Also in 1951, a trench was opened to investigate Building 20, east of the North Manor Area. Only the walls were exposed, showing that they had been constructed of chalk and reused sandstone blocks. It was 10-10.5m by 3.4-3.5m.

Site 8 (*Wharram VI*, 33-4, fig. 25)
This trench was opened in 1952 to investigate Area 5, Building 5. A two-phase building was revealed, composed of chalk blocks; no evidence of function was recorded. To the north was the northern end of a structure (Building 8) which may represent a narrower continuation of the second-phase structure of Building 5.

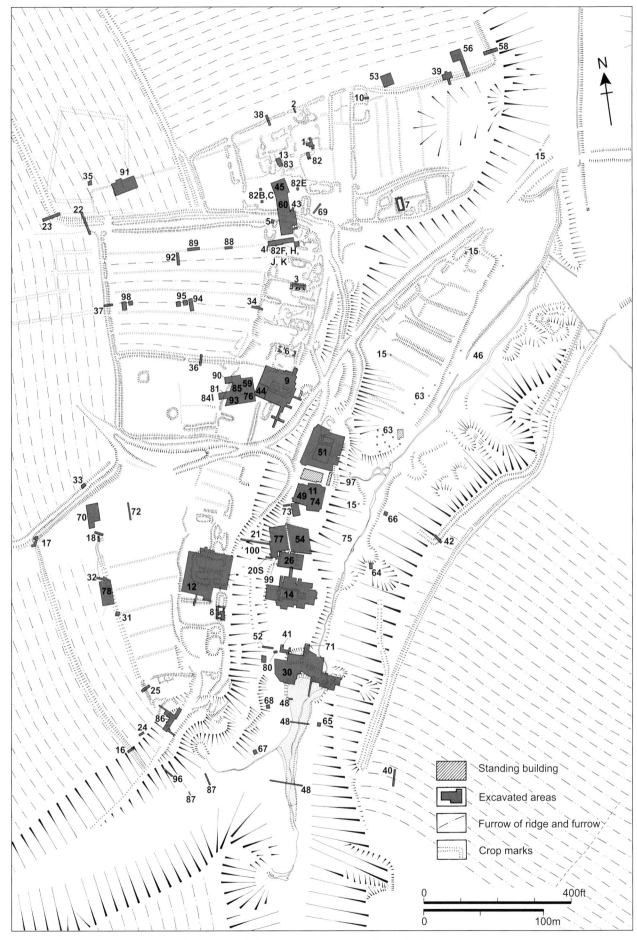

Fig. 2. Plan of Wharram Percy showing excavated sites. (C. Philo and E. Marlow-Mann)

Site 9 (*Wharram I*, 26-41, *VI*, 15, fig. 7 and *VIII*)
Area 10 was marked by the most prominent earthworks on the plateau and was chosen as an experiment in the open-area excavation of a complete medieval peasant house, beginning in 1953. The excavations unexpectedly revealed the undercroft of an earlier manorial complex (the South Manor), and evidence of extensive quarrying immediately after the manorial buildings had been abandoned.

Site 10 (unpublished)
In 1954, a small trench was excavated immediately east of the north-east corner of the North Manor enclosure. It revealed a chalk rubble bank.

Site 11 (*Wharram XII*, 64)
An ashlar wall was encountered during the digging of one of the excavation team's rubbish pits, which led to the subsequent exploration of this area as part of Sites 49 and 74.

Site 12 (*Wharram I*, 42-54 and *VI*, 23-33)
This investigation, begun in 1960, was part of the second major phase of peasant-house excavations and was focused on Area 6. It revealed a series of domestic and ancillary buildings which were subject to a wide range of structural changes throughout their use.

Site 13 (*Wharram IX*, 10-13 and *XIII*)
A trench was dug across the south side of one of the North Manor buildings to try to determine the date of this earthwork complex. A large Late Iron Age and Roman ditch was uncovered, along with a later burial which is reconsidered in Chapter 7 below.

Site 14 (*Wharram III, XI* and *XIII*)
In 1962 a major excavation began in the church of St Martin, to determine its full structural sequence from the erection of the earliest church building down to its post-medieval phases. Adjacent areas of the churchyard were also investigated to record medieval and later burials. A new analysis of the church fabric and a revised phasing of its structural history are presented in Chapter 15, below.

Site 15 (unpublished; Site Archive)
Four trenches were dug in advance of the installation of electricity pylons to bring power to Wharram Percy Farm. A small fragment of chalk walling was revealed in the trench for Pylon 2; the trench was too small for further interpretation.

Site 16 (unpublished; Site Archive)
The aim of Site 16 was to section the outer boundary bank to the west of the southern block of Plateau crofts. Two phases of linear features and banks were recorded; these were cut by a V-shaped ditch.

Site 17 (unpublished; Site Archive)
This site was opened to investigate the boundary which ran south-westwards from the south-west corner of the South Manorial enclosure. A series of ditches and banks was revealed but could not be accurately dated.

Site 18 (*Wharram XIII*, 130)
Three trenches were dug to investigate the line of the so-called 'inner boundary ditch' which delineated the ends of the southern block of crofts. A sequence of ditches suggested a boundary feature in use over a long period of time; they are recorded in Chapter 9 below.

Site 19 (unpublished; Site Archive; west of area shown on Fig. 2)
In 1970, a rectangular enclosure in the former open fields, west of the village site, was investigated before being levelled by ploughing. The south bank was sectioned and the south-east entrance excavated, identifying a possible post-medieval sheep enclosure.

Site 20 (*Wharram XI*, 57-8 and *XII*, 69 and finds)
Two trenches, Sites 20 and 21, were dug as part of a series of exploratory trenches down the hillside to the north-west of the church. A revetment wall and part of a stone stepped track (see Site 100) were revealed.

Site 21 (*Wharram XI*, 57-8 and *XII*, 69 and finds))
See Site 20 above.

Site 22 (*Wharram IX*, 297-300)
A trench was opened across the hollow way and boundary banks south of the North-West Enclosure to establish the chronological development of the village's principal boundaries. A Roman ditch was revealed, marking the southern boundary of the trackway along the south side of the North-West Enclosure.

Site 23 (*Wharram IX*, 300-302)
Site 23 was excavated at a point where the double-bank earthwork was replaced by a single broad bank. A Roman ditch, and a medieval wall and stone kerb were the principal features excavated at this site.

Site 24 (unpublished; Site Archive)
Site 24 was opened in order to investigate a feature identified by magnetometer survey. Excavation revealed a ditch aligned north-west to south-east lying between, and roughly parallel to, the inner and outer western boundaries of the southern block of Plateau crofts.

Site 25 (unpublished; Site Archive)
Site 25 was located across the 'inner western boundary' bank of the southern block of Plateau crofts. A north-south ditch was recorded, together with a later bank capped by a single course of chalk block walling.

Site 26 (*Wharram XI*, 30-64)
Site 26 was opened to investigate the northern part of the graveyard, and several phases of burials were uncovered. In other phases, however, structural remains and occupation debris rather than burials were revealed, indicating shifts in the graveyard's northern boundary.

Site 27 (unpublished)
This site code relates to finds recovered during the erection of the Guardianship fence.

Site 28 (unpublished)
Site codes 28 and 29 were allocated to objects found during ecological work in the valley.

Site 29 (unpublished)
See Site 28 above.

Site 30 (*Wharram X*, 26-69)
Parts of the pond and the dam at the southern end of the village site were excavated from 1972 to 1982. The evidence indicated Anglo-Saxon water management and milling, though the pond appears to have functioned as a general purpose village pond in the later Middle Ages.

Site 31 (unpublished; Site Archive)
A small trench was opened up in order to investigate the intersection of two features revealed on the magnetometer survey. A ditch, two post-holes and various linear features were recorded.

Site 32 (*Wharram XIII*, 130-33)
This east-west trench was excavated to investigate the anomalies recorded by geophysical survey. A sequence of north-south boundary ditches was revealed, some of them apparently Anglo-Saxon in date (see Ch. 9 below).

Site 33 (unpublished; Site Archive)
Site 33 was excavated on the headland which ran south-west to north-east beyond the north-west corner of the southern block of Plateau crofts. A boundary ditch and bank were recorded on a north-west to south-east alignment.

Site 34 (unpublished; Site Archive)
A trench was cut across the lynchet which separated the toft of House 13 from its croft with the aim of investigating the construction date and characteristics of the lynchet. Two linear features were recorded; these were later filled and the bank built up. On top of the bank a dry stone chalk wall or revetment was probably medieval.

Site 35 (unpublished)
A small area was excavated within the North-west Enclosure; no archaeological features were encountered.

Site 36 (unpublished; Site Archive)
Site 36 was located across the boundary bank on the north side of the South Manor enclosure. A sequence of successive boundary ditches was recorded, some overlain by an earthen bank, topped by a chalk block wall, which possibly originated as a ploughing ridge.

Site 37 (unpublished; Site Archive)
This trench was opened in order to section one of the main medieval boundary banks west of the West Row

(North) crofts. A V-shaped ditch was recorded, backfilled in Roman times. A further ditch and bank were revealed, associated with medieval pottery.

Site 38 (*Wharram IX*, 19)
A north-south trench was excavated across the northern boundary of the North Manorial Enclosure. At least four phases of this boundary were apparent, the final phase consisting of a wall footing set into the south side of the bank.

Site 39 (*Wharram VII*, 5-12)
This trench was excavated to establish the form of the northern boundary bank and the date of the enclosure. A Middle Saxon *Grubenhaus* was revealed, cut by a medieval east-west boundary ditch.

Site 40 (unpublished)
A trench was cut across the ridge and furrow east of the south end of the settlement area to make an assessment of manuring inclusions within a localised area of ridging. Only recent metalwork and brick were uncovered.

Site 41 (*Wharram XI*, 65-70)
Site 41 was investigated in order to ascertain the limits of the southern graveyard boundary. There was evidence of intermittent occupational activity, starting in Roman times, superseded by a series of medieval burials.

Site 42 (unpublished)
This trench cut through a bank and ditch earthwork which occupied the crest of the eastern valley side. The ditch had been cut through ploughsoil and its upcast was formed into a bank on its west side.

Site 43 (*Wharram IX*, 79-81)
A trench was cut to date the hollow way and to determine the date and construction of what appeared to be the southern boundary of the North Manor. Excavation revealed a sequence of Iron Age to Anglo-Saxon features.

Site 44 (*Wharram VIII*, 17-18)
This site was excavated with the aim of locating a timber hall associated with the undercroft building previously located in Site 9. In the event, no timber hall was identified, but a considerable amount of Anglo-Saxon pottery was recovered.

Site 45 (*Wharram IX*, 19-35)
In 1977 work began on an area within the North Manorial enclosure, south of the main group of medieval buildings marked by earthworks. The excavation revealed a concentration of features datable to the Later Iron Age and Early Roman periods.

Site 46 (unpublished; Site Archive)
A survey of the present-day soils around Wharram Percy was undertaken in order to produce a map of modern soils. This was generated to form a basis for comparison

with buried soils associated with the archaeological sites and also with ecological records.

Site 47 (unpublished)
This site code relates to finds recovered during repairs to the track leading down to the cottages.

Site 48 (unpublished)
This was a trench excavated across the southern end of the pond (Site 30).

Site 49 (*Wharram XII*, 62-6)
This site was excavated with the aim of uncovering the farmhouse yard and trackway shown on 19th-century maps. A much-repaired surface and trackway were revealed, together with post-medieval ditches and a complex of rubbish pits from the 1950s excavations.

Site 50 (unpublished)
This site code relates to finds recovered during concreting work.

Site 51 (*Wharram XII*, 42-56)
Site 51 was a series of excavations in the area of the 18th and early 19th-century outbuildings belonging to Wharram Percy Farm. Only one of the building ranges, that on the west, was reasonably well-preserved; it overlay medieval structural remains.

Site 52 (*Wharram XI*, 64-5)
The purpose of the excavation was to examine the line of the medieval and post-medieval terraced way which skirted the west boundary of the churchyard. No evidence of a trackway was revealed, but three medieval burials were excavated.

Site 53 (unpublished)
This site was excavated in advance of tree planting to the north of the village boundary. No archaeological features were revealed.

Site 54 (*Wharram XII*, 86-118)
The aim of the excavation was to continue the examination of the occupation sequence on the terrace around the church. The post-medieval vicarage was fully excavated and the site revealed a long sequence of earlier structures and buildings.

Site 55 (unpublished)
This site code relates to all stray surface finds recovered from the area of the village.

Site 56 (unpublished; Site Archive)
This site was opened in advance of tree planting to the north of the village boundary bank. A sequence of banks and ditches was revealed.

Site 57 (part published in *Wharram V*, 104-26)
This site code relates to finds recovered during fieldwalking.

Site 58 (unpublished; Site Archive)
A trench was cut across the boundary which ran northwards from the north-east corner of the village site. Two ditches and a bank were excavated but their relationships could not be established.

Site 59 (*Wharram VIII*, 32-35, 38-43 and 47)
Site 59 was the first of a series of adjacent areas excavated within the South Manor enclosure, beyond the south-west corner of Site 44. Sites 59, 76, 81, 84, 85, 90 and 93 uncovered extensive structural remains, including a smithy, dating to the Middle Saxon period, overlain by a layer of buried soil containing Late Saxon artefacts. Cut into the layer were features relating to the South Manor complex, and these were in turn overlain by later medieval peasant buildings. The Middle Saxon smithy and its products are further discussed below in Chapters 9 and 10.

Site 60 (*Wharram IX*, 35-103)
Site 60 extended southwards from Site 45 over the area considered to be the courtyard and southern boundary of the North Manor complex. Major ditch features were revealed, dating to the Iron Age and Roman periods, while a well-built stone structure with subterranean elements represented a later Roman oven. Two *Grubenhäuser* were also located.

Site 61 (*Wharram IV*, sections 15-28)
This number relates to the field survey and limited excavation of Wharram Grange Roman Villa.

Site 62 (*Wharram IV*, sections 1-14)
This number relates to the field survey and limited excavation of Wharram le Street Roman Villa.

Site 63 (unpublished; Site Archive)
Fifteen one metre square trenches were excavated in advance of tree planting. Two of the trenches revealed possible stony surfaces.

Site 64 (unpublished)
This site was excavated in advance of tree planting. No archaeological features were encountered.

Site 65 (unpublished)
Site 65 was excavated in advance of tree planting. Stake-holes were revealed, probably of 19th and 20th-century date.

Site 66 (unpublished)
This site was excavated in advance of tree planting. No archaeological features were encountered.

Site 67 (*Wharram X*, 71)
This test pit was dug to investigate the archaeology prior to tree planting. A series of chalk surfaces was excavated, some probably of late medieval date.

Site 68 (unpublished)
This excavation was undertaken in advance of tree planting. No archaeological features were revealed.

Site 69 (*Wharram IX*, 103-9)
Test trenches were located west, east and south of Site 60 to determine whether any substantial Roman structures were in the vicinity. A sequence of ditches from Iron Age or Roman to medieval times may have represented either a drainage or boundary function.

Site 70 (*Wharram XIII*, 125-30)
This excavation was undertaken in advance of tree planting and was specifically located to identify continuations of ditches and other features recorded on surrounding sites. A sequence of Middle Saxon boundary ditches and possible cart ruts was revealed (Ch. 9 below).

Site 71 (*Wharram X*, 26-69)
This area was opened in order to investigate the sequence of graveyard boundaries and to relate stratification to the excavations on Site 30. Excavation revealed water management channels and evidence of relatively high-status domestic occupation in the vicinity.

Site 72 (*Wharram XIII*, 130-33)
Site 72 was excavated in order to confirm the alignment of the road or track and other features revealed in Site 70. Three ditches were revealed, one probably of Middle Saxon date (see Ch. 9 below).

Site 73 (*Wharram XII*, 66-8)
The aim of excavation was to locate and interpret a small structure identified on maps of 1836-1855 as a stable. A number of surfaces and wall fragments indicated possible structures and yard surfaces. These were heavily disturbed by modern pits.

Site 74 (*Wharram XII*, 33-42)
Site 74, immediately south of the surviving cottages, was positioned in order to uncover the whole of the latest farmhouse on the village site. The early 19th-century building was uncovered, and it was found to overlay an earlier farmhouse occupied during the late 17th and 18th centuries.

Site 75 (unpublished)
This number relates to work on the valley side below the Vicarage.

Site 76 (*Wharram VIII*, 32-7, 45-6 and 52-6)
See Site 59 above.

Site 77 (*Wharram XII*, 69-86)
Excavations on Site 77 were undertaken to investigate the substantial building remains uncovered within earlier trenches on the western valley side (Sites 20 and 21). Excavation revealed many fragments of walling and floors relating to 15th, 16th and 17th-century vicarage buildings, few of them surviving in a coherent form.

Site 78 (*Wharram XIII*, 130-33)
Site 78 was investigated in advance of tree planting. A series of enclosure ditches, previously encountered on Site 32, was uncovered. Some of the ditches and apparently associated structural features are dated to the Middle Saxon period (see Ch. 9 below).

Site 79 (unpublished)
Two cesspits on the valley floor were excavated. Two pieces of glass and many fragments of pottery were recovered.

Site 80 (*Wharram XI*, 217)
This trench was excavated for the construction of a drainage sump, south of the churchyard gate. Excavation revealed an articulated human skeleton.

Site 81 (*Wharram VIII*, 26-32, 37-8, 55-6)
See Site 59 above.

Site 82 (*Wharram IX*, 109-138)
Site 82 consisted of a number of small trenches and test-holes dug around the periphery of Site 60. They revealed a series of major boundary ditches of Late Iron Age to Early Roman date, and parts of medieval peasant buildings towards the north end of the West Row (North) tofts.

Site 83 (*Wharram IX*, 13-19)
This was a re-excavation of Site 13, carried out to resolve ambiguities in the interpretation and dating of the recorded features. Considerable quantities of Late Iron Age and Early Roman pottery were recovered, along with a burial (p. 78 below) and medieval wall foundations.

Site 84 (*Wharram VIII*, 26)
The Site 84 trench was opened to check the alignment of the possibly Roman ditch extending westwards from Site 81. The ditch was uncovered.

Site 85 (*Wharram VIII*, 28-9, 32, 35-6, 37, 45-6, 55)
See Site 59 above.

Site 86 (*Wharram XIII*, 133-5 and unpublished; Site Archive)
Site 86 was opened to investigate the archaeological potential of the area prior to tree planting. A possible terracing cut was the earliest feature recorded on this site along with Anglo-Saxon artefacts (see Ch. 9 below). Above were the remains of walls probably representing a medieval outbuilding.

Site 87 (unpublished)
Two trenches were opened to investigate the archaeological potential of this area in advance of tree planting; no archaeological features were encountered.

Site 88 (unpublished; Site Archive)
Site 88 was opened up in order to calibrate the results of a magnetometer survey and to provide phasing information for the features it had revealed. A series of gullies and linear features was revealed.

Site 89 (unpublished; Site Archive)
This trench was opened to calibrate the results of the magnetometer survey and to provide phasing for the recorded features. A sequence of east-west and north-south ditches probably dated to the Late Iron Age and Roman periods.

Site 90 (*Wharram VIII*, fig. 30)
See Site 59 above. This site was only excavated to its late medieval occupation surfaces.

Site 91 (*Wharram IX*, 302-12)
This trench was opened to assess archaeological potential in advance of tree planting. It was located at the intersection of two linear features revealed by geophysical survey and aerial photography. Part of the boundary ditch of the North-west Enclosure was excavated and dated to the Roman period, along with other remains.

Site 92 (unpublished; Site Archive)
Site 92 was excavated to calibrate the results of the magnetometer survey and to provide phasing for the recorded features. Excavation revealed a series of ditches and surfaces, dating from the Iron Age to medieval periods.

Site 93 (*Wharram VIII*, 37, 43, 46 and 56)
See Site 59 above.

Site 94 (*Wharram VII*, 13-25 and *XIII*, 121-23)
Sites 94, 95A and 95B were excavated with the aim of investigating and calibrating intersecting linear features identified on the magnetometer survey. They revealed ditches dating to the Late Iron Age and Roman periods, and also uncovered a *Grubenhaus* dating to the Middle Saxon period, a structure that seems to have been a metal workshop on the basis of finds from its backfill. These remains are further discussed in Chapter 9 below.

Site 95 (*Wharram VII*, 13-25 and *XIII*, 121-23)
See Site 94 above for Sites 95A and 95B.

Site 96 (unpublished)
This trench was excavated in advance of tree planting on the slope of the plateau at its south end. Excavation revealed three ditches which probably functioned as drainage channels, running obliquely to the slope.

Site 97 (unpublished)
This number records work around the head of one of the springs issuing from the valley side.

Site 98 (*Wharram XIII*, 123-4)
The trenches recorded as Site 98A and Site 98B were opened in order to calibrate the results of the magnetometer survey and to provide phasing for the linear features identified in the survey. A series of ditches was dated to the Romano-British and Anglo-Saxon periods.

Site 99 (*Wharram XI*, 59-60 and *XII*)
Site 99 was opened as an extension trench in order to trace the line of a wall which was recorded on Site 77. The wall was a continuation of the major east-west wall recorded on Site 26.

Site 100 (*Wharram XI*, 58-9 and *XII*)
This extension trench was opened in order to investigate the substantial stone feature recorded in the south-west corner of Site 77. Several stone 'steps' were recorded, at the bottom of a hillside path leading up to the plateau.

Recording methodologies

The forty-year programme of excavations witnessed a wide variety of excavation and recording techniques. Though John Hurst, as the overall project director, determined the aims and objectives of the excavation programme, the methods of investigation were left very much in the hands of the individual site supervisors. Procedures for recording layers and structural features therefore varied according to the background of each supervisor: some chose single context recording because it was the method they used in the course of their employment outside Wharram; others did not.

Such procedural devolution was both a strength and a weakness: the project was not shackled to a single recording system that became gradually outdated during the course of the work; on the other hand, the variations resulted in some of the excavation sites being far more satisfactorily recorded than others. A similar devolution in the recording methodologies for artefacts and other finds was for the most part avoided, thanks to Ann Clark's introduction, in 1977, of a recording system based on that then used by the Central Excavation Unit of what was to become English Heritage. It was ultimately applied to all the sites, retrospectively where necessary.

During the course of the project there were several debates about excavation methodologies, one of the sharpest occurring in 1984, in relation to the application to Wharram of sampling strategies (see *Wharram IX*, 8, 103-16). One of the authors of this chapter was vigorously engaged with that debate, and it therefore seems best to leave a detailed review of the issues and outcomes to future researchers who have a greater distance from the arguments, and who can explore the relevant documentation in the Site Archive. No less controversial in its day was the introduction, in 1953, of open-area excavation techniques similar to those in contemporary use in Denmark; these form the subject of the next chapter.

2   The Danish Connection: Axel Steensberg and Wharram Percy

by Emma Bentz

Introduction

The archaeological investigations conducted at Wharram Percy over more than 40 years have made the site perhaps the best-known of all excavated English medieval rural settlements, particularly outside the British Isles. There are many reasons for this; one, obviously, being the extended lifespan of the project. The recurrent excavations taking place during a three-week season each summer from 1952 to 1990 offered students – many later to become professional archaeologists - a first insight into the technique of excavating medieval rural sites, and Wharram soon turned into 'an epicentre of activity for medieval archaeologists' (Gerrard 2003, 103), and a social institution. Traces of the latter can be seen in the Site Archive where manuscripts of theatre plays, invitations to the annual reunions at John Hurst's home and personal memories of time spent in Wharram have been filed. Yet another factor contributing to Wharram as a kind of 'collective memory' for medieval (rural) archaeology is the extensive production of the site's modern research history, mainly written by Maurice Beresford and John Hurst (e.g. Hurst 1956; 1985; 1988; Beresford and Hurst 1990).

This article focuses on one of the recurrent themes in these representations, forming a central part of the Wharram narrative, namely the Danish researcher Axel Steensberg and his methodological influence on early excavations at Wharram, resulting in the introduction of open area excavation. Until now there have not been any detailed attempts to investigate what this postulated methodological transfer looked like in practice and several questions arise. Why and how was the 'Danish connection' established? Which elements of Steensberg's archaeological practice were taken over and incorporated on the British site? What modifications were made? To answer these questions a comparison has been made between the excavations of the Danish site Store Valby (Zealand), where five historically known farmsteads were excavated in 1945-46 and 1949-53 under the direction of Steensberg, and the excavation of the peasant houses in Area 10 (1953-60: Site 9, see Fig. 2) at Wharram Percy. In order to do so, published material as well as archived material in the form of original field documentation and correspondence has been included in the study (Bentz 2008).

It is worth emphasising that the scope of this article does not include an attempt to re-evaluate original interpretations – something that has been done for parts of Steensberg's work (Foged Klemensen 1992; Svart Kristiansen 2009) and also in the case of Wharram Percy (*Wharram VI*). Rather, the main objective is to look in detail at the contacts between a group of researchers, their exchange of ideas - principally concerning the archaeological study of medieval rural settlements - and the consequences this interchange eventually had for excavation practice on the two sites of Store Valby and Wharram Percy.

Axel Steensberg (1906-1999) (Plate 2)

Plate 2. Axel Steensberg (1906-1999) guiding visitors at the Borup Ris site on Zealand, his last major excavation. (Grith Lerche, *c*. 1980, reproduced by permission of the Danish National Museum)

Although the non-Danish reader might already be acquainted with parts of Steensberg's life and work - due to Danish researchers' numerous publications in English and many international contacts and commitments - a biographical outline is given below. In accordance with the scope of this chapter, emphasis lies on Steensberg's archaeological activities.

Devoting a lifetime to the study of different aspects of farming and peasant life, Steensberg himself also had a rural background. He grew up on a farm in the parish of Sinding on west Jutland, where he worked as a peasant until the age of 20 (Lerche 1976; 2000; Rasmussen 1983; Engberg 1994; *Kraks Blå Bog* 1998). With the aim of becoming a teacher in history and geography, Steensberg entered the Askov Folk High School in 1926. These studies were continued in Copenhagen and led to a teacher's degree in 1930 (history) and 1932 (geography). Working as a teacher only for a short time, Steensberg continued his studies and enrolled at the University of

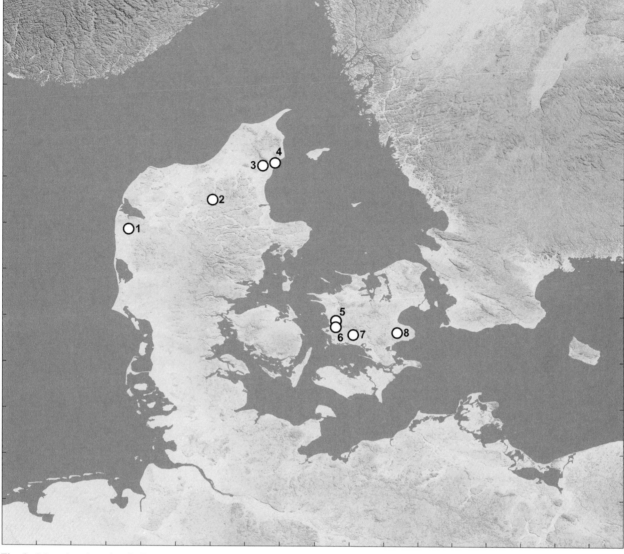

Fig. 3. Map showing sites in Denmark excavated by Axel Steensberg. (E. Bentz)

1 Alstrup Hede. Surveying and mapping of field systems in 1939 and 1950 (Steensberg 1957)
2 Nødskov Hede. Two medieval farmsteads and a wall feature investigated in 1942 (Steensberg 1952)
3 Bolle. Excavation of a mill, houses and an iron production site in 1938-9 (Steensberg 1952). Additionally, in 1946, the remains of two Roman Iron Age watermills were excavated.
4 Aså. Excavation of five buildings dating from the late 13th century to the 19th century (Steensberg 1952)
5 Store Valby. Five historically known medieval and post-medieval farmsteads excavated 1945-6 and 1949-53 (Steensberg and Østergaard Christensen 1974)
6 Hejninge. Excavation of two medieval and post-medieval farmsteads in 1941-2 (Steensberg 1986b)
7 Borup Ris. Surveying and mapping of field systems and excavation of medieval dwellings 1951-1983 (Steensberg 1968; 1983)
8 Pebringe. Documentation of the still standing farm before transfer to the open-air museum at Sorgenfri, Copenhagen, took place. This was followed by excavations on the site (Ludvigsen and Steensberg 1941; Steensberg 1986a)

Copenhagen. There he met a person who came to shape his early professional life: Gudmund Hatt (1884-1960), professor of human geography from 1929 to 1947 (Buciek 1999). During previous employment at the Danish National Museum, Hatt had become interested in Iron Age settlements and farming techniques. Sponsored by grants from the Carlsberg Foundation, Hatt conducted two long-lasting excavation campaigns devoted to the study of Iron Age Celtic fields and settlements in Jutland (e.g. Hatt 1928; 1936; 1937; Stummann Hansen 1984).

Steensberg was employed as Hatt's assistant in the second half of the 1930s, possibly from 1934 until 1937, joining him for fieldwork on the Jutland heaths. This work included the mapping and surveying of field systems as well as the excavation of prehistoric dwellings.

In this way Steensberg, who never took any university courses in archaeology, gained an insight into archaeological problems and excavation techniques. In later publications, Steensberg often emphasised his close relation to Hatt and the importance of the archaeological experiences he gained working alongside him (e.g. Steensberg 1952; 1955; 1974; 1982). The fact that Hatt, just like Steensberg, grew up in the countryside is put forward as a unifying link between the two researchers and Hatt occupies a central position in Steensberg's genealogy for the origin and development of open-area excavation in Denmark. It is an interesting fact that Hatt himself never published any detailed accounts of his methods of excavation. Rather it has been Steensberg who has presented Hatt's methods to a wider audience.

In 1936, Steensberg found employment at the National Museum in Copenhagen as an assistant at the Third Department, which was - and still is - responsible for collecting and documenting Danish cultural historical objects and buildings from 1660 to the present day. Thus, archaeological excavations did not make up one of the core activities of the department. Steensberg, however, soon had the opportunity to pursue his emerging interest in medieval rural settlements. In 1938 a farm building in the village of Pebringe on south-eastern Zealand had been sold to the Danish open-air museum, which was attached to the Third Department, and was to be dismantled and transported to Sorgenfri, near Copenhagen, where the museum was located. Together with architect Arne Ludvigsen, Steensberg was in charge of the project's realisation. In 1939, after having documented and prepared the farm for transport, Steensberg began excavating the site where the peasant houses had previously been standing. He had been encouraged to do so by museum inspector Kai Uldall, whose foremost interest was in the development of fireplaces, while Steensberg also was curious to trace predecessors of the post-medieval Pebringe farm, something he did successfully (Steensberg 1952, 197ff; 1986a).

Steensberg's positive results from the small-scale and low-budget excavation in Pebringe spurred him on to initiate archaeological investigations of other medieval rural sites in Denmark (Fig. 3). In parallel with work at Pebringe he excavated parts of the villages of Bolle and Aså on the north-eastern coast of Jutland in 1938-9 (Steensberg 1952). These excavations were followed by archaeological work in Alstrup Hede, Hejninge, Nødskov Hede, Store Valby and Borup Ris. Although, as previously stated, archaeological fieldwork did not traditionally belong to the activities of the Third Department, it is possible to view Steensberg's investigations of medieval rural villages as a natural extension of the ethnological research being conducted on rural buildings during the 1930s and 1940s, among other things seeking to fill in the gap between prehistoric dwellings and buildings that were still standing.

Having been appointed head of the Third Department in 1946, Steensberg remained at the National Museum for another sixteen years. In 1959 he left the museum to become the first professor of material folk culture at the University of Copenhagen. He kept this chair until he retired in 1970. As is so often the case, Steensberg's retirement did not mean a less productive phase in his life. On the contrary, several of the sites that he had been excavating during earlier decades were now published and made accessible in the form of monographs (Steensberg and Østergaard 1974; Steensberg 1983; 1986a; 1986b).

Although Steensberg conducted no less than eight excavations of medieval rural settlements in Denmark during his lifetime, it is worth emphasising that his research on the medieval peasant and his material remains constituted only *one* aspect of his broad scientific interest. During Steensberg's whole professional career, it was the conditions for rural populations at different times and in different geographical settings that formed the main theme of his research. Apart from being articulated in the excavation of medieval rural sites, this interest was further expressed by studies in experimental archaeology with agricultural tools: the subject of his dissertation had been ancient harvesting implements (Steensberg 1943). Numerous travels brought him to different corners of the world; his journeys to study agriculture in Papua New Guinea and Australia especially deserve mentioning (Steensberg 1986c).

Steensberg was eager to communicate his knowledge, and apart from a vast amount of scientific publications (cf. bibliographies in Lerche 1976; 1986; 1996), he featured frequently on radio and in the press commenting upon topics of current interest, contributing with an historical perspective. The epithet 'the last poly-historian', sometimes given to Steensberg, summarises well his ambitions: he was a researcher who believed in the possibility of generalisation and the grand narrative, drawing together knowledge and observations from several disciplines in order to do so. We shall now focus on Steensberg's initial contact with British researchers in the late 1940s and its consequences for the archaeology of medieval rural settlements.

Looking for 'a clever young archaeologist': first contacts with Britain

In 1947, the Cambridge economic historian Michael Postan had been invited to give lectures at the University of Copenhagen. His stay included a visit to the National Museum, where he met Steensberg, among others. The discussions that took place made Postan aware of the ongoing work on medieval rural sites in Denmark (Steensberg 1982, 28). Enthusiastic about what he heard, Postan invited Steensberg to come to England the same year. For various reasons the visit was postponed and it finally took place during three weeks in June 1948. Before that, Postan had paid a second visit to Denmark in May, among other activities taking part in excursions arranged by Steensberg.

Steensberg himself has published a detailed account of his activities during his stay in England, which apart from several visits to museums and archaeological sites also included meetings with archaeologists Gordon Childe, Grahame Clark and Glyn Daniel as well as historian W.G. Hoskins (Steensberg 1982; Steensberg 1948 *unpublished report*). Perhaps the best-known event during

Steensberg's stay is the meeting on deserted medieval villages that took place at Peterhouse in Cambridge on 17 June at Postan's initiative. This meeting was followed by excursions to the deserted medieval villages at Knaptoft and Hamilton, where Hoskins was then conducting small-scale fieldwork.

In the literature, this seminar at Peterhouse is often referred to as one of the decisive moments for medieval (rural) archaeology and thus occupies a prominent position in historiographical writings. Accordingly, Beresford and Hurst speak of 'a glorious June, 1948', referring to this meeting as well as to O.G.S. Crawford's aerial photographs of Wharram Percy that were taken during this same month; while Christopher Gerrard labels these events as 'A kind of genesis: 1948' and Matthew Johnson speaks of 'the famous 1948 meeting' (Beresford and Hurst 1990, 20; Gerrard 2003, 103; Johnson 2006, 63).

In Cambridge, Steensberg gave a talk on the archaeological methods he applied on medieval rural sites and thus introduced British colleagues to his ideas of open-area excavation. In the course of the meeting, there was a call for action also in England. In an unpublished report to the Rask-Ørsted Foundation, Steensberg writes: 'Dr Grahame Clark, one of the most important of the younger archaeologists in England - a man with an European outlook - soon concluded that a team should be set up, conducting rural excavations in England, similar to the Danish' (Steensberg 1948, *unpublished report*). A first step in this direction would be to send archaeologists to Denmark to get first-hand experience in excavating medieval rural settlements (Steensberg 1948, *unpublished report*).

The idea of an academic exchange had been loosely formulated already a year before, when Steensberg in a letter to Postan mentioned that he was looking for a 'clever young archaeologist, who should like to partake in my excavations', and that he was hoping that Clark, who was planning a visit to the Danish National Museum during the autumn of 1947, might come up with some names (letter to M.M. Postan, dated 25 July, 1947). This wish was expressed a second time at the meeting at Peterhouse in 1948, and as a result archaeologist Kenneth Dauncey went to Store Valby in 1949 on a recommendation from Clark. From archival sources, it is clear that Steensberg hoped, in return, for Danish researchers to get the opportunity to excavate villages in the former *Danelaw* (Steensberg 1948, *unpublished report*). For reasons unknown today, this exchange never came about.

Dauncey spent the months of September and October on the Zealand site. After having returned to Britain, Dauncey was planning to apply for a professorship of Anglo-Saxon archaeology at London University, but soon left archaeology to pursue a career in the steel industry. Thus, his experiences on the Danish site did not become incorporated into the British archaeological sphere. Instead it was Jack Golson, who worked in Store Valby for six months in 1952, who came to constitute the direct link between Danish excavation practice and early work in Wharram Percy.

The excavations in Store Valby 1945-46 and 1949-53

Before turning to the actual work that took place in Store Valby, a short introduction to the site and the circumstances that led to its investigation should be given. The village remains are located partly within forest and partly in open arable land on clay soil, approximately 4.5km north-west of the town of Slagelse on the Danish island Zealand (Fig. 3). There are no visible traces of the settlement and our knowledge of the medieval and post-medieval village structures thus comes from historical and archaeological sources. Store Valby ceased to exist in 1774, when the estate Valbygård was established nearby and the village was abandoned. According to Steensberg, the oldest traces of the village date back to the 9th to 10th centuries (Steensberg 1974, 385).

During seven field seasons in total, five of the seventeen historically known farmsteads were archaeologically investigated and approximately twenty buildings or part of buildings were identified (Fig. 4). Steensberg repeatedly expressed his ambition to uncover the whole village, but this wish was to remain unfulfilled (e.g. Steensberg 1952, 17). With an investigated area of approximately 7600 m², Store Valby – along with the excavations at Tårnby village on Amager in 1993-94 (Svart Kristiansen 2005) – remains today one of the most comprehensive excavations of a medieval and post-medieval rural settlement with preserved cultural layers in Denmark.

Guided by historical maps, Steensberg and his assistant Ole Højrup began work in Store Valby by opening up trial trenches in the autumn of 1945, trying to locate the remains of the abandoned village. Steensberg's motives for an excavation can be linked to earlier excavations that had taken place on the nearby site Trelleborg. Here, Poul Nørlund, who was later to become the director of the Danish National Museum, had begun excavations of a Viking Age fortress in 1934. On both sides of a circular earth and timber rampart, a hitherto unknown type of building was identified in large numbers: a ship-like house with convex walls and outer supporting posts (Nørlund 1936). Nørlund was curious to find out whether this mode of construction could be connected solely with the fortress or if it was a common building practice in the area (Steensberg 1974, 19). Accordingly, Steensberg initiated excavations in the nearby village of Hejninge in 1941-42, trying to identify possible Viking Age settlement traces (Steensberg 1986b). These aims were not achieved at Hejninge, since work was interrupted due to the farmer's rotation of crops; and once the excavation could be resumed, financial support was lacking. Because of these complications, the idea of further work in Hejninge was abandoned and when funds were again available, Steensberg decided to concentrate his efforts on a second site, also situated close to Trelleborg: Store Valby.

The search for possible parallels to the constructions identified in the Trelleborg fortress was by no means the

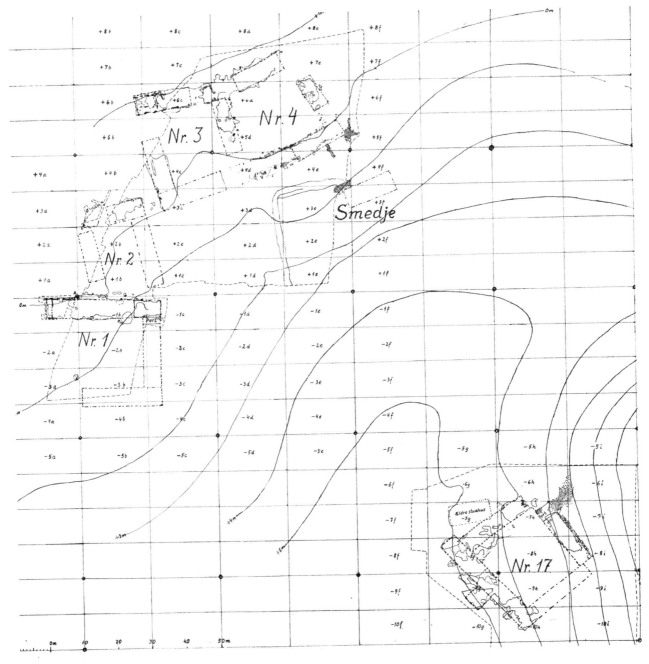

Fig. 4. Plan showing the remains of Store Valby. Dashed lines indicate excavated areas, and the dot-and-dash lines show the outlines of the post-medieval farmsteads as they appear on 18th-century maps. (Reproduced with the permission of the Royal Danish Academy of Sciences and Letters)

only motive for Steensberg, although it fitted well into his more general interest in the development of building techniques, an interest that he had pursued in previous excavations of medieval rural sites, during the late 1930s (Steensberg 1952). The excavations in Store Valby, however, came to differ from previous work undertaken by him. With Store Valby, the small-scale was abandoned as several farmsteads could be investigated. This opened up additional research topics, reaching beyond the evolution of the Danish peasant farm and taking into consideration also the surrounding field systems and landscape, as well as the documented history of the village.

After the first investigations in 1945-6, where traces of farmstead no. 1 had been identified, work was resumed and intensified in 1949 and continued until Spring 1953. Under the direction of Axel Steensberg the work force - mainly consisting of students and labourers provided by the unemployment agency - excavated and recorded traces of the abandoned settlement. It is a noteworthy fact that no Danish students of archaeology took part in the excavations. Instead, the only two students of archaeology came from Great Britain; namely Dauncey and Golson. As we have seen, Dauncey was the first British student to come to one of Steensberg's excavations, working on the remains of farmstead no. 3,

14

and Golson was the second, taking part in the excavation of farmstead no. 5. Golson came to Store Valby in late April 1952 and worked on the site for six months. Like Dauncey, he had been recommended by Clark and had been introduced to Steensberg at a conference held by The British Association for the Advancement of Science in Edinburgh in 1951.

Golson's arrival in Denmark on 24 April found its way into Steensberg's field diaries with the following entry: 'Picked up mr. J. Golson from Cambridge at the ferry from Newcastle at 10.30. Drove to St. Valby in the afternoon. Went over to Trelleborg. In the evening, the three of us went for a walk to Antvorskov.' (Steensberg, field diary 1/1952, Steensberg's emphasis). Golson returned to England by the end of October 1952. Apart from excavating on the Danish site he had been assisting Steensberg in producing an extensive English summary of *Farms and Water-mills in Denmark during Two Thousand Years*, making the results of Steensberg's early excavations available in condensed form also to an international audience (Steensberg 1952). This was one of the first books acquired by the newly formed Deserted Medieval Village Reseach Group (DMVRG *Annual Report* 1953, 4).

The following year, Golson spent one field season at Wharram Percy before leaving the British Isles in order to take up a position as a lecturer in Auckland, New Zealand. Steensberg and Golson however remained in touch and the Danish researcher was later invited to conduct fieldwork with Golson in Papua New Guinea (see Steensberg 1986c). Steensberg's decision to dedicate the monograph on Store Valby to Golson when it was finally published in 1974 can be seen as an expression of his appreciation of his foreign colleague.

Open area excavation in practice: fieldwork in Store Valby

In Store Valby, Axel Steensberg sought to uncover structures and layers without the limitations of the traditional grid system. Instead, he advocated stratigraphical digging on large, coherent surfaces without the interruption of baulks and sections (Plate 3). He thought this would be the best way to document extensive settlement remains in a landscape marked by cultivation, and where cultural layers were thin and traces scattered over large surfaces. Steensberg refers to this method as 'open area excavation' in English texts. He was however, far from alone in his reasoning, and before him - or parallel to his early activity in Denmark - archaeologists in different parts of Europe had applied similar trains of thought to single sites.

Plate 3. Open-area excavation at Store Valby, showing the excavation of farm no. 3 in 1949-50, viewed from the south-east. (Reproduced by permission of the Danish National Museum)

The move away from an emphasis on vertical stratigraphy towards greater attention to horizontal stratigraphy and surfaces goes hand in hand with the increased quantity of investigations of prehistoric settlements and can be seen for example in the excavations of the Neolithic *Bandkeramik*-site Köln-Lindenthal (1929-1934) in Germany, and Albert Egges van Giffen's many excavations of settlements in the Netherlands (Buttler and Haberey 1936; Waterbolk 1999).

In Britain, Gerhard Bersu's work at Little Woodbury and on the site of Vowlam on the Isle of Man is often put forward as early examples of open-area excavation (Bersu 1938; 1940). Bersu, however, practised a system using trenches that he had developed in Germany during excavations at Goldberg (Parzinger 1998, 13). Several parallel trenches were dug and the soil from the trenches was then placed on the surfaces between these trenches, before it was backfilled. The surfaces on which the soil had been stored was then excavated. These different steps cannot, however, be distinguished in the site plan which gives the impression that larger, coherent surfaces were contemporaneously exposed. This is the case with the records from Bersu's Little Woodbury excavation (Evans 1989).

In Steensberg's homeland, Gudmund Hatt was an important figure in this process and consequently he occupies a central role also in Steensberg's historiographical texts. What made Steensberg different from these other protagonists was that he was applying the technique of open area excavation to medieval and post-medieval rural settlements.

Since there is a gap of 21 years between the end of the excavations in Store Valby and the publishing of the monograph of the site, it seems relevant to turn also to the original field documentation when wishing to discuss Steensberg's method of excavation in detail. By studying the archived sources - in the case of Store Valby consisting of photographs, 1:50 and 1:25 drawings, find lists and 24 field diaries - you gain access to 'science in the making', i.e. the material as it was before it was put together and interpreted, published and thereby given its final form.

A second source of information is Steensberg's numerous publications, in which he put forward his method of excavation (e.g. Steensberg 1952; 1955; 1974; 1982). The reports all follow a similar pattern, starting off with an historical background followed by more concrete descriptions of the method applied on the rural settlements. At the same time as Steensberg is eager to point out the innovative character of the method applied by him, he is also careful to emphasise its close relationship to methods practised by Hatt in the 1930s. Steensberg hereby makes use of a well-known rhetoric where an older existing tradition is acknowledged at the same time as an innovative further development is presented. For instance, Steensberg stresses that he introduced a legend to be used on all Hatt's drawings as well as the millimetre drawing sheet (Steensberg 1982,

27). Taken together, the two categories of information give us a good basis for discussing Steensberg's excavation technique at Store Valby, focusing primarily on his ideas of stratigraphical digging, sectioning and finds recording.

The field diaries provide us with a good insight into daily work on the site, which consisted of levelling, drawing, find registration and taking photographs. Jack Golson recalls that the workmen often had started work on site before the archaeologists came, removing topsoil and cleaning surfaces (Golson, pers. comm., 13 October, 2005). Artefacts found during this process were left *in situ* to be drawn and levelled later by the assistants. This routine follows Steensberg's attitude towards fieldwork, where 'the co-workers will be left to investigate objects that are interesting but do not offer any excavation-technical problems…' (Steensberg 1974, 195). During fieldwork in Store Valby, Steensberg himself was often absent from the excavation due to other commitments, given his role as director of the Third Department. Entries in the field diaries have been made by the different assistants, however, not only during Steensberg's absence. This provides loose associations with the notion of 'reflexive archaeology', where all excavators are encouraged to take part in the interpretation of the site (e.g. Hodder 1989; Berggren and Burström 2002). Thus, much of the daily work was run by the workers and Steensberg's assistants. This is not an uncommon situation, but interesting when wishing to investigate Steensberg's role as a methodological innovator. To what extent assistants eventually contributed to modifications or refinements of Steensberg's technique of open-area excavation remains an open question.

The most challenging task at Store Valby was to identify and follow the thin and often diffuse cultural layers on the site; a difficulty that is reflected also in the diary entries. According to Steensberg, this procedure had to be led by the most experienced of the excavators. In the monograph, he speaks of the importance of a 'sensitive hand' that is capable of registering the slightest change in colour and consistency as well as texture (Steensberg 1974, 196). It is interesting to note that he refers to the children of farmers and their knowledge of different kinds of soil; knowledge acquired through the different tasks they had to conduct on the farm. This meant a special way of seeing that, according to Steensberg, Gudmund Hatt had achieved as he grew up in the countryside (Steensberg 1974, 185). Indirectly, Steensberg also ascribes to himself this skill, being the son of a farmer.

So how were the layers excavated and documented in Store Valby? As already stated, the thin and superimposed layers were often discontinuous and difficult to delimit horizontally as well as vertically. Steensberg's solution to this problem was to level layers and finds. When discontinuous layers could display identical levels they were seen as representing one contemporary layer. This - not unproblematic - method was then supplemented with the levelled finds material. All artefacts *inside* the buildings were meticulously three-dimensionally recorded. When sherds scattered in plan had identical positions vertically it was seen as an indication that they were in one and the same layer. The later refitting of sherds was seen as a last control of interpretations already made (Steensberg 1974, 384). This procedure explains why the exact documentation of finds was so important at Store Valby. On the plan drawings, find numbers and information on find types were recorded, something that has resulted in plans overloaded with information, and difficult to read (e.g. Steensberg 1974, 195).

One characteristic - as well as peculiarity - in Steensberg's excavation technique was his reluctance to work with sections. Based on experiences during his time as Hatt's field assistant in the 1930s, Steensberg chose not to make use of profiles, since the creation of (long) sections risked masking important stratigraphical relations. Thus, a reader might be confused when noticing that profiles can be found at the side of the published plans in the monograph (Steensberg and Østergaard 1974, Bilag VI-XVI). These are, however, schematic and do not represent actual measuring-up of profiles made on site during excavation; they are thus of limited value (cf. Foged Klemensen 1992, 4ff; Svart Kristiansen 2009). Instead, they have been *reconstructed* on the basis of plans and measurements.

As on every other site, it was of crucial importance to understand the stratigraphy in order to reconstruct the archaeological history of Store Valby and much time and detailed effort was spent on documenting layers and trying to relate them to each other. In the documentation, however, it is possible to distinguish a certain focus on more 'manifest' structures such as hearths, and to see that these objects have dominated excavation as well as interpretations and documentation (Svart Kristiansen 2009). For instance, while layers have not been assigned unique numbers, the more obvious features have. It should be added that Steensberg's preoccupation with hearths might partly be explained by his ethnological background, where the development of the fireplace over time was a key issue. As we have seen, the excavation of the Pebringe Farm in 1938-9 was initially spurred by a wish to investigate this problem (Steensberg 1940, 118).

Steensberg's ethnological background can also be seen in his treatment of the post-medieval remains in Store Valby. Today, these remains are often viewed as problematic from an antiquarian perspective and much discussed. There is a long tradition of searching for the oldest traces of a phenomenon (e.g. village formation, urbanisation), resulting in a find hierarchy where the more recent post-medieval remains frequently gain less attention. This kind of hierarchy is not visible in Store Valby, where dwellings from the 18th century enjoy the same attention as possible Viking Age settlement traces. It looks different when investigating another much discussed interrelationship, namely the relation between written sources and archaeological findings at Store Valby. Information from 18th-century written sources on dwelling structures and interiors is projected onto archaeological remains uncritically, setting the

frameworks and even furnishing the buildings (e.g. Steensberg 1974, 47, fig. 37). This displays a traditional pattern of trying to fit archaeological findings into historical frameworks.

It was with an insight into - and first hand experience of - the methods described and discussed above that Golson returned to England by the end of October 1952. What was his impression of Steensberg's way of investigating the deserted village? Before taking part in the excavation of the Danish site, Golson had gathered excavation practice of medieval archaeology in Norwich, documenting the town wall, and he had been excavating at Star Carr. Against this background of limited field experience he soberly concludes: 'I did not find what was happening at Store Valby in 1952, in the excavation of Farm 5, strange, just a different method for a different sort of site, which I was there to learn.' (Golson, pers. comm., 13 October, 2005). How this method was transferred and applied to the excavation of Area 10 at Wharram Percy the following year is the subject of the next section of this chapter.

An imported method? The excavation of Area 10 at Wharram Percy

By the time Golson returned to Britain, Beresford and Hurst had begun fieldwork at Wharram Percy. The story of how the economic historian with an interest in deserted medieval villages and the medieval archaeologist began their collaboration on the Yorkshire Wolds in the early 1950s has been told by the protagonists many times before (see e.g. Hurst 1985, 201; 1988, 201; Beresford and Hurst 1990, 29ff), and will thus only briefly be mentioned here.

In 1950-51, Beresford was digging trial trenches at Wharram, aiming to ascertain whether the visible earthworks really did constitute the remains of medieval dwellings and to determine their date of desertion. Beresford and Hurst had been in touch at the beginning of 1952, after Hurst together with Golson had decided to initiate a project on deserted medieval villages and needed the input of an historian. During the summer after Golson had left for Denmark, Hurst came out to Wharram to have a first look at the site (Beresford and Hurst 1990, 29). He soon realised that there had been more than one phase of occupation. It was this recognition of the site's stratigraphy that induced a methodological shift, away from chasing the walls of presumed peasant houses to the opening up of larger, coherent surfaces (Hurst 1971, 86ff). This new procedure was first practised in 1953 and was, as stated by Hurst, explicitly influenced by Steensberg's open-area excavation in Denmark: 'The method chosen for excavation was that used by Dr. Steensberg on similar sites in Denmark.' (Hurst 1956, 265-6). Both Beresford and Hurst had been introduced to Steensberg on different occasions during the Dane's repeated visits to England, but by this time it was only Golson who had any direct experience of Steensberg's excavation methods. He thus constituted the mediating link between a Danish practice and Wharram when he joined Hurst in the excavation of House 10 (Site 9), one of the most prominent earthworks on the site (Hurst 1956, 272).

With the aim of excavating a complete farmstead, work on House 10 began in May 1953 and was concluded in 1960, corresponding to approximately six months of continuous excavation (Hurst 1979a, 1). As in the case of Store Valby, information on the methods applied originates from field diaries and original documentation from the Site Archive as well as published accounts (Hurst 1956; 1971; 1979a; Hurst and Duckett 1954; Beresford and Hurst 1990).

The first season lasted fifteen days in total (Archaeological site diary House 10, 1953, Site Archive). During this time a grid was laid out and levelled over House 10. The excavation area, measuring approximately 23m x 14m, was then divided into three parts and de-turfed step by step, starting with the eastern grid. As the humus was removed, the chalk rubble became visible. This level was cleaned, drawn and photographed and designated as level 'A1'. This level was followed by 'A2', a stage reached when smaller stones, interpreted as not belonging to the walls, had been removed. Initially, the lack of any clearly laid or dressed stones made Hurst think of the remains as constituting parts of a cattle enclosure

rather than of a building (Hurst and Duckett 1954, 14). The next step in the search for wall footings was to remove also the larger blocks. Only those stones embedded in the clay platform were left in place when level 'A3' had been reached. The entries in the field diary for this first season reflect difficulties in tracing clear wall lines and when finally, on the last day of excavation, a wall base was distinguishable in the western grid it is commented upon with relief as 'a gratifying result after so much disappointment' (Archaeological Site Diary House 10, 1953, Site Archive).

As work on site proceeded during the following seasons, additional remains of building structures were identified and excavated as levels B1-3 (Hurst 1956, 273). Working with artificial levels was a procedure that differed from Steensberg's Danish method and should be seen as an adjustment to the British site, where Hurst and Golson could not identify any distinct layers. A second aspect that had no direct correspondence to Danish practice was the use of control baulks for vertical sections that were left across the excavation area (Plate 4).

At Wharram, larger surfaces were first opened up in 1953, during the excavation of House 10. Steensberg's technique of open-area excavation served as a source of inspiration and was mediated by Golson, who had spent six months in Store Valby the year before. The baulks left

Plate 4. Open-area excavation at Wharram, showing the excavation of House 10 in 1953, viewed from the north. Steensberg's techniques served as a source of inspiration and were mediated by Jack Golson who had spent six months at Store Valby the year before. The baulks left across the site did not correspond to Danish practice and can be seen as a compromise between established British excavation techniques and a new methodological input. (Wharram Site Archive, 1953)

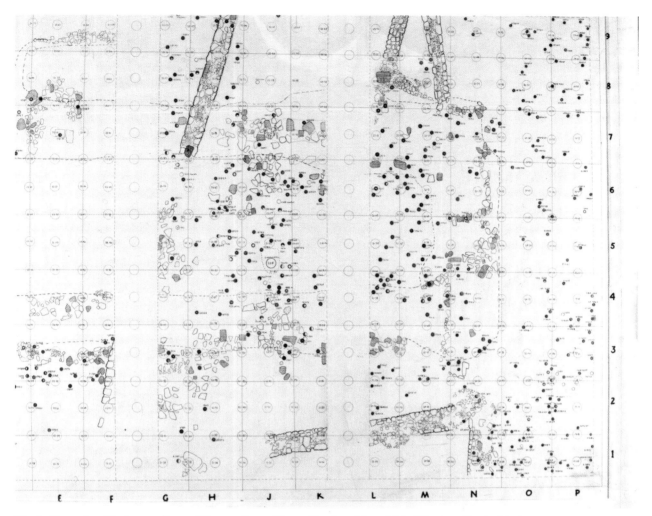

Fig. 5. Example of finds recording at Wharram Percy, House 10: plan of Level A3. (Wharram Site Archive)

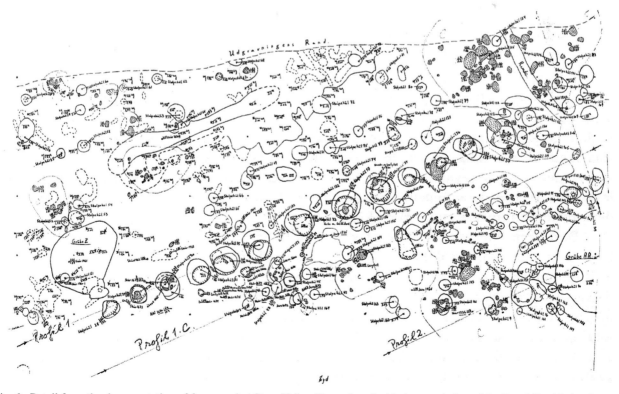

Fig. 6. Detail from the documentation of farm no. 4 at Store Valby. (Reproduced with the permission of the Royal Danish Academy of Sciences and Letters)

across the surface did not correspond to Danish practice and can be seen as a compromise between an established British excavation practice and a new methodical input delivered by the Danish researcher. It soon became clear that these could conceal evidence and that it was not an optimum method to apply when digging medieval rural sites (Hurst 1956, 272). It was not, however, until excavation of Area 6 (Site 12) began in 1961 that a different procedure was introduced, the sections now being continuously drawn and removed after each level had been dug. The existence - or non-existence - of baulks is a recurrent theme in the published literature on excavation techniques at Wharram and it seems to have been a somewhat sensitive topic at the time. In an interview from 1974, Hurst states that he, by the time of the excavation of House 10, '...was slightly cautious...as I had just been trained at Cambridge in the grid method' (*Current Archaeology* 1975, no 2, p. 41). Later, in 1990, he developed the subject further and related this hesitation to the then prevailing 'standard' archaeological practice and disciplinary norms within the subject, at a time when open-area excavation was seen as 'daring' (Beresford and Hurst 1990, 33). Golson, on the other hand, recalls that he and Hurst gave a lecture to the Royal Archaeological Institute in March 1953, presenting the work of the DMVRG, and the current open-area excavation at Wharram, in the presence of Mortimer Wheeler. According to Golson, Wheeler expressed only 'interest and encouragement' (Golson, pers. comm., 13 October, 2005).

In accordance with Steensberg's practice at Store Valby, single finds were recorded three-dimensionally and plotted onto the site plan (Figs 5 and 6). Following this practice, finds were left *in situ* when uncovered and later levelled, recorded and individually numbered and bagged. Not only was the exact position of each single find recorded but also the nature of the find was signalled on the plan in letters, e.g. (S) for pottery sherd and (F) for faunal remains. This, of course, resulted in plans that were overloaded with information and difficult to read, a fact of which Hurst was also well aware (Hurst 1956, 272). The meticulous documentation of finds was intended to help the excavators work out floor levels, something that Steensberg had been able to do in Store Valby. This did not however prove successful in the case of Wharram and the procedure was later modified (Hurst 1971, 88ff). When starting excavations in Area 6 in 1961, finds belonging to the same grid square were now sometimes bagged together. This was actually also the case with finds from level A1 in House 10, where finds were collected by 5ft squares (undated paper entitled 'Wharram Method of Excavation', Site Archive).

Before work began in Area 6, Hurst got the opportunity to work side by side with Steensberg in Denmark. In May 1960, Hurst came over to dig in Borup Ris on Zealand, where Steensberg and his co-workers were excavating dwellings and surveying and mapping field systems belonging to the village. Hurst took part in the excavation of farmstead no. 3 after having accepted

an invitation sent by Steensberg two years earlier. He summarises his experiences in a report and states: 'It was striking to see how close our methods are...and how several refinements and improvements to the method have been adopted independently both in Denmark and in England.' (Hurst 1960).

Within the academic sphere, the method of open-area excavation at Wharram was much advocated by the protagonists. From early on the novelty of the method was emphasised and Steensberg in particular was credited with its introduction in Britain, even if references to both Hatt and Bersu were made. This preoccupation with the method is reflected also in the daily press, reporting on work on site. It was reported that archaeologists at Wharram apply 'a technique never previously employed outside Scandinavia' (*Manchester Guardian* 1961) and headings such as 'Experiment in technique', 'New Technique' or 'Peeling the Wolds' all refer to the technique of open-area excavation being practised at Wharram (*Manchester Guardian* 1956; 1961; *Yorkshire Evening Post*, 22 May 1953). When asked to comment upon how revolutionary the method of open-area excavation was, Hurst himself has stated: 'It was certainly a very remarkable development, because there is no way that the Medieval peasant house, with its flimsy foundations, could have been understood by digging the grids and trenches of the Mortimer Wheeler school.' (Hurst interviewed in Smith 2004).

Conclusions

In retrospect, how should we view the role Steensberg played in British medieval rural archaeology? I propose to discuss the 'Danish connection' primarily on two levels. The first concerns the concrete excavation practice while the second seeks to understand the importance of Steensberg and his method of excavation in a wider disciplinary context. In conclusion, Steensberg's influence on medieval archaeology in his homeland is commented upon.

As we have seen, the process of excavating the medieval farmsteads in Area 10 bears several resemblances to the archaeological practice advocated by Steensberg; yet there existed a number of differences. This should not be surprising, since the two sites Store Valby and Wharram Percy have different characteristics and hence there were different prerequisites for the application of open-area excavation techniques. While the remains at Store Valby were situated on clay land and no surface indications of structures were visible prior to excavation, Wharram is a chalk site where the shapes of the remains are in many cases visible before excavating. The different building techniques left different traces, demanding different documentation methods. Due to these and other differences there can be no one-to-one relationship between the methods used on the sites. Therefore, rather than speaking of a direct methodological transfer, one should speak of inspiration and interpretation of a method that was adjusted to the prevailing characteristics of Wharram Percy. Steensberg's Danish excavation practice undoubtedly delivered a decisive input in the shift from trial trenches to open areas in Wharram, but as work proceeded local adjustments were made. In this context it should also be remembered that Golson in fact only spent a fortnight excavating in Wharram in 1953 and that from the next season and onwards, Hurst and his co-workers continued fieldwork without any further direct experience of Steensberg's methods. In the field diary from the 1953 campaign it is also clear that Hurst was not always present on site during these two weeks.

Still, Steensberg undoubtedly had an important influence on archaeological practice in the early excavations in Wharram, in that he delivered a manual and a tool-kit on how best to dig deserted medieval villages (Fig. 7). Until the early 1950s, few medieval rural settlements had been archaeologically investigated in Great Britain and there was a need for good examples, demonstrating the possibility as well as the necessity of investigating these remains archaeologically. Steensberg's excavations constituted important examples of how work was successfully conducted elsewhere, thus acting as 'model work'. In Denmark, Steensberg could in return put forward his international contacts and his influence in the Anglo-Saxon sphere to give additional weight to his own work and grant applications. In this way both parties benefited from the Danish-British contacts.

From early on there were ambitions to make fieldwork in Wharram Percy more than a 'unique experiment', as John Hurst characterised the initiation of the first excavations on the site (Hurst 1956, 251). Instead, with the establishment of the Deserted Medieval Village Research Group in 1952 and the recurrent excavations at Wharram, steps towards the formation of a new field of research were taken and gradually the archaeology of medieval rural settlements was put on the academic map. In this process, the existence of good examples and a suitable excavation technique formed important elements in a rhetoric, aimed at drawing attention to a previously neglected field of study and its scientific potential. By tradition, medieval archaeology had concentrated its efforts on the remains of the higher estates: castles, churches and monasteries being common objects of investigation (cf. Bruce-Mitford 1948). To investigate the archaeological remains of 'common' men and women, as reflected in peasant material culture, was no doubt an important motivation for early work at Wharram Percy, which various statements made by the protagonists indicate (cf. Hurst 1971, 76; Hurst in Smith 2004). It should be added that this ambition was shared also by Steensberg.

The prerequisites for the acceptance and spread of the excavation method, however, differed in the two countries. In the case of England, it is possible to distinguish at least three factors that promoted the spread of open-area excavation. First, as stated in the introduction, it is possible to view Wharram as a 'training camp' for medieval archaeologists at different stages of

their career. In the Site Archive, a list containing the names of those who volunteered at Wharram (until 1986) and then pursued archaeological or other academic careers records 45 people - and the list can surely be extended (file 'Visitors to Wharram', Site Archive). These people took field experiences from Wharram and applied them in other excavations.

Secondly, John Hurst himself played a mediating role, being the central figure at Wharram, a founder member of the DMVRG and an employee at the Ministry of Works (later English Heritage) from 1952 until his retirement in 1987. On his many visits to excavations all over Britain, he would have had the chance to spread knowledge about experiences of open-area excavation. For instance, Philip Rahtz recalls that Hurst convinced him to abandon the traditional grid method in favour of open area techniques and that Hurst was '…very influential in persuading a number of archaeologists to try this method.' (Rahtz 2003, 880). Also, Martin Biddle acknowledged Hurst's importance in the introduction of open-area excavation in Britain, as did Andrew Saunders (Biddle 2003; Saunders 2003).

Since field documentation from sites where archaeologists claim to have been inspired to try open-area excavation has not been investigated in detail within the framework of this study, it is not possible to comment more precisely upon which elements were actually incorporated. It should be added that, when discussing the influence of open-area excavation in Britain, we should note that Steensberg also had several contacts outside the immediate Wharram sphere, making possible a direct methodological influence that did not go via Wharram. This was for instance the case with Philip Barker, who first tried open-area excavation at Hen Domen (Barker 1969). Thirdly, the partly parallel technological development towards mechanical soil stripping on excavations was an additional component promoting open-area excavation, but on a different scale.

Contrary to the developments in Britain, Steensberg's excavations of medieval rural sites have had no significant influence on later archaeological practice in his homeland. He is repeatedly acknowledged as having pioneered village excavations in Denmark, but is never referred to as a source of inspiration regarding excavation techniques. Despite Steensberg's explicit ambitions to establish a new field of study (Steensberg 1952, 17), no-one followed in his footsteps. When mechanical soil stripping was introduced, step by step, in Denmark during the 1960s, the sites exposed in large open areas were primarily prehistoric ones (Becker 1987; Svart Kristiansen 2003a). Later, when new projects on medieval rural settlements were initiated during the second half of the 1970s, different questions - demanding methods different from Steensberg's - were formulated (cf. 'The origin and development of the medieval village on Funen', Grøngaard Jeppesen 1982; Porsmose 1977). With the risk of simplification, it is possible to state that the cultural historical approach, represented by Steensberg, was replaced by questions posed under the influence of processual archaeology. In a retrospective

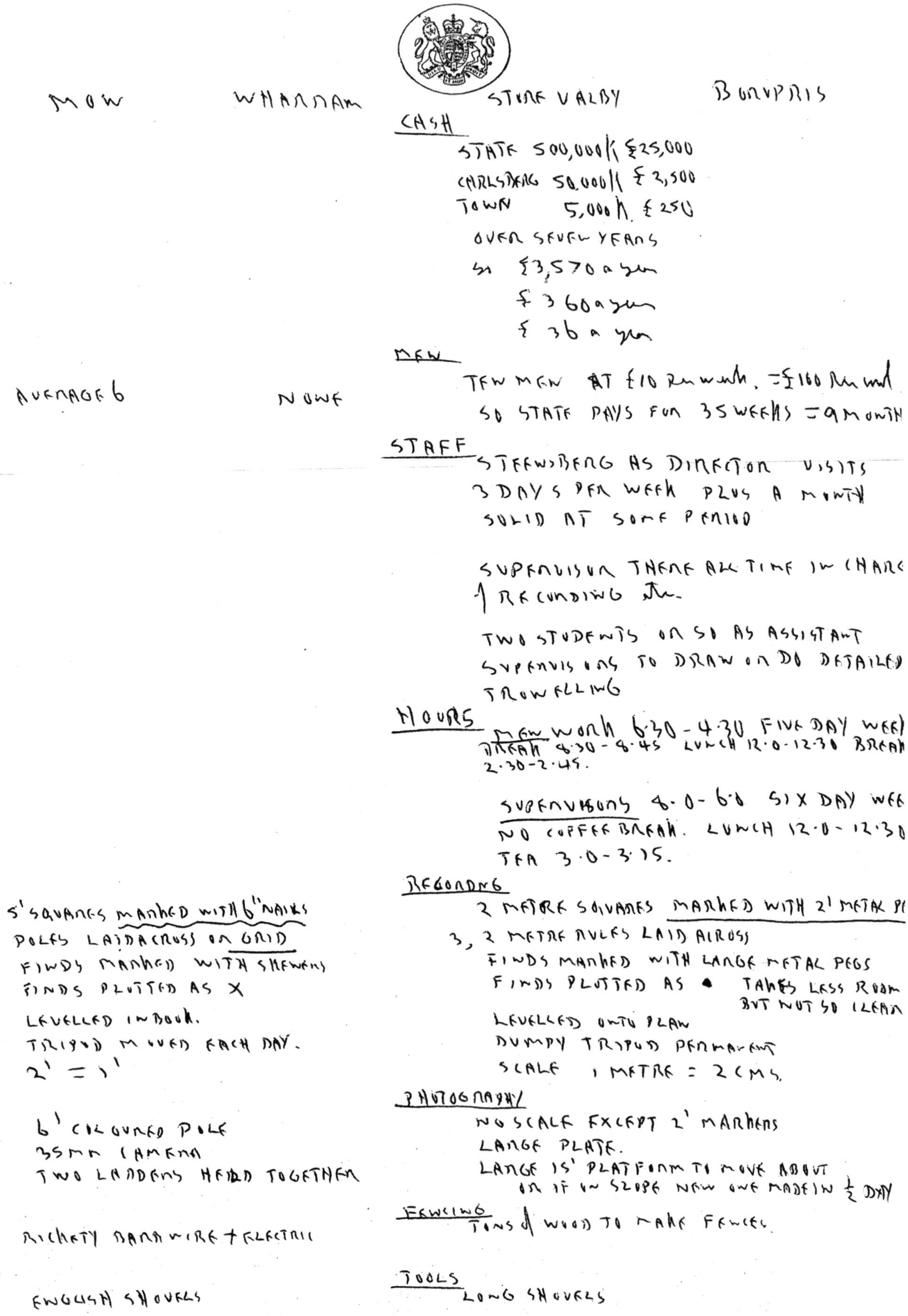

MOW   WHARRAM   STORE VALBY   BORUP RIS

CASH

STATE 500,000K £25,000
CARLSBERG 50,000K £2,500
TOWN 5,000K £250
OVER SEVEN YEARS
= £3,570 a year
£360 a year
£36 a year

MEN

TEN MEN AT £10 Per week = £100 Per week
SO STATE PAYS FOR 35 WEEKS = 9 MONTH

AVERAGE 6   NONE

STAFF

STEENSBERG AS DIRECTOR VISITS
3 DAYS PER WEEK PLUS A MONTH
SOLID AT SOME PERIOD

SUPERVISOR THERE ALL TIME IN CHARGE
OF RECORDING etc.

TWO STUDENTS ON SI AS ASSISTANT
SUPERVISORS TO DRAW OR DO DETAILED
TROWELLING

HOURS

MEN WORK 6.30 - 4.30 FIVE DAY WEEK
BREAK 8.30 - 8.45 LUNCH 12.0 - 12.30 BREAK
2.30 - 2.45.

SUPERVISORS 8.0 - 6.0 SIX DAY WEEK
NO COFFEE BREAK. LUNCH 12.0 - 12.30
TEA 3.0 - 3.15.

RECORDING

2 METRE SQUARES MARKED WITH 2' METAL Pt
3, 2 METRE RULES LAID ACROSS
FINDS MARKED WITH LARGE METAL PEGS
FINDS PLOTTED AS ● TAKES LESS ROOM
BUT NOT SO CLEAR
LEVELLED ONTO PLAN
DUMPY TRIPOD PERMANENT
SCALE 1 METRE = 2 CMS.

5' SQUARES MARKED WITH 6" NAILS
POLES LAID ACROSS ON GRID
FINDS MARKED WITH SKEWERS
FINDS PLOTTED AS X
LEVELLED IN BOOK.
TRIPOD MOVED EACH DAY.
2' = 1'

PHOTOGRAPHY

NO SCALE EXCEPT 2' MARKERS
LARGE PLATE.
LARGE 15' PLATFORM TO MOVE ABOUT
OR IF ON SLOPE NEW ONE MADE IN ½ DAY

6' COLOURED POLE
35mm CAMERA
TWO LADDERS HELD TOGETHER

FENCING

TONS of WOOD TO MAKE FENCES.

RICKETY BARB WIRE + ELECTRIC

TOOLS

LONG SHOVELS

ENOUGH SHOVELS

Fig. 7. Inspiration sheet compiled by John Hurst. Filed under the year 1961 are notes comparing the organisation of fieldwork conducted by the Ministry of Works and on the sites of Wharram, Store Valby and Borup Ris. (Wharram Site Archive)

article from 1982, Steensberg commented upon the situation, not without a hint of bitterness, and wrote: 'The younger generation of archaeologists excavating medieval village sites in Denmark has never worked with me. But it is at least encouraging that my methods are so widely accepted in Britain.' (Steensberg 1982, 30).

Other factors contributing to Steensberg's lack of practical influence might be explained by the criticisms of some of his interpretations of Pebringe, Store Valby and Borup Ris (e.g. Jespersen 1956; Gissel 1979; Stoklund 1986). The fact that much of Steensberg's archaeological work was conducted from a department within the National Museum whose main tasks did not include excavations might also have had a constraining effect. During Steensberg's employment, first as assistant and then later as head of the department, he managed to provide for excavations, but when he left the National Museum to take up a position at the University of Copenhagen in 1959, this focus disappeared (cf. Nielsen 1966, 187; Olsen 1977, 10). Existing subject boundaries may also have played a role in restricting Steensberg's archaeological influence. It is a noteworthy fact that his archaeological publications were exclusively reviewed in Scandinavian ethnological or historical journals (Berg 1975; Gissel 1979), not in the established archaeological forum. The situation is different in the Anglo-Saxon sphere, where, for instance, a review of the Store Valby monograph can be found in *Antiquity* (Wilson 1975). In a retrospective article, Wilson recalls that Store Valby was the first open-area excavation that he had ever seen and that it was an impressive experience (Wilson 2004, 906)

The work of the DMVRG and the excavations at Wharram Percy can be said to have been of vital importance to the establishment of medieval archaeology in Britain after the Second World War, but this development had no equivalent in Denmark. The archaeology of medieval rural sites long played a minor role within the discipline and this situation has only recently begun to alter (Svart Kristiansen 2003a; 2003b). In this process, a renewed interest in Steensberg and his work can be distinguished, given his role as pioneering the excavation of medieval and post-medieval settlements in Denmark.

3   A New Earthwork Survey of Wharram Percy
by Alastair Oswald

Introduction

The circumstances surrounding English Heritage's decision to carry out a new, comprehensive earthwork survey in 2002 have been outlined in the introduction to this part of the volume. The new plan resulting from this work is reproduced as Figure 8. By its nature, analytical earthwork survey of any intensively-used site tends to elucidate most clearly the latest phase of activity prior to the cessation of that intensive activity. Thus, in the case

of the Wharram Percy village site itself, the 500 years of active pastoral land-management responsible for ensuring the preservation of the medieval remains as earthworks offer negligible impediment - indeed vital assistance - to the attempt to detect the later phases of medieval settlement.

In terms of Wharram Percy's wider farmlands, the field boundaries established at the time of the estate's Improvement, mainly between 1775 and 1779 and depicted on Dykes' 1836 estate map (Ch. 22, Fig. 116; see *Wharram XII*, 11, fig. 5 and 27, fig. 7), can all be identified with confidence as low banks and shallow ditches, in several cases following the lines of medieval earthworks (notably the edges of hollow ways, suggesting that these were still in occasional use). In most cases, the boundaries are shown on historic Ordnance Survey maps as relict hedgelines, denoted by discontinuous lines of tree symbols, and one of the ancient hawthorns still survives, its trunk exhibiting evidence of traditional management by 'laying'. According to the 18th-century accounts, most if not all of the hedges were planted at intervals with standards of ash; one ancient pollarded ash still stands on the boundary of the garden of the Improvement farmstead. In addition, the development of a series of stratigraphically late trackways, which cut through medieval features including the boundary of the *curia* of the South Manor and, more tellingly, broad ridge and furrow, is also very probably attributable to the years after 1775.

As a result, most of the post-medieval earthworks can be straightforwardly filtered out of our perception of the medieval remains, if we so wish. Yet this exclusion may justifiably be regarded as detrimental to a holistic understanding of the earthwork evidence and the dynamic interplay of features and activities through time. For example, it was the demonstration through field survey that the construction of the earthen ramp up to the railway bridge must post-date spoil dumping associated with the construction of the Burdale railway tunnel in 1847-53 which allowed the earthwork to be ruled out as the prime candidate for the village's lost medieval mill dam (Oswald 2005, 13-15). For reasons of space, however, remains post-dating the abandonment of the village are not discussed in this précis (for description and discussion of these remains and for fuller descriptions of the medieval earthworks, the reader is referred to Oswald 2004).

To some extent, then, the medieval earthwork remains that are most readily detectable and intelligible do indeed relate to the horizon immediately predating the village's abandonment, as Beresford initially anticipated (Beresford 1954, 39). It is now clear, however, that desertion was not a single event but a long, drawn-out process which did not occur in the same way or at a uniform pace across the village. Therefore, through recognition of relative chronologies, as well as patterns and anomalies in plan form, earthwork survey, no differently from excavation, allows us to work backwards through time, framing questions about earlier phases and sometimes discerning possible answers 'through a glass, darkly'. Some of the most pressing research questions at Wharram, for example those concerning the foundation and early development of the village, are those for which analytical earthwork survey offers the fewest and least secure insights, but, again, it is no different from excavation in that respect. To emphasise this, the following description is structured as far as possible in reverse chronological order.

Settlement in the 16th and early 17th centuries

The documentary evidence relating to the depopulation of Wharram Percy has been considered in detail in a previous volume (Wrathmell 2010a, 1-3), and is summarised further below (Ch. 22). What the few late medieval records seem to show is a substantial decline in the number of holdings (perhaps by as much as 50%) between the late 13th century and the mid-15th century. Further farmholds were 'thrown down' at the end of that century, but others continued to be tenanted until around 1527, when the open fields were abolished and laid down to grass.

A case can also be made from the documentary sources for a number of houses in the township continuing in occupation into the mid-16th century, though probably as cottages for smallholders and shepherds, rather than as farmhouses. The discovery of two early 16th-century jettons and stoneware imported from Cologne, along with a modest quantity of other mid to late 16th-century material, may support this inference (Le Patourel 1979, 93-5; Didsbury 2010, 176-7). By 1605, and probably by the late 16th century, a 'chief messuage', or principal farmstead, was documented, apparently operating an infield-outfield system. The dating of the pottery and clay pipes recovered from the excavation of the late 17th-century farmhouse which was the direct predecessor of the 18th-century Improvement farm suggests that the early 17th-century farm was not on the same site (Wrathmell 2010c, 341-3).

It is seldom advisable to attempt to tie specific earthwork remains to specific documented events, but Building 5, near the southern end of the West Row (Fig. 9), is a very plausible candidate for the 'chief messuage' documented in 1605, notwithstanding the scant excavated evidence which would offer little support for the theory. One of the buildings first depicted on the *Ordnance Survey* (1890) 25-inch scale map, Building 5 is a relatively large and well preserved longhouse, with opposed central doorways and a clear tri-partite division of its interior. The wall-lines around the southern end of the building were trenched by Beresford in 1952 and it was here that excavation first revealed evidence for multiple constructional phases, as described below. The findings of this early investigation were re-evaluated subsequently (Wrathmell 1989b, 33-5) and both phases detected by Beresford can in fact be recognised from the surface traces.

The 2002 earthwork survey demonstrates that Building 5 falls very late in the sequence, for it not only encroaches northwards into the adjacent toft, but also eastwards beyond the original frontage of the row, hindering, if not impeding altogether, the passage of any traffic along the track that followed the brink of the escarpment giving access to all the tofts. Intriguingly, however, all the pottery recorded from the 1952 excavation dates to the 14th and 15th centuries, providing no suggestion that Building 5 was inhabited until at least the final years of the village, as might reasonably be concluded from the earthwork remains. However long it survived, Building 5 probably represents the last occupied farm holding in this part of the village.

The adjacent toft to the south contains the remains of two, or possibly three, fairly small buildings set around a rectangular sunken yard, which perhaps originated as a quarry. The enclosed yard is set within a larger enclosure linked to Building 5. The platforms around the yard were apparently not interpreted as the sites of buildings during the earthwork survey carried out in the course of the Wharram Research Project, although they had been depicted as such on the first edition 25-inch scale map (*Ordnance Survey* 1890). A ledge in the scarp that forms the western end of the sunken yard seems to represent the line of a footpath shown on the first edition 25-inch scale map (*Ordnance Survey* 1890).

The plan form of the yard enclosed by raised buildings is suggestive of livestock management and the apparent juxtaposition with Building 5 is reminiscent of the form of the late 17th-century farm revealed by excavation on the site of the Improvement farm. A series of four small quadrangular enclosures defined by low banks (presumably former hedgelines or fencelines) to the south and west of the sunken yard may represent associated pasture enclosures belonging to the same farm, since the ground within them shows no sign of having been ploughed. The southernmost of these paddocks encloses Building 4 and the northernmost, another (previously unrecognised) building, both of which could be barns or other agricultural outbuildings. Taken together, the complex seems to represent a late and relatively prosperous farmstead that would accord well with the 'chief messuage' documented in 1605.

The 1952 excavation of Building 5 unearthed the eastern wall of an earlier building on roughly the same site, but the vestigial earthworks of both this wall and the other three walls of the earlier building were not recognised until the 2002 investigation. The earlier building lies on the same north-south alignment as Building 5, but is confined within the width of the toft and adjoins the frontage, suggesting that it dates to a time when the structure of the village and the conventions governing acceptable redevelopment remained essentially intact.

Remarkably, the eastern wall of the earlier building, or perhaps the wall or bank that originally defined the frontage of the row, if this was a separate structure, can still be traced within the southern half of the interior of

Building 5. This does not seem to be attributable to the effects of the 1952 excavation, so may indicate that the feature was retained within the later building, perhaps providing the footings for a wall or partition that divided the southern end into two rooms, for it is otherwise difficult to account for its continued survival as an earthwork within the later house. At face value, however, the somewhat schematic record of the excavated section would not support this theory (Wrathmell 1989b, fig. 25). It is also tempting to speculate that the 14th and 15th-century pottery unearthed by Beresford might relate to the earlier building, but this possibility does not explain away the absence of 16th-century and later finds.

Although Building 5 has evidently shifted away from the earlier building on the same site, it undoubtedly represents a direct successor to it, in contrast to the excavated late 17th-century house on the site of the Improvement farm, which appears to have been a new foundation. This implies a dislocation or episode of discontinuity in the mid-17th century which can perhaps be characterised with greatest justification as the final desertion of the settlement, village life having stood on the threshold of extinction for nearly 200 years.

It is also possible to point, with varying degrees of confidence, to at least three groups of buildings which could still have been used in the mid-16th century, or might even represent the farmsteads from which the four families were evicted around 1500 (Fig. 9). The unusually large Building 23, and its neighbour Building 24, have previously been interpreted as a 'demesne farm', its occupants responsible for managing the manorial lands after the departure of the Percy family (Hurst 1984, 97). The two buildings, which seem to overlie the manorial earthworks (implying that they originated no earlier than the late 14th century), appear to define two sides of a courtyard tucked into the south-eastern corner of the *curia* of the North Manor. Buildings 23 and 24 share the same alignment as the alleged manorial solar block (see below), suggesting that this may also belong to a relatively late phase. The nearby Building 19 presents a plausible candidate for an associated farmhouse. The manorial *curia* may well have been maintained as a land parcel associated with the buildings; this suggests that the broad ridge and furrow which eventually encroached onto Track 1B never encroached into the *curia*. Building 24, though its form differs little from many buildings that are certainly of medieval date, also appears to overlie the bank which equates to the boundary between Great Hog Walk and Ings Meadow as shown on Dykes' 1836 map (Ch. 22, Fig. 115), hinting that this boundary may have been established well before 1777. Leases dating to the early 17th century refer to 'hedges and ditches sett with quickwood' (that is, hawthorn). The fact that some of these are described as 'nowe decayed' (see Wrathmell 2010a, 3), suggests that they may have been planted considerably earlier.

The sunken yard enclosed by Buildings 21 and 22, together with Building 20 which lies in the adjacent toft, seems to represent the hub of a courtyard farm complex which has aspects in common with that associated with Building 5 (Hurst 1984, fig. 4; Beresford and Hurst 1990, 47 and 80). In this instance, the associated dwelling is perhaps represented by Building 19 or a previously unrecognised building just to its north. Alternatively, Building 19 may be part of a separate unit encompassing what appears to have originated as one of two possible medieval village pounds. Some of the boundaries associated with Buildings 20, 21 and 22 show signs of having been remodelled, giving the impression that the paddocks associated with the farmstead equated almost exactly with the medieval village's northern row, but perhaps sub-divided into two along the line of one of the medieval croft boundaries. It seems likely, to judge from the degraded condition of the medieval earthworks, that ploughing continued within the amalgamated crofts. The western boundary of the land parcel as a whole, separates it from the *curia* of the North Manor (that is the holding putatively associated with Buildings 23 and 24) and equates to the boundary depicted on Dykes' map between Ings Meadow and Cow Pasture. Overall, this hints that the major land holdings associated with the last phase of the village's existence may have formed the bones of the 18th-century land divisions.

A similar pattern can be discerned in the northern half of the West Row, where the medieval crofts seem to have been amalgamated into two larger arable fields, separated by a boundary re-established on the line of one of the former croft boundaries. Building 18, at the north-eastern corner of the land parcel, is reminiscent in its siting, of the building at the north-eastern corner of the largest paddock associated with Building 5. In this case, it is difficult to single out a dwelling or an associated group of buildings, either because the medieval arrangement remained virtually unmodified or because the buildings lay at some remove (Building 19, for example, might once more be a candidate). Building 3 in the East Row is another very plausible candidate for a late building, probably a dwelling, set within its own enclosure, in this case formed by the amalgamation of two medieval tofts. It is worth noting that Buildings 3, 5 and 23 are amongst the largest recorded through earthwork survey.

The North Manor

At the northern end of the village, a distinctive cluster of mostly rectangular buildings of varying sizes has long been interpreted, undoubtedly correctly, as the site of the village's late 13th and 14th-century manor. The principal building remains of the complex were identified and recorded by the Ordnance Survey in 1851. Most previous attempts to marry the physical remains with the documentary evidence have concluded that the North Manor must represent that held by the Percy family, though a more recent discussion has shown greater caution in making this equation, pointing to the poor understanding of the physical development of the North Manor (Roffe 2000a, 3). On the other hand, the remarkable preservation of the North Manor alone suggests that it

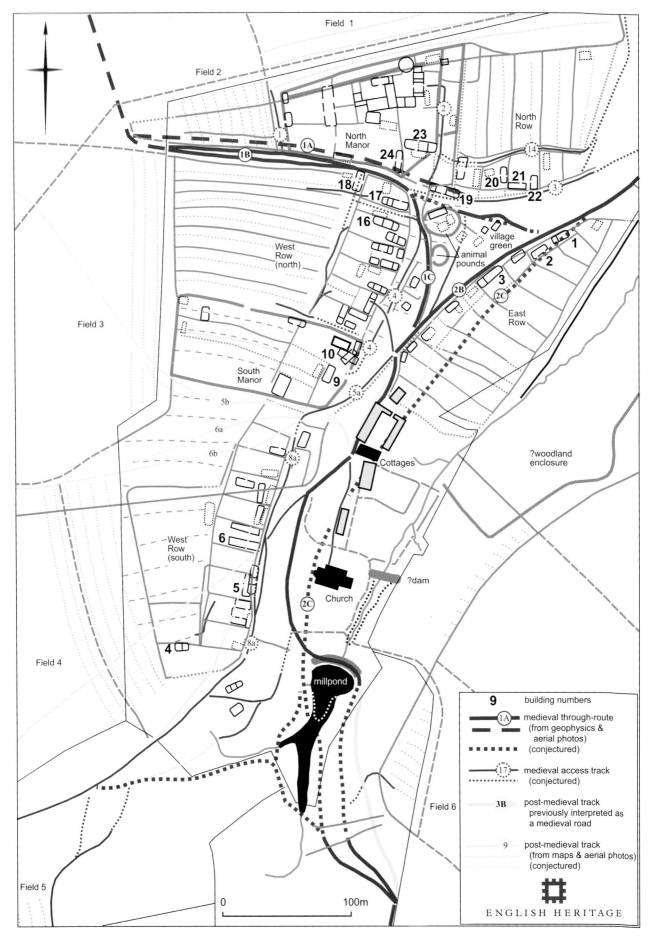

Fig. 9. Schematic plan of the network of roads and tracks. (English Heritage)

Fig. 10. Plan of the North Manor (reduced from original at 1:500 scale), with schematic plan without phasing. (English Heritage)

remained in use well after the destruction of the *camera* of the South Manor in the mid-13th century. None of the buildings has been fully excavated, but documents show that the manor was used well into the 14th century and earthwork traces of buildings post-dating the demise of the manor can also be identified (as described above).

Despite the paucity of excavated evidence, a bold attempt was made by John Hurst and Jean Le Patourel to interpret the disposition of specific rooms, based on a plan of the earthworks surveyed at a scale of 1:120 by W.J. Hopkins (Hurst 1985, fig. 4). In metrical terms, the new plan, surveyed at 1:500 scale, does not differ greatly from its predecessor, although there are a few important differences (Fig. 10). Perhaps the most significant is the addition of chronological depth to the previous interpretation, which treated the complex as a single, static entity. The new survey suggests that the manor underwent at least one major phase of expansion and that several of the buildings which might previously have been interpreted as part of the complex are more likely to represent later encroachment onto the site, as described above. The irregular trapezoid plan of the *curia*, which makes a striking contrast with the almost perfect rectangle of the South Manor, suggests that it was initially fitted into existing boundaries, specifically the hollow way on its south, whose longevity has been proved by excavation, and the northern boundary.

Within the manor precinct, a series of slight scarps on a north-south alignment may represent the vestiges of slight positive lynchets on the eastern (downslope) side of cultivation ridges, hinting that the complex may also have been laid out over what was once arable land. Therefore, the provision of access to the field to the north via Track 1 may be contemporary with the initial imposition of the manor (Fig. 9). This theory is supported by the observation that the alignment of many of the principal buildings and boundaries echoes that of the cultivation ridges in this field, which in turn replicate the north-north-west to south-south-east stretch of Road 1A/1B beyond the Guardianship Area. There is, however, no trace of these or later cultivation remains where they might be expected to survive best, in the large yards associated with the barn and immediately to the south of the manor house. This observation is also relevant in understanding the use of the *curia* after the demise of the actual manor house.

In both phases of its existence, the plan of the manorial buildings seems to have been more organised and regular in layout than has previously been appreciated (Fig. 11). Initially, the *curia* enclosure seems to have been a quadrangular area of about 0.47ha (1.16 acres), that is, somewhat smaller than that of the South Manor. At this stage, the main east-west range of the manor house, which has previously been interpreted as a solar, hall and buttery/pantry, seems to have formed the main range of an L-shaped building of modest size, with a major wing projecting to the north of the eastern end. A separate small building to the north of the western end of the east to west range was perhaps only connected by a broad corridor to

the main L-shaped building; this was originally interpreted as the private rooms of a solar block but is perhaps better seen as a possible kitchen (see below). These three arms defined three sides of a possible courtyard or enclosed garden of up to *c.* 300m². A building on the northern side of this has previously been interpreted as a bakehouse and brewery, partly because it shares the same east-west alignment of the manorial buildings. This structure is similar in size and form to the peasant houses found in other parts of the village. There is no clear-cut stratigraphic indication that the building is of different date from the manor, nor any reason why the cruck-truss construction technique employed by many of the peasant houses should not also have been used at the higher-status complex. The possibility that it represents encroachment by peasant houses onto the former site of the manorial complex after its destruction, cannot be dismissed.

The interior of the main east-west range was evidently divided into three parts, suggesting, in essence, a typical division into solar, open hall and service end, but the interpretation of the function of individual rooms is problematic. In its eventual form, the manor appears to have been approached from the east, and this would support the earlier theory that the private chambers of the solar block were towards the west, in the most private part of the complex. It is however, less clear how access was gained in the earlier phase - possibly from the west via the yards as concluded on the evidence of the earlier survey. A pronounced step within the range has previously been interpreted as the edge of a dais, whose identification seems optimistic. If proven, this would also support the identification of the western end of the building as its 'high' end. The new survey suggests that the step corresponds to the line of an underlying lynchet, although this observation in itself need not invalidate the previous interpretation.

The proximity of the barn (described below) to what has been seen as the private high-status solar block was regarded as somewhat awkward, but was justified by the apparent absence of doorways in the eastern side of the barn. The identification by the new survey of two doorways on this side, apparently blocked at some stage, again calls this theory into question. Access from such a utilitarian building to yards overlooked by service rooms seems more plausible. In this scenario, the building previously interpreted as a solar block might be a kitchen connected by a pentice. The wing extending northwards from the other end of the main range might represent the private rooms of a larger solar range. Although it might be assumed that a solar block should project southwards to enjoy the best light, ranges extending northwards were far from exceptional (see, for example, Pearson *et al.* 1994). In this form, the long south side of the main range might be said to have faced towards the church and the rest of the village, although how access was gained is unclear.

In the second major constructional phase identifiable from the earthworks, the *curia* seems to have been enlarged eastward and northward to encompass an overall

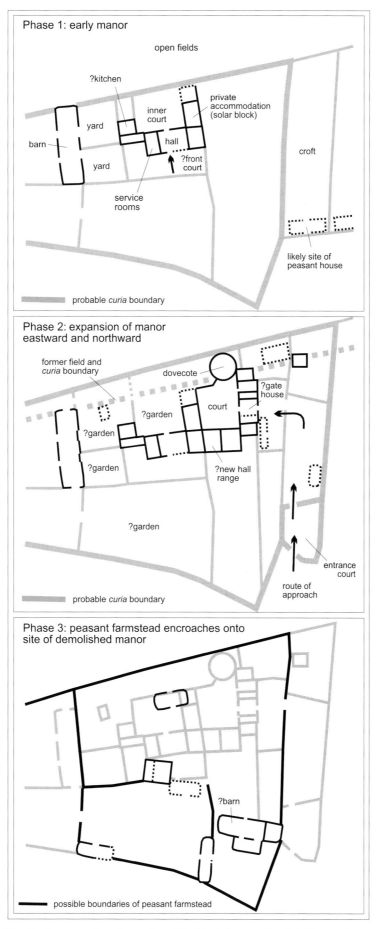

Phase 1: early manor

open fields

?kitchen

inner court

private accommodation (solar block)

yard

barn

hall

?front court

yard

croft

service rooms

likely site of peasant house

▨▨▨ probable *curia* boundary

Phase 2: expansion of manor eastward and northward

former field and *curia* boundary

dovecote

?gate house

?garden

court

?garden

?new hall range

?garden

?garden

entrance court

route of approach

▨▨▨ probable *curia* boundary

Phase 3: peasant farmstead encroaches onto site of demolished manor

?barn

▬▬▬ possible boundaries of peasant farmstead

Fig. 11. Interpretative phase plan of the North Manor. (English Heritage)

area of 0.90ha (2.22 acres). This expansion too seems to accord well with the theory that the North Manor was the property of the Percy family, plausibly representing the period between *c*.1254 and the early 14th century when Peter I and his son Robert III were probably investing considerably in the family's holdings at Wharram (see Ch. 14). To the east, the expansion demanded the reclamation of the westernmost toft and croft of the North Row, whose western boundary can still be discerned. To the north, it involved taking in a 10m wide strip of field land, so that the *curia* encroached on the former southern edge of the field. The narrowness of this strip is suggestive: if the cultivation ridges in the field were aligned north to south at the time when the expansion took place, as they may have been at some stage, it may have been the former headland of the field that was taken in. Alternatively, if the change to the eventual east to west alignment had already occurred, a single ridge may have been taken, but there is no surface trace of any continuation of either feature to the east of the *curia*.

In the same phase, the main east to west range of the building seems to have been extended eastwards to an overall length of 37m, encompassing what has previously been interpreted as a detached kitchen. This expansion is suggested in part by the fact that the eastern end of the range is on a fractionally different alignment from the wings that form the L-shaped portion. The addition may have created what might be interpreted as an outer courtyard, its eastern side formed by a range extending northwards, comprising what appears to be a gatehouse with adjoining rooms. An alternative interpretation might be that the extension was essentially the addition of a whole new hall, which replicated the rooms of the earlier hall, but in a location shifted to the east so as to stand more centrally within the extended *curia*. In this scenario, the outer court would be the main courtyard, and the south frontage of the hall range would have retained an unimpeded aspect. Another possibility is that the new hall was part of the north-south range overlooking the courtyard. In either scenario, the rooms in the Phase 1 building may have become more utilitarian in function and the surrounding compartments may have been converted to gardens at this stage. The dovecote (as previously interpreted, almost certainly correctly) overlooks the northern end of the new courtyard, an arrangement found widely in post-medieval manors. Despite damage done by stone-robbing, the structure remains one of the best preserved components of the manorial complex, with walls surviving to at least 0.5m high.

East of the gatehouse lay a small forecourt, with an opening in its eastern side opposite that in the gatehouse. The northern and southern sides of the forecourt continue the alignment of the rest of the main ranges to the west, while the eastern side follows the western boundary of the former toft. East of the forecourt lies a larger enclosure whose eastern side follows the eastern boundary of the former toft, an area effectively corresponding to the course of Track 2 as interpreted previously (see Fig. 9). The southern end of this outermost enclosure is formed

by a broad bank up to 0.4m high, with an original opening which would have given access on to the village green. Thus, while the focus and orientation of the complex as a whole had apparently shifted eastwards, the outermost entrance remained orientated towards the church and the heart of the village.

On the exterior of the bank that appears to have defined the western edge of the *curia* enclosure are the remains of a rectangular building aligned north-south with internal dimensions of 28m by 7.5m, which has been interpreted, entirely plausibly, as the manorial barn mentioned in a valuation of 1368 (Beresford M.W. 1979, 12). The barn was apparently one of three buildings standing within a yard, which was one of two such enclosures accessed from Track 1. The northern end of the barn initially seems to have lain against the earlier northern boundary, which may have been the headland of the adjacent field when the North Manor was first laid out (see above), and thus presumably allowed access to the barn from the cultivated land. Access from this direction was apparently blocked by the northward expansion of the manorial complex beyond this boundary. In the west side of the building are gaps which must represent broad doorways (as concluded by Hurst and Le Patourel), since both have slight traces of wear outside them. While the evidence for the doorway located centrally in the northern end is also secure, the gap in the southern end is not central and may be the product of later stone-robbing.

Arguably of greater importance is the identification by the new survey of two probable blocked doorways in the eastern wall of the barn, opposite those in the western wall. The gaps are much less clearly defined than those on the west side, and in both cases the blocking wall lies just inside the line of the rest of the wall, a misalignment reminiscent of the construction of the walls of cruck-truss buildings excavated elsewhere around the site. The pattern of opposing doorways, designed to funnel wind through the building to assist threshing, is widespread amongst medieval and later barns. As mentioned above, the identification of possible points of access into the main part of the manorial complex would tend to suggest that the area to the east is unlikely to have been used as a private garden, at least while the opposed doorways were in use. The function of the building after the probable blocking of the eastern doorways is uncertain, but it has been pointed out that doors are commonly located in the end of sheephouses in Yorkshire (Hurst 1984, fig. 4; Beresford and Hurst 1990, 47). It could be that doors were inserted into the north and south ends of the building at the time that the eastern doorways were blocked, signalling an important change in the function of the building and perhaps in the economic basis of the manor.

A series of grants in the 1320s mention the existence of a 'park', lying adjacent to an 'acre enclosed with a ditch', but they do not otherwise specify its size or location. On the assumption that any park would have been directly accessible from the North Manor, apparently the only manor in existence at that date, the enclosure has been equated by Hurst and Porter with the area of the North Row which, it has been deduced, must have been entirely cleared away in 1254, with the park extending beyond it, along the uncultivable valley sides, perhaps as far north as the parish boundary (Rahtz and Watts 2004, 4-5). The 2002 investigation did not securely identify the site or extent of the documented park, but it is worth noting that the bank which defines the northern sides of the extended manorial *curia* and North Row is accompanied on the north by a slight and poorly preserved ditch (though there are hints that this may have been recut in the post-medieval period). An equally slight ditch runs along the western edge of the lynchet that defines the eastern side of Field 1. In both cases, the placement of the ditch in relation to the bank could be compared to a conventional park pale, if the park occupied approximately the same area as Field 1.

The South Manor

In 1955, excavation of Area 10 (Site 9) revealed a sequence of peasant houses, beneath which lay the top of a major stone wall, which a trial trench proved to be set 3m into the ground. Further excavation in 1956 and 1957 showed that the wall was part of an elaborate rectangular stone-built undercroft, built *c.* 1180 on an east-west alignment. This was interpreted as part of the solar block, or *camera*, of a manor house and its outline was eventually laid out for display to visitors. Apart from various dressed stone blocks in the demolition rubble used to backfill the undercroft early in the second half of the 13th century, there was scant evidence for the form of

the upper storey and none at all for the remainder of the building, perhaps due to later disturbance. It has been speculated that the hall may have extended at right angles to the south, and was perhaps built primarily in timber (Beresford and Hurst 1990, plate 9); alternative interpretations are offered in the present volume (pp 232-4 and 264-5). Documentary evidence indicates that the Percy family acquired the rights of both manors in 1254 and since the *camera* had been demolished at about this date, the South Manor was initially linked to the Chamberlain family (Hurst 1979, 138-9). Caution about this conclusion has been expressed more recently (Roffe 2000, 3; see also Ch. 16 below).

With hindsight, the existence of the manorial complex might have been suspected prior to the 1955 excavation on the basis of the earthwork remains, although nothing of the backfilled undercroft itself could have been detected. The building lies within a rectangular *curia*, which is itself anomalous and encloses a number of other unusual features (Figs 12 and 13). The enclosure is defined on south, west and north sides by a substantial bank up to 0.7m high, presumably once surmounted by a wall or similar barrier. The bank is accompanied by an external ditch, now of negligible depth, which has previously only been detected as a discontinuous geophysical anomaly (Beresford and Hurst 1990, fig. 52). The ditch appears to form an integral part of the *curia* boundary, which contradicts the earlier interpretation of the ditch on the northern side as an element of the late Iron Age or Romano-British field system. The same conclusion has also been reached on the evidence of the

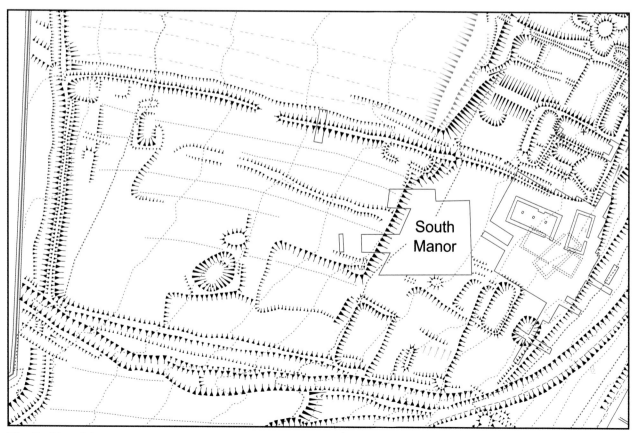

Fig. 12. Plan of the South Manor. Scale 1:1000 (English Heritage)

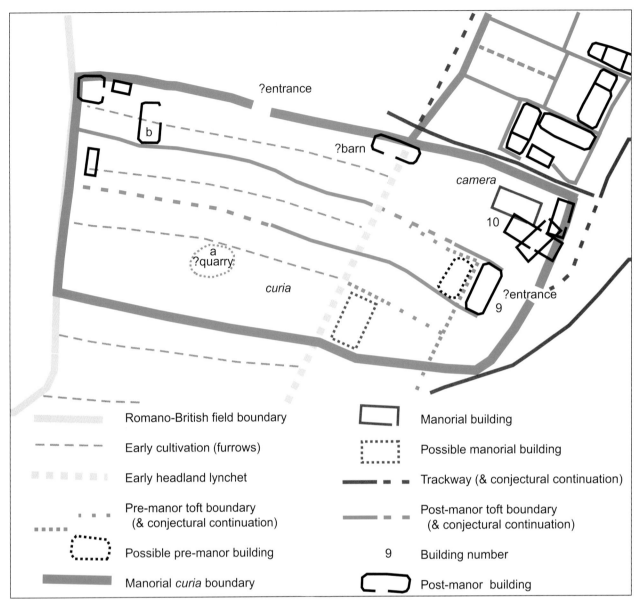

?entrance

?barn

camera

10

a
?quarry

curia

?entrance

9

Romano-British field boundary	
Early cultivation (furrows)	
Early headland lynchet	
Pre-manor toft boundary (& conjectural continuation)	
Possible pre-manor building	
Manorial *curia* boundary	

Manorial building	
Possible manorial building	
Trackway (& conjectural continuation)	
Post-manor toft boundary (& conjectural continuation)	
9 Building number	
Post-manor building	

Fig. 13. Interpretative plan of the South Manor. (English Heritage)

more recent geophysical survey (Linford and Linford 2003, fig. 8; Ch. 4 below). An examination of the four datable sherds recovered from the primary silt of the ditch has also indicated that while three are Roman, one is 12th-century 'Pimply ware' (information supplied by Ann Clark). If this single sherd can be taken as an indicator, the boundary of the *curia* would seem to have been built in the same century as the excavated *camera*. At its western end, however, the *curia* bank directly overlies part of a more extensive field boundary that may be of Romano-British or Late Iron Age origin.

The eastern end of the *curia* seems to have been defined by a ditch, the northern section of which was revealed by excavation in Area 10 (Site 9), continuing the line of the frontage of West Row (north). Although this was augmented by a wall after the demise of the manor, the excavation provided no evidence as to whether any wall existed while the manor still stood. A slight bank, obliquely sectioned by a trial trench extending southwards from the excavations in Area 10, probably

represents the continuation of the later wall rather than part of the original boundary. Interpretation of this bank is further complicated by the existence, apparently on a similar line, of a field boundary shown on the 1836 Dykes estate map and therefore probably laid out in the late 18th century. Nonetheless, given the lack of other possibilities, the point of entry into the manorial complex may have lain at the southern end of Track 4 (Fig. 9), roughly midway along the eastern end of the *curia*. A broad gap in the northern side of the *curia* boundary is also apparently an original opening, for the terminals of the bank on either side are slightly offset from each other, but this seems unlikely to have been a main entrance given its position. The *curia* as a whole would have measured 142m from west to east by 62m wide, with an internal area of 0.83 ha (2.05 acres).

What appears to be a large rectangular building platform is set into the corner formed by the so-called 'lynchet bank' and the southern side of the *curia*. This has not previously been interpreted as the site of a building.

The proportions and large size of the platform are unusual, measuring 17m long from north to south by 10m wide. The sharpness of the scarp along the western side of the platform, where it cuts into the foot of the lynchet bank, suggests that it may represent the line of a chalk wall. The slight scarp along the eastern side does not, however, immediately suggest the existence of any stone walling on this side, which may indicate that the building was a free-standing timber structure, or perhaps a building largely open on one side. In either case, the unusually large size of the building hints that it may have been a component of the manorial complex. Alternatively, given the thorough eradication of the *camera* in contrast to the apparently well-preserved condition of this building and taking into account its proximity to a number of late medieval or post-medieval routes, it may have been associated with one of the late courtyard farm complexes or with post-medieval livestock management.

Planned units of settlement within the village

Detailed descriptions and interpretations of the earthworks are presented elsewhere (Oswald 2004); more general observations about the form of the settlement are reproduced in this account. At an early stage in the Wharram Research Project, it was recognised that the plan of the village as a whole, together with the regular size and shape of many of the individual tofts and crofts, constituted strong evidence that the settlement had been deliberately planned at some stage, and initially it was assumed that there would have been a single episode of planning. From the late 1960s onwards it was, however, broadly accepted that the structure of the village as a whole was likely to represent the outcome of several planning events (e.g. Hurst 1971, fig. 25). Acceptance of this underpins the whole analysis of the settlement structure presented in this report, for it allows the differing characters of individual rows to be appreciated and a dynamic process of development to be inferred. In this report, the units of peasant settlement are distinguished for convenience as the East Row, the North Row, the West Row (north) and the West Row (south) (see Fig. 9).

The East Row

On circumstantial evidence, it seems likely that the East Row was the latest of the planned units of settlement to be established, occupying what had hitherto apparently been part of the northern end of a long village green (Fig. 14). The steeply sloping ground experiences considerable natural soil creep and is boggy in places, making the land inherently unattractive to settlement, and better suited to pasture than to arable agriculture, so that its inferred earlier use as part of the village green is easy to understand. Conversely, the very fact that the site was poorly suited to settlement is one of the strongest indications that the row was a relatively late addition to

the village plan. It would appear that, prior to the imposition of the row, Road 2C, a precursor of Road 2B, may have headed directly for the village church, following a typically gentle gradient across the slope and running through the heart of the village green (Fig. 9). The terraced lower edge of the track seems eventually to have formed the boundary between the tofts and crofts of the East Row. To gain the maximum space for the new row, this early route appears to have been realigned to run as close as possible to the foot of the steeper upper part of the slope, forcing travellers to climb and then descend again to reach the church.

One plausible context for this reorganisation is the quitclaim of the rights of the Chamberlains to the Percy family in 1254, at which time it has been argued that the North Manor underwent a considerable expansion, including an encroachment onto the westernmost plot of the North Row. The East Row could have included a holding for the evicted tenant family, but was also, perhaps, the location of new cottage holdings needed to support the expanded manorial facilities and status. More obviously, the establishment of the row could be seen as an attempt to increase the lord's income and stamp his newly acquired authority onto the form of the settlement through creation of something akin to a conventional two-row planned village, with its focus shifted closer to the gate of the North Manor's *curia*.

The East Row consists of as many as eleven tofts and crofts fronting onto the eastern side of Road 2B and stretching down to the foot of the western side of the valley. Earthwork traces of three buildings, numbered 1 to 3 on Figure 9, were recognised prior to English Heritage's surveys in 2002. Apart from buildings recognised in excavation beneath the Improvement farm, which may lie at or beyond the southernmost end of this row, this part of the settlement has not been investigated by excavation. It was first subjected to geophysical survey in 2002, with good results (Linford and Linford 2003, figs 3 and 6).

The plan of the southern end of the row has previously been reconstructed conjecturally as a rectangle whose southern end coincides with the boundary of the plots enclosing the parsonage and the church itself (Beresford and Hurst 1990, fig. 60). On paper, this gives a pleasing appearance of regularity comparable to the pattern of the other rows, but it ignores the irregular form of the natural topography. The steep-sided, scallop-shaped depression eroded into the valley side by the spring below Wharram Percy Cottages makes the achievement of such regularity impractical. The plan is more likely to have been confined within the triangular space formed by Road 2B on the west, the foot of the slope of the western side of the valley on the east, and the northern edge of the scallop-shaped depression on the south. Although the more southerly of the identifiable plots in this area are fairly long, regular rectangles aligned end-on to Road 2B, they become increasingly irregular in shape towards the northern apex of the triangle.

While the tofts are still set out at right angles to the road, the crofts are laid out perpendicular to the foot of

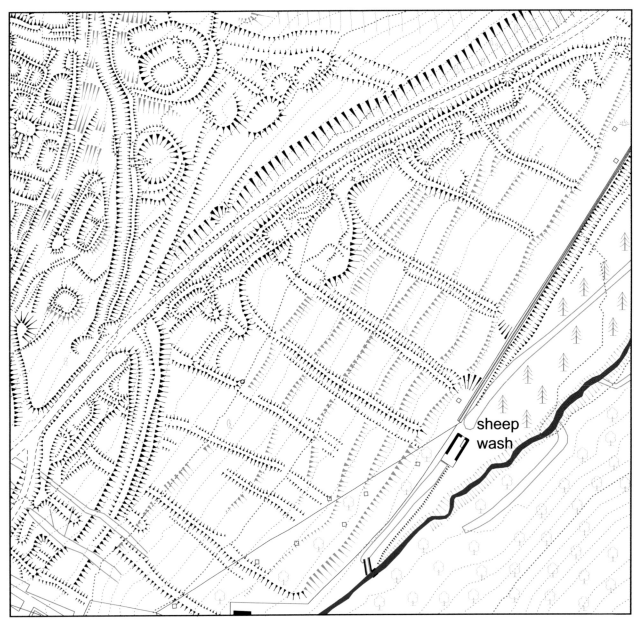

Fig. 14. Plan of the East Row. Scale 1:1000 (English Heritage)

the slope, creating a change of alignment at the junction of the tofts and crofts. From this pattern, it seems likely that Road 2B was established at the same time that the East Row was laid out, coinciding with the abandonment of the putative earlier and easier route, Road 2C. It was also evidently considered desirable, presumably for practical reasons to do with the cultivation of the ground, that the crofts should not be aligned obliquely to the contours. The eastern boundary of the crofts is marked by a continuous scarp up to 0.7m high, which presumably carried a hedge or fence. Its form is essentially that of a substantial lynchet, which presumably built up during the lifetime of the row, which would suggest that the interiors of all the crofts were used to some degree.

There may well have been a 'back lane', but the probable existence of such a route, which would have been little more than a footpath if it existed at all, does not fully account for the broad interval between the ends of

the crofts and the edge of the Wharram stream. Today, this part of the valley floor is dry and level and would apparently make useful cultivable land. The complete avoidance of the valley floor hints that it may once have been much more boggy. The bank that defines the frontage of the row continues beyond its junction with the scarp that defines the eastern side. This may have had the effect of blocking any back lane; there are other stratigraphic hints that the bank may have been rebuilt at some relatively late date, perhaps to carry a hedgeline in the post-medieval period, although no such boundary is depicted on historic maps.

The tofts are of more variable breadth than anywhere else around the village, ranging from 16m to 22m, but there is no sign that this was done deliberately in an attempt to maintain a constant area in the face of the unequal length of the plots. Towards the northern apex of the row, the alignment of the long boundaries, which are more or less parallel towards to the south, becomes less regular. This can only partly be accounted for by the natural topography, so it is tempting to infer that the planning of this part of the village was genuinely more piecemeal, contrasting with the evident regularity of design exhibited by the West Row (north) and the North Row. All the peasant houses that can be detected are aligned side-on to Road 2B, in striking contrast to the West Row (north) in particular, where most of the houses, in their eventual form, were aligned end-on to the frontage. Whether the side-on alignment of the buildings in the East Row simply respects the natural lie of the contours is doubtful, for a number of the tofts at the southern end of the row are sufficiently level to accommodate buildings aligned end-on to the road. It is tempting to draw a parallel with the West Row (north) in its early phase, where Wrathmell (1989a, 44) has suggested that most of the buildings may have been aligned side-on to Track 4. If so, it may follow that the East Row did not experience much modification subsequent to its establishment, as the West Row (north) clearly did. From this, it may be inferred that much of the East Row may also have been abandoned at a relatively early date, presumably for the same reasons that it is likely to have been the latest part of the village to come into existence.

The North Row

The North Row evidently existed in a planned form by the time the *curia* of the North Manor encroached onto its western end, an expansion which can plausibly be argued to have occurred soon after 1254. It has been suggested that the North Row originally comprised six tofts in a row aligned from west to east, but that all these were cleared away when the two manors were amalgamated in 1254. The earthwork investigation undertaken by English Heritage in 2002 supports the first of these observations, but suggests that only the westernmost of the tofts may have been cleared away and that the buildings that formed the courtyard farm may have been converted from surviving earlier buildings. There is further evidence that the sequence as a whole is likely to have been more complex (Fig. 15).

In the first place, it is possible that the ridged cultivation hinted at by possible positive lynchets underlying the North Manor may have extended eastwards to the edge of the western plateau. What may be the southern terminals of these ridges are preserved as positive lynchets on the very limit of the escarpment, to the south of the frontage of the row. In several cases, these more or less coincide with the more prominent positive lynchets that mark the divisions between the crofts of the row, hinting that earlier agriculture may have influenced

Fig. 15. Plan of the North Row. Scale 1:1000 (English Heritage)

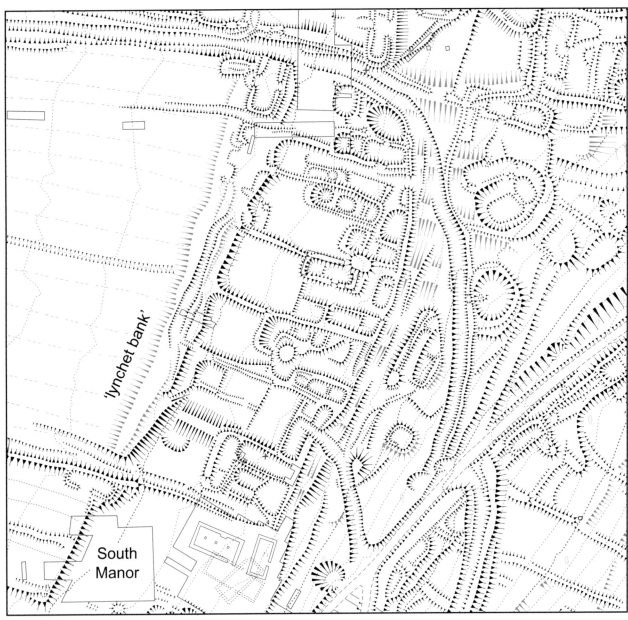

Fig. 16. Plan of the West Row (north). Scale 1:1000 (English Heritage)

the plan of the row. Earlier ploughing, however, might be expected to run perpendicular to the early northern boundary, or parallel to the crest of the western plateau. The alignment of the croft boundaries does not correspond precisely to either of these predictable alignments, so it could be inferred that they were set out with little regard to any pre-existing earthworks.

Secondly, the line of the western section of the frontage of the row may have been pushed back by up to 7m from the edge of the escarpment. This modification is suggested by a distinct change of angle towards the eastern edge of the toft containing Buildings 21 and 22 and a slight scarp which seems to represent a remnant of the earlier boundary. This apparent retraction from the edge of the escarpment may represent a reaction to the natural slumping that has evidently occurred in the locality. The survival of what seem to be the terminals of early cultivation ridges, mentioned above, would tend to

suggest, however, that slumping was not a problem at this point (unless the bulges interpreted as ridge terminals are, in fact, themselves the product of natural slumping). In this scenario, it is possible that the realignment reflects the incorporation of the westernmost toft in the row into the expanded *curia* enclosure of the North Manor, representing another major change to the layout of the row. The amalgamation of at least two of the peasant tofts to form a courtyard farm, in the very late medieval or early post-medieval period, is perhaps the latest of the significant developments. It is notable that at no point is there any sign of an entrance into any of the tofts from Track 3; this apparent absence seems to be due to the reconstruction of the frontage, with the addition of a shallow ditch along its outer edge, to form a continuous boundary around the late courtyard farm.

The dimensions of the tofts do not appear to have been as strictly laid out as those in the West Row (north), discussed below, their widths varying *c*. 2m on either side of 20m. There is similar variation in the width of the adjoining crofts, whose boundaries are easier to distinguish than those of the West Row (south and north) because the divisions are marked by positive lynchets. These boundary lynchets are slightly more pronounced than those associated solely with the cultivation ridges, two of which make up each croft. The lynchet that forms the boundary between the crofts behind Buildings 20 and 21 is accompanied by a shallow ditch, apparently a late subdivision of the land. This variation cannot be entirely accounted for by the constraints of the natural topography. Any variation in the length of the tofts is more difficult to detect, due partly to the putative realignment of the frontage and partly to the existence of Track 14, which seems, at least in the form that can now be seen on the surface, to be a relatively late development, although presumably approximately following the line of an earlier back lane.

The West Row (north)

The West Row (north) can be argued to have been established in its planned form at about the same time that the *curia* of the South Manor was laid out, probably at some point in the 12th century, rather than in the 13th century as suggested previously (Hurst 1971, fig. 25). In its earliest identifiable form, that is excluding the later encroachments into the *curia* of the South Manor, the row comprised six tofts of regular width (18.5m) and one of exactly half that width, all fronting onto a track (Fig. 16). As a whole, the row gives the impression of more regular

planning than any other component of the village. What may be the fragmentary remains of earlier broad ridges (discussed further below) have been identified east of the frontage of the row, and the toft boundaries seem generally to coincide with these, both in spacing and alignment. The form of this section of the so-called 'lynchet bank', which defines the boundary between the tofts and crofts, is also straight and regular, supporting its interpretation (at least of this section and in its initial form) as a deliberately constructed earthwork, contemporary with the laying-out of this part of the planned settlement. The lynchet is discussed further at the end of this chapter.

Six buildings have previously been identified within the tofts, with another (Building 18, Fig. 9) lying on top of the lynchet bank immediately west of the northernmost toft. The addition of the newly recognised buildings to those identified previously suggests that there was a common pattern in the layout of each toft. Buildings and/or boundaries were placed so as to enclose a central courtyard in the front half of each toft, with a more open half to the rear (presumably the 'garth'). Generally, as noted previously, there seems to be a pattern on the western plateau of buildings aligned end-on to the frontage, perhaps replacing an earlier norm of buildings placed side-on (Hurst 1971, 122-4; Wrathmell 1989a, 41-45).

The crofts of the West Row (north) were ultimately amalgamated into two larger fields - the boundary between the fields following a former croft boundary - and ploughed over, each croft being subdivided into two

Plate 5. Aerial photograph of the Wharram Percy village earthworks, viewed from the east in January 1970. (BAG 85. Copyright reserved Cambridge University Collection of Aerial Photography)

virtually flat ridges, echoing developments, perhaps at a similar date, in the North Row (Wrathmell 1989b, fig. 29). As described above, it seems likely that these fields were cultivated towards the end of the village's existence, possibly up until the early decades of the 16th century, from a farmstead somewhere within the West Row (north), whose location cannot be pin-pointed with confidence. As a result, the marginally more pronounced furrows which represent the ploughed-out ditches of the croft boundaries are easier to distinguish under optimum conditions from the air (Plate 5). It seems likely that banks once accompanied the ditches, as is the case with the croft boundaries of the East Row, but that all trace of these has been dug and, or ploughed away. It is possible that there were no hedges between the individual holdings, a pattern observed elsewhere (Roberts 1987, 3.7).

The relationship of the tofts in the West Row (north) to the northern boundary of the *curia* enclosure of the South Manor suggests that the remainder of this sector of the settlement is likely to have been laid out at the same time as the manorial compound, or within the period that it remained in active use. The width of the frontage of the southernmost toft, and consequently those of the tofts to its north, was evidently measured out with respect to the line of the north boundary of the manorial *curia*, for the only tofts whose frontages are of irregular size are the two northernmost in the row. The sides of the tofts, on the other hand, were apparently set out at right angles to the frontage rather than parallel to the northern boundary of the *curia*. As a result, the width of the southernmost toft was distorted and markedly broader at its western end.

It appears therefore, that the north boundary of the manorial enclosure was deliberately singled out as the starting point for the demarcation of the property boundaries. From this, it can again be inferred either that the row postdates the establishment of the manorial complex, or that the two were laid out at the same time. This might suggest a date for the planning and construction of the West Row (north) *c.* 1180, when the excavated *camera* block was constructed. On the other hand, it is entirely possible that this manorial site was in existence before the erection of the *camera* block.

The village green
The triangle of the steep valley side enclosed by the East Row, North Row and West Row (north), an area of about 1ha (2.47 acres), has been interpreted as a village green. The earthwork survey undertaken in parallel with the Wharram excavations depicted this steep ground as essentially an open area, though traversed by a number of trackways (Figs 9 and 14). While there is no reason to dispute the interpretation of the area as a green, the field investigation undertaken by English Heritage in 2002 has identified a number of important earthwork remains scattered across the area, which collectively give the impression of more intensive activity. The southern extent of the green is open to question. Unsurprisingly, the steep section of the valley side east of the West Row

(south) was evidently not settled, so it could be inferred that this formed part of the green. On the other hand, consideration of the overall plan suggests that the green proper would have extended no further south than Track 5a, allowing access from both manors and all three northern rows.

In the centre of this triangular area is a scatter of newly identified earthworks which probably represent the sites of small buildings. The clearest of these are approximately rectangular platforms, occasionally accompanied by slight suggestions of wall-lines, generally aligned along the contours. The largest are only slightly smaller than the houses and other buildings that constitute the rest of the domestic settlement. The earthworks are far slighter and much less crisply defined than the remains of the buildings on the western plateau, but it could not be ascertained whether this difference reflects the effects of soil-creep on the sloping ground, or a genuine difference in the age, function or form of the buildings. Indeed, some of the apparent platforms may be merely the products of small-scale quarrying.

Two circular enclosures, defined by what must formerly have been quite massive embankments (presumably originally supplemented by some form of upstanding barrier), suggest by their size and plan, common livestock pounds. Their existence was hinted at by the previous survey, but not made explicit. Why two should have existed is unclear; it may be that they were of different dates, or related in some way to the early division of the village between two manors. Alternatively, it is possible that one (or both) served a function other than a pound, for example as an arena for bear-baiting, bull-baiting or cock-fighting, or as a small show-ring. On Ham Hill in Somerset, a circular pit of similar size, enclosed by a penannular bank, appears to have served similar functions during fairs held on the hilltop in the post-medieval period, although the fairs originated early in the 12th century (RCHME 1997, 29-30). At Wharram Percy, both enclosures seem to have been sited adjacent to Road 1B and to have faced on to it, though the entrance into the more northerly one is not easy to discern. Both were evidently created by scooping into the natural slope and using the resulting material to augment the height of the surrounding bank.

The more southerly enclosure, with an internal area of 120m², is more clearly defined, but it is uncertain whether this is because it was constructed at a later date or simply because it was less affected by later activity. The internal area of the more northerly of the two enclosures, at 240m², is about twice that of the southern one. A slight kick in the course of Road 1B, which is otherwise a smooth curve, suggests that the construction of the pound may post-date the establishment of the route, forcing traffic to divert slightly to avoid its entrance. There is evidence for a fairly large rectangular building, apparently a later superimposition, occupying its northern side, with vestigial traces of what may be two more structures to its south, sharing a similar alignment. This hints that the pound enclosure may have eventually been converted into a toft-like unit. There is no way of telling whether this modification caused the construction of the second pound, or whether it was merely a piece of opportunism after the enclosure had already fallen into disuse. Either way, it is tempting to infer that the building which reused what had previously been a communal space might have retained some communal function, such as the common oven or the kiln, both of which are mentioned in a document of 1368 (see p. 342).

The West Row (south)

The character of the West Row (south) is so different that it is perhaps misleading even to term the unit a 'row', but that term will be used as a convenient shorthand. There is no convincing evidence for crofts adjoining the tofts, nor for conventional ridge-and-furrow cultivation in the area where crofts would normally be expected (Fig. 17). The scarp convincingly identified by Wrathmell as a continuation of the frontage of the West Row (south) extends well within the *curia* of the South Manor, which would imply the existence of more tofts prior to the imposition of the Manor and suggests a *terminus ante quem* for the foundation of the row of *c*.1180 at the latest. This suggests that the West Row (south) may represent the earliest planned element of the village, as first proposed early in the Wharram Research Project (Hurst 1971, fig. 25).

The bank that defines the northern side of the large building platform set against the foot of the lynchet bank and the southern boundary of the South Manor might represent the modification of the northern boundary of an earlier croft. This lies 20m north of the predicted position of the northern boundary of the next toft south, and there are hints that an earthwork may at one stage have extended eastwards from the building platform as far as the supposed frontage. The toft containing Building 9 may have been reoccupied and redefined after the demise of the South Manor, as described below. The southern boundary of the toft containing Building 10 would also fall neatly into the 20m pattern, and may represent the northern limit of that containing Building 9, perhaps the northernmost in the original layout of the West Row (south). This interpretation might help to explain the slight mismatch of orientations discussed below.

The West Row (north) and the West Row (south) appear, then, to have overlapped in these tofts, and they are crossed by two separate boundary banks, presumably defining the frontages at different dates. Wrathmell (1989a, 41) interprets the change in alignment of successive peasant houses excavated in Area 10 (Site 9), from north to south to north-east to south-west and finally to east to west, as a reaction to the misalignment of the frontages. In view of the complexity of the settlement record as a whole, he stops short of drawing any conclusion as to which is the earlier of the two units. The fact that these tofts lie within the *curia* of the South Manor implies further chronological depth. The relationship between the earthworks at the point where the frontage of the West Row (south) and the *curia*

boundary intersect at first suggests that the frontage of the row cuts through the manorial boundary and is therefore later. Closer inspection reveals however, that both earthworks have been dug away, the edge of this operation coinciding with the line of the frontage, so that the crucial relationship is unintelligible from the surface traces. The West Row (south) comprised as many as twelve tofts fronting onto Track 8a. While their lengths from west to east range from 34m to 42m, their widths are fairly regular, varying only a metre or two on either side of 20m.

The excavation trench known as Area 6 (Site 12), centred on a well-preserved longhouse initially identified from the earthworks and called Building 6. The entire area was interpreted as a single toft, but the investigations may in fact have sampled parts of three. The earliest stone buildings encountered, dating to the late 13th to late 14th centuries, were described as being '... clearly grouped around a courtyard', while the latest longhouse was said to have been '... built in the centre of the site' (Milne 1979b, 48 and 51). The earthwork investigation undertaken by English Heritage in 2002 suggests that parts of three tofts may actually have been examined and that several of the excavated buildings may have lain outside the toft occupied by the well-preserved longhouse. The overall pattern of toft boundaries identified by the new earthwork survey strongly suggests that two boundaries might be expected within the area of excavation (reinforcing the similar suggestion made in Wrathmell 1989b, 33 on the basis of refuse disposal).

Immediately to the west of the excavation trench, in the predictable positions, are what appear to be the stubs of two slight banks, running eastwards from the lynchet bank. Only the more northerly of these stubs was recorded by the earlier survey and neither was recorded as an earthwork within the excavated area. The levels survey undertaken prior to the excavations employed enhanced contours at 6-inch (0.15m) intervals and is therefore insufficient to determine in hindsight whether the earthworks actually continued further eastwards in a slighter form (Milne 1979b, fig. 12). Perhaps more surprisingly, no continuation of the stubs was detected during the excavations, except that the line of the more southerly one corresponds to that of an earthen bank, whose interpretation was left open, running along the southern side of the latest longhouse.

In terms of their dimensions, the two major excavated buildings in Area 6, often held up as examples of typical medieval peasant longhouses, are actually unusually large in the context of the other probable peasant buildings at Wharram, and one of them was probably not domestic. The later and better preserved of the two (that recognised first and referred to as Building 6) was the longhouse, its occupation dating to between the early 15th and early 16th centuries. The more northerly building, which might also have been recognised as an earthwork with hindsight, was a barn, probably demolished before the longhouse was abandoned to make way for an enlarged courtyard (Wrathmell 1989b, 32, fig. 23). The size of

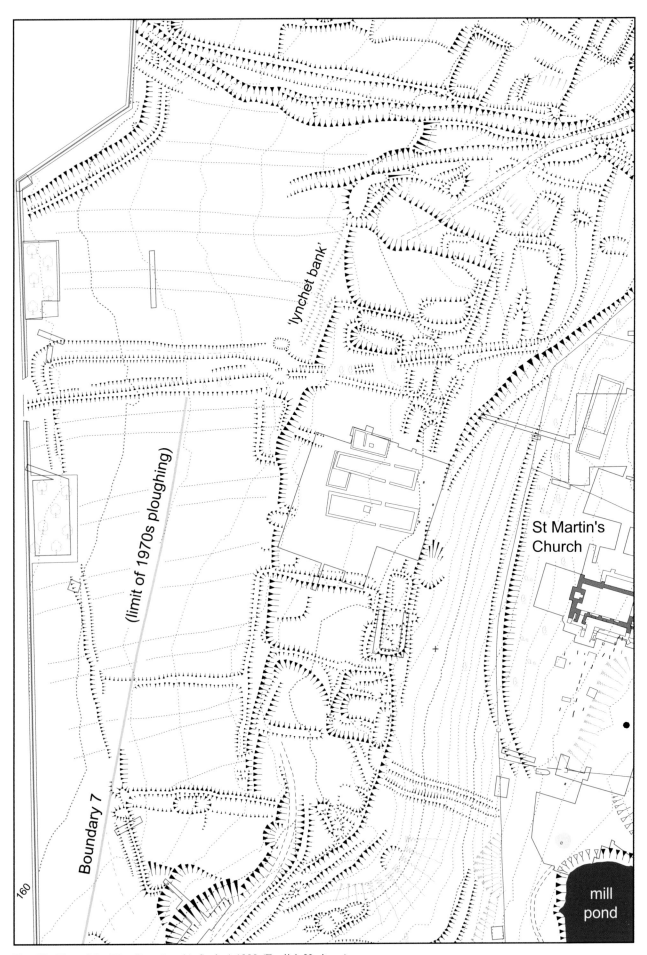

'lynchet bank'

(limit of 1970s ploughing)

Boundary 7

160

St Martin's
Church

mill
pond

Fig. 17. Plan of the West Row (south). Scale 1:1000 (English Heritage)

these buildings, carrying with it an implication of wealth and status, may well be significant.

The West Row (south) is distinctive in several respects, including its seeming isolation from the coherent core of the village plan, its lack of regularity, the absence of crofts, and the exceptionally large size (by comparison with the rest of the village) of some of the peasant houses. It has tentatively been suggested that this may be the earliest settlement unit of the village, as far as can be detected through analytical earthwork survey, apparently originating before the South Manor was established. This suggestion, and the possible association of this element of the village plan with free peasants of the Late Saxon period, is developed by Everson and Stocker in Chapter 13.

Early cultivation ridges
The new geophysical survey of Wharram Percy (Ch. 4) has identified a series of curvilinear enclosures on the plateau which, it is argued (Chs 9 and 11), constitute part of the Middle Saxon settlement. These enclosures provide long-overdue context for the puzzling distribution of Middle Saxon finds encountered by dispersed trial excavations; the excavated finds, in turn, offer dating evidence for the enclosures revealed through the geophysics. Earthwork survey makes its own indirect but important contribution to the picture. English Heritage's new fieldwork has independently identified extremely faint traces (at the very limits of what is perceptible with the naked eye) of unusually broad ridge-and-furrow ploughing, which apparently represents the mechanism by which the Middle Saxon enclosure ditches and (presumably) banks were erased, and seems to predate the establishment of much, and perhaps even all, of the medieval village proper.

The ridges, which survive best within and to the south of the *curia* of the South Manor, are up to 20m wide and gently cambered so that the intervening furrows also appear extraordinarily broad; their limits are consequently distinguished by pairs of dotted (rather than central dashed) lines on Figure 8. Were it not for the other archaeological evidence available, it would be easy to misinterpret them as periglacial soil stripes, similar in essence to those recorded in East Anglia (notably around Grimes Graves in Norfolk; Corbett 1973, figs 8 and 9). In the crofts adjoining the southern half of the West Row, the earlier survey recorded traces of the furrows from the 1946 RAF aerial photographs, on which they are clearly visible. Detailed examination on the ground under optimal conditions allows their alignment and extent to be more accurately plotted.

It is difficult now to gauge how far west the ridges extended, but they do seem to stretch at least as far as the present limit of arable cultivation. The fact that the ridges within the *curia* are in a similar condition to those outside it to the south suggests that they were already in that condition when the South Manor was laid out, that is, probably by the later 12th century. In relation to the layout of the southern half of the west row, there are three key observations: nowhere do the lines of the broad furrows coincide perfectly with the lines of the proposed toft boundaries; they do not share the same alignment; the so-called 'lynchet bank' (see below) cuts through the ridges.

North of the *curia* of the South Manor, conventional ridge and furrow in the crofts that make up the West Row (north) has apparently erased the early ridges, only leaving what appear to be remnants extending eastwards from the frontage of the row as far as the very edge of the plateau. There, the ridges seem to end in pronounced terminals, rather than on a conventional headland bank, perhaps indicating that the ploughing was not prolonged. Notably, several of the buildings on the village green and both livestock pounds seem to have made use of the relatively level platforms on the edge of the escarpment offered by the terminals of the ridges. The ridges are also apparently visible as a series of gentle undulations in the narrow interval between the frontage of the row and the course of Track 4 (Fig. 9). Significantly, unlike the West Row (south), the lines of the supposed ridges appear to coincide closely with the lateral boundaries of the tofts. Furthermore, Road 1C cuts through several of the ridges, suggesting that it is unlikely to have been part of the Romano-British route, but instead developed within the medieval period. The northernmost ridge seems to lie close against the side of Road 1B.

Taken together, the earthwork evidence seems to point to an episode of ploughing, which was perhaps brief but sufficiently intensive to erase enclosure banks and ditches across a wide expanse of the plateau. This took place somewhere between the abandonment of the Middle Saxon curvilinear enclosures, perhaps in the late 8th century or early 9th, and the final quarter of the 12th century – but probably in the earlier part of that broad time-frame. It is possible that the ploughing represents an unusual form of pre-Conquest ridge-and-furrow cultivation, though it may initially have been employed to level and prepare the site for the establishment of the rectilinear village in the Late Saxon period.

The 'lynchet bank'
The so-called lynchet bank is one of the most intriguing – and most discussed – earthworks at Wharram Percy. The main body of the bank appears to be a terrace-like accumulation of soil created by repeated ploughing (in other words, a 'positive lynchet'), which extends southwards for some 380m from the southern edge of Road 1B (Figs 16 and 17). It parallels the edge of the western plateau, following a sinuous curve that is reminiscent of the so-called 'reverse-S' pattern created by the use of teams of oxen to draw a plough. The steep face of the lynchet stands to a maximum height of 1.6m, even though the natural slope is not pronounced, and the sheer size of the earthwork has led to consideration of the possibility that it is actually a deliberate construction contemporary with the construction of the toft boundaries, perhaps a 'wall' made of turf and soil stripped from the rear of the tofts, possibly leaving a

surface of bare chalk (Beresford and Hurst 1990, 78). The size of the scarp does appear to have been enhanced in places by other features and by erosion within the tofts. For parts of its length, a broad bank, 0.2m high on average, runs along the top of the lynchet. This seems to have originated in the medieval period as a plough headland and may well have served as a path along the rear of the house plots. The earthwork as a whole, presumably surmounted by a hedge or fence, clearly served to divide the ends of the tofts from the adjacent crofts.

Although it was initially assumed that all the village earthworks were of broadly the same date, the 'lynchet bank' was soon recognised as being an anomaly of considerable importance to the understanding of the plan of the medieval village and potentially of earlier origin (Beresford M.W. 1979, 23). Following a visit to Wharram Percy in 1978 by Peter Fowler, then Secretary of the Royal Commission on the Historical Monuments of England, it was interpreted as a possible Bronze Age 'linear earthwork' boundary (information from Chris Dunn, retired RCHME field surveyor; Hurst 1984, 84-85 and fig.1; Beresford and Hurst 1990, 78). Excavations that were intended to settle the question produced only a single sherd of pottery which, although not strictly diagnostic, has been interpreted as pointing to a 12th-century date. The excavation seemed to show however, that the lynchet bank was stratigraphically later than features of Late Saxon date. Most recently, this evidence has also been questioned and it has been concluded that the origin of the earthwork remains uncertain: whether earlier than, contemporary with, or later than the toft boundaries that adjoin it (Stamper *et al.* 2000, 19).

It is easy to follow the deductive process by which Beresford and Fowler reached the conclusion that the earthwork predates the medieval village, for most of the observations are sound and are correctly depicted on the plan produced by the earlier survey. Firstly, the lynchet bank is clearly cut into by Tracks 5b and 6 (the former previously thought, erroneously, to be of Iron Age or Roman origin, Fig. 9), as well as by several minor hollows which apparently gave access to the headland from the rear of the tofts. One particular section is not adequately depicted on the earlier survey: the short surviving length of the lynchet bank between Tracks 5b and 6 maintains the same alignment as the rest of the earthwork, which would be almost inconceivable were the tracks earlier than the lynchet. Since the English Heritage investigation also suggests that Tracks 5b and 6 are probably of 18th-century date, this stratigraphic relationship does not in itself rule out a medieval origin for the lynchet bank.

Secondly, notwithstanding the most recent inconclusive appraisal of the evidence, in almost every instance the banks that form the medieval toft boundaries can be seen to ride over the lynchet bank. In the other instances, the relationship of one earthwork to the other is merely uncertain; none suggests that the lynchet bank is later. It could be argued that what is visible on the surface represents only the latest phase of the earthwork and that the toft boundaries were probably redefined many times, disguising or reversing the original stratigraphic relationship. Yet it may be significant that the boundary of the *curia* enclosure of the South Manor, which seems less likely to have been redefined after the *camera* of the South Manor was demolished, also rides over the lynchet bank. Similarly, a large platform that may well be the site of one of the manorial buildings, which has previously gone unrecognised, is cut into the foot of the lynchet bank. In short, were it not for the excavated evidence which apparently shows the contrary, there would be little hesitation in inferring that the lynchet bank is of earlier origin than the foundation of the manorial enclosure and the contemporary episode of planning.

It has however, been inherent in this and previous interpretations of the earthwork that the lynchet bank can be treated as a single feature. Although it describes a sinuous curve overall, close consideration reveals that there are slight differences in its form. Where it runs behind the West Row (north), the scarp is higher and sharper, running very straight and parallel to the frontage of the row. By contrast, where it runs behind the West Row (south), it is generally lower, making several minor changes of course and not running precisely parallel to the frontage, giving the impression of a more organic development.

This perception is sustained by the apparent existence of a series of very slight cultivation ridges of unusual form, which were discussed in the previous section of this chapter. To summarise, along the length of the West Row (south), these ridges are cut by the lynchet bank, but cannot be traced further east, suggesting that they may, in essence, be the manifestation of the ploughing responsible for creating the lynchet, though truncated by later activity within the tofts. If so, they may be contemporary in origin with the establishment of this part of the village though not necessarily the planned row. On the other hand, for the length of the West Row (north) the ridges seem to have extended beyond the lynchet bank and beyond the earthworks of the tofts themselves. Alternatively, it may be that the survival of the ridges beyond the frontage of the West Row (north) is a freak and that the whole settlement was laid out over the ridged cultivation. The more obvious inference, although the evidence is far from clear-cut, is that the southern half of the lynchet bank is in essence a genuine lynchet, though undoubtedly modified by the laying out of the West Row (south), while the northern half is a deliberately built boundary bank. It is difficult to pin-point precisely where these putatively different features join, but the line of the earthwork kicks westwards by some 7m at or near the northern side of the *curia* of the South Manor. As discussed earlier in this chapter, it has been argued that the West Row (south) and (north) joined at about the same place (Wrathmell 1989a, 41-2).

Fowler's early suggestion that the lynchet bank might follow the line of a Bronze Age linear earthwork can be firmly ruled out. There are many examples of such

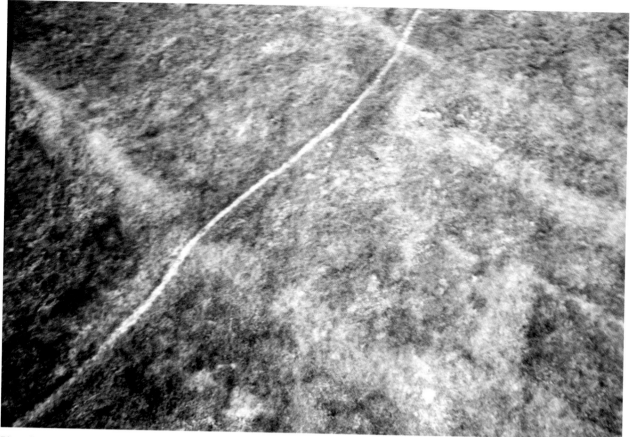

Plate 6. Foundations of buildings and toft boundaries in the West Row (north), showing as parch marks in 1986. Viewed from the south, the building at top right is Building 15 (Site 3) in *Wharram VI*, fig. 30. (English Heritage)

boundary earthworks on the Yorkshire Wolds, including one 900m south of Wharram Percy. Of this, a short stretch on the steep valley side survives well in earthwork form as a typical double bank with a medial ditch, while the remainder can be traced as a crop mark (Stoertz 1997, map 1; Ch. 7 below). Fowler suggested a Bronze Age date, in line with examples known at that date on the chalk uplands of Wessex, but it now seems likely that the earliest examples in Yorkshire, and perhaps beyond, date to the Late Neolithic, while in the Yorkshire region the tradition certainly continued well into the Iron Age (Spratt 1989; Vyner 1994; 2008). The relationships of such boundaries to the natural topography are distinctive, most running across relatively narrow necks of land, usually at right angles to the contours and often between the heads or junctions of valleys. The lynchet bank has none of these characteristics and its stratigraphic relationship to the early ridged cultivation renders a prehistoric date implausible. Its two distinct stretches probably reflect the development of adjacent cultivation and settlement activity between the late 8th and late 12th centuries.

Directions for future research
The essence of the method of analytical field survey - the process of observation, analysis and recording - has not changed significantly since the 19th century, but expectations of the technique's potential in its own right to deliver understanding, as opposed to merely a sterile

site plan on which to plot excavations, have progressed much further. Theories about the development of the village based on the surviving earthworks must of course be advanced with full awareness of the inherent limitations of the evidence. Yet, even at this stage in the long history of research at Wharram, it is unwise to assume that investigation through earthwork survey has no further potential to deliver useful insights.

It is too soon, as yet, to foresee what new contributions future field survey in the traditional mode might make. The limited objectives of the ground modelling undertaken in 2002 might be extended further and the resolution consequently increased, but possibly without yielding great dividends in terms of improved understanding. Airborne survey using Lidar, which at best currently offers resolution in the region of 0.25m, would be suitable for more comprehensive topographic modeling, but not (yet) for the recording of the slightest earthworks. Even terrestrial scanning, which offers much higher resolution recording than Lidar, disappointingly failed to pick out slighter earthworks that are clearly detectable with the naked eye during trials in the wake of the main fieldwork (again in part due to summer vegetation conditions).

Yet this technology might, in due course, be usefully applied to areas where earthworks are extremely slight and degraded, such as the site of supposed Middle Saxon settlement revealed by geophysical survey. The trained eye can recognise extremely subtle changes, yet it is drawn to sharper anomalies (scarps, in other words) while high resolution scanning could in theory detect form in micro-topography that appears unintelligibly amorphous to the naked eye. Extensive high-resolution geophysical surveys and low-level aerial photography carried out in drought conditions have already demonstrated their potential for recording sub-surface stonework with remarkable clarity (see Plate 6 and Wrathmell 1989a, 41 and fig. 30). The lesson of the new surveys, then, and indeed of the Wharram Research Project as a whole, is that dialogue between different research techniques is more likely to offer new insights than any single technique applied in isolation.

4 A New Geophysical Survey of Wharram Percy

by Paul Linford, Neil Linford and Andrew David

Introduction

The English Heritage Geophysics Team has been involved with the Wharram Research Project over much of its life. The first geophysical survey was undertaken in 1970 and visits to the site continued until 1989, the penultimate season of excavation, by which time a total of eight separate surveys had been carried out. During subsequent assessment of the survey evidence to produce this volume it was realised that the conclusions could be strengthened if magnetometer survey coverage were extended to the southern part of the plateau area which lies above the valley due west of St Martin's church. This part of the site had not previously been surveyed and the extent of pre-medieval occupation there was unclear. It was also noted that, between 1970 and 1989, several generations of magnetometer had been employed. Development of the technique over this period meant that the instrument used for the 1989 survey was ten times more sensitive than those used earlier. Furthermore, digital recording of the magnetometer results had only been possible for the 1987 and 1989 surveys owing to advances in computer technology. Prior to this, measurements were recorded as a continuous paper trace using a portable chart recorder, making the results almost impossible to re-analyse quantitatively or to integrate with other surveys. In addition, different grid alignments had been used over the course of the project and combining the results of the various, often overlapping, survey areas would not be straightforward.

It was thus decided that the most desirable course of action would be to carry out a new magnetometer survey, using modern instruments, over all parts of the Guardianship area where survey was practicable. Those areas of the arable fields adjacent to the Guardianship area would also be covered, so that, where necessary, archaeological anomalies could be traced beyond the immediate area of the medieval village. This strategy offered the benefit of providing a complete magnetic map for all the open areas of Wharram Percy referenced to a single survey grid established to a high degree of accuracy using modern satellite global positioning system (GPS) equipment. As a result, the site was visited by the Geophysics Team during the period 16 to 25 September 2002, when the entire site was surveyed. Full details of the 2002 survey have been reported by Linford and Linford (2003) where the results of the survey visits made in 1984, 1987 and 1989 are also summarised. Results of the five earlier surveys up until 1982 have been reported by David (1982). The following discussion focuses on the results of the 2002 magnetometer survey, which is by far the most extensive of the geophysical surveys so far carried out at Wharram Percy.

Results of the survey

The results of the fluxgate gradiometer survey are depicted as a greyscale plot in Figure 18. A schematic plan of all significant geophysical anomalies is presented in Figure 19 and it is clear that many of these might potentially have an archaeological cause. In several places, multiple anomalies overlie one another and the resulting dense palimpsest is difficult to interpret. For this reason, an attempt has been made to group the geophysical anomalies into four units. Three of these correlate approximately with different periods of occupation at the site; the fourth identifies anomalies likely to have a non-archaeological cause. The three archaeological groups are depicted separately in Figures 20-22, where the differentiation between them has been based upon four criteria: excavated evidence; geophysical character; correlation with earthworks, and alignment or contiguity.

Excavated evidence

In many parts of the site, anomalies detected in the magnetometer survey clearly correspond with features discovered in excavation trenches. In particular, between 1985 and 1990, Julian Richards undertook a series of excavations specifically to test the results of the 1984 and 1989 magnetometer surveys. Where such evidence was available at the time of the survey, it was possible to date anomalies to a specific period with a high degree of confidence. Since the publication of the survey report, the post-excavation analysis of the 'western plateau' sites (Sites 70, 78 etc.: see Ch. 9) has largely confirmed the inferences drawn on the basis of the information available in 2002.

Geophysical character

There is a distinct variation in the magnetic intensity of the detected anomalies. Those in the north-west of the survey area that appear to be related to the Iron Age and Roman settlement are relatively strongly magnetised, and exhibit peak magnitudes that are typically around 5-10nT and sometimes much higher. This is despite the amount of subsequent occupation activity overlying them, as attested by often substantial earthworks. By contrast, many of the anomalies that are clearly associated with extant medieval earthworks are typically only weakly magnetised, with peak magnitudes around 1-2nT. This variation in geophysical character is likely to reflect differences both in the form of the causative features and in the nature of the contemporary activities contributing to the enhancement of soil magnetisation.

Correlation with earthworks

Many of the detected anomalies clearly correspond in position and shape with earthworks visible on the ground. Such anomalies have been grouped into the medieval unit. Conversely, those anomalies that appear to be cut by the earthworks have been grouped into one of the other two units on the assumption that they could not be contemporary with the medieval layout of the village reflected in the earthwork plan.

Alignment and contiguity

Finally, where an anomaly is contiguous with, or on the same alignment as, anomalies that fall into one of the above classes, it has been assumed to be contemporary with them. Conversely, anomalies on different alignments or that overlie each other have been assumed to belong to different units.

The three archaeological units that result from this grouping are: 'Iron Age and Roman settlement', 'medieval settlement' and 'other settlement evidence'. The last unit contains many anomalies that may result from occupation at Wharram prior to the Late Iron Age/Roman settlement or in the Anglo-Saxon period, but a post-medieval origin for some of these may also be considered. The title of the unit reflects the inherent uncertainty in ascribing an archaeological period to this group.

Such a scheme obviously has its shortcomings, not least because medieval occupation at the site persisted for over 500 years, during which time many changes to the layout of the village occurred. Furthermore, it is likely that some geophysical anomalies have been misclassified. This is particularly likely in areas where alignments appear to have been preserved between periods, such as the superimposed Roman and medieval east-west trackways to the north-west of the site (identified as Road 1A and 1B in Ch. 3, Fig. 9). Nevertheless, the classification clarifies the presentation of the geophysical results and provides a framework for their discussion.

Anomalies relating to Iron Age and Roman settlement

The most intense magnetic anomalies at Wharram Percy are those forming a conjoined series of rectilinear enclosures at the north-western corner of the Guardianship area (Fig. 20). Where these have been investigated by excavation (see Chs 5 and 6 below) they have been found to be enclosure ditches cut into the underlying chalk and relating to Late Iron Age and Roman occupation at the site. This set of anomalies is not aligned with any of the earthworks visible on the ground and it is remarkable that they are still so clearly detectable given the extent of later occupation that has occurred in this area.

The most notable of these anomalies is the almost rectangular, North-west Enclosure where the peak magnetic anomaly strength is in excess of 10nT. This was first noticed as a crop-mark in aerial photographs (e.g.: NMR: SE8564/13 frame 149), although its significance was not recognised until the 1970s (Beresford and Hurst 1990, 19 fig. 4). An excavation across the anomaly was carried out in 1989 and 1990 (Site 91: Clark and Wrathmell 2004, 302-40) which revealed that it was caused by a ditch some 3.6 to 3.9m wide and about 1.8m deep which has been dated to the Late Roman period. Removal of the original, magnetically enhanced, ditch-fill in Site 91 has caused the apparent break in the line of the ditch visible in the magnetometer survey.

The features within the enclosure were thought possibly to represent the outbuildings of a villa, the main villa building being located towards the centre of the enclosure. This conjecture was partly based on a comparison with the geophysical evidence from the nearby Roman villa site at Wharram le Street (David 1980; Beresford and Hurst 1990, 87 fig. 64), excavated by Philip Rahtz (*Wharram IV*). There, the villa building was found to be in the centre of a central square enclosure of similar dimensions to the one at Wharram Percy. Furthermore, the pattern of magnetic anomalies within the Wharram le Street villa enclosure is similar to that revealed by the present survey. Unfortunately, the fields were being sown at the time of the 2002 survey and it was not possible to revisit the central part of this enclosure after the initial magnetometer survey. Subsequent excavations in the northern part of the enclosure, reported in Chapter 5 below, revealed material cultural traces more in keeping with a farmstead than a villa.

The Roman enclosure appears to be set within a larger rectangular enclosure, defined on three sides by a narrower ditch, running along the northern side of the main Roman east-west routeway through the settlement. Confirmation of its date was discovered during excavations in the North Manor area (Site 60) which indicated that the road was already in use in the Late Iron Age and Roman periods. Two *Grubenhäuser* were also found, dating either to the Early or the Middle Saxon periods (see Ch. 7 below); these were cut into a Roman metalled surface. It is interesting to compare the route of this Iron Age/Roman road with those of the later roadways in the medieval period, and their relationship is reviewed at some length in Chapter 7.

The easternmost of the Iron Age/Roman enclosures was investigated in the excavation of Sites 45 and 60, which revealed a ditched Late Iron Age and Early Roman enclosure with an entrance giving access from the

45

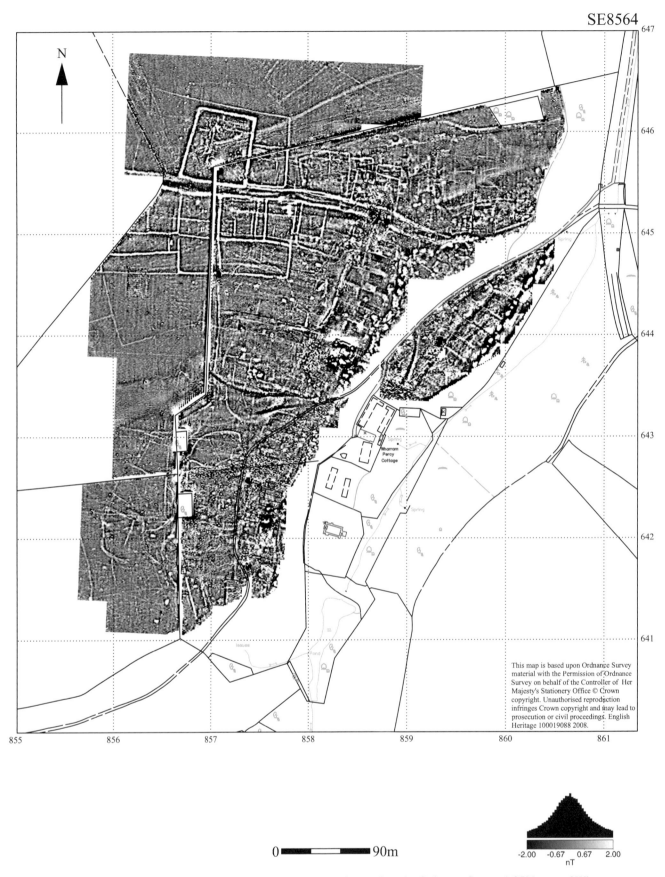

SE8564

This map is based upon Ordnance Survey material with the Permission of Ordnance Survey on behalf of the Controller of Her Majesty's Stationery Office © Crown copyright. Unauthorised reproduction infringes Crown copyright and may lead to prosecution or civil proceedings. English Heritage 100019088 2008.

0 ▬▬▬▬ 90m

-2.00   -0.67   0.67   2.00
nT

Fig. 18. Linear greyscale plot of the 2002 magnetometer survey superimposed on the Ordnance Survey 1:2500 map of Wharram Percy. (English Heritage)

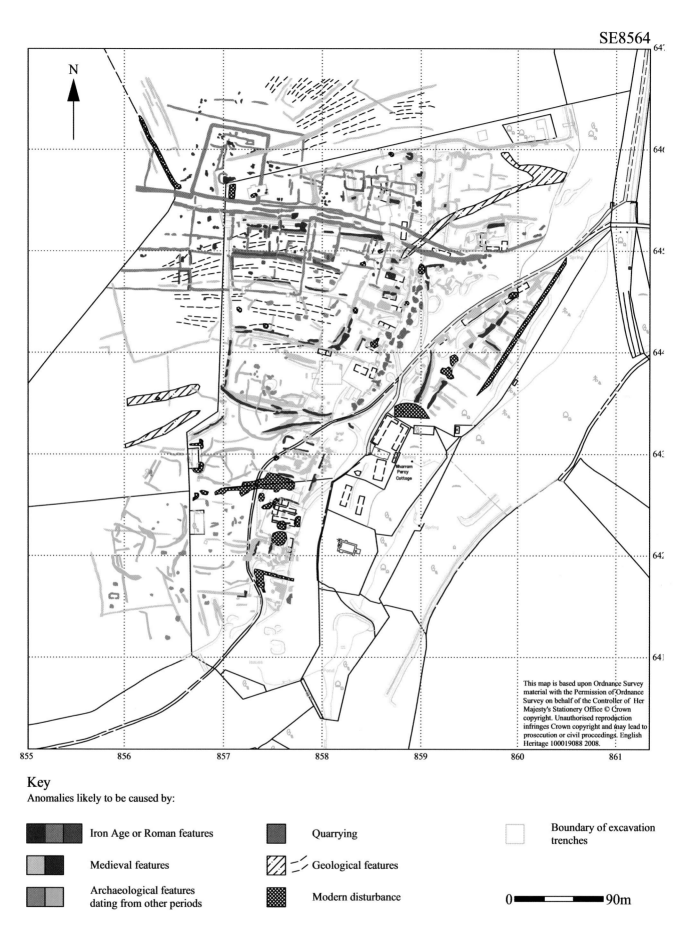

SE8564

This map is based upon Ordnance Survey material with the Permission of Ordnance Survey on behalf of the Controller of Her Majesty's Stationery Office © Crown copyright. Unauthorised reproduction infringes Crown copyright and may lead to prosecution or civil proceedings. English Heritage 100019088 2008.

Key

Anomalies likely to be caused by:

Iron Age or Roman features

Medieval features

Archaeological features dating from other periods

Quarrying

Geological features

Modern disturbance

Boundary of excavation trenches

0 ▬▬▬ 90m

Fig. 19. Interpretation of anomalies in the 2002 magnetometer survey superimposed on the Ordnance Survey 1:2500 map of Wharram Percy. Earthworks are shown in grey. (English Heritage)

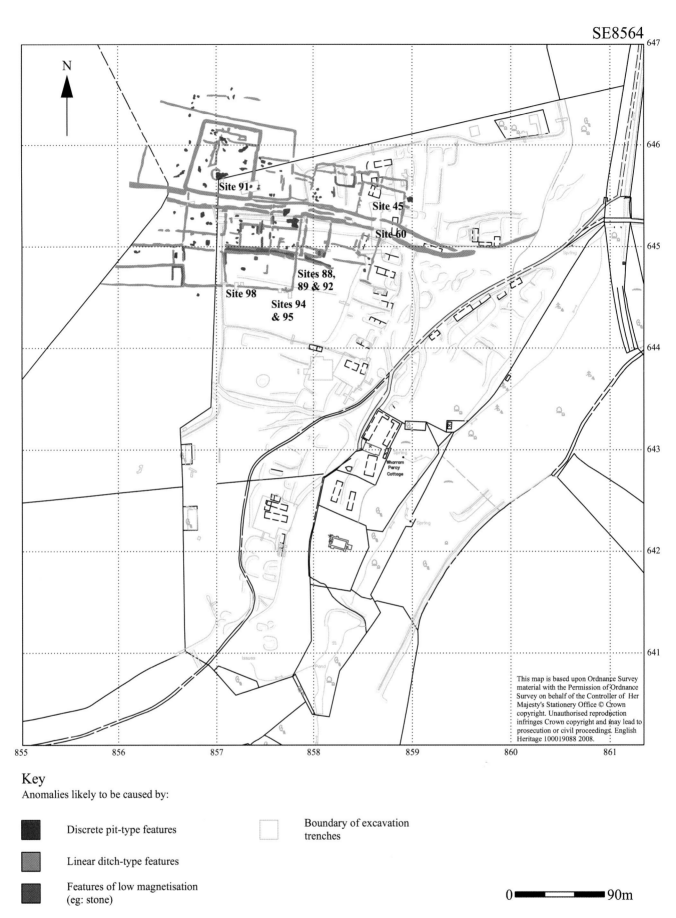

SE8564

Key

Anomalies likely to be caused by:

Discrete pit-type features

Linear ditch-type features

Features of low magnetisation (eg: stone)

Boundary of excavation trenches

0 ▬▬▬ 90m

Fig. 20. Interpretation of potential Iron Age and Roman anomalies detected in the 2002 magnetometer survey superimposed on the Ordnance Survey 1:2500 map of Wharram Percy. Earthworks are shown in grey. (English Heritage)

48

routeway on the south (Milne 2004, 19-35; Rahtz and Watts 2004, 35-66 and Ch. 6 below). The geophysical evidence for a complex series of interlinked rectilinear enclosures immediately north and north-west tends to support the inference that this enclosure was the focus of an Iron Age and Early Roman settlement. The excavations also show that this area continued to be utilised throughout the Roman period with a sequence of grain driers from the late Roman period being discovered. Further excavations at Sites 88, 89, 92, 94, 95 and 98 have confirmed that the sections of the ditch anomalies depicted in these locations in Figure 20 were in use during the Iron Age and Roman periods, increasing confidence in the map of Iron Age and Roman settlement that has been extrapolated from the geophysical evidence.

Anomalies relating to medieval settlement
The anomalies presumed to be due to medieval features are generally less strongly magnetised than the Iron Age and Roman ones just discussed, despite the fact that they often correlate in position with quite substantial surviving earthworks (Fig. 21). This is perhaps because the causative entities are often upstanding rather than cut features capable of holding large volumes of magnetically enhanced backfill. Furthermore, in the case of depressions and ditches dating from the medieval period, the soil backfill may have been subject to less anthropogenic enhancement. Steve Roskams suggests one possible explanation for such enhancement of earlier features: that it resulted from the specific refuse discard practices adopted by the people who made use of these enclosures (see Ch. 6).

Nevertheless, the magnetic survey has detected many medieval features at Wharram Percy. One notable example is the hollow way running west out of the village (Ch. 3, Plate 5). The banks to either side of this thoroughfare have been detected where they survive as earthworks. These run from Site 60 in the east, where the road was investigated by excavation, to a point some 30m south of Site 91 in the west. The peak magnitude of the magnetic anomalies is, however, much weaker (~2-3 nT) than those created by the parallel ditches running just north of the original prehistoric trackway (~7-10 nT).

Immediately north of Site 45 the magnetometer survey has detected anomalies caused by the remains of the complex of medieval buildings identified as the North Manor. It has been possible to distinguish these anomalies from those caused by earlier Iron Age and Roman enclosure ditches, upon which they are superimposed, owing to differences in alignment and peak anomaly strength. To the east of this area, a number of faint linear magnetic anomalies have been marked. They appear to run approximately east-west on an alignment similar to that of the manor complex. The surviving earthworks (Ch. 3) indicate the north-south aligned crofts behind the North Row of medieval dwellings in this area. The magnetic map suggests, however, another pattern of land division, perhaps originating during the late medieval period.

The enclosure bank running round the west and north sides of the North Manor *curia* has been detected in the magnetic map as two narrow, linear anomalies of positive magnetic field gradient separated by a band of slightly negative magnetic field gradient. The form of the magnetic anomaly over these banks reflects, at least in part, the topographic shape of the earthwork rather than differences in the magnetic susceptibility of subsurface features. A diminution in the magnetic gradient would be expected on the crest of an upstanding earthwork bank even if it were composed of soil of homogeneous magnetic susceptibility (Linington 1973).

Several other earthworks to the south also exhibit a similar magnetic signature including the so-called 'lynchet bank' (see Ch. 3, Figs 16 and 17), the western boundary of the West Row (north) crofts and the boundaries of the South Manor *curia* (particularly the northern and western boundaries). The magnetometer survey has detected only anomalies likely to result from the medieval earthworks rather than any strongly magnetised linear ditch responses like those exhibited by the Late Iron Age and Roman features discussed above. On the other hand, the topographical survey suggests that the western boundary may overlie a Romano-British boundary (Fig. 13), and the excavations at Site 37 further north revealed a ditch backfilled (on the evidence of the pottery it contained) before the end of the Roman period (Ch. 1). It may be that the discard practices suggested by Roskams (above) as the cause of the strong magnetic responses were focused on the habitation areas and not so common in the fields beyond.

As for the 'lynchet bank' itself, running south from Site 60, through the South Manor excavation Sites 81 and 90 and onwards to the southern end of the West Row, the currently available excavation evidence indicates a post-Roman origin (Stamper *et al.* 2000, 38). The most recent interpretation of the earthwork concurs (Ch. 3), and further suggests that it may not be the single feature previously identified, but formed from two separate elements. The magnetic map shows an anomaly similar to that of the North Manor *curia* boundary earthwork running south from about 40m south of Site 60 towards the South Manor *curia*. This then appears to turn west to run along the northern boundary of the latter, whilst the southern continuation of the 'lynchet bank' through Sites 81 and 90 and beyond is largely invisible to the magnetometer. Thus magnetic survey supports the suggestion that the earthwork may be composed of at least two different components along its length. No strongly magnetised linear anomalies similar to the Iron Age and Roman boundary ditches are apparent. Hence, the geophysical survey cannot offer any evidence to support a prehistoric origin for this boundary.

The medieval arrangement of croft boundaries has been detected most clearly in the East Row of the village (cf. Ch. 3, Fig. 14), as a series of parallel linear anomalies about 15m apart and approximately perpendicular to the eastern boundary fence of the guardianship area. Seven separate crofts can be distinguished. Also, a very faint

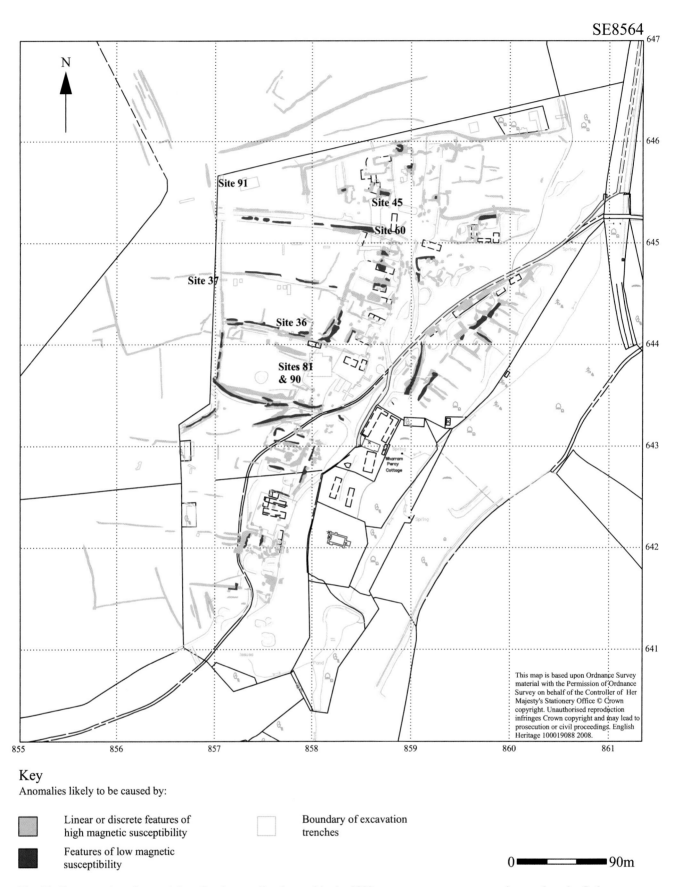

Key

Anomalies likely to be caused by:

Linear or discrete features of high magnetic susceptibility

Features of low magnetic susceptibility

Boundary of excavation trenches

0 ■■■■ 90m

Fig. 21. Interpretation of potential medieval anomalies detected in the 2002 magnetometer survey superimposed on the Ordnance Survey 1:2500 map of Wharram Percy. Earthworks are shown in grey. (English Heritage)

linear anomaly of negative magnetisation can be discerned running perpendicular to the croft boundaries beside their north-western ends. Comparison with the trackway anomalies just mentioned suggests that this may indicate the former presence of an access track, confirming the identification of Road 2C in the topographical survey (see Ch. 3, Fig. 9).

Outside the Guardianship area a number of linear anomalies have been indicated that are conjectured to be medieval or later enclosure boundaries. To the west, these anomalies appear to be continuations of features discernible as earthworks further east and it is on the basis of this continuity of alignment that they have been assumed to be medieval or post-medieval. One such anomaly to the west of Site 37 cuts across one of the characteristically strongly magnetised ditch anomalies of the Iron Age and Roman settlement (see Fig. 19) suggesting it is not contemporary with the Iron Age or Roman settlement. By extrapolation, other anomalies in the western fields with a similar geophysical signature are also unlikely to be of Iron Age or Roman date.

To the north of the Guardianship area, a number of linear anomalies have been identified that appear to run approximately parallel to the northern boundary earthwork of the North Manor *curia*. The longest and broadest of these, identifiable in aerial photography (Beresford and Hurst 1990, 19, fig. 4), cuts across the boundary ditch of the main Iron Age and Roman enclosure at the north-west of the site and so cannot have been contemporary with it. Hence, these anomalies have been classified as potential medieval boundary ditches. They appear, however, to run parallel to faint linear anomalies identified as possible periglacial features in the chalk surface (see Fig. 19) and so it is possible that these stronger and broader anomalies also have a natural, geological origin.

Anomalies relating to other settlement

Figure 22 depicts anomalies that are likely to be archaeological in origin but that cannot be confidently ascribed to any particular archaeological period. The difficulty may be illustrated by considering the arcing, linear anomaly running north-westwards through Site 94 where it crosses the east-west boundary ditch of the Iron Age and Roman settlement (see Fig. 19). Its northern end is extremely close to the east end of a second similar anomaly that arcs south-west to cross the same Iron Age and Roman boundary ditch in Site 98. It is tempting to assume that these two curving anomalies are caused by the same underlying feature, the slight break between them being simply due to limitations in the resolution of the magnetometer. Upon excavation, however, it was discovered that the anomaly in Site 94 was cut by the Roman ditch and was thus concluded to date from the Iron Age (Richards 1992a, 17), whilst the anomaly in Site 98 cuts it, suggesting an Anglo-Saxon date (Stamper 1991, 4). The reliability of the recorded stratigraphic sequence in Site 94 is reviewed below (Ch. 9). Nevertheless, it may be that the gap between the two

anomalies in the magnetometer plot is real and that two separate causative features exist. It is important to bear in mind that two anomalies with very similar magnetic signatures can have quite different dates.

The area to the south of the sites just discussed exhibits further concentrations of similar curvilinear anomalies stretching almost all the way down to Drue Dale both within and outside the Guardianship area. These anomalies do not align with any of the medieval features visible as earthworks and, in some cases, cross them. Excavation evidence from Sites 70 and 78 indicates that, whilst some of the straight ditches are probably part of the Roman field system, the curvilinear ditches enclose settlement activity that can be dated without doubt to the Middle Saxon period (see below, Chs 9 and 10).

A number of discrete anomalies have also been indicated, and these tend to cluster close to the curvilinear anomalies just discussed, particularly in the southern part of the survey area. Some of these have dimensions and magnetic signatures consistent with an interpretation as Anglo-Saxon *Grubenhäuser*. Such buildings have been discovered by excavation at Sites 39, 60 and 95 (Rahtz *et al.* 2004, 287-8; pp 118-23 below). Given the density of anomalies possibly caused by Anglo-Saxon structures in the southern part of the geophysical survey, it might be conjectured that the examples just discussed, lying to the north, are outliers from a main centre of settlement that developed on the plateau further south. This hypothesis is lent some weight by the extensive remains of the Middle Saxon period discovered in the South Manor Sites (Stamper *et al.* 2000, 27-37). Little Anglo-Saxon evidence was found in Site 12 (Milne 1979b), so any such settlement would have to have been situated further west, away from the edge of the plateau.

Along the eastern edge of the plateau, a number of magnetic anomalies that suggest quarrying pits, have been marked. Where these have been excavated, for instance at Site 9 (Wrathmell 1989b, 21), this is indeed what they have turned out to be. Much of this quarrying appears to have taken place in the 13th century, but there is some evidence for quarries dating from the Roman and Saxon periods as well. Hence the anomalies have been marked on Figure 22 rather than Figure 21.

At the far north of the survey area, beyond the northern Guardianship boundary, a linear anomaly has been detected that suggests a field boundary. It is not aligned, however, with any of the other anomalies or visible features on the site and it crosses the supposed medieval boundary anomalies in this area. Thus its interpretation and date remain enigmatic.

Conclusions

Magnetometer survey at Wharram Percy has been extremely successful in detecting anomalies likely to be of archaeological origin. Furthermore, the differing structures of features from various archaeological periods, along with differences in the occupation activities enhancing the magnetisation of the soil, have

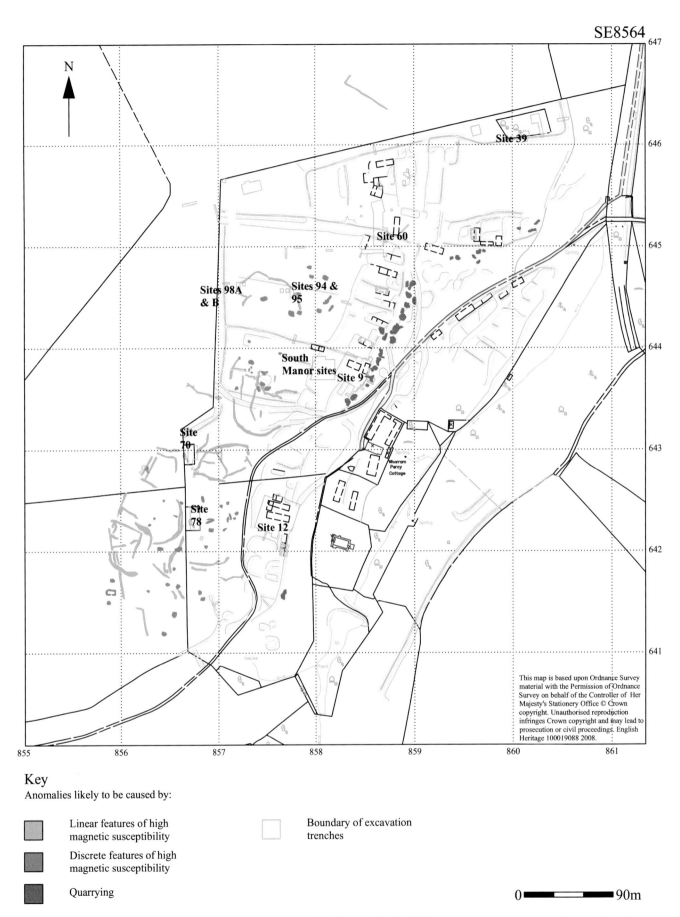

SE8564

Site 39

Site 60

Sites 98A & B

Sites 94 & 95

South Manor sites

Site 9

Site 70

Site 78

Site 12

Wharram Percy Cottage

This map is based upon Ordnance Survey material with the Permission of Ordnance Survey on behalf of the Controller of Her Majesty's Stationery Office © Crown copyright. Unauthorised reproduction infringes Crown copyright and may lead to prosecution or civil proceedings. English Heritage 100019088 2008.

Key

Anomalies likely to be caused by:

Linear features of high magnetic susceptibility

Discrete features of high magnetic susceptibility

Quarrying

Boundary of excavation trenches

0 ▬▬▬ 90m

Fig. 22. Interpretation of other potential archaeological anomalies detected in the 2002 magnetometer survey superimposed on the Ordnance Survey 1:2500 map of Wharram Percy. Earthworks are shown in grey. (English Heritage)

resulted in anomalies with distinctive magnetic signatures. It has thus been possible to produce an approximate phasing for the archaeological anomalies as depicted above. In particular, the Iron Age and Roman settlement at the northern end of the site has been clearly mapped, as have a complex series of possible Anglo-Saxon features in the south. It has not yet been possible to detect these remains using topographic survey.

Conversely, the magnetometer has responded only weakly to anomalies corresponding to extant topographic features, whilst oblique aerial photography and topographic survey have mapped features surviving as even slight earthworks in great detail. These features appear to relate almost exclusively to medieval settlement at the site and so the magnetic map has contributed relatively little new information to the understanding of occupation in this period. In this way, the magnetometer survey complements the information gained from other survey techniques.

Other geophysical techniques have been tested on small areas at the site, and the results of these trials suggest that the well drained soils of the western plateau offer good potential for both earth resistance and Ground Penetrating Radar (GPR) surveying. In both surveys, buried masonry wall footings, likely to date to the medieval period, have been detected clearly. They

contrast with the magnetic survey, which appears to have responded to cut features such as ditches rather than buried upstanding wall footings. GPR survey offers the additional benefit of providing relative depth information for the anomalies it detects. This has been demonstrated in the present instance through the location of a deeper building platform, undetected by topographical survey, in one of the tofts to the north of the South Manor (that of Building 13), indicating multiple phases of occupation during the medieval period. Although some evidence of buried wall footings has emerged from aerial photographs of parch marks (Plate 6, above; Wrathmell 1989a, 43 fig. 30), it is likely that electrical and GPR surveying could provide a more complete picture.

The list of geophysical surveys at Wharram Percy recorded in the introduction to this chapter represents in microcosm the history of development of geophysical survey techniques at the Ancient Monuments Laboratory. These developments have benefited immensely from the unique combination of exceptionally clear geophysical results and the feedback from extensive archaeological excavation afforded by the Research Project. Nevertheless, the trials have demonstrated that, despite the large amount of magnetometer survey already carried out, the potential for further discoveries to be made by geophysical survey using other techniques has not yet been exhausted.

Part Two

Wharram and the Wolds in Prehistoric, Roman and Early Anglo-Saxon Times

Though the principal focus of research at Wharram has always been the medieval settlement, it was recognised as early as 1961 that the village had been preceded in this location by homesteads of later prehistoric and Roman date, along with their associated trackways and fields. The discovery of such farmsteads at Wharram was hardly surprising given the crop mark evidence for their widespread distribution across the northern Wolds (Stoertz 1997), but their presence in this particular place invited questions relating to the origins of the medieval settlement: had the Wharram site been occupied continuously since prehistoric times; had the plan of the medieval village been determined by the layout of Roman period farmsteads and fields? The latter proposition was certainly accepted for a time: a 1976 publication contained a plan of Wharram 'showing Romano-British features which determined its later medieval development' (Beresford and Hurst 1976, 143). The pre-medieval features identified as having had a significant influence on the village plan included the so-called 'lynchet bank', thought then to be of prehistoric date, which has been reanalysed and reinterpreted in Chapter 3 of this volume.

Prehistoric and Roman Wharram were therefore important themes of research from the mid-1970s to the late 1980s, and the results were eventually brought together in a single volume, *Wharram IX*. A concurrent programme of fieldwalking and crop mark analysis, along with some geophysical survey, was carried out across all six townships in the parishes of Wharram Percy and Wharram le Street, and the prehistoric and Roman discoveries were reported in 1987 (*Wharram V*). They included two Roman 'villa' sites, one just beyond the south-east corner of Wharram le Street village, the other a short distance to the west of Wharram Grange Farm, about 1.5km north-west of Wharram Percy village site (see Fig. 27, below). These two villas were the subject of trial excavations, published in *Wharram IV*.

The formal cessation of excavation within the Guardianship area did not mark the end of fieldwork in the Wharram townships. A successor project under the direction of Colin Hayfield carried out several small-scale excavations in the parishes before, in 1995, embarking on a more extensive investigation of a group of Late Iron Age and Romano-British enclosures. These were located at Wharram Grange Crossroads, about half-way between the Wharram village site and the Wharram Grange villa. More recently still, the University of York Archaeology Department has carried out an excavation at the Wharram village site itself, in the so-called North-west Enclosure which was created and occupied in the Roman period. The Department's investigations focused on a part of the enclosure that lies outside the Guardianship area and therefore subject to continuing degradation by the plough. The results of this latest intervention on the Wharram site are summarised in this part of the volume (Chapter 5), and supplement the earlier excavation in the same enclosure, published in *Wharram IX*. Post-excavation analysis of the Wharram Grange Crossroads site is continuing, but some of its results have been made available for inclusion in Chapter 6.

Chapter 6 provides a description of the physical environment of the northern Wolds and then outlines the evidence for prehistoric activity in the region. This is followed by a detailed reassessment of the Late Iron Age and Roman remains found on the village site in the context of discoveries made elsewhere in the Wharram parishes, and more widely across the Wolds and along their margins. It draws on a new aerial photography survey commissioned in 2006 as part of an enhancement of survey data for this volume. The new survey was carried out by Alison Deegan and her full report is one of the documents available via the Archaeology Data Service (doi:10.5284/1000415). Figure 27 is her transcription of prehistoric and Roman aerial photograph evidence combined with the geophysical survey results.

As indicated above, one of the key issues for the Wharram Research Project over several decades was continuity of occupation on the village site from Late Roman to Anglo-Saxon times. It is one that is explored in Chapter 7, for the final time in this series of publications. Arguments both for and against continuity can find support in the published data, and we should acknowledge at the outset that neither side of the debate can as yet offer conclusive evidence. Here, the proposition is that the late Roman farmsteads and their extensive ditched field-systems did not survive beyond the late 4th or early 5th century, and that the northern Wolds generally reverted to open grazing grounds for communities located in the adjacent lowlands – or even further afield. The only cultural features to remain *in use* in the Wolds landscape from prehistoric times right through to the Anglo-Saxon period were routeways that had a continuing role to play in either crossing or giving access to the chalk uplands.

There appear to be three principal elements in the local communication network, and examples of each can be seen on Figure 23, a topographic model of the western part of the northern Wolds. The view is from above the Vale of York, facing eastwards towards the coast, with the lowlands of the Vale of Pickering to the left (north) and a corner of the low ground of Holderness towards the top right. It shows, first, four long-distance east-west routes (Routes 1-4), providing access between the coast and the

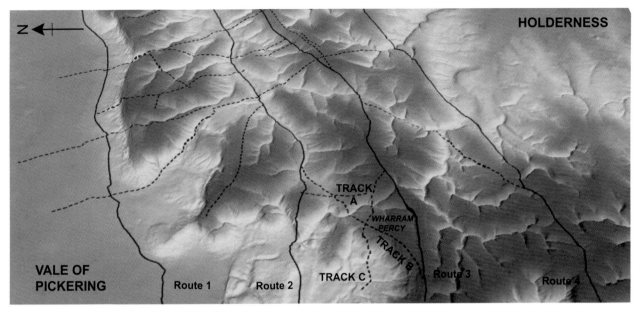

Fig. 23. Topographic model of the Wolds with main routeways, viewed from the west. (A. Deegan and E. Marlow-Mann)

Vale of York; secondly, a series of north-south routes linking this part of the Vale of Pickering to the Wolds and beyond, and thirdly, a selection of the numerous subsidiary tracks allowing traffic to cross from one major route to the next often in a diagonal fashion. Tracks A, B and C on Figure 23 are some of the subsidiary tracks identified in the Wharram area; their influence on settlement and land-use will be discussed in Chapter 6. The north-south routes, identified as potential droveways used in the early Anglo-Saxon period by the lowland communities to access grazing lands on the Wolds, will be discussed in Chapter 7. Here, a little more needs to be said about the east-west routes as their character and dating are fundamental to much of the discussion in both this and the next part of the volume.

In the area covered by the topographic model, Route 1 links a line of village settlements in the Vale of Pickering on the south side of the river Derwent. The present course of this route, the A64 road, is probably no older than the medieval village sites it serves, and highlights the difference between a route and its precise physical expression at any one time: a road or trackway. The course of the A64 seems to have replaced east-west ditched trackways that followed much the same alignment but ran a little further to the north in Roman times, closer to the fen edge. Indeed, part of the current course of Route 1 must be more recent in date than the Anglian cemetery it partly overlies at West Heslerton (Powlesland 2003a, 286, fig. 89).

The next route south, Route 2, links the medieval villages strung out along the Great Wold Valley. The present course may, again, therefore be coeval with the villages it serves, though the density of major prehistoric monuments along the valley suggests much earlier origins. This is certainly hinted at in the discussion, in Chapter 8, of Iron Age and Roman crop marks at Butterwick, one of the townships in this valley.

In contrast, Routes 3 and 4, traversing the most elevated parts of the Wolds, make use of the spines of

higher land running between the deep dales. They are marked for long stretches of their courses by prehistoric dykes, banks and ditches that indicate major land divisions, and were first discussed in detail, along with other similar 'boundary roads' elsewhere in Yorkshire, by May Pickles (1993, 66-7). It is difficult to establish which came first, the boundary dykes or the tracks, but both were probably in use before the later prehistoric period. A more recent exploration of the precise courses and antiquity of these two routes has been published by Chris Fenton-Thomas, who has argued that:

'In some cases, the boundaries that were laid out at the end of the Bronze Age appear to have followed these tracks, just as they followed the valleys and used barrows and ponds as markers and alignment points... Before 1000BC the mobile landscape was dotted with ceremonial monuments, meres, significant trees and other features, which would have been reached by a network of trackways. As the landscape became more ordered and enclosed, many of the trackways began to be used as boundaries. The tracks were already part of the way people organised the land and they would have made obvious boundaries as the landscape became more managed.' (Fenton-Thomas 2005, 49-50).

The western part of Route 3, named 'Towthorpe ridgeway' by Fenton-Thomas (2003, 41), was recorded by Colin Hayfield as a 'supposed prehistoric trackway', and a trackway of the Roman period (Hayfield 1987a, 124; 1987b, 186). Eastwards, it becomes the 'High Street', identified by Rev E. Maule Cole as a Roman road (Cole 1899, 41). Route 4, 'Sledmere Green Lane' (Fenton-Thomas 2003, 41), was identified by Phillips in the mid-19th century as a 'British' (prehistoric) trackway, though Maule Cole believed it would also have been used by the Romans (Cole 1899, 40).

Many of these routes and tracks – or at least their approximate courses – seem therefore to have been in use for millennia rather than centuries. Their presence and influence form a thread through many of the following chapters.

5   The 2005 Excavation of the North-west Enclosure

by Steve Roskams

Introduction

One of the key investigations in terms of understanding Late Roman occupation at Wharram was the excavation of Site 91 across the boundary of the so-called North-west Enclosure, carried out during the Wharram Research Project's last two seasons of fieldwork. The present chapter takes that investigation a stage further, summarising the results of a more recent excavation, carried out in 2005 as part of the University of York Archaeology Department's Yorkshire Wolds Project. This more recent work has in some respects confirmed the conclusions reached on the basis of the Site 91 work; but in others it offers new insights into what may have been happening in this part of the site both before the Roman period and – more significantly for later chapters – in post-Roman times.

The University's multi-period Yorkshire Wolds Project seeks to understand the interaction of human activity with the Wolds landscape at various levels of resolution in order to elucidate three types of issue: site visibility and landscape context, notably using crop mark evidence; settlement differentiation and evolution, involving surface mapping followed by more intensive sampling programmes to differentiate enclosure functions, room use etc.; and social and economic development, based initially on the systematic collection of both ecofactual and artefactual assemblages, then interpreting them in relation to the preceding contextual information (http://www.york.ac.uk/depts/arch/Wolds/index.html).

The project identified the Late Iron Age/Romano-British settlement transition as a key time of change on the Wolds, a period during which we might seek to understand archaeologically the landscape that Romano-British society inherited, and on which imperial authority endeavoured to impose itself. In particular, we proposed using archaeological fieldwork to answer a series of interlinked landscape questions:

How substantial were the changes between 100 bc and AD 500?

At which levels were they most intensive – in landholding across the Wolds, within settlement organisation or at more focused spatial levels?

In which spheres were the impacts felt most forcefully – in economic developments, or in social contexts such as gender relations or ritual activities?

Our specific work at Wharram Percy deployed a variety of fieldwork techniques in unison, including systematic fieldwalking, survey of surface topography, magnetometry and resistivity survey, and selective excavation. The overall aim was to establish the depth, extent and character of archaeological deposits, the spatial extent and more exact date of Roman landscape features and their relationship with pre-existing landscape divisions, and the character of activities within these different zones, using ecofactual and artefactual assemblages.

The site of the North-west Enclosure was chosen for investigation as it fulfilled a range of the above objectives. Previous geophysical surveys (Linford and Linford 2003, plus references) and aerial photography (Stoertz 1997) had shown that a large Roman enclosure developed here alongside a major, long-lived routeway which ran north-west from the Wharram Percy settlement to Wharram Crossroads and on to the proposed villa at Wharram Grange (Track C on Fig. 27; *Wharram IV*). This evidence could be complemented by a programme of fieldwalking undertaken by Hayfield (*Wharram V*) across

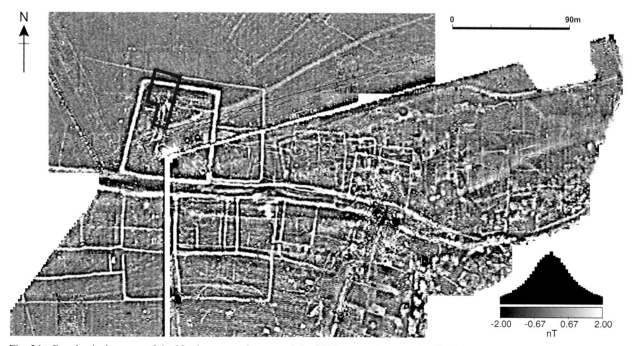

Fig. 24. Geophysical survey of the North-west enclosure and the 2005 excavation area (outlined in red). (English Heritage)

the whole area and by excavations of the North Manor site by this Department at Wharram Percy (*Wharram IX*). Finally, a trench had been laid across the eastern ditch of the enclosure in 1989 and 1990 in advance of tree planting (Clark and Wrathmell 2004, 297-340).

Our work in 2005 sought to enhance this existing, outline understanding, firstly by more detailed fieldwalking and a campaign of geophysical survey, then by excavation. The surface finds and geophysical prospection suggested that a concentration of features towards the north-west corner of the enclosure would be sufficiently complex to be diagnostic of the range of activities there, yet sufficiently dispersed to be properly evaluated in the available time. Thus an excavation area measuring 650m² was set out, positioned to intercept the northern ditch(es) of the North-west Enclosure and expose a zone within (Fig. 24). Despite its large extent, this work still constitutes, in essence, an *evaluation*, examining the surface encountered at the base of the ploughsoil, then recording and excavating a few selected areas.

Such work necessarily impacted on a site otherwise threatened only by the gradual attrition of modern ploughing: it lies beyond the north-west corner of the settlement area protected as a Scheduled Ancient Monument. We thought our more destructive strategy to be legitimate for three reasons. Firstly, it continued the selective testing of evidence from excavated features against that of non-intrusive methods (predictive geophysical maps were produced both before *and after* the area had been stripped of ploughsoil). Next, the distribution of finds encountered while cleaning below that ploughsoil could be compared with that of finds from more general fieldwalking. Finally, these analytical results could be related to those from a metal-detecting sweep across the whole of the natural chalk horizon. Excavation was, therefore, just one element of the continuing characterisation of the area. The following account concerns the specific results of our excavation work, rather than any more methodological aspects.

In terms of excavation procedures, the designated area was opened by mechanical excavator and deposits at the base of ploughsoil were then cleaned to sharpen the definition of underlying features and contexts. During this stage, all finds were plotted individually in three dimensions and the site and spoil heap were swept by metal detector. Although the process of feature definition proved problematic in unsettled and sometimes atrocious weather conditions, the resulting map is a sufficiently accurate representation of the archaeological remains within this part of the enclosure. Having identified and plotted a range of intrusive features, each was selectively excavated and recorded using multi-feature 'top plans' and sections of individual cuts; descriptions of every deposit (colour, soil matrix and inclusions) and cut (shape in plan, profile, and other relevant characteristics); and a stratigraphic diagram of all proven physical relationships between features.

As a result of this work, the major linear ditches within the trench have been reasonably sampled, although the deeper deposits in the central and southern areas could only be treated more summarily. Post-excavation analysis has allowed these to be rationalised into a number of elements (*Features 1-16*: F1-F16 on Fig. 25) which are employed in the description that follows. The trench was backfilled by mechanical excavator at the close of the work, the records and assemblages generated being housed presently in the Department of Archaeology, University of York.

Site development

The earliest human activity on the site, *Feature 1*, lay in the north-east corner of the trench and comprised the western part of a curvilinear ditch with a projected diameter of c. 18m (Fig. 25). No finds were recovered from it and this, plus the feature's circularity and the nature of its fill, all serve to differentiate it from later activity on the site. It is most reasonably interpreted as a round barrow, which had limited influence on the subsequent development of the site (although see Feature 15, pp 60-61).

To the east of F1, also adjacent to the limit of excavation, lay *Feature 2,* an insubstantial stone foundation set in a stepped trench, perhaps the masonry base for a timber superstructure. Accumulations to its north were overlapped by the fills of a large east-west ditch, *Feature 3*, which also cut the probable barrow. It was at least 20m long (both ends beyond the limits of excavation) and c. 3.5m wide but not bottomed in excavation. Its uppermost backfills took the form of rubble dumps alternating with the deposition of more culturally-rich materials, the former element perhaps derived from the demise of the superstructure associated with masonry F2. F3 represents a major landscape boundary: the creation of the North-west Enclosure ditch (see further below).

Feature 4 was a parallel, east-west cut 8m to the south of F3 (measured centre-to centre) which again cut the edge of proposed round barrow F1, elsewhere intruding into the natural chalk. At least 20m long and c. 2.0m wide, its shallow sides up to only 0.25m deep merged with a generally flat, locally undulating, base. Whilst this feature comprised a clear, if shallow, ditch in the eastern half of its exposed length, the western continuation was much more superficial and less sharply defined. This might suggest that here F4 took the form of an insubstantial boundary. Its fill throughout its length suggested initial weathering of its sides, before the deposition of more culturally rich material. Its common alignment with F3, and the fact that both post-dated F1, strongly imply that F4 was an internal feature of the North-west Enclosure.

A third east-west cut, *Feature 5*, lay 7m to the north F3, just within the limits of excavation. At least 13.5m long and c. 1.5m across, it had fairly steep, locally irregular, sides 0.70m deep curving to a rounded base. Its initial, stony fills seem likely to have been derived from weathering of its sides, their disposition in section

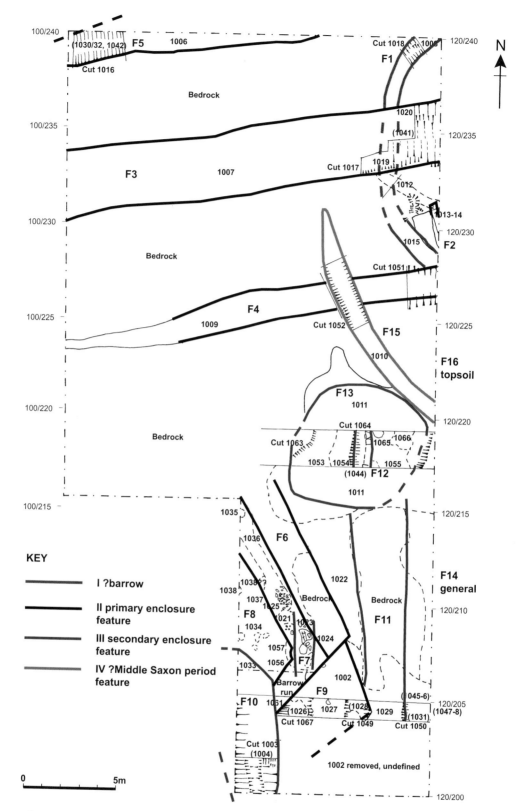

Fig. 25. Summary plan of the 2005 excavation, showing excavated features (F1-F16). (E. Marlow-Mann after S. Roskams)

perhaps suggesting the decay of a bank on its south side, with later, looser fills marking the ditch's final demise. Its alignment suggests it was in use with F3 and F4 as a third landscape division, although artefacts were noticeably less profuse here, perhaps implying that this ditch lay beyond the main centre of activity, fitting with the idea of there having been a bank on its south side.

Within the enclosure, towards the southern end of the excavation, lay a compact spread of small chalk fragments and occasional flat sandstone slabs above the natural chalk, forming a worn metalling. The chalk rubble could have been dumped in this position during disturbance of the natural geology, for example during pit digging, with a surface then formed during its use, whereas the sandstone slabs must have been deliberately laid to create such a surface. The two elements together created a pathway aligned roughly north-west to south-east, running for at least 4m across the site: *Feature 6*. A deposit of soft clay loam seems to have formed in a linear depression in the southern part of the feature, perhaps a product of that usage, whilst other stony spreads might imply its subsequent repair before further occupation took place. If the line of F6 is projected northwards, it meets ditch F4 where the latter changed from being a proper ditch to a less substantial boundary. This suggests that F4 and F6 were linked, and thus that the pathway was in use at the same time as the enclosure.

To the south of the pathway, partially exposed in a limited sondage, areas of compacted chalk fragments capped the natural chalk and were cut by two amorphous intrusions, the whole here labelled *Feature 9*. Its interpretation is problematic, given the limited exposure, but the alignment of its most clearly-defined edges and the nature of its backfill, comprising soft materials then possible ephemeral metallings, suggest an association with pathway F6. More broadly, the overall alignment of F9 and F6 matches those of the ditches to their north, suggesting that these features represent the initial use of the North-west Enclosure in this vicinity.

Three further features in the south of the site imply a second phase of activity after the initial development of the enclosure. Five limestone slabs, the largest up to 0.70m across, were laid flat above the accumulations on pathway F6 to form a foundation, *Feature 7*. The alignment of its eastern edge runs more north-south than that of the earlier pathway, suggesting a new stage of internal activity. Accumulations west of this foundation were cut for the insertion of a large, virtually complete, calcite-gritted ware pot. Subsequent dissection of its earth content recovered sherds from another vessel, one hobnail and one small fragment of burnt animal bone, but no human bone. Thus it seems to have acted as a buried storage vessel (a rudimentary *dolium*), rather than a cremation container.

Ditch *Feature 10* cut into F9 *c.* 2m west of foundation F7, but on a similar alignment to the latter. At least 5m long and *c.* 2.40m across, it had a sharp but undulating western edge, a more gently sloping eastern edge, with a subsidiary, steep-sided cut at the centre of its base *c.* 0.50m wide, giving a total depth of up to 0.71m. It was filled with compact, greyish brown clayey loam containing angular chalk fragments. The cut was not evident in intact stratigraphy in the central part of the trench and seems to have turned westwards some 5m into the excavation. It forms a major development of the site and, given its alignment, seems likely to mark the demise of suggested pathways F6 and F9, in turn implying that it was in use with the masonry foundation F7.

Approximately 4m to the east of the foundation F7 lay a parallel ditch *Feature 11*, also intruding into F9. Only its western edge could be securely defined, which was vertical and at least 0.20m deep. Given the differential exposure of the natural chalk bedrock to the north, it seems to have extended for as much as 11m in that direction before being obscured by later strata (see F13 and F14, below). Feature 11 thus marks a significant point in the site's development and, given its alignment, seems likely to have been in use at the same time as foundation F7 and ditch F10 to the west. The absence of visible bedrock in a parallel line *c.* 2.5m west of F11 might also suggest a similar north-south intrusion here, between ditch F11 and foundation F7.

Finally, in the area west of the earlier pathway F6 and foundation F7, a scatter of intrusions were suggested by disturbance of the natural chalk, here grouped together as *Feature 8*. Some comprised simple gaps in the bedrock, in one instance perhaps a double post-hole, others implied deeper cuts incorporating vertical packing stones. They showed no obvious alignments in themselves or in relation to adjacent features, so could be contemporary with either F6, or with the differently aligned F7 and its associated ditches. It is equally unclear whether these post-holes lay in an internal or external setting.

In an area subject only to limited excavation towards the centre of the site, the western edge of a possible north-south unmortared masonry foundation formed by five regularly placed, roughly worked stones was exposed in a sondage – *Feature 12*. Its alignment matches that of secondary intrusions F7, F10 and F11 to the south and it seems likely to be broadly contemporary with them. The base level of this foundation, below that of intact stratigraphy just to the south, suggests a localised feature. A large, irregular intrusion, *Feature 13*, cut the natural chalk in the vicinity of F12. Measuring 7.5m east-west by at least 2m north-south, it had a regular, shallow profile at least 0.20m deep (not bottomed) and contained a range of fills involving at least two actions: the deposition of dark brown soil and the later dumping of lighter, more stony material. Although no definitive relationship could be established between the cutting of F12 and F13, the latest of the latter's fills, which included a complete stone mortar, parts of a quernstone and a further number of flat-laid, tooled limestone slabs, sealed the former foundation and must mark its demise.

Taken together, the evidence indicates a major, non-linear feature confined to this area which incorporated water-sorted deposits in its filling. This suggests a well-head or pond. Masonry foundation F12 could be related to its initial construction, with the disturbed worked stones in later backfill derived either from the disturbance of this structure or, if the flat stones were deliberately placed, the consolidation of a muddy area to allow continued access to welled-up, standing water over an extended period of time. Spreads of friable, clayey deposits, *Feature 14*, covered the backfills of this pond/well-head, continuing south to seal the masonry foundation F7 and ditches F10 and F11. Although these deposits are likely to include more than one formation process, they mark the demise of all features in the centre and south of the site. Whether the main enclosure ditch F3 to the north was still in use at this point is unclear.

A curvilinear intrusion, *Feature 15*, cut into the general deposits F14 in the centre of the site, also intruding into ditch F4 to the north. At least 12.5m long and *c*. 1.20m wide with gradually sloping sides 0.35m deep curving gently to its dish-shaped base, it was filled with clayey silt. At its northern end, it was aligned north-south, running out towards the position of the main enclosure ditch, but it curved increasingly to the east further south, where it also deepened. Given its alignment, character and stratigraphic relationships, especially in cutting accumulations F14, this intrusion must belong to a later period of site activity. Its overall character, though not depth, resembles the sort of early medieval curvilinear enclosures seen further south at Wharram (Ch. 9 below), and elsewhere on the Wolds, an idea given some support from a single Anglian sherd recovered from its fill (M. Atha, pers. comm.). Most of the relatively profuse artefacts it contained, however, resemble those derived from earlier activity in the vicinity and it is assumed here that this material is redeposited from underlying strata, rather than generated in the use of F15 itself.

The position of the ditch is intriguing, running parallel to the much earlier barrow F1 and seeming to end in the north as it approached the enclosure ditch F3. These relationships may be simply coincidental but, if not, F15 may have been laid out to respect one or both earlier landscape components. That said, if barrow F1 was visible in the post-Roman period, it showed no sign of having, earlier, influenced the imposition of the Roman enclosure ditch on the landscape. The fact that an Anglo-Saxon curvilinear feature stopped opposite the line of a Roman ditch would be less surprising, however, given the substantial size of F3 at this point: although not bottomed in our own excavations, earlier work elsewhere showed it to be 1.8m deep (Herbert and Wrathmell 2004, fig. 152).

Finally, several layers of topsoil, *Feature 16*, covered not only the curvilinear ditch and the deposits below, but also continued south-east to seal the post-holes F8 and northwards over ditches F3 and F5. These, together with two modern burials of lambs, represent the final human activity falling within the excavation area.

General conclusions

Summary of sequence
Taken together, these findings imply the insertion of a Bronze Age round barrow in the landscape, then a major phase of Roman activity, followed by the cutting of a curvilinear feature, perhaps of early medieval date, below topsoil. Neither F1 nor F15 correlates securely with elements identified in geophysical prospection. The intervening, main period of occupation, however, can be related to this broader patterning and is focused on here. The first sign of activity comprised the insertion of three parallel ditches towards the north end of the site. Ditch F3, running east-west, can be shown from geophysics to be the northern arm of the North-west Enclosure and involved a substantial investment (excavation of its eastern counterpart showed a V-shaped profile with three recuts).

Ditch F5, to the north, represents a corresponding, outer enclosure, and F4 to its south an internal division, perhaps a hedge defining and retaining the inside edge of any enclosure bank in the east, with some sort of boundary fence continuing to the west. Given its alignment and northern termination, the foundation F2, although earlier than the backfilling of ditch F3, also seems likely to have been in use soon after the creation of the North-west Enclosure. As noted previously, this whole complex was set out on the north side of a major routeway running from Wharram Percy north-west to Wharram Crossroads, and then to the Wharram Grange 'villa' beyond. This route can be shown, elsewhere, to be in place well before the start of the Roman period.

Within the enclosure, initial occupation comprised pathway F6 and the associated metallings and insubstantial intrusions F9. A second phase of activity here, involving the setting out of masonry foundation and possible *dolium* F7 and the cutting of ditches F10 and F11, took place on a new alignment. Finally, a scatter of post-holes F8 in the south-west corner of the excavation could represent an insubstantial post-built structure belonging to either phase of activity. Between these elements and the enclosure boundary, a well or pond F12/13 was inserted, employing good quality, unmortared masonry and continuing in use for an extended period of time before being covered by a range of horizontal deposits F14. It is unclear, on purely stratigraphic grounds, whether all of these newly-aligned elements took place within an existing enclosure or after its demise, although the former seems more likely.

The total finds population from the excavation comprised 3,900 individual fragments. Of this total, 40% was pottery which, although not yet subject to detailed identification, has been roughly classified and 'spot-dated'. Over half comprises calcite-gritted wares, followed by grey ware (25%), then much smaller proportions of black burnished ware, oxidised wares, Huntcliff ware, Samian and mortaria fragments. Provably post-Roman artefacts were confined to a single sherd of Anglian pottery (found in F15 – see above), together with medieval green-glazed ware and stoneware. Some 40% of the finds were animal bone, although many of the latter are mere fragments and include elements of two modern lamb burials. The remaining finds include a considerable amount of iron slag and some lead residue, plus some metal finds (mainly iron nails, but also fourteen copper-alloy coins and other objects, including a bracelet and seal box lid), one whetstone, and the aforementioned fragments of a stone mortar and a quern found in association with the well/pond. Finally, some oyster shells were noted from the overlying topsoil. Although detailed analyses of these assemblages remains to be done, they can be considered at a general level for their dating and for their implications for the functioning of the North-west Enclosure.

Dating
When using finds to date activity represented by mostly intrusive features, the analyst faces two well-known

problems. On the one hand the material found within a feature is often dumped there at the end of its useful life. It thus marks its demise, whereas its creation could take place at a much earlier time. On the other hand, the datable material culture within any fill provides only a *terminus post quem* and could be residual. Thus the true date of the fill could be much later than the date of the assemblage it contains. That said, the chance of an intrusion being dug at a significantly earlier date than that of its earliest fills, for example by being cleaned out very systematically for many decades and then, suddenly, allowed to fill up, might be deemed unlikely, especially if adjacent features provide no clear indications of activity of such an earlier date. Equally, to suggest that *all* material within a feature is residual, especially when the character of later artefacts is known and none is apparent (see, for example, the material derived from late feature F15), becomes, at some point, special pleading. When one is seeking, as here, to establish only broad periods of use, not the date of specific features, it therefore seems legitimate to be guided by apparent dates, at least in the first instance.

The most accurate dating evidence in this case derives from the two identifiable coins (out of fourteen, all from spread F14 or overlying topsoil F16). These are attributed to Valens and Constantius, and thus to the third quarter of the 4th century, hence fitting with the ceramics, the vast majority of which date to the 3rd and 4th centuries AD. A little pottery, however, runs back as far as the Middle Iron Age, notably that found in association with main enclosure ditch F3, early intrusions F9, pond F13 and late spreads F14. This suggests that, for at least several centuries up to the 2nd century AD, there was a 'background noise' of occupation in the area, some material from which was redeposited into later strata when features of sufficient depth (F3, F9 and F13) or of sufficient extent (F14) intruded into the area.

On the basis of the main ceramic assemblages, the enclosure ditch F3 seems to have been dug in the 3rd century AD, with associated ditches F4 and F5 inserted at the same time or later in that century and appearing to continue in use into the 4th. This dating accords well with the earlier excavation of the enclosure circuit on its east side, which suggested a starting date in the later 2nd to early-3rd centuries on the basis of Samian and local wares (Herbert and Wrathmell 2004, 302). That said, the latter publication also noted later-3rd to mid-4th century material in the first recut of this ditch, interpreted there as intrusive (Herbert and Wrathmell 2004, 313). If intrusion is not assumed, it becomes possible to see the creation of the North-west Enclosure as taking place only at the tail end of the 3rd century, with consequent compression of the period of occupation as a whole.

A pathway and several amorphous cuts developed initially inside the enclosure, seemingly by the late 3rd century, perhaps with some form of timber structure to their west. The later phase of differently-aligned activity, in the form of an unmortared masonry foundation, two parallel ditches and a pond/well head, occurred in the early 4th century, occupation here continuing until the middle of that century, but perhaps not much beyond – the overlying surface spreads yielded mid-4th-century coins. This would correspond with Herbert and Wrathmell's suggestion (2004, 302) that occupation in the south-east of the enclosure ended by about AD 360. In short, the enclosure could have been occupied for over 150 years or for less than half that time, and there is currently no secure way of deciding between these two options. It seems fairly clear, however, that it fell out of use some decades before the formal 'end of Roman Britain'.

Enclosure function

The distribution of fieldwalking finds from across the whole area suggests that activity was concentrated within the North-west Enclosure, falling off markedly to its north and west, especially beyond the line of outer ditch F5. In this it resonates with the excavation on its eastern side, where the area beyond the main ditch was a more 'marginal' zone used, *inter alia*, for matters such as burial (Clark and Wrathmell 2004). To the south, however, concentrations of surface finds continued beyond the enclosure proper, into the line of the main routeway bounding it on that side. Clearly, that pre-existing feature continued in use for at least as long as the occupation within the enclosure.

The general impression from the stratified assemblages is of a resemblance with material derived from excavations elsewhere at Wharram: an area of predominantly rural activities and not of housing, still less of high-status housing. It is true that a few recovered items imply occupation of some prestige, for example the copper-alloy bracelet and seal box lid, together with a fragment of an Ebor red-painted ware, flanged bowl. In this, the north of the enclosure is paralleled by its south-east corner, which yielded another Ebor red-painted ware sherd, this time from a hemispherical bowl (which Evans notes there as 'surprising': Evans 2004, 316) alongside a couple of bone hair pins. Yet the vast majority of objects in both locales suggest the prominence of more mundane, straightforward agricultural activities. This is seen, for example with the whetstone, stone mortar and a quernstone from our work, alongside the ox goad and sickle blade to the south-east (Goodall and Clark 2004, 330) and with the quern fragments there, the vast majority being of local origin. The occurrence of smithing slag in each zone fits the same picture, one concentration of which occurred beside path F6. Over twenty lumps of lead residue from our own work, if correctly identified, might hint at more specialised metalworking at some point (G. McDonnell pers. comm.).

Taken alongside the physical evidence within the enclosure of pathways (areas of rough metalling, a pond/well, pits and drainage gullies, together with, at most, ephemeral timber structures) and with that beyond it (further pits and occasional cremations), there is little to lift the activities here above the farming seen elsewhere across the Wharram landscape or, for that matter, across wider parts of the Wolds.

6 Prehistoric and Roman Transitions at Wharram Percy

by Mick Atha and Steve Roskams

Introduction

This chapter concerns itself with prehistoric and Roman trajectories of development at Wharram, and has a two-fold purpose. Firstly, it seeks to characterise activities in this landscape in the prehistoric and Roman periods in order to provide a context for the more detailed consideration of occupation here in later epochs, the latter being the main focus of the remainder of this publication. Secondly, in describing these earlier changes, it aims to compare them to more general trajectories on the Wolds and beyond, in the process drawing out any implications this might have for contemporary changes within Yorkshire as a whole. The investigation of pre-medieval landscapes was not pivotal to the aims of the Wharram project at its outset, yet much material related to these early periods was generated during its subsequent fieldwork. As will be argued in detail below, this evidence has important things to say about the way in which territories were established here, 'ladder settlements' created, and larger enclosures then defined. In addition, the timing of these developments is significant in understanding transitions between the Bronze Age, Iron Age and Roman periods. These early periods have also attracted considerable interest in Yorkshire in general, and the Wolds in particular, thus generating a considerable body of evidence around the Wharram area. Some aspects are summarised next.

Prehistoric Yorkshire has been an object of study for many decades (Manby, King and Vyner 2003), such research suggesting an apparent dichotomy in the trajectory of social and economic development between the east and the west. It remains unclear whether these differences are real or a product of archaeological factors such as differential site visibility (better on the Wolds than in the adjacent Vales of York and Pickering) or the increased amount of fieldwork in the east. Either way, such differences mean that we have an understanding of late prehistory here which cannot be easily matched elsewhere in Yorkshire (compare, for example, Manby 2003 and Mackey 2003 on west and east respectively). This includes studies of burial (Stead 1979; 1991), settlement (Dent 1982; 1988; Mackey 1999) and, most recently, the theorisation of landscape settings to interpret meanings (Bevan 1997; Fenton-Thomas 2003; Giles 2000).

For the Roman period in eastern Yorkshire, towns, forts, villas and roads - the stuff of imperial discourse – have been the focus of attention for some time. Early antiquarian interest was consolidated in Kitson Clark's (1935) gazetteer, with subsequent work taking place at Malton fort and settlement (Robinson 1978; Wenham and Heywood 1997; Wilson 2006) and at various proposed 'villa' sites in the area (Corder and Kirk 1932; Stead 1980; Neal 1996), including the Wharram area itself (*Wharram IV*). Recent studies have addressed the full range of the rural economy, moving from essentially descriptive accounts to wider syntheses assessing the differing impact of imperial power on pre-Roman society (Branigan 1980; Dent 1983; 1988; Roskams 1999; Atha 2007).

Naturally, challenges remain in interpreting both periods. Accounts have suffered from the application of models to the Yorkshire region developed on the basis of evidence from south-east Britain, requiring the shoehorning of evidence into inappropriate categories and time slots. This has created narratives which fail to take full account of the diversity of evidence from the region. Recently, however, post-processualist critiques have created a welcome tendency to acknowledge the likelihood of diverse prehistoric social development, and of disparate responses to Roman rule in different parts of the region's landscapes.

The research undertaken at Wharram Percy has itself played an important role in opening up those agendas which promote the idea of understanding change at the landscape level. Thus prehistoric and Roman encounters may have happened initially as a chance by-product of excavations undertaken to investigate medieval levels. Yet, as indicated in the introduction to this part of the volume, once 'encountered' they became more central to the project as a whole. This generated not just an interest in these periods in their own right, for example on the North Manor, in the North-west Enclosure and at Wharram Crossroads, but it also enhanced the development of a 'landscape approach' to archaeology (see *Wharram V* for the start of this process, and Beresford and Hurst 1990 for setting medieval village against pre-existing landscape organisation). These early developments helped set in train more general advances in theory, which were eventually inherited by Giles, Fenton-Thomas and Atha and then applied back onto the Wolds. The development of new techniques at Wharram was part of this process – the large scale of excavated exposures, extensive geophysical survey (Chapter 4, above) and detailed topographic survey (Chapter 3, above).

This picture of developing interest in prehistoric and Roman matters is reflected in the project's publications over the years. Some early volumes (*Wharram II*; *Wharram VI*) barely mention such periods but the publishing of *Wharram IX* set them securely and equally beside their later counterparts. Hence the following discussion has much to draw on, whether in the form of 'background noise' of early occupation at Sites 6, 10 and 39, or the more concerted activities beneath the North Manor at Sites 45/60, 82 and 91. Inevitably, limitations remain. Excavations have been extensive, but still cover only a minute proportion of the whole landscape. In addition, full analysis of the recent work north of the scheduled area is incomplete, although the detailed research by one of the authors, Mick Atha, helps here. Finally, investigations have been published over a long period of time, so inconsistencies appear (the Roman fabric series for the North Manor had to be created afresh, rather than built out of that used earlier for other sites - fortunately, the two systems can be correlated).

Thus our evidence for landscape features is fragmented: differential survival makes comparison of assemblages across the area problematic whilst discard practices, and thus site formation processes, vary. For example, of the 13,000+ animal bones studied in *Wharram IX*, only 28% were identifiable to species and by element (*c.* 3,700), of which just 5% were either Late Iron Age (*c.* 180) and 11% Roman (*c.* 410) in date. More critically, it is reasonable to assume that an unknown, but probably large, proportion of the bones generated by occupation of the site were thrown into middens before being finally discarded when spread on fields during manuring - only a minority, and perhaps an unrepresentative minority, would have ended up in archaeological features.

By the same token, pottery was doubtless subject to the same complex processes, and must have been disturbed and redeposited in later levels. As ceramics can be dated, such material may give a better idea of the 'background noise' of ceramic use over time, even in situations where the majority of prehistoric and Roman material is actually recovered from post-Roman levels. Much of such 'scattered' prehistoric pottery can be dated by the presence of diagnostic rims to the Late Iron Age, suggesting increased ceramic use in the area from that date. Equally, Late Roman material is far more profuse in post-Roman levels than its Early Roman counterpart. In the South Manor area, for example, residual pottery in medieval layers comprises 90% Late Roman calcite-gritted and grey wares, with some 'Samian' tableware of Hadrianic or Antonine date and some colour-coated wares from the late 2nd/early 3rd century. Naturally, problems remain. The very nature of such redeposited assemblages means that they have limited spatial resolution and are similarly limited, therefore, in terms of their inferential value. In addition, even given the extent and intensity of fieldwork coverage at Wharram, it is mostly impossible to distinguish 'real' gaps in occupation areas from those zones simply subjected to later truncation or insufficient investigation thus far.

The three sections set out below discuss developments up to the 5th century AD in the vicinity of Wharram Percy. In line with the approach of other chapters here, they do not attempt a systematic synthesis of all the prehistoric and Roman evidence. Instead, they explore a series of questions: does this area reflect what is going on across the region or are different trajectories of change evident? How useful are 'conventional' chronological categories in explaining such processes? What forces for change are visible archaeologically in advance of period interfaces, and what implications do they have for the nature and timing of transitions between them? Finally, what does this evidence say about the interaction of the functional and ideological forces which influence human behaviour?

The following text is therefore structured around descriptive models drawn from across Yorkshire, each being first presented in outline, and then explored in more detail in relation to the Wharram datasets. The models are chronologically defined and ordered, their approximate dates being up to *c.* 200 bc (Prehistoric Territorialisation), from *c.* 200 bc to *c.* AD 200 (Late Iron Age and Early Roman Ladder Settlements), and from *c.* AD 200 to 'the end of the Roman period', here meaning probably within a generation or two of AD 400 (Discrete Late Roman Enclosures). It should be noted, however, that the changes at the end of each period described below raise questions concerning the nature of the transitions between them, in the process perhaps calling into question the viability of such neat chronological boundaries.

Finally, it is necessary to acknowledge the limitations of discussing Wharram evidence in relation to broader trends. When any case-study is related to a more wide-ranging synthesis, a number of problems inevitably arise if there is a 'lack of fit' between the two. Ultimately, it may be up to each reader to decide the implications of this for him/herself. On the one hand, new evidence may be considered an aberration from the norm (although none the less interesting for that). On the other, it may be that 'conventional wisdom' needs to be rethought. When considering the latter possibility, it is worth remembering three issues. First, whilst one might expect all proposed 'overviews' to be constructed on the basis of numerous specific studies, they frequently have less secure foundations. Second, even when generalised, descriptive models *are* developed on a sound basis, they may have drawn on evidence from one part of the country, to be deployed unquestioningly elsewhere (see Bradley 2007 and further below). Thirdly, the structures employed when creating general syntheses, especially their chronological divisions, may be derived from non-archaeological evidence (most obviously, documentary sources which define the start of 'the Roman period' and the dynamics involved in this take over). All of these factors must be borne in mind when thinking through the broader implications of the specific material from Wharram Percy.

The physical environment

Before describing these changes in detail it is useful to offer an overview of the physical environment represented by the Wolds, as it is an essential foundation upon which to contextualise any chronological discussion of cultural landscape development. The Yorkshire Wolds are the northernmost expanse of chalk in England, forming a 1350km^2 area between the Humber Estuary and Flamborough Head. Whilst this chalk landscape has some similarities to those of southern England (Lewin 1969, 1), it has many unique geological features (Lewin 1969, 56). These result from the juxtaposition of a series of striking environmental contrasts: pancake-flat lowlands abutting steep-scarped plateaux, relatively waterless uplands with thin permeable soils overlooking water-rich vales with deep impervious clays. Such diversity is largely concealed by the modern agricultural landscapes of the Vales and Wolds which, beyond the obvious topographic contrasts, look strikingly similar: uplands and lowlands alike are characterised by large, rectangular arable fields, but such apparent homogeneity is a recent phenomenon. Before modern large-scale manipulation of the environment, including the drainage of wetland areas, agricultural mechanisation and the industrialisation of farming using chemical fertilisers, the High Wolds and their peripheral lowlands were very different areas, both in terms of their physical geography and cultural potentials. The chalk uplands and, in particular, the clay-rich lowlands embodied a series of distinct environmental zones which, at their interfaces, offered access to a particularly wide range of resources.

On modern maps, the patterning of strip parishes around the High Wolds' periphery reflects a long-standing recognition by agricultural communities of the economic value of such interface areas. Each parish thus had access to a landscape transect encompassing the following zones: the natural resources of the central vale rivers and wetlands; the wet grazing at the latter's edge; a raised, freer-draining and spring-fed sub-scarp band suitable for arable and settlement, and the lush grazing

and furze scrubland of the Wolds' scarp and plateaux edge (see also Chs 7 and 8). The Wharram plateau, with its steep scarps and spring-fed valleys can thus be considered, in particular in concert with its surrounding flatlands, an exemplary case study of human-environmental interaction in a diverse but changing landscape. Before moving on to explore such interactions, however, some further discussion of the physical environment is necessary.

Wharram lies at around 150m above sea level in the north-west corner of the Wolds' crescent-shaped mass of uplifted and tilted Cretaceous chalk, which then sinks gently into the Holderness drift to the south and east (Figs 1 and 26). At the foot of the Wolds' scarp and in Wharram's deep valleys, the degree of uplift was sufficient to expose Jurassic strata in the form of Kimmeridge and Ampthill clays. The surrounding flatlands then formed during the Dimlington Stadial when the Vales of York and Pickering became filled with a combination of glacial drift, lacustrine and alluvial deposits (Catt 1990, 15-16). Within the High Wolds, the overall impression of a rounded, 'soft' landscape is interrupted by systems of interconnecting, steep-sided, sinuous dry valleys or slacks, which form dendritic patterns towards their upland heads. Although such

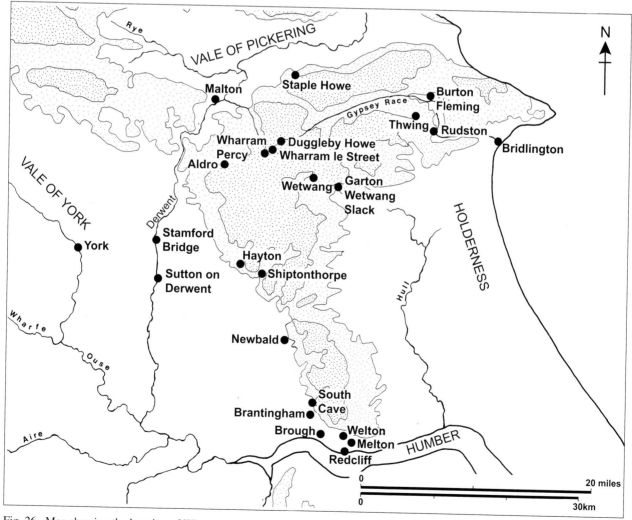

Fig. 26. Map showing the location of Wharram Percy and other places mentioned in Chapter 6. (C. Philo and E. Marlow-Mann)

valleys were created by periglacial freeze-thaw action and meltwater, the vast majority away from the Wolds edge now remain permanently dry except during extremely wet weather (Ellis 1990).

Around Wharram, in the region of greatest geological uplift, post and peri-glacial meltwaters carved down through the chalk and into the underlying impermeable clays. Spring lines at the chalk-clay interface were thus exposed and their streams have for millennia provided a reliable water supply for communities on and below the Wharram plateaux. The Gypsey Race, which rises from such a spring just to the east of Wharram le Street, is unique amongst surface streams in the Wharram area, in that it flows east down the Great Wold Valley towards Bridlington and not north or west into the Derwent.

The nature and patterning of soils across the Wharram area were, not surprisingly, strongly influenced by the underlying solid and drift geology. The rolling chalk plateaux are characterised by thin, free-draining calcareous soils, being either brown rendzinas in ploughed areas, or humic rendzinas in areas that are or were permanent pasture. East of Wharram le Street, the valley of the Gypsey Race contains calcareous brown earths, which exist where deeper soil profiles have developed, often through colluviation. The chalklands' soils also incorporate significant quantities of aeolian sands and silts that were redeposited on the chalk under dry periglacial conditions (Ellis 1990, 32). The seasonally waterlogged lower-lying hollows and main valleys at Wharram contain extensive tracts of pelo-stagnogley soils, which developed over the exposures of Jurassic clays in these areas. These latter soils at Wharram in fact mark the upland limit of such heavy, clay-rich gleys, which are far more characteristic of the surrounding flatlands. Thus the solid and drift geology created the basic patterning of soil types in the region, but it was the topography and drainage that determined to what use such soils might be put.

Prehistoric territorialisation

As set out above, the geological setting and natural resources of the High Wolds landscape are reasonably well known, although its specific character in early prehistory has been much debated. Previous conventional wisdom, that the Wolds were covered by argillic brown earths, has been questioned by Bush (1988), who argued for chalk grassland instead. This suggestion has itself been doubted (Thomas 1989), and perhaps a more mixed landscape should now be envisaged. Either way, the Wolds would not have been an obvious area of preferred settlement at this time. Yet there is no doubt that the region was exploited at an early stage, probably initially on a part-time, or even transhumant, basis linked to the Vales of York and Pickering, and the Humber wetlands which form its margins. Thereafter, a complex story emerges here of interactions between natural processes and cultural agencies.

A flint scatter from around the source of the Gypsey Race suggests Mesolithic activity there at this date, though most other flint assemblages from across the Wolds date to the Neolithic period or later. The latter include evidence for specialised production of knives, arrowheads and axes to the east, towards the coast (Durden 1995) and, much nearer to Wharram, scatters of material around Vessey Ponds (just to the east of Aldro on Fig. 26), employing Neolithic and Bronze Age hard hammer technology. Concentrations of material at such 'watering holes' could relate to contemporary habitation, or to concentrations of animals at these points, thus facilitating hunting (Hayfield et al. 1995).

In the course of the Neolithic period the site of Rudston, positioned in the Great Wold Valley at the centre of the Wolds, became a locus of activity as the setting for a series of *cursus* monuments (Chapman 2005; Dymond 1966; Stoertz 1997, fig. 10). The great barrow at Duggleby Howe may have provided a second focal point (Stoertz 1997, 60). Subsequently, there emerged a series of territorial claims on the surrounding landscape, based on the inserting of combinations of burial monuments and linear features at different times. This process, it has been argued, is most obvious in the distribution and positioning of Early Bronze Age round barrows (although see Woodward 2002 for alternative interpretations).

Whether barrows defined the first boundaries, or are merely the first definition which is clearly visible archaeologically can be debated (Fenton-Thomas 2005, 39ff). What *is* certain is that, by the Late Bronze Age, *c.* 1000 bc, earlier trackways across the Wolds, probably developed by mobile communities, had been replaced, or better reinforced, by the insertion alongside of single bank-and-ditch earthworks. These new forms of linear feature defined plateau areas, with further, double or triple-vallate features linking valley heads or articulating with the Wolds scarp. They incorporated gaps for access, probably to channel stock to particular points for access to lower water sources (especially for cattle which, unlike sheep, cannot manage on moisture derived solely from grazing: Giles 2007b; Johnston 2008, 282).

There is some debate over whether these earthworks simply controlled/directed movement across the landscape in the way just described, or rather were seeking to make territorial claims as part of a change from an open to enclosed landscape (Fenton-Thomas 2005, although, ultimately, this may come to much the same thing). Clearly the earthworks represented a major social investment when dug: inscribed in the white chalk, they would have been eminently visible, both to those few who oversaw their creation and to the many by whose labour a new socio-political reordering of the landscape was made manifest. Together with the barrows and natural components of the landscape such as meres, geological features, and even trees with which they seem to articulate (Giles 2007b), they have been interpreted as part of a ritual landscape in use for at least 1000 years, influencing the movement of people through the Wolds over time and linked to the Moraines crossing the Vale of York (Fenton-Thomas 2005, 47ff).

Alongside these earthworks, ditched enclosures at critical points such as Thwing/Paddock Hill, Staple Howe and nearby Devil's Hill become apparent by the end of the Bronze Age (the area around Aldro, an impressive, scarp-top promontory enclosed by earthworks to the south-west of Wharram, could represent another such focal point: Fig. 26). These are usually taken to suggest the existence of powerful aristocratic groups who inhabited this scattering of defended hilltop sites and concerned themselves with imported metalwork and grain storage facilities (Manby, King and Vyner 2003). Recent work by Giles (2007b) questions this interpretation, noting the diversity in size and apparent function which these sites embody. Whether or not they used such proposed 'hill forts', it is clear that late prehistoric social elites would have been helped in consolidating their social position by the physical structure of earthwork territorial divisions.

The evidence from around Wharram Percy matches, and elaborates, the picture outlined above. The water supply here, and the adjacent combination of dale and plateau plus grazing beyond, may have made it a focus for human occupation from an early date. The earliest *known* activity, however, lies further north, with the aforementioned finds of Mesolithic date near the source of the Gypsey Race, then the Neolithic remains at Duggleby Howe, to its north-east. At a later date, two major east-west linear features are evident to the north and south of the area that became Wharram Percy township. The northern one, numbered Route 2 in the introduction to this part of the volume (see Fig. 23), runs approximately east-west from the modern village of North Grimston, through Duggleby and along the Great Wold Valley. The next east-west route to the south, Route 3, runs along the ridgeway bounding the Wharram Percy township on the south. Its line is marked by clusters and strings of Early Bronze Age barrows as it passes along this plateau at constant height, linking contours at valley heads (Fig. 27).

Three further trackways developed between Routes 2 and 3, and are shown in Figure 27 along with possibly associated monuments. Track A ran northwards from the point where Route 3 skirted the top of Fairy Dale, and it continued past the east side Wharram le Street villa enclosures to Route 2, if not beyond; the villa enclosures may have impinged on its course (*Wharram IV*, fig. 7). It comprises at one place along its line a 25m-wide bank and ditch. Although essentially undated, two pieces of evidence suggest a Bronze Age date for its insertion (beyond its apparent articulation with Routes 2 and 3): near Wharram le Street village, a Middle Iron Age barrow was situated beside it and seemed to obey its line; and more convincingly, a cluster of Bronze Age barrows is located where its course meets Route 3 to the south. The latter group of burials, encircling a hill, are not inter-visible. This might imply that they were meant to be seen from different points elsewhere, most obviously by people moving along Route 3 and Track A, indicating that the latter feature may have been in use during the Bronze Age – or at least before the Middle Iron Age.

With Tracks B and C we can be a little more certain of date. The first of these bounds the Wharram Percy township on the north-west, running north-eastwards from the direction of Aldro to intersect Track C near the Crossroads sites. It continues along the south side of the Wharram le Street villa site to meet Route 2 near Duggleby Howe. To the south-west, in the vicinity of Aldro, two alignments of Bronze Age barrows combine to suggest that the route was in place by that time. In addition, research at Wharram Crossroads has shown that this boundary predates the Iron Age development of that area, forming the main spine of the ladder settlement of that date (see further below).

Track C appears to articulate with or cross Route 3 immediately to the north-east of Fairy Dale and from there it heads west-north-west to pass directly through the North Manor Area at Wharram Percy, before turning north-west to cross Track B at Wharram Crossroads. From there it continues its original line past Wharram Grange villa site, atop the peninsula formed between Birdsall Brow and Grimston Brow, where the crop mark evidence for this route disappears before the edge of the plateau. Either the trackway simply gave access to the end of this promontory, or it dropped down the Wolds scarp at this point. The feature has been shown to be fundamental to all pre-medieval development in the North Manor Area, and the earliest evidence for its existence comprises an alignment of several pits, severely truncated by later, Iron Age activity (Site 45/60). Although not directly dated, it is suggested that they belong to the Bronze Age on the basis of finds of that date redeposited here in later stratigraphy. In short, Track C was probably set out before the end of the Bronze Age, and then influenced developments in the area for many centuries thereafter.

Several important implications might be drawn from the detailed Wharram evidence. First, excavations along the line of Track B show that, by the end of the period under consideration here, a pair of flanking ditches defined the whole route explicitly and exactly (see further below). There are, however, subtle differences in its initial alignment, suggesting that it may have been created incrementally, with each length left to silt up thereafter: successive generations of Bronze Age society may have contributed to the creation of these major land divisions. In that sense, their elaboration over time makes them monuments to collective labour, creating the context in which encounters and interaction within contemporary communities were structured and performed (see further discussion below).

It is not possible, from the present evidence, to decide whether these subsidiary boundaries developed at the same time as major routes or later, yet such elaboration was certainly occurring within the Bronze Age (and these are only the elements seen in aerial photography – other, less visible, components may survive on the ground). This proliferation of ditches served to define a number of distinct zones of limited size, perhaps best seen as plots of land used by small groups of households. Clearly,

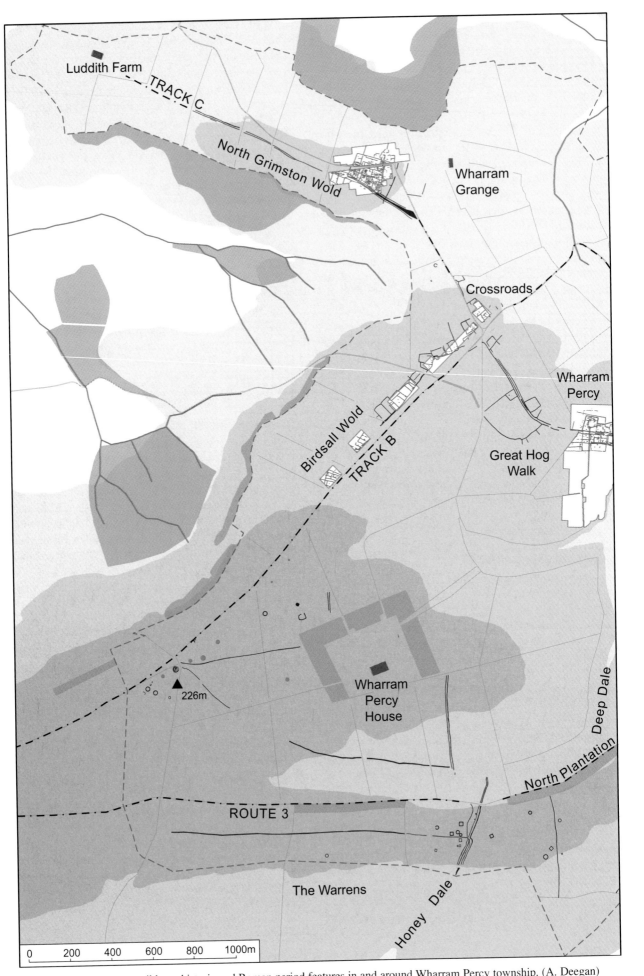

Fig. 27. Probable and possible prehistoric and Roman period features in and around Wharram Percy township. (A. Deegan)

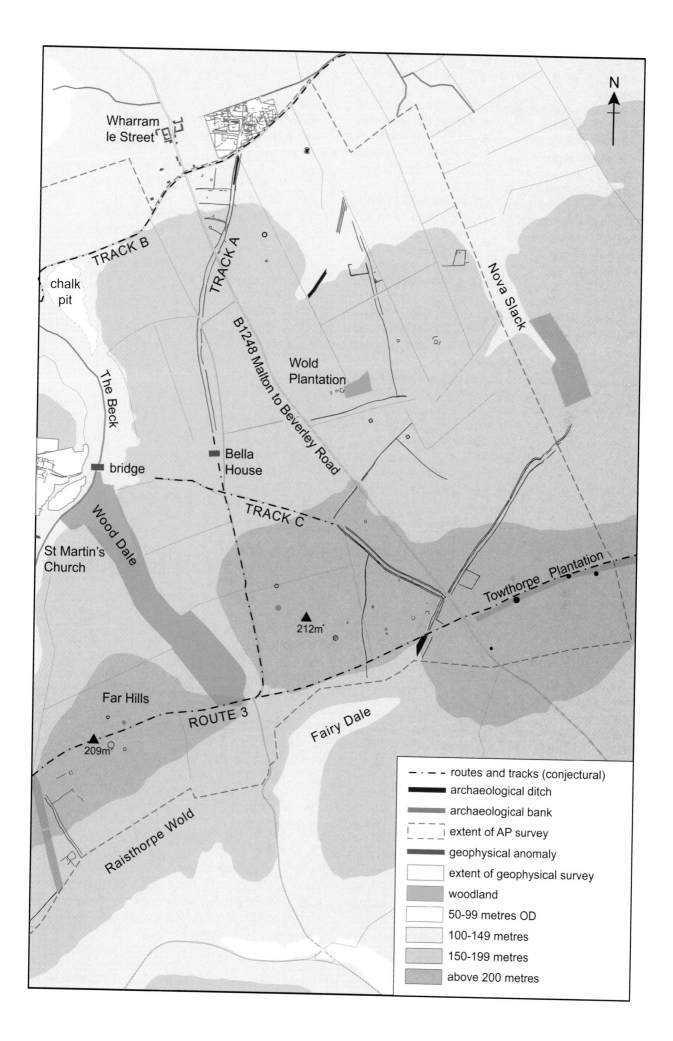

N

Wharram le Street

chalk pit

TRACK B

TRACK A

The Beck

B1248 Malton to Beverley Road

Nova Slack

Wold Plantation

bridge

Bella House

TRACK C

St Martin's Church

Wood Dale

Towthorpe Plantation

212m

Far Hills

ROUTE 3

Fairy Dale

209m

Raisthorpe Wold

- · - · - routes and tracks (conjectural)
  archaeological ditch
  archaeological bank
  - - - extent of AP survey
  geophysical anomaly
  extent of geophysical survey
  woodland
  50-99 metres OD
  100-149 metres
  150-199 metres
  above 200 metres

movement within 'territories' was being controlled to quite a low level. This suggests a comprehensive approach to landscape exploitation, perhaps along the lines of the 'estate' suggested for Vessey pastures just to the west of Wharram Percy (Hayfield *et al.* 1995). The conventional notion of Bronze Age society on the Wolds – that it comprised large, undifferentiated communities occupying only general territories – is called into question by such focused definition.

The above landscape divisions continued in use into the Iron Age, albeit becoming silted up over time. Yet, unfortunately, it is by no means clear what contemporary forms of occupation across the Wolds may have comprised, including the vexed question of where any associated housing might have lain. At Wharram, equally, material dating from before the Late Iron Age is very scarce. Early finds comprise a scatter of Bronze Age flints from under North Manor at Site 45/60, and a small amount of flint and Middle to Late Bronze Age pottery at Site 41 near the church, sealed by hillwash and so protected from later truncation (whether this represents *in situ* activity or was simply moved there by natural agencies cannot be determined). In addition, Middle Iron Age ceramics were present in certain assemblages in relatively small quantities. Finally, pit digging, including structured deposition at, for example, Wharram Crossroads, is the one clear indication of activity at this time.

Burial evidence, however, does allow us to say a little more about trajectories of change here within the Iron Age. The Middle Iron Age sees a significant innovation in mortuary practices across the region, in the form of the arrival of square-ditched barrows. These inhumations, often associated with water sources, have a complex relationship with pre-existing landscape features (see Bevan 1997 and Giles 2007b for different perspectives). Grave goods from such burials, for example at Garton Wetwang Slack, taken at face value, suggest increased social differentiation, whilst the well-known 'cart burials' from the region, a subset of this group (Dent 1983; Stead 1991), suggest the emergence of a further tier of elite within Middle Iron Age society. The most recent commentary has suggested, however, that these mortuary practices may be intended to help people '*rethink the realities of their own lives*' in particular localities (Giles 2007b, 115), rather than being a simple product of their status in life. To understand what sort of 'realities' might be envisaged here, we must turn to patterning in other types of archaeological evidence.

Some of the earlier hilltop enclosures were abandoned in the course of the Iron Age, perhaps signalling a move away from processing and storing surplus at a few fixed, strategic locations. The ideological role of these settings, it could be argued, was now replaced by the much more widely-distributed burials involving the commemoration of elite transport mentioned above Giles 2007b, 115. Could this be the point at which elite authority became much more integrated with local communities, the carts being promoted as the mechanism by which this new type of mobile authority could travel between them, to

consume products and reinforce their social position? If leaders were now increasingly locally-positioned in order to take direct advantage of the surpluses, it would come as no surprise that 'locale' became more important than 'region', both to the rural producers who created that surplus, and to those who sought to extract and consume it for themselves.

In the light of the above, it is interesting to consider the few Middle Iron Age burials encountered by aerial photography in the Wharram study area (see Archaeology Data Service, doi:10.5284/1000415, Deegan report). Differential site visibility may limit comparisons between Bronze Age and Iron Age practices, not least because the identified Middle Iron Age features lack any mound or confirmed existence of a central pit. Yet, taken at face value, these new barrows seem to lie adjacent to pre-existing landscape boundaries but, unlike their Bronze Age counterparts, are not placed to reinforce directly those adjacent routes. In the one case where a Middle Iron Age barrow 'cluster' can be identified (where Route 3 passes the head of Honey Dale: Fig. 27), they seem to define some form of 'cemetery area', not a linear arrangement. Although the earlier routes through the landscape were still in play, it could be argued that burials now took on a new role: providing more local identities rather than enhancing general divisions.

Late Iron Age and Early Roman ladder settlements

A diagnostic element of Late Iron Age society on the Wolds, and arguably beyond, comprises the creation of sets of contiguous enclosures, linked by ditch-flanked trackways (often referred to as 'droveways'), to form linear complexes. These, named 'ladder settlements', run for several kilometres in places (Stoertz 1997, 51ff and fig. 26). The relationship between pre-existing features and ladder settlements is clearly complex. That at Melton South Lawn (Fenton-Thomas forthcoming), for example, was laid out in relation to a Bronze Age division; whilst some respected the positions of Middle Iron Age burials and earlier monuments, others ignored these pre-existing features.

Their exact chronology has also been a matter of some debate. The best-preserved examples, for instance that south-east of Burton Fleming, are difficult to tie down. Stead (1980) has, however, put forward a pre-Roman date for the development of the 'ladder-like' features encountered beneath the Roman villa at Rudston. Subsequent work by Dent (1988 plus references) suggested that considerable quantities of Late Iron Age ceramics (or at least *proposed* Late Iron Age material – see below) are found in association with morphologically similar sites elsewhere. The problem lies in whether such material, particularly those wares tempered with calcite, is exclusively of that date or also used in the early Roman period.

Thus, there is a risk that some sites having such late calcareous-tempered pottery, but lacking provably Roman material, might be ascribed a Late Iron Age date, when they were really occupied later. Of course, the fact that we may not always be able to distinguish Late Iron Age from Early Roman activity on the basis of ceramics is itself of some significance in defining the close relationship between the two 'periods'. More importantly for present purposes, some sites may indeed have been founded only in the Roman period. Yet it seems special pleading to suppose that *all* were, even if some of those which started earlier may have continued in use for several centuries. Overall, whatever the exact proportions, it seems clear that some ladder settlements can now be seen as a creation of Late Iron Age communities (Giles 2007a). Thus, the form of landscape exploitation which they represent, once viewed solely as a Roman imposition, was in origin a product of pre-existing dynamics and needs.

It seems likely that the central components here are drove-ways, perhaps leading to areas of open pasture. The enclosures themselves may comprise agricultural fields or stock enclosures, areas of domestic activity or burial places, suggesting a mixed economy overall. Where subjected to detailed investigation, it is clear that adjacent enclosures were not created fully-fledged, in a single, planned development. Rather, they evolved over time as one element was added to another, perhaps a product of activity at 'slack' times in the agricultural calendar. As a result, they would have been formative in the construction of household identity for the groups which created them (Giles 2000). They vary considerably in size, those on the Wolds often being larger than elsewhere, as are their counterparts on its lowland edge. These more sizeable examples may be related to a more arable or transhumant economy, in contrast to smaller, irregular examples on narrow plateaux used for sheep farming. Recent work (Atha 2007) shows that this morphological form is evident beyond the Wolds, seen on its margins at Shiptonthorpe and Hayton and hypothesised at Stamford Bridge and Sutton-on-Derwent (Millett 2006), but also much further afield. These more widespread instances similarly suggest specialisation, for example an emphasis on cattle rearing alongside iron and pottery production in wetland areas.

Ladder settlements may provide some evidence for the continuity of certain activities from Middle Iron Age society. As noted, some respected the positions of earlier, square-ditched barrow cemeteries. In addition, ritual deposition in the form of infant burials is still evident at Garton Wetwang Slack in Late Iron Age contexts, something also hinted at with Late Iron Age or Early Roman neonate burials at Wharram Crossroads. Finally, the latter site saw the placement of a cattle skull, propped with chalk blocks, in a clay-lined, stone-capped Middle Iron Age pit, then the deposit of a fragmentary human humerus sealed by a burnt ashy deposit capped with close-set chalk blocks in a Late Iron Age feature. The pre-existing rules of ritual activity clearly had some continuing currency.

That said, when taken in the round, it is the differences that are most striking. These systems of enclosure represent a clear change to the way in which the landscape

was being organised and used, and thus to the economic underpinnings of society at the time. Furthermore, this process was clearly starting to occur in the centuries well before the Roman conquest of the region, although there is ample evidence that they continued in use after that point, most obviously at Wharram Percy itself, whose detailed data are considered next.

For Wharram, Late Iron Age and Early Roman evidence is more profuse than that of earlier periods and has far more explanatory potential, despite the aforementioned problems of interpreting it (limited feature excavation, differential finds survival, diverse discard practices, and complex processes of disturbance and redeposition). Late Iron Age and Early Roman activity can be definitely identified in two areas: one near the stream, beside the later church, and the second beneath the medieval North Manor. The latter is by far the more extensive, and can be linked to evidence from topographical and geophysical survey.

In the former area, the earliest evidence comprises the insertion of a Late Iron Age, south-facing crouched burial (80bc +- 60) of an arthritic female aged 25-35, without grave goods (Harding 2007, 31). Nearby chalk surfaces, of either Late Iron Age or Early Roman date, were sealed by clay which was then cut by a scatter of post-holes and slots with no obvious pattern. All seem broadly contemporary with the burial or slightly later, as do two east-west ditches backfilled with Early Roman pottery and residual Late Iron Age material (Harding and Marlow-Mann 2007, 22; Didsbury 2007, 246-7), and a hearth further south associated with Early Roman pottery and a glass bangle. (Given the stratigraphic sequence here, the fact that the hearth lay central to the later church seems, to the present writers, to be entirely coincidental: see Harding and Marlow-Mann 2007, 21, fig. 20).

Clearly there is activity here, starting in the Late Iron Age and seeming to run through to, perhaps, the mid-2nd century. Some quernstones with pecked, as opposed to furrowed, surfaces, one with upright handle hole, could be of Late Iron Age/Early Roman date, as, provably, are a disc brooch and trumpet-headed brooch. To interpret this as part of a substantial settlement, and even as a beck-side religious complex, which may have influenced medieval ecclesiastical development (see Harding and Wrathmell 2007, 329), seems much too large a claim. Far more important is the implication that Late Roman activity here either takes a very different form or is non-existent – there has been a sea-change by the end of the 2nd century AD.

More widespread evidence, both chronologically and spatially, comes from the North Manor, where there are more Late Iron Age/Early Roman finds than from the rest of the settlement, even if the proportions relative to later periods remain small. It is clear that an enclosure measuring 47m east-west by 31m north-south was set out on the north side of Track C, with a centrally-placed entrance on its south side and large, co-aligned ditches to east and west serving to reinforce the line of the pre-existing route way (Site 45/60: Fig. 28). Metallings laid out along the northern edge of these ditches obeyed their

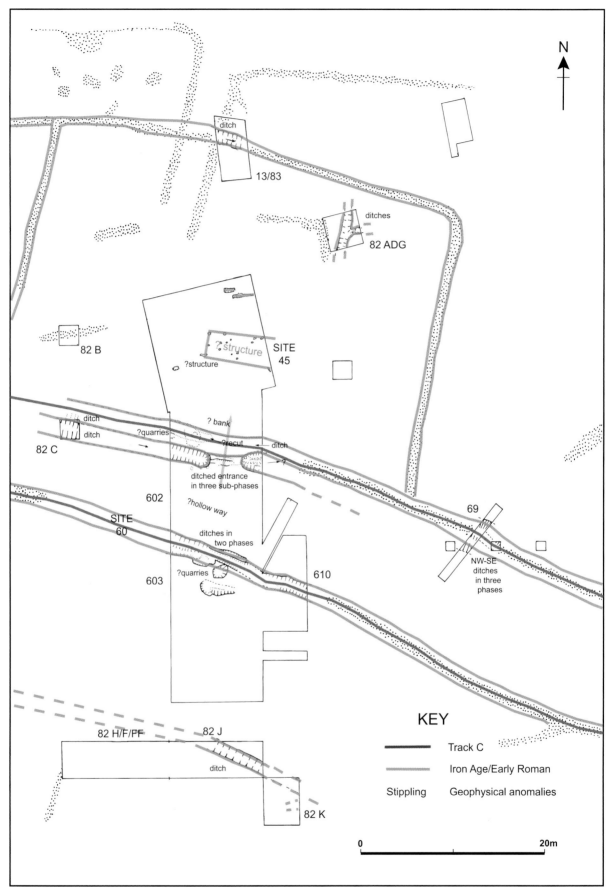

N

Fig. 28. Late prehistoric and early Roman features excavated in the vicinity of Sites 45/60, set beside evidence derived from geophysical survey. These elements created an enclosure, containing ditched subdivisions and evidence for structures, north of a pre-existing track (Track C on Fig. 27). Further enclosures may have been laid out south of that track. (E. Marlow-Mann after P. Rahtz)

line even after they had filled up, showing the long-term influence of this arrangement. Within the enclosure itself, several ditches further subdivided the area, whilst the zone directly north of the central entrance showed evidence of slots and post-holes associated with chalk surfaces, forming a rectangular structure co-aligned with the surrounding enclosure (G1-3, Site 45: Milne 2004, 22-3).

To the south of Track C, a second, contemporary ditch suggests another enclosure on this side, measuring 19m north to south (Site 82J: other limits unclear, Fig. 29). To the south-west, successive, broadly contemporary ditches imply corresponding development further along the pre-existing trackway, which clearly continued to be re-metalled and repaired at this time. More generally, geophysical prospection suggests the positions of a whole series of enclosures on both sides of Track C extending some 20-35m from it. Although direct dating evidence for these is lacking, their alignments and positions strongly suggest that a series of 'ladder-like' enclosures was set out beside Track C at this time, continuing west for at least 160m on its north side and for at least 250m on its south (see below, Fig. 30).

A second ladder settlement to the north-west, at Wharram Crossroads, has been identified by aerial photography and geophysical survey (Fig. 27). Set out along the north side of pre-existing Track B, it ran 1km south-westwards from where this crossed Track C. Although subject to only limited excavation, this site has undergone detailed analysis and interpretation by one of us (M. Atha), on which this summary is based. Dating evidence for its use is limited, but fieldwalking above its line yielded, for the most part, only material of Late Iron Age/Early Roman date.

In addition, limited excavation within an enclosure near its western limit, at Birdsall High Barn, exposed a proposed 'farmstead' of that date, which went out of use before 4th-century material accumulated on top of it. Finally, within another excavated enclosure towards its eastern end, gullies and post-holes indicate remains of structures, plus nearby deposits of domestic rubbish, one of which contained a coarse-toothed comb used in weaving. This matches hints from artefacts at Wharram Percy itself, for example burnt clay triangular loomweights, to suggest Late Iron Age/Early Roman textile production alongside the more dominant evidence of grain processing.

The evidence from Wharram itself supports the view that ladder settlements represent a radically new way of living within the Wolds landscape, albeit including mechanisms and elements inherited from earlier centuries, notably the trackways alongside which they were set out. They have been seen as a product of Late Iron Age population growth (Dent 1983), yet there is no evidence of any migration into the area. Critically, ladders do not involve the colonisation of land which was previously unoccupied, although they may, in part, have signalled a move away from its use purely for pasture, perhaps on a part-time basis.

In contrast to Dent, recent work by Giles (2007a) has focused on landscape ideology and exploitation to interpret this change. As noted above, ladders represented an important mechanism for defining individual households albeit in the context of larger communities. Thus they are strung out along single routeways, requiring common movement outside each enclosure and reinforcing interdependence. Yet there is an increased focus on the household itself, now secluded in enclosures with limited access. The banks, together with the hedges which probably topped them, ensured that it was not just activities within the house that were invisible to those beyond, as in Middle Iron Age organisation, but also in the household enclosure as a whole. The importance of access, expressed with the careful orientation of thresholds in earlier, unenclosed houses, was now augmented by the corresponding significance of gateways leading into these later enclosures.

In a wonderfully apposite turn of phrase, Giles (2000) has characterised this development as a move from 'open weave to close knit' communities, at the same time noting other changes in contemporary society. Mortuary practices, for example, may have moved from barrow burial to excarnation, perhaps taking place near individual enclosures and related to household histories. More generally, there is a greater emphasis on militarism in society, seen, for example, with the incidence of swords in burials. Locally, chalk figurines carrying swords on their backs were perhaps used in household shrines, and were then decapitated on the death of a family member.

Yet there remains a need to theorise more fully the material circumstances in which the change of emphasis, from community to household, was taking place. This must involve considering potentially separate household histories whilst, at the same time, contextualising the general, increased emphasis on military conflict. Certainly, more is involved with the establishment of household histories that just 'ideological' imperatives. The everyday slog of pit and ditch digging, repair of structures and so forth would also have been involved, together with the fundamentally important activity of landscape exploitation, now taking place in a more focused way than before.

Much recent writing on late prehistory has focused on the significance of everyday practices in establishing community identity. Here, Bourdieu's notion of *habitus*, set out in his Outline of a Theory of (everyday) Practice (1977), has become tremendously influential, particularly as articulated in Ingold's concept of 'the taskscape' (1993, 158ff; 2000, 194ff). It was the repetition of activities in both agriculture (Field 2008) and in animal husbandry (Johnston 2008; see also Chadwick 2007 for the interaction of human and animal movement around field systems in South Yorkshire) that structured the lives of the vast majority of the population. It is these processes, rather than single 'one-off' big events such as bringing together the labour needed to create a hillfort (Sharples 2007), which eventually came to define the

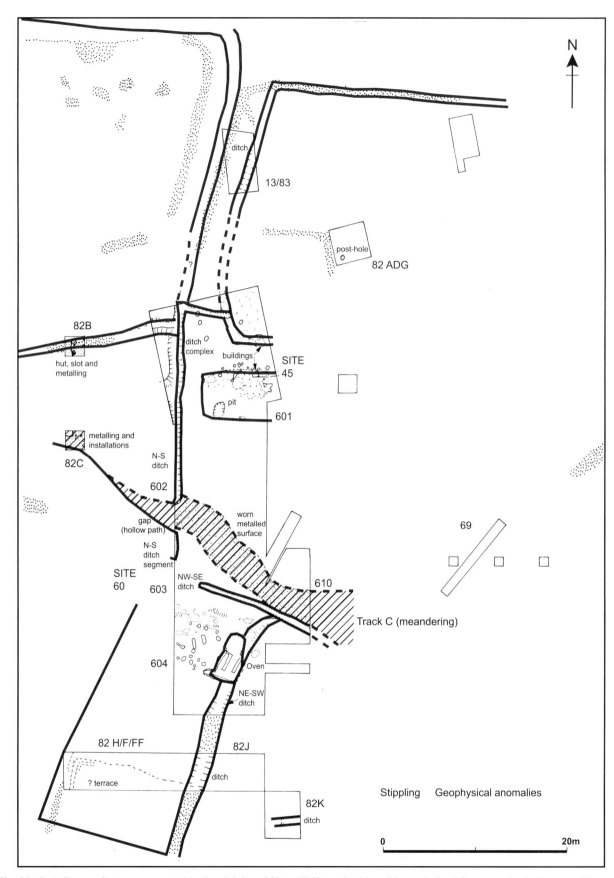

Fig. 29. Late Roman features excavated in the vicinity of Sites 45/60, set beside evidence derived from geophysical survey. The position of the latter is plotted here as in the original publication (*Wharram IX*, fig. 142; the lack of correspondence between the geophysics and the excavated evidence in the northern third of the diagram suggests an error in plotting). In this period, new enclosures and entrance arrangements replaced those in use from the later Iron Age on either side of Track C. The latter, in use from the Bronze Age, was retained in these new developments. In the Late Roman period it may have taken the form of a winding path, but for an alternative date for this path see Chapter 7. (E. Marlow-Mann after P. Rahtz)

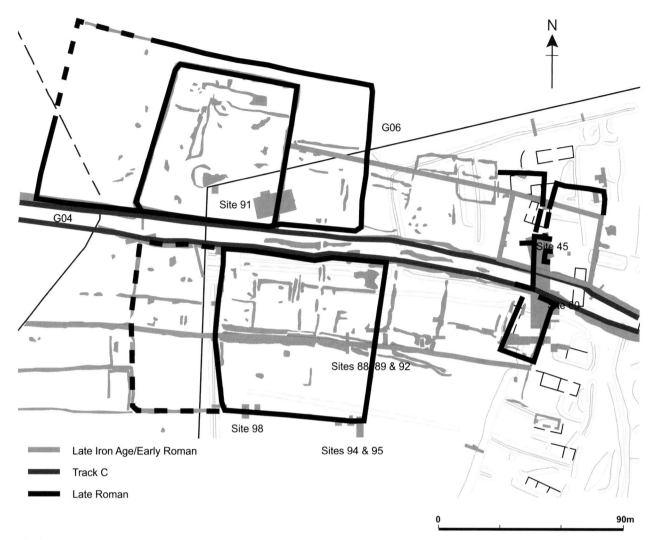

Fig. 30. Late Iron Age/Early Roman and Late Roman features across the North Manor area, revealed by a combination of limited excavation and geophysical survey. They suggest that the replacement of early 'ladder settlements' with larger, discrete enclosures beside Track C was more than a local phenomenon confined to Site 45/60. (E. Marlow-Mann after S. Roskams)

cosmological systems of the time. Such praxis, fitted within the context of generational, annual and even daily procedures, has led to the notion of 'the roll call and rhythm of routine' (Edmonds 1999) being fundamental to our understanding of these communities and the individuals within them, something which contrasts with modern notions of selfhood. Thus, for example, social identity would be created not only when ditches and other boundaries were first established, but also in their subsequent maintenance, repair and alteration (Chadwick 1999).

One of the most striking aspects of the ladder settlements, when surveyed geophysically, is a contrast between the uniformly strong magnetic responses of their boundaries and the lack of such signals inside the enclosures. This is matched by the excavated evidence, with little material found within them, yet considerable quantities derived from the adjacent ditches, implying that the latter functioned as middens. This interpretation is further supported by the evidence for successive recuts along their line, perhaps derived from filling, then clearing, them on a cyclical basis, presumably to spread

the now-decayed 'household waste' onto fields. The whole cycle would represent a rapid way in which household history was reproduced and reinforced during an activity which was critical to the agricultural functioning of that social unit. In contrast to earlier societies, whose linear boundaries were seemingly created incrementally by successive generations (see above), households were now defining their own, individualised identities on a regular, perhaps seasonal, basis.

Stepping beyond this detail, and incorporating the evidence of increased militarisation, this process can best be viewed as a classic case of increasing tensions derived from changes in the means of production conflicting with increasingly outmoded relations of production (see Roskams 2006, 498ff for explanations of this Marxist terminology and the argument in abstract). Late Iron Age society inherited a situation in which larger communities were the fundamental social unit, tied together by common burial and other practices. Given the evidence for social differentiation in the Middle Iron Age, it seems likely that some form of aristocratic authority survived thereafter, continuing to exploit local communities collectively through extraction of tribute. In contrast, however, to contemporary social elites in southern Britain, those in East Yorkshire seem to lack any obvious high-status settlement to articulate their interests in East Yorkshire, with the possible exception of Redcliff. Increasingly, however, the household became the fundamental unit of economic production within those communities: each unit may have remained part of a greater whole, but became more and more separate from it in terms of everyday production. Various factors would have allowed certain households to gain economic power at the expense of others. Differential access to landscape resources would have been inevitable, for example: a nearby water source or woodland, a more productive arable context than one's neighbours. In addition, the organisation of ladder settlements would ensure that some households had more direct relationships with other communities or itinerant groups. Being situated near to the crossing point of two routeways (for example Tracks B and C at Wharram) would increase one's ease of access to outsiders. It might even make such households better placed to take on a representative role in articulating relationships between different communities on the Wolds, or between those settled in, and those moving through, the region.

The exact outcomes of such situations need not be preordained, yet tensions would remain between more and less-favoured social units. These might surface in the context of everyday activities, for example in organising access to pasture or in maintaining boundaries between adjacent households, or in tasks which still required a communal level of organisation, for example the maintenance of the routeways beside which the enclosures were set out, but which also stretched across the landscape beyond. Further tensions might be expected to come to a head in negotiating relationships with those who stood above these details but still needed to take surplus from such settlements to retain their position – the tribute-extracting elite of Late Iron Age society. In such a situation, it is not surprising to find continuities of Middle Iron Age ritual practices – those activities which gave the larger community its sense of itself in former times – set beside new indicators of social tension such as the sword-carrying chalk figurines.

Little has been said thus far about the impact of Rome, and this for good reason. Clearly, the Roman conquest brought a whole new set of imperatives to Yorkshire, both soon after the Claudian conquest, when we find imports coming into the area via Redcliff and the local circulation of Corieltauvian coinage, and later when the legions moved across the Humber, creating short-term military needs with the setting up of nodal points at York and at Brough, Hayton, Malton and perhaps Stamford Bridge. Equally clearly, the Roman state would have endeavoured to impose its will on newly acquired territories, notably in the form of taxation using coins.

Yet within the Wolds landscape, as in areas at its periphery, change was patchy at best. It has been argued (Roskams 2007) that imperial rule brought a greater emphasis on roads and rivers, and the growth of some sites beyond the purely military *foci* related to these new networks. A road from *Petuaria* (Brough) to *Derventio* (Malton) skirted the Wolds to the west, whilst a second route can be reasonably suggested running west from the presumed Roman forerunner of Bridlington towards York (Stoertz 1997, 43-6).

This infrastructure had an impact on settlement development. Thus at Shiptonthorpe, on the interface between the Wolds and the wetlands to its west, enclosures stretched for 800m either side of a locally-maintained 'Roman' road, being utilised variously for habitation, stock rearing and as a cemetery. Initial supply mechanisms, though seemingly not militarily-dictated, still seem to have been linked directly to Lincolnshire, perhaps as administered activity rather than through economic integration. People would have been drawn to a place where the road crossed a stream, and roundhouses were built within the roadside enclosures into the 2nd century (Millett 2006).

Yet other settlements were affected only minimally by the conquest. The nearby Late Iron Age site at Hawling Road (Halkon and Millett 1999), for example, may lack any clear indications of agricultural activity but evidences woodland exploitation and pasture, plus loomweights and iron-working debris distributed in possible 'zones'. Such a combination of timber and bog ore allowed 'currency bars' to be produced on a scale which must have exceeded local needs. This intense level of production was past its peak by the Early Roman period but occupation here was largely unaffected: the pre-Roman barrows on the Wolds, still visible from this settlement, may have continued to be more relevant than the newly-arrived imperial authority down the road.

On the Wolds proper, especially around Wharram, the landscape seems to have changed very little initially. A Roman date has been claimed for a road thought to run south-east from Malton (Stoertz 1997, fig. 35) on the line of the modern B1248, passing through Wharram le Street east of Wharram Percy (see Fig. 27). The original suggestion (Cole 1899) was based on three factors: its articulation with 'street' place-names, notably Wharram le Street and High Street at Towthorpe; its alignment, in essence that it runs from the Roman site of *Derventio*; and its proximity to Roman sites, in particular a Roman cemetery at its proposed meeting with the York-Bridlington road mentioned above. This proposition has been followed in most subsequent discussion of Roman Yorkshire's road system but has to be treated with caution.

Such a date, although certainly possible, can be questioned on several grounds. First, place-name evidence of this sort is notoriously difficult to employ in such arguments. For example the suffix 'le Street' in the name Wharram le Street is not recorded by Smith (1937, 135-6) until the early 14th century, the two Wharrams having been differentiated in earlier centuries (if at all) as Greater and Lesser Wharram, as East and West Wharram, and as North and South Wharram. Secondly, Malton, although Roman in origin, also became a medieval settlement - hence a road leading from it could be of any date. In addition if a route was needed, for example, to move troops south-east soon after the Roman conquest, then it is by no means obvious where they would be heading. Without a clear destination, it seems unlikely that such a thoroughfare would remain in use in subsequent centuries. Thirdly, on the clustering of Roman sites on its line, there is considerable potential here for circular arguments: some sites are not securely dated, and others are not really near the route. The Roman cemetery just west of Wetwang, one of the few places which does not fall foul of the latter weaknesses, could just as easily be related only to the more securely-identified York-Bridlington road (Route 4 on Fig. 23), or even to no main road at all, rather than this route.

What can be said, then? Clearly, a road on this line influenced the layout of Wharram le Street village, and so presumably was in place by the 12th century at the latest. On the other hand, none of the known township boundaries of either of the two Wharrams follows it, and the course of the southern stretch of boundary separating the two townships might indicate that the road did not exist when the two Wharrams came into separate existence. Hayfield (*Wharram V*, 7) tends towards a Roman date for the feature by default, in that he thinks it unlikely to be of Anglo-Saxon origin (although his rationale for this is not stated).

If one demands a Roman context for its insertion, it has been shown above that several nearby prehistoric routeways were retained into the Roman period, notably Track A on which the Wharram le Street villa enclosures seem to be aligned; this would initially have made an additional thoroughfare unnecessary. Thus such a road is better linked to the large-scale 3rd-century changes described below, when new forms of dedicated surplus extraction were imposed on the Wharram landscape. A more direct route would have allowed easier supply of foodstuffs to Malton and transport of pottery from the kilns at Norton – all part of economic regionalisation at this time. This argument is, however, entirely circumstantial, and an equally strong case could be made for post-Roman dates up to, and including, the changes which occurred with the setting out of the Wharram le Street settlement, somewhere between the 9th and 12th centuries.

Stepping beyond communication networks and into the circulation of material culture, there is some evidence for wheel-made pots penetrating the Wolds area from the start of the Roman period. Yet, even these impacted differentially across the area. At Wharram Grange, for example, Early Roman imports of *amphorae*, decorated Samian, Ebor ware and North Lincolnshire fabrics were recovered. These indicate an early importance for this site, perhaps pre-figuring its role in subsequent centuries put forward below. Yet this implied status was only matched by structural development at a later date. More important, very little of this ceramic material reached other sites in the area.

Finally, we can turn to one of the fundamentals of the Early Roman landscape: food processing. Grain was now ground using a flatter type of quernstone, a change perhaps influenced by imported Mayen types. Yet the real change in crop processing came only with the use of the Late Roman corn drier described below. More generally, as far as can be seen archaeologically, the ladder settlements continued in use in much the same fashion as before, set beside long-existing routeways inherited from still earlier times. It is only, perhaps, a century or more after the military conquest of the region that significant changes are evident. These are discussed in the concluding section of this chapter.

Discrete Late Roman enclosures

In contrast to the Late Iron Age to Early Roman continuities emphasised above, the period of a generation or so either side of AD 200 can be identified throughout Yorkshire as a time of great change in many spheres (Roskams 1999): in urban or rural settlements (for example, systemic changes within the townscapes at York and Malton, and the arrival of villas on the Wolds – see further below); in developments in artefact production (glass, pottery and jet all see changes in the 3rd century); and in changed mortuary practices (the increased incidence of cremation in the countryside and a contrasting move towards inhumation in 'core' areas).

The previously-mentioned roadside settlement at Shiptonthorpe (Millett 2006) is a case illustrative of this transition at a more detailed level. The Early Roman roundhouses within its enclosures, though retained away from the road, were replaced by a horseshoe-shaped structure near it. Then a large, ten-bayed, rectangular building was imposed on top of all, associated with differential rubbish disposal (clean at the frontage, accumulations to its rear): the 3rd-century settlement was a very changed place. In the landscape beyond, farming practices developed here to a different level from those seen at nearby sites. Late Roman querns, some animal-powered, appear in considerable numbers, implying that crop surpluses from a wide region were being processed and shipped on as flour. A proliferation of knives suggests that larger domesticates, killed when mature, were being butchered in considerable numbers, perhaps to supply meat, especially sheep, to higher-order settlements such as York. Clearly, this settlement operated in a qualitatively different way from those surrounding it.

This picture of noticeable change contrasts with the evidence for ritual activity. For example, a large water hole, constructed *c*. AD 300 and screened from road, incorporated two phases of deliberate placement of faunal remains together with mistletoe and holly, suggesting a religious component integrated with more functional water supply (but also including a discarded writing implement - a role on the site for record keeping). In addition, neonates were buried near houses (adults were presumably interred elsewhere). Such deposition resonates with earlier, local practices: alongside the distinctive, profane farming practices, there was continuity of the sacred.

On the Wolds, notwithstanding the problems of definition and recognition, one might look to the creation of 'villas' as a way of judging the impact of Roman rule. Such establishments are usually interpreted as indigenous elites taking on board *Romanitas* which arrived on the back of military conquest. This timing is based on the finding of occasional glass bangles of early Roman date, but such artefacts could be heirlooms and/or there to be recycled (such production, using rudimentary technology, would be undetectable archaeologically). If one plays down their significance, and focuses instead on the much more voluminous ceramic and numismatic evidence, then few Wolds villas need date to before AD 200. The same applies to other nearby sites such as at Brantingham, Newbald and the possible example at South Cave (although Rudston might be argued to be important even before 'villa-like' structures developed there in the 3rd century, whilst the Welton villa is provably early, perhaps due to a relationship with nearby quarrying: Roskams 1999).

Two such important establishments lie near the study area and are thus worth looking at in more detail. The Wharram le Street site is set towards one end of a ladder settlement running along the line of Gypsey Race up to Duggleby Howe, near the former's water source. Its *tesserae*, stucco, *opus signinum* fragments, *tegulae* and *imbrices* show it is clearly a focus of high status activity, whether villa, religious complex, or something else. The main period of activity is from the 3rd century. The Wharram Grange settlement, positioned on a promontory with commanding views, is another site which may be significant before villa buildings were constructed there. Yet its heyday is clearly after the late 2nd century, when a major building complex was laid out, its north range having a tiled roof and mosaic pavement at its east end. The site may have been receiving rather less fine ware than the contemporary site at Wharram le Street, but the amounts involved still mark it out from other settlements in the vicinity. Furthermore, concentrations of such tablewares and cooking vessels at its centre, in contrast to amphorae on its periphery, suggest controlled rubbish disposal, as does the concentration of pitting south-east of the main enclosure. In short, structural characteristics, artefact status and levels of organisation all serve to mark these two sites out from the norm - and both are a product of Late Roman development.

In the landscape beyond these 'villas', Hayfield's survey defined two types of other settlements: villages and farmsteads (*Wharram V*, summarised in fig. 103). Most of them are known only from fieldwalking, which limits our interpretations to some extent. Nonetheless, some overall patterning seems clear. Villages were identified only at Wharram Percy, Burdale and Raisthorpe. The first site will be considered in detail below, but both of the other two were seemingly long-lived, being founded by the Late Iron Age and continuing in use throughout the Roman period and, arguably, beyond. Such longevity must relate to an adjacent water source at each and their sheltered positions. The available evidence cannot show how, if at all, they changed over these centuries. These larger settlements, however, stand in marked contrast to the eleven farmsteads which Hayfield also identified. All were occupied in the 3rd/4th centuries, yet few can be argued to exist much before that date: their floruit is clearly a Roman phenomenon, and then happening well within, rather than at the start, of that period. Hayfield saw the farmsteads as merely minor infilling of the earlier landscape, yet the numbers involved suggest to the present authors that they represent a more major transformation in landscape exploitation.

At Wharram Percy itself, there are myriad indications of a similar transformation at this time. If ceramic use is anything to go by, for example, there is a considerable increase in the density of occupation across the whole area: Late Roman material in post-Roman levels is far more profuse throughout than its Late Iron Age or Early Roman counterparts. Yet there are significant changes in the character of that occupation. For example, however one interprets the focus of Late Iron Age/Early Roman features near the stream and the medieval church, all have been sealed over by this point. The zone must be still in use, as the majority of pottery found here is 4th century, mostly coarse ware jars but also Crambeck types, and all six coins are of that date. Yet this later activity takes a quite different form.

In the core area, beneath the North Manor, there is also a fundamental shift in the organisation of occupation. Site 13/83 is pivotal to understanding these changes. Here the east-west ditch which formed the northern limit to the Late Iron Age/Early Roman ladder settlement fell into disuse, and was cut by a north-south ditch filled with Late Roman material (Fig. 29). When related to the results of geophysical survey in the vicinity, it is clear that a larger enclosure measuring over 30m north-south by at least 75m east-west (both limits are unclear from the geophysical survey) had replaced the original one. Entrance was from the north, formed by the excavated ditch in the east and a counterpart to the west, with a 4-5m wide metalled strip in between.

Cultivated soil is evident in several trenches in the eastern half of this new enclosure, but the area due south of the entrance track was occupied by several pebble-floored, rectangular structures and associated chalk surfaces, together with a possible kiln and cess pit, and further structures to the south (Site 45/60: G4 and G5). A late infant burial was then inserted in the main occupation area, perhaps linked to a much earlier brooch, dated to the 3rd to 1st century BC, recovered here (a deliberately placed heirloom?). Finally, further metallings lay to the west, plus traces of broadly contemporary structures (Site 82B). A ditch, seemingly cut across the entrance into the new enclosure, should mark its disuse (although, given its exclusively Early Roman pottery content, one wonders whether the stratigraphy may have been misinterpreted here: this feature would make much more sense in conjunction with the parallel Early Roman building just to its south-east). Overall, the burial and heirloom deposition may suggest continuity of ritual activity. The Late Roman landscape had, however, been entirely reorganised by this time, resulting in the complete demise of one element of the earlier ladder settlement.

A similar picture emerges to the south. The line of Track C was still obeyed, as Late Roman surfaces (Site 82C) run up to, but not beyond, the north edge of a backfilled Late Iron Age/Early Roman boundary ditch here. The long-existing droveway was now more meandering path than major thoroughfare (following *Wharram IX*, 283 and fig. 143; for an alternative dating and interpretation of the surface see Chapter 7, below). A new ditch defined part of its south side, but terminated in the west opposite the projected line of access into the northern enclosure. This, when set beside the sinuous character of the more ancient route at this time, might imply that north-south movement within the new, larger enclosure was now more important than east-west connections.

Beyond Track C to the south, two further north-south ditches formed either an access route or, more likely, a narrow second enclosure (Site 60). Either way, these insertions clearly mark the demise of ladder settlement on this side of the droveway. Another new Late Roman ditch to the east (Site 82K) suggests equivalent changes there. A large 'corn drier' was set up within this newly-defined southern enclosure, positioned along the line of the eastern ditch after the latter had become partially backfilled, but still apparently obeying its line (see Melton South Lawn: Fenton-Thomas forthcoming, for an exact equivalent there). This had successive phases, first T-shaped, then 'tuning fork' in plan form, and reused a number of stones from substantial structure(s) in its construction (see Rahtz and Watts 2004, 85-103).

It is this recycled material which has led to the suggestion that a villa must have existed nearby, the stones being thought too large to be brought from any great distance and the argument being reinforced by noting the evidence for vessel and window glass, *tegulae* and flue tile, plus a number of proposed *tesserae* (Rahtz *et al.* 2004, 283ff). Cool (2004, 343ff) has effectively critiqued this interpretation, noting how little tile, or indeed toilet or recreational equipment, has been recovered. Even accepting evidence of window glass, a stylus implying literacy, and connections to wider supply systems suggested by Kentish Ragstone and Mayen lava querns, she is surely right to conclude that the modest collection of small finds indicates a rural settlement with no great pretensions, rather than a villa.

That said, the debate about 'villa' status has tended to obscure the broader implications of the 'corn drier'. There is some dispute over whether such features were used to dry crops or as malting ovens. Either way, its construction implies an increased centralisation of crop processing. Indeed, the quernstone also reused in its construction, if it was part of a powered mill, suggests change before this date. Taken together, the evidence

indicates that agricultural surplus was being processed at an increased scale by this time, presumably to supply needs beyond the immediate environment (unless one believes, with Cool (2004, 345), that the driving force was simply to relieve locals of the more demanding work involved with hand milling - presumably by a suddenly more considerate landowner). It is interesting to note here that the demise of another substantial ladder settlement, this time off the Wolds at Melton South Lawn (Fenton-Thomas forthcoming), involved not only an entirely different form of landscape organisation, but also the insertion of a crop drier as part of these new arrangements.

Looking beyond the zone at Wharram subjected to extensive excavation, a combination of small trenches and geophysical prospection presents a similar picture of replacement of the ladder settlement with a series of larger, discrete enclosures (Fig. 30). Thus limited work *c.* 100m south-west of the above zone (Site 94/95: Richards 1992a, 17) uncovered a Late Roman ditch, associated with a profusion of contemporary ceramics, which can then be interpreted as at the south-east corner of a large enclosure, *c.* 75m square, set up against Track C, flanked by a possible subsidiary paddock. It crossed the projected line of the Late Iron Age/Early Roman ladder settlement here.

Opposite this element, the so-called North-west Enclosure (Ch. 5 above and Clark and Wrathmell 2004, 297-340) was also created in the 3rd century AD alongside the north edge of Track C, similarly obliterating the line of any ladder enclosures on this side. It contained pathways, a probable well, and other, more ephemeral traces of occupation. Despite a small number of more prestigious items, agricultural activities predominated here, typical of a Wolds farming establishment. The volume of smithing slag suggests blacksmithing close to the excavation area (G. McDonnell, pers. comm.)

Finally, much further along Track C to the north-west, at Wharram Crossroads, two large Late Roman enclosures were set up either side of that thoroughfare. They overrode and obscured the previously mentioned, now backfilled, ladder enclosures which ran west beside Track B, along Birdsall Brow. They would also have obliterated any earlier enclosures lying to the east of Track C, whose positions are hinted at in the geophysical survey of this area. These two new insertions in the landscape, each surrounded by very substantial ditches, would have dominated the crossing point of Tracks B and C. Two other, isolated enclosures lay alongside Track C between these developments at the crossroads and the contemporary Late Roman elements below the North Manor. Although visible only in aerial photographs, and so completely undated, they bear a striking resemblance in size and position to the other features described above.

When looked at across the landscape, a clear picture of change in the Late Roman period emerges. Larger enclosures replaced the two main strings of ladder settlements in the area, beneath the North Manor and on Birdsall Brow. When these elements were inserted, preceding arrangements were completely ignored: Late Iron Age/Early Roman ditches are rarely used for dumping Late Roman material, even within what had become a linear hollow. Furthermore, laying out these new enclosures impacted not only on the ladder enclosures in their immediate vicinity but, seemingly, on those at some distance. For example the Early Roman site at Birdsall High Barn, at the west end of the ladder settlement beside Track B and *c.* 1km beyond the new arrangements by the crossroads, also fell into disuse at this time, overlain by cultivated soil.

In the end, the impact must have been felt not only in terms of overall landscape organisation and thus movement within it, but also in terms of everyday practice. For example, the enclosure ditches of ladder settlements have been interpreted as short term repositories for future sources of manuring. The new arrangements, whether due to different farming practices and needs or otherwise, saw an end to this. As a result, a fundamental way in which household identities were constructed was under threat, or at least forced to express itself in a different way. Here it is interesting to note the increased scale of cereal processing implied by the corn drier and large millstone. Supplying needs beyond the immediate environment involved, seemingly, stepping beyond a household level of organisation.

In this new arrangement, Wharram Grange 'villa' marks itself out, both in size (covering an area half as big again as the next largest, the North-west enclosure) and in the character of activity (high status material, and a more organised approach to rubbish disposal than that seen elsewhere: see *Wharram IV*). Its critical position in the landscape is clearly of some significance: able to oversee, and thus monitor, not just traffic moving along both Tracks B and C, but also activities within the newly-created large enclosures themselves.

The artefactual and ecofactual assemblages from Wharram add another dimension to this picture. Ceramic use was at its most intensive by the 3rd century, and small finds present a similar picture of activity. It is the ecofactual material, however, which one might expect to provide most vibrant connections to the landscape developments. The paucity of carbonised materials means that changes in the cropping regimes, beyond those indicated by quernstones and corn driers, are mostly obscure to us, as are any alterations to the mix between pastoral and agrarian parts of the rural economy. We are mostly reliant on faunal evidence, although even here interpretations are clouded by the fact that most bones would have ended up on fields, not discarded in excavated features, and those which were excavated may be biased by specific activities taking place at particular points in the settlement.

Nonetheless, several significant patterns emerge. Wild fauna is never evident in great numbers in Iron Age and Roman levels beneath the North Manor: we see domestic fowl (chickens), rather than pheasant, and the larger domesticates rather than their hunted counterparts

(Richardson 2004a, table 63). Sheep become increasingly dominant over cattle between the Late Iron Age/Early Roman and Late Roman periods (Richardson 2004a, fig. 132: sheep then remain so into the high medieval period), and this transition also shows an increase in pig and a reduction in horse, although both of the latter two remained minority species throughout. This change from cattle to sheep, rather the opposite of what one might expect between Iron Age and Roman levels across Britain (Grant 1989), could be linked to changes in the Late Roman landscape. Were the individualised enclosures of that date acting as sheep folds?

Whatever the case, the trends established in the Late Roman period then remained stable through subsequent centuries, implying that animal husbandry practices fitted effectively within landscape potentials and community needs. Indeed, this picture only seems to alter in the late medieval period, with a considerable increase in the proportions of horse bones, a time at which one might have expected, a greater emphasis on sheep for wool. This final trend is probably a result of biases introduced by special activities within the settlement, notably the existence of a knackers' yard near the pond, and the slaughtering of horses to feed dogs on Site 82K (Jane Richardson, pers. comm.). Overall, therefore, stability seems to override change at this time.

When looked at in more detail, however, a more complex picture is apparent. Comparing domestic species from the North-west enclosure, with its greater chronological and spatial focus, with the more general datasets generated across the North Manor, the proportion of sheep is lower in the former area (*c.* 45% compared to *c.* 60% overall: Richardson 2004b, fig. 165): the 'specialised' enclosure does not suggest a greater concentration on sheep over cattle. The explanation for this patterning may relate to deposition practices, the larger cattle bones being dumped more often into the deep ditches around the North-west enclosure but occurring less often in the more diverse features in the area as a whole. This pattern, in turn, might relate to a tendency for slaughtered cattle to be consumed by bigger groups and bones deposited in larger, more public, contexts, with sheep eaten by smaller, household units and discarded accordingly (Mulville 2008). Alternatively, the greater proportion of cattle bones in the Late Roman enclosure could be a real reflection of meat production at the time. If true, this might be linked to the beef-dominated diet of Roman military and urban dwellers, and thus another sign of a more 'Romanised' approach to food in this newly-inserted landscape component.

The data generated by the excavations near the church (summarised in Richardson 2007, fig. 151), suggest a similarly high proportion of sheep to that recorded at the North Manor (just over 60%), though with much reduced cattle (*c.* 15%, even lower than the total for pig here). This total, however, amalgamates material from Late Iron Age/Early Roman occupation levels and overlying Late Roman dumps. Hence, without disaggregation of the data, it cannot be said if this represents a signature for early meat consumption, in place before imperial authority really imposed itself on the landscape (although see below on sheep fusion data). Either way, the age and sex data from the North-west Enclosure suggest that prime beef was being targeted there, with the remaining stock then being kept to maturity for breeding, and sometimes for traction. From the churchyard sites, fusion data for cattle (Richardson 2007, table 157) show that few died before 18 months, but 50% by 36 months plus, implying multi-purpose usage: not just meat, traction and herd maintenance, but also milk production, albeit probably of low intensity for domestic use.

Juvenile sheep were clearly killed for meat on some scale in the North-west Enclosure, with others retained for breeding and milk/wool. There is however, a greater emphasis here on meat than on the North Manor as a whole. The corresponding fusion data for sheep from the churchyard sites (Richardson 2007, fig. 154) show a contrast with both North Manor and, even more sharply, with the North-west Enclosure. This might suggest that the patterning here does, indeed, have a chronological implication. Few animals were slaughtered up to the age of 18-28 months, but that population halved by 30-42 months. As these animals would have provided only two fleeces, but not yet become part of a breeding population, it seems that they were being fattened over two years, perhaps for local consumption.

Taken as a whole, and notwithstanding the problems in amalgamating faunal assemblages from different periods, there is some indication of an important change in animal husbandry here. In the Late Iron Age/Early Roman period, it can be suggested that meat production met more localised demand, with a considerable emphasis on mutton and lamb but with an eye to fulfilling a range of food and, in the case of cattle, traction requirements. In the Late Roman period, there are indications of the more specialised production of both beef and lamb, maybe including more particular places to kill the animals and discard the resulting bones.

This picture matches wider landscape changes. In essence, we have moved from an Early Roman landscape of competing, yet communally integrated, households, still occupying ladder settlements inherited from the Late Iron Age, to a more focused and individualised process of defining rural communities, here under the surveillance of a single, higher-status settlement. The whole would have allowed for the food surpluses generated here to be consumed beyond the immediate locality on an increased scale. Perhaps this is the real point at which imperial authority was able to impose its will properly on this part of Wolds, the time after which its inhabitants were forced to face up to their responsibilities to the Roman state. Now, external obligations had become more important than internal dynamics. Corresponding change is evident in the immediate environs (the proliferation of farmsteads noted by Hayfield), elsewhere on the Wolds (the villas listed above), and in the surrounding margins (for

example the Shiptonthorpe site). All suggest a fundamental shift in the nature of imperial control at this time.

One final aspect of the evidence comprises a number of strands implying systemic change in the last decades of the 4th century. Burial is evident beside the North-west Enclosure, in the form of a cremation cemetery lasting into the 3rd century, however, neonates are being buried inside it at a late date (plus the structured deposition of a neo-natal calf, referring to a much longer tradition in the region). This corresponds with neonatal burials in the Late Roman enclosure beneath the North Manor at the end of its occupation (Site 45/60). The extended inhumation inserted into the access route to that same enclosure could represent the tail end of a Roman tradition there (Site 13/83: Hurst and Roskams 2004, 11-13).

Beside these important changes in burial practice, the history of development across the area becomes more fragmented in the course of the 4th century. Thus occupation within the North-west Enclosure falls away within that period, whereas the enclosure to its east, north of Track C, has a floruit then, at least in terms of pottery use (56% of ceramics date after AD 350), and may continue into the 5th century. Coins of the very end of the Roman period are, similarly, unusually well represented.

In short, whatever engendered this 3rd-century move to replace long-standing ladder settlements with larger, discrete enclosures under surveillance from Wharram Grange, it embodied dynamics which struggled to carry through to the 5th century. In this, Wharram corresponds with the occupation at Shiptonthorpe (Halkon and Millett 1999), which saw its earlier emphasis on individual enclosures running out by AD 350, its water hole, only inserted *c*. AD 300, also backfilled by that date, and then reduced density of occupation, seemingly accompanied by a very late/post-Roman move to subsistence. Hayton follows a different trajectory - but then complexity and diversity is to be expected during a process of fragmentation. Central authority was clearly able to impose its will around the start of the 3rd century, but could not sustain itself long-term. Archaeological evidence implies a splintering in this landscape some decades before the formal 'end of Roman Britain'.

Conclusions

Taken at a general level, the development of the Wharram Percy landscape before the medieval period presents a picture of increasingly sedentary societies exploiting the area in ways which match the story seen more generally in the region. 'The devil is in the detail' here however, in that the comprehensive archaeological data we have for this area does not simply strengthen 'conventional wisdom' but also raises some fundamental questions.

First, it calls into question some of the chronological categories deployed in the accepted story (Bradley 2007; Roskams 2007). Although the landscape and its resources here are *relatively* unchanging, even over the timescales considered above, there are clearly different ways in which cultural and natural dynamics interact. The fault lines for such changes fall within, rather than at, the boundaries defined by prehistoric technological change and Roman invasion: large territorial divisions are most clearly a product of Late Bronze Age society (although in part this clarity may be a product of our lack of Middle Bronze Age evidence); the development of ladder settlements happens towards the end of, but clearly well within, the Iron Age; and the impact of Rome, at a landscape level, is mostly a 3rd-century phenomenon, not an immediate result of military conquest.

Secondly, the changes embody a complex interaction of 'ideological' and 'material' factors – the sacred and profane are linked, but by an elastic band not a wire of predetermined length. This is most obvious in the case of burial practices, where the approaches to infant burial from earlier times (Late Iron Age contexts at Garton Wetwang Slack, related to Middle Iron Age practices; Late Iron Age or Early Roman neonate burials at Wharram Crossroads) have some currency later in the Roman period on the North Manor (and, indeed, might be said to return with more vibrancy in the transformations evident at the very end of the latter). It can be seen similarly with structured deposition. The deliberate placement of a cattle skull in a Middle Iron Age pit at Wharram Crossroads is matched by activities at Site 45/60, in one case involving an Iron Age heirloom from a much earlier social context. In contrast, innovative mortuary practices of the Middle Iron Age seem to prefigure some of the economic changes only seen later in landscape organisation – the increased importance of household over larger communities which the ladder settlements are argued here to express.

Thirdly, and related to this last point, there is consistent archaeological evidence for significant shifts in behaviour before the main thrust of change, and not only in Middle Iron Age burial practice anticipating later social development described above. It is also evident with the flow of Roman material culture into the landscape before 3rd-century change, notably into critical points such as Wharram Grange and, beyond this, Wharram le Street and Rudston before its villa was built. Imperial power may have taken over a century to impact fully, but some foundations were laid beforehand, alongside the development of transport infrastructure in Yorkshire. Furthermore, and perhaps most significant of all, there is evidence that central authority was falling away in the decades before the end of the 4th century, with significant implications for trajectories of development into the 'post/sub-Roman' period.

The challenge in coming to terms with all of the above trends is to acknowledge the real, local diversities, without losing sight of the commonalities - as much a matter of being aware of, and thinking through, our interpretative frameworks as it is simply a matter of attending to detail. This chapter has attempted to make a contribution to that process.

7 Early Anglo-Saxon Grazing Grounds
by Stuart Wrathmell

Continuity and discontinuity

We have seen in Chapters 5 and 6 that one of Wharram's Late Roman enclosures appears to have been abandoned some decades before the formal end of Roman Britain, but also that another may have seen use into the 5th century. Wharram has frequently been cited as providing evidence for continued occupation and farming extending from the late Roman period into Anglo-Saxon times, but too small an area has been explored to allow us to come to any reliable overall conclusion on the basis of excavation alone. To focus the debate more specifically, we should note the overwhelming evidence on the Wolds for an almost complete discontinuity in habitation sites, farm and field layouts, and even many trackways, at some point (or points) between the 4th and 12th centuries. It then becomes a question of when, rather than whether, discontinuity occurred.

One of the most dramatic demonstrations of discontinuity can be found in the township of Butterwick, some 15km to the north-east of Wharram in the Great Wold Valley (Fig. 31). In terms of its medieval layout, Mary Harvey's reconstruction of the settlement and its field system, based on the Dacre survey of 1563 (Castle Howard MS F4/14/3), shows that 'almost the entire township was occupied by open fields, the only enclosures being associated with the village' (Harvey 1982a, 30-31). The record is, of course, of post-medieval date, and the antiquity of such extensive arable systems is difficult to establish; but Harvey puts forward a case for their existence in the 12th and 13th centuries. She further notes that at the time of the Domesday survey in 1086, Butterwick may already have been almost as fully given over to arable cultivation as it was in 1563 (Harvey 1982a, 38).

Figure 31 shows Harvey's reconstruction of Butterwick township and its open-field furlongs in 1563 (Harvey 1982a, fig. 2), superimposed on the first edition six-inch Ordnance Survey map surveyed in 1850. It also records, in red, the crop marks plotted by Catherine Stoertz in her 1997 publication of the 'ancient landscapes' of the Wolds. Stoertz identified an extensive 'enclosed linear settlement' (Fig. 31, A) which she suggested belonged to the Late Iron Age, along with 'a large subdivided rectilinear enclosure' (B), which she suggested might be Roman, another comparable enclosure (C) and a 'double-ditched enclosure (D; Stoertz 1997, 77 and fig. 44). The morphological similarity of these records with the late Iron Age and Roman enclosure complexes at Wharram Percy (see Fig. 27) supports her identifications.

When these various datasets are superimposed, it becomes apparent that the medieval farming units – the township, its open-field holdings expressed as 'lands'

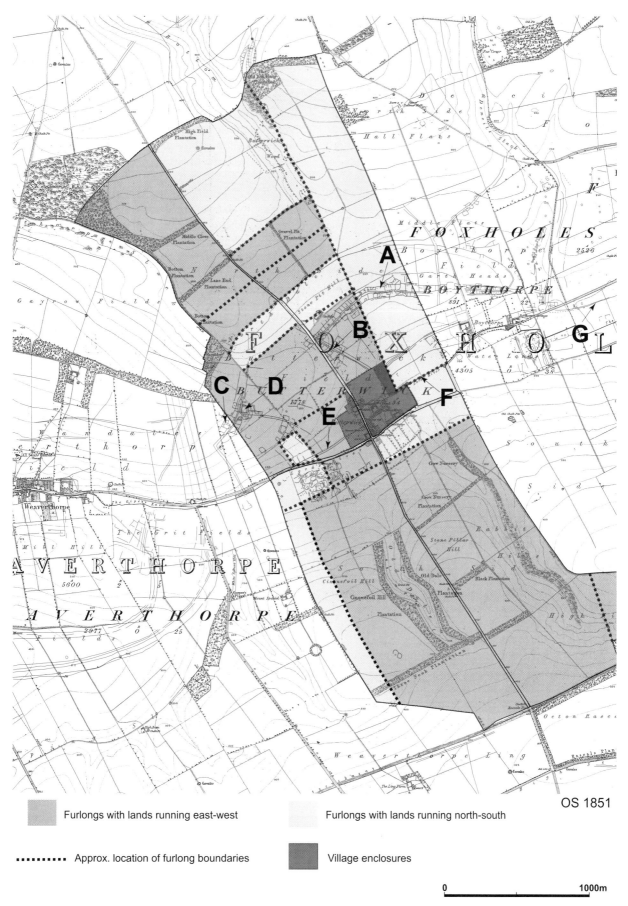

OS 1851

Furlongs with lands running east-west

Furlongs with lands running north-south

.... Approx. location of furlong boundaries

Village enclosures

0   1000m

Fig. 31. The open-field furlongs of the township of Butterwick, and crop marks of earlier enclosures and fields. (E. Marlow-Mann after C. Stoertz and M. Harvey)

grouped into furlongs, and the village settlement surrounded by its closes, bear absolutely no relationship to the later prehistoric and Roman farming units. The linear settlement (A) has been cut into two by the boundary between Butterwick and Boythorpe townships, and the subdivided rectilinear enclosure (C) is cut by the boundary between Butterwick and Weaverthorpe. Furthermore, the lanes and field boundaries associated with the settlement enclosures, and the enclosures themselves, quite clearly underlie the open-field lands, in locations and on alignments to which the furlong boundaries fail to conform in almost every respect. The medieval township boundaries and open-field lands – whichever came first – were laid out with no regard for the earlier farming units.

There is only one element of the later prehistoric and Roman farmscape that may in some sense have continued in use into medieval times: the east-west routeway along the bottom of the Great Wold Valley, the one defined in the introduction to this part of the volume as Route 2 (Fig. 23). Its precise course, as a track defined by ditches, seems to have changed over time – hence its partial visibility as a crop mark. The stretch at (E) on Figure 23 appears to have been replaced by the course of the modern road, which diverges from it to skirt the south side of the medieval village enclosures, and then returns north, following a stretch of the eastern township boundary. It seems likely that the earlier course of (E) had continued through the village settlement (or through what became the site of the village), and then along one of Harvey's furlong boundaries (F, still a pathway: see Stoertz 1997, fig. 44), to continue beneath the modern road into Boythorpe. An alternative, or perhaps even earlier course, may be marked by the crop mark trackway running eastwards from the north-east corner of Butterwick's village closes, taking a broadly parallel course to (F). East of Boythorpe Cottage, the modern road once more diverges from the earlier route (G), which seems to have taken a course through the site of the Boythorpe Cottage buildings.

Whatever the shifts in particular lengths of track or road, the general impression is that the more local 'access' tracks serving the Late Iron Age and Roman farming communities articulated with a pre-existing route along the valley floor that may have already existed for centuries if not millennia. For example, a stretch of ditched track from the Romano-British settlement enclosure (D) seems to curve south-eastwards to meet (E) at right-angles; and another stretch of track, which appears to form the eastern limit of the linear enclosure formation (A), runs southwards from that location to meet (G) (see Stoertz 1997, fig. 44).

If we compare the equivalent datasets for Wharram Percy township, the results, though not quite so unambiguous, seem to accommodate the same kinds of conclusions as those derived from the Butterwick analysis. The North-west Enclosure was unquestionably part of the open-field ploughlands in the Middle Ages (Clark and Wrathmell 2004, fig. 148; Herbert and Wrathmell 2004, 312,). Beyond the area of the village there are no clear conflicts, like those at Butterwick, between the positions of Romano-British enclosures and the course of township boundaries. Indeed, at first glance the Wharram Crossroads settlement shown in Figure 27 appears to bear some meaningful relationship to Wharram's western township boundary. This and similar relationships elsewhere on the Wolds are, however, indirect: the Late Iron Age and Roman enclosures, on the one hand, and the township boundaries on the other, are not actually related to each other; rather, each has a separate relationship to trackways which informed the alignments and positions of both. In this case the Late Iron Age/Early Roman enclosures were set alongside a pre-existing trackway, Track B, that linked the major Routes 2 and 3, and the same trackway was subsequently used to mark the western boundary of Wharram Percy township. On the other hand Track A on Figure 27, the one that had apparently linked the Wharram le Street villa to Route 3, disappeared beneath the open fields – like some of the local access tracks at Butterwick.

Having demonstrated the evidence for a major discontinuity between the 4th and the 12th centuries, it is then necessary to determine at what point within that time-frame the discontinuity may have occurred. Two alternative occasions have traditionally been proposed, both for Wharram and for rural settlement more widely. The break may have come in the 5th or early 6th century, after the collapse of Roman imperial authority, and coinciding with the first appearance of Early Anglo-Saxon material culture; or it may have come much later, at the time when nucleated medieval villages and open fields were being created between the 9th and the 12th centuries. It was the latter alternative that first seemed to be supported by the results of excavation at Wharram itself, and by the finds recovered from fieldwalking surveys across Wharram and neighbouring townships.

During the first half of the 1970s a series of trenches was excavated at Wharram Percy across the village earthwork boundaries on the plateau (Sites 16-18, 22-25, 31-39). The aim of this programme of work was 'to check the dating of the expansion of the village up from the lower terrace' (Beresford and Hurst 1976, 139): at the time, the growth of Anglo-Saxon settlement was still envisaged as an expansion of settlement from a core next to the church. Unexpectedly, it revealed extensive traces of Romano-British activity, augmenting the earlier discovery of a Romano-British building under the North Manor, the recognition from aerial photography of a Romano-British enclosure just beyond the north-west corner of the village site (the North-west Enclosure), and the scatter of Roman pottery from Areas 6 and 10 (Sites 9 and 12; Beresford and Hurst 1976, 139-41).

These discoveries, and the belief that the lynchet earthwork separating the tofts from the crofts in the West Row (North) was also of Romano-British and earlier date (see Ch. 3), led John Hurst for the first time to articulate what 'continuity' might mean at Wharram, in the light of the data then available:

'It is therefore beginning to look as though the basic plan of the medieval village was determined by the layout of the Romano-British fields. This immediately raises the question of continuity. The main objections to this are the lack of late Romano-British pottery of the third and fourth centuries and of datable early Anglo-Saxon finds. So far no structures of this date have been located. There are therefore two possibilities: either there was continuity from some, as yet unlocated, centres with the fields maintained under cultivation; or, when settlers returned after an interval, the outline of the Romano-British fields, and particularly the major lynchets, were still visible.'
(Beresford and Hurst 1976, 141-4)

This statement has framed much of the subsequent discourse on continuity at Wharram. It also articulated the view that Romano-British settlement in the village area consisted of a number of dispersed steadings:

'There was not a nucleated settlement but apparently a series of scattered farms set among the fields... So far, at least four farms (or more precisely, suggestive evidence for buildings) have been located.'
(Beresford and Hurst 1976, 144)

Though the concept of dispersed settlements across the village area applied only to Romano-British remains in 1976, by 1984 it was also used to characterise Anglo-Saxon occupation:

'The villa or farm in the N. manorial enclosure at Wharram Percy was by no means the only Romano-British settlement in the area of the future nucleated medieval village; there were at least four or five other settlement units... In the Anglo-Saxon period it is more difficult to identify the settlement pattern; it was clearly still scattered though perhaps with fewer sites and these not always in the same place as the Romano-British habitations... there is Saxon pottery and building evidence from three of the four possible Romano-British farm sites on the plateau, though as yet there is none from the terrace, which appears to have been unoccupied in the early and middle Saxon periods'
(Hurst 1984, 81-2)

Thus a picture was emerging of dispersed communities occupying and farming the Wharram area during the Roman and Anglo-Saxon periods, perhaps without a break though with the occasional relocation of some of the farmsteads; and of dispersed farmsteads and their landholdings being abandoned when the communities were eventually brought together (or when they decided to come together) to form a nucleated medieval village supported by an open-field system, in the centuries just before or just after the Norman conquest.

The hypothesis of 'continuity' from Roman to Anglo-Saxon times received a considerable impetus from the programme of fieldwalking across the Wharram parishes, carried out under the direction of Colin Hayfield. He identified a possible eleven Romano-British farmstead sites in the Wharram area, of which nine yielded fieldwalking assemblages. All nine produced pottery of the 3rd and 4th centuries, and six also produced 'Saxon' sherds (Hayfield 1988, 108-9; see also Hayfield 1987b, 177 fig. 103). One of the candidates for occupation from the Late Iron Age to the Middle Saxon period was the settlement site at Wharram Crossroads:

'Three separate elements have been identified around this crossroads, each of different date. The most recent lay in field 5 where the area of the field from the cropmarks northwards has produced a mixed scatter of Saxon and Roman pottery. The Roman sherds from this field were small, abraded and evenly scattered and most probably derive from manuring. The Saxon sherds, however, were more restricted in their distribution, and although also small and abraded, most probably derive from settlement'
(Hayfield 1988, 110)

Hayfield was more cautious about the precise form and layout of the Saxon settlement, but saw it as a single farmstead succeeding Roman predecessors:

'Elsewhere at Wharram the other farmsteads seem to have been remarkably stable in their location. However, the three settlement sites around Wharram Grange crossroads form a chronological sequence with little or no overlap between each and perhaps represent the migration of a single farmstead. The change in location from the 2nd to 4th-century farmstead site to the probable area of Saxon occupation was quite a small one, as they are immediately across the road from one another.'
(Hayfield 1988, 112)

Similarly on the site of Wharram Grange Roman villa, he revised his earlier conclusion (Hayfield 1986, 27.3) that the presence of Saxon pottery indicated stone robbing rather than settlement:

'The quantities of Saxon pottery now recovered from this site are such as to suggest that this activity took the form of settlement rather than stone robbing or looting from the already abandoned villa site'
(Hayfield 1987b, 177)

Though Hayfield rehearsed the difficulties of establishing the status of such settlement, he contended that 'this villa site would therefore seem to have been occupied for some eight hundred years, possibly as long as a thousand years' (Hayfield 1987b, 178), and he drew similar conclusions with regard to some of the other Romano-British farmstead sites: 'these farmsteads were an enduring feature of the Wharram landscape'
(Hayfield 1987b, 179)

Philip Rahtz's 1988 commentary on Hayfield's findings is rather more cautious, and begins with a useful definition of what, at the time, 'continuity' meant to him:

'continuous exploitation of resources in a given area, ranging from the use of a single field or house through to that of major sectors of Britain... Continuity is considered in relation to the basic landscape and

environment; to territorial boundaries, of field, farm, village or kingdom; to routes of communication; to the social or political entity of rural and urban settlements; to cemeteries and burial practice... Continuity implies that there is no major hiatus in the topic under consideration, such as the total abandonment of a tract of land and its reversion to a "natural" state'.
(Rahtz 1988, 130)

He noted the presence of 'Anglo-Saxon' pottery at Wharram Grange villa site, mainly from ploughsoil, and restated Hayfield's original conclusion that the few Saxon sherds found in the excavation might result from stone robbing activity. He also noted the absence of such pottery from the other nearby villa, at Wharram le Street, and raised the possibility that Anglo-Saxon pottery from other locations, where there had apparently been no Romano-British occupation, could be derived from manuring (Rahtz 1988, 132).

Despite Rahtz's obvious caution in relation to the hypothesis of continuous occupation at Wharram from the Late Roman to the Anglo-Saxon period, it was his own Site 60 excavations that appeared to provide the most secure structural evidence of Early Anglo-Saxon activity. He identified the hollows of two *Grubenhäuser*, initially dated to the 6th century, in the east-west routeway running alongside the North Manorial enclosure. This dating did not, however, go unchallenged: in the 1992 report on the Site 39 *Grubenhaus*, at the northern extremity of the village area, Gustav Milne argued that its occupation and disuse could be ascribed to the Middle Saxon period, and he suggested that the *Grubenhäuser* on Site 60 might be broadly contemporary.

In the definitive report on Site 60, published in 2004, Rahtz noted that 'nowhere in the excavations... is there any positive evidence of a continuum between Late Roman contexts and those assigned to MP4 [the Anglo-Saxon period]' (Rahtz *et al.* 2004, 289), yet he made the case that some of the Site 39 finds attributed by Milne to the Middle Saxon period *could* be of earlier date, including pottery and a bone comb (Rahtz *et al.* 2004, 290), and that other sherds of pottery and the iron strike-a-light from the Site 60 *Grubenhäuser* could also indicate Early Anglo-Saxon activity. He concluded:

'There is thus no clear evidence for or against continuity between the latest Roman levels and the SFBs [*Grubenhäuser*], though, if the latter are of the earlier Anglo-Saxon period, there would be less of a time-gap than in the case of Sites 39 or 94'
(Rahtz *et al.* 2004, 291)

It has to be acknowledged that, on the basis of current information in relation to both the structural and the artefactual evidence at Wharram, we cannot move beyond this debate. From the existing excavation evidence we can legitimately infer *either* that there was no major gap in occupation at Wharram in Early Anglo-Saxon times, *or* that there was such a gap; much depends on the personal preferences of those engaged in the debate. The results of the 20th-century investigations are intriguing, but too equivocal to use as a foundation for a chronological narrative – for a history of settlement at Wharram Percy in the Early Anglo-Saxon period.

It is for this reason that the next few chapters, those dealing with Wharram from the 5th to 11th centuries, have been approached from an entirely different point of view, one that was outlined in the preface to this volume. The approach has been to develop a hypothesis relating to the history of a larger area of the north Wolds, and to see how far the data available for that larger area – hereafter, the 'study area' – can be accommodated by the hypothesis. Only then are the Wharram data introduced to determine the extent to which these, too, conform (or fail to conform) to the hypothesis.

The Wolds as open grazing lands: a hypothesis

The chosen hypothesis involves a major discontinuity in the permanent occupation of the Wolds during the 6th to early 7th centuries, and its principal components can be expressed in the following statement:

Though an Iron Age and Roman settlement underlies at least part of the medieval village, it had been abandoned long before the first phase of substantive Anglo-Saxon occupation took place: there was a discontinuity in permanent settlement between the 6th and early 7th centuries, probably lasting until about 650AD. The people who then reoccupied Wharram made use of the Roman building materials they found there, along with the disused ditches of the abandoned field and farmstead enclosures which were convenient locations for their Grubenhäuser, *but they did not inherit late Roman territorial units or farming practices. When they decided (or were allowed) to occupy the place we know as Wharram on a continuous basis, it was not a pre-existing separate, defined administrative unit, but part of the broad sweep of north Wolds pastures used by lowland communities.*

Between the end of the Roman (or sub-Roman) period and the Middle Saxon re-occupation, people may, nevertheless, have lived in this place from time to time. They would probably have been herding livestock brought to the uplands on a seasonal basis, drawn to this spot where a trans-Wold trackway, established centuries earlier, crossed a small stream in a narrow wooded valley. It may even have been one of the places where animals were gathered to be driven back to the lowlands in the autumn, to graze the stubble of the communities' arable lands after harvest.

The broad ideas behind this hypothesis owe much to Harold Fox's stimulating essay on 'The People of the Wolds' (Fox 1989), which appeared in a festschrift for Maurice Beresford and John Hurst – a volume that was presented to them, appropriately enough, at Wharram Percy. Fox's study area was not, however, the wolds of Yorkshire, but those of Leicestershire, Northamptonshire, Nottinghamshire and Warwickshire.

He emphasised the pastoral character of wolds in Anglo-Saxon times, in contrast to regions already dominated by arable, but argued that, by the end of the 11th century, they supported only sparse and fragmented woodlands, in contrast to more densely wooded regions. They were 'countryside characterised by isolated stands of wood, perhaps amidst pasture and some cultivated land'; 'countrysides in which, between the arable lands, there were pastures supporting a scattering of trees, with larger stands here and there' (Fox 1989, 84-5). He commented that fragmentation of the woodland seems to have begun much earlier, given the number of Romano-British occupation sites in his study area, but also noted:

'This is not to contradict the suggestion… about a relatively late *intensification* of settlement on the wolds, for the Romano-British sites were hardly full villages and could well have existed in a semi-woodland setting, while continuity of occupation after the fifth century has not been proven'
(Fox 1989, 85, n. 26)

The theme of discontinuity is elaborated in Fox's discussion of evidence for the use of the wolds in the Anglo-Saxon period as seasonal grazing for communities living in the surrounding vales. Some of the evidence is in the form of place-names:

'the names of townships themselves, such as Somerby, Gotham and Harby, may take us back to even earlier forms of pastoral organisation when whole territories, later to become townships, within the wolds were used more exclusively, and perhaps seasonally, as grazing grounds'
(Fox 1989, 87)

Other evidence is provided by the network of broadly parallel lanes on the Nottinghamshire-Leicestershire border, some followed by parish boundaries, running from the Soar valley up to the High Leicestershire wolds:

'it is tempting to regard them as droveways connecting vale and wold'. Such linkages 'are not as common between vale and wold as they are between vale and woodland, perhaps because the links were more completely severed, and at an earlier date'
(Fox 1989, 87)

This last point gains greater emphasis from a more recent study of the longer-lived droveways in the Sussex Weald (Chatwin and Gardiner 2005).

Fox reiterated these arguments in a more recent publication, where he emphasised the attraction of upland wold pastures to lowland communities of the Middle Saxon period:

'Those who sent their animals into the wood-pastures were people from the adjacent vales who had not yet evolved classic "Midland" field systems with their great fallow fields for the safe-keeping of animals; all the more reason, therefore, for them to dispatch livestock into the fresh pastures of the wolds in springtime so that there was no risk of their trampling the growing crops at home'
(Fox 2000, 52)

There is one strand of evidence that might appear at first sight to run contrary to this view of the Wolds as largely uninhabited pasture grounds at this time: the presence of early Anglo-Saxon burials. Sam Lucy has identified trends in the location of burials through time: inhumation cemeteries around the margins of the Wolds in the 5th to 6th centuries, close to their associated settlements, with a shift in the 7th and 8th centuries towards burial on the higher areas of chalk. The Wolds burials seem frequently to have been associated with prehistoric monuments, for example as secondary interments in Bronze Age barrows, though as Lucy notes this may simply be because they have been uncovered incidentally, in the course of excavations that have targeted prehistoric monuments (Lucy 1998, 98-9).

Lucy did not, however, adduce a settlement shift to correspond to this shift in the location of burials; rather she saw it as a decision to increase the distance separating the dead from the living who continued to inhabit settlements on the lowland fringes of the Wolds:

'If the location of these settlements is an accurate reflection of their true distribution… It would seem as if the cemeteries were being deliberately placed at, sometimes great, distances from the main areas of settlement in the area, especially in the later periods'
(Lucy 1998, 100)

If at this time the Wolds were, indeed, open pastures belonging to lowland communities, the patterning in the location of burials may have a more intricate explanation: the dead, or some of them, may have been used to mark the affiliation of particular communities to particular stretches of pasture or woodland. The communities of the Vale will presumably have established routes on to the Wolds to specific locations which formed the hubs of their traditional grazing grounds, places where animals could be collected for management, or for the return journey to the Vale after harvest. Populating these locations and droveways with their dead may have given them a means of asserting their right to particular stretches of open countryside, or of guarding those grounds against natural or supernatural incursion without recourse to creating permanent settlements of the living.

Grazing grounds and droveways

Vale-wold routeways are one of the key indicators of transhumance, as Fox demonstrated in his studies of the Midlands. The introduction to this part of the volume identified a three-strand communications network across the northern Wolds (Fig. 23): the long-distance east-west routes linking the east coast with the vale of York (Routes 1-4); the north-south tracks traversing the Wolds at right-angles to these routes, linking the vale of Pickering to the High Wolds and beyond, and thirdly tracks such as those which intersected at Wharram (Tracks B and C), that gave access from one major track or routeway to another.

Figure 32 is another topographic model of the northern Wolds, one intended to focus on the north to south routeways. It is a view of the same area as that covered in Figure 23 but seen from the Vale of Pickering, looking southwards. It marks some of the trackways running from the marshes or carrs alongside the Derwent, through the arable lands of the vale that lay on either side of Route 1, and up on to the Wolds. The courses of these and the other routes and tracks are largely as shown on Greenwood's map of the County of York, surveyed 1815-17 and published in 1818. They have been plotted on the first edition 6 inch *Ordnance Survey* map surveyed in 1851, with appropriate adjustments to take account of changes that had occurred in the intervening years.

Also marked, in red, are medieval and post-medieval township boundaries, which demonstrate that in the main the north-south tracks run though the centres of known community territories, rather than forming their boundaries like Routes 3 and 4 and like some of the diagonal, interlinking tracks. This simple distinction itself might be taken as an indication that these tracks were droveways facilitating movement of livestock belonging to these communities, rather than being routes and tracks that provided passage for through traffic.

One of the most obvious of these putative droveways links the settlement at Sherburn with the place that became the village of Butterwick. It begins at the Derwent, runs south through Sherburn village and on to Butterwick on a fairly straight course. Harvey's map of Butterwick in 1563 shows its route through the open fields north of the village (Fig. 31), its intersection with Route 2 just south of the village, and its continuation through the South Field to the southern township boundary. Its straight course is, inevitably, a reflection of topography, in this case a lack of constraints that might have caused deviation in its line.

A track more obviously constrained by the terrain is the one from Wintringham to West Lutton. It starts at Wintringham Common, the township's carr lands, and runs south through the village settlement. Thence it takes a south-easterly direction, along a valley towards the area that became West Lutton township. It runs through West Lutton, and intersects with Routes 3 and 4 on its way towards Driffield, an Anglo-Saxon royal estate centre (Loveluck 1996, 43-5). This particular course will have been a trans-wold route between Driffield and the Vale of Pickering, but it probably also functioned as a droveway from the Vale to the Wold pastures.

One of the interesting questions that arises with regard to such putative droveways is whether there were communal or administrative linkages at one time between the settlements thus connected. Put at its simplest, were animals belonging to Sherburn once grazed at Butterwick; and were those of Wintringham out-pastured

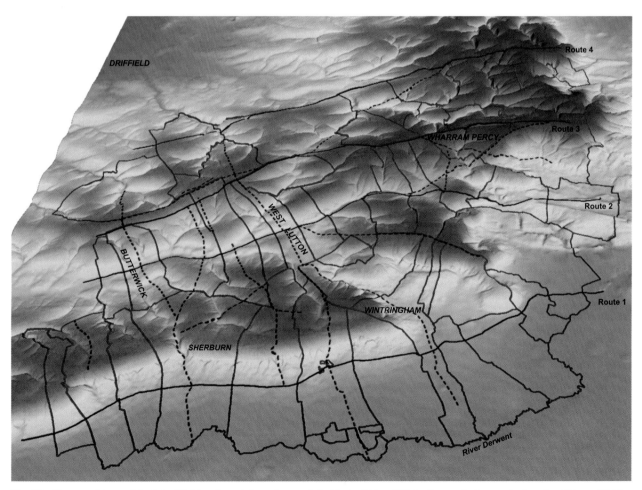

Fig. 32. Topographic model of the Wolds, viewed from the north (with the Vale of Pickering at the bottom), showing Vale to Wold routeways (dashed blue lines) and township boundaries (continuous red lines). (A. Deegan and E. Marlow-Mann)

at the place that became known as West Lutton? It is a question that will be considered in Chapter 8, in the context of place-name evidence (pp 103-4).

If we try to visualise the character of the Wolds at this time, we might see trackways leading from the surrounding lowland communities into the large upland expanses of rough grazing, mainly used for sheep but with localised cattle pastures where surface water was available, as at Wharram and in the Great Wold Valley. It was no doubt at such places in particular that seasonal settlements developed to house those whose job it was to guard the flocks and attend the herds. The people who were sent by the communities to supervise the livestock during their occupation of the Wolds will presumably have had to guard against theft by those using the east-west routes, particularly the 'boundary' roads, Routes 3 and 4. No doubt strangers who departed from the marked routes were as likely to be regarded as thieves as were those strayed from the woodland tracks in the territory of the West Saxon kings (see Whitelock 1979, 401: Ine, 20).

Plate 7. Sledmere Green Lane (Route 4) between Fimber and Wetwang, viewed from the west in 2008. (S. Wrathmell)

Fenton-Thomas (2003, 114-17) has emphasised the significance of these long-used routes as elements of the 'mythic landscape'. By Anglo-Saxon times they had been in existence for millennia, and their association with major prehistoric earthwork boundaries and burial mounds will have invested them with meanings that now elude us. At certain times through the seasons they may have borne significant traffic, particularly in terms of livestock movement; but at others they will have been desolate (Plate 7), and some places along their courses may have been shunned as the haunts of demons. This is wholly speculative, but it accords with traditions recorded in the early 19th century, when evangelical missions were sent to the Wolds by the Primitive Methodists. Woodcock's account of these missions describes some of the superstitions that had been current in Wolds communities, superstitions which the Methodists sought to stamp out:

'A century ago, more haunted houses could have been found on the Wolds than anywhere in England, within the same space. Ghosts and hob-goblins were nightly visitors, and travellers passing a lonely spot between Fimber and Wetwang, used to see a woman – now without a head, anon on horseback, rushing at a furious rate; many a Woldsman, with pale face and hair erect, has run from that spot as if running for his life'
(Woodcock 1889, 10)

The final part of this chapter turns from speculation to evidence, albeit limited evidence, for the development of trackways that passed through Wharram in the Early Anglo-Saxon period, and for the presence of seasonal settlement there.

Plate 8. Aerial photograph of the east-west trans-valley trackway (Track C), viewed from the east. It runs as a hollow way, in shadow, from the bottom of the photograph (left of Bella Farm), through the village and the snow-covered fields to the west, continuing as a modern track beyond the township boundary; January 1971. (BEP 38. Copyright reserved Cambridge University Collection of Aerial Photography)

Plate 9. The white chalk surface of Track C, seen in the distance from the North Manor area in 2008. (S. Wrathmell)

Wharram Percy in the 5th to mid-7th centuries

As we have seen earlier, two tracks linking the main east-west routes crossed near the site of Wharram Percy village. One of them (Track B in Fig. 27), was later followed by a stretch of the Wharram Percy township boundary to the north-west of the village site. It was described in a charter dated to between 1197 and 1210 as 'the road which leads to York [in one direction] and turns through Cranedale [in the other]' (Bond 1866, 321), Cranedale being the medieval name for the upper stretch of the Great Wold Valley which contained Route 2 (Smith 1937, 12-13).

The other (Track C in Fig. 27), the one that runs east-west through the northern half of the settlement area at Wharram Percy has been investigated in some detail. It is a cross-dale trackway, the course of which can be traced eastwards across the Beck, where it takes the form of a hollow way up the dale side towards the present farmhouse at Bella and beyond to a junction with Route 3 (Fig. 27). Westwards, it probably ran to Birdsall after its junction with the York-Cranedale routeway, at least in the 12th century when the Fossard lords of Birdsall were also the tenants in chief of Wharram le Street (Plate 8; see Wrathmell 2005a, 2-4). Though its course westwards from the village area has since become disused, that on the east side of the Beck is still used by visitors to the site who use the car park at Bella farm (Plates 9 and 10).

Plate 10. A stretch of the Track C hollow way descending from Bella towards the Beck and the village site, viewed in 2008. It is still used today by visitors approaching the village site from the Bella car park. (S. Wrathmell)

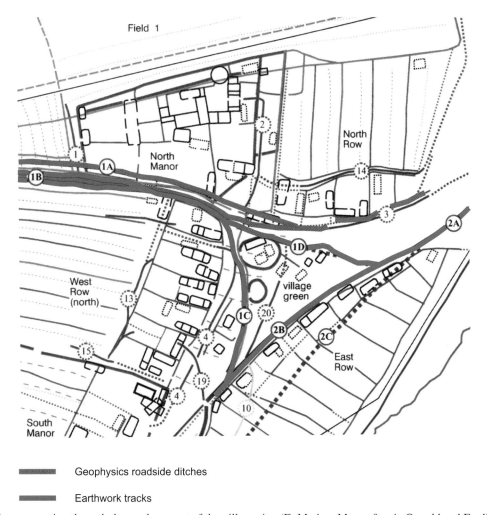

Field 1

North
Row

North
Manor

West
Row
(north)

village
green

East
Row

South
Manor

▧▧▧ Geophysics roadside ditches

▬▬ Earthwork tracks

Fig. 33. Trackways running through the northern part of the village site. (E. Marlow-Mann after A. Oswald and English Heritage)

Within the village area the geophysical survey marks its course clearly as a ditched trackway flanked by later prehistoric and Romano-British settlement and field enclosures on its north and south sides; these ditches are shown in red on Figure 33, where Tracks 1A and 1B are individual and chronologically distinct elements of Track C on Figure 27. The earthwork survey records the presence of this route in later centuries as a medieval hollow way running through the village on the south side of the North Manor enclosure. At that latter period, however, its course was to the south of the earlier line which had become buried beneath the southern boundary bank of the manorial enclosure; it is marked in blue on Figure 33.

The reason for this shift in alignment is not known precisely, but on the basis of Oswald's earthwork survey and analysis (Ch. 3 above), it is possible to make informed guesses. Eastwards of the north row of tofts and crofts, its course has been lost on the steep slope down the daleside, probably because of land slippage, a process at least partly associated with a spring at the foot of the slope. Past land slippage is evident today, and the problem continues: the trackway into the village site at the bottom of this slope was in 2006 again undermined by water flowing from the spring.

The later east-west route, 1B, turns southwards as it reaches the village green, providing (as 1C) access to the main part of the village. Oswald has also, however, identified an eastwards extension of 1B (as 1D) running through the northern part of the green. This may have been a replacement, on a more southerly course, of 1A. By the later Middle Ages, the dominant routes were 2B and 1C/1B, requiring through travellers to divert southwards along the east and west sides of the green. The conclusion here is that these shifts indicate increasing difficulties in following the direct route because of land slips and erosion caused by traffic, by cattle grazing on the green and by the spring and watercourse, difficulties magnified by the interaction of all three factors.

Stretches of both the Romano-British and the medieval trackways were exposed in Philip Rahtz's excavation of Site 60 (see Fig. 33); they are shown in Figure 34 and in section on Figure 35. The ditches flanking the Romano-British track (marked in red on Fig. 35), were revealed at the point where a break in the secondary northern flanking ditch 226/86 indicated an entrance to the adjoining settlement enclosure (Fig. 34B); this replaced an earlier continuous ditch (95: Rahtz and Watts 2004, 43, fig. 28). The southern flanking ditch 45 (= 606) was

91

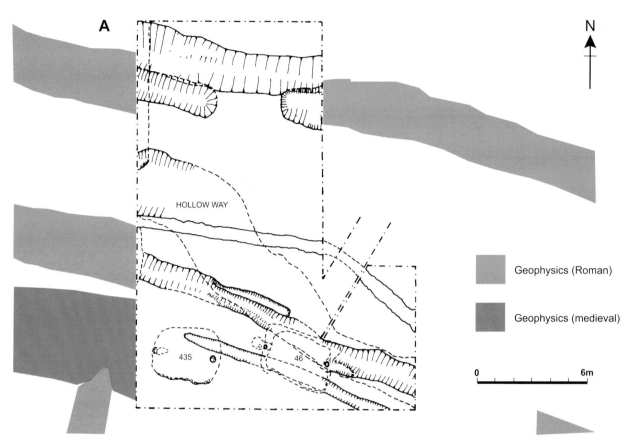

A

N

HOLLOW WAY

435   46

Geophysics (Roman)

Geophysics (medieval)

0   6m

Parallel east-west ditches, originally of Bronze Age date, defining a route across the landscape: Track C

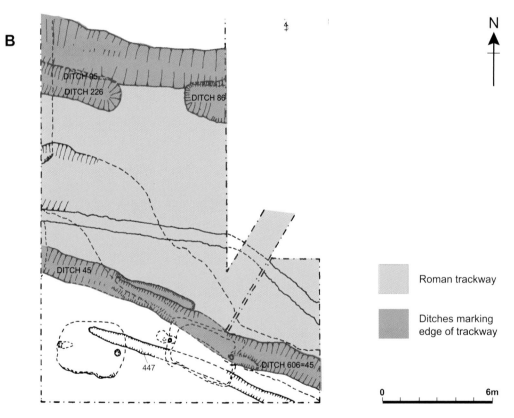

B

N

DITCH 95
DITCH 226   DITCH 86

DITCH 45

447   DITCH 606=45

Roman trackway

Ditches marking
edge of trackway

0   6m

By the late Iron Age, ditches reinforced the line of this track, which was metalled in the early Roman period. These ditches also formed boundaries to enclosures added to both sides of Track C. The 3.5m gap between 226 and 258 allowing access into the northern enclosure.

Fig. 34. The chronological development of the trackway running through Site 60 (Track C), from the Bronze Age to the medieval period. (E. Marlow-Mann after P. Rahtz)

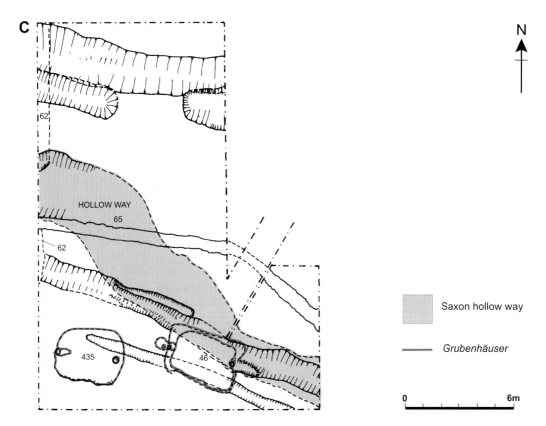

C

N

HOLLOW WAY

65

62

62

435

46

Saxon hollow way

Grubenhäuser

0   6m

In the late Roman period, when the flanking enclosures had fallen out of use, Track C became a winding pathway rather than a formal thoroughfare. It then evolved into a hollow way in the course the Saxon period, influencing the position of two *Grubenhäuser* which flanked it in the south.

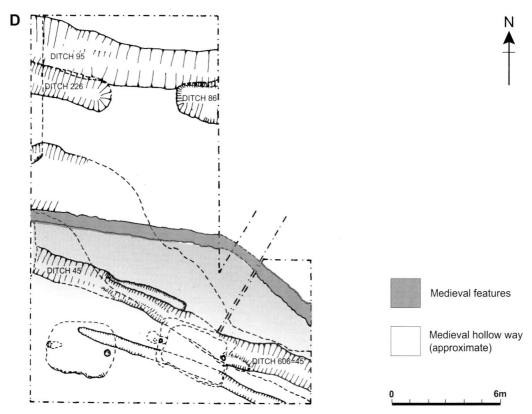

D

N

DITCH 95

DITCH 226

DITCH 86

DITCH 45

DITCH 606=45

Medieval features

Medieval hollow way
(approximate)

0   6m

By the medieval period a distinct hollow way had evolved from the Saxon trackway, and its fragmented surface extended over the *Grubenhäuser* located about 7m to the south. Its dimensions and profile were similar to those of the northern ditch 95, though it was narrower and shallower than ditch 09 in Site 22, its equivalent some 170m further east (Clark and Wrathmell 2004, 299, fig. 149). Ditch 45 seems at some point to have been replaced by a slighter ditch, 447(=609) following roughly the same course but further south (Rahtz and Watts 2004, 64, fig. 44).

The medieval routeway (Fig. 34D), a distinct hollow way marked in blue on Figure 35, provided plentiful evidence of fragmented surfacing and rutting. As would be expected with a track that gradually, over time, increased in depth through use, 'the first point at which its is possible to define the levels of the LMZ [linear movement zone] is at the end of its medieval use' (Rahtz and Watts 2004, 73). Most of the ruts were interpreted by Rahtz as marking the passage of wheeled vehicles.

In addition to the Roman and medieval manifestations of this routeway, the excavation of Site 60 revealed a further hollow way that appeared to represent intermediate use: a 'sinuous path [with a] worn or dished surface' (Rahtz and Watts 2004, 64, fig. 44). The north-west end of the exposed stretch of path 65, shown in green on Figure 34C and Figure 35, entered the western baulk of Site 60 at a point where two stretches of north south-ditch (62) appeared to cut across the Romano-British routeway. Rahtz argued that these features were contemporary, and that the path ran through a gap in the ditch:

'The upper fills of Ditch 62 (83 and 12 above it) both appeared to be cut by hollow way 65... This might lead to the conclusion that 65 is later than the fills of Ditch 62... As we have seen, however, it [65] passes through a gap between the ends of ditch segments which are probably contemporary, so is likely to have originated in Phase V [late Roman]'
(Rahtz and Watts 2004, 54)

A further indication of the contemporaneity of the hollow way and the ditch was claimed to be the recovery of a 'large unweathered sherd' of late Roman Huntcliff ware at the base of the lowest layer of hollow way fill (53a), although this layer also yielded eleven post-Roman sherds, including three of Torksey type:

'It would thus appear that, although we may still allow 65 to have originated in late Roman times or soon after (i.e. in the 5th century), the hollow way or path which it represents continued in use into later centuries (or came back into use)'.
(Rahtz and Watts 2004, 54-5)

If we really are dealing with a late Roman path running through a gap in a north-south ditch that otherwise blocked the routeway more or less completely, then its implications, in terms of control of traffic on this track, are intriguing. On the other hand, as Rahtz himself noted (Rahtz and Watts 2004, 55), the stratification in this area is rather vague and the limits of various layers and fills (including 53a) 'somewhat notional'; and there are additional reasons for questioning the supposed relationship of 65 with ditch 62.

In the first place, the profile of the base fill (53a) of hollow way 65 unequivocally cuts through (or lies above) the fill layers of ditch 62 on both its north and south sides (Fig. 35), so the alignment of the lowest part of 65 with the supposed gap in ditch 62 must be unintentional. On the south side of the hollow way, Rahtz's suggested course for the base of fill 53a may be slightly tenuous, but the alternative, flat course, following what was presumably once a surface scatter of burnt clay and charcoal debris, also seals the backfilled southern stretch of ditch 62. Secondly, the large sherd of Huntcliff ware at the base of 53a tells us nothing about when path 65 originated, as it presumably arrived in the soil that

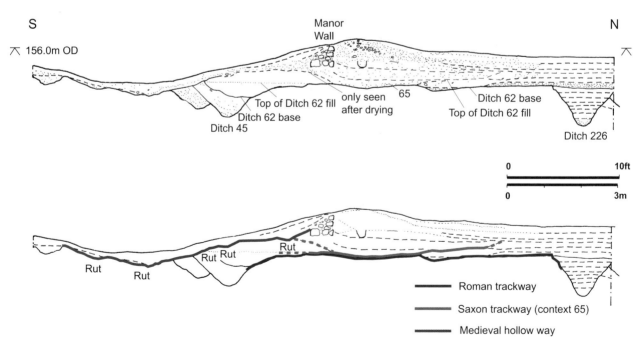

Fig. 35. Section along the west side of Site 60, with an interpretation of the various track surfaces. (E. Marlow-Mann after P. Rahtz)

covered the path after its disuse: it is hard to imagine that a large unweathered sherd lying on the path during its use, and close to a point where its course was constricted, would have remained in that condition for long.

The sinuous path seems, therefore, to represent traffic on this routeway at some period after the abandonment of the late Roman enclosures, and after the accumulation of soil over ditch 62, which is dated to the late Roman period (see Rahtz and Watts 2004, 54), but before the deposition of the soil which formed the southern bank of the North Manorial enclosure, for which Rahtz (Rahtz and Watts 2004, 71) suggests a pre-Conquest date. The path can plausibly be assigned, therefore, to the Early and/or Middle Saxon periods.

In plan (Fig. 34C) the sinuous path 65 can be seen to extend south-eastwards from the western baulk of Site 60, beneath the North Manor boundary bank and wall and across the line of the Roman ditch 45=606, into the main area of the medieval hollow way. This fits neatly with its intermediate chronological position, as land slippage on the steep slope to the east might have already caused a new track to be developed on the 1D line; whilst on the plateau, the Roman routeway could have continued in use.

There remains the question of the dates of the two *Grubenhäuser* (46 and 435) found on Site 60. The first point to emphasise is that there is no stratigraphic link between them: they may be contemporary, or of different dates. The only datable artefact that might be associated with the use of either was a firesteel in the base fill of 46, possibly attributable to the 6th or early 7th century (Rahtz and Watts 2004, 66 and 244, no. 25; see Ch. 10 below and Plate 15).

The key question is what relationship did these two structures have with the various phases of routeway? Both appear to have been later than the late Roman routeway, as both overlay the late Roman ?roadside ditch 447=609, and Building 46 also overlay the earlier flanking ditch 45=606. Both predated the medieval hollow way: it would have been impassable if they were standing, and the stratigraphic record shows medieval ruts cutting into the fill of Building 46 (Rahtz and Watts 2004, 65, fig. 45).

As far as the intermediate hollow way 65 – the sinuous path – is concerned, Building 435 could have been a contemporary structure by the side of the road; but on the basis of Rahtz's definition of the path's edges (Rahtz and Watts 2004, 64, fig. 44), Building 46 appears to have cut away part of the surface and blocked its course. On the other hand it is worth considering whether this building might actually have been earlier than the path: the relevant section (Rahtz and Watts 2004, 65, fig. 45) shows a small area of cobbles (42) attributed to path 65, just on the northern edge of the *Grubenhaus*, in a manner that does not seem to rule out the possibility of the cobbling once having extended across the site of the building, only to be eroded away by the passage of traffic across the fill of 46 in the later Middle Ages.

If Building 46 is later than hollow way 65, it is difficult to believe it was erected as early as the 6th century, given that 65 appears to have come into use long after the abandonment of the late Roman enclosures. On the other hand, if Building 46 is earlier than 65, it could well be of 6th-century date, representing a period when the routeway was little used.

Either way, the existence of these buildings in the 6th or 7th centuries would not invalidate the hypothesis put forward earlier in the chapter. The argument is not that the village area was completely devoid of human activity at this period, whether for short periods or for more prolonged seasonal occupation. It is that the kind of farming settlement evident at Wharram in the late Roman and Middle Saxon periods was absent in these centuries. *Grubenhäuser* might well represent (among a range of other functions) the sort of temporary accommodation required for seasonal pasturage. This was the suggested function of the three *Grubenhäuser* discovered beneath the medieval farmsteads of Houndtor, on Dartmoor (Beresford G. 1979, 110-12), and it might account for other isolated occurrences elsewhere, as at North Marden in West Sussex (Drewett *et al.* 1986, 110-13). More locally, it was perhaps also the function of the *Grubenhäuser* that seem to have been created in a rampart at the Roman military complex on Cawthorn East Moor, on the northern side of the Vale of Pickering (Tipper 2004, 80).

Apart from the firesteel there are few artefacts from Wharram that can be ascribed to the 6th or early 7th century with any degree of certainty. They are considered in detail by Ian Riddler below (Ch. 10). Colin Hayfield's parish survey, begun in 1974 and published in 1987, included extensive fieldwalking and limited excavations in both Wharram parishes. As indicated earlier in this chapter, 'Saxon' pottery recovered from the site of Wharram Grange Roman villa led him to conclude that 'activity on the site continued into the Saxon period' (Hayfield 1987b, 177); and for the village site he argued that 'the pottery sequence at Wharram Percy progresses unbroken throughout the Saxon period into the Late Saxon wheel-made wares' (Hayfield 1987b, 180, represented graphically on fig. 103).

Hayfield's conclusions would, therefore, seem to contradict the hypothesis which has guided this discussion. On the other hand his analysis was carried out before Anna Slowikowski's study of the pottery from *Grubenhäuser* in Sites 39 and 95, which led her to comment that 'it is possible that hand-made stamped pottery continued, in some areas of Yorkshire, into the 8th century' (Slowikowski 1992, 29), though it is clear that the ceramic evidence could be argued either way (Slowikowski 1992, 36-7). The interpretation of relevant types from the larger, South Manor Area assemblage is equally ambiguous (Slowikowski 2000, 81). It has not been possible to access the fieldwalking sherds for re-examination during the preparation of this volume, and so the ceramic evidence must be regarded as currently inconclusive as far as dating is concerned.

A more certain sign of 6th-century activity is represented by the two Frisian brooches found in the excavation of Sites 94 and 59. Though two in number they are, however, perhaps best regarded as representative of a single event; for Barry Ager argues that:

'Although the Wharram brooches neither form a matching pair nor come from the same site (though are not very far apart), their apparent uniqueness amongst Migration Period jewellery from Northumbria would suggest that they had probably been worn together' (Ager 1992, 49)

Various scenarios can be constructed to account for their presence at Wharram without assuming that they indicate 6th-century settlement here. They may have been heirlooms, curated in later centuries by people who identified themselves with a Frisian heritage: a number of Yorkshire place-names indicate the presence of groups of Frisians (Smith 1937, 24-5). Alternatively, they may have been collected at Wharram for recycling, to be used in the copper-alloy workshop identified in Site 95, especially as one of them came from the adjacent Site 94 (Richards 1992b, 82-3).

Evidence for the character of activity at Wharram in the 6th and early 7th centuries is, therefore, slight and open to competing interpretations. Evidence for activity from the mid-7th to 9th centuries is more prolific, although, as we shall see in the following chapters, this does not necessarily mean that it is more easy to interpret, or less amenable to competing interpretations.

Part Three

New Communities in the Middle and Late Saxon Periods

Part Two of this volume explored the hypothesis that the northern Wolds lacked permanently settled communities during the 6th and early 7th centuries, and that their function was to provide resources for communities in the surrounding lowlands. The resources discussed in Chapter 7 centred on the provision of rough grazing for sheep and, where surface water could be found, for cattle; but we should also consider a range of other uses for the Wolds in these and later centuries, notably for hunting and for industrial and craft activities. Even if the Wolds plateaux were largely kept clear of trees by summer grazing, the steep valley sides and the scarp would probably have supported scrub and woodland providing cover for game as well as fuel, in the form of charcoal, for furnaces.

Chapter 8, the first in Part Three, presents a hypothesis that complements the earlier one: that the northern Wolds began to be repopulated by settled communities in the period from the mid-7th to early 8th centuries. In fact, the discussion extends more widely, to the whole of what has been defined as the 'study area', stretching from the river Derwent in the north, to the watershed of the northern Wolds in the south, and from the townships of Langton and Birdsall in the west to Binnington and Boythorpe in the east (see Fig. 36). It identifies two parallel trends: the gradual division of the open Wolds grazing lands into township units, and the subdivision of large territorial units in the Vale of Pickering into the smaller townships that are recorded in Domesday Book.

The sources of information explored within the framework of this hypothesis are disparate in kind and varied in date: they range from township boundaries first mapped comprehensively in the early 19th century, through place-names first recorded in surviving documentation in the late 11th century, to the crop-mark signatures of curvilinear enclosure settlements that have, where excavated, indicated occupation in the Middle Saxon period. These strands have been combined in an exercise that seeks to map stratigraphic relationships between named vill territories, in a conscious attempt to find an alternative methodology to mapping place-names as point data – a procedure which, ultimately, reflects only the locations of the settlements to which those names are currently attached. All the names that appear in the Domesday survey are mapped on Figure 36 and are introduced in Chapter 8, though only those potentially coined in the Middle Saxon period are used to provide context for the Middle Saxon settlements. The names that reflect Scandinavian settlement are discussed in more detail in Chapter 12.

The review of Middle Saxon settlement in the study area is followed, in Chapters 9 and 10, by the detailed characterisation of Middle Saxon occupation at Wharram

Percy. As the curvilinear enclosure settlement at Wharram was not recognised until long after the end of excavations, it was not a target for investigation: elements of it were encountered fortuitously, and this has shaped what we currently know about it. Apart from the investigations in the South Manor Area, which were designed to explore the significance of a nearby concentration of Anglo-Saxon pottery, most of the Middle Saxon remains were uncovered in explorations of boundary ditches. Some of the ditches had been created to define Middle Saxon enclosures; others date to the Roman period but had proved to be convenient locations for Middle Saxon *Grubenhäuser*, which were in turn, the chosen locations for a significant amount of artefactual and faunal deposition after their abandonment.

It is partly because of such deposition strategies that the Middle Saxon artefact assemblage, reviewed comprehensively for the first time in Chapter 10, is so rich and varied. Some objects seem to emphasise Merovingian connections in the 7th and early 8th centuries; others point to links with Ireland in the later part of the Middle Saxon period. The Irish connections may find context in a range of artefacts with ecclesiastical associations, the significance of which is considered further in Chapters 11 and 12. The artefacts reviewed in Chapter 10 also evidence a range of craft activities pursued in Middle Saxon Wharram, including textile manufacture, wood and antler working and possibly comb manufacture. The record is, however, dominated by evidence of metalworking – mainly iron smithing, though with some evidence of non-ferrous metalworking.

The most extensively investigated assemblage of iron-working debris comes from the South Manor Area, and its precise significance is reviewed in the second half of Chapter 10. Significant quantities of iron-working debris have also been recovered from Site 78 (*c*. 6.3kg), about 200m to the south-west of the South Manor Area, hinting, perhaps, at a specialist smithing function at Wharram, one reflecting more than the settlement's own domestic requirements. This possibility takes on added significance in the light of evidence for metalworking recovered from Middle Saxon Burdale, summarised in Chapter 8. The Wolds seem, on the face of it, an unlikely home for communities specialising in the manufacture of iron and non-ferrous metal artefacts. Perhaps the steep-sided valleys still supported significant amounts of coppiced woodland to fuel industrial and craft activity in this period.

Some years ago, Christopher Dyer foresaw that framing the conclusions of the overall synthesis volume for Wharram 'will be no easy task, as there are so many rival interpretations and divergent opinions' (Dyer 2004, 40). Nowhere is this better reflected than in Chapter 11, which presents very different interpretations of the Middle Saxon curvilinear enclosures and *Grubenhäuser*, both at Wharram and elsewhere on the northern Wolds. Both sides of the debate have had full sight of the relevant data and each other's conclusions, but this has led to a refining rather than a coalescing of the two positions. Therefore it has been decided to give readers the opportunity to explore each of them in turn.

Chapter 12 moves Wharram from Middle Saxon to Late Saxon times, and it attempts to provide a context for the Scandinavian presence signified so spectacularly by the 10th-century Borre-style belt fittings found in the excavations. It does so on a rather broader canvas than the study area, as it became apparent during the course of research that Scandinavian influence could be best understood by extending the study area northwards as a transect across the Vale of Pickering and to the fringes of the North York Moors.

The themes considered in this chapter relate to more general questions about the character of Scandinavian settlement, questions which have been reviewed by Lesley Abrams and David Parsons (2004, 380-81, 387, 404). They have suggested that 'our understanding of these events will perhaps best be advanced by a series of micro-studies which treat small regions separately and co-ordinate the toponymic, archaeological, environmental, and landscape evidence'. Part of this agenda has been taken up in Chapter 12, and what emerges is in line with another of their propositions: that 'it may be dangerous to impose single interpretations on the whole of Britain, or England, or even eastern England' (Abrams and Parsons 2004, 422).

In the 10th and 11th centuries Wharram was unquestionably situated within a group of landholdings controlled by Scandinavian lords, but it seems very probable that these landholdings originated in an earlier 'multiple' estate controlled by one or more ecclesiastical institutions. It is suggested that the estate had been acquired by Vikings by right of conquest, and its subsequent history followed a very different trajectory from other estates in eastern Yorkshire which had different histories – for example the 'comital' estates that remained under the control of the king. The latter seem to have retained relatively stable organisational structures down to the Conquest; whereas the Scandinavian estate stretching across the central part of the Vale of Pickering and the northern Wolds was subject to fragmentation and disaggregation through sale (to the Archbishop and perhaps the Earl) and through partible inheritance among the kin group that controlled it.

Similarly, within these Scandinavian landholdings the communities recorded in Domesday could have had very different origins and trajectories. Some continued to be dominated numerically, though perhaps not economically and politically, by English inhabitants; others were new vills founded to house Norse-speaking communities during a period of massive expansion in cultivation. This strategy was pursued both through the extension of arable lands across existing townships, and through the formation of arable townships on former Wolds grazing lands. The context of such developments at Wharram and in its neighbourhood was a distinctly Scandinavian one; but this should not in any way be taken to imply that parallel developments were absent in surrounding estates that remained under the control of English lords.

Whatever the contribution to Wharram's development of specifically Scandinavian concepts of settlement planning and landholding, there is now little doubt that the Late Saxon period witnessed the creation of the earliest elements of the rectilinear medieval village and the large-scale, planned field system that was cultivated by its inhabitants. In the first part of Chapter 13 it is argued that the West Row of village enclosures may have succeeded the curvilinear enclosures between the mid-9th and mid-10th centuries. This conclusion is based, not on direct stratigraphic evidence, but on the indirect evidence of artefact distributions: shifts in the concentrations of both pottery and small finds from the area of the curvilinear enclosure settlement to the plateau edge, where the West Row enclosures were created, and the valley below.

Evidence for the creation in this period of the vast expanse of open-field ridge and furrow, extending as far as the township boundaries in all directions, is also indirect. In the faunal record the kill-off curves for both sheep and cattle, discussed in Chapter 11 (Figs 69 and 70), show some relatively subtle changes in slaughter patterns between the Middle and Late Saxon periods, with the Late Saxon profile being much closer to that of the 12th to 15th centuries. These changes may imply a move away from meat production to one focusing more on fleeces, manure and traction. They may not be very marked in the record, but this need not preclude them signalling a much greater change in Wharram's agricultural organisation: a rapid extension of cultivation, creating the vast expanses of open-field ridge and furrow that characterised the Wolds in the Middle Ages (see Ch. 17, below).

This expansion of cultivation, and the concomitant increased demand for labour to support it, will have generated many other changes in Wolds communities. One was probably a much greater reliance on water power to process grain, perhaps signalled at Wharram by the development of the excavated water-powered mill site: it seems to have been established in its known form in the late 9th or early 10th century. Another, wider impact may have been the carving out of small new communities, such as the *thorp* townships (Cullen *et al.* 2011), from larger vill territories, and the division of large vills, such as the original Wharram, into two smaller units.

The final part of Chapter 13 is the second contribution by David Stocker and Paul Everson. It addresses the morphological characteristics of Wharram's Late Saxon village and its church in the context of both the wider Vale-Wolds region and earlier studies in Lincolnshire. It explores the social and economic context of Wharram's 'village moment', building upon their earlier discussion in Chapter 11 and drawing upon their alternative vision of Wharram's development during the Middle and Late Saxon periods.

8 Resettlement of the Wolds

by Stuart Wrathmell, with contributions
from Alison Deegan, Julian Richards
and Steve Roskams

The resettlement hypothesis

From the mid to late 7th century onwards, the Wolds began
to be divided up into self-contained communities. These
were in the form of vill or township units, the significance
of which, both before and after the Conquest, was
summarised by Sir Paul Vinogradoff over a century ago:

'The fundamental union of the population, for
purposes of husbandry and local government, is not the
manor but the township. Townships are legally supposed,
in the feudal age, to cover the entire territory of the
kingdom... The same fundamental character of the
village or township unit is expressed in early records, and
in Domesday...'
(Vinogradoff 1908, 390-91)

It is the creation of townships on and around the Wolds
that is the subject of the second hypothesis:

*The 7th to 10th centuries were the period during which
the earlier large territorial units, centred in the vale but
with wide-ranging resources stretching from the carr lands
of the Derwent to the uplands of the High Wolds, were split
up into townships. The earliest wave of fragmentation
occurred in the vale, with the creation of townships with
names ending in* tun. *Where appropriate, they were
provided with their own shares of carr and wold.*

*The division of the Wolds themselves occurred rather
later, though the new units were in some cases centred on
pre-existing settlements – summer grazing stations,
dependent farmsteads, hunting lodges, craft and
industrial outposts and the like. Some of the townships
were either formed or re-formed under Scandinavian
influence, as evidenced by their place-names, but most
retained the topographical names that had long
distinguished specific locations and the resources they
had to offer, both for lowland communities and for long-
distance travellers using the main east-west routeways.
The north-south droveways, however, largely ceased to
function during the period of Wolds township formation.*

Once again these ideas owe much to Harold Fox's
vision of the Wolds at this period. He dated the creation of
independent townships there to the Anglo-Scandinavian
period, between the 9th and 11th centuries. He noted the
high density of Scandinavian and Scandinavian-
influenced place-names on the Wolds, especially names
ending in *by* and (on the Yorkshire Wolds) *thorp*, and the
paucity of 'the earliest strata of OE place name elements'.
He suggested that some Scandinavian place-names mark
new settlements; others, the Viking take-over of pre-
existing settlements, though he played down the role in
this of estate fragmentation (Fox 1989, 90-93):

'This is not to argue that these regions were ever an
unused void but to suggest that they were relatively little

favoured by early, seminal, settlement, leaving a good
deal of land for later colonisation.'...'For the wolds in the
Middle Saxon period, none of the evidence is inconsistent
with a picture of scattered minor sites with a good deal of
pasture and some wood in between them.'
(Fox 1989, 93 and n.51).

We can now return to the north Wolds study area, and
combine the earlier conclusions on long-established
routeways with township boundary and place-name data,
in order to establish whether the northern part of the
Yorkshire Wolds conforms to what would be expected
from Fox's general hypothesis.

Townships and township boundaries

Figure 36 is a map of the study area coloured to show the
various categories of place-name within the known
township boundaries. Two issues need clarification at the
outset. First, the names that appear on the map are the place-
names that were used to name vills, or townships, in
Domesday Book. Whatever they may originally have
signified, our earliest knowledge of them is as vill names.
So a name like Ganton may well at one time have meant
'*Galma*'s farmstead' (Smith 1937, 118), signifying a
settlement within a larger territory, but by the time we have
the name it refers to a community's territory, not to an
individual's farmstead; so it seems at least as logical to
colour the whole township, as it is known to us, to indicate
the name category, as it would be to put a dot on a map
where a modern settlement bearing that name happens to be
located. Secondly, it must be emphasised that the recorded
township boundaries are shown as they appear on the
earliest accurate maps: on Greenwood's map of 1818, and
on the first edition Ordnance Survey six-inch map
(surveyed 1851). It is assumed that they are for the most
part a faithful reflection of their medieval predecessors.

Since the time of Domesday Book there have clearly
been a few major modifications to the pattern of vills, as
evidenced by the loss of two of these units altogether. One is
a vill named Thoraldby, mentioned not only in 1086 but also
in a charter of *c.* 1157-70 which records the grant of land in
the western part of Mowthorpe vill between Aylnoth's croft
and the bounds of Thoraldby (*EYC II*, 387). The site of the
village has been identified by R.T. Porter with the 'site of old
buildings' immediately west of Thoroughby Hill, shown on
the first edition six-inch Ordnance Survey map. These
remains are discussed further in Chapter 18 (p. 310).

The other missing vill is Buckton, a soke centre at
Domesday (Roffe 2000a, 5). It was recorded in 1370 as
'iuxta Settrington'. Its name survives in Buckton Holmes
(Smith 1937, 140), shown on modern maps and also
recorded in a survey of 1600 immediately south of the
'Buckton garthes' (King and Harris 1962, 34 and map).
Buckton vill, which probably occupied the southern third
of what is now Settrington township, and the settlement
earthworks in Buckton Garths and at Kirk Hill, will also
be discussed in Chapter 18. It is worth noting that, given
their approximate locations, the addition of these two
townships to the map – if we knew the courses taken by

Fig. 36. Townships in the study area, showing the distributions of various categories of place-names and the relationship of township boundaries to routeways. The map is based on Ordnance Survey 1854 (surveyed 1848-50) and Greenwood 1818 (surveyed 1815-17). The Ordnance Survey has been followed except where townships have been amalgamated in the period between the Greenwood and Ordnance Survey maps, in which case Greenwood has been followed. Where there are other differences between the two maps, Ordnance Survey 1854 has been used except where there is good reason to suppose a change in boundary rather than an error in surveying or in information supplied to the surveyors. (E. Marlow-Mann)

100

their boundaries – would not affect the inferences drawn below in relation to the distribution of the various categories of township name.

There will also have been other, smaller-scale adjustments, such as that shown on an estate map of Kirby Grindalythe dated 1755 (British Library Add. MS 36899A). At the west end of the township, on the south side of the Gypsey Race, the property of L. Lillingston and S. Pierson included a field named 'Mowthorp Field', which had been part of the medieval township of Mowthorpe but came to be incorporated in Kirby after the division of Mowthorpe in 1622 (*VCH ER VIII*, 120). Similarly, a field called North Ings, on the boundary between Wharram Percy and Wharram le Street, was in the former vill during the Middle Ages and down to the early 18th century; but by the mid-19th century had become part of the latter township (see p. 294). Such changes are more likely to have occurred in post-medieval times than earlier, when townships still framed the activities of the local communities.

Despite such amalgamations and adjustments, the assumption here is that enough early 19th-century township boundaries follow courses established in the 7th to 10th centuries to make worthwhile the kind of analysis attempted here. As always, it is important to acknowledge the dangers of using 'late' evidence to analyse 'early' entities, a classic example being the reconstruction of Anglo-Saxon 'multiple' and 'minster' estates often on the basis of post-Conquest records of parochial hierarchies and far more recent delineations of parish boundaries (see e.g. Hadley 2000, 85-90).

Though doubts about the simplicity, uniformity and universality of multiple estates may be well-founded, there seems to be a broader consensus on the antiquity of the building blocks of those estates, the vill or township units. Dawn Hadley, for example, has accepted that their origins are to be found long before their names are first recorded in Domesday Book, and has also accepted the need to use post-medieval evidence to recover their boundaries (though to do this, she proposed using ecclesiastical parish boundaries as surrogates, whereas the present study uses the township boundaries themselves: Hadley 2000, 95-101).

Place-names and townships

The contribution of place-name studies to the debate on continuity or discontinuity from Roman to Middle Saxon times could be expressed succinctly with a quotation from Margaret Gelling's 2004 essay on the name 'Wharram', and on other Wolds place-names:

'In suggesting that the Wolds round Wharram are characterised by place-names likely to have come into use in the late 9th century, I am not putting forward a case for total depopulation after the Romano-British period, and total late recolonisation at the time of the Viking settlements. But a falling-off in the numbers of people living in the northern part of the Wolds, and an increase starting in the 8th century and continuing into the 10th century, is consistent with the archaeological record to date

at Wharram Percy; and it is noteworthy that the place-names fit such an hypothesis... Also, if there had been dense occupation in the earlier part of the Anglo-Saxon period, there would perhaps have been more English names of an early type on the Wolds, as opposed to in the sheltered valleys round the fringes.'
(Gelling 2004, 351)

To leave matters there, however, would be to forego an opportunity to link the place-name evidence to the record of trackways and township boundaries across the study area. In considering the relevant names in greater detail, it is important to be mindful of Gelling's warning, in the introduction to the first edition of her publication *Signposts to the Past*, to historians and archaeologists who might feel inclined to stray into the territory occupied by philologists (Gelling 1978, 11-12). It is a warning that that has been heeded here.

Though the English Place-name Society volume for the East Riding of Yorkshire was published before the Second World War (Smith 1937), Gelling herself contributed a more recent review, cited above, of place-names of the Wharram area (Gelling 2004, 347-51), as well as covering others in her ground-breaking book on *Place-names in the Landscape* (1984), rewritten as *The Landscape of Place-names* (Gelling and Cole 2000). This chapter follows precisely the word meanings given by Gelling and (by default) by Smith; though where alternatives are offered, the preference for one rather than another may have been selected to support this chapter's initial hypothesis.

That said, there is a world of difference between analysing the forms and meanings of words attached to places, and interpreting the social and economic significance of place-names attached to vills. The major strength of Gelling's work was her deployment of landscape analysis and archaeological evidence to give broader meaning to place-names, and it is here that the various relevant disciplines can engage with one another.

Place-name scholars have broadly divided their material into two main groupings: topographical names, which describe settlements according to their physical setting, and habitative names which have, as their main component, a word for farm, village or estate (Gelling and Cole 2000, xii), such as *ham*, *tun*, *ingtun*, *by* and *thorp*. Topographical names are now receiving much more attention from place-name scholars, and are thought often to represent the oldest stratum of surviving names. This suggestion appears to receive support from the numerous examples of a topographical name being used for the main settlement in a large conglomerate estate, with habitative names used for less important settlements within it (Gelling 1997, 123-5). On the other hand, Gelling also cited regions where topographical names mark areas of particularly late settlement:

'it looks as if a group of topographical settlement-names may be characteristic either of an area of exceptionally early or of one of exceptionally late English settlement; but such names should always be considered as potentially the earliest English ones in any region' (Gelling 1997, 126)

Such names are attached to over a quarter of the townships in the study area.

Among the Old English habitative names in the study area, the most common are those with the generic *tun*, qualified by a personal name to take the form 'x's *tun*'. They 'became overwhelmingly predominant after AD 730', though the number and range of personal name qualifiers is believed to have been overestimated (Gelling and Cole 2000, xx-xxi). They are thought to have referred not to new foundations, but to the arrival of an overlord in the life of a long-established farming community', which might previously have had a topographical name (Gelling 1997, unpaginated introduction to 3rd edition). They mark the granting by the king or a nobleman to a man or woman, and whilst there are examples that can be associated with documented persons in the 10th and 11th centuries, there are also examples as far back as the 8th century (Gelling 1997, 182). To these can be added the *ingtun* names which are also thought to have a genitive function, emphasising the association of a person with a place (Gelling 1997, 177-8).

Old Norse habitative names with *by* and *thorp* generics are also well-represented in the study area. The significance of *by* names on the Wolds and in other parts of eastern England has been a matter of lengthy debate, one that has been the subject of an important review by Lesley Abrams and David Parsons. They have concluded that *by* names were coined, perhaps mainly before the 11th century, by speakers of Old Norse who were present in sizeable communities in eastern England, and whose landholdings can be characterised as 'relatively marginal or low in status' (Abrams and Parsons 2004, 404): their significance will be further explored in Chapter 12 (pp 188-92). The *thorp* names, also the subject of recent review, are generally regarded as signifying dependent or outlying settlements, and were a later stratum of naming, perhaps associated with the rapid expansion of open-field farming (Cullen *et al.* 2011, 138-44)

Figure 36 maps the various categories of place-name in terms of township boundaries as they are known from 19th-century map sources. The origin of the relationship between township units and place-names is, of course, unknown. It may be that, as suggested earlier in this chapter, a community of some kind (large or small) was first named, and only later provided with a territory delineated by the known township boundaries. Alternatively, it may be that a community with a territory demarcated by the known township boundaries was at a later stage in its existence provided with the place-name which it now bears. A third possibility is that the name now attached to a settlement was given to that community at the time its township territory was first defined.

These three possible scenarios are themselves, of course, based on a number of assumptions, prominent among them the supposition that township boundaries have (with the qualifications noted earlier in this chapter) remained fossilised for a thousand years or more. Nevertheless, the alternative and more common place-name mapping strategy, of marking the various categories

of name as point data and comparing these to terrain, or to the distribution of early Anglo-Saxon or Scandinavian material culture, seems to offer no very clear way forward (see e.g. Baker 2005).

Taking first of all the townships bisected by Route 1, townships extending broadly from the marshlands in the north to the wolds scarp slope in the south, most of them have *tun* or *ingtun* generics. These are qualified by personal names, whether associated with an individual (Scampston) or a group of people (Knapton), and by words describing the character of the settlement or, perhaps, the land unit. (Potter) Brompton, for example, is rendered by Smith (1937, 119) as 'enclosure overgrown with gorse', but might it make more sense as the name of a territory whose chief characteristic was that it was overgrown with gorse at the time of its definition as a separate *tun*?

Of the other names in this zone, three have some claim to be early estate 'cores'. The first to be considered is the only topographical name in this zone: Sherburn, referring to a stream. Gelling suggested that its name is one of those 'most likely to date from the earliest period of English speech in the area' (Gelling 2004, 350), and it conforms to her class of topographically-named estate centres which have dependent settlements with habitative names (Gelling 1997, 123-5). The latter, however, are not necessarily an indicator of the later colonisation of previously unattributed lands. Rather, they represent the granting away of chunks of territory that had been part of the core.

Such a concept neatly circumvents the perceived problem of 'late' names ending in *tun* being located in regions where early Anglo-Saxon settlements and cemeteries are common. They do not necessarily indicate that *tun* names had a greater currency before *c*.730 than had previously been thought (cf. Baker 2005, 61); nor do they necessarily indicate that a whole stratum of place-names has been lost through replacement by *tun* names (cf. Gelling 1997, 125); merely that much of the original landholding unit was, in the 8th and, or 9th centuries, divided up into smaller estates.

Estate subdivision can be seen even more clearly in the case of two other names in this zone, both habitative, and both ending in *ingaham*, meaning 'village of x's followers' (Gelling 1997, 112). They are Yedingham and Wintringham, and Dr Gelling assigned their formation to the 7th century (Gelling 2004, 350). The chronological position of *ingaham* names, along with the related *ham* and *ingas* names, has been the subject of much debate, focused mainly (once again) on their distributions in relation to archaeological evidence.

The *ingas* ('x's followers') names, once thought to be an indicator of early folk migration, were removed from their primary position to a secondary one because of their lack of coincidence with areas containing the earliest Anglo-Saxon archaeology. This, however, follows only if the name was only ever given to a settlement. Alternatively, if the name denoted areas of, say, woodland or pasture, resources that had been allocated to a particular kin group, as suggested elsewhere (Roberts and Wrathmell 2002, 75), then the argument falls. It has, furthermore, been questioned more recently in a study of the Chilterns, which has also sought in part to uncouple the distribution of place-names and distributions of archaeological discoveries (Baker 2005, 60).

The argument in relation to *ingas* is, of course rather different from that concerning *ingaham*, which specifies habitation; but in the case of Yedingham and Wintringham this presents no difficulty, for they are both close to the extensive Early Anglo-Saxon settlement and cemetery remains, dating from *c*. AD 450 onwards, in what became the township of West Heslerton (Powlesland 2003a, 288). In terms of the relationship of their townships to neighbouring ones as seen on Figure 36, both have the appearance, even more than Sherburn, of cores truncated by the granting out of *tun* estates. Yedingham is merely a rump, passed over unnoticed in the Domesday survey, with bits of its territory intermixed with West Heslerton (including some adjacent to Route 1), indicating the latter vill territory's earlier affiliation. Wintringham, attenuated by grants of *tuns* from its east and west sides, retained a narrow passage from carr to wold, to give it access to the required range of resources. Figure 37 is a highly speculative attempt to delineate these early estates, their droveways, and the overlaying of *tun* vills.

Continuing this line of thinking, the two *thorps* in this zone, Scagglethorpe and Thorpe Bassett, probably represent a further stratum of naming. Both began, perhaps, as outlying settlements within existing vill territories. The affiliations of Thorpe Bassett are indicated by two features marked on the first edition six-inch Ordnance Survey map. The first is a strip of wold land on its east side, bordering on Wintringham, which constituted detached portions of the townships of Rillington and Scampston; the second is the apparent location of Thorpe Bassett village in the wolds droveway or 'outgang' of Rillington. Thorpe Bassett had been taken out of these *tun* territories before 1066, but they had retained some wolds pasture beyond the new township. Figure 37 shows the area occupied by Thorpe Bassett as having been *tun* territory before becoming *thorp* territory.

As Figure 36 indicates, the second zone of townships, those bisected by Route 2, has a very different mix of place-names. Excluding Langton and North Grimston, which form effectively an extension of the vale zone, there are only two *tun* names: East and West Lutton, which were presumably a single vill originally. Apart from the Luttons and Butterwick, the township names along Cranedale, and indeed further south, between Routes 3 and 4, are Old Norse habitative names and topographical names, with topographical names dominating the areas between and to the south of the main blocks of Scandinavian names.

Taking Lutton and Butterwick first: both lie north-south across Cranedale, encompassing a range of arable and pastoral resources in the same way as the vale *tuns*. Their Old English names may indicate that they were defined as townships earlier than their neighbours. Furthermore, both are bisected by north-south routeways, the one through Butterwick originating in Sherburn, the one through (West) Lutton providing links to Yedingham and Wintringham (Fig. 36). Are we seeing here early

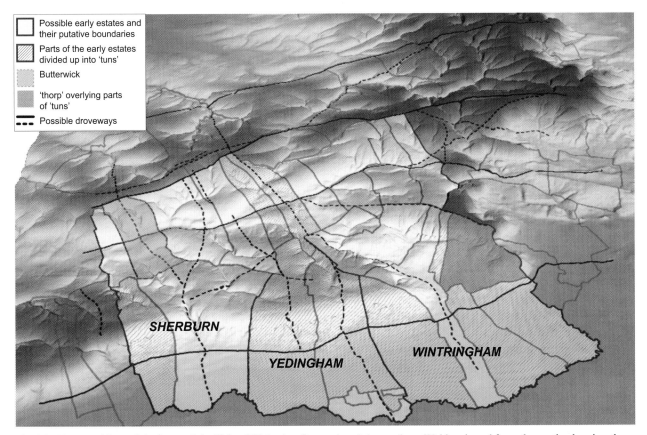

Fig. 37. Topographic model of part of the Vale of Pickering (bottom) and the northern Wolds, viewed from the north, showing three speculative early Anglo-Saxon estates and a selection of later vills carved out of their territories. (A. Deegan and E. Marlow-Mann)

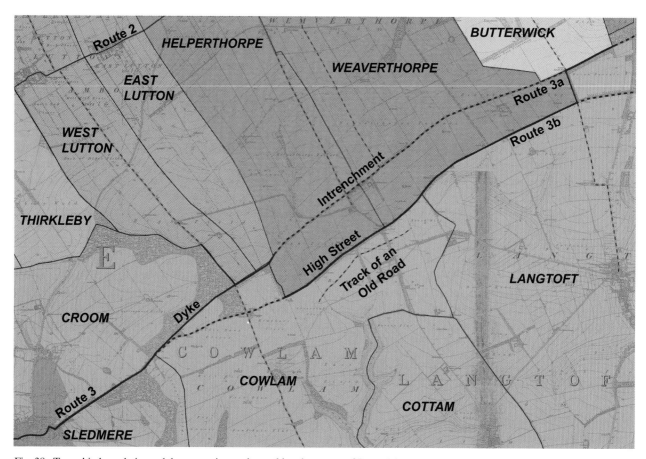

Fig. 38. Township boundaries and the successive tracks marking the course of Route 3 between Sledmere and Butterwick. (E. Marlow-Mann)

focal points for transhumance grazing for the three core estates in the vale, and perhaps subsequently for their offshoots? And were they subsequently, perhaps as a result of seasonal settlement and fertilisation of the surrounding soil, the first townships to be defined in Cranedale? The name Butterwick, denoting a farm where butter was made (Parsons and Styles 2000, 99), and presumably signifying its pre-eminent function, does not seem particularly appropriate to the almost exclusively arable township that we have seen in the 16th century (Fig. 31), and that had achieved this character, it has been argued, by the time of the Domesday survey (Harvey 1982a, 38); but it is one that might well have been suitable for an earlier dairy farm belonging to Sherburn, set beside the stream running through Cranedale.

To the west of the Luttons, Cranedale is occupied by a block of townships with *by* names: Kirby Grindalythe, Duggleby and Thirkleby together with the lost Thoraldby and a *thorp*, Mowthorpe. The significance of *by* names has already been noted briefly, and will be discussed in greater detail in Chapter 12, along with other aspects of the Scandinavian impact on this part of the Wolds. In terms of the broad chronological development of vills and place-names, it is suggested that the definition of these township units was linked to the creation of a cluster of Old Norse speaking communities.

In addition to Mowthorpe, there are three more *thorp* names bisected by Route 2, two of them, Helperthorpe and Weaverthorpe, filling the gap between the Luttons and Butterwick. If the townships bearing these names

were fully defined at the time these communities were established, then their southern boundaries provide an interesting contrast with those of the townships on each side of them, as can be seen in Figure 38. The boundary between the two Luttons and Cowlam follows the course of the Great Wold Dyke or a trackway along it (Route 3a); and the southern boundary of Butterwick takes the same line. The southern ends of Helperthorpe and Weaverthorpe, however, transgress that line and extend to the course of what appears on Figure 38 as Route 3b. Furthermore, just south of the boundary between Helperthorpe and Cowlam, the Ordnance Survey first edition six-inch map marks a short stretch of disused east-west track labelled 'Track of an Old Road'.

These observations fit neatly with May Pickles' discussion of the characteristics of the two 'boundary roads' which are numbered here Routes 3 and 4 (see pp 55-6). She noted (following Taylor 1979, 3) that they would once have been much broader lines of communication, later reduced to narrow trackways by expanding cultivation areas on each side. She also noted that the 'associated' boundaries might for a short distance follow a different but parallel course from the road, an indication of an earlier, superseded road line (Pickles 1993, 63, 72). Stretches of individual tracks would have been used from time to time, as passage along one was made more difficult through the trampling of animals, and an alternative course then came into use. It may be that a trackway along the Great Wold Dyke was in use when the Luttons and Butterwick were laid out, but had been superseded by the time the *thorp* townships were established. It has to be said, however, that the southern end of Boythorpe township, east of Butterwick, falls short of all these proposed routeways.

Between Routes 3 and 4 most of the township names are topographical, interspersed with a few *thorp* names. On the western scarp of the Wolds is another cluster of *by* names: Kirby Underdale and Uncleby, together with Garrowby which lies just outside the study area and another *thorp*. The similarity of the two clusters of *by* names, both focused on a church *by* and with associated *thorp* vills, is very striking. As will be argued later (pp 188-192), the clusters do not seem to delimit the extent of Scandinavian landholding and influence in the study area (as far as this can be inferred). They may, however, reflect a particular strategy followed by Scandinavian overlords who sought to intensify cultivation on the Wolds.

Turning to the topographical names which otherwise dominate the territory between Routes 3 and 4, Gelling has noted a number which are dative plural forms, some Old English, others Old Norse. Wharram itself is an example, meaning 'at the bends' or 'at the turns', along with Croom, 'at the nooks', Cowlam, 'at the hills' and Cottam, 'at the cottages' (Gelling 2004, 347-8). Gelling classified Cottam as a habitative name, though in this case the cottages are being picked out not to identify those who lived there, but because they were distinctive features in the landscape. In any case, they probably refer to 'relatively humble and sometimes impermanent structures' (Gelling 2004, 348), and like Arram and Bootham may indicate buildings occupied in the summer months during seasonal grazing on the Wolds.

Wharram's name has been taken to refer to the bends in the valley in which part of the village lies (Gelling 2004, 348), but it must be questionable whether the main Wharram valley and the dales which feed into it are distinctly more 'bendy' than those in neighbouring townships. The name may, alternatively, refer to the two streams which originate close together at Wharram le Street, and which then flow in different directions: Lord Carlisle's river (or the Gypsey Race) which flows eastwards along Cranedale from a spring just outside the south-eastern village crofts; and a stream that originates in a nearby spring – in 1810 feeding a pond in the centre of the village – and runs northwards and westwards into the Wharram Beck (Wrathmell 2005a, 1 and fig. 3). Given the spiritual significance of springs in general, the portentous qualities attributed to the Gypsey Race in particular, and the oddity of water issuing from neighbouring springs and flowing in completely different directions, this is perhaps a more distinctive attribute that would mark out 'Wharram' from surrounding places.

Among the other topographical names are those that refer to natural features at a particular location, such as the pool in the valley (Sledmere) or the pool by the heap of wood (Fimber: Gelling and Cole 2000, 27, 141, though a heap of wood seems a remarkably transitory landscape feature to be used in this way). As noted earlier, Gelling believed that these are the only two settlement names in

the northern part of the Wolds likely to have been coined before the mid-8th century (Gelling 2004, 350), and it is significant that they are both located close to Routes 3 and 4: their pools would have been important stopping-off points for those driving cattle along those routes. For Burdale, Smith offers 'house made of planks' or 'nook of land where planks were obtained', preferring the former (Smith 1937, 132). Gelling agreed with this preference (Gelling 2004, 348), though it could be argued that the alternative meaning fits better the view of the Wolds as a place which provided surrounding lowland communities with a range of resources – timber for planks might still have been available in this remote valley.

Underlying this reading of Burdale's name, and indeed this discussion as a whole, is a view that such topographical names may have become attached to places before they became settlements (or at least, before they became settlements in self-contained, permanent vills). As Gelling and Cole noted, this is a view that has been expressed by others, but it is not one that they themselves shared. The debate seems to focus on the earliest Old English topographical names, applied to places where settlements must already have existed when the Anglo-Saxons first reached them: 'the Anglo-Saxons were naming both site and settlement' (Gelling and Cole 2000, xvii). This may be an appropriate conclusion for some parts of the country, but there must be other areas, the Wolds among them, where the Anglo-Saxons who made use of these lands needed to name particular locations long before these places acquired permanent settlements.

Gelling and Cole emphasised that Anglo-Saxon topographical names distinguish subtle differences in the landscape, differences that are lost in modern vocabulary within broad terms such as 'hill' and 'valley'. They also emphasised that the Anglo-Saxon topographical naming system was country-wide, with the same terms being used to describe specific land-formations from one end of the country to the other, and that Anglo-Saxon travellers may have played a major role in creating this country-wide system. 'A country-wide system of topographical naming would certainly facilitate the giving of directions to travellers, and would also make it easy to know when a destination was in sight' (Gelling and Cole 2000, xv-xvi).

Signposting for long-distance travellers might well apply to the topographical names of the northern Wolds on routes 3 and 4; but with a change of scale they might equally be seen in the context of vale-wold droveways. If animals were driven from the vale to the wold, those who herded them would presumably have had in mind a specific target area for grazing, and certainly a gathering place where the animals could be collected at the end of the season and driven back to the lowlands. A nook of land, a pool or a winding valley could well mark such a gathering place, and these would need to be distinguished, one from another, by those who lived in the vale's farming communities.

This commentary on the place-names has sought to explore ways in which some aspects of naming may gain greater intelligibility through combining the relevant data with evidence for specific routeways and township boundaries, rather than in terms of broad and rather vague topographical frameworks. The next step is to see whether there is a body of archaeological data that can also be better understood when combined with place-name, routeway and boundary evidence.

Butterwick-type settlements in the study area and beyond

In the Royal Commission's major survey of crop mark evidence across the Yorkshire Wolds, Catherine Stoertz identified a distinct category of settlement remains that she named 'curvilinear enclosure complexes'. Here, they are referred to as 'Butterwick-type' sites, after one of the best examples, partly because it provides a less cumbersome reference, but also because curvilinear enclosures could be (and were) created at a wide variety of times in the history and prehistory of Britain. Butterwick-type sites have, on the other hand, been linked spatially to clusters of marks that are thought to represent Anglo-Saxon *Grubenhäuser*, and where excavation has taken place, they have demonstrated use in the Anglo-Saxon period.

A total of eleven such sites were identified by Stoertz on, and adjacent to the Wolds:

'Each site comprises a nucleated cluster of distinctive elongated and irregular curvilinear enclosures, tightly grouped and occasionally overlapping. They contain feint and superimposed traces of small internal features; rectangular pits are also found in association with these enclosures. The perimeter ditches appear to have been recut many times. Although [recti]linear features may be present in the vicinity of the curvilinear enclosure complexes, the two are not directly related.'
(Stoertz 1997, 55)

Stoertz went on to note 'the presence at each curvilinear complex of rectangular pits with rounded corners and typical dimensions of 6 x 4m, which strongly resemble sunken-floored buildings or *Grubenhäuser*' (Stoertz 1997, 59), suggesting a possible Anglo-Saxon date.

All but one of the eight clear examples that she illustrates (Stoertz 1997, fig. 30) are on the northern Wolds, and three of them are within the study area, at Butterwick, East Lutton and West Lutton – though as we shall see, Alison Deegan's fuller crop mark transcription indicates that the two Lutton settlements were in fact the two ends of a single large settlement. These and most of the others recorded by Stoertz lie in close proximity to medieval and later villages.

The type-site, at Butterwick, lies about 200m beyond the south-west corner of the medieval village envelope,

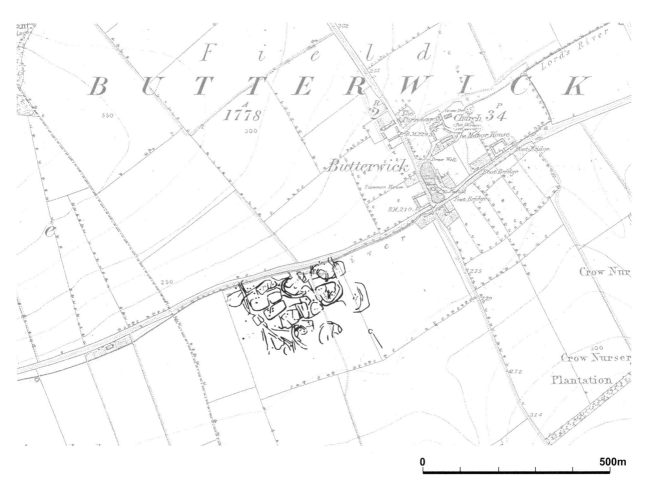

0   500m

Fig. 39. 'Butterwick-type' settlement enclosures south-west of Butterwick. (E. Marlow-Mann after C. Stoertz)

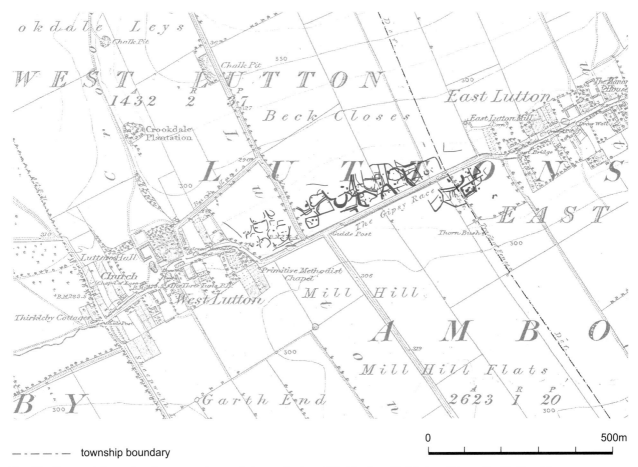

0   500m

Fig. 40. 'Butterwick-type' settlement enclosures between East and West Lutton. (E. Marlow-Mann after C. Stoertz)

and the relationship between the two can be seen on Figure 39. Several rectilinear boundary ditches in its vicinity are probably related to Romano-British field divisions, and most if not all of these have been removed from the accompanying illustration. The curvilinear enclosure settlement may have extended north of the present road, up to an earlier routeway along the Gypsey Race (Fig. 31, E), though there was no recorded crop mark evidence to demonstrate this. The record also seems incomplete to the south, where what is clearly only a part of a large enclosure has been recorded in the crop mark photograph.

The Butterwick-type settlement at Lutton (Fig. 40), was only partly recorded in the Royal Commission survey (Stoertz 1997, fig. 30, nos 7 and 8). The crop marks mapped there showed what appeared to be two separate, small groups of enclosures, one immediately to the east of West Lutton village, the other west of East Lutton. A more recent aerial photograph, taken by David MacLeod of English Heritage (Plate 11) has, however, indicated that the earlier record was simply of the two ends of a much larger Butterwick-type settlement that occupied the whole of the space between the two medieval villages. Again this emphasises that what has been recorded of any of these settlements may significantly under-estimate their full extent. Once more, the rectilinear ditches that are presumed to represent

prehistoric and/or Roman period settlement remains have been omitted (though a few may still remain).

What is of particular interest at Lutton is the relationship of the Butterwick-type remains to the territories of the two medieval vills and to the present village settlements. The vills were presumably at some stage carved out of a single territory called Lutton; and as the Butterwick-type settlement extends across the boundary separating the two vills, it is clearly a candidate for the settlement which had been supported by that earlier territory, replaced by the present village settlements at its east and west ends.

Domesday records only one Lutton, as part of the Archbishop of York's Weaverthorpe estate (*DB Yorks* 2B, 18), and it is tempting, therefore, to argue that the division of Lutton, the abandonment of the Butterwick-type enclosures and the creation of the medieval and later villages occurred after 1086. Yet (as with most things in rural settlement studies) the case is not as unambiguous as it might at first appear. David and Susan Neave note that the earliest reference to two Luttons occurs in *c*.1110, but they suggest that they were both subsumed in the single entry for Lutton in 1086. On the other hand, Domesday records only eight carucates in Lutton, whereas in the early 17th century the combined total of carucates in the two townships was over twelve (*VCH ER VIII*, 155, 161). Perhaps one of the two was omitted from the Domesday text in error.

Plate 11. Aerial photograph showing crop marks of 'Butterwick-type' settlement enclosures between East and West Lutton, viewed from the north. (NMR 17589/30, 9 July 2001. © English Heritage.NMR)

Further east, the Great Wold Valley contains at least two further Butterwick-type sites at Rudston and Low Caythorpe. The one at Rudston (Fig. 41) lies just north of the modern village enclosures (Stoertz 1997, 58-9). Figure 41 incorporates more recent geophysical survey data that have added to its known area, further south to the High Street (Milsted 2003). Indeed, it is conceivable that the roughly semi-circular village enclosure immediately south of the High Street, bounded by Middle Street and Church Lane and encompassing in its east end the medieval church and prehistoric standing stone, reflects the southern end of the earlier settlement. The monolith, which gives the village its name (Smith 1937, 98), would thus have been appropriate as the name of the Butterwick-type settlement as well as that of the more recent village.

The Butterwick-type complex called Low Caythorpe lies east of the earthworks of Low Caythorpe deserted medieval village, separated from them by just one field (Fig. 42). The course of a new pipeline running through the intervening field was excavated in 1992, and revealed part of an Anglo-Saxon *Grubenhaus* along with Romano-British remains (Abramson 1996, 24-6). An earlier excavation in the medieval manorial enclosure of Low Caythorpe, at the east end of the village site and therefore in the part closest to the Butterwick-type settlement, uncovered the remains of a rectilinear timber building

that was dated to the Late Saxon period (Coppack 1974, 35-6).

It would be easy enough, therefore, on archaeological grounds to assume a gradual shift westwards in the location of settlement at Low Caythorpe, with its origins in the Middle Saxon period. The 19th-century township boundaries, however, may point to a rather more complicated history, for the Butterwick-type settlement is in fact located within Boynton township rather than Low Caythorpe. It may, therefore have been the Middle Saxon settlement to which the name Boynton was originally attached, rather than a direct predecessor of medieval Low Caythorpe. In that case its abandonment would have reflected the introduction of the new township of Caythorpe within the territory of Boynton, and the transfer of Boynton's settlement to a new site further east.

Two other examples are located on the northern Wolds to the south of the study area, at Huggate and Garton (Stoertz 1997, fig. 30). The Butterwick-type settlement at Huggate (Fig. 43) is located beyond the north end of the present village, though earthworks indicate that the medieval village enclosures extended closer to it than does the present village. Garton (Fig. 44) is the only one of Stoertz's eight clear Butterwick-type settlements that is not in close proximity to a medieval village: it lies on the southern boundary of Sledmere township, apparently cutting or cut by the course of Sledmere Greenway (Route 4).

Fig. 41. 'Butterwick-type' settlement enclosures just north of Rudston. (E. Marlow-Mann after C. Stoertz)

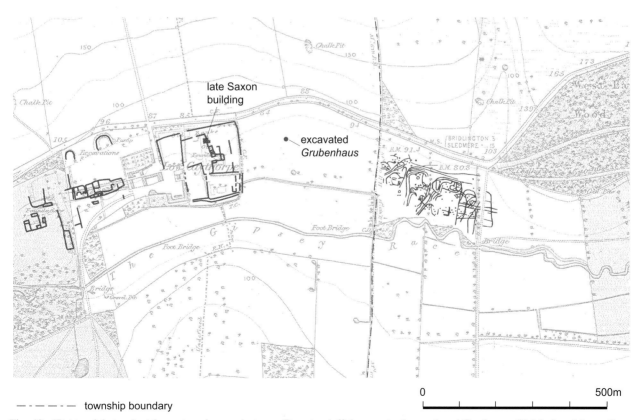

late Saxon
building

excavated
Grubenhaus

— · — · — township boundary

Fig. 42. 'Butterwick-type' settlement enclosures between Boynton (off the map to the east) and Caythorpe. (E. Marlow-Mann after C. Stoertz)

Fig. 43. 'Butterwick-type' settlement enclosures north of Huggate. (E. Marlow-Mann after C. Stoertz)

— · — · — township boundary

Fig. 44. 'Butterwick-type' settlement enclosures between Sledmere and Garton. (E. Marlow-Mann after C. Stoertz)

110

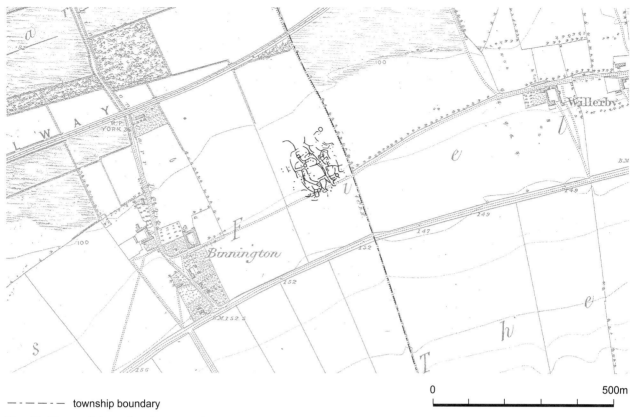

Fig. 45. 'Butterwick-type' settlement enclosures north-east of Binnington. (E. Marlow-Mann after C. Stoertz)

The remaining example illustrated by Stoertz demonstrates that Butterwick-type crop mark formations are not confined to the Wolds. It lies at the north-east corner of the study area, in the Vale of Pickering, and is recorded by Stoertz under the parish of Willerby (Stoertz 1997, 59). In terms of townships, however, it is located in the territory of Binnington, a short distance east of the existing settlement of the same name (Fig. 45). It is therefore a candidate for the predecessor of the medieval village of Binnington, the original *tun*, in the period before Willerby vill was carved out of its territory.

Beyond Stoertz's corpus, several other settlements with broadly similar morphological characteristics, and of broadly similar date, have been recorded in the study area by means of geophysical survey and excavation. Although Binnington is the only Stoertz site in this part of the Vale, there is an argument for adding to the list the Anglo-Saxon settlement site known as West Heslerton (Fig. 46). The impressive excavations have demonstrated that it was occupied from the mid-5th to 9th centuries, and that from about AD 450-650 it was accompanied by a cemetery a short distance to the north (Powlesland 2003a, 288). Ditched enclosures of curvilinear or sub-rectangular form existed only in the southern half of the settlement site: the post-hole buildings and *Grubenhäuser* of the northern half were not bounded by anything that survived in the archaeological record:

'Sub-zones represented by some of the enclosures seem to have functioned primarily as agricultural processing areas… The middle Anglo-Saxon enclosures

often re-use the earlier late Roman enclosures, but new boundaries are also defined which survive until the Anglo-Scandinavian period in the ninth century' (Powlesland 2000, 25 and fig. 3.2)

The Heslerton enclosures are, at their closest, within 150m of the mid-19th-century township boundary that divided West Heslerton from East Heslerton. As with Lutton the site is, therefore, a candidate for the original *tun* settlement, dating to the period before its territory was split into two vills served by the current village sites. More than that, its use in the early Anglo-Saxon period, combined with the use of the adjacent cemetery from the later 5th to early 7th centuries, may indicate that this was a settlement of 'Eada and his people' (Smith 1937, 121): Yedingham.

Among other Butterwick-type sites on the Wolds, the first that should be mentioned is Wharram Percy itself, though only briefly as it is the subject of the next two chapters. The curvilinear enclosure settlement identified by geophysical survey, marked in green on Figure 22, has been reproduced here at the same scale as the other sites (Fig. 47). Its signature is rather less coherent than the others, but it is the one that is still partly masked by permanent grassland; and even those parts under cultivation have not (to our knowledge) appeared as crop marks. Excavation has indicated that the enclosures are of Middle Saxon date, and that at least one contemporary *Grubenhaus* lies beyond the area of recorded enclosures, to the north (Site 39). Wharram is, of course, potentially another example of one large township being split into two.

— - — -— township boundary

Fig. 46. 'Butterwick-type' settlement enclosures east of West Heslerton. (E. Marlow-Mann after C. Stoertz)

Fig. 47. Butterwick-type' settlement enclosures just west of Wharram Percy. The large green dots mark concentrations of 'Saxon' pottery (with sherd numbers) recorded from fieldwalking (locations *very* approximate from Hayfield 1987a, 109-112). (E. Marlow-Mann after English Heritage and C. Hayfield)

In addition to Wharram, a few other curvilinear enclosure sites have been excavated on the Wolds, all seemingly datable to the Middle Saxon period. They include Paddock Hill, Thwing, where Terry Manby's excavations uncovered a small group of curvilinear enclosures representing 'a high status Middle Anglo-Saxon settlement' (Reynolds 2003, 128-9 and fig. 17), and Cottam B, where Julian Richards' excavations identified two separate and chronologically distinct foci of the Middle and Late Saxon periods. The Middle Saxon focus was a sub-rectangular enclosure with timber buildings occupied in the 8th and 9th centuries (Richards 1999a, 1-110; 2001, 271-2). It has been suggested that this may have been a high-status residence with a specific function – a hunting lodge (Fenton-Thomas 2005, 90).

Finally, Julian Richards and Steve Roskams have recently carried out excavations at another Butterwick-type site, at Burdale in Wharram Percy parish. Their investigations are as yet unpublished, and a summary report has therefore been included as the remaining section of this chapter.

Investigations of Anglo-Saxon occupation in Burdale: an interim note

by Julian Richards and Steve Roskams

Introduction

During 2005 to 2007 a team from the University of York investigated evidence for Anglo-Saxon activity in Burdale, *c.* 2km south-east of Wharram Percy. Post-excavation is ongoing but an interim summary is provided here because of its relevance to any general consideration of Anglo-Saxon settlement in the Wharram area, and specifically to the curvilinear enclosure settlements discussed in the previous section of this chapter.

The settlement (at SE 875623) is situated on the valley floor at *c.* 100m OD, along the main Thixendale-Fimber valley. Like most of the groups of remains described above, it is adjacent to the site of the medieval village and modern farm. The area comprises a long narrow level field, approximately 1km in a north-west to south-east orientation with an average width of 120m. Steep sides rise upwards from the field boundaries. The western end is not far from the convergence of Fairy Dale and Middle Dale at Burdale Crossroads, while Whaydale joins the northern side, about 500m from the western end. The valley bottom has a very slight upwards slope away from the Fimber boundary towards Burdale Crossroads. A natural spring rises above Burdale Crossroads and today runs as a subsurface stream towards Fimber. It feeds a pond which would have supplied both the settlement and animals in the surrounding pasture (Hayfield and Wagner 1995, 56).

The valley was included within Colin Hayfield's Wharram parish survey, and two sites were identified (Hayfield 1987c, 132-44). The first (B17: Burdale Crossroads – SE872623) was investigated on the triangular green formed by the road intersection at Burdale. A sequence of pottery spanning from the 3rd or 2nd century BC to the 17th century AD suggests this was

Plate 12. Aerial view showing crop marks of 'Butterwick-type' settlement enclosures at Burdale, viewed from the south. (NMR 20081/04, 22 July 2004. © English Heritage.NMR)

113

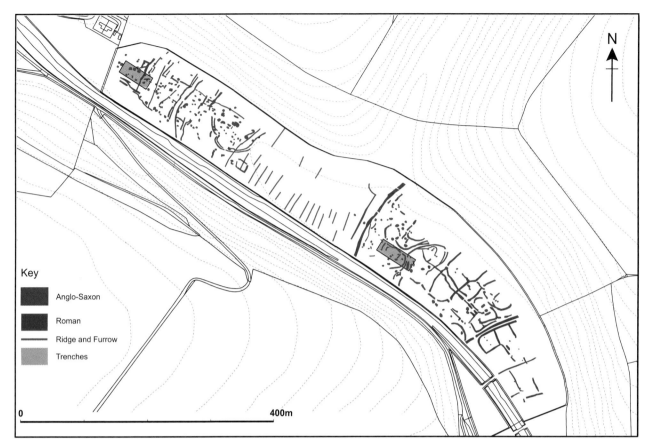

Fig. 48. Roman and 'Butterwick-type' settlement enclosures south-east of Burdale House Farm, transcribed and interpreted from aerial photographic and geophysical survey data. (© University of York)

a preferred settlement location, although there is no evidence to suggest it was permanently occupied. Hayfield's second site (B18: Burdale/Fimber Boundary farmstead - SE 881618) is at the other end of the valley. Crop marks appeared here in 1976 and were photographed by Tony Pacitto. Hayfield recovered predominantly Roman sherds and concluded that this was another Romano-British farmstead.

The RCHME National Mapping Programme Yorkshire Wolds survey (Stoertz 1997) indicates a linear boundary ditch crossing the eastern end of the valley floor and also plots a small number of poorly defined features. No other crop mark features were known at the time of Stoertz's survey, but a subsequent English Heritage sortie by David Macleod revealed a palimpsest of rectilinear and curvilinear features, including rectangular and curvilinear 'Butterwick-type' enclosures, trackways, and cut features (Plate 12 and Fig. 48). These may be interpreted as traces of the Romano-British farmstead (at the eastern end of the valley), with two Anglo-Saxon settlement enclosures with *Grubenhäuser* (one at the western end; the second east of Whaydale).

Burdale valley has been subject to metal-detecting over a number of years. With the co-operation of the finders Gary Parkin and David Wayper of the Dunelme Metal Detecting Club and the owner, Lord Middleton, Neil Campling deposited a number of items, including Romano-British and Anglo-Saxon artefacts, with the Yorkshire Museum in 2000 (YORYM: E2214). Most of

the metal-detecting has, however, been illegal night-hawking, focused on the eastern end of the valley away from Burdale House Farm. It is believed that this has produced material from the 1st century AD to the 8th century AD, including large numbers of Anglo-Saxon silver sceatta. There are also thought to be some burials, particularly inhumations. A limited metal-detector survey in September-October 2005 (Bambrook 2005) produced an Anglo-Saxon pin and strap-end. Three test pits and four auger transects were also undertaken in the mouth of Whaydale in 2005 (Neal 2006).

The site was selected for further investigation as part of a University of York research project to investigate Anglo-Saxon and Anglo-Scandinavian settlement on the Yorkshire Wolds. It was also included within the remit of the VASLE (Viking and Anglo-Saxon Landscape and Economy) project (Richards *et al.* 2009). Preliminary reconnaissance, including fieldwalking and magnetometry confirmed settlement activity.

The crop marks indicated two concentrations of Anglo-Saxon activity: the first, at the western end comprised enclosure ditches, trackways and various cut features, possibly buildings. Intercutting features demonstrated that several phases of activity were represented. Magnetometry yielded significant magnetic anomalies in this area, suggesting intense burning. There appeared to be a gap in activity to the south-east, with no crop marks at the junction of Whaydale and the main valley. Further east, however, there was the second concentration of activity with traces of several Butterwick-type enclosures, as well as more rectangular enclosures, most clearly visible at the eastern end – Hayfield's Burdale/Fimber boundary farmstead. Fieldwalking and metal-detecting confirmed this twin focus of activity, although there was a background scatter of artefacts across the valley. The soils within the western concentration were much darker and more loamy. Test pit excavations suggested that deposits were thicker here, and quantities of medieval pottery were recovered, possibly relating to middens associated within the village underlying Burdale House Farm. Two seasons of excavation were conducted, in 2006 and 2007, as student training exercises for the University of York.

Excavations in 2006

In 2006, a 20 x 60m trench was opened in the eastern crop mark group, close to the junction with Whaydale. The trench was positioned so as to provide a transect across the interior of the whole of one of the enclosures (Fig. 49).

The first signs of activity pre-dated the enclosure and comprised a gully and associated parallel feature, and a large pit. The gully and associated feature incorporated daub in their backfill, and may relate to more substantial activities off-site to the south-west, whilst the charcoal-rich pit implies some production activity. These features seem to have fallen into demise when the first enclosure (Enclosure 1) was set out in a single development of this part of the site, in the form of three parallel, curving ditches, plus presumed internal banks, its western side towards the west end of the trench. The creation of this enclosure, its projected dimensions at least 40m across, clearly represents a major development of the area.

A second curvilinear ditch was created within the area bounded by the ditches of Enclosure 1 to form a new episode, Enclosure 2, at least 20m across. The first enclosure, however, seems to have continued in use at this time. Indeed, Enclosure 2 might be better seen as a subdivision within 1, rather than something inserted after its disuse: insufficient was exposed within the excavated area to decide between these alternatives. Subsequently,

the northern end of this new enclosure was modified and recut several times, indicating an extended life for this component of the landscape.

Following the demise of Enclosure 2, Enclosure 3, comprising three co-aligned curving ditches, at least 25m in diameter, was set out close to the southern edge of the site, towards the centre. Several pits were seemingly used for rubbish disposal at the end of their life and either dug for this purpose or originally used for storage. Others seemed to have had a rather different function, being concerned with activity of a more 'industrial' character. Two features had hearths laid out in their base, whilst three further major pits lay nearby, two of which included substantial amounts of possible hearth residues in their backfill, and the other contained a channel or a slot of possible structural function in its base.

Finally, two sets of features, one late, the other early, lay at the southern corners of the excavation. A possible *Grubenhaus* in the south-west post-dates the demise of Enclosure 1, although could have been in use with later developments nearby, most obviously Enclosure 3. In the south-east corner, a second *Grubenhaus* with opposed posts on its long axis, plus several rubbish or storage pits, were inserted before the creation of Enclosure 4 here (see below). Thus, when in use, they must have either lain in an open landscape or been bounded by features lying beyond the excavation area.

In the east of the site, Enclosure 4 was created with the digging of three concentric ditches to define an area which would have been nearly 40m across in total, with its centre just beyond the north-east corner of the excavation. This new element was in use long enough for its innermost ditch to have been recut once. How Enclosure 4 relates to the creation and use of Enclosures 1-3 to the west could not be decided on stratigraphic grounds.

Within Enclosure 4, two adjacent pits containing a profusion of charcoal debris suggest production activity, probably associated with a second pair of pits to the north and an adjacent working area with stake-holes. This implies that the new zone became a production space, much as that defined within Enclosure 2 to the west.

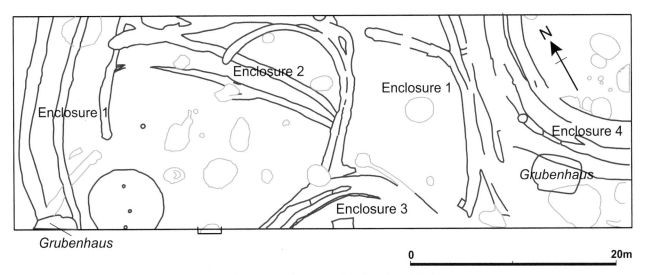

Fig. 49. Burdale 2006: composite phase plan of excavated features. (© University of York)

Finally, south of Enclosure 4 another, even larger 'production' pit was backfilled over an extended period of time, but was probably associated in its primary use with an adjacent channel and pit with a pebble-lined base. Hence, a diagnostically different set of production facilities is implied for this sphere. Overall, a highly structured use of space is indicated in each area lying inside each enclosure or within the interstices between them.

Preliminary dating places the settlement in the 8th and 9th centuries. The finds include several Anglo-Saxon combs, and copper-alloy buckles and dress pins. Iron objects include knives of various types, and part of an iron bell similar in construction to those found at Coppergate (Ottaway 1992, 557) although slightly larger in size. An iron pin with a polyhedral head is also similar to examples found at Coppergate from period 4B (*c.* 930/5-*c.* 975: Mainman and Rogers 2000, 2577) and may suggest that occupation continued into the early 10th century. There were also several fragments of lava quernstone found across the site, and a substantial animal bone assemblage which is compared with the equivalent assemblage from Wharram (pp 173-8 below). Very little ceramic material was recovered.

In associated work carried out as part of a doctoral investigation of soil formation in the Wolds a 3 x 12m trench was excavated across the lower slope of the valley mouth of Whaydale (Neal 2006).The transect showed a silty clay loam lying above solifluction gravels at a depth of 80-140cm. In the central part of the valley mouth the clay loam continued to a depth greater than the extent of the auger (1.5m). Very little artefactual material was found in this area however, confirming that Anglo-Saxon activity did not continue to the valley edge.

Excavations in 2007

In 2007 a second trench, 20m x 50m, was excavated at the western edge of the field, in the other crop mark concentration (Fig. 50). The precise location was chosen so as to include three of the more regular negative features, as well as areas with high magnetic anomalies. This confirmed that the rectangular cut features were each *Grubenhaus*-like structures, and that the magnetic anomalies were associated with a series of hearth bases in pits.

The first sign of activity in this trench occurred towards the eastern limit of the excavation area, comprising the insertion of a major north-south landscape division running across its full width. This had clearly been in use for an extended period of time, and probably represents a late prehistoric or Romano-British boundary. To the west of this, two further ditches with indications of a possible ankle-breaker in their base suggest the position of a subsidiary enclosure created against the larger ditch, seemingly associated with an amorphous pit to the north. Further west still, towards the centre of the site, another series of features represents a second enclosure, perhaps open to the west. The character of its initial backfill and alignment imply that this new insertion is broadly contemporary with those further east, with nearby post-holes suggesting installations, and perhaps even a fence line, within the area enclosed.

A number of pits, grouped loosely together here, were evident across the western half of the site. Some predated the setting out of curvilinear enclosures (see below), and the position of others appeared to articulate with the earlier, rectilinear ditches. Thus they are suggested to be in use early in the occupation of the area, comprising features for rubbish disposal followed by weathering, in

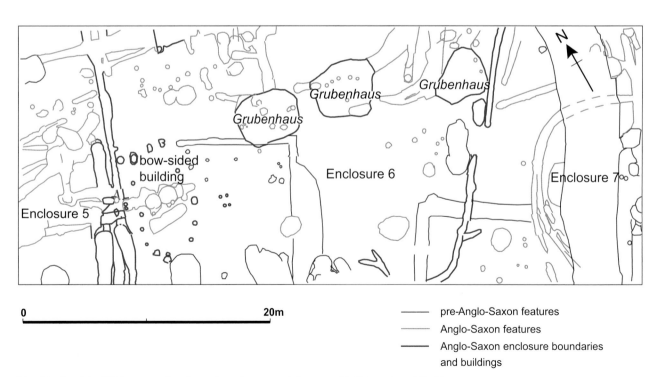

0   20m

——— pre-Anglo-Saxon features
——— Anglo-Saxon features
——— Anglo-Saxon enclosure boundaries and buildings

Fig. 50. Burdale 2007: composite phase plan of excavated features. (© University of York)

116

one case associated with dumping of butchering waste, and features related to quarrying of the natural chalk gravel. Taken as a whole, these components show that the first use of the site comprised a major boundary ditch and two rectilinear enclosures to its west, very different in character from the succeeding spatial organisation.

In the north-west corner of the excavation, ditches on a new alignment were inserted into the natural chalk, associated with pits further east. In this vicinity, a series of narrow and shallow ditches were cut into the earlier features, forming the sides of two enclosures with an entrance between the two. These strongly suggest that an entirely new system of landholding was created at this point, in the form of Enclosure 5 in the west and Enclosure 6 further east. To the east, another set of narrow and insubstantial ditches created a division between the centre of the site and its eastern zone, the latter therefore designated as Enclosure 7. From the surviving evidence, Enclosure 6 would have measured *c.* 28m east-west by 20m north-south. These three new zones marked the move from rectilinear to curvilinear spatial organisation on the site. They remained prominent in its subsequent use, although subsequent activity within each took different forms in different places.

At an early stage, further features were inserted in and around the access point between Enclosures 5 and 6, perhaps creating a new arrangement in the form of a gateway running into both zones. Within Enclosure 5, a roughly square structure 3m across was inserted just inside the north side of the entrance, perhaps to monitor movement into that zone, corresponding with a ditch channelling traffic on its south side.

Within Enclosure 5 proper, a major curvilinear ditch intruded obliquely across the edge of the square structure and up against the line of the enclosure's eastern limit. A number of smaller features to the north imply fence lines set out against the new ditch. Finally, a number of pits, perhaps for the disposal of organic waste, one of which may have been timber-lined, intruded into the above linear features, perhaps contemporary with a possible *Grubenhaus* to the south. Taken together, this suggests that, after the entrance arrangements east of Enclosure 5 were modified and developed, the internal space was then subdivided with a curvilinear ditch, subdivisions were reinforced with fence lines, and occupation and perhaps structural development then occurred across the area.

Enclosure 6 was also subdivided by a series of internal features soon after it had been set out, and three *Grubenhäuser* were then constructed within these subdivisions. The westernmost structure measured *c.* 5 x 4m and was 0.70m deep with a timber-framed structure in its base enclosing an area just under 4 x 3m and entrance arrangements along its southern side. Pebble metalling shows that occupation took place in the base of the feature, followed by weathering of its sides, then localised usage of a convenient hollow. The dumps above this, which contained the majority of cultural material, relate to general, later activities rather than those taking place within the structure itself.

Immediately to the east, a second building was slightly smaller than its western counterpart but was roughly the same depth and also incorporated a subsidiary area in its base, measuring 3 x 2.5m. The sides of the lower element, in this case, were revetted by planks held in place by posts seemingly separate from the superstructure of the building as a whole. In addition, access was via an entrance arrangement at its south-east corner. Otherwise, the two buildings bear a striking resemblance to each other in terms of position with respect to the pre-existing curvilinear ditches within Enclosure 6, their dimensions and alignment, the general character of their superstructure, and their backfilling processes.

Finally, some 6m east of the above structure, a third building, not completely excavated, was set within another subdivision of Enclosure 6. Slightly smaller than its western counterparts, measuring *c.* 4.5 x 2.5m, it also had a subsidiary cut just over 3 x 2m across, perhaps linked to the post-holes evident in its sides, and was of similar depth. Its entrance appears to have been on the long axis on its south-east side.

In the southern part of Enclosure 6 lay three pits and a scatter of post-holes. Two larger pits in the south may have been involved with the disposal of organic waste, though it is unclear whether this was their primary function, whilst the smaller pit and nearby post-holes could have been a structure set up just inside the eastern entrance into the enclosure. A fragment of an Arabic dirham was recovered from the upper fill of one of these pits.

Beside the western entrance to Enclosure 6 lay a scatter of eighteen post-holes, all of which cut into natural chalk and were sealed by topsoil and thus could belong to any period of occupation. Fourteen form the sides of a bow-sided building measuring *c.* 8m north-south by 4m east-west, symmetrically placed with respect to that entrance and so suggesting their broad contemporaneity. The four other post-holes imply a small structure further east. As the bow-sided building lies across the line of the access between Enclosures 5 and 6, it may have acted as a form of gatehouse, controlling movement by making it pass through a roofed area but not preventing it altogether.

In the north-west corner of Enclosure 6, a pair of pits and a scatter of post-holes cutting into natural chalk may be contemporary. Some of the post-holes form a rectangular configuration and may be ephemeral traces of former structures, although their shallow depth shows that the stone packing they contained must have been to support timber members which were part of a framed-superstructure, rather than freestanding vertical posts.

Just beyond the junction of Enclosures 5 and 6 in the north, two features forming an L-shaped junction seem to be inserted late in the history of the area. The character of their latest fills differs from that seen elsewhere, being markedly more stony. Hence, the two ditches either represent a new organisation of landscape, replacing the curvilinear systems or, if survival is better here than further south, a modification of what came before but with different, uppermost fills surviving intact.

Inside Enclosure 7, at the eastern extreme of the site, a curvilinear ditch with a 16m diameter was set out, with a second smaller curving feature set within its line. Both cut the early rectilinear divisions of the area and obeyed the line of the curvilinear enclosure, so clearly represent a new organisation of the zone within the latter. A probable *Grubenhaus* was inserted between them. Hence, as seen to the west, the sequence of subdivision then structural development seems also to apply to Enclosure 7.

Finally, a series of test pits dug to the north of the main excavation area for the purposes of evaluation generated some evidence for activities there. For the most part, this comprised indications of pits, gullies and some larger ditches which would not have been out of place in the fully excavated sequence. A number of stone-packed post-holes, mostly larger than those seen to the south, and stone footings for a possible masonry wall might imply a more substantial form of structural development here. This, together with the higher proportions of building materials, animal bone and pottery found in overlying strata, imply later medieval occupation.

The reorganisation of the landscape into a series of curvilinear enclosure mirrors activity in the eastern area, and also seems to have taken place in the 8th century. A number of residual Roman finds were found in many of the features but the earliest datable Anglo-Saxon finds are a Series D sceatta dated AD 700-715, and a Series E sceatta dated AD 710-60. Later finds include a styca of Aethelred II, dated AD 841-4. Other Anglo-Saxon finds include combs, 8th-century tweezers, brooches and pins, and a wide range of knives, including a pivoting knife (Ottaway 1992, 586). A copper-alloy faceted pin head is very similar to dress pins found in Anglo-Scandinavian contexts in York (Mainman and Rogers 2000, 2577) and, together with the dirham fragment (see above), these objects also suggest that activity may have continued into the early 10th century. As with the 2006 excavations, a substantial assemblage of faunal remains was recovered from the cut features. The assemblage has been analysed by Jane Richardson who summarises her overall findings in a later chapter.

Discussion

The process of transformation of an enclosed rectilinear organisation of the landscape evident in the Romano-British period and its replacement with a more open landscape and a number of Butterwick-type curvilinear enclosures is very similar to that observed or implied at the other sites, and, as we shall see, at Wharram Percy. The discrete negative features observed in and around Butterwick-type sites are confirmed at Burdale as *Grubenhäuser* and pits. Some of the pits at Burdale appear to have had an industrial function with hearth bases, and evidence for metalworking. Others may also have had a specialist function originally, but ended up as convenient rubbish pits.

The *Grubenhäuser* also appear to have had an industrial function, with activity taking place directly on the sunken floor area, as observed at West Heslerton. There is evidence for the organisation of space both within each excavation site, and also between the two concentrations of enclosures. Clearly both foci of activity were contemporary but they were *c.* 200m apart, with an open area in between them. This zoned use of the landscape parallels that observed at a larger scale at West Heslerton (Powlesland 2003a, 289-91). The curvilinear enclosures at Burdale were also reorganised through time. The stratigraphic evidence suggests that the enclosures were laid out first and later subdivided, in some cases after some of the ditches had already been filled, at least partially.

The nature of the relationship between Anglo-Saxon and Anglo-Scandinavian activity at Burdale requires further analysis. There appears to have been a complete break in settlement in the 10th century with no continuation of activity on the site of the Anglo-Saxon enclosures. Nor, as seen at Cottam (Richards 1999a), did Anglo-Scandinavian settlement precipitate a short-term 10th-century reorganisation. There is certainly evidence for some Anglo-Scandinavian activity at Burdale, but Anglo-Saxon settlement was abandoned rather than reorganised, and any later 10th-century activity must be assumed to be under the medieval village site.

9 Characterising Middle Saxon Wharram Percy: the Structural Evidence

by Stuart Wrathmell and Emmeline Marlow-Mann with contributions from Ann Clark and Justine Bayley

Introduction

Chapter 8 offered a hypothesis relating to Middle Saxon resettlement on the Wolds, the creation of bounded territories that we know as vills or townships, and the naming of the new communities. It also sought to link these communities to the crop mark remains of Butterwick-type settlement sites across the Wolds and beyond. The final section summarised the results of recent excavations at Burdale, which have clearly demonstrated that the Butterick-type remains identified there, including curvilinear enclosures, post-built structures and *Grubenhäuser* were in use during the Middle Saxon period.

The present chapter explores the character, components and dating of the Butterwick-type site at Wharram Percy itself. Some of the excavations that encountered Middle Saxon remains have been published fully in previous volumes, and their results are merely summarised here to provide a comprehensive picture. Other sites are described in more detail because they have not been published previously; full site reports can be accessed through the Archaeology Data Service (ADS), doi:10.5284/1000415. The locations of all the sites in question are shown in Figures 51, 52 and 56.

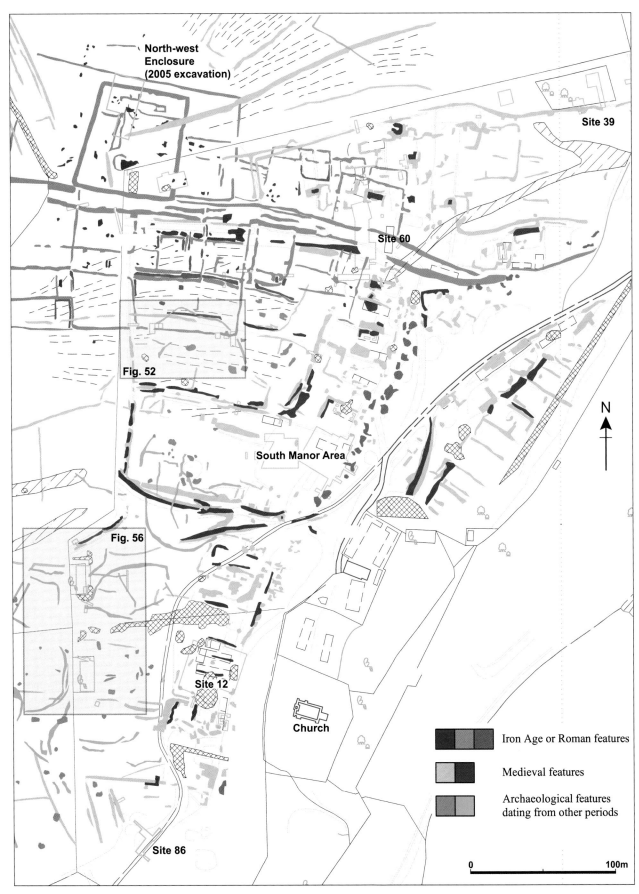

North-west
Enclosure
(2005 excavation)

Site 39

Site 60

Fig. 52

South Manor Area

Fig. 56

Site 12

Church

Site 86

N

Iron Age or Roman features

Medieval features

Archaeological features
dating from other periods

0   100m

Fig. 51. Interpretation of the 2002 geophysical survey and location of sites discussed in Chapter 9. (English Heritage and
E. Marlow-Mann)

At the northern end of the village area, the *Grubenhäuser* uncovered in Sites 39 and 60 were unanticipated discoveries. The excavation of Sites 94, 95 and 98 to the south-west of Site 60 was, on the other hand, an intentional investigation of a stretch of curvilinear ditch which had been recorded in the Ancient Monuments Laboratory's 1984 magnetometer survey (*Interim Report* 1986, fig. 2). In 1989-90 the curving ditch was trenched at two points where it intersected with a straight, east-west ditch. The latter was believed to belong to the later Iron Age and Roman 'ladder settlement' running alongside the east-west trackway. Before work began, the curvilinear ditch was thought likely to be the earlier of the two linear features (Richards 1992a 13).

To the south-east of Sites 94 and 95, Middle Saxon and later features had already been uncovered in the South Manor Area excavations (Sites 59, 76, 81, 85, 90 and 93). These investigations had focused on an area of ground immediately to the west of Site 44 where, in 1977-8, a significant quantity of Anglo-Saxon pottery had been recovered. The explicit aim of this work was to explore the settlement history of Wharram between the late Roman period and the Norman conquest in a part of the site where there might have been 'continuity' of settlement (Stamper *et al.* 2000, 17-18).

The same cannot be said for the area excavations south-west of the South Manor area. These were eventually found, a decade and more after the end of the Wharram excavations, to have fortuitously sampled parts of several curvilinear enclosures. Most of the small trenches in this part of the site were designed to investigate the boundary banks and ditches of the medieval settlement, with a view to determining when the village layout was created (Beresford and Hurst 1990, 68). Three larger areas (Sites 70, 78 and 86) were excavated, from 1981 onwards, for site management rather than research purposes: they were the planned locations for small plantations of trees. The recovery here of structural remains and significant quantities of Anglo-Saxon finds was inexplicable until the results of the Linfords' new geophysical survey became available.

The following brief descriptions are ordered in four groups, which are defined (purely for convenience) in terms of the topography of the later medieval village. The first covers sites within and to the north of the main east-west trackway separating the West Row (north) tofts and the North Manor and North Row. The second covers sites within and to the west of the West Row (north) tofts, including the South Manor area. The third deals with West Row (south) tofts and the largely unpublished sites to the west of them. The fourth deals with settlement remains in the valley which are potentially Middle Saxon. The site code is followed by the publication reference or, in the case of previously unpublished sites, by the reference to the relevant report held by the ADS (doi:10.5284/1000415).

Northern Plateau sites

Site 39 (Milne 1992a, 5-12, Milne 1992b, 80-82)
Excavation revealed a *Grubenhaus* (14) in Phase 2. It was 3.8m long and 2.4m wide, aligned east-west and terraced into the hillside. Two post-holes (41 and 42) were positioned slightly off-centre in the short sides of the feature. Slight ledges were noted on the east and west sides and these may have been used to support a timber floor; sharp flints were present in the base of the feature and the surface was not compact, indicating that it had not been used as a floor surface. No evidence of a hearth was noted and it was thought likely that the *Grubenhaus* was used as an outhouse rather than a domestic dwelling.

When the building was no longer in use, it was dismantled and levelled, apparently using the contents of a domestic midden. Gustav Milne's detailed analysis of the midden assemblage concluded that the artefacts it contained were 'a contemporary group of Middle Saxon finds which were in use *c.* AD 750-70. They were discarded some time later, and were subsequently thrown into the pit before too long a period had elapsed, perhaps by *c.* AD 780.' (Milne 1992b, 81). Rahtz has questioned whether in fact all the midden artefacts were in contemporary use, and has suggested the midden may have developed over a longer period before being dumped in the *Grubenhaus* hollow (Rahtz *et al.* 2004, 288). Whatever the precise status and dating of this material, its presence seems to indicate domestic occupation in the 8th century to the north of the east-west routeway. Finds include an antler comb for which a Middle Saxon date is preferred (39/SF778, p. 137 and Plate 16), an Early or Middle Saxon glass bead (39/SF807, Plate 15) and 209 sherds of Middle Saxon pottery.

Site 60 (Rahtz and Watts 2004, 66-71; Rahtz *et al.* 2004, 290-91)
The two *Grubenhäuser* identified in Site 60 have been discussed in print more frequently than most of the structures investigated at Wharram, and so are dealt with very briefly here. They could date to the 6th century, but it has also been argued that they may have been constructed, used and abandoned in the late 7th or 8th centuries, as part of the Middle Saxon settlement. In Chapter 7 above (p. 86), the two buildings and their relationship(s) to the various surfaces and tracks of the east-west routeway have been reviewed yet again, and it has been suggested that they may have had different dates of construction and use, one belonging to the 6th century, the other to the 7th or 8th century. Proximity does not necessarily imply contemporaneity.

Relevant finds include an iron firesteel which could be early 7th century rather than earlier (603/SF144, p. 137 and Plate 15), an antler spoon (603/SF143), a fragment from a pair of copper-alloy tweezers (610/SF185, Plate 16), a pin (610/SF184, Plate 16) and 68 sherds of Middle Saxon pottery.

Western Plateau (north) sites

Sites 94 and 95 (Figs 52 and 53; see Richards 1992a, 13-25)

Site 94 was excavated in 1989 with the specific aim of investigating two linear features that had been recorded in geophysical survey. One clearly represented a ditch delineating a rectangular enclosure belonging to the Iron Age/Early Roman 'ladder settlement'; the other, a curvilinear ditch intersecting the south-east corner of the enclosure, was thought possibly to be part of an earlier settlement enclosure.

The ladder settlement ditch was assigned to Phase 1. It was a large, V-shaped cut (2308), and its course westwards from Site 94 was recorded a year later in Sites 95A and 95B (2513). The curvilinear ditch (2309), appeared at the north-west corner of Site 94 and ran south-eastwards for a metre before intersecting with the edge of ditch 2308; it was not identified beyond that point, though the geophysical survey indicated its course should have continued south-eastwards. It was in the form of a small, shallow, steep-sided cut, and was recorded as having been cut by the rectilinear enclosure ditch. The reliability of this observation is re-examined below.

In Phase 2 the east-west rectilinear enclosure ditch fell out of use and became partly infilled. Phase 3 marked its reuse in Middle Saxon times, though not this time as a

ditch: in Site 95A its north and south sides were cut back to form the edges of a *Grubenhaus*. The structure was 3-3.6m wide, north to south, and its length must have been no greater than 7m, as it was not seen to extend into either Site 94 or Site 95B. An area of 'vitrified' chalk (2436) with patches of blue-green ash (2435) and compacted silty clay (2434) indicated the position of a central 'hearth'. Around this, the position of a three-sided screen was suggested by stake-holes; the functions of the remaining stake-holes remained unclear, but they were thought likely to represent internal partitions or equipment.

This building was interpreted as a non-ferrous metal workshop. Though the *in situ* features indicating use were limited to the 'hearth' and the ash deposits, the backfill of the *Grubenhaus* contained, among other refuse, fragments of clay crucibles, moulds and tuyère blocks indicative of non-ferrous metalworking (Bayley 1992, 59-65). Whilst Julian Richards acknowledged the possibility that the debris came from a different building (Richards 1992b, 82-3), he is surely right, in the light of the data currently available, to have suggested that the metalworking debris had been thrown out of the building during metalworking operations, and then reintroduced into its backfill when it was abandoned.

The precise significance of the 'hearth' is worth revisiting, particularly in the context of Gerry

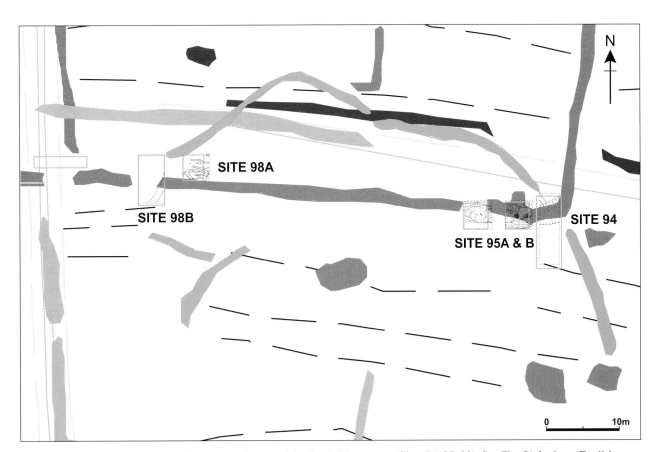

Fig. 52. Middle Saxon and earlier features north-west of the South Manor area (Sites 94, 95, 98). See Fig. 51 for key. (English Heritage and E. Marlow-Mann)

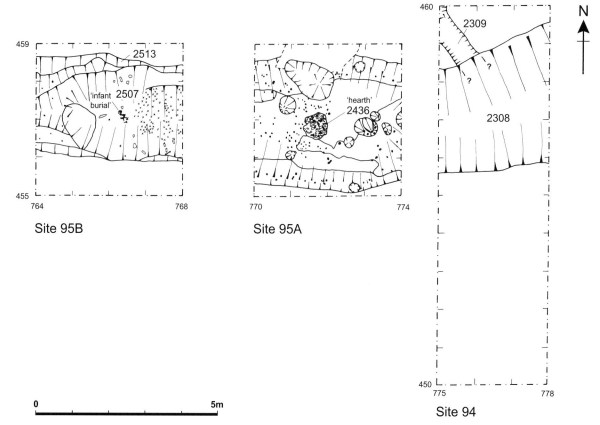

Fig. 53. Plan of excavated features in Sites 94 and 95. (E. Marlow-Mann)

McDonnell's review of the structural attributes of the Middle Saxon smithy in the South Manor Area (pp 157-8), where he postulates a waist-high hearth rather than one set on the floor. Justine Bayley has kindly provided an equivalent review of the structural evidence relating to the non-ferrous metal workshop in Site 95A:

'Secondary metalworking, such as melting and casting small quantities of copper alloys, would normally have been carried out indoors as the smith/craftsman would need to see the colour of the fire so he could judge when the metal had melted. It is thus quite likely that this metalworking was carried out in the *Grubenhaus*. The size of the hearth that was used to melt metal in crucibles like those found would probably have held a fire only 150-200mm across. The fuel used would have been charcoal, so some sort of container was required to stop the air blast from the bellows moving the fire about - the vitrified clay hearth lining and tuyère blocks would have been parts of such a structure.

Context 2436 (the 'hearth' in the base of the *Grubenhaus*) is about 0.7m across, and seems far too large to have been used to melt metals in the crucibles found. The chalk is not 'vitrified' in the normal meaning of the term, as vitrification is produced by reaction of an alkali, usually the ash in a fire, with a silica-rich material like clay or a silicate-containing rock/stone such as sandstone. Chalk is calcium carbonate and so contains nothing that would react with ash at high temperatures to produce a vitreous (glassy) surface.

The lack of any floor-level feature that can be positively identified as a hearth associated with the metalworking debris could be used to suggest a raised hearth, though arguing from lack of evidence is always questionable. The hearth would have been a relatively small structure, probably made of clay as there is no ready supply of local stone, that could have been constructed above the contemporary floor level. It might have been supported on some of the small stakes that have left holes in the floor, though a 'log cabin' type of structure with an earth-covered timber top could also have supported a raised hearth, and would have left no archaeological trace.

Wharram Percy is not alone in lacking good evidence for the form of the hearth used for metalworking. I can think of no example, of any date, where a hearth that can be positively associated with secondary metalworking has been identified. The relatively rare pictorial evidence from Roman and later times (e.g. gravestones, sarcophagi, carvings on churches, illuminated manuscripts) all suggests above-ground hearths were used by European metalworkers for most of the last two millennia. Against this can be set recent ethnographic evidence from other parts of the world which record hearths set on or into the ground.'

It is possible to take these suggestions a little further. The floor of the building around the 'hearth' contained numerous stake-holes, and whilst it is difficult to resolve them into coherent patterns (whether left by 'screens', as initially proposed, or otherwise), it is worth considering them in relation to the features of a well-preserved clay-built Roman oven found in excavations at Walton-le-Dale near Preston, Lancashire (personal observation; see Burnham *et al.* 1998, 390). The Roman oven had been constructed on a skeleton formed by vertical stakes with wattles woven around them. The stakes had been rammed into the ground not only in the positions marking the oven walls, but also into the floor within the structure. Wattles were woven around them, both to create the shape of the walls and to form the raised floor. Thick clay was applied to the skeleton, and the structure was then fired to harden the clay. This procedure left stake and wattle impressions in the clay walls, and holes in the surviving raised floor marking the former positions of the internal stakes, with stake-holes clearly visible in the ground directly below them. This method of construction, with frequent reconstruction on the same site, may account for clusters of stake-holes associated with other 'hearth'-type features, as in Site 95A.

Beyond the east and west ends of this *Grubenhaus*, in Sites 94 and 95B, the partly-filled former enclosure ditch contained layers of ash and burnt material that presumably represented debris from the metalworking processes: layers 2304 and 2306 in Site 94, and layer 2504 in Site 95B. Similar material (2305) built up in the north-west to south-east ditch (2309), and it is this (apparently a primary fill, see Richards 1992a, 23 and fig. 13) that suggests the recorded sequence of ditches (2308 cutting 2309) may be a misinterpretation, allowing ditch 2309 to be a length of curvilinear Middle Saxon ditch. It is difficult to believe that ditch 2309 could have been sufficiently empty to take deposit 2305 in Middle Saxon times if it had become disused at the time when the Iron Age/Early Roman ladder settlement ditch was dug.

The final aspect of these sites that is worth revisiting is the infant burial found in Site 95B near the disarticulated partial remains of a sheep (Richards 1992a, 20-23, fig. 11

and pl.14; Richards 1992b, 84-5). These remains appeared to have been placed on the surface of a layer (2507) which was similar to but less compact than the Phase 2 ditch fill. Though it contained only Roman pottery, layer 2507 was interpreted as redeposited ditch fill, dumped here when the *Grubenhaus* was created. If the infant and the sheep bones were deposited at the same time, their combined radiocarbon determinations would place *Grubenhaus* construction broadly in the first half of the 7th century (Richards 1992b, 84); yet the metalworking moulds have been dated no earlier than the 8th century and no later than the early 9th (Richards 1992b, 83). This suggests that the *Grubenhaus* may have been built for a purpose other than metalworking – perhaps a shepherd's hut in Wharram's transhumance phase – and maintained that purpose for more than half a century before being converted into a metalworking building.

Site 94 produced, among other items, one of the two Frisian brooches from Wharram thought to date to the 6th century (Goodall with Ager 1992, fig. 25, no.14), and one of four glass beads from these sites that could be Early Saxon (94/SF33, 95/SF73, 95/SF112, 95/SF132, Ch. 10 and Plate 15), along with a fragment of an 8th-century stone cross (Clark 1992, 43). Sites 94 and 95 together produced over 200 sherds of Middle Saxon pottery.

Sites 98A and 98B (Figs 52 and 54; see ADS report, doi:10.5284/1000415

Sites 98A and 98B were excavated in 1990 about 40m to the west of Sites 94, 95A and 95B, again on the line of the geophysical anomaly representing the Iron Age/Early Roman east-west enclosure ditch, and again at a point where that anomaly intersected with what appeared to be a stretch of curvilinear ditch, possibly a continuation of ditch 2309 in Site 94.

In Site 98A the south side of the trench exposed part of the northern edge of the enclosure ditch (2624). Site 98B, a longer trench extending further south, revealed the

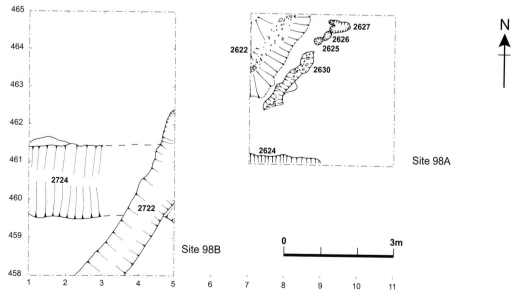

Fig. 54. Plan of excavated features in Sites 98a and 98B. (E. Marlow-Mann)

whole width of the same ditch (here 2724, and much the same width as in Site 95B). Before it had silted up fully the ditch in Site 98B had been cut by a narrower ditch (2722) which ran from south-west to north-east diagonally across the south-east corner of the site. The cut feature 2622 in the north-west corner of Site 98A was presumably part of the same ditch. A Middle Saxon sherd came from its primary fill (2617).

Immediately east of ditch 2622 in Site 98A, and on a comparable alignment, were a gully (2630) and three ovoid cut features (2625, 2626 and 2627). Because of their alignment these are likely to be contemporary with the ditch, and all are potentially part of the Middle Saxon curvilinear enclosure settlement. The two trenches produced only three sherds of Middle Saxon pottery.

Sites 59, 76, 81, 85, 90, 93 (South Manor Area) (Fig. 55; see *Wharram VIII*)

The excavations in the South Manor Area between 1981 and 1990 produced what is so far Wharram's largest assemblage of Middle Saxon and Anglo-Scandinavian finds, and it also produced some overall stratigraphy to help define successive phases of activity. Unfortunately, the interpretation of the stratigraphy is not entirely straightforward. There were two main layers running across most of these sites: an upper layer of dark brown to black loam, and beneath it a layer of yellow-brown

loam. Cut into the yellow-brown loam were two ditches (105/137/146 and 37/52), running east to west on roughly parallel courses. The more northerly ditch, 37/52, was the later of the two: it was recognised as soon as the dark brown/black loam had been removed, and one question to which there is no clear answer is whether it had been cut from this surface, or whether it had been cut, undetected, from a higher level. Ditch 105/137/146, in contrast, was revealed only after the removal of about 0.10m of yellow-brown loam (Stamper *et al.* 2000, 28).

The earlier ditch contained about fifty sherds of Anglo-Saxon pottery dating to the Middle Saxon period, with four post-Conquest, clearly intrusive pieces, and nothing in between. The two fills of the later ditch also contained mainly Middle Saxon sherds (excluding a large part of a Staxton ware jar: Stamper *et al.* 2000, 28), but with a greater proportion of later material, and including pottery of the Late Saxon period (e.g. Torksey-type ware). The profiles of the ceramic assemblages from the yellow-brown loam and the black loam were not dissimilar to those of, respectively, the earlier and later ditches (Slowikowski 2000, 85-6, table 10).

The issue of contamination through unrecorded intrusions into the loams and ditch fills is one that was discussed in the South Manor Area report (Stamper *et al.* 2000, 20 and figs 11 and 12), but its cause remained undetected, and its impact is therefore unmeasurable.

Fig. 55. Middle Saxon features in the South Manor area. (E. Marlow-Mann)

Contamination was inferred because layers that are assumed to be pre-Conquest in date contained post-Conquest artefacts. This may not, however, be the whole story, at least for the black loam. It is possible that this soil developed over a considerable time, starting in the Middle Saxon period, but that its constituent layers were at some point intermingled and homogenised through ploughing.

One further depositional characteristic is worth noting before the structural evidence is reviewed in detail. The surface of the yellow-brown loam was different in the northern halves of Sites 59 and 85, at the northern end of the excavations:

'The surface of the yellow-brown loam… contained relatively large sherds of pottery and whole bones such as sheep's jaws, material which, if exposed for any length of time, could have been expected to fragment. The conclusion is that, when occupation associated with the yellow-brown loam came to an end (perhaps in the 9th century), the surfaces were immediately covered with soil. (Stamper et al. 2000, 20)

The recorded line of the southern edge of the 'bone littered soils' follows quite closely the line of the later of the two east-west ditches (cf. Stamper et al. 2000, figs 8 and 16), which must surely open up the possibility that, when this ditch was being dug, its upcast was heaped on the north side, to form a spread or bank that quickly degraded. This in turn would strengthen the possibility, noted above, that the ditch was created for activities that occurred in the lowest part of the black loam deposit.

Large numbers of post-holes were recorded south of the east-west ditches, though most of them were unrecognised until the point at which they penetrated natural. Therefore the identification of buildings represented by post-holes was dependent on morphological characteristics, spacing and alignment, rather than stratification. One post-hole building was recognised during the excavations: Building A (Stamper et al. 2000, 29 and fig. 18); another was suggested in the excavation report (Stamper et al. 2000, 32), here termed Building B. It is possible to develop a chronological phasing for the buildings, and between the buildings and the main east-west ditches.

Figure 55 shows Building A as delineated in Stamper et al. 2000 (31, fig. 18), and the possible Building B. Only the west end and north side of Building B are clearly marked by alignments of post-holes, but the east end may have been formed (or obscured) by slot 63. The absence of post-holes forming a south side may be explained, as suggested in Stamper et al. 2000 (p. 32), by a loss of information at the junction of Sites 81 and 93 – witness the abrupt termination of the record of pit 118 on the boundary between the two sites. The east end of Building A is, similarly, unrecorded, though no reason for this can be suggested. Pit 124 was treated in the published report as an associated feature of Building A, located immediately east of the building's south-east corner. It was, nevertheless, allowed as possibly being earlier than Building A (Stamper et al. 2000, 31-2), an interpretation that is developed below.

It is clear from the plan that, if their forms were as shown on Figure 55, Buildings A and B could not have coexisted. Though there is no firm evidence as to which came first, there are circumstantial grounds for suggesting that Building B was the earlier of the two. Its alignment is close to that of the earlier east-west ditch, whereas Building A is not merely out of alignment; its north side is so close to the line of the earlier ditch that it is difficult to imagine the two having been in use at the same time – especially if ditch 69 continued the boundary westwards beyond the termination of ditch 105/137/146. Pit 124 could have been an internal feature of Building B, whatever its function.

The recovery of large amounts of hearth lining, smithing slag and cinder indicates that this part of the settlement was the location of a smithy, an identification confirmed by the presence of the smith's stock material – bars and rods of iron (McDonnell 2000, 162-3). In terms of structural features and deposits there was limited *in situ* evidence of smithing operations, save for a few isolated patches of burnt clay, ash and slag. Radiocarbon dates from charcoal associated with these patches indicated a possibly lengthy period of smithing, from the 7th to the 9th centuries. Charcoal from hollow 148, which cut the earlier east-west ditch, provided a date range of AD 780-1010 (Stamper et al. 2000, 35). It is noticeable that the *in situ* debris was largely confined to the upper fills of the earlier east-west ditch (Stamper et al. 2000, fig. 19, contexts 59/55 and 76/73), again suggesting that this area had been ploughed subsequently, and that the only patches to survive this were those that had sunk into the ditch or other hollows, below ploughing depth. Gerry McDonnell reviews the whole of the smithing evidence in Chapter 10 below, and suggests that the smithy itself may be represented by Building A, containing a structure supporting a waist-high hearth, built of stone or timber, and the hearth itself built of stone or timber lined with clay. We might also speculate that Building B was its predecessor.

Artefacts from associated layers and feature fills are discussed in Chapter 10. They include a copper-alloy belt fitting (59/SF466, Plate 15), eight pins (including 85/SF067, Plate 16; 85/SF118, Plate 16), fragments from four combs (including 59/SF348, Plate 16; 81/SF323, Plate 16; 85/SF242, Plate 15), a fragment of a glass vessel, a mount (59/SF303), a spearhead fragment (85/SF77), two spindle whorls (59/SF344, 76/SF293) and nine Early or Middle Saxon glass beads (59/SF293; 59/SF386; 59/SF482; 76/SF262; 81/SF29; 81/SF326; 81/SF334; 85/SF304; 93/SF33, all Plate 15). Excavations in the South Manor Area as a whole produced almost 2,500 sherds of Middle Saxon pottery.

Western Plateau (South) sites

Site 70 (Figs 56 -58; Plate 13; see ADS report, doi:10.5284/1000415)
Site 70 is one of the Plateau sites that has not previously been reported. It was excavated in 1981-3 in advance of tree-planting on the edge of the Guardianship area. Periods 1 and 2 were represented by possible tree-holes

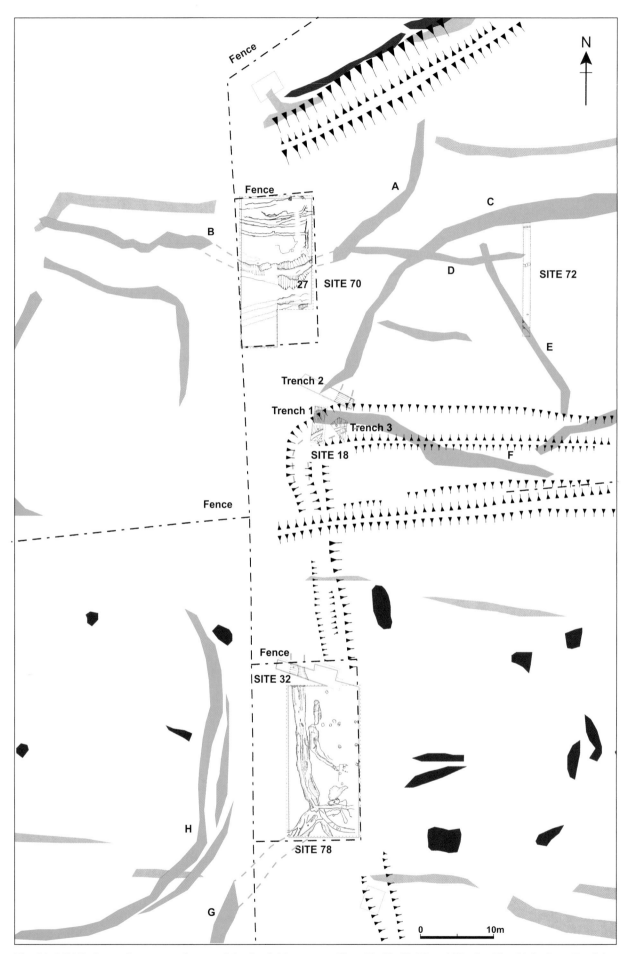

Fig. 56. Middle Saxon features south-west of the South Manor area (Sites 18, 32, 70, 72 and 78). See Fig. 51 for key. (English Heritage and E. Marlow-Mann)

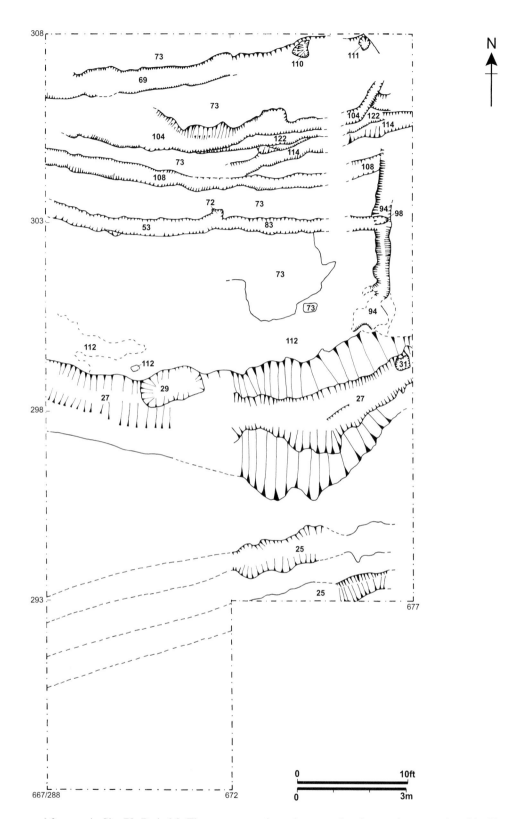

Fig. 57. Plan of excavated features in Site 70, Period 3. The context numbers shown on the plan are those mentioned in Chapters 9 and 10. (E. Marlow-Mann)

and a few post-holes of prehistoric and Roman date. Period 3 features, assigned a Middle Saxon date, were much more numerous. The earliest major linear feature uncovered was a ditch (27) which ran east to west on what appeared to be a curving course. It was undoubtedly a continuation of geophysical anomalies A and B on Figure 56, and if part of a curvilinear enclosure boundary would have enclosed the area to the north. It was 2m to 3.5m wide at the highest level at which it was visible, with a flat base about 0.5m wide.

North of ditch 27 was a series of narrower, shallower east-west gullies, some curving and all running generally in alignment with the ditch. Though believed by the excavator to be cart ruts, some at least may instead have been structural features relating either to successive buildings or to small compounds. Gullies 114 and 122 were both said to have near vertical sides and a flat base (though the recorded section of 114 has a more V-shaped profile). The positions of gullies 94 and 83, with post-hole 98, containing chalk packing, at their junction, again suggest roofed buildings or small compounds.

South of ditch 27 were two linear depressions of compacted chalk (25), their centres about 1.2m apart.

These were also interpreted as cart ruts. They appear to result from passing traffic of some sort, though they could be much later in date given the shallowness of the soil in this area (see Plate 13). Overall, Period 3 contexts produced 27 sherds of pottery, eleven being Late Roman and up to sixteen, Middle Saxon. Of the various gullies in the northern part of the trench, the fills of 69, 94, 114 and 122 produced twelve sherds of Middle Saxon pottery including one of Whitby-type ware.

The principal Period 4 features were three straight ditches, 67, 89 and 95 (Fig. 58). The earliest in the sequence was the north-south ditch 95, which produced only Roman sherds from its primary fill (105) but four sherds of 12th to 14th-century pottery from its secondary fill (81). The later east-west ditch 67, however, contained only Roman and Middle Saxon pottery, and the subsequent north-south ditch 89 contained Roman and Anglo-Saxon pottery with a single sherd of Late Saxon Torksey-type ware (fill 88). Given that ditch 95 was sectioned longitudinally by the eastern baulk of Site 70 it is conceivable that the High Medieval sherds from its secondary fill were either intrusive or were introduced at the time of the disuse of this sequence of features.

Plate 13. Site 70, general view of Period 3 and Period 4 features, from north-east (Wharram Site Archive)

128

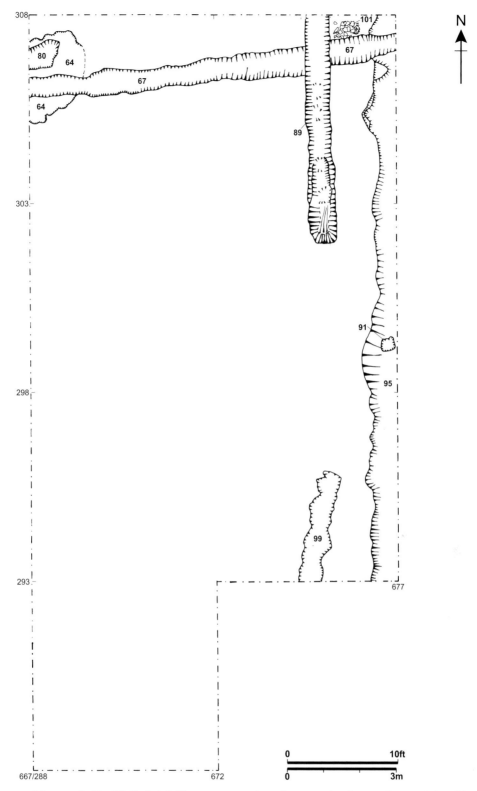

Fig. 58. Plan of excavated features in Site 70, Period 4. The context numbers shown on the plan are those mentioned in Chapters 9 and 10. (E. Marlow-Mann)

Also attributed to Period 4 was a hearth (101) at the north-east corner of the site. It was constructed from a broken rotary quernstone, the upper surface of which was burnt. There was no indication as to its function. It overlay the fill of Period 3 gully 69, and was therefore assigned to Period 4. On the other hand it is unlikely to have been in use with any of the three ditches in close proximity to it, and seems, indeed, to have possibly been truncated by ditch 67. It may therefore have been a secondary feature of Period 3, within the enclosure formed by ditch 27, rather than Period 4 in origin. Context 19, the soil that covered the Period 4 features, contained three Middle Saxon small finds: a copper-alloy buckle and plate (70/SF170, Plate 15), a pin (70/SF145,

Plate 16), a glass bead (70/SF49, Plate 15), and a sherd of Middle Saxon pottery out of a total of twenty for the site as a whole.

Thus, the overall sequence in Site 70 is a putative Middle Saxon curvilinear enclosure with some internal structures and a possible hearth (not necessarily domestic), followed by a series of ditches marking subsequent rectilinear enclosures or land divisions. Though the latter could not be linked directly to the geophysical plot, they perhaps echo the straighter linear anomalies. They were perhaps broadly contemporary with the Period 3 features in Site 78 (below) which appear to be Late Saxon or Norman in date.

Site 72 (Fig. 56; see ADS report, doi:10.5284/1000415)
Site 72 was excavated in 1982 in order to check the eastward continuation of various features recorded in Site 70. It uncovered three ditches, the northernmost, ditch 4, being part-sectioned longitudinally by the northern end of the trench. It produced no pottery. Despite a slight misalignment of recorded positions, there is no doubt that this represents the edge of another curvilinear enclosure ditch, ditch C on the geophysics plot on Figure 56.

Towards the centre of the trench, ditch 7 appeared to run into the excavation from the west and terminate close to the eastern side of the trench. Again, though the excavated ditch was on a more southerly alignment than geophysical anomaly D on Figure 56, the two records are undoubtedly derived from the same feature. The western end of D was obscured by anomaly A, but it may have formed a junction with the north-south ditch 95 in Site 70, being part of the rectilinear pattern of boundaries post-dating the curvilinear enclosures.

The remaining feature encountered in this trench was ditch 8, towards its southern end, running on a north-west to south-east alignment. This conformed to anomaly E on the geophysics plot. It was 0.5-0.6m wide and its fill (5) contained window glass. Only one sherd of Middle Saxon pottery was recovered from a later layer.

Site 18 (Fig. 56; ADS report, doi:10.5284/1000415)
The three small trenches grouped together as Site 18 were dug in 1970 to investigate the line of the so-called 'inner boundary ditch', a north-south ditch which delineated the ends of the West Row (south) crofts, at the point where that boundary turned eastwards. This ditch was recorded by the Ordnance Survey in the mid-19th century, and though ploughed in the early 1960s it can still be seen as a slight earthwork (see Ch. 3).

The earliest feature was ditch 3 (context 13 in trench 2 and 24 in trench 3), approximately 0.61m wide and 0.23m deep. It probably continued the course of geophysical anomaly C. It certainly predated the 'inner boundary ditch' which was recorded in trenches 1 and 3 on its anticipated course. The latter was only 0.3m to 0.5m wide and 0.13m deep. Its course eastwards may be marked by anomaly F.

Sites 32 and 78 (Figs 56 and 59-61; Plate 14; ADS report, doi:10.5284/1000415)
The Site 32 trench was excavated in 1972 to investigate two parallel, north-south anomalies recorded during the 1971 geophysical survey. It was also on the line of the 'inner boundary ditch' explored further north (see above, Site 18). Site 78, excavated between 1984 and 1986 immediately south of Site 32 in advance of tree-planting, provided an opportunity to explore a more extensive area of these same features. The results of the two investigations are described together.

The earliest features (Period 1) in Site 78 were two adjacent north-south ditches, numbered 117 and 119 (Fig. 59). They were not excavated because of time constraints, but their 'surface' widths ranged from 0.95m to 1.55m where they were visible as separate entities. Their fills were recorded as orange-grey clayey loam, probably equivalent to the dark red clay fills of ditches 2 and 3 in Site 32. In Site 78 they were overlain by a deposit of compacted chalk fragments in grey loam (59, 105-9) that contained (mainly) late Roman and earlier pottery. They represented presumably, successive phases of a field boundary relating to the later Iron Age to late Roman farm(s) further north, though the number of artefacts could indicate a further habitation site on this part of the plateau.

Cutting through layer 59 were Period 2 ditches, gullies, post-holes and other features less easy to categorise, all or most of which can be assigned to Wharram's Middle Saxon settlement (Fig. 60). Only one of them, a substantial ditch (56) running north-eastwards from the south-west corner of the excavation, seemed to be related to a geophysics linear anomaly (G on Fig. 56), but this is probably because of the proximity of the Guardianship area hedge and fence which masked responses in its vicinity. Ditch 56 produced two fragments of ceramic mould and a sherd of (?intrusive) late medieval pot from its fill (55). This ditch and anomaly G could mark stretches of the north-west sector of a curvilinear enclosure boundary, separated by a trackway from a neighbouring enclosure to the west which was itself marked by the roughly parallel anomalies labelled H.

Similarly, ditch 22 may have defined another enclosure on the east side of the boundary marked by anomaly H. It appeared initially to have a width ranging from 1.3m to 2.1m, but when excavated proved to have been formed from two narrower, parallel ditches, one presumably marking a recut. A similar phenomenon may also explain the form of the anomalies at H on Figure 56. Ditch 22 was represented by Ditch 1 in Site 32, where only one cut was observed. In Site 78, its fill (13) contained nine sherds of Middle Saxon pottery and a fragment of a Middle Saxon comb (78/SF399, Plate 16). It also produced evidence of nearby metalworking, in the form of hearth lining and slag.

It was not possible to determine the relationship of ditches 56 and 22, though if, as appears possible in terms of alignment, the more westerly manifestation of ditch 22

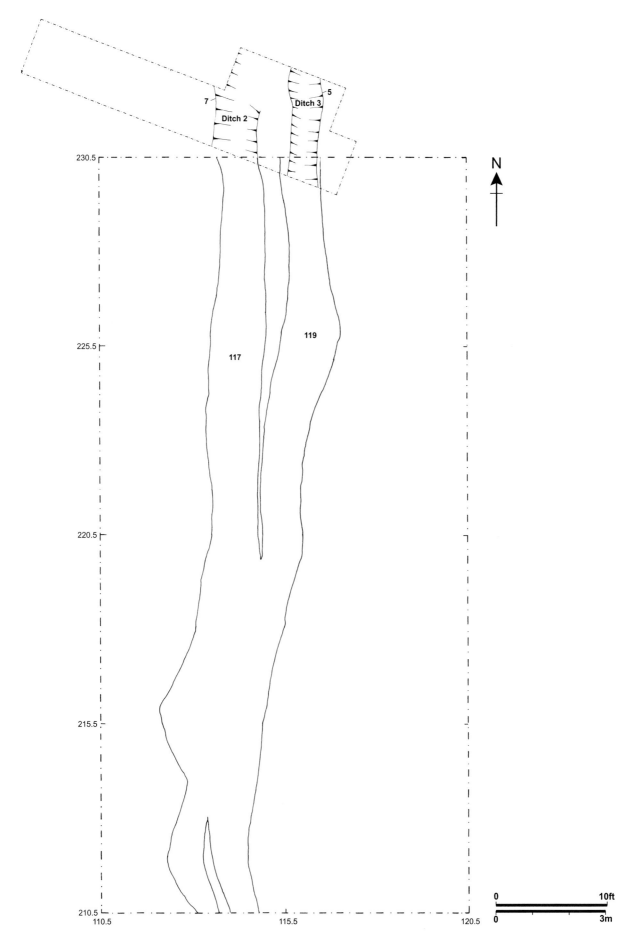

Fig. 59. Plan of excavated features in Site 78, Period 1 (including Site 32). (E. Marlow-Mann)

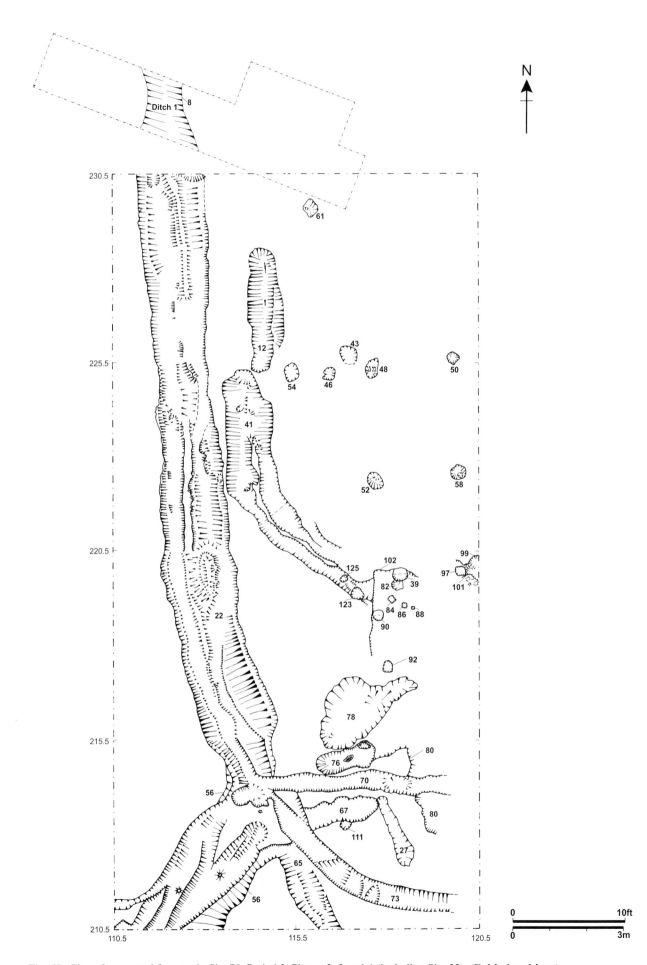

Fig. 60. Plan of excavated features in Site 78, Period 2, Phases 2, 3 and 4 (including Site 32). (E. Marlow-Mann)

curved eastwards as ditch 73 (Plate 14), and the more easterly cut continued south-eastwards as ditch 65, it would follow that ditch 56 bounds an addition to the original enclosure.

Plate 14. Site 78 general view of Period 2 features, from the north-west (Wharram Site Archive)

East of ditch 22, stretches of gullies, again of two phases each (12 and 41), may have bounded the western end of a timber building on an east-west alignment. Finds from deposit 40, the fill of 41, included two sherds of Middle Saxon pottery and one piece of Staxton ware. The building itself was represented by post-holes 48, 50, 52 and 58 (and possibly 54 as well). It ran presumably eastwards into the unexcavated ground. To the south were further post-holes, short lengths of gully and some cut edges with flat bases no more than 100mm deep. Some of these, in particular the cut edge 102 and post-holes within it, represent further structures, but their forms have not been resolved.

A layer of humic loam with chalk fragments containing large amounts of stone (29), including querns, appeared to cover the fills of the enclosure ditches in the southern half of the site, marking the disuse of the earlier features. It contained over twenty sherds of Middle Saxon pottery, including four of Whitby-type ware, a sherd of Torksey-type ware and a tiny chip of Brandsby-type pottery. The other Anglo-Saxon object was a Middle Saxon pin (78/SF413). Hearth bottom slag and hearth lining presumably derive from the metalworking operations already attested from debris in the fill of ditch 22.

Far fewer features were assigned to Period 3, which overlay deposit 29 (Fig. 61). In the southern half of the site towards the centre was a rather amorphous deposit (21) of medium and large fragments of limestone and 'lava stone', the latter presumably derived from a reused quern or millstone.

Further quernstone fragments are recorded (only photographically) from a more substantial structural feature at the southern edge of the site: a sandstone oven base (20), roughly oval in shape and measuring about 1.85m by 1.5m. It was surrounded by a thin deposit of light yellow daub fragments (34), presumably derived from the superstructure. An edge to the area of intense burning, running across the outermost fragmented floor slabs, marked the inner edge of the oven wall; the floor was presumably at waist height. A gap in the spread of deposit 34 on the south-west side, filled by layer 30 containing burnt daub and charcoal fragments, probably marked the position of the stoke-hole. Gully 113, with largely vertical sides and only 0.15m deep from the point where it was first observed, perhaps marks the position of a screen used to channel the wind into the fire. Its primary fill contained burnt debris similar to that associated with the hearth. Magnetic remanence dating indicated that final firing took place in AD 1110 +/- 60 at a 95% level of confidence (reported by Tony Clark, 5 July 1986).

The final feature assigned to Period 3 was another north-south ditch (28) running nearly parallel to the eastern side of the excavation. Its course shifted to a slightly more westerly alignment as it approached the northern end of Site 78 and, as Ditch 4 in Site 32, this shift became more pronounced. Its secondary fill (16) contained the burial of a dog, as well as nine sherds of Middle-Saxon pottery, two Late Saxon sherds and nine fragments of later vessels. The dating of the hearth indicates that Period 3 should be assigned to the late 11th or 12th century, perhaps broadly contemporary with the rectilinear ditches (Period 4) in Site 70.

The topsoil of Period 4 contained several Middle Saxon objects: two beads (78/SF057; 78/SF080 and 78/SF078, Plate 15), a bone comb (78/SF112 and 78/SF528), and two pins (78/SF1 Plate 16; 78/SF513). There was also a Middle Saxon pin from Site 31, a small square trench dug into the 'inner boundary' earthwork to the south of Site 78 (31/SF001, Plate 16). In total, the site produced more than 150 sherds of Middle Saxon pottery.

Site 86 (Fig. 51; ADS report, doi:10.5284/1000415)
Site 86, at the southern end of the Plateau on the slope down to Druedale, was another area investigated in advance of tree-planting. Two early structural features were uncovered. The first was a gully (84) running on a south-west to north-east course through a southwards extension of the trench at its south-west corner. This is undated. So, too, is a broad terrace cut (80) running east-west through the centre of the site; the northern, uphill side of which appeared to have been revetted by vertical timbers (76). Only two small areas of the cut and its filling layers were excavated. At some point the terrace seems to have been recut (79) through the fills. Cut 79 was itself then filled with a series of layers, probably the result of silting and hillwash.

None of this activity could be assigned with certainty to the Anglo-Saxon period, despite the significant quantity of Anglo-Saxon artefacts recovered from the

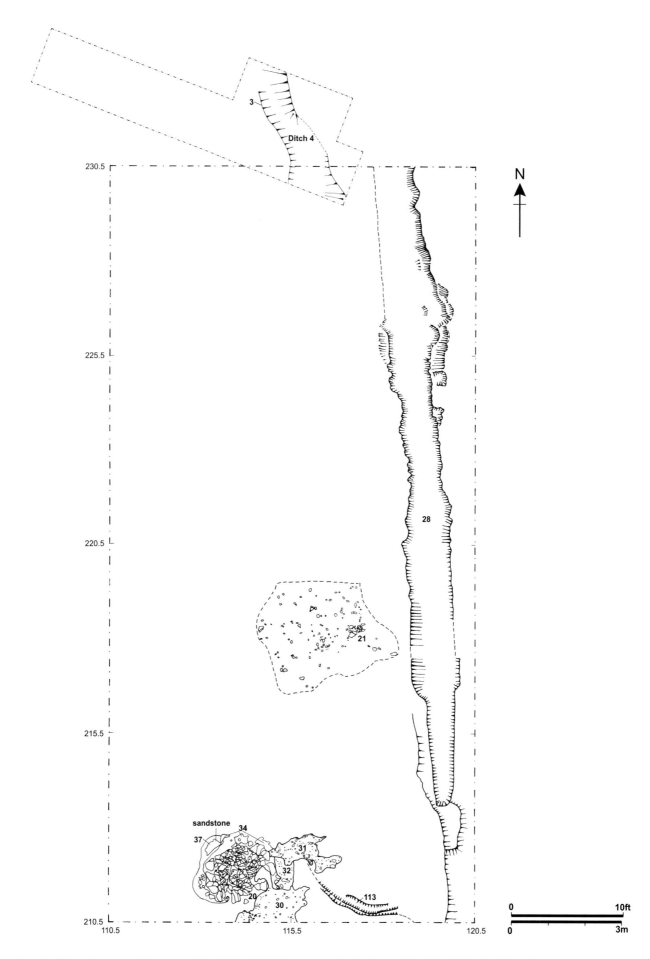

Fig. 61. Plan of excavated features in Site 78, Period 3, Phases 1 and 2 (including Site 32). (E. Marlow-Mann)

associated deposits and the site as a whole, including over a hundred sherds of Middle Saxon pottery. No pottery was recovered from the fills of the original terrace cut, though the fills of the recut contained Middle Saxon as well as later pottery. The next structure in the sequence was a post-Conquest building with stone foundations. Besides Middle Saxon and later pottery, the terrace recut fills also contained several fragments of lava quern. There were also numerous fragments of burnt daub with wattle impressions and several lumps of slag.

On current evidence it is impossible to say whether the primary features were Anglo-Saxon or later, or what precisely they signify. Given the quantity of Anglo-Saxon artefacts, however, they were either of this date, or close to an area of Anglo-Saxon activity, presumably on the uphill side of the site.

Site 12 (Area 6; Fig. 51; see Milne 1979b, 42-54)
Site 12, excavated and published as Area 6, is the only open-area excavation to have taken place within the West Row (south) tofts. It produced one of the most notable Middle Saxon stone artefacts: two joining pieces of Anglo-Saxon cross-arm dated to the late 8th century (Lang 1991, 222). It was, however, residual in its context – the fill of a 'Saxo-Norman' boundary ditch, and only about twenty pre-10th-century potsherds were recovered, all in contexts that also produced later pottery (Milne 1979b, 46; Le Patourel 1979, 77-80; Andrews 1979a, 124).

Valley sites

Sites 26, 41, Churchyard and Dam (see Harding and Marlow-Mann 2007, 29; Harding 2007, 34-6; Harding and Wrathmell 2007, 327-9)
The creation of the burial ground seems to have occurred in the second half of the 10th century, and the erection of the first stone church at a slightly later date. There are, however, some structures that indicate activity in this part of the valley earlier in the Anglo-Saxon period, though perhaps not much earlier, given the paucity of Middle Saxon artefacts from the valley when compared to the plateau sites (Ch. 10 below). These are a possible *Grubenhaus* north of the church and a structure indicated by substantial post-holes further north, in Site 26.

South-east of the burial ground, the radiocarbon determinations for successive structures associated with water management suggest that the earliest phase of dam construction should be assigned either to the later part of the Middle Saxon period or to the Late Saxon period. If in the latter period, it still seems likely to predate the creation of the burial ground (Bayliss 2005, 222). Middle Saxon finds from these sites include two pins (26/SF60, Plate 16; 26/SF30), a hooked tag (30/SF43, Plate 16), a strap end (26/SF115, Plate 16) and under ten sherds of pottery.

Having reviewed briefly the main groups of excavated structural remains that can be assigned with a fair degree of probability to the Middle Saxon period, it is now time to review Middle Saxon artefacts from across the whole village area in more detail.

10 Characterising Middle Saxon Wharram: Artefacts and the Iron Economy

Early and Middle Saxon artefacts
by Ian Riddler, with contributions from Ann Clark and Anna Slowikowski

Introduction
Anglo-Saxon objects have formed a significant part of the material culture of Wharram throughout its long period of excavation. Several were published in the first of the Wharram excavation monographs, alongside small quantities of Anglo-Saxon ceramics (*Wharram I*, 77-82 and figs 55.12, 66, 70 and 71) and they have appeared in almost every subsequent volume. An attempt has been made in this volume to bring together the evidence for material culture of the Anglo-Saxon period and to review it in terms of a series of research aims, which were agreed in advance of the study. These included confirmation (or otherwise) that the curvilinear enclosures and associated features are of Middle Saxon date; the characterisation of Middle Saxon settlement activity at Wharram; the date when the settlement was established and when it was replaced by the earliest elements of the medieval village as it is known from the surviving earthworks. The last of these questions is addressed in Chapter 13 below.

In order to address the research aims, it was necessary to look first of all at the Anglo-Saxon small finds from all the excavation sites and to examine the evidence for the intrinsic dating provided by the objects themselves, rather than the dating of the contexts in which they had been found. This included the Western Plateau sites which are published in summary form for the first time in this volume (Ch. 9). The context dating was then compared with the object dating, to provide a corpus of Anglo-Saxon material. The spatial distribution of the objects across the Wharram landscape has also been considered, in an attempt to map settlement activity. The Early and Middle Saxon material culture is considered in this chapter, whilst material assigned to the Late Saxon period is discussed in Chapter 13. The codes identifying individual objects are in the form: site number/small find number.

Relative and absolute chronologies
The majority of the Anglo-Saxon objects and ceramics from Wharram belong to the Middle Saxon period. Some of them were found in stratified deposits, whilst others are unstratified or residual in later contexts (a common problem at Wharram). Each individual site has been phased by its excavator, and in some cases, notably in the North Manor Area, phases for a series of sites have been amalgamated into a larger scheme, although there is no overall scheme for the entire landscape. The objects and ceramics have been considered in this volume in terms of

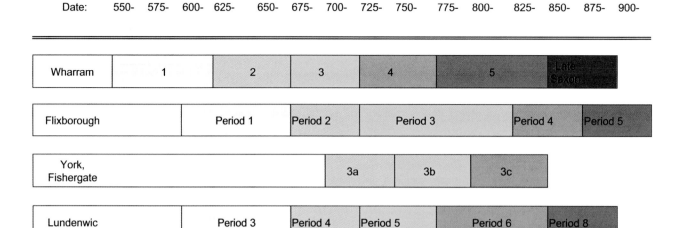

Fig. 62. Middle Saxon artefact phases at Wharram, and the equivalent phases or periods identified at other key sites. Note: *Lundenwic* Period 7 covers the entire period *c*. 600-900. Precise dates for the Wharram *Phases* are given below. (I. Riddler)

a single scheme, which begins in the Early Saxon period and continues to the 12th century. A concordance of objects, their site phases and overall phasing is provided in the Site Archive.

A series of publications dealing with Anglo-Saxon material culture formed the basis of the analysis, providing object dating and helping to establish the sequence of overall phases. The question of phases for the Middle Saxon period has inevitably been led by work on urban settlements (Fig. 62). The site at Fishergate in York was divided into three Middle Saxon phases spanning the 8th century and the first half of the 9th century, although the recent work on a nearby site simply identifies a single Middle Saxon period and an Anglo-Scandinavian period (Kemp 1996; Rogers 1993, 1205-11; Spall and Toop 2005). Five Middle Saxon periods were identified at Flixborough, as well as a number of phases within the periods (Loveluck and Atkinson 2007, fig. 2.21). Ceramics from the Royal Opera House excavations in *Lundenwic* formed the basis for the identification of six Middle Saxon periods there (Malcolm *et al.* 2003, 141-3). The *Lundenwic* phases have been adapted here in the light of recent work at both *Hamwic* and Ipswich, which has pushed the inception of these settlements back into the first half of the 7th century (Birbeck 2005; Scull 2009).

Comparisons have also be made with other Anglo-Saxon sites in the region, in terms of their phasing and material culture. Within Yorkshire, Naylor identified nine principal Middle Saxon sites, including Beverley, Caythorpe, Cottam, South Newbald, Thwing, West Heslerton, Whitby and York, as well as Wharram (Naylor 2004, 27-37). An extension of the study area a little to the south of the Humber allows Flixborough and Riby Cross Roads to be added to this list.

With these sequences in mind, a series of five artefact *Phases* (Italicised to distinguish them from the site phases) has been used for Wharram, as follows:

Phase 1	*c*. AD 550-630
Phase 2	*c*. AD 630-680
Phase 3	*c*. AD 680-725
Phase 4	*c*. AD 725-770
Phase 5	*c*. AD 770-850

Phase 1 covers the late 6th century and early 7th century, from *c*. AD 550-630. A reconsideration of the Wharram material culture indicates that there are very few objects that can be placed in this phase. *Phase 2* (*c*. AD 630-680) represents the period at which cemeteries first occur within the pre-Viking trading and production centres, notably at *Hamwic*, Ipswich and *Lundenwic* (Birbeck 2005; Scull 2009; Cowie and Blackmore forthcoming). Contemporary settlement evidence is also present at most of those sites. The Middle Saxon period was previously defined by the emergence of Ipswich ware, which was thought to begin around AD 650, but it is now thought to have begun somewhat later, closer to AD 700, or even later (Blinkhorn 2009, 359). On that basis, the beginning of the Middle Saxon period could be placed in the late 7th or early 8th century. On the other hand, if the *wic* sites also define Middle Saxon England, then its inception should accord with their origins, now thought to be *c*. AD 630.

The debate about whether *Phase 2* is an Early or a Middle Saxon phase is largely an academic one. More importantly, this is one of the last phases of accompanied burial, but equally one of the first phases at which such burials are seen across the Yorkshire Wolds. Prior to this phase, burial appears to fringe the Wolds and to be concentrated at major burial grounds like Sancton and West Heslerton (Lucy 1998, 85-99; Haughton and Powlesland 1999).

Phase 3 encompasses the period of the primary phase *sceattas* and the initial coinage of the secondary phase. It is also the period of the cessation of accompanied burial in cemeteries that are not linked to churches (Blair 2005, 228-45). Objects from this phase can, in some cases, be linked back to grave goods in late cemeteries, whereas those of later phases do not occur in burial contexts. *Phase 4* includes the secondary phase *sceattas* and witnesses significant changes in object types and artefact materials, allowing them to be distinguished from earlier forms. *Phase 5* is not as well understood at present for Wharram and is somewhat longer than any of *Phases 2-4*, whilst incorporating a smaller number of datable objects, as well as styca coins. As with *Phase 4*, it is defined in part by the introduction of new object types.

The limitations of the evidence

Placing objects into these *Phases* allows the development of Wharram to be studied across the Early and Middle Saxon periods, with the important caveat that by no means can all objects be dated with any precision, and the quantities of closely-dated objects attributable to a single *Phase*, rather than to two adjacent *Phases*, are often relatively small. This report therefore provides suggestions and ideas, rather than solutions. It is also a question of dealing initially with the specific dating of objects and not the contexts in which they were found, which are often considerably later in date. This feature of Wharram has been noted on several occasions (Stamper *et al.* 2000, 19-25). Some Middle Saxon objects have been found in stratified contexts and these are reviewed below and compared with the archaeological phases. Comparisons have also been drawn with the ceramic dating, where possible. Arguments for the dating of each of the relevant objects are discussed in an archive text and have been summarised in a spreadsheet file, also held in the Site Archive, ADS report (doi:10.5284/1000415).

Early Anglo-Saxon Wharram (*Phase 1*)

A small number of objects from Wharram have previously been placed in the early Anglo-Saxon period. They include a single-sided composite comb from Site 39, as well as two copper-alloy brooches of Frisian origin from Sites 59 and 94, and a firesteel from Site 603 (39/SF778: Plate 16 and MacGregor 1992, 54-5; 59/SF295 and 94/SF26: Ager 1992, 47-9; Goodall and Paterson 2000, 126 and fig. 60.1; 603/SF144: Plate 15 and Goodall and Clark 2004, 244 and fig. 127.25). Several small fragments of double-sided composite combs have also been placed cautiously into this period and are noted in the Site Archive.

It is immediately evident that characteristic elements of early Anglo-Saxon material culture are missing from Wharram. There are no cruciform, annular or square-headed brooches, sleeve-clasps, girdle-hangers or latch-lifters, and few buckles of copper alloy or iron, yet these are common finds within early Anglo-Saxon cemeteries of the region (Lucy 1998, 35-50; Drinkall and Foreman 1998; Haughton and Powlesland 1999). Objects from cemeteries, however, are not necessarily found within contemporary settlements (Richards 1992d, 136 and fig. 19). Accordingly, the arguments presented here are based on objects actually discovered in Wharram excavations, viewed alongside the ceramic evidence.

The Wharram ceramic evidence, analysed by Anna Slowikowski and discussed in previous volumes (e.g. Slowikowski 2000, 61-70; ADS Report, doi:10.5284/1000415), is important to these arguments. The earliest Anglo-Saxon ceramics in the South Manor Area have been separated into fabrics A01a-c and consist of organic-tempered sherds, combined either with quartz (A01b) or mica (A01c). These fabrics contributed just 0.5% of the total Anglo-Saxon assemblage from the site and were thought to continue in use into the 8th century – that is, well into the Middle Saxon period (Slowikowski 2000, 61). In Site 39, four sherds of this fabric, and in Site 94, one sherd, occurred in contexts of 8th-century date (Slowikowski 2000, 27, 36-7 and tables 1-2). The fabrics were poorly represented in the North Manor Area (Slowikowski 2004, tables 31 and 36). Although they may possibly go back to the early Anglo-Saxon period, their occurrence at Wharram appears largely to be within Middle Saxon contexts.

A further fabric may also have its origins in the early Anglo-Saxon period but continues into the Middle Saxon period. The temper used for ceramics of fabric A03 was identified as granite, a temper usually attributed to that period (Slowikowski 2000, 27-8; Slowikowski 2004, 184; Williams and Vince 1997; Young and Vince 2009, 346). It is a more common fabric at Wharram than fabrics A01a-c, extending to 10.4% of the Anglo-Saxon assemblage from the South Manor Area (Slowikowski 2000, 63). At the same time, it has been noted that its dating extends into the 7th century and that it also occurs consistently alongside fabrics of Middle Saxon date (Slowikowski 2000, 81; Naylor 2004, 63). It may possibly have been distributed from Leicestershire along the Trent valley (Slowikowski 2000, 99). Thus ceramics that are unequivocally Early Anglo-Saxon are hard to establish for Wharram, the fabric series continuing into the Middle Saxon period.

There is, therefore, very little material evidence for Early Anglo-Saxon activity at Wharram, and in fact less than has previously been suggested. The copper-alloy brooches can certainly be placed in this period but, as Ager noted, they are of late 6th-century date (Stamper *et al.* 2000, 47-8). The single-sided composite comb from Site 39 was found in a context of the second half of the 8th century and it is argued below that it is a comb of 8th-century date (39/SF778, Plate 16). Similarly, the firesteel is of a type essentially of 7th-century date, rather than any earlier period. It is an important object from Wharram because much of the dating for *Grubenhaus* 46 in the North Manor Area depends on its presence in a sealed context (Rahtz and Watts 2004, 69-71; Rahtz *et al.* 2004 290). The firesteel belongs to a common Anglo-Saxon type, which occurs in cemetery contexts of 7th-century date (Hawkes 1973, 195; Evison 1987, 111; Geake 1997, 79). This accords with Continental dating, which places the advent of this type in the late 6th to early 7th century (Reiß 1994, 142). The type continues into the second half of the 7th century, possibly being superseded thereafter by a form with long and sinuous arms to the terminals

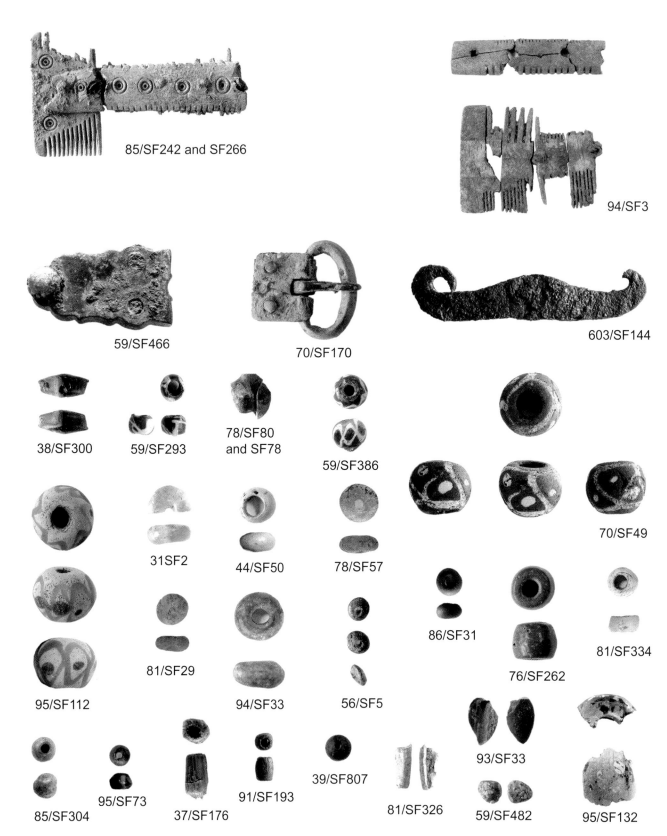

85/SF242 and SF266

94/SF3

59/SF466

70/SF170

603/SF144

38/SF300

59/SF293

78/SF80
and SF78

59/SF386

70/SF49

31SF2

44/SF50

78/SF57

95/SF112

81/SF29

94/SF33

56/SF5

86/SF31

76/SF262

81/SF334

85/SF304

95/SF73

37/SF176

91/SF193

39/SF807

81/SF326

93/SF33

59/SF482

95/SF132

Plate 15. Selected Early and Middle Saxon objects of *Phases 1-2*, and glass beads of *Phases 1-5*. 85/SF242 and SF266: double-sided composite comb, *Phase 2*; 94/SF3: double-sided composite comb, *Phase 1-2*; 59/SF466: Bern-Solothern type copper-alloy belt fitting, *Phase 2*; 70/SF170: copper-alloy buckle and plate, Type II.24a, *Phase 1-2*; 603/SF144: iron firesteel, elongated triangular form, *Phase 1-2*. 38/SF300: polychrome, elongated biconical mosaic bead, *Phase 1*; 59/SF293, 78/SF80 and SF78, 59/SF386, 70/SF49 and 95/SF112: polychrome beads of Koch type 34, *Phases 1-3*; 31/SF2, 44/SF50, 78/SF57, 81/SF29 and 94/SF33: monochrome, naturally coloured annular beads, *Phase 2-3*; 56/SF5, 86/SF31: monochrome, coloured annular beads, *Phase 2-3*; 76/SF262, 81/SF334, 85/SF304: monochrome spiral-wound beads, *Phase 2-3*; 95/SF73: monochrome biconical bead, *Phase 2-3*; 37/SF176: drawn, cylinder pentagonal bead, *Phase 3-4*; 91/SF193: monochrome cylindrical bead, *Phase 3-4*; 39/SF807: monochrome globular bead, *Phase 3-4*; 81/SF326, 93/SF33: beads with central copper-alloy tube, *Phase 3-4*; 59/SF482 and 95/SF132: bead fragments with random spots of colour, *Phase 3-5*. Bone combs and iron, Scale 2:3; copper alloy and beads, Scale 1:1 (I. Riddler)

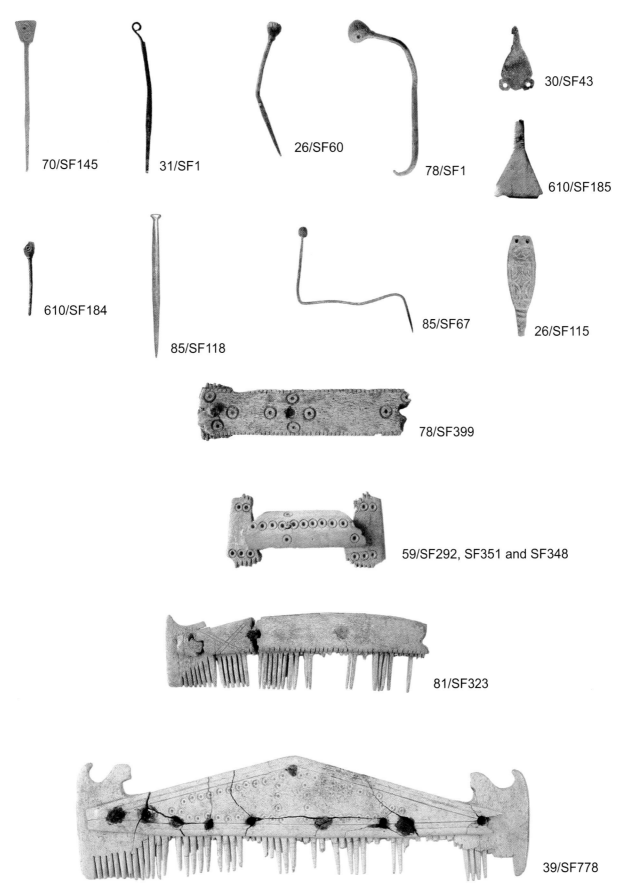

Plate 16. Middle Saxon Objects, *Phases 3-4*. 70/SF145: copper-alloy pin with spatulate head; 31/SF1: spiral-headed copper-alloy pin; 26/SF60 and 78/SF1: balloon-headed copper-alloy pins; 610/SF184: copper-alloy pin with polygonal head; 85/SF118: copper-alloy pin with T-shaped head; 86/SF67: copper-alloy pin with globular head; 30/SF43: copper-alloy hooked tag; 610/SF185: copper-alloy tweezers; 26/SF115: copper-alloy strap end; 78/SF399 and 59/SF348: Insular combs with broad connecting plates of trapezoidal section; 81/SF323 and 39/SF778: Anglo-Saxon single-sided composite combs. Scale 2:3 (I. Riddler)

(Penn 2000, 58). Its closest parallels lie with examples from 7th-century cemetery contexts (contemporary with the latest part of *Phase 1* at Wharram, and all of *Phase 2*).

A further item that can be placed in this period is an iron knife, from Site 83 in the North Manor Area (83/SF16), which has a straight back and curving cutting edge, allowing it to be placed in Drinkall's type B (Evison 1987, 113-15; Drinkall and Foreman 1998, 279-81). This is essentially an early Anglo-Saxon knife form, occurring in contexts of 5th and 6th-century date and rarely seen thereafter (Goodall and Clark 2004, 246 and fig. 127.30). Site 83, a trench about 3m by 6.5m, was an enlargement of an earlier trench (Site 13) that had uncovered an inhumation accompanied by a finger-ring, an unidentified iron object and a group of bird bones. The knife came from context 14, a ?cultivation soil that was probably equivalent to layer 2 in Site 13 – the layer of soil overlying the grave (Rahtz and Watts 2004, 11-12, 15). The burial has been variously dated to the Late Roman and post-Roman periods (Rahtz and Watts 2004, 13; Rahtz *et al.* 2004, 293; Cool 2004, 346), and it must be at least a possibility, therefore, that the knife was originally associated with an Early Anglo-Saxon inhumation.

Another important group of objects to be considered here is the beads of amber and glass. Small quantities in both materials, as well as in bone, chalk and coal, have come from Wharram excavations (Table 1; Plate 15). Amber beads occur in Early Anglo-Saxon contexts but are also found in those of Middle and Late Saxon date. There may have been a shortage in amber from the early 7th century onwards, or conceivably a change in fashion away from the use of the material (Geake 1997, 47; Walton Rogers 2007, 128) but it still continued in less frequent use. In consequence, amber beads are not closely datable as objects in their own right. Closer dating is provided by the glass beads, the majority of which (24 of

32) are monochrome. The predominance of monochrome beads is itself indicative of a 7th-century or later date and matches the situation seen at both *Hamwic* and Fishergate at York (Hunter and Heyworth 1998, 26; Rogers 1993, 1379). Most of the beads can be placed within the period from the late 6th century to the mid-8th century, the principal exception being an elongated biconical bead from Site 38 (38/SF300: Plate 15), a trench across the northern boundary of the North Manorial enclosure. It closely resembles beads from southern Germany recently placed by Koch into her group M96 and stemming from graves dating to *c.* 565-630 (Koch 1977, type M67; 2001, farbtafel 8), placing it within *Phase 1*.

In summary, therefore, there are four objects (two copper-alloy brooches, a knife and a glass bead) that can be placed with certainty in *Phase 1*, *c.* AD 550-630. A small number of additional objects *could* belong to this phase, but could equally well belong to the next. Amongst them are the fragments of a double-sided composite comb with undecorated, cylindrical connecting plates, an Early Anglo-Saxon comb form that continues into Wharram *Phase 2* (94/SF003, Plate 15; MacGregor 1992, fig. 30.5). Two fragments of a further comb from the South Manor (85/SF242 and SF266, Plate 15; MacGregor 2000, fig. 70.3 and 70.6) can also be placed in *Phases 1-2*. The ceramic evidence corroborates the detail provided by the small finds and suggests that intensive Anglo-Saxon activity at Wharram did not begin before the late 6th or early 7th century at the earliest. It is more likely to have begun in *Phase 2*, *c.* AD 630-680.

Establishing the Middle Saxon settlement (*Phase 2*)
Alongside the four objects attributable to *Phase 1*, and the comb fragments of *Phase 1* to *Phase 2,* a much larger number can be placed squarely in *Phase 2*, with an even greater assemblage attributable to the broader category of

Table 1. Anglo-Saxon glass beads from Wharram.

Type	Quantity	Phasing
Monochrome:		
Doughnut	4	1-3
Constricted segmented cylindrical	1	1-2
Drawn cylinder, pentagonal section	1	?2-3
Spirally wound	3	2-3
Copper-alloy tube at centre	2	3-4
Annular	3	Not closely datable
Globular	3	Not closely datable
Biconical	3	Not closely datable
Cylindrical	2	Not closely datable
Polychrome:		
Koch 34	5	1-3
Random colour spots	2	2-4
Koch M96 mosaic bead	1	1

Phases 2-3, effectively the 7th to early 8th centuries (see Fig. 63). As noted above, the assemblage of glass beads is largely indicative of a 7th-century date, with some examples extending into the 8th century. A copper-alloy belt fitting of Bern-Solothern type can be dated to *c.* AD 640-670 and recalls examples from cemetery contexts at *Hamwic*, Ipswich and London (59/SF466, Plate 15; Marzinzik 2003, 48-9).

The belt fitting can be set alongside an iron hilt guard (81/SF346) and two pommels (81/SF283; 93/SF32) from the South Manor Area, all of which are inlaid and of Frankish type (Goodall and Clark 2000, 139 and fig. 64.256 and 258-9). All of these are prestige objects, implying a high level of status. The glass beads are likely to be of Merovingian origin, whilst the belt fitting, hilt guard and pommels have certainly come from the Continent. Merovingian derived small finds are prominent in *Phases 2* and *3*, rather than the succeeding *Phase 4*, and that echoes the situation seen with the ceramics, with the imported fabrics of A10 also centred on the earlier part of the period, though extending into *Phase 4* (Slowikowski 2004, 184). The Anglo-Saxon comb sequence for Wharram develops in *Phases 2-3*, although it begins in *Phases 1-2*. It is dominated at this time by double-sided composite combs; the earliest single-sided composite combs are not seen before *Phase 3*. This echoes the situation seen across northern England in general. At Castledyke South, for example, nine combs are double-sided composites and just two are single-sided (Drinkall and Foreman 1998, 287-8).

The distribution of small finds attributable to *Phases 2-3* (Fig. 63) shows a concentration both in the South Manor Area sites and in the Western Plateau (south) sites (particularly when due allowance is given to the smaller volume of excavation in the latter sites). It strongly suggests that they form part of the same settlement. The Western Plateau (north) Sites 94 and 95 belong to the same settlement but there is little evidence of material of this period (*c.* AD 630-725) from the extensive excavations in the North Manor Area or the Churchyard. In terms of the ceramics, for example, fewer than 130 sherds of Middle Saxon pottery survive from the North Manor Area (excluding Site 82: see Table 13). Even smaller quantities came from the dam and ponds sites south of the Churchyard (three sherds: Slowikowski 2005 73). Larger quantities were recovered from Sites 39 and 94-5 (over 400 sherds), although the excavations were smaller; and over 2600 sherds of Middle Saxon ceramics came from the South Manor Area. Slowikowski has noted that 'Anglo-Saxon and Saxo-Norman pottery is sparse on Site 45, as elsewhere on the North Manor, and is unrelated to any of the structures' (Slowikowski 2004, 194).

Nonetheless, there was some occupation at the North Manor area at this time. The various fills of *Grubenhaus* 46 can be placed in this period at the latest, on the basis of the firesteel described above. There is also a small collection of iron knives, some of which may be of Middle Saxon date. The ceramics from those contexts do not survive, unfortunately (Slowikowski 2004, 197). An antler spoon (603/SF143) from one of the upper fills of 46 belongs to *Phases 4-5*, rather than earlier in the Middle Saxon period (Riddler 2004b, 254). This suggests an interval of time between the initial backfill and the later, secondary fills. The context containing the spoon may have formed part of an occupation surface of a later date, much in the manner envisaged by Tipper in his discussion of the nature of *Grubenhaus* fills (Tipper 2004, 106-7). Dating evidence for the second building in this area, *Grubenhaus* 435, is negligible (Rahtz and Watts 2004, 69). It is interesting to note that the percentage of organic-tempered ceramics from the North Manor Area is the highest at Wharram, albeit from a small sample, and bears comparison with the quantity from the South Manor Area, whilst the fabric is sparse at both Site 39 and in the Western Plateau (north) sites (Slowikowski 2000, 61; Slowikowski 2004, 184). There is no sign of occupation within the area of the Church or the Churchyard within *Phases 2-3*, in terms of both the small finds and the ceramics (*Wharram XI*, 255).

Having identified *Phases 2-3* from the small finds, can they be related to any of the archaeological phases of the settlement? Two phases of Middle Saxon occupation were identified in the South Manor Area sites (Stamper *et al.* 2000, 27-37). Approximately 25 small finds came from contexts of site phase 2 there, but not all of these objects fit neatly into the stratigraphic sequence. Amongst them is the *Phases 1-2* comb noted above (85/SF242 and SF266, Plate 15), found in two separate contexts, one the fill of post-hole 107, associated with Structure A. Some of the other post-holes assigned to Structure A also contained small finds, including context 121, the fill of pit 120 which incorporated a wound spiral glass bead attributable to *Phases 2-4* (and most likely to belong to *Phases 2-3*). A copper-alloy pin (85/SF247), a bone pin (81/SF445) and a fragment of an intermediate loomweight (85/SF251), all retrieved from phase 2 contexts elsewhere on the site, belong to *Phases 4-5* and further illustrate the difficulties of correlating small finds with site phases across the South Manor Area, where there are few sealed and undisturbed contexts of Middle Saxon date. The same problem can be seen from the distribution of the ceramics across features of the site, where no obvious pattern emerges for the Middle Saxon period (Slowikowski 2000, table 10).

The situation on the Western Plateau (south) is slightly better. The Anglo-Saxon small finds from Site 70 are largely from the clayey silt layer that covered the Period 4 features, but in Site 78, *Phase 3* objects were associated with the earliest Middle Saxon features, *Phase 4* objects with the later ones. In Site 86, Middle Saxon objects included a copper-alloy finger-ring (86/SF180) attributable to *Phase 5*, whilst several items of *Phase 3* are residual finds in post-medieval deposits. In summary, there is a reasonable quantity of small finds attributable to *Phases 2-3*, but relatively few well-stratified contexts that can be placed unequivocally in this period.

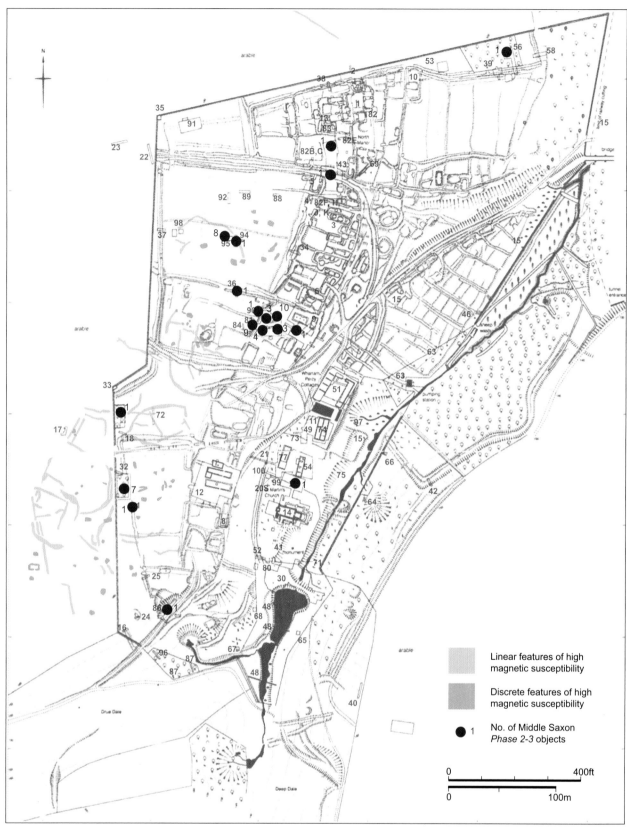

Fig. 63. Numbers and distribution of Middle Saxon objects from Wharram: *Phase 2-3* objects (*c.* 630-725). (English Heritage, E. Marlow-Mann and I. Riddler)

The late 7th to late 8th centuries *(Phases 3-4)*

The Anglo-Saxon coin sequence for Wharram has been summarised previously (Pirie 1992, 52-4; Knight and Pirie 2000, 124-6; Barclay 2007, 301-4). It consists of eight coins, four of which are sceattas, whilst four are 9th-century Northumbrian stycas. The sceattas include one of Series E (*c.* 700-710) and three of King Eadberht (737-758), one of which was minted *c.* AD 750 (Barclay 2007, 302-4). The Series E sceat came from the South Manor Area. One of the Eadberht coins came from the backfill of the *Grubenhaus* on Site 39, whilst the others were recovered from Church and Churchyard contexts. This may also be the period of the introduction of Ipswich ware at Wharram, five sherds of which came from the South Manor (Slowikowski 2000, 69-70). Its occurrence at Wharram has been placed in the period *c.* AD 725-850 but recent work suggests that it was not present in northern England in any quantities before the late 8th century (Loveluck 2007, 117).

Four bone combs can be placed in *Phase 3* (*c.* AD 680-730), with a larger group of 24 items falling into the combined *Phases 3-4*, which extend from the late 7th century to late 8th century. Many of the latter finds are bone pins (Table 2), the majority of which come from the South Manor Area, with a group also occurring in the backfill of the *Grubenhaus* on Site 95A. They occur with a variety of head forms, the majority of which can be placed in *Phase 2* or *Phase 3*. It is likely that small bone

pins of this type went out of favour at a point when copper-alloy pins were being produced in some numbers, during *Phase 4*.

One of the most distinctive features of *Phase 4* is the advent of copper-alloy pins with cast heads of globular, biconical or polyhedral shape. These are a type fossil of the Middle Saxon period, with evidence from Brandon, *Hamwic* and *Lundenwic* suggesting that they did not come into use before *c.* AD 720 (Riddler forthcoming a; Malcolm *et al.* 2003, 266-8). They continue into the 9th century with finds from Fishergate at York, in particular, demonstrating the transition to Late Saxon pin forms (Rogers 1993, 1361-7; Spall and Toop 2005). The majority of the sixteen copper-alloy pins from Wharram were retrieved from contexts of Late Saxon or medieval date (Plate 16), with the exception of two pins from Site 85. One of these came from a phase 2 context and the other from a phase 3 context; both contexts are probably of 8th-century date (Goodall and Paterson 2000, 126 and fig. 60.3 and 8).

Handled combs also belong to this period, the earliest examples again dating to *c.* AD 720. Four fragments of handled combs have come from Wharram and all of them are of Middle Saxon date, and were probably made in the 8th century. The comb sequence for Wharram extends to *Phase 4* and includes one of the most characteristic combs to have been recovered from the settlement (39/SF778, Plate 16; MacGregor 1992, fig. 29; Milne

Table 2. Bone pin head forms.

Type	Quantity	South Manor Area	Western Plateau (North)	Western Plateau (South)
Discoidal	10			
Hipped shaft		5	1	
Not hipped			2	
Fragmentary		2		
Triangular spatulate	1			
Hipped shaft		1		
Excrescent	4			
Hipped shaft			1	
Not hipped		1	2	
Headless	3	3		
Segmented	1		1	
Truncated conical	4			
Decorated head		1		2
Undecorated head		1		
Flat, rounded, perforated head	1			
Ipswich Group 11		1		
Gabled and perforated head	1			
Ipswich Group 5				1

1992a, pl. 4). It was recovered from the backfill of *Grubenhaus* 14 on Site 39, alongside a Northumbrian *sceat* issued *c.* AD 750, and a range of ceramics (Milne 1992b, 80-82). Although it has been suggested previously that the comb was manufactured in the 6th century (see above), elements of its design accord well with its date of deposition, and it is more likely to have been made in the first half of the 8th century. Milne's suggestion that the backfilling of the *Grubenhaus* took place between *c.* AD 760 and AD 780 remains the most plausible option, notwithstanding the presence there of sherds of A01 ceramics, which also occur in earlier deposits (cf Rahtz *et al.* 2004, 287-8). Pulling in the other direction and towards a later date, of course, is the single sherd of Tating ware, which remains an unusual find for a Middle Saxon rural settlement (Coutts and Hodges 1992, 38-9). The recent re-evaluation of the ceramic evidence for Ribe, however, again suggests that the sherd could be as early as *c.* AD 760-780. Sherds of Tating ware at Ribe have been found in phases 3 and 4 there, dating to between *c.* AD 760-825 (Madsen 2004, 256).

Several other fragments of single-sided composite combs can be placed in *Phases 3-4*, alongside three notable double-sided combs of Insular origin, recovered from the South Manor Area and Western Plateau (south) sites (see below). Some of these objects can be tied to specific structures. Like the one in Site 39, the *Grubenhaus* in Site 95A was probably backfilled in the 8th century, but a little earlier in date (Richards 1992b, 83-4). The intermediate loomweight (Clark 1992, fig. 23.26) found in that backfill could be as early as the 7th century, following a recent assessment of their dating (Walton Rogers 2007, 30), although an 8th-century date is more likely in this case. The presence of a spindle whorl made of bone, rather than antler, confirms that the backfill can be placed in the later 7th century or 8th century, rather than earlier in the 7th century (Riddler, Trzaska-Nartowski and Hatton forthcoming).

A number of bone pins also came from backfill contexts and these appear to have gone out of use by *c.* AD 750, suggesting that the main episode of backfilling occurred at some time between the late 7th century and the first half of the 8th century. Richards argued that the construction of this building took place in the first half of the 7th century, but a date in the second half of the century is equally likely, and may fit the evidence better (Richards 1992b, 83-4; Rahtz *et al.* 2004, 288-9).

Figure 63 shows the distribution of objects of *Phases 2-3* across the Wharram sites. There is a hint of an expansion in settlement beyond *Phases 1-2*, both to the Churchyard area and to the east of the North Manor Area, at Site 39. The first phase of the graveyard dates to the mid to late 10th century (Harding and Marlow-Mann 2007, 9). Alongside the coinage, 21 objects of Anglo-Saxon date have come from the Church and Churchyard. With the exception of one small comb fragment that can be placed in *Phase 2-3* (Riddler 2007, 314 and fig. 148.4) all of the remaining Middle Saxon objects, including copper-alloy pins, as well as bone and antler combs,

belong to *Phases 4-5*, equating well with the coin dating. This small collection hints at some form of activity in the Churchyard area, beginning *c.* AD 737-50. To the north-west, the principal phase 3 remains of the South Manor Area encompass smithing debris, which is difficult to date accurately. Radiocarbon dates suggest activity between the 7th and 9th centuries (Stamper *et al.* 2000, 35). There are no closely dated small finds from any of these contexts, unfortunately.

Whether or not the settlement expanded, the range of associated objects certainly did, extending to include stone sculpture and ceramic moulds, as well as bone or antler spoons. Fragments of Middle Saxon sculpture have been recovered from Area 6 (Site 12), from the Western Plateau (north) and from the North Manor Area. The cross-head fragment from the Western Plateau (north) has been compared with sculpture from Whitby of the first half of the 8th century, whilst the fragment from Area 6 has been placed in the late 8th or early 9th century (Andrews 1979, 124; Clark 1992, 43). Three small fragments from the North Manor Area may derive from crosses or architectural features (Clark and Gaunt 2004, 226). A newly identified fragment from a Western Plateau (north) site (94/SF124) may also derive from a cross.

Fragments of ceramic moulds and crucibles were found on Sites 94-5 and suggest that copper alloys were melted and cast there (Bayley with Lang 1992, 59-66). A small quantity of mould fragments also came from the South Manor Area and a single fragment was recovered from Site 43 in the North Manor Area (Bayley 2000, 121; Bayley 2004, 231). A mould fragment from Sites 94-5 shows a panel of interlace and it can be compared with a small fragment of a copper-alloy interlace panel, which came from the North Manor Area (Bayley with Lang 1992, fig. 32.13; Goodall 2004, fig. 126.25). Panels of this type are rectangular in shape and are unlikely, therefore, to have come from disc-headed pins or mounts. It is more likely that they would have adorned caskets, and quite possibly also ecclesiastical objects like decorated wooden crosses and book covers. Five examples of bone or antler spoons have come from Wharram (Riddler 2004b, 252). All five have come from Anglo-Saxon or later deposits, but can be placed in the Middle Saxon period on typological grounds. Comparable spoons belong to the 8th to 9th centuries, essentially *Phases 4-5*.

The 8th to mid-9th centuries *(Phases 4-5)*

The distribution of finds attributable to *Phases 2-3* can be contrasted with the reduced quantity of material for *Phases 4-5* (Figs 63-4). This diminution has to be treated with caution, however, given that there are numerous finds attributable only to *Phases 3-4*, and many of these have been considered above. Moreover, it is important to note the caution expressed by Loveluck in describing the site phasing for Flixborough (Loveluck and Atkinson 2007, 35). There is a greater range of datable material for the Middle Saxon period than for the Late Saxon period, both at Wharram and Flixborough. At Flixborough,

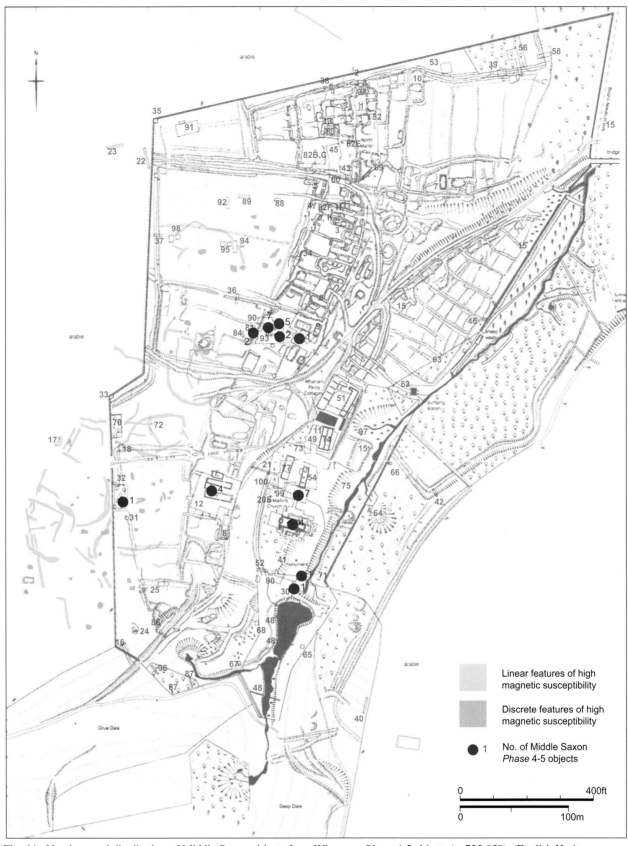

Fig. 64. Numbers and distribution of Middle Saxon objects from Wharram: *Phase 4-5* objects (*c.* 725-850). (English Heritage, E. Marlow-Mann and I. Riddler)

Linear features of high magnetic susceptibility

Discrete features of high magnetic susceptibility

● 1 No. of Middle Saxon *Phase* 4-5 objects

0   400ft

0   100m

however, the Late Saxon archaeological sequence was as prominent as that for earlier periods, despite the decrease in the quantity of datable small finds. The same cautious approach should be used for Wharram *Phase 5*. The diminution in the quantity of datable small finds does not necessarily mean that settlement itself contracted or declined. All of the *Grubenhäuser* at Wharram date to the 7th or 8th centuries and they formed useful spaces for the deposition of cultural material. There are no 9th-century *Grubenhäuser* from the site (unless the possible example, un-emptied, from the northern Churchyard is of this date: Harding and Marlow- Mann 2007, 22-7). Few other cut features of any size can be recognised for this period, and the absence of objects may, in part at least, relate to the corresponding absence of large cut features.

The four 9th-century coins from Wharram include two stycas of Eanred (810-41), one of Archbishop Uigmund (*c*. 837-54) and an irregular reflective issue of Aethelred II (*c*. 841-50: Barclay 2007, 303). One coin comes from Area 6 (Site 12) and the other three are from the area of the Church and the Churchyard. The forms of copper-alloy pin seen at Wharram continue into *Phase 5*, as do the bone or antler spoons. The most obvious addition to the material culture is the copper-alloy strap ends, three examples of which have come from Wharram, with a distribution clustering around the Churchyard (e.g. 26/SF115, Plate 16). They are supplemented by several examples of iron strap ends, most of which come from the South Manor Area (Table 3). The contrast in distributions between the copper-alloy and iron strap-ends is immediately noticeable and may possibly relate to the proximity of the iron finds to the smithy in the South Manor Area. It is worth noting in this respect that two iron strap-ends came from the Middle Saxon smelting site at Ramsbury (Evison 1980, 35). It is possible that iron strap-ends were being produced at the smithy, amongst numerous other items. The diagonal patterning and the single-rivet fastening seen on two of the iron strap-ends recall designs on copper-alloy strap-ends from Brandon and Coddenham (West 1998, fig. 21.29). These designs may pre-date the animal head series and belong to the late 8th century rather than the 9th century, according well with their presence in phase 2 and phase 3 contexts in the South Manor Area (Riddler forthcoming a). Nonetheless,

all of the Wharram strap-ends still belong to *Phases 4-5*. Alongside the strap-ends, the earlier of the two hooked tags from Wharram can also be placed in this phase (30/SF43, Plate 16; Goodall 2005 fig. 56.1). It came from the dam and pond area to the south of the churchyard, alongside two fragments of bun-shaped loomweights (30/SF20; 30/SF130) and a copper-alloy pin (71/SF19), all of which could conceivably belong to this phase as well.

The distribution of objects of *Phase 5*, together with the coins of that phase, is more restricted than that of earlier phases, as noted above. There is nothing of this date from the Western Plateau (south), which does include material of *Phase 4*, and Milne's dates for the end of Site 39 east of the North Manor Area still stand up well, as noted above. The evidence from the Western Plateau (north) Site 95 for *Phase 5* occupation is very tentative and consists merely of one bun-shaped loomweight (95/SF82), which could be as early as *c*. AD 770, but could equally well be later in date.

Trade, economy and activity: The nature of the Middle Saxon material culture

Wharram has provided a rich if not abundant material cultural assemblage. It is true that there is nothing of the quantity of material seen at Brandon, Carisbrooke, Flixborough, or the contemporary East Anglian sites of Barham and Coddenham (Carr and Tester forthcoming; Evans and Loveluck 2009; West 1998, 6-8 and 19-24; Newman 2003; Ulmschneider 2000a). On the other hand, Wharram stands up reasonably well against Yorkshire sites like Cottam and Thwing, for example (Richards 1999a; 2003; Leahy 2000, 71-2), whilst lacking the quantities of pins seen at the metal-detected sites of South Newbald and 'near York' described by Leahy (2000, fig. 6.11). Wharram has not been metal-detected, however, and that is an important consideration in attempting to compare site assemblages, despite Leahy's intriguing suggestion that the manner in which sites were investigated does not affect the number of coins found (Leahy 2000, 72). It does, of course, affect the number of copper-alloy objects recovered. Comparisons between Wharram and local settlement assemblages are made below, based on the earlier work by Richards (Richards 2000a, 198-200).

Table 3. Wharram strap-ends.

Area	Site	SF	Context	Period or Phase	Material	Illustration
West of Churchyard	Area 6	13811		Period VI	Copper alloy	*Wharram I*, fig. 55.12
Churchyard	26	115	539	Period 3 Phase 4	Copper alloy	*Wharram XI*, fig. 144.8
Churchyard	North Churchyard				Copper alloy	*Wharram III*, fig. 191.9
W. Plateau (South)	78	222			Iron	
South Manor	85	245	104	Phase 2	Iron	*Wharram VIII*, fig. 64.227
South Manor	85	227	74	Phase 3	Iron	*Wharram VIII*, fig. 64.228
South Manor	81	266	20	Phase 4	Iron	*Wharram VIII*, fig. 64.229
South Manor	76	368	28	Phase 4	Iron	*Wharram VIII*, fig. 64.230

Naylor has usefully included Wharram in his review of Middle Saxon sites of Yorkshire and its role within the Wolds can now be examined on the basis of the additional information provided by the North Manor Area and Churchyard sites, as well as those of the Western Plateau (Naylor 2004, 24-82). Wharram coins follow a local pattern that persists from the inception of post-Roman coinage in Yorkshire. Its single early sceat of series E places it in the company of other sites on the Wolds, including Cottam, Thwing and Kilham, as well as Flixborough to the south of the Humber (Naylor 2004, 40). It also follows the established pattern both in its restriction of later 8th-century coinage to issues of Eadberht and in its development as a settlement in *Phase 4*, particularly *c*. AD 725-770, at a point when Fishergate in York may possibly have been in decline and the focus in the Wolds may have shifted towards regional exchange networks (Naylor 2004, 43). Its 9th-century coinage reflects the continuing predominance of the Wolds sites and the continuation of settlement at the majority of them, with South Newbald, two Malton sites and Whitby seemingly abandoned around the middle or second half of the 9th century (Naylor 2004, 45; Leahy 2000, 72-4). At the same time, the relative lack of coinage, in comparison with other sites, has been related to Wharram's distance both from the coast and from York (Naylor 2004, 51). It may also reflect the relative standing of the settlement, as noted below.

It is clear also that small finds, principally from the Merovingian domains, were reaching the site at an earlier point in *Phases 1-2*, and both the belt mount and the sword fittings are conspicuous, prestige goods of this period. Small quantities of Merovingian ceramics extend this influence well into *Phase 2* and possibly into *Phase 3* (Slowikowski 1992, 29; Slowikowski 2000, 67-9; Slowikowski 2004, 184). Loveluck has noted the presence of Merovingian ceramics in cemeteries at Barton-on-Humber, Castledyke South and Driffield (Loveluck 2007, 113). A comb from Driffield grave 21 can be added to this list of Merovingian material (Mortimer 1905, 281 and fig. 799). Wharram is directly comparable with Flixborough for the presence of Merovingian objects in the 7th and early 8th centuries, which may have arrived via the Humber estuary, rather than via York.

As an aside, there is also an interesting point to be made about comparisons with metal-detected but unexcavated sites. Leahy understandably used the coin evidence to compare the start dates of his five sites (Leahy 2000, 72-4). But what about the period before the inception of coinage? The excavated sites of Wharram, Brandon and Flixborough all begin in the early 7th century, *c*. AD 650 or earlier. All three have also produced small quantities of early Anglo-Saxon material culture, which are absent from Leahy's sites (Leahy 2000, 74). But it should be noted that any site beginning *c*. AD 650 would have very few copper-alloy, silver or gold finds. They are noticeably scarce in contemporary cemeteries, as well as excavated settlements. At Wharram a single

copper-alloy pin is the only non-ferrous metal object of *Phase 3*, *c*. AD 680-725 and the Merovingian buckle plate is the only copper-alloy item of the previous one. Accordingly, the start dates of Middle Saxon settlements should be treated with considerable caution, if they stem from metal-detecting alone.

Whilst ample data for the region is available for the coinage, fewer can be presented for the ceramics, largely because the emphasis switches from metal-detected sites to those that have been excavated. In addition, some of the excavated sites, like Cottam, have produced very little pottery (Austin 1999, 49). The Wharram assemblage includes three fabrics from elsewhere in England, namely Maxey-type ware, Ipswich ware and Charnwood ware. Within Yorkshire, Maxey-type ware has been found also at Cottam, York and Beverley, and Ipswich ware is known from Beverley, Bridlington, Sewerby and York (Vince and Young 2005). Chris Scull (1997, 286) examined the distribution of Ipswich ware and suggested that the Middle Saxon settlement of York – the latter situated at Fishergate, Leadmill Lane and Clifford Street, as I have argued elsewhere (Riddler 2001a, 65-6) – exercised a measure of control over imported goods and was a point of redistribution, as is the case with sites in the south of England. This has been disputed by Naylor, whose distributions of coinage and ceramics seem to tell a different story, with the Wolds sites acting independently of York (Naylor 2004, 65-6). Charnwood ware is rare in Yorkshire and is known otherwise only from West Heslerton and the cemetery at Sancton; south of the Humber, it occurs at Flixborough (Naylor 2004, 62-4 and 67-8; Timby 1993, 268; Loveluck 2007, 113; Young and Vince 2009, 346-7). It is present in some quantities at Wharram but its function is unclear, although Williams and Vince (1997, 219-20) have suggested that it was traded as a commodity, rather than a container of goods.

The small quantity of imported ceramics from Wharram endorses Brown's view that demand for imports was rare and they are mostly – but not entirely – concentrated at the *wic* sites, which is certainly the case for York (Brown 1997, 108-12; Mainman 1993). Tating ware remains scarce in Yorkshire, outside York and Wharram (Hodges 1981, 43; Mainman 1993, 567). The presence of Whitby-type ware, on the other hand, links Wharram with the east coast (Slowikowski 2000, 61-3). Indeed, Whitby was another important site for traded goods at this time. Blair has emphasised the economic significance of *monasteria*, following the period of their foundation *c*. 670-730 (Blair 2005, 251-61). Whitby's role as a redistribution centre was not considered, however, by either Scull or Naylor. Most of the Middle Saxon sites on the Wolds are closer to Whitby than to York and may have benefited from that proximity. Wharram sits to the west of the Wolds group but nonetheless shares many characteristics of its material culture with them. The distribution of Whitby-type ware is of great interest, in this respect. Outside Whitby itself, it occurs also at Hartlepool, Jarrow, Newcastle, Norton-on-Tees and Wharram (Daniels 2007, 127; Jenner *et al.*

2006, 331; Slowikowski 2000, 61-3). Not all of these sites are documented monasteries, and one is an Anglo-Saxon cemetery; but the distribution has a distinctive, monastic flavour.

The imported objects of *Phases 3-4* from Wharram are of an entirely different character from those of *Phases 1-2*. Several are Insular in origin and were probably manufactured in Ireland. They consist of four combs, recovered from the South Manor Area and the Western Plateau (south) sites. All have connecting plates of trapezoidal section and two are decorated with ring-and-dot motifs arranged around the rivet spacing (78/SF399, 59/SF348, Plate 16). One of the combs also has an antler rivet. These are all characteristics of Dunlevy's class D1 combs, most of which are probably of 8th to 9th-century date (Dunlevy 1988, 358-9; Riddler, Trzaska-Nartowski and Barton forthcoming). There are few combs of Insular origin in Middle Saxon England and examples are limited to Canterbury, Thetford and Wigber Low (Blockley *et al.* 1995, fig. 509.1140; Andrews 1995, fig. 86.3; Collis 1983, fig. 40.3193). The only other double-sided composite comb of this date from England to include antler rivets – a distinctive Insular characteristic – comes from Whitby and forms another intriguing link with Wharram (Peers and Radford 1943, fig. 20.2). At least one fragment of stone sculpture also links Wharram with Whitby (Lang 1992, 43). The nature of the imported material has changed markedly at this point. Hodges had previously linked imported ceramics to the presence of merchants, but they are more likely to attest the movement of goods (Hodges 1981, 91; Brown 1997). Combs, however, do reflect the movement of individuals. Combs of ivory were exchanged between ecclesiastics, including Cuthbert and Alcuin, but the vast majority of antler and bone composite combs were produced locally and there is little evidence to suggest that they were traded widely at this period (Riddler, Trzaska-Nartowski and Hatton forthcoming).

A fragment of a vessel produced in a translucent brown glass can also be regarded as an import and added to Loveluck's list of sites with imported glass, which includes Beverley, Flixborough and York (Loveluck 2007, 113). The series E sceat also indicates contact, directly or indirectly, with Frisia, and to some extent,

Wharram appears as a scaled down version of Flixborough for imports of *Phases 3-4*, with smaller quantities of a similar range of material; but also with an Insular component, which is not seen elsewhere in Yorkshire or the hinterland of the Humber at this time, other than at Whitby.

Wharram shares a diminution in imported material from *Phase 5* onwards with both York and Flixborough. This also appears to be the period at which most of the Ipswich ware comes into northern England. There may, however, be one new commodity. Norwegian mica schist hones have been regarded as a Late Saxon implement type, reflecting trade with Norway from the late 9th century onwards (Ellis 1969, 149; Riddler and Walton Rogers 2006, 270) but one example from the South Manor Area at Wharram came from the upper fill of a phase 2 ditch, whilst another, of purple phyllite, was from what may have been in a Middle Saxon post-hole (Clark and Gaunt 2000, 106-7). These could be dismissed as intrusive objects (like many others that seem to have been in the South Manor Area assemblage: Stamper *et al.* 2000, 20) but a mica schist hone also came from a secure Middle Saxon context at *Lundenwic*, within a late phase there (Cowie *et al.* 1988, 134). The trade may just possibly have begun before the late ninth century, particularly when examples have reputedly been found at West Heslerton, which was apparently abandoned around the mid to late 9th century (Naylor 2004, 74).

Knives in Middle Saxon Wharram

Knives form one of the most common Anglo-Saxon iron implements recovered from Wharram. They have been recovered from practically all of the sites where Anglo-Saxon occupation has been identified, including the North Manor Area, where objects and ceramics of that period are otherwise scarce. All of them have whittle tangs. Few are complete and most survive only as fragments (Table 4).

In terms of their size, the Wharram knives are a little small, when compared with those from early Anglo-Saxon cemeteries. The blades vary in length from 40 to 85mm and most of their widths lie between 10 and 14mm. Härke grouped knives from early Anglo-Saxon cemeteries into three sizes, based on the length of their

Table 4. Anglo-Saxon knives.

	Western Plateau (South)	South Manor Area	Western Plateau (North)	North Manor Area
Blade fragment	12	6		1
Tang fragment	3			
Blade and tang fragment	3	10		2
Incomplete knife		1		3
Complete or near-complete knife	5	6	2	2
Total:	23	23	2	8

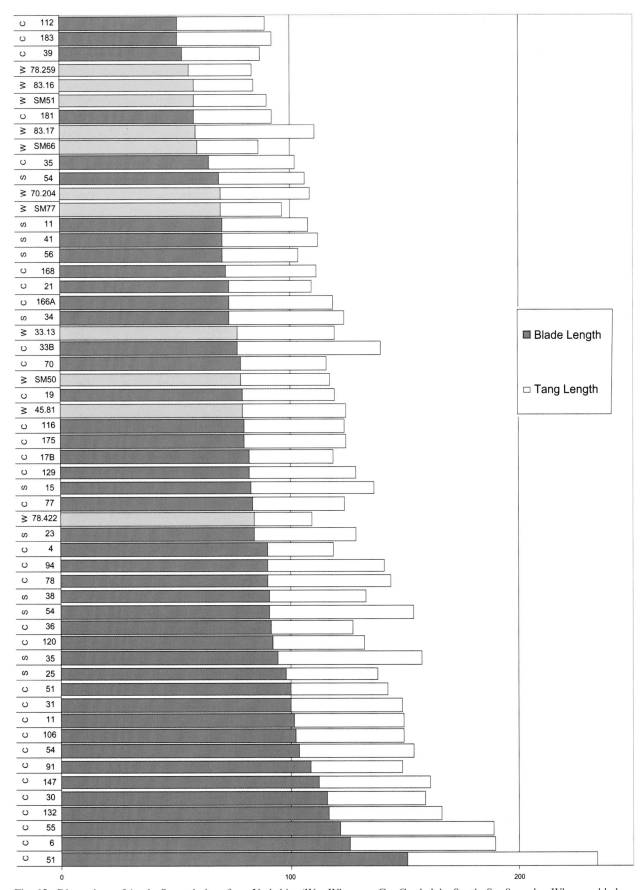

Fig. 65. Dimensions of Anglo-Saxon knives from Yorkshire (W = Wharram, C = Castledyke South, S = Sewerby; Wharram blades shown in yellow). (I. Riddler)

149

blades, with large knives and seaxes lying beyond these size bands (Härke 1989; 1992, 90-91). Large knives were defined by Härke as those with blades over 145mm in length, and by Siegmund as exceeding 150mm (Härke 1992, 90-91; Siegmund 1998, 112). No examples of knives of this size have been found at Wharram and all the Wharram knives would fall into Härke's smallest size class, with blades less than 100mm in length. It should be noted, however, that aggregating knives from across Anglo-Saxon England may conceal regional variations. Knives from Kent, for example, are larger than those buried in graves in East Anglia (Riddler forthcoming b).

The sizes of knives from Wharram are compared with those from the early Anglo-Saxon cemeteries of Sewerby and Castledyke South in Figure 65. In general, they are restricted to the upper part of the diagram, the area of the smaller knives, and there are longer examples than the Wharram sample from both cemeteries. All the long knives are found at Castledyke and it is essentially these that are missing at Wharram. Ottaway has argued that the longer and larger knives were used in butchery and hunting, as well as functioning as weapons, and Härke has noted the association between larger knives and the graves of males (Ottaway 1992, 583; Härke 1992, 90 and 188-9). The correlation relies entirely on attributions of gender from grave goods, however, and can be criticised on that basis. Larger knives become more common over time in the early Anglo-Saxon period, with their floruit occurring in the 7th century (Härke 1989, 145 and table 2; 1992, 189 and tab 31). Thereafter they are harder to find, and not only at Wharram. They are absent also at Fishergate in York, as well as *Sandtun*, although there are several from Shakenoak and a seax was found at Brandon, alongside a knife with a blade 121mm in length (Brodribb, Hands and Walker 1972, fig. 36; Nicky Rogers, *pers comm*). A seax also came from Flixborough (Evans and Loveluck 2009, 123 and fig. 3.1). A number of the knives from *Hamwic* have blades in excess of 100mm in length (Garner 2003, 125).

The shapes of knife blades fall neatly into a distinctive pattern emerging for Middle Saxon England. The principal classification schemes for Anglo-Saxon knives have been compiled by Evison and Ottaway, with Evison's scheme revised by Drinkall (Evison 1987, 113; Ottaway 1992, 558-72; Drinkall and Foreman 1998, 279-81). Evison considered early Anglo-Saxon knives, whilst Ottaway dealt initially with those of late Saxon date, subsequently extending his York scheme into the Middle Saxon period (Ottaway and Wiener 1993). The two schemes are aligned in Table 5. The revised Evison scheme has been adopted here as a means of comparing Wharram knives with those of early Anglo-Saxon date, as well as with contemporary examples.

Thirty-two of the Wharram knives can be assigned to type and most fall into types A, D and E. There are few knives of types B or C and this confirms, once again, the lack of early Anglo-Saxon occupation, given that these are knife forms of that early period. They tend to be less common even within early Anglo-Saxon assemblages. Type A occurs throughout the Anglo-Saxon period. Type B is essentially of 6th-century date, although a few examples may come from early 7th-century graves (Evison 1987, 115; Böhner 1958, 214-15; Riddler forthcoming b). The single example of a type B knife came from the North Manor Area (Goodall and Clark 2004, fig. 127.30) and has been noted above. Type C is of 6th to 7th-century date and it may have served as a precursor to the related Type E, although it is possible that both forms originated at roughly the same time (Evison 1987, 115). The three type C knives come from the North Manor Area, the Western Plateau (north) and the South Manor Area (Goodall I.H. 1992, fig. 27.59; Goodall and Clark 2000, fig. 64.49; Goodall and Clark 2004, fig. 127.33). Type D is of 7th-century and later date, with an emphasis on the second half of the 7th century onwards. Type E retains the angled back of the Type C knife but utilises a straight cutting edge. The type does not appear much before the 7th century and it increases in popularity thereafter, becoming one of the most common forms of the Middle and Late Saxon periods (Riddler 2001b, 232-4).

In many respects, the most interesting point to emerge from this survey of Yorkshire Anglo-Saxon knife forms relates to York rather than Wharram, and hints at a possible contrast between urban and rural sites. Sewerby and Castledyke South establish a standard for the early Anglo-Saxon period, with type A dominant and types D and E representing late forms, which occur in small quantities (Table 6). Wharram and Cottam, on the other hand, indicate the situation in the Middle Saxon period, with type E as common as type A, and type D well represented, at Wharram at least. The same situation has

Table 5. Concordance of knife typologies.

Blade shape	Drinkall and Foreman 1998	Ottaway 1992
Curved front section	A	C
Straight back, curved cutting edge	B	E
Angled back, curved cutting edge	C	
Curved back throughout	D	D
Angled back, straight cutting edge	E	A
Angled back, concave curve to front section	F	B

Table 6. Knife forms from Early and Middle Saxon settlements.

Evison Knife Type:	A	B	C	D	E	F	Total
Sewerby	9	3	2	4	2	1	21
Castledyke South	28	8	14	10	11	1	72
Wharram	12	1	3	5	11		32
York, Fishergate	23	1		6	3	1	34
York, Blue Bridge Lane	3			1	1		5
Cottam	13			1	21		35
Total:	88	13	19	27	49	3	

been noted for Thwing and elsewhere in rural Middle Saxon England, as at Brandon, and *Sandtun*, for example (Rogers 1993, 1275; Riddler 2001b, 232-4; Nicky Rogers, *pers comm*). The two samples from Middle Saxon York, on the other hand, show type A as dominant and type E comparatively scarce, which differs from other Middle Saxon sites and is essentially an early Anglo-Saxon pattern, rather than a pattern of the Middle Saxon period. Rogers has previously noted this peculiarity of the Fishergate sample (Rogers 1993, 1273-5). It is notable also that the sample of knives from the Royal Opera House excavation in *Lundenwic* follows the Fishergate pattern, with the majority of them belonging to type A and with few of any other type (Blackmore 2003, 255-6). There is the possibility, therefore, that the range of knives found within the *wic* sites differs from that seen at rural sites. The situation at *Hamwic* is a little difficult to establish, although greater quantities of type E knives may be present there, and type D knives were well represented at the St Mary's Stadium excavations (Birbeck 2005, 114-16). Wharram follows the common pattern for rural settlements in the Middle Saxon period, and particularly those in Yorkshire.

Knives of types D and E share the same characteristic of a straight cutting edge, which does not occur with the other forms, and it is possible that the smaller forms of these knives were used specifically in craft processes. At the same time, there is abundant evidence for craft working at Fishergate, but few knives of these types. Moreover, the illustration of 'Feasting in the Hall' in British Library MS Cotton Claudius B.IV, f63v includes a row of type E knives, held by men who are also carrying drinking horns and glass vessels, implying that these knives were used in feasting at the table (Loveluck 2007, fig. 9.2). The popularity of knives of types A and E during the Middle Saxon period reflects the use of knives by the majority of the population in utilitarian tasks. Blair has pointed out that knives were commonly placed in early Anglo-Saxon graves and that they were effectively the last object type to be deposited in graves, before accompanied burial ceased in the Middle Saxon period (Blair 2005, 240).

Middle Saxon artefacts with ecclesiastical associations

Determining the religious component of any Middle Saxon settlement on the basis of its material culture has become a fraught exercise. Earlier associations of Tating ware with ecclesiastical settlements are now regarded as overly simplistic and essentially incorrect (Hodges 1981, 65; Madsen 2004, 256). Its distribution encompasses sites of some status, relatively few of which have any monastic association (Blinkhorn 2009, 363; cf Coutts and Hodges 1992, 38-9). Both Loveluck and Pestell have also reduced the potential significance of styli, although Blair has attempted to reassert their ecclesiastical connections (Loveluck 2001, 112-13; 2007, 152; Pestell 2004, 40-47; 2009; Blair 2005, 209). Loveluck has taken these arguments further and suggested that a number of objects previously invested with religious and frequently monastic connotations can be interpreted in other ways. He has also drawn faunal remains into the argument (Loveluck 2001, 112-13). Wharram offers a chance to develop the arguments for material culture a little, in part by expanding the range of objects under consideration, and also by viewing them within phases of the Middle Saxon period, as wisely advocated for Flixborough (Loveluck 2007, 146). With this in mind, it is important to note that the table below deals specifically with the Middle Saxon period and not with Late Saxon developments. Early arguments for a monastic component at Wharram were brought together by Julian Richards and are reviewed here (Richards 1992c, 93-4).

The range of objects with possible ecclesiastical connotations is presented in Table 7 and their presence or absence at a range of sites is compared. A number of these object categories require a brief commentary, as does the selection of sites. Most of the items listed in the table would be acquired by excavation, rather than metal detecting. Both styli and Tating ware have been included, but only to indicate that they are unreliable attributes of ecclesiastical presence, particularly if used on their own. Stone sculpture and Middle Saxon window glass can be regarded as much more reliable indicators, although sculpture occurs largely north of the Humber and is rare

Table 7 Selected object categories from Middle Saxon sites.

Site	Window glass	Sculpture	Ceramic moulds	Inkwells	Whitby-type ware	Inscriptions	Large hand bells	Insular material	Tating ware	Styli
Hamwic	*		*	*		*		*	*	*
Sandtun										
Canterbury										
Outer Court	*		*							*
Dover										
Barking	*									*
Lundenwic									*	
Maidenhead									*	
Brandon	*			*		*	*		*	*
Middle Saxon									*	*
Ipswich										
Higham Ferrers										
Wharram Percy		*	*		*			*	*	
Beverley	*			*						
Jarrow	*	*	*		*	*			*	*
Hartlepool		*	*		*					
Whitby	*	*	*		*	*		*		*
Flixborough	*		*			*				*
Whithorn	*	*						*		*
York, Fishergate									*	
Cottam										

in East Anglia and southern England. Its presence at Wharram, with fragments there of both early and late 8th-century date, is therefore an important characteristic indicative of a monastic connection at that time. Stone sculpture is absent from Flixborough but window glass is present there within its late 8th to mid-9th-century phase. Outside Flixborough and Brandon, it is associated with large sites regarded by the majority of scholars as monasteries and much of it is contemporary with the Flixborough material, occurring late in the Middle Saxon period (Cramp 2000).

Ceramic moulds are not, in themselves, indicators of any ecclesiastical function and it is necessary to correlate them with the products they helped to form. Interlaced panels, like that from Site 94 (Bayley 1992, fig. 32.13), are more promising in this respect than the largely indistinct fragments retrieved from Flixborough, or those from Cook Street at *Hamwic* (Garner 1994, 111 and fig 13). Yet Cook Street at *Hamwic* lies a short distance to the west of the church of St Mary's, within southern *Hamwic*, an area which differs in character from the northern part of the settlement (Alan Morton, *pers comm*). Moreover,

the list of Middle Saxon sites that have produced ceramic mould fragments is an intriguing one, being otherwise limited to the Bayle at Folkestone, Hartlepool, Barrow-on-Humber and Canterbury (Bayley 1992, 64-5; Keith Parfitt, *pers comm*). All these sites have monastic associations, with the moulds belonging largely to the 8th century.

The distribution of Whitby-type ceramics has been noted above and, aside from finds at the Anglo-Saxon cemetery of Norton-on-Tees, and a sherd from Newcastle, it is confined to Whitby, Hartlepool, Jarrow and Wharram.

Inkwells may be the solution to two of the Old English Riddles of the Exeter Book, where they are described as made of antler (Jennifer Neville, *pers comm*: Krapp and Dobbie 1931-42, Riddles 88 and 93). Archaeological discoveries, however, are as yet limited to inkwell fragments of glass (Evison 2000, 82; and forthcoming). The distribution includes *Hamwic* once again, whose perceived role merely as a production and trading centre, without an ecclesiastical component, clearly needs to be questioned. The settlement included a minster in the 11th

152

century, possibly identifiable with St Mary's church (Morton 1992, 50-51). Inkwells return the argument to questions of literacy but whilst styli were used on tablets, ink was used on vellum and parchment. By no means were all written documents ecclesiastical but most *scriptoria* were attached to monasteries or churches.

Loveluck has drawn attention to the cetacean remains from Flixborough, as part of the feasting repertoire of the settlement (Loveluck 2007, 149). Almost all the cetacean remains stem from bottlenose dolphins, which it is argued were actively hunted in the Humber estuary (Dobney *et al*. 2007, 199-207). Whilst dolphins can be regarded as a food resource (if not necessarily an entirely palatable one), the skeletal remains of larger cetaceans have an ecclesiastical connection. Two distinct sets of whale remains are known from Middle Saxon England, which tend not to overlap. On the one hand, whale vertebrae have been recovered from *Hamwic*, Whitby, *Sandtun* and Lowestoft (Morton 1992, 144 and pl. 6; Riddler 1998; Riddler and Sabin 2009). Some of the vertebrae were used as working surfaces and include numerous knife marks (Riddler 1998). There is no connection between these working surfaces and anything ecclesiastical.

On the other hand, there is evidence for the use of whale bone as a substitute for ivory during the late 7th to 10th centuries. The most obvious examples of this use of the resource are the Franks and Gandersheim caskets (Webster and Backhouse 1991, 101 and 177-8). In addition, Pestell has illustrated the whale bone tablets from Blythburgh and the casket fragments from Larling and related these finds to minsters (Pestell 2004, 91-2, 94-6 and figs 18 and 20). Fragments of worked whale bone are known also from *Hamwic* and stem from opportunist strandings (Riddler and Trzaska-Nartowski forthcoming a; Riddler forthcoming c). They may have been used in casket manufacture, but no finished objects of this type survive from the settlement. They can, however, be related to several combs from the settlement, made of whale bone. There may have been a symbolic value in the use of this material in comb manufacture, given its substitute value for ivory. Combs with whale bone connecting plates are known from *Hamwic* and Brandon (Riddler forthcoming a).

Large hand bells of Insular origin have been described by Bourke (1980). They can be distinguished by their size from small iron bells, which are relatively common finds of the Early Anglo-Saxon and Middle Saxon periods, occurring in both cemeteries and settlements (Ottaway 1992, 557-8; 2009; Geake 1997, 102; Hinton 2000, 45-7). Most of the small bells were probably used with animals, although Hinton has suggested that some may have been rung by travellers to announce their presence (Hinton 2000, 47). Large hand bells are noticeably rare, however, and may form part of the Insular ecclesiastical tradition.

Insular material consists otherwise of combs, as well as glass bracelets and copper-alloy ring pins. A copper-alloy ring-headed pin has been found at *Hamwic*, which bemused David Hinton, and there is a possible example also from Brandon (Hinton 1996, 32). A small pin

(85/SF118, Plate 16) with a T-shaped head from the South Manor Area is difficult to parallel precisely, but the shape of the head does not fit well with Anglo-Saxon pin types, and is much more redolent of those from Ireland and Scotland. The length of the pin (60mm) and the decorated shaft also recall pins from that area assigned to Foster's LIA phase, of *c*. AD 600-800, with examples from Whithorn and the Broch of Burrian suggesting an 8th-century date (Foster 1990, 151 and fig. 9.2.2 and 11).

The distribution of Insular combs has been outlined above and includes both Wharram and Whitby. Whitby has also produced a glass bangle of Insular type and Carroll has drawn attention to the presence of Roman glass bangles on monastic sites, although it should be noted that they are relatively common in Romano-British contexts within northern Britain in general (Carroll 2001, 109). Several fragments of Romano-British glass bracelets have come from Wharram (Price *et al*. 2000, 123; Price 2004, 233; Price 2007, 300).

Reading across the rows of the table, and ignoring the columns for styli and Tating ware, Whitby includes six categories and most of the accepted monastic sites include either three or four, with the exception of Barking and Beverley. Brandon and Wharram include four categories, whilst Flixborough has three. They can be contrasted with the *wic* sites and the smaller, rural settlements, which have scarcely any of the categories at all. *Hamwic*, however, includes no less than five categories and is clearly different from the remaining *wics* in this respect. In reality, there should be no particular obstacle to endorsing an ecclesiastical and possibly monastic presence at Wharram, seen in objects of 8th-century date. This point was previously made by Julian Richards and is emphasised here once again (Richards 1992c, 93-4; Richards 2000a, 200). Whilst Tating ware and styli can be reduced in significance, the sculpture, ceramic moulds and objects of Insular origin are all redolent of 8th-century ecclesiastical associations. The character of these possible associations is explored further in Chapter 12 below.

Crafts and activities
Wharram follows a common pattern for Middle Saxon Wolds settlements in terms of its regional and imported material, although it differs from them in its ecclesiastical component. It provides also limited evidence for a range of crafts, including textile manufacture. The majority of the material evidence comes from the South Manor Area. Goodall noted that the relative proportion of tools and knives from the North Manor Area was greater than that from the South Manor Area, but this consists almost entirely of material of Roman and medieval date (Goodall and Clark 2004, 244). Similarly, the iron tools from the Churchyard sites all come from contexts post-dating the Norman conquest (Goodall and Clark 2007, 308). Whilst Wharram has produced good quantities of tools, and particularly of iron awls, almost all of these, too, have come from medieval or later contexts. Some could be residual in those contexts, but it is impossible to tell.

A small number of spoon bits, one of which came from a Middle Saxon context in the South Manor Area (Goodall and Clark 2000, 133), provide evidence for woodworking. A chisel also came from a Middle Saxon context there (Goodall and Clark 2000, 133). Several iron awls provide indirect evidence for leatherworking, although they may possibly have been used in woodworking. The fragment of a saw blade from a Late Saxon layer is more likely to have formed part of the toolkit of a comb maker than a woodworker. The quantity of bone pins recovered from the South Manor Area, as well as the Western Plateau (north) sites, suggests that a workshop was producing them at Wharram. Similar quantities are known only from an unpublished site at Swindon Hill, Wiltshire (Evison 1987, 84). Other sites have only produced them in small quantities. There is slight evidence also for comb making on site, with a single unfinished tooth segment coming from Site 59 in the South Manor Area. It is likely that the Middle Saxon workshop which manufactured the combs was also responsible for the bone pins (Riddler and Trzaska-Nartowski forthcoming a).

Although only a single red deer antler offcut has been recovered from the Plateau area (95/SF43), it is sufficient to indicate that antler working took place in the vicinity. There are few large assemblages of red deer antler dating to the Middle Saxon period and they are confined to the pre-Viking production and trading centres like *Hamwic* and York (Rogers 1993, 1245-63; Riddler 2001a). Rural settlements tend to produce very small assemblages of antler, or none at all. At Wharram, another antler offcut came from the South Manor and several were retrieved from contexts phased to the late medieval period at the North Manor (MacGregor 2000, 154; Richardson 2004a, 260-61). MacGregor has argued that red deer antler became increasingly difficult to obtain across the medieval period, which might suggest that the North Manor antler is residual and belongs to an earlier period (MacGregor 1989a, 113-14). On the other hand, red deer antler waste has appeared in well-stratified deposits of late medieval date, as at Norwich Castle, for example (Shepherd Popescu 2009, 632, 707 and 878-9).

Contemporary rural settlements are largely devoid of red deer antler remains. Flixborough merely produced a few 'possible antler fragments', whilst one fragment of red deer (not specified as bone or antler) is mentioned at Cottam (Dobney *et al.* 2007, 50; Richards 1999a, 85). A few fragments came from Bloodmoor Hill, Brandon, Higham Ferrers and Ramsbury (Higbee 2009, 302; Crabtree forthcoming; Evans 2007, 150; Coy 1980, 49). Monastic sites fair little better, with one fragment of antler from Hartlepool and a few from Wearmouth/Jarrow (Huntley and Rackham 2007, 120; Riddler 2006a, 268-9). 'Reindeer horn' came from the eastern area of the excavations at Whitby (Cramp 1976, 457). Other Middle Saxon sites have produced no red deer antler at all. All of this suggests that the mechanisms for the disposal of antler waste varied markedly between urban and rural sites of the Middle Saxon period. It is noticeable that the dense clustering of rubbish pits that effectively defines the landscapes of the pre-Viking production centres is absent in rural environments. Moreover, antler was not worked in every household and its distribution across settlements does not follow that of domestic animal bone, but may reflect the location of workshops, when found in sufficient quantities (Riddler 2001a; Haslam *et al.* forthcoming). Slightly greater quantities of antler waste have come from early Anglo-Saxon settlements, largely because it is usually concentrated in the backfills of *Grubenhäuser*, and these are less commonly found in the Middle Saxon period. Accordingly, this one small fragment of antler waste is a scarce indicator of a craft widely practised across Anglo-Saxon England, for which the evidence is often missing (Riddler and Trzaska-Nartowski forthcoming a).

By far the greatest quantity of evidence for industrial and craft activity is, of course, that related to the smithy found in the South Manor Area excavations (MacDonnell 2000, 155-66). Its character and significance are discussed in the next section of this chapter.

The iron economy of Wharram Percy
by Gerry McDonnell, Eleanor Blakelock and Samantha Rubinson with contributions from Nicolas Chabot, Allan Daoust and Vanessa Castagnino

Introduction
The 1981-90 excavations of Sites 59, 76, 84, 85, 90 and 93 in the South Manor Area recovered a substantial quantity of slag (113kg) that led to the identification of the location of a smithy of Middle Saxon date. Very few smithies have been investigated from any period, and only a few Anglo-Saxon examples can be quoted. The results were published a decade ago as a distinct chapter in the site publication (McDonnell 2000). This was an advance over many excavation reports in which the ironworking is presented as an appendix or in fiche, which belies the fundamental importance of iron to the society being researched. Nevertheless, the chapter was still a very routine publication reporting the finds and considering the spatial and chronological distribution of the slag with some limited reporting of the slag composition. In the last few years the evidence for ironworking has been assessed from other excavations at Wharram and significant archaeometallurgical research has been undertaken on the slag and iron artefacts from the smithy.

This section of the chapter will synthesise the new evidence gained from the analyses, in the context of the sequence of processes and activities required to create iron objects: the smelting of the ore to produce iron; the refining of the metal to trade iron, and then the smithing of the iron to forge the artefact (McDonnell 1987a). It reinterprets all the evidence in a more holistic way, setting the smithy in its landscape and considering how it functioned, and will, it is hoped, demonstrate to the non-specialist reader the potential of integrated archaeometallurgical research. The detailed results of the analyses are to be found in the full technical reports available through the Archaeology Data Service (doi:10.5284/1000415).

The present summary and discussion must, however, be prefaced by words of caution regarding the recovery of the ironworking assemblage from Wharram. In the late 1980s excavation strategies for ironworking sites were only in their infancy; in particular, hammerscale, now regarded as an absolute essential indicator of smithing, was only just being recognised and recovered. The first detailed recovery and recording of hammerscale took place at Burton Dassett in Warwickshire in 1991 (Mills and McDonnell 1992) – although one of us (McDonnell) has a strong memory of the late Leo Biek minutely examining the trowelled surface at Wharram with his magnifying lenses.

Three generic models can be proposed for the exploitation of iron. The first is the Self-sufficient Model, in which the whole process from the smelting of the ore to manufacturing the objects takes place entirely at the same settlement. This model allows for spatial separation of the processes, e.g. smelting in the 'outfield' and smithing within the settlement. The evidence for it includes the raw materials (e.g. ore, fuel and clay), the remains of a smelting furnace and the resulting smelting slag. In addition, evidence for the smithing of the artefact must also be present, including smithing hearth remains, smithing slag and stock iron.

The second model, the Complex Smithy Model, is one in which the settlement has a local smithy that is using imported stock iron in the form of bars to manufacture iron objects. The evidence consists of smithing hearth debris, smithing slag and stock iron. The level of smithing activity may vary from a full-time smithy to one used occasionally. The third model, the Basic Smithy Model, envisages all the iron artefacts being imported into the site from elsewhere, though some basic smithing is conducted, e.g. simple repairs, fettling of edged tools, and the manufacture of simple items such as hook, staples etc. from scrap. In this model there would be no evidence for smithing of new iron objects so there should be no stock iron present on the site.

While each of the above models could be independent of the others, it is equally likely that there could be a mixture of two or three models at any one settlement. For example, some rarer iron alloys such as high-quality high carbon steel may have been imported into some smithy sites to create composite iron artefacts, even though the same site is smelting its own bulk iron. In addition, the same site may also be importing some artefacts from sites elsewhere. With each of the above models it is possible that both repairing and recycling of iron objects was also taking place, leaving evidence in the form of smithing slag.

No smelting furnaces or smelting slag have been identified at Wharram Percy, therefore the first model, the fully self-sufficient model, can at present be excluded. There is, however, evidence for a smithy with stock iron at the site. Trade iron was imported into the site from elsewhere to supply the smithy, and there are several main scenarios with regard to its origins. The first is that the iron was being imported from the Jurassic Ridge sources in North Lincolnshire where smelting evidence has been recovered at Flixborough (Starley 1999) and Cherry Willingham (McDonnell 1987b). A slag block, typical of Anglo-Saxon smelting technology (see below), resides in the garden of Scunthorpe Museum (Leahy pers. comm.) and one is illustrated by Harold Dudley (1949). Secondly, the Wolds are surrounded by bog ores which were exploited in the Iron Age, e.g. North Cave (McDonnell 1988b) and further afield (Halkon and Millet 1999), and may have been exploited in the Anglo-Saxon period. A third option is that iron was sourced from further away, e.g. from the North York Moors or West Yorkshire via markets such as those at Malton or Driffield.

The production of iron
There are two methods of producing iron: the direct method in which iron metal is extracted from the ore in the solid state using a bloomery furnace, and the indirect process, which produces liquid steel or cast iron. In both processes the ore is reduced to metallic iron creating an iron slag of unwanted gangue material, but only in the indirect process does the iron become liquid (Buchwald and Wivel 1998, 45-6; Pleiner 2000, 131-3).

Smelting
The morphology of the slag produced during smelting often depends on the type of furnace used, which can also vary both regionally and chronologically, depending on the ore type (available and used), the available fuel and cultural traditions (Joosten 2004, 20-28; Pleiner 2000, 141-5). Very few Anglo-Saxon smelting sites have been identified in England. For example, there is no evidence for iron smelting in this period in the Forest of Dean, and only one site, Millbrook (Tebbutt 1982), in the Weald, although both areas were major centres for iron production in the preceding Roman and subsequent medieval periods. Excavations of the few iron smelting sites discovered have revealed three slag types based on slag morphology.

The first group consists of tapped slag similar to that present in other periods, found at Flixborough, North East Lincolnshire (Starley 1999). The second group comprises the raked slag at Millbrook, Sussex (Tebbutt 1982) and Cherry Willingham, North East Lincolnshire (McDonnell 1987b) and the furnace slag type recovered at Ramsbury, Wiltshire (Haslam *et al.* 1980). The third group has a distinct 'slag block' morphology similar to slag found in Southern Scandinavia, North Germany and Poland (McDonnell 1989). Examples of slag blocks have been found at Romsey (McDonnell 1988a), Mucking and Little Totham, Essex (Hamerow 2002, 189). Some rural smelting sites such as Ramsbury and Flixborough are high status centres (Hamerow 2002, 189; Loveluck

1998), whilst others such as Bestwall, Dorset are typical Anglo-Saxon rural settlements (Slater and McDonnell 2002). There is scant evidence for urban smelting in this period with very small amounts of smelting slag found at York (Ottaway 1992, 477-478; Rogers 1993) and no evidence found at *Hamwic*.

The sites that are known are predominantly single furnaces producing relatively small amounts of metal. Recent research has shown that phosphoric iron (see below) is present in significant quantities in most iron samples, suggesting that phosphoric iron was the product of many of the smelting sites. In contrast, iron with few alloying elements and steel appear to be rarer in the Anglo-Saxon period and may have been produced at specialised smelting sites.

Smithing

In contrast to the scarcity of evidence for smelting, smithing slag is the most common ironworking residue found on Anglo-Saxon settlement sites, suggesting that smithing was a craft carried out close to the consumer (McDonnell 1987a; Serneels and Perret 2003). This is to be expected, since smithies would have been required to manufacture and repair iron artefacts used by the communities. There are different levels of smithies, from permanent 'full-time' workshops to forges where occasional smithing operations were carried out. Even so, the evidence from this period is sparse, as, although there are numerous finds of iron smithing slag, very few smithy structures have been identified (McDonnell 1989; McDonnell 2000, 155-66).

Smithing slag has been found at a range of urban sites including York, London and Stamford but only at *Hamwic* has the smithy itself been identified (Andrews 1997; Ottaway 1992; Rogers 1993). Evidence for rural smithies has been found at a large number of settlements including West Stow (West 1985), West Heslerton, Catholme, Yarnton (Hey 2004) and Wharram Percy (McDonnell 2000, 155-166). Smithing slag has also been found associated with smelting sites such as Romsey, Ramsbury, Flixborough (Starley 1999), Mucking (McDonnell 1993; 1989), Little Totham and Bestwall (Slater and McDonnell 2002).

The inputs to the Wharram smithy

Stock iron

The smith, whether a specialist or a general village smith, required a stock of iron in the form of bars, billets and strips from which to produce iron objects. Bar, or trade iron, is the intermediate stage between the bloom and the finished artefact. It is created by consolidating and shaping the bloom into bars for trade and use. These bars are then used by blacksmiths in the manufacture of iron objects such as tools, fixtures and fittings etc. They have been variously termed as trade iron, bar, blank or strip (e.g. Ottaway 1992, 492). The bars recovered from the smithy are smaller than trade bars, which would probably have been about 40mm wide and 20mm thick, and of varying lengths. A bar fragment analysed from Coppergate (Ottaway 1992, 499, fig. 188, cat. no. 2073) is probably a scrap end of a typical trade bar. Thus, the material classified as bar at Wharram represents iron at an intermediary stage between the trade iron and a finished artefact.

Nine bars were found in the Wharram Percy smithy, averaging 76mm in length, with a 5mm width and 3mm thickness, with tapered or scrolled ends; they probably represent end of bar, i.e. that final portion of a bar that was discarded as being too short to use. The bars were different shapes and thicknesses providing a selection based on what the smithy needed (e.g. one, SF320 was a curved bar and two, SF260 and SF299, were classified as strip).

All the bars were sectioned and samples prepared; they were examined using optical and electron microscopy and micro-hardness testing. Elemental analysis of the metal indicated, in particular, the phosphorus content and the oxide composition of the slag inclusions trapped in the metal. Previous research has demonstrated that three alloys were used in the Anglo-Saxon period in England (McDonnell 1989; Blakelock and McDonnell 2007): ferritic iron, which contained few alloying elements (less than 0.1%); phosphoric iron, containing between 0.15 to 1% phosphorus; and steel which contains carbon as the main alloying element. A fourth type of iron, termed piled or composite iron, incorporates one, two or more of the single alloys (e.g. ferritic and phosphoric iron). The composite alloy may be formed 'naturally' by the traditional bloomery smelting furnace, or as a deliberate construction made by welding bars of the different alloys together. Thus an artefact may be manufactured from a single alloy or a combination of two or more alloys to make a composite artefact. In the case of bars, archaeometallurgical research was undertaken to test whether the bars are single or composite artefacts.

The Wharram bars represent a selection of alloys: one ferritic bar, three phosphoric bars, two steel bars and three composite bars (Fig. 66). The ferritic bar has a hardness of $116Hv_{200}$, compared to the highest value for the phosphoric bars of $205Hv_{200}$, which is harder than the low carbon steel bar ($130Hv_{200}$). Two of the phosphoric bars show a low concentration of slag inclusions (i.e. they are 'clean'), and the grain size of the phosphoric is larger than ferrite. A further attribute is that the phosphoric iron would colour differently, which leads to its use in pattern-welding. The steel bars are of particular interest. These bars fit into two different categories due to their different carbon contents. The high carbon steel (maximum 0.8%C) in SF359 had the potential to have been heat-treated to dramatically increase its hardness, making it ideal for the cutting edges of knives. The second steel bar (SF364) had a lower carbon content and would not have produced a cutting edge of the same quality.

Re-examination of some of the Anglo-Scandinavian bars recovered from the excavations from Coppergate, York (Fig. 66) shows that the composite bars dominate that assemblage, which can be interpreted as reflecting the heterogeneous nature of iron blooms produced by the

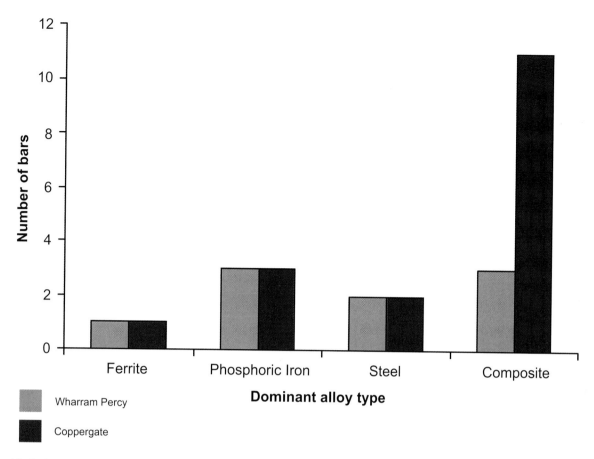

Fig. 66. Smithing bar compositions from Wharram and from Coppergate, York. (G. McDonnell)

bloomery process. This suggests that the single alloy bars were produced deliberately for specific functions, e.g. steel for cutting edges.

As part of a larger study (Chabot 2007), a detailed analysis of the slag inclusions in all nine bars from Wharram Percy was undertaken. The aim of this study was to test a model concerning the types of inclusion that may be found in iron artefacts. The model proposes that a simple object such as a bar is a small number of processes away from the smelting process. Each process in the production of the artefact will alter existing slag inclusions or introduce new slag inclusions into the metal. Thus, a simple artefact, such as a bar should contain a smaller range of compositions. In theory, the minimum number of inclusion types should be three, those deriving from the smelting process, the refining of the smelted iron, and those deriving from the smithing of the bar. Further characterising of the inclusion profile range within an assemblage of bars may indicate whether the bars derive from a single centre or multiple production centres. Bars generated by a single production would be expected to show the same range of inclusion profiles. The results suggested that the Wharram smithy was accessing iron from at least five production centres.

Other resources

There are many other resources involved in blacksmithing that are vital to the creation of the finished product, the most important being fuel and clay. Clay was

needed to make crucibles and moulds (two fragments were recovered from the smithy) for non-ferrous metalworking. Charcoal was the fuel in use in this period for both iron smelting and iron smithing. A working smithy would probably require several kilos of charcoal per day, giving a yearly requirement of less than half a tonne. The experimental charcoal burn conducted by Wheeler and Powell at Dalby Forest, North Yorkshire utilised 4 tonnes of chopped wood to produce one tonne of charcoal (Wheeler 2004; Powell *et al.* 2005); thus the smithy's annual needs could have been supplied by a single large burn.

A further resource is stone used for sharpening blades. Clark and Gaunt (2000, 104-109) reported on the hone stones from the South Manor Area excavations, which produced the largest quantity of hones stones from Wharram, with a particularly high concentration recovered from Sites 44, 59, and 76 (32 hones), associated with the smithy. This represents 44% of those recovered from the whole of the South Manor Area excavations. There was no evidence for preference of a particular stone type.

The smithy building

There are misconceptions about where ironworking, in particular smithing was conducted. It is essential that smithing is carried out inside a roofed structure, in low light levels to enable the smith to see the colour of the flame – and most importantly the metal – as this provides

157

the only temperature guide the smith has. It is envisaged that the Saxon forge comprised a roofed building dedicated to metalworking and containing a raised blacksmith's hearth, hand or foot powered bellows, an anvil, a range of tools, stock iron and fuel. It is probable that, other than fuel, the smithy of today is little changed from its Anglo-Saxon predecessor.

Clay was required for the construction of the hearth, providing its lining, especially around the tuyère (blow-hole) area which was subjected to the highest temperatures. The forge envisaged at Wharram would be a raised hearth, perhaps waist high, built of stone and/or timber, with the hearth itself built of stone or timber lined with clay, and perhaps a base layer of sand. The hearth would have a set of bellows to provide forced draught to raise the temperature required for welding (1100°C). Such a structure is illustrated in the 9th-century Utrecht Psalter (Clarke 1979, 106; http://psalter.library.uu.nl/).

The clay lining, especially around the tuyère, would have to be periodically replaced, perhaps weekly depending on the level of activity, as the internal hot face of the lining would fracture from the hearth due to chemical alteration of the clay and the high temperatures. A total of 14.2kg of hearth lining was recovered from the excavation; this quantity as a proportion of the total Wharram assemblage is comparable to other sites, though given the presence of a smithy dump, a higher proportion may have been expected.

Analysis of the distribution of slag on the South Manor sites shows a clear concentration in Sites 59 and 76, specifically within Phases 3, 4 and 5 (McDonnell 2000, 158-9, figs 74-5 and 160, table 23). In Phase 3 (Middle Saxon) the slag is distributed to the south of the main east-west ditches. This would suggest that it represents the smithy dump, outside the smithy building which was probably the structure identified as Building A, to the west (and perhaps Building B, its likely predecessor: see Fig. 55). The smithy was established in Phase 2, the early

part of the Middle Saxon period. How long it stood at this location is unknown as the slag spreads into Phases 4 (Late Saxon) and 5 (Medieval). The presence of large quantities of hearth lining is strong evidence for the proximity of the smithy to the dumps, rather than the dumps being of slag reused for foundations, levelling etc. Analysis of other assemblages indicates that the lining is friable and does not survive in recognisable form if transported and reused.

The argument against a smithy building within the excavation area is the absence of extensive quantities of hammerscale. As noted above, however, hammerscale was only beginning to be recognised in the mid-1980s, and it was only in the very late 1980s that strategies were introduced to recover these residues. Thus, some hammerscale was recovered from Site 76 (context 70) and analysed by McDonnell (1986, 188-93). Both flake and spheroidal hammerscale was recovered, indicative of the full range of iron smithing activity, the spheroidal hammerscale being generated during fire welding (McDonnell 1986, 146; Dungworth and Wilkes 2007).

Craft activity in the smithy

A wide variety of craft activities could have been carried out in an Anglo-Saxon smithy, ranging from ironworking, to non-ferrous metalworking and including other craft activities associated with the manufacture of metal artefacts. For example, all iron knives had a non-metallic handle, made from horn, antler, bone or wood, and these could have been produced by the smith, or a different craftsperson. This section focuses solely on iron smithing and outlines the different processes involved in the manufacture of iron artefacts.

Manufacture

Creating objects from iron is a process that can be very simple or incredibly complex, depending on the quality of iron used and the final product required, from a simple

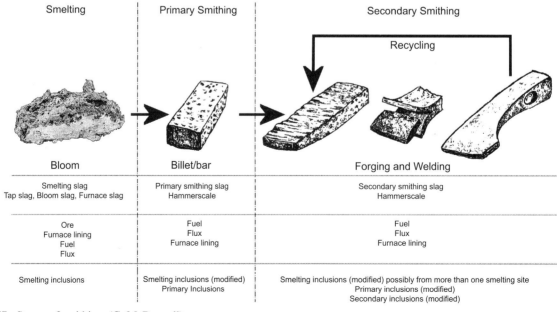

Smelting	Primary Smithing	Secondary Smithing	
		Recycling	
Bloom	Billet/bar	Forging and Welding	
Smelting slag Tap slag, Bloom slag, Furnace slag	Primary smithing slag Hammerscale	Secondary smithing slag Hammerscale	
Ore Furnace lining Fuel Flux	Fuel Flux Furnace lining	Fuel Flux Furnace lining	
Smelting inclusions	Smelting inclusions (modified) Primary Inclusions	Smelting inclusions (modified) possibly from more than one smelting site Primary inclusions (modified) Secondary inclusions (modified)	

Fig. 67. Stages of smithing. (G. McDonnell)

nail to an elaborate composite blade which has been heat treated and decorated (Serneels and Perret 2003). Therefore, in antiquity there were different levels of smith, from the general village blacksmith creating horseshoes to the master sword smith. The village blacksmith would have provided an important service to any community, both manufacturing and repairing iron items used either in the home or as agricultural equipment (Faull and Moorhouse 1981, 771-73). On the other hand, the skills and techniques required to manufacture a pattern welded sword may have been known only to a select few smiths (Anstee and Biek 1961; Peirce 2002; Tylecote and Gilmour 1986, 1-3).

There are two stages of smithing: primary and secondary (Fig. 67). Primary smithing is required to refine and consolidate the bloom and produce a billet. This is carried out by hammering the bloom, often while still hot, to remove adhering slag or to expel included slag and charcoal (Hedges and Salter 1979; Crew 1991; McDonnell 1991; Serneels and Perret 2003). Primary smithing or bloom smithing would almost certainly be carried out at, or close to the smelting site and is therefore considered not to have been conducted at Wharram. Secondary smithing or 'forging' is the operation where the billet is shaped into a trade iron or bar, and subsequently the bar is manufactured into artefacts. This process is carried out by repeatedly heating the iron in a hearth and hammering it on an anvil to form the artefact, and may involve welding to join two or more components, e.g. steel edges to tools.

Metallographic studies of knives and other objects have shown that there is a specific order used when manufacturing an object and therefore a 'chaîne opératoire' can be constructed. The manufacture of complex artefacts, in particular edged tools, utilises more than one type of alloy bar. In the case of edged tools, in particular knives, this enables a manufacturing typology to be established which demonstrates how the steel edge is introduced (Fig. 68; Blakelock and McDonnell 2007; Tylecote and Gilmour 1986, 2-7). The majority of these methods of manufacture require the different iron alloys

to be hot welded together. This occurs prior to the object being shaped, indicated by the large number of distorted weld lines found in knives. To weld pieces of iron together, it is vital that the metal is heated to a temperature at which it is soft but not molten (c. 1100°C). Weld lines joining metals are often visible due to slag inclusions which get trapped between the metals during the smithing process. Some weld lines even have a distinct white colour, which is due to arsenic and nickel enrichment, possibly indicating that during fire welding, a 'fluxing' compound was added to create a better quality weld (Castagnino 2007).

Once the object is the desired shape the smith has more decisions to make, depending on the required function (e.g. a knife requires a sharp and hard cutting edge). The speed of cooling can control the formation of certain microstructures which increase the hardness of the metal. The most common form of heat treatment is quenching, where the still hot object is plunged into a liquid to cool it rapidly and to create an extremely hard cutting edge (Pleiner 2006, 65-70; Samuels 1999, 5-37; Scott 1991, 31-32; Tylecote 1990). In modern smithies this is usually done with water, but other liquids such as oil, milk, urine and even blood would have been just as effective and may have been necessary for the ritual or 'secret recipe' aspect of the smith's work (Maddin 1987). Once quenched, the steel would also become brittle so it required tempering, heating to 500°C, which reduces the brittleness and its hardness (Samuels 1999, 5-37; Scott 1991, 31-32; Tylecote 1990). Cold working can also significantly increase the hardness of iron and its alloys (Swiss and McDonnell 2003).

Ironworking debris
All the smithing processes generate slag as a waste product. A total of 113kg of ironworking debris was recovered from the South Manor Area. In the original publication this was classified into four major groups: Hearth Bottoms, Smithing Slag Lumps, Hearth Lining and Cinder/Fuel Ash Slag (McDonnell 2000). A reassessment of some of the material in 2006-7 suggests

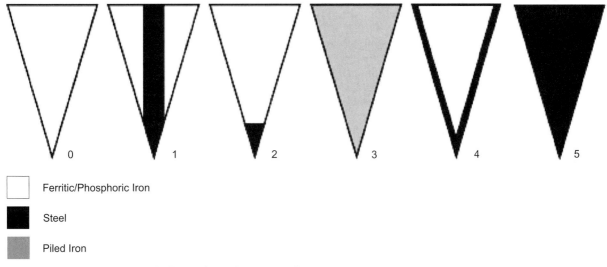

Ferritic/Phosphoric Iron

Steel

Piled Iron

Fig. 68. Manufacturing typology for iron knives. (G. McDonnell)

Table 8. Comparison of smithing slag debris from a range of sites. Mucking (McDonnell 1993), West Heslerton (Cowgill and McDonnell forthcoming), Yarnton (Hey 2004), Flixborough (Starley 1999) and Burton Dassett (McDonnell 1992a). Note Burton Dassett is medieval in date rather than Saxon.

Site	Hearth bottom		Smithing slag lumps		Hearth lining		Total
	(kg)	% of assemblage	(kg)	% of assemblage	(kg)	% of assemblage	
Wharram Percy Smithy	12.9	12	78.8	74	14.2	13	105.9
Hamwic (Site 31)	84.8	13	540.7	85	13.3	2	638.8
Mucking	69	33	115.4	56	22.3	11	206.7
West Heslerton	43.2	40	62.9	58	2.9	3	109
Yarnton	6.7	60	2.6	23	1.8	16	11.1
Flixborough	11.3	84	0	0	2.2	16	13.5
Burton Dassett	34.5	10	310.3	90	1.1	<1	345.9

that the identifications are correct, with the revision that the Cinder/Fuels Ash Slag would be reclassified as Smithing Slag/Cinder (i.e. it is smithing slag with a higher silica content). Other sites excavated at Wharram also produced slag but in small quantities.

Table 8 compares the Wharram slag assemblage with other sites, but all show marked differences. Four of the sites (Mucking, West Heslerton, Yarnton and Flixborough) display high or very high percentages of hearth bottoms compared to smithing slag lumps. This will be a function both of the archaeological site/deposits and researcher preference. Hearth bottoms are more likely to get widely dispersed from the smithy (e.g. through use for post packing), hence the large area excavations such as West Heslerton and Mucking will recover more of them, as opposed to the smaller fragments of smithing slag. There is also variability in researcher's typology: does a partly-formed hearth bottom count as smithing slag or a hearth bottom? The closest comparison for Wharram is with the medieval site of Burton Dassett (McDonnell 1992a), which was also the excavation of a smithy building and its associated slag dump.

Two samples of hearth bottom were analysed as part of the original research (McDonnell 1986, 158-62; McDonnell 2000, 156-7). The Wharram slag sections displayed a mineral texture of silicate laths with fine iron oxide dendrites in a glassy matrix that was more usually observed in iron-smelting slag. Daoust (2007) undertook further analysis of the Wharram Percy assemblage to explore composition relationships between smithing slag and weld lines which, supported by Chabot's (2007) analysis, provides an exceptional insight into macro-slag and metal inclusion composition relationships.

The archaeometallurgical analysis of the slag showed that both the hearth bottoms and the smithing slag lumps have similar compositions with two broad compositional groups emerging. This data set represents the largest analysis of a British assemblage of smithing debris. Previous studies have concentrated on hearth bottom analyses (e.g. McDonnell 1986, 150-87). Neither the mechanisms nor the reasons for the formation of hearth

bottoms and smithing slag lumps are fully understood (McDonnell 1991; Serneels and Perret 2003). Two key questions are: whether the formation of the slag is deliberate or is an accidental by-product of the process, and hence, whether the slag composition was controlled. The consistency of composition implies a high level of control. As smithing slag is regarded as a 'waste product' it can be argued that its composition would not be controlled, but would vary depending on many factors such as the type of smithing activity – for example one slag being formed during hot working to shape an artefact. These analyses suggest either that the composition was controlled irrespective of operation, or that the slag could tolerate changing operating conditions.

The Wharram hearth bottoms were originally examined in 1986 (McDonnell 1986, 158-61; McDonnell 2000). Since that date it has been noted on other sites (e.g. West Heslerton: Cowgill and McDonnell forthcoming) that some small hearth bottoms display particular characteristics. These include high density/fluidity and commonly occur as quarters of hearth bottoms, suggesting fracturing during cooling. These have been interpreted as possible evidence for steel making. Although the iron slag assemblage was not re-examined in full in the recent study, these features were not noted in the original examination. Daoust's selection, at random, of some hearth bottom examples did not encounter any such examples. Thus, this particular hearth bottom type appears to be absent from the Wharram assemblage.

There is only a little evidence that copper-alloy working was carried out in the smithy. Although two mould fragments are present there are no crucibles; and given the high level of preservation of hearth lining, crucibles would unquestionably have survived on the site.

The products of the Wharram smithy

More than 400 pieces of iron were recovered from the entire South Manor Area (Goodall and Clark 2000, 132). These included tools for crafts and agriculture, building ironwork, nails, decorative ironwork like pins and buckles, fittings for horses and swords as well as iron knives. To understand and investigate alloy use and smithing techniques in Middle Saxon Wharram Percy metallographic analysis was carried out on both knives and nails. Knives in the Middle Saxon period were essential, everyday tools, used for many purposes throughout the day, from eating to craft-working (Arnold 1997, 39), and their forms and functions have been discussed by Riddler in the first section of this chapter. Because of their ranges of size, shape and function, knives are also very suitable for archaeometallurgical analysis (Blakelock 2006; McDonnell 1992b). As there have been a number of studies of knives from both Anglo-Saxon cemeteries and settlements, there is a significant corpus of data available for comparison (Blakelock and McDonnell 2007).

Ten out of a total of twelve knives dating to the Middle Saxon period from the South Manor Area excavations were selected for analysis. To complement the study of the knives, seven nails were selected for analysis to examine the metallurgy of utilitarian ironwork. This comparison offers an opportunity to contrast the edged tool technology with lower skill ironwork. Both data sets can be compared to the data from the stock bars.

The archaeometallurgical analysis of the knives
The analysis of the knives shows that the manufacturing type 2, butt-welded blade (Fig. 68), was the commonest type (seven out of ten knives). Only one of the knives, however, had been heat-treated to exploit the steel to its maximum quality (SF159). Five of the other six type 2 butt-welded knives all had *c.* 0.8% carbon, suitable for quenching and tempering; but two of them were worn and found in the smithy, and could have been discarded as scrap. Hence they could have been normalised (i.e. heated) to remove the hardness of the cutting edge. The three knives not of manufacturing type 2 were less distinct in their typology: two (SFs134 and 307) were type 0 and the remaining knife consisted of piled iron (type 3). The knife backs were manufactured from a range of alloys: composite iron (six knives), phosphoric iron (two knives) and ferrite (one knife).

Three knives displayed 'white weld lines', which are due to enrichment in Arsenic (Castagnino 2007) and are indicative of high-quality steel welding. This supports the suggestion that lack of evidence for heat treatment is not a result of manufacture but due to subsequent use and mistreatment resulting in poorer quality edges. There is evidence at Wharram for re-edging in knife SF278, which had a low carbon strip welded to a quality type 2 knife.

Previous analysis of knives from both settlement and cemetery contexts has revealed significant trends (Blakelock and McDonnell 2007). There was a preferential use of manufacturing type 2, butt-welded knives in both urban and rural settlements (Blakelock and McDonnell 2007; Blakelock 2006). In total 79% of all knives examined from Anglo-Saxon settlements in England have been classified as of type 2 manufacture – although some knives classified as type 0 (plain ferritic iron) and 3 (piled iron) may have originally had steel cutting edges which have been subsequently lost due to

wear. The smiths in these settlements were making economical use of the high-quality steel which would have been time-consuming and expensive to make.

The Archaeometallurgical analyses of the nails
Nails are often overlooked because of their basic utilitarian uses and the quantities found. They are useful however, in the study of Saxon smithing techniques due to their simple nature and ease of creation. A total of 833 nails were recovered from the South Manor Area excavations (Watt 2000, 140-47), ranging in type from horseshoe to joinery nails. The largest quantity of unused nails from Wharram Percy was found at the smithy, which strongly suggests they were produced there.

Seven nails, of various types and usage, were sampled and underwent optical analysis and micro-hardness testing, along with elemental composition analysis. The composition and construction of the nails falls into three different categories: phosphoric, ferritic and a combination of phosphoric iron, ferritic and steel. The majority of nails are composed of phosphoric iron, an alloy which is both harder than ferrite and more corrosion resistant. The composite nails appear heterogeneous and have a banded structure of the different alloys present. There were no significant differences in the construction of the different types of nails: they all appear to have been constructed from one piece of thin bar with no evidence of welding. There is no evidence of heavy cold working, or shock in the microstructure of the nails.

The simple manufacture of the nails and the similarities of their alloys to the bars suggest that they were made from similar stock iron. It is very likely that the unused nails found in the smithy, very similar to the phosphoric iron bars, were constructed there.

Use and reuse
The function of an object can often be determined based on its shape and size. For example, the shape and size of the knife, especially that of the cutting edge and knife tip, would most likely determine its function. The handle length and materials used may also have affected the function (Cowgill *et al.* 1987, 51). Historic illustrations such as manuscripts and sculpture can also provide clues as to how objects were used in everyday life (Cowgill *et al.* 1987, 57). In other cases, the artefacts themselves may provide the evidence for how they were used – for example if a nail is still joining two pieces of wood together.

Whether an iron object was heavily used in antiquity can be determined by looking for evidence of wear, damage and repair. For example, as knives are used, the cutting edge will begin to wear down and blunt, so they are often re-sharpened, and this process can result in distortion of the original shape of the cutting edge. Ottaway has suggested that the way a knife was manufactured will affect how quickly the knife will be worn and how it will distort when sharpened, and this can also apply to other objects (Ottaway 1992, 598-9). The cutting edges of five out of the ten knives analysed were heavily worn with another four showing some evidence of wear. Only one knife, SF159, showed no evidence of wear, and this is the only heat-treated blade with a hard quenched and tempered cutting edge. This suggests that heat treatment affects the amount of wear, as knives with harder cutting edges are less prone to wear.

When a knife has been completely worn down and become unusable there is an alternative option to recycling or discard: the object could be repaired by adding more metal. This would be difficult for some iron objects but has been noted in a few of the knives from Wharram Percy and Coppergate, York (McDonnell 1992b). The metallurgical analysis revealed the presence of second weld lines in at least three of the knives from Wharram Percy (SFs237, 278 and 308). These factors suggest that the knives were continuously used, resharpened and repaired until they were no longer usable (for example if they had lost their steel cutting edge: knives SFs134 and 308).

Other rarer microstructures can also reveal information about the use of an artefact, such as Neumann Bands which are induced by shock. These have been identified in the Iron Age cart tyres from Ferrybridge (Swiss and McDonnell 2007), Roman knives from Carlisle (Swiss 2000, 18-23) and an anvil from Coppergate, York (McDonnell 1992b, 512-14). Recent research by the Archaeometallurgy Research Group has demonstrated that Neumann bands only form in very pure iron and that very low concentrations of alloying elements, phosphorus and carbon, inhibit their formation (Marufi 2007). Hence their absence in the Wharram assemblage reflects the metal composition rather than usage.

It is possible that Anglo-Saxon blacksmiths would have reused metals when the opportunity arose, as they still do today (Woodward 1985). It may have been particularly important in low status rural societies and those that were some distance from centres of iron production. It has been suggested that the piling effect seen in some iron is due to iron being recycled, although a more likely explanation for the piled structures seen in many iron knives is that it resulted accidentally when the heterogeneous bloom was worked, by bending and forging, into a bar (Tylecote 1986, 145). This piling effect can be seen in the three composite iron bars from the smithy, which have been interpreted as bar derived from the smelting operation, and not as a result of the welding together of scraps of bar. An underlying reason for taking this position is that when heating and welding takes place there will be a high loss of metal due to oxidation of the surface of the iron to form scale. It is therefore highly inefficient and prone to the law of rapidly diminishing returns to attempt to form small bars from smaller fragments. Thus a bar is drawn down from larger to smaller, rather than forging together pieces to make a larger one.

Conclusion

The archaeological and archaeometallurgical evidence of ironworking from all excavations at Wharram shows a general background scatter of slag on many sites with a clear focus of iron smithing in the South Manor Area. There is no clear evidence for iron smelting in Anglo-Saxon Wharram. Some possible fragments of tapped iron smelting slag have been recovered, but on the evidence of their morphology they are most likely to be of Romano-British date.

Detailed analysis of the South Manor Area data identified possible locations for a smithy building with its associated slag dump. A model can now be constructed of the Anglo-Saxon smithy. The smith imported bar iron to manufacture artefacts. It is probable that finished artefacts were also brought on to the site. The smith had access to all iron alloys available to the Anglo-Saxon smith, namely ferritic iron, phosphoric iron, steel and composite bars. The analysis of the slag inclusions strongly suggests that the iron came from a number of different smelting centres, but whether these were on the Wolds, on the Jurassic Ridge of North Lincolnshire, or even further afield in North or West Yorkshire cannot be determined. The smith most likely undertook the full range of smithing techniques from simple forging to fire welding.

There is a high degree of consistency of smithing techniques as indicated by the consistency of the two slag compositions. The expectation was that smithing slag compositions would vary, depending on operator and operation. Within the restrictions of the analysis however, the compositions indicate a high level of control. What the differences represent is unclear: they may be chronological, as the smithy perhaps operated for several centuries. The presence of fragments from at least two moulds for copper-alloy objects (Bayley 2000, 121), indicates some minor level of non-ferrous working. There is no evidence to support the smith manufacturing organic components of edged tools, e.g. bone or wooden blade handles.

The analysis of the knives demonstrates that the type 2 butt-welded method of applying the steel blade was in use in common with the practices of the day as evidenced by knife analyses from other sites (Blakelock and McDonnell 2007). The expectation was that the type 2 knives would be high quality with quenched and tempered steel cutting edges. Only one knife had such an edge, the remainder, although well manufactured in terms of alloy selection and welding, were not heat treated. The suggested interpretation is that the knives were originally of high quality with quenched and tempered steel cutting edges, giving optimum hardness and toughness, but that in the final stages of their life-cycle these knives were re-heated and cooled slowly, resulting in poorer quality cutting edges of low hardness.

Future studies must overcome the traditional post-excavation practice of taking the evidence of a highly skilled craft (even at a basic smithing level), and disseminating it to separate specialists, making the task of a holistic study of a smithy more difficult. This has been achieved to some extent with this new study of the Wharram smithy. It is essential that detailed archaeometallurgical investigations of all stages of the process are incorporated in such studies.

11 Wharram and its Neighbours in the Middle Saxon Period: a Debate and some Conclusions

Introduction
by Stuart Wrathmell

The previous three chapters have used various strands of evidence to characterise Middle Saxon occupation at Wharram and elsewhere on the northern Wolds and in the Vale of Pickering. In particular, they have sought to link the vill units recorded in Domesday Book, and the place-names attached to those vills, to the archaeological record of Butterwick-type settlement remains. It is now time to confront directly some of the assumptions and suppositions which underlie these attempted linkages.

The first supposition is that the township boundaries recorded largely for the first time in the early 19th century are broadly an accurate reflection of territorial units established in the Middle and Late Saxon periods. This may seem an unlikely, even a preposterous claim, but the map of township boundaries as delineated on Figure 36 does not 'read' as though they were created for those units at a single point in time; it looks like a chronological sequence that developed both through the extension of township units into territory that was previously unbounded, and by the subdivision of pre-existing units. Would it really look like this if boundaries had been laid out long after the creation of the *tun*s, *by*s and *thorp*s that they delineate?

A comparison of the vills named in Domesday with the township units named in the 19th century strongly suggests stability (with the few exceptions noted in Ch. 8) from the late 11th century onwards. There is no evidence that these vills were in existence any earlier than the mid-11th century, but the names they bore have been assigned by place-name scholars to earlier centuries. So if these vill units were not in existence before the mid-11th century, to what were these names attached? There is equally no evidence, to the writer's knowledge, for any alternative territorial units which might have framed the activities of Wolds communities in the Middle and Late Saxon periods – in marked contrast with the abundant evidence of very different field, farm and territorial boundaries of the Late Iron Age and Roman periods. Therefore, until such evidence emerges, the hypothesis of continuity in township structure seems as valid as any other, unless one argues, in company with David Stocker and Paul Everson below, that no territorial units existed on the Wolds until the Late Saxon period. The routeways and earthwork boundaries that came to play such an important part in the demarcation of township units on the Wolds had, of course, been in existence long before the Anglo-Saxon period.

Much the same line of thinking lies behind the supposition that the Butterwick-type remains represent the homes of the communities that occupied those named territories. All Butterwick-type remains must be located in townships (or in intercommoned land assigned to those townships), because medieval vills covered the entire landscape. Why should these remains be any more directly related to the known pattern of townships than, say, the late Roman farmsteads that preceded them? The reason is simple: archaeological investigation of Butterwick-type remains at Burdale, Wharram and West Heslerton have demonstrated that they were occupied in the Middle Saxon period when many of the known township names were coined. To what were these names attached if not to these communities and their homesteads? And if such associations are regarded as too speculative to be worthy of serious consideration, does this mean that place-name studies and archaeological research must forever run in parallel, never able to converge?

There are, too, some intriguing repetitions in the spatial relationship of Butterwick-type remains to medieval and later village settlements and to known township boundaries. One is the close proximity of several Butterwick-type settlements to medieval village sites, including Wharram where they partly overlap. Indeed it may be that similar groups of remains could be found directly beneath medieval village earthworks or modern villages. Another is the location of some Butterwick-type sites close to the partition boundaries of townships that seem, on the basis of their names, to have been single entities at an earlier period, as with East and West Heslerton and East and West Lutton.

These ideas were first presented at a seminar in 2008, which was attended by many of the contributors to this volume. Its aim was to provide authors with an indication of the likely shape of the volume as a whole, and to promote a greater coherence in the final product. The Wharram Research Project has, however, a long tradition of intellectual challenge and debate – Christopher Dyer once remarked that it 'has taken on the character of a continuous seminar' (Dyer 1990, 298) – and it is a tradition which has continued during the preparation of this volume. Earlier chapters have attempted to shape a story of 'settlement' in the study area which envisages the reoccupation of the northern Wolds by permanently settled communities during the Middle Saxon period, perhaps beginning in the 7th century and continuing until the creation of the earliest elements of the medieval villages that replaced them. It is a story with which two of the contributors, David Stocker and Paul Everson, profoundly disagree; and before moving on to discuss the creation of the medieval village at Wharram, it seems appropriate to share with readers their alternative vision of Wharram in the Middle Saxon period as a focus of seasonal activity, including a market function, rather than as a permanent settlement with monastic associations as envisaged in Chapters 9 and 10.

Wharram before the village moment

by Paul Everson and David Stocker

Sheep management and seasonal occupation

Archaeological evidence shows that there was an extensive spread of some form of occupation in the Early Anglo-Saxon and Middle Saxon periods on the Plateau to the west of what became St Martin's church. This conclusion is prompted both by the survey signatures of numerous *Grubenhäuser*, apparently associated with curvilinear ditches that perhaps amount to enclosures (Chs 4 and 9 above) and by a smaller number of similar structures encountered in excavations within the Guardianship site (especially *Wharram VII* and *Wharram IX*). This combination of *Grubenhäuser* and curvilinear ditches has been confidently described as a 'settlement' above, in the way that such agglomerations of *Grubenhäuser* and enclosure ditches usually are. They obviously represent the remains of considerable human activity, but in this section we wish to ask what character that activity might have had, and whether the term 'settlement' is really justified when applied to these remains.

Grubenhäuser are typically no more than 5m long (and often shorter) and are essentially a roofed hole in the ground. The roof was supported on a single ridge-piece supported by posts at either end. The roof coverings could have been of a variety of local materials including, one presumes, highly portable ones such as animal skins. The excellent typological study of buildings of this general character by Jess Tipper, published in 2004, brings together, for the first time, a full account of the evidence for these structures (Tipper 2004). To the dispassionate, uncommitted, observer several points seem worth making. First, architecturally speaking, the excavated remains clearly represent a category of building that was both contemporary with, and fundamentally different from, the principal building-types of the period that are known to have been permanent dwellings, which are rectangular structures with roofs of complex carpentry.

The *Grubenhäuser*, by contrast, are usually structures which could be erected by a couple of individuals without specialist carpentry skills. Secondly, unlike the contemporary dwellings, one presumes, the *Grubenhäuser* could be constructed rapidly; probably within a day. Thirdly, the extent to which they are frequently grouped together has often led to the assumption that *Grubenhäuser* commonly constituted densely occupied 'settlements'. Yet the remains of such buildings are often inter-cut and the evidence from most sites would, equally, support the interpretation that it is common for *Grubenhäuser* to be rapidly succeeded on the same spot by buildings of the same type. Fourthly, unlike the accompanying domestic structures, *Grubenhäuser* were frequently dismantled during the course of a process which involved the importation of domestic debris to backfill the hole where the building had been erected. Fifthly, the ethnographic evidence for this building type (i.e. holes in the ground covered with a simple roof-ridge supported by upright poles and without specialist carpentry skills) suggests that buildings of this type are frequently built for temporary occupation by groups occupied in specific activities. They are sometimes, though not always, topographically remote from the main centres of permanent settlement, and they are often built for seasonal occupation (Addy 1933; Innocent 1916).

Grubenhaus-type structures were constructed seasonally in the Lake District managed woodlands by charcoal burners well into the 20th century, for example. Here the buildings were dismantled at the end of each charcoal-burning season and the holes left over were backfilled with domestic debris, which had been accumulated throughout the season in a temporary midden, no doubt specifically for this purpose. For our purposes here, the critical point is that we believe that such *Grubenhäuser* often represent a type of building intended for temporary, specialised or occasional use and not for permanent occupation.

These observations have led one of us to propose that it may be incorrect to claim, as Jess Tipper has done (2004), that such *Grubenhäuser* always represent permanent 'settlement', but that they are just as likely to be signs of a temporary shelter associated with a specialised activity (Stocker 2006, 115-16). We suspect, indeed, that such buildings would have been called 'cotes' in the medieval period, and although they might occur adjacent to more clearly domestic buildings, and contemporaneously within the same enclosures, they also often occur in more remote parts of the landscape where seasonal occupation was required. Such a seasonal presence might have been part of an industrial economy (as in the case of the Lake District charcoal burners), but perhaps more frequently it was associated with the grazing of animals on remote pastures. In the later middle ages isolated shelters, in which shepherds could spend nights, are known to have been erected on the more remote pastures of the Cotswolds, for example (Dyer 1995, 161 and passim), and they are hypothesised on the Lindsey grazing marsh and in a number of other locations also.

For the period between the 5th and the 10th centuries, of course, we have little or no relevant documentary information to demonstrate that *Grubenhäuser* were used for such specialised purposes (amongst the many others which have been hypothesised) remote from permanent settlements. But the substantial body of archaeological evidence now accumulating might well reveal that *Grubenhäuser* did sometimes play the role of remote 'shelter' whilst a specialised agricultural or industrial process was being pursued. The most impressive recent archaeological discoveries relating to this type of building have been made at West Heslerton, where Dominic Powlesland's remarkable survey work has recently shown a line of hundreds of such *Grubenhaus* structures snaking along the contour that marks the southern boundary of the wetland along the southern side of the Vale of Pickering (Powlesland 1997; 2003b).

These structures have similar characteristics to those observed over and over again amongst this type of building. They are extensively inter-cut, and may not be long-lived, and each example could as easily represent a single isolated seasonal structure as a large contemporaneous community. They are backfilled with domestic debris, and many are remote from the centres of genuine permanent settlement which stand on the gravels about 1km to the south. As in many other cases, then, the more remote of the West Heslerton Project's *Grubenhäuser* can also be effectively explained as an indicator of temporary, specialised, occupation of a distant zone of the landscape, where a small number of *Grubenhäuser* were perhaps replaced season after season.

Which specialised activity necessitated the erection of such structures on the edge of the wetland along the south side of the Vale of Pickering remains to be explained, but several candidates apparently stand out. They could represent the management of seasonal grazing of cattle on wetland meadows. In such circumstances one might expect each community's herdsmen to erect a single shelter per year, and presumably occupy it for the summer months. This would save the labour of driving the cattle back to the settlement each night, with the associated risk that the cattle might eat arable crops they passed through. Alternatively, they might represent temporary buildings related to the exploitation of the wetlands themselves. Perhaps they were used by fowlers or fishermen?

If we bring this sort of understanding of *Grubenhäuser* to the evidence from Wharram, we might conclude, not that they represent something properly described as a 'settlement', but that they are more likely to represent a small seasonal population establishing themselves here for a period of time each year. Possibly, the evidence implies only a single group (perhaps only a pair?) establishing themselves here each year, but over a very extended period; conceivably over the several centuries that even the quite limited excavated material suggests (Richards 1992c, 90-94). Though it goes against the arguments put forward earlier in this volume, we also believe that this understanding of the *Grubenhäuser* in a location such as Wharram can also be applied to the lengths of curving 'enclosure' boundaries which have also been found here and elsewhere on the high Wolds of eastern Yorkshire.

It is a mistake to regard any large upland sheep flock as a single unit. Each part of the flock required a different management regime (e.g. Dyer 1995, 150-55; Hurst 2005, 43-9). Rams could not be kept together in a flock of ewes; the wether flock was also usually separated from the ewes; and ewes with lambs had to be separated out in the spring. Parts of the flock might be left out on the hill over winter (traditionally from Martinmas to Easter), whilst other operations, such as washing and shearing might be more easily undertaken near a marketing location or point of sale. Furthermore, if the flock was to be used for manuring the arable, the entire flock might be brought down off the permanent pasture, keeping its component parts separate. Throughout, animals would be separated from the flock for slaughter. All of these operations meant that managing sheep on the open wold would have been a constant round of assessing, dividing and reuniting elements of the flock. The archaeological traces that such operations have left in the landscape have long been discussed (e.g. Allcroft 1908, 231-2, 554; Dyer 1995) and they continue to contribute to the understanding of many projects in the uplands.

In the Wolds of eastern Yorkshire, Catherine Stoertz noted the correspondence between the crop marks of *Grubenhäuser* and sites with complexes of curvilinear enclosures, which are here called 'Butterwick-type', and demonstrated that they were likely to represent settlements of the period between the 5th and 10th centuries (Stoertz 1997, 55-9, fig. 30). This association is clearly correct; but our view is that neither the *Grubenhäuser* themselves nor the curvilinear ditches with which they are associated need be interpreted as permanent settlements. In fact they have several characteristics that argue to the contrary.

As interpreted and plotted from the aerial photographic evidence, these Butterwick-type remains are notably complex conglomerations of many small-scale compartments. These often exhibit what seem to be internal features and subdivisions, which Stoertz observes as being faint and superimposed. Other characteristics stand out as even more typical. It is far from obvious that the *Grubenhäuser* – which the rectangular pits or 'blobs' are surely correctly taken to represent – are surrounded by, or lie within, these enclosures. Many individuals and even groups of *Grubenhäuser* clearly do not, but rather stand outside the closes or even on the fringe of the complex as a whole. Even where they do appear to lie within the closes, it is sometimes in tight groupings of many examples and their distribution appears quite random in relation to the ditched boundaries. It might be argued – as Tipper would presumably wish to do (2004,162-3) – that this is precisely because the *Grubenhäuser* are only subsidiary facilities to unseen post-built structures. But (even allowing such an argument from absence of evidence) many of the enclosures here, and the over-busy layout generally, hardly provide adequate space for such sizeable putative structures. It is at least as plausible interpretation of this patterning – and one which we favour – that in these transcriptions we are looking at a palimpsest. Each typical 'Butterwick-type' is not a long-lived stable entity with a coherent layout, we suggest, but rather an accumulation involving repeated superimposition and local drift across the site. Thereby, abandoned and backfilled *Grubenhäuser* were 'captured' by new closes, and old closes randomly 'occupied' by new *Grubenhäuser*. Though the exceptional density of features in these complexes, and their small scale, tends to obscure it, there are clear cases of overlapping and intercutting, as Stoertz notes, which adds weight to this option.

A second characteristic, picked out as notable by Stoertz, is that 'the perimeter ditches appear to be recut many times'. For this to be evident in the aerial photograph evidence, as it is in runs of closely parallel ditches, it indicates not recutting of fixed, stable ditched systems as often encountered in excavation, but repeated relocation of ditches on similar but not quite identical alignments. The effect is the doubled or multiple ditched lines that contribute to the dense appearance of 'Butterwick-types'. We envisage this recutting as being a periodic matter, on a cycle measured in decades and relating perhaps to the maintenance of the sort of embanked hedges discussed below.

Pre-eminently, however, it is the sheer density of features of these complexes that stands out. As Stoertz's transcriptions amply demonstrate, they contrast with nearby settlements and field systems of later prehistoric and Roman date in this regard. Stoertz's coining of the phrase 'tightly grouped' as their headline characteristic reflects this. Somewhat counter-intuitively perhaps, this characteristic *in itself* suggests multiphased, repetitive use of a persistently similar type, on a much-revisited, traditional site: seasonal rather than permanent settlement, as we propose; and on a limited scale on any given occasion. Where the aerial photograph evidence is less dense, it may indicate less protracted use; and other examples may await identification because their remains lack that trademark density resulting from protracted reoccupation. The complete lack of planning in their layout and their lack of a coherent network of access routes or lanes is a further factor that suggests that they were accumulative, rather than laid out at a single moment, for a large group of occupiers. Not so much twenty discrete closes, then, but more likely a much smaller number were in operation at any one time, which were re-established repeatedly in the same location. In this way they 'drifted' across the landscape as each new close was re-established and apparently respected the locations of earlier closes.

Having indicated that the *Grubenhäuser* could represent temporary shelters, perhaps used seasonally by shepherds, we suggest that the patterns of curvilinear ditches and closes that surround them are also best seen as closes for sheep management. The eight examples documented by Stoertz (1997, fig. 30; see also above, Figs 39-45) exhibit some details which encourage that conclusion. First, two types of close are clearly visible amongst those plotted by Stoertz. The majority are curvilinear, of approximately similar sizes (about 0.25ha), but there is a substantial minority which form much smaller units (about 0.1 ha). Many of these smaller enclosures are near-circular and look very much like the circular stone-built 'pounds' that still survive in many upland areas today (Ramm *et al.* 1970, 12-14; Herring 1996; Smith 1999; Riley and Wilson-North 2001, 92; Riley 2006, 83-4). Another distinctive feature of the larger enclosures, though not the smaller 'pounds', is that few of them form enclosed spaces. Some have substantial gaps in their circuits, and some seem to represent only part of an enclosure.

Our suggested function as sheepfolds would imply the use of temporary and flexible barriers to block and adapt the gaps. Such barriers would likely be constructed from hurdles, as they still are today. Stuart Wrathmell reminds us that in the early 17th century Henry Best managed to control large flocks of sheep with temporary hurdles in Elmswell, on the south-facing Wolds (Woodward 1984, 18), folding them without the aid of other barriers on arable selions. A number of the curving, paired, parallel ditches that appear to form parts of larger enclosures, rather than being successive redigging, might have been contemporary ditches, dug either side of a bank. Ditches were required, in thin soils, to obtain the material to create banks; but the features represented were surely hedges, set on top of banks. Such permanent hedges, indeed, may never have been intended to be parts of closes at all. It has always been thought important to offer some form of shelter to grazing animals on the open wold, and still today – or within living memory – stone walls, or stells, are built on open moorland in the North York Moors purely to provide shelter for sheep where none other is available (Allcroft 1908, 554; Mortimer 1905, 388-96).

These then, in our understanding, are places of 'seasonal occupation on distant grazing'. Interestingly, this might be a legitimate – if, as David Parsons (pers comm.) advises us, somewhat contrived – derivation for the place-name Butterwick (OE *butan* [*buterra*], *wic* (3ii); Smith 1956a, 65; 1956b, 228, 259-60). But the name in the traditional understanding of its meaning has precisely similar connotations. The element 'wick' has its commonest sense as a temporary, seasonal settlement (Coates 1999); and, as Harold Fox has taught us from his studies in south-western England, the seasonal production of dairy products such as butter and cheese on the remote summer grazing slopes was a routine and well-documented function of established transhumance regimes (Fox 2008). As Fox also emphasises, sheep were as likely, or more likely, to be the milk source for such products than cattle, as numerous Shapwicks – let alone the vast flocks of *brébis* on the Grands Causses of central southern France, which supply the production of Roquefort cheese – suggest (Fox 2008, 360).

Stepping back, we find that the overall distribution of 'Butterwick-types' as represented by the examples currently known in fact defines a 'high Wolds' zone, a remote area encompassing the valley of the Gypsey Race. This zone has correlations with the patterning of place-name types and parish morphology discussed above. It is a zone which in traditional place-name terms might be thought of as characterised by 'late' settlement, with a suite of name forms consonant with a brief phase of settlement foundation and a notable Norse element (below, Ch. 12). In our archaeological terms, we suggest that it was a specialised upland grazing zone populated in the early medieval era by seasonal settlements appropriate to that important specialised function within the contemporary social and economic structure.

Significantly, it is a zone which in an earlier era was also evidently a specialist stock grazing resource and was then too characterised by quite distinctive (but different) archaeological signatures in the form of trackways and ranch boundaries. In an earlier and analogous cycle of change, these too were superseded – in the later Iron Age and Roman periods – by more intensive settlement and exploitation (Giles 2007a; see Ch. 6 above). Both the characteristic management of the Wolds as extensive grazing in the early medieval era and the longer-term cyclical pattern of their exploitation has been usefully explored across a wider canvas than is possible here by Chris Fenton-Thomas (2005). Part of our narrative, too, is the timing and circumstances of the recasting of the settlement and cultivation of high wold at Wharram and of the upper Gypsey Race, as part of a 'cereal revolution' (see Ch. 13 below).

One of the sets of Butterwick-type remains, that on the high wolds at Garton, has the parish boundary between Garton and Sledmere passing through it (Fig. 44); and the example at Butterwick itself has the township boundary with Weaverthorpe passing close to its western edge (Fig. 39). These are important indications that these complexes belong in a landscape pre-dating the formal subdivision of this zone by later medieval parishes and townships, with its recasting of the land use. In a similar way, a number of the Butterwick-type remains are – as at Wharram – situated near to medieval nucleations, at *c.* 150-300m distant, but we see no obvious reason to link the two types of landscape feature. The perception that one leads inevitably to the other is mere presumption, which at best places greater weight on proximity of non-contemporary features rather than on patterns of location in the contemporary landscape. In those pairs of cases that lie in the valley of the Gypsey Race, even the topographical proximity is made almost inevitable by the density of later settlements. But other 'Butterwicks' are much more removed from 10th-century and later settlements, as at Huggate (Fig. 43), and sometimes they have no later successor, as at Garton.

As Stoertz herself recognised, these crop marks are found in two distinctive types of location. Butterwick itself, Rudston, Low Caythorpe, and the two examples at East and West Lutton are all on the valley floors, right next to the stream. Huggate, by contrast, is high on the valley side, whereas Garton is on the wold top near the Tatton Sykes monument. The activity represented by these complexes is clearly very similar, then, but it is being performed in two distinct locations in the landscape: one on the open wolds, and the other on the valley floor very close to watercourses.

These two types of location in the landscape appear to match the two types of landscape locations recorded for the management of the sheep flocks of the Bishop of Worcester in the 13th and 14th century, for example. The bishop's substantial Cotswold flock was divided between manors such as Blockley (the organisational hub), Bredon and Withington with extensive upland pastures in locations such as Cleeve Hill and *Alrichesdoun*, and folds

for breeding flocks and young animals in and around lowland settlements (Dyer 1980, especially 69-70, 134-7, reported in Hurst 2005, 60). The same division into two topographical locations is also apparent in the better understood, later medieval Cotswold sheepcotes studied so effectively by Chris Dyer (1995, 147). Elsewhere, over 30% of the sheepcotes on the Bishop of Winchester's later medieval estates, for example, were in remote locations, on the open grazing and detached from their parent settlement (Dyer 1995, fn 40). It seems clear that such upland folds were used for managing the whole flock within their open grazing pastures, whereas those in the valley bottoms, set alongside a source of running water, were used for washing the various subdivisions of the flock: an operation that was undertaken in association with the annual shearing (Hurst 2005, 39-40).

Briefly, then, we suggest that the evidence both from the *Grubenhäuser* themselves and from the form taken by enclosures of the Butterwick-type crop marks is consistent with what we know of centres for management of sheep. Some of them represent various flock maintenance and management tasks undertaken on the grazing pastures themselves, whilst others are related to tasks undertaken in association with running water in the valley bottoms. The location that stands out as the most obvious candidate for the latter role, and perhaps as a focal point for the whole zone, is Rudston. Two of the 'Butterwicks' are located nearby, both in relatively low-lying topographical situation and (more importantly) with reliable access to water.

In Rudston itself we have a place – as signalled by its extraordinary assemblage of prehistoric monuments, including its standing stone and the focus of an array of cursuses – which has a long-established function as a place of assembly and congregation, to which a market is the typical early medieval successor (Sawyer 1981 etc.). We might envisage Rudston, then, as the obvious gateway between the upland grazing zone of the wolds to its west, with its seasonal transhumance occupation, and the permanent settlements and monastic communities of the lowland coastal zone to the east. Just such a sheep market with wide reach and significance survived into the early modern era at Kilham, where a market is documented at least from the early 13th century (*VCH ER II*, 258-9). Latterly it was a three-day November fair, probably held on a traditional site adjacent to the south of the village, at which farmers from Holderness bought sheep and in the 17th century it set the prices for stock and produce until the following spring.

At Wharram, being set on the plateau and substantially higher than the stream, rather than in the valley, a 'Butterwick-type settlement' would perhaps appear more directly analogous to the sites at Huggate and Garton, rather than to those in the Great Wold valley. But, in that it was *both* set on the high wolds with access to extensive grazing *and* had access to water for sheep washing as part of the process of preparing beasts and fleeces for market, it is possible that both types of activity were undertaken here and that the function of the total site was more complex. We go on (below) to argue that at Wharram the seasonal occupation was linked with a market on what subsequently became the village green area of the nucleated settlement. By comparison with the likely key role of Rudston at the eastern end of the grazing zone, Wharram performing a similar role was probably relatively small-scale. But importantly its connections were evidently to the north-west and north-east into Ryedale and the Derwent valley.

Can we pin down the character of this phase of occupation of the Wharram landscape further? We are unimpressed with the argument that the spread of *Grubenhäuser* at Wharram (and by association, at the other Butterwick-type sites) *must* have been accompanied by more substantial post-hole structures, which the remote sensing just does not pick up and which the excavation has been so piecemeal as to overlook or not recognise. This argument must surely be rejected, though it is quite explicitly espoused by Tipper. In his excellent and influential study, for example, he asserts that 'Large-scale open area excavation of Early Anglo-Saxon settlements has, *without exception* [our italics], shown that *Grubenhäuser* existed alongside ground-level post-hole buildings', and rejects the conclusion that, for example, a modern excavation like Old Down Farm on the high Wessex downland, in reporting six *Grubenhäuser* and no contemporary post-hole structures set within an Iron Age earthwork, had revealed the totality of a seasonal occupation site (Tipper 2004, 162-3; Davies 1979). The combination of this presumption with a disregard for the variety of landscape and resource-related contexts in which *Grubenhäuser* might occur reduces the question of their interpretation, for Tipper, to one of settlement scale - whether farmstead, hamlet or village, all presumptively with permanent, year-round occupation. We would wish to urge an alternative that allows for seasonal activity and envisages a more diversified settlement pattern as a result, which relates to demonstrable patterns of resource exploitation.

Although traces of mid-Saxon post-hole buildings are reported from Burdale (below), the fuller evidence from Wharram is clearly of a single, well-defined though small, post-hole building, which McDonnell has argued was probably a smithy. A smith would be an essential element of the settlement type we have in mind: both for the mundane tasks of sharpening and reworking sheep-shearing equipment, but also potentially for handling non-ferrous material in the process of recycling Roman *spolia* that might have been an ancillary activity of this seasonal cycle (below). What little we know of Middle Saxon smiths draws us towards an understanding, not that they were integrated members of permanently settled communities, but rather precisely that they occupied a liminal place within the settlement pattern. As David Hinton has said, a smith was 'an outsider both in the literal sense that he might have been brought in from afar to work for his lord, and in the spiritual sense that an aura of danger and "magic" hung around smiths' (Hinton 2000, 111-15, especially 113).

Hinton envisages smiths being supplied with shelter as part of their hire, perhaps of a distinctive form. He draws attention to the episode in the story of Wayland the Smith where his lord confined the smith to an island on the edge of his estate, adjacent to his workshop, from which Wayland magically escaped (Hinton 2000, 111-15; see also Hinton 1998). This cultural stereotype was well established. Wayland's story appears not only on the Frank's Casket, but also on monumental sculpture of the Viking age in Yorkshire, including at Sherburn (Bailey 1980, 103-16). Feature 59 at Wharram, located near the furnace and part of this phase, is reported as a ritual pit (Stamper *et al.* 2000, 36-7, pl. 4 and fig. 20; Richards 2000a, 197), which resonates with the magical aura of smiths.

Even if the structures represented by the *Grubenhäuser* were quite robust and capable of refurbishment in this part-time cycle of occupation for a decade or even a generation, for example, there may have been no more than one or two in use at any one time. Certainly, interpretation of the *Grubenhäuser* and ditches in this manner accounts for the very irregular layout of the supposed settlement, more or less completely lacking the intelligible patterns we recognise in permanent settlements. Occupation of this occasional and temporary character might also offer an explanation both for puzzling 'stragglers' outside what seems to be the focus of activity at Wharram, and for *Grubenhäuser* located in seemingly unsociable places, such as within the Romano-British hollow way. The question of whether the abandoned hollows of former buildings were filled at the end of the season or whether they were merely left to act as a convenient dumping place for a period, requires further consideration along the lines usefully laid out by Tipper (2004, 147-59).

Although we suggest that the principal specialist activity which resulted in this distinctive form of settlement, with its presumed occasional or seasonal occupation, was the maintenance and management of large sheep flocks on the open wold, it is quite possible that other specialist activities were also undertaken here. There was obviously potential in the area for the exploitation of woodland and/or scrub regeneration, following the abandonment of Roman cultivation regimes. We might ask, however, whether such activity would in itself require temporary shelters of such a substantial character, or what role the associated closes might have played. A more intensive activity, perhaps requiring the presence of more solid structures, would be the recovery and recycling of materials from the abandoned Roman complexes that lie on the north-western and western fringes of the Guardianship area. Certainly, the material evidence most distinctively associated with the *Grubenhäuser* in excavation, namely metalworking moulds and hearths etc. might suggest just such a recycling activity, which would, of course, require woodland and/or scrub to provide fuel. What began as a recycling operation may even have established itself in the seasonal routine and have come, in its later stages, to involve bringing in some of the raw materials.

Wharram's supposed 'monastic' associations

This explanation of the Early and Middle Saxon remains as representing temporary and seasonal activity on the high wold at Wharram, whether including the recycling of Roman materials or being related exclusively to the grazing of flocks, might also help explain the occasional burial here and its *ad hoc* treatment. An occasional death in this seasonal population may account for individual post-Roman burials that have been encountered by chance and unexplained in excavation; for example, a young adult in the North Manor area (Hurst and Roskams 2004, 11-13) and a new-born or stillborn infant, with a deposit of sheep bones on the plateau (Richards 1992b, 84-5). Such deaths might be expected throughout the proposed seasonal regime, which might have continued more or less continuously from the 4th to the 10th centuries, and the burial of these individuals in these detached locations, rather than in any formal graveyard, might even offer a line of explanation for the surprising discovery of two fragments of nominally early – i.e. pre-Viking – Anglo-Saxon stone sculpture from disparate contexts on the plateau part of the Guardianship area (Andrews 1979a, 124; Beresford and Hurst 1990, illustr. 62; Lang 1991, 222; Lang 1992, 43), which were discussed by Ian Riddler in the preceding chapter.

Both stones are residual, in that they were found in the backfill of hollow features (a ditch and a *Grubenhaus*). But the most telling aspects of these two items are, first, their small size – they are handy-sized chunks or chips and eminently portable – and, secondly, their very distinctive (and different) petrology, one from the Stonegrave area of the vale of Pickering the other from the Whitby area. Even without overt sculptural decoration – which the Whitby fragment lacks – their origins would recognisably have been two of the principal Christian centres of the region. These items, then, might be seen as tokens, brought to Wharram to place on a grave, to memorialise a burial which had not had the benefit of commemoration normal within the community, namely burial within a defined burial ground or churchyard. The neo-natal infant burial on the plateau was marked in just this way by a stone distinguished by its distinctive, though more locally sourced, geological patterning (Richards 1992b, 84-5).

Such a process would itself transform these objects *from* what we automatically think of and categorise as a fragment of a larger monument *into* an artefact in its own right within the new context. The same process might conceivably also account for the – equally surprising – incidence of a piece of Tating ware, excavated in the same type of context at Wharram (Coutts and Hodges 1992, 38-9). This ceramic is equally distinctive for its ecclesiastical associations, since it is typically found with metal foil crosses embedded in its surface as decoration and in a limited range of forms, which have caused some scholars to identify these as liturgical vessels, likely to be deployed only in contemporary Anglo-Saxon monasteries or churches (as proposed in Coutts and Hodges 1992, 38-

9 and above). But the broken fragment of such a vessel might become a valued artefact in its own right.

Such memorialisation might have happened at any time after death as long as the grave was still visible, of course, and it may not necessarily reflect the attitude or enthusiasm of the deceased, but of his/her kin at whatever remove. Furthermore, this phenomenon may have been most prevalent at that period when we know, from studying the micro-archaeology of the corpus of Anglo-Saxon sculpture, that there were incidents of its being deliberately smashed up (for example at Cherry Hinton in Cambridgeshire, where fragments were then incorporated in the structural foundations of a late pre-Conquest church: Everson and Stocker forthcoming b); and when, at the same time, tokens of belief were especially contentious, i.e. during the later 9th and early 10th centuries, following the arrival of the Vikings, but before they had assimilated indigenous Christianity.

Used as grave markers, such stone tokens would be vulnerable too, located away from the conventional protection of a formal graveyard and oversight of a resident community, and might more readily end up incorporated with other debris in hollow features – ultimately through the nucleation of settlement and initiation of cultivation over the whole area. An alternative is that such tokens might have originated in the temporary buildings themselves, as protective or apotropaic objects, in a usage that the ethnographical literature demonstrates is at least as common and significant as in burials, though more difficult to identify in the archaeological record (see helpfully Gilchrist 2008).

We wish to urge, then, that there are alternative understandings to be explored here, led by a consideration of these items of sculpture as artefacts themselves within broader archaeological contexts, and not solely as residual components in an art-historical narrative. For some scholars these scraps have been thought to imply an early religious community at Wharram in the pre-Viking era, and discussions of the diverse nature of contemporary monasteries have proliferated (Beresford and Hurst 1990, 84; Richards 1992c, 93-4; Blair 2005 offers a useful overview). Such discussion has influenced thinking about the church of St Martin, including whether its origin might lie within such a monastery, or as secondary ecclesiastical provision, i.e. as a 'private chapel' (Bell 1987b, 195-200); but we wish to note that other, more interesting, interpretations are possible, and that such claims about an early religious community are unjustified as well as improbable. As David Roffe remarks with characteristic restraint and understatement, having reviewed the early historical evidence for Wharram, 'the suggested possibility that there was an important church in the settlement in the 8th century [*sc* on the basis of the stone cross fragments] … is not immediately consistent with the social and tenurial structure of the late Anglo-Saxon period' (Roffe 2000a, 15). We suggest that it is not 'immediately consistent' with the archaeological evidence either.

These arguments that point to very special items being imported to this locale in the context of a seasonal settlement apply also to the presence of the range and quantity of mundane pottery. A major purpose of the vessels involved is quite clearly transporting and storing commodities: they are jugs, jars and bowls with relatively few cooking vessels (Slowikowski 2000, 95). In the sort of settlement we envisage, consumables would be brought every season in pots and that circumstance might lead to a relatively high level of breakage and discard. At those sites where production of butter and cheese was a feature – 'butterwicks' – that process would have included bringing salt, for example, as well as use of vessels in processing and storage (as later illustrated in the Luttrell Psalter, BL Add MSS 42130, f 163, and chosen for the cover of one of the standard textbooks on medieval pottery: McCarthy and Brooks 1988). The presence of marketing (as explored below) – though also not a function of permanent settlement – might have a similar effect.

An analogous point may be made about the animal bone assemblage. What would be the characteristic of such an assemblage in the sort of seasonal settlement we envisage? Would it resemble the profile of contemporary permanent settlements or might it be dominated by sheep? We suggest the former. As the faunal assemblage must be closely related to patterns of meat consumption at seasonal Wharram and as we should not expect the diet of any seasonal occupants to be markedly different from their fellows in the permanent settlements, we anticipate that both site types would exhibit similar profiles. Were the faunal assemblage on the seasonal settlement to be dominated by sheep remains, that would imply economic failure on the part of the shepherds. It would be like a sweet-shop owner living on his chocolate! Where we might expect a contrast in the faunal profile is following the abandonment of the economy represented by the open-wold sheep farming and its replacement by open-field village agriculture. Interestingly, just such a change occurs in the Wharram assemblage (below).

The place of Wharram on the established network of long-distance routes and droveways, both those lying east-west along the high spine of the Wolds and those lying north-south and linking the lowland resources of the Vale of Pickering with the complementary resources that the Wolds offered, is more consistent with our suggestion that Wharram prior to the nucleation was a sheep-station occupied temporarily than with a hypothetical monastic site. The evidence from later sources that Wrathmell brings together in Chapter 12, below, provides a context for these proposed grazing operations. In the same way that the great monasteries of the West Midlands had specialist stations for managing their flocks in the Cotswolds, so Wrathmell believes that Wharram too had early monastic contacts, 'perhaps as a sheep farm or stock collecting point', probably including links – even if only indirect – with distant Whitby.

While we do wish to reject the simplistic argument that specific finds or find types imply the presence of a

Middle Saxon monastery at Wharram, the specific nature of those sculptural artefacts in respect of their sources (whichever of our proffered interpretations about their use is preferred) actually encourages us to propose that the transhumance we envisage was a long-distance rather than a wholly local affair. It might, on this evidence, have plausibly included flocks of the great monastic establishments of the region, lying away to the north-west and north-east. In the context we have outlined – of transhumance to vast areas of open Wold – we see no impediment to there being more that one institution involved in the same location.

Furthermore, while the sheep-management activity we have envisaged is at one level functional and mundane, it may be worth recalling that, at the same time, there was a strong tradition in contemporary religious thought of the virtue of grappling with – of experiencing and overcoming – the place that was 'other', as Guthlac did at Crowland or Cuthbert on the Farnes, for example (Morris 1989, 113-20). The high Wolds landscape around Wharram was full not only of the ghosts of Roman buildings – which might later be dealt with in a pragmatic manner by recycling stone – but also held such a numinous presence as Duggleby Howe (or Thor's Howe and other ominous aliases), together with the spring sources of both the Wharram stream and the Gypsey Race, which seems to have been ritually marked from the earliest times (Rahtz *et al.* 2004, 275; Wrathmell 2005a, 1-2).

A market function

In summary, then, we suggest that our proposed understanding of pre-Viking Wharram as a seasonally occupied sheep-management station, rather than anything that we would wish to describe as a 'settlement', not only links many of our previous understandings, but also unites them into a coherent narrative. But the specialisation of the agricultural regime may not have been the only sense in which the high Wold was regarded as distinct and 'other' in the pre-Viking era, as revealed most clearly by its patterning of place-names (Ch. 8). It lay open and undivided, outside the early estates that Wrathmell reconstructs as based on centres along the vale edge, and its place-names could be characterised as typically denominating a particular uninhabited place some distance from the homes of the people who made use of it. The place-name at Wharram, in particular, might best be understood as distinctively identifying this zone of the Wolds for the distant visitor there.

By the common consent of recent scholarship the place-name *Wharram* means 'at the bends' (Smith 1937, 134-5; Gelling 2004, 347-51). Place-name scholars automatically refer this to bends in the river, but we might legitimately ask whether the riverine bends are actually any more notable or locally distinctive here at Wharram than elsewhere. Wrathmell, asking the same question, has suggested that the name refers to the very different directions taken by two streams that arise close together at Wharram le Street (p. 105). Might the name not refer, instead, to the dog-legging of the east-west road into and out of the valley; and to a trading place, located at a distinctive topographical feature? It would then, at least, have currency for people using that longer-distance trackway, rather than the local valley bottom road as a means of transit?

This strand of thought correlates very closely with Wrathmell's in Chapter 8 above (p. 105), where (tellingly) he evokes Gelling and Cole's view (2000, xv-xvi) that travellers' need to give directions to remote places has contributed significantly to this category of topographical place-names. At all events, the name is a locational rather than a habitative one, in an area where habitative names in *tun* are 'overwhelmingly preponderant', many of them of the so-called Grimston hybrid type (Gelling 2004, 350). The name *Wharram*, then, may itself actually predate the presence of a permanent, nucleated settlement, but still refer to a period when, nevertheless, there was a distinctive location worth identifying. While Gelling takes the name to have an Old Norse root, a plausibly conjectured form in Old English would have been almost identical (Gelling 2004, 348).

In addition, if we feel we can dispense with the 'early monastery' at Wharram, we should still ask why there was a particular concentration and persistence of such temporary, perhaps seasonal, occupation in this immediate vicinity, as opposed to any other on the open grazing of the Wold. Of course, it may be that we only know of the scattering of *Grubenhäuser* and ditches here because of the intensity of survey and other work devoted to this locale; but, presuming that the square kilometre around Wharram does represent an intensity of such features, we have to consider why they are grouped here and not elsewhere. Could it be because the seasonal activity, with its exploitation of specialised grazing resources, generated, incorporated, or came to be consolidated around, a marketing or trading function, which would naturally have taken place on the stream-side terrace and which subsequently became the focus of the nucleated settlement of the 10th century?

In fact there are indications of precisely this. It is here that the piecemeal interventions over many years have produced a particular concentration of early coinage: styccas and sceattas (p. 143, above). Once again there has been a temptation to jump from such finds to the presumption of a permanent settlement, but we have seen that our particular understanding of the *Grubenhäuser* and other features indicates temporary and perhaps seasonal occupation. As it happens, these characteristics of both temporary and seasonal occupation are also precisely the signature of the early trading places of which we know (Sawyer 1981; Pestell and Ulmschneider 2003). Albeit on a modest scale, do the remains from Wharram indicate, not just some seasonal agricultural and/or industrial activity, but a seasonal market as well?

In support of this proposition we should note that Richard Morris long ago pointed out that the church dedication to St Martin gives a feast day of 11 November,

which coincides with the season of the autumn cull of livestock, and suggested a connection specifically related to a traditional trading place (Morris 1991, 23-4). Perhaps such an event marked the end of seasonal occupation. Furthermore, earlier chapters have re-emphasised that major and long-established through routes serve the location, as they would a traditional market site, especially the east-west route that doglegs down into the valley and out again at Wharram. The church often colonised such markets, though not necessarily at the earliest stages of their existence. It would have been important for both the traders and the church authorities to ensure that the trading was legitimated by the church.

It seems, however, from the excavated evidence within the churchyard that whatever the nature of the church's contribution to this putative pre-Viking trading centre, it did not encompass either a building or a graveyard. It could, though, have been represented by a cross or crosses, and standing market crosses (or boundary markers, as at Yarnbury, below) represent another possible, and perhaps more straightforward, source for the fragments of pre-Viking sculpture discovered on the site. Is it possible that the two putative market crosses stood at the two principal points of access to the market area, north-west and north-east, the petrology, decoration and style of each signalling the long-distance destination of each route – Stonegrave and Whitby? This line of argument raises the rather startling possibility that, if it had been under plough in modern times, rather than such an iconic earthwork, perhaps Wharram would have figured as an example of the so-called 'prolific sites' of the Middle Saxon period which recent studies have made familiar (Leahy 2000; Ulmschneider 2000b; Richards 1999b).

We hope we have shown that our proposed understanding of the pre-nucleated settlement remains at Wharram – as the accumulated evidence of temporary, seasonal occupation that was principally concerned with exploiting the grazing monoculture of the high Wolds, but which came to be linked with a marketing function whose focus of congregation was the streamside terrace later occupied by the village green and communal church and which was serviced by ancient and long-distance routes – interconnects satisfactorily with several of the themes presented in earlier chapters, though it remains at odds with the proposition that Wharram was the location of a permanent settlement of the Middle Saxon era. We suggest that it does indeed represent a similar sort of place to the so-called Butterwick-type settlements but we are inclined to think that these too are not adequately described as 'settlements', as they are probably not of residential character. In our view, therefore, the nucleated arrangement of Wharram described in Chapter 13 below represents, not a replanning of an existing settlement and population, but rather a revolutionary change from a location occupied in a sporadic and specialist fashion to a fully rounded social place: a true 'village moment' – in this landscape.

It does not require much of a change of emphasis in the morphological arguments about the overall layout of the recorded field remains to shift from their interpretation as a permanent village to their interpretation as the sum of many phases of seasonal activity: to move, that is, from understanding them as an ever-expanding settlement, which became the equal in area of the later medieval nucleated Wharram, to a drift of seasonal occupation on a much more limited scale. Furthermore, we think we should ask whether the temporary structures, both the *Grubenhäuser* and the various fence and ditch lines, were not increasingly attracted here by the seasonal presence of the market on the riverside terrace below. Such a market would have had a distinctive character. In contrast to such events at places like Langton, in the Vale itself, the dealing in any early market at Wharram would have been related to the products of the grazing monoculture of the Wolds – the marketing of sheep, alive and dead, wool and wool-fells, and it would perhaps have taken place at specific seasons, perhaps synchronised with the autumnal cull prior to Martinmas.

We know of the existence of just such markets at, for example, the Winterbourne Stoke sheep fair, which is both well documented since it persisted as a twice yearly event until 1916, and is marked by a characteristic archaeological footprint of stalls and boundary stones within Yarnbury Iron Age hillfort in Wiltshire. Remotely situated, integrated with downland grazing regimes and occurring at a distinctive location within that resource zone, it was typically serviced by networks of long-established routeways (Bowden 1999, 116-17; NMR, unpublished archive report, ref. 922094). Furthermore, where grazing regimes survived into recent memory, as they did on the downlands of Salisbury Plain, it is clear that there were numbers of such traditional gathering sites and fairs, each with its own characteristics of timing and function (Hudson 1910, 25-6 (Salisbury), 73 (Britford), 139 (Weyhill), 251-2 (Yarnbury Camp), 326 (Wilton)).

Consequently, we suggest, 'the Middle Saxon village' of Wharram is a misnomer. It is a profoundly unhelpful category mistake, and we would like to suggest it should be changed to something like 'the Middle Saxon sheep-station and seasonal market'. Long ago, offering a commentary on the earliest stage of publication of Wharram results, Glanville Jones cited the medieval Welsh law codes, as he was wont to do, to the effect that 'buildings and tillage denote occupation' and that 'the tofts of the houses and barns … bear testimony to a person's title' (Jones 1980, 39). We can clearly see those factors to be present in the field evidence for Wharram nucleated around its green. It now seems less clear to us that this was the case before the 10th century. Or at the least, we suggest, the question is still open to debate. It is a debate, moreover, that needs not to be confined to positivist argument based on excavated data sets, but also to extend to (perhaps more theoretical) assessment of wider landscape issues – as indeed this volume has encouraged.

Wharram before the village moment: a response
by Stuart Wrathmell

The two sides of the debate about the character of Middle Saxon activity on the Wolds are not, perhaps, as far apart as might be imagined. Chapter 7 offered the hypothesis that in the Early Anglo-Saxon period the Wharram area, along with other parts of the northern Wolds, was used as summer pasturing by communities that lived in the Vale and perhaps beyond. Shepherds may have erected temporary dwellings for themselves in convenient locations; those locations may then have attracted other individuals (or families) who were 'marginal' to the main agriculturally-based communities in the Vale. They may have been engaged in crafts and industrial activities based to some extent, perhaps, on the recycling of stone and metalwork available on nearby Roman sites; they are, therefore, also likely to have been mobile in terms of their habitation. Thus Wharram may at some stage have been a temporary grazing settlement, or a 'squatter' settlement, or both in the Early Anglo-Saxon period. The debate therefore focuses on whether the Middle Saxon 'Butterwick-type' remains at Wharram, and by extension the others located elsewhere on the Wolds, were ever permanently occupied in the period before the creation of the medieval villages that continue to be inhabited or are, like Wharram, marked by earthwork remains.

As emphasised earlier in this chapter, Stoertz's 'curvilinear enclosure complexes' were also characterised by the presence of what appear from the crop mark records to be *Grubenhäuser* like the ones recorded in the geophysical survey of Wharram, and in the excavations. There is no doubt in the present writer's mind that such buildings would have been erected in temporary, seasonal settlements; but this does not mean that they would therefore have been inappropriate accessories of permanent settlements. The extensive intercutting of *Grubenhäuser* in some excavated settlements may, as Stocker and Everson argue, support the idea that they were very temporary structures, but it is worth noting that no intercutting was evident in the excavated examples at Wharram. Indeed, one possible interpretation of the example excavated in Site 95 is that it started as a seasonally occupied building and was converted to a workshop after some decades (see pp 121-23).

In terms of the density and character of structural features within (and without) the Middle Saxon curvilinear enclosures, it is also worth noting that, at Wharram, the excavated *Grubenhäuser* represent fortuitous investigations: in the main, they were uncovered in excavations designed to date boundaries which included ditches; and the ditches, when abandoned, had proved to be appropriate locations for creating *Grubenhäuser*. None of the interiors of the curvilinear enclosures was specifically targeted for excavation (not least, because most of them had not been recognised by the end of excavation in 1990). Yet the areas of Middle Saxon occupation that *were* investigated – the South Manor Area by design and Site 78 by accident – both produced post-hole structures, and quite high densities of cut features generally (see Richards 2000a, 196, fig. 96). Given the very small percentage of the settlement area so far excavated, this is quite an impressive strike rate. Combined with the quantity of material cultural debris – over 3500 sherds of Middle Saxon pottery, for example – it leads the present writer to conclude that, from the mid-7th century, the Butterwick-type site at Wharram was home to a growing, and permanent community.

Stocker and Everson also point to the very irregular layouts of the Wolds Butterwick-type sites, and suggest that they lack the intelligible patterns that can be recognised in the plans of permanent settlements. These settlements are certainly irregular in their layout, but they do in fact incorporate elements which can be read as indicating spatial order at an inter-enclosure, rather than merely an intra-enclosure level. A case in point is that part of the Wharram settlement shown in Figure 56, where it is not too difficult to recognise adjacent enclosures that have been laid out with a view to maintaining a space for livestock to be run between them. There is no denying that some crop mark signatures at these sites indicate the abandonment of enclosures and their replacement by successors, but this would not account for all or even most of the recorded morphological characteristics.

There is, furthermore, a wider argument to be made. The ditches will not, in themselves, have created a sheep-proof boundary. We can discount associated stone walls because of the geology, and we are left, as Stocker and Everson have pointed out, with fences or hedges. Though wattle fencing (or at least barriers formed of dead thorn bushes, cut from the valley sides) will have been required for the first few years to allow quick-set hedges to grow, it is much more likely that the long-term permanent barriers will have been such hedges. Whilst fences would have required the consumption of what might already have been diminishing woodland and scrubland resources, hedge maintenance would, in contrast, have offered a means of replenishing those resources. So the questions must be why, according to Stocker and Everson's reading of these remains, Wharram's shepherds chose so frequently to abandon ditches dug at great effort and replace them with new ones, and why hedges on the associated banks, that would take a number of years to mature into stock-proof barriers, were either uprooted or abandoned and left to grow into bushes.

One intriguing characteristic of these ditches to which Stocker and Everson have drawn attention is the way in which the alignments of some stretches seem to be replicated by other ditches just within, or just outside their courses, creating concentric runs of curvilinear ditches. If the sheep grazing operations were seasonal, then a new ditch might have been created each season. But why would the shepherds not simply have emptied the pre-existing ditches of their winter silts? The earlier ditches would still have been visible; otherwise their

replacements would not have replicated their alignments. Following Stocker and Everson, one answer to this phenomenon may be that, where there are two parallel curvilinear ditches set only a couple of metres apart, they had a hedged bank between them. Alternatively, if hedges were allowed to increase significantly in width over the years, it would then perhaps have been necessary to create a new ditch to generate new bank material outside the line of the original one, in order to prevent sheep penetrating the base of the hedge as it grew upwards.

The control of sheep did not, of course, require the creation of structures that would leave much of a permanent mark in or on the landscape – certainly not through the labour-intensive digging of ditches. Henry Best's instructions with regard to the folding of sheep on his arable lands, penned in by hurdles to manure specific ridges, would have left lines of stake-holes but nothing else in the archaeological record (Woodward 1984, 16-18); and though these instructions were written in the early 17th century they do not, on the face of it, imply husbandry techniques that would have been unknown in the Middle Saxon period, or inapplicable at that time.

Beyond the detailed interpretation of the structural remains, there is a further body of relevant data that has the potential to help define the character of activity in Middle Saxon Wharram: the faunal assemblage. It is common ground that in the Late Saxon period, and of course in post-Conquest times, Wharram Percy vill contained a permanently settled community that cultivated fields and maintained livestock – cattle and sheep. If activity in Middle Saxon Wharram had been of a very different kind – a focal point for transhumance practices, or a semi-permanent sheep station, for example – it is reasonable to anticipate that the differences would be visible in the faunal record. This is the question that was put to Jane Richardson, whose extensive analyses of Wharram's faunal assemblage are available through the Archaeology Data Service (doi:10.5284/1000415). Her response to this question is the basis for the next section of this chapter, which also makes comparison with the faunal assemblage from the excavated Middle and Late Saxon site at Burdale. This is followed by some observations, by Julian Richards, on the comparative characteristics of Middle Saxon material culture at Wharram and Burdale.

The Anglo-Saxon faunal assemblage of Wharram and its comparison with Burdale
by Jane Richardson

Introduction
Excavations at Wharram Percy have produced a significant multi-period animal bone assemblage of some 133,000 recorded elements. The village-wide assemblage can be grouped with relative ease into Iron Age/Roman, Roman, Anglo-Saxon, medieval and post-medieval phases, but unfortunately few well-dated discrete assemblages are available to allow finer temporal subtleties to be assessed. To this must be added the

inevitable mixing and redepositing of material that serves to temporally and spatially isolate the assemblages from their place of use. In addition, exporting animals to market on the hoof would remove any evidence of this section of the population from the retrievable assemblage and in doing so impact on the reconstruction of the village's livestock economy. Finally, given that various researchers have been involved with this long-term project, different methods of analysis have inevitably been used. Consequently, data are not always directly comparable and fluctuations may not necessarily be significant.

Despite these qualifications, the faunal assemblage has much to offer in terms of understanding the livestock management strategies employed by Wharram's inhabitants from later prehistoric times down to the post-medieval period. Many of the broader issues are considered later in this volume (Chs 19 and 20), in discussions based on a detailed analysis of the evidence relating specifically to the manorial and peasant households in the post-Conquest period. The present contribution focuses on one particular aspect: the role of sheep in the life of the Middle Saxon community, and more specifically whether there is any faunal evidence to support the hypothesis that the Middle Saxon 'settlement' was, as Stocker and Everson have proposed, a specialist and perhaps temporary sheep station rather than a more economically broadly-based community. It also considers whether, if this was the case, there is evidence of a shift to broader-based farming in the Late Saxon period, when the first elements of the medieval village were founded (see Ch. 13 below). In doing so it takes account both of Wharram's later faunal remains, and of Anglo-Saxon and later assemblages from other sites in the area. Among these is the assemblage from the unpublished Middle Saxon settlement excavations at Burdale, which have been described briefly in Chapter 8.

The South Manor Area in the Anglo-Saxon and post-Conquest periods

The faunal remains from the South Manor Area have already been reported by Pinter-Bellows (2000), and this section represents a brief revisiting of the data in light of subsequent analyses. Of particular importance is whether there is evidence at any period for an intensification of sheep farming. Sawyer, for example, has suggested that an 11th-century extension of settlement in the Wolds was due in large part to a growing demand for textiles

(Sawyer 1971, 174-5). This may be reflected in an increase in the proportion of sheep, a change in population dynamics as animals are kept to a greater age to maximise the number of fleeces obtained, or a change in body size as castrates are targeted for their superior fleeces. As a result, data assigned to the Middle Saxon, Late Saxon, and Norman to mid-13th-century periods are compared in order to investigate possible trends in animal husbandry over this critical period. Unfortunately, the data were not always subdivided thus, and on occasion a broader Norman to 15th-century period was used by Pinter-Bellows. The proportion of the main domestic animals, age data and metrical data are considered, with particular, but not exclusive, reference to sheep.

The proportion of the main domestic animals as a reflection of animal husbandry practices is a crude measure because factors such as the import/export of animals and differential disposal strategies can bias the recovered assemblage. Nevertheless, the data available highlight no significant increase in the proportion of sheep over time (Table 9); in fact the proportion of these four taxa show remarkable stability over nearly a millennium. If the inhabitants of Wharram Percy were at any period part of the drive for raw materials to feed the burgeoning textile industry, then they chose a different method to achieve this (e.g. a selective breeding programme) than simply increasing the number of sheep.

If sheep were not being maintained in greater numbers to supply the rapidly expanding wool trade, perhaps the flock was being targeted for fleeces more intensively (i.e. animals were kept to a greater age in order to recover a greater number of fleeces per individual). To test for such a change in the population dynamics, kill-off curves have been constructed by period, with comparative data from neighbouring Burdale (Fig. 69). Following Payne's (1973) kill-off models based on sheep raised for meat, milk or wool, all the slaughter curves fit most closely, but not precisely, with meat production. Certainly in the absence of any significant neonatal/juvenile slaughter, intensive milk production is not indicated, while a wether flock run for its wool should be reflected in a greater percentage survival through to old age, as indicated at medieval North Elmham (Noddle 1980, 396) and elsewhere (Thomas 2007, 144). Instead multi-purpose, low-intensity strategies are proposed for both Burdale and Wharram Percy, offering relatively low returns in terms of meat, milk and fleeces, but also relatively low risk.

Table 9. Proportion of the main domestic animals from the South Manor Area by period (numbers in parentheses are the total bone counts for these four taxa)

	Cattle	Sheep	Pig	Horse
Middle Saxon -buildings/smithy (6700)	34.6	55.2	8.6	1.7
Late Saxon - no structures (1773)	36.4	51.4	8.9	3.3
Earlier medieval - manorial (1609)	37.2	49.8	9.6	3.4
Later medieval - peasant (2194)	31.5	53.1	11.2	4.2

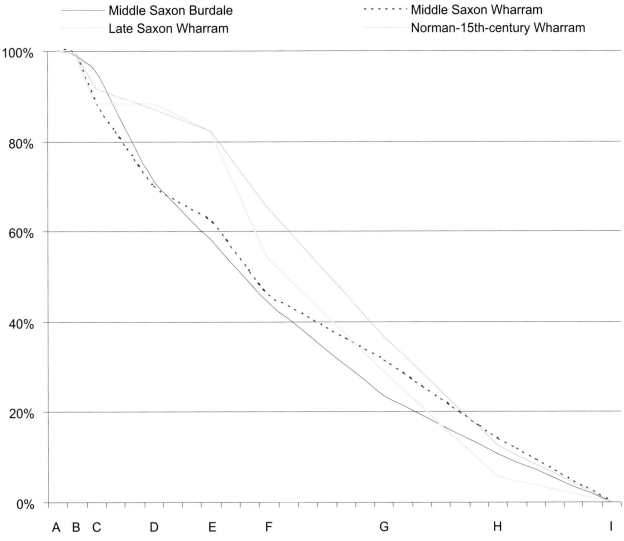

Fig. 69. Burdale and Wharram: kill-off curves for sheep by period and site (stages after Payne 1973). (J. Richardson)

Curiously, however, relatively subtle changes in the slaughter patterns at Wharram Percy from the Late Saxon period onwards are seen with the greater survival of sub-adults between the ages of one and four years (stages D-F) when compared to Middle Saxon Wharram and Middle Saxon Burdale (occupied *c.* 700 to early 900s AD). At stage E (2-3 years), for example, just under 20% of the sheep population had been slaughtered from Late Saxon and later medieval Wharram, compared to 38% from Middle Saxon Wharram and 42% from Burdale. Perhaps prime meat production was more prevalent at Middle Saxon Wharram and Burdale or alternatively prime meat animals were removed off site (whether traded, exchanged or as tribute) in greater numbers during later periods at Wharram. This shift of emphasis, however, appears to have occurred at too young an age to have impacted greatly on wool production, but clearly some change in sheep husbandry, dietary preferences and/or livestock movements had occurred by the Late Saxon period. Interestingly, the greatest potential for fleece production, as indicated by increased survivability of adult and mature animals, probably occurred at Norman and later Wharram, coinciding with the English wool

trade at maximum output (Sykes 2006b, 58; Ryder 1983, 455-7; Sawyer 1965, 161-3).

Unfortunately given Pinter-Bellow's method of recording cattle dental wear, comparison with data from other sites was extremely difficult and the same style of kill-off curve could not be constructed for cattle as for sheep. As such, only data from Wharram Percy are compared here (Fig. 70). Nevertheless, this graph highlights relatively stable husbandry practices, with some animals clearly raised specifically for slaughter at prime meat age and the remainder maintained as a breeding herd, for low-intensity milk production (in the absence of neonatal slaughter) and for traction. As with the data from sheep, however, the Middle Saxon slaughter pattern differs slightly, with a lower proportion of sub-adult cattle (between 2.5 to 4 years) surviving compared to later periods. Again a change in meat procurement might be indicated (proportionally more animals killed for prime beef during the Middle Saxon period, or perhaps proportionally more cattle at prime-beef age being moved off site during later periods). Whatever the reason, it is significant that changes in the slaughter patterns of both cattle and sheep, albeit subtle in nature, occurred at the same time.

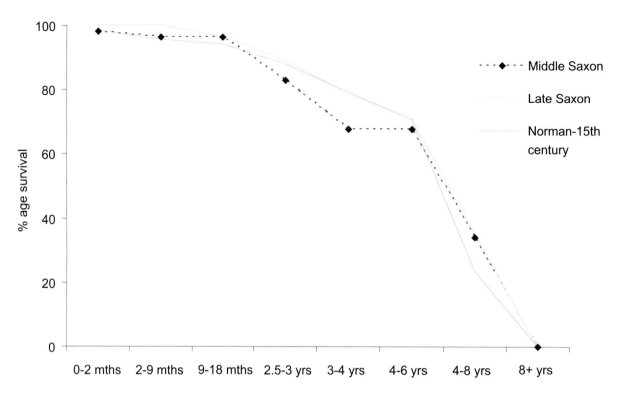

Fig. 70. Wharram: kill-off curves for cattle by period (using Pinter-Bellows' age ranges). (J. Richardson)

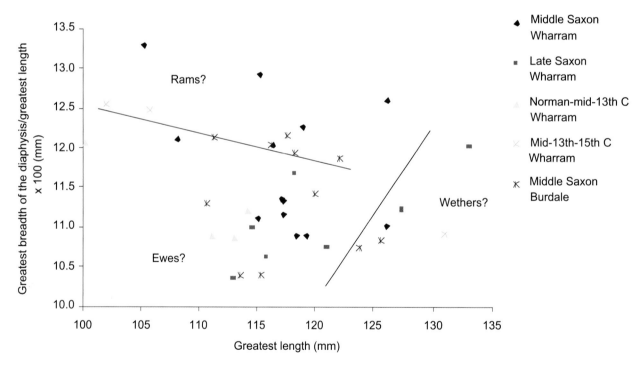

Fig. 71. Burdale and Wharram: scattergram of adult sheep metacarpals showing size variation by period and site (divisions based loosely on data from Davis 2000, fig. 8). (J. Richardson)

The final opportunity to clarify changes in animal husbandry practices over time lies with a reassessment of the metrical data. Comprehensive data interrogation by Pinter-Bellows (2000, 178-181) for cattle and sheep showed no significant difference in the size and shape of cattle by period but a size decrease for sheep over the same timeframe was indicated. A similar decrease in size has also been recognised from Anglo-Saxon to Anglo-Scandinavian/medieval Fishergate, York (O'Connor 1991, fig. 38) and Flaxengate, Lincoln (Dobney *et al.* 1996, 40). Rather than revisit the evidence for changes in size, the metrical data for sheep are assessed here for evidence of sexual polymorphism: can ewes, wethers and rams be separated on size? Shape variation due to sex,

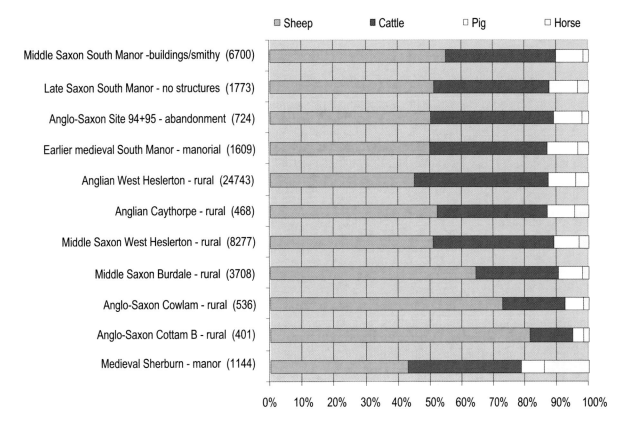

Legend: Sheep — Cattle — Pig — Horse

- Middle Saxon South Manor -buildings/smithy (6700)
- Late Saxon South Manor - no structures (1773)
- Anglo-Saxon Site 94+95 - abandonment (724)
- Earlier medieval South Manor - manorial (1609)
- Anglian West Heslerton - rural (24743)
- Anglian Caythorpe - rural (468)
- Middle Saxon West Heslerton - rural (8277)
- Middle Saxon Burdale - rural (3708)
- Anglo-Saxon Cowlam - rural (536)
- Anglo-Saxon Cottam B - rural (401)
- Medieval Sherburn - manor (1144)

0% 10% 20% 30% 40% 50% 60% 70% 80% 90% 100%

South Manor (Pinter-Bellows 2000), Site 94 and 95 (Pinter-Bellows 1992), West Heslerton (Richardson 2001), Caythorpe (Stallibrass 1996), Burdale (Richardson 2009a), Cowlam (Richardson 2009b), Cottam B (Dobney *et al.* 1999), Sherburn (Rushe *et al.* 1994)

Fig. 72. Proportion of the main domestic animals from Wharram by area and period, with comparison to nearby sites (numbers in parentheses are the total bone counts for these four taxa). (J. Richardson)

however, can be swamped by factors such as breed (O'Connor 1982, 28) and while diversity caused by different breeds has been investigated, in particular with reference to variation in the shape and size of horncores (O'Connor 1982, 20), this bone is relatively rare from Wharram. While an assessment of breeds is not attempted, therefore, the potential for different breeds to influence shape is acknowledged.

The premise here is that metrical data from a particular bone may allow the short, slender female to be separated from the tall, slender castrate and the short, stocky male, although overlap between the three groups is highlighted by previous studies (e.g. Davis 2000, 378). The metacarpal has been chosen as it often survives intact, although Davis (2000, 384) indicates that the pelvis (specifically the pubis) provides the best separation between the three sex groups. As Davis notes, however, this bone is poorly represented in the archaeological record, as is the case here. As might be anticipated, a reading of the data is not straight forward. As the bones of castrated animals fuse later (Davis 2000, 382), it is possible that wethers, important for their superior fleeces (Hagen 1995, 92), are underrepresented in the graph below as only adult (fused) bones were measured. Further, there remains the possibility that the perceived groups might reflect different breeds rather than sexual polymorphism. With these caveats in mind, the available data do indicate the presence of different groups, although given the small sample sizes, an increase in the proportion of the proposed wethers group over time cannot be proposed (Fig. 71).

Comparing Anglo-Saxon and post-Conquest South Manor, in the light of a proposed intensification of sheep farming from the 11th century (Sawyer 1971, 174-5) or perhaps even earlier (Sykes 2006b, 57-8), has highlighted interesting, if unexpected, results. Instead of evidence for intensive sheep husbandry (demonstrated by an increase in the proportion of sheep, an increase in the proportion of wethers and/or changes in the population dynamics), the farming regime established in the Anglo-Saxon period (and probably already adopted by the Romano-British inhabitants – see Richardson 2004a, 271) was deemed fit for purpose. It provided the Anglo-Saxon and medieval inhabitants of Wharram with lamb/mutton, beef, milk, fleeces and traction cattle, in addition to manure, skins and horn. The diet was also supplemented by pork, chicken, goose, fish and shellfish. Some relatively subtle changes in sheep and cattle slaughter patterns between the Middle and Late Saxon periods, however, were noted and these suggest that sub-adult animals were less likely to be slaughtered from later periods. This may imply a move away from meat production to one focusing more on fleeces, manure and traction. Conversely, slaughter patterns for adult and mature animals were largely unchanged over time.

On balance, while sheep, so well suited to the free-draining, chalk Wolds, predominated and no doubt provided an annual trade in fleeces, they formed only one part of a broad, multi-faceted economy from the Middle Saxon period onwards. Certainly no suggestion of a specialist sheep station can be made from the faunal assemblage at this time. Given Wharram's access to fresh water, which is relatively unusual for the Wolds, production of cattle with their high water requirements was also profitable. In this, Wharram's farming economy was more like Wold-edge sites such as West Heslerton, Caythorpe and Sherburn than those in the heart of the Wolds like Cowlam and Cottam (Fig. 72; Fenton-Thomas 2005, 87).

Burdale and Wharram Percy in Middle Saxon times: some comparisons
by Julian Richards

At Burdale there has been the opportunity to sample the interior of a number of the Anglo-Saxon enclosures. The negative features observed in the geophysical survey at Wharram Percy are confirmed at Burdale as *Grubenhäuser* and pits. Some of the pits at Burdale appear to have had an industrial function with hearth bases, and evidence for metalworking. Others may also have had a specialist function originally, but ended up as convenient rubbish pits. The *Grubenhäuser* also appear to have had an industrial function, with activity taking place directly on the sunken floor area, as observed at West Heslerton. There is evidence for the organisation of space both within each excavation site, but also between the two concentrations of enclosures. Clearly both foci of activity were contemporary but they were *c*. 200m apart, with an open area in between them. This zoned use of the landscape parallels that observed at a larger scale at West Heslerton (Powlesland 2003a, 290, fig. 91). The curvilinear enclosures at Burdale were also reorganised through time. The stratigraphic evidence suggests that the enclosures were laid out first and later subdivided, in some cases after some of the ditches had already been filled, at least partially. An intercutting sequence of backfilled ditches does not, by itself, however, provide evidence for seasonal activity.

At a landscape level, it is also very likely that the Middle and Late Saxon residents of Burdale were in contact with their contemporaries at Wharram Percy. Indeed, the proximity of the sites makes it likely that both were controlled from the same estate centre in the Middle Saxon period, although it is unclear what happened to this relationship with the changes in land ownership which came about as a result of Scandinavian settlement in the late 9th and 10th centuries. There is certainly evidence for some activity at Burdale in the Late Saxon period, but the settlement was soon abandoned rather than reorganised, and any later 10th-century activity must be assumed to be under the medieval vill.

If Burdale and Wharram Percy were managed as part of the same estate then analysis of the assemblages from each site will provide an important opportunity to examine the level of specialised activity taking place, such as one might expect from a 'multiple estate', where different settlements might each play a particular role. We should also be able to look at local networks of exchange and the extent of penetration of imported goods within Anglo-Saxon settlement hierarchies.

Preliminary analysis of the manufactured artefacts suggests that the site at Burdale was richer than Wharram Percy. Although much of the material has disappeared through night-hawking, the quantity of silver sceatta, including a number of possible hoards, indicates a wealthy settlement. Analysis of the artefact assemblages will throw further light on this but comparison of the knives already shows some intriguing differences.

In total 30 knives were recovered, including one pivoting knife, with eleven recovered during 2006 and nineteen in 2007; the most common forms were curved-back knives, closely followed by those with angle-backs, whereas angle-backed knives were more common at Wharram (Blakelock 2008). There is also a clear difference between the two Burdale sites, with all the angle-backed examples recovered from the 2007 excavation, and none from 2006. This may reflect a difference in date or site function. Metallographic analysis also revealed a difference in quality of the knives between Burdale and Wharram. The good quality manufacture and heat treatment of the Burdale knives is reflected in high hardness levels (473HV at Burdale compared to 261HV at Wharram). This must indicate that a different smith was operating at Burdale and it suggests localised differences in knives. There was also a number of surface features on the Burdale knives, whereas it is notable that at Wharram Percy no knives with transverse notches or indents were found, perhaps indicating a more limited range of craft activities (Blakelock 2008).

Preliminary examination of the comb assemblages also suggests that the combs from Burdale are of much higher quality than those at Wharram Percy (Ashby pers. comm.). This high level of differentiation in the quality of material culture at a local level is quite surprising. It demonstrates that, whilst the overall settlement morphology of each site may have been similar, there were significant differences in the types and quality of activity represented. Analysis of the finds assemblages is continuing and a full report on the fieldwork in Burdale is planned.

Conclusions
by Stuart Wrathmell

Richardson's faunal analysis has provided new and unanticipated insights into the character of Middle Saxon Wharram, especially in comparison with the contemporary settlement at Burdale. She has pointed out that Wharram's community, with access to relatively abundant water resources, may in some ways have been more closely comparable to its neighbours on the Wolds edge and in the Vale than to those in the interior of the northern Wolds. Richards' analysis, on the other hand, warns us not to assume that the settlements in the interior of the Wolds will necessarily have had a more impoverished material culture than those nearer the edge. Though there are clearly some changes to cattle and sheep slaughtering practices at Wharram at the end of the Middle Saxon period, neither faunal analysis specifically, nor the study of excavation data as a whole, provides support for the notion that specialist but temporary grazing facilities were replaced at this time by more broadly-based, permanently settled farming communities.

Stocker and Everson have argued, on the other hand, that neither the faunal record nor the substantial and wide-ranging assemblage of artefacts is incompatible with a seasonally occupied sheep-grazing facility. If they are not, it is legitimate to ask: what would be? We have also seen, in Chapter 8, that Stoertz recorded one Butterwick-type group of curvilinear enclosures in the Vale of Pickering, at Binnington (Fig. 45), and that these Butterwick-type signatures are not dissimilar in their broad structural characteristics and components to the settlement at West Heslerton (Fig. 46: compare for example Fig. 42). What, then, in the archaeological record differentiates seasonal grazing sites belonging to communities settled elsewhere, from the remains representing their permanent homes? It is hard to resist the conclusion that it is based solely on geographical distinctions: if they are on the Wolds they are to be assigned to the first category; if in the Vale, to the second.

Rejecting such an approach, it is worth looking in a little more detail at the similarities between Wharram and the one excavated Middle Saxon settlement in the Vale – West Heslerton. The principal elements of the Butterwick-type formation at Wharram are the groups of enclosure ditches which lie to the west of the medieval village's West Row of tofts. We cannot, however, discount the possibility that the enclosures continued eastwards up to the edge of the plateau, their full extent masked or obliterated by the medieval buildings, yards and toft boundaries of the West Row. On the other hand, they appear from the geophysical survey to be confined to the south side of the east-west trackway, despite the evidence from the Site 39 excavation that at least one contemporary *Grubenhaus* – or an abandoned *Grubenhaus* containing contemporary occupation material – lay on the north side of that trackway, some distance to the north-east of the visible curvilinear enclosures (Fig. 51 above; Milne 1992a, 5-12).

To this isolated record of Middle Saxon activity north of the trackway can be added a further piece of evidence: the results of fieldwalking in the fields, north of the Guardianship area, that are cultivated currently. Colin Hayfield's programme of fieldwalking was not comprehensive, and as noted earlier the assemblage of

'Saxon' pottery recovered in this exercise is not, currently, accessible. On the other hand, given the amount of Middle Saxon pottery recovered from the village excavations it seems reasonable to suppose that much of the 'Saxon' fieldwalking collection has a similar date range. Two transects in different parts of the field immediately to the north of the village site produced significant clusters of 'Saxon' pottery, totalling nearly 200 sherds (Hayfield 1987a, 109-12); their very approximate locations are shown on Figure 47.

It is just possible that curvilinear ditched enclosures also existed north of the trackway but remain undetected by aerial or geophysical survey: the stretch of possible post-Roman gully in the University of York's North-west Enclosure excavation could be cited in support of this view (see Fig. 25). Alternatively, the area north of the trackway may have been the location of an unenclosed zone of the Middle Saxon settlement area. This is, after all, the overall structure of West Heslerton: a zone of activity marked by tightly-grouped curvilinear enclosure ditches, and another without archaeologically detectable enclosures, but with *Grubenhäuser* and structures marked by post-holes (Powlesland 2003a, 290, fig. 91). Was Wharram also more extensive than its enclosure ditches suggest? Were its size and composition more closely comparable to Vale settlements such as West Heslerton, rather than those in the higher parts of the Wolds?

It is instructive to set the Wharram and neighbouring Butterwick-type remains in the context of the wider record of excavated Middle Saxon settlements, usefully assembled by Andrew Reynolds (2003) and Helena Hamerow (2010). The most closely comparable is perhaps the site at Riby Crossroads in Lincolnshire, where a long trench was excavated through Anglo-Saxon settlement remains in advance of pipeline construction. The site is adjacent to a routeway for which prehistoric origins have been postulated, and the excavated features assigned to two chronological groups on the basis of the pottery: 6th to 7th centuries, and late 7th to mid-9th centuries. The enclosures were separated by trackways; they could all have been in contemporary use, and the ditches of most of them had been redefined on several occasions. Several *Grubenhäuser* were ascribed to the Middle Saxon period, some set within the enclosures but at least one possibly outside. Some enclosures may have had a domestic use; others were perhaps livestock compounds (Steedman 1994, 214-28).

In terms of its plan form and components the Riby site seems by far the most comparable to the Butterwick-type remains of the Yorkshire Wolds, but this may be due in part to the nature of the record: it has been revealed, like the Yorkshire Butterwick-type sites (except Wharram), through crop mark signatures; whereas most of the other enclosed settlements recorded by Reynolds and Hamerow are known only from their excavated remains. Nevertheless, it shows that many of the characteristics of Middle Saxon enclosed settlements in the Vale of Pickering and on the Yorkshire Wolds are also to be found south of the Humber. In contrast, Hamerow's recent overview of excavated Middle Saxon sites seems to indicate that settlements south of the Wash may have exhibited a greater degree of rectilinearity than the Butterwick-type remains (Hamerow 2010, 10-17).

We should, however, be cautious about distinguishing regional variation in enclosure forms on the basis of current data. It is worth noting that, had the Wharram excavations *not* been accompanied by extensive geophysical survey, the Middle Saxon remains discovered in the South Manor Area would almost certainly have been cited in support of a settlement formed by rectilinear rather than curvilinear enclosures (Richards 2000a, 196, fig. 96): all Butterwick-type remains seem to include a number of straight-line ditches. Furthermore, the multiple curvilinear ditches excavated at West Stow, Suffolk, would not look out of place at Wharram, especially in Site 78 (Reynolds 2003, 112, fig. 6B; compare Fig. 60 above).

The curvilinear enclosure groups show wide variation in the numbers of enclosed units they contain. Some appear to have been single or small groups of enclosures, represented on the northern Wolds by Cottam and Thwing (Richards 1999a; Reynolds 2003, 111-12, 128-9). Both of these may have been high status sites, and Fenton-Thomas (2005, 90) has suggested that the former may have been a hunting lodge. Other groups were large agglomerations, sometimes extending beyond the enclosed areas and covering as much ground as the medieval and later villages that succeeded them. Though some of the enclosures in large agglomerations may have been cattle pounds, craft areas and the like, they are also likely to have provided accommodation for the rural population generally. They may have begun as small units, individual farmsteads, which then grew in size through the creation of additional enclosures.

Some of the Middle Saxon enclosed settlements on the northern Wolds continued to be occupied into the Late Saxon period, for example the small unit at Thwing (Reynolds 2003, 128-9). At Cottam there was a shift of focus in the late 9th century and again in the early 10th, before a further shift which may have seen the establishment of the medieval village before the end of the 10th century (Richards 2001b, 271-4). The Butterwick-type enclosures at Burdale also seem to have been abandoned at some point in the 10th century, presumably at the moment when the medieval village was established further to the north-west, on the site now occupied by the modern farm (Richards, above). Down in the Vale, however, the West Heslerton settlement is thought to have been abandoned earlier, at some stage in the 9th century (Powlesland 2003a, 288). After attempting in the next chapter to establish a context for changes in settlements and estates in the study area and beyond in the Late Saxon period, the final chapter in this part of the volume addresses two key questions relating to Wharram: when were its Butterwick-type enclosures abandoned, and what replaced them?

12 Lordship, Local Administration and Ecclesiastical Provision in the Late Saxon Period
by Stuart Wrathmell

Introduction

Chapter 8 envisaged, for the study area, a pattern of Early to Middle Saxon estate centres in the Vale, at Sherburn, Wintringham and Yedingham, and dependencies on the Wolds. If this hypothesis is correct, we might expect the entries in Domesday Book to reflect the linkages between these centres and their outliers, as they do in other parts of the East Riding. The estate centres of Market Weighton and Driffield, for example, were both associated in much earlier times with Anglo-Saxon kings, the latter being the place where Aldfrith king of Northumbria died in 705; and both are visible in Domesday Book as the centres of extensive estates, or 'sokes' (Hart 1992, 262 and map 8.7c; Loveluck 1996, 25-48). If we turn to the parts of the Survey that deal with Sherburn and Wintringham, however, there is no obvious sign of them having been centres of soke estates. Yedingham is entirely absent from Domesday Book: A.H. Smith records the earliest occurrence of the name in 1170-75 (Smith 1937, 121). Instead, the study area contains estate centres in three other vills, at Weaverthorpe, Buckton and Langton (see Figs 73 and 74), as well as a number of dependencies of two other soke centres to the west, at Kirkham and Howsham (*DB Yorks* 1Y 7).

The question that must be asked, therefore, is whether the initial hypothesis regarding estates is incorrect, or whether, by the mid-11th century, some major shift has taken place in the organisation of Vale and Wold estates. The latter explanation is the one preferred here, for several reasons. In the first place, the references to Sherburn in Domesday are inconsistent and incomplete – a feature of the Yorkshire survey as a whole, as David Roffe's analysis has shown (Roffe 1990, 310, 313-18). Domesday Book itself records two holdings there: a 3 carucate outlier or berewick belonging to the Weaverthorpe estate (*DB Yorks*, 2B 18), and another berewick of 9 carucates belonging to the Langton estate. The entry preceding the one for Langton, however, relates to a one carucate berewick at Fraisthorpe and records it as belonging to Sherburn (*DB Yorks*, 23E 13). Furthermore, the Summary records a third holding at Sherburn: 6 carucates belonging to the Count of Mortain (*DB Yorks*, Se Th1), which do not appear among the Count's holdings in this hundred in Domesday Book itself (*DB Yorks*, 5E 68-73). We may be seeing here a dismembered estate, misunderstood by the Domesday compilers and therefore poorly recorded.

Secondly, Sherburn church has produced by far the largest quantity of Anglo-Saxon stone sculpture of any in the study area (Lang 1991, 201-206). None of it appears to date to a period earlier than the late 9th century (most

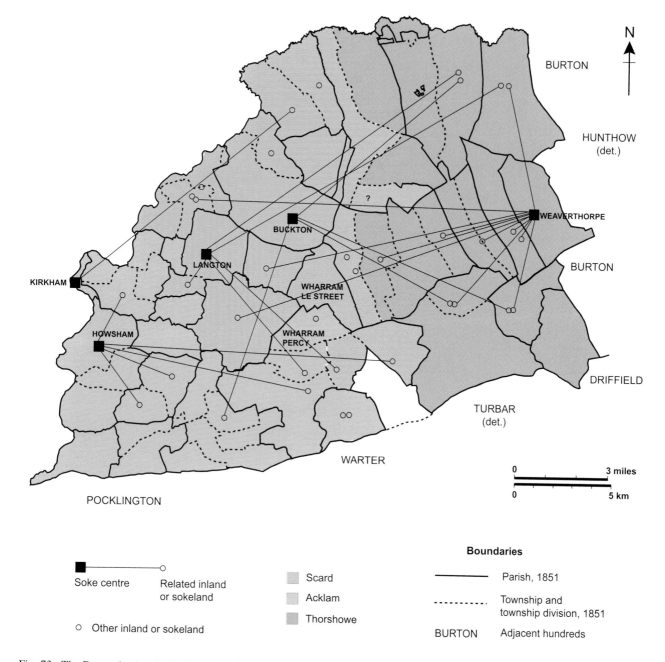

BURTON

HUNTHOW
(det.)

WEAVERTHORPE

BURTON

BUCKTON

LANGTON

KIRKHAM

WHARRAM
LE STREET

HOWSHAM

WHARRAM
PERCY

DRIFFIELD

TURBAR
(det.)

WARTER

POCKLINGTON

| 0 | | | | 3 miles |
| 0 | | | | 5 km |

Boundaries

■———○

Soke centre   Related inland
              or sokeland

○ Other inland or sokeland

Scard

Acklam

Thorshowe

——————— Parish, 1851

· · · · · · · · · Township and
                township division, 1851

BURTON   Adjacent hundreds

Fig. 73. The Domesday hundreds of Acklam, Scard and Thorshowe. (E. Marlow-Mann after M. Fossick)

of it to the first half of the 10th century according to David Stocker), but this still suggests an ecclesiastical establishment of more than local significance a century before the Conquest (see p. 217 below).

The final point relates to the Domesday soke centre of Weaverthorpe. As a *thorp* name, appropriate for a dependent settlement of the Late Saxon period, 'Weaverthorpe' seems unlikely to signify a 6th or 7th-century estate centre. It might be claimed that this vill could have had a quite different name before the 10th century, but this is a line of argument that should not be used selectively, simply to explain away what is otherwise difficult to explain. Renaming is a phenomenon that itself needs explanation and context before it can be invoked to resolve apparent naming anomalies. On the

face of it, Weaverthorpe is a vill that acquired its Domesday name before achieving its Domesday status.

Whatever their origins, the soke centres of Weaverthorpe, Buckton and Langton dominate the Domesday entries for vills in the study area, and the following accounts attempt to characterise the composition and lordship of these estates both before the Conquest and in the later 11th century. The summaries begin with Weaverthorpe, an estate of the archbishops of York, and continue with Buckton and Langton, which in 1066, it will be argued, had been held by members of an Anglo-Scandinavian kin group. These sokes were, however, only elements of a much larger grouping of estates held by this kin group, and some of the characteristics of these wider holdings are explored,

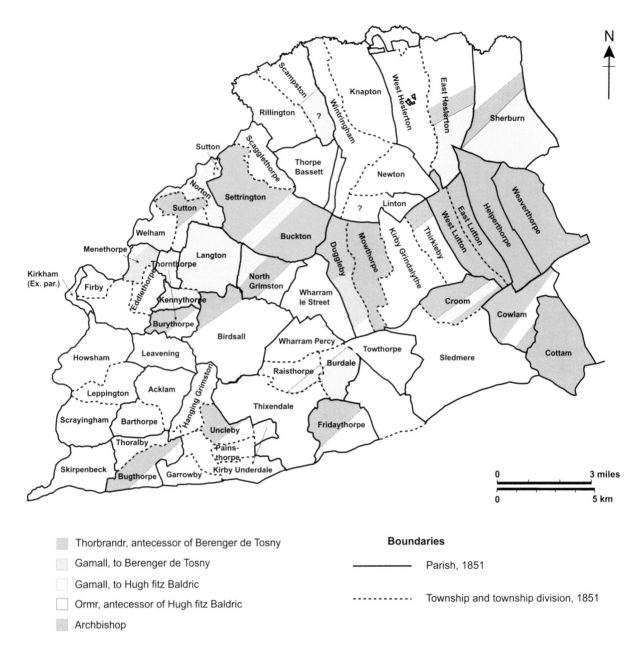

N

Thorbrandr, antecessor of Berenger de Tosny

Gamall, to Berenger de Tosny

Gamall, to Hugh fitz Baldric

Ormr, antecessor of Hugh fitz Baldric

Archbishop

Boundaries

—————— Parish, 1851

- - - - - - - - - - Township and township division, 1851

Fig. 74. Landholding in 1066 and 1086 in the hundreds of Acklam, Scard and Thorshowe. (E. Marlow-Mann after M. Fossick)

including aspects of ecclesiastical provision. After a discussion of the possible origins of the Anglo-Scandinavian landholdings, the chapter concludes with some comparisons between these and neighbouring Late Saxon sokes.

The soke estates: lordship and population

Weaverthorpe soke (Figs 73 and 74)
In 1066, in the time of Edward the Confessor (hereafter abbreviated to TRE), Weaverthorpe had belonged to Aldred, the last Anglo-Saxon archbishop. It was then assessed at 18 carucates, with berewicks of 5 carucates in Mowthorpe and 3 carucates in Sherburn, as noted above. In terms of the latter holding this is, of course, the reverse of the relationship that we might have expected in

Chapter 8. Also belonging to the estate was the jurisdiction, or soke of 12 carucates at Helperthorpe, 3½ at North Grimston, ½ at Sutton, 2½ at Birdsall, 4 at Croom, 1 at Thirkleby, 8 in Lutton and 1 in the lost *Ulchiltorp*. By 1086 these had passed to Archbishop Thomas I, along with the church and a ½ carucate at Cowlam (*DB Yorks*, 2B 18).

At some date between 1108 and 1114 Archbishop Thomas II made a feoffment of the whole estate in favour of Herbert of Winchester, the king's chamberlain (*EYC I*, 35-6, no. 25; Bilson 1922, 59-67; *VCH ER VIII*, 219). Soon after this, Herbert built a church at Weaverthorpe, a building that survives largely unaltered. Its erection is recorded in an inscription on a dial-stone set in the tympanum of the south doorway, which reads in part '*Herebertvs Wintonie hoc monasterivm fecit*' (Bilson

1922, 58, fig. 3). Between 1114 and 1121 his sons Herbert and William (later another archbishop of York) granted the church to the canons of Nostell (*EYC I*, 36-7, nos 26-28).

Weaverthorpe church stands on the northern slope of Cranedale, above and north of the present village. The east end of its graveyard appears to overlie the north-west corner of a manorial *curia*, a large rectangular enclosure bounded by a bank and ditch which survive in earthwork form (Plate 17; Brewster 1972, pl. 1). Though there is no sign of the west side bank and ditch within the churchyard, their projected course would have the church straddling the boundary, presumably sited in a break in the bank and ditch. This might indicate that, whilst the villagers could reach the nave without entering the *curia*, the lord had direct access to the chancel from his hall (see Morris 1989, 268-9).

In 1960, when T.C.M Brewster excavated part of the enclosure immediately east of the churchyard (in advance of the graveyard's expansion) he uncovered an 'early hall' which he dated to the 12th century, aligned with an east-west roadway (Brewster 1972, 117, 119-22, 125, 128). The roadway can be seen on the published aerial photograph to have run directly towards the east wall of the chancel (Brewster 1972, pl. 1). The enclosure boundary was also dated to the late 11th or early 12th

century, as Pimply ware (but no Staxton ware) sherds were recovered from beneath the bank (Brewster 1972, 118-19). Apart from a pit containing late Roman pottery, the only potentially pre-Conquest feature was a shallow scoop containing Stamford ware, and undated possible 'sleeper trenches' (Brewster 1972, 115, 118). In summary, there is nothing to suggest that, in this particular part of the vill, there was any occupation between the end of the 4th century and the 10th century, and therefore nothing (as yet) to indicate that its position as an estate centre was of long standing.

Buckton and Langton sokes (Figs 73 and 74)

Though Langton township survived to be recorded by the Ordnance Survey in the mid-19th century, Buckton vill had by then vanished from the map, its territory subsumed in the neighbouring township of Settrington. Some of Buckton's medieval homesteads survive as earthworks on both sides of Settrington Beck to the south of Settrington village, in the vicinity of Kirkhill and, further south, in an area called Buckton Garths in the survey and map of 1600. The vill's probable former bounds can be inferred from that map (see Fig. 109), despite the fact that it had ceased to be a separate entity by then.

Plate 17. Aerial photograph of Weaverthorpe's manorial *curia*, viewed from the north in 1990. The early 12th-century church appears to cross the line of the western enclosure bank near its northern end. (NMR CRA 16865/31, 2 March 1990. © Aeroscene Ltd)

In 1086 the Buckton soke estate was, along with the adjoining manor of Settrington, part of Berenger de Tosny's tenancy 'in chief' – the landholding that Berenger held directly from the king, rather than from another lord. Twenty years earlier both manors had been held by a tenant named Thorbrandr. Buckton had been assessed for geld as 10 carucates, and it included a church with a priest. Belonging to it was the soke of 4 carucates in Uncleby, 1½ in (East) Heslerton, 1 in Croom and 6 in Cowlam. Thorbrandr's Settrington holding was assessed at 9 carucates (*DB Yorks*, 8E 1, 3). The other soke centre, Langton, adjoined Buckton and Settrington to the south-west. In 1086 its tenant in chief was Hugh fitz Baldric, and in 1066 its tenant had been named Ormr. It had berewicks in Kennythorpe, Sherburn and East Heslerton, and within Wharram Percy parish in Burdale and Raisthorpe (*DB Yorks* 23E, 14).

Domesday tenures may at first sight seem unpromising material from which to construct a Late Saxon context for Wharram and its neighbours, especially given the partial and inconsistent nature of the record for Yorkshire. In fact, tenure is a vital, though ambiguous and sometimes, no doubt, misleading guide to establishing the local and regional context, as becomes clear when we examine the specific relationships between Thorbrandr and Ormr and their successors, Berenger and Hugh. As holders of extensive soke estates, Thorbrandr and Ormr were probably TRE overlords, rather than lesser lords of the kind that would be classed as tenants in demesne in later centuries (see Ch. 14). Furthermore, judging by their names they were Anglo-Scandinavian overlords. As David Roffe has commented, the Norman tenants in chief who replaced TRE overlords were typically 'granted the lands of a single pre-Conquest holder of land and they thereby succeeded to all the interests and obligations of this their predecessor' (Roffe 2000b, 20; see also Roffe 2007, 148). Thorbrandr, Ormr and their kind were the so-called *antecessors* of the 1086 tenants in chief: the people from whom the Norman tenants in chief derived 'seisin' as well as the jurisdiction of their estates (Roffe 1990, 331; see Ch. 14, pp 230-34, for a discussion of seisin).

The problem is that many of the TRE tenants recorded in Domesday were not overlords themselves, but were dependent tenants who held manors or sokeland from anonymous overlords. They may have held only for life, or for a term of lives, but their overlords would not usually, in such cases, be identified (Roffe 2000a, 8-9). Thus, manors that Thorbrandr had put in the hands of other lords, whether men who were themselves overlords of other manors, or lesser lords who held only dependent manors, would not appear to have any association with him in the relevant Domesday entries. On the other hand the occurrence of the same manors among Berenger de Tosny's 1086 tenancies in chief might in certain circumstances furnish grounds for supposing the former existence of such a connection.

It is just such an indicator that strengthens the suggestion made here, that the Buckton and Langton soke estates represent divisions of an earlier, single and much

larger territorial unit. There are several reasons for proposing this. One is the proximity of the two estate centres. Another is the way in which the dependencies of the two seem to have been scattered across the same geographical area (Fig. 74), and in the case of East Heslerton, interlocked at vill level. The third strand is the Domesday evidence that Buckton itself was divided into two manors. Thorbrandr's soke centre manor passed with Settrington and his other lands to Berenger de Tosny; but a separate three carucate manor in Buckton that had been held in 1066 by a tenant called Gamall did not. Instead, it had passed by 1086 to Hugh fitz Baldric, who took over Ormr's Langton estate (*DB Yorks* 23E, 16).

The combination of these characteristics leads us to infer that the two soke estates had been created through partition. Perhaps the likeliest explanation of partition lies in the division of an inheritance between heirs. The next task is therefore to explore the possible kinship links between Thorbrandr and Ormr.

The Domesday Thorbrandr, his kindred and estates

The Thorbrandr of 1066 can plausibly be identified as the eldest grandson of Thorbrandr the Hold, whose title, of Scandinavian origin, indicates a rank above a thegn but below an earl. Stenton noted that 'holds' were among the leaders of the Danish army that submitted to Edward the Elder in 914, and went on to comment:

'It is probable that many of the large and composite estates characteristic of the 11th-century Danelaw came into existence through the grouping of Danish colonists in village settlements around the residence of a nobleman of this class whom they regarded as their lord'.
(Stenton 1971, 509)

Thorbrandr the Hold, his son and grandsons were all involved in a blood-feud with earl Uhtred of Northumbria and his descendants, in what Stenton described as 'the most remarkable private feud in English history' (Stenton 1971, 390 n.1). It is recorded in the tract *De Obsessione Dunelmi*, which seems to have been compiled in the late 11th century: one of Thorbrandr's grandsons was said still to live at the time ('*Sumerlede, qui usque hodie superest*'). It survives in a manuscript dating to the second half of the 12th century (*SD I*, 215-20; Hart 1975, 143-50; Fletcher 2003, 4-5).

Uhtred, as part of a marriage settlement involving the daughter of a 'wealthy and prominent man', Styr son of Ulf, was said to have promised to kill Thorbrandr the Hold, Styr's enemy (Fletcher 2003, 52-3). Uhtred failed to carry out his promise, and in 1016 was himself murdered by Thorbrandr. Earl Ealdred, son of Uhtred, took his revenge by killing Thorbrandr, only to be himself killed by Thorbrandr's son, Karli, in *c*.1038 (Fletcher 2003, 118-22). Karli had entertained Ealdred sumptuously in his house, disguising his true intent, and had then killed him in the wood called Risewood. A small stone cross was erected at this spot to commemorate his death (*SD I*, 219). Rise in Holderness, presumably the location of the hall where Ealdred was entertained, lies about 12km east of

Beverley, and it is possible that Karli struck while they were hunting in the neighbouring woodland – not the first noble killer of the 11th century to use this strategem (e.g. see Fletcher 2003, 74-5).

The final round of killing recorded in *De Obsessione* took place in the winter of 1073-4. The instigator was earl Waltheof, grandson of Ealdred, and the victims were a number of Karli's sons and grandsons (or nephews). They were killed while the brothers were feasting at the house of the eldest of them, at Settrington. One brother, Knutr, was said to have been spared because of his innate goodness; another, Sumarlithi, was not present. Waltheof's men returned with a great quantity of booty of various kinds (*SD I*, 219).

Of the two named sons of Karli in this last record, Sumarlithi has been identified as the TRE tenant of Crambe, some 12km south-west of Settrington, where he held 4 carucates to geld (*DB Yorks*, 1N 92: Fletcher 2003, 190). Knutr has long been identified as the TRE tenant of that name who held Rise as a manor with 5½ carucates to geld (see Farrer in *VCH Yorks II*, 171). In 1086 it included wood-pasture 2 furlongs long and 2 wide (*DB Yorks*, 14E 37). It seems, therefore, as again suggested by Fletcher (2003, 189-90), that Knutr's father Karli had died before 1066, and his house and estate at Rise, where the murder of earl Ealdred had taken place, had passed to one of his younger sons. Karli has been identified by W.E. Kapelle with the *Karl minister* (or thegn) who began witnessing charters in 1024, and continued to do so until 1045 (Kapelle 1979, 23). It is possible that his death occurred soon after the latter date. A speculative attempt has been made in Figure 75 to chart these and other descendants of Thorbrandr the Hold.

If Karli's estate had been apportioned among his sons before 1066, then we might be able to trace holdings belonging to further sons: *De Obsessione* indicates that more than one son was killed in 1073, including presumably the eldest, as well as unnamed nephews, or grandsons (or possibly cousins). As indicated above, Domesday tells us that, seven or eight years before the killings, the holder of Settrington was called Thorbrandr; it seems probable, therefore, as again suggested by Farrer (*VCH Yorks II*, 160), that this was Karli's eldest son, named after his grandfather – in conformity with the naming practices evident among Scandinavian families in England at this period (see Townend 2007, 9-11). His portion also included the bulk of the adjoining Buckton estate centre and its dependencies.

Were there any other sons? The answer to this question is supplied by Orderic Vitalis, who enumerates them among the leaders of the 1069 revolt against the Normans at York: Marleswein, Gospatric, Edgar Atheling, Archill and the four sons of Karli (*et quatuor filii Karoli*: *Orderic II*, 222). Unfortunately he does not name the sons. Richard Fletcher ingeniously suggested that there may have been more than four, as the Latin could mean 'four sons of Karli' rather than '*the* four sons of Karli' (Fletcher 2003, 189). The same phrase recurs a little later, however, when *quattuor filii Karoli* were in the vanguard of the

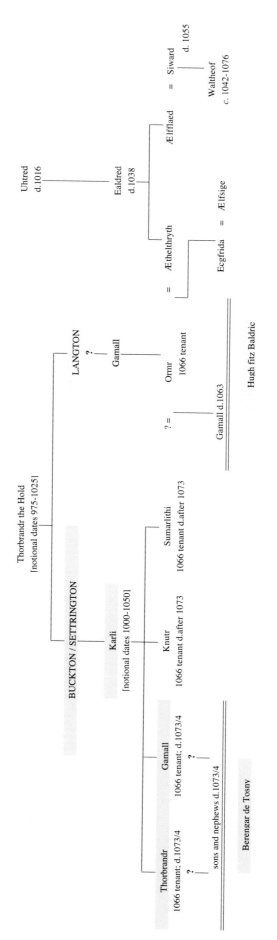

Fig. 75. The putative descendants of Thorbrandr the Hold. (S. Wrathmell)

Danish and Norse forces that took York on 20 September, 1069 (*Orderic II*, 228), a repetition that surely points to four sons in total, rather than to four from a larger number. Whatever the case, there is still, on the evidence of Orderic, one son missing, and of the two proposed by Fletcher, the more likely one is the Gamall who shared Duggleby with Thorbrandr and whose interest, along with Thorbrandr's, passed to Berenger (Fletcher 2003, 189; Williams 2000, 30).

Thorbrandr and Gamall's TRE vills extended well beyond the northern Wolds and the adjoining Vale: they were scattered across Holderness to the south, but were far more concentrated further north, on the far side of the river Derwent (Fig. 76). Berenger de Tosny failed to acquire most of their East Riding vills, but he gained many in the North Riding, in an area stretching from Oswaldkirk in the west to East Ayton in the east, and from the North York Moors in the north, to the Wolds in the south (see Fig. 76). Indeed, all of Berenger's lands in all three Ridings had been held TRE either by Thorbrandr or by Gamall (*DB Yorks*, 8N, 8W 8E).

The Domesday Ormr, his kindred and estates

Hugh fitz Baldric's antecessors were more diverse than Berenger's. He had acquired the soke estate of Langton held by Ormr TRE; and besides the three carucates at Buckton, a number of his other manors had also been held by 'Gamall' in 1066. Like Thorbrandr's manors, Ormr's landholding reached north of the Derwent, and included another major soke estate centred on Kirkby Moorside (*DB Yorks* 23N, 19-21). One of the soke dependencies was the vill of Welburn, where the church of Kirkdale is located, and there seems to be general agreement among scholars that the Domesday Ormr was the same person as Ormr son of Gamall who is recorded, on an inscription at Kirkdale church, as having rebuilt it 'in the days of King Edward and in the days of Earl Tosti' (see below); a poignant dedication, as Ormr was either the father or the son of the Gamall son of Ormr who was treacherously (and presumably subsequently) killed by Tosti in 1063 or 1064 (*SD II*, 178).

Fletcher (2003, 157-8) suggested that the Gamall slain by Tosti was the father of Ormr. Matthew Townend (2007, 28 n.11), however, has pointed out that Ormr son of Gamall, a 'Yorkshire thegn', is recorded in *De Obsessione* as having married Æthelthryth, one of the five daughters of earl Ealdred, at a time which seems to have been some years after the Norman conquest (*SD 1*, 220). If this was Ormr's first marriage, Tosti's victim could not have been his son.

For the purposes of Figure 75, however, the marriage to Æthelthryth has been assumed to be Ormr's second, perhaps contracted after he had lost his east Yorkshire estates to Hugh fitz Baldric. If they married after the Conquest, Æthelthryth must have been at least 30 years of age (her father having been killed by Karli in about 1038); and her sister Ælfflaed had been married to earl Siward who had died in 1055, and had borne him a son, the future earl Waltheof II, in the early 1040s (Fletcher

2003, 186). Tosti's victim could have been of the same generation as Waltheof. In any event, the naming conventions adopted by the Anglo-Scandinavians, referred to above, make it likely that both Ormr's father and (eldest) son were called Gamall.

There is a further piece of evidence, albeit even more tenuous and convoluted, that Ormr was a descendant of Thorbrandr the Hold. It is in the form of a charter which has been dated to 1142-3, formerly in St Mary's tower, York. It records a gift made by Roger Mowbray to the Augustinian canons who had migrated from Bridlington and had settled at Hood, near Sutton-under-Whitestonecliffe, until their new priory was built at Newburgh. For the souls of Nigel d'Aubigny his father and Gundreda his mother, and for the health of himself and his wife Alice, Roger gave the canons the church of St Andrew in York, located beyond the Fosse in Fishergate, and also a house which once belonged to Thurstan de Montfort and the man dwelling there called Thorbrandr: '*et cum mansura una que fuit Turstini de Munfort et hominem (sic) in ipsa manentem nomine Thorbrand*' (*EYC IX*, 205, no.118).

Clay identifies St Andrew Fishergate with the church of St Andrew bought by Hugh fitz Baldric before 1086 (*DB Yorks*, C11). Like most of Hugh's Yorkshire possessions it would have passed to Roger Stuteville I in the time of William Rufus, being then regranted by Henry I to Nigel d'Aubigny after the Stuteville forfeiture (see p. 222). The obviously tangled reference to the house where 'Thorbrand' lived is undoubtedly a misunderstanding of the traditional name of this house: 'Thurbrand's House'. It was a city landmark in the late 11th century, named in the record of privileges and legal titles held by archbishop Thomas I through the whole of York: 'that is to say, first Layerthorpe, and on the north Monkgate, and from Thurbrand's house all as far as Walmgate...' (Liebermann 1905, 415). Though Ann Williams suggested that the Thorbrandr in question was the 1066 tenant of that name (Williams 2000, 30, n.42), it is much more likely that the house had been built by and named after his grandfather, Thorbrandr the Hold.

In the first place, Thorbrandr the Hold was clearly of greater status and wealth than his grandsons, who had divided up his estates among them; he is the more likely candidate for builder of such a prominent house in the city. Secondly, the house, though it is not apparent among Hugh fitz Baldric's York properties (*DB Yorks*, C11), descended to the Mowbrays, as Hugh's property had; and Hugh's antecessor was Ormr, not the Thorbrandr of 1066. That the house was, indeed, once the property of Ormr is also implied by the reference to its possession by Thurstan Montfort; for it was Thurstan's descendants who laid claim to the Mowbrays' Langton soke that had been forfeited by the Stutevilles and regranted for a time to their own ancestor, Geoffrey Murdac (see p. 224). This further suggests that Ormr was in possession of part of the holdings of Thorbrandr the Hold; that he was a descendant of the Hold, though not one of the sons of Karli.

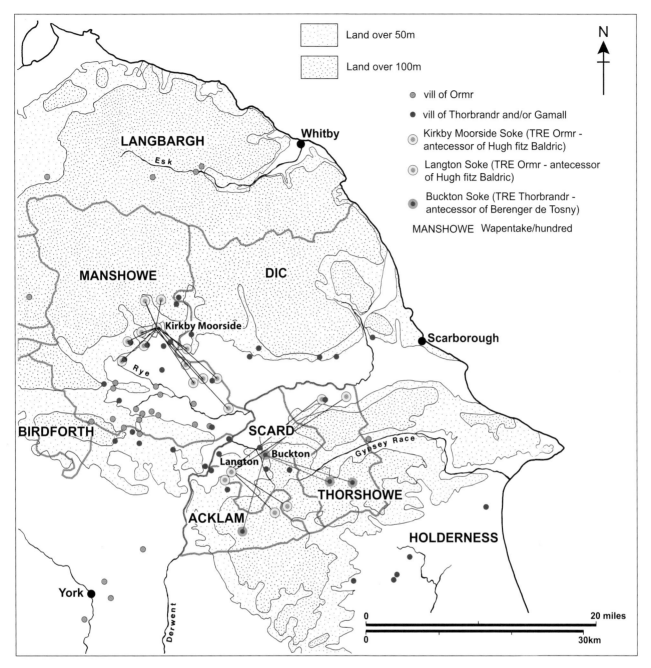

Fig. 76. The 1066 landholdings of Ormr and Thorbrandr/Gamall in and around the Vale of Pickering and the northern Wolds. (E. Marlow-Mann and C. Philo)

Whatever the weight that can be placed on the Mowbray charter – at most it seems to offer a distorted echo of earlier tenurial arrangements – there can be no doubt about the remarkable extent to which the manors and sokes of Ormr-Hugh and of Thorbrandr-Berenger were intermixed – not just in the study area but in the North Riding too. There are structural differences in the entries relating to the two estates: most of Thorbrandr's lands appear as separate manors, whereas large elements of Ormr's holdings were in the form of soke centres with recorded dependencies and jurisdictions in other vills (see Fig. 76). This may, however, have more to do with the forms of the documents supplied to the Domesday

inquisition by the 1086 tenants in chief (see Roffe 1990, 311), than with any real organisational differences in 1066.

The population of the Anglo-Scandinavian estates
We have reached the point where we believe we have defined an extensive group of Anglo-Scandinavian controlled soke estates occupying the central part of the Vale of Pickering and extending from the southern fringe of the North York Moors in the north, to the watershed of the northern Wolds in the south – including the Wharram area. The bulk of the lands held by Thorbrandr, Gamall and Ormr were concentrated in two groups of

administrative divisions: in the North Riding wapentake of Manshowe, and in the East Riding hundreds of Acklam, Scard and Thorshowe (Fig. 76). The relationship of hundreds to soke estates will be considered later, but at this point it is worth attempting to characterise the wider population of these linked Anglo-Scandinavian estates – at least as far as it can be glimpsed in the personal names provided by Domesday Book.

Building on the wider work of David Parsons, Matthew Townend (2007, 11-13) has examined the proportion of Old Norse to English personal names in Manshowe wapentake. Though Parsons' proportion of Old Norse to English names in Yorkshire as a whole (70:30) was the highest for any county, Townend's proportion in this particular wapentake (92:8) is far higher still. It emphasises two related points, and leads to a third. The first is that the county-wide figure clearly averages out marked variations within the region as a whole: if Manshowe has a much greater proportion of Old Norse names, other wapentakes and hundreds will have had much lower proportions.

Secondly, wapantake and hundred divisions may themselves even out more local variations – variations that are, perhaps, linked to estate overlordship. Manshowe is effectively formed from the northern part of the Ormr-Gamall-Thorbrandr holding and therefore avoids such discrepancies. Finally Townend's conclusion, that 'the local landholding elite in the district almost exclusively bore Scandinavian names… [and] that Scandinavian names probably indicate some form of Scandinavian ancestry and affiliations' (Townend 2007, 15), applies both to this wapentake and to this landholding, but primarily to the landholding.

It is clear that in the first half of the 11th century the estates identified as the inheritance of Thorbrandr the Hold were inhabited by landholders who emphasised their Scandinavian affinities by means of their choice of personal names, and that this applied not only to the overlords of these estates, but also to the lesser lords and perhaps even the leading sokemen.

Lordship in the Wharram parishes

The Scandinavian affiliations of Wharram itself are, of course, symbolised wonderfully by the early 10th-century Borre-style strap-end and belt-slide (see Goodall and Paterson 2000, 128-31 and p. 197 below); and a century or more later, the Domesday entries relating to the two Wharram vills and to the other vills in the medieval parish of Wharram Percy name Anglo-Scandinavian landholders. Unfortunately, the recorded landholders at Wharram Percy itself seem to have been dependent tenants rather than overlords (see Table 10). There are two entries for Wharram Percy. The first (*DB Yorks* 1E, 54), identifies two manors, held by Lagmann and Karli, together amounting to 8 carucates. The form of the entry, which is probably the TRE record although not specified as such (Roffe 2000a, 1-2), indicates that the manors were dependent holdings subordinate to a single overlord:

'The most obvious sign of dependence in the Yorkshire Domesday is the multiple-manor entry. Like the estates of Lagmann and Karli in Wharram, manors are frequently described together in single entries… there are grounds for believing that multiple-manor entries relate to groups of estates held from an overlord. Thus, although each of the thegns named often had his own hall, the holdings still had a common identity… The fact of such dependence, however, was of little interest to the Domesday commissioners – it is only explicit when it brought one tenant-in-chief into relationship with another – and overlords were therefore rarely identified. Nevertheless, it was through them that the Norman tenants-in-chief had title to their land' (Roffe 2000a, 8-9).

The other entry for Wharram Percy relates to a single carucate held from the king in 1086 by Ketilbjorn (*DB Yorks* 29E, 21). Although not specified as such,

'it has the form of a sokeland entry, that is of land which was subordinate to a second estate, and was therefore almost certainly attached to another manor. The tenant was probably the same Ketilbjorn who held manors in Wharram le Street, Birdsall, Mowthorpe, Kirby Grindalythe, and Carnaby in 1066, and it may have been to one of these estates that the land in Wharram was attached'.
(Roffe 2000a, 2-3)

Ketilbjorn probably held Wharram le Street and Birdsall from an unidentified antecessor of the Count of Mortain (Roffe 2000a, 16, note 13). On the evidence of the records for Thixendale and Towthorpe (Table 10), that antecessor may have been earl Waltheof, as of his soke estate of Howsham; though if Howsham was actually a 'comital' estate (see below), it may effectively have been the king's.

Two other vills, Burdale and Raisthorpe, contained berewicks of Ormr's soke of Langton; Howsham's Thixendale sokeland was held TRE by Gamall, and the Towthorpe sokeland by Ormr. Of the dependent manors, one in Raisthorpe was held by Ormr, and two in Thixendale by Ormr and Gamall. Thus, although the Domesday entries are opaque, there is no doubt that Ormr and Gamall had numerous interests in these vills, perhaps at different levels of engagement.

Ecclesiastical provision in the Anglo-Scandinavian estates

'Kirby' place-names and parishes (Fig. 77)

One of the characteristics of these Anglo-Scandinavian estates is their remarkable correlation with prominent Middle Saxon *monasteria*. Lastingham, founded by St Cedd in the 650s (Blair 2005, 191-2), and the source of both pre-Viking and Anglo-Scandinavian sculpture (Lang 1991, 167-74), is recorded TRE as a manor held by Gamall, antecessor of Berenger de Tosny (*DB Yorks* 8N, 3). Hovingham, also with pre-Viking and Anglo-Scandinavian sculpture (Lang 1991, 144-9), had been one

Table 10. The Wharram parishes: landholding recorded in Domesday Book.

VILL	1066 Estate	1066 Overlord	1086 Overlords	Status of Holdings	1066 Dependent Tenant(s)	Carucates and Bovates	DB Entry
Burdale	Langton	Ormr	Hugh fitz Baldric [Land of the king]	berewick not given	Ingifrithr	not given 10 bov	23E, 14 1E, 42
Raisthorpe	Langton	Ormr	Hugh fitz Baldric [Land of the king] Odo the Crossbowman	berewick 2 manors 1 manor	Hundingr & Grimr Ormr	not given 3 car 2 car	23E, 14 1E, 56 26E, 7
Thixendale	Howsham	Waltheof	Count of Mortain Odo the Crossbowman	soke 2 manors	Gamall Gamall & Ormr	5 car 6 bov 4 car 2 bov	5E, 67 26E, 5
Towthorpe	Howsham	Waltheof	Count of Mortain [Land of the king]	soke 2 manors	Ormr Lagmann & Sunnulfr	3 car 3 car 3 bov	5E, 60 1E, 40
Wharram le Street			Count of Mortain	1 manor	Ketilbjorn	12 car	5E, 59
Wharram Percy			[Land of the king] [King's thegns: Ketilbjorn]	2 manors ?soke	Lagmann & Karli not given	8 car 1 car	1E, 54 29E, 21

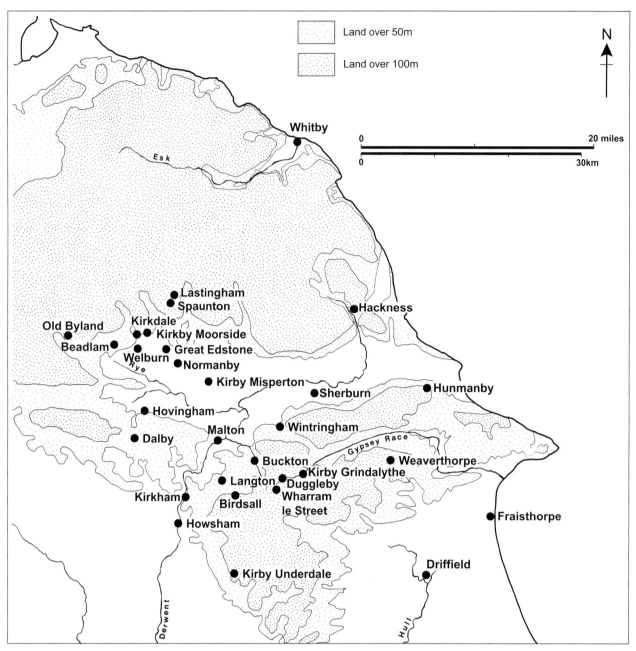

Fig. 77. Map showing places mentioned in Chapter 12. (E. Marlow-Mann and C. Philo)

of Ormr's soke estate centres, passing by 1086 to Hugh fitz Baldric (*DB Yorks* 23N, 23-24). Kirby Misperton, which has also produced early sculpture (Lang 1991, 152-4), is represented by two of Berenger de Tosny's 1086 holdings: *Chirchebi* which had been held TRE by Thorbrandr, and another *Chirchebi* which had been held by Gamall (*DB Yorks* 8N, 1-2). To complete the suite of potential family interests, one of the berewicks of Ormr's soke of Kirkby Moorside was also at Kirby Misperton (*DB Yorks* 23N 21). Whatever the mechanism by which they came to possess these lands – a topic explored later in this chapter – Thorbrandr the Hold and his heirs had acquired a number of important Middle Saxon monastic sites.

Two of these sites have Old Norse 'Kirby/Kirkby' names, presumably given to them by the Vikings who settled in or gained control over this part of the Vale in the late 9th or early 10th century. The significance of such names has long been debated. It has been suggested that they indicate settlements with churches that had existed at the time of the Viking settlement, ones which had some sort of elevated status to account for them occurring commonly in the landscape, but not in high numbers (Morris 1989, 160-61; Abrams and Parsons 2004, 395, n.82 and 421, n.205). This chapter is concerned with four of them: the two mentioned above – Kirby Misperton with its early sculpture and Kirkby Moorside, Ormr's 1066 soke centre – and also two others in the Wolds study area, at Kirby Grindalythe and Kirby Underdale.

Both Wolds 'Kirbys' were the centres of multi-vill parishes in the Middle Ages (Fig. 78). Moreover, as can be seen in Figure 36, they seem to have been the focus of two clusters of *by* vill names in an area where there were

190

no others. Kirby Grindalythe parish incorporated the townships of Kirby, Duggleby, Thirkleby, Mowthorpe, Croom and (at an early period) Sledmere (Lawrance 1985, 20, 52-3; *VCH ER VIII*, 121, 182). It had presumably also covered the lost Thoraldby between Mowthorpe and Duggleby (see p. 99). Kirby Grindalythe church has produced Viking-period sculpture, the earliest fragments being (late) 9th to 10th-century in date (Lang 1991, 150-52). At and beyond the south-west corner of the study area was Kirby Underdale, incorporating the vills of Kirby, Uncleby, Garrowby, Painsthorpe and Hanging Grimston (see Fig. 74).

If (and this is highly speculative) the *thorp* vills were actually later subdivisions of *by* vills, then in each case the *by*-named vills would initially have formed discrete blocks of land, perhaps constituting two distinct settlement projects. As in other parts of eastern England, the groups of

by names are associated with Old Norse personal names, suggesting the plantation of Norse speakers in two specific areas within an estate that was under the overall control of a Scandinavian Hold (cf. Abrams and Parsons 2004, 419-20). The Kirbys would in this case signify ecclesiastical provision for these projects, perhaps based upon pre-existing churches. Kirby Grindalythe church was, interestingly, called a *monasterium* in an early 12th-century charter (*VCH ER VIII*, 145), suggesting that new 'minster' formations might have continued to be created in the late 9th and 10th centuries, to add to those that had come through from the Middle Saxon period.

Paul Cullen, Richard Jones and David Parsons have recently argued that *by* and *thorp* settlements were established on very different types of soils: the *by* settlements on land suited to animal husbandry; the *thorp* settlements in arable areas (Cullen *et al.* 2011, 132, 136-

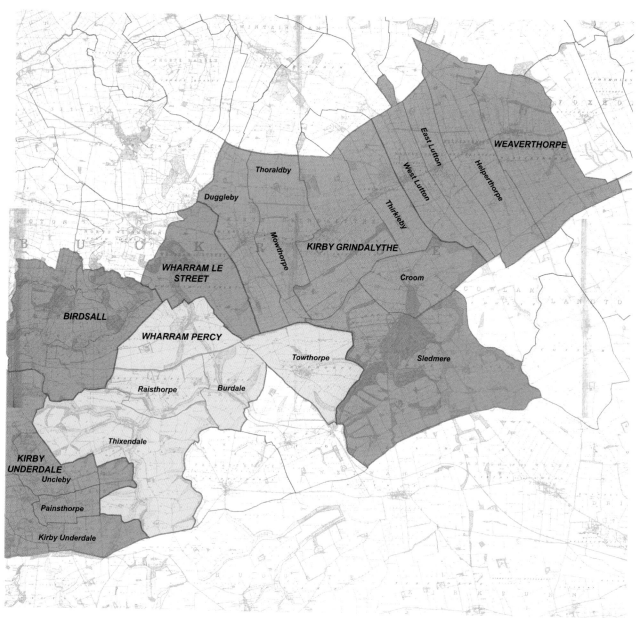

Fig. 78. Medieval parishes in the Wharram area. (E. Marlow-Mann)

7). At first sight the analysis presented here seems wholly to contradict their conclusions, but there is an alternative interpretation. It has been proposed in earlier chapters that the Wolds were early Anglo-Saxon grazing lands, and that the first permanent settlements, like Butterwick, may have begun as livestock farms. It is conceivable that the later *by* settlements had, in the first instance, a similar purpose, which they lost when the northern Wolds were almost wholly incorporated into open-field agriculture. This would have been the context in which *by* settlements were divested of the more distant parts of their extensive territories to create new, smaller townships. These would have facilitated the rapid expansion of open-field systems, not only in the new *thorp* units but also in the earlier and now smaller *by* townships.

Weaverthorpe was probably another Late Saxon 'minster' formation, but one which incorporated pre-existing vills that had earlier been attached to some other minster. There is no record of a church at Weaverthorpe before the present, early 12th-century structure built by Herbert of Winchester, but given that it had belonged to the Late Saxon archbishops of York it seems likely that the church and parish had been established before then (see *VCH ER VIII*, 13, 230). They were probably created when the soke estate was established, perhaps in the later 10th or early 11th century. The medieval parish included the vills of East and West Lutton and Helperthorpe, all of which contained dependent chapels (Lawrance 1985, 57; *VCH ER VIII*, 114, 154). We have already seen that Weaverthorpe church, like Kirby Grindalythe, was called a *monasterium* in the early 12th-century inscription recording its erection.

The other multi-vill parishes in the study area probably have very different origins. The formation of Wharram Percy parish may have been closely linked to the establishment of two other parishes in its immediate vicinity, parishes which stand in marked contrast to those discussed so far. Wharram le Street and Birdsall are coterminous with single vills and single manors: the community, its manorial superstructure and its ecclesiastical provision coincide in a way which suggests that the parish church was established from the outset as an estate church, an expression of the classic type of 'local church' created in the 10th and 11th centuries (Blair 2005, 385-8).

The Domesday entry for Birdsall records a 2½ carucate holding belonging to the archbishop's soke estate of Weaverthorpe, but also a manor (held TRE by Ketilbjorn) accounting for 13 carucates (*DB Yorks* 2B, 18, 5E, 58). Wharram le Street was a single manor, also held TRE by Ketilbjorn, and assessed at 12 carucates (*DB Yorks* 5E, 59). These manors differ markedly from the entries for the vills in Wharram Percy parish, listed along with Wharram le Street in Table 10, which evidence much smaller manorial holdings and a generally higher degree of tenurial fragmentation. As David Roffe has proposed, Wharram Percy parish may have been formed to serve the residue of communities after these larger manorial holdings had established their own local churches (Roffe 2000, 14-15).

Church building in the mid-11th century (Fig. 77)
Thorbrandr the Hold's putative descendants seem, by the middle years of the 11th century, to have been engaged in the erection, rebuilding or refurbishment of local churches designed to serve a single vill or a handful of adjacent vills: 'secularised' churches (see Townend 2007, 22-3). Several of these have 11th-century sundials with inscriptions built into their walls, the best known and most closely datable being at Kirkdale, near Kirkby Moorside.

As noted earlier in this chapter, an inscription to either side of a sundial above the south door of Kirkdale records that 'Orm, son of Gamal, bought St Gregory's church [*minster*] when it was completely ruined and collapsed, and he had it constructed recently from the ground to Christ and St Gregory, in the days of King Edward and in the days of Earl Tosti', (giving a date 1055 to *c.* 1065: Watts *et al.* 1997, 81). As indicated above, many scholars have identified the Orm who rebuilt Kirkdale church with the Domesday Ormr who had the Kirkby Moorside soke estate. It is an identification that can be strengthened and expanded.

'Kirkdale' does not itself appear in Domesday but, on the basis of the township boundaries shown on the mid-19th-century Ordnance Survey map, it was probably then located in the vill of Welburn immediately south-west of Kirkby Moorside township. Ormr's soke of Kirkby contained numerous berewicks (see Fig. 76), including one in Welburn (*DB Yorks* 23N, 21). A Mowbray grant of 1154-7 confirmed an earlier gift of '*ecclesia de Welburna*', long identified with Kirkdale church (*ECY IX*, 244 and n.1). In 1160-83 Robert Stuteville III confirmed a grant of *Hoveton*, a lost vill next to Kirkby Moorside and Welburn that had also been part of Ormr's soke estate (*DB Yorks* 23N, 20), which included in its bounds a reference to '*primam vallem que tendit contra orientem ab aquilonali parte ecclesie de Kirkdala*' (*EYC IX*, 90). We have seen that Ormr was the antecessor of the Stutevilles and the Mowbrays.

A further point worth noting in relation to the Kirkdale sundial is that, when it was taken out of the church wall in 1827, it was observed to be a large part of a stone coffin, 'having only the back part broken out and parts of the ends'. The stone is 2.35m long and 0.51m deep and the coffin was probably straight-sided (Watts *et al.* 1997, 89). It 'may have been consciously preserving part of an existing sarcophagus in memory of its former inhabitant' (Watts *et al.* 1997, 89); but might it equally have been a Roman sarcophagus, perhaps derived (by analogy with the Wharram Percy graveslabs: Stocker 2007a, 271-87) from the cemetery associated with the nearby villa at Beadlam (Neal 1996)? The place-name 'Beadlam' means 'at the buildings', perhaps a reference to the villa ruins (Watts 2001, 12).

Eastern Yorkshire has two other church inscriptions dated broadly to this period: at Great Edstone and Old Byland. These have been discussed, along with the one from Kirkdale and others from York and Aldbrough by Huggit (in Lang 1991, 46-7). The Great Edstone inscription and the form of the sundial show similarities to the one at Kirkdale (Lang 1991, 133-5), though the church's founder and dedication are not named. The mid-19th-century Ordnance Survey map shows that Great and Little Edston(e) townships adjoin Kirkby Moorside township on the south. There is, furthermore, almost a sense of inevitability in finding that the TRE tenants of Great and Little Edstone were, respsectively, Gamall and Thorbrandr, antecessors of Berenger de Tosny (*DB Yorks* 8N, 22-23).

The Old Byland inscribed sundial has been rendered in an unreliable 19th-century source as: 'Sumarlethi's house-servant (HVSCARL) made me'; but Townend has noted that the only really legible letters in the top line of the inscription, based on rubbings, are SVMAR[…]ARL (Townend 2007, 19 and 36 n.53). John Higgitt has identified [FE]CIT on the second half-line (Lang 1991, 195). Would it be too much to hope that it might refer to Sumarlithi son of Karli, or '[C]arl', rather than his housecarl? Sumarlithi was not, in fact, the antecessor of Robert Malet, the 1086 tenant-in-chief of Old Byland: this was Asketill. On the other hand, this lack of correspondence in landholding is matched by a lack of correspondence in building materials: the church recorded in 1086 is said specifically to be a timber church (*ecclesia lignea*: *DB Yorks*, 11N 17).There must be some doubt, therefore, as to which building this sundial originally adorned.

There is no evidence that Ormr or his wider kin were involved in church building on the Wolds, but it is interesting that the first stone church at Wharram may date to this same period. Even if its construction did not require the active participation of Ormr or his kin, it may signify that their initiatives in the Vale were being emulated by the lords of dependent manors, or by the local population more widely. This is a matter that will be considered further by Everson and Stocker in the next chapter.

The origins of the Anglo-Scandinavian landholdings

One of the most intriguing questions relating to these Anglo-Scandinavian soke estates concerns their origins. A case has been made that they were the result of partitioning, perhaps in successive stages, an earlier, more cohesive landholding that had extended northwards from the northern Wolds watershed, through the Vale of Pickering, and on to the North York Moors. How, and from what, was this putative estate formed? It might have been assembled from previously unconnected lands, held by diverse predecessors, who were simply dispossessed in an arbitrary fashion by Viking leaders. Alternatively, it may have been one or more pre-existing landholding units that had been specifically won by conquest, simply transferred from the control of one person or institution to another.

The putative original estate included, as we have seen, a number of earlier *monasteria* at Hovingham, Lastingham, Kirkby Moorside, and Kirkdale, and these remained important ecclesiastical centres during the Scandinavian period: they all have notable collections of both pre-Scandinavian and Anglo-Scandinavian sculpture (Blair 2005, 314-15). To this list, David Stocker would add Kirby Misperton, perhaps associated with Lastingham (D. Stocker, pers comm.). The hypothesis developed here is that the earliest manifestation of this estate was as a Middle Saxon monastic landholding, and that it had been acquired by Viking leaders by right of conquest.

An example of this kind of acquisition may be read (despite the chronological uncertainties) from Symeon of Durham's account of the fate of a group of vills in eastern Durham, between the Wear and the Tees, which belonged to the community of St Cuthbert. The group formed a unit defined by Brian Roberts (pers. comm.) as 'Easingtonshire', though that name does not appear in the sources. In the early 10th century bishop Cuthheard had leased these vills to Eadred, who was said to have come to the community to escape pirates.

Eadred was, however, killed at the first battle of Corbridge, fighting against the Norsemen under their leader Ragnald, and his vills were then shared out by the victorious Ragnald between two of his followers. The northern half of the estate, from Castle Eden (*Iodene*) to the Wear, was given to Onalafball, and the southern half, between Castle Eden and Billingham, to Scula (*SD I*, 73, 208-9; Hart 1975, 140-41; Roberts 2008, 156, 292; Abrams and Parsons 2004, 408).

In a similar fashion, the Scandinavians may have acquired, by right of conquest, the Yorkshire estates of monastic communities. Given that communities like St Hilda's, at Whitby and Hackness, and St Cedd's at Lastingham ceased to exist in the Scandinavian period, probably in the late 9th to early 10th centuries, someone must have taken over the estates that had formerly supported them. Indeed, it may have been this deprivation, rather than direct physical destruction, that ended their existence. The same point has been made in more general terms by Lesley Abrams (2001, 35).

Thorbrandr the Hold's ancestor may have been allocated former monastic lands in and around the Vale of Pickering before the mid-10th century. Furthermore, Wharram Percy may have been part of those lands. The archaeological evidence for a monastic 'interest' at Wharram is unambiguous: it was discussed in an earlier volume (Richards 1992c, 93-4), and has been reviewed once more in this (pp 151-3 and Table 7). Wharram may have been associated with one or other of the Middle Saxon *monasteria* in the Vale of Pickering. Alternatively, its associations might lie further afield, at Whitby, providing a context for the Anglo-Saxon cross fragments, for which an association with St Hilda's was suggested some years ago by Jim Lang, and for the Whitby-type ceramics from the site (Richards 1992c, 93-4). Debate continues as to whether Wharram was home to a monastic community of any kind; but we can suggest that at the very least it was a monastic asset, perhaps a distribution and collection centre for monastic sheep – even, we might speculate, St Hilda's sheep – grazing the Wolds. Furthermore, despite the arguments presented by Everson and Stocker in Chapter 11 (pp 169-70), we are still, in the present writer's view, unable to rule out the possibility of residential supervision by the community of St Hilda.

Taking a wider view, there is further support for the idea that these Scandinavian estates had been monastic at an earlier date. It is to be found in their history after the Anglo-Scandinavian overlords in this part of Yorkshire had been replaced by Norman tenants-in-chief (see Ch. 14), when monastic life was renewed at Whitby, Hackness and Lastingham, and was newly established at St Mary's York.

From the three diverse accounts of the refoundation of Whitby, Janet Burton has provided the following narrative. About 1074 Aldwin, prior of Winchcombe in Gloucestershire decided to travel north to live, in poverty, in the lost centres of Northumbrian monasticism. On his journey, at Evesham, he was joined by a priest, Aelfwig, and a monk, Reinfrid. For a time, the three of them lived in a shelter on the site of Bede's monastery at Jarrow.

In about 1077, Reinfrid travelled southwards alone, to the ruins of the pre-Viking *monasterium* at Whitby. He was allowed to occupy the site by William Percy, tenant of the earl of Chester. Reinfrid sought to live there as a hermit, but was willing to accept a group of like-minded men who wished to join him. One of them, Stephen, was elected Abbot soon afterwards (Burton 1999, 32-3). The formal grant by William Percy of the site of the abbey and two carucates of land was probably made to Abbot Stephen, accounting for its allocation to him in Domesday Book (Hamilton Thompson 1924, 395).

By 1086, however, Abbot Stephen was no longer at Whitby: he was abbot of York. He had left with a group of monks, perhaps after a dispute with William Percy, and had moved first to Lastingham, gaining the king's permission to settle on the site of the former *monasterium*. He then took his community to York before the time of the Survey, and in 1088 finally acquired the site of St Mary's abbey (Burton 1999, 34-9).

Other monks remained at Whitby under Reinfrid, but at some point they also moved away, this time to the site of the former *monasterium* at Hackness, reputedly to escape the destruction caused by pirates. When Reinfrid died he was buried at Hackness. In Domesday, the lands of this community were described as the land of St Hilda, and comprised 6 carucates in Hackness, Suffield and Everley. They were held of William Percy as part of his tenancy in chief (*DB Yorks*, 4N, 1; 13N, 13). Reinfrid's successor Serlo, brother of William Percy, eventually led this community back to Whitby (Burton 1999, 34-9).

The Lastingham/York and Hackness/Whitby communities may each have regarded themselves as heir to Reinfrid's original resettlement of Whitby. As Burton comments:

'The testimony of Domesday Book is that the abbey newly established at York claimed the initial endowment of Whitby and, by implication, saw itself as the legitimate successor of the community established by William Percy'.
(Burton 1999, 37)

It may be, however, that the Abbot of York's claim to succession was related not so much to the refounded Whitby community of the later 1070s, but to the pre-Viking *monasterium* of *Streanæshalch* and its estates, and perhaps to the former estates of other pre-Viking *monasteria* in the same region, such as those belonging to Lastingham. There may be an underlying narrative to the tale of monks and priests yearning to live in poverty, as hermits, on the long-ruined sites of Northumbria's Middle Saxon religious communities.

Medieval monastic communities had long memories when it came to the lands of which they had been dispossessed. Much monastic ink was used to retain a written record of such events; indeed, forged Anglo-Saxon charters were often designed to support claims by refounded communities to the lands belonging to their pre-Viking predecessors which the Church had lost to lay proprietors (Fleming 1985, 257-60). It may be that the late 11th-century monastic revival in Northumbria involved a policy of seeking to reclaim lands which had originally formed monastic endowments, but which had been seized by the Vikings, a policy of reacquisition comparable to that followed earlier by the community of St Cuthbert (see Abrams and Parsons 2004, 408). In eastern Yorkshire, the opportunity to do so came with the death and dispossession of the Scandinavian overlords themselves, in the five years following the suppression of the 1069 revolt (see above). It may be that records of the landholdings of Northumbrian *monasteria* had been transported to south-west England along with the relics of St Hilda (see Blair 2005, 314n), and that Prior Aldwin and his companions came north clutching not only Bede's *Ecclesiastical History* as their tour guide (see Burton 1999, 32), but also a shopping list.

There is an indication of this not only in the sites chosen as places of residence for the new communities – Whitby, Hackness and Lastingham – but also in the location of lands donated for their support, by the king and by some of his tenants in chief, in the decade or so after the refoundation of Whitby. In the Vale of Pickering, William the Conqueror's grant to the community that came to settle at St Mary's included 3 carucates at Lastingham, 3 at Normanby and 2 at Spaunton (*EYC I*, 264). The donation may have been made around 1080, at about the time the community settled at Lastingham (see Hamilton Thompson 1924, 395).

In the same part of the Vale, Berenger de Tosny gave 1 carucate in Lastingham, 6 in Spaunton, 8½ in Kirby Misperton and 3 in Dalby (*EYC I*, 265), all formerly held by his Anglo-Scandinavian antecessors Thorbrandr and Gamall. This grant predates the Survey, which records that these carucates were held of Berenger by the Abbot of York (*DB Yorks*, 8N, 1-5). Hugh son of Baldric's grants were 8 carucates in Hutton, 3 in Normanby and 3 in Misperton (*EYC IX*, 219), all part of the Kirkby Moorside soke that had been held by his Anglo-Scandinavian antecessor Ormr. The first witness to this grant, dating to the late 1080s, was Berenger de Tosny.

Such grants covered only small areas of the putative Anglo-Scandinavian estates in this part of Yorkshire, but they are, nevertheless, consistent with a partial re-formation of Middle Saxon monastic lands. As was emphasised at the beginning of this chapter, these strands of indirect and circumstantial evidence do not amount to a case *for* Wharram having been monastic property in Middle Saxon times. They do, however, provide a context for Wharram *as* a monastic property, if the archaeological evidence is deemed to indicate that it had such a status.

Stability and change in East Riding sokes

The flow of the argument above, maintained on its course by a liberal application of speculation, is that a vale, wold and moorland territory which had supported one or more Middle Saxon *monasteria* was acquired by Vikings, by right of conquest, and was then subject to fragmentation through the workings of partible inheritance, and through sales or other forms of alienation. The impact of partible inheritance can be seen more clearly in another Northumbrian estate: Bywell in Northumberland. There, the intermixed vills of two extensive ecclesiastical parishes, Bywell St Peter and Bywell St Andrew, together formed a single, coherent territory stretching from the Tyne valley southwards across the uplands and down to the river Derwent. It is clear that the configuration of the parishes reflects a pre-Conquest division of lordship, for they belonged to different Norman tenancies in chief: Bywell St Peter belonged to the barony of Baliol, and Bywell St Andrew to the barony of Bolbec. The split must have been made by the antecessors of Baliol and Bolbec in or before the 11th century: St Peter's was probably the original church and has been ascribed to the 8th century or earlier; whilst the tower of St Andrew's has been assigned to the late 10th or 11th century, but possibly incorporating an earlier porch (Taylor and Taylor 1965, 121-6; Wrathmell 1975, 74-7).

The history of the estate containing Wharram and its neighbours was clearly more complicated than Bywell's. Whilst the Langton and Buckton sokes probably represent divisions by inheritance, it is likely that Weaverthorpe was established through a grant of territory by one or other of the Anglo-Scandinavian lords to the archbishops of York (probably a purchase). The sokes of Howsham and Kirkham, to the west of the study area (see Fig. 73) were in 1066 held by Waltheof, presumably earl Waltheof who in 1073/4 instigated the Settrington massacre of Karli's sons, but who had earlier joined them in the 1069 revolt against William I (Williams 1995, 33-4). They occupied a strategic position at the western end of the northern Wolds, on the approach to York; they may have been acquired by the king, and then granted to the earl to provide control of the western boundary of the Anglo-Scandinavian lordships. They would thus have functioned in much the same way as comital estates created on the late 9th-century Anglo-Danish boundary in south-east England (Fleming 1985, 261-3; see Baxter 2007, 68-70).

'Comital' estates were those which were assigned to earls 'by the king on an "ex officio basis", for as long as they held office' (Baxter 2007, 150). Over the long term, therefore, they were under the control of the king, and probably achieved a much greater stability than the Anglo-Scandinavian estates delineated in this chapter. They would not, for example, have been subject to division through inheritance. The same, of course, applies to church estates. The East Riding sokes have been mapped by Hall (1993, 33) and Hart (1992, 256), and it is clear that many were, in the TRE Domesday entries, attributed either to the archbishop of York or to Morcar, earl of Northumbria, a son of the house of Leofwine and brother of the earl of Mercia (Baxter 2007, 18 and 260, fig. 6.4). He had been elevated to this position in 1065 after a rebellion against his predecessor, Earl Tosti (see Fletcher 2003, 160-61). Morcar's sokes were almost certainly comital, and in 1086 were back in the hands of the king.

There is one further way of measuring long-term estate stability: analysing the geographical relationship between the East Riding sokes and the hundreds – the units of local administration at the time of Domesday (see Fig. 73). Hadley described them as 'fundamentally unrelated institutions, both geographically and functionally' (Hadley 2000, 105), though in contrast Cyril Hart identified a close relationship (Hart 1992, 263). The middle ground has been occupied by Mary Hall (1993, 32-5). She found varying relationships between the two territorial units, in some instances close, in others less so. In a few areas, a major soke was effectively converted into a hundred, as at Driffield where the old Anglo-Saxon royal estate gave its name to the new unit. Elsewhere, the mutual inclusivity of soke and hundred was less precise, but again the geography of the hundred was clearly informed by the layout of a major soke (as with Hunmanby soke in Turbar hundred, for example: Hall 1993, 33, fig. 15).

Further south, Holderness presents a far more complex picture. Its three hundreds (North, Middle and South) were far less closely related to the distribution of sokes belonging to the major estate centres than in the examples so far discussed; but the sokelands of Holderness estates were also far more intermeshed than elsewhere. It may be that in this case the creation of workable hundred units based closely on the distribution of major sokes proved to be, quite simply, impossible; instead, distinctly more arbitrary divisions were created. The result was that the overarching administrative unit in Holderness, the wapentake, played a more prominent role in Domesday than it might otherwise have (see *DB Yorks*, CE34, SE Hol).

The same seems to be true of that part of the East Riding dominated by the sokes of Weaverthope, Buckton,

Langton, Kirkham and Howsham. Their overall territory was divided into the three hundreds of Thorshowe, Scard, and Acklam (Fig. 73). These appear, like Holderness, to owe much to arbitrary division, despite being apparently distributed so as to incorporate no more than two estate centres in each: Howsham and Kirkham in Acklam, Langton and Buckton in Scard and Weaverthorpe in Thorshowe. Though the dependencies of these centres are frequently to be found in the other two hundreds, it is noticeable that when the three hundreds are combined, linkages with centres or dependencies in adjacent hundreds are largely (but not entirely) absent.

As suggested earlier in this chapter, and in accordance with the ideas put forward in a previous volume by David Roffe, the sokes of these hundreds interlock in such a way as to suggest that the whole complex constituted a single estate or part thereof at an earlier period (Roffe 2000a, 14). Similarly, the disposition of the three hundreds suggests that they were formed out of an earlier, single wapentake that would have been coterminous with the estate (Roffe 2000a, 15), similar to the arrangements at Driffield. As in Holderness, the disintegration of this estate and the intermixture of the sokes that replaced it may have resulted in a need for new units of administration that paid relatively little regard to the distributions of soke dependencies.

When were the hundreds formed? Perhaps only a few decades before the Conquest, judging by the close correlation between the sizes of these hundreds and the carucation recorded in the Summary. Each of the hundreds contains a more or less equal share of the carucates belonging to the putative parent wapentake (around 190), suggesting that they were formed in a pragmatic fashion on the basis of the carucates attributed to each vill in current lists recording geld liability – lists which were then used to inform the Survey (see Roffe 2000a, 13).

Yet it may be that, as in Holderness, the parent wapentake retained some overarching functions. Just as the Domesday *clamores* refer to judgements of 'the men of Holderness', so too do they refer to 'Thorshowe wapentake' (*DB Yorks*, CE10: Roffe 2000a, 13), the name of which was retained for one of the successor hundreds. The name means 'Thor's mound'; it was not identified by Smith (1937, 120n), but there is one very prominent mound in the territory of these three hundreds: Duggleby Howe. Duggleby township is itself in Scard, and it would seem more likely that, if Duggleby Howe had been 'Thorshowe', the township would have been assigned to the hundred which continued to bear that name. On the other hand, the township of Mowthorpe, on the east side of Duggleby, *is* in Thorshowe hundred; as was the lost Thoraldby vill, which occupied territory between Duggleby and Mowthorpe. Thus, it is conceivable that Duggleby Howe was, in the 11th century, actually in Thoraldby and therefore in Thorshowe hundred; that it was the 'Thorshowe' from which the hundred was named, and the meeting place for the earlier wapentake.

13 The First Two Centuries of the Medieval Village: Wharram in the Late Saxon Period

by Ian Riddler, Paul Everson and David Stocker with contributions from Ann Clark, Anna Slowikowski, Martin Watts and Stuart Wrathmell

The Late Saxon material culture

by Ian Riddler

Wharram's Early and Middle Saxon material culture was reviewed in Chapter 10. The present chapter extends the study into the Late Saxon period. One of its objectives was, inevitably, to define the date when the Middle Saxon Butterwick-type settlement was abandoned, and the date when the earliest element of the medieval village, as known to us through its earthwork plan (Fig. 8), was created. The two dates may, of course, be the same; but they need not be. Another was to characterise the artefact assemblage that can be ascribed to the Late Saxon period (*c*. AD 850-1100/1150). The use of the term 'Anglo-Scandinavian' has been confined to objects that show Scandinavian influence but were produced in England, following similar usage by Richards and Hadley (Richards 2000b, 299-302; Hadley 2006, 120-28). A further distinction has been made relating to objects that can be defined as 'Hiberno-Scandinavian', objects whose origins are likely to be in Ireland during the period *c*. AD 850-1175.

The significance of Late Saxon settlement at Wharram has, along with the Middle Saxon, grown and developed over the years as the various Wharram monographs have been published. Objects of Anglo-Saxon date appeared in the first monograph; some of them belong to the Late Saxon period, and are discussed here. Others were recorded in the third volume, where the early phases of the graveyard and church were ascribed to the Late Saxon period (Bell 1987a, 52), a dating subsequently reflected in objects recovered from nearby excavations, as well as in the ceramic evidence. *Wharram VII-IX* focused on Early and Middle Saxon settlement, but objects of a slightly later date continued to be recorded across the landscape, if only in small numbers.

Whilst objects of Middle Saxon date are abundant at Wharram, those of Late Saxon date are not, although there is still an important assemblage attributable to this period. Their identification follows the same principles utilised for the Middle Saxon assemblage. Objects from well-dated contexts have been surveyed and form the basis for the corpus. To these can be added a small number of objects coming from later contexts but identifiable as of Late Saxon or Anglo-Scandinavian type, and therefore residual in those later deposits. Where objects could be Late Saxon but could equally well be of a later date, as with some of the mica schist hones for example, they have been included only if they come from contexts of the appropriate date.

A major difference in comparison to the Middle Saxon period is the quantity of material that cannot be closely dated. Of the 57 items that form the basis for this text, 45 can be attributed only to the Late Saxon period in general, and not to any specific phase within that period. Nevertheless, two artefact *Phases* (continuing the Middle Saxon sequence and italicised, like them, to distinguish them from site phases) can be tentatively identified:

Phase 6   *c.* AD 850-1000
Phase 7   *c.* AD 1000-1100/1150

Before attempting to answer the questions posed above, it is useful to summarise the objects of Late Saxon date from Wharram and they are briefly described here by category and material. It should be noted at this point that this text is dependent on the earlier work of other authors, notably Ann Clark, Alison Goodall, Ian Goodall, Caroline Paterson, Julian Richards and Anna Slowikowski.

Dress accessories

The small quantity of dress accessories includes a number of items that can be dated to one of the two Late Saxon *Phases* identified above. Attributable to *Phase 6* are the strap-end and a belt slide from the South Manor Area. They stem undoubtedly from the same belt set and represent two of the finest objects of the period from Wharram (85/SF015 and 85/SF111, Plate 18). They have been discussed in detail by Caroline Paterson, who noted that the two items could be of Scandinavian origin but might equally well be Anglo-Scandinavian, and could possibly have been made in York (Goodall and Paterson 2000, 128-31). She preferred a Scandinavian origin but equally strong arguments could be made for their production in England: the shape of the strap-end in particular suggests a 10th-century date and English provenance. A copper-alloy finger-ring from the Western Plateau (south) with tapered, entwined terminals (86/SF180), can also be placed in *Phase 6*, as can a pig fibula pin from the Western Plateau (south) with a gabled head (78/SF550).

A copper-alloy pin from the Churchyard is Hiberno-Scandinavian and dates to *Phase 7*. It was published briefly in the original Churchyard volume (Goodall A.R. 1987, 173 and fig. 191.43) and was mentioned by Fanning in his review of ring-headed pins (Fanning 1994, 45). It belongs to the stirrup-ringed class, which consists largely of pins of 11th-century date, possibly continuing in use into the early 12th century (Fanning 1994, 43-4). Earlier forms of ring-headed pin, going back to the 10th century, have been discovered at Chester, Meols and York, but the later stirrup-ringed class is rare in England (Lloyd Morgan 1994; Griffiths *et al.* 2007, 67-9; Mainman and Rogers 2000, 2580-82). A copper-alloy hooked tag from the Churchyard is also a Late Saxon type and is contemporary with the ringed pin (Goodall A.R. 1987, fig. 191.26).

Comparable examples from a number of sites have been discussed recently and their dating evidence centres on the 11th to 12th centuries (Riddler 2008, 331).

An antler or bone buckle frame from Site 9 (Area 10) came from a late medieval context and was originally thought to be of that date (Andrews 1979a, fig. 70.31; MacGregor 1985, 105). It includes, however, a small integral plate, which suggests that it is earlier in date, particularly on the basis of Hiberno-Scandinavian parallels. A related if slightly curious object from Cork is probably an integral buckle frame and plate with a separate metal spindle for the pin, which is now missing (Hurley 1997b, 268-9 and fig. 106.10). A complete buckle from Dublin High Street also has an integral frame and is thought to be of 11th-century date (Curriculum Development Unit 1978, 61). It can also be compared with a recent discovery from Golden Lane in Dublin, which also utilises an integral plate, a common device of the 11th and 12th centuries (Scully 2008, 96 and fig. 20.1307:1).

Personal items and weaponry

The range of personal items includes small numbers of combs, hones and knives. Four combs can be placed into this period. Amongst them is a small fragment of an animal rib connecting plate with saw marks surviving on one edge, which comes from a bone and horn composite comb (MacGregor 2000, 150, no. 52). The comb type was in use from the 9th to the 12th centuries and, as yet, no changes or developments in its form or technology can be seen across that period (Riddler 2005, 64). On the other hand, a single-sided composite comb from Site 12 (Area 6) can be assigned to *Phase 7*. It has the distinction of having been published twice (Andrews 1979a, fig. 71.36; MacGregor 1989b, fig. 38.36), and includes connecting plates of triangular section and alternating bands of vertical incised lines, set above and below paired horizontal medial lines. Single-sided composite combs with connecting plates of triangular section occurred at York in contexts of mid to late 11th-century date (MacGregor, Mainman and Rogers 1999, fig. 888.7601). Combs with connecting plates of this section can occur as early as the late 10th century but the presence of bands of vertical lines is much more redolent of a later phase and the comb is likely to be of 11th to early 12th-century date.

Another single-sided comb fragment, recovered from a medieval context, has been published in the Churchyard volume (Riddler 2007, fig. 148.3). It is a slightly peculiar comb, made of bone rather than antler, with connecting plates of trapezoidal section, which are indicative of a Late Saxon date. Most combs of this type come from contexts of 11th or 12th-century date (Riddler and Trzaska-Nartowski forthcoming b). A small fragment of an antler connecting plate from the South Manor Area (MacGregor 2000, fig. 70.44) was assigned to a phase 3 (Middle Saxon) context there but it has a trapezoidal section, which is not seen in Anglo-Saxon comb making before the 11th century. It could possibly be of Irish origin, alongside the other comb fragments noted above (pp 143-4); but it might equally well be of Late Saxon date.

85/SF15

85/SF111

81/SF202

85/SF275

85/SF44

26/SF148

Plate 18. Late Saxon objects from Wharram, *Phases 6-7*. 85/SF15: Anglo-Scandinavian strap-end, *Phase 6*; 85/SF111: Anglo-Scandinavian belt slide, *Phase 6*; 81/SF202 and 85/SF275: bone pin beaters; 85/SF44: iron knife, Ottaway type C; 26/SF148: Eidsborg Schist hone. Scale 1:1 (I. Riddler)

Table 11. Late Saxon hones.

Area	Site	Context	SF	Material	Site Phase	Reference
South Manor	81	19/21	231	Mica Schist	4	Clark and Gaunt 2000, 106 and fig. 51.29
South Manor	59	16/11	318	Mica Schist	4	Clark and Gaunt 2000, 107 and fig. 51.30
South Manor	85	74/6	225	Purple Phyllite	3	Clark and Gaunt 2000, 107 and fig. 51.33
North Manor	602	209	131	Purple Phyllite	MP3+	Clark and Gaunt 2004, 224, no. 43

Hones from Wharram were extensively discussed in the South Manor Area volume (Clark and Gaunt 2000, 104-10). The assemblage from the South Manor Area included six fragments of mica schist hones and five of purple phyllite. Two of these hones came from the black loam of phase 4 and one was even earlier, coming from a context of phase 3; the others were in later phases. Hones of these stone types continued in use well into the medieval period and only three can therefore be placed unequivocally into the Late Saxon period. Another hone of the same material from the North Manor Area can be added to this group. Their small find details are noted below (Table 11).

Schist hones appear in some numbers in contexts from the late 9th century onwards and their introduction has been related to Scandinavian commercial activities (Ellis 1969, 149; MacGregor 1982, 78; Mann 1982, 30). Their popularity continues until the 13th century at least, and they are reasonably common in some late medieval contexts (Margeson 1993, 197-202; Riddler and Walton Rogers 2006, 266-70). A number of examples came from medieval contexts at Wharram, including the joining fragments of Eidsborg Schist from the northern Churchyard, illustrated here (26/SF148, Plate 18).

A small number of knives are also of Late Saxon date. Stratified examples came from the South Manor Area, in particular. A knife of Ottaway type D came from a phase 4 context there, alongside two fragments of indeterminate type (Goodall and Clark 2000, 133, no. 69 and 134, nos 82 and 85; Ottaway 1992, 572). A further knife with a characteristically long tang was rightly identified by Goodall as a pre-Conquest form; it belongs to Ottaway's type C (85/SF044, Plate 18; Goodall and Clark 2000, 135 and fig. 62.76; Ottaway 1992, fig. 231.2841). Two knives of Ottaway's type A were recovered from separate sites at the Churchyard (Goodall and Clark 2007, 308 and fig. 147.10-11). It is surprising that so few knives can be attributed to this period, given that they are one of the most common objects to be found in Anglo-Saxon contexts. A lentoid iron hilt guard for a sword came from the South Manor Area and was found in a phase 4 context. It has been compared with a similar guard from Coppergate, York, and dated to the 9th to 10th centuries (*Phase 6*: Goodall and Clark 2000, 139 and fig. 64.257; Ottaway 1992, 797 and fig. 312.3941).

Household items

Virtually the only items that can be securely placed in this category are a number of quern fragments from the North and South Manor Areas, as well as several locks and keys. The high number of lava and Crinoid Grit fragments within phase MP5a, the early medieval phase in the North Manor Area, is perhaps indicative of Late Saxon use, although there are greater numbers from medieval contexts, a situation repeated also in the South Manor Area (Watts 2004, 221 and tables 55-6; Watts 2000, 111). Indeed, a number of the fragments can only be identified as broadly Anglo-Saxon in date. At the same time, there is a reasonable quantity from phase 4 deposits in the South Manor Area, all of which suggests usage during the Late Saxon period, although structural contexts for that phase could not be discerned easily.

Several sliding lock bolts came from the South Manor Area, mostly from phases 2 and 3, and a single example from phase 4 could also be residual and of Middle Saxon date (Goodall and Clark 2000, 135, no. 129). Three fragments of barrel padlocks from the same site came from phase 4 and phase 5 contexts (Goodall and Clark 2000, 135, nos 132-4), and all of these are likely to be Late Saxon and contemporary with examples from York and Haithabu (Ottaway 1992, 665-7; Westphalen 2002, 173-4 and taf 69). A key for a barrel padlock came from the Pond and Dam area (Goodall and Clark 2005, 134 and fig. 57.34) and further fragments of locks of this type are known from Site 12 (Area 6: Goodall, I.H. 1979, fig. 60.1-2) and Site 9 (Area 10), the latter found alongside a hasp of Late Saxon type (Goodall, I.H. 1979, fig. 64.84 and 87).

An unusual item from the North Manor Area is an unfinished antler cordage implement, retrieved from a post-medieval context (Riddler 2004b, 254 and fig. 131.13). Items of this type were used in the manufacture and repair of cordage and netting, and most examples are of 10th to 11th-century date (Riddler 2006b, 173).

Textile manufacturing implements

Annular loomweights are still largely a feature of Early Anglo-Saxon contexts, whilst both intermediate and bun-shaped loomweights can occur on Middle Saxon settlements and have been found on the same sites, if not in the same contexts (Riddler 2004a, 19-22; Walton Rogers 2007, 30). The bun-shaped loomweight, which can be associated with the warp-weighted loom, was going out of use in urban contexts as early as the 10th century, although it may have continued for a longer period in rural locations (Walton Rogers 1997, 1753 and 1799-1801). In searching for Late Saxon loomweights, therefore, only the bun-shaped form is relevant, and even when well-stratified in contexts of that date, there is the possibility that fragments of loomweight could be residual and of Middle Saxon date. A small number of fragments of bun-shaped loomweights came from the South Manor Area and the Pond and Dam area, and these could conceivably be of Late Saxon date; the majority were recovered from medieval contexts (Clark 2000c, 117-19; Clark 2005, 128). The actual number of loomweights of this type from Wharram is not entirely clear, given the fragmentation of the surviving pieces, but the quantities are certainly small.

The dating of spindle whorls from northern England has been established by Penelope Walton Rogers on the basis of their formal characteristics (Walton Rogers 1997, 1736-41). The discoidal form B, in particular, belongs mainly to the middle part of the Late Saxon period (*c.* 950-1050), although it may continue into the 12th century, and the earlier type A declines in use by the 11th century. Eight spindle whorls of the discoidal type B, coming either from Late Saxon or medieval contexts, can be identified as of Late Saxon date. They include one example from the Churchyard (Riddler 2007, fig. 148.9), four from Site 12 (Area 6), two from Site 9 (Area 10: Andrews 1979a, figs 68.11, 13, 15. 17-18 and fig. 70.24) and one from a post-*Grubenhaus* phase in Site 39 (Clark 1992, fig. 21.2).

Four pin-beaters can be identified as single pointed, and attributable, therefore, to the Late Saxon period. Two came from the South Manor Area (81/SF202 and 85/SF275, Plate 18: MacGregor 2000, fig. 71.103-4), one from the Churchyard, and one from a layer filling the Site 95 *Grubenhaus* (Riddler 2007, 314 and fig. 148.8: MacGregor 1992, fig. 30.21). The single pointed pin-beater is associated with the vertical two-beamed loom and occurs in England around the late 9th century (Walton Rogers 2007). The latest examples of the object type are of 12th to 13th-century date. The Churchyard example was a residual find in a post-medieval deposit. One of the South Manor Area finds is attributed to phase 2 there, which is a very early date for the type (perhaps another example of late intrusive items recorded in earlier deposits: Stamper *et al.* 2000, 20), whilst the other comes from a phase 4 context (MacGregor 2000, 152). A section of bird bone midshaft, trimmed at both ends, includes a central perforation (Andrews 1979a, fig. 70.33). It can be identified as a needle case of Late Saxon type. The earlier 9th to 11th-century form, seen here, has a perforation at the centre, whilst this is lacking on later examples of 12th to 13th-century date (MacGregor 1985, 193; Riddler 2005, 60-61; Riddler and Walton Rogers 2006, 282-5).

Recreation

A single *Tabula* counter has been produced from a cattle mandible and can be dated to the 11th to 13th centuries (Riddler 2007, fig. 148.11). It came from a period 2 phase 1 context on Site 26 at the Churchyard, in association with early medieval ceramics. Burial in this area is likely to have begun before the Conquest and impinged on earlier period 2 features (Bayliss *et al.* 2007, 211-12), all of which suggests that this gaming piece is relatively early in date and attributable to the 11th century rather than a later date. A further category of recreational object is represented by perforated pig metapodia, which formed 'buzz-bones'. Examples of this object type from Wharram have been discussed previously (MacGregor and Riddler 2005, 143-5). Their use continued into the medieval period and almost all of the Wharram examples have come from medieval contexts. The exception is a single example from a phase 3 context in the South Manor Area (MacGregor 2000, 153 and fig. 72.112).

Horse equipment

The South Manor Area produced a small but cohesive group of five iron mouthpiece links for bridle bits, all but one from phase 4 contexts (Goodall and Clark 2000, 139, nos 236-40). The one exception came from a phase 5A context but was noted as of a similar form to the remainder of the group. Three examples came from Site 76, one from Site 85 and one from Site 59. The type goes back to the Middle Saxon period but is also common in Late Saxon deposits (Ottaway 1992, 704-5). It corresponds with Westphalen's type A1 (Westphalen 2002, 254-5). A fragmentary horseshoe from the South Manor Area with countersunk nail holes belongs to Clark's type 1, a pre-Conquest form (Goodall and Clark 2000, 139 and fig. 64.242; Clark 1995, 85-6). A second example came from the North Manor Area (Goodall and Clark 2004, 247 and fig. 128.108). The type has been extensively discussed and dates essentially from the late 9th to the 11th centuries, being superseded by other forms in the 12th century (Clark 1995, 93-5; Ottaway 1992, 707-9; Westphalen 2002, 260).

Ceramics of the Late Saxon period
by Anna Slowikowski

Seven pottery types were identified and reported in previous Wharram publications under Ceramic Group 3 (Table 12). They are fully described in the publication of the South Manor Area (Slowikowski 2000). Pottery of this period makes up less than 1% of the total assemblage from the whole village and only 2.42% of the phased assemblage. Just over three quarters of it is residual in later contexts and only 13.15% was recovered from contexts phased to the Late Saxon period. Despite this, the pottery is still a significant assemblage.

The assemblage is generally very consistent in its make-up and there is little variety. It is relatively local and, unlike the ceramics of the Middle Saxon period, there are no imports from a great distance and certainly none from the Continent.

There is also a limited range of pottery types when compared to the preceding Middle Saxon period and the succeeding medieval periods. The most common fabrics in the Late Saxon assemblage are York, Torksey-type and Stamford wares (Fig. 79). The shelly wares make up a small proportion of the assemblage. Fifteen sherds of shelly ware were recorded and of these, eight have

Table 12. Ceramic Group 3 pottery types quantified by vessel, sherd and weight.

Fabric code	Common name/definition	Vessels	Sherds	Weight (g.)
B01	York type A	219	247	1234
B02	York type A (variant)	2	3	34
B03	York type D	41	45	160
B04	Torksey-type	274	322	1269
B05	Stamford	142	157	587
B06	Shelly	15	15	94
B40	Thetford-type	3	4	40
	Total	696	793	3418

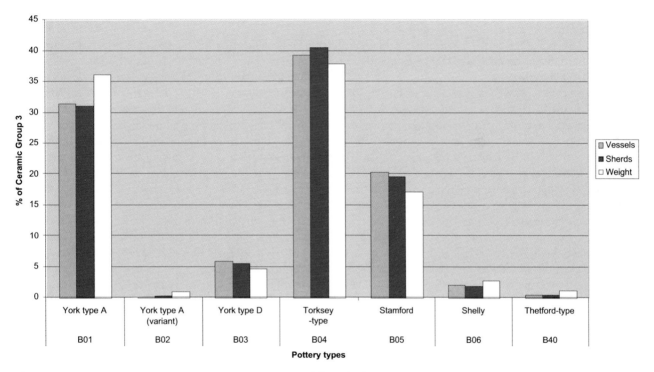

Fig. 79. Wharram: Late Saxon pottery types as a percentage of Ceramic Group 3. (A. Slowikowski)

identifiable sources. Five come from the Silver Street kilns in Lincoln (Lincoln Kiln-type Shelly ware (LKT)) and three are in Lincoln Shelly ware (LSH) (Young and Vince 2005, 47). Other unidentified shelly wares may also be Lincoln or Lincolnshire products: Wharram is very much on the periphery of the shelly ware distribution. With the exception of the York wares, most of the pottery appears to be reaching Wharram either from Lincolnshire or from more local production sites which are nevertheless producing similar pottery if not directly copying them.

Thetford and Thetford-type pottery occurred across most of eastern England in the 11th and 12th centuries (Vince 1991, 45). Although similar in fabric and form, these wares were not identical and were made on a number of kiln sites. The four sherds found at Wharram, if genuinely from the Thetford production site, may be incidental one-offs. Only one can be identified to form: it is a rim from a small jar.

The Stamford wares are both glazed and unglazed, with unglazed lid-seated jars predominating. Not all Stamford ware comes from Stamford. For example, kilns producing virtually indistinguishable pottery were in production in Northampton, although only for the immediate market, in the early to mid-10th century (Williams 1974). It was suggested at one time (Swinnerton 1959, 81) that there was another, northern source for Stamford wares, possibly York, although Le Patourel (1979, 81) believed those found at Wharram originated in Stamford itself. The existence of one or more northern sources has now been confirmed by the discovery of a kiln producing Stamford-type pottery in Pontefract, West Yorkshire (Roberts and Cumberpatch 2009). Unlike Northampton, the Pontefract kiln was producing both glazed and unglazed wares and its dating is slightly later, late 10th century to early 11th century (Roberts and Cumberpatch 2009, 376). Although it cannot be certain that the Wharram Stamford wares were coming from here, it does suggest the possibility of the existence of yet more production sites, of which York might still be one.

A similar situation pertains to Torksey ware. Despite the name, Torksey ware found at Wharram is not a product of the Lincolnshire Torksey kilns, something that was confirmed by neutron activation as far back as 1979 (Le Patourel 1979, 79) and it should more properly be called Torksey-type ware.

The two most common pottery types, the York and Torksey-type wares, both have similar characteristics: they are hard fired, gritty in texture and comprise mainly jars/cooking pots, some with deep lid seatings. Torksey-type ware is also made into bowls, some with inturned rims and rouletted decoration. Square-notch rouletting is also seen on the York wares; it was a common decorative motif found in many places across eastern England.

Late Saxon material culture in northern England

The most notable feature of the Late Saxon finds assemblage is the relative, small number of objects that can be assigned to it, when compared with its Middle Saxon counterpart, including the pottery. There are a few items of copper alloy and a good number of iron, as well as ceramics and stone. No items of glass can be attributed to this period with certainty but the localised manufacture of objects of antler and bone continued. In this respect, Wharram conforms with the overall image of Late Saxon England as summarised by Thomas (2000, 239-40).

At the same time, there is an impressive quantity of obviously imported objects, most of which may have been gathered from York, or possibly from an intermediate market centre closer to Wharram itself. They include the splendid Borre style belt set, alongside the ringed pin, which is more likely to have arrived via York than directly from Dublin or one of the other Hiberno-Scandinavian towns of Ireland. The antler or bone buckle frame from Site 9 (Area 10) may also have arrived from Dublin via York. Mica schist hones were now available in some quantity, largely obviating the need for hones of local stones, and there may have been access to lava querns, which are a common feature of the Late Saxon period. Ceramics from York, Lincoln, and Stamford were arriving at the site. It may be that by this time access was available to the market at York, something that was seemingly not happening during the Middle Saxon period. A similar situation has been envisaged for Cottam (Richards 1999a, 91, 97).

Comparisons can be drawn with other Late Saxon settlements of northern England, in terms of their material culture. Few finds were recovered from either Simy Folds or from Ribblehead, two upland sites, but these sites are scarcely representative of Late Saxon rural settlement (Coggins et al. 1983, 14-16; King 1978; Richards 2000b, 298-9; Hadley 2006, 104-6). The material culture of Wharram has much more in common with that seen at Goltho in Lincolnshire (Beresford G. 1987). There is a similar range of copper-alloy objects, including several important decorative items, but at both sites the balance

of material lies with the ironwork, including knives, box and barrel padlocks and horse fittings (Goodall I.H. 1987). Antler and bone objects include combs, pins, single-pointed pin-beaters and *Tabula* counters (MacGregor 1987). Only one mica-schist hone was found but there were fragments of Mayen lava querns (Beresford G. 1987, 195-6).

Closer to Wharram, the settlement at Cottam also produced sherds of York ware and particularly of Torksey-type ware, in an area that also included metalwork of 10th-century date (Austin 1999, 53 and 56). One mica schist hone was recovered, alongside fragments of lava querns; the latter could well be of Middle Saxon date, however (Richards 1999a, 64-5). Metal-detected finds include a Borre style buckle and a Jellinge style brooch (Richards 1999a, 94; Haldenby 1990 fig. 5; 1992 fig. 5.2).

It is interesting to note that, for all its Middle Saxon splendour, the site at Flixborough lacks anything of Anglo-Scandinavian character and, in terms of its material culture, it suffered a similar fate to Wharram, with a massive reduction in the quantity of ceramics and small finds attributable to the Late Saxon period (Evans and Loveluck 2009; Loveluck 2007, 28-9). Its resumption in the mid to late 9th century, or early 10th century, is on similar lines to Wharram (although Flixborough appears to be more impoverished), with the same transition to regional networks of trade.

Wharram fits very well into the patterns of development seen at both of these sites. Its Middle Saxon material culture has been described previously as 'high-status', although that is slightly debatable, given the overall richness of most sites across southern and eastern England (Richards 2001b, 274; Hadley 2006, 110; Ulmschneider 2000a; Naylor 2004). Anything below high status can be quite hard to find. Nonetheless, it has been noted above that Wharram has an appreciable quantity of high quality objects and Richards is quite right to stress how well the settlement was equipped, in comparison both with local sites and with those further afield (Richards 2001b, 274). If the Middle Saxon settlement achieved a reasonable standard of material wealth, what about the Late Saxon period?

Wharram does not include any explicitly early 9th-century Scandinavian or Anglo-Scandinavian objects, but in any case these are largely confined either to cemetery contexts or to urban centres, including Dublin, York and Ipswich. There are virtually no burials at Wharram before the later 10th century, although the settlement was occupied for three centuries prior to that date. Cemeteries remain to be discovered in the wider Wharram landscape, although discoveries of earlier Anglo-Saxon burials have been made over the last two centuries (Lucy 1999, 30).

Julian Richards has stressed that the South Manor Area is one part of the settlement that continued to be occupied in the Late Saxon period, and the Churchyard can be added to that list as a second focus at this period, particularly from the late 10th to 11th centuries onwards (see below). Site 12 (Area 6), on the Plateau west of the

Churchyard, has also produced material of the Late Saxon period. Overall, the Late Saxon small finds suggest a contraction of settlement, possibly beginning as early as the 9th century. The slender dating evidence, stemming from the ceramics in particular, indicates that these changes may have occurred in the period *c*. AD 850-950. A detailed analysis of these shifts of emphasis in the distribution of artefacts is offered in the next section of this chapter.

Dating the foundation of the medieval village

by Stuart Wrathmell

One of the research objectives agreed with Ian Riddler was, as indicated above, an attempt to achieve, through a record of the distributions of datable artefacts, a better chronological definition for the abandonment of Wharram's Butterwick-type settlement and its replacement by the earliest elements of the medieval village that survives in earthwork form. This simple statement is itself, of course, constructed on a series of assumptions which, in the future, may prove to have been foundations of sand rather than concrete. For example, the medieval village may not have been the immediate successor to the curvilinear enclosure settlement. Or again, the shifts in artefact distributions between the Middle and Late Saxon periods may reflect simply a shrinkage rather than an abandonment of the Butterwick-type site: there may have been similar curvilinear enclosures located where the medieval tofts of the West Row were later constructed, and the Late Saxon artefacts may have been associated with these rather than with the tofts that replaced and obscured them. For the current phase of research, however, the simplest hypothesis was chosen, and as the previous section of this chapter has shown, Riddler has achieved this objective.

Given that the date of medieval village creation, the village 'moment' as Christopher Taylor has called it (Taylor 2002, 68), is such a crucial issue for Wharram and for all who study medieval villages, it is worth exploring the detailed evidence in a little more depth. The date of village foundation was, of course, one of the key questions addressed during the excavations, and a programme of sectioning the earthwork boundary banks was begun for this purpose in 1970. Needless to say, matters were not so simply determined: enclosure banks have their own life cycles, phases of construction, depletion and re-establishment, with numerous opportunities for datable artefacts to be introduced at various times into various horizons. As shown in an earlier volume, toft banks may have become places where rubbish was dumped at regular or irregular intervals (Wrathmell 1989b, 32-3). The continuing ambiguity over the dating of the so-called 'lynchet bank' at Wharram (see pp 41-3) emphasises how difficult it is to attempt to date such boundary banks from the datable artefacts found at particular locations within them. Here, more general

dating has been attempted, based on the overall distribution of Middle and Late Saxon pottery and small finds, as comprehensively assembled by Riddler and Slowikowski.

In addition to the apparent chronological shifts in the distribution of finds, Riddler and Slowikowski have also noted, above, a reduction in the quantity of Late Saxon objects recovered, as compared with the number attributable to the Middle Saxon period. This may, of course, be a cultural phenomenon, but if it does reflect a real decrease in the overall population of Wharram Percy, a context can be found for it. It was noted in Chapter 8 that the two Wharram townships were presumably formed out of what had previously been a single territory named 'Wharram', just as East and West Lutton resulted from the division of a single 'Lutton'. In Wharram's case, this division may well have occurred in the Late Saxon period, and the creation of the vill of Greater Wharram (or Wharram le Street) might conceivably have been accompanied by the removal of a significant proportion of Lesser Wharram's inhabitants to populate the new village, and to cultivate its more expansive arable fields. Whatever the reason for the reduction, it has been analysed in Tables 13 and 14 which record, besides the overall quantities of pottery and small finds from the various parts of the village area, the percentages of Middle and Late Saxon artefacts from each of these areas.

Taking the pottery first, the overall distributions of Middle and Late Saxon types are shown in Figures 80A and 80B and tabulated in Table 13. The table shows that the database includes 3604 Middle Saxon sherds, but only 789 Late Saxon ones. The South Manor Area is dominant in both periods, producing almost three-quarters of the Middle Saxon sherds and nearly two-thirds of the Late Saxon ones; but beyond that there are some interesting differences. The next highest percentage (8.1%) of Middle Saxon sherds comes from the Western Plateau (south) sites – mainly Sites 70, 78 and 86 – and after that come the Western Plateau (north) sites with 6.7%. The latter, however, include the *Grubenhaus* fills in Site 95 which, like those of the one in Site 39, in the area east of the North Manor (6.1%), greatly inflate the numbers of artefacts. Three other areas of the village – the two parts of the West Row (north and south) of medieval tofts, and the Valley sites – each produced less than 1%.

In comparison, the second highest percentage of Late Saxon sherds, after the South Manor Area, came from the Valley sites (14.8%), followed by the North Manor Area (7.2%) and then the West Rows (south and north) with 4.2% each. The shift in weighting from the Western Plateau areas to the West Row areas and the Valley sites in and around the churchyard is quite marked.

The record of the small finds in Table 14 and Figures 80C and 80D shows similar patterns though with a few discrepancies; it is, of course, based on far fewer objects. The South Manor Area is again preponderant, providing over half the number of objects in each period. The Western Plateau (north, then south) areas were the next most productive for Middle Saxon small finds (16.1%

Table 13. Comparative numbers of Middle and Late Saxon pottery (sherd numbers) from various areas of the village site at Wharram.

	Western Plateau (South)	Western Plateau (North)	West Row (South)	South Manor Area	West Row (North)	North Manor Area	West of North Manor	East of North Manor	Valley	Total
Middle Saxon	293	*241	10	2667	24	124	8	*220	17	3604
	8.1%	*6.7%	0.3%	74%	0.7%	3.4%	0.2%	*6.1%	0.5%	100%
Late Saxon	26	1	33	510	33	57	2	10	117	789
	3.3%	0.1%	4.2%	64.6%	4.2%	7.2%	0.3%	1.3%	14.8%	100%

* includes artefacts from backfilled *Grubenhäuser* assemblages

Table 14. Comparative numbers of Middle and Late Saxon small finds from various areas of the village site at Wharram.

	Western Plateau (South)	Western Plateau (North)	West Row (South)	South Manor Area	West Row (North)	North Manor Area	West of North Manor	East of North Manor	Valley	Total
Middle Saxon	18	*38	4	139	0	13	1	*7	16	236
	7.6%	*16.1%	1.7%	58.9%	0%	5.5%	0.4%	*3%	6.8%	100%
Late Saxon	2	3	8	31	0	4	0	0	10	58
	3.4%	5.2%	13.8%	53.4%	0%	7%	0%	0%	17.2%	100%

* includes artefacts from backfilled *Grubenhäuser* assemblages

and 7.6%), though with the Valley sites in fourth place a short way behind (6.8%). The West Row tofts (south and north) again produced very low percentages of Middle Saxon objects (1.7% and 0%).

In the Late Saxon period there is again a shift of emphasis towards the Valley and the West Row (south), which occupy second and third place behind the South Manor Area, with 17.2% and 13.8%. The Western Plateau (south and north) areas again see a substantial decline (3.4% and 5.2%). In the two periods, the North Manor Area small-find record has much the same profile as the equivalent pottery record.

Overall, and with the reservations expressed above, the artefact evidence points to a shift from the Butterwick-type settlement enclosures to the West Row of tofts – generally agreed to be the earliest element in the village plan (see Ch. 3 and below) – at or soon after the transition from the Middle Saxon period to the Late Saxon period, or as Riddler has proposed, between *c*. 850 and 950. As usual at Wharram, however, matters are not quite as clear-cut as might be wished. For Riddler's distribution map of objects datable to the Middle Saxon *Phases 4-5* (Fig. 64) might be read as indicating that the transition had taken place somewhat earlier, perhaps even by the mid-8th century. On the other hand there are very few objects at all attributable to these phases, for reasons discussed in Chapter 10 above, and the preferred

hypothesis here is that the settlement transition should be dated to the second half of the 9th century or first half of the 10th century. It would then offer a satisfying but no less credible prospect of synchronic development with two other important changes in the facilities provided by and for this community: the harnessing of waterpower to mill grain, and the creation of the burial ground in and around what became the medieval graveyard – both at a time of increasing artefact evidence for activity in the Valley.

The earliest remains at the southern mill site were the crop-processing waste dumps, dated to the 9th or early 10th century, that had been incorporated into the earliest recorded dam (Wrathmell and Marlow-Mann 2005, 225). Though we cannot discount the possibility that earlier milling facilities await discovery further down the Beck, it is at least possible that what has been excavated represents the vill's first such milling facility, and signifies a change of scale in the community's arable production. Furthermore, Martin Watts' reflections on the type of facility created in the late 9th or early 10th century, outlined in the next section of this chapter, suggest that it was more of a communal development rather than a manorial imposition (though the milling capacity of the Beck was obviously at some point appropriated by the lords of Wharram). If he is right, the suggestion lends weight to the ideas of David Stocker and

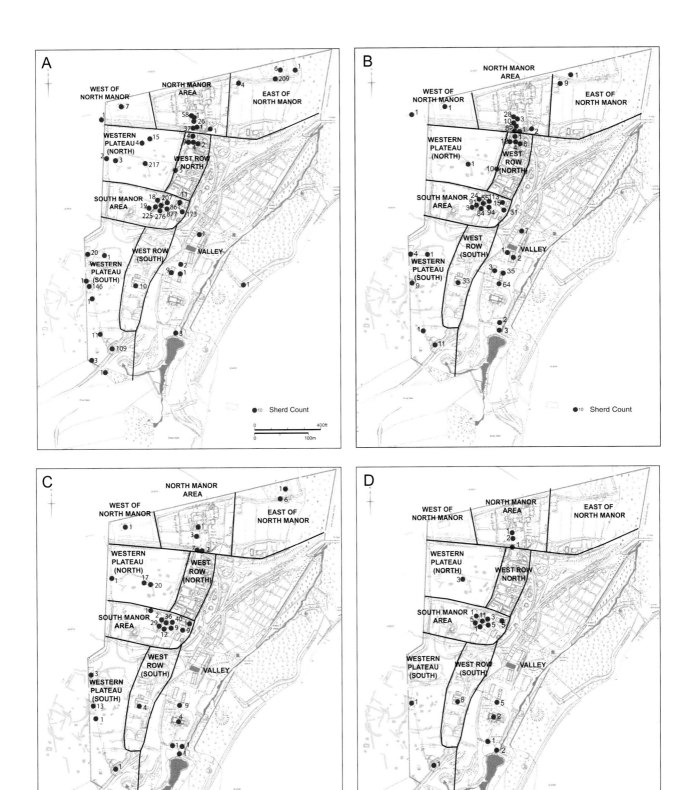

Fig. 80. Wharram: distribution of Middle Saxon pottery (A) and small finds (C) and Late Saxon pottery (B) and small finds (D). (English Heritage, I. Riddler, A. Slowikowski and E. Marlow-Mann)

205

Paul Everson with regard to the role of free peasantry in the creation of the earliest elements of the medieval village settlement, as developed in the final section of this chapter.

The Mill and Dam site at Wharram: some further thoughts
by Martin Watts

The archaeological and documentary evidence for watermills at Wharram Percy was presented and discussed in an earlier volume in this series (*Wharram X*). When considering the evidence for the mill site connected with the dam which was excavated between 1972 and 1983, and whether the mill was driven by a horizontal or a vertical waterwheel, my conclusion was open ended, to say the least (Watts 2005, 222-5). The archaeological evidence from the excavation of the dam suggests that a mill was probably established there in the late 9th or early 10th century. My reluctance to accept that it may have been driven by a horizontal waterwheel stemmed largely from the enigmatic nature of the excavated evidence and the strength of historical evidence, which has been interpreted as indicating that vertical-wheeled mills were closely associated with manorial development and that, by the beginning of the 13th century, they had completely replaced horizontal-wheeled mills on English manors (Holt 1988, 118).

The possible 9th or early 10th-century date for the establishment of a mill site at the dam may be taken as an indication that it is more likely to have been driven by a horizontal wheel. Although little comparable evidence has been excavated in England, the impressive corpus of material from early medieval Ireland indicates that both horizontal and vertical-wheeled mills existed contemporaneously and, sometimes, side by side (Rynne 2000). Analysis of the Irish sites suggests, however, that, for the period before 1100, vertical-wheeled mills form a relatively small proportion of the overall number of known and dated sites, probably less than ten per cent. Two early medieval vertical-wheeled mill sites have been excavated in England, at Old Windsor, Berkshire and West Cotton, Raunds, Northamptonshire.

Old Windsor was excavated in the 1950s and is as yet largely unpublished; its excavator considered that three leat-fed vertical wheels were superseded by a single horizontal wheel in the 10th century (Wilson and Hurst 1958, 184-5). The site appears to be high status, however, and is therefore likely to be atypical of early medieval village sites. At West Cotton, three phases of watermill development have been recognised (Chapman 2010). The earliest mill was established in the mid-10th century and, although the structural elements were only poorly preserved, it appears to have been driven by a vertical waterwheel, by comparison with the 8th-century vertical-wheeled site excavated at Morett, County Laois (see Lucas 1953). It is suggested that the two later phases of mill at West Cotton had horizontal wheels, although the

evidence presented does not clearly support such an interpretation (Chapman 2010, 113-151; Watts 2002, 79). The excavation of watermill sites at Tamworth, Staffordshire (Rahtz and Meeson 1992) and Northfleet, Kent (in prep.) prove the existence of horizontal-wheeled mills in England from at least the late 7th to the mid-9th centuries, and other less unambiguous evidence suggests that horizontal-wheeled mills still existed in the 10th century (at Corbridge, Northumberland, for example, see Snape 2003). So why should not the earliest phase of mill, built close to the downstream face of the dam at Wharram Percy, have worked with a horizontal waterwheel?

In my discussion of the dam site I drew analogy with the very few English horizontal-wheeled mill examples in terms of the plan size of the building, which suggested that the Wharram Percy evidence implied a small watermill with a single pair of stones. I further considered that if the mill was driven by a vertical waterwheel, it would appear to have been located beneath the milling floor, towards the centre of the building. While this may have been a feature of some Roman mills (Ickham, Kent, for example, see Spain 1984 and Bennett *et al.* 2010), it is not possible to be confident about such an interpretation for the Wharram Percy mill from the excavated evidence. A small rectangular building, its plan dictated by two post pads, an eroded post-hole and a possible bank bearing point for timber beams forming the south-west corner, appears just as likely to have housed a single pair of millstones driven directly by a horizontal waterwheel set below the building.

As noted, the relationship of the mill building to the dam would allow a horizontal wheel to be fed directly by an inclined timber pentrough (as found in many Irish examples, at Northfleet and so interpreted at Tamworth), and Oswald has made the perceptive observation that the configuration of the pond suggests that regulation of water pressure onto a wheel seems to have been more important than the creation of a large reservoir (Oswald 2005, 9-10). A further point is that in this period, referring to the scant evidence available from the sites at Morett and West Cotton, vertical waterwheels appear to have been more likely to be situated downstream of a dam and pond, and to have been leat-fed (see also Rynne 1989).

The earliest documentary reference to mills at Wharram Percy is in an IPM of 1323, which records two mills, both then out of use. One mill was recorded as working (again?) in 1368, and its millpond was said to lie on the north side of the town. The 1368 document also records another pond – though not as a millpond – on the south side of the town (Wrathmell 2005a, 8). The excavated pond and dam can be identified with some confidence as the pond on the south side of the town recorded in 1368. What is less certain, given the lack of firm dating evidence from the excavations, and the existence of other potential dam sites on the course of the Beck (Oswald 2005, figs 8 and 10), is that this was the location of the second (disused) mill recorded in 1323. The second 1323 mill may have been located elsewhere on the Beck, and the mill associated with the excavated dam may have gone out of use at a considerably earlier stage. This interpretation, based on a more rigorous assessment of the evidence than was achieved in its earlier publication (Wrathmell 2005a, 8), opens up the possibility that the excavated mill, if it had a horizontal wheel, may simply have been superseded at a much earlier date by a more technically advanced, and productive, vertical-wheeled mill on a different site, required to serve a growing community; it may also, and perhaps more significantly, provide tantalising evidence of a change from a communal village mill to a manorial one.

There is a little evidence from the late Anglo-Saxon period that in some areas mills were built, owned and worked communally. At St Dennis in Cornwall documentary evidence from the early 11th century clearly refers to a communally owned mill and it has been suggested that such an arrangement might account for the extremely low number of mills recorded in Cornwall in Domesday Book (Herring and Hooke 1993, 73). A changeover from communal to private and manorial mills may be reflected elsewhere in Domesday Book where the total number of recorded mills in some areas is low when compared with eastern, south eastern and southern counties. If similar conditions existed in the Yorkshire Wolds, then it is possible that a communal mill existed at Wharram Percy before changes in manorial administration after the Norman Conquest resulted in its demise.

The suggestion that watermills with horizontal wheels are a product of peasant culture was made by Curwen (1944, 130) and taken up by more recent commentators (for example, Holt 1988, 119). Their recent existence to serve the cereal grinding requirements of peasant and subsistence communities in marginal areas in many parts of the world perhaps reinforces this argument (see, for example, Hunter 1967; Gade 1971), although their mechanical simplicity should not be taken as an indicator that they are primitive or technologically regressive. Their simplicity of operation and their output make them a far better alternative to grinding grain by hand, using querns. Until the advent of a manorial system where mills were built at the behest and expense of the lord of the manor, and were seen as a valuable source of manorial income, the horizontal-wheeled mill was a viable milling machine for small communities. It had a further advantage in that it was straightforward to operate and did not require the specialist skill of a miller, an occupation which seems to have grown in importance with the widespread adoption of the technically more complex vertical-wheeled mill in the high medieval period. It is also possible that the need for a dedicated miller arose as part of feudal control, a manorial servant being appointed by the landlord to measure the grain input and ensure that toll was taken. In England the earliest reference so far found to a miller is to one Wine, *mylnere*, who was bequeathed along with an estate at Langford (Bedfordshire) in the late 10th-century will of Æthelgifu (Whitelock 1968, 6-7; 35). The nature of the bequest indicates that he was not a free man. Only six millers and

a mill keeper (*custos molini*) are recorded in Domesday Book, about 0.1% of the total number of mills listed (Darby 1977, 272).

Horizontal-wheeled mills were last used in Britain in the Northern and Western Isles of Scotland and in western Ireland. Their use in the Shetlands, where they were built and owned by small farmers and crofters, continued into the late 19th century and about a thousand sites have been identified (Goudie 1886; D. Flinn, pers comm). It is notable that on both Orkney and Lewis horizontal-wheeled mills were replaced by vertical-wheeled mills built by landlords, in order to control milling capability, and thus revenue. On Orkney this happened in the 16th century and on Lewis in the 19th (Clouston 1924-5, 49-50; Cheape 1984, 45-6; MacLeod 2009, 22-3). While it is acknowledged that there may not be a direct comparison between these events and those that took place in northern England in the 11th century, it is considered relevant to keep such parallels in mind when interpreting the slim evidence for the medieval milling sites at Wharram Percy.

Graveyard, church and parish
by Stuart Wrathmell

The other main developments in the Valley in the Late Saxon period were the creation of the burial ground and, somewhat later, the stone church. The chronology of churchyard development was established by means of a major programme of radiocarbon dating carried out on the skeletal remains from the graveyard and church, and the combination of its results with stratigraphic evidence to produce 'posterior density estimates' of the dates of archaeological 'events', as opposed to the simple calibrated dates of the samples. The detailed methodology and results have been published by Alex Bayliss (Bayliss *et al.* 2007, 193-215). Her conclusions as to the first use of the graveyard for burial, and its early development, are as follows:

'The model provides a posterior density estimate for the start of burial on the site of *cal AD 940-995 (95% probability…)…*burial extended to the identified limits of the cemetery very quickly, with the areas to the north of the church (including the area of Site 26), east of the church and south of the church all in use for adult burial before AD 1066 (at more than 95% probability). It is likely that the areas to the west of the church and right down to the southern boundary of the churchyard came into use, if not before the Conquest, shortly thereafter' (Bayliss *et al.* 2007, 213)

On the basis of these estimates it is highly probable that, within a century of the graveyard's first use, its boundaries were at their furthest limits. Indeed, the area designated for burial may have been planned at the outset to occupy its largest known area. This does not mean, of course, that burial was already continuous across the whole area by the time of the Conquest: various families or communities may have used designated plots scattered across the graveyard, separated by areas which were, at least in the first century or so, devoid of interments.

The archaeological investigations on the site of the present church – itself originating in the first half of the 12th century – recorded an earlier, much smaller two-cell stone church on the same site (Phase II), dated broadly to the early or mid-11th century (Bell 1987a, 57-61). They also identified the possible remains of a timber predecessor (Phase I: Bell 1987a, 55-6). The stone church was evidently erected at a later date than the start of burials in this area, as graves lay under its construction debris. On the basis of the radiocarbon dating of stratigraphically related skeletal remains, Bayliss has concluded that:

'the radiocarbon evidence is in good agreement with the architectural sequence. The model provides a posterior density estimate for the construction of the Phase II church of *cal AD 1010-1120 (68% probability)* or *cal AD 945-1185 (95% probability…)*. This is consistent with the late Saxon or Saxo-Norman date proposed by Bell…'
(Bayliss *et al.* 2007, 214)

Given that the Phase III church was itself built perhaps as early as the 1120s (pp 240-46), it seems unlikely that Phase II dates any later than the late 11th century. John Blair places it in the context of the 'Great Rebuilding' of churches focused on the 1050s and 1060s, which saw earlier timber structures replaced by stone buildings on the pattern of Odda's Chapel at Deerhurst (Glos.). He dates the church at Wharram to the period '*c*.1050-75?' (Blair 2005, 412-14 and fig. 48).

The date of the Phase I timber structure is entirely unknown, except that it preceded the Phase II church. Its plan form was not fully recovered (and not fully recoverable given the later use of this site), so we cannot even be certain that it was a church. On the other hand, *if* a church was associated with the pre-Phase II burials, these post-holes (or some of them) could well form the remains of such a building.

The medieval parish of Wharram Percy was, as we have seen in Chapter 12, a multi-vill parish, serving the communities of Burdale, Raisthorpe, Thixendale and Towthorpe as well as that of Wharram Percy itself. Though dependent chapels of ease were established in some of them (Beresford M.W. 1987, 6-7; Wrathmell 2010b, 16), their inhabitants were still required to use the Wharram Percy graveyard during the Middle Ages. Given that there was no apparent major expansion of the graveyard after the 11th century, it is at least a viable hypothesis that the area designated initially for burial was intended to supply the needs of the inhabitants in all five vills. In other words, the townships which we know as members of Wharram parish were either at this time, or soon after, (in the mid to late 10th century), grouped together for the purposes of ecclesiastical provision (Harding and Wrathmell 2007, 327). If the establishment of the burial ground was, indeed, the product of a decision to group together a number of vills for such provision,

then the effective formation of this parish should be dated a century earlier than Roffe suggested.

In the final section of this chapter, Everson and Stocker discuss in depth the scenarios that may have led to the foundation of the graveyard, church and parish. They note that the churchyard and church appear to have been established on 'public' space, towards the southern end of the village green, and argue that this would, in the light of their investigations in Lincolnshire, indicate a foundation by the sokemen of Wharram, as opposed to the lords of the dependent manors or their overlords. This would, of course, be difficult to reconcile with the suggestion made above, based on the archaeological evidence, that the graveyard was intended *ab initio* as a multi-vill facility. As with so much in this volume, it is for readers to weigh the evidence and decide which story they prefer.

Why at Wharram? The foundation of the nucleated settlement
by Paul Everson and David Stocker

Church on the green
At some point in the later Anglo-Saxon period, a nucleated settlement was created at Wharram Percy. This settlement developed into the recognisable village of the high medieval period which itself resulted in the famous earthwork remains, whose re-survey Alastair Oswald has described above (Ch. 3). Amongst other revelations, Oswald's survey shows beyond doubt that the framework for the settlement earthworks is mostly an artefact of this period of settlement establishment in the Late Saxon period. That is to say that what planners call the 'block structure' of the settlement – i.e. the outlines of blocks of properties defined by the system of route-ways – dates from this initial period of 'Anglo-Scandinavian' settlement-making, even though the detail of the properties within these blocks may have been revised at later periods.

The establishment of nucleated settlements in this period is frequently encountered in England's Central Province of settlement and is undoubtedly associated with a larger recasting of the landscape. Typically, the newly established nucleated settlement took the place of a scattering of smaller, more dispersed settlements, each with their own small-scale field systems, and was associated with the creation of large open fields, farmed in common, in the landscape around the new nucleation. This process of landscape transformation has been studied in various locations up and down the Central Province, and dates for its inauguration have been demonstrated from the later 9th century onwards (Hall 1995; Brown and Foard 1998; Lewis *et al.* 2001; Jones and Page 2006; Gerrard with Aston 2007; Audouy and Chapman 2008).

By far the most substantial and specific body of evidence bearing on this development locally arises from the long-running West Heslerton Landscape Project and relates to a 10km strip of prime lands along the south side of the Vale of Pickering, not 15km distant from Wharram (in summary, Powlesland 2003b). Here, it is plausibly asserted, the pre-existing well-established settlement and cultivation regime was swept away at a stroke in a co-ordinated action, in parish after adjacent parish, in a single season sometime in the late 9th century and replaced by a new pattern of nucleated settlements and open-field cultivation (Powlesland 1997; see further below).

Some scholars have proposed that the creation of a substantial number of Christian graveyards and churches could form a component of the same transformation (Everson and Stocker 1999, 76-80; and more generally Blair 2005, 368-74, 426-33). There seems little doubt that the landscape revolution represented by the nucleation of settlements and the creation of open fields, farmed in common around them, is also associated in some manner with the development of the parochial system, at least within the Central Province of settlement; not least because so many of the new parochial units (i.e. units of ecclesiastical taxation) define a single nucleated settlement and its associated common fields and other common resources. To this extent, the landscape revolution had a religious aspect as well as a social and economic one (Stocker 2007c, 220-21).

We suggest that this linkage can be seen at Wharram and the *effects* of nucleation there usefully studied by considering it and observing the similarities and contrasts exhibited by Wharram's neighbours. Though, in the distinctive topographical and land-use circumstances of the high Wolds, we do not presume that the *precursors* of nucleation were a series of dispersed farmsteads, as for example in Northamptonshire. Rather, as argued in Chapter 11, nucleation on the Wolds transformed an essentially non-arable landscape characterised by less numerous seasonal stations for sheep management, which appear in the archaeological record as Butterwick-type settlements.

In a recent major study in Lincolnshire (Stocker and Everson 2006), we have found that an approach to the relationship between settlement form, church location and tenure through simple morphological analysis has proved a powerful tool and can be very revealing about settlement and church foundation, and its social context. This study – which deployed what might be termed 'the Lincolnshire methodology' – revealed three major categories of church site within the sample group of 60 Lincolnshire churches. These major categories were, first, those parochial churches which had been established on sites which related to pre-existing locations, often near natural features such as outcrops or springs, prior to the establishment of nucleated settlements in the area. Secondly, we were able to identify a large group which were associated with the *curiae* of manors, and to define different sub-categories of relationship within this type. Finally, we were somewhat surprised to find a substantial group (amounting to well over 30% of the total sample) of churches that appeared to have been founded on greens (i.e. common open space) within nucleated settlements.

In Lincolnshire, these churches founded on the green were characterised by:
- The location of the church on an existing or former open space at the heart of the settlement;
- High or predominant numbers of residents holding their land by soke tenure, as free peasants, as recorded in Domesday Book;
- Often the presence of a priest's house also on the green alongside the church.

In Lincolnshire, we interpreted this combination of factors as indicating the investment of the community as a whole, rather than the dominance of any lord in the creation of the church, as reflected by its position on the common, public space rather than in a special relationship with any individual's property or residence.

At Wharram, as Oswald rehearses in his account of the results of the most recent topographic survey of the site, the location of St Martin's church has for long been a matter of concern and puzzlement. Brian Roberts has described it as 'a most curious siting, which raises many unanswerable questions' (Roberts 1987, 100). None of the various suggested reasons has proved convincing. They have included Richard Morris's relating it to the use of the stream for baptism at a particularly accessible point (Morris 1991, 23-4), the proposal that the church represents the Christianisation of an earlier, prehistoric burial and/or ritual site (Jones 1980; Bell 1987b, 199), and the concept that the church was the planned, southernmost, element in a regular eastern row of settlement (Beresford and Hurst 1990, 79-81).

By contrast, deploying 'the Lincolnshire methodology', we should like to suggest that St Martin's is a foundation of the 'church-on-the-green' type (Fig. 81A). It appears to have all three of the characteristics that we identified in the Lincolnshire study. At Wharram, the two topographical characteristics can be established quite straightforwardly and convincingly, taking its high medieval plan in the form of the surveyed earthworks as the basis for analysis. If the East Row is read as an encroachment of high-medieval date on what was formerly a large, integral open space – as a morphological reading would suggest, and both topographical survey and limited excavated evidence has confirmed – then a large open space, bounded on its east side by the stream or by steep slopes falling to the stream, is defined by a short settlement row on the north (the North Row) and a very long settlement row (the combination of the West Row elements, north and south, extending for perhaps a 350m length) on the west. The space defined had, on the arguments advanced by Oswald above (Ch. 3), an established role as public space and perhaps a tradition of public activities. St Martin's church was located well away from any settlement elements and prominently within this open space, albeit placed topographically towards its lower end, rather than its upper, and is consequently very similar to many examples of this group of foundations in the Lincolnshire study (e.g. Blyton, Brigsley or Corringham: Stocker and Everson 2006, 103-5, 120-1, 140-42).

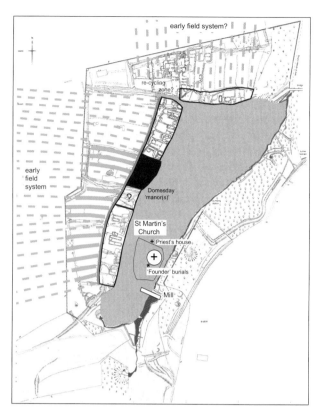

Fig. 81. Wharram: village development between the mid-10th and mid-11th centuries. (E. Marlow-Mann after P. Everson and D. Stocker)

This location of St Martin's within the green relates it more closely to the southern half of the West Row than to any other part of the settlement. But the specific location of the church within the green may be related, as Richard Morris signalled, to convenient provision for baptism in the stream, albeit of a purely parochial, rather than an early and centralised sort, as he envisaged. As is commonly the case with local parish churches, there is no evidence for baptismal provision within the church building at Wharram before the later 11th or beginning of the 12th century (pp 260-62). Previously, baptisms are likely to have been conducted in the living water of the stream or of the spring just below the church, using just the sort of resource that can sometimes be seen employed elsewhere in purely parochial contexts (see discussion in Stocker and Everson 2006, 64-5; Blair 2010).

Secondly, and with unusual confidence, we can demonstrate that the priest's house at Wharram was located adjacent to the church, despite the evidence for incumbents residing elsewhere in the village at various times (Beresford and Hurst 1990, 101-8; see Wrathmell 2010b, 16); it was thus 'on-the-green' just as much as the church. As we have noted, this is also a frequently found characteristic of churches in this category in Lincolnshire (Stocker and Everson 2006).

The last of the three characteristics we associated with church foundations of this 'on-the-green' type in our Lincolnshire study was the presence of evidence in the Domesday survey for a substantial percentage of the recorded population belonging to the 'sokeman' class.

The definition of such sokemen continues to be problematic, but most commentators agree that they represent a caste of upper peasantry, clinging tenaciously to certain rights and freedoms as the process of subinfeudation and manorialisation progressed in parallel with the parochialisation and nucleation of settlement through the period from the late 10th century to the late 11th century (Roffe 1992, 19-20; 2000b, 31-2; Faith 1997, 121-5).

The status of the population in these terms is more difficult to establish at Wharram than it was in many of the Lincolnshire cases within our previous study, as the Domesday entries for Yorkshire are much more terse (Roffe 2000a, 6). David Roffe's analysis has, however, shown that the Domesday entry for Wharram indicates tenure of sokeland type. Ketilbjorn's holding of one carucate 'has the form of a sokeland entry ... almost certainly attached to another manor' elsewhere; it is 'unlikely that Ketilbjorn maintained any sort of establishment with his holding' and had no demesne at Wharram but drew dues only (Roffe 2000a, 2, 8, 10). Furthermore, he comments that Lagmann and Karli's pair of manors, together rated at 8 carucates, had once been a single estate and were the type of thegnage holdings 'which would have appeared as soke in Lincolnshire'; it is 'unclear whether Lagmann and Karli [though probably resident] had truly seigneurial establishments in Wharram' (Roffe 2000a, 10). Although it is difficult to compare this evidence directly with the patterns of settlement plan and tenure in Lincolnshire, and even though we have here in Yorkshire no numbering of population, still it is possible to suggest that Wharram does have marked similarities with those Lincolnshire settlements that were dominated by 'sokemen'.

The best we can say about the social make-up of the newly nucleated community at Wharram is that the implication of 'the Lincolnshire model' might be that the foundation of the church 'on-the-green' was a physical and tenurial sign that an element of community initiative was involved, rather than its location being dictated by the autocratic will of a local lord insistent on his exclusive rights. This is also, of course, a conclusion supported by the excavations in the burial ground, where the 'lordly' graves occurred only after the burial of several generations of apparently undistinguished burials (Bell 1987a, fig. 11; Stocker 2007a, 285).

In short therefore, in terms of its plan-form morphology, St Martin's Wharram emerges as a church foundation of 'on-the-green' type and, furthermore, a good case can be made that the social structure of the village might also have been similar to those which generated church foundations in such locations in Lincolnshire as well. We should emphasise, however, that the strength of the Lincolnshire study's conclusions lay in the patterns that emerged from a sizeable sample, in a way that cannot apply so robustly to a one-off study.

As a foundation of this type, St Martin's Wharram would, on the Lincolnshire pattern, be merely of ordinary parochial status, new in the later pre-Conquest period. It was not a senior church, and actually nothing in its architectural form or development or in its later medieval documentation suggests otherwise. There is no justification, either in this understanding of its foundation or in its form or relationships, to sanction the use of the term 'minster' of St Martin's church.

This assessment of the ordinariness of St Martin's church and graveyard at Wharram and the communal character of its creation by free peasantry within the public space of the vill of Wharram envisages action by a 'community of the vill' similar to that recorded by a research-based conservation study of the green villages of Drenthe in northern Holland (Van der Vaart 1983). In many respects, the Dutch evidence, dating from at least the 12th to the late 19th centuries, matches what we might expect of the green at Wharram. There, greens were typically the communal property of the *bærschap* or 'entitled farmers'; functions of the green included the location of common meetings of the *bærschap* and of the local court. It was a place for ponds and stands of trees, for gathering of stock, for markets or fairs, and a place where – latterly – such communal buildings as the village school have been built. Traces of similar communal characteristics are recorded in eastern Yorkshire. In about 1524 at Newbald the inhabitants riotously assembled on the green, seeking to reverse infringements of customary rights; their common forge stood on the green (in a case cited by McDonagh 2007a, 216-18).

This understanding, that the driving force for the foundation of St Martin's church lay with the community of the vill, stands in sharp disagreement with the view that Wrathmell has developed in Chapter 12 above, where he identifies the tenurial overlord as the key factor in church foundation over a wide local area. He has brought forward fascinating evidence to suggest that the overlord at Wharram TRE, unnamed in the Domesday record, was in fact Ormr son of Gamall, one of the powerful kin-group who traced their origin back to the influential Thorbrandr the Hold. This suggestion replaces Roffe's more generic characterisation of the larger Wharram estate in the mid-11th century as 'comital' land; but is absolutely in line with the status he implied. It would make Wharram sokeland of Langton.

Ormr son of Gamal was named in the famous Kirkdale sundial's inscription as the re-founder of that ancient church. Wrathmell uses this evidence of Ormr's initiative in respect of an admittedly exceptional ancient foundation (as every aspect of Kirkdale's archaeology has proved it to have been: Lang 1991, 158-66 for sculpture; Rahtz and Watts 2003 for the site) as a springboard to propose that Ormr and his kin were agents, as overlords, for the series of new, later pre-Conquest church foundations in the settlements in which he held lordship in the area, including Wharram. Furthermore, he argues that this connection explains how and when and why the other vills in the greater, late-medieval parish of Wharram came to be attached to St Martin's.

We do not agree with the conclusions drawn from this evidence for three main reasons. First, in our wide-ranging Lincolnshire study we have explicitly tested the proposition that it is the overlords who are the influential figures in church foundation and building initiatives. The tenure of a particular tenant in chief proved, in our quite significant sample, to be a neutral factor (Stocker and Everson 2006, 72-3). This conclusion corresponds to the wholly inconclusive results of architectural and art historians working on other data-sets, when they have sought to identify patronage in this level of lordship (e.g. Thurlby 1999). By contrast, it is the local or mesne lords who are influential, and local free communities.

Secondly, Wrathmell's proposition would render the differentiation of siting of churches, observed through morphological analysis, wholly without explanation. This would apply to the most common circumstance of the juxtaposition of manor and church – where it is mesne lords and not overlords who are most typically resident. Thirdly, it would have a similar effect on the incidence of monumental sculpture, viewed as evidence of the influence of local lords (Everson and Stocker 1999, 76-9; Stocker and Everson 2001). By contrast, we can present cogent and interrelated arguments to account for the patterning visible amongst both local church locations and monumental sculpture (see below).

None of this is to deny the existence of lordship at that superior level of tenant in chief in the case of both minor local lordlings and of free communities. Nor is it to deny that that superior lordship had an interest and might have been consulted. But, no matter what the documents say, we still have to account for the archaeological observation that at one settlement where Ormr and his forebears were overlords – Wharram Percy – the church was located on the public space, whereas at others the church was intimately associated with the manor.

In practice, an overlord such as Ormr might have been most influential and pro-active in the establishment of the much larger, late-medieval parish attached to St Martin's church; rationalising, as it were, a deployment of resources that had emerged piecemeal 'from below'. Our model that St Martin's was founded through action by the community of the vill rather supports the proposition that St Martin's did *not* from the start serve all five vills that formed the high medieval parish. The community of Wharram Percy initially acted only for Wharram Percy vill and allocated Wharram communal land to the site of the church and graveyard and Wharram communal resources to support a priest. Consequently, this understanding of the nature and origins of St Martin's corresponds with the explanation of the formation of the greater Wharram parish as a pragmatic and tidying-up process that David Roffe suggests. He proposes that the large and irregular parish was an '*ad hoc* formation for payment of tithe' to an existing ecclesiastical entity (Roffe 2000a, 14-15).

St Martin's at Wharram was an established local, but not senior, church, without the fixed tithing arrangements that typified the private churches of booked estates like Wharram le Street, and to which, therefore, other tithing elements could be attached unproblematically. A sign of the late date and *ad hoc* character of this arrangement may be (*contra* Wrathmell, above) the circumstance that Burdale and Towthorpe lay in Scard hundred in contrast to Wharram, Raisthorpe, and Thixendale in Acklam. Roffe saw this establishment of the parish as occurring 'probably in the late 11th or early 12th century'. Such a retrospective or tidying-up process for the creation of the greater parish of Wharram as that proposed by Roffe might indeed have been the result of engagement by an overarching lordship, of the sort that Ormr could have brought to bear at this juncture, when he was a power in all these lands. In other words, might Ormr's standing in this group of vills have been a significant factor in the form and extent of the grouping, but at a later date than the creation of Wharram church and graveyard?

In the other townships of the greater Wharram parish, the closer ecclesiastical regulation of the late 11th and 12th centuries created a tidy, more uniform, arrangement, where all tenants now knew where they stood. Perhaps this process even prompted the sort of decisions between lords and their men about ecclesiastical provision which occasionally surface in the documentary record of this era, as at Little Sturton in Lincolnshire (Everson and Stocker 2005); or gave rise to enlargement of church fabric to accommodate the new parishioners, to regularisation of baptismal provisions, to raising of bell towers so that the occurrence of divine service might be more effectively perceived and acknowledged throughout the more extensive community – all of which we observe in St Martin's church in this era (Ch. 15).

Settlement and field system

The proposition that St Martin's foundation was of the church-on-the-green type, brings with it a series of questions about the settlement as a whole that might be explored and debated. Fortunately, with the great diversity of information now gathered about Wharram, we are able to explore these issues with rather more nuance than was possible in most of our Lincolnshire cases. One of the first questions raised by these observations relates to the date and context within which the church and graveyard were likely to have been founded. That is now quite closely calibrated to the mid to late 10th century (Bayliss *et al.* 2007, 193-215). Burials are cut by the foundations of the stone church and by the mid-11th-century grave group with stone covers. This group of decorated grave covers, most recently re-studied by Stocker (2007b, 271-87), is superimposed on these earlier generations of burials.

In their location as a close-knit group, with closely similar, simple decoration deployed on identical recycled Roman stone sarcophagus covers, these stone sculptures have the aspect of a so-called 'founder's grave' and kin group. Moreover, decoration of the covers is stylistically datable to the latest pre-Conquest decades, around the middle of the 11th century, and as a group they were located close to the south side of the chancel of the earliest stone church excavated, dates for which vary only slightly from the early to mid-11th century (*Wharram III*; Wrathmell, pp 207-8). Presumably, then, it was members of the generations represented by the first century of burials – i.e. those stratigraphically beneath this distinctive monumental group – who actually founded the church 'on-the-green'. This is very much in line with our established understanding of the chronology of such foundations in Lincolnshire, both from the earlier study and from further examples examined more recently (e.g. new work on Scothern and Reepham in Everson and Stocker forthcoming a), and was evidently focused on the modest timber church revealed by excavation (Bell 1987a, 56).

Although somewhat late in date relative to other examples in eastern Yorkshire (discussed below), the Wharram funerary monuments nevertheless fulfil all our expectations of a 'founder group', of the type excavated at Rounds (Boddington 1996) and hypothesised at many other locations up and down the Central Province of settlement (Everson and Stocker 1999, 76-9; Stocker and Everson 2001). In Stocker's substantial archaeological reassessment of this group of monuments, he proposed their identification with either Lagmann or Karli and their kin. But because they are superimposed on earlier burials, he suggested that they might be characterised, not as founders of the burial ground – as at Rounds and elsewhere – but as 're-founders' of St Martin's church, and that they might also have been responsible for rebuilding it in stone (Stocker 2007a, 284-7).

David Roffe defines this Domesday pair rather precisely as dependent tenants, the equivalent of *drengs* elsewhere in northern England; they probably held the estate for a term of one life, or at most several lives, and it is doubtful, he believes, whether they were any longer holding at Wharram in 1086, when the whole vill had reverted into the king's hands following the Harrying of the North and was not tenanted (Roffe 2000a, 10-11). Not enfeoffed or holding bookland, these were not 'lords of Wharram' in any simple, useful sense, rather they were more like 'principal tenants'. Nevertheless, it would be perverse not to read the archaeological evidence of the grave group and its relationship to the new stone church as a significant matter.

The Wharram funerary sculpture dates actually from several generations later than the 'founder' groups at places such as Folkton and Kirby Grindalythe (discussed further below). The sculptures at Wharram also reflect a slightly different tradition of memorialisation, comprising covers and thin slab-like grave markers, whilst the earlier monuments at Kirby, Folkton and Sherburn are mostly cross-shafts. These distinctions between Wharram and the material from Kirby, Folkton and Sherburn may permit us to draw distinctions between the status of the petty lords memorialised at the two groups of places. The monuments from Wharram could represent a family acting as '*primus inter pares*' and putting themselves forward as leaders of a community action; very much individuals like Lagmann and Karli, in fact.

Their form might be doubly appropriate perhaps, in the context of Wrathmell's identification of the overlord of Wharram TRE being Ormr son of Gamall, of Langton. It is an attractive thought – which he trails – that the Roman sarcophagi from which the Wharram grave-covers were manufactured were sourced from a cemetery associated with the Roman villa at Langton, rather than that at Wharram Grange which Stocker, on balance, favoured previously (Stocker 2007a, 281-4): not because they might represent the overlord directly, but because they might be an appropriate mechanism for aspirant local lordlings beholden to Ormr, Ormr's 'men', to exhibit their affinity. Perhaps this is indeed an instance – as is occasionally the case at Wharram – where we can see individual actions revealed in a complex archaeological sequence.

Combining Roffe's Domesday understanding with our own archaeological scenario, then, we can suggest that by the mid-11th century there was at least one resident family of aspirant lordlings at Wharram. This family (or pair of families) had, however, emerged from a similar 'sokemen' background to many of the resident peasants. By this time, peasant properties were organised in two estates. Much the smaller of these, and assessed at one carucate in the Domesday Survey, was held by Ketilbjorn in 1086. This was, to recap Roffe's understanding, a holding of sokeland type with little probability that Ketilbjorn had any focus of residence at Wharram from which to farm or regulate it. It may have been dependent on Ketilbjorn's manor in nearby Wharram le Street. Much the larger estate, and assessed at eight carucates in the Domesday Survey, was in 1066 subdivided and held in a form of dependent tenure, probably for a period of lives

rather than permanently 'by book'. This caused it to be described as two separate manors held by Lagmann and Karli. Roffe suggests that this implies that both Lagmann and Karli had residences at Wharram but that neither residence need have been (or was likely to have been) an *aula* or hall, or what would later have been thought of as 'manorial' in scale and distinctiveness.

Presuming that we are not overlooking a second suite of grave-furniture elsewhere in the unexcavated part of the graveyard, the known archaeology of St Martin's graveyard surely makes it clear, however, that one or other of these two petty lords was not only resident at Wharram but was putting himself forward as a leader in the community, and was doing so in a visibly assertive and symbolically articulate way. It might seem unlikely that his residence was not equally distinctive.

If we can discount as a late intrusion and encroachment on the green the East Row of the four planning units put forward by Oswald, it is tempting to equate these documented holdings in a simple way to the elements in the settlement morphology (Fig. 81B). First, the short section of North Row properties that forms the north end of the green (largely east of the later North Manor but including a westernmost plot that was superseded by that manor) could be associated with Ketilbjorn's relatively small holding in Wharram. We doubt that it included the North Manor, which may not have been established until the 12th or even the 13th century (see pp 270-72). This proposal does not, in fact, conflict either with the field survey evidence of the earthworks or with the evidence from York University's excavations, as reported by Rahtz. Indeed, Rahtz characterises the North Manor area as one – as so far investigated – which seems to be on the fringe of a major Romano-British complex and with evidence well into the medieval period of the dismantling and reprocessing of Roman materials (Rahtz *et al.* 2004, 289). Perhaps this was for an extended period a derelict Romano-British site within the early medieval landscape.

Secondly, the other, much larger holding (combining the later holdings of both Lagmann and Karli) might be associated with the long West Row – divided according to Oswald's analysis into a north and a south 'planning unit'. This holding was subsequently divided into the two dependent manor-like tenancies, and it might be that this documented subdivision was the factor that created or laid the foundations for the topographical or morphological division between north and south sectors of the West Row. At a simplistic viewing, it appears that a disjunction or change of direction in the row occurs roughly halfway along.

If there is any location in the row where one might anticipate a pre-eminent property corresponding to the evidence of the mid-11th-century 're-founders' grave group, it is this disjunction, which was also the locale for the 12th-century South Manor – perhaps a significant association. At the moment that the petty lord and his kin were establishing their priority in the graveyard, however, this property did not stand out in depth or otherwise from the row, except perhaps by engrossment of neighbouring plots. This, then, could plausibly be viewed as a property that was 'primus inter pares'; without the overt pre-eminence that might be associated with a demesne farm and the receipt of burdensome services. This assessment would fit comfortably with Roffe's understanding of the status of the two thegns of Wharram at Domesday, and also with our hypothesis on the origins of the settlement a few generations earlier, with its church on the green.

Some of the excavated finds from this locale do indeed point to some distinction for this location, within the Row as a whole. Especially notable is the Borre-style belt set, of course, which dates in its manufacture – outside the area and perhaps even outside England – to the 10th century (Riddler, p. 197; Goodall and Paterson 2000, 128-31). Old but cared for when lost in the remote Yorkshire Wolds, it had been repaired and perhaps adapted to a narrower belt than its original. This showy item of superior male dress might – as a gift or heirloom – have signalled the traditions and ethnic affinity suitable to the dependants of the house of Thorbrandr, a century later. But even the range of ceramics here – albeit recovered in small quantities – exhibits a notable diversity and reach, including all the contemporary advanced wheel-thrown product of eastern England: Thetford, Torksey, Lincoln and Stamford types as well as York ware (Slowikowski, p. 200-202). If one sought a second locale with any sign of difference, to correspond with the second of the two Domesday lordling holdings, it would probably be in the crofts immediately south of the South Manor, but perhaps only because the row further southwards is so remarkably regular and egalitarian. The location is here again at the end of a subsection of the row, but it is also undifferentiated from its neighbours in not standing out from the row in depth.

In fact, throughout its length this extended West Row of properties is held together by the lynchet bank that forms the back boundary of the crofts, in a notable feature extending nearly 400m in north-south linear extent. Formerly thought to be a single entity, this lynchet – in physical bulk the largest earthwork at Wharram – has proved problematic to interpret and place in the chronological sequence, as Oswald spells out more fully in his recent study (pp 41-2 above). Once thought to be of pre-medieval origin and a feature created principally by prehistoric and Roman cultivation on the plateau, it seems latterly to have been shown by excavation in the South Manor area to post-date the latest Middle Saxon, pre-nucleation occupation on the Plateau, but to be present by the 12th century (Stamper et al. 2000, 37-8). Its appearance – as a very broad, gently swelling bank – and location near the edge of the plateau and its generally uniform extent nevertheless recommend an interpretation as a product of cultivation.

Remarkably – and it is perhaps the most remarkable of all its fine observations – the new English Heritage survey has identified and planned very broad, shallow cultivation ridging preserved in the enclosed closes behind the West Row (south), and the West Row (north),

and lying at right angles (though a less than perfect right angle going southwards) to the crofts and to the lynchet bank. These fugitive and fragile traces are clearest in the south, where – in addition to being implausibly short to plough and therefore probably in their surviving form being truncated fragments of their original extent – they have been observed and recorded as being cut by the back boundaries of the rear closes behind the row (the so-called 'toft boundaries') and therefore predate them. These boundaries are 12th-century developments at Wharram rather than original features of nucleation, so the newly observed and fortuitously preserved early cultivation system would stand in a complementary relationship to the lynchet bank and might plausibly be its cause.

The recent English Heritage survey also proposes that what has most readily been understood as the north end of a continuous lynchet bank, extending to its northernmost 180m, is actually of a different form – most specifically straighter than the slightly curving aspect of the bank further south – and of completely later date. It also suggests that the early broad-and-shallow ridged ploughing extended eastwards to the very edge of the Plateau, where the ends of a series of the ridges can be perceived projecting east of the frontage of the later settlement row onto the green. In consequence, the northern section of the West Row is interpreted as a later planned development and not part of the early plan of nucleated Wharram.

As essentially the headland of the early ploughing, this section of the lynchet bank might perhaps have had a straighter configuration because the ridging here lay quite precisely at right angles to the headland, its orientation regulated by the close proximity of the ancient east-west hollow way to its north. By contrast, further south the orientation of the ridging is looser, itself responding to the lie of the plateau edge as it swings off in the side valley to the west, and produces a more curvilinear form to the headland. This, then, would seem to be excellent evidence for a form of open-field cultivation belonging to the late pre-Conquest estate. Whether there was originally a field system of analogous low, broad-ridged form lying on a north-south orientation behind the North Row seems less clear-cut from the new survey work, but probable (pp 35-7).

As an arable field system and form of cultivation, these remarkable remains are generically similar – in being permanently ridged – to the developed ridge-and-furrow patterns organised in interlocking furlongs that David Hall has so ably recorded at Wharram and elsewhere (pp 284-8); but they are significantly different. First, this earlier evidence bears no relationship to the later recorded cultivation patterns, which – whatever may have been claimed of their date of origin (Hall 1982) – might turn out most plausibly to have been a complete recasting of the 12th century (see p. 266). Secondly, although there may now be no way of telling because of the all-pervasive impact of later cultivation, it still seems improbable that this early cultivation extended throughout the parish in the manner of Hall's recorded ridge-and-furrow ploughing. It may rather have been a single bounded cultivation area, with pasture beyond, or even some form of infield-outfield arrangement. Indeed, the husbandry and general intensity of cultivation may in some respects have resembled the restricted regimes of the 17th century, when the arable was limited and carefully regulated because of what were considered to be poor soils (see Wrathmell 2010a, 3-10). Without systematic and assiduous and continuous manuring they may have been considered so in early times too, after an initial period of benefit from their post-Roman legacy of fallow and grazing. Maureen Girling's assessment of the pre-Conquest environmental evidence has identified a regime of 'mixed arable farming and grazing land' with very few trees (Hurst 1984, 87).

In Drenthe, where the land cultivated for arable was poor and sandy, the green stood at the communal heart of agricultural practice (Van der Vaart 1983). Large flocks of sheep were kept for production of dung to enrich the arable. The sheep spent overnight in the settlement, which was where the dung was gathered in byres, but the flock was assembled in the morning on the green to go out to the pastures of the vill, and divided on the green again on their return at evening. Whereas English medieval documentation relates principally to demesne regimes, there this was communal, peasant practice that lasted from at least the 12th century to the late 19th century. Perhaps something similar might have served pre-12th-century Wharram. It is tempting to look to the evidence of manuring scatters of pottery recovered from Wharram's fieldwalking survey (*Wharram V*) to define the extent of this early arable, but only a limited number of fields was walked. As Richard Jones has argued in explaining the absence of 10th and 11th-century ceramics from the manuring spreads in Whittlewood, though arable fields were undoubtedly present, the initial phase of common arable may have been sustained by dung from the community's folded livestock (Jones 2004). Only with the advent of intensification and commercialisation of arable from the 12th century was carting of domestic detritus added to the manuring strategy, in a pattern also seen at Wharram (Hurst 1984, 99; Hayfield 1987a, 109-19; Jones 2004, 186).

Thirdly, nevertheless, an early feature in the layout of nucleated Wharram was a mill on the stream, located to the south of the churchyard (see Watts, p. 206-7). As excavation has demonstrated, it was present by the later pre-Conquest period (though not, as its reassessment has confirmed, at an earlier date: cf. Hurst 1984, 101-2). Its function, milling cereal, itself implies a reasonable scale of sustained arable cultivation in the vill – just as its later enlargement implies an increase in that respect. This mill was established just as much 'on' the common, open space as the church, and was certainly not an appurtenance of any conceivable manorial *curia*. This might be taken as a further indication of a free peasant community organising their needs.

While the foregoing has explored the hypothesis of an early, common field system of a distinctive form, the suggestion has important implications for the form of the earliest properties, and probably through at least to the 12th century. Briefly, they were tofts only, rather than the toft and croft units that the orthodoxy of medieval settlement studies perhaps presumes. Is this in itself a surprising proposition? Flaxton, north-east of York, affords an excellent parallel, as well in its elongated triangular green, church and priest's house on the green, as in its long row of regular tofts separated by a back lane from the arable furlongs behind (Bourne 2006). It means at Wharram that in the first instance the large, sub-triangular public space was lined by rows of quite small private plots on the west and north, with very even but limited plot depth. It looks remarkably egalitarian.

Wharram in its context: other 10th and 11th-century settlements in Buckrose wapentake

Part of the evidence for the widespread foundation of parochial churches within the new nucleated settlements in the central and northern Danelaw is provided by the patterning of distribution of later Anglo-Scandinavian funeral sculpture (Stocker 2000; Stocker and Everson 2001). These monuments, it is argued, belong to a generation of 'graveyard-founders': a tier of lesser lords whose domains rarely extend to more than one or two of the new nucleated and parochial units. Current dating frameworks for the sculpted monuments on which these propositions are based suggest, however, that the foundation of many of the new parochial churches did not occur contemporaneously across Yorkshire and the East Midlands. In Yorkshire, Anglo-Scandinavian stone funerary sculpture of the type that might plausibly relate to the 'founders' graves', and those of their kin, have typically been given a broad date range from the late 9th century to the early 11th century (Lang 1991; 2001); whereas, in Lincolnshire, this material has been given a more restricted date-range between the mid-10th century and the early 11th century (Everson and Stocker 1999; Stocker 2000; Stocker and Everson 2001). This diversity in dates, though all occurring in the half-dozen generations between the late 9th and the early 11th centuries, need not be considered problematic for the overall hypothesis, but it does suggest that the process of parochial formation, along with the landscape revolution that accompanied it, is not likely to have occurred in all locations and topographies simultaneously.

We can use the results from Wharram to explore this apparent diversity in dates for the foundation of nucleated settlements, or at least for the establishment of the new parochial churches, by a 'founding generation' of lesser lords in the countryside. We can contrast, for example, the experience of Wharram with the line of settlements along the south side of the Vale of Pickering (see Fig. 82) and (in a different way) with the settlements of the Great Wold Valley. Those Vale communities shared common resources of wetland moor along their northern sides,

215

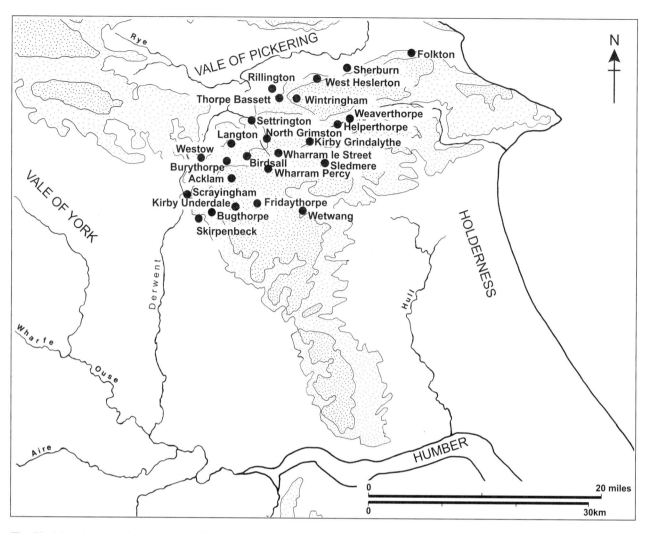

Fig. 82. Map showing places mentioned in Chapter 13. (E. Marlow-Mann and C. Philo)

good arable on the terraces, and upland grazing on the scarp and wold tops. As these valuable resources were all shared between the various dispersed settlements of the area in the period prior to nucleation, it is highly likely that all of these parishes, each with its discrete common-field system, will have been created at a single moment in time. This is because a division of common resources, in particular, cannot be achieved by piecemeal splitting up. Farmsteads set within their own field systems were abandoned, new farmsteads were collected together into a line of newly-planned 'villages' (which may or may not have been centred on one of the pre-existing farmsteads), common arable was established on the land adjacent to the new villages, whilst allocations of the common resources of wetland and grazing wold were made to each village and distinguished from the allocations of neighbouring villages. Finally a parochial church was established in each new village. It seems likely then, that the entire strip of parishes along the south side of the Vale of Pickering, from Malton to Folkton, was established at the same moment.

Despite the synchronous subdivision of resources along the south side of the Vale of Pickering, however, there is no inherent reason to presume that settlements

with a different economy, such as those in the deep wolds valleys like Wharram, would have been greatly affected. Here, because the arable would not have been contiguous with neighbouring settlements, as it was along the Vale edge, it would have been possible for the decision to create open fields farmed in common to have been made by a community in isolation, with its impact confined to that single community. As such wolds-top settlements sat like islands within a great sea of common grazing, the process of bringing the scattered and/or seasonal settlements of the area together in a 'village' and the creation of common arable fields around the new settlements could have occurred at much later dates and in isolation from each other. Although transhumance based in the line of Vale-edge settlements might have had some impact on the economies of the grazing zone on the high Wolds, we might be inclined to conjecture, on the basis of the subsequent parish boundaries, that the flocks of individual Vale settlements had been hefted within the grazing areas that were subsequently included within these Vale parishes.

The same assumptions would suggest that animals hefted on the upland wolds grazing in the area of the subsequent parish of Wharram would not belong to the

216

Vale-edge parishes, but rather to more distant places with a need for such resources. Alternative (and not necessarily mutually exclusive) possibilities might include lowland places like Langton that were quite nearby and linked to Wharram by the river valley but lacked extensive grazing resource immediately at hand, or more distant entities such as early monasteries. It may be that the hints of monastic linkages that Wrathmell (above) has gathered together from post-Conquest documentary sources, together with the early stone sculptural fragments at Wharram, bear witness to an early connection of just this type. Analogies lie with the much-studied organisation of the detached resources of the Weald in Kent, or of the salt marshes in Lincolnshire (e.g. Everitt 1986, 35-8; Owen 1984).

We seem, then, to be defining at least two discrete economic zones here: an area of mixed economy along the Vale edge, and a second on the Wold tops, where the process of landscape nucleation and parish formation need not have been contemporary. Most helpfully, the detached unity of the high Wolds area has been graphically picked out in Figure 36 above, through the incidence of a distinctive strand of place-naming which Wrathmell identifies as characterising a particular uninhabited place some distance from the homes of the people who made use of it (p. 170). It is significant, too, that he leaves this whole zone outside the boundaries of his reconstruction of early (sc. pre-Scandinavian) estates. A similar definition of this high Wolds area would no doubt arise from a simple morphological consideration – Conzen-like – of the shapes of the parishes. The Vale-edge parishes are narrow and greatly elongated; those on the Wold tops are markedly and consistently more 'blocky', not jostling for resource. A third zone – the parishes and townships in the Gypsey Race – are different again, as in origin extensions of the configuration of the Vale-edge parishes, but detached secondary creations (Wrathmell in Chapter 8) These observations might lead us to question any preconception that parochialisation in the East Riding or the diocese of York was uniform and of the same moment. It may not have been a single event, but rather a process of several phases with differences of timing and type of parochialisation – as we have indeed envisaged (from the inside out) in the case of Wharram itself.

The Anglo-Scandinavian funerary sculpture recovered from the first two economic areas seems to reinforce this distinction between these groups of settlements. The funerary sculpture associated with the putative parochial 'founder' burials within the Vale and that associated with the upland parishes is indeed of different character. Two of the 'ladder' parishes along the southern side of the vale of Pickering have generated pre-Conquest sculpture: Sherburn, within the study area, and Folkton, about 11km east of Sherburn (Fig. 82). At Folkton the remains of two cross-shafts have been recovered, which must be more or less contemporary and which probably date from the first half of the 10th century (Lang 1991, 131-2). At Sherburn, the church preserves the remains of perhaps five monuments (Lang 1991, 201-6; calculating the minimum number of monuments rather than counting the number of stones, as explained in Stocker 2000), of which all but one might also be dated to the first half of the 10th century, although Lang gives most of them the wide bracket of 'late 9th to 11th century'.

These monuments from the Vale-side settlements contrast with the three reused covers from Wharram (Stocker 2007a, 271-87), which are more comfortably dated to about a century later: the mid-11th century. Furthermore, the Vale-side monuments are mostly the remains of highly decorated cross-shafts, whereas the monuments from Wharram represent, principally, recumbent gravecovers. On the face of it, this evidence would suggest that the processes of parochial foundation in the two areas were separated by about a century and, more importantly, that the landscape reformation, the nucleation of settlement and the development of common field arable, which is so often linked with the process of parochial formation would therefore have been separated in time by about the same period.

This contrast in date and type between the funerary sculpture from Sherburn and Folkton and that from Wharram begs similar questions of the sculpture at nearby Kirby Grindalythe (Lang 1991, 150-52). Here the sculpture appears to belong to similar groups to the monuments from Sherburn and Folkton. Certainly it matches the late Anglo-Scandinavian art styles of Sherburn and Folkton; and, also like them, the sculpture from Kirby Grindalythe represents cross-shafts and not gravecovers. Consequently, it is also quite unlike that from Wharram in date and type.

Using such style-critical dating indicators for the sculpture as we have, then, it seems that this category of evidence is pointing towards the parochialisation – and therefore potentially the nucleation – of the southern Vale economies and those of the valley of the Gypsey Race at approximately contemporary moments, in – or shortly before – the first half of the 10th century. This material also suggests, however, that there may have been a difference of perhaps as much as a century between this phase and the parochialisation of the high wolds settlements like Wharram Percy.

Having said this, however, there are other factors which tend to bring the two groups of settlements closer together. First, as at Wharram, two stones from a single original monument at Kirby Grindalythe and one of the two monuments from Folkton are reused Roman material. Despite the distinctions between the two groups on style-critical grounds, this reuse of Roman material might suggest at least a continuous tradition of recovery and recycling over a period of a century or more, probably from several sources, and of its knowing redeployment.

Secondly, the excavation of the churchyard at Wharram demonstrated that, although the putative 'founder burials' marked by their distinctive sculpture might date from a period of 'refoundation' in the central part of the 11th century, actually the parochial graveyard was established considerably earlier. Indeed the signs are that the graveyard at Wharram was established at a

Table 15. Provisional categorisation of types of settlements in Buckrose wapentake, YER.

1 Related to pre-existing location	2 Manorial link	3 Church-on-the-Green
Acklam?	Cowlam?	Bugthorpe
Burythorpe?	Fridaythorpe	Langton
Sherburn	Helperthorpe	North Grimston?
Westow	Kirby Grindalythe	Rillington?
	Kirby Underdale?	West Heslerton?
	Scrayingham?	Wharram Percy
	Settrington	
	Skirpenbeck	
	Thorpe Bassett	
	Weaverthorpe	
	Wetwang	
	Wharram le Street	
	Wintringham	
4 of sample of 23 = 17.5%	13 of sample of 23 = 56.5%	6 of sample of 23 = 26%

Unassigned: Birdsall; Sledmere

Omitted from consideration: Norton; Yedingham

similar moment to those at Sherburn, Folkton and Kirby Grindalythe, judged on the basis of their sculpture, namely in the central parts of the 10th century. Although there may be a difference in date – between the first half of the 10th century and the second half – the greater difference between the two groups of settlements might have been more one of lordship. At Folkton, Sherburn and Kirby, our model for the origin of the sculpture in 'founder burial groups', would suggest that here we already have, in the mid-10th century, a dominant 'lordly' family wishing to demonstrate their patronage of the new parochial church within the newly nucleated landscape. By contrast, it seems that at Wharram no such family existed at this particular moment, though we have seen that just such a family did come forward in the following century. Furthermore, this distinction between the character of lordship in the two groups of settlement may also be visible in the topographical settings of the new parochial burial grounds within the new villages in the two areas as well.

An assessment of the relationship of church sites to their settlements offers another, complementary way into these issues. As with the sculpture, the plan-form morphology of the settlements containing sculpture indicates different types and circumstances of church foundation. The church at Sherburn is set well to the north of the main area of settlement, which (according to the first edition Ordnance Survey) was confined to clear tofts laid out against the road that leads from the modern A64 towards the church. On both sides the tofts run back to watercourses. Rather surprisingly, the land to the south of the A64 and around the junction with the road to Weaverthorpe and the Wolds, appears to be occupied by the manor house and its associated closes. According to the Lincolnshire scheme of classification, then, Sherburn would belong to category 1: those churches that were established with regard to some other feature in the settlement landscape, often a natural feature. In Lincolnshire these are often, also, the old-established churches, founded before the advent of settlement nucleation and the associated parochial system between the late 9th and 11th centuries.

Nearby, but actually outside Buckrose wapentake, Folkton is the easternmost of the comparable settlements along the southern side of the Vale of Pickering and the only other settlement in the area with Anglo-Scandinavian sculpture. Here, both Grange Farm and Manor Farm appear to occupy a group of rectangular enclosures at the south-west end of the village street, of which the graveyard is the north-easternmost. The medieval layout of the peasant plots running back from both sides of the street further north-east was clearly still visible on the first edition Ordnance Survey map. This type of morphology – with a manorial *curia* that either includes the church itself or where the church is located at its gates, and between the manor and the settlement – conforms to our Lincolnshire type 3a.

This plan-form appears, from a superficial inspection, to be much the most common in Buckrose wapentake (Table 15), accounting for at least eight and probably eleven out of the 25 parishes (excluding Yedingham and Norton). Furthermore, the preponderance of this type of village morphology can be increased by adding the three examples where the enclosure containing the manor house and parochial church are detached from the settlement units themselves, namely Thorpe Bassett, Weaverthorpe and, perhaps, Cowlam.

This preponderance of manor and church association seems also to have been the finding of Briony McDonagh's historical geographical study of settlement in the Yorkshire Wolds, deploying an analogous methodology of analysing the topographical relationship between manor, church and settlement. In practice, her focus was not on church location and deductions that might relate from patterning observable in that, but rather on the locations of manorial complexes themselves expressed in terms of proximate contrasted with peripheral or remote locations. This places the chronological emphasis of that study in the later medieval period and later. Also, since manors are inherently less stable than churches and tenurial structure might give rise to settlements with several manors, or none at all, and the processes of subinfeudation or amalgamation of holdings were additional variables, that study's discourse was rather different: sceptical about origins, and tending to the discursive and particular (McDonagh 2007a, especially chapter 4; 2007b).

At first sight, Kirby Grindalythe simply offers an example of this most numerous category of church site, both locally here and in the Lincolnshire study: those associated with manors. Combining the evidence of extensive settlement earthworks here (see Plate 34 below) with the 1st edition OS, we see that the village appears to be laid out as a series of properties running north-west to south-east from the valley-side roads along both sides of the valley towards the Gypsey Race itself, which occupies the valley bottom. It is a common plan-form found in many counties within the Central Province of settlement, not least in similar topographic settings in Lincolnshire (e.g. Croxby: Everson *et al.* 1991, 197-9). In this simple plan-form, the church sits within a large rectilinear enclosure, which is bounded along its eastern side by an even larger squarish enclosure containing the Manor House. It seems plausible, then, to categorise the church here as established within the manorial *curia*, adjacent to the manorial hall itself, and therefore conforming to our Lincolnshire type 3a.

But Kirby was a church, as the place-name reveals, with a wider significance in its topographical zone. Not only was its settlement distinctive amongst its neighbours as one with a church – a 'kirkby' – but also it was a church that was significant to the remote valley at large and perhaps served the developing communities there, Grindalythe reflecting the early district name for the upper valley of the Gypsey Race, now called the Great Wold Valley (Smith 1937, 12-13, 124-5). Until churches were founded at Weaverthorpe, Butterwick, and Wold Newton from the 12th century onwards, quite selectively among the numerous small communities along the valley, Kirby was *the* church of this larger landscape.

Furthermore, the location of Kirby church is topographically very distinctive. It is located at the point of the Gypsey Race valley where the landscape begins to open out somewhat. In the enclosed head of the valley to its west lies the strong, high spring which had been demarcated in earlier eras by the construction of the

Roman 'temple' east of Wharram le Street and by Duggleby Howe. Whether one portrays this church's siting as, as it were, 'bottling up' problematic ancient traditions of this locale (Semple 1998) or guarding and Christianising them, thereby transforming and passing on an origin myth or sense of local identity (Williams 1998; Stocker and Everson 2003) – and these are not mutually incompatible - Kirby church bears a similar relationship to the upper part of the Gypsey Race valley to that which prehistorians understand the complex at Duggleby Howe to have had (Kinnes *et al.* 1983, 103-5). More prosaically in terms of the Lincolnshire study, it has all the characteristics of churches founded in relation to some topographical or cultural feature (type 1 churches), but then subsumed or arrogated into a seigneurial context, becoming a type 3. In the Lincolnshire study, this was a not infrequent occurrence and one with a distinctive trajectory (Stocker and Everson 2006, 65-6, fig. 3.23).

At Kirby Grindalythe, then, it appears from the settlement morphology that the church was not newly built within the new seigneurial enclosure by the new Anglo-Scandinavian lords, like Folkton. Rather, it was a pre-existing church, adopted like Sherburn by local Anglo-Scandinavian lords, who marked their presence in a pre-existing churchyard by raising distinctive seigneurial monuments. At Kirby, in contrast to Sherburn, that adoption took the thoroughgoing form of encompassing the church within the new seigneurial enclosure, in a new settlement overseen by the dominant manor.

In terms of their plan-form morphology, there seems little to associate the four church sites in the locality which have produced Anglo-Scandinavian sculpture, with each other. In fact, they exhibit interestingly, four different forms of church inauguration and development. At Sherburn, the church in which the 'founder burials' of the first half of the 10th century were made, as indicated by that sculpture, appears to have been distanced from the nucleated settlement with which the new lord, presumably, was associated. It might have been an earlier church site – one of five potential examples in Buckrose wapentake (six including Kirby Grindalythe) – adopted as the parochial church site for the newly established nucleated settlement to the south, simply because there was already a church here. In such circumstances, it is not surprising that the local Anglo-Scandinavian lords should mark their presence in a pre-existing churchyard by raising distinctive seigneurial monuments. Kirby Grindalythe had a similar early origin, but was actually incorporated into a new lordly *curia* and its churchyard marked by monuments very similar in date and style. Folkton was evidently a straightforward lordly creation, newly built as an adjunct to the new seigneurial enclosure by the new Anglo-Scandinavian lords, with foundation sculpture to match.

By contrast, Wharram Percy stands as a clear example of a church founded 'on the green'. Our rapid scan of Buckrose wapentake has identified other *prima facie* instances of church-on-the-green morphologies, at

Bugthorpe, Langton and perhaps Rillington, West Heslerton and North Grimston, in addition to Wharram itself, as well as the manorial and 'pre-existing church' types. Wharram resembles none of these settlements, however. The monuments represented by its sculpture are of a different character compared with those at Sherburn, Kirby Grindalythe and Folkton, and they are also nearly a century later in date. Also, the earliest church here, apparently located on the early green or common space, suggests a greater degree of communal activity in its foundation, with less association with a specific lord. The developing impact of local lordship comes later; but then, in a petty form, it is reflected in the form and date of the early sculpture, and then, more decisively, by developments in the church fabric (Chs 15 and 16 below).

The combination of settlement morphology and resource zone considerations we have discussed, then, help us to nuance our understanding of the sculptural evidence, suggesting that different states of lordship are reflected in the different type, date and quality of sculpture. They also, in combination, throw light on the establishment of a comprehensive parochial system in this area. We might suggest that the zone around Wharram took a different route, on a different timetable, to that in the Vale of Pickering, and Kirby Grindalythe with the valley of the Gypsey Race, a different trajectory again.

The sculpture at Folkton represents a phase of lordly burials made at the inauguration of the graveyard. The nucleated settlement of which the graveyard is an integrated part may also have been related to the establishment of the parochial unit. As Folkton, like Sherburn, is an element in the run of 'ladder parishes' along the south side of the Vale, this line of reasoning might suggest that the parochialisation of this resource zone of eastern Yorkshire took place in the first half of the 10th century, just when the excellent evidence from West Heslerton demonstrates the wholesale recasting of a landscape that was already densely occupied. This process impacted on the pre-existing ecclesiastical provision (at Sherburn) as well as introducing new churches.

In the upland zone around Wharram there was no pre-existing ecclesiastical provision; and perhaps no permanent, year-round settlement (pp 164-72) and certainly nothing resembling that of the Vale. St Martin's church was founded, at no very different date to the new ones in the Vale, by the efforts of the Wharram community. Nearby communities, with their own township lands but no ecclesiastical provision, were attached to St Martin's, enlarging its parochial responsibilities, probably in the 12th century. Those arrangements persisted essentially until the impact of some new church building, piecemeal, in the 19th century.

In the valley of the Gypsey Race, there was an early ecclesiastical provision, at Kirby. Though like Sherburn in that respect, its function and place in local social networks may have been rather different, since this was a zone of seasonal pastoralism, perhaps with no permanent, year-round settlement (pp 164-8) and, again, certainly nothing resembling the density and complexity of the Vale. Here, the sole ecclesiastical provision was taken over and incorporated in a seigneurial complex and the early sculpted monuments reflect that; the wider landscape was divided into townships, each containing contiguous arable along the terrace land on the valley sides, along with meadow land in the valley floor and grazing on the wold tops, the latter abutting the Wold grazing of Heslerton, Rillington and Winteringham to their north and whose strip form they resembled.

As with the Vale-edge ladder, this sharing of local resources suggests synchronicity of the overall layout, but here with no permanent settlements and field systems to recast. These communities had a distinctively narrow suite of place-names, suggesting a close date bracket for their foundation. The several thorps display a high level of personal names as specifics, which are distinctively Norse (Gelling 2004, 350-51; Cullen *et al.* 2011, 71 usefully citing earlier work by Fellows-Jensen and Gelling). As a place-name type, Cullen and his co-workers assess them as evidence of 'Norse-speaking immigrant communities who would have arrived in the late 9th and 10th centuries', early within 'the thorp moment', which they associate with a large extension of arable in a so-called 'cereal revolution' (Cullen *et al.* 2011, 61, 107-8, 156).

In contrast to the Vale, however, there was evidently no contemporary burst of church provision before the Conquest. In this zone, that began in the 12th century only and was notably led by the Archbishop with the stylish church on his manor at Weaverthorpe. It is almost as though this church, with its prominent position high on the valley side, was deliberately intended to take over the role earlier filled by Kirby Grindalythe and give a lead to an area that was, and remained, rather backward in ecclesiastical provision and certainly never matched the density of the Vale-edge ladder of parishes.

Here, then, are three routes that parochialisation (and alongside it settlement nucleation) may have taken in this area of the Central Province around Wharram, three stages it seems to have reached, and three trails of evidence it seems to have left. The narrative is richer for considering more than the early sculpture alone. The combination suggests that we are right to look to social structure and the development of lordship as key drivers in providing a narrative from the physical evidence at Wharram.

Part Four

Wharram and the Wolds from the 12th to the 16th Centuries

Many of the themes explored in Part Three of this volume are taken up again in Part Four, but this time without any chronological subdivision. Chapters 14, 15 and 16 deal with themes relating to the lords of Wharram Percy, their lives and works. The first of them attempts to tease their personal histories out of the scraps of surviving documentary evidence – not an easy task given the paucity of relevant records. Yet we felt it was important, nevertheless, to try to assemble at least parts of their stories, and to locate them in a wider context of local lordship on the Wolds and in the Vale of Pickering, resuming the narrative of Chapter 12. Every medieval village excavation report is required to list the families that held it in lordship, but few seem to have gone beyond that to assess the possible wider impacts of the history of lordship, in terms of a lord's regional portfolio of holdings and rights, on that particular community and its physical appearance.

The parish church is one of the buildings that can have much to tell us about lordship, through its structural development and architectural elaboration. The results of the detailed recording of the standing fabric of St Martin's, supplemented by archaeological evidence, were published in *Wharram III*, and were therefore excluded from the recent analysis and publication phase of the project. During the preparation of this volume, however, it became clear that some of the interpretations offered in 1987 required significant revision. David Stocker and Paul Everson kindly agreed to extend their involvement in the project to encompass a review of the phasing and fabric development of the church, and the opportunity has been taken to present their findings in Chapter 15. They would be the first to point out that further, comprehensive and detailed recording of Wharram's architectural stonework, both loose items and blocks incorporated in the present building, is desirable; but this is for a future phase of research.

Chapter 16 deploys the discussions presented in the two previous chapters to relate the history of lordship to the development of the village. Essentially, the Everson-Stocker narrative flows on from their discussion of the pre-Conquest village in Chapter 13, and proposes that the late 12th century saw considerable architectural elaboration of St Martin's, accompanied by the erection of the South Manor buildings and the creation of the open-field ridge and furrow, all signifying the arrival of

the Percys as lords in demesne. Chapters 17 and 18 step back from Wharram, and take a wider view of field systems and village plans in eastern Yorkshire, in an attempt to provide, as in earlier chapters, a broader context which can in some respects fill the gaps in the record for Wharram Percy itself, and make more meaningful the fragments of information we have on Wharram – for example on the tenurial and physical structure of its open fields.

Chapters 19, 20 and 21 take a similar approach, but this time with respect to the lives of Wharram Percy's late medieval peasant farmers – on the land, around the farmstead and in the house. Yet again the stories are woven from the slight documentary record and the fuller archaeological evidence available for Wharram itself, combined with more informative written sources that have survived for neighbouring communities on and around the Wolds. The artist's impressions of the interiors of two peasant houses, which are the focal point of Chapter 21, are intended to stimulate debate rather than convey a message that we actually know what these interiors looked like. Their substantial virtue is that they make it almost impossible to do what is all too easy in written descriptions: to fudge or avoid decisions about presence or absence (except, of course, in terms of the chosen margins, viewpoint, scale and perspective!). Thus they stand firmly in the series of artists' impressions of Wharram that stretch back to Alan Sorrell's drawings of the 1970s (Sorrell 1981, 108-9), and will no doubt continue for decades to come as researchers construct new views of medieval Wharram.

This part of the volume ends with Chapter 22, which takes us back to the question that brought Maurice Beresford to Wharram in the first place: when was the village deserted? As with the earlier chapters devoted to documentary sources, few if any of the records cited in this volume were unknown to him. But having decided to write a history of Wharram, we have had the incentive to think very hard about the scarce sources of information that have survived, and to squeeze every scrap of information from them, as well as setting those scraps alongside the records of better documented neighbouring communities. It is for the reader to judge whether the effort, both in this and in the previous parts of the volume, has been worthwhile.

14 Lords and Manors from the 12th to the 15th Centuries

by Stuart Wrathmell, with contributions from Christopher Whittick

Tenancies in chief in the study area during the late 11th to 13th centuries

Chapter 12 was devoted to an attempt at constructing a broad tenurial context for Anglo-Scandinavian Wharram, in terms of the lordships which could be traced across the study area and more widely through the Vale of Pickering. It was argued that these lordships were under the jurisdiction of a Scandinavian kin group made up of the descendants of Thorbrandr the Hold. This kin group was dispossessed of its lands and rights during the four or five years that followed the suppression of the 1069 revolt, a rebellion that had numbered among its leaders four of Thorbrandr's grandsons, the sons of Karli. The present chapter outlines the subsequent history of the kin group's lands, as holdings of Norman tenants in chief (see Fig. 83), before focusing in on the fragmentary and confusing record of tenancies in Wharram Percy itself.

In the central part of the Vale of Pickering, including the soke of Buckton and the manor of Settrington, the lordships held by two of Karli's sons, Thorbrandr and Gamall, were handed over by the Conqueror to Berengar de Tosny, son of Robert de Tosny. It has been suggested that the transfer took place soon after 1073, following the killings at Settrington (Dalton 1994/2002, 54-8, 69 and map 11). Berengar was dead by c. 1115, evidently childless, as his lands then passed to his sister Albreda who had married Robert de L'Isle. Albreda also died childless, and Berengar's tenancy then passed to another sister Adelais and her husband Robert Bigod (Keats-Rohan 1999, 164; 2002, 43).

The Bigods' younger son Hugh, later earl of Norfolk, succeeded at the end of 1120 when still a minor, after the loss of his half-brother William, a member of the royal household, in the wreck of the White Ship (Keats-Rohan 2002, 175-6; Green 2006, 167). After the death without issue of the last Bigod earl of Norfolk in 1306, Settrington passed to his younger brother John, and it continued in the hands of his descendants until the mid-16th century, along with the dependent manor of Scagglethorpe (Moor 1935, 185-99, 201).

The other major element of what has been defined as Thorbrandr's inheritance was held in 1066 by Ormr son of Gamall. Its subsequent succession was interrupted by several forfeitures and re-grants, as its holders became caught up in the struggle for power among the sons of William the Conqueror. The tenancy in chief passed initially to Hugh Fitz Baldric, one of the men chosen by the Conqueror to restore order in Yorkshire in the aftermath of the 1069 rebellion; Hugh was sheriff between 1069 and about 1080 (Dalton 2002, 66, 102). The date at which Hugh replaced his antecessor is not known, but it may have been in the wake of the 1069 rebellion, even though Ormr is not recorded among its leading participants (pp 185-6).

Hugh was one of the tenants in chief who became involved in the rival claims to the throne of England after the death of William the Conqueror in 1087. William had quarrelled with his eldest son Robert Curthose, and though he had made him duke of Normandy, he gave the crown of England to his second son William Rufus (Green 2006, 21-8). This put his youngest son, Henry, subsequently king Henry I, in a difficult position, as it did the Norman barons who had estates in both Normandy and England. In 1088 a group of Normandy lords under the leadership of Odo of Bayeux aimed to put Robert on the throne of England; the rebellion was, however, unsuccessful. It seems that Hugh Fitz Baldric was an adherent to their cause, and thereby lost his Yorkshire estates (*EYC IX*, xii).

Hugh's estates were regranted to Robert Stuteville I (see *EYC IX*, 85); but he, too, subsequently forfeited these same lands in the struggle between Robert Curthose and Henry I, after the death of William Rufus (Green 2006, 42-4, 89-95). In 1106 Robert Stuteville I was involved in a failed attempt to entrap Henry I at Saint-Pierre, in Normandy, and then in September of the same year he was captured, along with his son Robert Stuteville II and Robert Curthose himself, by Henry I's army at the decisive battle of Tinchebray (Green 2006, 88-92). Robert Stuteville I and his son forfeited their estates as a consequence of their persistent support for Curthose (*EYC IX*, 116-17).

Henry I gave a large part of the Stuteville honour to Nigel d'Aubigny, one of his own key supporters , and it became part of the honour of Mowbray, passing to Nigel's son Roger Mowbray (Dalton 2002, 88-90; Green 2006, 100, 108; Greenway 1972, xvii-xviii). The date at which Nigel was given these lands is not known, but Henry I still retained at least some of them in the period 1109-14, when he gave the churches 'of three of my manors', Coxwold, Kirkby Moorside and Hovingham, to the bishop of Lincoln (Nigel d'Aubigny witnessing). The advowsons of the second two churches were the subject of a subsequent grant by Roger Mowbray (*EYC IX*, 85-6). Nigel had probably acquired the bulk of his lands in Yorkshire by c. 1118, but some of the old Stuteville lands were still retained by the king (Greenway 1972, xxiii-xxiv and 10, note to charter no. 3).

Orderic Vitalis records that at the end of November 1135 Henry I, on his death bed in the castle of Lyons-la-Forêt, and on the advice of the archbishop of Rouen, 'revoked all sentences of forfeiture pronounced on guilty men and allowed exiles to return and the disinherited to recover their ancestral inheritances' (*Orderic VI*, 449). It is not known whether the Stutevilles benefited specifically from this revocation, but in c.1135-40 a part of their fee was already back in the hands of Robert Stuteville III, son of Robert II, who confirmed a grant, made by his grandfather, after he had recovered his inheritance in England ('*postquam recuperavi*

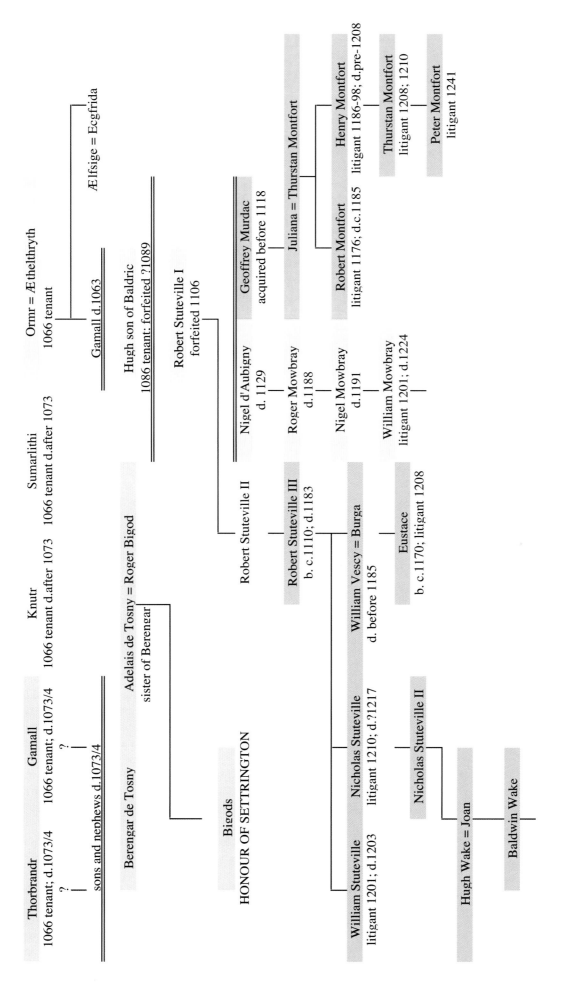

Fig. 83. The successors and rival claimants to the lands once held by the descendants of Thorbrandr the Hold.

223

hereditatem meam in Anglia': *EYC IX*, 86). He presumably regained Langton at the same time as it is not mentioned in his subsequent claims against the Mowbrays through which he attempted to regain the rest of his grandfather's estates (*EYC IX*, 5, n.5).

The Stutevilles continued to pursue their claims against the Mowbrays throughout the rest of the 12th century. In 1154-66, during Henry II's reign, a compromise between Roger Mowbray and Robert Stuteville III led to the former enfeoffing the latter with Kirkby Moorside and its appurtenances, to be held as a sub-infeudation of ten knights' fees. In the absence of royal confirmation, however, Robert III's son, William Stuteville, renewed his claim in the time of king John against William Mowbray, grandson of Roger (*EYC IX*, 116-19). In April 1200 king John gave notification that William Stuteville had made a fine of 3000 marks for confirmation of his charters, and for various other quittances and rights; and also for right ('*pro habendo recto*') in all the lands he claimed against William Mowbray, including Coxwold, Hovingham and Welburn (*EYC IX*, 114-5).

While the Stutevilles were attempting to recover further parts of their inheritance from the Mowbrays, the lands that they had already regained before 1140, including Langton, were themselves the subject of a dispute with another family, the Montforts. In 1208 Thurstan Montfort claimed a moiety of the vill of Langton against Eustace Vescy, son of Robert Stuteville III's daughter. Montfort's claim was based on his descent from Geoffrey Murdac '*qui inde fuit vestitus et saisitus*', through Juliana, Geoffrey's daughter, who had married the claimant's grandfather (see Fig. 83; *Curia Regis Rolls V*, 311; *EYC IX*, 66).

A claim for the other moiety was made by Thurstan against Nicholas Stuteville, younger son of Robert Stuteville III, and in 1210 Nicholas gave the king 300 marks and five palfreys to maintain his father's charter relating to certain lands claimed by Thurstan (*Curia Regis Rolls VI*, 40). The lands in question are specified in a Pipe Roll entry for 1208, when Thurstan was recorded as owing 50 marks for two writs, one against Nicholas for the restoration of a moiety of several vills including Langton (*EYC IX*, 66).

As Sir Charles Clay observed, these claims are most easily explained if, after Robert Stuteville I's forfeiture in 1106, a portion of his lands (including Langton) had been given by Henry I to Geoffrey Murdac, and if it was this portion that the Stutevilles recovered before 1140. This explanation is further supported by the record, in Robert Stuteville III's *carta* of 1166, that a tenant named Robert Murdac held of him a knight's fee of the old enfeoffment (that is, since before the death of Henry I: *Red Book I*, 429). Clay suggested that this fee included Kettleby Thorpe and Bigby, in Lincolnshire, and represents an enfeoffment of a younger branch of the Murdacs originally made by Geoffrey Murdac before its overlordship had passed to the Stutevilles as part of the initial restoration of their inheritance (*EYC IX*, 136). Kettleby Thorpe and Bigby had been in Geoffrey

Murdac's hands in 1115-18 (Keats-Rohan 1999, 84), and they had earlier been in the possession of Hugh Fitz Baldric (*EYC IX*, 65).

The claims of the Montforts were therefore in relation to lands which had been held in 1086 by Hugh Fitz Baldric, who himself had succeeded to the estates of his antecessor Ormr. The significance of this inference for the tenurial history of Wharram Percy will be considered in the next section of this chapter.

In this general survey of tenancies in chief in the study area we should, finally, mention those which had been held in 1086 by Robert, Count of Mortain (including Birdsall and Wharram le Street) and by the archbishop of York (the Weaverthorpe soke estate). Robert's tenancy passed to his son William in 1095 (Brian Golding, 'Robert, count of Mortain (*d.* 1095)', *Oxford Dictionary of National Biography* 2004), but the counts of Mortain were long-term supporters of Robert Curthose. William was said to have been jealous of his cousin Henry I, and it was outside the walls of his own castle, at Tinchebray, that he was captured along with the Stutevilles (Keats-Rohan 2002, 234; Green 2006, 50, 59, 63, 89-92). The Mortain estates were forfeited, but Henry did not bring in a new tenant in chief. Instead, a rung in the tenurial ladder was removed and the Fossards, who in 1086 had been tenants of Mortain, themselves became the tenants in chief of former Mortain estates including Birdsall and Wharram le Street (Dalton 2002, 91; *VCH ER VIII*, 15).

The Weaverthorpe soke manor, which had been held by the archbishop of York in 1086, came into the possession of the Fitz Herbert family through an enfeoffment, made between 1109 and 1112, by archbishop Thomas II to Herbert the chamberlain of Winchester, treasurer of Henry I (*EYC I*, 35-6). It has been argued that the grant was probably made to rescue the archbishop from financial problems, and to provide for Fitz Herbert's second son, William (later archbishop) who became treasurer of York minster at about this time (*VCH ER VIII*, 15).

Herbert's estates passed to his son, Herbert fitz Herbert, perhaps in 1129 or 1130 when the pipe roll records the younger Herbert paying a relief for his father's lands. Janet Burton has, however, suggested that Herbert the Chamberlain may have lost his lands much earlier, noting that there is no definite record of him after 1111, and that he could well have been the same person as 'H. the Chamberlain' whom Suger of St Denis named as the would-be assassin of Henry I in 1118, mutilated by Henry in punishment (Janet Burton, 'William of York (*d.* 1154)', *Oxford Dictionary of National Biography* 2004).

Tenancies at Wharram Percy in the 12th and 13th centuries

Introduction

As indicated in Chapter 12 (p. 188), the only record of tenancies in chief at Wharram Percy in 1086 is the single carucate held by Ketilbjorn of the king; and the Summary attributes this as well as the other eight carucates of

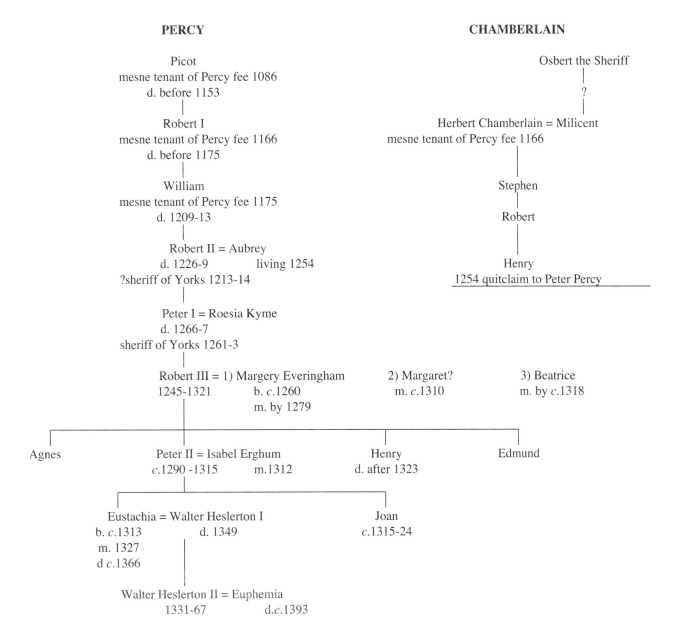

PERCY

Picot
mesne tenant of Percy fee 1086
d. before 1153
|
Robert I
mesne tenant of Percy fee 1166
d. before 1175
|
William
mesne tenant of Percy fee 1175
d. 1209-13
|
Robert II = Aubrey
d. 1226-9   living 1254
?sheriff of Yorks 1213-14
|
Peter I = Roesia Kyme
d. 1266-7
sheriff of Yorks 1261-3
|
Robert III = 1) Margery Everingham   2) Margaret?   3) Beatrice
1245-1321   b. *c.*1260   m. *c.*1310   m. by *c.*1318
                 m. by 1279

Agnes   Peter II = Isabel Erghum   Henry   Edmund
             *c.*1290 -1315   m.1312   d. after 1323

        Eustachia = Walter Heslerton I   Joan
        b. *c.*1313   d. 1349   *c.*1315-24
        m. 1327
        d *c.*1366

        Walter Heslerton II = Euphemia
        1331-67   d.*c.*1393

CHAMBERLAIN

Osbert the Sheriff
|
?
|
Herbert Chamberlain = Milicent
mesne tenant of Percy fee 1166
|
Stephen
|
Robert
|
Henry
1254 quitclaim to Peter Percy

Fig. 84. The Percys of Bolton Percy and the Chamberlains (from *EYC XI* and other sources cited in the text).

Wharram Percy to the king himself. Otherwise the earliest post-Conquest records of families with a tenurial interest in Wharram date to the later 12th and 13th centuries, and the families in question are Percy, Chamberlain and Montfort (Figs 83 and 84).

To avoid confusion, it is necessary to establish at the outset that this chapter contains references to two separate (though probably related) families that made use of the surname 'Percy'. One of them, the senior line, was descended from William Percy, a principal tenant in chief of William the Conqueror in Yorkshire, chosen by him, along with Hugh Fitz Baldric, to restore Norman authority there after the rebellion of 1069 (Dalton 2002, 66). Two of his extensive estates in the county were centred on Topcliffe in the North Riding and Spofforth in the West Riding; both contain castles that were probably established by him (Dalton 2002, 38-9 and map 3).

Hereafter, the family is distinguished as the Percys of Spofforth.

The other family with this surname descended from Picot, a Domesday tenant of William Percy of Spofforth (*EYC XI*, 105). Their holdings, which seem to have been built up over a number of years, included several widely scattered estates in Yorkshire held as mesne tenancies from the Percys of Spofforth – among them Bolton Percy, Carnaby, Ilkley and Sutton upon Derwent (Fig. 85; *EYC XI*, 104). The family is distinguished here as the Percys of Bolton Percy (Fig. 84). They also had tenurial interests in Wharram Percy, interests which are difficult to pin down until the mid-13th century, when they achieved an undisputed tenancy in chief of the whole of Wharram (with no mesne tenants). It was probably this acquisition that led to Wharram's name change: the disuse of the earlier prefixes 'Lesser', 'West' or 'South' (deployed in

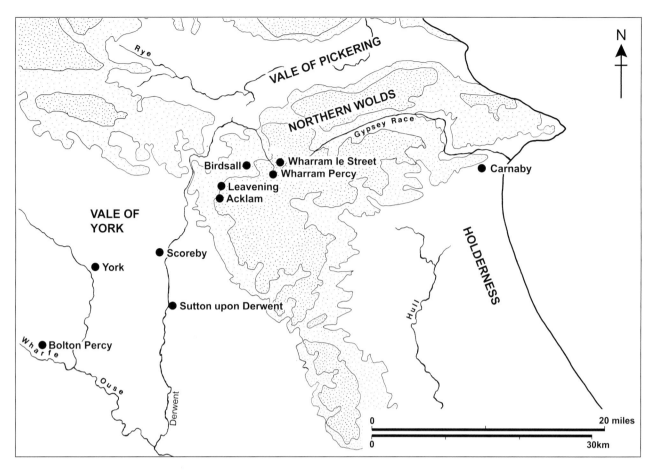

Fig. 85. Manors and lands in eastern Yorkshire held by the Chamberlains and by the Percys of Bolton Percy, and other places mentioned in Chapter 14. (C. Philo and E. Marlow-Mann)

contrast with the other Wharram's prefixes of 'Greater', 'East and 'North'), and their replacement by the suffix 'Percy'.

The Montforts (Fig. 83)

We have already met the Montforts through their dispute with the Stutevilles over the manor of Langton (Fig. 83). The earliest reference to their interest in Wharram is in the pipe roll for 1176-7, where William Percy (of Bolton Percy) is recorded as owing 100 marks for having his right of the land of Wharram against Robert Montfort: '*pro habendo recto de terra de Wharham*' (*Pipe Roll Soc*, 26 (1905), 78). In 1186 Robert's name was superseded by that of Henry Montfort and payments began; they were completed in 1198 (*Pipe Roll Soc*, NS 9 (1932), 28). There is no doubt that Henry was the younger brother of Robert, and father of Thurstan Montfort who prosecuted the claims against the Stutevilles.

There are two other references to Henry Montfort's interest in Wharram Percy, both derived from a charter he issued in favour of Meaux Abbey, a Cistercian community in Holderness which held a grange in Wharram le Street, on its boundary with Wharram Percy. The references occur in the writings of Thomas Burton, who compiled a chronicle of Meaux and became its 19th abbot in 1396. Burton extracted passages from charters in the Abbey's muniments, and then converted these extracts

into narrative texts, assembled in chronological order. The extracts survive as well as the more abbreviated narratives in the Chronicle, and they were discussed at length in an earlier volume (Wrathmell 2005a, 2-6). The Montfort charter relates to rights in a watercourse – the Beck – which ran northwards from the village site at Wharram Percy, and which towards the northern end of the township then formed the boundary between the vills of Wharram Percy and Wharram le Street (see Fig. 86; the course of the boundary had been modified by the mid-19th century).

The Meaux grange had been established by a donation made in the years 1150-60 by the tenant in chief of Wharram le Street, William Fossard. His grant included the site of the grange, around a spring called *halykeld* on the western boundary of Wharram le Street, and the adjoining watercourse for the purpose of erecting a mill. It appears, however, that the monks were unable to build a mill on the watercourse on the basis of this grant, because the bed of the stream belonged to Lesser Wharram and its lord, not to Greater Wharram and its lord William Fossard.

The monks therefore sought an alternative solution, building a mill within the grange precincts and diverting water from the Beck to run it. At some point they received a grant from Henry Montfort of the watercourse that descends from Lesser Wharram below the mills (of

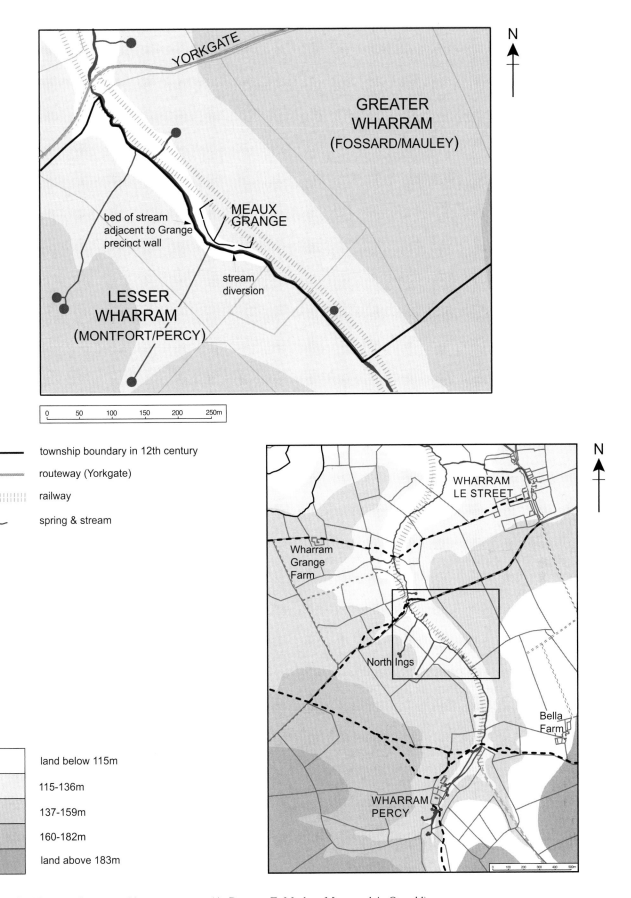

N

YORKGATE

GREATER
WHARRAM
(FOSSARD/MAULEY)

bed of stream
adjacent to Grange
precinct wall

MEAUX
GRANGE

stream
diversion

LESSER
WHARRAM
(MONTFORT/PERCY)

| 0 | 50 | 100 | 150 | 200 | 250m |

township boundary in 12th century

routeway (Yorkgate)

railway

spring & stream

land below 115m

115-136m

137-159m

160-182m

land above 183m

N

WHARRAM
LE STREET

Wharram
Grange
Farm

North Ings

Bella
Farm

WHARRAM
PERCY

Fig. 86. Wharram Grange and its watercourse. (A. Deegan, E. Marlow-Mann and A. Oswald)

227

Wharram Percy), together with the right to make a three-foot dam to divert the stream from its former channel through the middle court of the grange to the monks' mill. All this is evident from the Meaux Chronicle. The grant may date to the late 12th century or the early years of the 13th (if the completion of payments recorded in the Pipe Roll did not signify resolution of the Percy-Montfort dispute: cf Wrathmell 2005a, 6). It probably in any case predates 1208, when Henry's son Thurstan was in dispute with the Stutevilles over Langton (implying that Henry was dead by then).

Burton's lengthier extract of Henry's charter contains details that he omitted from the Chronicle, including the statement that a certain 'W de F' held the watercourse and the Wharram Percy mills from Henry. The identity of 'W de F' was considered at length in Wrathmell 2005a (p. 6), and no conclusion was reached. In the context of the dispute evident from the Pipe Roll entries, however, it is hard to escape the conclusion that the letter 'F' was written in error, and should have been 'P', to give W[illiam] de P[ercy]. It is a plausible error given that Burton was writing about William Fossard in the previous entry relating to the water mills.

Such a reading would supply a context for Henry Montfort's grant, in that it provided an opportunity for him to assert his overlordship of William Percy. It would also account for the persistent opposition to the diversion shown subsequently by Robert Percy: he 'claimed our watercourse', Burton says, and on account of this would frequently divert it (presumably by destroying the dam to allow the water to resume its original course) to the detriment of the brethren.

This Robert will have been Robert Percy II, son of the William who had paid 100 marks to have his right against Henry and who died in the period 1209-13 (see *EYC XI*, 106). Some of the interpretations here differ slightly from those given in Wrathmell 2005a (p. 6), including the identification of the destroyer of dams as Robert Percy II rather than Robert III. In 1269-70, however, it was indeed Robert Percy III, son of 'lord Percy' (Peter Percy I: see Fig. 84), who renounced any claim he or his antecessors had in the watercourse in favour of the monks, and in addition gave them a six-feet wide strip of land alongside the grange wall. This strip of land was presumably the original bed of the stream, granted to the monks to ensure that no future lord could re-channel the stream along its earlier course (Wrathmell 2005a, 5-6). By now the Percys had an undisputed tenancy in chief and so could afford to concede this right to the monks.

The key question here, and one that cannot be answered adequately in terms of direct evidence, is how the two parties to the dispute had acquired their competing interests in Wharram – or, indeed, what precisely those interests were. With respect to the Montforts, it is tempting to see this dispute in the context of their claims against the Stutevilles, and therefore based on the earlier seisin of Geoffrey Murdac. The problem is that Wharram was not, in 1086, recorded as part of Hugh Fitz Baldric's holdings; nor was it later part of the tenancy

in chief restored to the Stutevilles. Yet the Montforts' claim to both Langton and Wharram Percy, and the links, on the eve of the Conquest, between other vills in Wharram Percy parish and the soke centre of Langton, hint strongly at some earlier tenurial relationship.

The Chamberlains (Fig. 84)

The Chamberlain family was descended from Herbert, the chamberlain of the king of Scotland (not to be confused with Herbert, the chamberlain and treasurer of the king of England who had been enfeoffed with the Weaverthorpe estate: *EYC XI*, 214-5). Their interest in Wharram Percy is first specified in the feudal assessment of 1242-3, when Henry Chamberlain was recorded as holding, of the king in chief, a quarter of a knight's fee there, in addition to a knight's fee in Acklam and Leavening (*Book of Fees II*, 1200). There are no earlier records specifically linking the Chamberlains to Wharram, but such a link was adduced by Farrer from the *carta* of 1166 returned by Stephen son of Herbert Chamberlain. Stephen acknowledged that he held one knight's fee in chief, with which he had enfeoffed William Scures and others before the death of Henry I, and that he retained in demesne one carucate of land and six tenements or messuages (*masure*) over and above the aforesaid knight's service, which he owed to the king:

'*Remanet autem in dominio meo j carucata terre et vj masure super predictum servitium militis quod vobis debeo*' (*Red Book I*, 421)

Farrer identified the knight's fee as the Chamberlain holdings in Acklam and Leavening: in 1170-85 Stephen confirmed various grants of property in Acklam which had been made by the Scures family to Bridlington priory (*EYC II*, 169-70). If this is correct, then as Farrer also suggested, the single caurcate and the six *masure* were presumably located at Wharram Percy. They may be the reason why, in later centuries, the fee was sometimes assessed at six carucates (e.g. in 1302-3: *EYC XI*, 110: see Roffe 2000a, 3).

The fee of Stephen son of Herbert Chamberlain was therefore made up of lands which had been held at Domesday by the king's thegns, all in the hundred of Acklam. Though the vills of Acklam and Leavening lie to the west of the study area, they are close to Wharram Percy, separated from it only by the vill of Birdsall (see Fig. 74). The tenancy was presumably created by either William II or Henry I, as the Scures family had been enfeoffed in their lands by the antecessors of Stephen Chamberlain before Henry I's death.

In 1166 Stephen held, in addition to his tenancy in chief, two fees from William Percy of Spofforth (*Red Book I*, 425), and it is from records relating to this mesne tenancy as well as the lands held in chief that the early history of the family has been unravelled. Stephen's father Herbert was chamberlain of the king of Scotland, and his mother Milicent was granddaughter of Osbert the sheriff of Lincoln and York. Osbert had been enfeoffed by William Percy I with lands in Yorkshire and Lincolnshire, including Wickenby (*EYC XI*, 213-17), and Stephen was named as 'Stephen of Wickenby chamberlain' or 'Stephen chamberlain of Wickenby' in several charters dating to the period *c*.1175-84 (*EYC XI*, 219-20).

Osbert himself had been a priest, described as a most renowned priest; he was made sheriff of both Lincoln and York by Henry I, and he had acquired many lands from the earls and barons of England because of his service, and because he was a member of the royal household (Bond 1866, 85; Dalton 2002, 103-4). It seems probable, therefore, that a group of neighbouring holdings, attributed to the king's thegns in 1086, was granted by Henry I in the early years of the 12th century to Osbert the priest as a tenancy in chief, and that this was the origin of the Chamberlain fee of Wharram Percy.

The Chamberlain interest in Wharram seems to have been maintained until the mid-13th century, when it was sold to the Percys of Bolton Percy. As noted earlier, Henry Chamberlain, grandson of Stephen Chamberlain of Wickenby (*EYC XI*, 215), was recorded as holding a quarter knight's fee at Wharram in 1242-3. In 1254, however, he quitclaimed any rights he had, in demesne or in service, in all 8½ carucates in West Wharram in favour of Peter Percy I, in return for 40 marks (*Yorkshire Fines, 1246-72*, 98-9). A half carucate had been lost since the Domesday record: its fate is unknown.

In the second half of the 12th century the main residence of Stephen Chamberlain seems to have been at Wickenby in Lincolnshire, judging by the charters in which he refers to himself as 'Stephen of Wickenby' (see above). In 1175-84 he granted his whole demesne at Wickenby to Kirkstead abbey, excepting the ground of his house and specified pastures and woodland (*EYC XI*, 220). When his grandson Henry died in 1256 he was said to have held a capital messuage in Wickenby of Henry Percy (*EYC XI*, 218). Given that the Chamberlains' antecessors had apparently subinfeudated their other Yorkshire lands by the end of 1135, the vill that became Wharram Percy is the most likely location of any residence that the Chamberlains may have maintained in Yorkshire – if, of course, they had one.

Percys of Bolton Percy (Fig. 84)
As noted above, the Percys of Bolton Percy, descendants of Picot, were tenants of the Percys of Spofforth. Paul Dalton has noted that Picot's high status is indicated by the fact that he witnessed three of the surviving seven charters issued by his overlord Alan Percy, and that his name appears immediately after those of Alan's brothers, and before that of his steward (Dalton 2002, 126). They may even have represented a junior branch of the family, though a relationship has not been established from documentary sources. Their granting of a 'remainder' interest in Wharram to the Spofforth Percys at the time the tenancy in chief was entailed (see below) suggests that by then they at least thought they were related.

In 1166 Picot's son, Robert, was listed as holding three knights' fees of the old enfeoffment from William Percy (of Spofforth: *Red Book I*, 424). As noted earlier in this chapter,

William's *carta* also lists Stephen Chamberlain as tenant of two knights' fees of the old enfeoffment (*Red Book I*, 425). Of the Percy of Spofforth tenants in 1166, only five were descended from tenants of the William Percy who had been tenant in chief in 1086, and both the Percys of Bolton Percy and the Chamberlains were among them. It seems, therefore, that these families had been closely associated for the previous 80 years (Dalton 2002, 252).

Robert Percy of Bolton Percy had been succeeded before 1175 by his son William, who was described as William Percy of Carnaby in charters of 1191-1203, 1199 and 1209 (*EYC XI*, 107-8). It was he who disputed a tenancy at Wharram with the brothers Robert and Henry Montfort. The form of this interest, whether a tenancy in chief or a mesne tenancy, has not been determined. No tenancy in chief other than that of the Chamberlains can be found in the *Cartae Baronum* or in the *Testa de Nevill*. On the other hand, there is equally no clear evidence that the Percys of Bolton Percy had a mesne tenancy there, whether held from the Chamberlains or from some other family. David Roffe has suggested that part of the Percy interest was a mesne tenancy of the Chamberlains, part a holding that was independent of the Chamberlain fee (Roffe 2000a, 3).

Records of the 14th century, when the Percys of Bolton Percy held the tenancy in chief of the whole of Wharram Percy, provide conflicting evidence as to the type of tenure by which it was held: some records claim that Wharram Percy was held by knight service, others that it was a grand serjeanty – another military tenure, but one distinct from knight service. It is possible that the source of this confusion was the earlier existence of two tenancies in chief, and that William Percy and the Montforts had been in dispute over a grand serjeanty. An inquisition *ad quod damnum* in 1312 provides detail of the services supplied in return for the serjeanty. It involved providing one crossbowman at York Castle in time of war, for 40 days at the beginning of the war at the cost of those who held the manor and advowson, and afterwards at the king's expense for the whole duration of the war (TNA PRO C143/87/8).

By 1212 William had been succeeded by his son Robert II, who was probably the Robert Percy who served as sheriff of Yorkshire in 1213-14. In 1218-19 his house in York is mentioned as the location of an accidental death: William Aguillon, whose family held lands in Kirby Grindalythe (see Ch. 17, pp 296-7 below), killed Adam Moncell with a sword while they were playing ('*sicut ludebant*': Stenton 1937, 297). He was himself dead by 1229, and was succeeded by his son Peter Percy I, also a sheriff of Yorkshire for the years 1261-3 (*EYC XI*, 108-10). Peter's mother Aubrey survived her husband for at least a quarter of a century, and her dower interest was recorded in the Chamberlain quitclaim of 1254. Peter seems to have been the lord who decided to focus the family's attention on Wharram: in 1251 he obtained a grant of free warren in Wharram as well as in Carnaby and Ilkley, and this was perhaps followed by the creation of Wharram's park, recorded in a quitclaim of 1320

(Bodleian Library, Dodsworth 76, f.162r). In 1254, with Henry Chamberlain's quitclaim, Peter became sole possessor of the vill. When he died in 1267, to be succeeded by his son Robert Percy III, he was said to have held a quarter of a knight's fee there of the king, and the advowson of the church (*Cal IPM I*, 205, no. 653).

Robert Percy III entailed his lands on his son Peter Percy II, as detailed below. Peter, however, died before his father, and his inquisition *post mortem* records that he had demised a life interest in Wharram to Robert, as well as providing him with an annuity of £80 out of the much more valuable manor of Carnaby (*Cal IPM VI*, 82). It is probable, therefore, that it was father Robert who from time to time based himself and his household at Wharram, to which the name 'Percy' had now come to be attached (Smith 1937, 134). It would, though, be wrong to assume that Wharram was necessarily his only or even main residence: in 1300 Robert was living at Sutton on Derwent when he gave testimony in a proof of age inquisition (*Yorks Inq, IV*, YASRS 37 (1906), 2), and in 1312 he was described as Sir Robert Percy of Carnaby (TNA PRO E210/8364). His son Peter was perhaps based in the manorial *curia* at Carnaby, which seems to have been the long-term principal residence of the family, given the references in the early 13th century to Peter's great, great grandfather as William Percy of Carnaby (see above). It is likely that Wharram ceased to be a Percy residence after Robert's death, when the estate passed to other families through marriage.

There remains the question as to why Peter Percy I and Robert Percy III decided to develop Wharram as a residence with a hunting grounds and park attached. Its manorial revenues were evidently far smaller than those generated by Carnaby: during the 14th century the manor seems usually to have been valued at about £20 (e.g. *Cal IPM XII*, 182, though the church was worth far more: see below); moreover its area of emparked pasture and woodland was very limited (it was recorded as four acres of wood and four acres of pasture by an inquisition *ad quod damnum* of March 1321: TNA PRO C143/144). It may be that its attraction was simply its status: it was a tenancy in chief rather than a mesne tenancy – and in particular, a tenancy in chief rather than a mesne tenancy held (like Carnaby) from his kinsmen the Percys of Spofforth. This is, however, pure speculation.

The manorial topography of Wharram Percy and expressions of seisin

The tenurial interests in Wharram Percy, and their descent during the 12th and 13th centuries, have been explored in depth not because they will be of particular concern to most readers, but because they provide our only historical context for the developments which have been traced in the archaeology and architecture of its manorial homesteads. This section of the chapter attempts to tie together the historical, topographical and archaeological evidence; and whilst the results may not differ greatly from some of the suggestions put forward over thirty years ago (*Wharram I*), they are at least founded on a more substantial analysis.

The previous section of this chapter attempted to identify, on the basis of documentary evidence, the periods when the Chamberlains and the Percys might have had residences in the village. Archaeological evidence, from both earthwork survey and excavation, has so far revealed two manorial homesteads, called in previous reports the North and the South Manors. Of the two, it is the North Manor that is sited, presumably intentionally, in a location where it commands views across most of the village area, and where it could therefore be seen from most of the village area. Its siting would also, of course, have facilitated direct access to the park and hunting grounds if these were (as previously assumed) to the north of the village (see Rahtz and Watts 2004, 4).

The North Manor's 'dominant' siting at Wharram is, however, far less dominant than that of another manorial *curia* in the study area: the one that belonged to the archbishops of York and their successors, the Fitz Herberts. At Weaverthorpe, the *curia* is positioned to have long-distance views westwards, over the line of vills along Cranedale which were all part of the Weaverthorpe estate (see Plate 19). Eastwards there are no long-distance views because of the bends in the valley; but eastwards, the lords of Weaverthorpe had no lands.

It would be easy enough to see the location of the Weaverthorpe *curia*, and to a lesser extent that of the North Manor at Wharram Percy, as an expression of lordly dominance over the servile peasantry. But there is, in fact, no reason to suppose that the Norman lords would have felt any need to express their dominance over their serfs. That is modern thinking. What mattered to Norman and later lords was 'seisin' of their estates, a concept that does not quite equate to the modern term 'possession', but was close to it at least in the 12th century. A.W.B. Simpson said of this period that 'the person seised of land was simply the person in obvious occupation, the person "sitting" on the land' (Simpson 1961, 37). The visible expression of seisin was probably an important determinant in the location of manorial homesteads, though it is a factor that has received little attention from archaeologists.

The emphasis on obvious occupation meant that if the lands of a feudal tenant were taken over by a rival claimant to them – if the tenant were 'disseised' by another – the disseisor thereby gained some sort of title to the land in question, good against all but the person disseised. It was then a matter of determining whether the disseised or the disseisor had the better title, and this was often achieved with reference to the seisin held by the claimants' ancestors: which of them could bring forward an ancestor who could be shown to have had seisin earlier than the other's ancestor (Simpson 1961, 35-6). In general, the earliest seisin provided the best title. This is why the Montforts had to demonstrate their descent from Geoffrey Murdac to support their claim to Langton (and probably also to Wharram).

Plate 19. Weaverthorpe soke estate, looking westwards along the Great Wold valley from Weaverthorpe *curia*. (S. Wrathmell)

These two elements – obvious occupation, and seisin derived from a remote ancestor or antecessor – were in some circumstances combined. Thus the continued occupation of a pre-Conquest manor or burh in the period of Norman settlement was intended to represent 'continuity' in a very specific, tenurial sense: the outward sign of a tenant in chief's rightful succession to the lands of his antecessor. It is a concept that has been explored by Robert Liddiard in relation to the siting of Norman castles on the residences of pre-Conquest antecessors (Liddiard 2005, 26-38). Of course the castle not only represented, in its siting, an opportunity to emphasise seisin based on rightful succession in a tangible way; it was also a visually impressive and tangible sign of the conceptual idea of seisin. Moreover, it provided protection against disseisin, particularly during times of weak royal control, as in the reign of Stephen.

A more local example of disseisin occurred at the end of the 12th century. Robert Turneham, who had married Joan, daughter and heir of William Fossard and became the lord of Wharram le Street on William's death, ejected the monks from Wharram Grange and removed all their domestic and ancillary buildings, including the mill, the bakehouse and barn, and carried them away to Birdsall. There, he used the building materials to construct his own houses (Bond 1866, 291). The large timbers, at least,

would no doubt have been valuable enough to warrant reuse elsewhere, whatever other considerations were in play; but in this case, the removal of these buildings from the grange site would have been a useful means of eradicating the visual signs of former monastic seisin.

Seisin applied not only to tenants of land (to those at the bottom of the feudal ladder, who were seised in demesne), but also to tenants in chief and mesne lords whose interests were based on the exaction of services from the tenants whom they had enfeoffed: they were 'seised in service' (Hudson 2004 Reprint, 7). This time, the key concept was not visible occupation, but the visible exercise of rights (Simpson 1961, 45), and it is again one that can be exemplified at Wharram. When Henry Montfort granted the watercourse to Meaux Abbey, noting that '*W de F*' was his tenant, he was exercising his rights as overlord of '*W de F*', and thereby reinforcing his claim to that overlordship.

In the light of these comments we can now return to the issue of the North Manor's location and date of foundation. The architectural evidence for its buildings is currently limited to a single block of stone with mouldings dating it to the second half of the 13th century (Clark and Gaunt 2004, 228). Even without this, however, the positioning of the North Manor *curia* is most readily construed as a wish to express seisin of the whole vill,

231

especially when seen by outsiders using the routeways into and through the village. This is true both for the main east-west through route, passing immediately in front of the gates into the *curia* (the view of this routeway eastwards *from* the manorial site is shown in Plate 9, above), and for the route leading into the village from the south – the one that would have been taken by the lords of Raisthorpe and Thixendale when they came to attend the parish church. Such an expression would have been appropriate after the Percy acquisition of the tenancy in chief of the whole of Wharram, but not, perhaps, before. The probable layout of the manorial buildings, in terms of the earthwork evidence, has been discussed in depth in Chapter 3.

As for the South Manor, its position and layout specifically express seisin of the block of tofts known as the West Row (North) (see pp 37-8), rather than of the village as a whole. It is tempting, therefore, to see it as the Chamberlain holding with its six tenements or *masure*. Its date of abandonment, in the mid-13th century (Milne 1979a, 33), would support this identification. On the other hand, the date of its erection, in the later 12th century (p. 264 below and Thorn 1979, 60), coincides with the dispute between the Percys and the Montforts, and this might be seen as an alternative context. For it is entirely possible, as argued by Everson and Stocker (pp 362-3 below), that soon after 1166 the Chamberlains had subinfeudated their holding to the Percys, and that the erection of the South Manor was an expression of the Percys' seisin in demesne, at a time when their claims were under attack from the Montforts. It also has a far closer visual relationship with St Martin's church than does the North Manor, which is in keeping with the

phasing of new works at the church. The extensive remodelling of the church in the third quarter of the 12th century coincides with the erection of the undercroft and chamber/hall block in the South Manor, but there is no sign of significant work on the church fabric in the second half of the 13th or early 14th century (see pp 246-254 below and Fig. 87).

Though this is not the place for a long digression on the archaeological and architectural evidence relating to the South Manor, which is discussed further in Chapter 16, there are a couple of points that should be made in relation to previous interpretations. In the first place, there must be some doubt as to the form and layout of its buildings. The only *in situ* structural remains were those of the semi-subterranean undercroft and the chamber (or hall) that it supported. It has usually been argued that there must have been a large ground-floor hall attached to its south side, and that all traces of such a hall would have been obliterated by the subsequent quarrying in this area. A speculative illustration of such a hall was published in 1990 with, outside its north-east corner, a ramp running down from ground level to the undercroft entrance (Beresford and Hurst 1990, colour plate 9). The overall effect seems rather odd.

When the area outside the undercroft entrance was excavated, there was no sign of any ramp; indeed, as far as could be established (given the quarrying disturbance), the chalk further south had been cut away to form a surface at the same level as that of the undercroft floor (see Plates 20-22). This certainly seems to have been the view held by the excavators at the time of these investigations. In 1956 three depressions south of the

Plate 20. The South Manor undercroft from the south-east. (Wharram Site Archive)

Plate 21. The South Manor undercroft from the north-west. (Wharram Site Archive)

Plate 22. The South Manor undercroft entrance from the south. (Wharram Site Archive)

undercroft were investigated: 'The central one appears to be a form of entrance to the cellar of the manor either from another room or an open courtyard on the same level as the base of the cellar' (*Interim Report* 4 (1956), 2). A further report says:

'In 1957 it was found that the undercroft of the 12th century manor house was entered at its south-west [*recte*: south-east] corner from a courtyard at the same low level, six feet down. This courtyard was excavated in 1958 in an attempt to find how large it was and how it was entered from ground level. The search was frustrated by the fact that during the 13th century two quarries, each about six feet across and fifteen feet deep had been dug into the chalk. It is hard to see why these quarries were dug in this position at that time because the manor house was apparently still standing. After the quarries had been dug, and filled into the level of the courtyard, a revetment wall was built to hold up the chalk on either side.'
(*Interim Report* 6 (1958), 1)

This interpretation was somewhat modified during later investigations of these quarries: 'They seem to lie in groups with at least one balk of undisturbed chalk coming to the surface in each group; within each group the quarries seem to be dug individually with narrow ridges dividing quarry from quarry and the depth of these ridges from the surface is very varied' (*Interim Report* 7 (1959), 1), and by the time of the first definitive report the ramp had made an appearance:

'Outside the cellar were two walls which revetted the natural chalk of the hillside and flanked the ramped passage-way down to the cellar entrance... Later quarrying had destroyed the southern end of this passage-way.'
(Milne 1979a, 31 and fig. 5)

If, on the other hand, more areas to the south of the undercroft had been cut down to the same level, there may have been a group of buildings with rock-cut basements, rather like the ones at Spofforth Castle (which was, of course, one of the principal residences of the senior line of the Percy family). This is, inevitably, only one of a number of possibilities. An alternative layout of *camera* block and hall is suggested by Stocker and Everson in Chapter 16 (pp 264-5).

The second point relates to the quarries themselves: who dug them, and why. In 1959 it was admitted that they were not really understood: 'The purpose of the quarries has been a great puzzle, for the buildings which are known in this medieval village would hardly have needed all this volume of chalk in so short a time: all the quarries except one date within about 50 years [on the evidence of pottery in their backfills] (*Interim Report* 7 (1959), 1). In the first definitive report they were linked, in terms of their dating, to the demolition of the manor house:

'Sandstone fragments in the filling of the quarries suggest that they were open at the same time as, or soon after, the dismantling of [the undercroft building]. Furthermore, all but one of the quarries contained similar groups of pottery belonging to the second half of the 13th

century... They were probably worked and filled within a very short period, perhaps a year or so, as little weathering was observed on their faces' (Milne 1979a, 35). The discussion continues with regard to the purpose of the quarrying, and two of the suggestions relate to the extraction of building materials, and lime-burning (a possible lime kiln was discovered) to make mortar. 'As demand for the latter at Wharram would have been limited to buildings other than those belonging to peasants the quarries would have had to be linked to an important phase of stone building elsewhere in the village' (Milne 1979a, 35)

These conclusions lead almost inevitably to the suggestion that the quarrying on this site was carried out by those engaged in erecting a new group of manorial buildings, in the area we call the North Manor, soon after the Percys acquired total control of Wharram through purchase of the Chamberlain interest. The buildings on the old manor site were dismantled and removed, and the chalk for wall cores and mortar was quarried from the floors of the old buildings, obviating the need to clear overburden from another part of the village area. Such a strategy would also (to return to an earlier theme) remove from the landscape the visual evidence of seisin that the South Manor buildings had expressed, and the sense of more than one manorial interest.

The Percy family and Wharram from the end of the 13th century

Family disasters: the descent of the manor

We have seen that by the late 13th century, the Percys of Bolton Percy had secured the whole of West Wharram as an unchallenged tenancy in chief. A new or remodelled manorial *curia* had been established, and a manor house of architectural pretension had been built. The next step was to settle the descent of Wharram through succeeding generations of the family, and Robert Percy III sought to do this by entailing the manor on his son Peter II and Peter's heirs, thereby limiting the inheritance to Peter's lineal descendants. At the same time Robert himself took a life interest and so would remain seised of Wharram until his death. Should Peter's line fail, Robert assigned the remainder interest to his kinsman Henry Percy of Spofforth: Henry and his descendants would become lords of the manor.

Robert Percy III's first known actions in relation to the settlement of his estate are summarised in the records resulting from an inquisition held much later, in February 1368. About 70 years before the inquisition (in *c*.1298), Robert Percy had given the manor of Wharram and the advowson of the church to Adam fitz William and Bertram Doughty, chaplains, and they had subsequently enfeoffed Robert for the term of his life, with successive remainders to Peter Percy his son, and the heirs of his body, and to Henry Percy of Spofforth (*Cal IPM XII*, 182, no. 202). There is nothing to indicate what triggered this move, but Robert would have been over fifty years old by then (see Fig. 84), and the appointment of trustees may suggest that Peter was still a minor. Our understanding is not helped by a contradictory record of events in the Court of Common Pleas, in 1371, which places the grant to Adam fitz William and Bertram Doughty in the reign of Edward II (after 1307: TNA PRO CP40/444, m.174).

By early 1312 Peter had reached majority, and on 19 February in that year Robert settled Carnaby, Wharram with the advowson of the church, Sutton upon Derwent and other lands on Peter and Peter's heirs (TNA PRO E210/8364). On 13 March in the same year, Peter granted to his father in return a life estate in the same lands (TNA PRO E210/8308). Robert may have felt that the family's future was now secured. If so he was mistaken, for some three-and-a half years later Peter died, and the escheator, acting on behalf of Robert's overlord, the king, removed Robert from the manor. The reason for the ejection is clear: whilst Robert had, in March 1312, obtained licence from the king to grant in fee to Peter the manor and advowson on payment of a fine of 20 marks (*Cal PR 1307-13*, 436), a separate licence had not been obtained for Peter to convey a life interest to his father. Robert complained to the king about his ejection, and the king issued a writ which resulted in an inquisition (*Cal IPM V*, 390, no. 609). Matters were settled in February 1316, when the king ordered the escheator to deliver to Robert:

'the manor of Wharram, co. York, and the advowson of the church thereof, with the issues received, the king, for a fine of 100s [£5], having pardoned the said Robert his trespass in acquiring for life the said manor and advowson of Peter de Percy, who held the same in chief, and in entering therein without licence'
(*Cal Fine Rolls II*, 272)

The early death of Peter Percy II was clearly a disaster for the family. Peter had married Isabel Erghum in 1312 (Fig. 84), and she had produced two daughters: Eustachia, who was no more than two or three years old at her father's death, and Joan, who was probably only a few months old. The escheator no doubt saw an opportunity for imposing wardship. If a tenant died leaving an heir who was still a minor, his lord (in this instance the king) had right to wardship of the heir, the right to sell his marriage and to custody of the lands until the heir attained majority. The overlord did not have to account for the profits of the land: 'wardships were bought and sold as investments and were the most lucrative of the incidents of tenure' (Simpson 1961, 18); hence the challenge to Robert's life tenancy. In the event, Robert regularised his position by payment of a fine, and wardship was delayed until Robert himself died.

Robert Percy III died in 1321, aged about 76, when Eustachia was still under ten years of age (*Cal IPM VI*, 237). Robert's inquisition *post mortem* was held at York in June 1323, and in the following month the king committed the keeping of the manor of Wharram into the hands of Geoffrey Scrope, in return for Scrope paying 10 marks a year into the Exchequer (*Cal Fine Rolls III*, 230). This sum represented nearly a third of Wharram's annual revenue, excluding the church, and Scrope would have pocketed the other two-thirds. With wardship went the right to sell the marriage of the ward, and in the case of both knight's service and grand sergeanty, the lord had custody of a female heir's lands until she reached sixteen years of age if unmarried, or fourteen years if married (Simpson 1961, 18).

Although there are some contradictions in her recorded age, Eustachia would have reached fourteen years in about 1327, and it was probably in that year that Scrope sold her marriage to Walter Heslerton I, taking a final profit from the wardship. They were certainly married by 8 July 1328, when Scrope made a quitclaim in their favour regarding his right in the manor of Sutton upon Derwent (TNA PRO E210/7170). The deed was enrolled on the plea roll of the court of the king's bench (TNA PRO KB27/237 m. 106d); Scrope was the chief justice of the court. After the marriage, Walter claimed custody of her Wharram lands from the king, as she was of full age: the writ for a proof of her age, dating to 1 Edward III (January 1327 - January 1328) survives, but not the inquest (TNA PRO C135/9/11; *Cal IPM 8* 705). Scrope was ordered to be present to show why, if she were of full age, her inheritance should not be delivered to her (and Walter); he, of course, failed to contest the claim.

In 1331 Eustachia gave birth to a son, Walter Heslerton II. Once again fate intervened: Eustachia's husband died of the Black Death in 1349, when their son was still a minor, aged 17. A further round of minority wardship was avoided because Wharram was Eustachia's inheritance, not his. An inquisition taken at Kilham in 1351 found that Walter Heslerton I:

'held no other lands &c in the county in his demesne as of fee; but he held, by reason of coverture, of the right and inheritance of the aforesaid Eustachia, daughter and heir of Peter de Percy... the manor of Wharram Percy of the king in chief, as of the crown, by service of a knight's fee. Eustachia still holds...
(*Cal IPM IX*, 431, no. 639)

Nevertheless, the escheator was instructed to enquire further as to any lands that Walter I had held in chief on the day of his death. If he found any he was to take custody of Walter II, should Walter have been a minor and unmarried on the day of his father's death (as he was). The escheator's second inquisition found no other lands, but this was not the end of the matter.

In July 1352 John Gaunt, representing the king in chancery against Henry Percy of Spofforth, said that Walter I had acquired other lands etc in Wharram, 'which are held of the king in chief and died seised thereof, whereby the custody of all his lands etc ought to belong to the king'. A jury was empanelled at York to take a third inquisition, but it came to the same conclusion as before: all Walter I's lands at Wharram had been 'of the right and inheritance of Eustachia his wife, who survives... and the said Eustachia now holds it' (*Cal IPM IX*, 431-2, no. 639).

The royal officials were, however, able to introduce another line of attack. Eustachia was found by inquisition to have been 'an idiot from birth' (*Cal IPM XII*, 125), and so another form of wardship came into play. Since the late

13th century congenital idiots had been under the protection of the king, with the result that he could once again benefit financially by granting out their wardship (Roffe and Roffe 1995). In the case of Eustachia, her congenital condition (if she really had one) may have been concealed by her husband during his lifetime, and perhaps also by Geoffrey Scrope beforehand. After Walter I's death, however, she seems to have been taken into the king's protection, and Sir Thomas Ughtred, Martin Skirne and Walter Cotes took possession of Wharram.

Eustachia died in about 1366 and Walter II, who had reached majority, became seised of the manor. He, however, was also dead within the year. He was childless: his uncle was his heir, and by the terms of Robert Percy III's entail, the remainder interest in the Wharram fee passed to Henry Percy of Spofforth. Walter's widow, Euphemia, was granted a third of Wharram for life, as her dower.

It was at this point that the royal officials swooped again. This time, they focused on the documents relating to the 1298 settlement, which had been uncovered during the inquisition held as a result of Walter's death. A certificate by the escheator, following an *ex officio* inquisition, found that Robert Percy's enfeoffment of Adam son of William and Bertram Dughty, and their subsequent enfeoffment of Robert Percy for life, had both taken place without the king's licence; 'therefore the escheator took all the premises into the king's hand, and they are still there' (*Cal IPM XII*, 182, no. 202).

Henry Percy himself died on 12 May 1368, and an inquisition found that he had been seised of two-thirds of the manor of Wharram Percy, with the advowson of the church and reversion of the third part now held by Euphemia late wife of Walter Heslerton II, the whole manor held of the king in chief by a moiety of a knight's service and suit to the county court every six weeks (*Cal IPM XII*, 222, no. 242). Henry Percy 'le piere' was succeeded immediately by his son Henry, who had reached majority. On 15 May the king finally pardoned the unlicensed 1298 settlement, in return for a payment of £40 (*Percy Chart* 1911, 216-17). By 1402 the manor and vill had come into the hands of the Hilton family of Durham, having been exchanged by the Percys for property in Northumberland (Beresford M.W. 1979, 19-20; *Feudal Aids VI*, 260; *Percy Chart* 1911, 457).

Family disputes: the advowson and rectory

The inquisitions *post mortem* relating to the manor of Wharram Percy suggest that Peter Percy II, son of Robert III and heir to the tenancy in chief, would have reached the age of 21 in about 1311, placing his date of birth around 1290. His father would then have been about 45 years old (see Fig. 84). Another son, Henry Percy, who became rector of Wharram, seems to have been born around the same time, perhaps a few years earlier: it was subsequently claimed that he had still not reached 25 years of age in January 1312, the date at which a challenge was made to his institution. He was perhaps born around 1288. In 1309-10 Robert granted another son, Edmund, probably the youngest of the three, a life

interest in the manor of Stainborough, near Barnsley. The manor had been given to Robert in free marriage by Adam Everingham at the time of Robert's marriage to Adam's daughter Margery. The date of the marriage is not recorded (*Yorks Deeds I*, YASRS 39 for 1907 (1909), 155 n.3). This Edmund is recorded as having incurred a debt of £2 in 1306 (TNA PRO C241/53/218).

One other child, a daughter called Agnes, was evidently born before her three recorded brothers. In 1300 Robert Percy III gave testimony at a proof of age inquisition concerning Adam, son and heir of Robert Everingham, himself son of the Adam Everingham who was Robert Percy's father-in-law. Robert said he knew that the younger Adam had been born in 1279 because his daughter Agnes had been born the following September. The elder Adam Everingham was one of Agnes' godfathers (*Yorks Inq IV*, YASRS 37 (1906), 2). The implication of these records is that Robert Percy III and Margery Everingham were married before 1279, that Agnes, Henry, Peter and Edmund were all Margery's children, and that Margery was perhaps born around 1260.

We cannot be certain that Henry was older than Peter. Sir Charles Clay identified him as the elder of the two, but this seems to have been based on the dates (1270-80) incorrectly assigned by Turner and Coxe to a quitclaim made in Henry's favour by his father (*EYC XI*, 111 and n. 9). Nevertheless, the share of Wharram that came to Henry – the rectory (combined with the vicarage), and later the advowson (the right to present a nominee to a vacant church living) – was a valuable one because the church still drew in tithes and other revenues from all five townships that made up the parish. Indeed, the church was far more valuable than the manor: in 1368 the manor was valued at £20 (*Cal IPM XII*, 182), whereas the church was worth £40 (TNA PRO C135/194/5: *Cal IPM XII*, no. 147, 125).

The archbishop's register records, in January 1308, the institution and induction of Henry Percy, clerk, to the church of Wharram Percy on the presentation of Sir Robert Percy (*Reg Greenfield III*, 128). He was appointed as rector of Wharram Percy, the rectory and vicarage having been consolidated during the incumbency of his predecessor, William Skeldergate (*Reg Corbridge I*, 165). The consolidation of the vicarage with the rectory had been permitted on the grounds that Skeldergate 'resides and intends to reside' (*Reg Corbridge I*, 165), and could therefore exercise the cure of souls in the parish. The same could not be said of his successor.

Three months after Henry's induction, archbishop Greenfield gave notice to his official not to molest Henry for his failure to appear in person at the York synod, and in the following September Greenfield licensed Henry to study (at a university) for seven years from the day of his institution, 'and in the meantime he was not to be compelled to reside or be ordained priest' (*Reg Greenfield III*, 128 n. 2). Presumably Henry was required, like other incumbents given dispensations for non-residence, to make provision for the cure of souls in his absence (see *Reg Greenfield III*, xlvi), but any such arrangements are unrecorded.

What we do know is that Henry was soon indebted to Master Michael Harclay, the brother of Andrew Harclay, earl of Carlisle. Michael was a senior churchman, and became the official of the Archdeacon of Richmond in 1316 (TNA PRO SC8/296/147633); he was also a moneylender (Summerson 1993, 249 and 254). In October 1309 Henry acknowledged a debt of £19 1s 8d that he owed to Harclay, and the king ordered it to be levied on Henry's lands and chattels in Yorkshire in default of payment (*Cal Close R 1307-13*, 234). Evidently no payment was forthcoming, and in February 1310 the king issued a writ to the archbishop to levy the amount owed from Henry's ecclesiastical goods (*Reg Greenfield IV*, 94). The reason for Henry's indebtedness is not known, but we might speculate that he was not the first nor last student to find himself in financial difficulties.

Whatever provision Henry made for the cure of souls, the arrangements clearly did not meet with the approval of one powerful parishioner, Gerard Salvayn, lord of Burdale and Thixendale and sheriff of York. On 17 January 1312 a number of clerics including the rector of Sutton upon Derwent were commissioned to judge in a case between Sir George Salvayn, clerk, presented to Wharram, and Sir Henry Percy in possession. George, the son of Gerard, claimed to have been presented by Robert Percy, who at this date still held the advowson in fee simple: Robert granted it along with the manor to his other son, Peter in the following month, before receiving both back as an estate for life.

On 21 January the same clerics were also commissioned to deal with a petition from Sir Gerard Salvayn himself. He claimed that Henry was neglecting the needs of his parishioners, including Gerard himself, and in particular had been under age at the time of his institution. He had been 'in truth, a minor of 24 years of age, neither then nor yet reaching his 25th year' (*Reg Greenfield III*, 199). If, however, the date of his induction is correct, he must have been well under 24 years at that time. The Second Council of Lyons (1274), referred to by Gerard in his submission, had confirmed that no person should be appointed parish priest until he had reached 25 years. The deliberations of the clerics appointed to judge the case presumably failed to reach a satisfactory outcome, as on the following 24 September the archbishop's vicar-general and his official were given a further commission to try the case (*Reg Greenfield III*, 204-5).

By this time, the dispute had reached the level of personal violence. In July 1312 the king commissioned John Neville and others, on complaint by Gerard Salvayn, sheriff, that Henry, 'parson of the church of Wharram, Roger Grymet and Walter his brother with others assaulted him at Wharram Percy when executing his office' (*Cal PR 1307-1313*, 478). Henry put his side of the story in a petition to the king's council, dated only to Salvayn's shrievalty (1311-14), but perhaps soon after the above event:

'whereas Gerard Salvayn, sheriff of Yorkshire, procured his son George Salvayn to be presented to the church of Wharram, for which he [GS] caused him [HP] to be impleaded in Court Christian, so because the said sheriff could not attain his will by means of law, he maliciously accused the parson of various trespasses to have a pretext against him by colour of his office to harm him by imprisonment; by which the sheriff and others with him by force and arms assaulted the parson in the buildings belonging to the said church, beat him, wounded him and ill-treated him, bound him, seated him on a mare without a saddle and thus ignominiously took him to York castle, like a thief; and the sheriff kept him there in the vilest prison that there is in the castle, among thieves, not willing to let him be bailed by any bail that man could tender, but kept him there in prison against all manner of law and reason to force him to resign the said church.' (TNA PRO SC 8/327/E789)

A further twist in the story is revealed by a citation issued on 23 September 1312 to Margaret, wife of Robert Percy III, who was accused of adultery with Sir Gerard Salvayn (*Reg Greenfield III*, 205). She had been warned to stop, and had contumaciously refused; the commission was to compel her, under pain of excommunication, to abjure the sin and be corrected. It seems likely that she had run off with Salvayn – not the only such case dealt with by the ecclesiastical courts at this time (another being the wife of Robert Everingham: *Reg Greenfield III*, xlix). We can speculate that she was the one who persuaded or tricked Robert, now in his late 60s, into presenting George to the incumbency. Acknowledging the dangers of imposing modern prejudices on this narrative, it is hard to imagine that the woman who behaved in this way was Margery Everingham, Henry's mother who would now have been over 50 years old. Had Margery Everingham died and been replaced by a much younger Margaret? If so, Robert had acquired yet another replacement wife, named Beatrice, by 1318-19 (TNA PRO E210/6972).

A further commission followed in December 1312 (*Reg Greenfield III*, 205 n.1). As the dispute continued, Henry was at one point fined 100s [£5] for non-residence. In February 1314, however, the fine was remitted when the record of the licence to study was uncovered in the register and found to have almost two years to run (*Reg Greenfield III*, 215).

In March 1315 sentences were finally delivered: Henry was cleared of all charges and Gerard and George Salvayn were to pay £50 costs each, under pain of excommunication to be denounced in every parish church in the archdeaconry (*Reg Greenfield III*, 247-52). Nevertheless, after the death of archbishop Greenfield the Salvayns tried again: an entry in the register for February 1317 commissioned the official of York to try the case commenced before archbishop Greenfield between Gerard Salvayn, parishioner of Wharram Percy and George Salvayn, presented to the same church, plaintiffs, and Sir Henry Percy, rector of the same church, defendant (*Reg Greenfield V*, 269). In April 1318 and February 1322 Henry was again licensed for absence 'in a fit and honest place where a *studium generale* favourable to the study of letters flourishes' (BIA, Reg 9, f.267v; Reg 9, f.286).

Whatever Robert Percy's intentions with regard to the presentation of George Salvayn, he was clearly supporting his son by September 1320, when he quitclaimed to Henry all his rights in the park of Wharram Percy, and in the pool which William Skeldergate, former rector, had held of him, and in an acre of land as it was enclosed with ditches, next to the park, and in the advowson of the church, all previously held for a life term by Henry by a chirograph deed, and now recovered by Henry by an assize of novel disseisin (Bodleian Library, Dodsworth 76, f.162r). An inquisition *ad quod damnum*, held in March 1321, found that the property had been granted without the king's licence and had been taken into the king's hands, but that there would be no detriment to the king. It recorded that the 4 acres of land (worth 16d) and 4 acres of wood (worth no less than 2 shillings) were once parcel of the manor held of the king in serjeanty. The church was valued at 50 marks (TNA PRO C143/144/20).

Robert himself was dead before the year was out, and in 1322 Henry disposed of his interest in the park (now described as 8 acres of land and 6 acres of wood), and in the pond (now described as the millpond), together with the advowson of the church to Geoffrey Scrope for the sum of £200 (Roper and Kitchen 2006). The necessary licence was issued by the king in June of that year, after another inquisition *ad quod damnum*, which gave the value of the land as 10s 6d and of the advowson as £40 (*Cal PR 1321-4*, 136; TNA PRO C143/149/7 (2-3)). By May 1323 the living was vacant because Henry Percy had resigned (BIA, Reg 9, f.290).

A month after Scrope obtained the king's licence to purchase Henry Percy's interest in the advowson, he also acquired the wardship of Eustachia, as described above, and thus acquired control of both the manor and the church. His interest in the advowson was not long-lived; indeed, he may have purchased it in the first place with a view to transferring the church to the priory of Haltemprice, near Hull, newly founded by his friend Thomas Wake of Liddell. In 1320 Wake had obtained papal licence to found an Augustinian priory at Cottingham, and had begun to erect buildings there; but a secure title to the site could not be assured. In June 1322, therefore, the king gave licence for Wake to confer a messuage in nearby Newton on a religious house of whatever order he wished to build there, and in January, 1326 the pope licensed the removal of Haltemprice from Cottingham to Newton (*VCH Yorks III*, 213).

Wake's foundation charter, issued towards the end of January 1326, included grants to Haltemprice of the advowsons of Cottingham, Kirk Ella, Belton and Wharram Percy churches. Kirk Ella was not yet his to give: the advowson belonged to Selby Abbey, and was not transferred to Wake until 1331 (*VCH Yorks III*, 213-14). The grant of Wharram may have been similarly prospective rather than effective, as it was another year before (in February 1327) the king licensed Scrope to grant in free alms to Haltemprice, at the request of Wake, a wood, a fishery and the advowson of Wharram (*Cal PR 1327-30*, 14). Scrope covenanted with Haltemprice that upon the grant they should provide two chaplains at

Wharram, one to say masses for the souls of various members of Scrope's family (Lawrance 1985, 67).

Scrope's interest in Wharram came to an end when Eustachia and Walter Heslerton I took possession of her inheritance in about 1327. Nevertheless, Thomas Wake evidently still had the manor in his sights to provide a further endowment for his priory. For in 1336 the king licensed Eustachia and Walter I to enfeoff Wake in the manor of Wharram, and for him to assign it in free alms to Haltemprice (*Cal PR 1334-38*, 277). The licence was not, however, acted upon.

In 1368 Edward III's officials made a final attempt to assert his rights over the advowson, based on the failure of Robert Percy to obtain a licence to alienate the property. The prior of Haltemprice was summoned to answer the king in a plea that he should permit the king to present a parson to Wharram Percy church, then vacant and in the king's gift. Judgement was eventually given against the Crown (Baildon 1895, 81-2).

Family debts: the finances of Robert Percy III

There is one other aspect of Robert Percy's affairs that is relatively well documented: his debts. The earliest record is in May 1271 when a debt of £30 owed by Robert to Aaron of York was assigned by the king to Martin fitz Peter after Aaron had been killed (*Cal CR 1268-72*, 344). Aaron was pre-eminent among the Anglo-Jewish financiers of the 13th century, but he was, like other Jews in York, persecuted and ruined by punitive taxation (*VCH ER I*, 48). In 1273 Hagin son of Cresse or Deulacres acknowledged an obligation to acquit Robert with respect to a debt of £100 (*Cal PREJ II*, 117). In 1275 another Jew named Deudone Crespyn petitioned the king that he should be acquitted of the arrears of a charter of £200 which was delivered to Robert without anything being paid; the justices of the Jews were ordered to acquit Deudone of the tallage assessed on him out of the debt (TNA PRO SC 8/311/15531; *Cal CR* 1272-9, 185).

Robert was also indebted in this period to Gilbert Louth, a prominent citizen of York and one of those who, in 1282, lent Edward I over a thousand marks (*Kirkby's Inquest*, Surtees Soc 49 (1867), 65n). In June 1276 Robert demised to Gilbert the manor of Scoreby for £30 yearly, 'for everything that can be exacted from the manor', excepting the windmill and the lands that William Clervaux held of Robert on the day of making the charter. This was evidently a means of securing a loan, as twelve years' worth of dues, amounting to £360, were paid in advance (*EYC XI*, 111; *Cal CR* 1279-88, 49). The grant resulted, in 1279-80, in an assize of novel disseisin as Gilbert then appropriated tenements at Scoreby with which Robert had enfeoffed German the Goldsmith of York three years before his enfeoffment of Gilbert (TNA PRO JUST 1/1055, m.26d). Gilbert himself used the lands he had by gift of Robert to secure a debt of £100 which he owed to Anthony Beck, and which he acknowledged in 1280, excepting the lands that Anthony bought of German the Goldsmith (*Cal CR* 1279-88, 49). Scoreby lies close to York, between the city and Stamford Bridge, and it looks as though Robert made specific use of it to raise loans from the merchants of York. It was not, however, the only manor used in this way.

Also in 1280 Gilbert Louth and John the Spicer petitioned that Robert had leased them the manor of Carnaby, worth £66 a year, for six years for a debt of 250 marks, but that the sheriff had seized the manor into the king's hands, to their great damage (TNA PRO SC 8/220/10969; *Cal CR 1279-88*, 14). The reason for Robert's indebtedness at this period is unknown, but the sums were substantial and were secured on his lands. Were they the result of raising capital to erect buildings in the North Manor *curia*?

In contrast, a series of much smaller debts incurred between 1286 and 1294 might well have been part of everyday commercial transactions. Ranging in value from £3 10s to £73 5s 8d (but mainly under £15), they are recorded in the certificates of debt produced under the Acton Burnell Statute of 1283 (TNA PRO C241; see Nightingale 2000, 38). The creditors were almost all citizens and merchants of York, some of them repeat lenders, including Nicholas Langton (2 debts), Peter Appleby (3 debts), Master Robert Gra (3 debts) and Rayner Sperry (4 debts: TNA PRO C241/7/339B, C; C241/7/141, C241/17/19, C241/17/26, among others). A more distant source of cash was a partnership of Italian bankers known as the Riccardi of Lucca, whose better known clients included the pope and the kings of England and France. In 1289 they lent Robert £10 5s 4d (TNA PRO C241/9/227).

The certificates dating between 1284 and 1311 have been analysed by Pamela Nightingale. Though there was no rule that certificates should indicate what the debt was incurred for, 87 of them record knights as debtors for wool, and 34 of them relate to Yorkshire knights. The debts were probably advance payments for wool yet to be delivered (Nightingale 2000, 38-9). Though Robert Percy is not recorded specifically as owing debts for wool, it is very possible that he was one of the knights taking an active role in the wool trade, particularly in the first decade of the 14th century when the export trade boomed. In 1284 a knight of Westmorland was recorded as owing five sacks of wool, worth 6o marks, to Peter Appleby of York who, as we have seen, was one Robert's repeat creditors. In 1294 Sir John Bulmer of Bulmer the North Riding owed six sacks of wool worth 60 marks to Nicholas Langton of York, another Percy creditor; Bulmer also later also dealt with a merchant of Lucca (Nightingale 2000, 39-40).

Though we lose sight of Robert Percy's commercial activity in 1311, when the certificates were limited to merchants (Nightingale 2000, 38), his borrowings seem to have continued. An inquisition of 1327 records that, after the death of Robert's son, Peter Percy II, Peter's wife and daughter Eustachia entered the manor of Sutton upon Derwent and tenements in *Cathewaite*, as the right of Eustachia, and held them undisturbed for three months; but afterwards Robert intruded on the manor and tenements, and his widow Beatrice still held them in 1327. Robert also intruded on tenements in Hull, held them for two years and then gave them as security for a debt to William Gra of York, 'who still holds them, until

he should have levied the debt'. William was probably related to Robert Gra, one of Robert Percy's earlier creditors. He also intruded upon rents in the city of York, received them for two years and similarly granted then to Thomas Horneby and Katherine his wife as security for a debt (*Cal IPM VI*, 83). These actions suggest that Robert had a need for loans in 1317.

The last of Robert's creditors to be recorded was Thomas Alwarthope of York, clerk. By writ of 14 November 1321, an inquisition *ad quod damnum* was held to determine whether Thomas could retain £10 worth of rent for life issuing from the manor of Wharram Percy, granted him by Robert Percy, which he had acquired without licence, and which had been taken into the king's hands on account of the trespass (TNA PRO C143/149/7 (1-2). This was the free tenement which had been subject to an assize of novel disseisin, permitted at the beginning of 1319 to be taken between Thomas and Robert (BIA, Melton Reg, fo. 274). The charge was again recorded in the inquisition *post mortem* of Robert Percy in 1323, when the reduced value of the manor, as a result of most of the demesne being uncultivated, meant that Thomas's £10 left a clear yield from the manor of only £2 6s 4d (TNA PRO C134/75/15).

Conclusions

As acknowledged at the beginning of this chapter, the additional documentary research on the lords and manors of Wharram Percy has provided relatively little new information to help us interpret the results of archaeological investigations in the village. It has, however, provided us with circumstantial evidence for Wharram's development both in terms of what was happening elsewhere in the neighbourhood, and what was happening in the wider estates of the lords of Wharram. It is possible to infer that in the 13th century Wharram was a relatively minor and unimportant vill in comparison with some of its neighbours, whilst at the same time it was a favoured residence of the Percy family – its seisin the prize of a lengthy dispute at the end of the previous century. On the other hand its rectory and advowson were exceptionally valuable, covering as they did a total of five vills, and particularly as they had not yet been appropriated by a monastic community even in the early 1320s.

The manor's financial position is likely to have deteriorated considerably in the first half of the 14th century, and not just because of the stresses that were felt more widely by England's rural population. Wharram will, in addition, have suffered the impact of the Percy family's misfortunes, starting perhaps with Robert Percy's debts, but mainly during the subsequent lengthy wardships which allowed Scrope and others to drain the manor's resources for personal benefit, and for pet projects such as the endowment of Haltemprice. In the event, Haltemprice remained financially unstable, a circumstance no doubt reflected in the development of St Martin's during the 14th and 15th centuries. It is to the evidence for St Martin's structural development from the 11th to the 16th centuries that we now turn.

15 A New Understanding of the Church Fabric

by David Stocker with contributions from Paul Everson

Introduction

The standing fabric of St Martin's church is exceptionally complex, no doubt partly because of the many small repairs evidently necessary to keep it standing that have been made since the 16th century. Maurice Beresford showed that there were still plenty of parishioners during the 15th to 18th centuries, but it seems clear that they were not prepared, either as individuals or as a group, to sponsor thoroughgoing rebuildings of the fabric, preferring to make-do-and-mend.

The excavations carried out between 1962 and 1974 both within and around the extant church were sufficiently well recorded to generate complex phase plans, and to enable broad dates to be assigned to these phases (Bell 1987a). The publication of that work also required a statement about the standing fabric of the church, and this was provided by Jim Thorn (1987). The recording of the wall elevations was carried out manually by Thorn between 1978 and 1980 (*Wharram III*, xvi). Though some inaccuracies are evident in the drawings, it is a testament to their overall quality that it is now possible to return to the church structure and its record, and to suggest revisions and alterations to the proposed development sequence – revisions which match the excavation results better, and for which both the standing fabric and the loose architectural fragments provide evidence. The loose architectural stonework has been reviewed, and the pieces tabulated with cross-references to Thorn's catalogue and drawings. The table and drawings constitute one of the reports available electronically via the Archaeology Data Service (ADS) (doi:10.5284/1000415).

This chapter is accompanied by a new set of phase plans (Fig. 87), a smaller number than appeared in previous versions but one which, we believe, provides a rather more coherent story of structural development. To distinguish these structural phases from those used in *Wharram III*, they have been given Arabic rather than Roman numerals. The elevation drawings (Figs 88-91) are those published in *Wharram III*, but coloured to indicate which parts of the wall faces belonged to which phases. The same colours are referred to in the headings of the following phase descriptions. The post-medieval phases (8 and 9) have not been reassessed in detail for this volume given its focus and chronological range, but will be dealt with at a later date.

Phase 3: early 12th century (ochre)

Substantial standing fabric for the church designated Phase 3 still survives 'on the surface' of the walls of today's nave, and doubtless there is more within the cores of refaced walls. The largest areas of visible fabric of this phase are at the western end of the building (Fig. 89), where it includes the tall narrow tower arch cocooned within the later tower. It is a fine architectural feature with simple chamfered imposts, which are returned onto the interior (east) face, and a ring of well-constructed radial voussoirs, without mouldings. The arch is founded on the remains of a plinth course, surviving as two chamfered stones on either side, which both project slightly from the wall line and line up with the straight joint marking the western face of the tower arch. Neither of these plinth courses is shown on the elevations.

The presence of this arch confirms the intention to build a western tower in Phase 3, but it is clear from the excavations that no such tower was in fact built (Harding and Marlow-Mann 2007, 16-17). We can presume that the tower arch was constructed to be integral with the west wall, but was then filled with rubble, pending the raising of funds for the construction of the tower. Such forward planning is far from unusual in medieval church building programmes (perhaps most famously at Beauvais Cathedral, where the westernmost arch in the uncompleted nave still retains its 13th-century temporary blocking), and continues today. In the case of St Martin's, however, by the time that work was started on the tower, and for whatever reason, the plans had changed (Phase 4 below).

Phase 3 fabric is visible to a considerable height in the west wall, to the north and south of the Phase 4 tower. On the east face, masonry of this period survives to the same approximate height as the crown of the Phase 3 tower arch. Presumably masonry above this point was taken down when the tower was inserted in Phase 4. The Phase 3 wall is founded on a plinth with a chamfered offset at about 1m above the ground surface. The level of this chamfered plinth is continuous with the fragmentary plinth courses at the bases of the jambs of the Phase 3 tower arch. On the exterior, west face, however, the Phase 3 fabric has been re-fronted; to the south partly by masonry which is probably quite early in date (Phase 4) whilst, to the north, the masonry is of later date (Phase 7).

The nave's north wall also contains a substantial amount of Phase 3 fabric, especially at its western end, west of the inserted arcade. This wall retains the rerearch of the tall narrow north doorway of Phase 3, which was later adapted to take a more up-to-date external architrave (In Phase 5). Within the replaced architrave, however, the western impost for the Phase 3 doorway arch seems to have been left *in situ*. It is a substantial block with a simple chamfer running along its underside. The rerearch to the Phase 3 doorway is clearly original *in situ* work (a reading that contradicts Wrathmell's interpretation in Harding and Wrathmell 2007, 330, fig. 157), and above it, the Phase 3 wall rises almost to the final wall plate. Early fabric can also be clearly seen in both reveals of the doorway, where its striated tooling contrasts with the claw tooling of the inserted masonry. In the central and eastern parts of the north wall, the insertion of the arcade required demolition of the Phase 3 fabric, and it appears to survive only at foundation level.

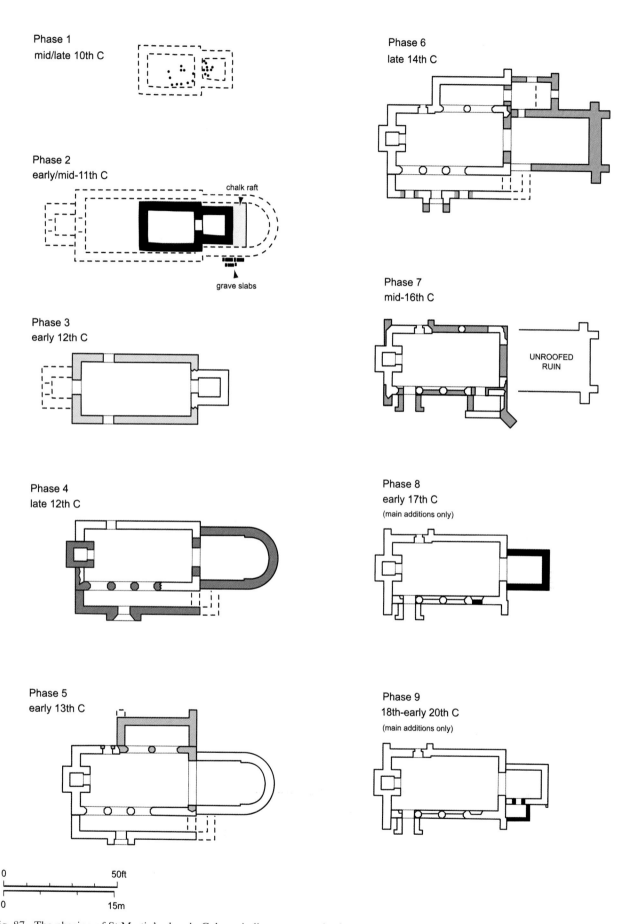

Phase 1
mid/late 10th C

Phase 2
early/mid-11th C

chalk raft

grave slabs

Phase 3
early 12th C

Phase 4
late 12th C

Phase 5
early 13th C

Phase 6
late 14th C

Phase 7
mid-16th C

UNROOFED
RUIN

Phase 8
early 17th C
(main additions only)

Phase 9
18th-early 20th C
(main additions only)

0   50ft

0   15m

Fig. 87. The phasing of St Martin's church. Colours indicate new work of each phase. (J. Prudhoe after D. Stocker)

241

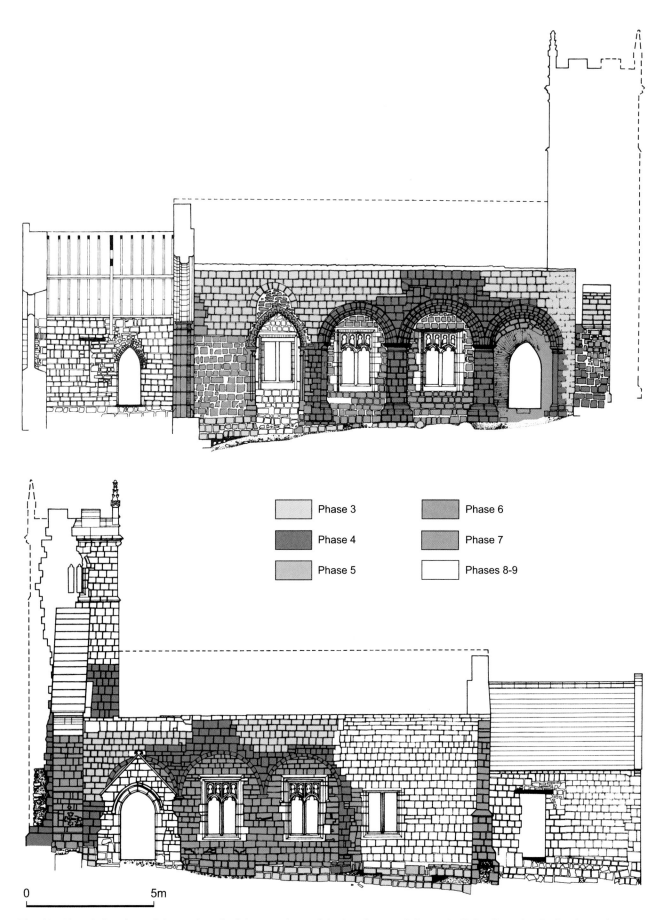

Fig. 88. Phased elevations of the south wall of the nave: internal (top) and external (bottom). (J. Prudhoe after D. Stocker, using elevation drawings by J. Thorn)

Phase 3

Phase 4

Phase 5

Phase 6

Phase 7

Phases 8-9

0　　　　　　　　5m

Fig. 89. Phased elevations of the west wall of the nave and the tower: east face (top) and west face (bottom). The external elevation of the west wall of the tower is from photographs taken prior to its collapse in 1959. (J. Prudhoe after D. Stocker, using elevation drawings by J. Thorn)

243

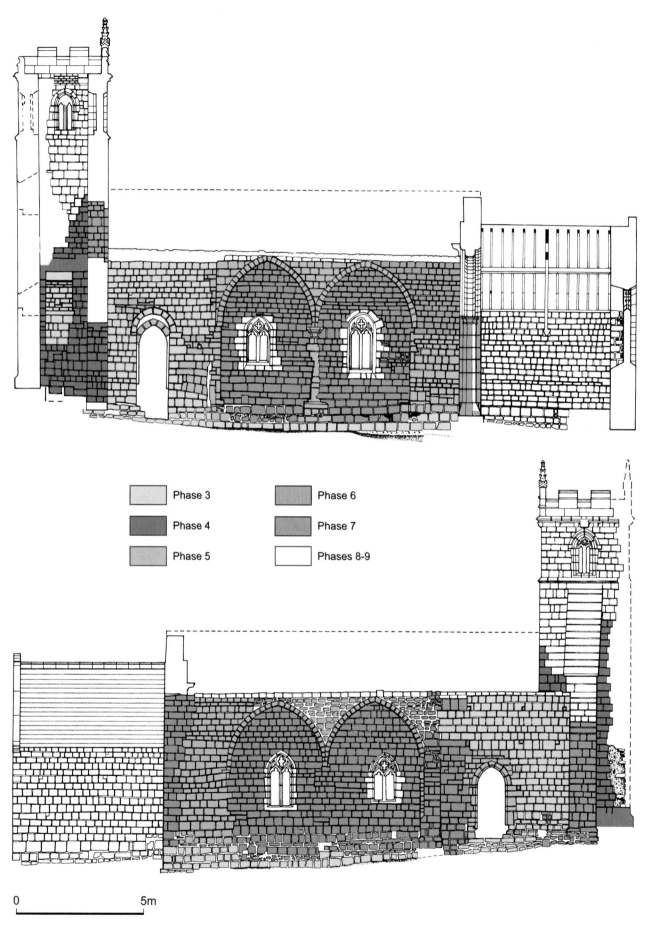

Phase 3

Phase 4

Phase 5

Phase 6

Phase 7

Phases 8-9

0   5m

Fig. 90. Phased elevations of the north wall of the nave: internal (top) and external (bottom). (J. Prudhoe after D. Stocker, using elevation drawings by J. Thorn)

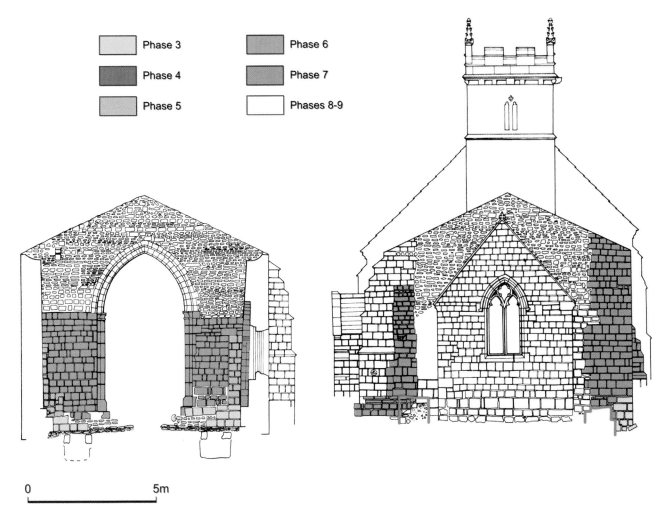

Fig. 91. Phased elevations of the east wall of the nave: internal (left) and external (right). (J. Prudhoe after D. Stocker, using elevation drawings by J. Thorn)

In the nave's south wall there are also substantial remains from the Phase 3 fabric, clearly earlier in date than the Phase 4 south arcade (Fig. 88). This fabric includes the rerearch of a blocked original nave window above the Phase 7 archway, and an area of Phase 4 fabric above the second bay from the west in the south arcade which is very likely to mark the location of a second Phase 3 window. We will see that the architrave of this window might have been relocated in the west tower during its construction in Phase 4.

Also in the south wall, some sections of simple chamfered set-off were recovered by the excavations. These were apparently *in situ*, and had presumably been buried by the ground works of the south aisle in Phase 4. They were, however, not all present: gaps in the western part of the sequence might indicate where some of these stones had been robbed to provide a plinth of the base of the Phase 4 tower, which appears to have been of precisely the same proportions. Unfortunately, the simple chamfered plinth is not intrinsically closely datable, and can only be placed in Phase 3 because of its archaeological context.

The surviving foundations of Phase 3 identified in excavations at the south-west and south-east corners of the nave indicate a building with clasping buttress at the

angles. The unexplained projection from the foundations at a point approximately two-thirds of the way along the south wall might indicate the location of another buttress, though it appears not to have been contemporary with the original footings, and it did not divide the south into symmetrical bays. A more plausible explanation for this feature will be offered later.

We can say very little that is positive about the east wall of the Phase 3 nave. The contemporary chancel arch is represented by some of the lowest of the blocks excavated along this line (Fig. 91), but frankly phasing is not easy to establish here, and the footings of the earlier, Phase 2 church are not easy to distinguish from Phase 3. It seems likely, however, that there would have been a new chancel arch at Phase 3, because a new east wall would be required to support the new nave roof, but it is not certain that the chancel fabric itself was rebuilt at this period.

The excavation account makes it quite clear that the Phase 2 chancel was still standing up to the point when the impressive apsidal chancel and sanctuary were erected (Bell 1987a, 70-73). The unwritten assumption seems to have been that this was simply a matter of practicality, with the old chancel surviving only for a year or two whilst the new chancel was constructed around it.

This is not, however, a necessary requirement of the stratigraphic sequence or the pottery and we will explore, later, the possibility that there was a substantial gap of a generation or two between the construction of the nave and the erection of an elaborate new chancel.

Phase 3: dating evidence

The style of the masonry, with its distinctive well-squared ashlar and broad joints must point towards a construction date relatively early in the 12th century. The fabric is very similar in character, for example, to the church at Weaverthorpe, dated to the second and third decades of the 12th century (see Fig. 95, below and Plate 19, above). The Weaverthorpe window rerearches also bear close comparison to those at Wharram, as does the external architrave of the upper window formerly in the west wall of the Phase 4 tower (reconstructed in Fig. 89), if that detail really was reused from a Phase 3 window. It is also possible that both the Phase 4 tower arch and the voussoirs of the arch forming the western face of the high-level doorway are reused features from the Phase 3 church. The masonry of the tower arch is of such similar form to the *in situ* rerearch of the Phase 3 nave north doorway that we suggest it had originally formed the rerearch of the nave south doorway. This doorway was perhaps also the origin of the sections of tympanum (ADS Report, doi:10.5284/1000415, table 1, stone I) which were discovered among the rubble of the tower. This tympanum, and the doorway of which it formed part also dates from the first few decades of the 12th century on the strength of local parallels such as that at Braithwell (West Riding); a national list of similar examples (based on Keyser 1927) has now been published (Wood 2001, list 3). In her study of such tympana in Yorkshire, Wood suggests that they all date from before 1135 (Wood 1994, 61; see also Keyser 1909, 167-70). Finally, the voussoirs forming the western face of the high level doorway might be related to the missing Phase 3 window in the south wall, though this would necessitate their having been adapted to fit in their present position.

Phase 4: late 12th century (brown)

The excavations suggested that the insertion of the arcade in the south nave wall and the construction of the west tower, belonged to the same phase of activity (Bell 1987a, 93; Thorn 1987; 111, fig. 36). The following analysis of the fabric and its architectural details confirms that connection.

The south arcade and aisle

The inserted fabric surrounding the three bay arcade of Phase 4 is quite clear in the phased elevations (Fig. 88), as is the disturbance above the central arch of the arcade which must indicate where a second Phase 3 window in the south wall has been removed. Because of the reuse of Phase 3 ashlars in the Phase 4 work, however, there remains some doubt about the extent to which the Phase 3 fabric at the western end of the south wall was rebuilt,

but it seems clear that a substantial panel of Phase 3 masonry was retained above the western arch in the new arcade.

At the eastern end of the arcade the later insertion of a fourth arcade arch (in Phase 7) has made matters more complicated. We simply cannot be certain whether or not the easternmost Phase 3 window in the south wall was blocked when the aisle was built, as its blocking is now of Phase 7. But the answer to this question would have lain in the plan of the new aisle itself. If it is true, as the excavators eventually decided (Bell 1987a, 85-92), that the new south aisle extended the whole length of the nave, and perhaps also overlapped the chancel by half a bay, then it is most unlikely that this window remained open in Phase 4. If, however, the south aisle of Phase 4 originally only extended for the length of the south arcade, then this window would have remained open in Phase 4, only becoming blocked in Phase 7. This latter sequence was thought unlikely by the excavators, and a similar conclusion has been reached during this reconsideration; therefore it is suggested (*contra* Thorn 1987, 119-21) that this window was blocked with masonry in Phase 4, and then re-blocked when the Phase 7 archway was inserted.

The original Phase 4 arcade was of three bays, and of considerable architectural sophistication. The three semi-circular arches stand on two substantial piers of circular section with responds of semi-circular section. The crown of the central arch stands slightly taller than those to either side. This central bay was most likely emphasised because this was the archway by which entrants through the south aisle doorway, whose location was discovered during excavation, emerged into the body of the church. All the piers stand on square sub-bases, with chamfered upper angles. The bases themselves, for both piers and the two responds, are all of attic sequence, with a pronounced fillet to either side of the *torus*, which stands nearly upright.

The capitals for the two responds and the easternmost pier are identical, and are of 'chalice' profile. They have a pronounced double-chamfered astragal, a tall neck which develops towards the simply chamfered abacus by means of simple chamfer and a vertical band. The upper part of the capital, above the neck, and the abacus itself, however, are octagonal in plan, in all four capitals including the more highly developed example above the western pier. Although this pier has the same base moulding as its fellow, its capital has an astragal of semi-circular profile and a more complex abacus moulding with a rounded extrados (i.e. an upper roll) above a dropped fillet, a hollow-chamfer and a lower fillet. The arcade arches throughout are of two orders, each with a bold chamfer. There is no label to either side.

As noted above, excavation revealed the footings of the original, Phase 4 south doorway of the demolished south aisle. The distinction between the original projections either side of the doorway and the later porch was clearly visible (Bell 1987a, 86-88, fig. 22), and it has been reconstructed in the consolidated remains. These

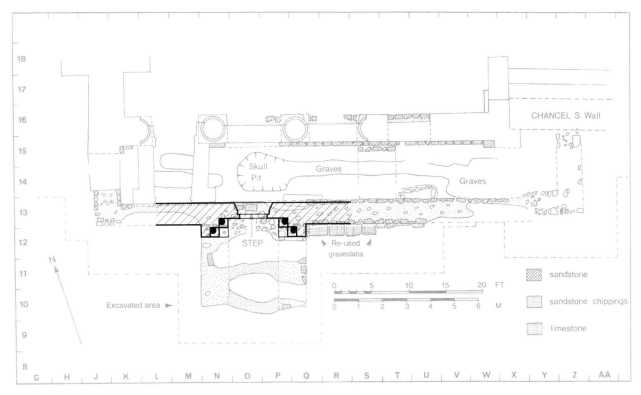

Fig. 92. Location and plan form of the late 12th-century south doorway. (J Prudhoe after D. Stocker)

projections were interpreted as buttresses in *Wharram III* (Bell 1987a, 89-90), a role which is entirely implausible for two reasons. First, they are not located symmetrically within the aisle façade so, even if other similar projections had existed and were missed in excavation, they are incorrectly placed. Secondly, the aisle wall itself is unlikely to have been of greater height than about 3m, and such a wall would not usually be buttressed at this date.

Symmetrically located around the south doorway, these footings are unquestionably the remains of a projecting doorway canopy, of the kind seen in association with many elaborate doorways with multiple orders (Fig. 92). Such an explanation would account for the mass of masonry found between the two projections, but not to either side. Locally, an example of exactly this type of projection can be seen surrounding both doorways into the aisleless nave at the magnificent church at Newbald (20km south: see Fig. 95), where the north door is, like that at Wharram, of three orders (Keyser 1909, 175-6; Bilson 1911). But, being a doorway through an aisle wall, the original arrangement at Wharram would have more closely resembled the contemporary doorway at Brayton (West Riding) where a door of three orders, through a south aisle wall, was also placed in a projecting canopy of this type (Keyser 1909, 194-5).

The same circumstances prevail at the north nave doorway of the great abbey church of Kirkstall (West Riding), where the three-order doorway is also built into a projection from the aisle wall. The Kirkstall building, however, is enormously more substantial of course than would have been the case at Wharram. Of the other Yorkshire examples of three orders (Wood 1994), most are either set within two-storey walls (such as Kirkburn or

Birkin) or have been reset in the post-medieval period (Riccall, York St Lawrence). In relatively thin aisle walls, such as Wharram, such a projection was inevitable when a doorway of three orders, or more, was to be achieved, as the recession of orders inevitably takes up more space than the thickness of the wall itself can accommodate. Sometimes, as at Adel (West Riding, of four orders), this projection is so deep as to become almost like a porch canopy in its own right. This feature is certainly not confined to Yorkshire, however, and five similar projections surrounding 12th-century doorways were catalogued by James Bond in Worcestershire, where they are mostly of two orders (Bond 1988, 145-9).

The conclusion of this review is that the doorway set within this canopy was very probably of three orders, and that its original form can be reconstituted from two later architectural features that seem to have been formed out of its elements: the present south doorway, set within the Phase 7 blocking of the westernmost arch of the Phase 4 south aisle arcade; and the Phase 7 archway punched through the wall to the east of the Phase 4 arcade. To these remains can be added various pieces of loose architectural stonework recovered from the excavations and from the debris of the partial collapse of the tower.

The present south doorway has a single moulded order that looks most uncomfortable in its original relationship to the capital blocks that support it (Plate 23). The western surviving capital is set beneath an integral abacus with a well-executed quirk and chamfer moulding above a roll, of conventional type. The capital itself is a precisely cut 'waterleaf' type, with tightly curled whorls and a precisely drilled hole between the leaves. Waterleaf capitals were new in Yorkshire in the 1160s and continued

Plate 23. The present south doorway of St Martin's, viewed from the south. (P. Gwilliam)

to be produced for a generation, until at least the 1180s. The drilled hole detail occurs, amongst many other places in Yorkshire and the North, at both the chapter house of Fountains Abbey (West Riding), built in the 1160s; at Burton Agnes Hall (East Riding), where it is usually associated with the tenure of Roger Stuteville and is dated to *c*.1170, and at the chapel of the new keep at Newcastle Castle, which was built between 1172 and 1177.

The eastern capital belongs to the same original arch, and sits beneath an abacus of the same dimensions, with the same moulding, though it represents a different tradition of capital sculpture. It is decorated with 'wings' of finely carved acanthus foliage, with the gap between the two fronds filled with a third frond whose leaves fall forward. This is a capital type less frequently met with in Yorkshire, although very fine examples of the type were used in the arcade on the western façade of the chapter-house at St Mary's Abbey, York in the third quarter of the 12th century. It is more common in Lincolnshire buildings dating from the same decades (Stocker 1991, 33-7), though the type continues in use for a couple more decades and is found, for example, amongst the chevet capitals at Abbey Dore (Herefordshire) in the subsequent generation (e.g. Fergusson 1984, 94-100).

The arch order from which the voussoirs, now set above these capitals, were derived, was deeply moulded with a pronounced central roll of keeled form, flanked by

two quirks and hollow chamfers followed by further quirks and, to one side, only a half-roll. Thorn reconstructed this arch as having a width of somewhat less than 2m. Though precision is not possible, as there are clearly some voussoirs missing, this calculation would make this arch a suitable candidate for the next order outwards from the architrave in our reconstructed doorway, as Thorn had it (Thorn 1987, fig. 41). But given the known dimensions of the projection to house the porch, we must conclude that both an inner and an outer order are missing in Thorn's reconstruction.

The collection of architectural fragments from the site reveals the former existence of four other late-Romanesque arches. Most of these fragments are singletons, however, and we will explore where they might have originated subsequently. But one of the fragments (ADS Report, doi:10.5284/1000415, table 1, stone T) from an order decorated with a simple chevron moulding which is, nevertheless, confined to the forward face of the arch, belongs to the same original arch as the seventeen examples reused in the Phase 7 archway inserted east of the Phase 4 arcade (Plate 24). These stones are all of the same depth, demonstrating clearly that they were originally set beneath a hood-moulding or another arch order.

Can this chevron-decorated arch order also be associated with the Phase 4 south doorway? First of all, with a diameter of something over 3m, it would fit comfortably in the outer order of the projection containing the doorway in the south aisle wall. Secondly, it seems likely that the feature from which these chevron moulded voussoirs originally came was indeed a doorway, rather than any other category of architectural feature, because the jambs and the integral capital blocks with which they are reused are of a distinctive narrow and upright type, usually found in the inner orders of elaborate, late Romanesque doorways.

Furthermore, although the stones have been rearranged and placed in 'side-alternate' fashion in their reused positions, the moulded jamb blocks themselves all have one face which extends to a very similar depth, a detail which suggests that it could have formed the rebate against which the original door closed. The finely moulded, yet deeply cut shafts running up the arrises of the jambs are flanked by hollows, but are integral with them. The shafts stand on bases, which in the case of the westernmost here, still survives, reused in its correct relationship with the shaft above. Though now badly damaged, the base is of attic sequence with a near-vertical *torus*; in effect a simplified version of the bases to the arcade piers further west. The deep hollows flanking the arris shafts are also terminated within both base and capital blocks with characteristic 'scoops'.

The capitals themselves are decorated with a similar repertoire of foliage motifs to those in the existing south door. That to the west has a distinctive astragal decorated with a zig-zag fillet, beneath a tall neck carved with vertical acanthus fronds, not dissimilar to the western of the two capitals still within the south doorway. That to the

Plate 24. The blocked south arcade of St Martin's, viewed from the north-east. (P. Gwilliam)

east has a type of leaf resembling more the 'waterleaf' form of the western capital in the surviving south doorway, but with the leaves themselves decorated and subdivided by acanthus sprays. It is almost a cross-fertilisation between the designs seen in the two capitals in the surviving doorway. The leaves are divided by tall 'lollypop'-like motifs, and the whole design sits above a semi-circular astragal. The *abaci* above both capitals are crude replacements, probably inserted when the components were reused here in Phase 7.

These are all good reasons to think that all the masonry reused to form this eastern arch in Phase 7 originated in two separate orders of the south aisle doorway. For this explanation to be correct, however, we must accept that the understanding of the development of the south aisle put forward in *Wharram III* is defective. This is not unlikely, however, as Bell himself confirmed that the excavation of the eastern end of the aisle had presented problems of phasing and understanding which the excavators did not feel they had resolved. To take the issues one by one: first the foundations of the south aisle south wall do not terminate at, or even near, the eastern respond of the arcade. They continue eastwards for at least another 6m before they run into an area of disturbed masonry and clear evidence that the south-east quoin, and perhaps lengths of wall to either side, has been comprehensively rebuilt. It seems clear, therefore, that as originally suggested, there was a substantial eastern space, enclosed on three sides in the original design of the

south aisle. *Inter alia* this must imply, as indicated above, that the easternmost of the Phase 3 windows in the former nave south wall was blocked at this time, even though its current blocking belongs to a later Phase.

There seems no reason to doubt that this situation persisted until the eastern end of the aisle; in *Wharram III*, that part beyond the Phase 4 arcade respond was separated from the westernmost part by means of an architectural feature which postdates the arcade. The excavators were unsure what this feature represented, and they chose to interpret it as the footings for a respond to support an inserted arch across the aisle. Photographs of the excavation, however (e.g. *Wharram III*, pl. ix a), seem to show not 'a few blocks' but a substantial mortared foundation, which has been cut through in the aisle space itself by many graves.

What could this feature represent? The suggestion that it represents an archway inserted within the aisle, when that aisle was still in use, seems most implausible. This is quite a major piece of construction and one would have to ask why such work, which would appear to be more or less unparalleled, might have been undertaken? A preferable explanation might be that this foundation represents all that is left of the footings for a newly constructed wall, across the line of the former aisle, intended to provide a western gable to support the roof of a chapel or chamber, and permit the remainder of the aisle, west of the foundation, to be demolished. In such circumstances, orders of the former south aisle doorway would become available for reuse as a newly fashioned archway to provide access between the newly created chapel or chamber and the nave.

It seems possible that these substantial works at the western end of this newly created space were the counterpart of the works identified as Phase VIII in *Wharram III*, which consisted largely of the reconstruction of the east wall of this building, and the provision of an enormous new south-eastern buttress. What might have been created, then, out of the east end of the south-aisle, when the rest was demolished, was a small 'chapel' some 5.25m by 6m.

Finally, then, it seems likely that the original Phase 4 south aisle did extend at least as far as the line of the chancel arch. Foundations continued the wall line beyond that point, but they were of a quite different character and on a different alignment. For reasons that the excavation report does make specific, it was thought that despite their differences, these foundations indicated that the aisle originally continued to the east, overlapping the chancel (Bell 1987a, 86-8). From the records that have come down to us it seems equally likely that the original east wall of the Phase 4 south aisle was to be found on the same line as the chancel arch, and was replaced in this location by the large heavily buttressed wall (Phase 7).

We are now in a position to reconstruct the likely appearance of the south door of the Phase 4 south aisle (Fig. 93). It was of three orders, housed within a projection from the wall itself. It was decorated with fine capitals and two decorated orders, outside the plain inner order which served as the frame for the door-leaf itself. Beyond the outer order of chevron moulding, which would have sat in the plane of the projection's façade, it is likely that there would have been a decorated hoodmoulding. A fragment from just such a hood moulding, of a distinctive type decorated with isolated rosettes, was recovered from a destruction layer in the Chancel (*Wharram III*, fiche fig. 155, no. 17; ADS Report, doi:10.5284/1000415, table 1, stone KK). Although it is hard to gauge the precise curvature of the arch from the single fragment, it appears to match the reconstructed chevron-moulded archway, and it is highly likely that this is the final remnant of the hoodmoulding of the south doorway.

The south arcade and aisle: dating

The arcade, and the south aisle which accompanied it, are precisely dated by the architectural details in the reconstructed south door and by those of the south arcade. All four capitals clearly belong to the third quarter of the 12th century. The arcade itself can also be dated to exactly the same period, and therefore so is the aisle to which it gave access. The base mouldings, of attic sequence, are precisely what one would expect at this date and compare with examples at many Yorkshire buildings of the third quarter of the 12th century from York Minster downwards (Rigold 1977, 127ff; Stocker 1999, 284 no. 126). They have a very upright *scotia* and a rounded lower *torus*. Similarly, the simple chalice

capitals can be allocated to the same period, though the more developed abacus on the westernmost pier is undoubtedly an advanced feature, and this detail, and indeed the extended form of the lower *torus* in the base, might suggest a date towards 1180 rather than one nearer 1150.

The west tower

When it was finally built, in Phase 4, the tower bore little resemblance to that intended for the Phase 3 church. Indeed, we might ask whether the original provision for a standard west tower of the Weaverthorpe type represented a realistic aspiration at Wharram, given the narrow space available west of the church. This might suggest, firstly, that the Phase 3 church was a design taken 'off the shelf', without much regard for its local context, and secondly that the aspiration to provide a tower had been important for the original commissioners of the Phase 3 building.

The new Phase 4 tower, however, involved the demolition of the central part of the west gable, which had been carefully prepared to accommodate a tower during its construction in Phase 3, retaining only the Phase 3 tower arch as an internal support for the first floor of the new tower. The walls of the Phase 4 tower were simply built through this gap in the gable, extending both inside and outside the line of the original gable wall. Although the excavators found a stratigraphic distinction between the footings to the west wall and those of the east wall (Thorn 1987, 111-12), the difference in dates can hardly have been significant.

The lower parts of the new tower were constructed using ashlar of very similar grade to that used in Phase 3 and it is likely that a good proportion of it was reused from the fabric taken from the upper parts of the west gable and from the former south wall where the new arcade was driven through (Fig. 89). It has already been argued that the new tower arch was probably built from reused components from the former south door of the Phase 3 church, and is therefore not a reliable dating indicator. Otherwise, the small simple tower is remarkably featureless. There had clearly been two round-headed lancets in the west wall. That lighting the ground floor was a very small loop (the head of which was recovered from the rubble after the wall's collapse), whereas that higher up, lighting the ringing chamber, was a more substantial window. It too, we have argued, could have been reused from Phase 3. Similarly, it seems likely that the simple chamfered plinth on which the west wall of the Phase 4 tower was founded was also built of reused stones from the south nave wall, where the excavations found some plinth stones of the same proportions still *in situ*.

Subsequent reconstructions of the upper parts of the Phase 4 tower also carefully reused the Phase 3 ashlars for a second time. Consequently, it is hard to tell how high the undisturbed Phase 4 tower fabric rises or rose. In both west and north walls, clear building breaks are visible, but in the east wall the belfry fabric (Phase 6) may extend as low as the head of the upper lancet window lighting the ringing chamber.

Fig. 93. Reconstruction of the late 12th-century south doorway. The reconstruction cannot be assumed to have precise metrical accuracy because there is uncertainty over the radius of the arch. (J Prudhoe after D. Stocker, based mainly on the published drawings of J. Thorn)

In the west nave wall there is clear evidence for the reveals of two window apertures placed high up in the interior face. The external reveals of these windows would have fallen perilously close to the estimated lines of the north and south walls of the intended Phase 3 western tower. This presumably suggests that they were not constructed until the original plan for the tower footprint had been abandoned in favour of the modified one that was

actually built; and that they should therefore be assigned to Phase 4. The west nave wall south of the tower retains much of its Phase 4 masonry. Although it is possible that parts of this surface date from Phase 3, there appears to be a clear break line in the coursing close to the present ground surface. To the north of the tower, however, the greater part of the wall facing clearly dates from the same Phase (7) as the reconstruction of the north-west quoin.

The west tower: dating

If it is true, as suggested, that most of the architectural details in the tower are reused from elsewhere, they cannot be employed to date its construction. The small loop in the west wall, which might have been made for this location, is so simple as to defy accurate dating. The Phase 4 tower fabric, however, contained a tympanum fragment that, we have argued, probably came from the south doorway of the Phase 3 church. As the replacement south doorway of Phase 4 can be precisely dated to the third quarter of the 12th century, the Phase 3 doorway must have become available for reuse at that time. The construction of the tower is, therefore, most likely to have taken place at the same time: in the third quarter of the 12th century. It would be remiss of us not to note, however, that there is something of a contrast in quality between the expansive and expensive new south aisle, with its up-to-the-minute architectural details, and the narrow, featureless tower, which apparently relied on reused architectural features for its decoration. The aisle must have come first, but it may be that the tower was completed somewhat later, and in a rush, with minimum expense.

The chancel

As already explained, the precise sequence of construction within the chancel arch was not elucidated during the excavations and the relationship between the Phase 3 nave and the elaborate Norman chancel was not investigated in detail. The large chalk raft constructed to support its eastern apse did not produce precisely datable artefacts. There is no reason to presume, however, that the new chancel and apse belong to Phase 3; and indeed, if they do, they leave us with a considerable puzzle regarding the original location for the remaining four large chevron-decorated arches for which we have evidence amongst the architectural fragments collection (ADS Report, doi:10.5284/1000415, table 1, stones B, F/R, O and V).

There is no doubt that these fragments represent four different orders from major archways (much larger in scale than the Phase 4 south doorway). Furthermore, whilst all of them are likely to date from the third quarter of the 12th century, two of them (ADS Report, doi:10.5284/1000415, table 1, stones O and V) belong to a group of the latest period of chevron-moulded architectural details, in which the complexity of the moulding is achieved by incorporating a deeply-undercut ariss roll. Such details, and therefore the arches from which they derive, undoubtedly belong to the second half of the 12th century and probably nearer 1175 than 1150. In other words, they indicate the presence within the church of three further orders, from a large arch or arches, which would be happily grouped along with features such as the westernmost pier in the south arcade and the capitals in the south doorway. Such arches belong to a major structural work of Phase 4, and not Phase 3.

If these orders came from a single arch it would have been of colossal size. It is more likely that they came from two separate arches, and the only possible locations

that we know about which could have accommodated arches of this size and quality are the two great arches implied by the ground plan of the new Romanesque chancel: one at the crossing arch and the other at the chord of the apse. It is theoretically possible that all four orders could have come from the same arch, but in practice the footings for an arch of such depth were not found in excavation. If it is accepted that these fragments do date the chancel, then it clearly belonged to Phase 4 not Phase 3, and to a similar date as the south arcade and south aisle. Indeed, if the extension of the south aisle beyond the line of the chancel arch is thought likely (though we have expressed reservations about this suggestion above), it might make better sense if it was built at the same time as the new chancel south wall.

There are a number of other architectural fragments from the third quarter of the 12th century which also presumably date from this Phase. These are catalogued in the ADS Report on the loose architectural stonework (doi:10.5284/1000415, table 1).

Phase 5: early 13th century (red)

The next substantial phase of datable work at St Martin's includes a north chapel and a new chancel arch. The aisle, or chapel, added to the north of the Phase 3 nave was not large, of only some 10m by 2.5m. Foundations survived reasonably well beneath the surface, especially in its eastern parts, where evidence for an altar platform was discovered against the eastern wall. There was a contemporary buttress extending northwards from the north-east corner, although any matching buttress extending eastwards would have been removed by the Phase 7 chapel. Such an eastwards buttress may not have existed as there was no equivalent feature at the north-western angle, where a buttress extending northwards was also suspected but not actually recorded (Bell 1987a, 81, fig. 21).

The aisle was divided from the former nave by an arcade of two bays with a single centrally placed pier. We can presume two windows in the north wall, one in the east, and probably one in the west also. We will see (below) that we can date the aisle's construction and we should note that the two windows inserted in the masonry with which the arcade was blocked in Phase 7, are a century or more later in date. These windows, then, were probably not simply transferred from the external aisle walls at that time, but must have come from elsewhere.

The arcade pier is circular in plan and sits on a square sub-base with a chamfered upper surface. The capital is of simple form, set above a simple astragal of semi-circular section. The neck is simply flared, and circular in section, but it supports an octagonal abacus, which is simply chamfered. The base mouldings are in very poor condition, but appear to be of simple form: a single astragal, set above a fat half-roll with little or no *torus*. The pier is reduced in diameter and the capital's flared neck lies at a considerably greater angle, and has quite different proportions, compared with those in the south arcade; but apart from that detail indicating a later date, taken as a whole the pier appears to be an imitation of the design of the more complex piers of the south arcade.

The arcade responds are both buried in the fabric of the blocking, but they appear to have been simple, perhaps so simple that they did not repeat the profile of the pier. Little of the arcade arches is visible beneath the blocking, but they are pointed in profile, and they were of two simply chamfered orders (revealed on the northern side). These arches also, then, are similar in form to those in the south arcade. Fragments of painted mural decoration were applied to the arcade pier in the centre of the arcade, which survived behind the blocking masonry of Phase VII (Thorn 1987, 134-6).

The masonry associated with the construction of the new arcade is clearly visible in the Phased elevations (Fig. 90), and, unlike the south arcade (which was inserted underneath the existing masonry), it was constructed by demolishing a whole length of the former nave wall and rebuilding it completely from foundations to wall-plate. When rebuilt it was considerably reduced in width, compared with the Phase 3 wall to the west. The lower parts of this inserted Phase 5 masonry can be traced right into the north-east corner of the nave where it turns south and forms the lower part of the east wall (Fig. 91). Here the Phase 5 masonry terminates against a simple chamfer (of the same proportions as that which can be seen against the western respond of the arcade). A precisely similar arrangement can be seen on the southern side of the chancel arch, where this masonry is clearly stratigraphically earlier than the masonry associated with the insertion of the archway east of the south arcade in Phase 7. This evidence in the nave east wall must indicate that the whole east wall of the nave was reconstructed at this moment.

The Phase 3 chancel arch must have been removed and presumably the gable was rebuilt. Unfortunately, there is very little evidence for the form of the chancel arch inserted at this date. Thorn's reconstruction (Thorn 1987, 128, fig. 46) is unlikely to be valid, however, as the visible chamfer is likely to have been merely the start of a sequence of half-shafts supporting the respond. All this detail was removed when the chancel arch was replaced with a narrower one in the following century (Phase 6), and this itself might indicate that the Phase 5 chancel arch was over-ambitious.

A final architectural detail which can be associated with Phase 5 is the conservative reconstruction of the north doorway (Plate 25). This was a very cheap and cautious piece of work. The external face of the Phase 3 door was removed and replaced with a new architrave which forms a simple arched doorway, decorated with a single simple chamfer. There is no other elaboration. On the interior face of the doorway, the Phase 3 rerearch was left *in situ*, although there was some patching of Phase 5 above and to the west. As has been mentioned, it seems that the simply chamfered western impost to the Phase 3 doorway was left *in situ* during the course of this work, indicating that this arch had sprung from a low-level relative to external ground level, which appears to have risen by about half a metre between Phases 3 and 5. It may be, therefore, that the doorway was reconstructed in Phase 5 simply to provide more adequate headroom, to ensure that those entering would no longer have to bow their heads (see Harding and Wrathmell 2007, 329-30).

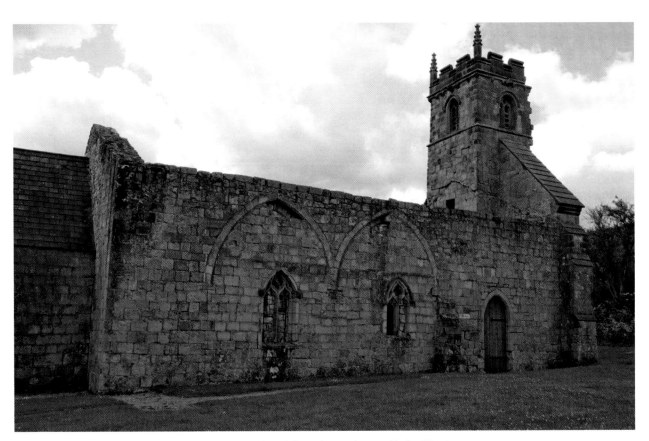

Plate 25. The blocked north arcade of St Martin's, viewed from the north-east. (P. Gwilliam)

Given the size of the aisle extension and its date, it is perhaps most likely that it was roofed with a single slope, extending the line of the nave roof downwards towards the churchyard. This implies that the windows in the north wall would have been small in size, probably no more than simple lancets, and that the aisle would have had no independent gable. In its turn, this suggests that the fragmentary gable cross (*Wharram III*, fiche fig. 160, no. 41; ADS Report, doi:10.5284/1000415, table 1, stone A) which is one of the finest of the architectural fragments discovered during clearance, is likely to have come from the east nave gable, above the chancel arch (which we have deduced from other indications in the fabric, must have been rebuilt). The base and socket stone for a gable cross (*Wharram III*, fiche fig. 159, no. 37; ADS Report, doi:10.5284/1000415, table 1, stone DDD), with its four simple gablets, represents a feature of precisely the same period, and indeed is of an appropriate size to have been the base for the gable cross.

Phase 5: dating evidence

We have noted several details in the north aisle arcade which might suggest that the masons were taking as their model the south arcade across the nave. But the details used, the simplified base (which is not of attic sequence), the flared profile of the simple capital and the pointed profile of the arcade arches, all indicate a somewhat later date. The arcade, and therefore the whole aisle, surely dates from the first half of the 13th century, perhaps from the first quarter, though the details are so simple that precision is not really possible on these grounds. Similarly, apart from its simple two-centred profile, there is no distinctive detail in the north doorway which would allow this phase to be dated with any greater precision.

If the arguments for associating the highly decorated gable cross and the new east gable of the nave with this phase are accepted then a much more precise date for this work might be obtained. The cross has four arms composed of bundled fronds, with pronounced vertical bindings, around a central boss, but the arms do not turn over at the tips in the fashion of the earlier 'bracelet-headed' crosses usually dated to the later 12th century (Butler 1964). This cross form can be dated from its occurrence on monumental gravecovers to the early 13th century and is used, for example, on the gravecover of Abbot Alanus of Tewkesbury who died in 1202, though the monument might not have been installed immediately (Cutts 1849, pl. XLII; Morris and Shoesmith 2003, 44-5, 162, 211). Closer to home is a cover at Tadcaster, West Riding, which Boutell (1854, 34) dated to *c.* 1225.

Phase 6: late 14th to early 15th centuries (green)

The chancel and north-east chapel

After six major phases in three hundred years, it may have been as long as another century before a further major phase of reconstruction was undertaken at St Martin's. But when it came, this new work represented a considerable investment in the church: this time at the eastern end and presumably, therefore, by the rector and/or the benefactor of the small chapel built to its north (Fig. 87). Once again, the wall along the line of the chancel arch was extensively modified, as it had been in almost every other phase of work previously, suggesting a continuing instability in this part of the fabric, which none of the earlier interventions had succeeded in neutralising.

The replacement of the chancel arch was merely one component of the complete reconstruction of the chancel itself. With the possible exception of a length of wall at the eastern end of the south wall, where it adjoined the overlapping south aisle, the former Phase 4 chancel was demolished and rebuilt on a slightly larger plan with a squared off east end, supported by buttresses at right angles to the north-east and south-east corners standing on the chalk raft foundation. Unfortunately, the excavators found very little of the fabric of the chancel intact, and the entire south wall foundations had been removed at later dates. The new chancel arch itself was narrower than the Phase 5 example it replaced. The arch itself is two centred, and of two chamfered orders, composed of well-cut, radially-jointed, voussoirs. The entirely distinct character of the masonry in which the arch is now set, however, demonstrates that the arch itself has been taken down and reset, no doubt during the reconstruction of the church in the 19th century. Nevertheless, it seems that traces of original wall painting consisting of red ochre sexfoils were discovered on the west face of the arch between 1958 and 1962 (Thorn 1987, 134-5).

The jambs, or responds, of the arch do not appear to have been greatly disturbed since their original construction. They too are simple semi-octagonal piers with a simple capital also of semi-octagonal form. They sit above an astragal with a slightly 'nibbed' profile, which might once have been an ogival fillet, whilst the simple hollowed neck supports an abacus component with a rounded extrados and a fillet. The fillet divides the lower half-roll from the upper component. The half-roll also appears to have a slightly 'nibbed' profile, which is marginally undercut by the neck itself. The base moulding is more simple. It sits above a square sub-base which is converted to an octagonal section by means of two simple lumpy broaches. The base consists of a simple roll moulding, between two quirks. The arch itself preserves the mortices and other details permitting Thorn to reconstruct the locations of screens and the rood-beam.

To the north of the chancel, and extending eastwards about half the length of it, lay a new north-east chapel. This small structure survived better beneath the ground surface than the chancel, with which it communicated by means of a simple doorway, the threshold of which was revealed in excavation. The chapel was supported by a large square buttress at the north-east corner, although only the foundation platform for this feature was recorded, and not the buttress itself. Towards its western end, there was a doorway through the north wall, providing access to the chapel independently from the remainder of the church (Bell 1987a, 80-83). Inside the chapel, the eastern third was occupied by a solid masonry altar platform, and a pit-like feature in the foundations of the north wall, towards its eastern end, was identified as a *piscina*. This last identification must be considered doubtful as *piscinae* are usually located in the south wall, to facilitate their use during the preparations for an aftermath of the mass, when the celebrant stands to the south of the altar.

The two windows now reset in the Phase 7 blocking of the north arcade were thought by Thorn to have originated in the north aisle wall (Thorn 1987, 123-7; see Plate 25). We have seen, however, that this structure, at least as originally constructed, probably had a cat-slide roof and its north wall would have been too low to accommodate windows of this size. They could, however, have come from the north-east chapel of Phase 6, and this suggestion is made more plausible by the fact that they are interestingly different from each other. Although the tracery designs are similar, they are not identical: the principal difference is that the westernmost is a smaller window, with main lights about 300mm shorter than its fellow. They probably represent, then, two windows cut for the same building at the same time, but cut for different locations within that building. Given that we think it unlikely that they will have come from the aisle itself, the north-eastern chapel looks like an obvious alternative.

Furthermore, their slight differences suggest that the taller, easternmost might have been cut for the tall northern wall of the chapel, whereas the shorter, westernmost was perhaps cut for the east gable wall – the reduced height being necessary to accommodate an altar and reredos beneath it. The windows themselves are of two glazed lights each under cusped heads of ogival form. Each has a single symmetrical tracery unit consisting of a single cusped quatrefoil, again with ogival foils. The westernmost window preserves its external hoodmoulding, which is an extremely simple form, and both windows have been reset in the company of some outsized stops (on the north face only), which clearly do not belong with these windows, and those on the western window do not match the hoodmoulding. These are, however, fine decorative sculptures, and presumably also came from within the chancel or, perhaps more likely, given they are reused with these windows, from the north-east chapel.

The chancel and north-east chapel dating evidence
The work in the chancel and chapel to its north can be dated relatively precisely through the survival of three datable components: the two windows reused in the blocking of the north nave arcade and the chancel arch. The window tracery designs are simple ogival forms, using a simple double-chamfered mullion section, but they are easily dated to the mid or later 14th century (perhaps to the third quarter). All four decorative stops, now reused as dripstones on the northern faces of the reset windows in the blocking of the north arcade, are of mid or later 14th-century character, with one lady's hair-

do in particular (westernmost window, eastern stop) being quite closely datable as it is the type seen on the tombs of Blanche of the Tower (d.1342) and Philippa of Hainault (d.1369), whose monuments in Westminster Abbey both date from the 1370s (Duffy 2003, 131, 133-7). A broadly similar date is implied by the simple mouldings on the chancel arch itself, where the slight 'nibbing' on the rolls (created from ogival curves of course) also indicates a date in the 14th century. There might have been a difference in the dates of construction between the chancel and north-east chapel of about a generation, however. A circumstantial case can be made for the construction of the chancel between *c.* 1308 and *c.* 1327, one explored in Chapter 16 (pp 273-4).

The west tower and south aisle
Thorn attributed the reconstruction of the upper parts of the west tower, including the provision of a new belfry, to the same phase as these works on the choir and north-east chapel (Thorn 1987, 112-14). As he recognised, although much of the masonry in the upper parts of the tower derives from earlier structures, it was actually erected in its present form (or at least in its form prior to 1959) in the 19th century. The phasing of the fabric shows, however, that there was a campaign of later medieval work on the west wall of the nave and in the first floor of the tower which, although it has no fixed relationship to the work on the chancel, might date from this same general period. These works included the blocking up of the two Phase 4 windows to either side of the tower and the reconstruction of the upper parts of the high level doorway. The work in the high-level doorway included replacing the lintel on the eastern face and the stones forming the upper parts of the jambs that supported it. This repair work might suggest that the original lintel had failed, but taken along with the blocking of the two windows to either side of the tower, it might rather indicate a general strengthening of the tower in preparation for the provision of a new belfry; no doubt one equipped with cage-mounted bells suitable for change-ringing.

Also belonging to this general late medieval period, but clearly of a somewhat different date to the chancel and north-east chapel, was the refurbishment associated with the two fine traceried windows which are now located within the Phase 7 blocking walls beneath the south aisle arcades. These windows are more or less identical, and stand under simple square lintels with plain labels, now on the southern sides of the windows. These labels have a simple quarter-circle profile. The windows are each of two triple-cusped lights (under arch-heads which are struck from a single centre, i.e. they are semicircular) with simple tracery above. The central mullions (of simple double chamfered section) are carried up to divide the tracery panels into two, each of which is then equally subdivided. The tracery lights themselves have cusped lights struck from a single centre. It is a simple form of tracery, which sits comfortably within windows under square lintels, but it results in the distinctive feature of a vertical mullion rising from the centre of the head of the major light below, in what is often thought to be a 'Perpendicular' fashion.

Thorn and others have argued that these two windows were relocated under the blocked south arcade in Phase 7, when that blocking was itself first executed, and this is clearly correct. They have then proceeded to suggest that these windows, like the components of the south door (see above), were relocated from the original south aisle wall a few metres to the south, when that was demolished in this same phase (Thorn 1987, 121). Certainly this form of window, with its diminished height and square lintel, would be of an appropriate size to have come from the relatively low external wall of the south aisle, and this, rather than any other detail, suggests that this conjecture is probably correct. Because the doorway to the aisle was placed centrally, however, these two windows would have been placed opposite the first and third arches of the arcade.

The windows, then, presumably represent a substantial refurbishment of the aisle during Phase 6, which will have offered not just a more up-to-date and impressive façade to the south but also the opportunity for some stained glass imagery to enhance the ritual and didactic uses of the building. Such enhancement of the south aisle might also be associated with the construction of a south porch, the plan of which was recovered during the excavations (Bell 1987a, 88), but there is no formal link between the two embellishments and they could have been separated in time by many decades. So little of the porch footings was recorded that we can say little about it, but it seems quite likely that the reused arch stones that form the southern arch of the present porch (which is presumed by Bell to have been rebuilt in the early 17th century: Bell 1987a, 91) were originally located in the same location but in the Phase 6 porch, some 10m to the south.

The porch's two-centred archway (which is heavily weathered) is decorated with a minimal hollow chamfer between fillets, which is a moulding detail not often found in isolation, being more usually a component of arches of more than one order. The moulding is continuous into the arch-head, which is provided with a simple hood-moulding (also decorated with a hollow chamfer between two broad fillets) standing on two stops, both once elaborately carved, but now unrecognisable. Although it is not entirely clear, it seems likely that the fine decorated gable-cross base (ADS Report, doi:10.5284/1000415, table 1, stone EEE) which now sits above the gable at the south end of the reconstructed porch, was located there in the late 1950s when the archaeologists first arrived at Wharram. It does not quite fit this location, suggesting that it too could have come from the Phase 6 porch, but as we will see below, it is possible that it comes from a larger gable at the eastern end of the church and could have been added to the south porch for example at the time when the gable above the chancel arch was reconstructed in the 18th or 19th century.

The west tower and south aisle dating evidence

The renewal of the south aisle can be dated relatively precisely to the period around the year 1400 by the distinctive tracery design in the windows. Windows of this type, with mullions rising from the heads of the lights beneath, are ultimately derived from the new tracery designs used in the new east end of York Minster. This work began in 1361, but its full effects were not really seen in local buildings until the end of the century, when such lights become widespread in Yorkshire (e.g. Stocker 2001, 595).

On the other hand, the gable-cross base on the present porch has a somewhat weathered decorative detail on one face (no doubt originally its eastward-facing face), which incorporates a trefoil-headed gablet with a central ogival light. This ogival detail associates it not so much with the fenestration of the south aisle but with that of the north aisle, which might suggest that it dates from a decade or two earlier in the 14th century. This slight stylistic discrepancy might make us question whether the gable cross did originate from the new Phase 6 south porch, or whether it might have come from elsewhere in the building. We cannot be certain how the north-east chapel was roofed, and whether or not it had a ridged roof. Gables at either end of the new building are a possibility, with the cat-slide of the north aisle terminating against the western gable, but there is no evidence in the excavated remains for such an arrangement.

A more likely location, then, for the elaborate gable cross represented by this fine decorative base might be the chancel itself: either from the east gable, or from a newly reconstructed eastern gable to the nave, over the reconstructed chancel arch. In our revised understanding of Phase 7 below, we suggest that the chancel was indeed demolished at the time we suspect that the present south porch was constructed (i.e. within Phase 6 and not in the 17th century when Thorn thought was most likely), and therefore such an original location for the gable-cross would be feasible. This stylistic link between the gable-cross base and the windows in the north-aisle is a tenuous one, however, and if we are suggesting that other material for the reconstructed south porch came from the Phase 6 south porch, such as the southern archway, we might presume that this was the most likely origin for the gable-cross base also. As for the moulding around the south porch archway itself, that is less precisely datable, but a date in the late 14th century would be entirely appropriate.

Dating the reconstruction of the upper parts of the tower, providing a new belfry and spire appears, on the face of it, to be relatively straightforward. Although the masonry of the upper parts of the tower that survived to be drawn during the project represented a wholesale reconstruction of 1881-2, Thorn demonstrated that this reconstruction had not only reused walling masonry from the late medieval tower, but had also reset a number of architectural details, including a series of masks within the undercut string supporting the battlements, fragments from merlons (decorated with incised cross-bottonnée), coping stones, three water-spouts and blocks decorated with the heraldic arms of the Hilton family (*Wharram III*, fiche figs 157-8; ADS Report, doi:10.5284/1000415, table 1, stones SS, TT, UU, VV, WW, XX, YY, ZZ, AAA, BBB and CCC). The Hiltons acquired Wharram around 1403 (Beresford M.W. 1979, 19-20) and their interest in the site seems to have faded within a generation. It is highly likely, then, that the reconstruction of the tower with its new bell-chamber and intended spire dated from the first decade or so of the 15th century. As it happens, we have seen that such a date would also be very appropriate for the refurbishment of the south aisle with its new windows and added south porch.

Phase 7: mid-16th century (blue)

After several centuries of expansion, the next marked phase of work at St Martin's represents a radical contraction of the fabric. The floor-area of the church was reduced by more than half, and the resulting 'box' would have offered only the minimum accommodation for services. Work of this phase occurs throughout the nave fabric, and is marked primarily by demolitions and the building up of arcades, wall-stubs and scars to make the remaining standing fabric sound.

At the western end of the nave, two areas of rebuilding, probably mostly consisting of a refacing of earlier core-work, are clearly visible, incorporating reconstructions of both north-west and south-west nave buttresses. Both buttresses have set-offs and their associated sloping and chamfered stones, which create an oddly matched pair, disregard the usual design rules for such architectural features and are also quite different from each other. These design oddities establish that both are reconstructions of earlier features and that they reuse the cut and moulded stones in a haphazard manner. There was probably always a buttress of some sort on the north-west corner of the nave, which has merely been rebuilt in this phase, and probably had its footprint extended to the north. That to the south-west angle of the nave, however, was evidently newly constructed in this phase, and the core of this masonry must be the remains of the former west wall of the south aisle. This south-western buttress establishes that this phase of work at the west end is contemporary with the demolition of the south aisle of Phase 4.

The demolition of the west and south walls of the south aisle at this phase was a major matter. The two eastern bays of the south arcade were blocked up with reused masonry, which was almost certainly derived from the former south aisle south and west walls, and pierced with the two windows of Phase 6. They were evidently relocated in the new arcade blocking without modifications, and were probably reglazed with the glass with which they had originally been provided in their original locations. The former south doorway into the south aisle (originally created during Phase 4) was dismantled when the wall was demolished and the stones from its two outer orders were reused in two new arches.

First, the stones from the original roll-moulded order were reset within the blocking of the westernmost bay of the former south arcade to form the arch head of the new south doorway (Plate 23). The head of the archway, which was formerly circular, had to be squeezed laterally to fit into the new space and so the reset arch is nearly two centred, but without a clearly pointed apex. Instead, a cut-down moulded voussoir section had to be inserted here to form a flat top to the arch.

The two fine later 12th-century capitals, originally supported by nook-shafts were also relocated to support this order, but in their new location they evidently had to be recut to fit. They have probably also been transposed, i.e. that to the east was probably on the western side of the original embrasure and vice-versa. The original form taken by the jambs below the shafts in their reconstruction of Phase 7 is somewhat obscured by the replacement of the two nook-shafts and their associated bases in recent times. Beneath these inserted nook-shafts and bases, behind the bench of the later porch, the jambs of the Phase 7 doorway continue in a different form, apparently reusing chamfered sections.

Other elements from the original south doorway of Phase 4, however, were reused in what was probably an entirely new archway further east in the original nave south wall (Plate 24). As we have explained, the excavations in the eastern end of the south aisle revealed the evidence for a complex series of alterations which were not entirely understood, but none of these results suggested that there was an opening through the south nave wall this far east (leading into the eastern bay of the aisle) prior to Phase 7. As the opening is formed entirely from reused sections of late 12th-century masonry, therefore, it is likely that it was first created during Phase 7. The masonry involved is the outer of the two moulded orders of the archway of the original south doorway (which was decorated with a distinctive two-dimensional chevron) and the innermost order of its jambs, along with its integral angle-shaft moulding and etiolated capitals.

There can be no doubt that this masonry is reused in this location, as the mouldings merely terminated above loose rubble at the latest floor-levels within the church, but there are many other tell-tale signs, such as the discrete recutting of several voussoirs and the insertion of an entirely new voussoir at the head of the arch to give it its arcuate profile. Both *abaci* have been lost in the transfer from the Phase 4 south doorway to their new location, as they have been replaced by a simply fashioned moulded stone, which makes only a slight effort to imitate the original moulding and also seems to be in a slightly different petrology.

Some of the masonry surrounding the archway is also of the period of this insertion in Phase 7. As one would expect, cutting a hole through the original wall and inserting the moulded components from the original south doorway would create quite a mess either side of the new feature, and the panels of refacing dating from Phase 7 are clearly visible in the elevation, especially to the east. It is notable that much of the masonry used for this refacing work is reused late 12th-century ashlar, almost certainly derived, like the architectural details themselves, from the south aisle south wall. The blocking of the Phase 3 window above the new archway is likely to derive from this period also, but as explained above, because of the uncertainties surrounding the phasing of changes in the east end of the south aisle, it is not clear whether this window was first blocked at an earlier phase.

Although it is interesting and worthwhile to chart the reuse of stone from the demolished south aisle in the newly created 'box' of Phase 7, the most intriguing question is why, at a time when the church was contracting, a new archway was considered necessary at the east end of the south nave wall at all, especially as the former south arcade further west was being walled up at the same moment. Unfortunately, the complexities revealed by the excavations in the south aisle in this area demonstrate only that this end of the aisle was rebuilt on various occasions in the later middle ages and subsequently.

At one stage, however, a substantial footing was constructed north to south across the aisle at a point a small distance to the west of the western jamb of the newly inserted archway. This wall has already been discussed and is puzzling, not only for its location but also for its considerable scale. It looks very much like the foundation for a load-bearing wall across the aisle at the point. It was added to the Phase 3 nave and might have supported the original eastern terminal wall of the south aisle in Phase 4, before the former was extended eastwards. Logically, its use as a foundation should be placed stratigraphically at this same Phase 7, as it is only at this point that we have any evidence that the eastern end of the aisle is being used in a different manner from the aisle further west.

It seems most satisfactory, then, to associate this excavated foundation with the insertion of the new archway through the south nave wall in Phase 7 and to suggest that it was intended to support the western wall of a new chamber, fashioned out of the eastern end of the aisle once the remainder of the aisle to the west had been demolished. Such an explanation would also provide a justification for the apparent continuation of alterations to the south-east corner of the aisle into and beyond Phase 7 and the addition of a substantial, but apparently very crude, diagonal buttress in the south-east corner, at a period when the remainder of the aisle was apparently being demolished.

The evidence in the fabric, then, points towards a complex situation at the eastern end of the south aisle in Phase 7. It appears that even though the nave was being reduced greatly in size, nevertheless the eastern end of the south aisle was not demolished but instead its east and south walls, along with a new western wall, were incorporated into a small rectangular chamber. It was accessed from the nave via a newly created archway which was composed entirely of decorated late 12th-century masonry derived from the former south doorway of the south aisle. With the exception of the room beneath

the tower, which would be required for bell-ringing, this would have created the only space within the reconstructed building which could be screened off, for example as a vestry or parish room.

The date at which the present south porch was added remains unclear. In stratigraphic terms, it appeared later in date than the blocking of the westernmost bay of the south porch, but although it was placed in a 17th-century phase in *Wharram III* (Bell 1987a, 91), no positive evidence for this was reported. It is, however, still entered via a reused open archway, which has not been greatly damaged during its reuse and is of 14th-century date. It is hard to envisage where this archway could have come from to be reused in this location except for the equivalent arch of the earlier porch, which we have ascribed (largely on the basis of the date of the arch itself) to Phase 6 (above). Surely the assumption must be that this porch was demolished at the same time that the aisle itself was demolished, in Phase 7, and that its component archway was reused very shortly after the blinding wall in the south arcade, against which it was set, was inserted?

On the north side of the nave, further demolitions were in progress, and were probably undertaken as part of the same campaign of reconstruction as those we have identified in the south aisle. Here the mid-13th-century north aisle was also demolished and its two-bay arcade was walled up. Again, the masonry used for the blocking work is reused ashlar, and once again we can suggest that it derives from the fabric of the former north aisle wall. We have already seen, however, that the two simple traceried windows that were reset in the new blocking walls were probably not from the aisle itself, but from the north-east chapel that was attached to its eastern end. This must imply that the north-east chapel was demolished at the same time as the north-aisle, which might be a logical deduction anyway, although there was no clear evidence for the association in the excavations.

As the two windows of the north-east chapel were carefully removed for reuse, it is likely that the walls of the chapel were taken down, probably to the ground, and this leaves the question of what happened to the chancel fabric during the major reconstruction of Phase 7. Once again, the excavations did not elucidate the sequence of events here. It was originally presumed (*Wharram III*) that the chancel of Phase 6 continued in use until replaced by the surviving structure in the earlier part of the 17th century, by which date wall-paintings were being applied to its interior.

The post-excavation analysis of a socketed stone associated with a burial high up in the stratigraphic sequence, suggested that burials were taking place within the area of the Phase 6 chancel at a time when this was an exterior space (Ryder 2007, 293-4). This must imply that at some date between its construction in the 14th century and its replacement in the 17th century, the chancel was open to the elements, perhaps as a ruin rather than having been completely demolished, and that this space became part of the burial ground. It is perhaps most likely that the closure of the chancel, accompanied, presumably, by the blocking of the Phase 6 chancel arch, for which no clear evidence was reported in the excavations, occurred during the phase of radical contraction we have called Phase 7.

There is, in fact, good evidence from our fabric analysis that the chancel was at least partly demolished during Phase 7. The reconstruction of the north-east angle of the building included a buttress (with reused cut details) very similar to those at the south-west and north-west angles. But critically, this refacing of the Phase 6 wall in Phase 7 continued across the northern part of the eastern face of the east nave wall and across the lines of the north chancel wall. In other words, when the north-east corner of the building was reconstructed, it seems that not only did the work to remove the scars of the former north-east chapel disappear beneath the refacing, but so did the scar left by the demolition of the north chancel wall. In fact it is highly likely that there was also similar refacing of the scar left by the demolition of the south chancel wall, but we cannot associate the panel of masonry here directly with Phase 7, as the intervening south-eastern buttress has been extensively rebuilt in a post-medieval phase.

Phase 7: dating evidence

There is no independent archaeological argument for the date of these major works to the fabric, although a 16th-century book-clasp was found in the demolition rubble associated with the north-east chapel (Bell 1987a, 84-5). All the newly-constructed features of this date were built reusing earlier architectural features. Nevertheless, the comprehensive nature of the contractions, aimed at producing a square 'box', very likely with an entirely new roof, marks such a break with the liturgy of late-medieval England that we are very much inclined to think that it must post-date the Reformation. In particular, the demolition of the north-east chapel, which as we have seen was probably associated with the contemporary demolition of the choir, is unlikely to have become functionally redundant before the dissolution of chantries in 1547, but equally will have been completely redundant after that event. Similarly, whilst the late medieval Church had assumptions about maintaining distinctions between the laity in the nave and the clergy in the choir, these requirements were simply removed in the course of the Reformation, when even moderate protestants would prefer the altar to have been brought into the same space as the communicants.

Furthermore, the Phase 7 alterations seem very purposeful, and directed towards the single end of constructing a simple 'box'. All four quoins were rebuilt, for example, and this probably suggests that all this demolition and reconstruction took place in a single moment, perhaps within a single year. Bell noted that the chapels at Towthorpe, Raisthorpe and Thixendale were all demolished c. 1550 (Beresford M.W. 1987, 6-7; Bell 1987a, 84), and it may be that reconstruction of the parochial church at Wharram Percy was an integral part of this same rationalisation of ecclesiastical provision.

Some circumstantial support for a date of around 1550 for the reduction of the medieval church to a simple box can be extracted from the sequence of wall paintings identified within the building between 1958 and 1962. This study revealed that the nave of the church was redecorated after the blocking of the arcades, when a clear painted surface (Surface II) was identified (Thorn 1987, 136). Presumably, this surface would have been necessary immediately after the blocking of the arcades, as that operation itself would have damaged existing decorations considerably. Surface II carried indecipherable black-letter scripts which, although not conclusive evidence, is a sign that the contraction and reconstruction might belong to the period after the Reformation, when such decorations became much more common, especially following Elizabeth I's instructions to her Church Commissioners in 1560 (Cox and Harvey 1907, 356).

Furthermore, the detailed assessment of the decorative surfaces identified second, third and fourth redecorations, all overlaid on Surface II (Surfaces III, IV and V). The final one of these surfaces not only extended into the chancel, but carried a decorative roundel which can be dated style-critically to the period 'late 16th to early 17th century'. Presuming that the church was redecorated about once every generation (i.e. about 25 years), and presuming that the box-like building of Phase 7 was created c.1550, this implies that the chancel of Phase 8 was rebuilt in about 1625. The distinctive marked burial reported in *Wharram XI* (Ryder 2007, 293-4) already mentioned, would thus have been of an Elizabethan or early Jacobean individual, who took advantage of the period of something like two or three generations, when the space of the former medieval chancel was thrown into the burial ground, to be buried on or near the site of the medieval high altar in his prominently marked grave. Such an act must have represented a strong statement of religious and political position on the part of the deceased and/or his family, and must have represented a considerable determination to mark the site where the medieval mass had been performed.

Phases 8-9

For the purposes of the present volume, the reconsideration of the phasing and the fabric of St Martin's stops at the newly defined Phase 7. There were, however, at least four further major interventions in the fabric between the close of Phase 7 and the 1950s: the construction of the existing chancel (c. 1620-30?); the re-roofing and reconstruction of the east nave gable; the reconstruction of the tower following its collapse in 1882, and the reconstruction of the east end of south nave wall following its collapse in 1923.

It is possible that the lowering of the pitch of the nave roof and the associated reconstruction of the eastern gable of the nave was undertaken in the later 18th or early 19th century. It is equally possible, however, that it was undertaken as part of the reconstruction of the western gable during the process of propping the west tower after its collapse in 1881. The details of all these reconstructions were not explored in detail as part of the excavation and structural recording projects, and the reader is referred to *Wharram III* (Bell 1987a, 47-97; Thorn 1987, 98-140) for what information is available.

A note on the fonts of Wharram

Jim Thorn was greatly interested in the font he found at St Martin's in the late 1950s and devoted a short section to it in *Wharram III* (129-30, fig. 47). It appears, however, that evidence for two Wharram fonts was actually recovered, with the evidence for the second one going unnoticed until the recent reassessment work.

The first Wharram font

The evidence for an earlier font than that recorded by Thorn in such detail is a pair of small fragments, which Thorn catalogued in his fiche as two fragments from the head of a Romanesque window (*Wharram III*, fiche fig. 155, no. 16; ADS Report, doi:10.5284/1000415, table 1, stone W). They represent a (sub)circular feature cut on three sides, with a bold cable-moulding along the outside of the curvature, set above a quirk, which itself stands above a worked face which has been broken away beneath. 'Inside' the cable-moulding, along the edge of the interior surface, is an irregular, incised, wavy line. The interior surface at right-angles to this plane is also finely worked and is parallel to the 'external' face. There is no way these two stones can be reconstructed as an architectural feature. They are clearly two fragments from the rim of a font bowl (Fig. 94). In such a reconstruction the font bowl would have been in the order of 45cm in diameter, though not enough survives to say how deep it was, nor how high the artefact stood above the church floor.

The two fragments represent a 'tub' font of a type that is quite familiar from examples across the country (examples from Canterbury, St Martin, Avington (Berkshire) and Lullington (Somerset) to Ilam (Staffordshire) and Kirkby (Lancashire) (e.g. Bond 1908 passim). A very similar fragment was recovered from the church site of unknown dedication that was excavated in the north-east bailey of Norwich Castle in 1979 (Ayers 1985). In his analysis of these fragments (nos 1 and 2), Stephen Heywood dismissed the possibility that they came from an early Norman font in favour of an explanation of the stones as fragments of an Anglo-Saxon arcaded screen of a type usually associated with capital buildings of much earlier date (despite the fact that the church itself was only of late 10th or 11th-century date: Heywood 1985, 41-4).

The type of font is particularly common, however, in the old East Riding (Fig. 95), where Norman fonts are reported in more than 40 churches by Pevsner and Neave (1995). Of these East Riding examples, the great majority take this earlier 'tub' or 'drum' form (ADS Report, doi:10.5284/1000415, table 2) and at least sixteen of these have a cable-moulded rim matching that at

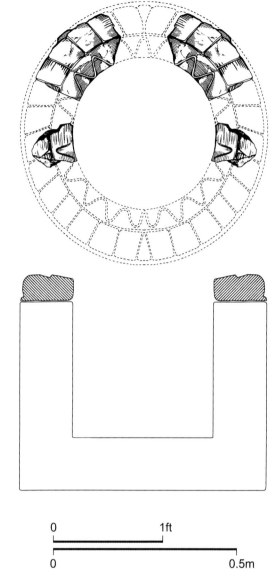

Fig. 94. Reconstruction of the early 12th-century 'tub' font. (J Prudhoe after D. Stocker, based on published drawings of J. Thorn)

Wharram, in twelve of which the cable takes the simplex form represented here. All of these fonts are cut, like the Wharram example, in a similar-looking yellow Jurassic limestone, and their distribution is tightly grouped, in the northern Wolds, especially along the southern edge of the hills between Flamborough and the hills above Middleton-on-the-Wolds, although there are also a number in the Great Wold Valley.

The new example from Wharram is towards the western edge of the known distribution, but it emphasises that, in the early 12th century at least, trading patterns in stone extended to Wharram's east and south, and not to the north-west, although there are plenty of cable-moulded fonts in the North Riding. The distinctive feature of the new Wharram font is the wavy line on the inside edge of the bowl. This feature has not been noted elsewhere, but every single one of the fonts still in use has had a rebate cut into this upper edge at a later date to

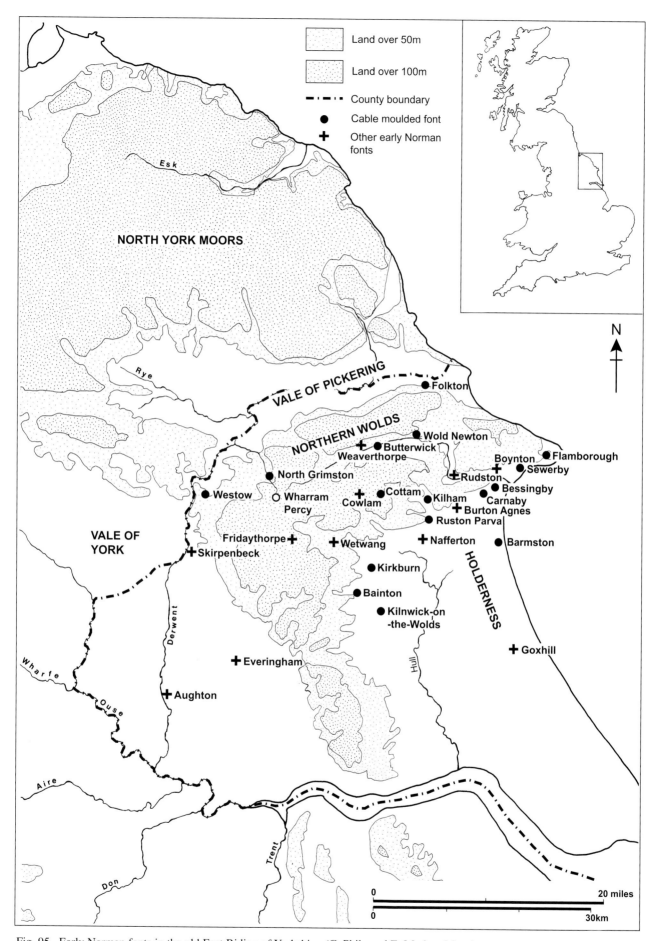

Fig. 95. Early Norman fonts in the old East Riding of Yorkshire. (C. Philo and E. Marlow-Mann)

261

provide a seating for the font cover. It is consequently difficult to say whether this is an unusual feature or common place. Its survival, however, might indicate that the font at Wharram was not in use at the time of the famous edict of 1236 that fonts should be kept with a locked lid (Bond 1908, 281). It is possible, however, that the wavy line might not have represented pure decoration, being related perhaps to the sealing of the flange of the lead lining within the bowl over the rim itself.

The identification of this earlier font fills in the gap left in Thorn's analysis of the font which was found in the church in the late 1950s. As we shall see, that font is unlikely to be much earlier in date than the late 12th century, yet we know that the church had been there for at least a century and a half by then. The church is known to have had burial rights since around the turn of the millennium, which is very likely to indicate its foundation as a parish church at that period, and how early baptism was conducted in the parish at this stage remains a matter of speculation. So many parochial churches were provided with internal fonts following the Norman Conquest that, without this new discovery, we would be searching for an explanation for Wharram's lack of a font during the 12th century. Unfortunately, we have little indication of the archaeological context of the fragment. Thorn reported that it was discovered 'discarded in the 1962 clearance', without any further detail (Thorn, Site Archive, p. 330).

Fonts were regarded as having a special status amongst ecclesiastical furnishings, because of their direct contact with consecrated water. It is notable, for example, that Wharram's second font has an inscribed cross on one of its faces (*Wharram III*, fiche, p. 283), which was almost certainly made during a consecration ceremony (Stocker 1997, 21). The disposal of redundant fonts has therefore always presented a liturgical problem (Stocker 1997). Typically, the solution was to bury the old font beneath the new one. Sometimes the old font was broken up ('ritually killed') before this process took place. It is possible, therefore, that these two fragments represent evidence for the disposal of Wharram's early Norman font within the church floor, perhaps as part of a rubble footing for its replacement, and that they became detached from their archaeological context during the 1962 clearance process.

There is, for example, a circular feature located centrally within St Martin's nave and seemingly filled with rubble (visible in *Wharram III*, pl. V and reported on p.66). In *Wharram III* this feature is associated with the adjacent furnace and bell-casting pit, but the fact that there was no burning associated with it, and that it was much shallower than either industrial feature, caused puzzlement. It is conceivable that this feature was a footing for a font (presumably the second font, below) and that the rubble with which it was filled included fragments of the early Norman font, of which, only these two stones have come down to us. In his archive report, Thorn was unable to suggest where the font had been originally located within the church (Thorn, Site Archive, p. 286).

St Martin's surviving font

Jim Thorn wrote a very extensive account of the surviving Wharram font, which is still housed in the church of St Michael and All Angels, Orchard Park Road, Hull (Thorn, Site Archive, pp 282-87). The description he generated in 1979 is still entirely valid and the reader is referred to it. Thorn pointed out the similarities between this font and later Norman members of the East Riding group, such as Fridaythorpe and Langton locally, both of which include blind arcading of approximately similar type decorated with comparable 'nailhead' decoration. He also pointed to the font at Belton (Lincolnshire) which, though octagonal in plan, nevertheless has panels with similar segmental arches outlined in 'nailhead' to those at Wharram, though here the panels are more elaborately formed, with fully formed architectural detailing, and are filled with interesting, though recut, figures. Thorn suggested that these parallels all indicated that Wharram's second font was set up around the year 1200. He was probably correct in his assessment.

16 Who at Wharram?
by Paul Everson and David Stocker

Development of the nucleated settlement in the 12th century

The nucleated settlement at Wharram underwent great change before its eventual desertion, and within, the patterns of its property plots and lanes, as well as its buildings, were also enhanced, changed and demolished. In the following section we will consider how some of these changes in the physical shape and appearance of the settlement and its buildings relate to changes in ownership and leadership during the late 11th and 12th centuries, which we can understand from the fragmentary documentary history and the record of church rebuilding that have been unravelled in the two previous chapters. In particular, we wish to explore the relationship between changes in the physical character of the settlement and its buildings, and the development of resident lordship (as opposed to lordship exercised at a distance), suggesting eventually that there is a close relationship between the one and the other.

In trying to bridge the historically obscure century following Domesday Book in the absence of the useful aid that Lincolnshire enjoys with the Lindsey Survey, David Roffe proposes that, in 1086, Lagmann and Karli no longer held their dependent tenancies in Wharram, and that their reunited estate (which was in the king's hands in 1086) was alienated to Osbert the Sheriff in the late 11th or early 12th century. According to him, in 1086 'it would seem that the two estates in Wharram, though not necessarily waste, were untenanted and in consequence were probably loosely administered by the sheriff' (Roffe 2000a, 10). As a single estate, the former double manor became part of the Chamberlain fee, though it was not formally enfeoffed until shortly after 1166 and by 1176-7 the Percy family had become mesne tenants of the Chamberlains.

There is, however, no sign that the Chamberlains actually held court themselves at Wharram between 1066 and 1166; Wharram was only a small component of a large estate, and it is entirely credible that the successors of Lagmann and/or Karli would have continued to act as the Chamberlains' representatives in the manor, exercising seigneurial power from their hall(s) until the establishment of the Percy's mesne tenancy shortly after 1166. Even so, lordly patronage was probably not absent at Wharram in the late 11th and early 12th centuries, but we have some difficulty assessing the extent of its influence. The small two-celled church (which remains Phase 2 in our reassessment: Chapter 15, Fig. 87) was probably erected in the first half of the 11th century and is associated with the earliest phases of elite burials in the graveyard outside (Stocker 2007a, 271-87). But neither church nor burial group reflects any status higher than the lord's 'representative', and the burials are unlikely to be of shrieval rank (Stocker 2007a, 285-7). In the same reassessment of St Martin's church, however, it seems clear that the major reconstruction of the nave, and the provision that was made for a great west tower (which we have now re-designated Phase 3), belongs to the first or second decade of the 12th century, i.e. it falls into this period when the manor was probably held by the Chamberlains, and might therefore be seen as evidence for the intervention of a remote lord in the fabric of his outlying estate.

The Phase 3 church resembles in several respects that surviving at Weaverthorpe, a few miles to the east. Like Weaverthorpe (Plate 19), it seems that St Martin's Wharram was originally intended to be equipped with a large west tower. This structure was perhaps intended for use in the latest elaboration of the burial rite, which was ordained by the new ecclesiastical regime of Archbishop Lanfranc after the Conquest, and which we have suggested lay behind the construction of so many similar contemporary towers in Lincolnshire (Stocker and Everson 2006). Weaverthorpe was also equipped with a new tub font at this date, and it now seems clear that Wharram acquired one of similar type at this date also (pp 260-62 and Figs 94-5). Both tower and font indicate a Wharram community, and any external patron, keeping abreast of the latest advances in liturgical practice, and they point towards Wharram's participation in the symbolism of the new lordly world of Henry I's reign.

Of course, we do not know how much influence the Chamberlains might have had over the decision to undertake this major building project. In our study of late 11th and early 12th-century churches in Lincolnshire, we noted that many churches of the 'on-the-green' type exemplified by Wharram existed in vills with large numbers of sokemen at Domesday, and we speculated that such settlements, whilst not being without direction and guidance from their lords and their officials, might nevertheless have been more independent in their actions,

and that the resident sokemen might have been more influential in undertaking building projects in these vills than they would have been in those with resident lordship (pp 210-11). If this line of reasoning has any merit, it might suggest that, at Wharram, the major works at St Martin's might have been undertaken, on their common open space, by the large population of resident free peasantry here; no doubt with the consent of the Chamberlains, but perhaps without the very active participation of that family. This is not to suggest a change in social composition in the vill between Phases 2 and 3, however. We have already argued that Lagmann and Karli, who led the vill during the early 11th century, were of no more than sokeman rank, and we are only suggesting that the leading sokemen of the early 12th-century vill, probably the descendants of Lagmann and Karli, remained just as influential in respect of community decisions, such as the reconstruction of community assets like the church.

Nevertheless, the Phase 3 church was a major architectural statement, especially compared with the cramped and unambitious building which preceded it. The new liturgies exemplified by the tower and the font, introduced by Archbishop Lanfranc at the end of the 11th century, owe their existence to the Hildebrandine reforms in Rome and to the reforms of the English church undertaken in the generations following the Norman conquest. For a church community such as Wharram, and specifically for its architectural patrons, adopting such distinctive and demonstrative structural forms would have been making a very clear declaration of religious and therefore political allegiances. In our view, however, we see no need to presume that this positioning was a gesture on the part of the tenant in chief; and in Lincolnshire we made a strong case that gestures of this type were more likely representative of a slightly inferior level of society.

This situation, where we suggest that the sokemen held considerable sway within village decision making, however, would have been radically altered after 1166, when the Percy family is thought to have entered into a mesne tenancy of the Chamberlain manor. According to Roffe's analysis, the Percys already held the second, smaller, estate in Wharram by this time, which Ketilbjorn had held in 1066. As a form of sokeland holding, probably dependent on the manor at Wharram le Street in Ketilbjorn's time, this estate is unlikely to have included an aristocratic residence in Wharram Percy; especially as the Percys appear to have transferred the dependency of their Wharram Percy holding to Carnaby at this stage, which was the main centre of their fee in the East Riding (Roffe 2000a, 3-4). Furthermore, the fact that the Percys entered a mesne tenancy under the Chamberlains 'shortly after' 1166 probably also suggests that there was no Percy house on the Ketilbjorn holding, as otherwise they would not need the additional demesne. But after this decade, holding both the larger share and the smaller, in an established tenure, the Percys of Wharram must have become the dominant force in the vill. Furthermore, their new tenure as *mesne* lords clearly implies a demesne calling for their physical presence in a manorial residence at Wharram. What appears in the archaeology of Wharram at precisely this juncture is the stone range of the South Manor (Plates 20-22), which can be dated to this very moment by means of its architectural detail.

The stone range, or *camera* as it has been called, has been discussed in *Wharram I* and has been reconstructed in some detail, using both architectural fragments recovered from excavations and parallels (Thorn 1979). Some of Thorn's descriptions of the architectural remains might benefit from modernisation, but the dates proposed for the small number of precisely datable architectural details remains acceptable (*c.* 1165-90). In fact, modern opinion on the precise date of some items might refine Thorn's date even further, and bring it more closely into line with the acquisition of the mesne tenancy by the Percys 'shortly after' 1166. The single 'waterleaf' type capital (Thorn 1979, fig. 23, no. 33), from a door or window reveal, and the 'stemmed' base of attic sequence (Thorn 1979, fig. 23, no. 36), evidently from a rather fine internal architectural fitting such as a fireplace hood, both suggest a date between *c.* 1160 and *c.* 1180, and other less precisely datable details would match such a date comfortably.

As Thorn recognised, the *camera* is very likely to have been associated with a ground-floor hall, although he stated that no traces of this structure were identified during the excavations (Thorn 1979, 60). But, at the very least, the details in plan of the *camera* show that the hall is likely to have been to its south and east when it was first constructed (Fig. 96), as the north wall contains a substantial chimney breast (a feature usually applied to external walls at this date). The excavation report (Milne 1979a, 29-33) devotes scant discussion to this matter, but Beresford and Hurst (1990, 44-7) suggested that the west wall of the sunken passageway leading to the doorway into the cellar in the south wall of the *camera* represented the *east* wall of the associated hall. A reconstruction of such a building generates, however, a very odd-looking structure (Beresford and Hurst 1990, pl. 9). In fact, the results published in *Wharram I* seem to suggest that the *camera* was abutted by substantial stone walls at both its north-east and south-east corners, and, if these are used to generate a reconstruction of a stone-founded hall (the superstructure of which is still most likely to have been of timber), then we can suggest that the associated hall extended southwards from the east end of the *camera*, and enveloped the cellar door (Fig. 96). The sloping passage-way (if there was one: see pp 232-4), would have risen within the floor of the hall and given direct access to the cellar itself, which otherwise seems to have no access.

This cellar, then, related not to the use of the *camera* but to the hall, perhaps as storage, but it could also have played some 'public' role as a 'presence chamber' where

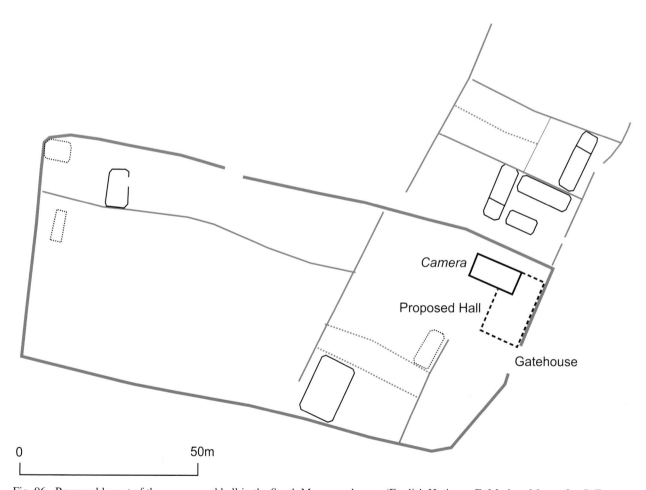

0   50m

Fig. 96. Proposed layout of the *camera* and hall in the South Manor enclosure. (English Heritage, E. Marlow-Mann after P. Everson and D. Stocker)

264

the lord might hold council with advisors before issuing judgement in the hall next door. It might be objected that there is plenty of room for a detached hall elsewhere within the putative South Manor enclosure at Wharram, but no other candidate structures for the missing hall have been discovered in excavation. If the hall was located south-east of the *camera*, however, it would have lain partly beneath the buildings designated 1, 2 and 4, but mostly within the area seriously affected by quarrying in period III (later 13th century). Any or all of these intrusions might have cut away hall features. Access to the *camera* from the hall in such an arrangement would be through the east wall at first-floor level, and the stair might well have been housed within an 'air-lock' chamber at the hall's north end. Is it possible that some of the slots and gullies excavated in this area and associated with this phase (Milne 1979a, 29-33), belong to such a 'staircase chamber'?

Regardless of the lack of clear archaeological information about the hall, however, it is highly likely that such a contemporary hall existed, and the reconstruction of the *camera* implies a hall, at right-angles to it and probably extending southwards from its east end. The hall would therefore be on the right as visitors entered the South Manor *curia* and, as they turned northwards, they would be presented with the most impressive two-storied stone façade of the *camera*, speculatively reconstructed by Thorn (1979, fig. 19). Such a layout would also place the broad side of the putative hall along the 'skyline', as it were, when viewed from the green below: a clear statement of mastery of the community space represented by the green, by the family of the new resident lord, and perhaps offering a second, preferable, indoor meeting place for community decision-making, only now under his patronage and supervision. The newly arrived *demesne* lord was palpably now 'in residence'.

Many manor houses and larger establishments of the later 12th and early 13th centuries were planned with their halls and chambers at right-angles to each other, often as part of a courtyard, or semi-courtyard plan (Blair 1993, 10-14). Blair makes a case that the plan was disseminated outwards into wider aristocratic and gentry society from a series of influential examples at bishops' palaces, and by the turn of the 13th century such layouts are in evidence at otherwise undistinguished manors houses, such as Jacobstow (Beresford 1974).

It is scarcely surprising that the unexpected discovery of this major new building complex has subsequently become identified with the establishment of the Percy manor (Roffe 2000a, 3). Of course, Roffe and Wrathmell (p. 232) are quite right to remind us that, on the evidence presented thus far, it is quite conceivable that the newly reconstructed manor building represents a new assertion of the superior rights of the Chamberlains in Wharram and of their continuing relevance, as overlords of the Percys, in this manor. As such it would, as Roffe characterises it, be a base for preserving and managing any residual interests of the Chamberlains; and in that

case the Percys' new residence would have been sited elsewhere; presumably on the North Manor plot. But this argument simply shifts the problem to a location where there is no evidence for a 12th-century manorial phase at all (below) and one has seriously to question whether it would have been entertained if, following the South Manor excavations, there had not been two easily identifiable manor house sites.

We have already suggested, however, that the power-politics within the vill changed with the arrival of the Percys and the construction of the South Manor, and we propose, instead, that several features in the field archaeology relating to the South Manor may, cumulatively, suggest that we can adopt a more positive position, and associate the spectacular construction of the South Manor with the arrival of the Percys as resident mesne lords. First, the South Manor is located centrally within the West Row, and this row may represent the early royal estate that was recorded as subdivided in 1066, but had been reunited in 1086. Furthermore, we have also noted above (p. 214) that the South Manor may reoccupy the location of one of the two Late Saxon quasi-manorial properties. Perhaps it was the one whose occupier had aspired to leadership of the vill in the first half of the 11th century, and asserted those pretensions through the 'founder's' grave-group of decorated stone covers in St Martin's churchyard (Stocker 2007a, 271-87).

As can be read in the earthworks (Fig. 97a), the extent of the manorial complex associated with this increasingly powerful family is remarkably clear, and it persisted as a structural plan element despite becoming redundant and (as it appears) being partially recast into peasant plots. The manor house and associated buildings occupy a position at the south end of West Row (north). The manor's court extended westwards, maintaining a similar width, over the lynchet bank and taking in what had formerly been open-field (or infield) arable, thereby fossilising part of the ultra-broad-ridged mode of cultivation. On the north side of this core a rather larger rectangular block was defined, also with a well-marked bank on its west and north sides. It had the same depth from the frontage onto the green as the South Manor's court and the north edge lay along the main east-west route through the village. The strip of crofts to the east of the lynchet bank were defined or redefined as an extremely regular formal row of seven (or six and a half) peasant properties (see p. 37 above); but the large close behind them was accessed from the rear part of the South Manor court, via a very well-defined and apparently long-lasting gap in the north boundary of the manorial court, which remains a prominent feature in the earthworks.

This close may have been divided in two, but it, too, probably took in and fossilised a section of ultra-broad-ridged mode of cultivation, as the published earthwork survey proposes (Fig. 8). Traces of the ridge and furrow of later medieval cultivation within the close(s) is understood from the field evidence to be a development secondary to the creation of this close. If this area was ever divided into crofts corresponding to the tofts along

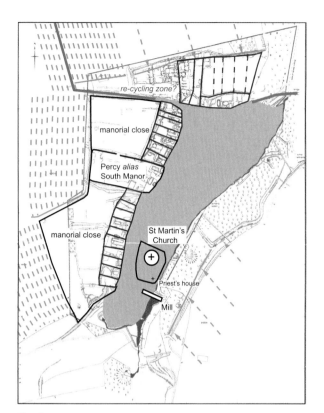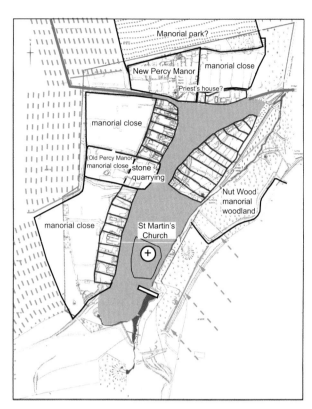

Fig. 97. The South Manor and the late 12th-century village (left); the North Manor and the mid-13th-century village (right). (E. Marlow-Mann after P. Everson and D. Stocker)

the frontage – as has traditionally been assumed – it was a secondary step and the evidence for it was not observable by ground survey. At best it would sit awkwardly with the entrance gap as long as the South Manor was active.

The area behind the West Row (south) was also taken in from the former early arable in what might be thought a similar fashion. A bank-and-ditch west boundary similar to that to the north enclosed what seems to have been a single large close extending south to the edge of the plateau against the side valley; and in consequence the relatively large area of fossilised ultra-broad-ridged cultivation is as well-preserved and coherent as it is anywhere. Here it is cut through by everything except the lynchet bank and the settlement row, but including the close boundary; and there are no plausible traces of long peasant tofts going with or extending the plots on the row fronting the green. Though there is no direct link with the South Manor court to match the entrance gap going north, it seems possible – even probable – that the rather similar southern close was also an appurtenance of the South Manor. Perhaps it is even to a 12th-century replanning, initiated as part of this same process, that the regularity of the plot pattern of the West Row (south) can be ascribed.

In contrast to this remarkable survival of early cultivation within these big closes, beyond their boundaries it is ridge and furrow of normal high medieval type, organised in furlong bundles that can be plotted, and all trace of the early form of cultivation has been obliterated. That familiar evidence extends to the furthest boundaries of the vill (see pp 292-5 and Fig. 106, below)

and tells of an initiative that aspired to exploit its arable potential in a highly-organised way. It was evidently a profound change. The field evidence for the creation and form of the South Manor, the closes attached to it and the way they fossilise the old arable cultivation regime, and the complementary incidence of ridge-and-furrow cultivation, carry the implication that now, for the first time in the mid to late 12th century, new, open and common fields superseded the old. The reorganisation of the arable, which we feel is patent in the earthwork evidence, was probably, we suggest, also undertaken at the instigation of the newly resident lord who now held the manorial demesne.

We feel that the field evidence is quite clear in this sequence and in its implication; but perhaps we should entertain some alternatives. The most plausible, perhaps, is the proposal that the open fields of the high medieval type might have been created earlier, replacing the ultra-broad-ridged cultivation, but not have included that precise area that became the demesne court and closes. A sort of set-aside was created – at an unknown date, of unknown status and function, of irregular shape and with boundaries that have left no trace except the 12th-century ones – over the end of the early arable and against the back of the village properties, which the demesne in the mid to late 12th century simply engrossed. This might be hypothetically a possible scenario, but introducing an extraneous phase in an archaeological narrative, in the complete absence of direct evidence, represents poor practice (and Occam's Razor and the taint of special pleading forbid it). In contrast to the interpretation offered, too, the proposition lacks context or explanation. Another formulation – approaching the issue from the form of the cultivation ridges – might say that it is possible that the common field was created earlier but had broad ridge and furrow. From the field survey evidence, the 'earlier' (i.e. pre-12th-century) aspect of this depends on the same hypothesis as the previous proposition; the 'broad ridge and furrow' is simply another stage, a view on whose presence or absence depends on the sort of excellent fieldwork and analysis that David Hall has done so often. Broad ridge and furrow of this type is absent from the demesne closes.

As part of these developments in the common fields, it seems from the excavations that the main watermill lying south of the church may have been enlarged and refurbished at the same time (Watts 2005, 222-5; Wrathmell and Marlow-Mann 2005, 225-6). The very act of reconstructing the mill in this manner, of course, reflects a new, more extensive and more efficient arable regime. Furthermore, it could be that such a development reflects the newly resident mesne lord's take-over and recasting of what had earlier been a community asset, fulfilling a need for capital investment in the community's common plant, as it were. The new field survey has also suggested the possible presence of a second mill, below the first, on the stream immediately east of the church (Oswald 2004, fig. 27). While the observation has been neither validated nor dated it may be another indication of a growing need for milling capacity.

It is also worth reporting other, less obvious, indications of the impact of the recasting of the South Manor and the agricultural regime associated with it. For example, with the north boundary of the West Row (north) and its backlands (the large close behind) closely defined over quite a length, the alignment of the main east-west routeway over the plateau from the west becomes more permanently fixed, taking it away from its prehistoric and Roman alignment and tending to leave the frontage of the North Row rather set back from the effective medieval highway (see also p. 84).

More spectacularly, perhaps, we can also suggest that this programme of development aimed at demonstrating both the dominance of the newly resident lordly family and the vitality of the new manorial community they headed - both indispensable parts of the feudal bargain - resulted in substantial reconstruction at St Martin's church in what we have called Phase 4 (pp 246-52 above; formerly called phases IV and V in Bell 1987, 63-5, 93-5). Although we have noted the previous churches here, and although social distinctions had already been drawn within the graveyard community (Stocker 2007a, 284-7), nevertheless there was clearly a discrete phase of lordly patronage at St Martin's at precisely the same date that we see great investment in the South Manor buildings, and also perhaps, the reorganisation of the arable: i.e. in the third quarter of the 12th century. Once again it seems likely that the work at St Martin's is related to the arrival in residence of the new demesne lord and his family.

We have seen in Chapter 15 (pp 246-52) that a south aisle, a new chancel and a tower were all added at precisely this time. The tower, of course, was a rather impoverished version of that originally intended for the Phase 3 church, before the Percys arrived, but the chancel and south aisle represented significant novel additions to the church at this moment. A quite precise date for these works is obtainable from the architectural detailing of the blocked south aisle arcade, the south door and a whole range of loose fragments. Although any date between the 1160s and the 1190s is possible, the details point to a date in the 1170s or 1180s for all these works. At the same time as the Percy's were constructing an impressive manorial complex with hall and stone-built *camera*, then, they were also embarking on a major programme of extension at St Martin's. The architectural details at both buildings may even be sufficiently similar to permit the suggestion that the same gang of masons was involved.

We have also seen in Chapter 15 (pp 246-50) that the architectural details of the new work at Wharram associate it with the group of Yorkshire doorways and other structures connected with the programme of reconstruction undertaken at York Minster under Archbishop Roger of Pont l'Eveque from the mid-1150s until *c.* 1180 (Butler 1982; Hearn 1983; Wilson 1986). They seem to indicate that the new patrons of architecture responsible for the later 12th-century work at the South Manor and at St Martin's were in the mainstream of architectural patronage locally, and could afford the most up-to-date craftsmanship, which linked their renovation of St Martin's to the renovation work at the Minster itself. This showy initiative targets a part of the church structure – the main entrance to the building – that the whole community of the extended parish at Wharram will have encountered regularly: the focus and setting also of certain specific liturgies, such as marriage and death. Unsurprisingly, it was a particularly popular locus of patronage in the later 12th century, not only in Yorkshire where it aligned the patron with many of his peers in the local gentry, but more widely too (e.g. Keyser 1909; Kahn 1980).

An architectural link and close similarity in date between the construction of the stone *camera* of the South Manor and the reconstructed south doorway of the church has long been recognised; but the costly elaboration and architectural affinities of the doorway, the connection with other works elsewhere in the church, and the significance of the development of the south aisle with its eastern chapel have not. In addition, the South Manor stands proximate to the church, and certainly within sight of it (though the view is now partly obscured by trees). Not to associate the two buildings, and not to recognise the work at both as representing a newly assertive display of lordship would be perverse.

Those attending the new enlarged church, entering through the new south door into the new south aisle and admiring the fine new chancel to the east, would have been in no doubt that the growth and prosperity of the church was under the patronage of the newly ensconced local lord, in the same manner that the growth and prosperity of the wider community also lay in his hands. But the south aisle might have been more personally related to the new lord's family. We have seen in Chapter 15 (p. 246) that there remains some uncertainty about the form of the eastern part of the aisle, but we believe that the most likely reconstruction includes a deep chapel at its eastern end, discretely tucked away to the east of the arcade itself. In *Wharram XI* (Stocker 2007a, 271-81) the proximity of the eastern chapel at the end of the south aisle to the earliest lordly monuments in the graveyard was noted. It abutted and incorporated, but did not disturb, the lordly grave group of the mid-11th century, and it was observed that one of these early monuments appeared to have been reverently 'built into' the footings of its east wall. Furthermore, the monuments of previous lordly families were literally embedded in the fabric of the church's new extension: the new aisle deliberately reused their gravecover sections in the foundations of the new south wall (Bell 1987, 58, 86-8; Stocker 2007a, 276, fig. 134).

These coped covers are likely to have been no more than a generation or two old when they were reused in this fashion, and this treatment should probably be seen as a deliberate act by the patrons of the new aisle associating themselves directly with the elite families who had formerly been patrons of the church. Not only did the south aisle pay this self-conscious homage to earlier elite families who had resided at Wharram, but all these, surely deliberate, acts of structural reuse and recognition of earlier burials strongly suggest that the east end of the new south aisle was contrived to provide a distinctive and prominent burial space for the new elite family of Wharram, who were now resident in the vill and therefore burying in this church, as opposed to the others of their holding. Furthermore, they were concerned to identify themselves in the minds of the community as legitimate successors to the lords of the latest pre-Conquest era and publicly to arrogate their role. The building subtly emphasises their links with previous lordlings in the vill, but at the same time draws an architectural distinction, between themselves and their predecessors, by erecting a much richer structure than had been seen here before.

Instead of a grand tower of the Weaverthorpe variety, which was clearly planned for the Phase 3 church, however, we have seen that a much smaller tower was actually constructed, in a wholly exceptional position, astride the west gable wall. Furthermore, most of its architectural details and the masonry of which it was built seem to have been salvaged from reconstruction work associated with the south aisle. The several arguments that seem to associate its construction with the Phase 4 church seem to us to be robust however, and we presume that the tower was a further addition of the later 12th century, made at the same time or just after the south aisle.

Jim Thorn reconstructed the belfry stage of the 12th-century tower using the section of shaft found in the rubble of the tower collapse in 1959 (Thorn 1987, 133,

fig. 49). He presumed that it came from a belfry window opening of late 12th-century date. This is simply not the case (pp 250-52; ADS Report, doi:10.5284/1000415, Architectural Stone Catalogue, stone U). Firstly, the window indicated by the shaft is quite small, with lights only about 1m tall, unfeasibly small for belfry openings. Secondly, the shaft is not in fact the 'mid-wall shaft' that Thorn reported, but rather a half shaft which has a pair of rebates behind, no doubt to receive shutters. Thorn suggested that the rebates were for louvres such as might be found in a belfry, but in practice not a single one of the 11th or 12th-century belfry shafts studied in our Lincolnshire survey is rebated in this fashion. Those which have integral accommodation for louvres (such as Little Bytham) seat the louvres in a back plate behind the shaft. Both the form of rebate and the size of the architectural feature represented by this stone suggest, in fact, that it is a domestic detail. Furthermore, this form of detail is characteristic of the later 12th and early 13th centuries, so we should presume, not that it originated in the fabric of the tower during its original construction during Phase 4, but rather that it belongs to one of its reconstructions, presumably being reused casually as building rubble.

This observation raises the question of the location for which the shaft was originally cut, and this returns us to the *camera* on the South Manor. This is the only stone-built domestic building of which we know at Wharram at this date, and the window it represents would sit well with the other architectural details of *c*.1160-80 that have been identified there. Indeed it would fit well (better than Thorn's proposed shaft) into the window reconstructed in *Wharram I* (fig. 22). This is particularly so, as Thorn's shaft sections, and the neck of the associated capital, clearly belong to the 'stemmed' base block (illustrated in *Wharram I*, fig. 23 no. 36), which itself probably comes from the support for a fireplace hood and not this window. We have seen that the South Manor had been demolished by *c*.1260, and like John Hurst (1979b, 139) we shall argue that it was demolished as a result of a shift of the manor site to the North Manor after 1254. In its turn, this would suggest that the fragment of domestic window was not available for reuse in the fabric of St Martin's tower until *c*. 1260 at the earliest. Presumably, then, if the shaft section did come from the South Manor, it must have been reused in a later 13th-century reconstruction of the upper parts of the tower (below). It also suggests that we can say nothing about the form of the original Phase 4 belfry.

We might legitimately doubt whether the new Phase 4 tower, of *c*.1160-80, would have played the same liturgical role within the church as that envisaged for the much larger tower of Phase 3, for which it was substituted. We have already noted that, had it been constructed, the Phase 3 tower would have been comparable with those which formed the subject of our study in Lincolnshire (above; Stocker and Everson 2006). In this study we proposed that the original liturgical use for which such towers had been constructed (for the performance of the *vigil* during the elaborated burial rite) had been short-lived. We suggested that, after the end of the 12th century, during the burial services, the coffin of the deceased was placed more frequently in front of the high altar, rather than within the tower base. The Phase 4 tower at St Martin's was simply too small to have played this role, so we can suggest that, in the period between the planning of the original Phase 3 tower in the early 12th century and the construction of the Phase 4 tower towards its end, the performance of the burial rite at Wharram had changed substantially. We would argue, on the basis of our Lincolnshire study that, in the course of the 12th century, the location of the *vigil* had been moved from the tower space to the high altar. Furthermore, in our Lincolnshire study we also suggested that the exit from the early 12th-century towers to the churchyard had been an important aspect of the burial ceremony, and we also observed that west doors had lost their importance by the 13th century; the aisle doors, presumably, being used in their place. Whereas, we cannot know what was intended for the Phase 3 tower at Wharram, but it is notable that the Phase 4 tower had no west door. This detail suggests that, although the Phase 4 tower might have resembled a smaller version of that proposed for Phase 3, it was not intended to fulfil the same liturgical function, being devoted now almost entirely to the ringing of bells. Perhaps even more than the construction of the south aisle, however, this innovation of bells hung on high and housed within a prominent architectural feature would have been a very distinctive symbol of the vitality of the community and of the feudal bargain with their newly resident lords.

The new apse, within which we might suggest that the *vigil* was now performed, also reflects the use of an up-to-date liturgy, in which the host was presented eastwards during the celebration of the Mass, as opposed to earlier practice when it was presented towards the congregation to the west (Taylor 1973). The great enlargement of the chancel itself reflects the clergy's rise in prestige since the 11th century, constantly promoted by Rome and by reforming English bishops, like Pont L'Eveque. Not only were the clergy now to be given an architecturally splendid setting in which to perform the mystery of the Mass, but they were also, to some extent, separated off from the laity in the nave within their new splendidly decorated sacerdotal world, east of the new chancel arch (e.g. Barnwell 2004).

The interconnections between the development of elements of village economic infrastructure, the changes in the plan form of the settlement that they reflect, alongside the reconstruction work at the church and South Manor at this same moment are remarkable. Furthermore, the architectural developments, at least, can be dated very precisely to the generation between about 1160 and 1180, through the various architectural remains at both St Martin's and the South Manor. We can see here, perhaps, the radical changes one might expect following the arrival of one of the aristocratic families, long associated with the vill, actually to live on the site and

work its demesne, as the Percys did soon after 1166. But it is important to note that it is *not* their actual lordship of the vill that was the significant factor in bringing about all these developments; they had perhaps been both senior and junior lords in the two holdings in the vill for a considerable period of time. No, it was their arrival within the village community to live and work the demesne 'in person' that was the critical factor in stimulating all this activity.

In fact, this picture is not unfamiliar in studies of medieval settlement up and down the country in the 11th and 12th centuries. In many cases it is just such mesne lords who play the dominant part in moulding their settlements and their buildings, rather than their feudal superiors. These local men have often been their lord's 'man' in the place; sometimes they assumed the place-name as their family name. It is these figures who are found creating developed manorial complexes and impacting influentially on their community (Everson *et al.* 1991, 41-3, 48-50; Stocker and Everson 2006, 70-76).

Developments at Wharram, as we understand them, are not an exceptional case, then, but a highly typical one. At Wharram we have difficulty putting names to the leading sokemen of the century between 1066 and 1166, who will have led the reconstruction of the church in Phase 3, though we might presume that they were the successors of Lagmann and Karli; but the works at St Martin's undertaken in Phase 3 were relatively restrained by comparison with those of Phase 4, and they appear to have been left unfinished. The Phase 3 church can be contrasted, then, with the reconstruction of the church in the later 12th century. The works to the church undertaken in the third quarter of the 12th century by the newly resident Percy lord, were not only of a different order of ambition; in terms of architectural form and sculptural decoration they also linked this remote place to movements in both architecture and liturgy which extended across Europe.

Furthermore, it was not just the Percys' works in the church that were radical; they were one part of a package which included major new construction at the manor and, perhaps, reorganisation of the agricultural economy. Today, perhaps, we load the Percy name with connotations of the highest status, but we must beware of thinking that it was the sheer importance of the family which brought about this radical transformation of Wharram. We would suggest, rather, that it is not so much the importance of the family to which the new manorial tenants belonged, but the fact that they were resident in the vill that made the difference. We have no reason to think that any of the three families who contested the lordship of the vill throughout the century from 1086 to the 1160s were resident, or would have been particularly concerned in the detail of ecclesiastical provision within this community.

Once the Percys entered into their mesne tenancy, the situation changed rapidly; it was their presence, and not their ownership, that made the difference. They wished to be seen by their own tenants to live in a fine house. They wished their court to be held in a fine hall, they wished to hear services performed according to the most up-to-date liturgical thinking, and in an architecturally appropriate setting, and they wished to commemorate their dead in a suitably appointed reserved space within the church. The message conveyed by the 12th-century remains from Wharram may be that it is not the tenant in chief who is most influential in shaping the fabric of the vill, but the resident lord. This is also the conclusion we arrived at in out consideration of our sample of Lincolnshire churches and their vills in the period between 1066 and 1150 (Stocker and Everson 2006, 76).

Development of Wharram in the 13th century and subsequently

The move to the North Manor

Prior to our suggesting, in the previous section, that the creation of the South Manor was intricately connected to the arrival of the Percy family as resident tenants 'shortly after' 1166, attention had been focused not so much on the arrival of the South Manor in the pattern of development of the vill, but on its removal. Typically, commentators have thought that the formative event in the development of the nucleated settlement at Wharram during the later medieval period was the removal of the South Manor from its location in the West Row and the occupation, it is supposed, of an already existing North Manor site in the North Row. This relocation has been allocated a date in the third quarter of the 13th century, following the Percys' final acquisition of the whole lordship in 1254 (Hurst 1979a, 138-9). Most previous commentators have presumed that it was the reduction in number of manors, from two to one, and the concomitant shift of the surviving manor site from the South Manor to the North Manor, that brought with it, or gave rise to, most of the other changes in the plan-form of the settlement. It was this move, it was thought, that gave the settlement its final appearance prior to the long process of shrinkage.

Here we have tried to redress the balance; but it is true, nevertheless, that though they had held influence at Wharram for more than a century previously, and though they may have lived at and worked the South Manor *demesne* for more than 80 years, the Percy family's undisputed tenure of Wharram dates only from 1254 when Henry Chamberlain of Wickenby quitclaimed his rights to Peter Percy (p. 229). Therefore, at least in theory, the Percys had been subject to some local competition within the vill in the 12th and early 13th centuries. We have already noted that the extent to which that competition from the Chamberlains was manifest on the ground is debatable. Although it is true that lordship was not just manifested in the erection of buildings, but also had a critical, tangible, aspect in the paying of rents and the hearing of suits at the manorial court, nevertheless we would argue that the Percys had stood between the manorial tenants (paying their rents and pleading their suits) and the Chamberlains.

Following 1254, however, 'the whole vill of Wharram Percy was held by the Percys of Bolton Percy, in chief, of the king by a service which is variously described as a quarter of a knight's fee, or grand sergeancy' (Roffe 2000a, 3). In just the same way that their acquisition of the mesne lordship of the South Manor had been the stimulus for changes in the organisation, planning and buildings of the settlement, so their final acquisition of outright lordship in 1254 had equivalent impact on the fabric of the vill and on some its buildings. Many others have noted that it seems probable that the major direct result of the 1254 quitclaim was the upgrading of the North Manor *curia*. Given our analysis of the South Manor (above), however, in our view this is more likely to have consisted, not of upgrading an existing North Manor site, but of the removal of the Percy manor to an unoccupied location at the west end of the North Row. Although vacant in the 13th century, however, in the Roman period the plot had been occupied by a complex, whose core lay principally to the west, well into the 4th century (Fig. 97b).

Though not the only candidate, the site to which we suggest the manor was moved after 1254 might even have been the source for Roman masonry that is occasionally reused in and around Wharram; already in the 4th century the corn-drier that has been excavated in the eastern part of the plot was recycling substantial masonry blocks from a major building (Rahtz and Watts 2004, 100). Indeed Rahtz's overall assessment of his excavations across this zone of the settlement was that they revealed 'much late Roman material related to substantial structures of 'villa-type'', but not directly; rather through the activities of 'the wrecking and dismantling of them'. These were activities which, on his assessment, continued well into the medieval period.

There is, then, no real evidence for the North Manor site being occupied by any pre-existing high-status activity prior to our suggested relocation to it of the South Manor. Furthermore, the excavated evidence that directly related to walls of buildings of the medieval manorial complex at the North Manor indicates a date span from the mid-13th century to the early 15th century, which correlates rather closely with the evidence from documentary sources, and seems to support the proposal that the manor was moved here, from elsewhere, only in the mid-13th century (Rahtz *et al.* 2004, 295-6).

Such is the quality of those North Manor earthworks that relate both to its main buildings and to its ancillary structures (which, – unlike those on much of the remainder of the site, – are generated by substantial stone walls), that close interpretation of the manorial complex has been attempted in previous publications (e.g. Beresford M.W. 1979, 17-20; Rahtz and Watts 2004, 2-4), and has been reconsidered in the present volume by Oswald (pp 26-31), who offers plausible identifications of the individual structures and a narrative for the development of the manor buildings.

Why was the shift made, then, and why to this location? The extent to which its Roman background might have lent the new site in the North Row some caché in the 13th century is debatable, and ultimately unknowable, but it is not impossible that it was a location singled out within the vill for exceptional treatment at the lord's behest, and the Percys' use of it for their new manor house at this precise moment might be seen in that context. By the mid-13th century, no doubt, the old-fashioned form and limited accommodation of the South Manor made it a poor residence for the permanent occupation of the household of a lord of any pretensions, still less one who had recently secured the status of tenant in chief and might wish to assert it (see pp 231-2). Quite apart from any such perceived internal limitations, the re-siting of the manor house from the West Row to the North Row removed it from the midst of a row of peasant properties. Prior to relocation, its frontage was no doubt pre-eminent in the row, but it was still limited in width, affording little room for an imposing gateway for example, and we may doubt how pleasant a setting this was.

Moving to the western end of the North Row placed the manorial residence, not marginally, but prominently alongside one of the principal and long-established access routes into Wharram, and at the same time at the upper and topographically higher end of the settlement (*pace* McDonagh 2007a, table 4.1; 2007b, 195-9). The principal motive was surely a desire to celebrate and actualise the Percys' new lordly status in currently conventional and recognisable ways. The mere location was furthermore dressed up in a variety of ways; and specifically in ways that would be meaningful to the Percys' social peers and superiors.

The appearance of those closes immediately adjacent to the new manor site, as revealed in the recent survey, seems to have included garden and orchard plots; but their extent may be better understood when we have looked at a slightly wider canvas. A park is a documented appurtenance in the early 14th century; and if Oswald is right in identifying its likely location behind the new manorial complex to its north, such a development would have consolidated the amenity and seclusion, as well as the facilities, of what became, for the Percys, a major family residence. Such a park was a rarity for manors on the Wolds (Neave 1991, 18-19) and need not have been large. The densely settled and intensively farmed Yorkshire Wolds of the later 13th century did not lend themselves to an extensive, 'wild' form of hunting such as might be afforded on the North York Moors, and were not everywhere adapted topographically to the sort of display park or 'Little Park' under the windows of the greater manorial residences seen at Helmsley or Ravensworth, for example (Everson and Barnwell 2004; Everson 2003, 27-9).

Nevertheless, creating a park, at whatever scale, must have entailed removal of land from the common arable cultivation cycle of the community of the vill and its reservation to exclusive lordly uses of pleasure. This 'privatisation' of the landscape demonstrates a priority of interests, and a level of dominant control that allowed it to happen; and that apparently at a time before the major

population falls of the mid and later 14th century. It is not without documented parallel, however, and was certainly not confined to the crown or the senior aristocracy, but involved lords of local, aspirant standing like the Percys (Mileson 2009, 53-9, 163-4). Andrew Luttrell(I), for example, in just this era, created a park at Irnham in Lincolnshire in 1246, enclosing farming land, while at the same time rebuilding the parish church alongside his hall where, in time, dependent members of the Luttrell family were installed as rector (Brown 2006, 74-6).

A further development in the adjacent landscape that might also be viewed as elaborating the setting of reinvigorated lordship, associated with the new North Manor, is the creation of a block of managed woodland – Nut Wood – on the steep, facing bank to the east of the village. The earthworks of its typical boundary banks have now been recorded in the new site survey (Figs 8-9). Though rather unimpressive in plan and apparently just another practical or economic resource, in fact this woodland spread down the valley side directly across from the North Manor and at a level with it, and it must have formed a backdrop or screen to views in that direction.

There are strong indications, then, not just that the Percys took the opportunity to resite and aggrandise their own accommodation following their achievement of enhanced status in Wharram after 1254, but also that they enhanced its setting, with appurtenances of modest style and amenity. Even if the two functions are not mutually exclusive, of course, it may be that we should consider this manor and its constituent features as much (or more) in the light of a country house as in that of a working farm complex. With the park probably extending right along the north boundary of North Row eastwards to the eastern lip of the plateau, where the boundary bank along the north of the North Manor is recorded as turning north, it seems legitimate to question whether the back plots are in fact 'tofts' (Oswald 2004, fig. 16, nos 22-6). It seems at least worth asking whether these squarish closes might not have been paddocks etc. in this phase of development, constructed to service the park and manor itself (for horses, for example). Is it even possible that the peasant plots fronting onto the green in this area were engrossed into the North Manor in this era, so that the whole of the north side of the green in this period was Percy manor, perhaps with home farm and agricultural facilities on the eastern frontage? The latter would then emerge, as Oswald proposes, as one of the handful of large late medieval farms in the village plan.

A reflex of just such a process of 'reserving' the northern end of the settlement for the lordly family might be a more 'public' reconfiguration of the remainder of the settlement, as the recent survey report hints (pp 26-31; see Oswald 2004, 101-2). For, at the same period that the North Manor took over the North Row (partially if not wholly), in the mid-13th century, the East Row was laid out in a regular pattern of tofts and crofts extending down the valley side, effectively terminating against the low-lying fringe of the stream. As Dyer has commented (pp 318, and

324), from their form and buildings these properties could be new cottage holdings created to support the resited and expanded manor. They shaped and formalised a triangular green within the northern part of the old public open space. This green lay quite clearly at the gate of the new North Manor, and must have enhanced the impression of a community attached to, and beholden to, the manor; both for those resident and to those visiting or passing through.

These developments no doubt generated the strong impression of a single-manor settlement; and this seems to have been reinforced by the location of new communal assets like the livestock pounds – themselves features bespeaking good regulation of the community – which the topographical survey has identified, located on this northern triangular space rather than further south as earlier common assets had been. By contrast, when milling ceased at the pond south of the church, in its situation remote from the display of the North Manor, it was apparently not developed as a fish pond but turned into a village pond. Significantly, it is also in the later 13th century when the place-name 'Wharram Percy' has its first documented occurrence. It was the highpoint of Percy influence and the most visible moment for resident lordship.

Oswald has commented that these new developments must have resulted in the 'exclusion' of the southern half of the West Row from the closed triangle of the northern sector, and has conjectured that it reflects a different origin for this part of the settlement, in a different tenure outside the Percy manor. This is not the sequence of development and origins that we have reconstructed or described above; and the alleged exclusion may have been more apparent than real: more an effect of the plan in two dimensions than the settlement in reality. On the ground, the topography was always likely to have resulted in the continuous line of houses of the West Row (south), especially when viewed from the green, rather than an excluded, non-manorial sector. If anything was 'excluded' through these reorganisations of the vill after 1254, it was perhaps the church and its priest's house. The church did indeed have a role that was greater than the vill of Wharram Percy alone, servicing the needs of the other four vills in the parish, as well in life as in death, with its extensive graveyard. We will explore the major late medieval works implemented in St Martin's church by the Percys and their successors in the following section.

Together, then, these alterations amounted in combination to a purposeful outward assertion of seisin, as described in Chapter 14 (pp 230-34). In the other branch of the family, Sir Henry de Percy can be observed deploying a similar range of strategies when raised to the status of Lord Percy in 1298/9, in creating a new moated residence at Leconfield with licence to crenellate and a hunting park enclosing former arable (McDonagh 2007a, 202-3). Unfortunately, in contrast to the church, no clear dating or phasing can be identified in the wider landscape

changes we have explored. Oswald can identify two clear phases in the earthworks of the North Manor, however, including major structural changes to the house and access arrangements. He favours the view that this represents a periodic upgrading within the era of Percy residence up to the early 14th century (pp 26-31), rather than works associated with later transfers of lordship. Barns and a dovecote can be identified amongst the North Manor earthworks; both are symbols of lordly residence, of course. The main residential building, the focus of all this lordly display, was presumably the new manor house built after 1254, aligned east-west and looking southwards towards the green. Just as we have argued was the case with its South Manor predecessor, then, the North Manor presented a long façade towards the public space, giving the tenantry the full effect of its tall hall windows, symbolic of the household, and of the end elevations of its cross wings, denoting the lord's private family (e.g. Stocker forthcoming). For much of the day the sun would sparkle on the stonework and bring out colour and detail. These buildings are also set back somewhat within the plot, reserved behind some form of court or garden closes without obvious buildings, and removed from the passing bustle. But the lie of the land meant that the wall did not screen the new building from view. Indeed it gave the hall itself some elevation (as was recognised in the reconstruction on the cover illustration of Beresford and Hurst 1990), and consequently a wide outlook, including a view southwards over the wall across the upper green.

Late medieval reconstructions at St Martin's

From the North Manor, the uppermost storey of the west tower of St Martin's church could also be seen. Today, of course, the view is of the ruin of the Perpendicular belfry stage, which, thanks to the survival of the Hilton arms on architectural fragments (ADS Report, doi:10.5284/1000415, Architectural Stonework, stone SS), we can date quite precisely to the years immediately after 1400 (see pp 256-7). The prominent interest in heraldry betokened by the shields in the parapet, offers a direct comparison with other Hilton properties which were also bedecked with heraldry. It can be no coincidence that the Hilton lord who acquired the manor (William Hilton, 1376-1435) was also the patron of the massive new gatehouse (finished in 1410) at the family's main *caput*, at Hylton County Durham, which is notable for the prodigious display of family heraldry on its west wall (Morley 1979). The Hiltons did not become lords of Wharram until around 1403, and their interest in the estate faded in less than a generation; but this period coincides with William Hilton's interest in heraldry and suggests that their replacement of the upper storey of the tower, so prominently adorned with their own family arms, was probably undertaken in the first decade or two of the 15th century. It is also possible that they never took up residence here (Beresford M.W. 1987, 15), yet even so, the fact that they chose to adorn the upper stages of the tower suggests that its view from the North Manor was important to them, and we can guess that it had been equally important to the Percys before them.

We have seen in Chapter 15 (pp 255-7), indeed, that there are indications of a second, somewhat earlier phase of work on the tower (which we have allocated to Phase 6) in the reconstruction of the high-level doorway and in the blocking of the two Phase 4 windows to north and south of the tower. Furthermore, we have already seen that the section of late 12th or early 13th-century domestic window mullion (ADS Report, doi:10.5284/1000415, Architectural Stonework, stone U), discovered in the rubble of the 1959 tower collapse, may have come originally from the *camera* at the South Manor. It seems quite clear that the South Manor buildings had been deliberately swept away in the later 13th century (Milne 1979, 33) and consequently we have to presume either that this stone was reused somewhere else during the intermediate period between the 1250s and *c*.1400, or alternatively that the Percys used some of the rubble from their South Manor in a building project enhancing the tower of St Martin's in the later 13th century. The upper part of St Martin's tower, then, may have been altered to give it a more attractive or meaningful appearance in the later 13th century, now that it stood so squarely in the view from the new North Manor. Jim Thorn reports, indeed, that one of the bells dated from the early 14th century (1987, 116-17). It might have been cast in the excavated late-medieval bell-founding pit and perhaps represented the culmination of this intermediate phase of re-edification.

The Percy and Hilton families evidently placed their mark on the church in Phase 6 not just physically then, in the form of alterations to the fabric of St Martin's tower; they also put their mark on the auditory landscape, through new belfries. These were designed to accommodate groups of bells, perhaps (in the Hiltons' case) for the newly introduced communal activity of change-ringing, which would both enliven leisure periods and regulate so many community activities, much like the clock-towers provided as gestures of philanthropy by so many northern mill owners at the town halls of new manufacturing towns in the 19th century.

Yet the Percy and Hilton interest in the late medieval fabric of St Martin's extended far beyond its diminutive western tower. We have already seen in Chapter 15 (pp 252-4) that the north aisle of the church (Phase 5) dates from the 13th century, and we should ask whether its construction is also related to the Percys' acquisition of the tenancy in chief in 1254. It would certainly make a satisfying narrative to propose that one element in their celebration of acquisition of the whole of the vill was the construction of a new north aisle to the church; possibly to provide additional burial space to that available in a family chapel at the east end of the south aisle, and on the north side of the church facing the newly established North Manor site.

In such a narrative, the 'upgrading' of the north door as a door of entrance would also fall into place, as a new access door for the lordly family coming from their new manor site. Unfortunately, our assessment of the date of the new aisle proposes an earlier date than 1254 for its construction. The architectural details themselves are so simple as to defy accurate dating, and on these grounds alone a date in the 1250s would be as plausible as one in the first two decades of the century. The fragment from a gable cross (ADS Report, doi:10.5284/1000415, Architectural Stonework, stone A) is however, much more precisely datable and suggests a date between *c*. 1200 and *c*. 1220; and it is thought likely that the only gable on which it might have sat is that over the rebuilt chancel arch, which was contemporary with the construction of the north aisle. Thus, unless an alternative location for the gable cross can be suggested, it seems likely that our proposal, though superficially attractive, cannot be substantiated.

Even so, it is clear that the reconstruction of the chancel and the erection of the north-east chapel must correspond with the Percy occupation of the North Manor. In Chapter 15 (pp 254-5) we argued that the windows now reset in the north wall probably originated in the north-east chapel and, although they have nondescript tracery units, it is possible to date them to the second half of the 14th century. Furthermore, it seems likely that, even though archaeological evidence for the connection is thin, the construction of this chapel was not far separated in time from the total reconstruction of the chancel itself in Phase 6.

Reconstruction of the chancel by the Percys in the 14th century might perhaps be expected. In 1254 they acquired not only the manor in chief, but also the advowson (pp 229-30). This acquisition should be seen as another critical symbol of their ascent into the outright tenure of the manor in that year, and their contemporary relocation to the new North Manor site. During their residence at Wharram, at least one member of the Percy family was appointed to the rectory, and one strong indication that the chancel was rebuilt by them may be the discovery that the high-status burial placed in the position of honour within the new chancel, in the 'founders' position north of the high altar, was a priest. We might doubt whether a priest would have been accorded this honorific position if he had not also been the lord of the church, or at least a member of the lord's family.

When the manor passed into the hands of Sir Geoffrey Scrope of Masham in 1323 (on his acquisition of the lunatic Percy heiress's wardship: see p. 235), he evidently set in train arrangements to make the advowson of Wharram part of the foundation endowment of Haltemprice Priory (a transfer completed by 1327: Beresford M.W. 1987, 21-3; Wrathmell 2010b, 16-17). Thereafter, canons of the priory served the cure, or they appointed vicars in their stead. As Beresford noted, Haltemprice Priory was never in a good financial state, and it seems highly unlikely to have instigated even a relatively modest building programme on one of its more remote holdings (Beresford M.W. 1987, 22). This, in turn, adds weight to the argument that the chancel was probably rebuilt in the period when the Percys held both the manor and the advowson, between 1254 and 1327. In this connection we should also note that the chancel had 'defects' in 1308 (Beresford M.W. 1987, 29), suggesting perhaps an early 14th-century date (between 1308 and 1327) for its construction.

Indeed, it is possible, perhaps even likely, that the chancel was rebuilt by the Percys (or by their proxy Sir Geoffrey Scrope) shortly before the advowson passed into the hands of Haltemprice Priory, as a gesture of family piety and as an item of patronage towards the newly founded Priory. This would place the construction of St Martin's chancel alongside contemporary examples such as that at Heckington (Lincs.), where (on a much grander scale) Edward I's chaplain, Richard Potesgrave, erected a magnificent new chancel whilst he was both rector and vicar, in the full knowledge that the advowson would pass to Bardney Abbey on his death. Like the priest at Wharram, Potesgrave was buried – with his patten and chalice – in the honorific 'founder's' location, north of the high altar (Wilson 1980).

If this line of thinking, and the parallel with examples such as Heckington is valid, then we might even go so far as to suggest that the ecclesiastic found in the critical 'founders' position within the newly rebuilt choir at St Martin's was in fact Sir Henry de Percy, who was both a son of the Percy lords of Wharram and the incumbent between 1308 and 1322 (Beresford M.W. 1987, 21-22; Wrathmell 2010b, 16). In 1320, indeed, the advowson was quitclaimed by Robert Percy to Sir Henry (Wrathmell 2010b, 16), a move which would have ensured that the advowson would no longer descend through family inheritance and perhaps indicating an intention, at this stage, to alienate it to a monastic institution. Alienation did not occur, however, immediately following Sir Henry's presumed death in about 1322, as the advowson had been caught up in the complexities of transfer of ownership of the manor from the lunatic heiress to Sir Geoffrey de Scrope, to whom Sir Henry sold the advowson in 1322. It was not until 1327, and after he had presented a further three (no doubt absentee) rectors, that the advowson was finally granted to Haltemprice Priory by Sir Geoffrey (Wrathmell 2010b, 16).

This grant, finally, affords a little further circumstantial evidence for the chancel's enlargement, as the grant of the rectory of Wharram was intended to permit Haltemprice to support four chaplains, two at their mother church and two at Wharram itself. These new chantry chaplains were to pray daily for the souls of William and Constance Percy, their sons Thomas and William, and for Sir Geoffrey himself, his wife Yvette, Sir Henry Scrope and Master Stephen Scrope (Wrathmell 2010b, 16). Such an impressive new chantry might well have required an architectural setting, and it has been suggested that the new north-east chapel added to St Martin's might have been associated with its endowment

(Beresford M.W. 1987, 29 fn; Bell 1987a, 82-4). But given that we feel confident enough to date the north-east chapel on the strength of its window tracery to the period after *c*.1350 we are saying, at the very least, that any such separate chantry building had to wait for a generation to be glazed.

On the other hand there was no requirement, of course, for the newly established chantry to be performed in a self-contained building at all. It might be preferable to pursue the analogy with chantries such as Potesgrave's at Heckington further, and suggest that a new architectural setting for the chantry was provided by the reconstructed choir of Phase 6, and the entire operation, reconstruction of the chancel, burial of a family priest (possibly Sir Henry Percy?) and the donation of the advowson to Haltemprice along with the property to support the chaplains, was part of an elaborate plan that originated amongst the Percy family sometime after 1308 and was only brought to fruition on the death of Sir Geoffrey Scrope.

But, if so, what of the north-east chapel, perhaps built as much as 50 years later (judging by its window tracery), and with all the appearance of having been constructed to house a chantry? It is not unheard of for chantry buildings to remain under construction for a generation following the establishment of the endowments for the chantry priest, so the north-east chapel could have been the final result of several generations' fund-raising to provide a building within which the Scrope chantry could be accommodated. There were certainly further adjustments to the ritual layout within the church in the second half of the 14th century. The finely carved statue bracket (Thorn 1987, 126 fig. 45, now at Birdsall), which was subsequently built into the blocking of the north arcade, and which we might therefore presume also came originally from the north aisle or north-east chapel, like the windows, is evidence for a cult statue probably placed above or near to a subsidiary altar. *Contra* Thorn (Thorn 1987, 127), this item is certainly not from a piscina, and it has such a slender platform that it is unlikely to be a corbel. The buttoned sleeves on display to either side of the boldly-carved face were in vogue in the second half of the 14th century, although they were also still in widespread use around 1400. It seems clear, then, that a new altar, with its cult statue, was inaugurated somewhere within the north aisle, north-east chapel or chancel during the second half of the 14th century, and it is perhaps likely that this altar was within the north-east chapel. If so it would confirm the later 14th-century date for the structure indicated by the two surviving windows.

Another possibility worth considering, however, is that the north-east chapel was erected to house an entirely distinct chantry within the church. Thanks to the untangling of the references to Towthorpe chapel and its chantry (Wrathmell 2010b, 17), we now know that, in addition to there being a chapel at Towthorpe itself (dedicated to St Katherine) there was also a Towthorpe chantry at St Martin's before the Dissolution. Because it is not mentioned in the ordination that reordered Haltemprice's responsibilities in St Martin's in 1440, Wrathmell makes the assumption that the chantry came into existence after that date. But this is not a necessary conclusion, and the north-east chapel could easily have dated from the foundation of this Towthorpe chantry; a date in the third quarter of the 14th century on the evidence of its window tracery. It is perhaps most likely that the chantry, whether housed in the north-east chapel or elsewhere in the church, was aimed at celebrating masses for a family called Towthorpe, as we have no indication of any sort of communal guild at Towthorpe vill who might have sponsored such an institution at St Martin's.

Once the rectory and advowson had been transferred to Haltemprice, and with it the patronage of the chancel, we might expect, perhaps, the focus of patronage by the resident lord at St Martin's to shift back to the nave, and indeed this seems to have been the case. We have already seen that the Hilton's patronage after their acquisition of the manor in c.1403 was focused, at least in part, on the re-embellishment of the upper storey of the west tower. The final major medieval gifts to the church fabric, however, might also be associated with the Hiltons. These are the new windows in the south aisle. We have already seen (pp 255-6) that the two surviving windows in today's south wall originated in the south wall of the Romanesque south aisle. They have a distinctive mullion rising from the shallow apex of the two main lights, which is seen in many tracery designs in Yorkshire around 1400, and which derives ultimately from the reconstruction of the York Minster Lady Chapel in the final decades of the 14th century (Stocker 2001, 595; Brown 2003, 144-68). As Thorn first suggested, then, this dating may suggest that they represent further embellishment of the church by the Hiltons.

The fact that the Hiltons chose to insert new windows here, in the, no doubt, cramped and dark south aisle, is a reminder that the south wall still contained the main access door into the church. Furthermore, this aisle probably still contained memorials to the early Percy lords of the manor in the chapel at its eastern end. There would have been the practical need to bring light into the aisle, and indirectly into the nave, and there would no doubt have been a liturgical need to provide stained glass images for the lay devotion. But it is also likely that the Hiltons wished to associate themselves with previous lordly families who had held the manor before them, by paying this architectural compliment to their predecessors. There is, at any rate, no clear sign of their demarcating a new mausoleum space for their family that distinguished them, in any way, from their predecessors as lords of the manor. Like the Percys themselves in the 12th and early 13th centuries, perhaps, they intended to use existing mausoleum space in the south aisle which, although closely identified with the Percys by 1400, was also associated with the 11th-century lordly families buried outside to the east, when the Percys were

themselves newly arrived. It is also possible, however, that the Hiltons had no such 'dynastic' pretensions: they had acquired the manor through purchase and exchange (Beresford M.W. 1979, 19-20) and we might forgive them for not creating a new structural mausoleum within the church envelope.

Like the late 12th-century Percys before them, then, the Hiltons also wished to place their mark as lords and patrons on the south side of the church, by which the congregation presumably still approached, at least on formal occasions, and remarkably this tradition was continued, by coincidence or design, in the mid-16th century when gravecover fragments of 12th, 13th and 14th-century dates were recycled in the blocking of the south nave arcade (Phase 7: Thorn 1987, 121; Ryder 2007, 287-93). The proximate source of the gravecovers reused in this way would have been high-status burials in the south aisle floor, although it is true that they could have been brought here from the chancel floor or even from the north aisle and north-east chapel in Phase 7. Even so, accidentally or otherwise, the initial lordly monuments of Lagmann and Karli began a tradition of associating the lords of the vill with the south side of the church that was not only respected by the Percys and the Hiltons but was also continued by their Protestant successors.

But the south aisle of St Martin's also faced away from the recast village. The most convenient entry would never have been the south door, even at periods when the properties at the southern end of the West Row were fully occupied. This continuing focus of attention on the south door, rather than the north, which would be so much more convenient for the villagers, probably originated at an early stage in the development of the fabric, before the arrival of the resident lords in the later 12th century. At that stage (i.e. at the date of the first doorway of which we know in this location in the Phase 3 church) this door would have welcomed not just residents from Wharram but also those of the townships of Burdale, Raisthorpe, Thixendale and Towthorpe, who, throughout St Martin's life, were probably in a considerable majority (Beresford M.W. 1979, 5-16). This is the Phase 3 door, of course, from which we suspect that the carved tympanum (ADS Report, doi:10.5284/1000415, Architectural Stonework, stone I) came, which seems to mark it out as the more important. Had there been a resident lord from the foundation of the church, of course, the north door might have been established as the more important.

The south door had been aggrandised in the late 12th century, when the South Manor was being upgraded, and in a similar architectural style, but the transfer of the manor site to the North Manor in 1254 did not have the effect of reorientating the church around a principal north entrance. Indeed, although upgraded in Phase 5, the north door always remained very much a private entry, quite unsuitable for elaborate ceremonial. Perhaps a sensible approach to the church from the South Manor (and possibly from its predecessor halls of Lagmann and

Karli?) would have taken a route southwards from the gate along the West Row to the end of the terrace before turning northwards to approach the church from the south. If we take this functionalist view, that the south door became the dominant one for practical reasons, though, it was probably retained in the period after 1254 for reasons of its symbolic associations with previous lords.

Generations of Wharram lords had, then, asserted their local lordship in the space to the south of St Martin's church nave. In the 11th century the 're-founders group' was the first to colonise this space, and in the early 12th century their successors' churchyard monuments were brought within the church by the Percys' new enveloping south aisle, with a new family burial chapel at its east end. Indeed, the reused bracelet-headed gravecover discovered amongst the loose masonry cleared from St Martin's church might have marked a lord's grave contemporary with this new south aisle (ADS Report, doi:10.5284/1000415 Architectural Stonework, stone H; Ryder 2007, 292, no. 34). Furthermore, we might suggest that the dozen or so reused gravecovers in the south wall of the Phase 7 church, mostly dating from the 13th and 14th centuries (Ryder 2007, 287-93), could also have come from the floor of the abandoned south aisle, although it is also possible that they came from the abandoned chancel. Amongst their numbers are probably also memorials to members of the Percy family buried in the church between *c.* 1200 and *c.* 1400. As late as 1400, the Hiltons still saw the south aisle as an important site for demonstrating patronage, in the form of a new suite of windows. We should modify Beresford's remarks on these matters, then. Whilst he asserted that 'there is no evidence of family tombs or other Percy burials at Wharram' (Beresford M.W. 1987, 22), we would say that both the chancel and the south side of the church embodied Percy lordship, and can probably identify Percy family burials in the south-east chapel. But the Percys were preceded in their occupation of the space south of the church by earlier lordlings of Wharram, Lagmann and Karli, and even if they were not succeeded here by the burials of later lords, such as the Hiltons, such evidence as we have suggests that they continued to respect the lordly associations of this part of the church through their continuing patronage.

The Hiltons, however, may never have been in residence, and certainly not after 1406 (Beresford M.W. 1987, 15), and the fabric of St Martin's entered a long period of decline. Yet our new understanding of this fabric (pp 256-9) suggests that a massive contraction and reconstruction of the fabric did not occur for over a century, until after the Reformation; a conclusion based primarily on liturgical considerations. In fact, the documentary history (richer now of course) offers a circumstantial narrative into which the archaeological features of Phase 7 can be fitted. The rectory and advowson of St Martin's passed to the crown from Haltemprice Priory in 1536, and we have no reason to think that the crown would have invested in the church building. Similarly, 16th-century lords of the manor, now absentee, clearly did not feel any greater onus to cater for the dwindling population of the five settlements. Towthorpe chapel had vanished by 1556, whilst those at Raisthorpe and Thixendale had gone a decade later. In 1573 the manor had also been sold by the Hiltons to Matthew Hutton, the Dean of York, but he did not take an immediate interest in the spiritual comforts of his newly acquired tenants either. In 1555, whilst the manor still belonged to the Hiltons, and the rectory and advowson still belonged to the crown, the chancel of St Martin's was said to be 'ruined'. In 1575, after the manor had passed into the Dean's hands, the chancel remained 'utterlie decaid so that in winter the people ar like to perishe with colde'(Beresford M.W. 1987, 24). Indeed, for all that he was a committed protestant who whitewashed the Minster and equipped it with Geneva Bibles (Cross 1977, 205-6), and despite the fact that he had added the rectory (i.e. great tithes) and the advowson of St Martin's to his manor in 1582, Hutton had still taken no steps to rectify matters by 1586. In the latter year he was presented for neglect by the Archdeacon following a formal visitation, when it was said,

'the chauncell is fallen downe and the churchwardens and vicar be authorized to sell the leade which covered the same chauncell and to bestowe the money upon the repaire of the said chauncell'
(Beresford M.W. 1987, 24*)*

Given our archaeological analysis of the Phase 7 fabric, we must surely conclude that Hutton's very public admonition by his colleagues, and with the authority of the Archbishop, stimulated him finally to attend to St Martin's defective fabric, with the spectacular contraction of the fabric we have documented in Chapter 15 (pp 256-9). As we have noted, the result of his work was an avowedly 'reformed' building, with no chancel where the priest could be separated from the laity. Yet even so, the priest was accorded, we suspect, the dignity of a small vestry fashioned from the remains of the south aisle. Would such a thoughtful touch have been provided had the patron of this work not been a clergyman himself?

Though greatly respected, Matthew Hutton was also a controversial figure, at least within Yorkshire recusant circles, and that recusant voice seems to have been given expression in Phase 7 at Wharram also, with the intriguing burial and its prominent gravemarker, placed centrally within the area of the former chancel, on the site of what had once been St Martin's high altar (p. 259 above; Stocker 2007b, 293-4). One of us has argued that this burial was marked with a standing wooden cross, mounted in a socket stone fashioned from a reused fragment of architectural masonry (Stocker 2007b, 293-4). The deliberate placement of such a monument in this significant location, within the ruins of the chancel, was making a very explicit declaration of sympathy with a more conservative style of religion than would have been to Hutton's taste. Presuming that the burial was made with knowledge and understanding of recent history, indeed, it might even have been intended as an implied criticism of the Dean and of the manner in which he had 'reformed' the church fabric. Can we make any progress in attempting to identify the individual involved?

The burial itself and its monument cannot be dated any more closely than *c.* 1550-1650 (Stocker 2007b, 294), but we have shown that the area of the former chancel would have been part of the churchyard when the burial was made and so a date between the late 1580s and *c.*1650 is consistent with the known facts. This gesture need not necessarily have been made by a priest, of course, though the circumstances must suggest that this is at least a possibility. During this period only two men held the vicarage at Wharram Percy. Thomas Pereson (vicar from 1576-1618) might have had little time for Hutton, as he was in residence during the visitation of 1586, and it is possible to read that presentation as a belligerent act by a disaffected incumbent against his ecclesiastical superior. Pereson, however, was buried at Wharram le Street in 1618 (Beresford M.W. 1987, 30). His successor, Edward Lowthorpe, was buried at St Martin's in 1642/3, but we can say little about his doctrinal position and, by then, Matthew Hutton had been dead for 30 years and the manor had been sold by his grandson in 1634. Intriguingly, perhaps, several families named Pereson appear on the list of recusants in the County of York for 1604 (Peacock 1872), but none of them appears local to Wharram and they may have been unconnected with Thomas Pereson of Wharram le Street. Some slight indication of Thomas' doctrinal position, however, might be revealed by his charging his tenant, Leonard Weddel, with irreverent behaviour by allowing his dog to cause a disturbance in the churchyard (Wrathmell 2010b, 24); an event which brings to mind the Laudian injunctions against dogs in churchyards of a generation later. Perhaps, then, the burial at the high altar of medieval St Martin's was one of Pereson's parishioners wishing to make such a strong 'high Anglican' point with the location and form of his own burial monument. Although the Weddels do not appear in the 1604 list of recusants, there are a number of Milner families (Peacock 1872) and Michael Milner of Mowthorpe was a joint tenant with Leonard Weddel of Wharram Percy in 1604.

Conclusion

Unsurprisingly, the evidence from the church fabric in the later medieval period is more complex and finer-grained than that emanating from the village plan and wider landscape. There, the broad-brush picture reveals a thoroughgoing recasting of the village consequent on the relocation of the manorial *curia* from the South Manor to the new North Manor. Altogether, the new landscape amounts both to a visible display of seisin, as envisaged in Chapter 14 (pp 230-234), which is impressively legible in the archaeological record in a way closely comparable to the equally radical changes of the later 12th century. Yet we might also be able to perceive, very dimly, less tangible aspects of this display of lordship (the soundscape of the new bells, the strike of sunlight on

stone, the hazy recollections of the Roman past) which hint at more complex contemporary perceptions of that landscape and would have given it qualities of richness and depth.

In the fabric of St Martin's church, we also read the impact of the Percys in the 13th century, in the tower, and perhaps a new attention to the north side of the church. But their patronage must have been particularly visible in the fine new chancel, the symbol of their acquisition of the advowson in 1254. Furthermore, the Percys' work on the tower is linked to that in the chancel by the import of a 12th-century voussoir from one of the arches within the chancel to be reused as a corbel in the upper floor of the tower (Thorn 1987, 114). Even though the 14th century is a period of tenurial complexity and disruption caused by failures in the Percy line, nevertheless fabric history suggests that there remained important lords in residence in the North Manor, and that they were still active in patronising the church fabric. The justification for such a bold conclusion is to be found in the apparently close links we have observed between *resident* lordship and the erection of fine capital buildings such as the manor houses and the various phases of work at the church, and in the landscape that we have identified in earlier phases. It is this apparent link that represents the principal lesson of this study. Taken as a whole, many changes to the layout and fabric of Wharram seem to have been ephemeral and long-term, except at moments when the resident lord had a position to establish, an income to bolster or a reputation to renew. These moments may be small-scale examples of what have been called 'rupture points' (Johnson 2007, 149-50) and at those moments, it seems that the archaeological record at Wharram also demonstrates major changes.

It is also significant, of course, that these 'rupture points' seem to bear no relationship at all to the broader economic history of the settlement. Such mechanistic links between the floor area of churches and the sizes of the population of their vills are not now made as frequently as they once were. Beresford was aware of this, of course, and noted in 1987, that 'the relationship between the size of the parish population and the demise of the parish church is not a simple one' (Beresford M.W. 1987, 19). Following the much more nuanced and sensitive discussion in Richard Morris's seminal book (1989), which sets out the case that no such simplistic conclusions should be drawn, subsequent studies have been more careful not to draw simplistic parallels between numbers of parishioners and floor area of the church. The Wharram case would seem to exemplify the complexity to which Morris points: in a general sense large vills often have large churches, but there is no direct causal link between numbers of parishioners and total floor area. Although the Phase 3 church of the early 12th century might reflect the community's aspirations more directly, later phases at Wharram seem to offer more evidence for the impact of elite patronage by resident lordship on the growth of the church plan, regardless of the growth or decline of the community of the vill.

17 Field Systems and Landholdings

by David Hall with contributions from Stuart Wrathmell

Introduction

In the previous chapter, David Stocker and Paul Everson argued that Wharram's open fields – insofar as we know them from field investigations and documentary sources – were among the many aspects of community life that were transformed by the arrival of the Percys as mesne tenants in the late 12th century. Allowing that the creation of such a mesne tenancy is an inference rather than a documented event, it is still a plausible hypothesis that Wharram's mix of tenanted strips and blocks of demesne ridges, described in the final section of this chapter, were created in that period. Whether the ridges themselves were also created at that time, as Stocker and Everson argue, is a different matter. The numbers of carucates recorded for the vill in Domesday and in later sources do not support the notion that there was a massive expansion of arable between the late 11th and 13th centuries, and some would assign the near complete ridging of Wolds vills to the period before the Norman conquest.

The documentary evidence for the character of Wharram's field system and for the patterns of landholding within it is highly fragmentary, and completely nonexistent for many centuries. Once again, therefore, we have decided to set such information as we have within a broader regional context. The first three sections of this chapter deal with the general characteristics of field systems in Yorkshire, and particularly in eastern Yorkshire – in the Vale of Pickering, the Wolds and Holderness (Fig. 98). These are followed by a section that focuses on the physical and documentary evidence for open-field systems in a range of townships in the study area, drawn from a largely unpublished survey carried out thirty years ago as part of the Wharram Research Project. After a short review of evidence for the survival of permanent pastures in the study area into the 12th and 13th centuries, the final section focuses on the evidence for Wharram Percy's own open fields, and speculates on their possible origins.

Field systems in Yorkshire

H.L. Gray's study of English field systems placed all the county lying east of the Pennines within the area where two-field and three-field systems predominated. Under this system of agriculture, one or two fields were cropped each year and the remaining one left as fallow. The fallow field was used for grazing after harvest and subsequently ploughed and harrowed several times to kill weeds, followed by manuring. Three-field systems are found on fertile soils, and two-fields on poorer soils that needed longer resting to regain fertility. Two-field and three-field arrangements form an extensive central belt running approximately from Durham through the Midlands to Dorset and Hampshire (Gray 1915, frontispiece). Yorkshire field systems are, however, far more diverse than indicated by Gray, reflecting the county's wide topographical variations. In the Dales and the Pennines on the west, and the North York Moors on the north-east, townships lying on or near high ground often had small and irregular field systems. These were generally enclosed at an early date, and so records of them are relatively few. In such areas, it is commonly found that the terms 'field' and 'furlong' – furlongs being the components of fields in classic open-field systems – are interchangeable names and have nothing to do with cropping arrangements.

Such townships had an abundance of common pasture grounds, and as a result pieces of pasture were occasionally ploughed and cropped for one or a few years and then allowed to revert to pasture again for several years until fertility recovered. The practice is known as convertible husbandry or infield-outfield, depending on how it was managed. Under such an arrangement the long period of rest allowed the land to recover. The core arable lands were grazed after harvest, and could also have been manured from accumulations in winter byres. It is possible that many south-western Yorkshire townships were organised in this way and so appear in documents as 'one-field' systems like Sheldon in northern Derbyshire, and various places in Lancashire (Youd 1962, 20-34).

An early example of these practices can be found at Hitchells in Bessacar, where part of the common could be brought into tillage in 1187 (*EYC II*, 163). Late examples are recorded in the East Riding at Walkington, where oxgangs in 1729 were partly under tillage and partly ley (Harris 1955, 533). Bishop Wilton, towards the west end of the northern Wolds, had three fields on the low ground in 1772, but in 1611 the Wold itself (about half the total area) had been sown only once in ten or twelve years (Sheppard 1973, 153-4, plan). Late infield-outfield cultivation also seems to have been established at Wharram Percy after the depopulation of the village and the abolition of open-field agriculture (see pp 356-9).

The importance of arable versus pasture can also be assessed through data provided by probate inventories. A study of early 17th-century inventories found that corn was the most highly valued item on the Wolds, whereas it was low on the North York Moors where cattle were the most valuable component of the farm stock. The Dales and Craven had similar high cattle valuations. As would be expected, the corn growing areas of the Wolds and lowlands had more ploughs and harrows than the regions where cattle were predominant (Harwood Long 1960, 103-15).

The field systems of eastern Yorkshire

Two-field and three-field arrangements

Two-field and three-field systems predominated in the Vales of York and Pickering, on the Wolds and in Holderness. Their late survival in these areas ensured that

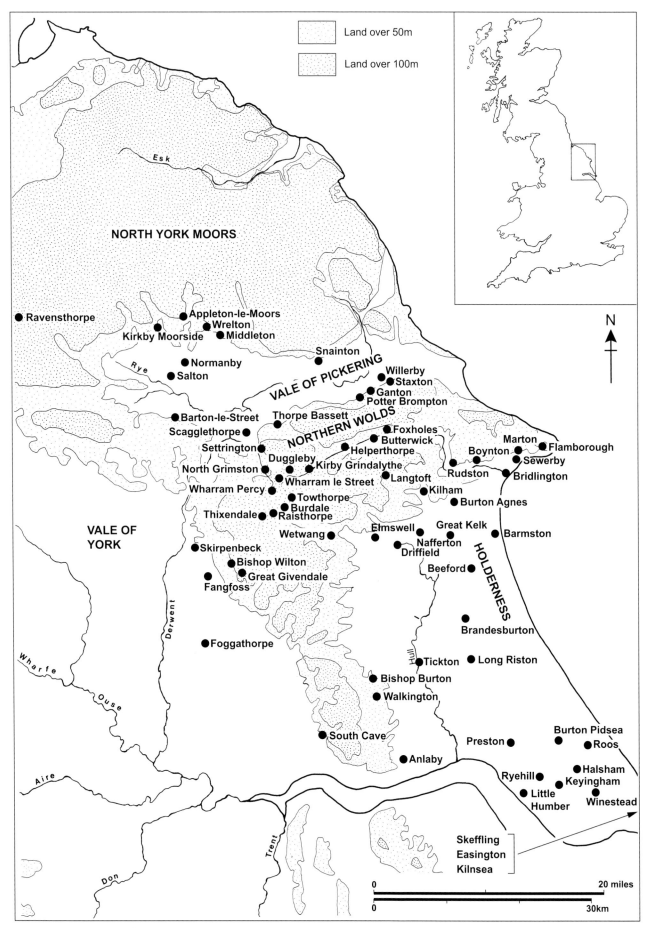

Fig. 98. Map showing places mentioned in Chapter 17. (E. Marlow-Mann and C. Philo)

279

records about them are abundant. Gray (1915, 504-9) found ten townships with satisfactory evidence of two fields before 1510, six of them being demesne; and he recorded 25 examples of three fields before 1610, of which twelve were samples of demesne lands.

More detailed research on East Riding open-field systems was carried out in the 1950s by Alan Harris (1959; 1961). He identified many two-field systems in the Wolds and Holderness regions, including Tickton in the 17th century and Burton Pidsea in 1862 (Harris 1961, 38-43); he also published an outline plan of Beeford as it appeared in 1766, when it had had two arable fields occupying 2000 acres with 1,100 acres of meadow and pasture, and a linear village lying in the middle (Harris 1962, 120). Furthermore, some late 16th-century two-field Holderness townships are recorded as having a two-tilth crop rotation, spring and winter crops being sown on one field while the other was fallow (Sheppard 1973, 152). A study of 44 places in Holderness has shown that 36 of them were two field and, on the Wolds, a sample of 47 places included 27 three-field and 14 two-field townships (Harris 1959, 2).

Two and three fields are also recorded or implied for earlier dates. Flamborough had a three-course tilth in 1377 with one third fallow (*VCH ER I*, 157), and in the 13th century Keyingham Marsh demesne, near Hull, was run as a three-tilth system, with 306 out of 459 acres sown (Brown 1892, 78 and 80). On the other hand, Kilham on the Wolds had two fields in 1320 (*VCH ER I*, 256), as did Marton, near Bridlington, in *c.* 1188, when there were 20 acres 'on each side' (*EYC III*, 462). Marton was still two-field in the 13th century (Brown 1894a, 10-14). Little Humber demesne was run as two tilths in the 13th century (Brown 1892, 79). Two fields are known in Brandesburton in the 14th century, where one of them lay idle each year (Siddle 1967, 42).

Further north, in the Vale of Pickering there is evidence for some three-field systems in the 14th century, for example at Snainton and Appleton-le-Moors. Kirkby Moorside demesne had a three-course tilth in 1352 (Allerston 1970, 104). Skirpenbeck, lying east of York on the Derwent, had three fields in 1446 with 8 bovates distributed between them as 39, 33 and 26.5 acres (Atkinson 1878, 328-9).

The frequent survival into post-medieval times of two and three-field systems in eastern Yorkshire can be seen in Maurice Beresford's study of glebe terriers, principally dating to the 17th century, for the county as a whole (Beresford 1951, 348-9). As would be expected at that date, there were few open fields in the upland parishes of the north-east and west of the county; Cleveland deanery, for example, had only 12 per cent of its parishes in the open state. The East Riding, in contrast, had most surviving open fields, the parishes of its four deaneries ranging from 57 to 74 per cent open. In terms of named fields, satisfactory information was supplied by 157 places, of which there were 20 (13%) with one field, 46 (29%) with two fields, 66 (42%) three, 19 (11%) four, and

3 (2%) with five fields and more than five fields. Without more analysis it cannot be determined whether places with four named fields had two fields grouped together to make a three-course tilth or whether there was a Cotswold type four-field system.

Oxgang holdings

The medieval farmholding consisted of a number of individual strips of arable land called *selions* (or *riggs*, *doles*, *acres*, or simply *lands*) dispersed with other similar holdings among the *furlongs* (or *flats*, *falls*, *faughs*, and occasionally *wandales* or *bydales*) of the township's arable fields. The unit of landholding was called an oxgang (or 'bovate' from the Latin) and normally there were 8 oxgangs to a carucate. The size, and therefore the number of strips involved, varied from township to township. Early records of sizes of oxgang are known for a number of Yorkshire vills, and they generally range between about 7 and 20 acres. For example at Ravensthorpe in Felixkirk, 10 acres of land and meadow made an oxgang (Brown 1892, 15-51).

The range of possible dispositions of oxgangs in the fields is well illustrated in the 1446 record of Skirpenbeck noted above. Two oxgangs lay in a block next to the vill of '*Pontebelli*' (Stamford Bridge), four others lay in groups of one or two selions next to the lord's demesne, and another 8 oxgangs lay adjacent to each other but dispersed in the flatts of the three fields of the vill (Atkinson 1878, 328-9). The first were therefore (presumably) part of a block of demesne lands, the second were dispersed among demesne furlongs, and the third were completely dispersed as shown by a terrier naming all the flatts. Most of the oxgangs recorded in medieval charters were completely dispersed rather than being located in blocks (e.g. *EYC III*, 1916, 289; Atkinson 1878, 109; Anon. 1903, 97-8; Brown 1889, 278).

Long lands and tenurial cycles

During the late 1970s and early 1980s a number of historical geographers explored the characteristics of field systems in eastern Yorkshire, mainly in Holderness and on the Wolds but also extending into the Vale of Pickering. Their overall conclusions have been usefully assembled by Mary Harvey (1982, 29). Field structures in Holderness and on parts of the Wolds were remarkably simple. Lands were long, commonly over 1000 metres and often extending across an entire open field from the village enclosures to the township boundary. They rarely changed orientation; therefore furlongs or falls were few in number, and again were not necessarily marked by changes in orientation. As noted above, many of these townships had their furlongs grouped into just two fields, despite the great extent of the arable lands.

Land holding was also simple and regular: the parcels belonging to each bovate or oxgang lay in the same relative positions, with the same neighbouring strips, in all the furlongs of a township. Though there was variation in each furlong, the variations were repeated consistently in each other furlong. These 'regular' characteristics were already in place by *c.*1250 when documents become detailed enough to enable some topographical reconstruction. As Harvey also noted, these distinctive characteristics are to be found in two regions – the Wolds and Holderness – that could hardly provide a greater contrast in terms of terrain and soils. This method of organising and using land was clearly neither terrain nor soil specific.

All the characteristics can be seen in Figure 99, a plan of the Holderness township of Great Kelk. The original is dated 1842, and this version is based on a redrawing by Alan Harris which was published by Matzat (1988, 134, fig. 2 and n.1). The plan shows that, apart from some short furlongs with intermixed orientations in the carr lands at the extreme east end of the township, the arable strips stretched from east to west across the entire township, from the boundary with Lowthorpe to the boundary with Gransmoor. Their sinuous sweep was bisected by a line of settlement enclosures that itself stretched from one end of the township to the other, from the boundary with Little Kelk in the north to that with Gembling in the south.

The related photograph (Plate 26), shows two widths of ridges which can be related to the broad and narrow lands distinguished on the map by the different widths between the dashed lines. In post-medieval times mixes of broad and narrow lands are recorded in many townships across the East Riding (Harris 1955, 529), and in the early 17th century Henry Best's broad lands at Elmswell, near Driffield, were 28 feet wide (Woodward 1984, 18, 317). Narrow lands were half the width, perhaps formed by splitting broad lands in two lengthwise to create smaller farmholds, accounting for the difficulty in recognising them where the ridges have been truncated by modern ploughing. Harvey (1983, 91) has linked broad lands to two-oxgang holdings, narrow lands to single oxgang holdings.

The other aspect demonstrated succinctly on the Great Kelk map is the regular distribution of holdings through the furlongs. Philip Boynton's holding of one broad and two narrow lands forms, on Figure 99, a repetitive pattern through the furlongs on both sides of the village enclosures, with only a limited amount of fragmentation in the south-eastern part of the township. Similar repetition can be seen in an earlier map of Great Kelk, dating to 1789, which shows the holding of Rev Thomas Preston. In this case it appears that a number of adjacent broad and/or narrow lands have been amalgamated to form long closes on each side of the village enclosures, presumably created through exchange; but the repetitious patterning of closes and neighbouring unenclosed strips in each co-aligned furlong is very marked (Sheppard 1973, 150, fig. 4.2).

Much of Holderness remained open until the 18th century and contemporary maps record long lands, some up to a mile or more in length, in various other townships including Skeffling (1721) and Preston (1750). Similarly, there is evidence for long lands in the Middle Ages: Long

Riston and East Halsham both had strips extending from the village closes to the neighbouring townships in the 13th century (Harvey 1981). Others are recorded at Kilnsea, Winestead, Ryehill and Roos (Harvey 1980, 4-5, with plans).

Long lands also occurred over most of the Wolds, although Kilham is the only township with an open field map (Sheppard 1973, 149). Wetwang had strips about 1.2 miles long, and a plan of Butterwick, reconstructed from a field book of 1563 (Castle Howard MS F4/14/3: see Fig. 31), suggests further strips of great length. They can be found, too, in the Vale of Pickering to the north. Ordnance Survey plans of enclosed field systems west of Pickering show patterns of walls and hedges lying in narrow fields that make up very long curved lines, suggesting that they reflect similar simple strip fields (e.g. Middleton, Aislaby and Wrelton on Ordnance Survey Sheet SE 78, scale 1: 25,000: illustrated in Hall 1982, 51 and Roberts 2008, 99-101). There is also medieval evidence for long lands in several townships immediately below the northern Wolds scarp, for example at Ganton, Potter Brompton, Willerby and Staxton (Harvey 1982a).

In other parts of the county, such as the Vale of York, and in other regions, pre-eminently the East Midlands, simple, uniform planned systems have been subsequently subdivided into smaller units, creating the characteristic chequer-board patterns of furlongs, even though the overall alignment and original large-scale planning can in some places still be detected by detailed analysis (e.g. at Hardingstone, Northamptonshire: Hall 1980, 126-7). In contrast, the early systems of long, uniform riggs on the Wolds and in Holderness were not, on the whole, subsequently broken up, as can be seen in the examples from the Wharram area presented later in this chapter.

In the case of the Wolds, soils are well drained by the underlying chalk, and the plateaux slope into the nearby dales, so that a complicated fall pattern was not required to achieve surface drainage. For Holderness, the often near-flat terrain had to be drained with furrows running across the contours, according to the gentle slope available. Any attempt to introduce smaller 'cross falls' lying along the contours would introduce undesirable waterlogged furrows.

Tenurial cycles of landholding

Regular tenurial cycles of lands, like those evident at Great Kelk, are found in abundance in the field systems of the Wolds and Holderness. One of the clearest examples of an ordered structure in a 13th-century field system is to be found in the abbot of Selby's holding at Foggathorpe, about ten miles to the north-east of the abbey. Six oxgangs consisted of 135 strips lying in 45 flatts grouped into three named fields. Each of the 45 flatts contained six strips lying together, three of the abbot and three of the fee of Peter Mauley (who held all the sets of six). Throughout all the fields the strips had the land of Robert Skrykenbek on one side, and the land of John Pothow, holding of the Mauley fee, on the other (Fowler

Plate 26. Broad and narrow ridges in the fields of Great Kelk, Holderness in 1946 (RAF/CPE/UK/1839 Frame 3015; CAM.RP; LN516; 13/11/46. English Heritage (NMR) RAF Photography)

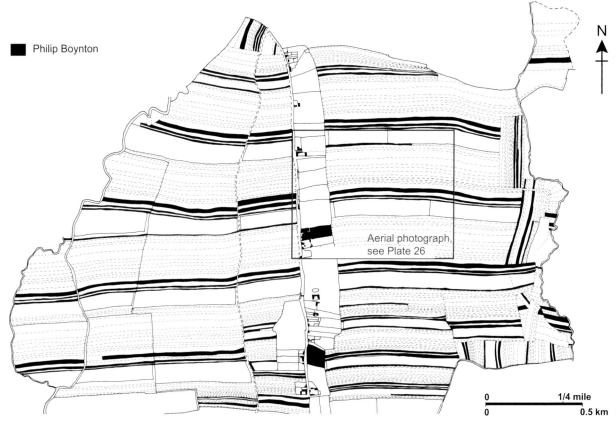

Philip Boynton

N

Aerial photograph, see Plate 26

| 0 | | 1/4 mile |
| 0 | | 0.5 km |

Fig. 99. The fields of Great Kelk, Holderness, as shown on a plan of 1842. (E. Marlow-Mann, after W. Matzat and A. Harris)

1893, 42). The regular disposition of the oxgangs in the two fees proves that it was not the result of a private partition arrangement, but a fundamental part of the field structure.

Similar, though often later evidence is found in many other townships in these regions. The regular distribution of oxgangs was, for example, identified at Burton Agnes (Göransson 1961, 85-7), using an 1809 open-field plan of the northern part of the township (published by E. G. Taylor in 1888 and reproduced in Göransson 1961, 87). There was a regular distribution of small blocks of glebe, which consisted of strips lying together, stated to be 8 oxgangs in 1685; in 1285 the glebe had been described as one carucate.

Beresford found clear evidence of a regular order at Langtoft, Wetwang and Great Givendale in the 16th and 17th centuries. In 1698, the glebe of Foxholes was dispersed, being 4 oxgangs of arable and pasture in every fall (Beresford 1951, 334). This probably implies that there was convertible husbandry. Glebe terriers give several examples of a fixed regular order of lands. Six oxgangs at Langtoft were dispersed in 1726 as the 11th, 12th, 26th, 27th and 30th and 31st [lands] from the bank on the south side of the flat through out the fields. At Wetwang two oxangs lay 'throughout all the fields lying next one oxgang of land of William Moores' (Beresford 1951, 337).

Harvey (1982, 28-39) identified other examples of regular tenurial order in terriers and furlongs on the Wolds, with holders having the same positions in the furlongs or the same neighbours throughout the field systems in the 18th century (North Grimston, Sewerby, Rudston and Walkington). The field books of Butterwick and Thorpe Bassett, both dated 1563 (Castle Howard MS F4/14/3), had regular tenurial cycles throughout their furlongs. For the 13th century, at Kirby Grindalythe and Nafferton small groups of oxgangs lay together throughout the fields and at Boynton and Rudston oxgangs were defined as lying between the same two neighbours.

Harvey (1980; 1981, 192-7) also found evidence for a regular ordering of oxgangs through the fields of some Holderness townships (Easington, Ryehill and Kilnsea). At Barmston it could be traced back to 1473, and at Preston, to *c*. 1250. An approximate relationship was shown between township areas and the carucate areas of 1086, and was used to suggest that in at least some cases there may be a relationship between taxation and the area of the field system (Harvey 1978).

Management of the fields

Open-field by-laws of East Yorkshire, ranging in date from 1594-1856, were studied by M.W. Barley (1943, 35-60) who discussed the social aspects as well as open-field control. At Burton Agnes in 1625 there were grazing rights for twenty sheep to the oxgang, and twenty for the husbandman's house. Cottagers also had twenty sheep allowed for their houses. In some villages, cottagers were not allowed to let unused commons to non-residents. At Anlaby in the 17th century the ends of lands were left as grass and were mowed for hay (Barley 1943, 42). Fences were to be maintained around the Ings (meadows) and Carr at Burton Agnes in 1632. At Driffield drainage grips (small ditches) were dug between the wheat and rye fields. Balks and headlands were not to be encroached by the plough (Burton Agnes 1641). Animals were tethered on the balks. Rings were to be put on pigs' snouts. There were regulations about gleaning and wool gathering. Harris (1955, 530-31) also studied East Riding field orders of 17th and 18th-century date. All lands at South Cave were to be gripped (drained) to prevent water lying in the furrows (1693). Similar gripping orders were made at Bishop Burton in 1719.

At Bridlington, detailed rules were written down in the 17th century regarding the common rights of various classes of tenants on different commons and moors. For instance a cottager could have two beast gates on the moors and ten sheep gates on another moor called 'sheep huntow' and on the fallow fields and wastes. Oxgangs of demesne could have twenty sheep on the same pasture and fallow. Courts during the same century recorded orders and presentments of tenants for breaking them. Common offences were animals trespassing in the cornfield, tethering horses on the balks and breaches of the fold (i.e. the pound, to recover stray animals and avoid a fine: Purvis 1926, 110-111, 242-3).

Sheep folding at Elmswell in 1641 was practised on the stubble after harvest. The folds were constructed of willow stakes. At corn harvest one man bound the loose corn into sheaves and set up twelve to a stook. He kept up with six to eight reapers. The stooks were left for about one week to dry, if weed free. The strongest shearers were placed on the ridge where the corn was rankest (Robinson 1857, 14, 43-5). Part of Elmswell carr was used for hay crops and had been enclosed into small parcels by 1628; demesne pasture closes there were let to the tenants (Robinson 1857, 128-31). At Normanby in 1716, sheaves were bound and gathered twelve to a stook, placed on the ridges (Beresford 1951, 344). Low carr ground in the Hull region was used for rough grazing and produced an inferior hay. Mowing times were fixed by village by-laws (Harris 1961, 37).

The great extent of arable in the Wold townships created a shortage of pasture. This was partly compensated for at Wetwang where farmers leased meadows lying 7 miles distant in the early 18th century (Harris 1959, 11). The serious absence of pasture and meadow for hay was probably ameliorated to a certain extent by practising convertible husbandry or outfield, as was done at Helperthorpe and Kilham in the 18th century (Harris 1959, 6-7). A tithe dispute at Risby in 1591 referred to lands left as ley for almost 20 years (Harris 1962, 122). Oxgangs at Walkington were partly arable and partly ley in a survey of 1726 (Harris 1955, 533). Kirby Grindalythe had large areas of leys and pasture on the high ground (Harris 1961, 23). Butterwick had no pasture and cut off a corner of the fields for the purpose

(Harris 1961, 30). Staxton township straddles the Wold and the Vale of Pickering, having meadows and carrs at the north. In 1803 there was still some open-field cultivation of the Wold ground. It was ploughed once in about six years, and so formed part of a convertible husbandry system (Loughborough 1965, 106).

Field systems in the Wharram parishes and the study area

Introduction

During the winters of 1976-82 the writer and P. Martin mapped and reconstructed from fieldwork the patterns of ridge and furrow in all the townships of the two Wharram parishes: Burdale, Raisthorpe, Towthorpe, Thixendale, Wharram Percy and Wharram le Street. The results of these investigations, which were originally intended to be part of a projected volume on the two parishes in the Middle Ages, are contained in the fuller version of this report which is available via the Archaeology Data Service (doi:10.5284/1000415), along with examples from elsewhere in the study area: Butterwick, North Grimston and Settrington. The following four townships – Burdale, Towthorpe, Wharram le Street and Settrington – have been selected for inclusion in this chapter because they typify the range of variation in the physical form of open fields to be found in the High Wolds, in Wold-edge townships, and in the Vale.

The fieldwork techniques for mapping open-field systems have been fully described elsewhere (Hall 1982, 25-36; 1995, 39-42). In summary, ploughing of individual lands to create ridges also moved small quantities of soil along the strips forming small heaps at each end, called heads. When ridge and furrow is destroyed by modern ploughing, the ridges disappear rapidly, but the soil piled up at the ends of all the lands merges to form a long smooth bank lying along the edge of the furlong. Hence the physical pattern of open-field furlongs is preserved in the landscape by earthwork remains that allow reconstruction using archaeological fieldwork techniques.

On the Wolds there are very few furlong or flatt boundaries, because the strips stretch from dale to dale over plateaux of high, fairly level ground. The field mapping consisted of recording what few linear boundaries there were and noting where there was surviving ridge and furrow in spinneys and in farm paddocks that still lay in pasture. Additional information was obtained by ground observation of bare weathered ploughland in January or February. Long parallel belts of flinty soil represented the former ridges where post-enclosure ploughing had cut into previously undisturbed subsoil under the ridges (the 1970s agricultural system used bare winter ploughland with little autumn planting).

The field results were checked against evidence recorded on aerial photographs, primarily those taken in the late 1940s by the RAF. All plans shown here have the furlong boundaries accurately drawn but the lands are marked schematically. They have the correct orientation as far as can be estimated, but only about a quarter of the actual number of lands is reproduced to ensure clarity. The working maps were prepared at a scale of 1:10,560.

The accompanying illustrations show the survey record of ridge and furrow within the boundaries of each township and against a topographical background. North is at the top in each case, and the relative sizes of the townships can be determined on Figure 36. The plans of the Wharram townships show a uniform simple pattern of strips, often of great length, running across the Wolds, dissected by the dales which are deeply incised into the chalk bedrock. The pattern is mainly controlled by the topography and suggests large scale planning. All are very similar to plans revealed by manuscript maps elsewhere on the Wolds and in Holderness, at Kilham (Sheppard 1973, 149, referring to East Riding RO, DDDU/12/54) and Burton Agnes (Harris 1961, fig. 19).

Settrington, in contrast, has a plan intermediate between that of the Wolds proper and a Midland type chequerboard of small furlongs. There are some long strips and some smaller furlongs. Aerial photographs reveal more of the intermediate pattern at Barton le Street near Malton (SE 72 83), where hedges have reverse-S curves about 1200 yards long (RAF/106G/UK/1417 frame 4389, 15 April 1946: NMR).

Field patterns of townships further down the Derwent valley have furlongs much more like Midland type with strips about 220 yards in length. Fangfoss, near Stamford Bridge, was studied as an example. There were some furlongs with lands 200-300 yards long, the pattern interrupted in places by small areas of meadow ground. There was still, however, an element of planning to be seen where strips were rather long or furlongs were in alignment. The furlong with the longest strips had ones extending to 800 yards.

None of the Wharram townships has a fieldbook that would fully elucidate the field structure. The most useful sources are the Dacre Survey and Field Book of 1562 and 1563 (Castle Howard MS F4/14/3 and F4/14/1) which cover several townships in the Wharram area. Each township has a variable amount of information that relates to its fields, which is summarised below. Settrington does have a detailed survey, although the information about the fields is limited (see also pp 302-4 below). There is, nevertheless, sufficient information in various sources to indicate that the northern Wolds and adjacent parts of the Vale of Pickering were marked by a regular tenurial order in the fields, as with the rest of the East Riding. Further information is given under each township.

Burdale (Fig. 100)

This township was surveyed in 1978. No archaeological remains of the medieval village survived. Truncated ridge and furrow ends were preserved in Middle Dale. The pattern of furlongs is broken by many small dales. There is a simple layout with the longest strips being 600 yards.

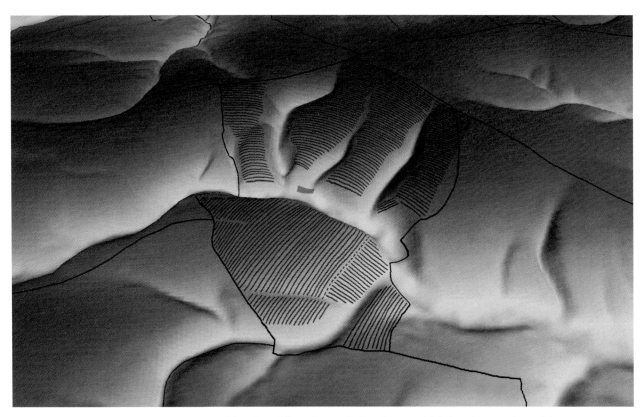

Fig. 100. Ridge and furrow in Burdale township, viewed from the south. For the township's location see Figure 36. (A. Deegan and D. Hall)

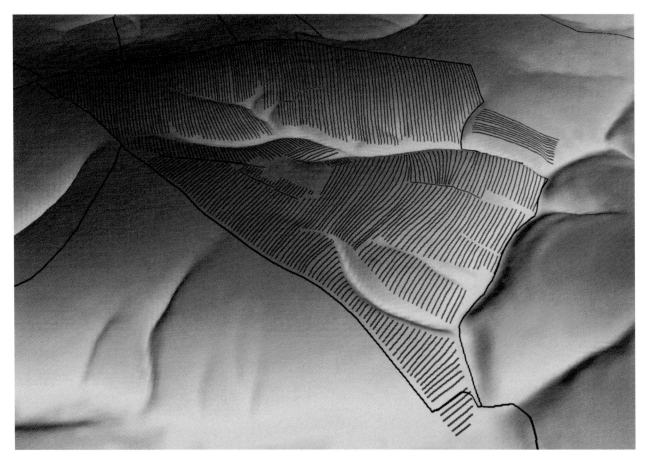

Fig. 101. Ridge and furrow in Towthorpe township, viewed from the south. For the township's location see Figure 36. (A. Deegan and D. Hall)

St Mary's Abbey, York had possessions in Burdale, referred to in its cartulary (John Rylands Library Latin MS 221 f.372). Several charters refer to 40 oxgangs, four belonging to the capital messuage. A regular order of strips is indicated by a grant of four oxgangs lying 'towards the sun', and a grant of six oxgangs with pasture rights, made in 1272, had strips with the same neighbours 'everywhere in the furlongs'. Burdale seems to have been reduced to a single farm in the later Middle Ages (see p. 362 below). In 1548 a grant to Thomas Heneage recorded pastures and sheepgates called *rigges* on the wold of Thixendale, lately belonging to St Mary's York, and sheep pasture called two oxgangs in Burdale on the Wold lately belonging to Malton Priory (*Cal Pat Rolls Edward VI*, ii, 122). This suggests that formerly cultivated lands had been converted to sheep pasture – a trend seen in other townships.

Towthorpe (Fig. 101)

The township was surveyed in 1980. There was a fine set of village earthworks with some ridge and furrow adjacent to them at the west and north (see Plate 39, below). The ends of ridges survived in the long belt of woodland at the northern township boundary. The furlong pattern is fairly simple, aligned either side of an east-west dale. Some strips were of great length – up to 1100 yards.

In 1310 Robert Ughtred's manorial holding consisted of fifteen tofts and 32 oxgangs (*Cal IPM V*, no. 204). In 1524 Thomas Heneage became lord of the manor which then included 36 oxgangs (Hull Univ DD KP 9/3). The village, which had still contained eleven households in 1672 was depopulated during the next three decades by a resident yeoman farming family (Neave 1990, 172; see p. 362 below). A plan of the enclosed township was made in 1772 (Allison 1976, 107); by that date it was being run as a single farm and the extent of arable across the former open fields was very limited.

Wharram le Street (Fig. 102)

Surveyed in 1980, Wharram le Street had a good set of earthworks, with small quantities of ridge and furrow at the west and north, on the east side of Cow Cliff which formed the eastern valley side of the Beck. Ridges also survived in the small Wold Plantation at the south. It has a remarkable field system, with most strips lying on a north-east to south-west alignment. Four furlongs make up most of the system, and the strips are as long as 1000-1200 yards in places.

Long riggs are implied by the Dacre survey. This covered a holding of four oxgangs comprising 59 selions in 27 furlongs. Of these, fourteen lands were 1.5 acres in area and two extended to 1.75 acres. If the latter were one rood wide, then their length would be 1540 yards and if two roods 775 yards, thus agreeing with the great length of the lands as suggested by field survey. The four oxgangs totalled 45.375 acres, or 11.344 per oxgang. Each oxgang had a stint of twenty sheep. The 27 furlongs were grouped into four areas called fields, and this holding had the following arable acres in each on them: South Field, 10¼ acres, Haverfield, 8 acres, West Field, 4 acres, North Field, 22¼ acres, plus Oxcroft, 1 acre. It is not obvious how these would relate to a cropping arrangement; perhaps North Field was run with the others together as a two-year tilth.

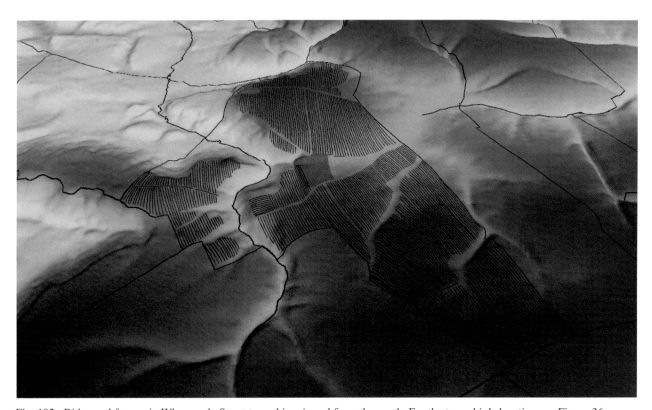

Fig. 102. Ridge and furrow in Wharram le Street township, viewed from the south. For the township's location see Figure 36. (A. Deegan and D. Hall)

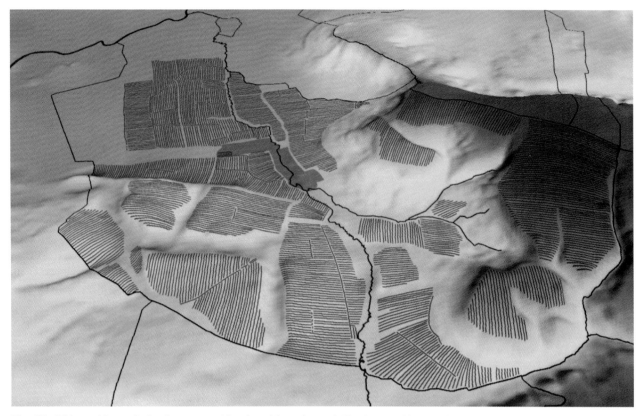

Fig. 103. Ridge and furrow in Settrington township, viewed from the south. For the township's location see Figure 36. (A. Deegan and D. Hall)

Settrington (Fig. 103)

The township was surveyed in 1983. There were a few village earthworks at the Town Green (Plate 29). Ridge and furrow survived in Screed Plantation (formerly part of the Great Wold demesne pasture), to the west of Settrington Wood around Low Bellmanear (formerly a demesne pasture close), and around Cross Cliff House (formerly the Town Wold pasture: Fig. 109). There were also small pieces north of the Town Green (formerly the Low Field arable). The furlong pattern as a whole is fragmented by the scarp. The high ground of the Wold in the east had strips up to 1100 yards long, typical of the Wold townships. On the low ground at the north there are many furlongs of 200-300 yards, however, four of them have an exact alignment extending to 1700 yards, suggesting a large scale layout before later subdivision.

Settrington, covering nearly 5,000 acres, has a detailed manorial survey made in 1600 accompanied by maps (King and Harris 1962; see below, pp 302-4). The landuse of blocks of land is given, but no detail of the furlongs and strips is provided. There were three named fields recorded as arable (total 1698 acres) and many large areas of open pasture (916 acres), most of them belonging to the town, and stinted. Part of Lee Moor pasture lying on the west was intercommoned by Settrington, Norton and Sutton. There was meadow called the Ings next to the Derwent (61 acres) as well as other smaller meadows. A large part of the south-east consisted of enclosed demesne pastures with woods on the steep scarp (235 acres). The high wold land was still open and was shared as a sheep pasture between the lord and the town. There was some demesne land dispersed in the open fields and meadows.

The arable fields contained scattered strip holdings, but differed appreciably in size, the High Field being nearly twice the size of the other two. There is no statement about the cultivation system in terms of seasons. Limited common rights existed in a few of the demesne closes and woods. The stint per 'ancient husband rent' (the holdings were called 'husbandries') was one oxgate in the ox pasture, two kyegates on the cow pasture and twenty sheep in the sheep pasture. Cottagers were allowed two kyegates and twenty sheepgates. The rectorial glebe possessed 99 acres unequally dispersed in two fields, with 14 acres of meadow. In 1663 it consisted of closes and lands lying in two open fields, with 32 cowgates and 240 sheepgates on the Town Wold from Michaelmas to Lady Day in Beresford (1951, 333).

There were in all fifteen husbandries that averaged 54 acres of arable. Smaller holdings were called grass farms, there being fourteen, averaging 6 acres of arable, and there were twenty cottagers who held 22 acres of arable in total, but ten of them had no arable. The husbandries' total of open-field land including pasture was 1392 acres, so that each holding averaged 93 acres, i.e. the arable amounted to only 58 per cent. It seems, therefore, that at the end of the 16th century there was no shortage of pasture for the farming economy.

Comparison of the published 1600 map with the field survey suggests that a much greater part of the parish had previously been arable, including most of the demesne cattle pastures in the south-east of the township and significant parts of the wolds sheep pastures adjoining them. Medieval pasture lay in The Marrs and Ings at the north next to the Derwent (about 270 acres, the meadow and cow pasture in 1600), and at the Moor pasture on the west (Lee Moor Pasture in 1600). There was no evidence of ridge-and-furrow ploughing on the ground in these areas, much of which were alluviated. The glacially fractured wooded scarp was unploughable.

The field survey also revealed part of the neighbouring settlement of Buckton (see pp 302-4 below). It was visible as a concentrated scatter of pottery, stone and dark soil lying along the west side of Settrington Beck towards North Grimston, centred SE 8420 6938. The area is linear about 800 by 60 metres (26 acres).

Permanent pastures on the northern Wolds

by Stuart Wrathmell

David Hall's ridge-and-furrow surveys of townships such as Burdale and Towthorpe give the impression that the whole of the northern Wolds was covered in ploughing ridges, apart from the steep-sided valleys that could not be ploughed, or areas like Lund in Wharram le Street (see Wrathmell 2005a, 4-5), where the ground has suffered from land slippage on a long-term basis. This impression is confirmed by early township surveys, such as the one for Butterwick. In systems such as these, the grazing of fallow, and of arable fields after harvest, was clearly vital not only for the management of livestock but also for maintaining the fertility of the arable land. Henry Best's description of arrangements for folding sheep on specific ridged lands in the early 17th century demonstrates how manure could be targeted at particular furlongs in advance of growing specific crops (Woodward 1984, 19); such practices may then have been centuries old.

There were, however, a few strips of permanent pasture surviving into the 12th and 13th centuries, which Chris Fenton-Thomas has discussed at length. The Introduction to Part Two of this volume (pp 55-6) defined several long-distance, east-west routeways, including two which traversed the high Wolds (Fig. 104): the Towthorpe Ridgeway (Route 3) and Sledmere Green Lane (Route 4). We have noted that these routes were more in the nature of communication corridors rather than single tracks, and the broad strips of ground crossed by successive tracks were presumably areas of permanent pasture. Fenton-Thomas has mapped a number of these along both routeways.

On the north side of Route 4, the south-east part of Thixendale township was occupied by a distinct area, defined on Figure 104, called Pluckham or Pluckholme on early 19th-century maps. It was marked as a separate administrative division (e.g. on Bryant's map of the East Riding published in 1829) and was almost certainly permanent pasture in the Middle Ages: it constitutes, notably, the only wold-top land in the whole of Thixendale where David Hall was unable to record the former existence of ridge and furrow. Further strips of pasture seem to have existed along the south side of the Route, immediately south of our study area (named but not defined on Fig. 104). One was called Wetwang Rakes, a detached portion of Wetwang township, which originated as an intercommon for both this township and Bishop Wilton to the west. Adjoining it to the east were further strips in Huggate township: Huggate Tongue and Huggate Wold (Fenton-Thomas 2003, 77, 81 and 231 fig. 96).

Fenton-Thomas also notes that some of these remnants of permanent pasture were granted to monastic institutions in the late 12th and early 13th centuries, and were subject to improvement at that time (Fenton-Thomas 2003, 82). For example in Huggate township there is reference to a 'half carucate upon the new improvement (*frussura*) on the "wald" in Huggate', and a further four acres of arable were said to be '*in Waldo versus Fridatorp* [Fridaythorpe]' (*EYC II*, 525), locating at least part of the 'wold' in the vicinity of Route 4. His suggestion that the use of *versus* indicates lands without permanently fixed boundaries at that period, an 'open buffer zone between the neighbouring townships' (Fenton-Thomas 2003, 82), must be open to doubt. There are plenty of references to precisely located arable lands that use similar qualifications to aid identification.

There were further strips of permanent grassland along Route 3, Towthorpe Ridgeway, also mapped on Figure 104. Towards the east end of the study area is a territory called Burrow, in the north-east corner of Cowlam township, where the courses of Routes 3a and 3b converge. Fenton-Thomas described it as a 'smaller township/hamlet' (Fenton-Thomas 2003, 84), though the evidence for it having been a separate unit of medieval administration is lacking. It was, nevertheless, a distinct area of land with its own name, like Pluckholme on Route 4, and was also, like Pluckholme, defined on early 19th-century county maps as a separate administrative division (e.g. on Bryant's map). Its 19th-century status and its location, together with the record of an old trackway running through it (Fig. 104), make it a strong candidate for another strip of late surviving permanent pasture.

There is, furthermore, an indication that the name Burrow referred to an area of ground that extended into adjoining townships. An inquisition of 1286 records that Reginald fitz Peter held Weaverthorpe from the archbishop by knight's service (see p. 182 above), and that he had in demesne 24 bovates and a pasture called *Burrehou* that was reckoned to be worth 30 shillings a year (the equivalent of the value of three of the demesne bovates: *Yorks Inqs II* YASRS 23 (1898), 48).

Further west were other areas of 'wold': *Hornhouwald* and *Houstwald* (the latter meaning East Wold according to Smith 1937, 125). In *c*.1157-70 William Aguillun gave to the canons of Malton a croft of four acres in the western part of Mowthorpe, and arable land that ran southwards as far as *Sutdale* (perhaps 'Crowtree Slack' on the OS Six Inch map), and through the middle of *Sutdale* and beyond the road to the south (*et ultra iter versus meridiem*); and the whole of *Hornhouwald* by the bounds made between us, that is to say between the land of Mathew and the bounds of Thoraldby as far as the bounds of Sledmere and Towthorpe, for pasture or crops, whichever they wished. He further gave them whatever

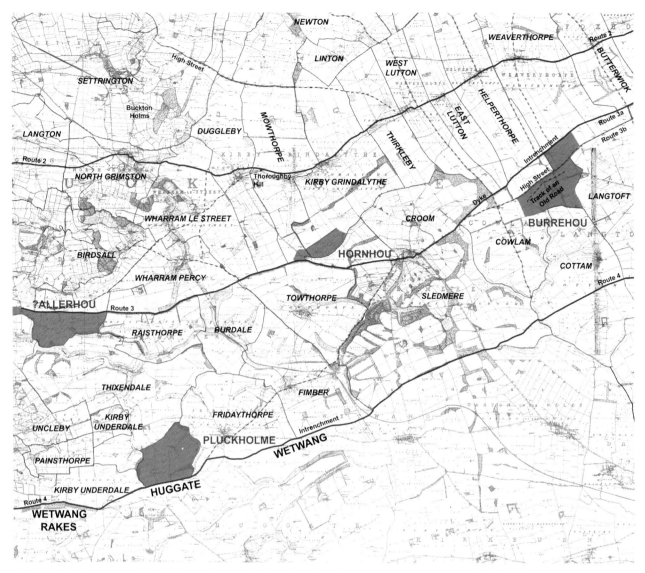

Fig. 104. Southern part of the Wolds study area, showing stretches of permanent pasture recorded in the 13th century along Route 3, and surviving later along Route 4 (E. Marlow-Mann)

he had in *Houstwald* between the ditch and *Dreusgate* (*EYC II*, 387). The grant is not evidence that the *Hornhouwald* recorded here was outside the township structure (cf. Fenton-Thomas 2005, 109), as Mowthorpe is not included among the vills that defined it externally.

Although *Dreusgate* has not been identified, it is probable that *Houstwald*, like *Hornhouwald*, adjoined the north side of Towthorpe Ridgeway, which formed the boundary between Mowthorpe and Towthorpe, and that the term 'wold' was employed for remaining areas of permanent grassland, as proposed by Fenton-Thomas (2005, 102). It may be that the granting of such lands to monastic institutions in the late 12th and early 13th centuries led to the rapid diminution of such remnants (see Waites 1968, 137-8).

One of the best recorded areas of late surviving permanent grassland along Route 3 lay at the western end of the study area, on the boundary between Birdsall and Thixendale townships. The survival of a detailed description of this land is the result of a dispute over its

seisin. The plaintiffs were the abbot of St Mary's, York, the prior of Kirkham and Dionise Montchesney, who claimed it was part of Thixendale. The defendant was Peter Mauley, lord of Birdsall, 'he having taken more than belongs to him'. Peter acknowledged that he had taken possession of this land, amounting to 480 acres of pasture and heath, and offered to defend it by the body of his freeman Hubert son of William Hoyland (an offer which Hubert, who was present, confirmed). One of his sureties was Robert Percy, presumably Robert Percy III who had recently inherited Wharram Percy. Hubert's opponent, representing the abbot, the prior and Dionise was to be John son of Adam Burstal.

The duel took place on 12 June 1268 at the Old Bailey, York. John son of Adam was adjudged the victor by the four justiciars; but the winning side (*pars convincens*) gave to Peter Mauley (*parti convicte*) 60 (or 70) marks for a surrender and a quitclaim on behalf of Peter himself and his heirs (Craster and Thornton 1934, 12; *Yorkshire Fines 1246-72* (1932), 150-51).

The ground was described as 'pasture and heath', and could be identified by its metes and bounds. The plaintiffs claimed that the bounds between the disputed lands and those of Peter (i.e Birdsall) 'should be from a place called Pilesdale and so by the King's way, on the south side as the King's way extends to the east, as far as the bounds of R[a]isthorp[e], so that between these bounds Peter should have nothing to the south' (YASRS 82, 150).

Maurice Beresford identified this area of pasture and heath as the extension of Birdsall township and parish which lies south of Towthorpe Ridgeway (Fig. 104; Beresford M.W. 1987 6). He was undoubtedly correct. What is remarkable, however, is that this territory should still have been adjudged to be part Birdsall township in the 19th century, despite the outcome of the duel. Unfortunately, Birdsall township was not part of David Hall's survey of ridge and furrow in the Wharram area, so we do not know whether this land was ridged at any time.

The name of this area of pasture is unknown, but at its west end is Aldro, a name recorded in the early 15th century as *Allerhow*. Like *Burrehou* and *Hornhou*, it incorporates the Old Norse *haugr*, referring either to named hills, or to prehistoric barrows that are found in the vicinity of the Ridgeway (Smith 1937, 126, 142, 324; Fenton-Thomas 2003, 107). In Chapter 7 (p. 87) we considered the significance of these barrows, and in particular their use for secondary interments in the Early Saxon period, in terms of the way in which communities in the Vale may have used the then undivided Wolds as grazing grounds. It may not be too fanciful to suggest that in the high wolds specific areas of grazing were named with reference to groups of barrows, and that such naming practices continued into the Late Saxon period and remained current over subsequent centuries.

Despite these occasional references to permanent pasture on the Wolds, it is clear that almost all the wold plateaux were at some point brought into cultivation during the Middle Ages, and probably before the 14th century. Thereafter, there are clear indications of retreat of cultivation, and the reconversion of wold top land to sheep pasture. This is very much the picture that emerges from the fragmentary records of open fields at Wharram Percy.

Open fields and land holdings at Wharram Percy
by Stuart Wrathmell with contributions from Alison Deegan

Open-field holdings in the 14th and 15th centuries
There are just a few medieval documents that provide glimpses of the organisation of farm holdings at Wharram Percy, all of them associated with inquisitions *post mortem* of the 14th and 15th centuries. The earliest is the extent of the manor made in July 1323, some two years after the death of Robert Percy III (TNA PRO C134/75/15; see p. 235).

The extent records 27 demesne bovates, though at that time only a third of them were under cultivation, the remainder being 'fallow and uncultivated'. It is clear that these other 18 bovates had not been purposefully left fallow, as each of them was given a standard, notional value of 5 shillings 'if it could be let'. A single tenant at will held 4 bovates, and nine customary tenants held a further 37, giving a total of 41 tenanted bovates. The demesne and tenanted bovates amount to an overall vill total of 68 bovates, which is equivalent to the $8^{1}/_{2}$ carucates quitclaimed in favour of Peter Percy I, Robert's father, in 1254 (see p. 229). Furthermore, as indicated below, this was the same assessment as that which informed a dower assignment of 1368.

When Robert Percy's great grandson, Walter Heslerton II, died without issue 'before Michaelmas' 1367, the manor and vill passed through a remainder interest to his mother's distant kinsman Henry Percy of Spofforth (see p. 225). Walter's wife Euphemia, however, survived him, and in April 1368 she was assigned a third of the manor as her dower share. It might be assumed that this involved simply the attribution of a third of the overall profits of the manor, and in terms of the profits 'in common' from the mill and the manor court, for example, this was indeed the case; but where feasible Euphemia was given specific landholdings that would make up her third.

Furthermore, the way in which the assignment sets out the lands which should be attributed to Euphemia suggests that the allocation was made on site, no doubt with rent and account rolls to hand. The bailiff and reeve would have been involved, perhaps along with another official from Spofforth (given that Henry Percy had only recently acquired the manor), and a representative of Euphemia. The original record of assignment is now very difficult to read (TNA PRO C135/198/12), so the relevant entries from the calendar of inquisitions *post mortem* have been set out *verbatim* below, but in a series of itemised entries rather than in the continuous narrative of the calendar (*Cal IPM XII*, 183). The other entries, which relate to the composition and topography of the village settlement, are discussed in Chapter 21 (see p. 342) .

The eight entries recorded here relate to the allocation of Euphemia's third share of the demesne and tenanted bovates. The assessors made the allocation by visiting a furlong ('shot' in the calendar; '*cultura*' in the original) named Middlegates. It was perhaps somewhere to the west of the manorial *curia*, in the area framed on the south by the routeway running east-west through the village, just outside the southern boundary of the *curia*, and on the north and west by Yorkgate, the routeway running from Cranedale towards Malton and York. The hypothetical layout of dower lands in this (and therefore in all the other open-field furlongs) is shown in Figure 105.

The assessors identified the path that separated the demesne and tenanted bovates in this and in every other furlong in the open fields, and allocated to Euphemia the 9 demesne bovates lying nearest the path, out of the overall block of 27 demesne bovates:

WEST	BOVATES
demesne allocated to Henry Percy	18
	27 demesne bovates
demesne allocated to Euphemia Heslerton	9
path between the demesne lands and lands of the tenants at will	
formerly in tenure of Reynold Martynson allocated to Euphemia Heslerton	3
in tenure of John son of Robert two-thirds to Euphemia Heslerton; one third to Henry Percy	?3
[tenure unrecorded] [allocated to Henry Percy]	?3
[tenure unrecorded] [allocated to Henry Percy]	?3
[tenure unrecorded] [allocated to Henry Percy]	?3
in tenure of Walter del Hill; to Euphemia	2
[tenure unrecorded; allocated to Henry Percy]	?2
[tenure unrecorded; allocated to Henry Percy]	?2
in tenure of Reynold Cawod; to Euphemia	2
[tenure unrecorded; allocated to Henry Percy]	?2
[tenure unrecorded; allocated to Henry Percy]	?2
in tenure of John Pryket and Alice his mother; to Euphemia	2
[tenure unrecorded; allocated to Henry Percy]	?2
[tenure unrecorded; allocated to Henry Percy]	?2
in tenure of William del Hill; to Euphemia	2
[tenure unrecorded; allocated to Henry Percy]	?2
[tenure unrecorded; allocated to Henry Percy]	?2
in tenure of William son of Geoffrey: one third to Euphemia	2
EAST (*propinquiores sole*)	68

41 tenanted bovates

Fig. 105. The bovate holdings in Middlegates furlong, Wharram Percy, recorded in 1368. (S. Wrathmell)

[1] *9 bovates of the demesne lands lying throughout the whole field along the paths between the demesne lands and the lands of the tenants at will on the west side in a shot* (cultura) *called 'Medelgates', and so in the same way throughout the whole field;*

It is clear from the first two entries that the furlong's ridges – the physical representation of these bovate lands – ran north to south, because the allocation of lands belonging to specified holdings runs from west to east, with the demesne at the west end of the furlong. To the east of the path, Euphemia was allocated in whole or in part a series of tenanted bovates on a 'one for Euphemia, two for Henry' basis as the assessors walked down the headland at right-angles to the path. The aim was to provide Euphemia with 13²/₃ bovates, a third of the 41 tenanted bovates.

The first five holdings probably contained 3 bovates each; there are other possible combinations, but this is the simplest hypothesis that achieves the required totals. We are told the location of the first two holdings in terms of what they adjoined:

[2] *a messuage formerly in the tenure of Reynold Martynson, with 3 bovates of land thereto belonging next to the metes dividing the demesnes from the lands of the tenants at will on the east side in the same shot, and so throughout the whole field;*

[3] *... bovates of land in the tenure of John son of Robert adjoining the last named 3 bovates throughout the field;*

As we shall see, the next entry [4] is not described as adjoining [3], so we can identify a gap in the allocation.

Though the number of bovates in holding [3] was unreadable to the compilers of the calendar, we can suggest it was 3, and that the allocation to Euphemia was a $2/3$ part of the holding, giving her 5 bovates out of the lands of five tenants who held 3 bovates each. The allocation then moved on to the 2 bovate holdings, from which she needed a further $8^2/3$ bovates:

[4] *a messuage and 2 bovates of land in the tenure of Walter del Hill;*

In neither the above entry nor in any of the succeeding ones is the adjoining bovate holding mentioned, again implying that the allocated 2 bovate holdings were separated from each other by a couple of 2 bovate holdings that remained with Henry:

[5] *a messuage and 2 bovates of land in the tenure of Reynold de Cawod;*
[6] *the like in the tenure of John Pryket (?) and Alice his mother;*
[7] *the like in the tenure of William del Hill;*

The assessors had now reached the final 2 bovate holding in the furlong, and having achieved already an allocation of 8 bovates, this one had to be split into $1/3$ and $2/3$ shares, Euphemia's $1/3$ of 2 bovates providing the required $2/3$ of a bovate. Though the calendar translates '*propinquiores sole*' as 'the south side', it is clearly the east side that is meant, given the orientation of the furlong. The final statement 'and so throughout the whole field' is a reminder that all the allocations in Middlegates were repeated in every other furlong:

[8] *a third part of 2 bovates of land in the tenure of William son of Geoffrey lying on the south [*recte '*east*'] side in Medelgates and so throughout the whole field;*

Clearly the pattern of holdings in 1368 has changed somewhat since 1323, but there has been no formal break with the past. The 1368 record stills describes a community assessed at $8^1/2$ carucates, unchanged therefore since the mid-13th century and apparently little changed since 1086. At some point within the seventy years following the dower assignment, however, there was a complete reassessment of the vill's arable potential.

The next inquisition *post mortem* with any detail on Wharram Percy was one of 1436 (TNA PRO C139/80/22), carried out after the death of William Hilton, who had acquired the manor by exchange with the Percys of Spofforth (see p. 236). There were 16 bovates of arable land worth 4s each, and 6 acres of meadow worth 20d each. A further inquisition of 1458 (TNA PRO C139/168/8) repeated this information.

On the face of it, the period 1368-1436 saw a major reduction in cultivation at Wharram, and the new bovate assessment presumably signified a reordering of holdings in the open fields. There is no record of the disposition of holdings at this time, as there had been in 1368, but some indication of the extent and composition of the arable lands in the 15th and early 16th centuries can be gleaned from later terriers recording the glebe lands, in the context of the known distribution of ridge and furrow across the township (Fig. 106). The results of David Hall's survey indicate once more that, apart from the steep valley sides, almost the entire territory was at some point ridged. These have been supplemented by additional information drawn from Alison Deegan's more recent aerial photograph survey.

Glebe lands and the extent of the late medieval open fields

A new ordination of the vicarage, approved by the archbishop in 1440, allocated to the vicar, in lieu of tithes, 2 bovates of land in the open fields which belonged to the prior and convent of Haltemprice. The priory had appropriated the church in 1327 (Wrathmell 2010a, 12). As we will see in Chapter 22 (p. 356), these bovates, along with 2 others that supported Towthorpe chantry in the parish church, continued to be cultivated for some decades after the general conversion of the open fields to pasture in about 1527; and even after they, too, were put down to grass, the glebe bovates continued to be recorded into the 18th century in the terriers, though with increasing uncertainty as to where these lands were precisely located (BIA, Ter. K Wharram Percy).

The earliest terrier is undated, but can be assigned to the mid-17th century as it is signed by Edward Carlisle who was vicar from 1643-68 (Beresford M.W. 1987, 30). It includes information on the locations of eight lands belonging to the glebe, entitled 'A copy of the two oxgangs of glebe land…'. It is presumably copied from an earlier document, rather than being based on field observations of lands that were still physically marked. The next terrier, also undated but compiled during the incumbency of Robert Luck (1668-92: Beresford M.W. 1987, 30-31), briefly mentions the general locations of the lands: 'on the Bella, the Hogwalk, the Ewpasture and in the new piece…[along with] Hay Ground lying in the Ings.' The third terrier, dated 1716, says simply: 'Tis not known where the Glebe land lies. But in lieu thereof the vicar receives from the Farmer Nine Pounds yearly…'; the fourth says much the same. The compilers of the fifth terrier, however, in 1743, seem to have gained access to the earlier record used in the first terrier, as they list the same lands, in the same order, though they give a fuller description that indicates the glebe was made up of a single land in each of eight furlongs or 'falls'.

The original document containing these details seems then to have been lost once more, as the 1749 terrier, and later ones, simply repeat that the location of the glebe lands is unknown. The lost document may have been one of the 'old Papers and Terriers relating to the Living of Wharram Percy' that were recovered in 1779 by David Lambert, agent of Wharram's then landowner, Sir Charles Buck, from a Mr John Taylor of Kennythorpe. Lambert conveyed the papers to Bella, the farm then newly created in the eastern part of the township, so they could be perused by Sir Charles and Mr Rousby, the vicar (NYCRO IQG XIII/11/2). Their fate beyond that point is unknown.

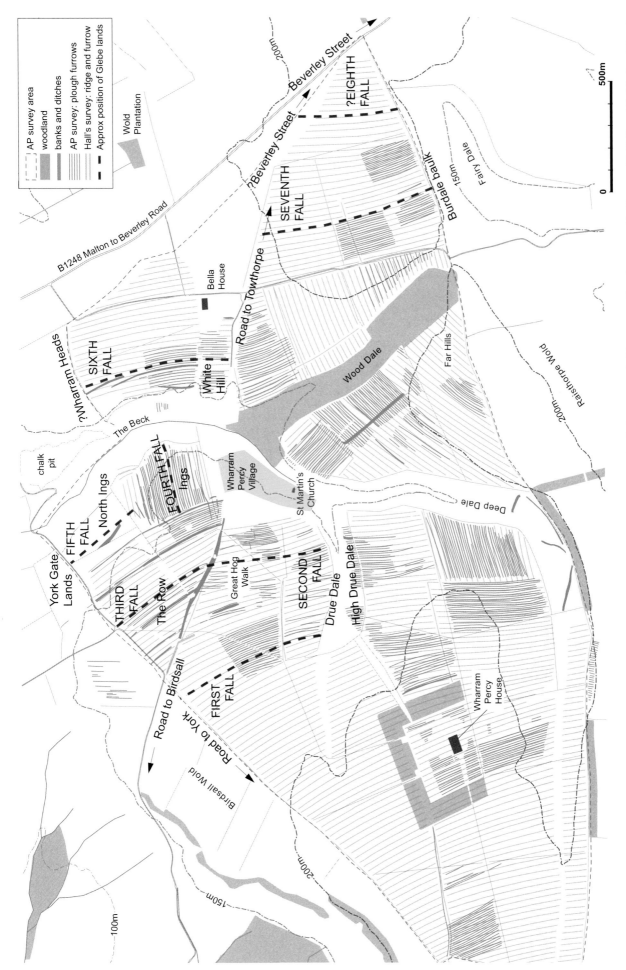

Fig. 106. Ridge and furrow in Wharram Percy township, and the approximate positions of glebe lands in the furlongs recorded in post-medieval sources. (A. Deegan, D. Hall and E. Marlow-Mann)

293

The information on the vicar's lands contained in the mid-17th-century terrier has been interlined below (in *Italics*) with the fuller descriptions from the 1743 terrier. These are followed by notes which attempt to give approximate locations to the lands and, therefore, to the falls or furlongs; the results are shown on the accompanying map, Figure 106. This map is based on documented topographical names, particularly the field names recorded in 1836 (see Fig. 115), and on the evidence from aerial photograph transcriptions prepared by Deegan and ground survey of the township's ridge and furrow carried out by Hall. Broadly speaking, it seems that the record from which the terrier descriptions were taken was compiled on a geographical basis, the entries running from west to east. The first three falls all have locational details indicating that they were to the west of the village site. The fourth and fifth are in the Ing grounds which lay north of the village site, and the sixth to eighth have names relating to the eastern part of the township, east of the Beck.

Most of the lands (excluding the ings) were said to be marked by holes at the ends of the ridges. In a part of Yorkshire where stones suitable for marking lands or boundaries were hard to find, holes or 'hutts' (heaps of turf or earth: see Woodward 1984, 301) were all that was available. In 1616 the only physical boundary separating the townships of Wharram le Street and Duggleby was a 'green baulk' (BIA CP H1175).

First Fall: *'one near the old swarth, with a short land on drudale top'*
'One land near the Old Swarth about 12 Lands within the new-enclosure having a Baulk on the west side of it and reaching from the York Road to Drudale Top markt with two Holes at the North End of it, with a short Land on Drudale Top'.

The main land was, broadly speaking, orientated north to south, its northern end against the north-west township boundary that was formed by the routeway from Cranedale to York (known also as Yorkgate, a name attached to two adjacent fields further to the north-east, marked on Fig. 115). Its southern end was presumably on the brow of Drue Dale (Drewdale in 1836). The record of ridges in this part of the township provides confirmation of this orientation. The short land has not been identified.

Second Fall: *'one land from the row end to drudale top'*
'One Land from the Row End to Drudale Top mark't with two Holes at the North end of it'.
This is once again a land running north to south. It is evident from the third fall description, below, that the Row was a furlong occupying the triangular area formed by the road to Birdsall (the east-west routeway through the northern end of the former village site), the road to York (already described) and the Ing Meadows (fourth and fifth falls, below). This land presumably ran from the south side of the Birdsall road southwards to Drue Dale.

Third Fall: *'one within the row to york gate'*
'One Broad Land within the Row commonly called

New Piece reaching from Birdsall Road to York Road near the York Gate markt with two Holes at the South End of it'.

The location of the Row has already been discussed. This is another land running approximately north to south, with the Birdsall road at its south end and the York road near York Gate at its northern end. York Gate Lands, named on the 1836 map, adjoined the York road on its north side, and were part of Wharram Grange Farm. It is possible that it is this furlong that was 'Middlegates' in 1368. The reference to a 'broad' land recalls the evidence from both Holderness and the Wolds of broad and narrow lands in open-field furlongs (see above).

Fourth Fall: *'one in the rigs next quickwood stack'*
'A Piece of Meadow Ground in the Great Ings commonly called Priest's Flat or Priest's Lands reaching from the Headland to the Beck having Cobler Flat on the North and a Land joining on the Quick wood-Stack on the South'.

The Great Ings is presumably the Ings Meadow of 1836, bounded on the north by the smaller North Ings Meadow, and on the south by the site of the village. The reference to the Beck being at one end of the land (and to other lands being to the north and south of this piece) indicates an east-west orientation (very much the minority orientation in the ridges at Wharram and in many other Wolds townships). It is confirmed by the observed orientation of the ridges here.

Fifth Fall: *'one above the farr ing spring'*
'One Meadow Land in the Far Little Ings having the Land next the Spring Head on the east and reaching from the Great Ings Hedge to the Hedge opposite to it'.

Far Little Ings is assumed to be the North Ings of 1836, and the description suggests a north to south orientation. The spring head is perhaps the one towards the centre of this field shown on the Ordnance Survey map surveyed in 1850-51.

Sixth Fall: *'one land on white hill from towthropway to Wharram heads'*
'In the Pasture called Bellow One Land on White Hill from Towthorpe Way to Wharram Heads mark't with two Holes at the South end of it'

This land is on the east side of the Beck, in the area which later gave its name to Bella Farm. White Hill is the name given on the OS 1850-51 map to an area of land to the west of Bella House, and Towthorpe way is presumably the routeway that runs eastwards from Wharram Percy village site and then turns south-eastwards towards Towthorpe. It is assumed here that Wharram Heads is the boundary between Wharram Percy and Wharram le Street, marking the northern end of the land, though this is purely supposition.

Seventh Fall: *'one on white hill near burdale baulk'*
'One Land on White Hill near Burdale Baulke mark't with two Holes at the South end of it'.

The White Hill mentioned in this entry seems to be a different one from that recorded in the previous one (unless its area was far more extensive than suggested by the OS), as Burdale baulk must be on the southern boundary of Wharram Percy, where it met the township of Burdale. The land was once more orientated north to south.

Eighth Fall: *'one in goosdale to Beverly Street'*
'One land in Goosdale to Beverley Street'

The location of the eighth fall is the most problematic, as Goosdale has not been identified, and Beverley Street, presumably the modern Malton to Beverley road (B1248) coincides with Wharram's township boundary only at the south-east corner of the township. It is, however, possible that Beverley Street was (in terms of routes out of Wharram) an alternative name for Towthorpe Way.

These lands were, presumably, the ones allocated to the vicar in 1440, and therefore give us a clue as to the distribution of open-field lands supporting the late medieval village. It has been suggested above that there had been a significant reduction in the extent of arable at some point in the early 15th century, but we do not know whether the lands forming the 2 glebe bovates were assigned at this time, or whether these bovates (acquired, presumably, by Haltemprice in the early 14th century), had been unaffected by such changes. What is noticeable, however, is that the glebe strips are not distributed across the whole of the township, even though almost the whole township seems to have been covered in ridge and furrow.

In the eastern half of the township, the distribution of glebe strips seems to have been confined to the area east of Wood Dale, and in the western half their distribution was even more limited: none was recorded south of Drue Dale. It is intriguing to find, moreover, that the distribution of strips to the west of the village site mirrors the putative extent of 'ingrounds' belonging to the 17th and early 18th-century farm at Wharram (cf. p. 359, Fig. 115). Perhaps it was less fertile and higher grounds towards the southern and western ends of the township that were withdrawn from cultivation in the 15th century.

It is worth noting, also, that the reassessment of Wharram's bovate tenements in the 15th century is not unique. In Northumberland, far harder hit by Scottish devastations and subject to recurrent plagues, the surviving inquisitions and monastic surveys continued throughout the 14th century to record the compositions of vills in terms of the notional numbers of bondage and cottage holdings that had existed in the 13th century, even though many had clearly been untenanted and waste for decades. By the time of the Dissolution, however, they had been completely reorganised in terms of the number and size of holdings: evidently there had been a realisation that the old structure of the farming community could never be recreated, and that a new allocation of land was required, one that would match the smaller number of available husbandland tenants (Wrathmell 1975, 154-5).

Discussion

At some point in the early 15th century, then, Wharram Percy's arable lands were significantly reduced in size, and the riggs that remained under cultivation were presumably redistributed among the smaller number of bovate holdings. These changes do not, however, seem to have extended to a wholesale recasting of the field-system's physical structure. If Wharram Percy's riggs had a uniform north-south alignment when first laid out – as in neighbouring Wharram le Street – then a minority of furlongs had, at some stage, been broken up and their ridges realigned east-west, in developments comparable to, though far less comprehensive than, those inferred by Hall (1980) at Hardingstone and elsewhere in the East Midlands.

Wharram Percy's basic field structure remained, nevertheless, intact. Though not recorded in surviving sources until the 14th century, it may well have been created before the Norman conquest: the vill's overall assessment in terms of carucates and bovates was little changed between the mid-11th and 14th centuries. Given that the base orientation of ridging on the east side of the township is co-aligned with the ridges of Wharram le Street (Fig. 102), it is conceivable that the formation of the 'Wharram' territory's field system predated or at least accompanied its division into two vills. It is impossible on current evidence to determine whether the early east-west ridging behind the village's West Row of enclosures, identified in the earthwork survey (p. 41), predates the creation of the comprehensive field planning on the north-south alignment; but as the early ridges run right up to the edge of the recorded north-south ridging (compare Figs 2 and 8), this is a strong possibility. It would, in turn, suggest that the wholesale north-south replanning took place after the creation of the West Row (south). The early east-west riggs overlie, and must therefore post-date, the Middle Saxon Butterwick-type settlement enclosures.

The tenurial cycle recorded in Middlegates furlong was anchored, on the ground, by the reference to William son of Geoffrey's two bovates as lying nearer the sun. The use of the direction taken by the sun across the sky to specify the direction in which the tenurial cycle should be read is a common feature of northern Wolds townships. In Wharram Percy parish itself, Beresford recorded references in three of the four other townships. At Burdale and Thixendale, the term *'propinquiores sole'* was used in connection with the lands of Kirkham Priory and St Mary's Abbey (Beresford and Hurst 1990, 99-100); and in Raisthorpe a 1384 grant to the vicar of Wharram Percy gave him two bovates *'iuxta solem'* in each of the two fields (*Yorks Deeds IV*, 117; YAS RS 65 (1924).

These references have frequently been cited as evidence for the presence in England of *solskifte*, a system of land allocation recorded (later) in Sweden (e.g. Beresford M.W. 1979, 22), with the implication that it was introduced into northern England by Scandinavian settlers. There is, however, a further layer to *solskifte*: the order of lands in the furlongs was a replication of the ordering of the tofts in the village, which were themselves ordered in relation to the direction taken by the sun. It is this layer that is hard to find in the English sources (see Homans 1941, 98-9; Roberts 2008, 82-4); and at Wharram it evidently did not exist in the 14th century, for if it had, there would have been no need to use the Middlegate furlong as a model. As Gardiner has pointed out, the use of the sun's direction to orientate the tenurial cycle hardly justifies an assumption that such arrangements were brought to England by Scandinavians, especially when they are found in England well beyond the regions of known Scandinavian settlement (Gardiner 2009, 11; see Homans 1941, 101).

There is, furthermore, an underlying assumption in some discussions that the large-scale division of the landscape into long strips and the creation of tenurial cycles occurred only once in the lifetime of a community, and was then subject to gradual deformation over succeeding centuries as the realities of landholding and farming practices gradually diverged from the model. Whilst gradual deformation may have been common, it is conceivable that there was a series of large-scale planning and replanning events before the one we now see – as suggested by Mary Harvey in her detailed study of Preston in Holderness.

Preston was, like Great Kelk, a township with two massive open fields on each side of a linear village settlement, the lands running continuously from the township boundaries to the village enclosures. The two fields were each divided into seven subdivisions equivalent to furlongs, called *bydales* (Harvey 1981, 187, fig. 24), a term that seems to refer to the land shares allocated to individual farms: *by* meaning farm and *deill* referring to a share (Gardiner 2009, 8). Harvey noted that the surnames of late 13th and 14th-century Preston tenants seem still to have been attached to lands in the *bydales* recorded in the 18th century. But as she pointed out, this need not signal the date at which the *bydales* were initially formed; rather, it may mark the point at which a process of intermittent reallocation of *bydale* lands ceased to operate (Harvey 1980, 4-6, 13-15). The framework could have been established at a much earlier time, and indeed it may have been preceded by earlier frameworks. This is particularly the case in townships like Preston where the number of carucates increased significantly after the Conquest. Here, the 93 oxgangs of its Domesday assessment were later expanded to 130 oxgangs (Harvey 1978, 19-21).

The term *bydale* has not been found in the northern Wold vills, but its equivalent seems to be *wandale* from Old Norse *vondr* meaning a wand or measure and *deill*, again a share of land (Smith 1937, 107). June Sheppard argued that *wandales* is a furlong name that occurs once in a large proportion of Wolds townships, suggesting that the furlong had a special significance. In twelve of the fifteen townships where she could record its precise location as a field name, it abutted the tofts, and could

have been the furlong where agreed shares were measured out, and which then formed the model for the allocation of lands in the other furlongs (Sheppard 1973, 185) – in much the same way that Middlegates operated in 14th-century Wharram.

The difficulty is that the name *wandales* is, like Preston's *bydales*, attached in some cases not just to small areas of arable acting as models for much larger stretches of lands, but to significant proportions of the townfields. The first edition Ordnance Survey six-inch map of Duggleby has two groups of fields called 'Wandales', names which, from their mapped positions, look as though they might originally have been given to furlongs covering the western third of the township, running both northwards and southwards from the village enclosures. Medieval records of Wharram le Street are indicative of equally extensive areas of arable called *wandales*. Thomas Burton's version of a document he entitled '*Antiqua mensuracio terrarum*', undated but perhaps drawn up in the late 13th or early 14th century, has three groups of entries relating to arable lands (perhaps indicating a three-field system). All three have numerous references to *wandales*, including a great furlong (*cultura magna*) called *Wandayles*, *les Wandaeles* towards Duggleby, and *Wandaylflat ad Oustkeld* (BL Cotton Vit. C vi, ff 229-229v).

The spread of *wandale* and *bydale* names suggests, then, that they were attached to significant numbers of furlongs, making it difficult to see them simply as the keys to the wider ordering of open-field lands. In fact a reference to *wandales* in a charter of *c.*1193-1205 seems to turn the argument on its head. The document records William Aguillon's confirmation of the grant by Juliana, daughter of Gerald Kirkby, of three bovates of her demesne in Kirby Gridalythe, of which one was next to Juliana's furlong (*culture*) on the western side of the vill of Thirkleby, another was next to her furlong of *Aldithehou* (Dollith Howe, on the south side of the Race: Smith 1937, 125), and the third was next to her furlong on the south side of Kirby. The grant also included such *wandales* as pertained to three bovates of that fee ('*et tot wandailes quot pertinent ad tres bovatas ejusdem feudi*': *EYC II*, 384) The three bovates 'next to' Juliana's furlongs were presumably originally part of those demesne furlongs: the grant simply separated off the outermost lands to avoid unwelcome traffic across the remainder – in much the same way that Euphemia's dower share of demesne at Wharram Percy has been the outermost nine next to the path between the demesne and the tenants' lands.

Whereas the *bydales* of Preston occupied the whole of the open fields, it seems that the *wandales* of Kirby Grindalythe were the shares of tenanted lands attributed to demesne holdings. Furthermore, Juliana's furlongs were clearly blocks of demesne lands, just as the demesne lands of Wharram Percy were also in blocks, at least in the 14th century. It may be that the fields of Kirby Grindalythe were structured by two types of furlong: those wholly given over to blocks of demesne lands, and those in which the manorial tenants held dispersed shares of lands, ordered in a tenurial cycle and of a size equivalent to the proportionate assessment of their farms – one oxgang, two oxgangs, or three. At Wharram Percy the demesne was again in blocks of land, but in furlongs that were shared with tenanted lands. George Homans noted the occurrence of blocks of demesne at Salton in the Vale of Pickering, where eight demesne bovates lay in four flats, the flats being in severalty (*sunt seperales*), while eight other demesne bovates were intermixed with the lands of the tenants (Homans 1941, 100 and 426, n. 31). There seems to have been a good deal of variation in the arrangement of demesne holdings and tenant lands both on the Wolds and in the Vale.

Gardiner has argued that the large-scale replanning of arable fields, and the allocation of proportionate shares in them through the creation of tenurial cycles, could have been accomplished by the vill communities themselves, in particular by the 'substantial communities of free sokemen' in Lincolnshire and Yorkshire, rather than through the agency of seigneurial action (Gardiner 2009, 12-13). It is an argument that gains support from the way in which, at Wharram and elsewhere, the proportionate shares of oxgang land on the ground can be combined to generate the number of carucates for the vill as a whole, the number that was used for assessment of geld liability, whatever manorial units it contained. It suggests, further, that the creation of block demesnes at Wharram and Kirby Grindalythe may belong to a later restructuring of the fields resulting from an increased manorial involvement on the ground, an observation that would go some way to meeting the Stocker-Everson position on the putative late 12th-century transformation of Wharram.

18 Rural Settlement in Eastern Yorkshire
by Stuart Wrathmell with contributions from Alison Deegan

Introduction

Chapter 17 outlined the characteristics of medieval field systems in eastern Yorkshire, in terms of the management of agrarian resources, the physical forms of furlongs and fields and aspects of landholding. The present chapter turns to the morphological characteristics of some of the settlements supported by these field systems, again with the aim of providing context for, and a better understanding of the village plan at Wharram Percy. It is followed by three chapters which focus in greater depth on the village's individual farmsteads and their occupants, on the lives of Wharram's inhabitants both on their lands and in their homes.

We have seen that eastern Yorkshire, despite its very marked topographical variations, was in the Middle Ages a region of extensive arable farming, pursued within a framework of regular, planned two and three-field systems. In other English regions field systems of this sort were accompanied by village settlements rather than by dispersed farmsteads, and this is, on the whole, also true of eastern Yorkshire. Yet, as we have also seen, such generalisations can mask significant variations in form, and this is certainly the case with regard to villages in the Vale of Pickering, in Holderness and on the Wolds.

Regular row villages

Northern England has been characterised as a region of geometrically regular villages. Brian Roberts has estimated that 'an overall figure of 80% may not be unrealistic' for the percentage of settlements of all kinds exhibiting 'planning' through underlying regularities and uniform structural geometry (Roberts 2008, xii-xiii). One settlement form frequently encountered in the North is the 'regular row' village, in which the farmsteads were constructed in rows of tofts, often taking the form of two rows facing each other across a street or green. The compartments formed by the rows were frequently separated from the open-field furlongs behind them by back lanes (Roberts 2008, 8, 41).

Regularity is primarily achieved through uniformity; and uniformity in the length and width of tofts suggests an attempt to create a series of holdings of equal size. Just as the 'regular row' village is a prominent feature of northern medieval settlements, so is the occurrence, in medieval records, of holdings of equal size – or at least, holdings that were assessed equally in terms of the number of oxgangs or bovates attributed to them. One of the classic demonstrations of the relationship between assessment and toft size is Roberts' analysis of the Merringtons in County Durham, where the physical structure of Middle Merrington, a regular row village with two facing compartments of tofts, has been linked to its assessment, in *c*.1200, as twelve bondage holdings each containing two bovates (or 30 customary acres: Roberts 2008, 136-8).

At a more general level, June Sheppard attempted to link the overall assessment of the number of carucates in a vill with the lengths of the toft rows in its village. Her work built on studies of the regular row villages or *radby* of southern Sweden and Denmark, and on the identification there of a link between fiscal assessments and the length of toft rows (Sheppard 1974, 124-34). Whilst it is easy enough to point to the potential for circularities in some of the arguments, as she herself acknowledged (Sheppard 1974, 126-7), there is no reason to doubt that the communities which, as we have seen in Chapter 17 (p. 280), created proportionate shares of land on uniform base field structures, could equally well have managed to express those proportions and uniformities in their village plans – if they felt the need to do so.

Whether they did or not, it is clear that the carucate assessment of a vill for tax purposes was directly linked at some point to the arable capacity of that vill; and it is also clear that the carucate assessment of a vill such as Wharram Percy was the sum of the oxagang or bovate assessments of the individual farmholds worked from the village tofts. The characteristics of villages in three

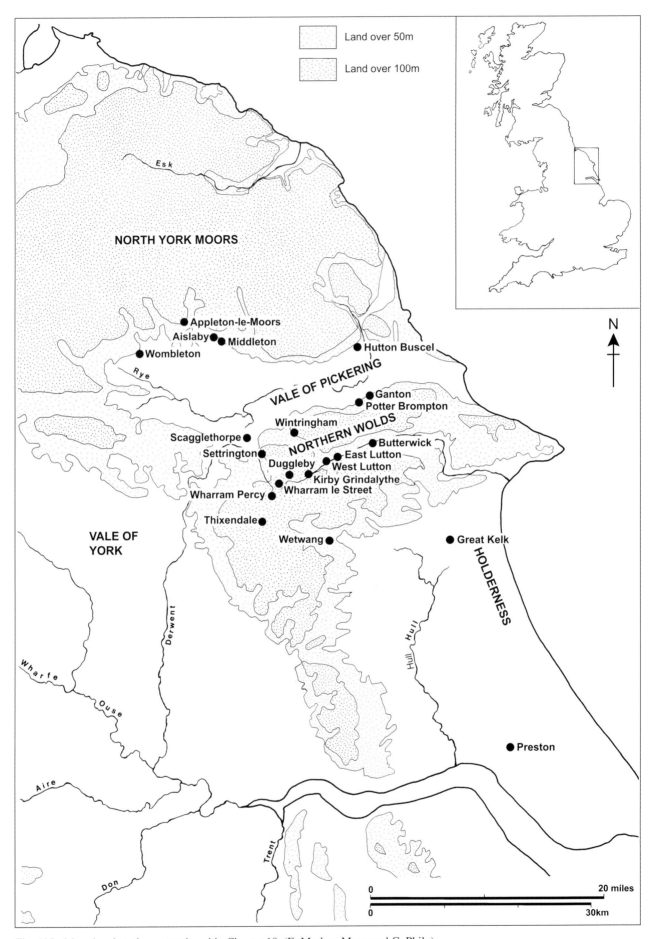

Land over 50m

Land over 100m

N

Esk

NORTH YORK MOORS

Appleton-le-Moors
Aislaby ● Middleton
Wombleton
Rye
Hutton Buscel

VALE OF PICKERING

Ganton
Potter Brompton
Wintringham
Scagglethorpe ● NORTHERN WOLDS
Settrington ● Butterwick
Duggleby ● East Lutton
West Lutton
Kirby Grindalythe
Wharram Percy ● Wharram le Street
Thixendale ●
Wetwang ● Great Kelk

VALE OF
YORK

Derwent

Wharfe

Ouse

Hull Hull

HOLDERNESS

Preston

Aire

Trent

Don

0   20 miles
0   30km

Fig. 107. Map showing places mentioned in Chapter 18. (E. Marlow-Mann and C. Philo)

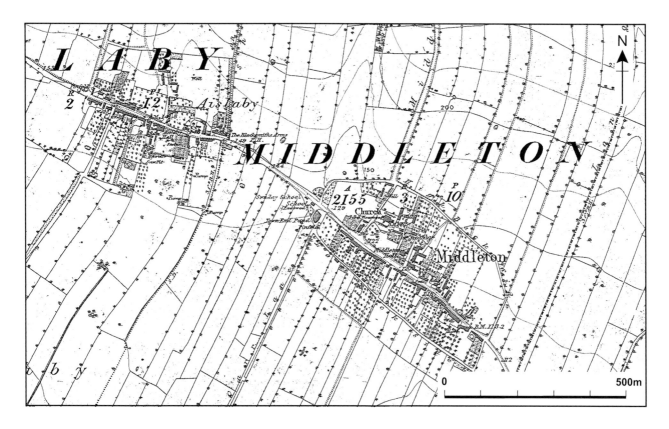

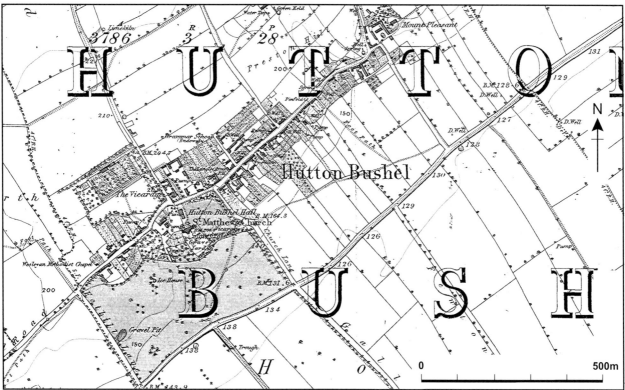

Fig. 108. Village settlements in the Vale of Pickering in the mid-19th century, from the first edition Ordnance Survey six-inch map. (E. Marlow-Mann)

regions, the Vale of Pickering, Holderness and the Wolds (Fig. 107), are explored in turn – mainly, of necessity, through 19th-century maps – and are compared and contrasted. This chapter is not, it must be stressed, based on any systematic survey; its purpose is to highlight issues that may warrant further investigation.

The Vale of Pickering

Villages in the Vale of Pickering north of the river Derwent, and in the Tabular Hills flanking the Vale, have been the subject of studies by a number of historical geographers, most recently by Roberts, who has

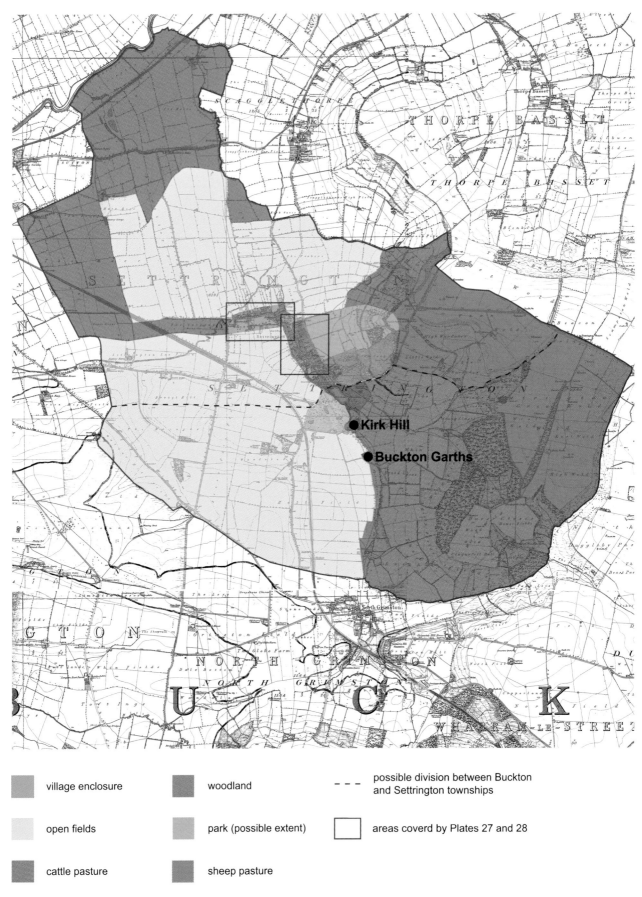

Fig. 109. Settrington and Buckton townships: information recorded on, and inferred from, the plan of 1600. (E. Marlow-Mann)

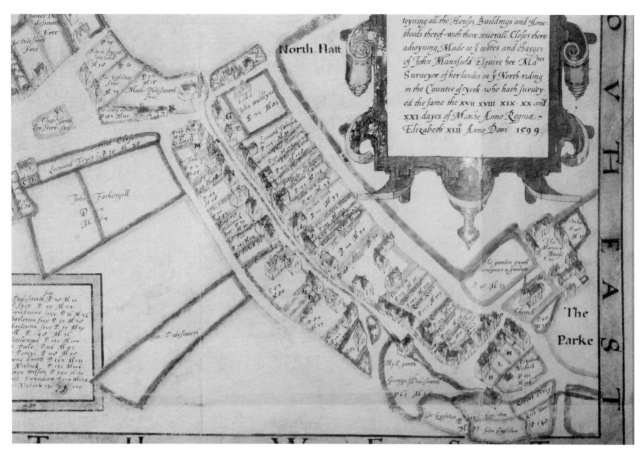

Plate 27. Settrington village, the north-south rows along the Beck, depicted on the plan of 1600. The location of this part of the map is shown on Figure 109. (P. Gwilliam; by permission of Sir Richard Storey, Bt)

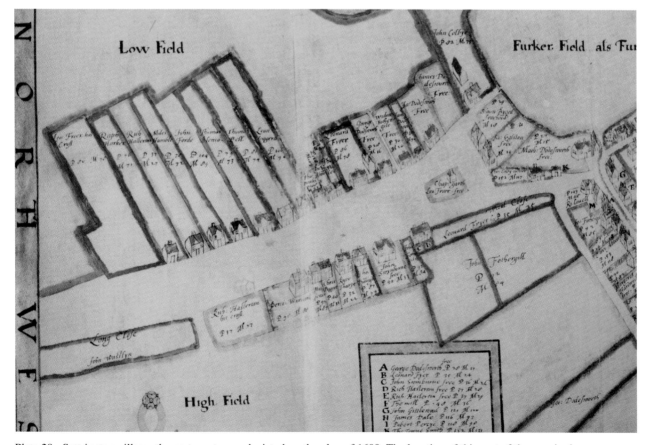

Plate 28. Settrington village, the east-west rows depicted on the plan of 1600. The location of this part of the map is shown on Figure 109. (P. Gwilliam; by permission of Sir Richard Storey, Bt)

concluded that row plans tend to be the dominant form here, and that regular rows are common (Roberts 2008, 30-31, fig. 2.1 and 41). The form is most clearly expressed at Appleton-le-Moors (Roberts 2008, 59, 61, 65), where the back lanes dividing the ends of the tofts from the field strips run parallel to the axis of the toft compartments and at right-angles to the toft partition boundaries. It can also be seen at Wombleton and Middleton, where the row compartments and back lanes are less precisely rectangular (Allerston 1970, 97, fig. 2). Given the large-scale, uniform planning evident in some of the associated former open-field systems, it is perhaps surprising that an even greater degree of integration between settlements and field systems is not apparent.

Middleton, just west of Pickering, is a case in point (Fig. 108, top). Here, the alignment of the field strips north and south of the village can be seen to flow through it, leading to the suggestion that the village was laid out over part of the field system; yet it has also been acknowledged that 'few, if any, of the [19th-century] strip boundaries flow directly into the toft lands' (Roberts 2008, 101). Much the same could be said of the neighbouring village of Aislaby, where the alignment of the north-south strips has shifted slightly from the course of those running through Middleton, and where the axis of the village, at right-angles to the strips, has also changed to reflect the shift.

Villages such as Middleton and Aislaby were quite distinct entities despite being adjacent settlements on the same routeway and conforming to a broadly uniform orientation of field strips. The same cannot be said for a line of small villages to the east of Pickering, in what is now Hutton Buscel (Fig. 108, bottom). In the Domesday survey, Hutton, Preston and Newton were three distinct vills, all soke of Falsgrave manor (*DB Yorks* 1Y3). By the mid-19th century, however, they had all coalesced into a single ribbon of settlement, formed by tofts along the south side of the road; only the bands of fields north of the road retained the names of the earlier vills (Allerston 1970, 103; Roberts 2008, 101-2 and fig. 4.7). They represent a settlement trajectory that finds echoes both in Holderness and on the Wolds.

On the south side of the Vale of Pickering, two-row villages are again frequently encountered in the study area. The mid-19th-century Ordnance Survey maps show two facing rows at Scagglethorpe, Ganton and Potter Brompton, and exceptionally long ones at Wintringham. Settrington is another example, but with a difference. The township was surveyed in considerable detail in March 1600, and the written survey, published by King and Harris (1962), is accompanied by a series of plans showing the township, village and manor house. Figure 109 illustrates land-use in the township as recorded in 1600, together with the positions of the two principal elements of the village: two adjacent two-row elements set at right-angles to each other.

The accompanying photographs of these two elements of the village are reproduced here by kind permission of Sir Richard Storey, Bt. Plate 27 shows the north-south element which was itself composed of two distinct parts:

two short rows at the south end, aligned on the church and manor house, and two long, very regular rows aligned on Settrington Beck – the beck that originates at Wharram Percy. The long rows have back lanes separating them from the adjacent fields, but the toft partition boundaries in the west row appear to be aligned with the few parcels of land marked in the open field to the west of the village, and with the ridge and furrow recorded in this area by David Hall (Fig. 103).

The rows on each side of the Beck have different depths of toft, perhaps indicating different dates of formation. That on the east side may have been created on land taken out of the edge of the medieval park: this suggestion is based on the pattern of field boundaries shown on the plans, though by 1600 the area encompassed by the park pale was much smaller and further south. There is one early reference to a toft in Settrington: in *c*.1185-1208 Alfred son of William Settrington granted a toft twelve perches in length and four in width (*EYC* I, 493). If the perches were northern 18ft perches (see Sheppard 1974, 119 and Roberts 2008, 60), the row that appears to conform most closely in depth is the west row, as determined both from the plan of 1600 and from the Ordnance Survey map of the mid-19th century. This assumes, of course, that the toft was in one of these two rows and not in another part of the settlement.

The second main element of Settrington is, in effect, a second two-row village (Plate 28), which seems to have been constructed along the two sides of the driftway or 'outgang' along which cattle could pass between two of the open fields to the meadows located in the low ground beside the Derwent (Fig. 109). The outgang can also be clearly seen in Hall's survey as a gap in the coverage of ridge and furrow (Fig. 103). Furthermore, the tofts associated with the two rows appear to have been formed out of the ends of north-south field strips, most obviously in the western half of the north row where much longer strips have, for some reason, been enclosed. In the centre of the outgang towards its east end was an enclosure called Chapel Garth or Kirkclose 'lying in the common way there called the Highstreet', according to the survey. Another entry refers to the stretch of ground between the rows as the Common Green (King and Harris 1962, 20-21). The aerial photograph (Plate 29) confirms the location of the chapel garth and the orientation of ridge and furrow behind the north row. It also shows the ridges within the south row recorded in Hall's survey. Less easy to interpret are the numerous earthworks between the rows, set within the outgang.

The presence of what is, in effect, a second village may be connected to another phenomenon: the disappearance of the township of Buckton, at Domesday a separate vill and soke estate centre (see pp 183-4 above). An indication of the former location of Buckton can be established on the evidence of field names. *Buckton Garths* and *Buckton Holmes* were pieces of meadow named in the survey of 1600, and they can be identified on one of the maps that accompany the survey, to the south of Settrington village

Plate 29. Aerial photograph of the east-west rows of Settrington, marked by surviving farmsteads and earthworks, viewed from the west. (NMR 12328/18, 21 October 1992. © Crown copyright.NMR)

Plate 30. Aerial photograph of farmstead earthworks at Buckton Garths, Settrington, viewed from the west (NMR 17435/06, 26 January 2000. © English Heritage.NMR)

(King and Harris 1962, 34-5 and frontispiece). Both are adjacent to Settrington Beck (Fig. 109), and Buckton Garths contains the earthwork remains of buildings that appear to form a courtyard-plan farmstead (Plate 30), of unknown date. It is probably medieval, given that it does not appear on the plan of 1600, but on current information we cannot discount entirely the possibility that it was a short-lived creation of the 17th or 18th century. During his ridge-and-furrow survey Hall identified a spread of medieval pottery in dark ploughsoil running northwards from this point on the west side of Beck, presumably part of the village (p. 288, above).

Immediately north of the pottery spread, the Beck, where it curves around Kirk Hill and the modern farmstead that sits there, is flanked by a number of earthworks marking further buildings and enclosures. More extensive remains may have been obscured by levelling that took place around the farmstead within living memory (Peter Grice, *pers. comm.*). On the other hand, the 'Church (Site of)' to the east of the farmstead, marked on the OS Six Inch map revision of 1926 (1938), is located in a field covered in what appears to be medieval ridge and furrow (not recorded on Fig. 103).

The date at which Buckton disappeared as a unit of territory and administration is not known. The last reference cited by Smith in his place-names volume is in 1406 (Smith 1937, 140), but it seems long before then to have become simply an appendage of Settrington, as indicated by the following references kindly supplied by David and Susan Neave. In 1305 Buckton was said to be a member of Settrington manor (*Cal IPM IV*, no. 320), and an inquisition relating to Roger Bigod dated 1 August 1359 refers to a toft in the 'hamlet' of Buckton that had been held by Thomas Noddyng, a victim of the Black Death (*Cal. Inq Misc III*, no. 345).

It is possible that at some point after the 11th century the eastern half of the Buckton township, including its extensive woodlands on the steep slopes rising to the Wolds at the eastern extremity of the township (see Fig. 109), had been incorporated into the demesne lands of Settrington manor, with the lord's cattle pastures below the woods, and his sheep pastures above. All these resources were certainly part of the demesne in 1600. The arable fields belonging to the two vills may have been regrouped into a single, new three-field system, discussed above by Hall (pp 278-80), and the farmsteads of Buckton's manorial tenants may have been relocated to the northern end of Settrington village, accounting for the second two-row village.

If these various speculations have any validity, they prompt a number of observations on village morphology. First, in the Vale of Pickering the tofts containing the homesteads of tenant farmers were frequently arranged in regular rows, though we must not assume that all were: it is the row villages that have received a good deal of scholarly attention. Secondly, the presence of two rows facing each other does not necessarily mean they were

304

created at the same time, especially if they exhibit dimensional variations. Thirdly, even where such variations are not apparent, facing rows could well have been established at different dates if both used the same template for toft formation: the ends of open-field furlongs with ridges of identical width.

Holderness

The villages of Holderness, on the other side of the northern Wolds, appear to have very different characteristics from those of the compact, two-row villages in the Vale of Pickering. Harvey described them as being remarkable for both their irregularity and their linearity: 'Villages over one mile in length are not uncommon, and some extend almost from one township boundary to another' (Harvey 1982b, 65). She also observed that many of them were composite: they included several clusters of tofts linked together by lines of irregular enclosures, suggesting that they resulted from linking together two or more once separate clusters of farmsteads and larger nuclei.

Preston is the classic and frequently cited example of this form of settlement, in a township which is otherwise notable for the regularity of its field system and distribution of oxgangs through uniform series of *bydales* stretching to the township boundaries (see pp 278-81 above). The fields extended from both sides of 'a string of tofts of irregular shape and size, extending east-west for over two miles' (Harvey 1978, 23). There were two settlement 'ends', West End and East End, and between them was a separate, more compact 'row' village exhibiting, on the basis of

alignments, at least three separate planning elements. All this is evident on the first edition Ordnance Survey six-inch map of the mid-19th century (Fig. 110). Also on the map are hints that the row of compartments was not originally continuous: that there may have been gaps filled at various times by new settlement units (Harvey 1982b, 65).

Much the same form is evident at Great Kelk, which has been discussed and illustrated in Chapter 17 (pp 281-2). What is striking about the sample land holding marked in black on Figure 99, that held by Philip Boynton, is not so much the repetitive distribution of his broad and narrow lands in each half of the township, but the way in which the alignment of a number of these lands 'runs through' the line of settlement enclosures, as though the enclosures, or some of them, overlie a sweep of lands that originally ran continuously across the township. The same characteristic is evident on the part of an earlier plan of Great Kelk, dated 1789, published by Sheppard (1973, 150, fig. 4.2). On it, the closes then belonging to Rev. Thomas Preston, represented by some of the wide, blank strips on Figure 99, are also interrupted by the village enclosures. The aerial photograph (Plate 26) shows some patches of ridge and furrow within the village enclosures which might represent underlying continuations; but elsewhere, confusingly, the closes contain small areas of ridge and furrow running at right-angles to the grain of the open fields.

Three other points should be made about the settlement enclosures shown on the Great Kelk plan. First, though they form a continuous run of rectilinear compartments, there are some variations in width and alignment that may indicate more than one phase of

Fig. 110. The village of Preston in Holderness in the mid-19th century, from the first edition Ordnance Survey six-inch map. (E. Marlow-Mann)

development. Secondly, the shapes and sizes of the compartments are markedly different from the usual dimensions of tofts in northern 'regular' villages, though there is one cluster of the more usual toft-shaped enclosures at the southern end of the vill. Thirdly, the fields immediately surrounding this southern end are the only ones that exhibit evidence of some kind of replanning, through a deformation of the pattern of holdings which seems otherwise to be remarkably uniform throughout the rest of the township.

How could such patterns emerge? In relation to Preston, Harvey suggested that at least some of the clusters of farmsteads may once have cultivated their own distinct fields, and that there had been a fundamental reorganisation of the fields (but not, evidently, of the associated farmsteads and tofts: Harvey 1982b, 68). Yet, as appears to have been recorded at Great Kelk, there seem also to have been occasions when the overall uniformity of field layout could be disturbed by changes associated with particular elements in a township's complex settlement structure. Having confused rather than clarified the range of village development to be found in Holderness, it is time to do the same for settlements on the Wolds.

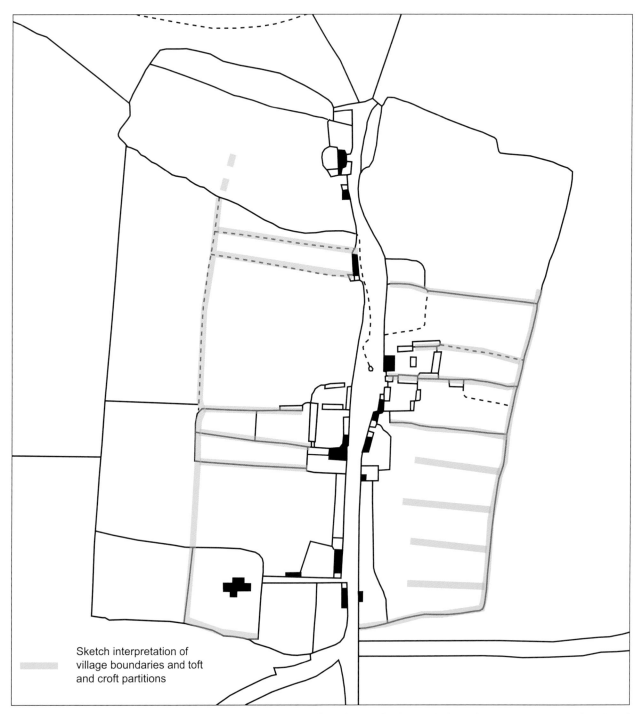

Sketch interpretation of village boundaries and toft and croft partitions

Fig. 111. Reconstruction of the original village boundaries and toft partitions of Wharram le Street based on the survey of 1810 and on aerial photographs. (E. Marlow-Mann)

Plate 31. Aerial photograph of Wharram le Street village, viewed from the north. (NMR CRA 16866/12, 2 March 1990. ©
Aeroscene Ltd)

The Wolds

Harvey proposed a sharp contrast between the settlement forms in Holderness and those on the Wolds. The former were, as we have seen 'linear, comprising ribbons of irregularly-shaped enclosures which were often of considerable length… [with] one or more denser clusters of enclosures'. The latter had simpler layouts, 'nucleated around an open space or a road junction, or else arranged in two rows facing each other across a street' (Harvey 1983, 95). Thus, she would presumably have seen Wolds village morphology as a continuation of what we have encountered in the Vale of Pickering, and very different from the plans of Holderness settlements.

There are, indeed, some regular two-row village plans on the Wolds, for example at Wetwang where there were also back lanes (Sheppard 1976, 4, fig. 1). In the two Wharram parishes, Beresford has suggested a regular row layout for medieval Thixendale (Beresford and Hurst 1990, 96, fig. 72), and Wharram Percy itself, of course, is composed of rows. But the clearest example of regularity

in settlement formation is Wharram le Street, a village of two rows, on the east and west sides of a road which was itself bisected by a spring, pond and stream (Fig. 111; Plate 31). Though the village enclosures on the west side seem at first glance to be much wider than those on the east, there are clear indications from the boundaries shown on two Birdsall Estate Office plans, based on Rawson's 1810 survey, and on aerial photographs, that the tofts and crofts had once been more uniform in their dimensions. Indeed, there is much on the plans to suggest that the village was laid out as a single event, perhaps when the coterminous manor and ecclesiastical parish were carved out of the larger territory of Wharram.

Elsewhere in the study area there are, however, settlements more reminiscent of the long ribbons of village enclosures in Holderness. The settlements in question are those that lie in the Great Wold Valley, or Cranedale. As would perhaps be anticipated from the layout of townships in the valley (Fig. 36 above), the pattern is one of villages set by the side of the Gypsey Race, with extensive open fields running up the valley

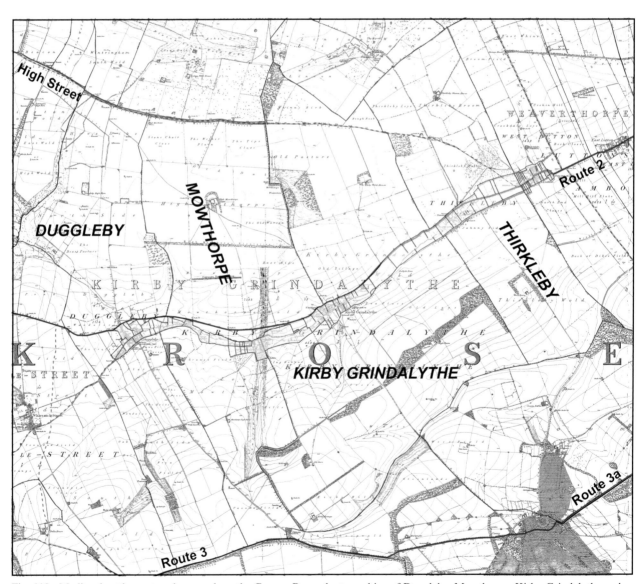

Fig. 112. Medieval settlement enclosures along the Gypsey Race: the townships of Duggleby, Mowthorpe, Kirby Grindalythe and Thirkleby. (E. Marlow-Mann)

Plate 32. Aerial photograph of Thirkleby deserted village, viewed from the north-east (NMR 17048/07, 7 November 1997. © Crown copyright.NMR)

sides to the north and south. As far as they can be determined, the furlongs and lands within those fields were mainly orientated north-south, as indicated by field boundaries recorded on the 19th-century Ordnance Survey maps, and on the one earlier estate map: a 1755 map of Kirby Grindalythe (BL Add MS 36899).

As David and Susan Neave have noted (*VCH ER VIII*, 120, 121 fig. 47 and 123), linear formations of settlement enclosures seem to have run more or less continuously along this stretch of the Gypsey Race (Fig. 112), through Duggleby, the lost Thoraldby, Mowthorpe, Kirby Grindalythe and Thirkleby and eastwards into the Luttons. Besides the villages and farms still occupied in the mid-19th century, the first edition Ordnance Survey six-inch map marks numerous 'Old Foundations' and 'Sites of Old Buildings' in the gaps between them.

The homesteads contained within these enclosures were by no means evenly distributed. As in the Holderness townships discussed above, the 19th-century mapping shows clusters of tofts and crofts in small blocks or 'rows', as at Thirkleby (Plate 32), and gaps between them. Some of the gaps, though, contain archaeological traces of groups of building foundations that appear to represent courtyard-plan farmsteads rather like the one at Buckton. They can be seen best in Duggleby, just west of Thoroughby Hill and close to the boundary with Mowthorpe; these were perhaps originally located in the lost Thoraldby vill, which seems formerly to have occupied a strip of land between Duggleby and Mowthorpe (Plate 33; see Fig. 36). Another

courtyard-plan farmstead may be marked by the earthworks of buildings and enclosures at Kirby Grindalythe to the west of the church there (Plate 34; see *VCH ER VIII*, 124, fig. 49), and there may be others at the east end of Thirkelby settlement (Cambridge University Collection of Aerial Photographs AUD 17).

John Hurst suggested that the Duggleby farmsteads might be 16th-century in origin, accounting for the absence of similar courtyard-plan farmsteads at Wharram Percy which had been deserted by then (Beresford and Hurst 1976, 128). An alternative explanation is that at least some of the courtyard plans mark medieval farmsteads held in free tenure, whereas the blocks of narrower tofts and crofts were laid out for groups of villein tenants. A couple of the bigger units no doubt represent the two largest monastic holdings in Cranedale. Malton priory established a grange in Mowthorpe on the basis of a late 12th-century grant of land on the west side of the township, next to Thoraldby. The buildings of the grange may be those evident in the large enclosure to the west of the modern Low Mowthorpe farmstead, visible as a soil mark on aerial photographs (e.g. Cambridge University Collection of Aerial Photographs AXH 43). In the 13th century the grange farmed 32 bovates in Thoraldby and rented out two tofts (*VCH ER VIII*, 127).

Kirkham priory also established a grange in these townships. It was in Kirby Grindalythe, and originated from a three bovate holding which had been granted to Newburgh priory, and which Newburgh had granted on to

Plate 33. Aerial photograph of farmstead earthworks east of Duggleby village, viewed from the north. (NMR ALP 2831/06, 21 July 1976. © The Anthony Laughton Pacitto Collection)

Plate 34. Aerial photograph of farmstead earthworks at Kirby Grindalythe, viewed from the south-west (NMR 12610/01, 24 November 1994. © Crown copyright.NMR)

Kirkham. The site of the grange may have been on the eastern boundary of the township, next to Thirkleby, where a house called Kirby Grange was located in 1755, and where the remains of rectangular buildings and medieval pottery have been revealed by ploughing (*VCH ER VIII*, 121 fig. 47, 125, 131).

Other similar units may have been in lay hands. It is, perhaps, too easy to assume that medieval rural settlements in the Central Province were in the form of compact villages comprising simply a manorial *curia*, the farmsteads of the villeins attached to the manor, and a number of cottage holdings. In Cranedale we are perhaps seeing a greater variety of farmstead units established by the 13th century. There are a few surviving records of late 12th and early 13th-century grants relating to these vills, and it is clear that there had, by then, been fragmentation of landholding through subinfeudation as well as through donations to monastic institutions. At Butterwick, for example, an extent of 1360 recorded nine holdings of a few bovates each that were held by knight's service: William Ergum held a messuage and four bovates in return for homage and service of one twenty-fourth part of a knight's fee; and one of the three holdings of John Gemelyng was a messuage and two bovates held for one forty-eighth part of a knight's fee (*Cal IPM X*, no.524, p. 426). It may be the small freehold homesteads created for holdings such as these that are, along with minor granges, represented by the courtyard-plan earthworks.

Village plan forms and their dating

This brief discussion of settlement forms in and around the study area has served merely to highlight a few characteristics relating to a small number of townships for which information can be readily accessed: it is no substitute for a comprehensive investigation of settlement plans on the northern Wolds. Nevertheless, it suggests that the widely accepted picture of uniform, compact nucleated villages and open fields may mask a more varied and less easily classifiable mix of homesteads and holdings.

There has also, frequently, been an assumption of uniformity with regard to the origins of Yorkshire's regular villages. Traditionally the most popular date and occasion have been the late 11th to 12th centuries, and the aftermath of William the Conqueror's supposedly widespread devastation of Yorkshire in 1069-70. Sheppard, for example, argued that 'the majority of regular village layouts in Yorkshire are likely to have originated during the late 11th or 12th centuries' and that 'the devastation of 1069-70 makes the chances of survival... of any such pre-Conquest plans very small' (Sheppard 1976, 4-5, 16-20). Others have been less dogmatic, but historically documented devastations, both pre-Conquest and post-Conquest, still have a strong grip on the imagination of settlement scholars, as Roberts (2008, 142-3) has acknowledged.

There is in fact no reason to suppose that the generation of regular village plans was triggered wholesale by major events such as these; though Roberts is of course correct to say that they would have provided opportunities for settlement planning 'but not the certainty of this taking place' (Roberts 2008, 144). As the morphological analysis of Settrington and Wharram Percy has shown, 'planned' elements within a single settlement might be created on a variety of occasions in widely differing contexts; or alternatively, as seems to be indicated at Wharram le Street, a planned village may have been created at one time and modified little over subsequent centuries. We need far more data, assembled on a systematic basis, before we can say which of these histories is the more frequently encountered on the Wolds, and therefore whether Wharram Percy's record of apparent incremental growth is typical or unusual.

19 The Late Medieval Village of Wharram Percy: Farming the Land

by Christopher Dyer with contributions from Ann Clark, Jane Richardson and Anna Slowikowski

During the 60 years of the Wharram Percy project we have learnt much about the village, the peasant houses and the way of life of its inhabitants. Meanwhile, substantial progress has been made in understanding the late medieval peasantry in general. This chapter and the next one will bring these fields of inquiry together. The work based on Wharram, meaning the excavations and the constant debate that accompanied them, has contributed to the opening of new questions and enquiries. Discussion of such universal problems as village origins, the planning of medieval villages, the layout and durability of peasant houses, and the causes of village desertion have been much influenced by the Wharram research. This chapter has been conceived as a contribution to the study of peasant farming and production, using the Wharram research as its principal example. The questions that will be addressed concern the organisation of farming, the effectiveness of the techniques of husbandry, the degree to which peasants produced for exchange and the market, and the long-term changes between c. 1200 and c. 1550.

The interpretation will be influenced by recent historical research from other places and other regions. Its special feature, however, is its consideration of the evidence from both archaeology and documents. This is not easily accomplished in the specific case of Wharram, because there is a mass of archaeological material, not just the raw data but high quality interpretation of the finds and structures; the documents specifically relating to Wharram, however, are relatively few and uninformative. As is the case with many lay estates, no archive of manorial records for Wharram has survived, and only very few deeds, and

instead we have to make do with some Inquisitions *post mortem* and tax records. We do not know the names of many Wharram inhabitants, let alone have information about their buying and selling of land, marriages and deaths, debts and quarrels, as are documented for other villages. The balance can to some degree be redressed from the written evidence from other manors and villages in the vicinity of Wharram in the north-west Wolds (Fig. 113). There are manorial records for Wetwang and Bishop Wilton, both part of the estate of the archbishops of York, and a few rentals. From a dozen places within 10km of Wharram many deeds survive because they were copied into monastic cartularies. The foundation in east Yorkshire of monastic houses of the new orders (especially Augustinians), mainly in the 12th century, led to their acquisition of pieces of land and groups of holdings in many villages where they were not themselves the main lord. The monks and canons kept systematic records of their evidence of title to these properties, to the lasting benefit of historians (Jurkowski *et al.* 2007).

Organising farming

In order to investigate the framework within which medieval peasant farming was carried out, we will begin with houses and agricultural buildings, and then move to the yards, gardens, tofts and crofts. The inquiry will expand further to examine the peasant holdings in the fields, pastures, meadows, woods and wastes in the territory of the village and beyond its boundaries. This follows quite closely the sequence of the original progress of the Wharram project, which began with quite a close focus on the houses which were visible as earthworks, and then probed the croft and village boundaries away from the centre of settlement. The landscape history of the remoter parts of the village's territory came later in the research programme.

When the scientific excavations at Wharram began, the research questions posed by John Hurst were in accordance with the progressive agenda of that time. The intention was to reveal the form and structure of village houses, and to investigate the material culture of the medieval peasants (Beresford and Hurst 1990, 31-44). The term 'peasant house' was constantly applied and in the 1950s and early 1960s the excavation was concentrated on two buildings visible as earthworks on Site 9 (Area 10) and Site 12 (Area 6). The discovery of the undercroft of the South Manor at Area 10 was an accidental distraction from the main programme. The peasant buildings seemed clumsily impermanent, and the relatively flimsy structures were apparently rebuilt in each generation. The assumption of a succession of young heirs rebuilding the house that had passed down to them fitted well with assumptions about medieval family continuities, and the belief that a close bond existed between each holding and the family that possessed it. The unimpressively ragged lines of chalk blocks of the walls were thought appropriate for insubstantial superstructures based on branches rather than timber

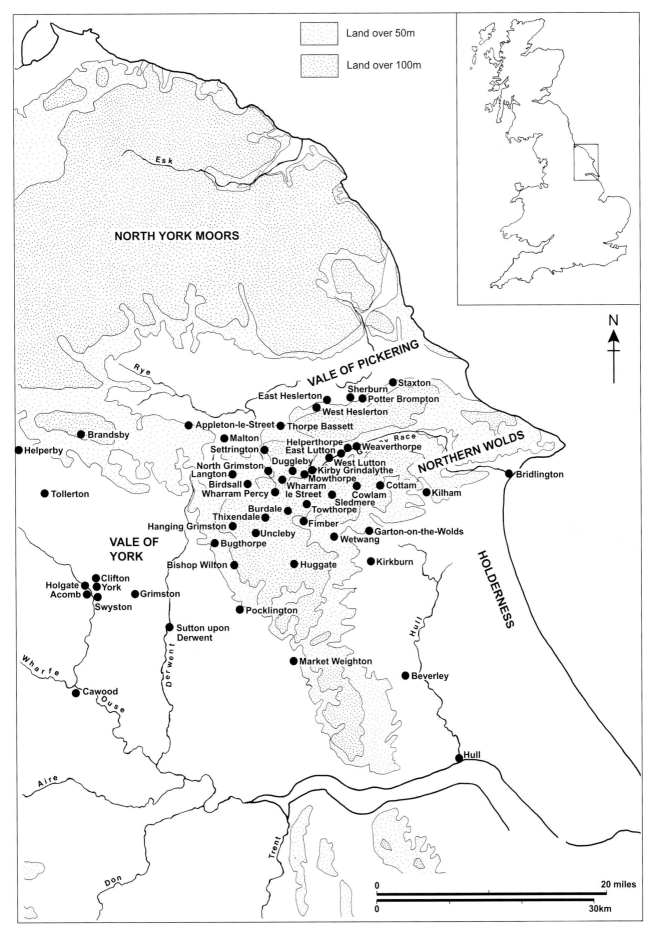

Fig. 113. Map showing places mentioned in Chapters 19 and 20. (E. Marlow-Mann and C. Philo)

framing. All of these observations accorded with the characterisation of peasants as afflicted by grinding poverty. The larger buildings were thought to have been longhouses, which combined domestic and agricultural functions, with a byre occupying the lower end. The only outbuildings would have been quite small stores. This again reflected the apparent poverty of peasants, who could afford only one large multifunctional building. The discovery of longhouses in Yorkshire and the Midlands showed that building types once thought to have been confined to remote parts of the highland zone had extended over much of England.

Now we understand that peasant houses throughout England in the 13th, 14th and 15th centuries often functioned solely as dwelling houses, without animal stalls at one end (Astill 1988, 54-6). They were accompanied at such sites as Barton Blount, Caldecote and Hound Tor by buildings dedicated to agriculture, which most commonly were barns, but might have included byres, stables, pigsties and sheepcotes, and also subsidiary domestic buildings such as bakehouses or detached kitchens. A range of peasant buildings are recorded in manorial court rolls of the period c. 1380-1520 (Dyer 1986, 25, 33-4). Surviving buildings, in Sussex for example, include barns and detached kitchens, and occasionally granaries and animal houses (Martin and Martin 2006, 33-8; see also p. 342 below). These discoveries prevent us from accepting the idea, once current at Wharram, that the farm, with house and agricultural buildings arranged around a yard, developed only at a very late phase, or even after 1500. Peasant holdings with yards lying between buildings are found throughout the later middle ages, and indeed before 1200. Even when longhouses contained accommodation for people and animals under the same roof, they would be accompanied by other buildings, one of which would be a barn.

The new approach to buildings suggests that some parallels can be observed between the peasant way of life and that of their lords. Both lords and peasants built specialised domestic and agricultural buildings, and both grouped them around yards. The manorial buildings, as can be seen at the North Manor at Wharram, were of course larger, more numerous, and better built than those of the peasants. In many cases the farmyard was separated from the residential courtyard adjoining the hall and kitchen. But there was a generic resemblance between the structures and spaces built and used by peasants and aristocrats.

At Wharram, from the excavated sites and from observation of the earthworks marking the foundations of buildings, in a recurring pattern, houses were paired with long buildings which were probably barns, often facing one another across a sunken yard (Wrathmell 1989a, 41-5). On Site 12 (Area 6) Building 1 was an exceptionally long structure (28m), with accommodation for people at the west end and, it has been suggested, for animals at the east. Across the yard and running in parallel was Building 4, which was also long, at 25m, and is best interpreted as

a barn, because of its narrowness, its lack of a hearth, and its floor which did not show signs of intensive use or cleaning (Wrathmell 1989b, 23-33). The less thoroughly excavated Building 8 on Site 8 (Area 5) was probably a barn, suggested by its narrowness and its round corner which would have been associated with a roof with a gavel fork at the end (Wrathmell 1989b, 35). Barns tended to lack finds such as metalwork, as in the case of Building 4 on Site 12. They were mainly designed for storing crops in straw awaiting threshing, but the stacks of crops would not always have occupied the whole space, and the buildings had other functions. Judging from the distribution of fragments of coal, part of Building 4 on Site 12 was used to store fuel at some period of its life. We can assume that implements, including carts and ploughs could have been sheltered in the building, and space might have been found for livestock in bad weather.

The association between houses and barns is recorded in a deed from nearby Fimber in the 13th century. A house and barn which were 11 feet apart had been built by a tenant a few feet on the wrong side of a property boundary dividing two tofts, and the problem was resolved by a grant of a small strip of land by the tenant who had suffered the encroachment, for which a compensatory payment was made. The barn had a stone wall, presumably a low foundation wall (John Rylands Lib Latin MS 221, f. 366r-366v). One could imagine that such an encroachment might arise in one of the rows of tofts at Wharram, if a toft was left vacant for a time and the boundary became unclear.

Specialist agricultural buildings included Building 1 on Site 9 (Area 10) which probably served as a stable, in view of its relatively small size and finds of horse shoes and a spur (Wrathmell 1989b, 17, 21). On Site 76 Building 1 was another relatively small structure, 4m by 10m-12m, which had good quality foundations and a roof of stone slates and ceramic tiles, perhaps in succession. Its lack of internal features appropriate to a dwelling or animal house suggested that it served as a cart shed with an open front (Stamper et al. 2000, 52-4).

Small buildings (one measured 3.7 m by 4.3m) were excavated on both Site 12 (Area 6) and Site 9 (Area 10), which were once identified as outhouses or stores (Milne 1979a 41; Milne 1979b, 51). Small outbuildings are a plausible part of the stock of buildings, and there are parallels on other village sites, but they are not much mentioned in documents anywhere (Wrathmell 1989c, 14). The Wharram examples may have been pigsties or poultry houses. No excavated village building at Wharram has been suggested as a sheepcote, but there were at least four buildings located at the back of tofts in the West Row, and two or three set at the western end of the crofts attached to the South Manor, which might have been placed to give animals kept in these buildings access to the crofts (Dyer 1995, 158-60).

All the foundations of these buildings show signs of alteration, reconstruction, repair, extension in length or shortening. Such modifications may be associated with changes of function, and just as documents tell us that, throughout the country, a carthouse or a bakehouse could be converted to a dwelling, or a dwelling made into an animal house, so the Wharram buildings may have gone through such a transformation. One of the cottages listed in the inquisition survey of 1368 was called 'the Stable'. (*Cal IPM* XI, 183).

A particular uncertainty surrounds the Wharram longhouses. Positive identification of the lower end of a house as a byre end remains elusive, as Wharram buildings in general lack the well-built drains which suggest on other sites the presence of animal stalls. It was originally supposed that longhouses were a normal feature of the village; but then it was argued that Building 1 at Site 12 (Area 6) was an example of a longhouse being introduced at a late stage, in the 15th century. Buildings 9 and 5 (Area 7) were adjacent structures which may originally have been a single building, the west end of which was a dwelling, and the east end may have had a 'non-domestic' use, perhaps for animals, in the 14th century. Building 9 was shortened in length, and eventually was abandoned and Building 5 continued in 'non-domestic' use (Wrathmell 1989b, 38-40). This combined building, and Building 1 on Site 12, were both more than 20m long, and therefore provided sufficient space for a byre end. Most of the houses visible as earthworks were about 15m long, presumably built in three bays with four pairs of crucks. They provided enough room for a household of five people or so, but very limited space for livestock.

A positive conclusion emerges from these difficulties in identifying the function of buildings. If the remains of a dwelling house cannot be distinguished easily from those of a farm building, and if buildings could be converted from one purpose to another, then this tells us that the farm buildings were not all being constructed to a low standard. The apparent cart shed on Site 76, with its roof of ceramic and stone tiles, must be regarded as a building of good quality, because in addition to having waterproof roofing material, the heavy tiles could only have been carried on the walls of a well-constructed timber frame. We know from later evidence from Settrington that barns as well as dwelling houses were cruck-built. The peasants of Wharram seem to have regarded farm buildings as important assets, and devoted some of their scarce resources to providing good timber and other materials to keep crops out of harm's way, and to protect equipment and livestock. To put the point in more modern economic terms, they were investing in order to gain profit from their holdings. We must allow, however, for a type of building which is usually hidden from us because it has left no earthworks, and therefore would not have attracted excavation. Building 3 on Site 82K (North Manor) had some chalk foundations but was 'insubstantial', and it may be that peasants had different standards of construction for their barns, which seem to have been carefully built, and cheaper and less robust structures to shelter carts, or livestock in bad weather, or less valuable crops, such as peas (Roskams and Richards

2004, 133, 138). Such buildings may have been especially a feature of the tofts of the East Row, where there is less visible earthwork evidence for outbuildings than in any other part of the village.

Peasants' productive activity was concentrated in the toft and the croft. The typical toft in the northern part of the West Row of Wharram village was roughly 40m by 20m, in which, as we have seen, stood the house and barn, with a yard between them. The toft boundaries were sometimes defined by chalk walls, which are recorded in documents from other wolds villages such as Kilham (BL Harleian rolls, H12). The west end of Site 12 (Area 6) and the east end of Site 9 (Area 10) were bounded by walls of chalk, but other toft boundaries around the village were apparently marked by a ditch and bank, which may have been surmounted by a hedge. These were apparently secure, and at Site 12, a gate set in a barrier, which may have been a wall or fence, was hinged on a socketed stone (Wrathmell 1989b 33).

The buildings were set very near to the toft boundaries, to gain shelter from the elements, and to leave a maximum of open space (Stamper *et al.* 2000, 50). The yard on Site 12 (Area 6) was cobbled, and the sunken profiles of the yards in general suggests, as at Goltho (Lincs.) that cattle were kept in them at night, especially in the winter, and their trampling, together with the periodic scraping of the surface for manure would have eroded the ground surface (Beresford 1975, 13-18). The dunghill would have been sited in the yard, according to the excavators, based on the distribution of finds, against the wall of a building. On this heap would be thrown animal manure, soiled litter, and also domestic refuse. The absence of rubbish pits at Wharram suggests that waste and ordure of all kinds were deposited onto the dunghill. This valuable accumulation was spread onto the fields at the appropriate seasons, leaving tell-tale signs in the soil in the form of a scatter of pot sherds (Jones 2004, 159-88). The apparent tidiness of the Wharram peasants has been remarked, and most strikingly reflected in the dished profile of the repeatedly swept house floors, but cleanliness was linked to the recycling of wastes in order to maximise agricultural returns.

The yard could also have been the place for stacks of unthreshed grain or legumes, or hay, if there was no room in the barn. In the yard of Site 9 (Area 10) a circular platform of stone about 1.5m in diameter may have been a stand for a small stack, though a threshing floor would be an alternative explanation (Stamper *et al.* 2000, 21).

Production went on throughout the toft. The labour force lived in the house: that is members of the family and for the better-off peasants, one or two servants. Elsewhere in the toft the crops were stored and some of the animals kept; horses, oxen and cows must have spent much time near the house or barn, ready to be harnessed, or to be milked. The implements such as ploughs, harrows, carts and hand tools were stored in the barn or specialised buildings, together with dairying equipment such as wooden and ceramic vessels. Cheese-making or butter-churning probably went on in the house, the domain of women who were responsible for this work. Brewing, also a preserve of women, must have taken place in the house as there is no evidence from Wharram of separate brew houses. Bread seems not to have been baked at home in view of the uncertain evidence for ovens. The dough it seems was taken to the common oven.

There was limited room in the toft for a garden. On Site 9 (Area 10), a plot of dark earth north-west of the building was identified as garden soil, and one can observe spaces in the tofts now visible as earthworks which had the potential for use as gardens as large as 15m by 15m. Adequate room for gardening is most clearly present on the western side of the tofts in the West Row, with much less available space in the North Row and East Row plots, although the latter was the likely location of the cottages, the inhabitants of which had most need of garden produce. The garden plot would have been reduced when new buildings were added, but gardening could be extended over ground left vacant, as apparently happened after the abandonment of Site 9 in *c.* 1500, when a garden soil accumulated over the ruins of the buildings.

Documents record the plants grown in gardens in general throughout England, mostly the various members of the onion family (onions, leeks, and garlic) and brassicas such as cabbage, with fruits and especially apples and pears. Botanical material from Wharram includes cherry stones, the pollen of the cabbage family, and flax and hemp, and also the rather negative evidence of pollen from weeds likely to have grown in gardens (Wrathmell 1989b, 22; Bush 2005, 184; Carruthers 2005, 217). Flax and hemp are also named in documents regarding tithe from the wold villages of Garton and Kirby Grindalythe, together with vague references to tithe of gardens and bushes (Bodl Lib Fairfax 7, f. xv r). The peas found quite frequently (in a charred condition) at Wharram may have originated as garden crops, but most legumes (peas and beans) would have been grown in the fields. Flax and hemp, however, would have been cultivated either in gardens in the tofts or in plots set aside for that purpose near to the village.

It cannot be said that there is an abundance of evidence for gardening at Wharram, and we have to assume that the villagers would not have neglected the opportunity for horticulture. An early 16th-century rental for Settrington, a very comparable settlement, records no less than 42 gardens on a total of 50 holdings (TNA:PRO SC12/23/13), and the tithe agreements from Garton and Kirby were based on the understanding that horticultural products had a significant value. In the common speech of Yorkshire, gardens were called garths, which is recorded at Towthorpe in 1536, and in the poll tax of 1381 for Settrington the name Alice Garthwoman suggests that tending a garden could have been a specialist occupation, the work left to women as one of their many poorly documented but important activities. Two iron spade shoes show that land was dug, but this need not always have happened in a garden (TNA:PRO SC6 Henry VIII/4505; Fenwick 2005, 210).

Women also traditionally tended poultry, and this dimension of peasant production is well attested at Wharram. The bones of fowls and geese are scattered over the peasant house Sites 9 and 12 in greater number than any other type of bird, and egg shells were recovered from Site 9. The tenants are recorded in 1323 as owing an annual rent of a cock and two hens, which would have been a surplus from the larger flock which would normally have been kept on each holding. Hens and cocks gained their sustenance in the toft and croft, but the geese grazed on the common pasture, and the 13th-century stints that regulated the commons at Mowthorpe, Thixendale and other villages in the neighbourhood (Table 16) attempted to limit each oxgang to keep their number of adult geese to four or five, though at Kirby Grindalythe the three female geese could be accompanied by their goslings. Geese, said in 1379 to have trespassed at Bishop Wilton were kept in flocks which numbered between six and sixteen for each offender, all women from prominent families in the village (Hull UL DDSY/4/2 1084; Table 17).

Beehives are another likely part of the garden economy, and tithes of bees and honey were paid in Wharram parish in 1548-9; elsewhere on the Wolds bees are mentioned in a tithe agreement from Thirkleby, and they were a feature of the nearby village of Wetwang in the early 17th century (Purvis 1949, 37; Bodl Lib Fairfax 7, f. xv r; VCH 8, 249-50).

Behind the tofts lay the long crofts, some of which stretched more than 100m in the northern part of the West Row, but half that length in the East Row. The purpose of the crofts could have been as enclosures for livestock. According to standard open-field custom, those with rights of common pasture could only graze as many animals on the fields as they could keep on their own land in the winter. The limited amount of grass would have been supplemented with straw, hay, peas and oats (some of these latter still in straw, that is unthreshed) which were being stored in the barn or in stacks in the toft. There is evidence for cultivation of the crofts, however, at least in a late phase of the life of the village (Richards 1992a, 24). This would not have prevented livestock being kept on the stubble in the winter if the next year's planting was delayed until the spring. At some stage, in bad weather for example, the animals were brought into the toft, perhaps in the yard, or accommodated in the sheepcotes which have been tentatively identified in or near the croft, or in less substantial buildings of the type excavated on the North Manor site (see above, p. 30).

To sum up the role of the toft and the croft in peasant production, this was the part of the tenant's assets over which he or she exercised most control. The house, barn and other structures were built on the peasant's own initiative, and some choice was exercised, always within the inevitable limitations on resources. The produce from the toft – vegetables, fruit, bacon, honey, eggs and poultry – were no doubt primarily a contribution to the household's diet, and added not just to its nutritional quality but also to the pleasure and satisfaction of those

Table 16. Stints on common pasture for one oxgang (bovate) in the vicinity of Wharram Percy.

Place	Date	Horses	Oxen	Cows	Calves	Sheep	Pigs	Poultry
Kirby Grindalythe	13th century	-	1	1	-	16 with lambs	1*	3 geese with goslings
Mowthorpe	1259	1	-	1	-	15 ewes with lambs	1	5 geese (1m 4f)
Thirkleby	1259	1	-	2	-	20 sheep with lambs	3	5 geese (1m, 4f)
Thixendale	1252	2 large animals			-	30 sheep with lambs	2	4 geese (1m, 3f)

Sources: *EYC* 2, 382-3; BL Cott Claudius DXI , f. 196v.; Bodl. Fairfax 7, f.8r.
Notes: * or 1 sow with litter until weaning

Table 17. Animals attached for trespassing at Bishop Wilton, 1379-80

Horses	Cattle	Sheep	Pigs	Geese	Total
67	69	894	0	53	1083
6%	6%	83%		5%	100%

Source: Hull UL DD57/4/2/1084

eating them. The more enterprising women producers would have taken the surplus of their produce to market, walking with baskets to such towns as Malton, and they would in consequence have been able to contribute a shilling or two to a holding's annual income. Occasionally, the scale of production rose to a point where a woman like Joan Hambald of Bishop Wilton, who had sixteen geese in 1379, must be regarded as a petty entrepreneur. The flax and hemp grown at Wharram were most likely to have been sold, often in the form of spun thread, thanks again to women's labour.

The principal foodstuffs and most of any saleable surplus, came from the land out in the common fields. The villages of the north-west Wolds at first sight followed a common pattern. The oxgang was used everywhere as the standard unit of tenure, which in theory contained about 15 acres of arable land, but varied from 4 to 20 acres (p. 280 above). The oxgangs were usually distributed over two fields, so half the land was cultivated each year. When a holding was conveyed by deed in the 13th or 14th century a number of standard formulae described a 'messuage' (house and buildings) or a 'toft and croft', with an oxgang (bovate) in the 'territory of the village', and 'all of the appurtenances within and without the vill'. The oxgang referred to the arable strips in the fields, and the appurtenances to the common rights of pasture, and a share of the meadow and woodland.

The idea, however, that the toft and croft were always bound strongly to the field land and the appurtenant pasture rights, is only partly supported by the written sources. Not infrequently the deeds conveying an oxgang make no mention of a messuage or toft, or tofts and crofts are conveyed without reference to an attached oxgang. Sometimes it is stated quite clearly that the oxgang is 'without a toft'. Such a state of detachment between the tofts and crofts and the units of land holding is found in examples at Duggleby, North Grimston, Mowthorpe, Sledmere and Thixendale or in other words through all Wharram's neighbours for which documents survive. This separation is implied in the survey of Wharram attached to the Inquisition *post mortem* of 1436, which gives the value of sixteen messuages and of sixteen oxgangs as distinct items. One reason for this division between oxgangs, messuages, tofts and crofts was the development of a land market, which is readily apparent in east Yorkshire (and the rest of England) in the 13th century. In that century we often find two oxgangs being held by a single tenant, implying that a once separate oxgang had been sold to a tenant who already held one. He or she only needed one toft and croft, and spare tofts and crofts could be held by people who lived mainly from wage work. The land market is visibly recorded in deeds, fines, and court rolls, but some sub-letting might be hidden from view. In spite of these irregularities, it can still be assumed that the toft and croft served as the base from which land in the fields was worked. This discussion of the farming of oxgangs at Wharram will presume that these standard units were managed from the tofts and crofts lining the streets of the village, even if they were not bound to one another tenurially.

The land of Wharram was divided into 68 oxgangs (see pp 280 and 284-8). The whole township contains in modern times 1459 acres, and the modern boundaries are believed to resemble closely though not competely those of the middle ages. The ridge and furrow is very extensive, and the only land that does not carry the marks of cultivation are the steep valleys (dales) which could not be ploughed, and the village itself (Fig. 106). The ploughed area at its greatest extent was about 1250 acres, which would suggest an oxgang of 18 acres. No medieval document indicates the size of the oxgang at Wharram Percy, but at Wharram le Street the oxgang carried a rent of 10s while a 3-acre holding paid 4s, suggesting an oxgang acreage of only a little more than 10 acres (BL Cot Vit. Cvi, f. 215r and 215v). These were probably customary acres.

We can hopefully be more certain about the number of oxgangs held by the tenants. Of the total of 68, 27 lay in demesne, which leaves 41 for the tenants. The surveys of the 14th century assign two, three or four oxgangs to each of the tenants (excluding the cottagers), but this is likely to reflect an amalgamation of holdings after the Scottish raids of 1322 and the Great Famine of 1315-17. The village earthworks contain about 37 tofts, 26 in the West and North Rows, and eleven in the East Row. The latter row can probably be equated with the cottars, in view of the restricted space in their tofts and crofts, so that 26 tenants located in the other two rows in the 13th century probably cultivated the 41 tenant oxgangs, suggesting individual holdings of one or two each.

In the 13th century the main (non-cottar) households at Wharram lived on either 18 or 36 acres of arable land. In the following century there were larger holdings amounting to 54 and 72 acres, and indeed with the division of the 27 oxgangs of demesne among the tenants, the holdings had grown further in size. The layout of the fields is discussed in detail above, in Chapter 17 (pp 284-8), which means that here no more than a reminder is needed that the land of the oxgangs was distributed over the culturae, shots, flats and falls of the field system, and that the strips were arranged in the orderly fashion which prevailed throughout the north-west Wolds. The arable land of Wharram was divided into two cropping areas, so that half the land was fallowed each year, and the fallow field gave the livestock of the village access to about 625 acres of vegetation which had grown in the stubble of the previous year's corn.

The regular structure of tenements and fields dates back well before the 13th century, and the origins of these institutions are not a direct concern of this chapter, but of course they had a great impact on the late medieval peasants as they worked within a well-established framework. The system was partly designed to make life easier for the lords and higher authorities, because the number of oxgangs was related to the obligations of the village to pay rents and services to the lord and taxes to the state. It was in the lords' interest to make sure that the oxgang survived as a unit, and was not subdivided or fragmented. The effectiveness of the lords' exploitation depended on the peasants who occupied the oxgangs having sufficient resources to pay the rent and perform the services. They would not be able to carry out their obligations on the demesne if they lacked ploughs, carts and draught animals. They even contributed their experience and skill, as the tenants were expected to act as graves (reeves in other parts of England) entrusted with the management of the demesne. On the other hand, there would be obvious dangers for those in authority if the tenants became too prosperous and independent.

The communal principles of the fields allowed 40 households to live on limited resources. All the villagers were bound into paying some respect to the common good, as selfish behaviour could upset the balance between crops and livestock. If a very high proportion of the land was cultivated, finding enough fodder for the animals posed a problem. The grass growing in the valleys of Drue Dale, Deep Dale and Wood Dale, and the stream valley provided some permanent pasture, but that had to be supplemented by the seasonal grazing of the fallows and stubble field. Wharram lacked a large area of high quality hay meadow, which ideally would occupy a flat-bottomed stream valley, yet hay was the main winter feed for livestock.

Woodland, another desirable resource, was also in short supply. Wharram had 20 acres in 1436, and this was probably exploited by coppicing to provide fuel, fencing wood and wattles rather than large building timber. Wood and timber must have come from outside the township, perhaps from Settrington which had 80 acres of wood in 1305 and 120 acres in 1536 (Allison 1976, 66; TNA:PRO, SC12/23/13). Timber must have come from a distance, as the crucks which formed the frame of the houses and barns could only be cut out of substantial trees which would not have been obtainable in the immediate neighbourhood. More than 500 cruck blades would have been used in Wharram's peasant buildings in c. 1300, and although they were very durable, they would occasionally have needed replacement. What other resources were brought into the township? Were cartloads of hay (at a price) carried from the 'ings' around Malton in the Derwent valley? Or was there a custom which allowed Wharram's sheep to be driven to intercommon on one of the remaining permanent pastures and heaths on the high wolds (see pp 288-90)? In the 16th century a tithe dispute revealed a pasture called 'Great Wharram' in Thixendale parish, to the tithes of which both Wharram Percy and Kirby Underdale's churches laid claim. This may have been an intercommoned upland to which Wharram's livestock had access. Great Wharram may have occupied the south-east corner of Thixendale, where Riggs Farm and Pluckham now stand (Purvis 1949, 23-37; Bodleian Lib. Fairfax 7, 7v-7ar; see Fig. 104 above).

Having seen the buildings, tofts, crofts, oxgangs and commons of Wharram itself, and speculated about possible assets outside the township, we can explore the effectiveness of peasant agriculture.

Farming and producing

Let us focus on Wharram in the late 13th century, before it was beset with a series of crises, and when most tenants were holding either 18 or 36 acres of arable land in the form of one or two oxgangs. They worked within the constraints of the landscape and the institutions inherited from previous generations, but it is useful to see their methods of cultivation and management in terms of decisions, some of which they could make for themselves, but which had often been made by their predecessors and had become enshrined in custom and tradition.

The first choice concerned which crops to grow. Preserved grain has been recovered in quantity from the South Manor area and from the pond site. Negligible quantities of rye were present in these and all other samples, so the main crops were wheat, barley and oats. In two samples, wheat and barley each accounted for between 25% and 44% of the total, and oats from 13% to 20%. Quantities of peas, and some vetch, were also recovered but were not included in the calculations because the analysis was concentrated on grain (Carruthers 2005, 219). The documentary records of crops grown on the demesne at Wetwang in the 14th century provide a helpful comparison because Wharram and Wetwang cultivated similar soils under comparable conditions. As Table 18 shows, on the basis of figures for crops harvested and acreage sown, wheat accounted for about a third of the crops (24 % to 36%), barley for rather more than a third (29% to 41%), oats for 8% to 20%, and peas and beans between 3% and 23%. Drage (a barley and oats mixture which was grown both for brewing corn and for animal feed), if added to the barley would bring the barley and barley mixture total of the harvested crops

in 1303-4 to 61%. These were demesne crops, but those grown by the peasants may not have been very different. At Bishop Wilton, which straddles the western edge of the Wolds, for 1298 the production of the demesne and grain tithe receipts can be compared. The tithe was collected mainly from the peasant holdings, and their crops were similar to those of the demesne, except that the demesne grew a higher proportion of peas and beans, because the lord probably had a greater interest in fodder crops.

The selection of crops depended on a combination of factors. Barley usually did well on chalk and limestone soils, and was an obvious staple for peasants because of its versatility as a bread and brewing corn. It could be used in the household, and might be sold though not at a very high price. Rye was normally grown on sandy soils, which are not found on the Wolds, so wheat was the main winter sown grain, and it was desirable because wheat bread was preferred to any other, and it commanded the highest price at market. Small quantities of oats and peas were consumed in peasant households as pottage corn, and the rest was destined for animal feed or sale. Vetch had only one use, as animal feed. The spring sown crops (barley, oats and legumes) were grown in greater quantity than winter sown wheat, which gave the cultivators crops with a relatively low market value, but with a greater variety of uses.

A secondary consideration, once the balance between wheat, barley, oats and peas had been fixed, was to decide which variety of these crops to plant. The administrative documents make no reference to this aspect of the crops, and much of our knowledge depends on the skill of palaeobotanists in their analysis of preserved grains, straw and other plant remains. The grain deposited at the pond site in the 14th and 15th centuries included both

Table 18. Crops from manors in the vicinity of Wharram Percy.

Manor	Date	Wheat	Barley	Drage	Oats	Peas/beans	Total
Wetwang (1)	1304-5	62q 3b	65q 5b	40q 1b	-	6q	174q 1b
		36	38	23		3	100%
Wetwang (2)	1315-16	34ac	58ac	-	28.5ac	22ac	142.5ac
		24	41	-	20	15	100%
Wetwang (2)	1316-17	57ac	48ac	13ac	23 ac	24.75ac	165.75ac
		34	29	8	14	15	100%
Wetwang (2)	1373-4	53ac	67.5ac	-	14.25ac	41.25ac	176
		30	38	-	8	24	100%
Bishop Wilton demesne (1)	1298	130q	60q	50q		30q	270q
		48	22	19		11	100%
Bishop Wilton tithe (1)	1298	60q	35q	30q		10q	135q
		45	26	22		7	100%

Notes: (1) quantities harvested or collected; (2) acreage sown
q = quarters; b = bushels
Sources: TNA:PRO SC6 1141/1;1144/2;1144/4; 1144/10; Pratt 2005, 4-6

bread wheat and rivet wheat (Jones 2005, 195). Each had its own virtues and drawbacks. For example, bread wheat made the best bread, but the awns (spikes on the ear) of rivet wheat discouraged predation by birds. They reacted differently to soil and weather condition, which might explain why both were grown as an insurance against poor yields. Two-row and six-row barley were grown at Wharram; the former yields better, but the latter has a higher protein content (Jones 2005, 195, 199; Moffett 2006, 47-50).

The third set of choices concerned the method of cultivation. The routines of ploughing, sowing, harrowing, weeding and harvesting are well documented in the manorial records. The ploughsoil excavated on Sites 94 and 95, was between 6 and 10cm thick, presumably the product of repeated ploughing and harrowing sufficient to form a seed bed (Richards 1992a, 24-5). The ploughs, if they followed the types employed on the Wetwang demesne, were 'foot ploughs', which were unwheeled implements, each fitted at the end of the beam with a 'foot' of wood strengthened with iron. This device helped the ploughman to maintain an even depth of furrow (Langdon 1986, 129). The excavated evidence from Wharram, as is commonly the case elsewhere, tells us little about ploughs, as the most important iron fittings, the share and coulter, were large and expensive enough to be constantly refashioned and never discarded. Some miscellaneous iron bindings, rings and other fragments may once have been attached to ploughs (Goodall, I.H., 1989, 51).

The East Riding was one of those regions which has been identified as adopting horses as plough beasts at a relatively early date, and Wharram may have participated in that movement. From the 13th century, ploughing on the demesne at Wetwang was done by horses, four for each plough, and there were plough horses at Market Weighton in 1403 (TNA: PRO, SC6/1144/4; BIA D and C wills 1403 Scarle). At Wharram, the proportion of horse bones is rather higher than on other comparable sites, rising near to 10% in some samples, and there were two remarkable deposits, one at the pond and the other at the North Manor, which suggest that these were specialised places of slaughter and butchery. There may have been a 'knacker's yard' near the pond, where many horse shoes and horse shoe nails were found as well as bones (Richardson 2004a, 268-71; Goodall and Clark 2005, 132-8). In addition to horse shoes, excavations at Wharram have produced a considerable quantity of metalwork linked with the harnessing and riding of horses, including parts of bridles, spurs, and curry combs. We have seen that one of the peasant buildings has been identified as a stable. Although the horses were quite small, with an average height of twelve hands (Richardson 2004a, 268; Richardson 2005a, 164; Richardson 2005b, 237), they were capable of hauling ploughs, and a number of horse bones shows signs of stress from haulage work (Richardson 2004a, 271).

On the other hand, oxen were engaged in fieldwork, as their bones also demonstrate trauma resulting from arduous labour. There was no shortage of cattle of the required age – over two years – to be trained as oxen, and at least 28 ox shoes have been found. Both oxen and horses are likely to have pulled ploughs on the fields of the township, as they did at Wharram le Street, where in 1511 the vicar's probate inventory included both eight oxen and eight stotts (plough horses) (BIA D and C wills 1511 Grissaker). This late reference to plough oxen does not suggest that horses gradually replaced oxen, and at Wharram Percy four ox shoes were found in the last phase of Site 9, at the time of its abandonment.

The fourth area of decision-making related to the use of fertilisers and soil improvers. We know that great sheep flocks were kept on the Wolds, at Mowthorpe and Thixendale for example, and that at the latter in 1255 the flocks grazed over the arable, on the stubble after the corn was carried, and on the fallow (John Rylands Lib Latin MS 221, 263v). This was not often recorded in any detail because it was a commonplace of the agriculture of the Wolds, a region of 'sheep and corn' husbandry, where the sheep gained nutrition from the corn fields after the corn had been carried, but also virtuously returned the vegetation that they had eaten in the form of manure. Demesne and tenant sheep would have been folded on much of the arable at Wharram, but part of the field would have been manured 'by the cart', and this practice can be inferred from the scatter of medieval pottery found by fieldwalking on the modern arable fields of the township. The pot sherds signal the presence of cartloads of dung and refuse, which has otherwise left no trace. The pottery scatter is concentrated on fields to the north of the village's territory, which suggests that the peasants selected parts of the fields with good land which they regarded as most likely to benefit from this more intensive application of manure.

The cultivation of legumes, especially peas, by the Wharram peasants increased the fertility of their land in two ways. The nodules attached to the roots of the plants added nitrogen to the soil for the advantage of subsequent crops; and if fed in stalls or sheepcotes to livestock, would result in concentrated accumulations of droppings for convenient carting to the field.

The fifth dilemma facing peasant cultivators was how to counter weeds among the growing corn. Analysis of surviving seeds and pollen reveals a good range of troublesome plants, such as poppy, charlock and corncockle in deposits from the early medieval period. In the later centuries corn marigold and corn chickweed grew among spring-planted crops, and stinking chamomile was found in the wheat field. The most effective remedy was to plough the arable repeatedly before planting, in order to kill weeds and destroy their root systems, but we do not know if the Wharram fallows were double or triple ploughed. Perhaps the ploughing was not always done thoroughly, because the particular mixture of weeds found at the pond site suggested that a light plough, an ard, was being used and therefore weed growth was not being controlled effectively (Hillman and Arthur 2005, 190; Jones 2005, 191-200). As the crops were growing the weeds could be removed by hand, which is recorded on the demesnes of Wetwang and Bishop Wilton. The peasants of Wharram did the same judging from the finds of weed hooks and spuds, small iron blades which were attached to long hafts and wielded to cut the weeds off at the roots (Goodall, I.H. 1989, 52; Goodall and Clark 2000, 133-4; Goodall and Clark 2004, 244-5). This laborious procedure was practised sparingly on demesnes, but may have commended itself to peasants who could deploy reserves of family workers. Weeding (from the perspective of an adult male) was an ideal task for women and children.

A sixth point requiring choices in the corn-growing cycle was encountered in the harvest field. Should the corn be cut with small reaping hooks or sickles, which meant grasping a bunch of ears in one hand and cutting the stalks near the top with a sawing motion? Or should scythes be used to cut the corn near the roots in a sweeping motion? Blades from sickles and reaping hook have been found at Wharram, and so have pieces of scythe (Goodall I.H. 1979, 121; Goodall I.H. 1989 49, 52; Goodall and Clark 2000, 133). This does not reveal which was the predominant harvesting technique, because worn-out scythes, having large blades made from a quantity of iron, were more likely than small sickles to be returned to the smith for reworking. In any case, many households would own a scythe for mowing hay, and a scythe might be brought into use in the harvest field after the upper part of the plant had been removed with the sickle in order to cut straw for various uses, including bedding for animals, thatching and fuel. Straw was fed in large quantities to oxen at Bishop Wilton in the 14th century, and the agricultural writers of the 13th century advocated straw as winter feed for sheep (TNA:PRO SC6 1144/7; Oschinsky 1971, 339).

The sickle was often wielded by women workers, and the scythe by men, which added a further dimension to the choice. Women always made a contribution to harvest labour, but this increased in significance after the Black Death of 1349 and the long-term fall in population (Astill and Langdon 1997, 24-5, 48, 58-9, 126, 136-9, 164). The choice of implement was determined partly by the wealth of the household, as scythes were relatively expensive. William Akclum, a poor husbandman of Wharram le Street, in 1481 had two sickles and no scythe, while a better off contemporary from Grimston near York in 1464 owned four sickles and four scythes (BIA D and C wills. 1481 Akclum; 1464 Jakson). The Wharram finds include an abundance of whetstones, which were used to sharpen knives, shears and other blades throughout the year, but their most intensive use would have been in the months of August and September with so much depending on the efficiency of the harvest implements.

Sheaves were brought back to the toft by horse-drawn carts. They have left little direct trace in the material record apart from pieces of iron that may have been used to bind their bodies or strengthen their wheels. Their passage past the North Manor is attested by ruts, which shows that they conformed to standard dimensions with wheels c. 1.5m apart (Rahtz and Watts 2004, 74). Peasant inventories of the 15th century from villages around York show that horse-drawn carts and ox-drawn wains were especially costly pieces of equipment, usually ranging in value from 12s to 23s 4d.

Finally, the peasants were still faced with problems and dilemmas after the harvest had been gathered, because the benefit of their husbandry practices would be lost if crops were not properly stored. A number of mouse and rat bones, including a complete rat skeleton from Site 12 (Area 6) confirms the presence of one threat (Ryder 1974, 44). Examination of cereal grains reveals holes bored by insect pests, and the observation that some grain had sprouted before it was carbonised suggest that stores were not always sufficiently dry (Hillman and Arthur 2005, 189).

One way to protect crops was to build barns robustly with chalk foundations, timber-framed superstructures, secure thatched roofs and carpentered doors, of which the large barn at Site 12 (Area 6) is an example. The storage capacity of the Wharram barns can be calculated with the help of a formula given in a 13th-century accounting treatise. This states that a stack of unthreshed wheat 30 feet long, 15 feet wide and 10 feet high would contain 40 quarters of grain, so a quarter of grain would have occupied 112.5 cubic feet (Oschinshky 1971, 475). The long barn on Site 12 had a capacity of 7000 cubic feet, assuming that sheaves stacked inside it would not reach any higher than 8 feet, because a narrow cruck building would have a lower roof than the large seigneurial barn which the treatise envisaged. More typical barns, though unexcavated, can be seen as well-defined earthworks in the West Row, for example in the toft immediately to the north of Site 12. This building is near to the standard dimensions of a three-bay cruck structure, 45 feet by 15 feet, which had a capacity of more than 5000 cubic feet. The large barn then could have contained 62 quarters of grain, and a smaller barn 44 quarters. A two-oxgang holding might have produced in an average year 32 quarters (see Table 19), so both of these buildings could have stored the crops from a large holding, and left some space for other purposes, such as sheltering implements, or storing fuel or hay. The crop would not have remained in sheaf for long, but would have been threshed a few bushels at a time through the autumn and winter as the corn was needed for consumption, seed or sale.

The pastoral side of Wharram's peasant farming can be investigated using animal bones, buildings, small finds and documents from nearby villages. The stints from four villages declared in the 13th century show that an oxgang could keep between fifteen and 30 adult sheep (with their lambs), two or three larger animals (cattle and horses), between one and three pigs, and four or five adult geese (Table 16). These were legal limits, designed to prevent the overburdening of common pastures with excessive numbers. As more tenants through the 14th and 15th centuries held multiple holdings with two, three and more oxgangs, flocks and herds could become much larger without breaking any rules. A wealthy tenant of

Table 19. Crops on an oxgang holding at Wharram Percy *c.* 1300. A speculation. The oxgang is presumed to be 18 ac., and that on a two course rotation 9 ac. are sown each year.

Description	Wheat	Barley	Oats	Peas/beans	Total of all crops
Acres planted(1)	3	3.5	1.5	1	9
Seed per acre(2)	3b	4.5b	7b	3.5b	
Total sown	9b	16b	10.5b	3.5b	39b
Yield ratio(3)	3.85	3.77	2.35	2.30	
Harvested	35b	60b	25b	8b	128b
Seed	9b	16b	10.5b	3.5b	39b
Crop – seed	26b	44b	14.5b	4.5b	89b
Food (4)	20b	30b	2b	1b	53b
Mill toll (1/16) (5)	1b	2b			3b
Surplus	5b	12b	12.5b	3.5b	33b
Rent (10s) (6)	5b (3s)	8b (3s 7d)	12.5b (3s 2d)	1b (3d)	26.5b
Remaining	0	4b	0	2.5b	6.5b

Notes: 1. The planted acres have been based on the crops on the demesne of Wetwang; 2. Seed per acre is based on Wetwang; 3. Yield ratios are based on a national average for the period, based on the assumption that tithe had been taken; 4. The food is based on peasant budgets in Dyer 1998; 5. Mill tolls are those for Birdsall, Yorkshire; 6. Rent is assumed to be 10s per annum, based on the 9s annual value put on an oxgang in the 1323 inquisition, assuming extra payments such as amercements. Some of the totals have been rounded up and down to the nearest bushel, as the whole calculation is very speculative.
Sources: TNA:PRO SC6 1144/1;1144/2;1144/4; 1144/10; Campbell 2000, 320; Dyer 1998, 114, 134-5; Holt 1988, 81

Fridaythorpe in 1392 probably was exceeding his limit with 180 sheep, six cows and two horses (*Cal Inq Misc* 6, 2). Tenants at Bishop Wilton in 1379-80, who were fined for allowing their animals to graze illicitly, owned flocks of sheep as large as 60, 80 and 100, and in some cases we learn about their other animals; one offender trespassed with four horses and 40 sheep. The proportions of different types of animal (Table 17) indicate the overwhelming preponderance of sheep, but this cannot be an accurate census of livestock, as pigs do not appear at all (Hull UL DD57/4/2/1084).

The relative importance of different types of livestock at Wharram emerges from the numbers of animal bones identified, with sheep leading the list, followed by cattle and pig (Richardson, ADS Report, doi:10.5284/1000415, Table 3). But these are a guide to consumption rather than the numbers kept, and are not strictly comparable with the figures derived from documents (Table 16). As horse meat was not normally eaten by humans, the horse bones should not be included in the sample, and their numbers might be distorted by the excavation, as we have seen, of specialist deposits. Goose bones cannot be expected to survive in large numbers, or be fully recorded, in view of their size and fragility.

A positive story can be told about the complementary role of livestock in the agrarian economy of Wharram and other villages which it resembles. Animals contributed to the efficiency of cultivation with their power of traction and supplies of manure. They needed less labour than corn growing, and the big events of the pastoral year, such as

lambing and shearing, did not clash with peaks of intense work in the corn field. Dairying, mostly between May and October, required mainly female labour, though for a time in late summer the corn harvest and cheese making must have competed for attention. The household enjoyed a varied diet because the preserved cheese and bacon could be eaten throughout the year, and the better-off households kept a store of salted beef or mutton, which may explain the pieces of wooden barrels from the pond site, though ale may have been kept in them (Morris 2005, 140-41). The livestock also helped the cash economy of the household through the sale of wool and cheese. In about 1300 a fleece from the wolds fetched about 8d, so a better-off peasant with twenty adult sheep could hope for an annual income of 13s 4d. Wolds wool growers had the advantage over others at the time because their fleeces were quite heavy, at about 2lbs each, and they fetched a price towards the higher end of the scale (TNA:PRO SC6 1144/2, 1144/4). When the lactage of ewes was rented out at Bishop Wilton in the 14th century each animal was rated at 2½d in each milking season, so ten ewes were worth about 2s per annum (TNA:PRO SC6 1144/2).

This happy picture of pastoral and arable farming working together for the good of the peasant community needs some qualifications. We have already seen that the Wharram township contained limited amounts of land for permanent pasture and meadow. Other villages countered this problem by gaining access to pastures outside their boundaries, like the peasants of Duggleby who rented a piece of wold land in the parish of Settrington, and the wold pasture of Wetwang Rakes which was intercommoned by the villagers of Wetwang and Bishop Wilton (TNA: PRO SC12 23/13; VCH 8, 249). Wharram people might have been able to rent grazing or buy hay; for example, the sale of hay and herbage from Bishop Wilton is recorded, and this was probably the practice on a number of Wold edge manors, and so in theory grass and hay were available to people from the higher ground. Part of the grain crop was fed to animals. At Wetwang in 1316-17, when exceptionally wet weather in the summer spoiled the hay, the affers were given peas 'in place of hay'(TNA: PRO 1144/4). Lords fed their animals sparingly with peas, oats and drage in normal years, and we must suppose that peasants also fed some crops to livestock, but in even smaller quantities because their supplies were more limited. At every point animal husbandry underlined the social stratification of the village. The stints defined the limits on an oxgang, and we suspect that smallholders owned few or no animals. The most successful keepers of flocks and herds must have been those who could afford to grow crops for fodder.

The stress of finding feed for livestock is apparent in all the written sources. The 13th-century stints show that villages and their lords were concerned that the limited grazing might be overburdened. The court rolls of Bishop Wilton of 1379-80 contain dozens of actions taken against peasants who allowed their animals to graze beyond the customary limits, and in March 1380 special measures were taken to catch the offenders when five leading peasants were appointed as a 'plebiscite'(Hull UL DD 57/4/2/1084).

The bones from the Wharram excavations show that the animals were small in size. Horses, for example, attained a maximum of fifteen hands and more commonly stood at about twelve hands, so they resembled modern ponies. Even the poultry was small, and the hens were no bigger than modern bantams (Ryder 1974, 48). Their size may have been appropriate for the local breeds, but it may also reflect the standard of nutrition. Some of the molar teeth of horses were pitted by a condition that has been linked with poor feeding (Ryder 1974, 45).

Setting aside the problems of grazing and fodder, only a little is known about the methods of animal husbandry practised by peasants. Our fragmentary evidence for byres and stables suggest that larger animals were likely to be housed, but were the sheep kept indoors in the winter? A pasture at Thixendale belonging to St Mary's Abbey York had a *bercaria*, a sheephouse or sheepcote, built on it, and a sheephouse attached to Wharram Grange belonged to the monks of Meaux. These buildings figure regularly in the documents for other seigneurial sheep pastures on the Wolds. If the flocks of the lords were normally provided with them, did peasants build smaller versions, as was the case in the Gloucestershire Cotswolds, for example? Mention has already been made of buildings located at the rear of the Wharram tofts, of which the best example is a rectangular structure just outside the west boundary of Site 12 (Area 6). This measures approximately 18m by 6m, and using the formula that each sheep that was 'cotted' needed a square yard of floor space, it had the capacity for at least 80 sheep, which is the size of flock that the tenant of a large holding (four oxgangs) is likely to have owned.

Some methods of pastoral farming found on demesnes may have been practised by peasants. The managers running the estates of the archbishops of York supplemented the diet of lambs by buying cows' milk, perhaps as part of a strategy of maximising production of sheep's milk. Peasants may also have valued the income from the sale of sheep's cheese and did something similar. We do not know if peasant sheep were treated with grease and tar to protect them from disease, which was standard practice for demesne flocks. Nor does any document record that sheep belonging to peasants were washed before shearing, which would be necessary if the wool was going to be sold alongside that of the demesne flocks. The Wharram peasants had access to running water in the stream which flowed on the eastern side of the village. In two small respects we have more information about peasant sheep than exists for the demesne flocks. The purchase of a bell for a sheep leading the flock is rarely mentioned in manorial accounts, but examples of such bells have been found at Wharram (for example Goodall I.H. 1979, 121), and there are parallels from other village sites. Neither do dogs feature in the manorial documents, but the bones from Wharram and other villages show that they were kept in some numbers, and finds of swivel rings may have come from dog chains. Keeping these animals might have been to the advantage of good sheep husbandry, if dogs were trained to drive them to the pasture, but if they were not obedient, the worrying of sheep could have been a problem.

Documents can sometimes unwittingly reveal commonplaces of thought and life normally hidden from view. When Yorkshire peasants made their wills, they wished to identify precisely the animal which should go to a particular individual. Richard de Ley, a husbandman of Huggate, a Wolds village south of Wetwang, in 1461 bequeathed a horse called Bosse; other wills mention animals' distinguishing marks like a filly with a white forehead (Raine 1855, 249; York Minster Library L2/4, f.353v). Peasants clearly knew their stock well, and this encourages us to have high expectations of the standard of care that the animals received.

A final point about the villagers' relationship with animals is to observe the very small contribution that hunting made to peasants' incomes, judging from the few finds of arrow heads of the type suitable for shooting wild animals and birds, and the limited number of bones of deer or wild birds.

An assessment needs to be made of the contribution of labour to production on the peasant holding. During the lifecycle of a peasant family the bulk of the labour necessary for cultivating the 18 acres of an oxgang could have come from the resources of the household, if the father of the house and a son of working age were both available, but in many circumstances extra resources were needed. This might be necessary if the children were young, or no sons were born to a couple, or if young people left for employment elsewhere. Outward migration, mainly by young women, was a particular problem in the western Wolds because the bright lights and employment prospects of York beckoned.

Other reasons for a household's deficit of labour included illness or death, which might leave a wife or widow in charge of the land, or indeed a widower without the essential aid of an active female in the garden and dairy. Even if a 'nuclear' family of parents and children were working the land, the harvest would put them under pressure. If a substantial burden of labour service on the lord's demesne was required, the household might have to find the 50 or more days of work to fulfil its obligations. These problems would be felt more acutely if the holding consisted of two or more oxgangs (Fox 1996).

A source of employable labour would have come from the cottagers, of whom six are recorded in 1323, and twelve in 1368. There are eleven tofts in the East Row which is likely to have been the section of the village where the cottagers lived, though by 1368 cottage holdings seem to have been scattered around the settlement. They would have been hired by the day, and in the period before 1349 when they could expect not much more than 1d per day a man would have to work for many months each year to earn enough to feed a family. Many holdings, especially those which contained two or three oxgangs, would have taken in young people as servants. At Thixendale, where a 1381 poll tax assessment guides us to the likely content of the missing Wharram return, there were sixteen substantial households, that is married couples among whom were the employers of labour, especially the wealthy six who paid 2s 6d to 3s 6d rather than the norm of 2s as the tax was supposed to yield 12d per head (Fenwick 2005, 212). Of the nineteen single people, nine contributed only 4d to the tax suggesting their modest means, almost certainly because they were working as servants, living in their employers' houses and receiving most of their pay in the form of board and lodging. They would agree to a contract which committed them for a whole year.

The family was often not self-sufficient in labour, and nor was the village itself. Workers were frequently in movement, especially in the harvest season. This became controversial after 1349 because the law forbade workers to refuse an offer of employment in order to leave the village. But this was precisely the complaint against Sibilla, daughter of Alice del Holm, who left Fimber in 1361 to find work (and better wages). A married couple from the small town of Pocklington went off in the harvest season 'up to the wold', and York workers followed suit, enjoying the break from city life as well as the good money and ample food with which harvest workers were rewarded (Goldberg 1995, 105). Workers like Emma Cave of Langton refused to accept an annual contract as a servant, but preferred the freedom, independence and better pay of working by the day (Putnam 1939, 59, 69-70, 72).

The serious labour problem of the later middle ages made it very difficult to maintain the intensive and laborious tasks that had been taken for granted in earlier centuries, such as weeding and dairying. Workers were better paid, and peasants probably gained higher incomes from their larger holdings, but the productivity of each acre of land must have fallen as peasants skimped on ploughing, weeding and processing flax and hemp. The problem of labour went deeper than the number of workers and their rates of pay. Family labour was presumably well motivated, but workers who resented annual contracts and who were tempted by better prospects in other villages and towns may not always have been enthusiastic and productive.

Exchanging and marketing

Were the Wharram peasants producing for their own use, or for exchange and sale? When the Wharram research began, self-sufficiency was emphasised; now we expect to find that villages like Wharram were integrated into the late medieval commercial world. The reconstruction of the production of a Wharram oxgang (Table 19) shows that in a normal year a modest surplus of 33 bushels of grain would be left after seed was deducted, and after an allowance has been made for the crops consumed as food by the family, and the mill toll. If rent money (conservatively estimated at 10s) had to come from the sale of this grain, then virtually none would be left for any other purpose. But in practice the rent money is much more likely to have come from the sale of animal produce, such as wool, dairy produce and animals, in which case part of the surplus grain could have been used for brewing ale for the family. Some of the oats and legumes may also have been set aside to feed animals. Any money to spend on buildings, purchase of animals, equipment, utensils or clothing and so on would also have come from the sale of animal products, and we may doubt if many holdings had much cash to spare – we estimated above that wool and cheese might bring in about 15s. In other words, tenure of an oxgang provided its tenants with a living, but no great rewards.

We have seen, however, that some Wharram tenants in the 13th century held two oxgangs, and multiple holdings became more common in the 14th century. A reconstruction of the 'bottom line' of such a holding gives a more optimistic picture. All the figures in Table 19 should be doubled to reflect the 18 acres under crops, giving a total of produce after the seed has been deducted amounting to 178 bushels. The family, however, might be rather larger, and a servant might be employed, but food consumption would not be double that of the oxgang holder's household. If 65 bushels were used in food and four bushels consequently went in mill tolls, the tenant would still have a surplus of 109 bushels, or more than thirteen quarters. The household could have drunk ale regularly, fed their animals with a share of the crops, and still sent six quarters to market with a possible return of 30s, to which can be added the rewards of selling twice as many fleeces and cheeses as the single oxgang holder, as the stint of animals would be double. A two-oxgang tenant in a good year could have gained an income in excess of £3, though £1 of this would be paid in rent, and he would be liable to pay a shilling or two in taxes.

Grain and cheese would have been taken to market by cart, and animals driven there, but the smaller quantities of garden produce, eggs and butter, and the yarn from spinning flax and hemp, may have been carried in baskets by the women producers. Malton was the nearest market town, but the various records of contacts between wold villages around Wharram and towns also make mention of Pocklington to the south, Kilham to the east, and of course Beverley and York.

Wool was handled by specialist traders, some of whom operated in official markets such as Malton, but they also came to the villages. In a typical transaction recorded in the early 1360s William Hugot of Pocklington bought a half sack of wool from John Holm of Fridaythorpe. Those who sold the wool must have been middlemen, as a number of them disposed of a sack or two, representing 180-360 fleeces, which came from more sheep than an average non-seigneurial wool grower would keep. The traders who bought the wool, who came from Beverley and York as well as from Pocklington and Malton, probably sold it to a local cloth maker, or it was exported through Hull (Putnam 1939, 13-16, 23).

Some exchange was confined within the village. The cottagers whose main income came from wages would have bought grain and other foodstuffs from their neighbours. This type of sale would explain the possession of a bushel measure by a peasant, such as William Akclum of Wharram le Street (see p. 342). Brewing ale for sale would have been an extension of household brewing. A pattern of ale selling at Bishop Wilton in 1379 resembles that found in many villages and may have been practised at Wharram. Six women were amerced for charging too high a price (breaking the assize) and for failing to erect a sign. The sign (or ale stake) was necessary as the house selling ale was a peasant dwelling, temporarily converted. Some of the women came from better-off households, and were adding value to the holding's surplus of barley (Hull UL DD57/4/2/1084).

Meat was also processed and exchanged between villagers. Animals may have been sent to market for sale to urban butchers, from whom peasants could buy joints of meat. The bones, however, show that animals were slaughtered and butchered in the village, as the skull and bones from the other less palatable parts are found. Those who cut up the animals did not follow the usual practices of the urban craft, which began by splitting the carcase, which shows that the job was carried out either by an untrained rural butcher, or by a peasant (Richardson 2005b, 238). The fresh meat would presumably have been distributed among village households within a short time, for money which under normal procedures would not necessarily be paid immediately. The practice of salting beef and mutton has already been mentioned, and bacon would be salted and smoked. The by-products of butchery, the hides and horns for example, would have been sold to town traders; and the tallow too, but it could have been processed into candles in the village.

Perhaps peasants did not so much sell their produce for cash, but practised exchange and barter among themselves? Peasants who made their wills, which tended to be the wealthier individuals, apparently had few coins to bequeath, and instead left goods to their relatives and friends – Richard de Ley of Huggate for example, in 1461, left six stones of wool, eight wethers, two horses, a bullock and five quarters and two bushels of barley (Raine 1855, 249). Villagers had to handle some cash, as external demands from the lords and the state would only be satisfied by payments in money. At Wharram a rent of 9s per oxgang is mentioned in 1323, and 7s per annum in 1436 for a messuage and oxgang. These rents are recorded after a period of some difficulty and likely reductions in rent. In 1279 other oxgangs in the Wolds villages of Garton and Birdsall were paying as much as 12s 8d and 13s 4d, and at Wharram le Street in 1397 the standard rent for an oxgang was 10s (Brown 1892, 187-8, 195; BL Cott Vit C vi, 215r-215v). Extra charges included entry fines which might be more than a year's rent, such as the fine levied at Bishop Wilton for 23s 4d for an oxgang (Hull UL DD57/4/2/1084). The state required less money, and not every year, but the peasant still had to dig into his purse or sell produce to obtain the cash – 1s 11d for the leading tax payer at Wharram Percy in 1297 for example. From 1334 the whole village was expected to find 18s every time that the lay subsidy was levied (Brown 1894b, 147, 149).

Finds of coins from the excavations show that money was part of the village's material culture, but does not suggest that it played a very important role. Only eighteen coins of the period 1100-1500, mostly pennies and halfpence, have been found, of which only two came from the main peasant house excavations in Site 9 and Site 12 (Barclay 2007, 301-4). A hundred pennies must have passed through the hands of each Wharram peasant each year, but each was so valuable that they were kept safely, and any loss was followed by a thorough search. A hint of the presence of coins which are not found comes from the coin weight which was used to check the weight of gold nobles, worth 6s 8d each, much used at the end of the middle ages, and metal hooks for hanging a purse on to a belt again show that money was a presence in the village (Barclay 2007, 304; Goodall A.R 1989, 46-7; Goodall I.H. 1979, 123). Jettons (counters for use in financial calculations) may have circulated as informal small change.

The circulation of coins was not incompatible with a good deal of bartering and complex credit arrangements, as the latter depended on an acceptance by all parties of money as a means of assigning values to good and services. At Bishop Wilton, William Keen had bought cloth from Richard Taillour, and in 1379 they fell into dispute because Keen had failed to pay. They both seem to have agreed that the cloth was worth 2s 4d. If two parties who exchanged labour and goods trusted one another they could wait for months and years until a 'reckoning' established the balance that was due for payment. This practice was recorded in the 15th century in the archives of Fountains Abbey (Fowler 1918, 201-47). Two wills from Wharram le Street dated to 1481 and 1511 provide ample evidence of money lending as well as delayed payments forming part of networks of credit. These had a negative dimension, as unfortunate borrowers might end their days in serious financial difficulty, but credit also helped healthy and active tenants to build houses and barns, buy livestock and implements, and engage successfully in the market (see p. 347).

In an age when much industry was located in the countryside, the Wharram villagers depended almost entirely on agriculture. Some leather working was indicated by a few offcuts preserved in the damp conditions of the pond, awls and specialised knives from the peasant house sites, and some iron smelting and smithing was practised over a number of sites. Tools such as a chisel and a bit suggest some contact with the more specialised aspects of woodworking. The main participation in craft work must have been the preparation and spinning of yarn from flax, hemp and wool, which is attested by finds of teeth from wool and flax combs, and spindle whorls of which 22 came from the two main peasant sites. This was women's work – which could be combined with other tasks in the house or yard. It is always possible that some cloth was made at Wharram, but it is more likely that the yarn was sold for weaving in a town or specialist manufacturing centre in the countryside. Clothes could be made at home, judging from finds of a thimble, pins, needles and a pair of scissors. An unexpected and rather inexplicable pair of finds – a weight for a net and large fish hook – could mean that a Wharram peasant also worked as a fisherman on the coast.

Although the peasants of Wharram sold commodities and made a profit, advanced credit and borrowed money, invested in buildings and livestock, and even through their sales of quite highly priced wool contributed to international trade, they cannot be regarded as belonging to a capitalist economy. They produced without specialisation with an eye on household consumption, and inhabited a world dominated by family, lordship and community. Wharram's peasants had a strong sense of private ownership, which led them to define precisely their toft boundaries, and to keep chests and doors locked, yet they still belonged to a community which ruled over many aspects of their lives, including the use of the common fields and their access to grazing. They shared assets, such as the pinfold, pond and oven. And at various stages the peasant community built or maintained the fabric of the community's most important asset, the parish church.

Changing and declining

This exploration of the peasants and production should lead us to a convincing explanation of Wharram's decline, but this is not possible. Many comparisons have been made between Wharram and other villages, especially those in its vicinity. All of them have a generic similarity, in topography, fields, tenures and much else, yet they diverged dramatically. Wharram was deserted, along with Burdale, Mowthorpe, Raisthorpe, Towthorpe and others. Thixendale, however, together with Duggleby, Fimber, North Grimston, Wharram le Street and the rest have survived. Explaining Wharram's decline has to be attempted in a comparative light, with reference to the numerous deserted villages throughout England as well as the settlements on the Yorkshire wolds (see further, pp 359-64).

We are tempted to pick out small, ill-favoured, underprivileged places such as Raisthorpe, which seemed doomed to disintegrate as troubled times exposed their weaknesses. Such small, outlying settlements without a parish church or other assets figure prominently among deserted villages everywhere, but not all deserted villages fit that model. Wharram Percy appeared to enjoy many advantages. It was large, with almost 40 houses at its height; it had a substantial parish church and at various times its lords were resident. It must have looked impressive with its planned lines of houses along the edge of the valley, which would have been a matter for pride for its lords, and indeed for the inhabitants. The villagers included a majority of tenants of oxgangs and multiples of that unit, with good land in the well-ordered fields characteristic of the district. Unlike other villages it had a steady water supply and water-mills.

Wharram does not seem to have suffered from fundamental problems. It was not provided with much pasture, meadow and woodland, but some arrangement must have enabled the villagers to gain access to fuel and fodder. Most of the villagers were customary tenants, but they were not heavily burdened with rents and services. At the point when the village was going downhill in the early 15th century an annual rent of 7s for a messuage and oxgang looks far from a deterrent for tenants or would-be tenants. Cottars were in short supply, which may have caused labour problems. Although Wharram was not as remote in relation to the road system as is now the case, the journey to a market town was inconveniently long. Apart from some spinning among the women, the villagers lived entirely from agriculture.

The last 250 years of Wharram's history poses problems and presents us with a series of paradoxes. Firstly, here was a big village, an important place in its district, and well provided with corn and sheep. This is difficult to reconcile with its miserable poverty as depicted in the tax records. In 1297 it could muster only five tax payers. Duggleby had seven, and Wetwang fourteen. Wharram made a contribution of 6s 1$\frac{1}{2}$d, which places it at 40th position in the 49 villages in Buckrose wapentake (Brown 1894b, 144-9). If the earthworks are a guide to the number of families at the end of the 13th century, more than 30 households were judged too poor to pay anything. It was no better in 1334, when Wharram's tax quota was fixed at 18s when neighbouring villages were thought capable of paying on average 33s

(Beresford M.W. 1979, 11). The poverty of the village in the 1330s can be blamed on the Scottish raids, but those attacks were a distant memory in the 1360s and 1370s. Then there is a discrepancy in the poll tax of 1377, when wealth was not assessed – everyone paid 4d, but at Wharram only 30 people did so, implying a dozen inhabited houses, as two or three individuals would be liable to tax from each household. The survey of 1368 would lead us to expect double that number. Rents seem to confirm the story of the tax assessments. In 1436 an oxgang and messuage at Wharram Percy was paying 7s per annum, when the equivalent at Wharram le Street was charged with 10s to 12s. Even higher figures are found at Settrington and North Grimston (BL Cott Vit C vi, f 229r-229v; TNA:PRO SC12/23/13; Tringham 2002, 97). Lords did not charitably lower the rents of prosperous tenants. So, inexplicably, a village which bulks large, even rather grandly in material terms, looks small and poor in the written records.

This might prompt us to attribute Wharram's desertion to this apparent poverty. A second paradox, however, appears on the eve of the village's terminal phase, in which individual prosperity has to be reconciled with the decay of the settlement. The documents show that tenants were acquiring three-oxgang (54 acre) holdings in the 14th century, and later larger farms are revealed by the archaeological evidence. The house measuring 25m on Site 12 (Area 6), which at some stage of its life stood next to a long barn, represents the messuage to which one of these larger units was attached, and we have seen that it shows many signs of its tenant's relative affluence. The existence of at least three more large holdings have been proposed in other parts of the village on the strength of their earthworks. The tenants presumably diverged from the traditional husbandry by converting part of the arable in their oxgangs to grazing land. An early 16th-century holding of 52 acres at Settrington was described as consisting of arable, pasture and meadow, while nearer to home, land in the fields of Wharram le Street had been converted in 1397 to leys, that is pasture on former arable (TNA:PRO SC12/23/13; BL Cott Vit C vi, f. 229r-229v). These technical changes in the use of land were linked in other Wolds villages with the rise of a notable peasant elite, such as the eight tenants with three to four oxgangs at Settrington in 1536 accounting for a sixth of the holdings in that manor.

The settlement at Wharram was being remodelled, no doubt on the initiative of its tenants as we find elsewhere, and the settlement probably had a future as a relatively small village with a group of large holdings served by labourers and servants. This happened at Hazleton (Glos.) and the village has survived (Dyer and Aldred 2009). At Wharram in the first half of the 16th century, a reversal in fortune left the large farms abandoned, and brought in large-scale specialist sheep farming, as we shall see in Chapter 22 (pp 356-9). Peasant cultivation, even the yeoman production of the last generations which combined arable and pasture, had come to an end.

20 The Late Medieval Village of Wharram Percy: Living and Consuming

by Christopher Dyer with contributions from Ann Clark, Jane Richardson and Anna Slowikowski

This chapter will explore the inner life of the village and its inhabitants. The Wharram villagers of the period 1200-1550 will be examined in their various roles: as members of families, as inhabitants of houses, as a human population, as consumers of food, fuel and other goods, and as members of a community. At the end, the villagers' own perceptions of their lives will be explored. Neighbouring communities cited in this chapter are located on Figure 113.

Living in houses

Families and households are rightly regarded as the fundamental building blocks from which medieval society was constructed. The two words were almost interchangeable, but from the modern perspective the 'family' refers to a group of people related to one another, whereas the 'household' includes relatives and non-relatives (who were usually servants) living together. A proportion of the houses at Wharram at any one time are likely to have contained a simple 'nuclear family' consisting of parents and a few children. The poll taxes of 1381 for nearby villages do not record many complete families because children evaded or were exempted from payment, but occasionally we glimpse a family with children over the age of fifteen, who were liable for tax. At Thirkleby, William Maw and his wife were listed with a son, John, and a daughter, Agnes. They shared out their tax liability of 4s: the parents contributed 3s 0d and the children 6d each, reflecting their limited contribution to the family's income.

Servants were listed more frequently than children. Among the tax-paying households at Helperthorpe, John Sumervyle and his wife, who were relatively wealthy, had two servants, Robert and Thomas, both of whom paid the minimal tax of 4d. The Sumervyles may have had children too young to pay tax, or to work on the land, so the servants would have been engaged to join the household until the children were old enough; alternatively there may have been no children, or they had died, or left home. Richard de Ley of Huggate similarly mentions in his will of 1461 his wife Elizabeth and two male servants, but no children. At Wetwang in 1381, 23 of the 103 people paying poll tax were single, thirteen of them female, who in most cases would have lived as servants in their employers' houses. Some of the single people listed at Wetwang and other villages represent one person households, such as those of widows (Fenwick 2005, 209, 213, 214; Raine 1855, 249). We can be confident that the houses at Wharram would have contained conventional nuclear families, households with one or two servants, and single person households.

Families might have consisted of three generations, when grandparents or a grandparent became dependent on a married son or daughter, who themselves had children. The connection between the older generation and their offspring is recorded in contracts for maintenance in manorial court rolls, for example those from the 14th century from the Yorkshire manor of Hatfield (Poos and Bonfield 1998, 65-6). Often, the retired peasants, having surrendered their holding of land to a successor, were provided with separate accommodation, which might be a converted farm building (see pp 314-15). Some of the smaller buildings visible at the rear of tofts at Wharram may have served this purpose at some stage of their existence.

Outsiders expected that each household would be headed by an adult male, or if he had died, by a widow, and these individuals had obligations on behalf of the whole domestic group. They would be responsible for the payment of rent and services to the lord, taxes to the state, and church dues (such as tithe), and they were expected to ensure that members of the household behaved in an orderly fashion. The head would call on the rest of the household to work on the holding, and he or she would negotiate with neighbours over lending and borrowing equipment or animals, and they might arrange with outsiders the sale of produce and hiring of labour. Young people were integrated into society and the workforce through experience gained in the household, which meant that boys learnt how to farm, and girls were trained in brewing and cheese-making as well as acquiring domestic skills (Goldberg 1992, 158-94).

In the 13th century most holdings consisted of an oxgang or two, which makes the village appear rather uniform and egalitarian. There was always, however, a hierarchy, and from the heads of households an elite emerged who acted as manorial officials, like the individuals who took it in turn to administer the manor as grave (reeve), and the twelve who served as jurors in the manor court. The hierarchical tendency would have increased with the growth of larger land holdings in the 14th century. A minority of peasants could expand their holdings and rise to the top, but villages also provided a safety net to prevent extreme poverty and deprivation. The open-field system worked through allocating land, both good land and less fertile, to everyone, and the cultivators followed the same routines so that all those involved had a good chance at least of a modest living. People buried in the churchyard include a few who suffered from some permanent disability since infancy, who clearly received care adequate for them to survive into adulthood in spite of their disadvantages (Mays 2007, 150-53). They were presumably helped by their family. Also, from the evidence of the churchyard, families, or sometimes perhaps the community, ensured that everyone received a decent burial.

Villages and traditional societies have a reputation for enforcing conventions of behaviour. In a medieval parish, for example, those who failed to attend church, or who worked on the Sabbath or saints' days, or who committed sins such as fornication or adultery, would be reported to the church courts (Poos 2001). In the secular courts, not just offences against the rules of the open-field system, but also irregular behaviour such as playing illicit games, gossiping or scolding would have been presented and punished (McIntosh 1998). The Wharram evidence, again from analysis of the cemetery, suggests a tolerance of some deviant behaviour. Left-handedness is apparent in 16 per cent of the population, judging from the development of left and right arms visible from the skeleton, suggesting that the right-handed majority allowed a degree of non-conformity (Mays 2007, 118).

Young people were not generally given too much freedom in their sexual relations or in their choice of marriage partners. A church court in 1312 heard that Matilda Nunn of Bugthorp and Walter Cobbe of North Grimston, an unmarried couple, were notorious for their carnal relationship, and Alice le Bakester, aged 60, had through a window observed them together, alone and naked, in a chamber in Bugthorp, a village just to the west of Wharram (BIA, CP.E.6). The courts also heard many matrimonial cases, to which they applied strict rules on the forms of words and actions which established a valid marriage. If uncontrolled sexual contacts and early and casual marriages were permitted, the very fabric of agrarian society was threatened. Marriage was delayed by general agreement until the parties to the union had acquired the skills and the land on which family life and child-bearing could be based. Holdings could not be divided, and the rules of primogeniture meant that a younger son could not inherit part of the core holding, but would have to find land or a job elsewhere. The hereditary succession had to be clearly based on legitimate offspring.

The village plan at Wharram, with its orderly rows of tofts and crofts, represents much more than a neat settlement plan. It reflected at the core of the village territory the conservative tenurial pattern of oxgangs which applied to all the land around it. New holdings, we might imagine, could be added only in a controlled way, and existing units remained intact; they served as an insurance policy against overpopulation and impoverishment. The plan and the orderly arrangement of tenures would in practice have been changed and subverted – land could have been sublet, and lodgers and landless workers accommodated in corners of the toft, just as families and households varied from the ideal nuclear model (Fox 1996). The occasional insubstantial buildings, like that excavated on the North Manor site, may be a material reflection of these departures from the conventional social structures (see p. 315).

Were women constrained by this hierarchical and regulated society? They could hold land, by inheritance or when they acquired a joint tenancy with a husband, as became increasingly common in the late 14th century in Yorkshire, as in the rest of England (Smith 1991). They became tenants and heads of household in widowhood, as long as they did not remarry. At Bishop Wilton (on the edge of the Wolds) for which manorial court rolls have survived, a number of women brewed ale for sale, and were themselves held responsible for their breaches of rules (rather than their husbands, as happened sometimes). Women also appeared on their own behalf in litigation about debt, and they kept flocks of geese apparently on their own account. There seems to have been a defined sphere of female activity, centred on the house, garden and toft, where they worked and took initiatives. We suspect that wives played a part in decisions about the purchase of household items, such as furnishings and ceramics. The assumption by all around them that widows could take over the holding when their husbands died suggests that they had become familiar with the management of the land during their husbands' life time, implying some element of partnership between husband and wife.

On a more negative note, females were expected to do chores connected with the preparation of food and drink, such as fetching water from the pond or stream. Bone studies for Wharram show that their arms were well developed through hard labour, a feature which they did not share with women living in towns in the same period (Mays 2007, 122-3). Their leg bones bear traces of the squatting posture that they repeatedly adopted while cooking, laundering and performing other household tasks (Mays 2007, 125-6). They were excluded from office in manor and village, although they played a part in public events such as church services. In many aspects and stages of their lives they were subordinated to males – fathers, brothers, husbands and even sons – but nonetheless they have left their marks on the material remains of the village (Bennett 1987).

The houses that provided living space for peasant families present modern scholars with numerous problems. Longhouses, in which people and animals were accommodated under the same roof, have caused much debate (p. 315), and for many years it was believed that, apart from the byres at the end of longhouses, there were few buildings designed entirely for agricultural use. Now we are satisfied, mainly by analogy with other settlements, that Wharram houses were often specialised dwellings, without any byre end, but there are still difficulties in distinguishing between these and the barns and other agricultural structures. The presence of a hearth is an important clue to a building's domestic use, though some rooms intended for human occupation were traditionally unheated.

The conventional classification of medieval peasant rooms emphasises the divide between hall and chamber, with other less well defined spaces or separate buildings for services, storage or food preparation. The hall must be the focus of our attention because the presence of the hearth ought to make it relatively easy to identify. The best example of a hall is that in Building 1 on Site 12 (Area 6), which was a large house abandoned in the last stages of Wharram's desertion, leaving the internal arrangements relatively undisturbed and therefore discoverable by excavation (see pp 340-42). A cross passage between opposed doorways shows that it conformed to a conventional house plan, and the first hearth was placed close to the passage and near to the centre of the house. Later it was moved to the side, still near to the screen which defined one side of the cross passage, and it was fitted with a smoke hood or timber-framed chimney. Various features around the hearth, such as a broken stone mortar and a pot set into the floor, suggest that some food preparation was carried out near to the hearth (Wrathmell 1989b 23-30).

There is no clear evidence at Wharram for specialised kitchens or bakehouses, though Building 9 in Site 12 (Area 7) had two hearths (or a hearth and an oven according to another version), and a pit for water storage at one stage of its use. Building 4 on Site 9 (Area 10) also had two hearths, one of which again is a suggested oven, though it does not conform to the normal oven form (Wrathmell 1989b, 17-19, 38-40). Chambers are almost impossible to identify, as they contained no hearth or other distinguishing feature. The end of the incomplete Building 8 on Site 8 (Area 5) contained a group of broken jugs of the 15th century, which might suggest that the space was used for the storage or serving of drink, and there are parallels for such pottery groups in or near to chambers on other sites (Wrathmell 1989b, 33-8; Moorhouse 1986).

Inventories from Wharram le Street throw light on the likely arrangements of rooms and furnishings at Wharram Percy. William Akclum in 1481 had a chamber with bedding, a chest, household textiles and pots. The inventory then has another heading of the 'house', which shows that those listing the dead man's possessions had moved to another room. The list begins with the expected contents of a hall, with a chair, table, dishes, a spit, but then without a break moves on to livestock, farm equipment and crops, and one does not know when the description of the hall ends (pp 342-3 and Plate 35; BIA, D and C wills, 1481, Akclum). A better-ordered inventory of 1511 is for Thomas Grissaker. He was vicar of Wharram le Street, which puts him into a social category superior to the peasantry, but his house may not have been so much grander. He had a chamber with bedding and chests, and equipment for carding and spinning yarn. His hall had a chair, table, cupboard and preserved meat, bacon and beef. The cooking equipment was kept in a separate kitchen (BIA D and C wills, 1511, Grissaker). The division between hall and chamber, and sometimes with a separate kitchen is repeated in a number of peasant inventories of the late 15th century which have survived, unusually for the period, for the inhabitants of villages in the vicinity of York (see pp 345-7).

The quality of the Wharram buildings has also been a matter for controversy. The rather ragged lines of chalk blocks which appear in excavations look very inferior to the neat stone walling, sometimes rising to at least six courses, which are found when peasant buildings are excavated on Dartmoor, or in the Cotswolds, or in the uplands of Northumberland. The Wharram peasants were conscious of the inferior quality of their building materials, and interspersed among the pieces of chalk, they placed sandstone blocks many of which had been taken from the ruinous 12th-century manor house. In view of the amateurish and fragile nature of the foundations, we can understand the assumptions that developed among the Wharram excavators that the superstructure would have been roughly assembled from branches by the peasants themselves, and that at regular intervals the whole structure needed to be rebuilt.

It is now believed that the Wharram houses in the 13th century went through the same transition as in the rest of England from buildings depending on vertical timbers set in the ground, to framed structures based on horizontal sills on stone foundations, or trusses standing on padstones. Chalk blocks, the only easily available and plentiful local stone, were adequate means of raising the timbers above the ground. The chalk walls were not the most important or durable part of the building – the timber frame with its substantial crucks could have been long lived, and periodically the underpinning of chalk could be rearranged and renewed under the beams, while the timbers were propped, without rebuilding the whole structure (Wrathmell 1989c, 3-14). The Wharram houses resembled those found throughout late medieval England, built in two or three bays in most cases, so measuring approximately 10-15m in length and 5m in width.

Like peasant houses elsewhere, smoke hoods and internal chimneys were being fitted in the 15th century. The roof around the smoke hole was provided with a patch of slates or ceramic tiles to protect the thatch from sparks (Milne 1979c, 72; Andrews 1979a, 131-2). Windows, which would have been small, were equipped with wooden shutters on iron hinges. Doors might be swung on pivot stones rather than hinges. The Wharram houses occasionally have features not encountered everywhere, such as a gavel fork at the end of a building, that is, an extra lateral cruck supporting a hipped roof, rather than gables. Building 1 on Site 12 (Area 6) with its ten bays is one of the largest village houses known in England, and it was apparently fitted with some window glass in lead cames (Goodall A.R. 1979 , 115), which did not spread generally to ordinary rural houses until well into the 16th century. Other examples of rather superior building materials include the tile and slate roof (probably built in succession) on Building 1 on Site 76, and the plentiful nails in the roof of Building 1 on Site 9 (Area 10), though these may not have been dwellings.

Some features of peasant houses in other regions have not been noted at Wharram. Upper rooms, for example, have left no trace and may not have existed. And chalk walls on other sites also built in the 15th century, such as those at nearby Cowlam, seem superior to those at Wharram, with neatly squared blocks surviving up to six courses high (Hayfield and Brewster 1988, 21-109). There is no reason, however, to regard Wharram houses as much inferior to those in other villages. They would, for example, have had their timber frames built by specialist carpenters, with timber brought from a distance, which would have incurred considerable expense, usually for the tenant. As an indication of cost, in order to encourage a tenant to carry out repairs to a messuage at Kilham (a Wolds settlement) in the early 15th century the lord made a grant of 40s or £2 (BL Harleian rolls, H12). The full outlay for rebuilding would have been much more than this.

The Wharram houses might be judged to have various deficiencies, but they provided those who inhabited them with adequate space for sleeping and eating. A three-bay house gave each of its occupants an area in excess of 100 sq feet, which was more spacious than many working-class houses of the 19th century (Dyer 1986). They had a sense of privacy and were able to exclude outsiders by surrounding the toft with walls and hedges, and kept their possessions behind locked doors and shuttered windows, and in locked chests. The hall, however, had a purpose as a public room, and the records of the church court sometimes contain reports of ceremonies in the hall. When Nicholas Thomson, alias Wilson, of Wharram Percy exchanged marriage vows with Katherine Pynkney of Uncleby in January the couple and, presumably, the more important guests stood in the hall, and a large crowd overflowed into the garden or yard outside and watched and listened through the open door (the case was heard in 1526). In better weather, at Whitsun at Settrington, the whole ceremony for Katherine Anger's marriage was held in the garden, a court was told in 1489 (BIA, CP G. 180; CP. F.273).

Living and dying

Normally, a discussion of the daily life of medieval peasants has to assess their health and welfare from the indirect evidence of housing and diet. Wharram's population, however, is uniquely well documented through the bones of the inhabitants, which have been recovered in greater numbers than from any other English village, and have been subjected to an especially rigorous and searching analysis. The chronology of the burials does not quite match that of the peasant buildings, environmental material and artefacts highlighted in this chapter. The excavated houses were occupied between the 13th and early 16th centuries, whereas the cemetery was in use by the 11th century and continued well after 1500. The people buried in the churchyard included people from other villages in Wharram's large parish, and not all of them were peasants – for example, the graves of the parish clergy can be recognised from the chalices and pattens deposited as grave goods. Having made these qualifications, it is still the case that the burials (which were most numerous in the period 1100-1400) can be associated closely with the village – some of the skeletons excavated may have been the remains of the inhabitants of the houses on Sites 9 and 12, on which this chapter is focused.

The evidence of the Wharram burials can be compared with documentary testimony, but often the bones tell us about aspects of the population which are normally hidden from demographic historians. For example, historians have to presume high rates of infant and child mortality, because of the relatively few children recorded in medieval censuses or wills. Often parents in their later years are recorded as having between one and four living children, after a period of potential child bearing when perhaps seven births could be expected. One explanation lies in the high mortality among the very young. In the second half of the 16th century, when parish registers provide a guide, in a sample of English parishes just over 200 of every thousand children died before they reached the age of ten, and this level of mortality continued and tended to increase through the next two centuries (Wrigley and Schofield 1989, 248-54). In the sample from the Wharram churchyard 45% of the burials were of individuals under the age of sixteen, which suggests a relatively high rate of mortality among the young. On the other hand, the rate of infant mortality, that is deaths within the first year, seems comparatively low at 11%-15% according to the bones. Once Wharram villagers had reached the age of eighteen, they had a good chance of survival for another 20-30 years, as 21% of those buried had died between the ages of 18-29, followed by 39% in the age group 30-49, and 40% at 50 and over (Mays 2007, 84-93).

The large numbers of burials of young people has allowed a glimpse of the crucial early stages of the life cycle, for which there is little evidence in other sources. Stable isotope analysis shows that babies were breast fed for a year, and were weaned in their second year. This gave babies a healthy start in life, and had the further benefit that the mother would be unlikely to conceive while lactating, which would give her a chance of an interval between pregnancies (Mays 2007, 94). In childhood, the nutritional standards seem to have declined, as children between the ages of four and eight ate less meat and fish than did adults (Mays 2007, 95). The deficiencies in the diet did not, however, result in many conditions visible in the bones, so only eight individuals showed signs of rickets (Mays 2007, 176-7). Wharram's teenagers had a rate of growth which was notably slower than that of modern populations, with the result that a fourteen-year-old was no taller than a ten-year-old in the United States in the 1950s. Such an example might seem unrealistic as a comparison, but young villagers at Wharram had an inferior rate of growth to the not very privileged population of early 19th-century Manchester, which is likely to reflect a low standard of nutrition. Modern young people cease to grow around the age of twenty – at Wharram growth continued after that age in a prolonged adolescence (Mays 2007, 97-100).

Adult heights, with a mean of 1.69m (5ft 7in) for men and 1.58m (5ft 2in) for women, place our late medieval peasants a little below samples from the first millennium AD (both Roman and Anglo-Saxon), and not very different from the medieval and modern urban poor. The urban working class in the midst of the industrial revolution in the early 19th century attained a rather slighter stature (Mays 2007, 118-20; Dyer 1998, 316)

The whole population faced deficiencies in diet and disease, and their sufferings were etched on to their bones. Episodes of hunger left Harris lines, and dental enamel hypoplasias. Study of the former shows not just that people experienced food shortages or diseases which limited their capacity to digest food, but that they took some time to catch up after these episodes. The Wharram population were engaged in hard work in agriculture, and the physical stress of their occupation left its mark on the skeletons. In 118 individuals, a condition of the vertebra can be associated with lifting heavy weights. An arduous life can also be linked with osteoarthritis, and a number show signs of the formation of sub-chondral cysts (Mays 2007, 153-63)

Human bones do not provide much evidence for infectious disease, though there are traces of tuberculosis among the Wharram burials, and a case of leprosy (Mays 2007, 153-63). Further signs of traumas arising from illnesses such as dysentery come from bones that were pitted with periostosis and porotic hyperostosis (Mays 2007, 166-70, 172-4). A positive conclusion about the well-being of Wharram's population can be reached by comparing the Wharram bones with those recovered from a churchyard in a rather poor district of the city of York, St Helen-on-the-Walls, where signs of infections seem to have been more prevalent and there is evidence for severe levels of sinusitis (Mays 2007, 101-2, 138-40; Roberts 2009, 312-13). The Wharram population gained some advantages from their relatively healthy sanitary conditions, lack of overcrowding and clean air.

Other material evidence however alerts us to environmental hazards which must have contributed to the spread of disease. The village was dependent on the pond and stream for its water, as is demonstrated by the large number of jugs of all kinds and periods found in the pond excavations, the result of loss and breakage by the many females who walked from the village daily to fetch water (Wrathmell and Marlow-Mann 2005, 227). The pond, however, served as a dump for rubbish, and its mud contained at one time pieces of horse carcass, and at another a dead dog (Richardson 2005a, 155-64, 167). Rubbish disposal was not usually done carelessly, and the cleanliness of houses has already been mentioned. Any farming community which practised dairying had to observe basic rules of hygiene lest the cheese and butter spoil. The deposit of human ordure on the fields contributed to good husbandry and took waste matter away from the settlement, but at the same time it must have attracted flies at some intermediate stage of its collection and dispersal. There were rubbish dumps in agreed places, such as a corner of the churchyard, or the collection of horse carcasses near the North Manor, but this did not prevent animal bones lying exposed for dogs to find, as a minority of them show signs of having been gnawed.

We have a chronological sequence for the Wharram burials, but that cannot be precise enough to match them with specific historical famines or epidemics. The famine of 1315-17 is well documented at nearby Wetwang where corn was scarce and prices very high. Some of the Harris lines and other physiological signs of nutritional deprivation may well have come from individuals who lived through those years of severe food shortage, and the Wharram clergy would have been conducting many funerals in those hard years. There is no obvious trace of the epidemic of 1349 in the churchyard, though it must have had its effects on Wharram as it did on other parts of Yorkshire (Thompson 1914). In the long term the threat of hunger receded, though infectious disease would have continued, and cultural restraints on early marriage would have prevented the population from increasing rapidly in spite of the easy availability of holdings of land and well-paid employment.

Eating and drinking

Both the bones and the documents tell us about quantitative aspects of diet, both the availability of food for those with adequate holdings, and the problems of food shortages. There is much more information available for a qualitative approach to food and drink, which means examining the varieties of foods consumed, and the food culture. When the consumption of a family living on an oxgang was analysed (Table 19), it was assumed that they ate some wheat bread, but also consumed barley, presumably as bread, and used smaller quantities of oats and legumes as pottage corn.

They could in addition have brewed some of the barley, or barley and oats, though tenants with two oxgangs would have found it easier to spare grain for this purpose. The farm servants working on the demesnes of the archbishops of York's manors of Bishop Wilton and Wetwang received in normal years an allowance of grain that consisted of wheat and barley in approximately equal proportions. In the famine years the wheat disappeared from the allowance, and the servants were provided mainly with barley, supplemented with peas and beans which accounted for a proportion of between 5% and 12% (TNA:PRO SC6/1144/1-7). We can assume that peasant households made similar adjustments in hard times. Pottage (made of oat meal or pulses) figured more prominently in their diet when grain was in short supply, and some of the barley may have been boiled also in pottages or puddings, though much was doubtless baked into bread.

The documentary evidence for crops and diet can be compared with the botanical evidence, which is more likely to relate to the consumption of grain and legumes rather than to their production (see Table 20). The accidental burning which has led to the preservation of plant remains in carbonised form was most likely to happen when grain was being dried in preparation for its use as food, or for storage. Another circumstance in which burning might occur would be if overheating damaged grain that was being malted, which would bias the sample in favour of brewing grains such as barley and oats. The second sample is heavily biased in favour of wheat, suggesting that grain for bread making was accidentally burnt; an alternative explanation could be that wheat straw was being used as fuel or was by misfortune set on fire, and the grain came from the unthreshed ears left in the straw. The other samples did not exactly match the crops sown and harvested at Wetwang, but they stand comparison with the combination of cereals issued to farm servants and estimated in the budget of a model oxgang (Table 19).

Peasants ate much bread and cereal-based pottage, and we do not know how much protein in their diet derived from meat, dairy produce and fish. We know that milk, cheese, eggs, bacon and meat were being produced on the holding, but the need for cash must have led peasants to send a proportion to market. Stable isotope analysis tells us that meat and dairy products did form part of their diet, but a larger quantity is found in samples from urban inhabitants, such as the people buried in and near the friary at Warrington and in the cathedral close in Hereford (Müldner and Richards 2006, 230-31, 235-7). On the basis of the estimation of an oxgang's income and outgoings (Table 19), there should have been a considerable difference between those with one oxgang and a family living on a two oxgang holding who could have consumed some meat and cheese regularly.

Food preparation took up much time and resources, and here we will follow the food from field to table. Once harvested, the grain was threshed and winnowed over a period of months after the harvest, and then as it was needed, milled. Wharram villagers had access at various times to three water-mills, of which at least one must have been working at any one time, except in the aftermath of the Scots raid of 1322 (Wrathmell 2005a, 1-8; Oswald 2005, 9-19; Wrathmell 2005b, 19-22). The advantage of the water-mill lay in the saving of labour, and the speed with which the grain went through the hopper. The disadvantages were the toll (one sixteenth of the grain at

Table 20. Carbonised grain from samples most likely to reflect peasant crops (percentages).

Location	Date	Wheat	Barley	Oats	Peas/beans	Unidentified	Total
Site 71	14th-15th-century	44	25	11	present	20	100
S. Manor	13th-century	83	3	13		0	100
S. Manor	12th-century	37	43	20		0	100

Sources: Jones 2005, 200; Carruthers 2005, 218

Table 21. Animal bones from Wharram Percy.

Site	Date	Cattle	Sheep/goat	Pig	Horse	Fowl	Total
Site 9*	12th-15th-century	877	1640	454	279	72	3322
(Area 10)		26	49	14	8	2	100%
Site 12*	13th-15th-century	1122	3216	659	523	71	5591
(Area 6)		20	58	12	9	1	100%
Sites 9+ and 12	12th-15th-century	77	18	5			100%
Site 71*	Late medieval	130	292	112	45	56	635
		20	46	18	7	9	100%

Notes: * based on a count of bones and bone fragments, domestic species only; + a percentage based on estimation of meat weights of edible animals.
Source : Richardson 2005b, 230; Ryder 1974

Birdsall, for example) and the extra grain that the miller was suspected of stealing for himself (Holt 1988, 81, 103-6). The mill might not have been regarded as a convenience if a member of the household (often a woman) had to spend a long time in a queue with her sack of grain. The alternative lay in home milling, which required the expense of buying a quern, the risk of a fine because avoiding suit of the lord's mill was a breach of customary law, and the drudgery of the process for a member of the household, again usually a woman. We know that the home milling option was sometimes taken, because pieces of millstone are found scattered over Wharram; 27 fragments on Site 12 (Area 6) for example. Wharram peasants sometimes bought the best imported German lava stones. The quern may have been used to mill malt, while the bread corn was taken to the water-mill.

The dough was mixed and kneaded in the peasants' houses, but in view of the uncertain evidence that any of the houses had ovens, the loaves must often have been taken to the common oven, which was a seigneurial monopoly, like the mill. The tolls on bread provided an income for the baker, who would be a tenant paying a rent to the lord. The common kiln was presumably for malting, again with a toll taken, but we do not know how the kiln monopoly worked. The oven and kiln were set up to add to the lords' profits, not as a public service, but in one respect they were advantageous for villagers in an area with scarce fuel supplies.

The malt would have been brewed in the ale-wives' houses, or perhaps in separate brewhouses or bakehouses, though as we have seen these have not been positively identified among the various Wharram buildings. Individuals would go to the ale house to drink and enjoy the society, games and other pleasures available, but households would also provide themselves with ale to serve at home. Wooden vessels would have been used to transport and store the ale, as ceramic cisterns are rather rare, and at table it might have been poured from ceramic jugs into wooden cups or bowls, but in the 13th-century jugs are not plentiful on the peasant house sites. Towards the end of the village's life German stoneware mugs were in use on Site 12 and lobed cups on Site 9, but neither they nor the jugs have been found in such quantity or quality to match the drinking culture implied by the variety of cisterns, jugs and drinking vessels found in late medieval Oxfordshire (Mellor 1994, 111-40).

With the bread baked and the ale on the table - or in poorer households, milk or water – the household was ready for its meal. Meat-eating was permitted on five days of the week in 46 weeks of the year, but the limited resources of the household would reduce its consumption to a much greater degree.

Animal bones inform us about the consumption of meat, rather than its production, as most of the bones that are found were the by-products of food preparation. Counts of bones and fragments of bones (Table 21) give the impression that sheep were the most numerous animals that were butchered and therefore the main source of meat, but when a calculation is made for the number of individuals represented by the bones, and the amount of meat that the carcasses contained, beef emerges as dominant. The bones also tell us about the selection of animals for slaughter. They were not always elderly, because pigs were usually killed within two years, and more young sheep seem to have been consumed on Site 12 than Site 9, perhaps indicating the superior status of the household (Richardson 2005b, 232-7). In general, sheep were too valuable as wool, lamb, milk and manure producers to be killed young for their meat, and likewise cattle were needed for dairy, breeding and draught purposes. When they were killed the butchery methods, as we have seen (p. 235), suggest a lack of urban professionalism, as the task was carried out by the peasants themselves or by a 'country butcher'. Poultry tended to be eaten on special occasions, and meat-eating events punctuated the peasants' year. They could look forward to the celebration of the reapgoose at the end of the harvest; or eating the perishable parts of the slaughtered pig in early November; and we can suppose that peasants owed a rent of poultry to their lord at Christmas because everyone who could afford to do so ate poultry at that time of year.

A specialised item of kitchen equipment, shared with aristocratic households, was the stone mortar, suggesting that food was ground into a paste (Andrews and MacGregor 1979, 128; Smith 1989, 54-5). Perhaps ambitious peasant wives, who might have acquired knowledge of aristocratic cooking while serving in manor house kitchens, attempted a dish like *mortrews*, in which meat was ground in a mortar and cooked in a broth with such ingredients as bread-crumbs and egg yolks. Puddings, sausages and other offal-based foods are likely to have featured in the peasant diet. Pottages were the typical peasant dish, in which a common ingredient for the better-off would be meat preserved by salting or smoking, such as bacon or salt beef, boiled with oat meal, peas, beans or barley, and with garden vegetables such as cabbage, leeks or garlic. Fresh meat could have been roasted on a spit, a utensil which appears in 15th-century Yorkshire peasant inventories, like that of William Akclum of Wharram le Street (BIA D and C wills, 1481, Akclum). There are traces of posts for supporting a spit near the hearth in Building 1, Site 12 (Area 6) and a broken mortar set into the floor perhaps to catch the drips of fat. Boiling in a brass pot or one of the numerous ceramic cooking pots was more frequently practised. Stewing was an appropriate way of dealing with the meat of rather old cows, oxen, ewes and wethers, which formed a high proportion of the animals consumed, and this cooking method economised on fuel.

The bones of an especially wide range of sea fish species have been found near the Wharram rectory, but on the peasant house Sites 9 and 12 cod, ling and haddock bones have been recovered, and the shells of whelks and oysters (Ryder 1974, 45; Clark 2000a, 205; Barrett 2005, 169-75). We may suspect that more very small bones, such as those of herring, were not recovered by the excavators. These fish would have reached the site in dried or salted form, and large cod in particular would have been brought to Wharram as stockfish which had been caught in the North Sea or imported from Norway to Hull and then traded overland. Stable isotope analysis suggests that a small but significant amount of the villagers' dietary protein came from marine sources, but this is not accepted by all authorities, who refer to sea fish providing a 'very minor part of peasant diet' (Mays 2007, 94-5; Müldner and Richards, 230-31). An inland trade in sea fish is to be expected after the extension of the marketing network in the 13th century, and some types of fish, such as stockfish, were inexpensive enough to be bought by peasants. We know that in the 14th century people at Wetwang ate sea fish, because when the tenants there did a special ploughing service and a harvest service for their lord, he rewarded them with a meal consisting of a loaf of bread and two herrings for each worker. The fish were cheap enough for the lord, at ten for 1d in 1316-17

(TNA:PRO SC6/1144/4). The meals presumably provided the workers with foods with which they were familiar in their everyday lives. Purchases of fish by peasants were most likely in the six weeks of Lent, when no meat could be eaten.

Cheese-making was a major activity, judging from the number of shallow pottery bowls found which would have been used in the process. Both cows and ewes would have been milked, but a proportion of the produce would have been sent to market, and we do not know how much was available for the consumption of the household.

The meal was served on a trestle table in the hall, with a table cloth. The household sat down together, its head in some position of dignity on a chair, his wife, children and servants on benches, each with his or her own knife, though the household would have kept spoons of wood or bone – metal spoons only appear in the late 15th century. The meal of course had much more significance than merely providing an opportunity to ingest food. This was the time when the household came together, asserting its unity but also observing its internal hierarchy.

Consuming

Food and drink account for a very high proportion of peasant consumption, and most of the ingredients of their diet were obtained within the village territory. When our inquiry expands to include non-food items, we become increasingly concerned with commercial contacts and sources of supply from further afield.

Some fuel was available from the twenty-acre wood recorded in 1436, but whether the villagers had common rights there is not known. Another local resource might have been dried cows' dung, which is known to have been burnt in domestic hearths on the wolds in the 19th century (see pp 352-3). Otherwise various sources of energy came from a distance. The early medieval wattle fences found in the pond excavation contained wood from alder, ash, birch, hazel, and willow, which had probably been grown in coppicing systems. These would also have been used to produce firewood, and charcoal deposits include the same species (Morgan 2005, 200-210; *Wharram X*, 242). Likely sources were the large woods at Settrington, and parcels of woodland on the slopes of the wolds edge, within a distance of 12km, but as far as we know these cart loads and pack loads of firewood, and occasional pieces of building timber, were purchased and not obtained as part of customary rights. Coal has been found on a number of sites, from contexts as early as the 13th century; a large concentration of 738 fragments came from Site 9 (Area 10) and 32kg were found at Site 12 (Area 6). Increasing quantities of the fuel were being brought to Wharram in the 15th century (Andrews *et al.* 1979, 133-4; Clark 2000b, 206). The likely source was Methley near Leeds, which required a journey of 60km, partly by boat on the Ouse, but still taking a challenging road journey from York to Wharram. Coal was often used for industrial purposes, such as lime burning at Bishop Wilton in 1316-17, and a smith working at Wharram would have needed the fuel, but on Site 12 it seems to have been burnt on a domestic hearth, which underlines the problems of obtaining firewood. Turf (peat) was another fuel obtainable at a distance, though the only evidence was the presence at Wharram in the 13th century of shallow pots of Staxton ware, which are known as 'peat pots' because they were well suited to cooking on a peat fire. The fuel could have been carried from the moors in the valley to the east of Malton, from Willerby for example, where we know that thousands of turfs were being dug in the 13th century (Lancaster 1912, 102, 131).

Lighting came from tallow candles, for which both socketed and pricket candlesticks were provided (Goodall I.H. 1979, 117-18, Goodall I.H. 1989, 51). The small number of candleholders that have been found does not suggest a great quantity of artificial lighting, though tallow must have been in regular supply when sheep and cattle were killed and butchered. Candle-making, however, is known from other villages to have been a specialist occupation, as the price of candles was subject to regulation. A ceramic lamp which would have had a wick floating on oil, came from Site 51.

Clothing and footwear would have been acquired by the peasants of Wharram, but the only items recovered from the excavation were five shoes or pieces of shoe preserved in waterlogged conditions in the pond. These suggest that shoes were scarce and renewing them was so costly that they were subject to repeated mending. One child's shoe had received four patches, and had only been discarded when further repair was impossible. Pieces of leather found with the shoes suggest that shoe repairs were carried out in the village, but an urban craftsman is likely to have made the child's shoe as its upper was probably made of goat's skin: the famous cordwain (originally from Córdoba) imported from Spain (Mould 2005, 145-9).

Linen material, made into shrouds, has been recovered from three of the Wharram graves, and the living wore the same cloth, together with harden textiles (made from hemp rather than flax) which were cheaper but had similar functions. Men's shirts and women's shifts were made from linen, and also sheets, towels and table-cloths. Outer garments were usually woollen, which like the linen would have been made in towns or specialist rural centres of manufacture many miles away. The potential cost and sophistication of peasant clothes is brought home to us by the purchase, by the lord of the prebendal manor of Bishop Wilton, for six farm servants, of liveries (sets of clothing) in 1368-9 (Hull UL, DD57/4/3). Each received 3 yards of woollen cloth, one being issued with sanguine (red) at 2s 2d per yard, and the others 'mixed blue' at 2s. This belongs to a period when servants were criticised for demanding excessive rewards, both cash, and the various perks such as food and clothing. Under the sumptuary law of 1363 (which soon lapsed) farm servants were not allowed to wear cloth costing more than 1s 1d per yard (Dyer 1998, 88-9). The Wilton ploughmen, who were dressed like members of the gentry, prove the

lengths that employers took to attract scarce labour. The peasants probably wore cheaper cloth, like a piece worth 10d per ell which was taken in distraint from a man significantly called Wever in the course of a law suit at Bishop Wilton in 1379 (Hull UL DD SY/4/2/1084).

At Wharram, the cloth may not survive or be recorded in documents, but excavation has produced a wide range of metal fittings often attached to clothes, which, like woollen cloth, were manufactured by specialists, usually in the case of copper-alloy objects in larger towns, and distributed through local market towns or itinerant pedlars. The fastenings and fittings included buckles, strap-ends, mounts, pendants and plaques, some of which belonged to leather belts, textile girdles and other dress accessories. Some were decorated with mouldings and coated with tin to make them shine in imitation of silver, and we can detect signs of fashion consciousness, and the adoption of new styles as country people kept up with changes in dress. The tags from the ends of laces, for example, may relate to the tighter clothing and body-hugging fashions that developed after the mid-14th century (Egan and Pritchard 1991, 281-90).

Inventories show the importance of textiles in furnishing the peasant house, with bedding (sheets, blankets, coverlets) in the chamber, and cushions, table-cloths, and wall coverings ('painted cloths') in the hall. None of these survives in the ground, but among the Wharram iron objects are found more durable parts of chests including iron straps, hinges, locks and keys (Goodall I.H. 1979, 115-18). Peasants protected their private property, with locked doors on the outside, and locked chests within. They also presented visitors with public images of the dignified and hierarchical dinner table already described, and of the opulence of the coloured cloths and cushions. Some households made displays of their superior status. The family who lived in Building 1 on Site 12 (Area 6) were able to afford German stoneware drinking vessels and a few glass vessels around 1500 (Le Patourel 1979, 94; Andrews 1979a, 130; Slowikowski 2000, 95). The inhabitants of Site 9 (Area 10) owned chafing dishes, showily glazed in yellow and decorated with red pellets (Slowikowski 2000, 95). These small luxuries stood out from the rather drab and functional cooking pots which predominated among the Wharram ceramics.

A few of the possessions of the inhabitants of Wharram hint at their aspirations to a higher social status. Among those who rode horses, individuals provided themselves with elaborate rowel spurs, and as well as the mundane harness buckles and fittings were found six copper-alloy pendants, one of which, gilded, was in a scallop shape, and another had a heraldic design (Goodall I.H. 1979, 123; Goodall A.R. 1989, 46-7; Goodall and Clark 2005, 130-31). A few pieces of weapons, such as a lance head, military-style arrow heads, a dagger pommel and the tip of the blade of a sword or dagger could be dismissed as strays from the inhabitants of the manor house, or losses by passing knights or soldiers (Goodall A.R. 1989, 46-7, Goodall I.H. 1979, 120-21). Inventories of Yorkshire peasants of the 15th century, however, include more weapons than are found among the possessions of their southern or Midland equivalents. Perhaps the experience of the Scottish incursions in the early 14th century, and the continuing threats from north of the border, made Yorkshire peasants especially prepared to engage in war.

The daily lives of the villagers should not be represented entirely as a grim struggle for survival in a routine of hard labour, unpalatable eating, and sleep. Though unimpressive in their number, some Wharram artefacts are associated with entertainment and leisure, such as musical pipes made from bones, two jews' harps, a die, and a board for playing nine-men's morris scratched on a stone (Goodall I.H. 1979, 120-21; Andrews 1979a, 128-9; Clark and Gaunt 2005, 123-4). As well as four of the usual square dice, a *teetotum* or spinning dice was found. There was also a bone tuning peg from a box-like musical instrument (Site Archive: Bone Objects 27 and 26). Simple entertainment came from buzz bones – a pig's foot bone, through which a hole was bored, which was twisted on a thong in order to produce a diverting noise when released (MacGregor 2000, 153; MacGregor and Riddler 2005, 143-5). Other more sophisticated dimensions of popular culture, such as singing, story telling, dancing and team sports, leave no material trace.

In summing up the consumption patterns of peasants revealed by research into Wharram, we are torn between an optimistic view of their integration into a wider world of consumption and opportunity, and a more realistic appreciation of the many limits on their ability to spend money or improve themselves. We will look at both sides of the argument.

In favour of an expansive view of peasant engagement with the market, the inhabitants of Wharram can be seen in constant contact with the outside world. Their main sources of pottery included Staxton and Brompton to the north-east at a distance of 10 miles or 16km; Brandsby in the north-west (27km) and the Humber estuary (50km). During the later middle ages, trading patterns shifted their orientation as Humber ware became more prominent, as if the villagers, or at least the trading patterns which served their needs, looked more to the south. Their wood and timber came from such places as Settrington, and their coal probably from Methley. Stone roofing slates and some of their hand millstones were brought from other parts of Yorkshire, but their lava hand mills were quarried in Germany and some of their whetstones in Norway. Stockfish, some of it originating in Norway, came through Hull (Barrett *et al.* 2008, 850-61). Copper-alloy pots and dress accessories, and more complicated ironmongery, such as locks and knives, were all probably made in towns, and often in the larger centres such as York and Beverley. The York connection is reinforced by the occurrence of York wares among the pottery. Peasants' shoes were urban products, and their cloth came from towns such as York or from specialist rural textile centres, such as those established in west Yorkshire by the 15th century.

Wharram peasants would have hired skilled artisans from other villages or local towns to erect timber-framed buildings, or to tailor their better clothes. The immediate source for most of these goods and services would have been markets and fairs held in nearby market towns, such as Malton and Pocklington, though for an expensive item they might have occasionally travelled to York. Pedlars would have visited villages like Wharram with smaller items. This consumerism is imperfectly represented in the material evidence, because the perishable commodities, such as cloth, have decayed, and the larger metal items such as brass pots, and the spits and cart tyres of iron have been recycled. These were the more costly peasant possessions, as we are reminded by a legal dispute at nearby Fimber in 1395, when an official wishing to bring maximum pressure to bear on the tenants to pay money, seized their 'carts and horse harness, and linen and woollen cloth and brass vessels' (Jn Rylands Lib Latin MS 221, f. 242r, 248r-248v).

On the other side of the argument, peasants were careful and frugal consumers, especially when they bought an expensive utensil, such as a brass pot, which cost 3s 4d or perhaps more. Often they acquired such goods outside the market, as pots would be given as part of a dowry or in a bequest. They preserved them, and if they broke they had them mended if possible, or took them to the urban potter or brazier for recycling, so reducing the cost of a replacement. Recycling was not a matter of conscience or fashion, but a sheer necessity for reducing costs. They reused even the cheapest objects, as a broken pot could still have a function, and roughly-shaped pieces of building stone could be added to a building foundation. They chose pottery at the lower end of the market, notably cheap Staxton ware cooking pots, with a minimum of jugs and small quantities of decorated or colourful vessels. The by-products of their own farming could be put to good use, such as the straw that was left after the harvest or after threshing, which for them had a dozen valuable functions, as fodder, bedding for animals and people, to make mats and ropes, as a roofing material, as fuel, and much else.

In house and outbuildings, wooden vessels (troughs and tubs), with no doubt many baskets, fulfilled useful functions at low cost, but have left little trace. 'Make do and mend' was taken to extremes, like the shoe with four patches, or the Staxton ware pot (worth no more than 1d) which was repaired with five rivets (Wrathmell 1989b, 39). Needles, thimbles and scissors suggest that they mended clothes, or made their own to reduce tailors' bills. They could not dispose of resources without good reason. For example, some dignity had to be accorded to the dead, so corpses would not be put naked into the earth. Coffins were however not so essential, and timber scarce, so peasants went to their graves in linen shrouds. Wealth and standards of living changed through the period, as has already been noted with the new developments in house construction in the 13th century, and the emergence in the 15th century of superior dwellings such as the large longhouse on site 12. Among the pottery finds, a rising trend is apparent in the use of glazed wares, such as those from York and Scarborough from the mid-14th century onwards.

Living in a community

The discussion of houses, health, diet and consumption has focused on individuals and households, but to what extent did Wharram people belong to a community and devote time and resources to collective activities? They had strong formal commitments to the village through imposition from those in authority. Their lord insisted that they all use the mill, oven and kiln, and he would expect them to attend the manor court and take on official roles such as that of the grave (administrator of the manor from day to day) and hayward. Lord and village together managed the pound or pinfold where stray animals were kept. The state expected the village to assist in maintaining law and order. In 1274-5 'Wharram' (which one is not known) was said to have allowed the escape of a woman arrested for felony, and the whole community had to contribute to a collective fine of £8 (English 1996, 77). From 1334 the village was charged by the state with assessing and levying from the inhabitants its contribution to the main tax, the lay subsidy.

The church authorities expected the laity of the parish to look after the fabric of the church and to keep the churchyard in order. It has been argued that the lords of the manor sometimes paid for church building, but their interest was episodic and the ordinary parishioners, through the churchwardens, were responsible for much building work. Wharram's large parish contained five villages, each in its own separate township, which made co-operation among the laity complicated to organise. When Thixendale, Towthorpe and Raisthorpe all acquired their own chapels a greater burden must have fallen on Wharram itself.

Villagers did not need to be ordered to take account of the common good, as this was essential for the management of the field system and the pastures. The surviving elements of the village plan suggest many ways in which co-ordination of effort maintained boundaries, roads and watercourses. The adjacent village of Wharram le Street had a guildhouse according to a chance reference in 1397, and a fraternity may have been involved in the management of almshouses at Settrington which are revealed in the early 16th century (BL Cotton Vit C vi, f. 215r; TNA: PRO SC12/23/13). Such village institutions may have existed at Wharram Percy, but there is no evidence for them.

The community, or parts of it, also met more informally for social events. The churchyard was a natural focus for gatherings, unofficial markets or games, hence the modest concentration of coins, and scattered finds of pottery, buckles, horse shoes, spindle whorls and a dice, from a place that we might expect to be empty and silent. At the pond, where so many jugs were lost while water was collected, the women of the village naturally took advantage of a meeting-place where gossip was exchanged. At night the ale houses would attract groups, mainly but not exclusively of men, who would drink, talk and gamble. There would always have been elements who resisted the community – the anti-social underclass who stole wood from their neighbours' hedges, and worse, and the ambitious would-be entrepreneurs who broke the rules to maximise their profits.

While the Wharram peasants were clearly attached to their village, they also took part in the great movement of people that has been found throughout medieval England. Villagers recorded at Wharram in the 13th and 14th centuries can be shown from their surnames (or those that they inherited from their forebears) to have originated in places called Barkby, Cawood and Sutton, of which the last lies south of Malton, and the second is the village on the river Ouse down river from York (Brown 1894b, 147; *Cal IPM XI*, 183). Movement out of the village is indicated by the surname 'de Warrum', which could refer to Wharram le Street, but that is unlikely to account for all of the occurrences. In 1301 the name is recorded in Malton and York, and later in the 14th century it is found in the villages of Birdsall, Bishop Wilton, Fridaythorpe, Kirkburn, Thixendale and Wetwang (Brown 1897, 53, 119, 121; *York Inqs III*, 166; Fenwick 2005, 211-14). York is known to have attracted migrants from the Wolds, especially young women who became servants, and this movement has been plausibly linked with the high proportion of male burials in the churchyard (Goldberg 1992, 293; Mays 2007, 92). The shortage of women in the village might have driven young men to look elsewhere for marriage partners, but this was a common pattern whether or not there was a gender imbalance. Migration is found everywhere, but presented real problems of maintaining tenant numbers if a village's land was regarded as unattractive. To indicate the scale of movement, Settrington was a village which kept its numbers yet only five of the twenty surnames recorded in 1297 reappear in the 1381 poll tax, and of the 32 names legible in 1381 not a single one can be seen in the rental of *c.* 1536 (Brown 1894b, 144, 148; Fenwick 2005, 210; TNA:PRO SC12/23/13).

How did the villagers regard their lords? The successive lords of the manor were often absent, so the villagers encountered them mainly through itinerant estate officials who would hold courts and receive money. Rents and other payments such as entry fines and heriots (payable on death) were likely points of contention, as were the restrictions on the movement and marriage of the many Wharram villagers who in the 13th century were included among the bondsmen or unfree. The Scottish raid of 1322 must have caused resentment directed against lords, just as the people of Cumberland are known to have protested after destructive attacks (Briggs 2005). The aristocracy claimed to be the military elite whose function was to protect society, and in view of their failure, peasants may well have acquired arms with the intention of defending themselves.

Three pieces of material evidence have been used to show that the Wharram peasants resisted the privileges of lordship. One was the purloining of pieces of sandstone from the ruins of the 12th-century South Manor to be built into the foundations of peasant houses. We cannot be sure, however, that the authorities were especially protective of this stone, and the new lords may not have cared about a collapsed building that had perhaps belonged to their Chamberlain predecessors. More convincing is the widespread use of hand mills in apparent defiance of the lords' milling monopoly. Also subversive of a seigneurial privilege was the peasants' possession of arrows with heads suitable for hunting game, and the scatter of deer bones showing that they occasionally ate venison. The early 16th-century rental for Settrington includes a prohibition against unauthorised hunting, fowling and fishing, which suggests that these were current causes of controversy (Smith 2009, 396-410; TNA:PRO SC12/23/13).

In other nearby villages we find robust peasant attitudes towards their lords, including a serious dispute at Fimber which led an official of St Mary's Abbey York in 1395 to seize peasant property to force them to pay arrears of rent totalling 79s 9d. Direct action was taken at Wetwang in 1540 by villagers who pulled down an enclosure hedge (Jn Rylands Lib Latin MS 221, 242r, 248r-248v; *VCH ER VIII*, 250). This was one of a succession of enclosure disputes in which hedges were destroyed and pastures ploughed on the Wolds in the 16th century (Macdonagh 2009). Not enough of a village was left at Wharram in the early 16th century to mount such actions, but the community was surely capable of defending its interests in earlier centuries.

Working together in communities, and resisting the powers of lords, are familiar elements in peasant society, and archaeological evidence for ritual practices strengthens the idea that peasants had their own distinctive culture. In the 14th century in Building 9 on Site 12 (Area 7), seven pots were broken and put into a pit in a way that suggests a deliberate deposit (Wrathmell 1989b, 39). This ceremonial disposal of goods may well have followed a death or change of tenancy.

On a number of medieval sites, prehistoric and Roman artefacts have been found in circumstances which suggest that they had been deliberately collected and kept. At Wharram the six Roman coins at Site 9 (Area 10) may have been the result of bringing finds in from the fields, either as curiosities, or as a commemoration of some kind, or even because such an object served as a talisman (Sitch 2004, 235; Gerrard 2007).

In the churchyard, various burial practices seem to have been following local traditions. One was to concentrate children's graves in one area of the churchyard. Another was to set stones around the corpse in the grave, or to put stones on either side of the head. Various objects were found in graves that may have been deliberately placed for some purpose unclear to modern observers: these include pebbles, a fossil, part of a Roman glass bangle, and a bone stylus (for writing). The last, placed in the grave of a teenage boy, might have commemorated his educational progress (Clark 2007,

269-70). These deposits are not confined to rural cemeteries, but still suggest the currency of unofficial beliefs among peasants.

The Wharram peasants spoke a regional dialect of English, and as they looked to York as well as to Malton, they were not cut off from urban society and educated people. Late medieval documents survive with detailed topographical descriptions which locate boundaries and describe pieces of land in Thixendale and Wharram le Street. These were written by clerks who came from outside the area, but the coinage of the names arose from the daily speech of the local people. They employed words which were not unique to the Wharram area. They called the steep-sided valleys which are such a marked feature of the area dales, (*dall*) but the word *cumb* is also found in Thixendale. *Nab* described a sharp hill, and *dic* an earthwork. A *flat* was a subdivision of an open field, called a furlong further south in England, and grassland was described as *ing* or *eng* (Jn Rylands Lib Latin MS 221, f. 248v-263v; 363v- 365r; BL Cotton Vit C vi, f.229r-229v; Bodleian Lib. Fairfax 7, 7v-8r; Smith 1937). Wharram Percy itself was not always known by that name, as a witness in a church court proceeding in 1410 said that he lived in Wharram on the Wold (*Wharrom super le Wald*: BIA, CP.F. 59).

The documents produced for the church courts which have survived in great numbers for York diocese contain reports of speech recalled by witnesses in matrimonial cases. The sentences and phrases were very conventional, because certain formulaic expressions of consent to a marriage contract were crucial in establishing that a valid marriage had taken place. At Settrington, reported in 1489, Richard Watson and Katherine Anger expressed their 'luf' for their future 'wif' and husband, and both parties plighted their 'trought' (troth: BIA, CP.F.273).

Experiencing life in Wharram

The unique combination of abundant archaeological evidence with some written sources allows us at least to map an outline of a social world at Wharram that was closed almost five centuries ago. So far, this chapter has been written from the perspective of 20th and 21st-century archaeologists and historians. Now we can attempt to sum up this enquiry by visualising the late medieval villagers' perception of Wharram and their role within it.

They would locate themselves in families, in houses and households, and in the village community. Their names signal their sense of lineage, because unlike their contemporaries in other regions, but like many northerners, their names were often formed as patronymics – like Reynold Martynson and Emma Henrykesson who lived in the village in 1368 (*Cal IPM XIII*, no. 202, p. 183). Their contemporaries in other villages and towns, when they migrated, named them 'de Warrum', because their place of origin was an important part of their identity. Even young people were fully aware of the formal structures in which they were pigeon-holed by officialdom – they belonged to the household of their father or their employer. That household was based on possession of an oxgang or a number of oxgangs, which had specific obligations to the lord, to the community, and perhaps also to the parish. They saw the formal structure of the village displayed in the village plan, with its orderly rows of tofts. Villagers all had individual experiences and circumstances. The houses, though generically similar, differed in size and layout, and were not arranged uniformly in relation to farm buildings and the tofts. Households varied in size and composition – some had a female head, some had servants, some were extended to include relatives not in the nuclear family – and they changed as they went through their lifecycles.

Villagers did not have a uniform perception of their role within the community. An acquisitive minority exceeded their stint of grazing on the common, put their animals to pasture on their neighbours' land, and invested in stock and buildings in order to seek market profits. They had access to credit, took advantage of the land market, and may have sublet land which eroded the unity of the oxgangs. Others conformed to the rules, and benefited from their neighbours' assistance, in borrowing equipment and animals, for example. Both types of cultivator were capable of seeking improvement by modifying agricultural methods, in choosing particular varieties of grain to plant, growing fodder crops, and storing the harvest safely.

Wharram's inhabitants were aware of three social hierarchies: within the household, within the village; and between lords and peasants. In the household everyone could see the head seated on a chair at table, and the young were trained and socialised in that setting. To turn to the village as a whole, in 1368 Reynold Martynson held three oxgangs (see p. 280), and could have lived comfortably on their produce: he might have looked down on John le Schephird who only had a cottage, but he valued him as an employee; Schephird, while doubtless resenting his wealthy neighbour, needed work. The inequalities of wealth within the village meant that the wealthy ate wheat bread with some ale, meat and cheese, while the poor depended above all on pottage. The rich exploited the poor by employing them, and supplying them with food and credit. The social hierarchy also depended on privilege (free and unfree), on gender, and on age. The villagers regarded the lord of the manor warily, and they would all be united in resentment if he raised rents or curtailed their rights. At the same time they looked up to the lords as setting standards, and we see peasant households modelling themselves on arrangements in the manor house, and peasants following aristocratic styles in their dress or their horse riding.

Everyone knew the parish and its boundary. They would be united in indignant protest if Birdsall or Wharram le Street people let their animals invade Wharram's fields. The landscape – the divisions of the fields, the dales, the boundaries, roads and paths – were well known and ingrained on their consciousness. These features were all named, because they were important for the common welfare, and especially vital was the stream, which filled the pond, powered the mills, watered the stock and provided water for the villagers.

The peasants were constantly engaged in meetings and discussions. They set high value on the lord's court, although it served the lord's interest, because it also functioned as a meeting of the community, and the leading villagers would have decided beforehand to raise matters of common concern, relating to such issues as the management of the fields, and keeping the peace. Women met in their own unofficial assemblies, perhaps by the pond or in the queue for the mill, or gathered around the oven. Young people encountered one another on the green by the pound, or in the churchyard. Adults drank, talked and played dice in the ale houses. At these gatherings gossip would be exchanged, in which the church courts took an interest because sinful behaviour or a marriage might be attested by 'the fame in the parish' or the 'common fame', or the 'public voice and fame… in the vills of Uncleby and Wharram Percy'. The unfree status of an employee of Meaux Abbey at Wharram Grange was 'commonly reputed in the parish of Wharram' in 1410 (BIA, CP.G. 180; CP. F 59). Gossip was not just a source of evidence for those in authority; it could be used as a means of expressing strong local opinion and exerting pressure on those who had offended the community.

The villagers were fully aware of the precariousness of life. Many of them had aches and pains, and periodically suffered serious illnesses. Families experienced deaths every few years, particularly among those under ten and over 50. They expected to endure deficient harvests, and epidemic diseases among animals, but suffered severe shocks from which recovery was difficult, like the catastrophe of the 1315-17 famine, the Scottish raid of 1322, and the Black Death of 1349. Individuals and families had their own uncertainties – the death of a family member, or just of a horse, or the deterioration of a barn - all could bring hardships.

The congregation saw the church as a community asset. Masses and celebrations of holy days would help to bring the villagers together, and space was provided for this in the large nave and aisles. The dedication to St Martin, who gave half his cloak to a beggar, made them aware of charity, and almsgiving such as the collection and distribution of 'holy loaves' gave that concern practical expression. For the peasants, St Martin's day on 11 November had an agricultural significance as animals and particularly pigs were killed. It marked the end of the growing season, so pasture would henceforth be diminished in value for grazing, and servants' contracts began and ended. Even if the peasants performed rituals and perpetuated non-Christian superstitions, the sincerity of their commitment to religion should not be doubted. They participated in services and willingly contributed to church funds.

Villagers' lives were focused on their own community, with its fields and church, but that did not make them unaware of a world beyond the parish boundary. They knew from the teachings of the clergy about Jerusalem and Rome. They were drawn into national politics because they were expected to take legal responsibilities (holding prisoners, for example), pay taxes, and be available for military service. They could scarcely see their village as cut off from the outside world, above all because of their many contacts with the market. One imagines a peasant sitting by a hearth burning firewood from Settrington, heating pottage in a pot from Staxton, while he sharpened a knife bought at York with a whetstone imported from Norway. All of them knew the world beyond the village, and many joined it by moving to another village or town.

The peasants of Wharram lived within a framework of ideas which began with a concern for the welfare of the community and respect for local customs which regulated tenancy and the use of land. They expected to be mutually supportive in such matters as relief of poverty and defence of common interests. They looked up to a king who upheld the law and was concerned for his subjects' welfare. They co-operated with the church courts and reported sinners to the church officials, because they valued morality and stability in marriage. They had learned the main tenets of Christianity and expected, if they led a good life and performed good works, to save their souls and progress through purgatory to a better world.

21 The Houses of Wharram's Tenant Farmers at the end of the Middle Ages

Introduction

In Chapters 19 and 20 Christopher Dyer reviewed the domestic and working lives of the late medieval farming families at Wharram and in some neighbouring communities. The present chapter explores, in more detail, aspects of their lives that are particularly amenable to archaeological investigation: the construction, form and contents of their houses. In terms of the first two of these aspects, the most important remains at Wharram are unquestionably those of Building 1 in Area 6 (Site 12). Yet as we have seen in Chapters 3 and 20, there are reasons for questioning whether this building is truly representative of the kinds of farmhouses occupied by most of Wharram's families during the 14th and 15th centuries. As for its contents, it has to be acknowledged (as always) that the recovered artefacts provide only a fragmentary and very partial picture of the house's furnishings and fittings.

In the case of other medieval villages we might anticipate being able to supplement the archaeological evidence with surviving documentary sources, but as we have seen in Chapters 14, 19 and 20, these are very sparse for Wharram Percy, and those that remain are of the sort that tell us very little about the daily lives of its farming

families. It has been decided, therefore, and in keeping with the approach taken in earlier chapters, to draw into this exploration a surviving probate inventory for Wharram le Street, one dating to the 1480s. The inventory provides a good deal of information about the contents of one house in Wharram le Street on one specific day (though in distinctly abnormal circumstances), and emphasises how many of its furnishings and fittings could *not* be expected to be identified through archaeological excavation. Here again, of course, our understanding of what the record tells us – and does not tell us – depends upon detailed contextual analysis, both of this specific document and of similar near contemporary records from the region.

The final section of this chapter takes the accumulated evidence from the two Wharrams for the internal arrangements of late medieval houses and their contents, and relates it to the broader Wolds traditions of housing and domestic routines recorded in early post-medieval sources. Acknowledging that there will have been some significant changes over this period we can, at least in terms of house plan and construction, demonstrate a gradual evolution which encourages us to locate the late 15th and early 16th-century data within longer-term trends. The analysis is accompanied by two new images: the first an impression of Building 1, Area 6, at the beginning of the 16th century; the second, a more speculative impression of the kind of house that might have accommodated the items listed in the 1480s inventory.

Observations on the structure and form of Wharram's late medieval farmhouses
by Stuart Wrathmell

It is one of the ironies of the Wharram Research Project that 40 years of archaeological investigations, intended almost from the start to explore the lives of medieval peasant farmers, uncovered so few coherent plans of medieval farm buildings, and even fewer that could claim to represent the homes of the village's tenant farmers. The best preserved farmstead, one in which a house and barn faced each other across a central courtyard, was extensively (but not completely) explored in Area 6 (Site 12), and in the late 1980s a review of the findings in Area 6 contributed much to the development of hypotheses relating to the structural characteristics and durability of Wharram's peasant houses (*Wharram VI*).

It is, therefore, a matter of concern that the house in question, Building 1, seems to have been exceptional on at least two counts. In the first place, as Oswald has emphasised, it was much larger than the average buildings in Wharram's farmsteads (Oswald 2004, fig. 17, A); and secondly it was clearly home to a prospering family, perhaps right up to the final destruction of the open fields in the late 1520s. Compared with the range and quantities of distinctively late 15th and early 16th-century pottery from the village as a whole, and in particular from the late medieval vicarage which survived until its destruction by fire in the 1550s (Didsbury 2010, 176-7), the assemblage of Cistercian wares, along with Langerwehe, Raeren and Cologne imports recovered from Building 1 is quite impressive, and stands alongside evidence for glazed windows (Le Patourel 1979, 94-5; Andrews 1979a, 130).

Was it wrong, then, to place so much emphasis on the structural evidence from Building 1 when trying to create a model for medieval peasant house construction more generally? Inevitably perhaps, the present writer thinks not, if only because the model has since been applied to many other excavated medieval peasant buildings (both houses and barns) constructed and occupied at varying periods in widely differing locations, and it seems to account adequately for their observed characteristics (Wrathmell 2002). The main area of contention now appears to be the date at which such buildings were first erected. Nick Hill has argued that cruck construction developed 'in the thirteenth century, as an integral part of the development of innovative, well-carpentered houses' (Hill 2005, 12, also 3-4), and a similar date was proposed some time ago by Dyer, for whom 'building methods changed with the introduction of stone walls' (Dyer 1986, 36; 1989, 161).

A perennial problem for archaeologists is that major changes in the character of excavated structural remains are invariably assumed to result from major changes in techniques of construction. Thus the first appearance of stone walls – even if only low stone sills to support a timber superstructure – must mark a radical departure from earlier techniques requiring earthfast posts. The writer believes this is not necessarily the case: the first appearance of padstones, stone sills and stone walls was not inevitably accompanied by new superstructures built using new techniques. Earthfast uprights, whether vertical posts or cruck blades, could be underpinned with stone to extend their longevity, the extent of underpinning dependent upon the local availability of stone (see Gardiner 2000, 159-60 and 178).

It is clear from Mark Gardiner's assembly of house plans of the 11th and 12th centuries that the modest dwellings of Domesday's villeins and bordars are hard to spot. Apart from two at Monkton in Kent, which could be indicative of the smaller houses of this period (in that region), his examples are all probably manorial or sub-manorial in status (Gardiner 2000, 168-74). Does this mean that the Late Saxon and Norman peasantry continued to erect dwellings that would have been indistinguishable from those of earlier centuries, with walls formed by closely set, substantial earthfast uprights of the kind evidenced by the Middle Saxon building in the South Manor Area (Fig. 55), or had there already been a shift in structural techniques?

The hypothesis proposed here and elsewhere (Wrathmell 1994, 189-90; Wrathmell 2002, 183-4), is that the emergence of manors and the development of lord-villein relations in the Late Saxon and Norman periods created a context for change. The lords would have provided the main timbers needed by the villeins to construct their houses and barns; in later centuries customary tenants were fined for allowing their buildings to fall into disrepair – not because the sight of wrecked buildings would have been displeasing to their lords, but because the failure to maintain roof coverings and walls presented a threat to the condition of the main timbers, the lord's assets. It would equally have been in the lord's interest to reduce to a minimum the amount of building timber he had to provide for each villein dwelling, and it may have been this consideration, against a background of diminishing timber resources, that led to the development of the post-and-truss and cruck-truss techniques of construction. The quantities of building timber required for their houses could have been significantly reduced through the use of widely-spaced, transverse trusses forming bays, and more sophisticated carpentry joints to fasten them together.

The plan forms of the Wharram houses have been discussed at length too many times to require further detailed consideration here, but in summary Building 1 in Area 6 can be accommodated comfortably in the contemporary and later vernacular traditions of the Wolds (Wrathmell 1989c, 10-11; cf. Cowlam: Wrathmell 1988, 106). It had a hearth-passage plan, with an entry passage running across the building in a position immediately behind the main hearth place. West of the passage was the 'non-domestic' end; on its east side was a door leading into the main living room by the side of the hearth. The living room itself provided access to a sleeping parlour beyond.

The position of the hearth, backing on to the partition that separated the living room from the entry passage, implies that it had been furnished with a firehood that funnelled smoke through the roof space. Hearths in such locations seem to have replaced hearths positioned in the centre of the floor in earlier houses, the latter possibly represented at Wharram by Building 4 in Area 10 (Site 9: Wrathmell 1989b, 18-19). The transition was more clearly recorded at West Whelpington in Northumberland (Jarrett and Wrathmell 1977, 115-17). Such shifts in position, with the accompanying introduction of a firehood, would have enabled much of the living room to be lofted over, to create a chamber for storing equipment and farm produce, or perhaps a place where servants could sleep. In earlier buildings with central hearths, the extent of lofts would have been more restricted.

As we have seen in Chapter 19 (p. 315), debate continues in relation to the function of the 'non-domestic' ends in such buildings, along with the associated arguments about the former distribution of the 'longhouse', with a living room and byre under one roof, and a common entry passage between them (see also Gardiner 2000, 163-8). For the present writer, the discussion seems to involve too great a polarisation of functions and too rigid a classification of plan forms to be of real relevance to the lives of the families who occupied these buildings. As Dyer has pointed out, buildings or rooms erected for one purpose would be converted to another when circumstances required, including the conversion of domestic to non-domestic functions, and *vice versa*. Furthermore – and a point that seems rather lost in the debate – functions will have changed over the course of the annual farming cycle on a recurrent basis. In the traditional Northumberland longhouse, the 'non-domestic' end or *out-bye* served as a byre in winter and a bedroom in the summer (Hodgson 1827, 189), no doubt to the relief of the farmer and his wife who could put some nocturnal distance between themselves and their children. It is very possible that similar variations in function on a seasonal basis were experienced in Building 1, Area 6 at Wharram Percy.

Another topic of debate has been the identification, in both excavated and surviving structures, of ancillary domestic buildings – detached kitchens, bakehouses and brewhouses. It is one that has again already been touched on by Dyer (see pp 314-15 and 329 above), and a little more can be said on the basis of one of the few detailed (though partial) records of the vill: the assignment of dower, made in April, 1368 which provided Euphemia, widow of the lord of Wharram, with a third share of the manorial assets (TNA PRO C135/198/12). Such assets as could be physically divided were allocated in a ratio of 1:2 (see pp 290-92), but others could not. Euphemia was allocated a third part of the profit of the common oven and a third part 'del kylne' with suit etc. in common (*Cal IPM XII*, 183).

The common oven was presumably used for baking bread, and the kiln seems likely to have been for malting, in which case we might anticipate that the individual farmsteads (or many of them) would not, in the 14th century, have contained their own bakehouses or brewhouses. The continued existence of such manorial facilities (we can say nothing about their use) might be a sign of the strength of lordly control, but it could equally be an indication of the scarcity of fuel: it was presumably more fuel-efficient to run a single large facility than numerous small ones, even if the tenants would otherwise have taken it in turns to supply the rest of the village. The village bread oven and kiln will presumably have been large structures located on the green or on other common land in the village.

In other parts of the country, bakehouses and, or brewhouses were clearly appurtenances of individual farmsteads. For example, the deserted settlements of Hound Tor and Hutholes in south-west England produced four similar sized ancillary buildings, each with a stone platform at one end containing a kiln and an oven (Beresford G. 1979, fig. 24); these are readily identifiable as facilities of this sort (Wrathmell 1989c, 14). The writer has previously suggested a bakehouse function for a couple of small, two-bay structures with ovens mounted on stone platforms, excavated in the deserted village of Hangleton, Sussex (Buildings 3 and 11: Holden 1963, 85-91; Hurst and Hurst 1964, 108-11; see Wrathmell 1989c, 14). This still seems to him a more likely identification than that of 'detached kitchen', as subsequently suggested

(Martin and Martin 1997, 87). Clearly this is another topic in need of systematic regional analysis. As far as Wharram Percy is concerned, all we can say is that there is no obvious candidate for a detached bakehouse or brewhouse associated with Building 1 – unless it is represented by Building 8, a narrow structure set at right-angles, to the south of its eastern end (Wrathmell 1989b, 34-5 and fig. 29).

The inventory of William Akclum and its context
by Christopher Dyer

The Akclum inventory
Though we lack detailed documents which tell us about individual Wharram Percy villagers, an inventory for 1481 has survived for William Akclum, a peasant from the adjoining village of Wharram le Street (Plate 35: BIA, D&C wills, 1481, Akclum). The following is a calendar/translation rather than a transcript of the document. Where possible the modern English word is given (sometimes with the original in parentheses) after). If there is uncertainty about the modern equivalent, or the meaning is known but this cannot be conveyed in a single word, the original spelling in italics is given. Items in [ ] had been crossed out in the original.

Inventory of all of the goods of William Akclum of Wharram in Street, made the penultimate day of the month of May (30 May) in the year 1481, valued by Robert Maneby, Roger Carter, Robert Allynger and William Robynson of the same.

In the chamber (*In camera*)
Firstly, one ....; 1 mattress; 1 pair of linen sheets (*lynshettis*), 8d.; 2 pairs harden sheets (*harden shettis*), 8d.; 2 pillows (*coodis*), 1d.; 2 table cloths (*bordclothis*) and 1 towel, at least 5d.; 2 blankets (*Blankydis*), 3d.; 1 chest (*arke*), 4d.; 3 *tabbys*, 12d.; 4 pots (*potts*) and 1 *ston* de..., 4d.   .....3d.; ....; in s ...and..............

　　　　Total ....

In the house (*In domo*)
1 chair (*cheyre*), 2d.; 1 meat board (*metburde*), 1d.; 1 mat (*nate*), 1d. ; 1 cupboard (*awmery*), 2s.; 1 *calle*, ?d.; 1 *pate* and 1 kettle, 20d.; 1 pan, 4d.; 1 candlestick, 1d.; 1 *skele* and dishes, 2d.; 1 lead (*lede*), 16d.; 1 *braik* and 1 *swynkelstok* , 3d.; 2 *garnwyndels fote* and 1 *cob stol*, 1d.; 1 board and 1 stock, 1d.; 1 *raken* and 1 pair *klpes*, 2d.; 1 spit and 2 wombles, 6d.; 2 sickles and 1 *lowke roke* , 2d.; 2 *rokkes* and 2 *relles*, 1/2d.; 1 *?leknyffe*, 1/2d.; 1 pair shears, 1/2d.; 1 heckle, 1d.; 1 *temes*, 2d.; 1 *skote* and 1 *syffe* and a *batildor* , 2d.; 1 bushel and 1 *strekile*, 2d.; 1 *mannger* and 1 *horesheke*, 1d.; 14 hens and 1 cock, 14d.; 6 birds, 2d.; 1 pig (*swyne*), 20d.; 1 pair plough irons, 4d.; 2 yokes, 3d.; 1 pair hames, 1d.; 1 *leye* and 1 iron fork,

2d.; manure (*moke*), 8d.; wheat in the field, 8 acres, 26s.
8d.; 5¹/₂ acres of spring corn (*war corn*) , 11s.

Total 50s. 5¹/₂d.

Sum total of goods 56s. 11¹/₂d.

Debts which the said William owes

To Wharram church (*Wharrum kirke*),   12s.3d.

To lord William Ryngros, vicar of same, 4s.10 ¹/₂d.

To lord John Kirsagar, 16s.

[To Robert Nalton, 12s.]

To William Sharp, 13s.4d. [40s.]

To the wife of Wilbefosse, 28s.

To Richard Smyth, 11s.

To Richard Dikson, 4s. [10s.]

To Rage of Neswick (*Nesewik*), 10s. [12s.]

To Thomas Skern, 7s.

To Edward Bigot, 4s.

To John Lutton, 3s.4d.

To Edmund Dawlton, 7s.

To Hasilwood of York, 3s.

To Robert Gilson, 3s. [4d.]

To John Cottes of York, 18s. [20s.]

To John Dobson, 10s. [16s.]

To William Key, 10d. [10d.] (*sic*)

To John Leppyngton, 4s. [7s.]

To [John] same Leppyngton, 6s.

To Thomas Horesley, 4s.

To William Howntrode, 14d.

To Thomas Molfyrde, 15d. [16d.]

To Thomas Acklom, 13s.

To Dove of Duffield (*Duffeld*), 3d.

To Richard Yngrham, 9d.

To Robert Hanc, 6d.

[Garnumwar, 4s.]

To Robert Manby, 5d.

Total £12 14s. 0 ¹/₂d.

Debt exceeds goods by £9 17s. 1d.

Which makes default, to be paid at 2s. for
each 6s. 8d. [6s in the pound]

The inventory as a source for life in the village of Wharram Percy

Probate inventories are available in large numbers throughout England from the mid-16th century onwards, but they are scarce before 1530. It was a common procedure when wills were proved before a church court for possessions to be listed after death, as the valuation of the goods showed how much was available to pay the debts, expenses and bequests of the deceased. Unfortunately for historians, before the Reformation the inventories, though often compiled, were not usually preserved. There is however an important collection of inventories for southern England mainly for the period after 1480 in the archives of the Prerogative Court of Canterbury, and a group for an earlier period, mainly after about 1420, are found in the Diocesan and Dean and

Plate 35. William Akclum's inventory of 1481. (D&C wills, 1481, Akclum. Reproduced from an original in the Borthwick Institute for Archives, University of York)

343

Table 22. Inventories of Yorkshire peasants, dated 1438-94.

Name	Robert Connyg (1)	William Atkynson (2)	John Scott	John Crosby	John Faysby	John Jakson (3)	John Hall	Thomas Smyth	Thomas Kyrkeby	John Gaythird	William Akelum
Date	1438	1456	1456	1458	1463	1464	1468	1479	1482	1494	1481
Place	Helperby	Helperby	Acomb	Tollerton	Huby	Grimston	Holgate	Swyston	Clifton	Acomb	Wharram le Street
Cash (£ s d)	0 11 8 (3%)	-	0 1 4 (3%)	-	0 1 0 (0%)	0 0 2	0 0 6 (0%)	-	11 12 0 (38%)	-	-
Clothing & weapons	0 3 4 (1%)	-	0 6 8 (13%)	-	-	0 15 7 (7%)	-	-	-	-	-
Household goods	3 9 6 (15%)	1 15 8 (15%)	1 2 8 (46%)	0 1 6 (13%)	0 18 2 (5%)	1 9 11 (14%)	2 8 0 (27%)	1 2 7 (10%)	3 9 2 (11%)	2 6 1 (14%)	0 13 8 (24%)
Implements	1 5 4 (5%)	1 5 4 (10%)	0 3 0 (6%)	0 5 0 (11%)	0 2 0 (1%)	0 19 3 (9%)	1 6 8 (15%)		1 2 0 (4%)	2 4 5 (13%)	0 1 11½ (4%)
Hay, muck and wood	0 2 0 (1%)	0 1 8 (1%)	-	0 16 0 (35%)	0 2 0 (1%)	0 7 0 (3%)	0 12 0 (7%)	-	0 15 0 (2%)	-	0 0 8 (1%)
Crops	8 6 0 (36%)	4 5 8 (35%)	0 9 0 (18%)		1 18 0 (11%)	2 18 4 (27%)	2 1 0 (23%)	2 16 6 (24%)	4 13 1 (15%)	5 11 1 (33%)	1 17 8 (66%)
Animals	8 2 6½ (35%)	4 11 4 (38%)	0 7 0 (14%)	0 19 0 (41%)	14 12 0 (83%)	4 1 2 (38%)	2 7 8 (27%)	7 16 0 (66%)	9 5 4 (30)	6 10 10 (39%)	0 3 0 (5%)
Total of Inventory	23 2 0½ (100%)	12 2 8 (100%)	2 9 8 (100%)	2 6 1 (100%)	17 13 2 (100%)	10 13 1 (100%)	8 15 10 (100%)	11 15 1 (100%)	30 16 7 (100%)	16 12 5 (100%)	2 16 11½ (100%)
Debts owed to deceased	-	-	3 6 8	0 2 3	-	0 15 2	0 4 0	0 14 6	1 19 0	16 6 4	-
Debts owed by deceased	2 9 4	2 12 10	0 18 7	3 5 0	-	3 7 4½	2 3 1	10 18 1	-	9 13 11½	12 14 0½

Notes; 1 With 1s 8d for 'various items not valued', £1 for wool; 2 With 3s for salt meat; 3 With 1s 8d for bacon flitcher

Chapter archive in York, and from the archives of various peculiar jurisdictions, including the district around Northallerton now kept in the archives of Durham Cathedral.

In the final part of this chapter Peter Brears uses his profound knowledge of the terminology of domestic furnishings and kitchen equipment to explain the meaning of the names of the (to us) obscure objects owned by Akclum, which help to show what the interior of his kind of house may have looked like, especially around its hearth, in the late 15th century. This short contribution seeks to assess Akclum's resources, consumption and wealth by comparing his inventory with those of ten other peasants who lived in other parts of Yorkshire, dated from 1438 to 1494 (see Table 22). They came from villages near York and to the north-west of that city, and they occupied low-lying alluvial or clay soils, quite different from Wharram's chalk wolds. That part of Yorkshire was not very densely populated or prosperous, and rather inferior in those respects to the north-west wolds where Akclum lived (Campbell and Bartley 2006, maps 18.5, 18.6, 18.10 and 18.15). Although the inventories used for comparison have been chosen because they were made for peasants, they tend to relate to the better-off individuals within that group.

The first point, to state the obvious, is that William Akclum was very poor, and faced heavy debts. The total value of his inventory, £2 16s 11½d, was equivalent to a fully employed northern carpenter's earnings in about 6 to 7 months, while his debts approximated to the same carpenter's wages for three years (Woodward 1995, 181-3). His household goods, though numerous, were each assigned very low values, which meant that together they were worth less than those included in nine of the ten

inventories in the sample. He owned very few animals or agricultural implements. His 13½ acres of crops were given quite a high price considering that they were valued in May, ahead of the harvest, and accounted for two-thirds of the total assessment of all of his goods. There were many people in his position of poverty, but it is unusual to find detailed documentation of the plight of the poor because they did not often have inventories made for them. Among the ten peasant inventories being used here for comparison, only that of John Scott of Acomb resembles Akclum's in the low overall value and the lack of livestock, though his debts came only to 18s 7d, which gave a surplus for his widow and two children. John Crosby of Tollerton generally lacked goods of all kinds, which left him with an overall total similar to Akclum's, and like Akclum his debts exceeded the value of his inventory, and his heirs would have suffered in consequence.

A probate inventory provides a snapshot of a lifetime at its worst moment, when it ended. For those who were cut off in the midst of an active life by an infection or accident, the inventory reflects their productive resources and healthy finances, but for many the inventory was made after a period of illness or old age, when holdings were run down and implements and furnishings had become worn and shabby. Neither Akclum nor Crosby were life-long paupers. There are signs that not long before their deaths they did not lack resources. Among Crosby's debts is listed an annual rent of £1, which suggests that his holding contained at least 20 acres of land and more probably 40 acres, because land in 1458 commonly paid 6d per acre. Akclum had 13½ acres sown with corn. Of these 5½ acres had been sown in the spring, and one suspects that he had intended to sow

Table 23. Crops in selected inventories.

Inventory	Wheat	Rye	Barley	Peas/beans	Oats	Total
Connyg		9 ac 45%	8ac 40%	1ac 5%	2ac 10%	20ac 100%
Atkynson	7ac 41%		7ac 41%	3ac 18%		17ac 100%
Hall		8ac 73%		3ac 27%		11ac 100%
Smyth	10ac 37%	-	3ac 11%	7ac 26%	7ac 26%	27ac 100%
Gaythird		15.6ac 43%	17 46%	4 11%		36.6ac 100%
Akclum	8ac 59%		5.5 41%			13.5ac 100%

more. Even 13½ acres, however, represents the amount of sown land we would expect to find in a holding of two oxgangs or bovates totalling about 30 acres, of which a half would have been left fallow. Two oxgangs would place him among the more substantial. The other inventories in the sample, which depict holdings which were functioning more or less at full potential, were compiled for peasants with acreages comparable with Akclum's and Crosby's: John Jakson had only 6 acres under crops, but he had rented out another 10 acres, so his holding in total was similar to Acklum's. Others were cultivating 11, 17, 20, 27 and 36.6 acres (Table 23).

Akclum had an adequate amount of land, but he was not properly equipped to cultivate it. His plough irons (share and coulter) were valued at 4d., compared with 14d. for those owned by John Jakson, which suggests that Akclum's were defective or inferior in some way. He seems to have had no plough, when seven of the ten peasants whose inventories were sampled owned at least one. No vehicle is mentioned in Akclum's inventory, though eight of the sample contained either a cart or a wain, or both in two cases. They were expensive items, and John Hall of Holgate's smart new iron bound cart (*biga*) was valued at £1 3s.4d. Carts were pulled by horses, and wains by oxen, and the number of wains recorded around York suggests that oxen were being employed there as draught animals, when there was greater use of horses on the wolds (Langdon 1986, 256). Akclum's implements were small items of low value, such as sickles, a fork and shears. His bushel suggests that he had once sold corn, from the profits of which he could have paid his rent, invested in the farm, and bought clothing and shoes for himself and his family, household furnishings and kitchen utensils. But he could not use his shears to obtain wool for sale, as he had no sheep, and his yokes and hames were left over from the time when he had oxen and horses to serve as draught animals.

The most likely explanation of this incomplete inventory is that the holding was fully equipped with livestock and implements some time before May 1481.

William might himself have ploughed and planted the acres under crops, and then through some disability or misfortune had to dispose of all of his more valuable animals and equipment in a matter of weeks. A more plausible reconstruction of events would be that because he was unable to do heavy work himself, he arranged for his land to be cultivated by hired labour in the autumn of 1480 and the spring of 1481, and that he had been compelled by his debts to sell his plough, cart, oxen and horses at least a year before his death. If we read between the lines of the inventory, it records the sad long-term decline of a once substantial peasant, who had fallen ill or had suffered an injury.

The profile of Akclum's agricultural production before he suffered a setback can be reconstructed by reference to the sample of ten inventories. His corn consisted of 8 acres of wheat, sown in the autumn, and 5½ acres of spring sown corn, probably barley and peas. The preponderance of winter sown crops is unusual among the inventories as often about two-thirds of the crops consisted of barley, peas and oats (Table 23). To some extent the crops of the comparative sample reflect the farming practices of the lowlands, in their cultivation of rye as one of the winter grains, for example, but a bias towards spring crops is found everywhere (Dodds 2007, 34-5). Wheat brought a better price at market, but could only be used for bread, and the same tendency to grow the more versatile spring-sown crops has been observed in the 14th-century records of demesne crops on the Wolds, and those collected as tithes (Table 18).

Akclum's livestock was restricted to the bare minimum, a pig and some poultry. Only three other inventories mention poultry, perhaps because a few hens were not worth valuing, but they were an important asset for a poorer household. Almost every household had at least one pig, and one, that of John Faysby, kept enough to make a substantial profit in the market (Table 24). Akclum's yokes and hames show that he had recently used larger animals, and most peasants in the sample of inventories owned between two and five horses, and five

Table 24. Livestock in inventories. (*=partly legible)

Inventory	Horses	Oxen	Cows	Other cattle	Sheep	Pigs	Poultry	Other
Connyg	2		15		40	2	24	-
Atkynson	5	4	2	7	-	3	16	-
Scott	-	-	1	-	-	1	-	-
Crosby	4	-	-	2	-	1	-	-
Faysby	16	3	5	6	80	63	-	-
Jakson	2	4	1	2	6	6	7	bees
Hall	4	-	1	4	-	1	-	-
Smyth	2	8	7	-	60	-	-	-
Kirkeby*	3	-	4	1	9	3	-	-
Gaythird	7	6	1	6	11	6	-	-
Akclum	-	-	-	-	-	1	21	-

Sources for Tables 23 and 24: York Minster Library, Probate Jurisdiction, Inventories, L1 (17) 19; BIA, D&C wills 1456 Atkynson; BIA Acomb Peculiar Court Probate Index; BIA Alne and Tollerton Peculiar Probate Index, 1458-1601; BIA Exchequer Wills, 15th century; BIA, D&C wills 1464 Jakson; BIA, D&C wills 1468 Hall; BIA, Arch. Reg. 22, fo. 354v; BIA, D&C wills 1482 Kirkeby; BIA, D&C wills 1494 Gaythird. For Akclum see above.

to fifteen cattle. Horses were for pulling carts and for riding, and some were reared for sale, while the cattle included oxen for draught, cows for dairying, and younger male castrates to be sold for beef. Most households kept at least one cow, and the four which kept four or more would probably have been producing surplus butter and cheese for the market, and were rearing beasts for sale. The sample of inventories reflects the cattle orientated farming of the vale. Sheep were very unevenly distributed, with three flocks of between 40 and 80, and a number of peasants leaving inventories kept none at all. A consideration, as well as the absence of upland pasture, must have been the labour for looking after them, which was only justified if the flock contained 40 animals. It would be reasonable to suppose that a year or two before he died, Akclum had owned at least two horses, four cattle, some sheep, a plough and either a cart or wain.

Although Akclum's inventory is the only example from the Wolds, the stints recorded for Wolds manors in the 13th century suggest that in that region the overall balance between animals of different species was not dissimilar, except that sheep were probably kept by a higher proportion of peasants (Table 16). The numbers of animals were not so different, remembering that the stints applied to a single oxgang, while the inventories were compiled for tenants with two or three oxgangs. The late medieval shift towards pastoral farming may be reflected in the inventories of Connyg, Faysby and Smyth with numbers well over the level envisaged in the stints, but of course stints were attempting to establish maximum numbers, and in the real world of the 13th century as in the 15th, a few ambitious peasants would have disobeyed the rules.

In his decline Akclum could barely have maintained the peasant ideal of self-sufficiency as his own produce of grain, eggs and bacon would have fed his family, with little to spare after rent had been paid. In his prime, he would have been able to sell a surplus of grain and animal products. His furnishings and household goods were given very low values by the appraisers, as if they were old and worn. A chest would often have been worth more than 12d, but Akclum's was said to be appraised at 4d. A pan was assigned the same low value, when those belonging to other peasants were often said to be worth three times that sum. In one respect Akclum was well provided, with equipment for preparing and spinning flax fibres. Perhaps this had always been a side line, practised by his wife, but it may also be another indication of poverty, as such crafts were often pursued by cottagers rather than those with two oxgangs of land. Two other inventories in the sample mention heckles and other tools used in processing flax.

The absence of cattle and horses, and a cart, and perhaps also of a cast bronze cooking pot or a coverlet for his bed suggests that Akclum had kept his household going by selling everything of value. His large debts might show that he had borrowed money, or that he had not paid promptly for goods and services. His debt to the vicar of Wharram le Street may have originated as a consumption loan, as the beneficed clergy often acted as money lenders. One of William Ryngros's successors, Thomas Grissaker when he died in 1511 had made at least six loans (BIA, D&C Wills, 1511, Grissaker). But we should not jump to the conclusion that Akclum's debts reflect simply his miserable poverty and inability to pay back his creditors. Many of the other inventories indicate levels of debt comparable with our Wharram le Street peasant, such as those of Thomas Smyth and John Gaythird, and neither of them have any hints that they were sinking into penury. Five others left debts in the region of £2 to £3.

Debts were a normal part of peasant life, as they were buying (and not paying immediately), investing in buildings and animals, and lending money for profit. Their engagement in networks of credit should not be seen as a sign of poverty or desperation, but rather that they were active in a world, including the urban world, in which money played a major role (Briggs 2009, 214-223). Part of Akclum's debts could have been accumulated when he was leading a normal busy life, when for example he had dealings with two people in York, though there must also be an element in his list of obligations of dangerous and even reckless borrowing on the strength of limited assets and income, which would eventually ruin his family. His debts also caused hardship to his creditors who according to a note at the end of the inventory would receive only 2s for each 6s 8d that they were owed.

In one aspect, Akclum's inventory leaves us in uncertainty, as it begins to describe the goods with a room-by-room survey, beginning with the chamber with its bedding and furnishing, and its pots which may well have been ceramic vessels, and then moves vaguely to the 'house', with the usual contents of the hall which was also used for cooking, and then describes farming equipment and livestock. These cannot all have been housed in one all-purpose space, but the appraisers seem to have lost sight of their aim to identify each room. At some point they moved into an out-building or barn, and then walked into the fields. Other inventories tend to divide the goods between a hall and chamber (in six of the ten inventories). Four mention a kitchen, two a *seler* which seems to be an upper room, and individuals were recorded as having goods in a brewhouse, a barn and a 'house of husbandry'. One took the same course as Akclum's appraisers, and used the single inadequate heading of the 'hall and other necessaries'. Clearly in the Yorkshire lowlands, as at Wharram Percy as demonstrated by survey and excavation, peasant dwellings were normally divided into a hall and chamber, and could be accompanied by a room or building for food preparation, and space for agricultural use.

The Wharram le Street inventory, in spite of the rather special circumstances in which it was produced, if compared with others from Yorkshire helps us in many ways to visualise aspects of the peasant economy of Wharram Percy: crops, animals, farming equipment, household possessions, domestic crafts, credit arrangements, and the ups and downs of life.

Plate 36. Artist's impression of the interior of Building 1 in Area 6 (Site 12) in the early 16th century. (© Peter Brears)

348

The interiors of Wharram's farmhouses and their contents: two artist's impressions and a commentary

by Peter Brears

Plate 36 is an impression of the interior of the main room of a Wharram farmhouse – of Building 1 in Area 6 (Site 12) – in the early 16th century, in what was to be the last generation of the village's existence (see Ch. 22 below). It is based partly on the archaeological discoveries at Wharram itself and partly on the Akclum inventory discussed above, and in terms of its structural aspects it represents, perhaps, the final stage in the transformation of our ideas of medieval peasant houses, from flimsy, short-lived buildings to the types of structure that are known to have formed the traditional dwellings of this region down to the 19th century (see Wrathmell 1989c, 3-5). The focus of this chapter is, however, the furnishings and equipment of the room, and here the excavations of Building 1 were less revealing, and perhaps less revealing than they might have been.

For the past fifteen years the writer has studied the service areas of numerous historic houses, many of which have been completely stripped of their furniture and fixtures. The accurate reconstruction of these interiors looks impossible at first, faced with only hard-paved floors and bare walls; however, regular cleaning and the passage of feet causes varying degrees of wear and changes in texture. Normal archaeological techniques usually fail to record such subtleties, but stroking with the fingertips can reveal a wealth of detail – for example, the slight dome where a table leg has protected the floor from erosion or the slight trough where feet have shuffled at table or bench. Seeing the completely exposed floors of Wharram houses in the early 1960s was a revelation at a period when trenches and baulks were the norm. With hindsight, it is possible that the floors still retained evidence, even of the scantiest nature, of the furnishings and activities they originally supported. Such information would have been invaluable in recreating the lives of their last inhabitants.

Nevertheless, there are some pointers to furnishings and equipment in the form of artefacts recovered from the excavations, some of which were of types current at this time. Furthermore, much can be gleaned from later social history sources: Henry Best's *Farming and Memorandum Book* of 1642, George Meriton's *In Praise of Yorkshire Ale* of 1684, and even Woodcock's *Primitive Methodism on the Yorkshire Wolds* of 1889, can all offer insights into the ways in which the population of the Wolds used their natural resources throughout the centuries. Wharram Percy may have been depopulated, but other Wolds villages have continued to the present day.

As noted in several previous chapters and earlier in this, Building 1 in Area 6 appears to have been an exceptional house: it was perhaps the largest in the village; it had been equipped with glazed windows, and its table had been furnished with imported ceramic drinking vessels (Le Patourel 1979, 94-5; Andrews 1979a, 130). Some of the vessels are shown in Plate 36 which is based on archaeological evidence and inferences. As suggested earlier in this chapter, it may have been fully lofted over, having a firehood, but the illustration shows only a loft over the entry passage.

Plate 37 shows a house interior of earlier date, with a central, open hearth to provide contrast with the firehood arrangement in Building 1. It is furnished with the items of loose furniture and equipment recorded in William Akclum's inventory, and these items are individually identified in Figure 114. As we have seen, the inventory lists the contents of, first the chamber (*camera*) and then the hall or 'house' (*domus*). Though these two are differentiated, it is clear that the list then runs from the domestic end of the hall, on to its lower end, which housed mangers, plough irons, yokes, hames etc., along with hens and a pig, before viewing the crops in the fields. Modern niceties often assume that a wall separated the human and animal compartments of the 'longhouse', but boarded screens four to five feet high were still performing this function in the 1870s (Atkinson 1891, 19).

Floor coverings

The inventory does not mention any overall covering on what are presumed to have been earthen floors, but as *Juncus* rushes were available in the valley bottom (Jones 2005, 191-5), it should be expected that they were regularly cut for scattering in the halls or living rooms of the houses, being periodically cleaned out to serve as animal bedding etc. Pleasantly moist and aromatic when cut in summer, they then dried to provide good insulation between the earthen floors and the occupants' feet during the cold autumn and winter months.

The document does, however, itemise a *nate*, located in the hall and valued at 1d. Nates appear in the halls of a number of Yorkshire peasant households. Besides William Akclum's nate, John Jackson of Grimston had one in an inventory of 1464, which was valued, along with two cushions, at 2d. In 1479 Thomas Smyth of Swyston had a nate also valued at 1d (Stell and Hampson 1998, 240, 275, 280). All are listed adjacent to the hall table.

References such as 'making a natt for the wyves to knele on when they come to be churched' in 1597 (Barmby 1888, 43), or for 'covering the seates with natting in the Dean's closet' at York Minster in 1669 (Raine 1859, 348), show them to have been relatively thick and soft. William Marshall's glossary of 1788, based on usage around the Vale of Pickering, defines a 'nat' as a straw mattress, probably made by stitching together lengths of plaited straw or twisted straw rope (Marshall 1788, 'nat'). The presence of a straw mattress in the hall suggests that the practical and comfortable practice of sleeping snug and warm by the fire, rather than in the cold, unheated chamber, was customary for at least some members of the household – or perhaps even for William himself during his final months of illness. In

Plate 37. Artist's impression of the interior of a late medieval house, largely furnished with items listed in William Akclum's inventory, see Figure 114. (© Peter Brears)

the daytime it might have been rolled up and stowed away, or else left in place to serve as a low-level seat/lounger in this household of only a single chair and a low stool.

Furniture

William Akclum's inventory lists a mattress and bedding in the chamber, but not a bed. This is unlikely to mean that the mattress was laid on the ground, since this would be uncomfortable, damp and dirty, but may indicate that the bed frame had its posts set into the ground, and so became part of the freehold, rather than goods movable.

Also listed in the chamber was an *arke*, valued at 4d. Up to the 16th century, arks were used to securely hold personal possessions in a chamber, rather than to hold corn and/or meal in a service room; 37 of them are indexed by Stell and Hampson (1998). In rural communities, it was usual up to comparatively recently to leave outer doors open in all but bad weather, only bolting them when it became dark, and the occupants were about to retire to bed. There was therefore as much need for hasps and locks on the lids of arks as on outer doors, especially since the latter need only be locked on the outside if the family were to be absent for some time. It is therefore probable that the looped hasps, such as those found in Area 6 (Goodall I.H. 1979, 116-18), are as likely

to come from arks as from doors. The same form is seen on an oak ark of 15th-century date illustrated in Chinnery (1979, fig. 2, 121).

In the hall, the inventory lists a *cheyre* and *metburde*, a chair and a meat board – a table at which meals were taken. The latter would probably have followed the simplest contemporary designs, the board being supported on trestles so as to be easily moved or dismantled when not in actual use. The 1413 Ordinances of the York Joiners' Company (Morrell 1949, 23) state that a dining table should be of the length of one wainscot (imported oak plank) by 1 inch in thickness, or if 45 inches long, of a $^1/_2$ inch thickness, with legs 1 inch thick.

There was also an *awmery* or aumbry. Meriton (1684, 81) records that 'An Aumry; is a Cupboard to put bread or meat in'. Akclum's was valued at 2s, when most others in contemporary inventories ranged from 6d to 1s 8d, so this must have been a good quality piece. The 1413 Ordinances of the York Joiners' Company (Morrell 1949, 23) state that cupboards were to be made of 2 wainscots formed into 4 posts with a main body of $^1/_2$ inch, $^3/_4$ inch and 1 inch boards. Most aumbrys take the form of a plank-built cupboard, its door and planks usually being pierced with small window-like openings for ventilation, and its interior fitted with shelves to hold foodstuffs and tableware; 62 aumbrys are listed in the index to Stell and Hampson (1998).

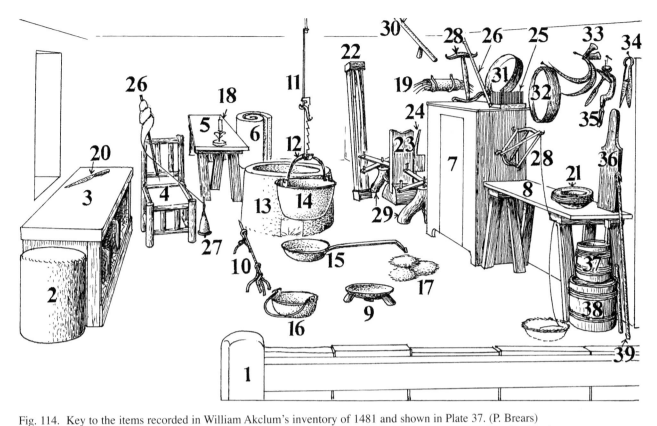

Fig. 114. Key to the items recorded in William Akclum's inventory of 1481 and shown in Plate 37. (P. Brears)
Fittings 1. heck: partition between the doors, separating humans from animals. *Furniture* 2. stock: chopping block;
3. cawl: dresser-cum-chicken coop; 4. chair; 5. meatboard: dining table; 6. nate: straw mattress; 7. aumbry: food cupboard;
8. board: table; 9. cobstool: low stool. *Cooking and lighting* 10. spit; 11. raken: adjustable pot-hook;
12. pot kilps: adjustable pot hanger; 13. lead: boiling furnace; 14. kettle; 15. patel: frying pan; 16. pan; 17. cassons: dried cow dung;
18. candlestick; 19. candle-bark: candle and rushlight holder, of birch bark; 20. knife; 21. dishes. *Linen production* 22. brake;
23. swinglestock: swingletree; 24. swingletree dagger; 25. heckle; 26. rocks: distaffs; 27. spindle; 28. reels: niddy-noddies;
29. garnwindles. *Agricultural and general equipment* 30. ley: scythe; 31. temse: sieve for meal or brewing; 32. sieve; 33. sickles;
34. shears; 35. wombles: spoon-bit augers or drills; 36. battledore: laundry bat; 37. skeel;
38. bushel and strickle: bushel measure and stick to remove any surplus; 39. lowkeroke (lowk-crook): hooked knife for weeding
corn.

A further item of furniture in the hall, a *calle*, is of particular interest. No furniture with this name is recorded in the OED, but Ross *et al.* (1877, 'Cawl') record the east Yorkshire word 'cawl' as a kitchen dresser with hutches underneath for young chickens and ducks in cold weather. This presumably provided a warm and fox-free home for some of his fourteen hens, especially when broody or being fattened for the table. The hens shown in Plate 37 are probably oversized: faunal remains suggest that the hens at Wharram were no bigger than modern bantams (see p. 323).

The remaining board would be another table, but not used for dining, while the 'stock', a word with a variety of meanings, was probably a simple length of tree stump, used as a chopping block for culinary purposes and firewood etc. Even though simply furnished, such houses had everything required for a basic but practical lifestyle.

Akclum had also owned a *cob stol*, a cobstool or 'coppy-stool'. It was a low three-legged stool, probably used when tending the pots etc. on the hearth. Simon Mays' analysis of human remains has indicated a greater prevalence of 'squatting facets' in females than males, and he ascribes this to women's role in tasks such as

preparing food and tending the fire (Mays 2007, 125-7). Though women may have squatted for long periods for other reasons, hyperdorsiflexion of the feet was perhaps also the result of using cobstools, particularly at the fireside.

Lighting

The only reference to the means of lighting William Akclum's house is to a candlestick, valued at 1d. This is, however, unlikely to have been the only means of illuminating the building. There may also have been rush lights, described by Meriton (1684, 106) thus: 'A seave is a Rush that is drawn through in grease, which in ordinary poor houses, they light up and burn instead of a Candle'. This description reflects a practice already of considerable antiquity. The rush was not bullrush, or reed-mace, but the *Juncus* soft or common rush, with long tapering cylindrical stems a few millimetres in diameter. When harvested in high summer, they were soaked in water, so that all their smooth green peel could be stripped off their absorbent pith, leaving just one narrow strip to provide support. They were then dipped in molten grease, i.e. rendered pig fat or lard, rather than tallow, and stored for winter use. A cylinder of stripped birch-bark made an ideal container, giving the name candle bark to its later tinplate replacement (Wright 1923, 165). They burned quite rapidly, the rate being determined by the angle at which they were set, the more vertical, the slower.

Rush-light holders cater for this property, by having tapering notches into which lengths of rushlight could be jammed at the required angle. A pricket candlestick excavated from Site 12 (Goodall I.H. 1979, 117, fig. 61, no. 20) has an upwards spike to hold a candle, and a downwards one to secure it on to a wooden base or foot, the former spike being flanked by a pair of scrolls to give it a fleur-de-lis silhouette. The angular notches between the spike and the scrolls would have been ideal for holding lengths of rush, and probably served as rush light holders when no candle was being burned.

Candles represent a more expensive form of lighting, since they require linen wicks, and larger quantities of hard sheep or ox-tallow. They were usually made by repeatedly dipping the wick in barely melted tallow, until it had taken up an almost cylindrical form. Two iron socket-candlesticks from Site 12 (Goodall I.H. 1979, 117, fig. 61, nos 21 and 22), show that the candles here were about half an inch (1.3cm) in diameter. Being of iron, they were probably similar to William Akclum's candlestick.

Utensils for food preparation
Of the objects recovered from the sites of medieval farmhouses at Wharram, the larger knives would have been used for cutting meat, fish and vegetables ready for cooking. The other significant utensil in food preparation was the mortar, and again examples have been recovered from the excavations (e.g. Smith 1989, fig. 36). In the kitchens of major households mortars might be used for reducing a wide variety of ingredients to smooth pastes, but this is not the basic cookery of rural households such as those at Wharram. One of the oldest methods of converting cereal grains into easily digestible food was to thresh them from the ear, winnow off the chaff, then grind off the husk by pounding them with a little water in a mortar, before rinsing off the debris, to leave them smooth and pearled. After soaking and stewing, they turned into a highly nutritious, glutinous and satisfying dish called frumenty, from the Latin for corn, *frumentum*. It had the advantage that it could be made without having access to either a quern or a mill. Its earlier popularity is confirmed by its continuity, a number of East Riding families still making a batch every Christmas at the present time.

Mortars are not recorded in Akclum's inventory, but it does contain other items related to food preparation, including a bushel and *strekile* valued at 2d, a *temes* or tempse, also valued at 2d and a *syffe*, or sieve. It was usual to grind small quantities of corn in a quern or at the mill shortly before it was required for use, since the meal might rapidly spoil due to mildew etc. A bushel measure would be filled to overflowing with the corn, the surplus

being swept off level with the top of the measure, using a cylindrical rod called a strickle. The meal was measured again after it had returned to the house, to check that the miller had not taken too much as his 'mulcture' or fee. Before use, the coarser bran was removed using a coarse-meshed cloth stretched across a wooden hoop called a tempse. The function of Akclum's sieve, valued with his *batildor* (battle dore or laundry bat) is uncertain, but it may have separated dust and grit from grain, spent malt grains from wort when brewing, or fine flour from coarse, along with other culinary operations.

Most late medieval sites produce a number of bowls/basins which would be used for dairy activities, mixing doughs etc. Wharram has relatively few of these, which suggests that their place may have been taken by turned wooden vessels. A wide range of ceramic jugs have, however, been found. These will have had multiple uses but the presence of handles at the pond suggests their use for collecting water. The significance of the springs supplying water to the two Wharram townships has been discussed in Wrathmell 2005a (1, 2) and vessels of pottery and other materials would have been used to collect it. Another significant observation is no drip-lines were found around the houses; indeed accumulations of rubbish were found in the areas where they might have been expected (Wrathmell 1989b, 32-3). This suggests that wooden gutters and rainwater butts may have been used, as in the post-medieval period.

Fuel
There was insufficient woodland in the township of Wharram Percy to enable wood fires to burn permanently in its houses. Similarly the transport of peats from the moors would have been prohibitively expensive. It is most probable that small fires were only lit as and when required for cooking one, or perhaps two meals each day, day-long fires for room-heating only being provided in the cold winter months. Even major households, such as those of the Percys at Wressle and Leconfield, only provided fires in their halls from All Hallows on 1st November to Lady Day on 25th March (Percy 1905, 99).

The Wolds have been relatively short of fuel throughout recorded history. The banks enclosing the various plots at Wharram Percy would have been useless unless topped by well maintained hedges, presumably of thorn, which would have provided a regular if limited source of rapidly-burning trimmings, both for domestic use and for heating the communal bread oven. Straw and chaff would be suitable for heating the communal malt kiln, but were hardly practical for home cooking. An alternative was cassons. Meriton (1684, 83) records that 'Cassons, are dryed cow turds'. The English expression to 'clap cassons' is almost identical to the Danish *klapkassen*, used to describe the clapping of cassons into balls as fuel, just as the Swedish *klappertorv* refers to doing the same thing with peats. This suggests a Scandinavian introduction of this practice into this area, or alternatively a renaming of pre-existing practice.

J.R. Mortimer remembered that in the 1830s the cottage wives of Fimber collected semi-dried cow-pats from the surrounding lanes and pastures for use as fuel. In wet weather they collected them soft, clapped them on the sunny sides of their cottages and left them there until they were removed for use, and replaced with a new supply (Mortimer 1978, 5). Alternatively, they were spread out as a two or three-inch thick solid mass on the ground, cut into diamonds or squares, left to dry, and stored away for use. Clay was sometimes mixed in, or it was burnt with lumps of chalk to make an excellent fire, long lasting, giving a good heat, little smoke and a pleasant perfume. This practice is probably borne out at Wharram by the presence of numerous fragments of burnt chalk on most excavated sites. The writer, having used cassons as a fuel for both boiling and baking on the hearth, can confirm its efficiency. They must have provided the main fuel at Wharram Percy, and we should picture the south or west-facing walls of its houses pelted with the bovine equivalent of snowballs (Brears 1987, 46-7; Brears 2008, 60).

The presence of 'charcoal' in an archaeological deposit is not necessarily an indicator of the use of charcoal as a fuel there, since pieces of firewood smothered by ashes as a fire burns out might be converted into charcoal, providing a scatter of charcoal in a situation where intentionally kilned charcoal was never used. The charcoals found here, however, include oak, ash, hazel, alder, willow/poplar, field maple and birch, most of which species are not found in the Wolds, but are common in the Vale of Pickering and its Marshes to the north (Andrews et al. 1979, 133). Including both twigs and large sections, they almost certainly represent charcoals kilned there, their lighter weight and high calorific value making them ideal for transport up to villages such as Wharram, and for regular use there. Charcoal works best with an under-draught, such as that provided by a chafing dish (e.g. Le Patourel 1979, 94, fig. 42). It is most probable that the chafing dishes found here were used as primary cooking utensils, rather than as dining-table reheaters of more fuel-rich areas. Food placed in cooking pots balanced on their three projecting knobs could be readily boiled or fried without having to light a fire on the hearth, thus making great savings in fuel. Ceramic chafing dishes remained in regular use in the East Riding through to the mid-19th century, one collected at Eske near Beverley being given to the Yorkshire Museum in 1888 (Brears 1963, 27, no.78a).

The long-term shortage of fuel at Wharram is clearly indicated by the presence of coal here, starting in the 13th to 14th centuries, and expanding in the 15th century. Given the presence of the major Newcastle-London collier shipping trade passing by Bridlington, and the established Bridlington-York road via Wharram, it might be expected that the coals found there came from the North-east. The analysis of samples suggests that the coal came from the Methley area, at the junction of the Aire and the Calder to the east of Leeds (Andrews et al. 1979, 133-4). From here it may have been possible to partly barge supplies down the Aire towards Howden, up the Ouse, and then follow the Derwent towards Malton, but this route was not made fully navigable until the late 18th century. The only alternative would have been to transfer the coal from barge to pack-horse at York, then follow the busy pannierman's route for the seventeen miles to Wharram.

It is interesting to speculate how the coal was burned. The Wharram hearths are all level with the ground, not sunken to provide an under-draught-cum-ashpit as is seen in the hall at Warkworth Castle, for example. No evidence for ranges or grates is provided either by archives or by archaeology, and so it must be assumed that the coal was burned on the flat hearths, probably as a mixed fire with local firewood. Since most shallow-mined coal, especially if dampened by rain en route, produces volumes of stinking grey-yellow smoke, it is unsuitable for cooking other than for roasting or for boiling in covered pots. Its use may therefore have been largely restricted to room-heating over the winter period, unless no other fuels were available.

Cooking on the hearth

Medieval hearths at Wharram were set in the centre of the hall, the main living room of each house. Only in the late 15th to 16th-century Building 1, Area 6 does the hearth move off-centre, apparently to introduce a hearth passage and effectively to convert the bay between the opposed doors into a cross-passage. It is probable that this change was associated with the introduction of a timber-framed smoke hood. Such hoods remained in use in this part of Yorkshire through into the 20th century.

The hearths are usually made up of stones, either slabs or smaller blocks, laid horizontally at or close to ground level. It might have been expected that post-holes would have been found at each side of the hearths, to support forked uprights holding a horizontal gallows-bar, for the suspension of cooking vessels. There was, however, no evidence for these in any house, showing that some alternative form of suspension was in use.

On any hearth, but especially on those where economy in fuel consumption was important, as here, the use of a boiling vessel hung over the fire was inefficient. Only a limited amount of heat was transferred to the vessel, most being either diverted by draughts, or dispersed as it rushed up the sides of the vessel, and lost into the air. It was far better to build a square or circular clay or clay-bound masonry wall around the vessel, into the top of which the rim fitted snugly. When burning fuel was thrust in, through a single floor-level firemouth, its heat was concentrated around the cooking vessel, ensuring a much higher level of transfer to its contents, before the smoke issued from the upper part of the firemouth. Such furnaces are found in medieval kitchens of every size and status, and are mentioned in contemporary documentation either as furnaces, or as 'leads', even though their vessels had been made of copper alloys rather than lead from the early medieval period. William Aklums' *lede*, or lead was, at 16d, one of his more valuable possessions.

In Area 6, a yard-square perimeter of stone blocks to the right, south side of the hearth of Building 1, and opening onto it (Wrathmell 1989b, fig. 15), may represent the base of a furnace; similarly, the stone-slabbed hearth of Building 4, Area 10 (Site 9), has a *c.* 3ft by 4ft 6ins burnt area to its south-west (Wrathmell 1989b, fig. 8). This has been interpreted as a possible oven, but ovens were never, ever, set at floor level, since they were impossible to use in that position. It is the base of a furnace, showing that furnaces with inset 'leads' were in use here from the late 13th century onwards. In use, such furnaces would have been ideal for boiling larger quantities of liquid, such as water for brewing, laundry, or textile finishing.

Moving on to metal cooking pots, Akclum's inventory lists a *pate* and a kettle, valued together at no less than 20d. He also had a pan, worth 4d. The *pate* is a 'patel', or frying-pan, as confirmed by an entry in the Durham Account Rolls of 1481 for '2 friyng patyls ferr' (Fowler 1898, 97). Akclum would therefore have had a frying pan in which to fry his bacon and eggs, fish and fritters. The kettle would be an open-topped vessel, made of beaten metal sheet, most probably copper alloy, with its rim rolled over an iron hoop, and with loops or a bail-handle for suspension. It would be hung over the fire from his *raken* and a pair of *klpes*, worth 2d.

The 'rackan', or rack and crook, was a long iron crook hung from the roof over the hearth, a narrow loop at its base engaging with the row of notches along the long edge of rack below, so that it could be rapidly adjusted up or down as required. A hook forged at the bottom of the rack supported the 'kelps'. These were single bow handles, with loops at each end to slip into the hanging loops of pots or kettles, and a hinge in the middle, so that they could be used on vessels of many diameters. The kettle on its adjustable hanger would be Akclum's main cooking vessel, in which all his meat, fish and vegetable pottages would be simmered. The form of his 'pan' is less certain, but it would most probably be smaller than the kettle, have no means of suspension, be shallower, and be made of beaten copper-alloy sheet. Evidence for the use of sheet-metal vessels at Wharram is provided by patches and fragments of rim and body sherds (for example Goodall A.R. 1979, 110, fig. 56, no. 51 and 113, fig. 57, nos 60 and 61).

The more prosperous households might also have a cast copper-alloy pot, of the form now known as a cauldron, with bulbous body, flared rim, pair of hanging loops, and three legs. The leg of one of these was retrieved from Site 12 (Goodall A.R. 1979, 110, fig. 56, no. 52).

Ceramic cooking vessels do not feature in the Akclum inventory, but Wharram excavations demonstrated that they were prevalent in earlier centuries. From the 12th to the 14th centuries they were usually the local Staxton wares, and were of two forms: one with a height some 60-85% of its diameter, and the other only 30%. Both have rims some 7/8 inches (20mm) wide, with a high external outer edge which falls at a concave 30° to the inner lip, suitable for receiving a flat wooden lid. In capacity, the

deeper vessels would be suitable for cooking two gallons, the shallower around 1 or 1.25 gallons. Their different shapes probably represent two different cooking operations. The deeper would be ideal for liquid pottages, such as meat, fish or vegetables simmered in water, while the shallower would be better for either cereal pottages, including oatmeal gruel and wheat frumenty which had to be regularly stirred, or for simmering fish, which could more easily be removed from them in larger pieces. The broad, relatively flat bases of these pots would absorb more heat from the fire than those of narrower vessels, suggesting that the potters had purposely designed their wares to meet the needs of this fuel-impoverished environment.

Although the 12th-century bakestone from the North Manor Area showed that circular brandreths (three-legged iron supports) were then used to hold vessels over the fire in that period (see Clark and Gaunt 2004, 216-19), there appears to be neither archival nor archaeological evidence for their use in the later Middle Ages. It is most probable, however, that brandreths did continue, the only alternative being that the vessels were placed directly on the fire on the hearth stones.

The excavations have produced no evidence of the flesh-hooks, ladles, skimmers, slices (pot sticks) or skewers necessary for cooking. These may all have been of wood, which would not have survived on this site. It seems more likely, however, that implements such as these were recycled when they ceased to be serviceable, or were taken away by departing tenants if still usable.

Given the lack of domestic ovens at Wharram, and the lack of evidence for bakestones from the 13th century onwards, it is probable that breads were home-baked on the hearth, using an upturned cooking pot. The traditional technique involved lighting a fire on the hearth until it was hot, moving the embers to one side, setting the bread either directly on the hearth or on a thin slab on the hearth, then covering the bread with a cooking pot, heaping the embers around and over it, and leaving it until it was completely baked. Trials carried out using both peat and cassons have shown this to be an effective technique.

Compared to boiling, roasting is an expensive and time-consuming method of cookery. It requires a brighter, radiant fire of dry wood, the better-quality cuts of meat (fish rarely being roasted), and the constant attention of someone to keep the spit rotating, for if left stationary for even a minute or two the joint is charred and spoiled. In addition, it fails to produce the flavoursome stocks required for pottages. There is good evidence, however, for roasting being carried out at Wharram, from both archival and archaeological sources. William Akclum's inventory valued his spit and two wombles or 'wimbles' (i.e. gimlets or augers) at 6d. In 1485 a moderately-sized spit might be valued at 1s to 2s 6d, and small spits at 3d each, showing that his was a small spit, and one not supported on racks (Stell and Hampson 1998, 298).

Before the introduction of dripping pans, either cooking pots or old mortars were sometimes set into one end of the hearth, rim at floor level, to collect the fat dripping from the roasting joints. They have been found in this position in a number of medieval hearths such as the York Bedern (Richards 2001a, 205), and a fine example is to be seen in the hall kitchen at Warkworth Castle. At Wharram, a mortar was set into the side of the hearth in the latest phase of Building 1 on Site 12, presumably to fulfil the same function (Wrathmell 1989b, fig. 15).

Domestic industries: textile production

The best evidence for textile production in the late medieval Wharram townships is provided by Akclum's inventory. His pair of *lynchettis*, or linen sheets, and two pairs of *harden shettis* (coarse linen sheets) could have been home-produced, along with his two *coodis*, 'cods' or pillowcases, two *bordeclothis* or tablecloths, towel, and presumably his underclothes too. His 'house' or main living room, was provided with all the equipment necessary for manufacturing such linens. Following the instructions in *The English Hus-wife* (Markham 1615, 90-104), it is possible to envisage how linen was produced at villages such as Wharram Percy and Wharram le Street with a relatively high level of confidence.

Having used harrows or beetles (mallets) to break up the soil three times commencing at the end of February, the seed retained from the previous flax crop was sown broadcast at the end of April, harrowed in, and the birds scared off until its stalks emerged. At the end of July the flax was pulled up by the roots, laid on the ground for 24-36 hours, tied into bundles or 'bats', and left vertical to dry out and wither for a week. It was then 'rippled' through an iron-toothed comb to remove all the seeds, which were kept in a dry vessel for the next year's crop (see Robinson 1857, 171, 'one peare of reple combs'). The bundles were then submerged in a pond, ditch or pit for three nights, being secured there by stakes driven into the bed, horizontal bars tied down across them, and heavy stones placed on top. After being 'watered' in this way, each bundle was washed clean of all its leaves and dirt, and carried back to the house, where it stood vertically in the sun until it was perfectly dry and brittle, and could be stored indoors. If the weather was inclement, the bundles might alternatively be dried in the malt kiln.

The various stages of extracting the 'bun' or coarse fibres from the finer filaments required for linen production could now commence in late summer. Choosing a sunny day, the bundles were laid out until tinder-dry, and then worked with a *braik* or 'brake'. This was a frame with two closely-set horizontal bars about two feet from the floor, between which a sharp and notched-edged board was hinged, so as to break up and remove the coarsest bun with a chopping action. The bundles were then transferred to the *swynkelstok*, or swinglestock, a half-inch thick board supported on a strong foot or stock. As each bundle was progressively pushed over the edge of the stock, it was beaten with a long, blunt-edged length of wood called a swingle-tree dagger, this scissor-like action removing most of the bun, and softening the linen fibres. The coarse 'hards' or bun left after breaking and swingling could be worked

between wool-cards and then spun to produce harden, the coarsest of the linen cloths – such as Akclum's *harden shettis*. Any surplus bundles were sent to market at this stage, the remainder being swingled again, to make the linen fibres finer and softer, and extract more coarse fibres for making a finer harden. Now the linen was ready for heckling, the heckle being a board from which rows of close-set straight iron teeth projected vertically, through which each bundle or 'strike' was now pulled. The remaining hards made 'middling' cloth, while the fine 'tear' were now ready for spinning.

Although spinning on the Great Wheel had probably been introduced into England from Flanders in the early 14th century, it did not produce a thread as fine as that spun on the slower drop-spindle and distaff (Baines 1982, 54). These remained in use in Yorkshire up to the late 17th century, George Meriton's *Clavis* (1684, 103 and 167) informing us that 'A Rock, is a Distaffe, and 'A Sneauskin, is a leather which Women have fast at their Distaff, and lay upon their thigh to twirle their spindle upon'. The resulting thread had then to be wound into skeins on a reel, which Markham (1615) says is hardly two feet long, with two contrary crossbars. This is the 'niddy-noddy' of the West Riding textile industry, which had hook-ended crossbars set at 90° to each other at each end of the shaft, around which the thread could be rapidly wound from the spindle into a skein (Baines 1982, 219). Acklum's two *rokkes* and two *relles*, or two rocks and two reels, were valued at a halfpenny. Each eighty turns of the yarn were tied together to form a 'ley', and twenty such leys formed a 'slipping'.

On being removed from the reel, the skeins were soaked in water for three or four days, being wrung out and plunged into fresh water each day and finally rinsed in a well or stream. They were then transferred to bucking-tubs of wood-ashes and water, which together produced a strong alkaline lye which bleached them to whiteness. Once dried, the skeins were stretched on a garnwindle – Akclum had two *garnwyndels* – from which the thread was wound into balls, weighted, and sent off to the weaver. After the web or piece of probably yard-wide cloth had been returned to the house, it had to be steeped, bucked in ash-lye, and stretched out on the grass, with stakes driven through loops sewn on to the selvedges. Here it was left for some three weeks to bleach, with periodic bucking and rinsing, only being allowed to dry and be taken indoors when sufficiently white. The best months for bleaching were April and May, by which time the seeds from last year's crop had been sown, to restart the annual cycle of cloth production.

It is significant that all the above information is available almost solely from a range of archival and later published sources. In terms of archaeological evidence, all that might be expected to survive would be a few post-holes in the mill-pond or stream-bed, organic remains of flax seeds, and the few small pieces of metalwork used in the entire process. No ripple combs have been found, but numerous heckle teeth have been recovered from village. Two from Site 12 (Goodall I.H. 1979, 119, fig. 62, nos

53-54) are each some 4ins long by $1/4$ inch square (100mm x 6mm) and taper towards their points.

Akclum's two *blankydis*, or blankets valued at 3d, and presumably his outer clothing, would all be of wool. His sheep, after being washed in late June, would be clipped about ten days later, each fleece then having the soiled 'dags' around the rump clipped away, so that it could be folded and rolled either for sale or for storage. Since this was not a specialised worsted area (such as York or Beverley) there were no woolcombs in Wolds inventories. Rather more surprisingly, there were none of the cards, spinning wheels and looms required for the production of woollens. The archaeological record tends to confirm this, having provided nothing related to domestic wool processing. It therefore appears that most or even all the wool produced on the Wolds was sold as a cash crop to weavers in the towns, the finished cloth being bought as required from their markets. In fact this conforms with the later 16th-century inventories of South Cave, at the south end of the Wolds (see Kaner 1994, 26), where the local linen industry also predominated. This may be an unexpected conclusion for an area in which sheep and wool were so prominent, but unless archaeological or archival evidence for wool-cards is found here – carding being the essential pre-spinning process – there is nothing to suggest that the locally-grown wool was even spun on the Wolds.

22 The Desertion of Wharram Percy Village
by Stuart Wrathmell

The end of the medieval community

The starting point for discussing the desertion of Wharram Percy is the same as it was in the first volume in this series: the findings of the government's 1517 commission of enquiry into depopulation. They indicated that 'four messuages and four ploughs were thrown down' at Wharram Percy between Michaelmas 1488 and 1517. Beresford suggested a rather shorter timescale, 1488 to 1506, on the basis that the entry named the current tenant in chief, the Baron Hilton who had inherited the lordship in 1506, but did not ascribe the depopulation to him (Beresford M.W. 1979, 6-7).

The second critical piece of evidence was discussed in detail in a more recent volume. It is a statement by one of the deponents in a 1555 law suit or 'cause', brought in the court of the archbishops of York, relating to alleged dilapidations at Wharram Percy vicarage (Wrathmell 2010b, 17-22). The witness was Robert Pickering of Raisthorpe, aged about 70, who claimed that the 'towne' of Wharram Percy had been laid to grass 28 years earlier (that is, in about 1527: Plate 38). Whatever the reliability of Pickering's memory of the precise year, the final abolition of open-field agriculture seems to have come a decade at least, and perhaps nearer half a century after the depopulation recorded by the 1517 commission.

The implication of the 1555 record is that, until 1527, significant numbers of bovate holdings were still in the hands of manorial tenants, and were still under open-field cultivation. There is, moreover, a further indication that Wharram supported a stable population until this time, in the records of another cause, dating to 1526 (BIA CP G.180: information kindly supplied by Christopher Dyer). The cause related to the marriage of Nicholas Thomson alias Wilson of Wharram Percy and Katherine Pynkney of Uncleby. One of the deponents was another resident of Wharram Percy, George Marshall, aged 60, who claimed to have known Nicholas since his birth. George may well have been one of the tenants evicted soon afterwards.

Other depositions in the 1555 cause indicate that, after 1527, the pair of two-bovate holdings outside manorial control – the glebe and chantry lands – were still cultivated for a time, though evidently with their yields much reduced by contamination from the surrounding grasslands (Wrathmell 2010a, 1-2). By the middle of the century these, too, had finally succumbed, and Wharram Percy had become a classic example of open-field 'enclosure' carried out to effect the wholesale conversion of arable lands to permanent pasture. It is the type of enclosure that did not involve the definition and fencing of new fields: the whole township remained 'open', but as a sheepwalk rather than as a territory that was largely under cultivation.

This does not, however, mean that the four messuages and ploughs thrown down before 1517 were necessarily the first stages of some grand plan to achieve such an outcome. Engrossing – the amalgamation of two or more holdings – was of as much concern for the government as was enclosure for the conversion of arable to pasture, whether for animal husbandry or for sustaining wild animals in parks (see Thirsk 1967, 200-217). It is possible that these four Wharram holdings were simply absorbed by neighbouring farmers. It may, indeed, be wrong to suppose that the Hiltons were driving forward such changes at that time: engrossing may have been a tenant initiative, as it was at Filey, where William Battom occupied three husband-holdings, causing the dereliction of two messuages (Leadam 1893, 250).

Some indication of what replaced the open-field tenements can be gleaned from another cause heard in the archbishop's court, a dispute over tithes. In 1543/4 Marmaduke Atkinson, vicar of Wharram Percy, was in dispute with John Thorpe of Appleton over tithes of fleeces, lambs and hay. Atkinson, as farmer of the Wharram rectory tithes, claimed he had been given an insufficient share given the number and value of sheep pastured by Thorpe in the parish, and given the number of loads of hay that Thorpe had made there. The arguments therefore centred on quantities and values.

The surviving record of the proceedings consists of a set of Articles on a sheet of parchment in which Atkinson set out his charges, and a series of six Depositions, on paper, detailing the evidence given by a number of local farmers and farm-workers in relation to each of the

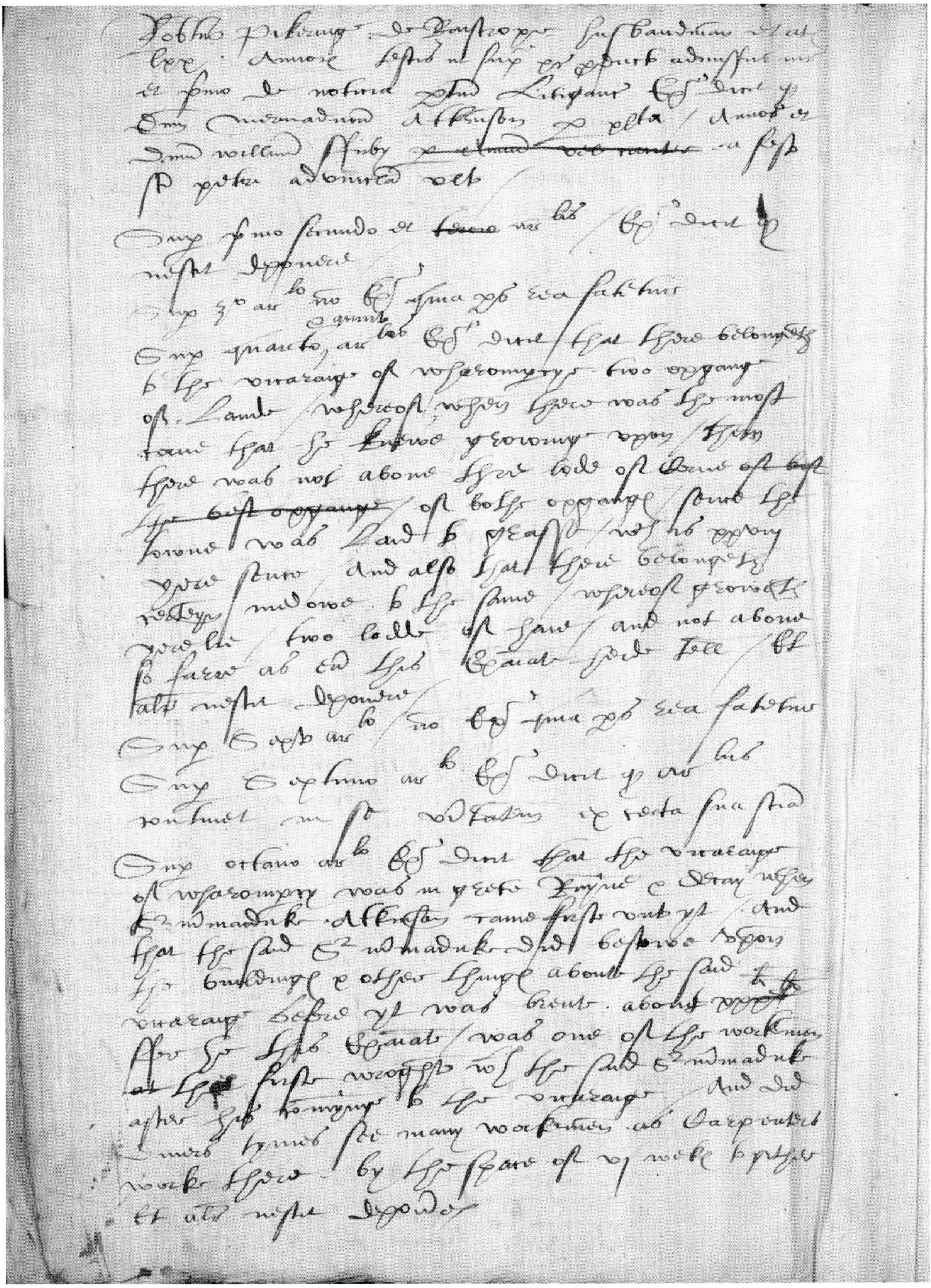

Plate 38. Deposition of 1555 referring to Wharram township having been laid to grass. (CP G.917. Reproduced from an original in the Borthwick Institute, University of York)

Articles. Thorpe's responses to the charges are interlined with the Articles (BIA CP G.314). The documents do not specify the townships in which the flocks and hay grounds were located, since all that mattered was that they were within the parish. As noted in a previous volume, however, there is a good circumstantial case for suggesting that Wharram Percy township had provided much, if not all, of the pasture grounds and hay 'ings' in question (Wrathmell 2010a, 2-3).

One of the witnesses, Thomas Carter, was resident at Towthope at the time he made his Deposition, but stated that he had been an inhabitant of the 'towne' of Wharram Percy until the previous November. He had kept ten sheep of his own in a pasture where John Thorpe's sheep went, and he 'saith that he could neither go to nor fro to Fodder his said sheep but he must needs see them...': that is, he knew the numbers of sheep Thorpe kept there because, when he was resident in the township, he walked through them to tend his own sheep.

Atkinson's Articles recite the successive owners and farmers of the rectory and its tithes, from Haltemprice Priory to the King, and then to Atkinson who farmed them from the King. They then give the number of Mr Thorpe's sheep that Atkinson claimed had grazed in the parish, and how long they had been there. Atkinson's case was that from January to March 1542[/3], and from April to December 1543, Mr Thorpe had pastured there 26 score ewes, three hundred wethers and three hundred hogs. As Henry Best tells us a century later, sheep were counted 'sixe score to the hundreth' (i.e. to the 'long hundred' of 120: Woodward 1984, 19), so the total number of animals was 1240.

Thorpe's response gave, inevitably, a rather lower total (1100). The two deponents who made a stab at the figures gave numbers even lower than Thorpe's: they varied slightly as to the individual categories (perhaps to avoid the appearance of collusion?), but achieved identical totals (1080). They also stated that the hogs (the young sheep still to experience their first shearing) had been removed from Wharram to 'Yastrope' between St Andrew's Day and Lady Day (that is, for the winter months). Yastrope can be identified as Easthorpe, a township adjacent to John Thorpe's place of residence, Appleton-le-Street, some 6 miles north-west of Malton (Fig. 113). According to Dodsworth, 'Yestrop' or 'Yaresthorp' was 'walled and imparked this present yere 1620' (Clay J.W. 1904, 163).

'Mr Thorpe', as he was called by the deponents, may have been a sheep-master of the sort that had been targeted by government legislation a decade earlier. The ineffective 1533 Act had sought to limit the number of sheep one man might keep to two thousand by the long hundred (i.e. 2,400: Beresford 1954, 111; Thirsk 1967, 217), and Thorpe's Wharram operation may have represented only a part of wider grazing interests. Whatever the actual size of his total stock of sheep, the more interesting question in a Wharram context is whether he was party to the laying down to grass of the township some sixteen years earlier, or whether he had simply moved more recently into an already vacant township.

It seems, on the face of it, a distinct possibility that Thorpe was the person who offered sufficient money to the Hiltons to encourage them to evict the township's remaining open-field tenants. The 1543/4 deponent who has already been quoted, Thomas Carter, said that he had known Thorpe for only four years – a period coinciding with Carter's residence in Wharram Percy township which had ended the previous November. Of the other witnesses, however, John Wilson, a current inhabitant of Wharram Percy township, said he had known Thorpe for eleven years, Michael Tailor of Towthorpe had known him for ten years, Richard Hodgson of Towthorpe for 18 years, and William Hogg of Raisthorpe for 20 years. Perhaps most significantly of all, Mathew Morwen, the farmer of Wharram Grange, had known him for 16 years.

No doubt a man like Thorpe, a rich grazier who lived only about 12 miles from Wharram, would have been widely known in the local farming community, not least through his presence at nearby markets and fairs, such as those at Malton. Nevertheless, it remains a distinct possibility that he was known locally for more than a decade because, in about 1527, he had played a major part in the abolition of open-field farming at Wharram, and had continued to pasture his sheep in the township ever since.

In the first Wharram volume it was suggested that Thorpe's residence at Appleton 'may explain why not even the shepherd of *Utopia* was living at Wharram and available as a witness in 1555-6 [in the vicarage dilapidations cause]' (Beresford M.W. 1979, 9). Whatever the reason for the failure of Wharram Percy's inhabitants to make an appearance among the 1555-6 deponents, it is now clear that the township had a few residents in the mid-16th century, even if they were short-term small-holders or cottagers. Indeed, it may have been their short-term residency that made them unsuitable witnesses in the Dilapidations cause. We know the names of Mr Thorpe's shepherds there in 1543: George Alan and George Gurwell were cited by Thomas Carter, who claimed to know how many fleeces they had given in for the king's tax.

Wharram Percy was not just an outlying and transitory area of grazing; it was clearly a territory where flocks were pastured and managed on a long-term basis – many perhaps for the whole of 1543. The ewes and wethers will have been shorn there in May or June, after being washed in the Beck. In the 1640s Henry Best of Elmswell described the method of constructing a sheepwash in a stream by creating a dam, 'for a sheep-dyke shoulde allwayes bee of that depth that it may take a man to the buttockes'. It was often necessary to 'sette downe broade and close doore or coupe-lynings against some hecke or bridge', but he preferred a stream deep enough for washing without damming, in order to cleanse the fleece more thoroughly:

'Yette the dyke that is deepe enough of itself, that needeth neither stoppinge nor damminge but runnes continually and lettes the scumme and dirty water passe away – that, I say is the onely Sheep-dyke' (Woodward 1984, 19-20).

It may be that, in the 16th century, the Wharram Beck offered such an advantage: some of the banks and mounds recorded by the stream in the earthwork survey may be the remains of constrictions in its course which had subsequently been removed. Furthermore, once the village had gone, the stream would have ceased to be contaminated by the tenants' cattle treading the margins of the south pond (see Wrathmell and Marlow-Mann 2005, 226).

With this sort of facility, Wharram Percy would have been far more attractive for commercial sheep-farming than many other Wolds townships, especially those on the High Wolds that depended on just one or two rain-fed ponds for the whole of their water supply (see Wrathmell 2005a, 1). It may have been targeted by Thorpe for this reason, as well as for its accessibility from the Vale. The conversion of its arable lands to pasture does not necessarily imply that the bovate holdings had become too infertile to be worth cultivating; only that, in the 1520s to 1540s, the returns from renting out to a grazier were better than those that could be extracted from the open-field tenants.

The middle years of the 16th century may have marked a rare moment in the township's history when there was no arable cultivation at all at Wharram; but it is unlikely to have lasted for long. By the early 17th century, and probably in fact by the 1570s, Wharram Percy had become an infield-outfield farm (Wrathmell 2010a, 3-7; see Harris 1961, 24-5). The bulk of its territory was still undivided pasture, and a probate inventory of 1699 suggests that the chalk plateaux were still primarily sheep pasture, but there was also a core area of intensively cultivated arable land, the infield, that was supplemented by occasional intakes from the pastures beyond.

Figure 115 is a reconstruction of the putative areas of infield and outfield based on a rental of the second quarter of the 18th century, and on the field shapes and field names shown on Dykes' plan of 1836. It is very speculative, but reflects broadly those areas that were recorded as 'closes' in the rental (see Beresford and Hurst 1990, 113, fig. 84). In 1776, however, Improvement came to Wharram, with the subdivision of the outfield into fenced, hedged and ditched fields (Wrathmell 2010a, 10-13). As the 1836 plan shows (Fig. 116), the areas of former outfield were put under cultivation, whereas the former infield was put down to grass. At a time when its many neighbouring open-field townships were also being enclosed, Wharram Percy came once more to resemble them.

Settlement shrinkage and desertion in the study area and beyond (Fig. 113)

Overall, the 1517 commission of enquiry found relatively few cases of depopulation in the East Riding: the total number of houses recorded as being decayed, including the four at Wharram, was just 41 (Leadam 1893, 219 and table 8). Furthermore, few of these were located in the vicinity of Wharram. The wapentake of Buckrose furnished only two records: Wharram itself and Hanging Grimston, where St Mary's Abbey had converted 40 acres of arable to pasture, resulting in the decay of two messuages (Leadam 1893, 248). On the evidence of the surviving records it seems that, between 1488 and 1517, the northern Wolds saw very little depopulation as a result of either engrossing or the conversion of arable to pasture. Wharram Percy was atypical.

There is one other nearby township that appears, like Wharram, to have been wholly depopulated and its lands converted to pasture. Eastburn, now a completely deserted site in Kirkburn parish, on the Wolds dipslope just south of the study area, was acquired by John Heron of Beverley who pulled down most if not all its houses and turned the entire township into a sheepwalk. Eastburn was, however, acquired by Heron in 1664-6, and his activities are recorded in a Tithe cause that came before the archbishop's court in 1682 (Neave 1993, 133). As we shall see below, the parallels with Wharram Percy are striking; but the depopulation of Eastburn came no less than a century and a half after the desertion of Wharram.

Most townships in the study area continued, like Eastburn, to support villages farming open-field systems for another century or two after the pastoral conversion of Wharram. Except for Kirby Underdale, where the whole township was enclosed in 1583, the first to succumb to general enclosure were those on the fringes of the Wolds. Birdsall, Langton, Scagglethorpe and Thorpe Bassett were largely or entirely enclosed by private agreement between 1650 and 1726. Many more study area townships, including ones on the high Wolds, saw general enclosure in the second half of the 18th century, among them Duggleby, the Heslertons, Kirby Grindalythe, North Grimston, Rillington, Settrington, Sherburn, Sledmere, Thixendale and Wharram le Street; whilst Fimber, Helperthorpe, the Luttons and Weaverthorpe lingered on into the early 19th century (Alexander 1994, 50-51 and 218: Appendix III).

Susan Neave has identified the later 17th and early 18th centuries as a period in which many long-established Wolds villages experienced significant shrinkage, and some of them near total depopulation. Her calculations indicate that it was a period when the rural population of the East Riding as a whole fell by almost 19%, and when Buckrose wapentake experienced a reduction of almost 27% (Neave 1993, 128). The vulnerability of individual settlements to contraction was linked to landownership:

'The majority of settlements under the control of only one or a small number of landowners experienced substantial contraction, and in some cases had been reduced to one or two farms by the mid-eighteenth century. This suggested that settlement contraction could be a direct result of changes in land use or agricultural practice, such as emparking, enclosure, or an increase in the size of farms, initiated by major landowners.' (Neave 1993, 130)

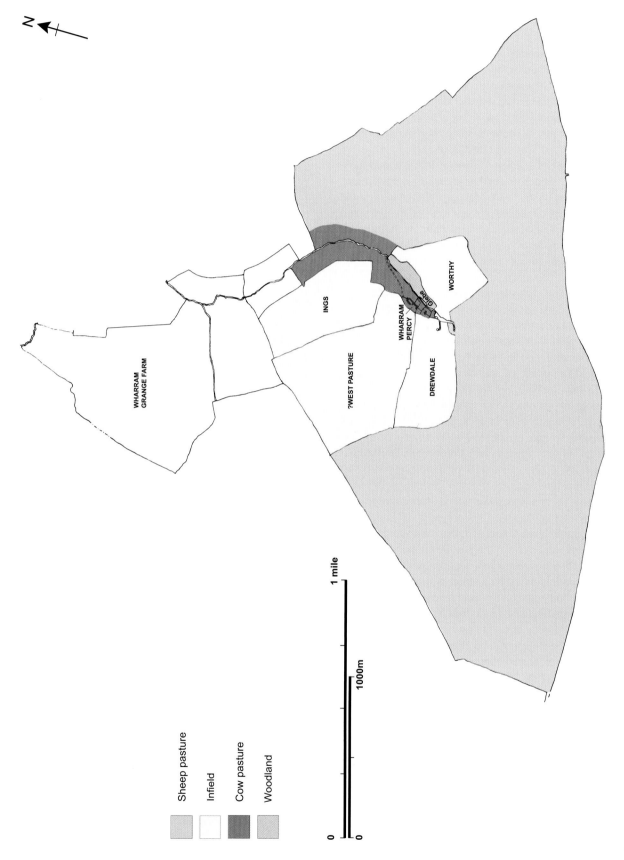

Fig. 115. Reconstruction of the 17th and 18th-century infield and outfield of Wharram Percy. (E. Marlow-Mann after W. Dykes)

Sheep pasture

Infield

Cow pasture

Woodland

WHARRAM
GRANGE FARM

INGS

?WEST PASTURE

WHARRAM
PERCY

Glebe

DREWDALE

WORTHY

1 mile

1000m

N

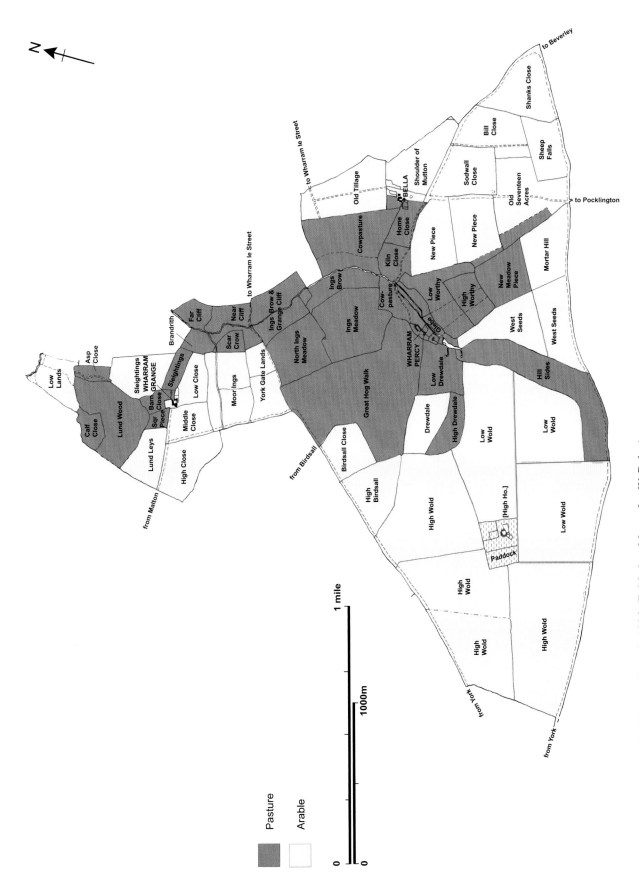

Fig. 116. Arable and pasture lands in Wharram Percy in 1836. (E. Marlow-Mann after W. Dykes)

The impact of such changes can be seen at Birdsall, where the open fields were enclosed in 1691-2. The number of households declined from 70 in 1672 to 37 in 1764 (Neave 1993, 133). North-east of Birdsall, the village of Settrington is shown on a map of 1600 as a substantial settlement formed by two distinct two-row units, one running north to south, the other east to west (p. 302 and Fig. 109 above; King and Harris 1962, frontispiece). By the mid-19th century, the first edition Ordnance Survey six-inch map shows that the southern row of the east-west element has been almost entirely abandoned (cf. Plates 28 and 29).

The vill of Buckton, a soke-centre at Domesday (see pp 183-4), adjoined Settrington on its south side, but by the time of the 1600 map had ceased to exist as a separate township. Some farmstead earthworks have been recorded in the vicinity of a field called Buckton Garths in 1600; but by that date the farmsteads no longer existed. It is possible, as suggested in Chapter 18 (pp 302-4), that the farmers of Buckton were removed to a new settlement – the east-west element of Settrington village – when the townships were amalgamated at some point in the later Middle Ages. If this hypothesis is correct, then Buckton has the distinction of experiencing the complete desertion of its first village site, and major shrinkage on its second.

Townships in the Great Wold Valley also witnessed population decline during the 17th and 18th centuries. At Duggleby and Kirby Grindalythe both village settlements contracted (Plate 34), and the settlements of

Mowthorpe and Thirkleby were reduced to single farms with cottages. Thoraldby disappeared altogether, like Buckton, both as a settlement and as a township, and both Mowthorpe and Thoraldby were probably largely deserted by the end of the Middle Ages. Thirkleby survived, though much reduced, as late as 1672, but it was probably finally depopulated by the end of that century (Plate 32: *VCH ER VIII*, 125).

A similar pattern, of a few desertions by the mid-16th century, with more general shrinkage and some near complete desertion in the late 17th and early 18th centuries, has been traced in other parts of the study area. In 1719 a new lessee of the Dean and Chapter of York's estate at Cottam was encouraged to amalgamate existing holdings and demolish redundant houses and cottages. The number of dwellings reduced from nine in 1706, to one by 1743 (Neave 1993, 134). Cowlam was reduced from fourteen households in 1672 to one in 1743 (Neave 1990, 52, table 10; *VCH ER VIII*, 53-5).

In Wharram Percy parish, Burdale may have experienced desertion in the early 16th-century, like Wharram itself, but the remaining villages continued to be occupied. At Towthorpe the resident yeoman farmers, William Taylor and his son Thomas, purchased various freeholds between 1660 and 1709, depopulating a village which had contained eleven households in 1672. The former tofts and crofts are recorded on a map of 1772 (Neave 1990, 172), and have been confirmed by aerial photography (Plate 39). Raisthorpe seems to have been

Plate 39. Aerial photograph of Towthorpe deserted village, viewed from the north-east (NMR 12609/39, 24 November 1994. © Crown copyright.NMR)

depopulated at the same period, in about 1680 (Beresford M.W. 1987, 13; *Wharram III,* 221). The village of Thixendale, which has survived, still contained 28 houses in 1801 (Beresford M.W. 1987, 10).

Many of these post-medieval desertions on the Wolds, including the 17th-century conversion of Eastburn to a sheepwalk, had been recorded by Alan Harris in the 1950s, early enough to be noted by Maurice Beresford in *Deserted Medieval Villages: Studies* (Beresford and Hurst 1971, 43); but they seem not to have disturbed Beresford's conviction that, except in the case of emparking, village desertion was a phenomenon largely pre-dating the mid-16th century, and that it was primarily associated with the conversion of open-field townships to sheepwalks. The writer's attempt to rekindle debate within the Medieval Village Research Group (Wrathmell 1978, 52-4) made no impact, and a decade later Susan Neave was still able to comment on 'a reluctance amongst some academics to accept post-medieval village desertion as an important phenomenon' (Neave 1990, 259). Although the main thrust of rural settlement research has moved on from desertion (and to some extent from villages), this final volume in the Wharram series seems an appropriate place to re-examine the key tenets of Beresford's hypothesis.

The first is the distinction that he made between deserted and shrunken medieval villages. It was expressed on the first page of the introduction in *Lost Villages*:

'There are many villages still alive whose changes of fortunes in the last few centuries have meant that more people might be found in the Poll Tax lists of 1377 than in the Census of 1951. These shrunken villages are another story, and we must resist the temptation to turn our attention to them or to include them in our definition of depopulation. It may be that forces similar to those described in this book assisted in their shrinkage, but the crucial fact is that they did not result in the total destruction of human settlements, and our care is with those settlements which were destroyed'
(Beresford 1954, 21)

He went on to define the deserted village as one 'where we now have no more than (at most) a manor house and a farm and a church' (Beresford 1954, 21), a threshold which came to be enshrined in the Deserted Medieval Village Research Group's classification of sites (*Annual Report*, 5 (1957), Appendix A).

The second tenet, providing a chronological dimension to each of these phenomena, is that the activities which led to village desertion belong to the early 16th century and earlier, whereas shrunken villages are later. The third is causal: desertion resulted from the conversion of arable townships to sheep pasture, whereas the shrunken village was the result of open-field enclosure that led to more efficient but still mainly arable farming. These aspects of the hypothesis were clearly expressed in *Lost Villages* (Beresford 1954, 141-2), and were reaffirmed in *Deserted medieval Villages: Studies*:

'The encloser after *c.*1550... certainly shared one aim with the depopulating grazier of earlier times: that is, the elimination of the open fields and the complete transformation of the landscape to hedged fields. But no more... Both grain and meat could most profitably be produced in enclosed fields... [Enclosure] was still the enemy of Habitation, in the sense that some reduction in the village labour-force was part of the cost of greater efficiency, but did not produce total depopulation... If these later enclosures have an archaeological product, it is not the depopulated but the shrunken village.'
(Beresford and Hurst 1971, 18-19)

It is now clear from Susan Neave's research that, for the East Riding at least, the classification of deserted and shrunken villages as distinct phenomena, with distinct chronologies and causes, is misplaced. Desertion could and did occur in the 17th and 18th centuries, often (but not always) in villages that had become reduced in size since the 14th century. It was usually accompanied by enclosure designed to create improved arable farming rather than sheep-walks. Whether a village was wholly 'deserted' (as defined by the Deserted Medieval Village Research Group) or merely further reduced in size depended upon many factors, including landownership and the extent of prior shrinkage (Neave 1990, 265-72). She also demonstrated that no less than 28 of the 'deserted medieval villages' recorded in the East Riding still contained four or more households in 1670-73 (cf. Beresford and Hurst 1971, 207-09 and Neave 1990, 263).

Was the East Riding's chronology of depopulation very different from that in the Midlands, in those counties that figured most prominently in Tudor enquiries and legislation? It may have been; but it is worth reflecting on the strength of feeling generated in the arguments over Tudor depopulation – fact or fantasy, now as well as then – which can be sensed in Beresford's review of historical research to 1968 (Beresford and Hurst 1971, 3-75). The more bitterly contested the debate, the more polarised the intellectual positions, the less room there is for ambiguity and modification. Thus, while Beresford's 'probable periods of desertion' in Northamptonshire, Leicestershire, Oxfordshire and Warwickshire record a preponderance of cases in his Period 4 (*c.*1450-1700), there is no real consideration of whether a proportion of them might have occurred after the first hundred years of this timespan. Economics, in the form of price movements in grain relative to wool and livestock, rule this out (Beresford and Hurst 1971, 12-13, table 2 and fig.1):

'One could therefore explain the empty townships and the visible village earthworks in a county where little or nothing emerged in [the depopulation inquiries of] 1517-18, by the fact that virtually all its conversion to pasture had taken place before [the first anti-enclosure legislation of] 1488'
(Beresford and Hurst 1971, 40)

The default position for deserted medieval villages whose depopulation history is currently unknown, and which did not figure in the enquiries of 1517-18, is therefore pre-1488 rather than post-1518. Yet even one of the cornerstones of Beresford's hypothesis, John Rous' late 15th-century list of depopulated villages in Warwickshire (with a few in Worcestershire) is not as clear-cut as Beresford implied, when he wrote:

'This list is, I think, unique, No other county, even others as badly hit by the conversion to sheep pasture, can boast such first hand, incontrovertible evidence' (Beresford and Hurst 1971, 82)

James Bond's analysis of Rous' record of depopulated villages came to the conclusion that 'it needs to be treated with rather greater caution than hitherto' (Bond 1982, 151). In the first place, four of the 60 places listed seem never to have been villages at all, and in four other cases the evidence for nucleated settlements is flimsy. Secondly, as Rous himself notes, destruction was not always complete: almost 20% of the places listed by him do not seem to have been completely depopulated at the time he wrote. Thirdly, the causes and chronology are also questionable: in a number of cases examined in detail, the villages seem to have been wholly or substantially depopulated before the 15th century (Bond 1982, 150-52). Some of the villages are said by Rous to have been emparked, or enclosed though greed and avarice, but without actually mentioning sheep or sheepwalks (C.J. Bond, pers. comm.).

In addition, Joan Thirsk urged caution in terms of creating a chronology for desertion from the price movements of agricultural produce:

'Farming is not a highly flexible business which can twist and change direction at every trick and turn of the price curve. The land and its buildings impose severe limitations on most farmers. Moreover, within the framework of what is practicable, the successful farm business is a union of several interlocking enterprises.

Complex problems arise for the man who makes a change in any one of them. Even if he can reorganise and rearrange them satisfactorily, he may find the short-term benefits cancelled out by the long-term disadvantages.' (Thirsk 1967, 212)

The issue of short and long-term benefits is a crucial one, because the various farmers in a township may well have had different levels of interest in the land, and therefore differing horizons and objectives. Both Susan Neave's study of depopulation in the East Riding, and the writer's in Northumberland, have emphasised the varying trajectories of townships which had, one the one hand, an all-powerful landlord, and on the other, numerous small proprietors (Neave 1990, 266-72; Wrathmell 1980, 123-4). Township communities will have responded differently to the same economic and social stimuli, depending on their existing social and economic structure and the mix of interests and objectives represented among their inhabitants.

Maurice Beresford, John Hurst and their fellow researchers in the late 1940s and 1950s opened up an enormous new vista of settlement research. Their card indexes and lists of deserted and shrunken village earthworks, however inadequate we may now consider them to be as research tools, ensured the preservation of a significant number of such sites, and promoted the investigation of dozens of medieval settlements across the length and breadth of England. Discourse has moved on: the topics that have concerned rural settlement archaeologists and historians over the past few decades relate to the circumstances surrounding the formation and early development of medieval villages, rather than their dissolution. Nevertheless, the ability we now have to interrogate rapidly large quantities of data could generate a far more sophisticated analysis of settlement shrinkage and depopulation than was possible during the early decades of deserted village studies.

Part Five

Wharram and the Wolds: Future Research Potential

Wharram XIII has no concluding chapter: with only about 6.5% of the Scheduled area so far excavated, any 'conclusions' would be distinctly premature. Instead, this final part of the volume aims to bring together a few of the most significant topics investigated both on and off the site over the past sixty years, and to suggest ways in which they could be explored further by means of both additional fieldwork and research in the Site Archive.

In terms of the large-scale questions addressed in this volume, the ones that have in general preoccupied students of medieval settlement over the past thirty years concern village origins – when were villages created, and what did they replace? As far as Wharram and its neighbours are concerned, the chapters in Part Three have offered several competing answers to these questions, because of the divergence of opinion regarding the purpose and significance of what have been termed Butterwick-type settlement sites. For the present discussion, the preferred hypothesis is that Butterwick-type formations represent the permanent homes of distinct communities; that on the Wolds some had been established by the 8th century (in the case of Wharram probably by the mid-7th century), and that several, perhaps most, were sited at the locations of earlier seasonal grazing settlements.

Many of the Butterwick-type clusters of curvilinear ditched enclosures in the northern Wolds seem, on morphological grounds, to have expanded through agglomeration, presumably in response to population increase. Some did not: the Middle Saxon site known as Cottam B appears, on the evidence of crop marks and finds distributions, to have remained a small settlement during the 8th and 9th centuries, perhaps within the confines of a single ditched enclosure. It was replaced in the late 9th century by another small and distinct Anglo-Scandinavian settlement a little further north (Haldenby and Richards 2009, 309-12). On the other hand, the extent of the enclosure complexes at Lutton, Wharram and various other places within the study area is sufficient to warrant the use of the term 'village' to describe them.

In a recent overview of settlement in France in the period AD 300-1100, Elisabeth Zadora-Rio has made a number of perceptive comments regarding the unwillingness of modern scholars to use the term 'village' for multi-homestead settlements occupied before the 11th century (Zadora-Rio 2009, 77). She has assembled the results of recent excavations of settlement sites in northern France and notes that 'villages' were established from the 7th century onwards, 'including ditch-systems delineating house-plots and fields, with some areas devoted to specific activities such as craftmanship or corn processing and storage' (Zadora-Rio 2009, 86). One of the settlements, at Saint-Ouen-des-Besaces (Calvados), has revealed evidence of conjoined curvilinear enclosures (E. Zadora-Rio, pers. comm.), but the excavated gullies seem to be much narrower than the Butterwick-type ditches.

Reluctance to use the term 'village' for extensive settlement sites of this period can be matched in England (e.g. Powlesland 1999, esp. p. 64), and reflects the intellectual swing away from the supposition that the earliest manifestations of existing villages in some parts of England were created as the initial form of Anglo-Saxon settlement (cf. Stenton 1971, 285-7). That swing developed momentum through the identification, in some East Midlands counties, particularly Northamptonshire, of dispersed Anglo-Saxon settlements which had been abandoned well before the mid-9th century, their occupants presumed to have been displaced and moved 'to those settlements which later became villages' (Brown and Foard 1998, 67, 73, 76). This model came to be applied much more widely, and shaped ideas about Anglo-Saxon settlement in the Wharram area (see *Wharram V*).

The pendulum may now be swinging back in the opposite direction. The circumstances of investigating existing villages are such that it can be difficult to estimate reliably the extent of Middle Saxon settlement beneath them. It is, however, significant that Tony Brown and Glen Foard describe some of the Northamptonshire 'settlements which later became villages' as having been more important places from an early phase than those dispersed settlements that were deserted; and they note that 'far greater quantities of pottery have been recovered from the examination of the early-middle Saxon settlements which underlie such medieval villages... than have been retrieved from the deserted outlying Saxon settlements in the same townships' (Brown and Foard 1998, 76). It is interesting that their plot of Early and Middle Saxon sherds from fieldwalking at Higham Ferrers shows concentrations adjacent to the later village (Brown and Foard 1998, fig. 15), suggesting either a shrinkage in settlement area or (as suggested at Wharram) a slight shift to facilitate replanning. Surely the 'settlements which later became villages' could themselves have been villages, indicating that nucleation was already proceeding in key locations before the abandonment of dispersed farmsteads.

A more recent field project has provided us with further variations in the early history of nucleation. When the Wharram Project completed its fieldwork phase in 1990, the Medieval Settlement Research Group, under the leadership of Christopher Dyer, began the search for a successor project, and a lengthy selection process resulted in the Whittlewood Project. It is, perhaps, the supreme irony of the Wharram Project that the researchers who drove forward its successor managed to gallop through their field investigations, analyse the results and publish their findings within the space of six years, leaving Wharram trailing far behind. As a result, Wharram's settlement history must now be evaluated in relation to Whittlewood's, rather than *vice versa* – as was originally intended; and in the present context the most striking conclusion from the latter project is in relation to the process and timing of nucleation.

Richard Jones and Mark Page have concluded that Whittlewood's settlement history does not conform to the Brown and Foard model, with its emphasis on the creation of nucleated settlements before AD 850 through a concentration of previously dispersed farmsteads. They have argued instead, that in the Whittlewood area there is little evidence of nucleation before AD 850, and that 'both nucleated villages and dispersed settlements grew after AD 850 from small nuclei', the villages from pre-existing settlements called 'pre-village nuclei' (Jones and Page 2006, 12, 25). They present a picture of settlement that emphasises stability, in contrast to the Brown and Foard model that emphasises mobility, and they see nucleation as the result of expansion from existing cores, rather than as the concentration of previously dispersed elements. The process of expansion from pre-village nuclei into villages occurred in some places in the period AD 850-1000, but elsewhere rather later, from the late 10th century (Jones and Page 2006, 88-91).

The data so far accumulated for the northern Yorkshire Wolds seem to indicate yet another variation: the growth of village-size communities during the 8th to 10th centuries but without, as yet, any clear indication that expansion was facilitated by the abandonment of previously dispersed homesteads. Substantial regional variation is perhaps to be expected, but before the hypotheses developed in this volume can be built into the standard interpretations of settlement in this period, more detailed and focused field investigation should be carried out.

In the 1980s the exploration of Wharram's Butterwick-type settlement enclosures was largely fortuitous. Now, when we have a much better appreciation of their extent and characteristics, it would be possible to construct a research design to analyse more purposefully the relationships and functions of the individual curvilinear enclosures, and to determine more closely when they were abandoned and replaced by the rows of homesteads that delineate the 'medieval village'. We have suggested that the transformation had occurred by *c.* AD 900 on the basis of the pottery and small finds distributions, but on current evidence it could conceivably have taken place a century or more before that date. Did the transformation take place at a time when Wharram was probably under the control of a Middle Saxon monastic institution, or did it occur after the monastic lands had been taken over by Scandinavian lords?

In terms of the rows of homesteads constituting the 'medieval village', there seems to be a greater degree of consensus as to their likely overall development, but it has to be said that archaeological evidence for the proposed sequence is again very limited. For example the suggested 'late' insertion of the East Row, coinciding with the (assumed) creation of the North Manor *curia* in the 13th century, is a very attractive hypothesis, but one that has simply not yet been tested by excavation – either in the East Row or in the North Manor. Similarly, it seems to the writer that the northern half of the West Row may have been created or refashioned to accompany the erection of the South Manor buildings in the period 1160-80, but additional, closely-focused excavation would be needed to explore this possibility in a more meaningful way.

An understanding of the origins and development of medieval village plans has, of course, been one of the principal concerns for medieval rural settlement archaeologists over the past fifty years, and it is clearly the view of Sally Smith that the emphasis on 'large-scale processes of development' (she cites the distribution of village plan forms and the emergence of nucleated settlement) has stultified exploration of the lives of the peasants who occupied these villages (Smith 2009, 392-4). She focuses her own analysis of the archaeological data for Wharram on the concepts of power and resistance, and the supposed 'resistance practices' she has identified in Wharram's archaeological record. These include the activities that led to the incorporation of reused dressed stone blocks into peasant house foundations, the quarrying of the former South Manor area in the later 13th century, the evidence for poaching of game and the use of hand-powered querns (Smith 2009, 404-10). This is not the place to address the strengths and weaknesses of her arguments in detail, but it is appropriate to acknowledge the wider value of her comments; they remind us that John Hurst's primary objective at Wharram was to understand, not the development of Wharram's settlement plan, but the lives of its medieval peasant farming families.

In this volume the chapters by Chris Dyer have addressed Hurst's objective directly, but whilst they make use of the structural and artefact evidence from Wharram itself, they also rely heavily on the surviving late medieval documentation relating to surrounding communities. As will be apparent from Part Four of this volume, the only 'peasant' farmstead excavated extensively at Wharram now seems to be anomalous in terms of its size, status and date. We still need to excavate a farmstead that would typify the later medieval community more widely, using modern recording methods: the three-dimensional recording of all 'finds' (without, this time, the intrusion of Steensberg's 'levels'); a more detailed dissection of the structural remains, and computer modelling of surfaces within the buildings to explore the kind of issues raised in Chapter 21 by Peter Brears.

Given that funding for further major excavations at Wharram is unlikely to be available in the near future, there is still a good deal of research potential in the Site Archive – both the finds and paper archive currently being assembled at English Heritage's store at Helmsley, and the records made available in digital format through the Archaeology Data Service (doi:10.5284/1000415). The latter include data relating to excavation sites which have not been fully published in this series of monographs, as well as records of enormous quantities of finds – 110,00 objects of various kinds, plus 220,000 fragments of animal bone – enabling future researchers to explore what lies behind some of the hypotheses offered in this volume.

It has long been a principle of archaeological practice that excavation records, along with relevant artefacts and other 'finds', should be preserved to enable future generations to re-interrogate the data in the light of new theories and techniques. How often does this actually happen? How often are new archaeological syntheses based on anything more than the conclusions reached in print by the original excavators? Not often enough, perhaps; but given the costs of storing and keeping accessible such material (whether artefacts, samples, paper records or digital data) it is an issue that archaeologists will have to address in the near future. Perhaps Wharram will, once again, play a key role in the debate.

Bibliography

Abbreviations

BIA, Borthwick Institute for Archives, University of York

Bodl Lib, Bodleian Library, Oxford

Cal Close R 1307-13, Calendar of Close Rolls

Cal CR 1268-72, Calendar of Charter Rolls

Cal Fine Rolls II, Calendar of Fine Rolls

Cal Inq Misc, Calendar of Inquisitions Miscellaneous

Cal IPM, Calendar of Inquisitions Post Mortem

Cal PR, Calendar of Patent Rolls

CalPREJ II, Rigg, J.M. (ed.), 1910, *Calendar of the Plea Rolls of the Exchequer of the Jews II*, Jewish Hist. Soc. Engl.

CH MS, Castle Howard MS

DB Yorks, Faull, M.L. and Stinson, M. (eds), 1986, *Domesday Book. Yorkshire*

DMVRG, Deserted Medieval Village Research Group, *Annual Reports*

EYC I, Farrer, W., 1914, *Early Yorkshire Charters, I* (Edinburgh)

EYC II, Farrer, W., 1915, *Early Yorkshire Charters*, II (Edinburgh)

EYC IX, Clay, C.T., 1952, *Early Yorkshire Charters IX. The Stuteville Fee*, Yorkshire Archaeol. Soc. Rec. Ser.

EYC XI, Clay, C.T., 1963, *Early Yorkshire Charters, XI. The Percy Fee*, Yorkshire Archaeol. Soc. Rec. Ser., Extra Ser. 9

Interim Reports, Interim reports on each year's work from 1953-1990. A full set of these reports is held in the Archive

Orderic II, Chibnall, M., 1969, *The Ecclesiastical History of Orderic Vitalis, II. Books III and IV*

Orderic VI, Chibnall, M., 1978, *The Ecclesiastical History of Orderic Vitalis VI, Books XI, XII and XIII*

Percy Chart 1911, Martin, M.T. (ed.), *The Percy Chartulary*, Surtees Society, 117 (for 1909)

Pipe Roll Soc, Publications of the Pipe Roll Society

Red Book I, Hall, H. (ed.), 1896, *The Red Book of the Exchequer, part I*, Rolls Series 99

Reg Corbridge I, Brown, W. (ed.), *The Register of Thomas Corbridge, Lord Archbishop of York (1286-1296)*

Reg Greenfield III, IV and V, Brown, W. and Thompson, A.H. (ed.), *The Register of William Greenfield, Lord Archbishop of York 1306-1315*

SD I, Arnold, T. (ed.), 1882, *Symeonis Monachi Opera Omnia I*, Rolls Ser.

SD II, Arnold, T. (ed.), 1885, *Symeonis Monachi Opera Omnia II*, Rolls Ser. 75

TNA PRO, The National Archives, Public Record Office

VCH ER I, Allison, K.J. (ed.), 1969, *A History of the County of York: East Riding, Volume I. The City of Kingston upon Hull*

VCH ER II, Pugh, R.B. (ed.), 1974, *A History of the County of York: East Riding Volume 2 Dickering wapentake*

VCH ER VIII, Neave, D. and Neave, S. 2008, *A History of the County of York: East Riding, Volume VIII. East Buckrose: Sledmere and the Northern Wolds*

VCH Yorks II, Page, W. (ed.), 1912, *The Victoria History of the County of York*, II

VCH Yorks III, Page, W. (ed.), 1913, *The Victoria History of the County of York*, III

Wharram I (Andrews, D.D. and Milne, G., 1979) *Wharram. A Study of Settlement on the Yorkshire Wolds, I. Domestic Settlement 1: Areas 10 and 6*, Soc. Medieval Archaeol. Monogr. 8

Wharram II (Rahtz, P.A. and Watts, L., 1983) *Wharram: A Study of Settlement on the Yorkshire Wolds, II. Wharram Percy. The Memorial Stones of the Churchyard*, York Univ. Archaeol. Publ. 1

Wharram III (Bell, R.D., Beresford, M.W. and others, 1987) *Wharram. A Study of Settlement on the Yorkshire Wolds, III. Wharram Percy: The Church of St Martin*, Soc. Medieval Archaeaol. Monogr. 11

Wharram IV (Rahtz, P.A., Hayfield, C. and Bateman, J., 1986) *Wharram: A Study of Settlement on the Yorkshire Wolds, IV. Two Roman Villas at Wharram le Street*, York Univ. Archaeol. Publ. 2

Wharram V (Hayfield, C., 1987) *Wharram: A Study of Settlement on the Yorkshire Wolds, V. An Archaeological Survey of the Parish of Wharram Percy, East Yorkshire: 1. The evolution of the Roman landscape*, Br. Archaeol. Rep. Br. Ser., 172

Wharram VI (Wrathmell, S., 1989) *Wharram. A Study of Settlement on the Yorkshire Wolds, VI. Domestic Settlement 2: Medieval Peasant Farmsteads*, York Univ. Archaeol. Publ. 8

Wharram VII (Milne, G. and Richards, J.D., 1992) *Wharram. A Study of Settlement on the Yorkshire Wolds, VII. Two Anglo-Saxon Buildings and Associated Finds*, York Univ. Archaeol. Publ. 9

Wharram VIII (Stamper, P.A. and Croft, R.A., 2000) *Wharram. A Study of Settlement on the Yorkshire Wolds, VIII. The South Manor Area*, York Univ. Archaeol. Publ. 10

Wharram IX (Rahtz, P.A. and Watts, L., 2004) *Wharram. A Study of Settlement on the Yorkshire Wolds, IX. The North Manor Area and North-West Enclosure*, York Univ. Archaeol. Publ. 11

Wharram X (Treen, C. and Atkin, M., 2005) *Wharram. A Study of Settlement on the Yorkshire Wolds, X. Water Resources and their Management*, York Univ. Archaeol. Publ. 12

Wharram XI (Mays, S., Harding, C. and Heighway, C., 2007) *Wharram. A Study of Settlement on the Yorkshire Wolds, XI. The Churchyard,* York Univ. Archaeol. Publ. 13

*Wharram XII (*Harding, C. and Wrathmell, S., 2010) *Wharram: A Study of Settlement on the Yorkshire Wolds, XII. The Post-medieval Farm and Vicarage Sites,* York Univ. Archaeol. Publ. 14

Yorks Deeds I, Brown, W. (ed.), 1909, *Yokshire Deeds. Volume I, Yorkshire Archaeol. Soc. Rec. Ser.* 39 (for 1907)

Yorks Deeds IV, Clay, C.T. (ed.), 1924, *Yorkshire Deeds. Volume IV*

Yorkshire Fines, 1246-72, Parker, J., 1932, *Feet of Fines for the County of York 1246-72,* Yorkshire Archaeol. Soc. Rec. Ser. 82

Yorks Inqs II, Brown, W., 1898, *Yorkshire Inquisitions, II,* Yorkshire Archaeol. Soc. Rec. Ser. 23 (for 1897)

Yorks Inqs III, Brown, W. (ed.), 1902, *Yorkshire Inquisitions III* , Yorkshire Archaeol. Soc. Rec. Ser., 31

Yorks Inqs IV, Brown, W., 1906, *Yorkshire Inquisitions in the Reigns of Henry III and Edward I,* IV, Yorkshire Archaeol. Soc. Rec. Ser. 37

References

Abrams L., 2001, 'The conversion of the Danelaw', in Graham-Campbell, J. *et al.* (eds), *Vikings and the Danelaw. Select Papers from the Proceedings of the Thirteenth Viking Congress, Nottingham and York, 21-30 August 1997,* 31-44

Abrams, L. and Parsons, D., 2004, 'Place-names and the history of Scandinavian settlement in England', in Hines, J., Lane, A. and Redknap, M. (eds), *Land, Sea and Home. Settlement in the Viking Period,* Soc. Medieval Archaeol. Monogr. 20

Abramson, P., 1996, 'Excavations along the Caythorpe Gas Pipeline, North Humberside', *Yorkshire Archaeol. J.,* 68, 1-88

Addy, S.O.,1933, *The Evolution of the English House,* revised and enlarged by J. Summerson

Ager, B., 1992, 'Discussion', in Goodall with Ager, 47-9

Ainsworth, S., Bowden, M. and McOmish, D., 2007, *Understanding the Archaeology of Landscapes. A guide to good recording practice*

Alexander, A., 1994, 'Enclosure by agreement in east Yorkshire: four seventeenth-century examples from the wapentake of Buckrose', MPhil. thesis, Univ. Hull

Allcroft, A.H., 1908, *Earthwork of England: Prehistoric, Roman, Saxon, Danish, Norman and Medieval*

Allerston, P., 1970, 'English village development', *Inst. Br. Geogr. Trans.* 51, 95-109

Allison, K.J., 1976, *The East Riding of Yorkshire Landscape*

Andrews, D.D., 1979a, 'Miscellaneous small finds', in *Wharram I,* 124-32

Andrews, D.D., 1979b, 'Tiles', in *Wharram I,* 131-2

Andrews, D.D. and MacGregor, A., 1979, 'Bone objects', in *Wharram I,* 128-130

Andrews, D.D., Arthur, J.R.B., Bayley, J., Biek, L., Evans, J.G., Keepax, C.A., Morgan, G.C., Ryder, M.L. and Smith, A.H.V., 1979, 'Environmental and technological evidence', in *Wharram I,* 133-37

Andrews, P., 1995, *Excavations at Redcastle Furze, Thetford, 1988-9,* East Anglian Archaeol. 72

Andrews, P., 1997, *Excavations at Hamwic. Volume 2: Excavations at Six Dials,* Counc. Br. Archaeol. Res. Rep. 109

Anon, Yorkshire Deeds, *Yorkshire Archaeol. J. 13,* 1903, 97-8

Anstee, J.W. and Biek L., 1961, 'A Study of Pattern-Welding', *Medieval Archaeol.* 5, 71-93

Arnold, C.J., 1997, *An archaeology of the early Anglo-Saxon kingdoms* (2nd ed.)

Astill, G. and Grant, A., 1988, *The Countryside of Medieval England*

Astill, G. and Langdon, J. (eds), 1997, *Medieval Farming and Technology. The Impact of Agricultural Change in Northwest Europe* (Leiden)

Aston, M., Austin, D. and Dyer, C. (eds), 1989, *The Rural Settlements of Medieval England: Studies dedicated to Maurice Beresford and John Hurst*

Atha, M., 2007, *Late Iron Age Regionality and Early Roman Trajectories (100BC-AD200): a landscape perspective from eastern Yorkshire,* unpubl. PhD thesis, Univ. York

Atkinson, J.C., 1878, *Chartulary of Whitby* 1, Surtees Soc. 69

Atkinson, J.C., 1891, *Forty Years in a Moorland Parish*

Audouy, M. and Chapman, A. (eds), 2008, *Raunds: the origin and growth of a Midland village, AD 450-1500*

Austin, D., 1989, *The Deserted Medieval Village of Thrislington, County Durham. Excavations 1973-4,* Soc. Medieval Archaeol. Monogr. 12

Austin, T., 1999, 'The Pottery', in Richards 1999a, 49-60

Ayers, B., 1985, *Excavations within the North-East Bailey of Norwich Castle, 1979,* East Anglian Archaeol. 28

Baildon, W.P., 1895, *Notes on the Religious and Secular Houses of Yorkshire I,* Yorkshire Archaeol. Soc. Rec. Ser. 17 (for 1894)

Bailey, R.N., 1980, *Viking Age Sculpture*

Baines, P., 1982, *Spinning Wheels, Spinners and Spinning*

Baker, J.T., 2005, 'Topographical place-names and the distribution of *Tun* and *Ham* in the Chilterns and Essex region', *Anglo-Saxon Stud. Archaeol. Hist* 13, 50-62

Bambrook, G., 2005, *Burdale Survey report,* unpubl. Historia Detectum

Barclay, C., 2007, 'A review of the medieval coins and jetons from Wharram Percy', in *Wharram XI,* 301-4

Barker, P., 1969, 'Some aspects of the excavation of timber buildings', *World Archaeol.* 1, 220-35

Barley, M.W., 1943, 'East Yorkshire Manorial By-laws' *Yorkshire Archaeol. J.* 35, 35-60

Barmby, (ed.), 1888, *'Churchwardens' Accounts of Pittington and other Parishes in the Diocese of Durham*, Surtees Soc. 84

Barnwell, P., 2004, 'The Laity, the Clergy and the Divine Presence: The Use of Space in Smaller Churches of the Eleventh and Twelfth Centuries', *J. Br. Archaeol. Assoc.* 157, 41-60

Barrett, J.H., 2005, 'The fish bone', in *Wharram X*, 169-175

Barrett, J.H., Johnstone, C., Harland, J., Van Neer, W., Ervinck, A., Makowiecki, D., Heinrich, D. and others, 2008, 'Detecting the medieval cod trade: a new method and first results', *J. Archaeol. Sci.* 35, 850-61

Baxter, S., 2007, *The Earls of Mercia. Lordship and Power in Late Anglo-Saxon England*

Bayley, J. 1992, 'The metalworking evidence', in *Wharram VII*, 59-66

Bayley, J. 2000, 'Evidence for copper-alloy working', in *Wharram VIII*, 121

Bayley, J. 2004, 'Objects used for copper-alloy working', in Elsdon, S., Clark, E.A. and Gaunt, G.D., 'Fired clay objects', in *Wharram IX*, 231

Bayley, J. with Lang, J.T., 1992, 'The metalworking evidence', in *Wharram VII*, 59-66

Bayliss, A., 2005, 'Radiocarbon dates from the dam', in *Wharram X*, 221-22

Bayliss, A., Cook, G. and Heighway, C., 2007, 'Radiocarbon dating', in *Wharram XI*, 193-215

Becker, C.J., 1987, 'Farms and villages in Denmark from the Late Bronze Age to the Viking Period', *Proc. Br. Acad.* 73, 69-96

Bell, R.D., 1987a, 'The excavations', in *Wharram III*, 47-97

Bell, R.D., 1987b, 'Conclusions', in *Wharram III*, 189-220

Bennett, J.M., 1987, *Women in the Medieval English Countryside: Gender and Household in Brigstock before the Plague* (New York)

Bennett, P., Riddler, I. and Sparey-Green, C., 2010, *The Roman Watermills and Settlement at Ickham, Kent*

Bentz, E., 2008, *I stadens skugga. Den medeltida landsbygden som arkeologiskt forskningsfält*, Lund Stud. Hist. Archaeol. 8 (Lund)

Beresford, G, 1974, 'The Medieval Manor of Penhallam, Jacobstow, Cornwall', *Medieval Archaeol.* 18, 90-145

Beresford, G., 1975, *The medieval clay-land village: excavations at Goltho and Barton Blount*, Soc. Medieval Archaeol. Monogr. 6

Beresford, G., 1979, 'Three deserted medieval settlements on Dartmoor: a report on the late E. Marie Minter's excavations', *Medieval Archaeol.* 23, 98-158

Beresford, G., 1987, *Goltho. The Development of an Early Medieval Manor, c 850 – 1150*, Engl. Heritage Archaeol. Rep. 4

Beresford, M.W., 1951, 'Glebe Terriers and the Open Field', *Yorkshire Archaeol. J.* 37, 325-68

Beresford, M.W., 1954 (1983 ed.), *The Lost Villages of England*

Beresford, M.W., 1979, 'Documentary evidence for the history of Wharram Percy', in *Wharram I*, 5-25

Beresford, M.W., 1987, 'The Documentary Evidence', in *Wharram III*, 5-46

Beresford, M. and Hurst, J.G. (eds), 1971, *Deserted Medieval Villages: Studies*

Beresford, M.W. and Hurst, J.G., 1976, 'Wharram Percy: a case study in microtopography', in Sawyer, P.H. (ed.), *Medieval Settlement. Continuity and Change*, 114-144

Beresford, M. and Hurst, J.G., 1990, *Wharram Percy: Deserted Medieval Village*

Berg, G., 1975, 'A destroyed Danish village reconstructed. Axel Steensberg and J. L. Östergaard Christensen, Store Valby. Historisk-arkæologisk undersøgelse af en nedlagt landsby på Sjælland', *Ethnologia Scandinavica* 5, 181-3

Berggren, Å. and Burström, M., 2002, *Reflexiv fältarkeologi? Återsken av ett seminarium* (Stockholm/Malmö)

Bersu, G., 1938, 'The Excavation at Woodbury, Wiltshire during 1938', *Proc. Prehist. Soc.* 4, 308-13

Bersu, G., 1940, 'Excavations at Little Woodbury, Wiltshire', *Proc. Prehist. Soc.,* 6, 30-111

Bevan, B., 1997, 'Bounding the landscape: place and identity during the Yorkshire Wolds Iron Age', in Gwilt, A. and Haselgrove, C. (eds), *Reconstructing Iron Age societies: new approaches to the British Iron Age*, 181-191, Oxbow Monogr. 71

Biddle, M., 2003, 'John Hurst', *The Times*, 15 May 2003

Bilson, J., 1911, 'Newbald Church', *Yorkshire Archaeol. J.* 21, 1-43

Bilson, J, 1922, 'Weaverthorpe church and its builder', *Archaeologia* 72, 51-70

Birbeck, V., 2005, *The Origins of Mid-Saxon Southampton. Excavations at the Friends Provident St Mary's Stadium 1998 – 2000,* Wessex Archaeol.

Blair, J., 1993, 'Hall and Chamber: English Domestic Planning 1000-1250', in Meiron-Jones, G. and Jones, M. (eds), *Manorial Domestic Buildings in England and Northern France*, Soc. Antiq. London Occas. Pap.15, 1-21

Blair, J., 2005, *The Church in Anglo-Saxon Society*

Blair, J., 2010, 'The prehistory of English fonts', in Henig, M. and Ramsay, N. (eds), *Intersections: the archaeology and history of Christianity in England, 400-1200. Papers in honour of Martin Biddle and Birthe Kjølbye-Biddle*, Br. Archaeol. Rep. Br. Ser. 505, 149-77

Blakelock, E.S., 2006, *Analysis of knives from the Middle Saxon Rural Settlement of Wharram Percy, Yorkshire*, unpubl. undergrad. diss., Univ. Bradford

Blakelock, E., 2008, *Burdale E-Radiograph and Metallographic analysis report*, unpubl. archive rep., Univ. Bradford

Blakelock, E. and McDonnell, G., 2007, 'A Review of the Metallographic Analysis of Early Medieval Knives', *Hist. Metall.* 41, 40-56

Blackmore, L., 2003, 'The Iron Objects', in Malcolm, G., Bowsher, D. and Cowie, R. (eds), *Middle Saxon London. Excavations at the Royal Opera House 1989-99*, Mus. London Archaeol. Serv. Monogr. 15, 251-64

Blinkhorn, P., 2009, 'Ipswich Ware', in. Evans, D.H and Loveluck, C., *Life and Economy at Early Medieval Flixborough c AD 600 – 1000*, Excavations at Flixborough 2, 357-63

Blockley, K., Blockley, M., Blockley, P., Frere, S.S. and. Stow, S., 1995, *Excavations in the Marlowe Car Park and Surrounding Areas*, Archaeol. Canterbury 5

Boddington, A., 1996, *Raunds Furnells. The Anglo-Saxon church and churchyard*, Engl. Heritage Archaeol. Rep. Ser. 7

Böhner, K., 1958, *Die Fränkischen Altertümer des Trierer Landes*, Germanische Denkmäler der Völkerwanderungszeit, serie B1 (Berlin)

Bond, C.J., 1982, 'Deserted medieval villages in Warwickshire and Worcestershire', in Slater, T.R. and Jarvis, P.J. (eds), *Field and Forest: an Historical Geography of Warwickshire and Worcestershire*, 147-71

Bond, C.J., 1988, 'Church and Parish in Norman Worcestershire', in Blair, J. (ed.), *Minsters and Parish Churches. The Local Church in Transition 950-1200*, OUCA Monogr. 17, 119-158

Bond E.A., 1866, *Chronica Monasterii de Melsa I*, Rolls Ser.

Bond, F., 1908, *Fonts and Font Covers*

Bourdieu, P., 1977, *Outline of a Theory of Practice*

Bourke, C., 1980, 'Early Irish Hand Bells', *J. Royal Soc. Antiq. Ireland* 110, 52-66

Bourne, D., 2006, 'Flaxton – the layout of the original planned settlement', *Yorkshire Archaeol. J.* 78, 61-83

Boutell, C., 1854, *Christian Monuments of England and Wales …,*

Bowden, M. (ed.), 1999, *Unravelling the Landscape: an inquisitive approach to archaeology*

Bradley, R., 2007, *The Prehistory of Britain and Ireland*

Branigan, K., 1980, 'Villas in the North: change in the rural landscape' in Branigan, K. (ed.), *Rome and the Brigantes,* 18-27

Brears, P., 1963, *A Catalogue of English Country Pottery Houses in the Yorkshire Museum, York*

Brears, P., 1987, *Traditional Food in Yorkshire*

Brears, P., 2008, *Cooking and Dining in Medieval England*

Brewster, T.C.M, 1972, 'An excavation at Weaverthorpe Manor, East Riding, 1960', *Yorkshire Archaeol. J.* 44, 114-33

Briggs, C., 2005, 'Taxation, warfare, and the early fourteenth century 'crisis' in the north: Cumberland lay subsidies, 1332-1348', *Econ. Hist. Rev.* 58, 639-72

Briggs, C., 2009, *Credit and Village Society in Fourteenth-Century England*, Br. Acad.

Brodribb, A.C.C., Hands, A.R. and Walker, D.R., 1972, *Excavations at Shakenoak Farm, near Wilcote, Oxfordshire. Part III: Site F*

Brown, A.E. and Foard, G., 1998, 'The Saxon landscape: a regional perspective', in Everson, P. and Williamson, T. (eds), *The archaeology of landscape*, 67-94

Brown, D.H., 1997, 'The Social Significance of Imported Medieval Pottery', in Cumberpatch, C.G. and Blinkhorn, P.W., *Not So Much a Pot, More a Way of Life*, Oxbow Monogr. 83, 95-112

Brown, M.P., 2006, *The World of the Luttrell Psalter*

Brown, S., 2003, *'Our Magnificent Fabrick' York Minster: An Architectural History c 1220-1500*

Brown, W., 1889, *Cartularium Prioratus de Gysburne*, Surtees Soc. 86

Brown, W., 1892, *Yorkshire Inquisitions Post Mortem*, Yorkshire Archaeol. Rec. Ser. 12

Brown, W., 1894a, *Cart Prioratus de Gysburne* 2, Surtees Soc. 86

Brown, W. (ed.), 1894b, *Yorkshire Lay Subsidy. Being a Ninth collected in …1297*, Yorkshire Archaeol. Soc. Rec. Ser. 16

Brown, W. (ed.), 1897, *Yorkshire Lay Subsidy. Being a Fifteenth collected …1301*, Yorkshire Archaeol. Soc. Rec. Ser. 21

Bruce-Mitford, R.L.S., 1948, 'Medieval Archaeology', *Archaeol. Newsletter* 6, 1-4

Buchwald, V.F. and Wivel, H., 1998, 'Slag analysis as a method for the characterization and provenancing of ancient iron objects' *Mater. Charact.* 40, 73-96

Buciek, K., 1999, 'Aage Gudmund Hatt (1884-1960) - mellem forskning og ideologi. En forskerbiografi', in Illeris, S. (ed.), *Danske geografiske forskere*, 75-88 (Fredriksberg)

Burnham, B.C., Keppie, L.J.F., Esmonde Cleary, A.S., Hassall, M.W.C. and Tomlin, R.S.O., 1998, 'Roman Britain in 1997', *Britannia 29*, 365-445

Burton, J., 1999, *The Monastic Order in Yorkshire, 1069-1215*

Bush, M., 1988, 'Early Mesolithic disturbance: a force on the landscape', *J. Archaeol. Sci. 14*, 453-64

Bush, M.B., 2005, 'The post-Saxon vegetational history of Wharram Percy: a palynological account', in *Wharram X*, 175-184

Butler, L.A.S., 1964, 'Minor medieval monumental sculpture in the East Midlands', *Archaeol. J.* 121, 111-53

Butler, L.A.S., 1982, 'The Labours of the Months and "The Haunted Tanglewood": Aspects of late twelfth-century sculpture in Yorkshire', in Thompson, R.L. (ed.), *A Medieval Miscellany in Honour of Professor John le Patourel*, Proc. Leeds Philos. Lit. Soc. 18, 79-95

Buttler, W. and Haberey, W., 1936, *Die Bandkeramische Ansiedlung bei Köln-Lindenthal*. Römisch-Germanische Forschungen 11 (Berlin)

Campbell, B.M.S., 2000, *English Seigniorial Agriculture 1250-1450*

Campbell, B.M.S. and Bartley, K., 2006, *England on the Eve of the Black Death. An Atlas of Lay Lordship, Land and Wealth, 1300-49*

Carr, R. and Tester, A., forthcoming, *A High Status Middle Saxon Settlement at Staunch Meadow, Brandon, Suffolk,* East Anglian Archaeol.

Carroll, J., 2001, 'Glass Bangles as a Regional Development in Early Medieval Ireland', in Redknap, M., Edwards, N., Youngs, S., Lane, A. and Knight, J., *Pattern and Purpose in Insular Art,* 101-116

Carruthers, W.J., 2005, 'Environment and economy at Wharram Percy: evidence fron the pond and dam samples', in *Wharram X,* 214-19

Castagnino, V., 2007, 'An investigation of the white weld line phenomenon', unpubl. MSc diss. Univ. Bradford

Catt, J 1990, 'Geology and relief' in Ellis, S. and Crowther, D. (eds), *Humber perspectives: a region through the ages,* 13-28

Chabot, N., 2007, 'Modeling of inclusions in forged iron artefacts', unpubl. MSc diss. Univ. Bradford

Chadwick, A., 1999, 'Digging ditches, but missing riches? Ways into the Iron Age and Romano-British cropmark landscapes of the north midlands', in Bevan, B. (ed.), *Northern Exposure: interpretative devolution and the Iron Ages in Britain,* Univ. Leicester Archaeol. Monogr. 4, 149-71

Chadwick, A., 2007, 'Trackways, hooves and memory-days: human and animal memories and movements around the Iron Age and Romano-British rural landscapes', in Cummings, V. and Johnston, R. (eds), *Prehistoric Journeys,* 131-52

Chapman, H., 2005, 'Rethinking the "Cursus Problem" – investigating the Neolithic landscape archaeology of Rudston, East Yorkshire, UK using GIS' in *Proc. Prehist. Soc. 71,* 159-70

Chapman, A., 2010, *West Cotton, Raunds. A study of medieval settlement dynamics AD 450-1450*

Chatwin D. and Gardiner, M., 2005, 'Rethinking the early medieval settlement of woodlands: evidence from the western Sussex Weald', *Landscape Hist.* 27, 31-49

Cheape, H., 1984, *Kirtomy Mill and Kiln,* Scott. Vernacular Build. Work. Group

Chinnery, V., 1979, *Oak Furniture: The British Tradition* III

Christie, N. and Stamper, P., 2012, *Medieval Rural Settlement: Britain and Ireland, AD 800-1600*

Clark, E.A. (ed.), 1992, 'The finds assemblage', in *Wharram VII,* 40-58

Clark, E.A., 2000a, 'Mollusca', in *Wharrram VIII,* 205

Clark, E.A., 2000b, 'Coal and charcoal', in *Wharrram VIII,* 206

Clark, E.A., 2000c, 'Fired clay objects', in *Wharrram VIII,* 117-121

Clark, E.A., 2005, 'Clay objects', in *Wharrram X,* 128-9

Clark, E.A., 2007, 'Introduction', in *Wharram XI,* 269-70

Clark, E.A. and Gaunt, G.D., 2000, 'Stone objects', in *Wharram VIII,* 101-117

Clark, E.A. and Gaunt, G.D., 2004, 'Stone objects', in *Wharram IX,* 213-30

Clark, E.A. and Gaunt, G.D., 2005, 'Stone objects', in *Wharram X,* 123-8

Clark, E.A. and Wrathmell, S. (eds), 2004, 'The North-west Enclosure', in *Wharram IX,* 297-340

Clark, J., 1995, *The Medieval Horse and its Equipment, c. 1150 - c. 1450,* Medieval Finds from Excavations in London 5

Clarke, H., 1979, *Iron and Man in Prehistoric Sweden* (Stockholm)

Clay, J.W., 1904, *Yorkshire Church Notes 1619-31, by Roger Dodsworth,* Yorkshire Archaeol. Soc. Rec. Ser. 34

Clouston, H.S., 1924-5, 'The Old Orkney Mills', *Proc. Orkney Antiq. Soc. 3,* 49-54

Coates, R, 1999, 'New lights from old wicks: the progeny of Latin vicus', *Nomina,* 22, 75-116

Coggins, D., Fairless, K. J. and Batey, C.E., 1983, 'Simy Folds: an Early Medieval Settlement Site in Upper Teesdale', *Medieval Archaeol.* 27, 1-26

Cole, E. Maule, 1899, 'On Roman roads in the East Riding', in *Trans. East Riding Antiq. Soc.* 7, 37-46

Collis, J., 1983, *Wigber Low, Derbyshire: A Bronze Age and Anglian Burial Site in the White Peak*

Cool, H.E.M., 2004, 'An overview of the sites', in *Wharram IX,* 341-46

Coppack, G., 1974, 'Low Caythorpe, east Yorkshire. The manor site', *Yorkshire Archaeol. J.* 46, 34-41

Corbett, W.M., 1973, *Breckland Forest Soils*

Corder, P. and Kirk, J., 1932, *A Roman Villa at Langton, near Malton, East Yorkshire,* Roman Malton Dist. Rep. 4

Coutts, C. and Hodges, R., 1992, 'Tating-type ware: a review with particular reference to the Wharram sherd', in *Wharram VII,* 38-9

Cowgill, J. and McDonnell G., forthcoming, 'The slags and other metal-working debris', in Powesland, D., *Excavations at West Heslerton*

Cowgill, J., Neergaard, M.D. and Griffiths, N., 1987, *Knives and scabbards,* Medieval Finds from Excavations in London 1

Cowie, R. and Blackmore, L. (eds), forthcoming, *Lundenwic: Excavations in Middle Saxon London 1987-2000,* Mus. London Archaeol. Monogr.

Cowie, R., Whytehead, R.L. and Blackmore, L., 1988, 'Two Middle Saxon Occupation Sites: Excavations at Jubilee Hall and 21-22 Maiden Lane', *Trans. London Middlesex Archaeol. Soc.* 39, 47-164

Cox, J.C. and Harvey, A., 1907, *English Church Furniture*

Coy, J., 1980, 'The Animal Bones', in Haslam, J., 'A Middle Saxon Iron Smelting Site at Ramsbury, Wiltshire', *Medieval Archaeol.* 24, 41-51

Crabtree, P.J., forthcoming, 'The Mammal and Bird Remains from Brandon', in Tester, A., Anderson, S., Riddler, I. and Carr, R., *Brandon, Staunch Meadow. A High Status Middle Saxon Settlement Site,* East Anglian Archaeol.

Cramp, R.J., 1976, 'Analysis of the Finds Register and Location Plan of Whitby Abbey', in Wilson, D.M., *The Archaeology of Anglo-Saxon England,* Cambridge, 453-7

Cramp, R.J., 2000, 'Anglo-Saxon Window Glass', in Price, J., *Glass in Britain and Ireland AD 350-1100,* Br. Mus. Occas. Pap. 127, 105-114

Craster, H.H.E. and Thornton, M.E., 1934, *Chronicle of St Mary's Abbey, York,* Surtees Soc. 148

Crew, P., 1991, 'The Experimental production of prehistoric bar iron', *J. Hist. Metall. Soc.* 25(1), 21-36

Cross, C., 1977, *Church and People: England 1450-1660* (1st ed. 1976)

Cullen, P., Jones, R. and Parsons, D.N., 2011, *Thorps in a Changing Landscape,* Explor. Local Reg. Hist. 4

Current Archaeology 49, 1975, 'Wharram Percy', 39-49

Curriculum Development Unit, 1978, *Viking Settlement to Medieval Dublin. Daily Life 840-1540* (Dublin)

Curwen, E.C., 1944, 'The Problem of Early Water Mills', *Antiquity* 18, 130-36

Cutts, E.L., 1849, *A Manual for the study of the Sepulchral Slabs and Crosses of the Middle Ages*

Dalton, P., 1994 (reprint 2002), *Conquest, Anarchy and Lordship. Yorkshire, 1066-1154*

Daniels, R., 2007, *Anglo-Saxon Hartlepool and the Foundations of English Christianity. An Archaeology of the Anglo-Saxon Monastery,* Tees Archaeol. Monogr. 3

Daoust, A. B., 2007, *The nature and composition of blacksmithing residues and their connection to weld-line slag inclusions,* unpubl. Masters diss. Univ. Bradford

Darby, H.C., 1977, *Domesday England*

David, A., 1980, 'Wharram-le-Street: Geophysics', Ancient Monuments Lab. Old Ser. Rep. 3053

David, A., 1982, *'Wharram Percy: Report on Geophysical Surveys 1970-1982',* Ancient Monuments Lab. Old Ser. Rep. 3959

Davies, S.M., 1979, 'Excavations at Old Down Farm, Andover. Part 1: Saxon', *Proc. Hampshire Field Club Archaeol. Soc.* 36, 161-80

Davis, S.J.M., 2000, 'The effect of castration and age on the development of the Shetland sheep skeleton and a metric comparison between bones of males, females and castrates', *J. Archaeol. Sci.* 27, 373-390

Dent, J., 1982, 'Cemeteries and settlement patterns of the Iron Age on the Yorkshire Wolds' *Proc. Prehist. Soc.* 48, 437-57

Dent, J., 1983, 'The impact of Roman rule on native society in the territory of the Parisi', *Britannia* 14, 35-44

Dent, J., 1988, 'Some problems of continuity in rural settlement' in Manby, T. (ed.), *Archaeology in Eastern Yorkshire: essays in honour of T C M Brewster,* 94-100

Didsbury, P., 2007, 'The prehistoric, Iron Age and Roman pottery', in *Wharram XI,* 243-51

Didsbury, P., 2010, 'The post-medieval pottery', in *Wharram XII,* 155-98

Dobney, K.M., Jaques, S.D. and Irving, B.G., 1996, *Of Butchers and Breeds: Report on Vertebrate Remains from Various Sites in the City of Lincoln,* Lincoln Archaeol. Stud. 5

Dobney, K., Jaques, D. and Brothwell, D., 1999, 'Assessment of the bone assemblage from COT93', in Richards, 1-110

Dobney, K., Jaques, D., Barrett, J. and Johnstone, C., 2007, *Farmers, Monks and Aristocrats. The Environmental Archaeology of Anglo-Saxon Flixborough,* Excavations at Flixborough 3

Dodds, B., 2007, *Peasants and Production in the Medieval North-East. The Evidence from Tithes, 1270-1536*

Drewett, P., Holgate, B., Foster, S. and Ellerby, H., 1986, 'The excavation of a Saxon sunken building at North Marden, West Sussex, 1982', *Sussex Archaeol. Collect.* 124

Drinkall, G. and Foreman, M., 1998, *The Anglo-Saxon Cemetery at Castledyke South, Barton-on-Humber,* Sheffield Excavation Rep. 6

Dudley, H.E., 1949, *Early Days in North-West Lincolnshire*

Duffy, M., 2003, *Royal Tombs of Medieval England*

Dungworth, D. and Wilkes, R., 2007, *An investigation of hammerscale,* Portsmouth Res. Dep. Rep. 26/2007

Dunlevy, M., 1988, 'A Classification of Early Irish Combs', *Proc. R. Ir. Acad.* 88C, 341-422

Durden, T., 1995, 'The production of specialised flint work in the later Neolithic: a case study from the Yorkshire Wolds', *Proc. Prehist. Soc.* 61, 409-32

Dyer, C., 1980, *Lords and Peasants in a Changing Society: the estates of the bishopric of Worcester 680-1540*

Dyer, C., 1986, 'English peasant buildings in the later middle ages', *Medieval Archaeol.* 30, 19-45

Dyer C., 1989, *Standards of Living in the Later Middle Ages*

Dyer, C., 1990, 'Review... [of *Wharram VI*], *Medieval Archaeol.* 34, 297-8

Dyer, C., 1995, 'Sheepcotes: evidence for medieval sheepfarming', *Medieval Archaeol.* 39, 136-64

Dyer, C., 1998, *Standards of Living in the Later Middle Ages. Social Change in England c. 1200-1520*

Dyer, C., 2004, 'Review [of *Wharram VIII* and *Wharram IX*]...', *Medieval Settlement Res. Group Annual Rep.* 19, 39-40

Dyer, C. and Aldred, D., 2009, 'Changing landscape and society in a Cotswold village: Hazleton, Gloucestershire, to c. 1600', *Trans. Bristol Gloucestershire Archaeol. Soc.* 127, 235-70

Dykes, W., 1836, 'Plan of an Estate comprising Wharram le Street (sic), Bella and Wharram Grange in the East Riding of the County of York, the Property of Henry Willoughby Esqre', surveyed 1836, Borthwick PR WP 9/5

Dymond, P., 1966, 'Ritual monuments at Rudston, East Yorkshire, England' in *Proc. Prehist. Soc.* 32, 86-95

Edmonds, M., 1999, *Ancestral Geographies of the Neolithic: landscape, monuments and memory*

Egan, G. and Pritchard, F., 1991, *Dress Accessories 1150-1450*

Ellis, S.E., 1969, 'The Petrography and Provenance of Anglo-Saxon and Medieval English Honestones, with Notes on some other Hones', *Bull. Br. Mus. (Natural History) (Mineralogy)* 2, 135-187

Ellis, S., 1990, 'Soils', in Ellis, S. and Crowther, D. (eds,) *Humber perspectives: a region through the ages*, 29-42

Engberg, N., 1994, 'Resultater og tendenser i dansk landsbyarkæologi', *Hikuin* 21, 10-20

English, B. (ed.), 1996, *Yorkshire Hundred and Quo Warranto Rolls*, Yorkshire Archaeol. Soc. Rec. Ser. 151

Evans, C., 1989, 'Archaeology and modern times: Bersu's Woodbury 1938 & 1939' *Antiquity* 63, 436-450

Evans, D.H. and Loveluck, C., 2009, *Life and Economy at Early Medieval Flixborough c. AD 600-1000. The Artefact Evidence*, Excavations at Flixborough 2

Evans, E-J., 2007, 'Animal Bone', in Hardy, A., Charles, B.M. and Williams, R.J., *Death and Taxes. The Archaeology of a Middle Saxon Estate Centre at Higham Ferrers, Northamptonshire*, 145-57

Evans, J., 2004, 'The Iron Age and Roman pottery', in Clark and Wrathmell, 312-24

Evans, D.H. and Loveluck, C. (eds), 2009, *Life and Economy at Early Medieval Flixborough c. A.D. 600-1000. The Artefact Evidence*, Excavations at Flixborough 2

Everitt, A., 1986, *Continuity and colonization: the evolution of Kentish settlement*

Everson, P., 2003, 'Medieval gardens and designed landscapes', in Wilson-North, R. (ed.), *The Lie of the Land. Aspects of the archaeology and history of the designed landscapes in the South West of England*, 24-33

Everson, P. and Barnwell, P.S., 2004, 'Landscapes of Lordship and Pleasure: the castle in its landscape setting', in Clark, J., *Helmsley Castle*, 24-5

Everson, P. and Stocker, D., 1999, *Corpus of Anglo-Saxon Stone Sculpture in England, Volume 5: Lincolnshire*

Everson, P. and Stocker, D., 2005, 'Little Sturton Rediscovered. Part 1: the grange of Kirkstead Abbey', *Lincolnshire Hist. Archaeol.* 40, 7-14

Everson, P. and Stocker, D., forthcoming a, *Custodians of Continuity: the Premonstratensian abbey of Barlings in its landscape*

Everson, P. and Stocker, D., forthcoming b, *Corpus of Anglo-Saxon Stone Sculpture in England: Cambridgeshire*

Everson, P.L., Taylor, C.C. and Dunn, C.J., 1991, *Change and Continuity: Rural Settlement in North-West Lincolnshire*

Evison, V.I., 1980, 'Iron objects', in 'A Middle Saxon iron smelting site at Ramsbury, Wiltshire', *Medieval Archaeol.* 24, 35-9

Evison, V.I., 1987, *Dover: the Buckland Anglo-Saxon Cemetery*, Hist. Build. Mon. Comm. Archaeol. Rep. 3

Evison, V.I., 2000, 'Glass Vessels in England, AD 400-1100', in Price, J., *Glass in Britain and Ireland AD 350-1100*, Br. Mus. Occas. Pap. 127, 47-104

Evison, V.I., forthcoming, 'The Vessel Glass', in Carr, R. and Tester, A., *A High Status Middle Saxon Settlement at Staunch Meadow, Brandon, Suffolk*, East Anglian Archaeol.

Faith, R., 1997, *The English Peasantry and the Growth of Lordship*, Stud. Early Hist. Br.

Fanning, T., 1994, *Viking Age Ringed Pins from Dublin*, Medieval Dublin Excavations 1962-81, Series B Volume 4 (Dublin)

Faull, M.L. and Moorhouse, S.A., 1981, *West Yorkshire: an archaeological survey to A.D. 1500, Vol 3*

Fenton-Thomas, C., 2003, *Late Prehistoric and Early Historic Landscapes on the Yorkshire Chalk*, Br. Archaeol. Rep. Br. Ser. 350

Fenton-Thomas, C., 2005, *The Forgotten Landscapes of the Yorkshire Wolds*

Fenton-Thomas, C., forthcoming, *'Where sky and Yorkshire water meet': the story of the Melton landscape from prehistory to the present*, On-Site Archaeol. Monogr. 2

Fenwick, C., 2005, *The Poll Taxes of 1377, 1379 and 1381, Part 3 Wiltshire-Yorkshire*, Br. Acad. Rec. Soc. Econ. Hist., New Ser 37

Fergusson, P., 1984, *The Architecture of Solitude. Cistercian Abbeys in Twelfth-Century England* (Princeton)

Field, D., 2008, 'The development of an agricultural countryside' in Pollard, J. (ed.), 202-24

Fleming, R., 1985, 'Monastic lands and England's defence in the Viking Age' *English Hist. Rev.* 100, 247-65

Fletcher, R., 2003, *Bloodfeud. Murder and Revenge in Anglo-Saxon England*

Foged Klemensen, M., 1992, *Middelalderlige bondehuse. En diskussion af Axel Steensbergs husrekonstruktioner på bakgrund af de senere års landsbyundersøgelser*, Middelalder arkæologisk nyhedsbrev (Aarhus)

Foster, S.M., 1990, 'Pins, Combs and the Chronology of Later Atlantic Iron Age Settlement', in Armit, I., *Beyond the Brochs. Changing Perspectives on the Atlantic Scottish Iron Age*, 143-74

Fowler, F.J., 1898, 'Extracts of the Account Rolls of the Abbey of Durham I', *Surtees Soc.* 99

Fowler, J.T., 1893, *The Coucher Book of Selby* 2, Yorkshire Archaeol. Soc. Rec. Ser. 13

Fowler, J.T., 1918, *Memorials of the Abbey of Fountains*, Surtees Soc., 130

Fox, H.S.A., 1989, 'The people of the Wolds in settlement history', in Aston *et al.* (eds), 77-101

Fox, H.S.A., 1996, 'Exploitation of the landless by lords and tenants in early medieval England', in Razi, Z. and Smith, R. (eds), *Medieval Society and the Manor Court*, 518-68

Fox, H.S.A., 2000, 'The Wolds before *c*.1500', in Thirsk, J. (ed.), *Rural England. An Illustrated History of the Landscape*, 50-61

Fox, H., 2008, 'Butter place-names and transhumance', in Padel, O.J. and Parsons, David N. (eds), *A Commodity of Good Names: essays in honour of Margaret Gelling*, 352-64

Gade, D.W., 1971, 'Grist Milling with the Horizontal Waterwheel in the Central Andes', *Technol. Cult.* 12, 43-51

Gardiner, M., 2000, 'Vernacular buildings and the development of the later medieval domestic plan in England', *Medieval Archaeol.* 44, 159-79

Gardiner, M., 2009, 'Dales, long lands, and the medieval division of land in eastern England', *Agric. Hist. Rev.* 57, pt 1, 1-14

Garner, M.F., 1994, 'Middle Saxon Evidence at Cook Street, Southampton (SOU 254)', *Proc. Hampshire Field Club Archaeol. Soc.* 49, 77-127

Garner, M., 2003, 'Excavation at St Mary's Road, Southampton (SOU 379 and SOU 1112)', *Proc. Hampshire Field Club Archaeol. Soc.* 58, 106-29

Geake, H., 1997, *The Use of Grave-Goods in Conversion-Period England, c. 600-c. 850,* Br. Archaeol. Rep., Br. Ser. 261

Geake, H. and Kenny, J., 2000 (eds), *Early Deira. Archaeological Studies of the East Riding in the Fourth to Ninth Centuries AD*

Gelling, M., 1978, *Signposts to the Past,* (1st ed.), 11-12

Gelling, M., 1984, *Place-names in the Landscape*

Gelling, M., 1997, *Signposts to the Past* (3rd ed.)

Gelling, M, 2004, 'A regional review of place-names', in *Wharram IX*, 347-51

Gelling, M. and Cole, A., 2000, *The Landscape of Place-names*

Gerrard, C., 2003, *Medieval Archaeology. Understanding traditions and contemporary approaches*

Gerrard, C., 2007, 'Not all archaeology is rubbish: the elusive life histories of three artefacts from Shapwick, Somerset', in Costen, M. (ed.), *People and Places. Essays in Honour of Mick Aston*, 166-80

Gerrard, C. with Aston, M., 2007, *The Shapwick Project, Somerset. A rural landscape explored*, Soc. Medieval Archaeol. Monogr. 25

Gilchrist, R., 2008, 'Magic for the Dead? The archaeology of magic in later medievial burials', *Medieval Archaeol.* 52, 119-60

Giles, M., 2000, *Open Weave, Close Knit: archaeologies of identity in the later prehistoric landscape of East Yorkshire*, unpubl. PhD thesis Univ. Sheffield

Giles, M., 2007a, 'Good fences make good neighbours? Exploring the ladder enclosures of late Iron Age East Yorkshire' in Haselgrove, C. and Moore, T. (eds), *The Later Iron Age in Britain and Beyond*, 235-49

Giles, M., 2007b, 'Refiguring rights in the Early Iron Age landscapes of East Yorkshire' in Haselgrove, C. and Pope, R. (eds), *The Earlier Iron Age in Britain and the Near Continent*, 103-18

Gissel, S., 1979, Review: 'Axel Steensberg, og J L Østergaard Christensen:Store Valby. Historisk-arkeologisk undersøgelse af en nedlagt landsby på Sjælland', *Historisk Tidsskrift*, 13 række, band VI, 124-134

Goldberg, P.J.P., 1992, *Women, Work and Lifecycle in a Medieval Economy. Women in York and Yorkshire c.1300-1520*

Goldberg, P.J.P., 1995, *Women in England c.1275-1525*

Goodall, A.R., 1979, 'Copper-alloy objects', in *Wharram I*, 108-114

Goodall, A.R., 1987 'Copper-alloy objects', in *Wharram III*, 171-3

Goodall, A.R., 1989, 'Copper-alloy objects in *Wharram VI*, 46-9

Goodall, A.R., 2004, 'Non-ferrous metal objects', in *Wharram IX*, 240-43

Goodall, A.R., 2005, 'Non-ferrous metal objects', in Clark, E.A. (ed.), 'The small finds', in *Wharram X*, 129-31

Goodall, A.R. with Ager, B., 1992, 'Non-ferrous metal objects', in *Wharram VII*, 47-9

Goodall, A.R. and Paterson, C., 2000, 'Non-ferrous metal objects', in *Wharram VIII*, 126-32

Goodall, I.H., 1979, 'Iron objects', in *Wharram I*, 115-123

Goodall, I.H., 1987, 'Objects of Iron', in Beresford, G., 177-87

Goodall, I.H., 1989, 'Iron objects', in *Wharram VI*, 49-53

Goodall, I.H., 1992, 'Iron objects', in *Wharram VII*, 49-51

Goodall, I.H. and Clark, E.A., 2000, 'Iron objects', in *Wharram VIII*, 132-47

Goodall, I.H. and Clark, E.A., 2004, 'Iron objects', in *Wharram IX*, 244-51

Goodall, I.H. and Clark, E.A., 2005, 'Iron objects', in *Wharram X*, 132-9

Goodall, I.H. and Clark, E.A., 2007, 'The Iron objects', in *Wharram XI*, 308-313

Goransson, S., 1961, 'Regular open-field pattern in England, and the Scandinavian Solskifte', *Geografiska Annaler* 43

Goudie, G., 1886, 'On the Horizontal Mills of Shetland', *Proc. Soc. Antiq. Scotl.* 20, 257-97

Grant, A., 1989, 'Animals in Roman Britain', in Todd, M. (ed.), *Research on Roman Britain, 1960-89*, 135-46

Grassam, A., 2010, 'A report on the excavations undertaken in 1980 at Hillam Burchard, Parlington, West Yorkshire: Archaeological Excavation', draft ASWYAS rep.

Gray, H.L., 1915, *English Field Systems*

Green, J.A., 2006, *Henry I. King of England and Duke of Normandy*

Greenway, D.E., (ed.), 1972 (reprint 2006), *Charters of the Honour of Mowbray 1107-1191*, Rec. Soc. Econ. Hist. New Ser. 1

Greenwood, C., 1818, 'Map of the County of Yorkshire', surveyed 1815-17

Griffiths, D., Philpott, R.A. and Egan, G., 2007, *Meols. The Archaeology of the North Wirral Coast*, Oxford Univ. Sch. Archaeol. Monogr. 68

Grøngaard Jeppesen, T.G., 1982, 'Arkæologiske metoder anvendt ved fynske landsbyundersøgelser', *META* 2, 2-10

Hadley, D.M., 2000, *The Northern Danelaw. Its Social Structure, c. 800-1100*

Hadley, D.M., 2006, *The Vikings in England. Settlement, Society and Culture*

Hadley, D.M. and Richards, J.D., 2000, *Cultures in Contact. Scandinavian Settlement in England in the Ninth and Tenth Centuries*, Stud. Early Middle Ages 2 (Turnhout)

Hagen, A., 1995, *The Second Handbook of Anglo-Saxon Food and Drink. Production and Distribution*

Haldenby, D., 1990, 'An Anglian Site on the Yorkshire Wolds', *Yorkshire Archaeol. J.* 62, 51-63

Haldenby, D., 1992, 'An Anglian Site on the Yorkshire Wolds. Part Two', *Yorkshire Archaeol. J.* 64, 25-39

Haldenby, D. and Richards, J.D., 2009, 'Settlement shift at Cottam, East Riding of Yorkshire, and the chronology of Anglo-Saxon copper-alloy pins', *Medieval Archaeol.* 53, 309-14

Halkon, P. and Millett, M. (eds), 1999, *Rural Settlement and Industry: studies in the Iron Age and Roman archaeology of lowland East Yorkshire*, Yorkshire Archaeol. Rep. 4

Hall, D.N., 1980, 'Hardingstone Parish Survey', *Northamptonshire Archaeol.* 15, 119-30

Hall, D., 1982, *Medieval Fields*

Hall, D., 1995, *The Open Fields of Northamptonshire*, Northamptonshire Rec. Soc. 38

Hall, K.M., 1993, 'Pre-Conquest estates in Yorkshire', in Le Patourel *et al.*, 25-38

Hamerow, H., 2002, *Early medieval settlements: the archaeology of rural communities in North-West Europe, 400-900*

Hamerow, H., 2010, 'The development of Anglo-Saxon rural settlement forms', *Landscape Hist.* 31, issue 1, 5-22

Hamilton-Thompson, A., 1924, 'The monastic settlement at Hackness and its relation to the abbey of Whitby', *Yorkshire Archaeol. J.,* 27, 388-405

Harding, C., 2007, 'Excavations in the northern graveyard area', in *Wharram XI*, 30-64

Harding, C. and Marlow-Mann, E., 2007, 'Excavations in the central graveyard area', in *Wharram XI*, 9-30

Harding, C. and Wrathmell, S., 2007, 'Discussion', in *Wharram XI*, 327-35

Härke, H., 1989, 'Knives in early Saxon burials: blade length and age at death', *Medieval Archaeol.* 33, 144-8

Härke, H., 1992, *Angelsächsische Waffengräber des 5. bis 7. Jahrhunderts*, Zeitschrift für Archäologie des Mittelalters, Beiheft 6 (Cologne)

Harris, A. 1955, '"Land" and oxgang in the East Riding of Yorkshire', *Yorkshire Archaeol. J.* 38, 529-35

Harris, A., 1959, *The Open Fields of East Yorkshire*

Harris, A., 1961, *The Rural Landscape of the East Riding of Yorkshire*

Harris, A., 1962, 'The Agriculture of the East Riding of Yorkshire before Parliamentary Enclosures', *Yorkshire Archaeol. J.* 40, 119-28

Hart, C.R., 1975, *The Early Charters of Northern England and the North Midlands*

Hart, C., 1992, *The Danelaw*

Harvey, M., 1978, *The Morphological and Tenurial Structure of a Yorks Township; Preston in Holderness 1066-1750*; Queen Mary College Occ. Pap. Geogr. 13

Harvey, M., 1980, 'Regular field and tenurial arrangements in Holderness, Yorkshire', *J. Hist. Geogr.* 6, 3-16

Harvey, M., 1981, 'The origin of planned field systems in Holderness, Yorkshire' in Rowley, T. (ed.), *The Origins of Open-field Agriculture*, 184-201

Harvey, M., 1982a, 'Regular open-field systems on the Yorkshire Wolds', *Landscape Hist.* 4, 29-39

Harvey, M., 1982b, 'Irregular villages in Holderness, Yorkshire: some thoughts on their origin', *Yorkshire Archaeol. J,* 54, 63-71

Harvey, M., 1983, 'Planned field systems in eastern Yorkshire: some thoughts on their origin', *Agric. Hist. Rev.* 31, 91-103

Haslam, A., Riddler, I.D. and Trzaska-Nartowski, N.I.A., forthcoming, 'Middle Saxon Comb Manufacture in *Lundenwic*, and Post-Medieval Covent Garden', *Trans. London Middlesex Archaeol. Soc.*

Haslam, J., with Biek, L. and Tylecote, R.F., 1980, 'A Middle Saxon Iron Smelting Site at Ramsbury, Wiltshire', *Medieval Archaeol.* 24, 1-68

Hatt, G., 1928, 'To bopladsfund fra ældre jernalder, fra Mors og Himmerland', *Aarbog for nordisk Oldkyndighed og Historie*, 219-60

Hatt, G., 1936, 'Oldtidens Landsby i Danmark', *Fortid og Nutid* 11, 97-129

Hatt, G., 1937, 'Dwelling-houses in Jutland in the Iron Age', *Antiquity* 42, 162-73

Haughton, C. and Powlesland, D., 1999, *West Heslerton. The Anglian Cemetery I*, Landscape Res. Centre Archaeol. Monogr. Ser. 1

Hawkes, S.C., 1973, 'The Dating and Social Significance of the Burials in the Polhill Cemetery', in Philp, B., *Excavations in West Kent 1960-1970*, 186-201

Hayfield, C., 1986, 'Wharram Grange Roman villa', in *Wharram IV*, sections 15-38

Hayfield, C., 1987a, 'Wharram Percy Township', in *Wharram V*, 104-126

Hayfield, C., 1987b, 'Discussion', in *Wharram V*, 176-201

Hayfield, C., 1987c, 'Burdale township', in *Wharram V*, 127-44

Hayfield, C., 1987d, 'Introduction', in *Wharram V*, 1-28

Hayfield, C., 1988, 'The origins of the Roman landscape around Wharram Percy, east Yorkshire' in Price, J. and Wilson, P.R. (eds), *Recent Research in Roman Yorkshire*, Br. Archaeol. Rep. Br. Ser 193, 99-121

Hayfield, C. and Brewster, T.,1988, 'Cowlam deserted village: a case study of post-medieval village desertion', *Post-Medieval Archaeol.* 22, 21-109

Hayfield, C. and Wagner, P. 1995, 'From dolines to dewponds: a study of water supplies on the Yorkshire Wolds', *Landscape Hist.* 17, 49-64

Hayfield, C., Pouncett, J. and Wagner, P., 1995, 'Vessey Ponds: a "prehistoric" water supply in East Yorkshire?', in *Proc. Prehist. Soc. 61*, 393-408

Hearn, M.F., 1983, 'Ripon Minster: the beginning of Gothic style in Northern England', *Trans. American Philos. Soc.* 73, pt 6, 1-140

Hedges, R.E.M. and Salter, C.J., 1979, 'Source determination of iron currency bars through analysis of the slag inclusions', *Archaeometry* 21,161-175

Herbert, P. and Wrathmell, S., 2004, 'Site 91 excavations', in *Wharram IX*, 302-12

Herring, P., 1996, 'Transhumance in medieval Cornwall' in Fox, H.A.S. (ed.), *Seasonal Settlement*, 35-44

Herring, P. and Hooke, D., 1993, 'Interrogating Anglo-Saxons in St Dennis', *Cornish Archaeol.* 32, 67-75

Hey, G., 2004, *Yarnton: Saxon and Medieval settlement and landscape*

Heywood, S, 1985, 'VIII. The Stone Fragments', in Ayers (ed.), 41-44

Higbee, L., 2009, 'Mammal and Bird Bone', in Lucy, S., Tipper, J. and Dickens, A., *The Anglo-Saxon Settlement and Cemetery at Bloodmoor Hill, Carlton Colville, Suffolk,* East Anglian Archaeol. 131, 279-304

Hill, N., 2005, 'On the origins of crucks: an Innocent notion', *Vernacular Archit.* 36, 1-14

Hillman, G. and Arthur, J.R.B. (revised Caruthers, W.J.), 2005, 'Charred plant remains from Site 30', in *Wharram X*, 185-91

Hinton, D.A., 1996, *The Gold, Silver and other Non-Ferrous Alloy Objects from Hamwic, and the Non-Ferrous Metalworking Evidence*, Southampton Finds 2

Hinton, D.A., 1998, 'Anglo-Saxon smiths and myths (T Northcote Toller Memorial Lecture 1997)', *Bull. John Rylands Univ. Libr. Manchester* 80: 1, 3-21

Hinton, D.A., 2000, *A Smith in Lindsey. The Anglo-Saxon Grave at Tattershall Thorpe, Lincolnshire,* Soc. Medieval Archaeol. Monogr. 16

Hodder, I., 1989, 'Writing archaeology: site reports in context', *Antiquity* 63, 268-74

Hodges, R., 1981, *The Hamwih Pottery: the local and imported wares from 30 years' excavations at Middle Saxon Southampton and their European context*, Counc. Br. Archaeol. Res. Rep. 37

Hodgson, J., 1827, *A History of Northumberland, Part 2,* Vol. 1

Holden, E.W., 1963, 'Excavations at the deserted medieval village of Hangleton', *Sussex Archaeol. Collect.* 101, 54-181

Holt, R., 1988, *The Mills of Medieval England*

Homans, G.C., 1941, *English Villagers of the Thirteenth Century*

Hudson, J., 1994 (reprint 2004), *Land, Law and Lordship in Anglo-Norman England*

Hudson, W.H., 1910, *A Shepherd's Life: impressions of the South Wiltshire Downs*

Hunter, J.R. and Heyworth, M.P., 1998, *The Hamwic Glass,* Counc. Br. Archaeol. Res. Rep.116

Hunter, L.C., 1967, 'The Living Past in the Appalachias of Europe: Water-Mills in Southern Europe', *Technol. Cult.* 8, 446-66

Huntley, J. and Rackham, J., 2007, 'The Environmental Setting and Provisioning of the Anglo-Saxon Monastery', in Daniels, R., *Anglo-Saxon Hartlepool and the Foundations of English Christianity. An Archaeology of the Anglo-Saxon Monastery*, Tees Archaeol. Monogr. 3, 108-23

Hurley, M.F., 1997, *Excavations at the North Gate, Cork, 1994* (Cork)

Hurst, J.D., 2005, *Sheep in the Cotswolds: the medieval wool trade*

Hurst, J.G., 1955, 'Wharram Percy, Yorkshire - D.M.V.R.G. Excavations 1953/5', *Deserted Medieval Village Res. Group Ann. Rep.* 3, 9-12

Hurst, J.G., 1956, 'Deserted Medieval Villages and the Excavations at Wharram Percy, Yorkshire', in Bruce-Mitford, R.L.S. (ed.), *Recent Archaeological Excavations in Britain*, 251-273

Hurst, J.G., 1960, 'Report by J.G. Hurst on a Visit to Denmark, May 1960', *Deserted Medieval Village Res. Group Ann. Rep.* 8, Appendix C

Hurst, J.G., 1971, 'A Review of Archaeological Research (to 1968)', in Beresford and Hurst (eds), 76-144

Hurst, J.G., 1979a, 'History of the excavation', in *Wharram I*, 1-4

Hurst, J.G., 1979b, 'Conclusions', in *Wharram I*, 138-41

Hurst, J.G., 1984, 'The Wharram Research Project: Results to 1983', *Medieval Archaeol.* 28, 77-111

Hurst, J.G., 1985, 'The Wharram Research Project: Problem Orientation and Strategy 1950-1990', in Hooke, D. (ed.), *Medieval Villages. A Review of Current Work*, Oxford Monogr. 5, 201-204

Hurst, J.G., 1988, 'The Medieval Countryside', in Longworth, I. and Cherry, J., (eds), *Archaeology in Britain since 1945. New Directions*, (1st ed. 1986), 197-236

Hurst, J.G. and Duckett, D.G., 1954, 'Wharram Percy Excavations, 1953-4', *Deserted Medieval Village Res. Group Ann. Rep.* 2, 14-15

Hurst, J.G. and Hurst, D.G., 1964, 'Excavations at the deserted village of Hangleton' *Sussex Archaeol. Collect.* 102, 94-142

Hurst, J.G. and Roskams, S.P., 2004, 'Sites 13 and 83', in Rahtz and Watts, 10-19

Ingold, T., 1993, 'The temporality of landscape', *World Archaeol.* 25/2, 152-74

Ingold, T., 2000, *The Perception of Environment: essays in livelihood, dwelling and skill*

Innocent, C.F., 1916, *The development of English building construction*

Jarrett, M.G. and Wrathmell, S., 1977, 'Sixteenth- and seventeenth-century farmsteads: West Whelpington, Northumberland', *Agric. Hist. Rev.* 25, 108-19

Jenner, A., Mills, S. and Burke, B., 2006, 'The Anglo-Saxon and Medieval Pottery', in Cramp, R.J., *Wearmouth and Jarrow Monastic Sites. Volume 2*, 327-423

Jespersen, S., 1956, 'Et nordisk gårdproblem', *Fortid og Nutid* 19, 342-56

Johnson, M., 2006, *Ideas of landscape*

Johnston, R., 2008, 'Later prehistoric landscapes and habitation' in Pollard, J. (ed.), 268-87

Jones, G.R.J.,1980, 'Review Article: Wharram perceived', Medieval Village Research Group, 28th annual report, 39-41

Jones, J., 2005, 'Plant macrofossil remains from Site 71', in *Wharram X*, 191-200

Jones, R., 2004, 'Signatures in the soil: the use of pottery in manure scatters in the identification of medieval arable farming regimes', *Archaeol. J.* 161, 159-88

Jones, R. and Page, M., 2006, *Medieval Villages in an English Landscape. Beginnings and Ends*

Joosten, I., 2004, *Technology of Early Historical Iron Production in the Netherlands.* Geoarchaeological and Bioarchaeological Studies, Amsterdam Institute for Geo- and Bioarchaeology, Vrije Universiteit

Jurkowski, M., Ramsay, N. and Renton, S., 2007, *English Monastic Estates, 1066-1540*, List Index Soc. Spec. Ser. 40-42

Kahn, D., 1980, 'The Romanesque sculpture of the Church of St Mary at Halford, Warwickshire', *J. Br. Archaeol. Assoc.* 133, 64-73

Kaner, J., 1994, *Goods and Chattels 1552-1642*

Kapelle, W.E., 1979, *The Norman Conquest of the North. The Region and its Transformation, 1000-1135*

Keats-Rohan, K.S.B., 1999, *Domesday People. A Prosopography of Persons Occurring in English Documents 1066-1166, I. Domesday Book*

Keats-Rohan, K.S.B., 2002, *Domesday Descendants. A Prosopography of Persons Occurring in English Documents 1066-1166, II. Pipe Rolls to* Cartae Baronum

Kemp, R.L., 1996, *Anglian Settlement at 46-54 Fishergate*, Archaeol. York 7/1

Keyser, C.E., 1909, 'The Norman Doorways of Yorkshire', in Fallow, T.M., *Memorials of Old Yorkshire*, 165-219

Keyser, C.E., 1927, *A List of Norman Tympana and Lintels …*,

King, A., 1978, 'Gauber High Pasture, Ribblehead – an Interim Report, in Hall, R.A., *Viking Age York and the North*, Counc. Br. Archaeol. Res. Rep. 27, 21-5

King, H. and Harris, A. (eds), 1962, *A Survey of the Manor of Settrington*, Yorkshire Archaeol Soc. Rec. Ser. 126 (for 1960)

Kinnes, I., Scadla-Hall, T., Chadwick, P. and Dean, P., 1983, 'Duggleby Howe reconsidered', *Archaeol. J.* 140, 83-108

Kitson Clark, M., 1935, *A Gazetteer of Roman Remains in East Yorkshire*, Roman Malton Dist. Rep. 5

Knight, B. and Pirie, E.J.E., 2000, 'Coins', in *Wharram VIII*, 124-6

Koch, U., 1977, *Das Reihengräberfeld von Schretzheim*, Germanische Denkmäler der Völkerwanderungszeit, serie A13 (Berlin)

Koch, U., 2001, *Das alamannische-fränkische Gräberfeld bei Pleidelsheim*, Forschungen und Berichte zur Vor- und Frühgeschichte in Baden-Württemberg 60 (Stuttgart)

Kraks Blå Bog, 1998, Axel Steensberg, 1169-1170 (Copenhagen)

Krapp, G.P. and Dobbie, E.V.K., 1931-42, *The Anglo-Saxon Poetic Records*, volume 3 (New York)

Lancaster, W.T. (ed.), 1912, *Chartulary of the Priory of Bridlington*

Lang, J.T., 1991, *Corpus of Anglo-Saxon Stone Sculpture in England, Volume 3 York and Eastern Yorkshire*

Lang, J.T., 1992, 'Fragment of cross-head. 94/2302 SF29', in Clark, 'Miscellaneous small finds of stone, clay, jet, amber and glass', in *Wharram VII*, 43

Lang, J.T., 2001, *Corpus of Anglo-Saxon Stone Sculpture in England, Volume 6: Northern Yorkshire*

Langdon, J., 1986, *Horses, Oxen and Technological Innovation: the Use of Draught Animals in English Farming from 1066-1500*

Lawrance, N.A.H., 1985, *Fasti Parochiales V. Deanery of Buckrose*, Yorkshire Archaeol. Soc. Rec. Ser. 143 (for 1983)

Leadam, I.S., 1893, 'The Inquisition of 1517. Inclosures and evictions, part II', *Trans. R. Hist. Soc.*, New Ser. 7 (for 1893), 219-53

Leahy, K., 2000, 'Middle Anglo-Saxon Metalwork from South Newbald and the "Productive Site" Phenomenon in Yorkshire', in Geake and Kenny (eds), 51-82

Le Patourel, H.E.J., 1979, 'Medieval pottery', in *Wharram I*, 74-107

Le Patourel, H.E.J., Long, M.H. and Pickles, M.F. (eds), 1993, *Yorkshire Boundaries*, Yorkshire Archaeol. Soc.

Lerche, G. (ed.), 1976, *The common fields of culture. Axel Steensberg 1 June 1976* (Copenhagen)

Lerche, G. (ed.), 1986, *A birthday bibliographic supplement 1976-1986. Axel Steensberg eighty years 1 June 1986* (Copenhagen)

Lerche, G., 1996, *A birthday bibliographic supplement 1986-1996. Axel Steensberg ninety years 1 June 1996* (Copenhagen)

Lerche, G., 2000, 'Axel Steensberg 1906-1999', *Ethnologia Scandinavica* 30, 115-16

Lewin, J., 1969, *The Yorkshire Wolds: a study in geomorphology*

Lewis, C., Mitchell-Fox, P. and Dyer, C., 2001, *Village, Hamlet and Field. Changing medieval settlements in Central England*

Liddiard, R., 2005, *Castles in Context. Power, Symbolism and Landscape, 1066 to 1500*

Liebermann, F., 1905, 'An English document of about 1080', *Yorkshire Archaeol. J.* 18, 412-16

Linford, P. and Linford, N., 2003, 'Wharram Percy, North Yorkshire: Report on Geophysical Surveys, 1984-2002' Engl. Heritage Centre Archaeol. Rep. 28/2003

Linington, R.E., 1973, 'A Summary of Simple Theory Applicable to Magnetic Prospecting in Archaeology', *Prospezioni Archeologiche* 7-8, 61-84

Lloyd Morgan, G., 1994, 'Ring-Headed Pins', in Ward, S., *Excavations at Chester. Saxon Occupation within the Roman Fortress. Sites Excavated 1971 – 1981*, Archaeol. Serv. Excavation Surv. Rep. 7, 104

Long, W.H., 1960, 'Regional Farming in Seventeenth-century Yorkshire', *Agric. Hist. Rev.* 8, 103-15

Loughborough, B., 1965, 'An account of a Yorkshire Enclosure', *Agric. Hist. Rev.* 13, 106-115

Loveluck, C.P., 1996, 'The development of the Anglo-Saxon landscape, economy and society 'On Driffield', east Yorkshire, 400-750 AD', *Anglo-Saxon Stud. Archaeol. Hist.* 9, 25-48

Loveluck, C.P., 1998, 'A high-status Anglo-Saxon settlement at Flixborough, Lincolnshire', *Antiquity* 72, 146-161

Loveluck, C.P., 2001, 'Wealth, waste and conspicuous consumption: Flixborough and its importance for Middle and Late Saxon rural settlement studies', in Hamerow, H. and MacGregor, A. (eds), *Image and Power in the Archaeology of Early Medieval Britain - Essays in honour of Rosemary Cramp*, 78-130

Loveluck, C., 2007, *Rural Settlement, Lifestyles and Social Change in the later First Millenium AD. Anglo-Saxon Flixborough in its Wider Context*, Excavations at Flixborough 4

Loveluck, C. and Atkinson, D., 2007, *The Early Medieval Settlement Remains from Flixborough, Lincolnshire. The Occupation Sequence, c AD 600-1000*, Excavations at Flixborough 1

Lucas, A.T., 1953, 'The Horizontal Mill in Ireland', *J. R. Soc. Antiq. Ir.* 83, 1-36

Lucy, S., 1998, *The Early Anglo-Saxon Cemeteries of East Yorkshire. An Analysis and Reinterpretation*, Br. Archaeol. Rep. Br. Ser. 272

Lucy, S., 1999, 'Changing Burial Rites in Northumbria AD 500-750', in Hawkes, J. and Mills, S., *Northumbria's Golden Age*, 12-43

Ludvigsen, A. and Steensberg, A., 1941, 'En dansk Bondegaard gennem 2000 Aar', *Fra Nationalmuseets Arbejdsmark 1941*, 5-24

MacGregor, A., 1982, *Anglo-Scandinavian Finds from Lloyds Bank, Pavement and other Sites*, Archaeology York 17/3

MacGregor, A., 1985, *Bone, Antler, Ivory and Horn. The technology of skeletal materials since the Roman period*

MacGregor, A., 1987, 'Objects of Bone and Antler', in Beresford, G., *Goltho. The Development of an Early Medieval Manor, c 850-1150*, Engl. Heritage Archaeol. Rep. 4, 188-93

MacGregor, A., 1989a, 'Bone, Antler and Horn Industries in the Urban Context', in Serjeantson, D. and Waldron, T., *Diet and Crafts in Towns*, Br. Archaeol. Rep., Br. Ser. 199, 107-128

MacGregor, A., 1989b, 'Bone and antler objects', in *Wharram VI*, 56

MacGregor, A., 1992, 'Bone and antler objects', in *Wharram VII*, 54-8

MacGregor, A.G., 2000, 'Bone and antler objects', in *Wharram VIII*, 148-54

MacGregor, A.G. and Riddler, I., 2005, 'Bone and ivory objects', in *Wharram X*, 143-5

MacGregor, A., Mainman, A.J. and Rogers, N.S.H., 1999, *Craft, Industry and Everyday Life: Bone, Antler, Ivory and Horn from Anglo-Scandinavian and Medieval York*, Archaeol. York 17/12

Mackey, R., 1999, 'The Welton Villa - a view of social and economic change during the Roman period in East Yorkshire', in Halkon, P. (ed.), *Further light on the Parisi*, 21-32

Mackey, R., 2003, 'The Iron Age in East Yorkshire: a summary of current knowledge and recommendations for future research', in Manby *et al.*, 117-21

MacLeod, F., 2009, *The Norse Mills of Lewis*

Maddin, R., 1987, 'The Early Blacksmith', in Scott *et al.* (eds)

Madsen, H.J., 2004, 'Pottery from the 8th-9th Centuries', in Bencard, M., Rasmussen, A.K. and Madsen, H.B., *Ribe Excavations 1970-76. Volume 5*, Jutland Archaeol. Soc. Publ. 46, 223-70 (Aarhus)

Mainman, A.J., 1993, *Pottery from 46-54 Fishergate*, Archaeol. York, The Pottery 16/6

Mainman, A.J. and Rogers, N., 2000, *Craft, Industry and Everyday Life: Finds from Anglo-Scandinavian York*, Archaeol. York, 17/14

Malcolm, G., Bowsher, D. and Cowie, B., 2003, *Middle Saxon London. Excavations at the Royal Opera House 1989-99*, Mus. London Archaeol. Monogr. 15

Manby, T., 2003, 'The Iron Age of Central and Pennine Yorkshire', in Manby *et al.* (eds), 121-24

Manby, T., King, A. and Vyner, B., 2003, 'The Neolithic and Bronze Ages: a time of early agriculture', in Manby *et al.* (eds), 35-116

Manby, T., Moorhouse, S. and Ottaway, P. (eds), 2003, *The Archaeology of Yorkshire: an assessment at the beginning of the 21st century*, Yorkshire Archaeol. Soc. Occas. Pap. 3

Mann, J., 1982, *Early Medieval Finds from Flaxengate. I: Objects of Antler, Bone, Stone, Horn, Ivory, Amber and Jet*, Archaeol. Lincoln 14-1

Margeson, S., 1993, *Norwich Households. Medieval and Post-Medieval Finds from Norwich Survey Excavations 1971-8*, East Anglian Archaeol. 58

Markham, G., 1615, *The English Hus-wife*

Marshall, W.H., 1788, *Provincialisms of East Yorkshire*

Martin, D. and Martin, B. 1997, 'Detached kitchens in eastern Sussex: a re-assessment of the evidence', *Vernacular Archit.* 28, 85-91

Martin, D. and Martin, B., 2006, *Farm Buildings of the Weald 1450-1750*

Marufi, I., 2007, 'An investigation into the occurrence of Neumann bands in archaeological iron', unpubl. MSc diss. Univ. Bradford

Marzinzik, S., 2003, *Early Anglo-Saxon Belt Buckles (late 5th to early 8th centuries AD). Their Classification and Context*, Br. Archaeol. Rep. Br. Ser. 357

Mays, S., 2007, 'The human remains in *Wharram XI*', 77-192

Maztat, M., 1988, 'Long strip field layouts and their later subdivisions', *Geografiska Annaler* 70B, 133-47

McCarthy, M.R.and Brooks, C.M, 1988, *Medieval Pottery in Britain, AD 900-1600*

McDonagh, B.A.K., 2007a, 'Manor houses, churches and settlements: historical geographies of the Yorkshire Wolds before 1600', unpubl. PhD thesis, Univ. Nottingham

McDonagh, B.A.K., 2007b, '"Powerhouses" of the Wolds landscape: manor houses and churches in late medieval and early modern England', in Gardiner, M. and Rippon, S. (eds), *Medieval Landscapes, Landscape after Hoskins Volume 2*, 185-200

McDonagh, B.A.K., 2009, 'Subverting the ground: private property and public protest in the sixteenth-century Yorkshire Wolds', *Agric. Hist. Rev.* 57 (2), 191-206

McDonnell, G., 1986, 'The classification of early ironworking slags', unpubl. PhD thesis, Univ. Aston

McDonnell, G., 1987a, 'The study of Early Iron Smelting Residues', in Scott *et al.*

McDonnell, G., 1987b, 'The ironworking residues from Cherry Willingham, Lincolnshire', Ancient Monuments Lab. Rep. 92/87

McDonnell, G., 1988a, 'The ironworking residues from Romsey, Hampshire', Ancient Monuments Lab. Rep. 72/88

McDonnell, G., 1988b, 'The ironworking slags from North Cave, North Humberside' Ancient Monuments Lab. Rep. 91/88

McDonnell, G., 1989, 'Iron and its alloys in the fifth to eleventh centuries AD in England', *World Archaeol.* 20, 373-381

McDonnell, G., 1991, 'A model for the formation of smithing slags' *Materialy Archeologiczne* 26, 23-26

McDonnell, G., 1992a, 'The identification and analysis of the slags from Burton Dassett, Warwickshire', Ancient Monuments Lab. Rep. 46/92

McDonnell, G., 1992b, 'Metallography of the Coppergate knives', in Ottaway, P. (ed.), *Anglo-Scandinavian ironwork from 16-22 Coppergate*, 591-599, York Archaeol.

McDonnell, G., 1993, 'The examination of the slags and residues from Mucking, Essex. London', Ancient Monuments Lab. Rep. 4/93

McDonnell, G., 2000, 'The ironworking evidence', in *Wharram VIII*, 155-66

McIntosh, M., 1998, *Controlling Misbehavior in England, 1370-1600*

Mellor, M., 1994, 'A synthesis of middle and late Saxon, medieval and early post-medieval pottery in the Oxford region', *Oxoniensia* 59, 17-217

Meriton, G., 1684, *In Praise of Yorkshire Ale*

Mileson, S.A., 2009, *Parks in Medieval England*

Millett, M. (ed.), 2006, *Shiptonthorpe, East Yorkshire: archaeological studies of a Romano-British roadside settlement*, Yorkshire Archaeol. Rep. 5

Mills, A. and McDonnell, J.G., 1992, 'The identification and analysis of the hammerscale from Burton Dassett, Warwickshire', Ancient Monuments Lab. Rep. 1992/47

Milne, G., 1979a, 'Area 10', in *Wharram I*, 26-41

Milne, G., 1979b, 'Area 6', in *Wharram I*, 42-54

Milne, G., 1979c, 'The peasant houses', in *Wharram I*, 67-73

Milne, G., 1992a, 'Site 39', in *Wharram VII*, 5-12

Milne, G., 1992b, 'Site 39', in 'Characterisation and dating of the assemblages', in *Wharram VII*, 80-82

Milne, G., 2004, 'Site 45', in Rahtz and Watts, 67-73

Milsted, I.D., 2003, 'Pathways into the Neolithic? Cursus Monuments and Remote Sensing, Rudston, East Yorkshire', unpubl. MA diss., Univ. York

Moffett, L., 2006, 'The archaeology of medieval plant foods', in Woolgar *et al.* (eds), 41-55

Moor, C., 1935, 'The Bygods, earls of Norfolk', *Yorkshire Archaeol. J.* 32, 172-213

Moorhouse, S., 1986, 'Non-dating uses of medieval pottery', *Medieval Ceram.* 10, 85-123

Morgan, R., 2005, 'Tree-ring analysis of wattling from the millpond and graveyard', in *Wharram X*, 200-210

Morley, B., 1979, *Hylton Castle*, Dep. Environ. guidebook

Morrell, J.B., 1949, *Woodwork in York*

Morris, C.A., 2005, 'Wooden objects', in *Wharram X*, 140-43

Morris, R., 1989, *Churches in the Landscape*

Morris, R.K., 1991, 'Baptismal places 600-800', in Wood, I. and Lund, N. (eds), *People and Places in Northern Europe 500-1600. Essays in honour of Peter Sawyer*, 15-24

Morris, R., and Shoesmith, R., (eds), 2003, *Tewkesbury Abbey, History, Art & Architecture*

Mortimer, J.R.,1905, *Forty Years' Researches in British and Saxon Burial Mounds of East Yorkshire*

Mortimer, J.R., 1978, *A Victorian Boyhood on the Wolds*

Morton, A.D., 1992, *Excavations at Hamwic. Volume 1: excavations 1946-83, excluding Six Dials and Melbourne Street*, Counc. Br. Archaeol. Res. Rep. 84

Mould, Q., 2005, 'The heather', in *Wharram X*, 145-9

Müldner, G. and Richards, M.P., 2006, 'Diet in medieval England: the evidence from stable isotopes', in Woolgar *et al.* (eds.), 228-38

Mulville, J., 2008, 'Foodways and social ecologies from the Middle Bronze Age to the Late Iron Age', in Pollard (ed.), 225-47

Naylor, J., 2004, *An Archaeology of Trade in Middle Saxon England*, Br. Archaeol. Rep., Br. Ser. 376

Neal, C., 2006, *Geoarchaeological Report Burdale 2006*, unpubl. archive rep., Univ. York

Neal, D.S., 1996, *Excavations on the Roman Villa at Beadlam, Yorkshire*, Yorkshire Archaeol. Rep. 2

Neave, S., 1990, 'Rural settlement contraction in the East Riding of Yorkshire, *c*.1660-1760 with particular reference to the Bainton Beacon division', PhD thesis, Univ. Hull

Neave, S. 1991, *Medieval Parks of East Yorkshire*

Neave, S., 1993, 'Rural settlement contraction in the East Riding of Yorkshire between the mid-seventeenth and mid-eighteenth centuries', *Agric. Hist. Rev.* 41, 124-36

Newman, J., 2003, 'Exceptional Finds, Exceptional Sites? Barham and Coddenham, Suffolk', in Pestell and Ulmschneider (eds), 97-109

Nielsen, S., 1966, 'Village archaeology', in Rasmussen, H. (ed.), *Dansk Folkemuseum & Frilandsmuseet. History and activities*, 167-88 (Copenhagen)

Nightingale, P., 2000, 'Knights and merchants: trade, politics and the gentry in late medieval England', *Past & Present* 169, 36-62

Noddle, B., 1980, 'Identification and interpretation of the mammal bones', in Wade-Martins, P., *Excavations at North Elmham Park 1967-72*, East Anglian Archaeol. 9, Volume II, 377-409

Nørlund, P., 1936, 'Trelleborg ved Slagelse. Hvad der er fundet og hvad det har været', *Fra Nationalmuseets Arbejdsmark 1936*, 55-66

O'Connor, T.P., 1982, *Animal Bones from Flaxengate, Lincoln c 870-1500*, Counc. Br. Archaeol., Archaeol. Lincoln 18/1

O'Connor, T.P., 1991, *Bones from 46-54 Fishergate*, Archaeol. York 15/4

Olsen, O., 1977, 'Perspektiver for dansk middelalderforskning' *Hikuin* 3, 5-12

Ordnance Survey 1854, First Edition six-inch scale map. (East Riding) Yorkshire, CXLIII SW, surveyed 1850-51

Ordnance Survey 1890, First Edition 25-inch scale map, Sheet Yorkshire (East Riding) CXLIII.9, surveyed 1888

Oschinsky, D. (ed.), 1971, *Walter of Henley and other Treatises on Estate Management and Accounting*

Oswald, A., 2004, 'Wharram Percy deserted medieval village, North Yorkshire: archaeological investigation and survey', Engl. Heritage Archaeol. Investigation Rep. Ser. A1/19/2004

Oswald, A., 2005, 'The field evidence', in *Wharram X*, 9-19

Ottaway, P., 1992, *Anglo-Scandinavian Ironwork from 16-22 Coppergate*, Archaeol. York, The Small Finds 17/6

Ottaway, P., 2009, 'Possible Liturgical Objects: Iron Bells and Bell Clappers', in Evans and Loveluck (eds), 141-2

Ottaway, P. and Wiener, K., 1993, 'Comparative Data', in Rogers, 1304-8

Owen, A.E.B., 1984, 'Salt, sea banks and medieval settlement on the Lindsey coast', in Field, F.N. and White, A.J. (eds), *A Prospect of Lincolnshire. Being articles on the history and traditions of Lincolnshire in honour of Ethel H Rudkin*, 46-9

Parsons, D. and Styles, T., 2000, *The Vocabulary of English Place-names, BRACE-CÆSTER*

Parzinger, H., 1998, *Der Goldberg. Die metallzeitliche Besiedlung*, Römisch-Germanische Forschungen 57 (Mainz am Rhein)

Payne, S., 1973, 'Kill-off patterns in sheep and goats: the mandibles from Asvan Kale', *Anatolian Stud.* 23, 281-283

Peacock, E., 1872, *A List of Roman Catholics in the County of York 1604*

Pearson, S., Barnwell, P.S. and Adams, A.T., 1994, *A Gazetteer of Medieval Houses in Kent*

Peers, C. and Radford, C.A.R., 1943, 'The Saxon Monastery of Whitby', *Archaeologia* 89, 27-88

Peirce, I.G., 2002, *Swords of the Viking age*

Penn, K., 2000, *Excavations on the Norwich Southern Bypass, 1989 – 91 Part II: The Anglo-Saxon Cemetery at Harford Farm, Caistor St Edmund, Norfolk*, East Anglian Archaeol. 92

Percy, T., 1905, *The Northumberland Household Book*

Pestell, T., 2004, *Landscapes of Monastic Foundation. The Establishment of Religious Houses in East Anglia, c 650-1200*, Anglo-Saxon Stud. 5

Pestell, T., 2009, 'The Styli', in Evans and Loveluck (eds), 123-37

Pestell, T and Ulmschneider, K. (eds), 2003, *Markets in early medieval Europe: trading and productive sites, 650-850*

Pevsner, N. and Neave, D., 1995, *The Buildings of England. Yorkshire: York and the East Riding* (2nd ed.)

Pickles, M.F., 1993, 'The significance of boundary roads in Yorkshire', in Le Patourel *et al.* (eds), 59-74

Pinter-Bellows, S., 1992, 'The vertebrate remains from Sites 94 and 95', in *Wharram VII*, 69-79

Pinter-Bellows, S., 2000, 'The animal remains', in *Wharram VIII*

Pirie, E.J.E., 1992, 'Northumbrian Sceat', in *Wharram VII*, 52-4

Pleiner, R., 2000, *Iron in archaeology: the European bloomery smelters*. Archaeologický Ústav Avĕr

Pleiner, R. 2006. *Iron in archaeology: Early European Blacksmiths*. Archaeologický Ústav Avĕr

Pollard, J. (ed.), 2008, *Prehistoric Britain*

Poos, L.R. (ed.), 2001, *Lower Ecclesiastical Jurisdiction in Late-Medieval England*, Br. Acad. Rec. Soc. Econ. Hist., New Ser., 32

Poos, L.R. and Bonfield, L. (eds), 1998, *Select Cases in Manorial Courts 1250-1550. Property and Family Law*, Selden Soc. 114

Porsmose, E., 1977, 'Den stationære landsbys opståen. Overvejelser omkring den fynske bebyggelse på overgangen mellem oldtid og middelalder', in Thrane, H. (ed.), *Kontinuitet og bebyggelse. Beretning fra et symposium d. 12.-14. maj 1977 afholdt af Odense universitet*, Skrifter fra Institut for historie og samfundsvidenskab, Odense universitet, historie, 22, 66-75 (Odense)

Postles, D., 1979, 'Rural Economy on the Grits and Sandstones of the South Yorkshire Pennines, 1086-1348' *Northern Hist.* 15, 1-23

Powell, A., Baumann, J. and Vernon, R., 2005, 'Experimental charcoal burn at Dalby Forest, North Yorkshire' *Counc. Br. Archaeol. Yorkshire Forum*, 7-10

Powlesland, D., 1997, 'Early Anglo-Saxon settlements, structures, form and layout', in Hines, J. (ed.), *The Anglo-Saxons from the Migration Period in the Eighth Century: an ethnographic perspective*, 101-24

Powlesland, D., 1999, 'The Anglo-Saxon settlement at West Heslerton, North Yorkshire', in Hawkes, J. and Mills, S., *Northumbria's Golden Age*, 55-66

Powlesland D. 2000, 'West Heslerton settlement mobility: a case of static development', in Geake and Kenny (eds), 19-26

Powlesland D., 2003a, 'The Heslerton parish project: 20 years of archaeological research in the Vale of Pickering', in Manby *et al.* (eds), 275-91

Powlesland, D., 2003b, *25 years of archaeological research on the sands and gravels of Heslerton*

Price, J., 2004, 'The Roman glass', in Clark, E.A. (ed.), 'The North Manor Area small finds', in *Wharram IX*, 232-3

Price, J., 2007, 'Roman glass', in Price, J., Wilmott, H. and Clark, E.A., 'Glass objects', in *Wharram XI*, 299-300

Price, J., Clark., E.A. and Joseph, A., 2000, 'Glass objects', in *Wharram VIII*, 121-24

Purvis , J.S., 1926, *Bridlington Charters, Court Rolls and Papers*

Purvis, J.S., 1947, 'A note on 16th century farming in Yorkshire', *Yorkshire Archaeol. Soc.* 36, 435-54

Purvis, J.S. (ed.), 1949, *Select XVI Century Causes in Tithe*, Yorkshire Archaeol. Soc. Rec. Ser. 114

Putnam, B.H. (ed.), 1939, *Yorkshire Sessions of the Peace 1361-1364*, Yorkshire Archaeol. Soc. Rec. Ser. 100

Rahtz, P.A., 1988, 'From Roman to Saxon at Wharram Percy' in Price, J. and Wilson, P.R. (eds), *Recent Research in Roman Yorkshire*, Br. Archaeol. Rep. Br. Ser. 193, 123-37

Rahtz, P.A., 2003, 'Obituary. John Hurst 1927-2003', *Antiquity* 77, No. 298, 880-81

Rahtz, P. and Meeson, R., 1992, *An Anglo-Saxon Watermill at Tamworth*, Counc. Br. Archaeol. Res. Rep. 83

Rahtz, P. and Watts, L., 2003, 'Three Ages of Conversion at Kirkdale, North Yorkshire' in Carver, M. (ed.), *The Cross Goes North: processes of conversion in northern Europe, AD 300-1300*, 289-309

Rahtz, P.A.and Watts, L., 2004, 'The North Manor area excavations', in *Wharram IX*, 1-138

Rahtz, P.A., Richards, J.D. and Roskams, S.P., 2004, 'The North Manor Area excavations', in *Wharram IX*, 273-96

Raine, J. (ed.), 1855, *Testamenta Eboracensia*, Surtees Soc. 30

Raine, J. (ed.), 1859, *Fabric Rolls of York Minster*, Surtees Soc. 35

Ramm, H.G., McDowall, R.W. and Mercer, E., 1970, *Shielings and Bastles*

Rasmussen, H., 1983, 'Axel Steensberg', *Dansk biografisk leksikon*, band 14, 23-4 (Copenhagen)

RCHME, 1997, 'Ham Hill, Somerset', unpubl. field surv. rep.

Reiß, R., 1994, *Der merowingerzeitliche Reihengräberfriedhof von Westheim (Kreis Weißenburg-Gunzenhausen)* (Nürnberg)

Reynolds A., 2003, 'Boundaries and settlements in later sixth to eleventh-century England', *Anglo-Saxon Stud. Archaeol. Hist.* 12, 98-136

Richards, J.D., 1992a, 'Sites 94 and 95', in *Wharram VII*, 13-25

Richards, J.D., 1992b, 'Sites 94 and 95', in 'Characterisation and dating of the assemblages', in *Wharram VII*, 82-85

Richards, J.D., 1992c, 'Anglo-Saxon Settlement at Wharram Percy: a general introduction', in *Wharram VII*, 89-94

Richards, J.D., 1992d, 'Anglo-Saxon Symbolism', in Carver, M.O.H., *The Age of Sutton Hoo. The Seventh Century in North-Western Europe*, Woodbridge, 131-48

Richards, J.D., 1999a, 'Cottam: An Anglian and Anglo-Scandinavian settlement on the Yorkshire Wolds', *Archaeol. J.* 156, 1-111

Richards, J.D., 1999b, 'What is so special about "productive sites"? Middle Saxon settlements in Northumbria', *Anglo-Saxon Studies Archaeol. Hist.* 10, 71-80

Richards, J.D., 2000a, 'The Anglo-Saxon and Anglo-Scandinavian Evidence', in *Wharram VIII*, 195-200

Richards, J.D., 2000b, 'Identifying Anglo-Scandinavian Settlements', in Hadley and Richards, 295-310

Richards, J.D., 2001a, *The Vicars Choral of York Minster: The College at Bedern*, Archaeol. York 10/5

Richards, J.D., 2001b, 'Finding the Vikings: the search for Anglo-Scandinavian rural settlement in the northern Danelaw', in Graham-Campbell, J., Hall, R., Jesch, J. and Parsons, D.N., *Vikings and the Danelaw. Select Papers from the Proceedings of the Thirteenth Viking Congress*, Nottingham and York, 21-30 August 1997, 269-77

Richards, J.D., 2003, 'The Anglian and Anglo-Scandinavian Sites at Cottam, East Yorkshire', in Pestell and Ulmschneider (eds), 155-67

Richards, J.D, Naylor, J. and Holas-Clark, C., 2009, 'Anglo-Saxon landscape and economy: using portable antiquities to study Anglo-Saxon and Viking Age England', *Internet Archaeol.* 25 http://intarch.ac.uk/journal/issue25/vasle_index.html

Richardson, J., 2001, 'The animal bones from West Heslerton - The Anglian Settlement', unpubl. rep. for D. Powlesland, Landscape Research Centre

Richardson, J., 2004a, 'The animal remains', in *Wharram IX*, 257-72

Richardson, J., 2004b, 'The animal remains', in Clark and Wrathmell (eds), 332-39

Richardson, J., 2005a, 'The animal remains', in *Wharram X*, 153-169

Richardson, J., 2005b, 'The animal remains from Sites 9 and 12 (Houses 10 and 6), in *Wharram X*, 229-42

Richardson, J., 2007, 'The animal remains', in *Wharram XI*, 319-26

Richardson, J., 2009a. 'Burdale animal bone', prepared for Julian Richards, Univ. York

Richardson, J., 2009b. 'Cowlam animal bone', prepared for Julian Richards, Univ. York

Riddler, I.D., 1998, 'Worked Whale Vertebrae', *Archaeol. Cantiana* 118, 205-15

Riddler, I.D., 2001a, 'The Spatial Organisation of Bone and Antler working in Trading Centres', in Hill, D. and Cowie, R., *Wics. The Early Medieval Trading Centres of Northern Europe,* Sheffield Archaeol. Rep. 14, 61-6

Riddler, I.D., 2001b, 'The Small Finds', in Gardiner, M., Cross, R., Macpherson-Grant, N. and Riddler, I., 'Continental Trade and Non-Urban Ports in Mid-Anglo-Saxon England: Excavations at *Sandtun,* West Hythe, Kent', *Archaeol. J.* 158, 228-52

Riddler, I.D., 2004a, 'The Small Finds', in Leary, J., *Tatberht's Lundenwic. Archaeological Excavations in Middle Saxon London,* Proc. Cambridge Antiq. Monogr. 2, 19-26, 52-61 and 98-102

Riddler, I.D., 2004b, 'Bone, antler and ivory objects', in *Wharram IX*, 251-4

Riddler, I.D., 2005, 'Bone and Antler', in Wallis, H., *Excavations at Mill Lane, Thetford,* East Anglian Archaeol. 108, 58-66

Riddler, I.D., 2006a, 'Objects and Waste of Bone and Antler', in Cramp, R.J., *Wearmouth and Jarrow Monastic Sites. Volume 2,* 267-81

Riddler, I.D., 2006b, 'Early Medieval Fishing Implements of Bone and Antler', in Pieters, M., Verhaege, F. and Gevaert, G., *Fishing, Trade and Piracy. Fishermen and Fishermen's Settlements in and around the North Sea Area in the Middle Ages and Later,* Archeologie in Vlaanderen 6, 171-80 (Brussels)

Riddler, I., 2007, 'Objects of antler and bone', in *Wharram XI*, 313-17

Riddler, I.D., 2008, 'The Small Finds', in Bennett, P. Clark, P., Hicks, A., Rady, J. and Riddler, I., *At the Great Crossroads. Prehistoric, Roman and Medieval Discoveries on the Isle of Thanet 1994-95,* Canterbury Archaeol. Trust Occas. Pap. 4, 331-3

Riddler, I.D., forthcoming a, 'Objects of Silver and Copper Alloy', in Carr and Tester

Riddler, I.D., forthcoming b, 'The Knives', in Parfitt, K. and Anderson, T., *The Anglo-Saxon Cemetery at Dover Buckland, Kent. The 1994 Excavations,* Archaeology Canterbury, New Ser.

Riddler, I.D., forthcoming c, 'The Archaeology of the Anglo-Saxon Whale', in Klein, S.S., Lewis-Simpson, S. and Schipper, W., *The Maritime World of the Anglo-Saxons,* ISAS Monogr. (New York)

Riddler, I.D. and Sabin, R., 2009, 'Whalebone Chopping Boards', in Lucy, S.J., Tipper, J. and Dickens, A., *The Anglo-Saxon Settlement and Cemetery at Bloodmoor Hill, Carlton Coleville, Suffolk,* East Anglian Archaeol. 131, 191-3

Riddler, I.D. and Trzaska-Nartowski, N.I.A., forthcoming a, 'Chanting upon a Dunghill: Working Skeletal Materials in Anglo-Saxon England,' in Hyer, M.C. and Owen-Crocker, G., *The Material Culture of Daily Life in Anglo-Saxon England*

Riddler, I.D. and Trzaska-Nartowski, N.I.A., forthcoming b, *Combs and Comb Making in Viking and Medieval Dublin,* Medieval Dublin Excavations 1962-81, Series B (Dublin)

Riddler, I.D. and Walton Rogers, P., 2006, 'Early Medieval Small Finds', in Parfitt, K Corke, B. and Cotter, J., *Townwall Street, Dover. Excavations 1996,* Archaeol. Canterbury. New Series 3, Canterbury, 256-307

Riddler, I.D., Trzaska-Nartowski, N.I.A. and Barton, R., forthcoming, 'The Knowth Combs', in Eogan, G., *Knowth. The Early Medieval Settlement,* Excavations at Knowth 5, R. Ir. Acad. (Dublin)

Riddler, I.D., Trzaska-Nartowski, N.I.A. and Hatton, S., forthcoming, *An Early Medieval Craft. Antler and Boneworking from Ipswich Excavations 1974-1994,* East Anglian Archaeol.

Rigold, S., 1977, 'Romanesque Bases in and South-east of the Limestone Belt', in Apted, M.R., Gilyard Beer, R. and Saunders, A.D. (eds), *Ancient Monuments and their Interpretation: Essays presented to A.J. Taylor,* 99-137

Riley, H., 2006, *The Historic Landscape of the Quantock Hills*

Riley, H. and Wilson-North, R., 2001, *The Field Archaeology of Exmoor*

Roberts, C., 2009, 'Health and welfare in medieval England: the human skeletal remains contextualised', in Gilchrist, R. and Reynolds, A. (eds), *Reflections: 50 Years of Medieval Archaeology 1957-2007,* Soc. Medieval Archaeol.Monogr. 30, 307-26

Roberts, B.K., 1987, *The Making of the English Village*

Roberts, B.K., 2008, *Landscapes, Documents and Maps. Villages in Northern England and Beyond, AD 900-1250*

Roberts, B.K. and Wrathmell, S., 2002, *Region and Place. A Study of English Rural Settlement*

Roberts, I. and Cumberpatch, C.G., 2009, 'A Stamford ware kiln in Pontefract', *Medieval Archaeol.* 53, 45-50

Robinson, C.B. (ed.), 1857, *Rural Economy in Yorkshire in 1641: being the Farming and Account Books of Henry Best of Elmswell, in the East Riding of the County of York,* Surtees Soc. 33

Robinson, J., 1978, *The Archaeology of Malton and Norton*

Roffe, D., 1990, 'Domesday Book and northern society: a reassessment', *Engl. Hist. Rev.* 105, 310-36

Roffe, D.R., 1992, 'An introduction to the Lincolnshire Domesday', in Williams, A. and Martin, G. (eds), *The Lincolnshire Domesday* (Alecto County ed.), 1-42

Roffe, D., 2000a, 'The early history of Wharram Percy, in *Wharram VIII*, 1-16

Roffe, D., 2000b, *Domesday. The Inquest and the Book*

Roffe, A., 2007, *Decoding Domesday*

Roffe, D. and Roffe, C., 1995, 'Madness and care in the community: a medieval perspective', *Br. Med. J.* 311, 1708-12

Rogers, N.S.H., 1993, *Anglian and other Finds from 46-54 Fishergate,* Archaeol. York 17/9

Roper, M. and Kitchen, C. (ed.), 2006, *Feet of Fines for the County of York from 1314 to 1326*, Yorkshire Archaeol. Soc. Rec. Ser. 158

Roskams, S., 1999, 'The hinterlands of Roman York: present patterns and future strategies', in Hurst, H. (ed.), *The coloniae of Roman Britain: new studies and a review*, J. Roman Archaeol., Suppl. Ser. 36, 45-72 (Portsmouth, Rhode Island)

Roskams, S., 2006, 'The urban poor: finding the marginalised', in Bowden, W., Gutteridge, A. and Machado, C. (eds), *Social and Political Life in Late Antiquity*, Late Antique Archaeol. 3.1, 487-531 (Leiden/Boston)

Roskams, S. with Whyman, M., 2007, 'Categorising the Past: lessons from the archaeological resource assessment for Yorkshire' *Internet Archaeol.* 23. http://intarch.ac.uk/journal/issue23/roskams_index.html

Roskams, S.P. and Richards, J.D., 2004, 'Site 82', in Rahtz and Watts, 109-38

Ross, F., Stead, R. and Holderness, T., 1877, *A Glossary of Words used in the East Riding of Yorkshire*

Rushe, C.M., Smith, H. and Halstead, P., 1994, 'The animal bone' in Brewster, T.C.M. and Hayfield, C., 'Excavations at Sherburn, East Yorkshire', *Yorkshire Archaeol. J.* 66, 143-146

Ryder, M.L., 1974, 'Animal remains from Wharram Percy', *Yorkshire Archaeol. J.* 46, 42-52

Ryder, M.L., 1983, *Sheep and Man*

Ryder, P.F., 2007, 'Post-conquest stonework - medieval cross slab grave-covers', in *Wharram XI*, 287-94

Rynne, C., 1989, 'The Introduction of the Vertical Watermill into Ireland: Some Recent Archaeological Evidence', *Medieval Archaeol.* 33, 21-31

Rynne, C., 2000, 'Waterpower in Medieval Ireland', in Squatriti, P. (ed.), *Working with Water in Medieval Europe*, 1-50 (Leiden/Boston/Koln)

Samuels, L.E., 1999, *Light microscopy of carbon steels*, ASM (Ohio)

Saunders, A., 2003, 'John Hurst. Medieval archaeologist and inspector of ancient monuments', *The Independent*, 9 May 2003

Sawyer, P.H, 1965, 'The wealth of England in the eleventh century', *Trans. R. Hist. Soc.* 15, 145-164

Sawyer, P.H, 1971, *The Age of the Vikings* (2nd ed.)

Sawyer, P., 1981, 'Fairs and markets in early medieval England', in Skyum-Neilsen, N. and Lund, N. (eds), *Danish Medieval History: New Currents*, 153-68 (Copenhagen)

Scott, B.G., Cleere, H. and Tylecote, R.F. (eds), 1987, *The crafts of the blacksmith : essays presented to R.F. Tylecote at the 1984 symposium of the UISPP Comitâe pour la Sidâerurgie ancienne*, 7-17, UISPP Comitâe pour la Sidâerurgie ancienne, in conjunction with Ulster Museum (Belfast)

Scott, D.A., 1991, *Metallography and microstructure of ancient and historic metals*, The J. Paul Getty Trust (United States)

Scull, C., 1997, 'Urban Centres in pre-Viking England', in Hines, J., *The Anglo-Saxons from the Migration Period to the Eighth Century. An Ethnographic Perspective*, 269-98

Scull, C., 2009, *Early Medieval (Late 5th – Early 8th Centuries AD) Cemeteries at Boss Hall and Buttermarket, Ipswich, Suffolk*, Soc. Medieval Archaeol. Monogr. 27

Scully, S., 2008, 'The Medieval Small Finds from Golden Lane', in O'Donovan, E., 'The Irish, the Vikings and the English: New Archaeological Evidence from Excavations at Golden Lane, Dublin', *Medieval Dublin* 8, 71-99 (Dublin)

Semple, S., 1998, 'A fear of the past: the place of the prehistoric burial mound in the ideology of middle and later Anglo-Saxon England', *World Archaeol,* 30 pt 1, 109-26

Serneels, V. and Perret, S., 2003, 'Quantification of Smithing Activities based on the Investigation of Slag and Other Material Remains', in *Proc. Int. Conf. Archaeometallurgy Europe*, 469-479, Associazione Italiana di Metallurgia (Milano)

Sharples, N., 2007, 'Building communities and creating identities in the first millennium BC', in Haselgrove, C. and Pope, R. (eds), *The Earlier Iron Age in Britain and the near Continent*, 174-84

Sheppard, J.A., 1973, 'The Field Systems of Yorkshire, in Baker, A.R.H. and Butlin, R.A. (eds), 1973, *Field Systems in British Isles,* 145-87

Sheppard, J., 1974, 'Metrological analysis of regular village plans in Yorkshire', *Agric. Hist. Rev.* 22, 118-35

Sheppard, J., 1976, 'Medieval village planning in northern England: some evidence from Yorkshire', *J. Hist. Geogr.* 2, 3-20

Shepherd Popescu, E., 2009, *Norwich Castle: Excavations and Historical Survey, 1987-98. Part II: c 1345 to Modern*, East Anglian Archaeol. 132

Siddle, D.J., 1967, 'The Rural Economy of Medieval Holderness', *Agric. Hist. Rev.* 15, 40-45

Siegmund, F., 1998, *Merovingerzeit am Niederrhein: Die Frühmittelalterliche Funde aus dem Regierungsbezirke Düsseldorf und dem Kreis Heinsberg* (Cologne)

Simpson, A.W.B., 1961, *An Introduction to the History of the Land Law*

Sitch, B., 2004, 'Coins: a review of the Iron Age and Roman coins from Wharram', in *Wharram IX*, 234-40

Slater, R. and McDonnell, G., 2002, 'Bestwall Quarry Slag Assemblage', unpubl. rep. Bestwall Aggregates Levy Project Engl. Heritage

Slowikowski, A.M., 1992, 'Anglo-Saxon and medieval pottery', in *Wharram VII*, 27-38

Slowikowski, A.M., 2000, 'The Anglo-Saxon and medieval pottery', in *Wharram VIII*, 60-100

Slowikowski, A.M., 2004, 'The Anglo-Saxon and medieval pottery', in *Wharram IX*, 183-212

Slowikowski, A.M., 2005, 'The Anglo-Saxon and medieval pottery', in *Wharram X*, 73-121

Smith, A.H., 1937, *The Place-names of the East Riding of Yorkshire and York,* Engl. Place-Name Soc. 14

Smith, A.H., 1956a, *English Place-Name Elements. Part 1 A-IW*, Engl. Place-Name Soc. 25

Smith, A.H., 1956b, *English Place-Name Elements. Part 2 JAFN-YTRI*, Engl. Place-Name Soc. 26

Smith, D.T., 1989, 'Stone mortars', in *Wharram VI*, 53-6

Smith, N., 1999, 'The earthwork remains of enclosure in the New Forest', *Proc. Hampshire Field Club Archaeol. Soc.* 54, 1-56

Smith, P.J., 2004, *A splendid idiosyncrasy: Prehistory at Cambridge, 1915-50*, Http://www.arch.cam.uk/~pjs1011/publications.html#thesis

Smith, R.M., 1991, 'Coping with uncertainty: women's tenure of customary land in England c.1370-1430', in Kermode, J. (ed.), *Enterprise and Individuals in Fifteenth-Century England*, 43- 67

Smith, S., 2009, 'Towards a social archaeology of the late medieval English peasantry: Power and resistance at Wharram Percy', *J. Soc. Archeol.* 9, 391-416

Snape, M.E., 2003, 'A Horizontal-Wheeled Watermill of the Anglo-Saxon Period at Corbridge, Northumberland, and its River Environment', *Archaeol. Aeliana* 32, 37-72

Sorrell, M., (ed.), 1981, *Alan Sorrell. Reconstructing the Past*

Spain, R.J., 1984, 'The Second Century Romano-British Watermill at Ickham, Kent', *Hist. Technol.* 9, 143-80

Spall, C.A. and Toop, N.J., 2005, 'Blue Bridge Lane and Fishergate House. Report on Excavations, July 2000 to July 2002', Archaeol. Plan. Consultancy Monogr. 1. Accessed at www.archaeologicalplanningconsultancy.co.uk/mono/001, July 2008

Spratt, D.A. 1989, 'Linear Earthworks of the Tabular Hills of Northeast Yorkshire', Univ. Sheffield

Stallibrass, S., 1996, 'The animal bones', in Abramson, P., 'Excavations along the Caythorpe Gas Pipeline, North Humberside', *Yorkshire Archaeol. J.* 68, 1-88

Stamper, P.A., 1991, *'Interim Report on the 41st Season of the Wharram Percy Research Project, 7th July to 4th August 1990'*, Medieval Settlement Res. Group

Stamper, P.A., Croft, R.A. and Andrews, D.D., 2000, 'The excavations', in *Wharram VIII*, 17-56

Starley, D., 1999, *The analysis of Middle Saxon ironwork and ironworking debris from Flixborough, Humberside*, Ancient Monuments Lab. Rep. 35/99

Stead, I.,1979, *The Arras Culture*

Stead, I., 1980, *Rudston Roman Villa*

Stead, I., 1991, *Iron Age Cemeteries in East Yorkshire*, Engl. Heritage Archaeol. Rep. Ser. 22

Steedman K., 1994, 'Excavation of a Saxon site at Riby Cross Roads, Lincolnshire', *Archaeol. J.* 151, 212-306

Steensberg, A., 1940, 'Middelalderens og Renaissancetidens Bondeboliger', *Naturens Verden*, 109-121

Steensberg, A., 1943, *Ancient Harvesting Implements. A study in archaeology and human geography*, Nationalmuseets skrifter, Arkæologisk-historisk række 1 (Copenhagen)

Steensberg, A., 1952, *Bondehuse og Vandmøller i Danmark gennem 2000 år.* Arkæologiske Landsbyundersøgelser 1 (Copenhagen)

Steensberg, A., 1955, 'Medieval and Later Village Excavation in Denmark', *Archaeol. NewsLetter*, 1955: 2, 182-184

Steensberg, A., 1957, 'Jorddyrkning i Middelalderen' *Fra Nationalmuseets Arbejdsmark 1957*, 83-96

Steensberg, A., 1968, *Atlas over en del af middelalderlandsbyen Borups agre i Borup Ris skov ved Tystrup Sø, Sjælland. Textband: Borups agre 1000-1200 e.Kr*, Det kongelige danske videnskabernes selskabs kommission til udforskning af landbrugsredskabernes og agerstrukturernes historie 1 (Copenhagen)

Steensberg, A., 1974, 'Landsbyen Store Valby i historisk og forhistorisk tid', in Steensberg, A. and Østergaard Christensen, J.L., *Store Valby. Historisk-arkæologisk undersøgelse af en nedlagt landsby på Sjælland*, Band 1 Det Kongelige Danske Videnskabernes Selskab, Historisk-Filosofiske Skrifter 8, 1 (Copenhagen)

Steensberg, A., 1982, 'The development of open-area excavation and its introduction into medieval archaeology. A historical survey', *Deserted Medieval Village Res. Group Ann. Rep.* 30, 27-30

Steensberg, A., 1983, *Borup, A.D. 700-1400. A deserted settlement and its fields in south Zealand, Denmark.* R. Danish Acad. Sci. Letters' Comm. Res. Hist. Agric. Implements Field Struct. 3 (Copenhagen)

Steensberg, A., 1986a, *Pebringegården. Folk og dagværk fra oldtid til nutid* (Aarhus)

Steensberg, A., 1986b, *Hal og gård i Hejninge. En arkæologisk undersøgelse af to sjællandske gårdtomter*, Historisk-filosofiske Skrifter 11. Det Kongelige Danske Videnskabernes Selskab (Copenhagen)

Steensberg, A., 1986c, *Man the Manipulator. An Ethno-Archaeological Basis for Reconstructing the Past*, R. Danish Acad. Sci. Letters' Comm. Res. Hist. Agric. Implements Field Struct. Publ. 5 (Copenhagen)

Steensberg, A and Østergaard Christensen, J.L., 1974, *Store Valby. Historisk-arkæologisk undersøgelse af en nedlagt landsby på Sjælland*, Det Kongelige Danske Videnskabernes Selskab, Historisk-Filosofiske Skrifter 8, 1 (Copenhagen)

Stell, P.M. and Hampson, L., 1998, *Probate Inventories of the Diocese of York 1350-1500*

Stenton, D.M., 1937, *Rolls of the Justices in Eyre for Yorkshire*, Selden Soc. 56

Stenton, F.M., 1971, *Anglo-Saxon England* (3rd ed.)

Stocker, D, 1991, *St Mary's Guildhall, Lincoln. The Survey and Excavation of a Medieval Building Complex*, Archaeol. Lincoln 12-1

Stocker, D., 1997, '*Fons et Origo*, The symbolic death, burial and resurrection of English font stones', *Church Archaeol.* 1, 17-25

Stocker, D, 1999, *The College of the Vicars Choral of York Minster at Bedern: Architectural Fragments*, Archaeol. York 10/4

Stocker, D., 2000, 'Monuments and Merchants; irregularities in the distribution of stone sculpture in Lincolnshire and Yorkshire in the tenth century', in Hadley and Richards (eds), 179-212

Stocker, D., 2001, 'Architectural Description of Bedern Hall', in Richards 2001a, 583-602

Stocker, D., 2006, *England's landscape: the East Midlands*

Stocker, D., 2007a, 'Pre-Conquest stonework - the early graveyard in context', in *Wharram XI*, 271-87

Stocker, D., 2007b, 'Stone associated with burial EE120', in Ryder, 293-4

Stocker, D., 2007c, 'This bless'd plot ...', unpubl. seminar pap. in the POMLAS ser., given at York 21 September 2007 [see abstract on website; Dyer published roundup]

Stocker, D., forthcoming, 'Enclosures and Extensions. Exploring relationships between urban building types and medieval town planning', *Vernacular Archit.*

Stocker, D. and Everson, P., 2001, 'Five Towns Funerals: decoding diversity in Danelaw stone sculpture', in Graham-Campbell, J., Hall, R., Jesch, J. and Parsons, D.N. (eds), *Vikings and the Danelaw. Select Papers from the Proceedings of the Thirteenth Viking Congress, Nottingham and York, 21-30 August 1997*, 223-43

Stocker, D. and Everson, P., 2003, 'The straight and narrow way: Fenland causeways and the conversion of the landscape in the Witham Valley, Lincolnshire', in Carver, M. (ed.), *The Cross Goes North: Processes of Conversion in Northern Europe, AD 300-1300*, 271-88

Stocker, D. and Everson, P., 2006, *Summoning St Michael*

Stoertz, C., 1997, *Ancient Landscapes of the Yorkshire Wolds: aerial photographic transcription and analysis*

Stoklund, B., 1986, 'Gensyn med Pebringegården', *Fortid og Nutid* 33, 303-310

Stummann Hansen, S., 1984, 'Gudmund Hatt – The Individualist against his Time', *J. Danish Archaeol.* 3, 164-169

Summerson, H., 1993, *Medieval Carlisle. The City and the Borders, from the Late Eleventh to the Mid-sixteenth Century 1*, Cumberland Westmorland Antiq. Archaeol. Soc.

Svart Kristiansen, M., 2003a, 'Arkæologiske undersøgelser af den middelalderlige landsbebyggelse – metodiske problemer og prioriteringer i fortiden, nutiden og fremtiden', *Bol og By. Landbohistorisk tidsskrift* 1-2, 9-29

Svart Kristiansen, M., 2003b, 'Boligindretning i middelaldergårde', in Roesdahl, E. (ed.), *Bolig og familie i Danmarks middelalder*, Jysk Arkæologisk Selskabs Skrifter 89-99 (Højbjerg)

Svart Kristiansen, M., (ed.) 2005, *Tårnby. En gård og landsby gennem 1000 år*. Jysk Arkæologisk Selskabs Skrifter, 54 (Højbjerg)

Svart Kristiansen, M., 2009, Axel Steensbergs udgravning i Store Valby set med nutidens øjne. En analyse og dekonstruktion af de arkæologiske metoder og resultater, *Aarbøger for nordisk Oldkyndighed og Historie 2006* (Copenhagen)

Swinnerton, H.H., 1959, 'Note on Glazed Stamford Ware sherds' in Richardson, K.M., 'Excavations in Hungate, York', *Archaeol. J.* 116, 81

Swiss, A.J., 2000, 'The metallographic analysis of selected Roman ferrous edged tools from Castle Street Carlisle, unpubl. MSc diss. Univ. Bradford

Swiss, A.J. and McDonnell, J.G., 2003, *Evidence and interpretation of cold working in ferritic iron: Proceedings of the International Conference on Archaeometallurgy in Europe Volume 1*

Swiss, A.J. and McDonnell, G., 2007, 'Metallurgical analysis of the iron tyres from the chariot burial', in Brown, F., Howard-Davis, C., Brennand, M., Boyle, A., Evans, T., O'Connor, S., Spence, A., Heawood, R. and Lupton, A., *The Archaeology of the A1 (M) Darrington to Dishforth DBFO Road Scheme*, Lancaster Imprints, 463-498

Sykes, N.J., 2006b, 'From *Cu* and *Sceap* to *Beffe* and *Motton*', in Woolgar *et al.* (eds), 56-71

Taylor, C., 1979, *Roads and Tracks of Britain*

Taylor, C.C., 2002, 'Nucleated settlement: a view from the frontier', *Landscape Hist.* 24, 53-71

Taylor, C., 2010, 'The origins and development of deserted village studies', in Dyer, C. and Jones, R., *Deserted Villages Revisited*, Explorations Local Regional Hist. 3, 1-7

Taylor, E.G., 1888, 'Domesday Survivals' in Dove, P.E. (ed.), *Domesday Studies* I

Taylor, H.M., 1973, 'The position of the altar in early Anglo-Saxon churches', *Antiq. J.* 53, 52-8

Taylor, H.M. and Taylor, J., 1965, *Anglo-Saxon Architecture*

Tebbutt, C.F., 1982, 'A Middle Saxon iron smelting site at Milbrook, Ashdown Forest, Sussex', *Sussex Archaeol. Collect.* 120, 19-36

Thirsk, J,. 1967, 'Enclosing and engrossing', in Thirsk, J. (ed.), *The Agrarian History of England and Wales, IV, 1500-1640*, 200-255

Thomas, G., 2000, 'Anglo-Scandinavian Metalwork from the Danelaw: Exploring Social and Cultural Interaction', in Hadley and Richards (eds), 237-55

Thomas, K., 1989, 'Vegetation on the British Chalklands in the Flandrian Period: a response to Bush', in *J. Archaeol. Sci. 16*, 549-53

Thomas, R., 2007, 'Maintaining social boundaries through the consumption of food in medieval England', in Twiss, K. (ed.), *The Archaeology of Food and Identity,* Center Archaeol. Invest. Occas. Publ. 34, 130-151 (Carbondale)

Thompson, A.H., 1914, 'The pestilences of the fourteenth century in the diocese of York', *Archaeol. J.* 71, 97-154

Thorn, J.C., 1979, 'The *camera* in Area 10', in *Wharram I*, 55-66

Thorn, J.C., 1987, 'The structural history of the church', in *Wharram III*, 98-140

Thurlby, M., 1999, *The Herefordshire School of Romanesque Sculpture*

Timby, J.R., 1993, 'Sancton I Anglo-Saxon Cemetery. Excavations carried out between 1976 and 1980', *Archaeol. J.* 150, 243-365

Tipper, J., 2004, *The* Grubenhaus *in Anglo-Saxon England. An analysis and interpretation of the evidence from a most distinctive building type*

Townend, M., 2007, *Scandinavian Culture in Eleventh-century Yorkshire. The 2007 Kirkdale Lecture*

Tringham, N. (ed.), 2002, *Charters of the Vicars Choral of York Minster*, Yorkshire Archaeol. Soc. Rec. Ser. 156

Tylecote, R.F., 1986, *The prehistory of metallurgy in the British Isles*, Instit. Metals

Tylecote, R.F., 1990, 'Scientific examination and analysis of iron objects', in Biddle, M. (ed.,) *Object and economy in medieval Winchester*: 140-154

Tylecote, R.F. and Gilmour, B. J. J., 1986, *The metallography of early ferrous edge tools and edged weapons*, Br. Archaeol. Rep. 155

Ulmschneider, K., 2000a, *Markets, Minsters, and Metal-Detectors. The Archaeology of Middle Saxon Lincolnshire and Hampshire compared*, Br. Archaeol. Rep., Br. Ser. 307

Ulmschneider, K., 2000b, 'Settlement, economy, and the "productive" site: middle Anglo-Saxon Lincolnshire, AD 650-780', *Medieval Archaeol.* 44, 53-79

Van der Vaart, J.H.P., 1983, 'The brink or village green in brink villages in the province of Drenthe (The Netherlands); its development, contemporary value and prospect', in Roberts, B.K. and Glasscock, R.E. (eds), *Villages, Fields and Frontiers: studies in European rural settlement in the medieval and early modern periods*, Br. Archaeol. Rep. Int. Ser. 185, 61-70

Vince, A. (ed.), 1991, *Finds and Environmental Evidence*, Aspects of Saxo-Norman London 2, London Middlesex Archaeol. Soc. Spec. Pap. 12

Vince, A. and Young, J., 2005, 'The Period 3 Pottery', in Spall and Toop

Vince, A. and Young, J., 2009, 'The Anglo-Saxon Pottery from Flixborough within the context of the East Midlands of England, A.D. 650-1000', in Evans and Loveluck (eds), 392-401

Vinogradoff, P., 1908, *English Society in the Eleventh Century*

Vyner, B., 1994, 'The territory of ritual: cross-ridge boundaries and the prehistoric landscape of the Cleveland Hills, northeast England', *Antiquity* 68, 27-38

Vyner, B., 2008, 'Research Agenda: The Neolithic, Bronze Age and Iron Age in West Yorkshire' published on-line by the West Yorkshire Archaeology Service, http://www.archaeology.wyjs.org.uk/documents/archaeology/Revised-SW-Later-Prehistoric_Neo-BA-IA.pdf

Waites, B., 1968, 'Aspects of thirteenth and fourteenth century arable farming on the Yorkshire Wolds' *Yorkshire Archaeol. J* 42, 136-42

Walton Rogers, P., 1997, *Textile Production at 16-22 Coppergate*, Archaeol. York 17/11

Walton Rogers, P., 2007, *Cloth and Clothing in Early Anglo-Saxon England, AD 450-700*, Counc. Br. Archaeol. Res. Rep. 145

Waterbolk, H.T., 1999, 'Albert Egges van Giffen (1884-1973)', in Murray, T., (ed.), *Encyclopedia of Archaeology, P. 1, The Great Archaeologists, vol. I.*, 335-356 (Santa Barbara)

Watt, J.G., 2000, 'Iron nails', in Goodall and Clark, 140-47

Watts, L., Rahtz, P., Okasha, E., Bradley, S.A.J. and Higgitt, J., 1997, 'Kirkdale – the inscriptions', *Medieval Archaeol.* 41, 51-99

Watts, M., 2002, *The Archaeology of Mills and Milling*

Watts, M., 2005, 'The evidence for milling sites', in *Wharram X*, 222-5

Watts, S.R., 2000, 'Grinding stones', in Clark and Gaunt, 111-115

Watts, S.R., 2004, 'Querns', in Clark and Gaunt, 219-224

Watts, V., 2001, 'Some Ryedale place-names', *Ryedale Hist.* 20, (for 2000-2001),11-14

Webster, L. and Backhouse, J., 1991, *The Making of England. Anglo-Saxon Art and Culture AD 600-900*

Wenham, P. and Heywood, B, 1997, *The 1968 to 1970 Excavations in the Vicus at Malton, North Yorkshire,* Yorkshire Archaeol. Rep. 3

West, S., 1985, *West Stow: the Anglo-Saxon village Vol.1, Text.* East Anglian Archaeol. Rep. 24

West, S., 1998, *A Corpus of Anglo-Saxon Material from Suffolk,* East Anglian Archaeol. 84

Westphalen, P., 2002, *Die Eisenfunde von Haithabu,* Die Ausgrabungen in Haithabu 10, (Neumünster)

Wheeler, J., 2004, Secrets of the sooty stack, *Planet Earth,* Winter Volume 10-11

Whitelock, D., 1968, *The Will of Aethelgifu, A Tenth Century Anglo-Saxon Manuscript*

Whitelock, D., 1979, *English Historical Documents, c. 500-1042* (2nd ed.)

Willard, J.F., 1908, 'The Scotch raids and the fourteenth-century taxation of northern England', *Univ. Colorado Stud.* 5, 237-42

Williams, A., 1995, (reprint 2000), *The English and the Norman Conquest*

Williams, D. and Vince, A., 1997, 'The Characterisation and Interpretation of early to middle Saxon granitic tempered pottery in England', *Medieval Archaeol.* 41, 214-20

Williams, H., 1998, 'Monuments and the past in early Anglo-Saxon England', *World Archaeol.* 30 pt 1, 90-108

Williams, J.H., 1974, 'A Saxo-Norman kiln group from Northampton', *Northamptonshire Archaeol.* 9, 46-56

Wilson, C., 1986, 'The Cistercians as "missionaries of Gothic" in Northern England', in Norton, C. and Park, D. (eds), *Cistercian Art and Architecture in the British Isles,* 86-116

Wilson, D.M., 1975, Review of Axel Steensberg and J. L. Østergaard Christensen: Store Valby. Historisk-arkæologisk undersøgelse af en nedlagt landsby på Sjælland, *Antiquity* 49, 66-67

Wilson, D.M and Hurst, J.G., 1958, 'Medieval Britain in 1957', *Medieval Archaeol.* 2, 183-5

Wilson, D., 2004, 'Retrospect' *Antiquity* 78, 904-913

Wilson, P., 2006, 'A Yorkshire fort and "small town": Roman Malton and Norton reviewed, *Yorkshire Archaeol. J.* 78, 35-60

Wilson, W.D., 1980, 'The Work of the Heckington Lodge of Masons, 1315-1345', *Lincolnshire Hist. Archaeol.* 15, 21-8

Wood, R., 1994, 'The Romanesque Doorways of Yorkshire, with special reference to that at St Mary's church Riccall', *Yorkshire Archaeol. J.* 69

Wood, R., 2001, 'Geometric Patterns in English Romanesque Sculpture', *J. Br. Archaeol. Assoc.* 154, 1-39

Woodcock H., 1889, *Piety among the Peasantry: being Sketches of Primitive Methodism on the Yorkshire Wolds*

Woodward, A. 2002, *British Barrows : a matter of life and death*

Woodward, D., (ed.), 1984, (reprint 2006), *The Farming and Memorandum Books of Henry Best of Elmswell 1642,* Rec. Soc. Econ. Hist. New Ser. 8

Woodward, D., 1985, Swords into ploughs - recycling in pre industrial England, *Econ. Hist. Rev.,* 38, 175-91

Woodward, D., 1995, *Men at Work. Labourers and Building Craftsmen in the Towns of Northern England*

Woolgar, C.M., Serjeantson, D. and Waldron, T. (eds), 2006, *Food in Medieval England. Diet and Nutrition*

Wrathmell, S., 1975, 'Deserted and shrunken villages in southern Northumberland from the twelfth to the twentieth centuries', PhD thesis, Univ. Wales

Wrathmell, S., 1978, 'Desertion, shrinkage and depopulation', *Medieval Village Res. Group Rep.* 25, 52-4

Wrathmell, S., 1980, 'Village depopulation in the 17th and 18th centuries: examples from Northumberland', *Post-medieval Archaeol.* 14, 113-26

Wrathmell, S., 1988, 'Comments on the structural evidence of the excavated buildings', in Hayfield and Brewster, 106-7

Wrathmell, S., 1989a, 'The plateau farmsteads: plans, arrangement and composition', in *Wharram VI,* 41-5

Wrathmell, S., 1989b, 'The excavated peasant farmstead', in *Wharram VI,* 15-40

Wrathmell, S., 1989c, 'The peasant buildings: a model', in *Wharram VI,* 3-14

Wrathmell, S., 1989d, 'Peasant Houses, Farmsteads and Villages in North-East England' in Aston *et al.* (eds), 247-67

Wrathmell, S., 1994, 'Rural settlements in medieval England: perspectives and perceptions', in Vyner, B. (ed.), *Building on the Past,* R. Archaeol. Inst., 178-94

Wrathmell, S., 2002, 'Some general hypotheses on English medieval peasant house construction from the 7th to the 17th centuries', in Klápště, J. (ed.), *The Rural House,* Inst. Archaeol., Acad. Sci. Czech Republic, Památky Archeologické, Supplementum 15, Ruralia IV, 175-86 (Prague)

Wrathmell, S., 2005a, 'The documentary evidence', in *Wharram X,* 1-8

Wrathmell, S., 2005b, 'Discussion', in *Wharram X,* 19-22

Wrathmell, S., 2010a, 'Farming, farmers and farmsteads from the 16th to 19th centuries', in *Wharram XII,* 1-15

Wrathmell, S., 2010b, 'The Rectory, Chantry House and vicarage from the 14th to 19th centuries', in *Wharram XII,* 15-25

Wrathmell, S., 2010c, 'The post-medieval settlement and its buildings', in *Wharram XII,* 341-55

Wrathmell, S. and Herbert, P., 2004, 'Conclusion', in *Wharram IX,* 340

Wrathmell, S. and Marlow-Mann, E., 2005, 'Discussion' in *Wharram X,* 225-8

Wright, J. (ed.), 1923, *The English Dialect Dictionary*

Wrigley, E.A. and Schofield, R., 1989, *Population History of England 1541-1871*

Youd, G., 1962, 'The Common fields of Lancashire, *Trans. Hist. Soc. Lancashire Cheshire* 113, 1-41

Young, J. and Vince, A., 2005, *A Corpus of Anglo-Saxon and Medieval Pottery from Lincoln*, Lincoln Archaeol. Stud. 7

Young, J. and Vince, A., 2009, 'The Anglo-Saxon Pottery', in Evans and Loveluck, 339-401

Zadora-Rio, E., 2009, 'Early medieval villages and estate centres in France (c. 300-1100)', in Castillo, J.A.Q., *The Archaeology of Early Medieval Villages in Europe*, 77-98 (Bilbao)

Index
compiled by Hilary Cool

Page numbers in *italics* refer to figures and plates.
Modern individuals are indexed with surname first, medieval individuals with Christian name first.
Place-names without a county/authority are either unitary authorities or are in North Yorkshire.

Abbey Dore, Herefords., 248
Acklam hundred, *181-2*, 188, 212, 218, 228
Acomb, York, 345
Adel, W. Yorks., 247
aerial photography, 284, 305, 310
Aethelred II, coin of, 118, 146
Alcuin, 148
Aldbrough, 192
Aldred, 182
ale, 322, 337, 349, *see also* brewing
almshouse, 337
Alstrup, Denmark 11, 12
amber, *see* beads
Anglo-Saxon occupation, *see* Site 30, 32, 43, 44, 86, 98A/B
Anglo-Scandinavian, finds, 196, 197
    overlords, 184, 188, 193, 366
    see also Omar, Thorbrandr the Hold
animal bone, 3, 367, 64, 77, 80, 170, 173-8, 322, 332, 337
antler working, 154
apple, 316
Appleton-le-Moors, 280, 302
Appleton-le-Street, 358
arce (storage), 350
Archaeological Data Service, 3, 284, 367
Archbishop Uigmund, coin of, 146
Area 5, *see* Site 8
Area 6, *see* Site 12
Area 10, 10, 17, *see* also Site 9
Area 12, *see* Site 6
Area 15, *see* Site 3
arrowhead, 323, 335, 337
Aså, Jutland, Denmark, 12
aumbry, 350
Avington, Berks., 260

bacon, 325, 332, 334, 347
bakehouse, 314, 329, 342
bakestone, 354
bangle, glass, Insular, 153
    Romano-British, 71, 78, 153, 338
baptism, 210, 262, *see also* tub fonts
Barham, Suffolk, finds from, 146
Barker, Philip, 21
Barking, Gr. London, 152, 153
barley, 319, 320, 322, 325, 332, 334, 345, 346
Barmston, E. Yorks., 283
barn, 272, 314, 321, 329
barrel, 322
barrel padlock, 199

barrows, 76, *see also* Iron Age barrow; round barrow
barter, 325-6
Barton-on-Humber, N. Lincs., 147, 152
basket, 336
baulks, 20
bead, amber, 140
bead, glass, 120, 123, 125, 130
    Anglo-Saxon, *138-9,* 140, 141
Beadlam, 192
bean, 316, 319, 320, 321, 332, 334, 345
bee, 316
beef, 322, 325, 333, 334, 347, *see also* cattle
Beeford, E. Yorks., 280
bell, iron, 153
    animal, 323
    from Burdale, 116
    Insular, large hand, 152, 153
belt fitting, 125
    Bern Solothern type, *138*, 141
    Borre-style, 197, *198*, 202, 214
    see also buckle
Belton, Lincs., 238, 262
Berenger de Tosny, 184, 186, 188, 190, 193, 194-5, 222
Beresford, Maurice, 10, 13, 17, 221, 364
Bersu, Gerhard, 16
Bestwall, Dorset, 156
Beverley, E. Yorks., 36, 147, 148, 152, 153, 325, 336
Biddle, Martin, 21
Bigby, Lincs, 224
Binnington township, 111
bird bone, modified, 200
Birdsall, 73, 79, 90, 182, 188, 192, 224, 228, 231, 289, 322, 325, 333, 337, 359, 362
Bishop Wilton, E. Yorks., 278, 312, 316, 319, 321, 322, 323, 325, 329, 332, 334, 335, 337
bit (woodworking), 326
Black Death, 304, 321, 339
blacksmithing, 79, *see also* iron working
Blockley, Glos., 167
Blythburgh, Suffolk, 153
Bolle, Jutland, 12
book-clasp, 259
Borup Ris, Denmark, 11, 12, 20, *22,* 23
bovates, 290-95, 310-11, *see also* oxgang
Boynton, E. Yorks.,108, *109,* 283
Boythorpe township, 84, 105
bracelet, copper alloy, 61-2
Braithwell, W. Yorks, 246
Brandesburton, 280
Brandon, Suff., 143, 146, 150-54 *passim*

Brantingham, E. Yorks., 78
Brayton, 247
bread, 316, 319, 332, 333, 346
bread oven, 352
Bredon, Worcs., 167
brewhouse, 342
brewing, 316, 319, 324, 325, 328, 329, 332, 333
bridle bit, iron, 200, 320
Bridlington, E. Yorks., 147, 283, 353
Broch of Burrian, 153
Brompton, 102
Bronze Age activity, at Wharram, 67-70
    on the Wolds, 56, 66-7, 82, 87
    see also round barrow
brooch, Anglo-Saxon, 118
    Iron Age, 78
    Frisian, 96, 123, 137
    Roman, 71
Brough, E. Yorks., 76
buckles, 337
    Anglo-Saxon, 116, 129, 140
    antler/bone, 197
Buckrose wapentake, 215, 218, 359
Buckton (missing vill), 99, 180, 181, 183-4, 195, 288, *300*, 302, 304, 362
Buckton Garths, 99, 302, 304, 362
Bugthorpe, E. Yorks., 218, 220, 328
Building 1 (Site 9), 314, 315, 330
Building 1 (Site 12), 314, 329, 330, 334. 335, 340-42, *348*, 349, 353, 354, 355
Building 1 (Site 76), 314, 330
Building 3, 26
Building 3 (Site 82), 315
Building 4 (Site 9), 329, 341, 354
Building 4 (Site 12), 314
Building 5 (Area 7), 314
Building 5 (Site 8), 24-26
Building 6, 39
Building 8 (Site 8), 314, 329
Building 9, 39
Building 9 (Site 12), 315, 329, 338
Building 10, 39
Building 12 (Site 6), 3
Building 13, 53
Building 15 (Site 3), 3
Building 18, 37
Building 19, 26
Building 20, (Site 7), 3, 26, 37
Building 21, 26, 36, 37
Building 22, 26, 36
Building 23, 26
Building 24, 26
Building 46, 95
Building A, 125
Building B, 125
building techniques, 329-30
bullock, 325
Burdale, 78, 113, 184, 208, 212, 275, 275, 284-6, 295, 326, 362

animal bone from, 116, 174, 175
'Butterwick-type' settlement at, 118, 163, 178, 180
dress pin from, 116, 118
excavations at, 115-8, 168
place-name evidence, 105
burials, 169
    Anglo-Saxon, 87, 140, 290
    cart, 70
    children, 338
    dog, 133
    infant, 71, 77-8, 123, 169
    Iron Age, 71
    priest, 273, 274, 330
    Roman, 81
    sword, 73
    unusual objects in, 338
    see also St Martin's, round barrows; Sites 13, 41, 52, 80, 83
Burton Agnes, E. Yorks., 283, 284
Burton Dassett, Warwickshire, 155, 160
Burton Fleming, E. Yorks., 70
Burton Pidsea, E. Yorks., 280
Burythorpe, 218
bushel measure, 325, 352
butchery, 325, 333
butter, *see* dairy products
Butterwick, 56, 82-4, 88, 106-7, 219, 281, 283, 284, 288, 311
    Middle Saxon occupation at
    place-name evidence, 103, 104, 105, 166
    Roman field systems at, 107
'Butterwick-type' settlement, 106-16, 365
    hedges at, 166, 173
    permanent occupation at, 172-3
    seasonal occupation at, 163-7, 209
buzz-bone, 200, 336
bydale, 305
by names, 99, 101, 102, 103, 104, 163, 190, 191, 192,
Bywell, Northumberland, 195

cabbage, 316, 334
candle, 325, 335, 352
candlestick, 335, 351, 352
Canterbury, Kent, 148, 152, 260
Carisbrooke, I of W, 146
Carnaby, E. Yorks., 229, 230, 263
cart, 315, 321, 346, 347
cash economy, 317, 322, 324-6
casket, 144
Castledyke South, N. Lincs., 141, 147, 149-50
cattle, 80, 175-6, 317, 346, 347
    cowpats as fuel, 352-3, 354
    grazing 287, 321, 322
    see also animal bone, bullock, ox
cauldron, 354
Cawood, 337
Cawthorn East Moor, 95
Caythorpe, E. Yorks., 136
cetacean remains, 153

chafing dish, 335, 353

Chamberlain family, 31, 33, 228-9, 230, 263, 265, 270, 338

       at South Manor, 232-4

       Osbert, 262

change-ringing, 273

charcoal, 157, 334, 353

charlock, 320

cheese, *see* dairy products

cherry, 316

Cherry Hinton, Cambs, 169

Cherry Willingham, Lincs., 155

Chester, Chesh., 197

chisel, 326

chocolate, 170

church-on-the-green, 209-11 *passim*, 263

clay pipe, 24

clothing, 335

coal, 314, 334, 336, 353

cod, 334

Coddenham, Suffolk, 146

coins, Anglo-Saxon, 114, 118, 136-7, 143, 144, 147, 178

       Arabic dirham, 117, 118

       Corieltauvian, 76

       medieval. 325, 337

       Roman, 62, 78, 338

coin weight, 325

comb, Anglo-Saxon, 125, 130, 197

       as gifts, 148

  double-sided composite, 137, *138,* 140, 141

       from Burdale, 116, 178

       handled, 143

       single-sided composite, 137, *138,* 141, 144, 197

comb, antler, 120

comb, bone, 86, 133, 197

comb, Insular, *139,* 148, 153

       double-sided, 144

comb, Merovingian, 147

comb, weaving, 73

'comital' estates, 195, 211

convertible husbandry, 278, 283, 284

coppicing, 334

Corbridge, Northumberland, 206

cordage implement, antler, 199

cordwain, 335

corn chickweed, 320

corncockle, 320

corn drier, 79, 270

corn marigold, 320

cottagers, 324, 325, 347

Cottam, E. Yorks., 113, 118, 136, 146, 147, 150, 152, 154, 180, 202, 180, 362, 365

Cottingham, E. Yorks. 238

Cowlam, E. Yorks., 182, 184, 218, 330

Coxwold, 222, 224

Crambe, 185

Croom, 182, 184, 191

crop yields, 319

cross-shaft, 213, 217

cross, stone, 123, 135, 144, 193

       possible market cross, 171

crucible, 121, 144

cruck-built buildings, 315, 318, 330, 341

curry comb, 320

curvilinear enclosure complex *see* Butterwick-type settlement, sheep flock management

cushion, 349

Dacre survey (1563), 82, 88, 281, 283, 284, 286

dagger, 335

dairy products, 166, 315, 322, 325, 328, 331, 332, 334, 347, 352

Danelaw, 215

Danish archaeology, 10-15

Dauncey, Kenneth, 13, 14

day labourers, 324

debt, 347

Deerhurst, Glos., 208

depopulation, 356, 359, 362, 364

Deserted Medieval Village Research Group, (DMVRG) 15, 20, 21, 23, 363

deserted villages, 362-4

die, 336, 337

dog, 323

dolphin remains, 153

Domesday survey, 82, 99, 101, 103, 104, 107, 163, 180, 184, 185, 188, 192, 194, 207, 209, 262, 302, 341, 362

domestic fowl, 80, 316, *see also* animal bone, kitchen dresser

dovecote, 272

Dover, finds from, 152

drage, 319, 323

Drenthe, The Netherlands, 211, 215

Driffield, E. Yorks., 88, 147, 180, 195, 283

drinking horn, in manuscript, 151

dripping pan, 354

droveways, 88, *see also* Routes

Dublin, Ireland, 197, 202

Duggleby, 104, 191, 196, 294, 296, *308-9,* 310, 317, 322, 326, 359, 362

Duggleby Howe, 66, 196, 219

dunghill, 315

Eadberht, coin of, 143, 147

Eanred, coin of, 146

earthwork surveys, 1, 23-44

East Ayton, 186

East Halsham, E. Yorks., 281

East Heslerton, 184,

East Lutton, 106, *see also* Lutton(s)

East Row, 38. 209, 271, 315, 316, 318, 366

       earthwork survey, 33-5

       magnetometer survey, 49

ecclesiastical objects, 144, 151-3, *see also* cross

egg, 316, 325, 332, 347

Eidsborg Schist, *198,* 199

Elmswell, E. Yorks., 281, 283

enamel hypoplasia, 331

enclosure, 359, 362, 363
Eustace Vescy, *see* Stuteville family
Eustachia Percy, *see* Percys of Bolton Percy
excavation methodology, 1, 9, *see also* open-area
  excavation

famine (1315-17), 318, 332, 339
feasting, 151, 153
fence, 318, 334
Field 1, 31
field systems, *see* ladder settlements, open field
figurine, chalk, 73, 76
Fimber, E. Yorks., 105, 314, 324, 326, 336, 353, 359
finds recording, 20
finger-ring, 140, 141, 197
firesteel, 86, 95, 120, 137-40
fish, 332, 334
fishing, 338
fish hook, 326
Fitz Herbert family, 182, 183, 192, 224
Flamborough, E. Yorks., 280
flax, 316, 317, 325, 326, 347, 355
flax comb, 326
Flaxton, 215
fleece, 323, 325, 356, 358
Flixborough, N. Lincs., 136, 144-54 *passim*, 155, 156,
  160, 202
Foggathorpe, E. Yorks., 281
Folkestone, Kent, 152
Folkton, 213, 217, 220
Fossard family, 224, 226, 228
Fountains Abbey, 248, 326
fowling, 337
Frankish finds, 141
Frank's Casket, 153, 168
Fridaythorpe, E. Yorks., 218, 262, 322, 325, 337
Frisian finds, 148, *see also* brooch
frumenty, 352, 354
frying pan, 354
fuel supplies, 168, 318, 332, 334, 352-3, 354 , *see also*
  charcoal, peat
furlong, 84, 278, 280, 281, 286, 288, 290, 295, 296, 310
furnace (kitchen), 353-4

Gamall, *see* Thorbrandr the Hold
gaming counter, 200
Gandersheim casket, 153
Ganton, 281, 302
garden, 316
garlic, 316, 334
garth, *see* garden
Garton, E. Yorks., 108, *110*, 167, 316, 325
Garton Wetwang Slack, E. Yorks., 71, 82
geese, 316, 317, 321, 329, 333
Geoffrey Murdac, 224, 228, 230
Geoffrey Scope, 235, 238, 273, 274
geophysical survey, 2
glass, *see* bead, vessel
gleaning, 283

Goldberg, Germany, 16
Golson, Jack, 13-21 *passim*
Goltho, Lincs., 202, 315
grain, preserved, 319, 321, 332
grain driers, 49
grain storage, 315, 321
grave (reeve), 318, 328, 337
grave covers, 212, 275, 276
grave markers, 169
graveyard, 207-8, *see also* St Martin's Church, Site 26, 71
grazing, 86-9, 165-8, 172, 220, 316-8, 320, 321, 323
Great Edstone, 192, 193
Great Givendale, E. Yorks., 283
Great Kelk, E. Yorks., 281, *282*, 296, 305-6
Grimes Grave, Norfolk, 41
Grimston, York, 321
Ground Penetrating Radar, 53
Grubenhäuser, 106, 146, 154, 171, 172
  as temporary settlements, 164-8
  at Burdale, 114-8 *passim*, 178
  at Low Caythorpe, 108
  at West Heslerton, 111, 118, 164-5, 178
  ethnographic parallels for, 164
  function of, 168
  Grubenhaus 14, *see* Site 39
  Grubenhaus 46, *see* Site 60
  Grubenhaus 435, *see* Site 60
  Site 26, 135
  Site 39, 6, 51, 86, 95, 111, 120, 144, 200, 203
  Site 60, 7, 45, 51, 86, 120, 137, 141
  Site 94, 9, 51, 121-3
  Site 95A, 143, 144, 203
guildhouse, 337
gutter, 352
Gypsey Race, 66, 101, 105, 166, 167, 170, 217, 219,
  308, 310

Hackness, 194
haddock, 334
hair pin, bone, 62
Haithabu, Germany, 199
Haltemprice Priory, E. Yorks., 238, 273, 274, 276, 295,
  358
ham names, 101, 102
Ham Hill, Somerset, 38
hammerscale, 155
Hamwic, Hants., 136, 140, 143, 150, 151, 152, 153, 154
  iron working at, 156, 160
hand mill *see* quern
Hanging Grimston, 191, 359
harden (textile), 335, 355
Hardingstone, Northants., 281
harness fitting, 335
Harris lines, 331, 332
Hartlepool, 147, 152, 154
Hatt, G., 11-2, 16
Hawling Road, E. Yorks., 76
hay, 283, 315, 316, 318, 321, 323, 356
Hayfield, Colin, 55, 56, 85, 95, 113-4, 215

Hayton, E. Yorks., 71, 76, 84
hearth, cooking, 329, 353-4
hearth, metalworking, 121-3
hearth bottom, 160
hearth lining, 158
Heckington, Lincs., 274
heckle, 347, 355
Hejninge, Zealand, Denmark 12, 13
Helperthorpe, 104, 182, 192, 218, 283, 327
hemp, 316, 317, 325, 326
Hen Domen, Powys, 21
Henry I, 222
Henry Chamberlain, *see* Chamberlain family
Henry Montfort, *see* Montfort family
Henry Percy, *see* rectors of Wharram
Henry Percy, *see* Percys of Spofforth
heraldry, 272
Herbert, Chamberlain of the King of Scotland, *see*
 Chamberlain family
Herbert Fitz Herbert see Fitz Herbert family
Herbert of Winchester (Chamberlain of Henry I), *see*
 Fitz Herbert family
Hereford, Herefords., 332
herring, 334
Heslertons, 359, *see also* East Heslerton, West Heslerton
Hiberno-Scandinavian finds, 197
hides, 325
Higham Ferrers, Northamptons., 152, 154, 365
Hillam, W. Yorks., 3
hilt guard, iron, 141, 199, *see also* dagger
Hilton family, 236, 272, 273, 275, 276, 292, 356, 358
hobnail, 60
Holderness, 195, 278, 280, 281, 281, 283, 305-6, *see
 also* Meaux
hollow way, 49, 214
holly, 77
hone, stone, 148, 157, *198*, 199, 202
honey, 316
hooked tag, copper alloy, 135, 146, 197
horn, 325
horse, 80, 317, 320, 321, 322, 323, 325, 346, 347, *see
 also* animal bone
horseshoe, iron, 200, 320, 337
Højrup, Ole, Denmark, 13
Houndtor, Devon, 95
House 6, *1*
House 10, 18, 19, 20
House 13, see Site 34
Hovingham, 188, 193, 222, 224
Howsham, 180, 195, 196
Huggate, E. Yorks., 108, *110*, 167, 288, 323, 325, 327
Hugh Bigod, 222
Hugh Fitz Baldric, 184, 186, 188, 222, 224, 225 , 228
Hull, 325, 334
hundreds, formation of, 195
hunting, 323, 337
Hurst, J., 1, 9, 10, 13, 17-18, 20, 21, 28, 312, 364, 366
Hutton Buscel, 302
Hylton family, 257

Ickham, Kent, 206
Ilham, Staffs., 260
Ilkley, W. Yorks., 229
infield-outfield, *see* convertible husbandry
ingaham names, 102, 103
ingas names, 102, 103
ingtun names, 101
inkwell, 152-3
inquisition *post mortem*, 230, 235, 236, 290-92, 312,
 317
inspect pests, 321
Insular articles, 153, *see also* combs
inventories, 329, 334, 342-7
Ipswich, Suffolk, 136, 152
iron, composition of, 156, 161
 quantity found, 3
 models of production, 155
 source of, 155, 162
 see also bell, bridle bit, hit guard, horseshoe,
 knives, iron working, locks, nails, saw blade,
 smithy, spade shoe, spoon bit
Iron Age activity, at Wharram, 70, 71
 barrows, 67, 70
 magnetometer survey evidence, 45-49
 on Wolds, 70
 re-dating of remains, 31
 see also ladder-settlements, Sites 13, 43, 45, 60,
 69, 82, 83, 89, 92, 94
iron working, manuscript illustration, 158
 smelting, 155-6, 326
 smithing, 156, 326
 stock bars, 156-7
 see also charcoal, hammerscale

Jarrow, Tyne, 147, 152, 154, 194
jetton, 24, 325
jews' harp, 336
John Thorpe of Appleton, 356, 358-9

Karli, *see* Thorbrandr the Hold
Karli, landholder at Wharram, 188-9, 210-211, 262, 263,
 275, 276
Kennythorpe, 184
Ketilbjorn, 188, 192, 210, 213, 224, 263
kettle, 354
Kettleby Thorpe, Lincs., 224
Keyingham Marsh, E. Yorks., 280
Kilham, E. Yorks., 147, 167, 280, 283, 284, 325, 330
Kilnsea, E. Yorks., 281
Kirby Grindalythe, 104, 190, 191, 192, 213, 217, 218,
 219, 220, 283, 296-7, *308*, 310, *311*, 316, 317, 359,
 362
Kirby Underdale, E. Yorks., 105, 190, 191, 218, 318,
 359
Kirkburn, E. Yorks., 337, 359
Kirkby, 191
Kirkby, Lancs., 260
Kirkby Misperton, 190, 193
Kirkby Moorside, 190, 192, 193, 222, 224, 280

'*kirkby*' place-names, 188-93
Kirkdale, 192, 193, 211
Kirk Ella, E. Yorks., 238
Kirk Halls, 99
Kirkham, 180, 195, 196
Kirkham Priory, 295, 310-11
Kirkstall Abbey, W. Yorks., 247
kitchen, 314, 329, 329, 342, 353-4
kitchen dresser, 351
knives, iron, 77, 116, 118, 141, 148-51, 161. 162, 178, *198*, 199, 321, 334, 352
Köln-Lindenthal, Germany, 16

ladder settlements, 64, 70-76, 79, 82, 121
Lagmann, landholder at Wharram, 188-9, 210, 211-2, 262, 263, 275, 276
lamp, 335
lance, 335
lands (field division), 82, 280, 281, 310
Langtoft, E. Yorks., 283
Langton, 103, 180, 181, 183-4, 195, 196, 213, 218, 220, 224, 226, 228, 262, 359
Larling, Norfolk, 153
Lastingham, 188, 193, 194
Late Saxon, change in animal husbandry, 175
    changes in finds, 202
    finds phasing, 197
    Minster formations, 191, 192
    transformation of landscape, 209
    see also Site 59
lead working, 62
leather working, 326, 335
leavening, 228
Leconfield, E. Yorkshire, 272
leek, 316, 334
left-handedness, 328
legumes, 315, 324, *see also* bean, pea, vetch
Le Patourel, Jean, 28
leprosy, 331
lighting, 335
Lincoln, Lincs, 176, 222
linen, 335, 355
ling, 334
Little Sturton, Lincs., 212
Little Totham, Essex, 155, 156
locks, iron, 199, 335, 336, 350
London, 156, *see also Lundenwic*
longhouses, 39, 314, 315, 329, 341, 342, 349
Long Riston, E. Yorks., 281
loomweight, 141, 144, 146, 199-200
looped hasp, 350
Low Caythorpe, E. Yorks., 108, *109*, 167
Lowestoft, Norfolk, 153
Lullington, Somerset, 260
Lundenwic, finds from, 136, 143, 148, 151, 152
Lutton(s), 103, 104, 107, *108*, 111, 167, 182, 192, 310, 359, 365
'lynchet bank', 37, 41-3, 49, 84, 203, 214, 265-7

magnetic remanence dating, 133
magnetometer survey, 2, 44, 144
Maidenhead, Windsor, 152
malting, 333
malt kiln, 352
Malton, 76, 77, 147, 288, 318, 325, 336, 337
Malton Priory, 286, 310
Manshowe hundred, 188
manuring, 315, 320, 331
maps, Kirkby Grindalythe (1755), 101, 310
        Greenwood (1818), 88, 99, *100*
        Ordnance Survey (1854), 99, *100*, 103, 130, 192, 193, 218, 219, 294, 296, *299*, 302, 305, 310, 362
        Ordnance Survey (1938), 304
        Settrington 1600, 183, 287, *300-301*, 302, 362
        see also Dacre Survey, Dykes' plan
market, 167, 172
    in land, 317
Market Weighton, E. Yorks., 180
marriage, 330, 337, 338
Marton, 280
Matthew Hutton, 276, 277
mattress, 349, 350
meadow, 317
Meaux, E. Yorks., 226-8, 323, 339
Meols, Merseyside, 197
Merovingian finds, 141, 147
Mesolithic activity, 66
metal-detecting, 114-5, 146, 147
metalworking, 130, 133
metal workshop, 121-3, *see also* Site 94, smithy
Methley, W. Yorks., 334, 336, 353
mica schist, 199, 202
mice, 321
Middle Merrington, Co. Durham, 297
Middle Saxon, 86, 178-80
    classification of knives, 150
    earthwork survey evidence, 41
    finds phasing, 136-7
    magnetometer survey evidence, 51
    'prolific sites', 171
    urban/rural distribution patterns 151, 154
    see also antler working, beads, belt fitting, Butterwick-type settlements, combs, ecclesiastical objects, firesteel, hilt guard, Insular articles, iron working, knives, pommel, pottery, saw blade, Sites 39, 70, 78, 59, 70, 72, 78, 94, smithy, spoon, spoon bit,
Middleton, 302
migration, 337
mill, 204, 206-7, 215, 226-8, 267, 332
    Lord's prerogative, 333, 338
Millbrook, E. Sussex, 155
miller, 207, 333
millpond, 238
millstones, 79-80
mistletoe, 77
monastery, 147-8, 169, 170, 191

Anglo-Scandinavian estates at, 188-90, 193-5
  record keeping, 194, 312
  re-foundations of, 194-5
money lender, 347
Monkton, Kent, 341
Montfort family, 224, 226-8, 230, 231
Morett, Ireland, 206
mortar, stone, 60, 61, 329, 334, 352, 354, 355
mortrews, 334
mould, ceramic, 121, 130, 144, 152, 160, 162
Mowbray family, 186, 222, 224
Mowthorpe, 99, 101, 104, 191, 196, 288, 289, *308,* 310,
  316, 317, 320, 326, 362
Mucking, Thuruck, 155, 156, 160
mutton, 322, 325

Nafferton, E. Yorks., 283
nails, iron, 161
needle, 326, 336
needle case, bone, 200
Neolithic activity, 66
Newbald, 78, 247
Newburgh Priory, 310
Newcastle-upon-Tyne, Tyne, 147, 248
Nicolas Stuteville, *see* Stuteville family
niddy-noddy, *350-51,* 355
Nigel d'Aubigny, see Mowbray family
nine-men's morris, 336
Nødskov Hede, Denmark, 11, 12
Nørlund, Poul, 13
Northfleet, Kent, 206
North Grimston, 182, 218, 220, 283, 284, 317, 326,
  327, 328, 359
North Manor, development of, 28, 36
    earthwork survey of, 26-31
    foundation of, 231-2, 366
    Iron Age occupation in area, 71
    magnetometer survey at, 49
    lordly residence at, 71-2
    Roman occupation in area, 45,71, 78, 82, 270
    ruts, 321
    yard at, 314
    see also Percys of Bolton Percy, Site 1, 2, 13, 60
North Manorial Enclosure, *see* Sites 38, 45
North Marden, W. Sussex, 95
North Row, 31, 35-7, 38, 267, 271, 318
North-west Enclosure, 45, 58-62, 79
  see also Site 13, 91, Wharram Crossroads
Norton, 77
Norton, Stockton-on-Tees, 147
Norwegian mica schist, 148
Norwich, Norfolk, 17, 154, 260

oats, 316, 319, 322, 323, 324, 331, 334, 345, 346
Old Byland, 192, 193
Old Windsor, Windsor, 206
onion, 316
open-area excavation, 9, 12, 15-23 *passim*
open fields, 209, 214, 265-7, 278, 280, 282-97 *passim,*

302, 305, 317, 328, 359, 362
  see also convertible husbandry
Ormr, 184, 187, 188, 190, 192, 193.211-13, 222
Osbert, sheriff of Lincoln and York, *see* Chamberlain
  family
osteoarthritis, 331
Oswaldkirk, 186
oven, 316, 333
oyster, 61, 334
oxen, 320, 346
oxgang, 278, 280, 281, 283, 286, 305, 316, 317, 318,
  332
    see also, rent
ox goad, 62
ox shoe, 320

Painsthorpe, E. Yorks., 191
pea, 315, 316, 319, 320, 321, 323, 332, 334, 345, 346
pear, 315
peasant house, 312
peat, 354
Pebringe, Zealand, Denmark, 12, 17, *23*
pedlar, 336
Percy family, 26, 30, 31, 33
Percys of Bolton Percy, 225, 228, 229-30, 234-6, 263-74
  passim, 289, 290, 296
    at North Manor, 234, 270-72
    at South Manor, 264-7
    debts of, 237
Percys of Spofforth, 225, 228, 230, 234, 236, 272, 290
periglacial features, 41, 51, 66
Peterhouse seminar, 13
Peter Percy I-II see Percys of Bolton Percy
pig, 80, 283, 317, 321, 334, 346, *see also* animal bone,
  buzz bone
pigsty, 314
pin, Anglo-Saxon, 114, 118, 125, 129, 133, 135, *139,*
  141
    bone, 141, 143, 144, 154, 197
    copper alloy, 143, 146, 147, 197
    Insular, 153
    pig fibula, 197
    ring-headed, 197
    sewing, 326
pin beater, *198,* 200
place-names, 102-4, 188
Plateau crofts, *see* Sites 16, 24, 25, 33
plough, 320, 346
Pocklington, E. Yorks, 324, 325, 336
pommel, 141
Pontefract, W. Yorks., 201
poppy, 320
Postman, Michael, 12-3
pottage, 332, 334, 339, 354
Potter Brompton, 108, 281, 302
pottery, Anglian, 61
pottery, Anglo-Saxon, 6, 95, 135, 203-5, 214
    assemblage composition, 170
    Brandsby-type, 133

Charnwood ware, 147
Ipswich Ware, 136, 143, 147
Maxey-type, 147
Middle Saxon, 120, 123, 124, 125, 128, 130, 133, 135, 137, 141,
shelly ware, 200-201
Stamford Ware, 183, 200-201
Staxton ware, 124, 133
Tating ware, 144, 147, 151, 153, 169
Thetford ware, 201
Torksey ware, 94, 124, 133, 200-202
Whitby-type, 147, 152, 193
York, 200-201
pottery, Iron Age, 62, 70
pottery, medieval, 42, 115, 128, 130
Cistercian ware, 341
glazed, 337
Pimply ware, 32, 183
Staxton ware, 335, 336, 354
use of, 329, 331, 333, 334, 335, 337, 352, 354
York wares, 336
pottery, Merovingian, 147
pottery, post-medieval, 24, 333, 335, 341, 349
pottery, Roman, 32, 64, 81, 130
calcite-gritted ware, 60
Crambeck, 78
Ebor ware, 62
from Burdale, 61, 62
from Weaverthorpe, 183
from Wharram Grange, 77
Huntcliffe ware, 94
poultry, 316, 323, 334, 346
Preston, E. Yorks., 281, 283, 296, 305-6
Primitive Methodists, 89, 349
probate see inventory
purple phyllite, 148, 199

quarry pits, 51
quernstone, 60, 61, 77, 207, 338, 352
Crinoid Grit, 199
lava, 116, 133, 199, 333, 336
rotary, 129

radiocarbon dates, 123, 125, 135, 144, 207-8
Rahtz, P., 21
rainwater butt, 352
Raisthorpe, 78, 184, 208, 212, 259, 274, 276, 284, 295, 326, 336, 362
Ramsbury, Wilts., 146, 154, 155, 156
rat, 321
Raunds, Northants., 212
Ravensthorpe, W. Yorks., 280
reaping hook, 321
rectors, of Wharram,
Henry Percy, 236-8, 274
William Skeldergate, 236, 238
Redcliffe, E. Yorks., 76
red deer, 154
Reepham, Lincs., 212

reeve see grave
rent, 324, 325, 326-7, 337, 338, 346, 347
Ribe, Denmark, 144
rickets, 331
ridge and furrow ploughing, 41, 214-5, 265-7, 284-8, 292, 293, 304, 305, 318,
Rillington, 103, 218, 220, 359
Risby, E. Yorks., 283
Rise, 185
ritual deposit, 71, 77, 82, 168, 338
Road 1A/B, 28, 38, 41, 45
Road 1C, 41
Road 2B, 33, 34, 35
Road 2C, 33, 34, 51
Robert, Count of Mortain, 224
Robert Montfort see Montfort family
Robert Percy II-III see Percys of Bolton Percy
Robert Turneham see Fossard family
Robert Stuteville I-III see Stuteville family
Roger Mowbray, see Mowbray family
Roman occupation, at Burdale, 114, 116
field systems, 71, 107
magnetometer survey evidence, 45-49
re-dating of remains, 31-2
roads, 76-7
remains at Burdale, 114
reuse of sarcophagus, 192, 212, 217
reuse of spolia, 168, 172,
villa development, 78
see also Sites 13, 22, 23, 37, 41, 45, 60, 61, 62, 69, 82, 83, 84, 89, 91, 94, 98A/B, Wharram Grange villa, Wharram Crossroads, Wharram le Street villa
Romsey, Hants., 155, 156
roofs, 314, 315, 330
Roos, E. Yorks., 281
Roquefort cheese, 166
round barrow, 58, 61, 66, 87, 290
Route (long distance), 55-6, 87
Route 1, 88, 102, 103
Route 2, 67, 84, 103, 104
Route 3, 67, 84, 88, 89, 90, 104, 105, 288, 289
Route 4, 88, 89, 104, 105, 288
rubbish pits, 315
Rudston, E. Yorks., 66, 70, 78, 108, 109, 167, 283
rushes, 349
rushlight, 351-2
rye, 319, 345, 346
Ryehill, E. Yorks., 281

St Cedd, see Lastingham
St Cuthbert, 148, 193, 194
St Dennis, Cornwall, 207
St Hilda, 193-4
St Martin's church, advowson of, 236, 238, 239, 273, 275
arcade, 246
belfry, 212, 255, 256, 268, 273, 273
burials in chancel area, 258, 259, 273, 276-7

burials in churchyard, 338
chancel, 245, 252, 254-5, 273, 276
chantry chapel, 274
churchyard, activities in, 337
contraction of, 257-9, 276
dating of phases, 246, 250, 252, 254, 255, 259
elite burials, 212-13, 217-8, 263, 265, 268, 275-6
fonts at, 260-62
gable cross, 254
liturgy, influence of, 263, 268-9, 275, 276
location of, 209-10
nave, 240, 242-5
north chapel, 252
north door, 253, 273, 275
north-east chapel, 254-5, 256, 273,
origins of, 169, 171, 208, 211, 212, 219-20
Perpendicular refurbishment of, 256
Percy family influence on, 267-8
post-medieval reconstruction, 259-60
reuse of monuments in, 268
Reformation, influence of, 259, 276
Romanesque arches at, 248, 252
south aisle door 246-9
south door, 247, *251*, 267
south porch, 258
tithes, 236, 318, 356
tower, 240, *243*, 250-52, 255, 263, 267, 268-9,
    272-3
wall paintings, 253, 259
see also rectors, Site 14, vicars
Sancton, E. Yorks, 147
Sandtun, 151
Saunders, Andrew, 21
saw blade, iron, 154
Scagglethorpe, 103, 222, 302, 359
Scampston, 102, 103
Scandinavian influence, 104, 105
Scard hundred, *181-2*, 188, 196, 212
sceatta, 114, 118, 137, 143, 144, 147, 148, 171, 178
scissors, 336
Scothern, Lincs., 212
Scottish Raid (1322), 318, 327, 332, 337
Scrayingham, 218
sculpture, 144, 151-2, 180, 211
    at monastic sites, 188-90, 193
    funerary, 215, 217, 220
    reuse, 168, 169
    Viking period, 191
    see also cross
Scures family, 228
scythe, 321
seal box, 61
seax, 150
seed beds, 320
seisin, 184, 230-31, 272, 289
servants, 324, 327, 332, 335, 337, 339
Settrington, 99, 183-4, 195, 218, 222, 284, 287-8, 300-
    303, 315, 316, 318, 322, 327, 334, 337, 338, 359, 362
Sewerby, E. Yorks., 147, 149-50, 283

Shakenoak, Oxon, 150
shears, 321
sheep, 80-81
    as dairy animals, 323
    ecclesiastical flocks, 167
    exploitation of 174-8
    farming, large-scale, 327, 356, 357
    flock management, 165-7, 173
    grazing in open fields, 283, 317, 320, 321, 322
    in inventories, 346, 347
    pasture, 286, 287
    station, 170, 172, 178, 209
    see also animal bone, mutton, wether
sheepcote, 314, 316, 323
sheepwalk, 359, 363, 364
Sheldon, Derbys., 278
Sherburn, N. Yorks., 88, 102, 103, 104,168, 180, 184,
    213, 217, 218, 220, 359
Shiptonthorpe, E. Yorks., 71, 76, 77, 81
shoe, 335
shroud, 335, 336
shrunken villages, 363
sickle, 62, 321
sinusitis, 331
Site 1, 3
Site 2, 3
Site 3, 3
Site 4, 3
Site 5, 3
Site 6, 3, 63
Site 7, 3
Site 8, 3, 314
Site 9, 5, 31, 32, 39, 200, 312, 314, 315, 325, 333, 334,
    335, 338, *see also* Area 10, Site 44
Site 10, 5, 63
Site 11, 5, *see also* Sites 49 and 74
Site 12, *1*, 5, 20, 39, 135, 144, 146, 197, 200, 202, 312,
    314, 315, 321, 323, 325, 327, 333, 334, 335, 336, 355
Site 13, 5, 78, 81, 140, *see also* Site 83
Site 14, 5
Site 15, 5
Site 16, 5, 84
Site 17, 5, 84
Site 18, 5, 84, *126,* 130
Site 19, 5
Site 20, 5, *see also* Site 77
Site 21, *see* Site 20
Site 22, 5, 84,
Site 23, 5, 84
Site 24, 5, 84
Site 25, 5, 84
Site 26, 5, 135, 200, 207, *see also* Site 99
Site 27, 6
Site 28, 6
Site 29, 6
Site 30, 6, *see also* Site 48, 71
Site 31, 6, 84
Site 32, 6, 84, *126,* 130-33, *see also* Site 78
Site 33, 6, 84

Site 34, 6, 84
Site 35, 6, 84
Site 36, 6, 84
Site 37, 6, 49, 84
Site 38, 6, 84
Site 39, 6, 63, 84, 86, 94, 111, 120, 137, 200, *see also*
  Grubenhäuser
Site 40, 6
Site 41, 6, 70, 135
Site 42, 6
Site 43, 6
Site 44, 6, 157, *see also* Site 9
Site 45, 6, 45. 63, 70, 71-3, 78, 81
Site 46, 6
Site 47, 7
Site 48, 7, *see also* Site 30
Site 49, 7
Site 50, 7
Site 51, 7
Site 52, 7
Site 53, 7
Site 54, 7
Site 55, 7
Site 56, 7
Site 57, 7
Site 58, 7
Site 59, 7, 96, 124, 137, 154, 157, 200, *see also* Site 93
Site 60, 7, 49, 91, 94
  Roman occupation at, 45, 63, 70-79 *passim,* 81
  see also Grubenhäuser, Site 82
Site 61, 7
Site 62, 7
Site 63, 7
Site 64, 7
Site 65, 7
Site 66, 7
Site 67, 7
Site 68, 8
Site 69, 8
Site 70, 2, 8, 51, 125-30
Site 71, 8, *see also* Site 30
Site 72, 8, *126,* 130
Site 73, 8
Site 74, 8
Site 75, 8
Site 76, 124, 154, 157, 200, 314, 315, *see also* Site 59
Site 77, 8, *see also* Sites 20, 21, 99, 100
Site 78, 2, 8, 51, *126,* 130-34, *see also* Site 32
Site 79, 8
Site 80, 8
Site 81, 49, 124, *see also* Site 59, 84
Site 82, 8, 63, 79, 315, *see also* Site 60
Site 83, 8, 78, 81, 140, *see also* Site 13
Site 84, 8, 154, *see also* Site 81
Site 85, 124, 154, 200, *see also* Site 59
Site 86, 8, 133-5
Site 87, 8
Site 88, 9
Site 89, 9

Site 90, 9, 49, 124, 154
Site 91, 9, 45, 49, 57, 63
Site 92, 9
Site 93, 9, 124, 154, *see also* Site 59
Site 94, 9, 79, 96, 121, 137, 144, 320, *see also*
  Grubenhäuser
Site 95, 95A, 95B, 9, 95, 96, 320, *see also* Site 94
Site 96, 9
Site 97, 9
Site 98A/B, 9, 51, 123-4
Site 99, 9, *see also* Sites 26, 77
Site 100, 9, *see also* Site 77
Skeffling, E. Yorks., 281
Skirpenbeck, E. Yorks., 218, 280
Sledmere, E. Yorks, 105, 108, 167, 191, 288, 317, 359
smithing debris, 144
smithy, 7, 125, 146, 154, 157-8, 168
smoke hood, 329, 330, 341, 349, 353
Snainton, 280
social identity, 75
soke, 180, 182-4
sokemen, 210, 263, 297
solskifte, 295-6
South Cave, E. Yorks., 78
South Manor, 23, 37, 41, 232-4, 264-5, 273, 319, 338,
  366
    earthwork survey of, 31-33
    Late Saxon occupation, 202-4
    Middle Saxon occupation, 120, 141, 153-4, 203-4,
      341
    pottery from, 95
    underlain by cultivation traces, 41
    see also Chamberlain family, Percy of Bolton
      Percy family Site 9, 36, 59
South Newbald, E. Yorks., 136, 147
spade shoe, iron, 316
spearhead, 125
spindle whorl, 125, 144, 200, 326, 337
spinning, 355
spit, 334, 354
spoon, 334
    antler, 120, 141, 144, 146
spoon bit, iron, 154
spud, 321
spur, 320, 335
stable isotope analysis, 332, 334
stables, 314, 320, 323
Stamford, Lincs., 156
Stamford Bridge, E. Yorks., 71, 76, 280, 284
Staple Howe, 67
Star Carr, 17
Staxton, 281, 284
steel, 160, 161
Steensberg, A., 1, 10-23
Steven Chamberlain, *see* Chamberlain family
stinking chamomile, 320
stockfish, 334, 336
stone, sources of, 169
stool, 351

Store Valby, Zealand, Denmark, 10, 12, 13-7, *19*, 20, *22*, 23
strap-end, Anglo-Saxon, 114, 135,
    Borre-style, 188
    copper alloy, 146
    iron, 146
straw, 316, 321
strike-a-light, *see* firesteel
structured deposition, *see* ritual deposits
Stuteville family, 186, 222, 224, 228, 248
stycas, 143, 171,
stylus, 151, 153, 338
sub chondral cysts, 331
sundial, on churches, 182, 192, 193, 211
Sutton, 182, 337
Sutton-on-Derwent, 71
Swindon Hill, Wiltshire, 154
sword, 335

table, 350
Tabula counter, 200
tallow, 335, 351, 352
Tamworth, Staffs., 206
Tårnby, Amager, Denmark, 13
tax, 297, 325, 326-8, 337
tenants in chief, 222-4
textiles, 335, 336, 355-6
Thetford, Norfolk, 148
thimble, 326, 336
Thirkleby, 104, 182, 191, 296, *308-9*, 310, 316, 317, 327, 362
Thixendale, 208, 212, 259, 275, 276, 284, 288, 289, 295, 308, 316, 317, 320, 322, 324, 326, 337, 338, 359, 363
Thoraldby, 99, 104, 191, 288, 310, 362
Thorbrandr the Hold, 184-5, 188, 190, 211, 214, 222
    church building by family (?), 192, 211-2
    Gamall, (grandson?) 184, 186, 187, 190, 193
    Karli (son), 184-5, 188
    Knut (grandson), 185
    origins of land holdings, 193
    Sumarlithi (grandson), 185, 193
    Thorbrandr (grandson?) 184, 186, 187, 188, 190, 193
    see also Berenger de Tosny, Ormr
thorp names, 98, 99, 101, 102, 103, 104, 105, 163, 181, 191, 192, 220
Thorpe Bassett, 103, 218, 283, 359
Thorshowe hundred, *181-2*, 188
Thrislington, Co. Durham, 3
Thurstan Montfort, *see* Montfort family
Thwing, E. Yorks., 67, 113, 136, 146, 147, 180
Tickton, E. Yorks., 280
timber, 341
tithe, 319
Tollerton, 345
townships, 99-106, 163
Towthorpe, East York, 76, 208, 212, 259, 274, 275, 276, 284-6, 288, 289, 316, 326, 337, 362

Track 1 (A-D), 26, 28, 30, 91
Track 2 (B), 30, 91
Track 3, 36
Track 4, 32, 35, 41
Track 5a, 38
Track 5b, 42
Track 6, 42
Track 8a
Track 14, 37
Track A, 67, 77
Track B, 67, 76, 84, 87, 90
Track C, 67, 71-3, 76, 79, 81, 87, 90, 91
Trelleborg, Zealand, Denmark, 13, 15
tuberculosis, 331
tub fonts, 260-62, 263
tun, 99, 101, 102, 103, 111, 163, 171
tuning peg, 336
turf, 335
tuyère, 121, 122, 158
tweezers, Anglo-Saxon, 118

Ulchiltorp, 182
Uncleby, 105, 184, 191
Utrecht Psalter, 158

Vale of Pickering, 278, 280, 281, 284, 299-305
Vale of York, 278
venison, 337
vessel, copper alloy, 336, 347, 354
vessel, glass, Anglo-Saxon, 125, 148, 151
    post-medieval, 335,
vessel, wood, 333, 336, 352
Vessey Ponds, 66
vetch, 319, 320
vicarage, *see* Site 54, 77
vicars of Wharram,
    Marmaduke Atkinson, 356
    Edward Lowthorpe, 277
    Thomas Pereson, 277
vigil, 268-9
village green, 208, 211
    church on, 209-10
    earthwork survey of, 38-9
    possible origin of, 171
village origins, 365-6
village plans, 297-312, 366
village pond, 267, 272, 319, 331, 337, 352 *see all* Site 30
village pound, 337
Vowlam, I. of Man, 16

wain, 321, 346, 347
Walkington, E. Yorks., 278, 283
Walter Heslerton I-II *see* Percys of Bolton Percy
wandale, 296
wapentake, 195-6
wardship, 235
Warkworth, Northumberland, 353, 355
Warrington, 332
water management, *see* Site 30

Wayland the Smith, 168
Wearmouth, Tyne and Wear, 154
Weaverthorpe, 104, 107, 167, 180, 181, 182-3, 192, 195, 218, 219, 224, 230, 246, 250, 263, 288, 359
weed hook, 321
weeds, 320-21
weight (net), 326
Welburn, 192, 224
West Cotton, Northants., 206, *see also* Raunds
West Heslerton, 56, 103, 111, *112*, 136, 147, 148, 156, 160, 163, 180
West Lutton, 88-9, *see also* Lutton(s)
Westminster Abbey, 255
Westow, 218
West Plateau (north), 203-4
West Plateau (south), 141, 203-4
West Row (north), 24, 26, 32, 35, *36*, 37-8, 39, 42, *43*, 203-4, 213-14, 265, 272, 316, 318, 366, *see also* Site 37, 82
West Row (south), 39-41, 42, 266, 295, 316, 318, 321
West Stow, Suffolk, 156, 180
West Whelpington, Northumberland, 341
wether, 325
Wetwang, 218, 281, 283, 288, 312, 316, 319, 321, 321, 323, 327, 332, 337, 338
whale remains, 153
Wharram, 101, 105, 203, 212, 225-6, 318
Wharram Crossroads, 55, 70, 71, 73, 79, 82, 85
Wharram Grange, 339
    monks at, 226-8, 231
    villa, 55, 67, 78, 80, 82, 85, 86, 213
    pottery at, 77, 85-6, 95
    see also Site 61
Wharram Grange Farm, 294
Wharram le Street, 105, 170, 188, 203, 219, 227, 326, 338, 359
    boundary of, 226, 294
    church provision at, 192, 212
    manor at, 213, 218, 224, 231
    rent at, 318, 327
    ridge and furrow at, 284, 286, 288, 295
    villa, 45, 55, 76-8, 82, 84, 86
    village plan, 306-8
    see also guildhouse, inventories, Site 62, William Akclum
Wharram site archive, 2, 367
Wharram Percy, adultery at, 237, 328
    aerial photographs of, 13, *37*, 44, 55, 70, 73
    burials (Iron Age) at, 71
    burials (medieval), 330-32
    Butterwick-type settlement at, 111, *112*, 118, 203, 204, 295
    Churchyard, 144, 202
    coin use at, 325
    cottagers at, 324, 358
    decline of, 24, 326-7
    dialect spoken at, 338
    Dykes' plan (1836), 359, *360-61*
    ecclesiastical changes, 259
    emigration from, 337, 338
    enclosure at, 356
    evictions from (*c.* 1500), 26
    formation of parish, 192
    founder's graves at, 212, 215
    graziers at, 326-9
    health of population, 331
    hedges at, 23, 352
    impact of Percys at, 263-70
    improvement of farmland at, 23, 359
    infield-outfield at, 359, *360*
    initial excavations at, 17
    landscape, perceptions of, 272, 277
    Late Saxon occupation focus, 202
    marriages at, 330
    monastery at 147, 193, 195, 217, 366
    mortality rates, 331
    name, 272
    open field, destruction of, 340, 356
    open-field systems at, 278, 290-95,
    park at, 229, 238
    parish origins of, 208, 217
    place-name, 105, 170-71
    poverty of, 326-7, 339
    priest's house, 210
    priests' graves, 273, 274, 330
    reduction of arable at, 295
    resistance practices, 337-8, 366
    Roman/Anglo-Saxon continuity at, 84-6
    sheep market at (?), 167-8
    tenants at, 318, 324, 326-7, 337, 356, 358
    vicarage, 341
    village origin models, 203, 208
    village plan, 308, 328
    woodlands at, 271, 318
    see also Percys of Bolton Percy, rectors, rents, St Martin's church, sheep station, tax, vicars
Wharram Percy Farm, *see* Site 15, 51
wheat, 319, 320, 322, 332, 345, 346
Wheeler, Mortimer, 20
whelk, 334
whetstone, 321, *see also* hone
Whitby, 136, 144, 147, 152, 153, 154, 194
    see also St Hilda
Whithorn, Dumfries, 152, 153
Whittlewood Project, 366
wic sites, 136, 147, 153
widows, 327, 328, 329, 341
Wigber Low, Derbys., 148
Willerby, 111, 281, 335
William Acklum, *see* inventories
William Fossard, *see* Fossard family
William Fitz Herbert, see Fitz Herbert family
William Mowbray, *see* Mowbray family
William Percy, *see* Percys of Bolton Percy
William Percy, *see* Percys of Spofforth
William Scures, *see* Scures family
William Stuteville, *see* Stuteville family
wills, 325, 326, 343, *see also* inventories

window glass, 130, 151-2, 330, 349
windows, 330
Winestead, E. Yorks., 281
Wintringham, 88, 102, 103, 180, 218, 302
Withington, Glos., 167
Wold Newton, 219
Wombleton, E. Yorks., 302
women's rights, 328-9
woodland, 271, 317, 318
woodworking, 326
wool, 325, 326
    cloth, 335
    comb, 326
    trade, 239, 322, 324, 356
    see also fleece
work, children's, 321
    paid, 324, 346
    women's, 315-16, 317, 321, 322, 324, 325, 326,
        329, 331, 351
written sources, use of, 17

yard, 314, 315, 316
yarn, 325, 326, 355
Yarnbury, Wilts., 171, 172
Yarnton, Oxon., 156, 160
Yedingham, 102. 103, 111, 180
York, 76, 77, 156, 162, 176, 192, 197, 199, 202, 325,
   331, 336, 337, 338, 350, 355
      Archbishops of, 182-3, 192, 224, 312, 323, 332,
        356
      finds from, 136, 140, 143, 147, 151, 152, 162, 199
      Minster, 256, 267, 275
      St Mary's Abbey, 194, 248, 286, 289, 295, 323,
        338, 359
Yorkshire Wolds, 105, 147, 170, 136, 163, 192, 209
    cultivation of, 278, 280, 281, 284
    geology, 64-6
    permanent pasture, 288-90
    village plans, 308-11
    see also seasonal grazing, townships
Yorkshire Wolds Project, 57